PRENTICE HALL

WORLD HISTORY

PART 2

Elisabeth Gaynor Ellis

Anthony Esler

PEARSON

Authors

Elisabeth Gaynor Ellis

Elisabeth Gaynor Ellis holds a BS from Smith College and an MA and MS from Columbia University. Before she began writing textbooks, Ms. Ellis taught World Cultures, European History, and Russian Studies in Ardsley, New York. Ms. Ellis co-authored Prentice Hall's *World Cultures: A Global Mosaic*, and *World History: Connections to Today* with Dr. Anthony Esler. Ms. Ellis has also written other social studies materials, including *America's Holidays*, individual state histories, and a variety of Teacher's Edition materials. Ms. Ellis is currently working on a middle grades curriculum on Korea as well as a historical novel.

Anthony Esler

Anthony Esler is an emeritus professor of history at the College of William and Mary in Williamsburg, Virginia. His books include several studies of the conflict of generations in world history, half a dozen historical novels, and two other surveys of world and Western history besides this one. He is a member of the American Historical Association, the World History Association, and the Authors Guild. He has received Fulbright, Social Science Research Council, and other research grants, and is listed in the *Directory of American Scholars*, the *Directory of Poets and Fiction Writers*, and *Who's Who in America*. Books by Dr. Esler include *Bombs, Beards, and Barricades*, *Forbidden City*, and *The Human Venture*.

Senior Consultant

Burton F. Beers

Burton F. Beers is a retired professor of history from North Carolina State University. He has taught European history, Asian history, and American history. Dr. Beers has published numerous articles in historical journals and several books, including *The Far East: A History of Western Impacts and Eastern Responses*, with Paul H. Clyde, and *World History: Patterns of Civilization*.

Program Consultant

Grant Wiggins

Grant Wiggins, Ed.D., is the President of Authentic Education in Hopewell, New Jersey. He earned his Ed.D. from Harvard University and his B.A. from St. John's College in Annapolis. Wiggins consults with schools, districts, and state education departments on a variety of reform matters; organizes conferences, workshops, and develops print materials and Web resources on curricular change. He is the co-author, with Jay McTighe, of *Understanding by Design* and the *Understanding by Design Handbook*, the award-winning and highly successful material on curriculum.

The Association for Supervision of Curriculum Development (ASCD), publisher of the "Understanding by Design Handbook" co-authored by Grant Wiggins and registered owner of the trademark "Understanding by Design," has not authorized, approved, or sponsored this work and is in no way affiliated with Pearson or its products.

Cover Art: Terracotta sculpture of Ife king, c. 12th century
Taken from:
Prentice Hall, World History
By Elisabeth Gaynor Ellis & Anthony Esler
Copyright © 2011 by Pearson Education, Inc.
Published by Pearson Prentice Hall
Upper Saddle River, New Jersey 07458

Pearson Learning Solutions, 501 Boylston Street, Suite 900, Boston, MA 02116
A Pearson Education Company
www.pearsoned.com

Printed in the United States of America

3 16

000200010271276407

EG

ISBN 10: 1-256-46792-8
ISBN 13: 978-1-256-46792-2

Academic Reviewers

Africa
Barbara B. Brown, PhD
African Studies Center
Boston University
Boston, Massachusetts

Ancient World
Maud W. Gleason
Department of Classics
Stanford University
Stanford, California

Evelyn DeLong Mangie, PhD
Department of History
University of South Florida
Tampa, Florida

David Pilbeam
Henry Ford II
Professor of Human Evolution
Peabody Museum
Harvard University
Cambridge, Massachusetts

Chicano/a Studies
Shirlene Soto
Chicano/a Studies
California State University, Northridge
Northridge, California

East Asia
Mark Arlen Peterson
Coordinator of Asian Studies
Brigham Young University
Provo, Utah

Economics
Mark V. Siegler
Professor of Economics
California State University,
 Sacramento
Sacramento, California

Medieval Europe
Kathryn Reyerson
Department of History
University of Minnesota
Minneapolis, Minnesota

Modern Europe
Douglas R. Skopp, PhD
Distinguished University Teaching Pro-
 fessor of History, *emeritus* and Col-
 lege Historian
State University of New York at
 Plattsburgh
Plattsburgh, New York

Religion
Susan Douglass
Education Consultant
Falls Church, Virginia

Shabbir Mansuri
Founding Director
Institute on Religious
 and Civic Values (IRCV)
Fountain Valley, California

Gordon D. Newby
Middle Eastern and South Asian
 Studies
Emory University
Atlanta, Georgia

William L. Pitts, Jr.
Director of Graduate Studies
Religion Department
Baylor University
Waco, Texas

Benjamin Ravid
Near Eastern and Judaic Studies
Brandeis University
Waltham, Massachusetts

Russia and Eastern Europe
Bradley F. Abrams
Department of History
Columbia University
New York, New York

South Asia
Susan S. Wadley
Anthropology Department
Syracuse University
Syracuse, New York

Southeast Asia and the Pacific Rim
Barbara S. Gaerlan
Center for Southeast Asian Studies
University of California, Los Angeles
Los Angeles, California

Southwest Asia
Palmira Brummett
Department of History
University of Tennessee
Knoxville, Tennessee

Women's History
Lyn Reese, Director
Women in World History Curriculum
Berkeley, California

Teacher Reviewers

Jonathan Barnett
John Adams High School
Ozone Park, New York

Stephen Bullick
Mt. Lebanon School District
Pittsburgh, Pennsylvania

Elizabeth DeFreitas
East Islip HS 1
Islip Terrace, New York

Todd E. Gibson
Muncie Central High School
Muncie, Indiana

Mayrene A. Graef
Heritage High School
Newport News, Virginia

Sheila Hanley
James Madison High School
Brooklyn, New York

Geraldine L. Hayes
Louis D. Brandeis High School
New York, New York

Jennifer Herman
Winters Mill High School
Westminster, Maryland

Aimee Horowitz, JD
College of Staten Island High School
 for International Studies
Staten Island, New York

David Kenewell
Utica Community Schools
Sterling Heights, Michigan

Mary Oppegard
Oklahoma Baptist University
Shawnee, Oklahoma

Richard Renyer
Eleanor Roosevelt High School
Greenbelt, Maryland

James A. Weidemoyer
School District of Lancaster
Lancaster, Pennsylvania

The Concept Connector Solution

The Concept Connector Solution is an engaging way for you to connect with World History. As you study different civilizations, you will again and again encounter enduring Essential Questions and issues that people have wrestled with throughout history and that still challenge us today. The Concept Connector Solution will help you:

- **Connect to experience the past**
- **Connect to succeed today**
- **Connect to understand today and tomorrow**

Connect to Experience the Past

Experience the excitement of history for yourself. Video, audio, and digital interactivities make history come alive as you experience and interact with people and events of the past.

WITNESS HISTORY 🔊 AUDIO

Audio symbols throughout your text let you know when you can listen to primary sources, music, and sounds from the past on your Witness History Audio CD or Interactive Textbook.

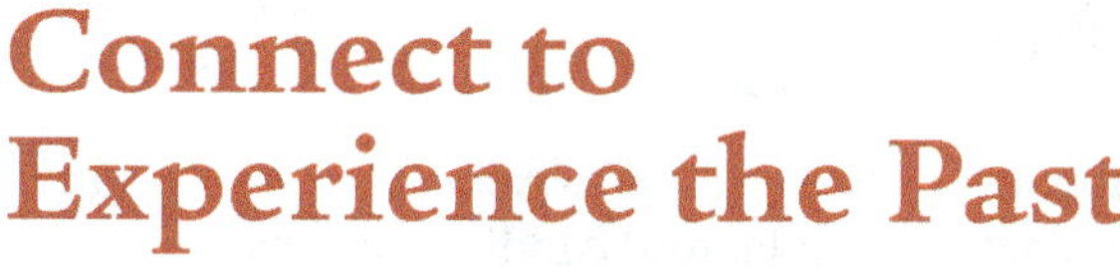

Use the Web Codes to go online for interactive animations, maps, timelines, and more. Listen to the people who were there and see dramatic images of the past.

Go Online at PHSchool.com

History Interactive

For: Interactive map, audio, and more
Visit: PHSchool.com
Web Code: nap-2941

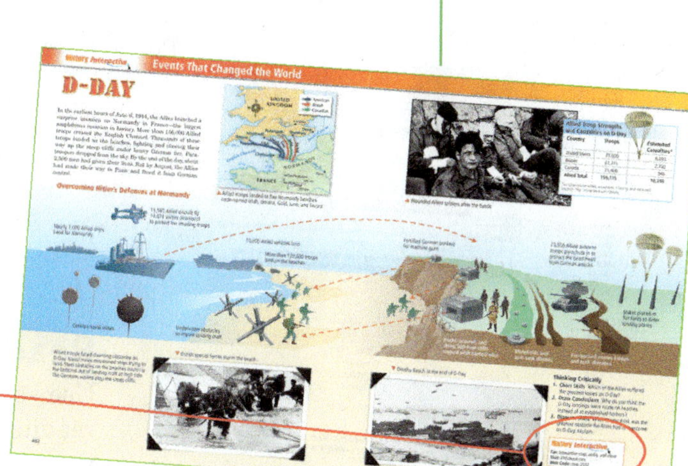

Connect to Succeed Today

Prentice Hall World History's Concept Connector Solution provides you with a variety of strategies and tools to help you truly understand the past, demonstrate your knowledge of world history, and succeed on quizzes, projects, and high-stakes tests.

21st Century Skills Handbook

The 21st Century Skills Handbook at the front of your textbook lets you brush up on important skills that you will use throughout your World History course and throughout your life. With 21st century knowledge and skills, you will succeed in school and succeed in life. Skills instruction to help you read, learn, and demonstrate your knowledge of world history includes:

- Reading Informational Texts
- Writing Handbook
- Geography Skills Handbook
- Critical Thinking About Texts, Visuals, and Media Sources
- Speaking and Listening

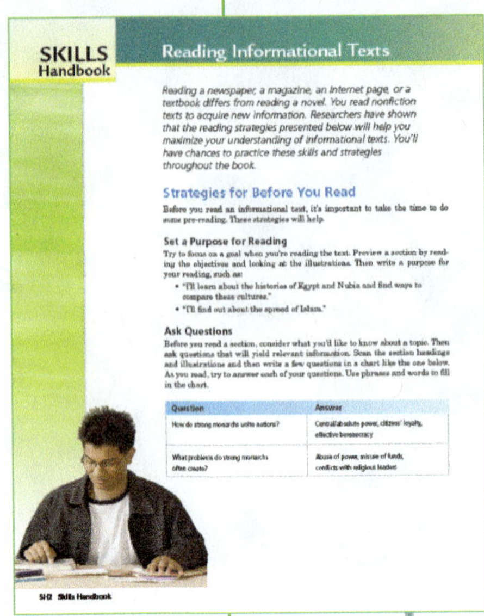

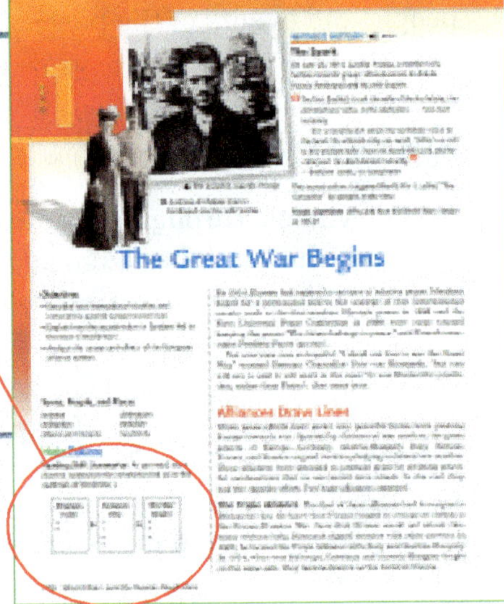

Note Taking

At the start of every section, you'll find suggestions on how to take notes using graphic organizers, timelines, and outlines. Use these to take notes in your own notebook, in your Reading and Note Taking Study Guide, or on the Note Taking Worksheets which you can download.

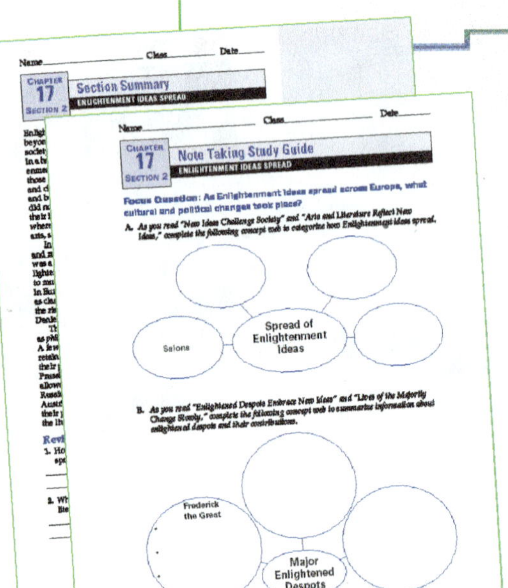

Reading and Note Taking Study Guide

Use your print or online study guide to develop vocabulary, practice reading and note taking skills, and record main ideas in different graphic formats. Use the easy-to-read summaries to help you learn the main ideas.

Progress Monitoring Online

Web codes at the end of every section take you to online quizzes with multiple choice questions on section content and vocabulary. At the end of each chapter, you'll find an online self-test on chapter content and a crossword puzzle to test your vocabulary mastery.

Go Online at PHSchool.com

Progress Monitoring *Online*
For: Self-test with vocabulary practice
Web Code: naa-2961

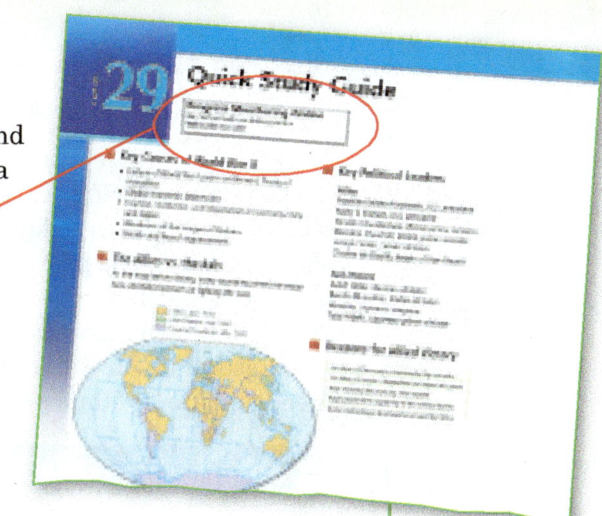

Quick Study Guides

At the end of each chapter, use the Quick Study Guide to make sure you have mastered the chapter contents and are ready for tests. Each Quick Study Guide organizes and reviews main ideas in a variety of formats, including:

- charts, graphs, and tables
- maps and illustrations
- graphic organizers and concept webs
- outlines and summaries
- timelines (Interactive timelines available online at PHSchool.com)

Document-Based Assessment

At the end of each chapter, the Document-Based Assessment contains several documents followed by multiple-choice questions that help you analyze documents and practice your map, graph, visual learning, and critical reading skills. A writing task helps you compare, contrast, and draw conclusions about the various documents.

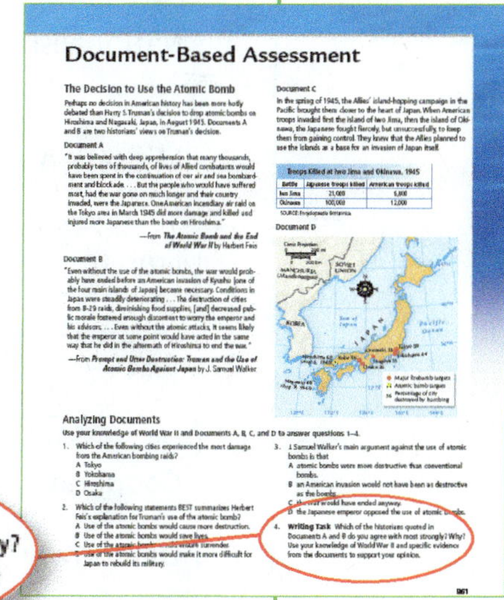

Connect to Understand Today and Tomorrow

Explore 18 enduring concepts and Essential Questions that people are still wrestling with today. In each chapter, you can explore how people and civilizations of the past dealt with these tough questions. You can record what you learn in your Concept Connector Journal, as you gradually build your own answers to these Essential Questions. By learning about the Essential Questions of world history, you will develop the knowledge needed to understand your world today and tomorrow.

Concept	Essential Question
Belief Systems	How do religions and belief systems affect society?
Geography's Impact	How do geography and people affect one another?
Conflict	When, if ever, should people go to war?
Cultural Diffusion	How does cultural diffusion occur?
Trade	What are the intended and unintended effects of trade?
Science and Technology	What are the benefits and costs of science and technology?
Political Systems	How do political systems rise, develop, and decline?
Impact of the Individual	How can an individual change the world?
Economic Systems	How should resources and wealth be distributed?
Revolution	Why do political revolutions occur?
Nationalism	How can nationalism be both a positive force and a negative force?
Migration	Why do large groups of people move from one place to another?
Empire	What factors allow empires to rise and cause them to fall?
Dictatorship	Why do people sometimes support dictators?
Genocide	Why do people sometimes commit the crime of genocide?
Cooperation	With whom should we cooperate and why?
Democracy	Under what conditions is democracy most likely to succeed?
Human Rights	How are human rights won or lost?

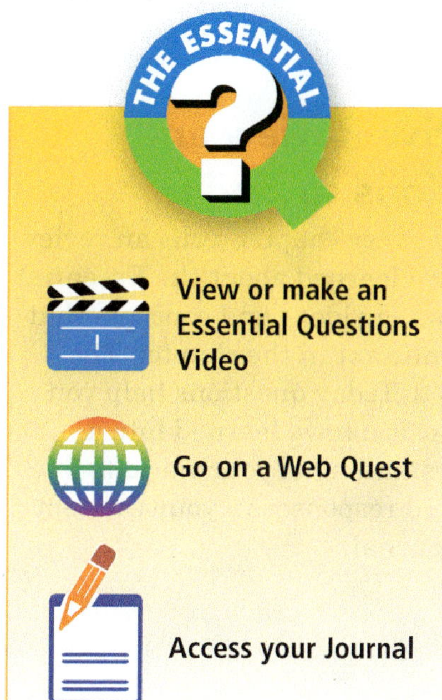

View or make an **Essential Questions Video**

Go on a Web Quest

Access your Journal

View Concept Connector Online

It's all here! As you start or finish a chapter, you can go online to find out which Essential Questions are most pertinent to the chapter. For each Essential Question, you can explore a full-page feature, engage in various interactivities, pursue a Web Quest, or make and submit your own video or digital presentation. You will record what you learn in your Concept Connector Journal. Finally, you will transfer your knowledge of the past into a better understanding of your world today and tomorrow.

Go Online at PHSchool.com
Web Code: nah-3008

Concept Connector Feature Pages

Each of the 18 Essential Questions is highlighted in a full-page feature. Suppose the question is "When, if ever, should people go to war?" The full-page feature in the chapter you are studying will show you how people of that time dealt with conflict. A timeline will give you ideas on why people of other times and places went to war or avoided war. Most importantly, you will transfer your knowledge and explore how people today are still dealing with conflict and war.

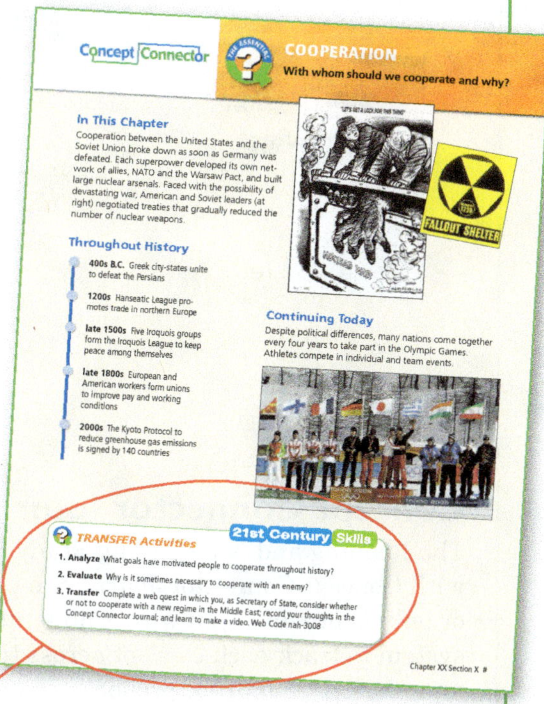

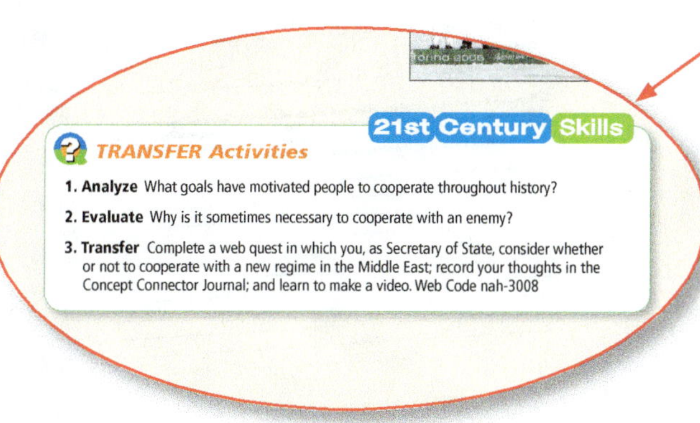

Transfer Activities and Student-Made Projects Online

After working with the full-page feature, you can go online to transfer what you have learned about the past into a clearer understanding of what's happening in your world today. You might go on a Web Quest, play a role-playing game, interact with digital primary resources, or make and submit your own video or digital presentation.

Cumulative Review and Connections to Today

At the end of every chapter, you can review what you have learned about the Essential Questions and big ideas and concepts that are most significant in the chapter. The Connections to Today questions help you transfer what you have learned into a better understanding of your world today. You can record responses in your Concept Connector Journal.

Concept Connector Journal

The Reading and Note Taking Study Guide with Concept Connector Journal, in print or online, provides you with a note taking system to track each concept across time and place. The Journal prepares you for Essential Question Web Quests, activities, and essays. The essays are just like thematic essays on high-stakes tests. In your essays, you will respond to enduring Essential Questions on big ideas and concepts by drawing on your knowledge of different historical eras and civilizations.

A message for you from Grant Wiggins

The Concept Connector Solution will help you gain understanding of big ideas—not just for "the test," but for life. Essential Questions are the foundation of the system. Each Essential Question is designed to guide your inquiry into important ideas of World History. How is an essential question different from any other question?

There are three basic kinds of questions that you face as a student.

1. **The factual question:** *When did World War II begin?* The answer is in the textbook.

2. **The opinion question:** *Should the United States have dropped the atomic bomb on Japan?* The answer is your personal response, based on your values and the facts that you know.

3. **The Essential Question:** *When, if ever, should people go to war?* This is clearly an important and timeless question that is not linked to only one chapter or era. You will build an answer to this question as you study history, do research, and complete a Web Quest. But, in some ways, you will never be finished answering the question because it is a question that every generation must face, from your great grandparents who lived through major wars in the twentieth century to you who will face the conflicts of the twenty-first century.

Essential Questions are challenging, but need not be overwhelming. Take a step-by-step approach.

Step 1. Don't become buried by a blizzard of facts. Look for the key ideas, themes, and trends implied by the question, around which facts are presented. What is the key issue or dispute? What matters to us in the present about this past event? Use the Concept Connector Journal to take notes not only on the facts, but also on ideas about the question that are sparked by those facts in the text. Think about the question throughout the course and note details related to it regularly in your journal.

Step 2. You often need to question the question itself. Consider the question above: *When, if ever, should people go to war?* Does *when* refer to events outside the country? For example, someone might say that we should go to war when our allies are invaded. Or does *when* refer to the politics inside our own country in terms of the decision-making process? Then, the answer to *when* might be that we should only go to war when all citizens strongly support the cause. The question refers to both meanings, and both should be carefully considered.

Step 3. Consider the alternatives, weigh the evidence and arguments, and reach a thoughtful conclusion—like a jury member. All important historical and political questions can be looked at from different points of view. The best historians carefully explore alternative narratives, theories, and arguments. They know all sides of an argument, and they can offer good reasons why their argument is a better explanation than the alternatives. By exploring Essential Questions in this way, you will build understandings that will have lasting value beyond the classroom—and be more thoughtful about issues that you will face in the future.

"I want you to really see the value of history! That's our aim here: to help you achieve useful and interesting insight. We want you to understand . . . the goal is understanding, not superficial knowledge." —Grant Wiggins, World History Program Consultant

▲ Catherine the Great

◄ Shuttles for the fly shuttle loom, introduced in 1733

▲ Sepoy fighter in India

▶ Nazi dictator Adolph Hitler with member of Nazi Youth, 1930s

▼ Mother Teresa

▼ Mongolian yurt with satellite dish

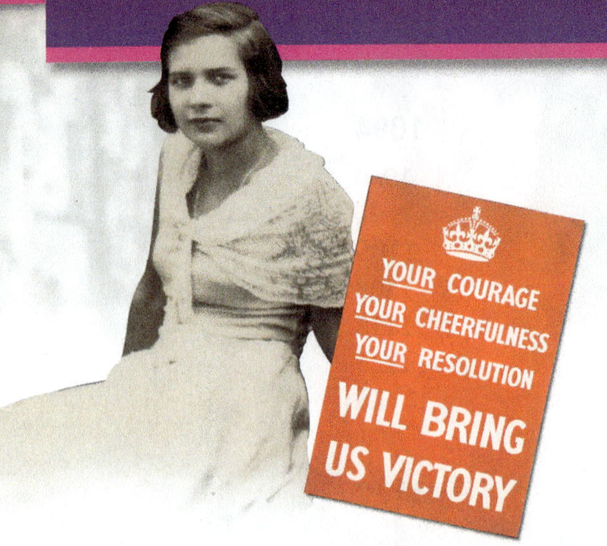

Witness History: Janina's War Story

"It was 10:30 in the morning and I was helping my mother and a servant girl with bags and baskets as they set out for the market. . . . Suddenly the high-pitch scream of diving planes caused everyone to freeze. . . . Countless explosions shook our house followed by the *rat-tat-tat* of strafing machine guns. We could only stare at each other in horror. Later reports would confirm that several German Stukas had screamed out of a blue sky and . . . dropped several bombs along the main street—and then returned to strafe the market. The carnage was terrible." 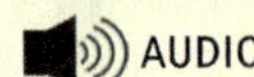 AUDIO

—Janina Sulkowska,
Krzemieniec, Poland,
September 12, 1939

WITNESS HISTORY AUDIO

Primary source audio accounts throughout the text bring the voices and sounds of history to life.*

*Available on Witness History Audio CD and online at PHSchool.com

NASA seal

Astronaut on the moon

History Interactive — Events That Changed the World

Audio, video, and animation-filled features help you explore major turning points in history.

Concept Connector

Explore World History's essential questions and go beyond the facts to connect with the issues that people are still wrestling with today.

Primary Sources

Full page excerpts allow you to relive history through eyewitness accounts and documents.

In-text Primary Sources

Gain insights as you read by reading the words of people who were there.

Matthew Perry arrives in Japan.

Traveler's Tales

View historic places through the eyes of those who traveled there.

COMPARING VIEWPOINTS

Explore issues by analyzing two opposing viewpoints.

HUMANITIES

Experience great literature and arts from around the world.

BIOGRAPHIES

Meet fascinating history makers.

Marie and
Pierre Curie

● INFOGRAPHICS

Photographs, maps, charts, illustrations, audio, and text help you understand the significance of important historical events and developments.

● INFOGRAPHIC

Taiping Rebellion

Taiping Rebellion leader Hong Xiuquan (at right), was a village schoolteacher. Inspired by religious visions and Christian missionaries, he wanted to establish a "Heavenly Kingdom of Peace"—the Taiping. Hong endorsed ideas that Chinese leaders considered radical, including community ownership of property and the equality of women and men.

◀ Chinese coins *c.*1850

● INFOGRAPHICS

▼ Battle scene of the
Taiping Rebellion

Julius Caesar

Document Based Assessment

Practice the art and science of a historian by analyzing an event by examining multiple historical documents, data, and images.

Cause and Effect

Diagrams help you see the short- and long-term causes and effects of history's most important events.

Charts and Graphs

Diagrams and data help you understand history through visuals.

Charts and Graphs

Charts and Graphs

Daily Life in the United States, 1920s

	1922	1929
Households with radios	60,000	10.25 million
Local telephone calls	36,831	61,034
Motion picture attendance per week	40 million	80 million
Dwellings with electricity	40%	68%

SOURCE: *Historical Statistics of the United States, Colonial Times to 1970*

Maps Geography Interactive

Interactive maps and Audio Guided Tours for each map with a Web code help you understand where history happened.

Maps Geography *Interactive*

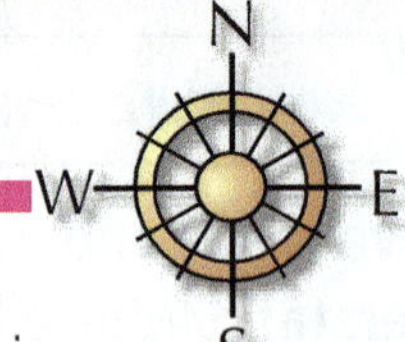

SKILLS Handbook

Contents

A series of handbooks provide skills instruction to help you read, learn, and demonstrate your knowledge of world history.

Reading Informational Texts

Writing Handbook

Geography Skills Handbook

Critical Thinking About Texts, Visuals, and Media Sources

Speaking and Listening

Reading Informational Texts

Reading a newspaper, a magazine, an Internet page, or a textbook differs from reading a novel. You read nonfiction texts to acquire new information. Researchers have shown that the reading strategies presented below will help you maximize your understanding of informational texts. You'll have chances to practice these skills and strategies throughout the book.

Strategies for Before You Read

Before you read an informational text, it's important to take the time to do some pre-reading. These strategies will help.

Set a Purpose for Reading

Try to focus on a goal when you're reading the text. Preview a section by reading the objectives and looking at the illustrations. Then write a purpose for your reading, such as:

- "I'll learn about the histories of Egypt and Nubia and find ways to compare these cultures."
- "I'll find out about the spread of Islam."

Ask Questions

Before you read a section, consider what you'd like to know about a topic. Then ask questions that will yield relevant information. Scan the section headings and illustrations and then write a few questions in a chart like the one below. As you read, try to answer each of your questions. Use phrases and words to fill in the chart.

Question	Answer
How do strong monarchs unite nations?	Central/absolute power, citizens' loyalty, effective bureaucracy
What problems do strong monarchs often create?	Abuse of power, misuse of funds, conflicts with religious leaders

Predict

Engage in the reading process by making predictions about what you are preparing to learn. Scan the section headings and the visuals. Then write a prediction, such as:

- "I will find out what caused feudalism in Europe to develop and later to disappear."

Keep your predictions in mind as you read—do they turn out to be accurate or do you need to revise them?

Use Prior Knowledge

Research shows that if you connect the new information in your reading to your prior knowledge, you'll be more likely to remember the new information. You'll also see the value of studying history if you see how it connects to the present. After previewing a section, create a chart like this one. Complete the chart as you read the section.

What I Know	What I Want to Know	What I Learned
Many people today are Calvinists or Lutherans.	How and when did these religions begin?	John Calvin and Martin Luther led people to start new Protestant churches during the sixteenth-century Reformation.

Strategies for During Reading

It's important to be an active reader. Use these strategies as you read an informational text.

Reread or Read Ahead

If you don't understand a certain passage, reread it to look for connections among the words and sentences. For example, look for cause-and-effect words that link ideas, or sequence words that show when events took place. Or, try reading ahead to see if the ideas are clarified later on. Once you find new clarifying information, return to the confusing text and read it again with the new information in mind.

Paraphrase

To paraphrase is to restate information in your own words, as in the example below. Paraphrasing is a good way to check your understanding of the reading. Think of it this way—if you can explain it to someone else, you understand it.

Original Paragraph	Paraphrase
When Ireland won independence in 1922, Britain retained control of six northern counties where there was a Protestant majority. Faced with widespread discrimination, Catholics demanded civil rights and the reunification of Ireland. Protestants wanted to remain part of Britain.	After Irish independence in 1922, Britain controlled six Protestant-dominated counties in the north. People in these counties divided along religious lines: Catholics called for both civil rights and reunification of the Irish nation; Protestants supported British control.

Summarize

Summarizing—a version of paraphrasing—can also help you confirm your understanding of the text. Summarizing focuses on restating the main ideas of a passage, as you can see in the example below. Include a few important details, such as the time period, to orient yourself or other readers to the text.

Original Paragraph	Summary
Ottoman expansion threatened the crumbling Byzantine empire. After several failed attempts to capture Constantinople, Muhammad II finally succeeded in 1453. Over the next 200 years, the Ottoman empire continued to expand.	The Byzantine empire gave way to the Ottoman empire around 1453, resulting in 200 years of Ottoman rule.

Identify Main Ideas and Details

A main idea is the most important point in a paragraph or section of text. Some main ideas are stated directly, but others are implied. You must determine these yourself by reading carefully. Pause occasionally to make sure you can identify the main idea.

Main idea

Europeans continued to seek new routes around or through the Americas. In 1513, the Spanish adventurer Vasco Núñez de Balboa, with the help of Native Americans, hacked a passage through the tropical forests of Panama to reach what he called the South Sea. In November 1529, Spanish nobleman Ferdinand Magellan sailed through a passage at the tip of South America. After a difficult journey filled with brutal storms, rushing tides, and unpredictable winds, Magellan's ships emerged into Balboa's South Sea, which Magellan renamed the Pacific—that is, peaceful—Ocean.

Main ideas are supported by details. Record main ideas and details in an outline format like the one shown here.

Main idea

Details

European Exploration in the Americas
I. Continued as Europeans sought new routes around or through the Americas
    A. Balboa and Native Americans found a passage across Panama.
    B. Balboa named the South Sea.
    C. Magellan found passage around tip of South America.
    D. Magellan reached the South Sea and renamed it the Pacific Ocean.

Vocabulary

Here are several strategies to help you understand the meaning of a word you do not recognize.

Use Context Clues You can often define an unfamiliar word with clues from the surrounding text. For example, in the sentence "Crusaders fought on and off for more than 200 years, and many died for their cause," the words *fought* and *died* are clues indicating that a Crusader was someone who fought wars. Context clues can be in the same sentence as the unfamiliar word or in nearby sentences or paragraphs.

Analyze Word Parts Use your knowledge of word parts to help you define unfamiliar words. Break the word into its parts—root, prefix, suffix. What do you know about these parts? For example, the suffixes *–ify* and *–ation* mean "make into" and "action or process." The word *desertify* means "turn into a desert." *Desertification* means "the process of turning into a desert."

Recognize Word Origins Another way to figure out the meaning of an unfamiliar word is to understand the word's origins. Use your knowledge of Greek or Latin roots, for example, to build meaning. The words *formation* and *reformation* contain the Latin root *form,* which means "shape." *Formation* is the shape in which something is arranged. *Reformation* is a change in the shape of an idea or institution.

Analyze the Text's Structure

Just as you organize a story about your weekend to highlight the most important parts, authors will organize their writing to stress their key ideas. Analyzing text structure can help you tap into this organization. In a social studies text, the author frequently uses one of the structures listed in the chart at right to organize information. Learn to identify structures in texts and you'll remember text information more effectively.

Analyze the Author's Purpose

Different reading materials are written with different goals, or purposes. For example, this book is written to teach you about world history. The technical manual that accompanies computer software is written to teach readers how to use the product. In a newspaper, some articles will be written to inform readers about news events, while editorials will be written to persuade readers to accept a particular view about those events.

An author's purpose influences not only how the material is presented but also how you read it. Thus you must identify the purpose, whether it is stated directly or merely suggested. If it is not directly stated, use clues in the text—such as opinion words in an editorial—to identify the author's purpose.

Structures for Organizing Information

Compare and Contrast Here, an author highlights similarities and differences between two or more ideas, cultures, processes, people, etc. Look for clue words such as *on the other hand* or *similarly*.

Sequence Here, an author recounts the order in which events occurred or steps were taken. History is often told in chronological sequence but can also involve flashbacks from later times to earlier times. Look for sequence words such as *initially*, *later*, and *ultimately*.

Cause and Effect Here, an author highlights the impact of one event on another or the effects of key events. Cause and effect is critical to understanding history because events in one time often strongly influence those in later times. Look for clue words such as *because, so,* or *as a result*.

Distinguish Between Facts and Opinions/Recognize Bias

It's important to read actively, especially when reading informational texts. Decide whether information is factual—which means it can be proven—or if it includes opinions or bias—that is, people's views or evaluations.

Anytime you read material that conveys opinions, such as an editorial, keep an eye out for author bias. This bias might be revealed in the use of emotionally charged words or faulty logic. For example, the newspaper editorial below includes factual statements (in blue) and opinion statements (in red). Underlined words are emotionally charged words—they'll get a rise out of people. Faulty logic (in green) may include circular reasoning that returns to its beginning and either/or arguments that ignore other possibilities.

Editorial

In 1993, the people of Brazil voted to keep their government a republic rather than revert to a monarchy. Voters chose between the two options in a special election. Clearly, anyone who favored monarchy was a reactionary dinosaur who maliciously wanted to undermine Brazil's progress. The republican format allows Brazilians to vote for their leaders directly. As a result, our brilliant leader Fernando Henrique Carlosa spearheaded life-saving reforms to Brazil's dying and antiquated economic system. In a monarchy, this would be impossible.

Identify Evidence

Read critically. Don't accept an author's conclusion automatically. Identify and evaluate the author's evidence. Does it justify the conclusion in quantity and content? An author may present facts to support a claim, but there may be more to the story than facts. For example, what evidence does the writer of the editorial above present to support the claim that a monarch could not help Brazil's economy? Perhaps a monarch would use his or her more centralized authority to achieve more sweeping and rapid reforms.

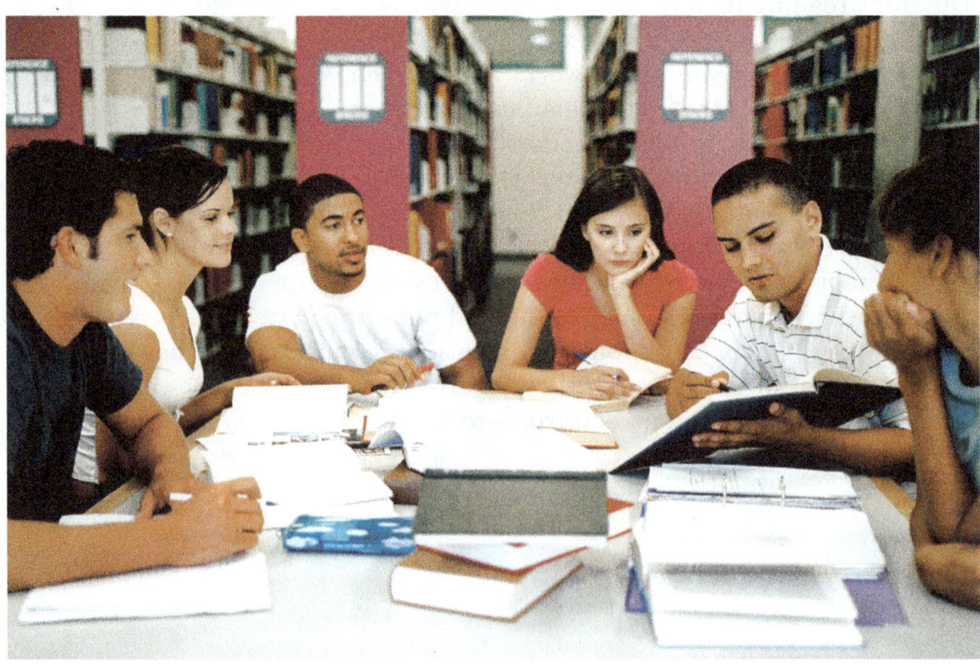

Evaluate Credibility

After you evaluate evidence, check an author's credentials. Consider his or her level of experience and expertise about the topic. Is he or she likely to be knowledgeable *and* objective about the topic? Evaluating credibility is especially important with sites you may visit on the Internet. Ask the following questions to determine if a site and its author are reliable.

- Who sponsors the Web site? Is it a respected organization, a discussion group of individuals, or a single person?

- What is the source of the Web site's information? Does the site list sources for facts and statements?

- Does the Web site creator include his or her name and credentials?

- Is the information on the Web site balanced and objective or biased to reflect only one point of view?

- Can you verify the Web site's information using two other sources, such as an encyclopedia or news agency?

- Is the information current? Is there a date on the Web site to show when it was created or last updated?

Strategies for After Reading

Evaluate Understanding

Evaluate how well you understand what you've read.

- Go back to the questions you asked yourself before reading. Try to answer each of them.
- Check the predictions you made and revise them if appropriate.
- Draw a conclusion about the author's evidence and credibility.
- Check meanings of unfamiliar words in the dictionary to confirm your definitions.

Recall Information

Before moving on to new material, you should be able to answer the following questions fully:

- What is the text about?
- What is the purpose of the text?
- How is the text structured?

You should also be able to place the new information in the context of your prior knowledge of the topic.

Writing Handbook

Writing is one of the most powerful communication tools you will use for the rest of your life. Research shows that writing about what you read actually helps you learn new information and ideas. A systematic approach to writing—including prewriting, drafting, revising, and proofing—can help you write better, whether you're writing an essay or a research paper.

Narrative Essay

Narrative writing tells a story, often about a personal experience. In social studies, this story might be a narrative essay that recounts how a recent or historical event affected you or your family.

1 Prewriting

Choose a topic. The focus of your essay should be an experience of significance to you. Use these ideas as a guide.

- **Look at photos** that show you and/or your family. Perhaps you attended a political rally or visited an important historical monument.
- **Scan the news** in print or through electronic media. Consider how current events relate to you and your family.
- **Brainstorm** with family or friends about recent events. How did you respond to these events? Jot down ideas like the ones below.

> Connections to History This Year
> — trip to art museum: Renaissance painters
> — historical books: World War II Africa
> — mock debate: Vietnam War

Consider audience and purpose.

- Keep your **audience's** knowledge and experience level in mind. Make sure you provide any necessary background information.
- Choose a **purpose** as well. If you want to entertain, include humorous details. To convey how the experience changed you, you might share more serious insights.

Gather details. Collect the facts and details you need to tell your story.

- **Research** any background about the historical event that readers might need to know about.
- **List details** about your own experience as it relates to the event.

❷ Drafting

Identify the climax, or most interesting part of your story. Then logically organize your story into a beginning, middle, and end. Narratives are usually told in chronological order.

Open strongly with an engaging sentence, such as the one below, that will catch your reader's attention.

Use sensory details, such as sights, sounds, or smells, to make the story vivid for readers. Describe people's actions and gestures. Pinpoint and describe locations.

Write a conclusion that sums up the significance of the event or situation you have experienced.

> I never expected to find myself arguing to support America's role in Vietnam. Our recent mock debate on the Vietnam War gave me new insight about this complex time in my nation's history. Research took me inside the perspective of those who supported the War and its goals. On the day of the debate, my hands were covered in sweat and my heart pounded as I stood to explain this currently unpopular position.

Strong opening engages the reader.

Insight or significance tells the reader what this event means to you.

Sensory details help the reader envision the experience.

❸ Revising

Add dialogue or description. Dialogue, or conveying a person's thoughts or feelings in his or her own words, can make a narrative more effective. Look for places where the emotions are especially intense. In the model, this might be when the writer's opponents respond to the debate position.

First Draft	Revised Original
At the debate, my hands were wet and my heart beat fast.	On the day of the debate, my hands were covered in sweat and my heart pounded.

Revise word choice. Replace general words with more specific, colorful ones. Choose vivid action verbs, precise adjectives, and specific nouns to convey your meaning. Look at the example above. Notice how much more effective the revised version is at conveying the experience.

Read your draft aloud. Listen for grammatical errors and statements that are unclear. Revise your sentences as necessary.

❹ Publishing and Presenting

Share by reading aloud. Highlight text you want to emphasize and then read your essay aloud to the class. Invite and respond to questions.

21st Century Skills

SKILLS HANDBOOK

Expository Writing

Expository writing explains ideas or information in detail. The strategies on these pages examine each of several expository writing styles.

 Prewriting

Choose a topic. In social studies, the focus of your writing might be explaining a historical process, comparing and contrasting cultural trends, explaining causes and effects of current events, or exploring problems societies have faced and the solutions they have sought. These ideas are a guide.

- **Ask questions.** For process writing, consider the question *how*. Think about *how* people in history have accomplished their goals, such as building a giant monument. Identify the steps and procedures involved.

> Question: How did great thinkers of the 1600s change people's view of the world?
>
> Answer: They developed the scientific method.

- **Create a compare/contrast grab bag.** With a small group, write on separate slips of paper examples from each category: ideas, cultures, or time periods. Mix the slips in a bag and choose two. Compare and contrast the two ideas, cultures, or time periods.

- **Interview** someone who made a major change in lifestyle, such as moving from one culture to another. Find out how and why the person did this. Understanding *why* is the basis of any cause and effect essay.

- **Take a mental walk.** Study a map and envision taking a tour of the region. Think about problems each area you visit might face, such as armed conflict, natural disaster, or governmental change. Choose a problem and suggest solutions for it.

Consider audience and purpose. Consider how much your readers know about the problem, comparison, event, or process you will address. Suit your writing to your audience's knowledge or plan to give explanations of unfamiliar terms and concepts.

Gather details. Collect the facts and details you need to write your essay.

Research the topic. Use books, the Internet, or interviews of local experts. List facts, details, and other evidence related to your topic. Also consider your personal experience. For example, you might know about a process from personal experience or have witnessed the effects of a historic legal decision.

Create a graphic organizer. For cause-and-effect or problem-solution essays, use a two-column chart. Process writing can be listed as a bulleted list of steps. A Venn diagram can help you compare and contrast.

World War I
- new weapons used: machine guns, poison gas, submarines
- 8.5 million military deaths

fought by two powerful alliances
- began in Europe, then spread

World War II
- new weapon used: atomic bomb
- 20 million military deaths

Identify causes and effects. List possible explanations for events. Remember that many events result from multiple causes. Identify effects both large and small. Note that some events may have effects that in turn cause other events. Look for causes and effects in all your expository essays. For example, in a process explanation, one step often causes the next.

Fine-tune your ideas. For a problem-solution essay, decide what you will suggest as a solution. Keep your solution narrow to be achievable in cost, effort, and timing. Make sure no one has tried it before, or if it has been tried and it failed, address the failure.

❷ Drafting

Match structure to purpose. Typically, process writing and cause-and-effect writing are written in sequence order. Problem-solution essays benefit from block organization, which presents the entire problem and proposes a solution. For compare/contrast essays, you can organize by subject or by point.

> By subject: Discuss the events and outcomes of World War I, and then compare and contrast these with those of World War II.
> By point: Introduce a category, such as use of new weapons. Relate both wars to this category, comparing or contrasting them along the way.

Give background. To discuss events from history, first orient the reader to time and place. Choose the important facts but don't overwhelm the reader with detail. If you need to, return to prewriting to narrow your topic further.

Elaborate for interest and emphasis. Give details about each point in your essay. For example, add facts that make the link between events so that a cause-and-effect relationship is clear. Also, readers will support proposed solutions more if your details clearly show how these solutions will solve the stated problem. Use facts and human experiences to make your essay vivid.

Connect to today. Even when you write about historical events, you may find links to today. Explore these links in your essay.

> Mexico's population underwent great change during the mid-twentieth century. Population shifted from rural areas to urban areas. The nation's society went from largely agricultural to largely industrial and urban. Urban populations exploded, with Mexico City alone growing from 1.5 million people in 1940 to nearly 20 million later in the century. These changes resulted from several causes.
>
> First, land reform begun in the 1930s failed. The millions of acres redistributed by then–President Lázaro Cárdenas proved arid and unproductive. Second, the rural population was growing rapidly. This placed increased demands on the land. The land became even more depleted and unproductive. Finally, several Mexican governments in turn shifted their attention from the small rural peasant farmer toward larger scale farming operations.
>
> Mexico's shifting population and changing economic patterns yielded new problems for its leaders by late in the twentieth century.

Identify the topic to orient readers.

Chronological order walks readers through the cause-effect sequence.

Elaboration supports the relationship you are highlighting.

Connection to today tells readers why this matters to them.

③ Revising

Add transition words. Make cause-and-effect relationships clear with words such as *because, as a result,* and *so.* To compare or contrast ideas, use linking words, such as *similarly, both, equally* or *in contrast, instead, yet.* Use words such as *first, second, next,* and *finally* to help readers follow steps in a process. Look at the following examples. In the revised version, a reader knows the correct order in which to perform the steps.

First Draft	Revised
Scientists form an educated guess called a hypothesis. They test that hypothesis with an experiment.	<u>Next</u>, scientists form an educated guess called a hypothesis. <u>Then</u>, they test that hypothesis with an experiment.

Remember purpose. Shape your draft so that it answers the question or thesis you began with. For a problem-solution essay—in which your purpose is to sell your solution—that means anticipating opposing arguments and responding to them. For cause-and-effect, you want to stress the way one event leads to the next. Always tell readers *why* they should care about your topic.

Review organization. Confirm that your ideas flow in a logical order. Write main points on index cards. Reorganize these until you are satisfied that the order best strengthens your essay.

Add details. Make sure you haven't left out any steps in your essay, and don't assume readers will make the connections. For example, you might forget to state explicitly that a process must be repeated in order to produce accurate results. Add more background if necessary for clarity.

Revise sentences and words. Look at your sentence length. Vary it to include both short and long sentences. Then scan for vague words, such as *good.* Replace them with specific and vibrant words, such as *effective.* Use technical terms only when necessary, and then define them.

Peer review. Ask a peer to read your draft. Is it clear? Can he or she follow your ideas? Revise areas of confusion.

④ Publishing and Presenting

Collect in a class manual. Contribute your process explanation to a class manual of *History How-To's.*

Submit to a library. Find a specialized library, such as a presidential library. Mail your essay to the library's publications or public relations department.

Seek publication. If your historical events or issues are local, seek publication in a local historical magazine or contact a historical society. You might speak to their members.

Mail to an advocacy group. Find a local, national, or international organization that is concerned with your topic. Send them your essay and ask for comments on its ideas. Make sure to include a self-addressed stamped envelope and a note explaining your essay and offering thanks for its review.

Research Writing

1 Prewriting

Choose a topic. Often, a teacher will assign your research topic. You may have flexibility in choosing your focus or you may have the opportunity to completely define your topic. These ideas are a guide.

- **Catalog scan.** Using a card or electronic catalog, search for topics that interest you. When a title looks promising, find the book on the shelves. Libraries usually use the Dewey Decimal Classification system to group research materials by subject, so you should find other books on similar subjects nearby. You can use them all to decide on your final topic.

- **Notes review.** Review your social studies notes from the last month or so. Jot down topics that you found interesting. Then repeat the process with your other classes. For example, you might find a starting point for research into the Scientific Revolution from a math theorem.

- **Social studies categories game.** With a group, brainstorm categories in social studies. For example, you might list key world leaders or important wars. Within each category, take turns adding subtopics. The chart below looks at different transportation topics.

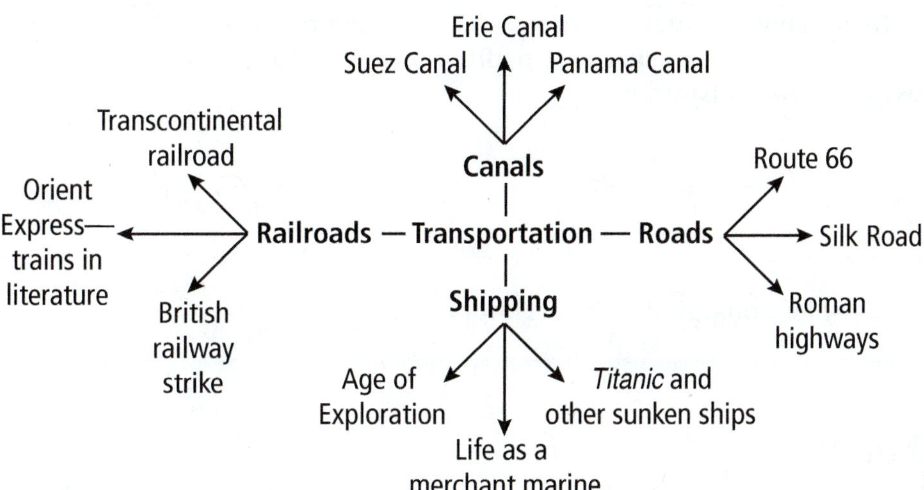

You can use sources such as newspapers to get ideas.

Analyze the audience. Your research and your paper should be strongly influenced by the audience. How much will readers know about this topic and how much will you have to teach them?

Gather details. Collect the facts and details you need to write your paper. Use resources beyond the typical history books. Look at nonfiction books such as memoirs or collections of letters. Also look at magazine and newspaper articles. Consider news magazines, as well as those focused on topics such as history or travel. You may find interviews with experts on your topic or travel articles about a region that interests you. Search the Internet, starting with online encyclopedias, news organizations, and history Web sites.

Organize evidence and ideas. Use note cards to record information and to help you organize your thoughts. Start with a general thesis statement in mind. Then begin reading and taking notes. Write a heading at the top of each note card to group it under a subtopic. Note a number or title to identify the information source. In the examples below, the number 3 is used. Use the same number for an additional source card containing the bibliographic information you will need.

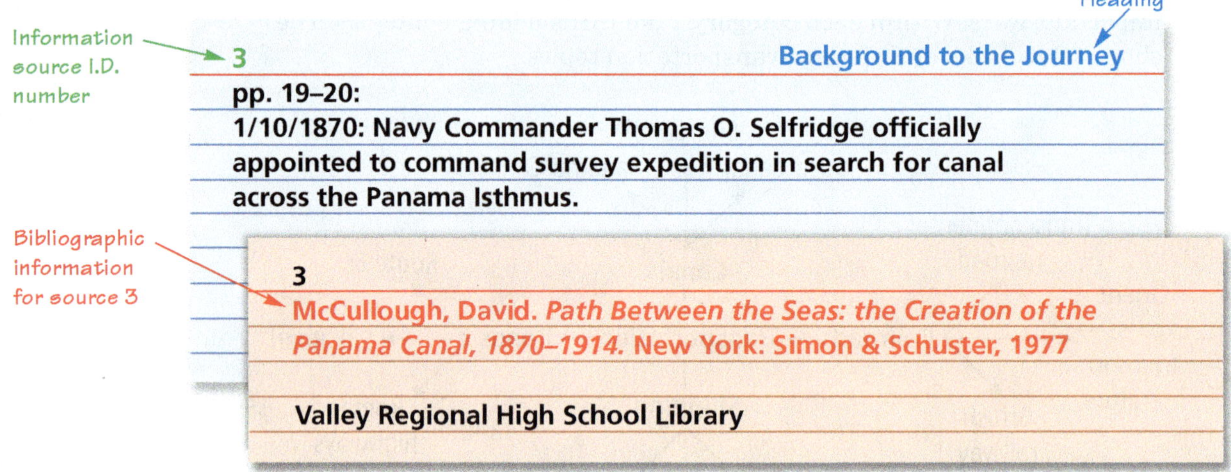

2 Drafting

Fine-tune your thesis. Review your notes to find relationships between ideas. Shape a thesis that is supported by the majority of your information, then check that it is narrow enough to address thoroughly in the allotted time and space. Remember, you can fine-tune your thesis further as you draft or even when you revise.

Organize to fit your purpose. Do you want to persuade readers of a particular position about your topic, compare and contrast aspects of the topic, or show a cause-and-effect relationship? Organize appropriately—for example, by looking at parts of a whole to examine events leading to building and completing the Panama Canal.

Make an outline. Create an outline in which you identify each topic and subtopic in a single phrase. You can then turn these phrases into sentences and later into the topic sentences of your draft paragraphs. Study the example at the top of the next page to see how to do this well.

Write by paragraph. Write an introduction, at least three body paragraphs, and a conclusion. Address a subtopic of your main topic in each body paragraph. Support all your statements with the facts and details you gathered.

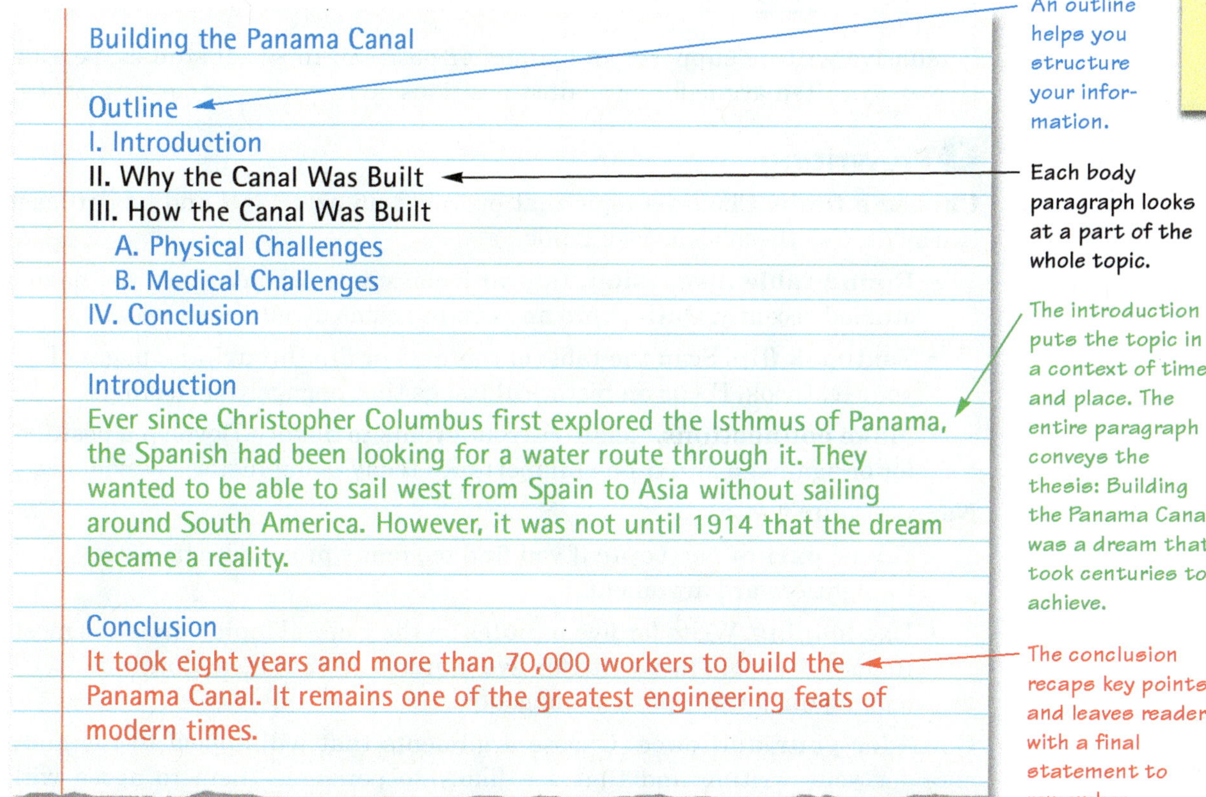

An outline helps you structure your information.

Each body paragraph looks at a part of the whole topic.

The introduction puts the topic in a context of time and place. The entire paragraph conveys the thesis: Building the Panama Canal was a dream that took centuries to achieve.

The conclusion recaps key points and leaves readers with a final statement to remember.

3 Revising

Add detail. Mark points where more details would strengthen your statements. Look at the following examples. Notice the added details in the revised version. When adding facts, make certain that they are accurate.

First Draft	Revised
The Navy excursion was a huge undertaking. Supplies were gathered to support the team for many months.	The Navy excursion was a huge undertaking. Supplies were gathered to support the team for many months, including more than 600 pairs of shoes, 100 miles of telegraph wire, 2,500 pounds of coffee, and 10,000 pounds of bread! (McCullough 20).

Make the connection for readers. Help readers find their way through your ideas. First, check that your body paragraphs and the information within them flow in a logical sequence. If they do not, revise to correct this. Then add transition words to link ideas and paragraphs.

Give credit. Check that you have used your own words or given proper credit for borrowed words. You can give credit easily with parenthetical notes. These include the author's last name and the relevant page number from the source. For example, you could cite the note card here as (McCullough 19–20).

4 Publishing and Presenting

Plan a conference. Gather a group of classmates and present your research projects. You may each wish to create visual materials to accompany your presentations. After you share your papers, hold a question and answer session.

Persuasive Essay

Persuasive writing supports an opinion or position. In social studies, persuasive essays often argue for or against positions on historical or current issues.

 Prewriting

Choose a topic. Choose a topic that provokes an argument and has at least two sides. Use these ideas as a guide.

- **Round-table discussion.** Talk with classmates about issues you have studied recently. Outline pro and con positions about these issues.
- **Textbook flip.** Scan the table of contents or flip through the pages of your textbook. Focus on historical issues that engage your feelings.
- **Make connections.** Relate current events to history. Develop a position for or against a situation of importance today using historical evidence.

Narrow your topic.

- **Cover part of the topic** if you find too many pros and cons for a straightforward argument.
- **Use looping.** Write for five minutes on the general topic. Circle the most important idea. Then write for five minutes on that idea. Continue looping until the topic is manageable.

Consider your audience. Choose arguments that will appeal to the audience for your writing and that are likely to persuade them to agree with your views.

Gather evidence. Collect the evidence to support your position convincingly.

- **Identify pros and cons.** Use a graphic organizer like the one below to list points on both sides of the issue.

Position: Education is key to improving life in developing nations.	
Pro	**Con**
• Education allows people to get higher-paying jobs. • With more money, people can help boost the economy. • With education, people can better handle disease and disaster.	• Building new schools may cost more than the government has available for education. • Some countries have other large problems to handle, such as serious diseases.

- **Interview** adults who have lived or worked in developing nations. What do they think? Ask them for reasons to support their views.
- **Research** to get your facts straight. Read articles or books about life in developing nations.

 Drafting

State your thesis. Clearly state your position, as in this example:

> Education is the key to revitalizing developing nations. Once many people are educated, many other problems can be solved.

Use your introduction to provide a context for the issue. Tell your readers when and why the issue arose, and identify the important people involved.

Sequence your arguments. Open or close with your strongest argument. If you close with the strongest argument, open with the second-best argument.

Acknowledge opposition. State, and then refute, opposing arguments.

Use facts and details. Include quotations, statistics, or comparisons to build your case. Include personal experiences or reactions to the topic, such as those a family member might have shared when interviewed.

Write a conclusion that restates your thesis and closes with a strong, compelling argument.

> Many people living in developing nations want to improve life in their countries. They want the people to have everything they need, such as food and clean water, electricity, medicines, and even fun items like televisions and bicycles. Education is the key to revitalizing developing nations. Once many people are educated, many other problems can be solved.
>
> Education allows people to get higher-paying jobs. With more money, people can help boost the economy. As well, education is an added tool people can use to deal with other problems. It's true that building new schools costs a lot. And in some places, people face many other major problems such as serious diseases. But education will only help them handle these issues....

Background orients readers.

Thesis identifies your main argument.

Supporting argument clarifies your thesis.

Opposing argument, noted and refuted, adds to your position.

③ Revising

Add information. Extra details can generate interest in your topic. For example, add a quotation from a news article that assesses the role of education in a developing nation or a poor area.

Review arguments. Make sure your arguments are logically sound and clearly developed. Avoid faulty logic such as circular reasoning (arguing a point by merely restating it differently). Evidence is the best way to support your points. Look at the following examples. Notice how much more effectively the revised version supports the argument.

First Draft	Revised
Education allows people to make more money, which is helpful.	Education allows people to get higher-paying jobs. With more money, people can help boost the economy.

Use transition words to guide readers through your ideas.

- To show contrast: *however, although, despite*
- To point out a reason: *since, because, if*
- To signal conclusion: *therefore, consequently, so, then*

④ Publishing and Presenting

Persuasive Speech. Many persuasive essays are delivered orally. Prepare your essay as a speech, highlighting words for emphasis and adding changes in tone, volume, or speed.

Biographical Writing

 **Prewriting**

Choose a topic. Biographical writing tells the story of a real person's life. For social studies, you should focus on the life of an important historical or current figure. The following ideas are a guide.

- **Find a hero.** Think about a person from history whom you admire—for example, a world leader, a great thinker, or an inventor. Remember to choose someone about whom information is easily available.

- **Name game.** On an index card, write the name of a person in the news today. Write a sentence or phrase explaining what makes this person interesting to you, as on the examples below. With a group, shuffle all the cards and then take turns drawing topics. If you like, trade your topic with a friend.

Martin Luther	Wangari Maathai
He thought the Bible—not the pope—should guide a person's actions.	She thinks preserving the environment can improve people's lives.

- **Table of Contents scan.** Your history book lists the short biographies that are included in the text. Scan this listing in the book's Table of Contents for three possible subjects. Read the biography of each subject before you make a final choice.

Focus your approach. Decide how you want to approach your subject. For example, you could emphasize the person's influence on historical events, or you could show how personal experiences affected his or her achievements.

Gather details. Collect the facts and details you need to write your paper. Use the research methods for gathering information explained on page SH14. In particular, check biographical source materials in the reference section of the library.

Isolate episodes. As you learn about your subject, focus on the particular episodes that seem to be most important. Then learn more about the events surrounding these episodes and take notes on them, as in the example below.

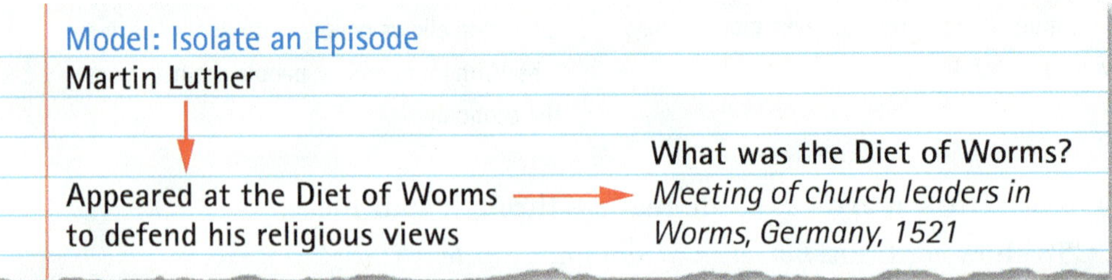

Focus your fact-gathering. Your goal is to bring this person's life to readers—to share facts and opinions relating to that life and respond to them with your own conclusions. As you determine the main points you wish to make about this person, find facts to support your assertions. Make sure to give enough factual background for readers to appreciate your points.

Drafting

Focus your essay. In a single paper, you will probably need to focus on an aspect of your subject's life or on a quick overview of major events in that life.

Organize important events. Choose the events you will discuss, and then order them in a logical way. Biographies are usually organized chronologically.

Reveal your subject. Include direct description of your subject, which allows you to convey information quickly. Balance this with quotations or examples of the person's actions, which lend color and authenticity to your essay.

Open strongly. Get readers' attention immediately with an engaging quotation, an interesting fact about your subject, or an anecdote that sets the tone.

> "Here I stand, I cannot do otherwise." Martin Luther spoke these words at the Diet of Worms in 1521. The Diet, a conference of religious leaders, had summoned Luther to explain his controversial religious views.
>
> Martin Luther was born in 1483 into a German family. Raised a Catholic, Luther entered a monastery after experiencing a religious calling. He became both devout and committed to strict observance. Over time, this approach brought him into conflict with the Church. For example, Luther felt that the Catholic Church should not sell indulgences, or guarantees of good grace after death.
>
> Luther developed new ideas about the Church and its leadership. At the core were his beliefs that people should have a direct relationship to the Bible and that the Church and the pope stood in the way of this. In his 95 Theses, Luther called for widespread reforms in the Catholic Church and later in the German government. Because his views were contrary to accepted beliefs, Luther was called in front of the Diet of Worms. He refused to back down, so the Church expelled him in 1521.

A quote gets the readers' attention and quickly establishes the subject's personality.

The biography will focus on this aspect of Luther's life.

Chronological organization helps readers see the development of Luther's ideas.

The conclusion brings the biography back to its initial anecdote.

 **Revising**

Examine word choice. Bring your subject to life with vivid adjectives, specific verbs, and precise nouns. Then link your chronological organization with words that show sequence. The draft above uses dates as well as phrases such as *over time* to show the sequence of Luther's life and religious growth.

Make connections for readers. For example, the sentence below connects Luther's life to current times by linking it to the modern Lutheran Church.

> Although Luther himself never called for a new church, today the Protestant branch named for him claims more than 5 million members in America alone.

Give credit. Cite sources for any facts, statistics, or quotations you include. If several pieces of information in a paragraph come from a single source, you may cite the source once at the end of the paragraph. Always check with your teacher for specific bibliographic requirements.

 **Publishing and Presenting**

Create a biographical character. Use what you've learned about this person's life to appear as that person. If you wish, wear a costume. Explain who you are and what is most important to you. Ask and answer questions.

Writing for Assessment

Assessment writing differs from all other writing that you do. You have fewer choices as a writer, and you almost always face a time limit. In social studies, you'll need to write both short answers and extended responses for tests. While these contrast in some ways, they share many requirements.

❶ Prewriting

Choose a topic. Short-answer questions seldom offer a topic choice. For extended response, however, you may have a choice of more than one question. Use the following strategies to help you navigate that choice.

- **Examine the question.** To choose a question you can answer effectively, analyze what each question is asking. Use key words such as those listed below to help you choose topics and respond to short-answer questions in which the topic is given.

Key Words	What You Need in an Answer
Explain	Give a clear, complete account of how something works or why something happened.
Compare/Contrast	Show how two or more things are alike and different.
Define	Give examples to explain meaning.
Argue, Convince, Support, Persuade	Take a position on an issue and present strong reasons to support your side of the issue.
Summarize	Provide the most important elements of a subject.
Evaluate/Judge	Assign a value or explain an opinion.
Interpret	Support a thesis with examples from the text.

Notice in the examples below that the key words are underlined:

Short answer: <u>Describe</u> one way that Chief Joseph showed his <u>military expertise</u>.

Extended response: According to the author of this article, Chief Joseph was both a <u>peace chief</u> and a <u>military genius</u>. Use information from the article to <u>support this conclusion</u>.

- **Plot your answer.** After choosing a question, quickly plot the answer in your mind. Do you have the information to answer this question? If the answer is *no*, try another question.

Measure your time. Your goal is to show the instructor that you've mastered the material. To stay focused on this goal, divide your time: one-quarter on prewriting; half on drafting; one-quarter on revising. For short-answer questions, determine how much of the overall test time you can spend on each question. Don't spend more than that.

Gather details. Organize the facts and details you need to write your answer. For short-answer questions, this usually involves identifying exactly what information is required.

Use a graphic organizer. For extended response, divide your topic into subtopics that fit the type of question. Jot down facts and details for each. For the question on Chief Joseph, the following organizer would be effective:

Chief Joseph of the Nez Percé
Peace Chief
- traded peacefully with white settlers (1)
- reluctantly went to war (2)
- famous speech, "I will fight no more forever." (3)

Military Genius
- won battles with fewer warriors than opposing troops had (a)
- avoided capture for many months (b)
- led his people more than 1,000 miles (c)
- knew when to surrender for the good of his people (c)

2 Drafting

Choose an organization that fits the question. With a short-answer question, write one to three complete sentences. With extended response, you'll need more elaborate organization. For the question on Chief Joseph, organize your points by importance within each subtopic. For a summary or explanation, use chronological order. For compare/contrast, present similarities first, then differences.

Open and close strongly. Start your answer by restating the question or using its language to state your position. This helps you focus and shows the instructor that you understand the question. Finish with a strong conclusion that restates your position. For short answer, include some language from the question in your response.

One way that Chief Joseph showed his military expertise was by defeating U.S. Army troops despite having fewer warriors than they had.

Support your ideas. Each paragraph should directly or indirectly support your main idea. Choose facts that build a cohesive argument. The numbered sentences in the draft below show how this writer organized support.

Chief Joseph was both a peace chief and a military genius. He was a peace chief because he traded peacefully with white settlers for many years. (1) He went to war reluctantly after the government ordered his people to move to a reservation. (2) When he finally surrendered, he said in a famous speech, "I will fight no more forever." (3) Chief Joseph was also a military genius. He fought off U.S. Army forces with fewer warriors than they had, (a) and he avoided capture for many months. (b) He led his people more than 1,000 miles (c) before he made the decision to surrender. Chief Joseph will long be remembered for his dual roles as peace chief and military genius.

The opening restates the question and presents the main idea.

The writer uses information from the graphic organizer, in order of importance.

The writer supports the second subtopic.

The conclusion recaps the main idea and again uses the question's language.

❸ Revising

Examine word choice. Replace general words with specific words. Add transitions where these improve clarity. Read the following examples. The revised version shows the relative importance of the writer's supporting evidence.

First Draft	Revised
Chief Joseph was both a peace chief and a military genius. He was a peace chief because he traded peacefully with white settlers for many years. He went to war reluctantly...	Chief Joseph was both a peace chief and a military genius. He was a peace chief for several reasons. First, he traded peacefully with white settlers for many years. Second, he went to war reluctantly...

Check organization. Make sure your introduction includes a main idea and defines subtopics. Review each paragraph for a single main idea. Check that your conclusion summarizes the information you've presented.

❹ Publishing and Presenting

Edit and proof. Check spelling, grammar, and mechanics. Make sure that tenses match, that subjects agree with verbs, and that sentences are not too long. Finally, confirm that you have responded to all the questions you were asked to answer.

Use this chart, or rubric, to evaluate your writing.

SAT

SCORE OF 6	SCORE OF 3
An essay in this category is **outstanding**, demonstrating **clear and consistent mastery**, although it may have a few minor errors. A typical essay • effectively and insightfully develops a point of view on the issue and demonstrates outstanding critical thinking, using clearly appropriate examples, reasons, and other evidence to support its position • is well organized and clearly focused, demonstrating clear coherence and smooth progression of ideas • exhibits skillful use of language, using a varied, accurate, and apt vocabulary • demonstrates meaningful variety in sentence structure • is free of most errors in grammar, usage, and mechanics	An essay in this category is **inadequate**, but demonstrates **developing mastery**, and is marked by **one or more** of the following weaknesses: • develops a point of view on the issue, demonstrating some critical thinking, but may do so inconsistently or use inadequate examples, reasons, or other evidence to support its position • is limited in its organization or focus, but may demonstrate some lapses in coherence or progression of ideas • displays developing facility in the use of language, but sometimes uses weak vocabulary or inappropriate word choice • lacks variety or demonstrates problems in sentence structure • contains an accumulation of errors in grammar, usage, and mechanics
SCORE OF 5	SCORE OF 2
An essay in this category is **effective**, demonstrating **reasonably consistent mastery**, although it will have occasional errors or lapses in quality. A typical essay • effectively develops a point of view on the issue and demonstrates strong critical thinking, generally using appropriate examples, reasons, and other evidence to support its position • is well organized and focused, demonstrating coherence and progression of ideas • exhibits facility in the use of language, using appropriate vocabulary • demonstrates variety in sentence structure • is generally free of most errors in grammar, usage, and mechanics	An essay in this category is **seriously limited**, demonstrating **little mastery**, and is flawed by **one or more** of the following weaknesses: • develops a point of view on the issue that is vague or seriously limited, demonstrating weak critical thinking, providing inappropriate or insufficient examples, reasons, or other evidence to support its position • is poorly organized and/or focused, or demonstrates serious problems with coherence or progression of ideas • displays very little facility in the use of language, using very limited vocabulary or incorrect word choice • demonstrates frequent problems in sentence structure • contains errors in grammar, usage, and mechanics so serious that meaning is somewhat obscured
SCORE OF 4	SCORE OF 1
An essay in this category is **competent**, demonstrating **adequate mastery**, although it will have lapses in quality. A typical essay • develops a point of view on the issue and demonstrates competent critical thinking, using adequate examples, reasons, and other evidence to support its position • is generally organized and focused, demonstrating some coherence and progression of ideas • exhibits adequate but inconsistent facility in the use of language, using generally appropriate vocabulary • demonstrates some variety in sentence structure • has some errors in grammar, usage, and mechanics	An essay in this category is **fundamentally lacking**, demonstrating **very little** or **no mastery**, and is severely flawed by one or more of the following weaknesses: • develops no viable point of view on the issue, or provides little or no evidence to support its position • is disorganized or unfocused, resulting in a disjointed or incoherent essay • displays fundamental errors in vocabulary • demonstrates severe flaws in sentence structure • contains pervasive errors in grammar, usage, or mechanics that persistently interfere with meaning
	SCORE OF 0 Essays not written on the essay assignment will receive a score of zero.

Geography Skills Handbook

Analyze the Five Themes of Geography

The five themes of geography are tools you can use to analyze geographic information given in photographs, charts, maps, and text.

- **Location** answers the question "Where is it?" The answer might be an absolute location, such as 167 River Lane, or a relative location, such as six miles west of Mill City.

- **Regions** are areas that share at least one common feature. Climate, culture, and government are features that can be used to define a region.

- **Place** identifies natural and human features that make a place different from other places. Landforms, climate, plants, animals, people, culture, and languages are features that can be used to identify a specific place.

- **Movement** answers the question "How do people, goods, and ideas move from place to place?"

- **Human-Environment Interaction** focuses on the relationship between people and the environment. Humans often make changes to the environment, and the environment often affects how humans live.

Use the photograph and steps that follow to analyze the five themes of geography.

The Nile River in Egypt

Read supporting information such as a caption or key. Use this information and your own knowledge of the world to determine location and region.

Analyze the content. Consider the elements of the visual or text to develop ideas about region, place, movement, and human-environment interaction.

Practice and Apply the Skill

Use the photograph above to answer the following questions:

1. How might you describe the relative location of the fields of crops?

2. What is the climate region shown here? How do you know?

3. What elements in the scene identify this specific place?

4. How do you think people, goods, and ideas move to and from this place?

5. How have the people of this area changed their environment?

Understand Latitude and Longitude

Geographers divide the globe along imaginary horizontal lines called parallels of latitude. They measure these parallels in degrees (°) north or south of the Equator, which itself is a line of latitude. Geographers also divide the globe along imaginary vertical lines called meridians of longitude. They measure these meridians in degrees east or west of the Prime Meridian, a line of longitude running through Greenwich, England. All meridians intersect at the North Pole and the South Pole. Together, the lines of latitude and longitude form a grid that gives an absolute location for every place on Earth. Use the globes and the steps that follow to understand latitude and longitude.

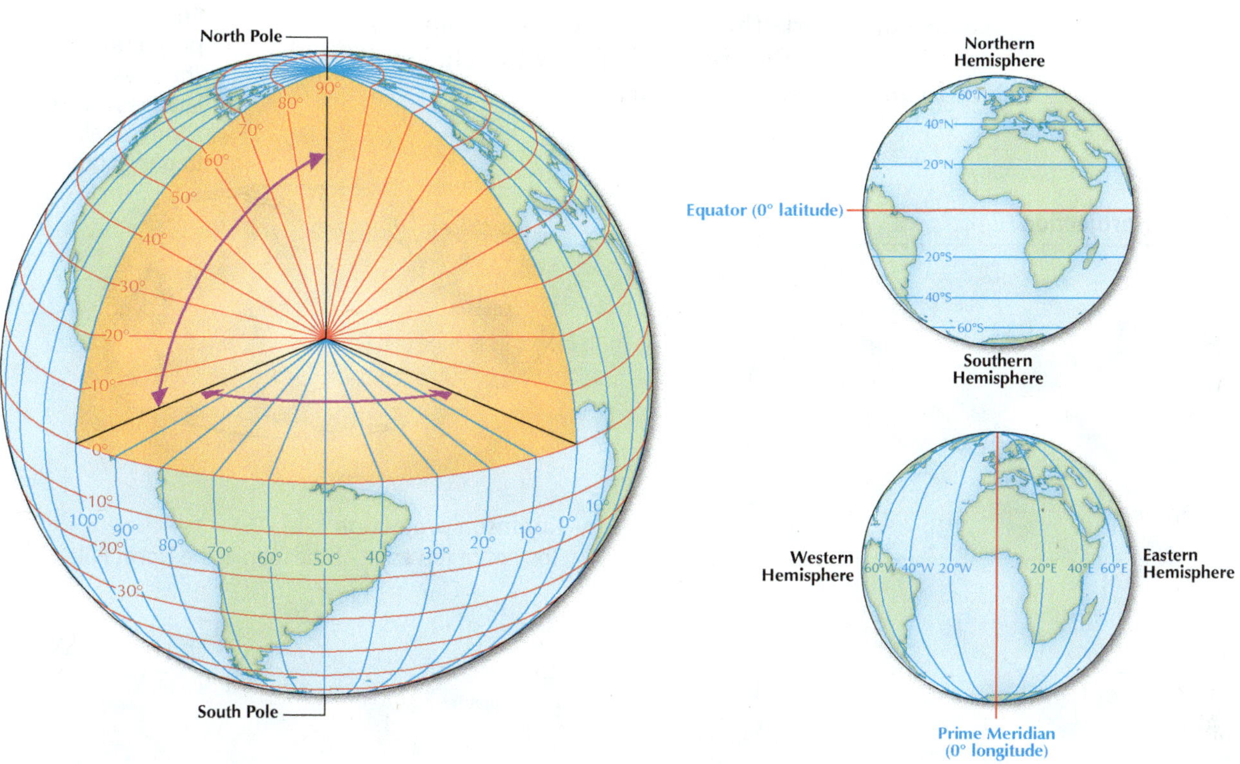

Study purpose. Study the two main globes to understand why geographers divide the globe into parallels and meridians. Study the two smaller globes to understand the role of the Equator and the Prime Meridian as starting points for measuring parallels and meridians.

Read labels and captions. Read the labels and captions to understand how to determine the latitude and longitude of a given location, as well as to identify which hemispheres it sits in.

Identify absolute location. You can use lines of latitude and longitude together to identify the absolute location of any spot on Earth.

Practice and Apply the Skill

Use the text and globes above to answer the following questions:

1. Which part of the location 67° N, 55° E represents the longitude?
2. What line of latitude lies halfway from the Equator to the North Pole?
3. Do lines of latitude ever intersect one another? Explain.
4. If you followed the 70° W line of longitude north to the North Pole and then continued on the same line south, what line of longitude would you be on? (Hint: The globe, like a circle, has a total of 360 degrees.)

Analyze Map Projections

Because maps are flat, they cannot show the correct size and shape of every feature on Earth's curved surface. Mapmakers must shrink some places and stretch others. Different types of map projections distort Earth's surface in different ways. Mapmakers choose the projection that has the least distortion for the information they are presenting.

Same-shape map projections such as the Mercator projection accurately show the shapes of landmasses. However, they distort sizes and distances. Equal-area map projections show the correct size of landmasses but distort shapes, especially at the edges of a map. The Robinson projection keeps the size and shape relationships of most continents and oceans but distorts the size of the polar regions. Use the maps below and the steps that follow to help you learn how to analyze map projections.

Mercator projection

The greatest distortion is at the far northern and southern latitudes.

Equal-area projection
The sizes of landmasses are accurate relative to one another.

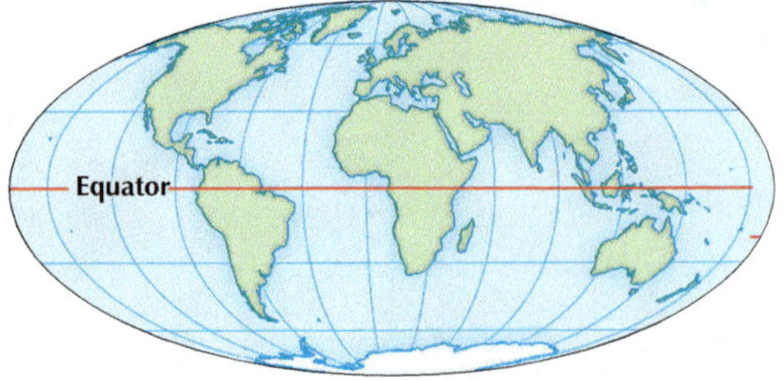

Robinson projection
The entire top edge of the map is the North Pole.

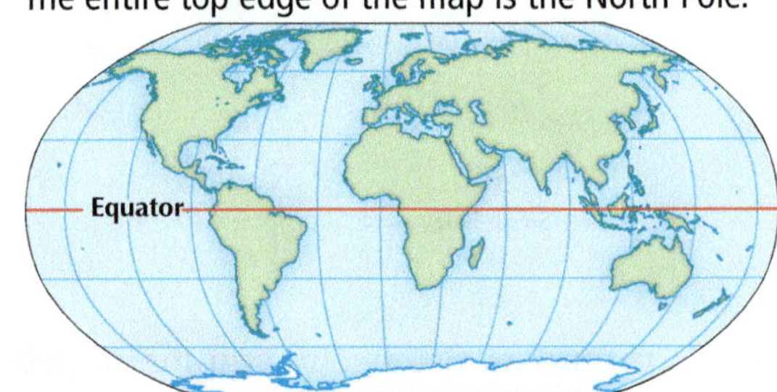

The entire bottom edge of the map is the South Pole.

Identify each projection. Study the appearance of each type of projection.

Read labels and captions. Read the labels and captions to understand the important details of each projection.

Compare the maps. Compare the shape of the maps and then the shapes of landmasses on them. Last, compare the amount of curvature of the lines of latitude and longitude on the maps.

Practice and Apply the Skill

Use the maps above to answer the following questions:

1. If you wanted to plot a course to sail from one port to another on the most direct route, which map projection would work best? Why?

2. Which map shows the most accurate relative size of Antarctica, the white region on each map? Why?

3. How do the grid lines on the Mercator projection vary from a globe's?

4. Why do you think many maps in this book use the Robinson projection?

Read Maps

Maps can show many different kinds of information. A physical map represents what a region looks like by showing its major physical features, such as mountains and plains. A political map focuses on elements related to government, such as nations, borders, and cities. Special-purpose maps provide information on a specific subject—for example, land use, population distribution, or trade routes. Road maps and weather maps are two kinds of special purpose maps.

Mapmakers provide clues to help you read maps and gather the information they offer. Use the map below and the steps that follow to practice reading a map.

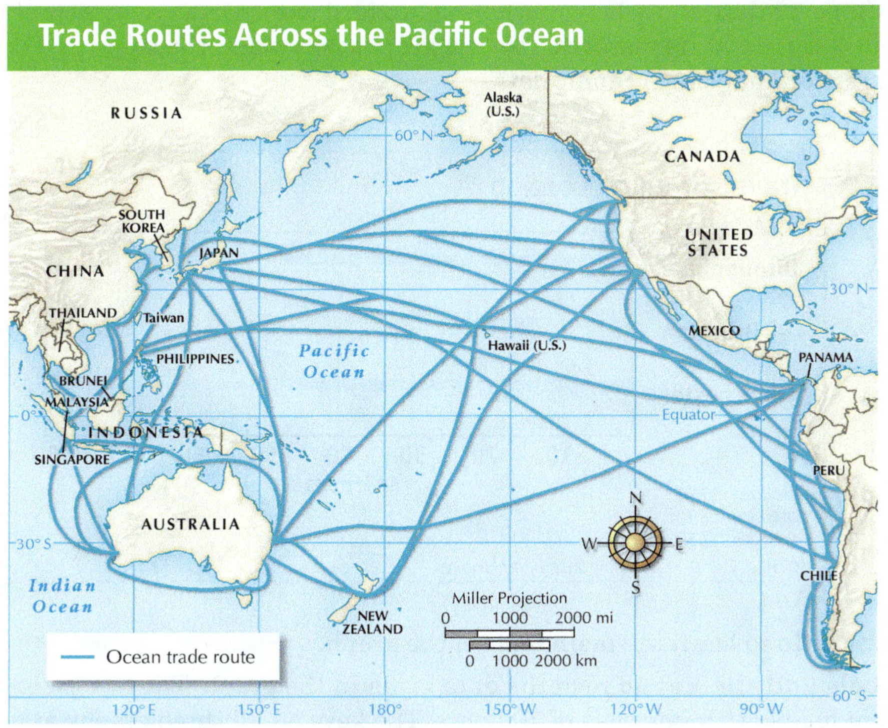

Read the title. The title tells you the subject of the map.

Read the key. The key explains the symbols, lines, and colors and the map.

Use the scale bar and compass rose. Use the scale bar to determine distances between places on the map. Use the compass rose to determine the relative directions of places on the map.

Practice and Apply the Skill

Use the map above to answer the following questions.

1. What is the purpose of this map? What part of the world does it show?

2. What do the blue lines represent?

3. How many trade routes go through New Zealand?

4. When goods travel from the United States to Australia, in what direction do they travel?

5. What generalization could you make about trade across the Pacific Ocean based on this map?

Analyze Graphic Data

The study of history requires that you think critically about the text you're reading as well as any visuals or media sources. This section of the Skills Handbook will allow you to practice and apply some important skills for critical thinking.

Graphs show numerical facts in picture form. Bar graphs and line graphs compare things at different times or places, such as changes in school enrollment. Circle graphs show how a whole is divided into parts. To interpret a graph, look closely at its features. Use the graphs below and the steps that follow to practice analyzing graphic data.

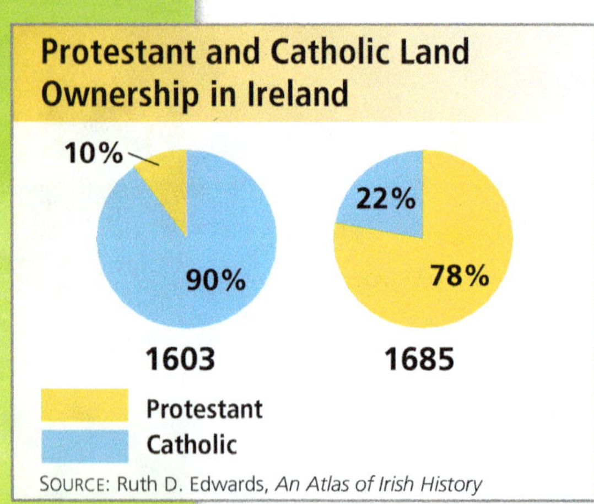

SOURCE: Ruth D. Edwards, *An Atlas of Irish History*

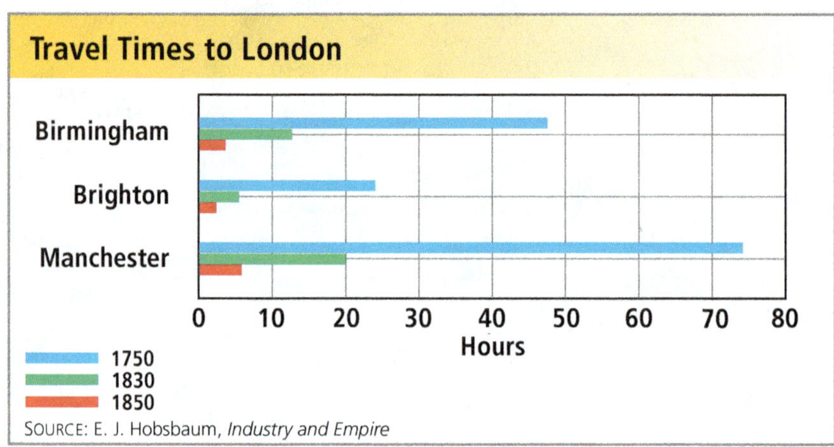

SOURCE: E. J. Hobsbaum, *Industry and Empire*

Read the title to learn the main topic of the graph.

Use labels and the key to read the data given in the graph. The bar graph is labeled in hours, with intervals of 10 hours. The keys on all three graphs assign different colors to different groups or dates.

Interpret the graph. Look for interesting patterns in the data. Look at changes over time or compare information for different groups.

Practice and Apply the Skill

Use the graphs above to answer the following questions:

1. What is the title of the bar graph? What is its topic?

2. Which cities show the longest travel times to London, and in which years? What does this tell you about changes in transportation?

3. What color on the circle graphs shows Catholic land ownership? How did Irish land ownership change over time? What might explain this change?

4. Could the information in the circle graph be shown as a bar graph? Explain.

Analyze Images

Television, film, the Internet, and print media all carry images that seek to convey information or influence attitudes. To respond, you must develop the ability to understand and interpret visuals. Use the photograph below and the steps that follow to practice analyzing images.

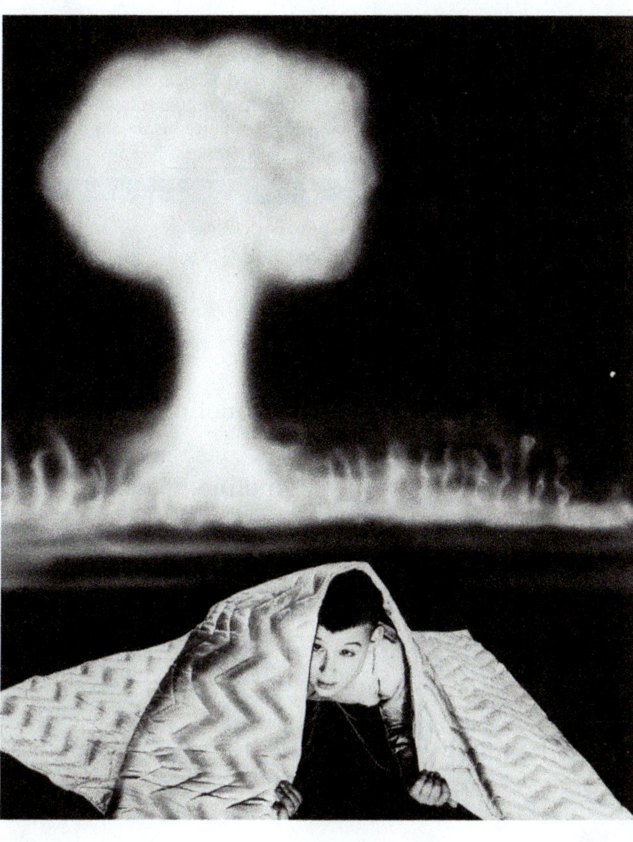

In the 1950s, people everywhere worried about nuclear attack. This 1954 image advertised a bogus "radiation-resistant" blanket.

Identify the content. Look at all parts of the image and determine which are most important.

Note emotions. Study facial expressions and body positions. Consider the emotions they may suggest.

Read captions/credits. Gather information about the image, such as when it was produced.

Study purpose. Consider who might have created this image. Decide if the purpose was to entertain, inform, or persuade.

Consider context. Determine the context in which the image was created—in this case, the Cold War between the United States and the Soviet Union.

Respond. Decide if a visual's impact achieves its purpose—to inform, to entertain, or to persuade.

Practice and Apply the Skill

Use the photograph above to answer the following questions:

1. What are the three main images in this photograph?
2. What feelings are conveyed by the boy's facial expression?
3. What do you think the photograph's purpose is?
4. When was this image produced? How did historical context influence its production?

Analyze Timelines

Timelines show the order in which events occur as well as the amount of time that passes between events. To understand a timeline, study its labels and captions carefully. Use the timeline below and the steps that follow to practice analyzing timelines

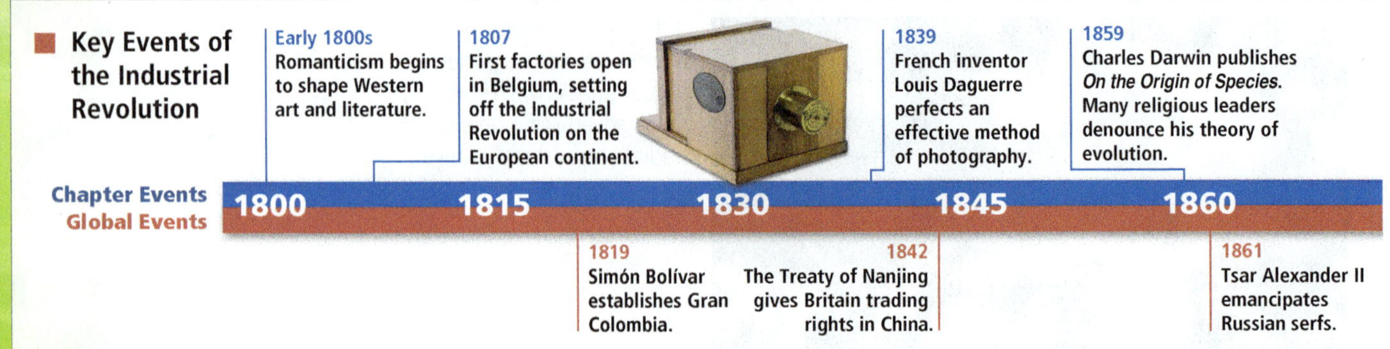

Identify time units. Find the main time units of the timeline. Determine how much time is represented by the entire timeline.

Read each entry. Read each of the entries on the timeline. Connect each entry to the events before and after it.

Look for patterns among the events shown. Determine if any of the entries fall into a common category. Think about whether the events might be causes and/or effects.

Practice and Apply the Skill

Use the timeline above to answer the following questions.

1. What is the most recent event on the timeline? When did it take place?
2. When did the first factories open in Belgium?
3. How many years after the first factories opened did Louis Daguerre perfect his method of photography?
4. What happened in 1859?

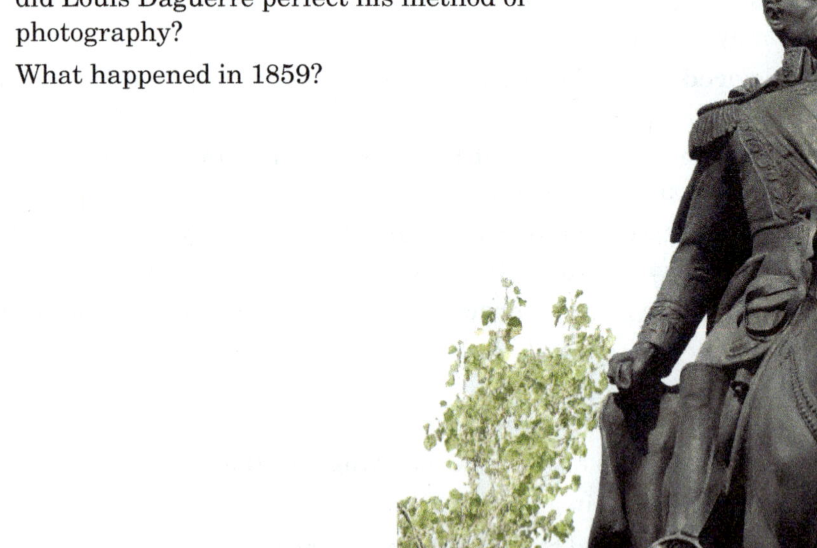

Simón Bolívar

Analyze Primary Sources

Primary sources include official documents and firsthand accounts of events or visual evidence such as photographs, paintings, and political cartoons. Such sources provide valuable information about the past. Use the excerpt below and the steps that follow to learn to analyze primary sources.

The following excerpt is a translation from *The Satires*, a series of poems written in Latin by Juvenal about life in Rome in the first century A.D. In this excerpt, Juvenal recounts a friend's reasons for moving away from Rome.

Primary Source

> "Since at Rome there is no place for honest pursuits, no profit to be got by honest toil—my fortune is less to-day than it was yesterday. . . .
>
> What shall *I* do at Rome? I can not lie; if a book is bad, I can not praise it and beg a copy. I know not the motions of the stars. . . . no one shall be a thief by my co-operation. . . .
>
> Who, now-a-days, is beloved except the confidant of crime. . .?"
>
> —Juvenal, *The Satires of Juvenal, Persius, Sulpicia, and Lucilius*

Read the headnote, caption, or attribution line. Determine the source's historical context—who wrote it, when, and why.

Read the primary source. Identify and define unfamiliar words. Then look for the writer's main point.

Identify facts and opinions. Facts can be proven. Opinions reflect a person's views or feelings. Use opinion clues to help: exaggeration, phrases such as "I think," or descriptive words such as "gorgeous."

Identify bias and evaluate credibility. Consider whether the author's opinions suggest bias. Evaluate other factors that might lead to author bias, such as his or her previous experiences. Decide if the author knows enough to be credible and was objective enough to be reliable. Determine whether the source might be propaganda, that is, material published to promote a policy, idea, or cause.

Practice and Apply the Skill

Political cartoons reflect an artist's observations about events of the time. They often use symbols to represent things or exaggeration to make a point. Use the cartoon at right to answer the following questions.

1. Who is the author of this primary source?
2. What does the bulldozer represent?
3. What is exaggerated in this cartoon?
4. What opinion is the cartoonist expressing?
5. Do you think the cartoonist's opinion is valid? Why or why not?

This cartoon by Arcadio Esquivel of Costa Rica comments on environmental destruction.

Compare Viewpoints

A person's viewpoint is shaped by subjective influences such as feelings, prejudices, and past experiences. Two politicians will recommend different policies to address the same problem. Comparing such viewpoints will help you understand issues and form your own views. The excerpts below offer two different views on the purpose of education. Use the excerpts and the steps that follow to learn about comparing viewpoints.

King Henri Christophe of Haiti set up schools for outstanding students. He believed these schools would secure Haiti's new and hard-won freedom. In 1817, he wrote:

Primary Source

"To form good citizens we must educate our children. From our national institutions will proceed a race of men capable of defending by their knowledge and talents those rights so long denied by tyrants. It is from these sources that light will be diffused among the whole mass of the population."

—Henri Christophe, 1817

Leo Tolstoy, a Russian aristocrat of the late 1800s, became a famous novelist as a young man. As he grew older, he increasingly focused on social issues in his writing. In 1902, he wrote:

Primary Source

"You can take a puppy and feed him, and teach him to carry something, and enjoy the sight of him; but it is not enough to rear and bring up a man, and teach him Greek: he has to be taught to live, that is, to take less from others, and give more."

—Leo Tolstoy, 1902

Identify the authors. Determine when and where the authors lived.

Examine the viewpoints. Identify the author's main idea and evaluate his or her supporting arguments. Determine whether the arguments are logical and the evidence is sufficient to support the main idea. Confirm that the evidence is valid by doing research if necessary.

Determine the author's frame of reference. Consider how the author's attitudes, beliefs, and past experiences might affect his or her viewpoint.

Recognize facts and opinions. Identify which statements are opinions and which are facts. Opinions represent the author's viewpoint.

Evaluate each viewpoint's validity. Decide whether the viewpoints are based on facts and/or reasonable arguments. Consider whether or not you agree with the viewpoints.

Practice and Apply the Skill

Use the excerpts above to answer the following questions.

1. Who are the authors of these two documents? Where and when did each one live?

2. What is each man's main argument about education? What evidence or supporting arguments does each provide?

3. How might each man's frame of reference affect his viewpoint?

4. How does Tolstoy's phrase "he has to be taught to live" signal an opinion?

5. Are these two viewpoints based on reasonable arguments? Explain.

Synthesize Information

Just as you might ask several friends about a movie before deciding to see it, you can combine information from different sources to develop a fuller understanding of any topic. This process, called synthesizing, will help you become better informed. Study the documents below about developments in the 1400s and 1500s. Then use the steps that follow to learn to synthesize information.

Document A

This caravel helped Europeans sail across and into the wind.

Document B

Improved Technology

Several improvements in technology helped Europeans navigate the vast oceans of the world. Cartographers, or mapmakers, created more accurate maps and sea charts. European sailors learned to use the astrolabe, an instrument developed by the ancient Greeks and perfected by the Arabs, to determine their latitude at sea.

Europeans also designed larger and better ships. The Portuguese developed the caravel, which combined the square sails of European ships with Arab lateen, or triangular, sails. Caravels also adapted the sternpost rudder and numerous masts used on Chinese ships. The new rigging made it easier to sail across or even into the wind.

Document C

Hardships on the Uncharted Sea

In his journal, Italian sailor Antonio Pigafetta detailed the desperate conditions Magellan's sailors experienced as they crossed the Pacific Ocean:

Primary Source

66We remained three months and twenty days without taking in provisions or other refreshments, and we only ate old biscuit reduced to powder, and full of grubs, and stinking from the dirt which the rats had made on it. . . . we drank water that was yellow and stinking. We also ate the ox hides which were under the main-yard [and] were very hard on account of the sun, rain, and wind. . . .99

—Journal of Antonio Pigafetta

Identify thesis statements. Before you can synthesize, you must understand the thesis, or main idea, of each source.

Compare and contrast. Analyze how the information and ideas in the sources are the same or different. When several sources agree, the information is more reliable and thus more significant.

Draw conclusions and generalize. Look at all the information. Use it to draw conclusions that form a single picture of the topic. Make a generalization, or statement that applies to all the sources.

Practice and Apply the Skill

Use the documents above to answer the following questions.

1. What is the main idea of each source?
2. Which sources support the idea that European sailors became better equipped to sail the seas?
3. What view does Antonio Pigafetta contribute to the topic?
4. Draw a conclusion about European ocean exploration in the early 1500s.

Analyze Cause and Effect

One of a historian's main tasks is to understand the causes and effects of the event he or she is studying. Study the facts below, which are listed in random order. Then use the steps that follow to learn how to analyze cause and effect.

> In the 1980s and 1990s, the Soviet Union underwent a major change in its economy and government. As a result, the Soviet Union ceased to exist. This list shows key elements in that change.
>
> - Low output of crops and consumer goods
> - Soviets want to ensure influence in neighboring Afghanistan, so they invade that nation in 1979
> - Soviet Union breaks up into 15 republics after its central government collapses
> - Changeover to market economy in Russia
> - Ethnic and nationalist movements to achieve independence from Soviet Union
> - Cold War with United States leads to high military spending
> - Food and fuel shortages
> - Rise to power of Mikhail Gorbachev in 1985
> - Russian republic approves a new constitution
> - Baltic states of Estonia, Latvia, and Lithuania demonstrate for independence
> - Cold War ends

Identify the central event. Determine to what event or issue all the facts listed relate.

Locate clue words. Use words such as *because, so,* and *due to* to spot causes and effects.

Identify causes and effects. Causes precede the central event and contribute to its occurrence. Effects come after the central event. They occur or emerge as a result of it.

Consider timeframe. Decide if causes have existed for a long period of time or emerged just prior to the central event. Short-term causes are usually single or narrowly defined events. Long-term causes usually arise from ongoing conditions.

Make recommendations. Use what you've learned to suggest actions or make predictions.

Practice and Apply the Skill

Use the list above to answer the following questions:

1. Which item on the list describes the central event whose causes and effects can be determined?

2. Name three facts that are long-term causes.

3. Name three facts that are probably short-term causes.

4. Name three facts that were most likely effects of the central event.

Problem Solving and Decision Making

You will face many problems in your life, from disputes with friends to how to vote on issues facing your nation. You will be most likely to find solutions if you make decisions in a logical way. Study the situation outlined below. Then use the steps that follow to learn the skills of problem solving and decision making.

A Problem for Japan and China

In the 1800s, Japan and China faced a problem. Industrialized nations had developed machinery and weapons that were superior to those that the Japanese and Chinese had. Some industrialized nations used their new power to demand special trading privileges in Asia.

Options for Japan and China

Option	Advantages	Disadvantages
1. Give in to demands of the industrialized powers.	• Avoid conflict. •	• Native merchants lose profits to foreigners. •
2. Give in to demands, but also build modern machines and weapons.	• •	• •
3. Refuse the demands and reject much of the new technology.	• •	• •

The Decisions
- The Japanese government decided to follow option 2.
- The Chinese government decided to follow option 3.

Effects of the Decisions
- Japan quickly became a modern industrial and military power. Although it demilitarized after suffering defeat in World War II, it remains one of the world's leading industrial powers.
- China was weakened by a century of conflict with Great Britain and other major powers, and was invaded and occupied by Japan. Foreign nations gained special privileges in China. Today, China is still struggling to become a leading industrial power.

Identify the problem. You cannot solve a problem until you examine it and understand it.

Gather information and identify options. Most problems have many solutions. Identify as many solution options as possible.

Consider advantages and disadvantages. Analyze each option by predicting benefits and drawbacks.

Decide on and implement the solution. Pick the option with the most desirable benefits and least important drawbacks.

Evaluate the decision. After time, reexamine your solution. If necessary, make a new decision.

Practice and Apply the Skill

Use information from the box above to answer the following questions:

1. What problem did China and Japan face? What caused this problem?
2. Describe an option that Japan or China could have chosen other than those in the list.
3. Identify two advantages and two disadvantages for options 2 and 3.
4. Why do you think China and Japan chose the options they did?

Draw Inferences and Conclusions

Text and artwork may not contain all the facts and ideas you need to understand a topic. You may need to add information from your own experience or knowledge, or use information that is implied but not directly stated in the text or artwork. Study the biography below. Then use the steps that follow to learn how to draw inferences and conclusions.

BIOGRAPHY

James Watt

How did a clever Scottish engineer become the "Father of the Industrial Revolution"? After repairing a Newcomen steam engine, James Watt (1736–1819) had become fascinated with the idea of improving the device. Within a few months, he knew he had a product that would sell. Still, Watt lacked the money needed to produce and market it.

Fortunately, he was able to form a partnership with the shrewd manufacturer Matthew Boulton. They then founded Soho Engineering Works in Birmingham, England, to manufacture steam engines. Watt's version of the steam engine shown here had a separate condensing chamber and was patented in 1769. Eventually, a measure of mechanical and electrical power, the watt, would be named for James Watt. **How might the Industrial Revolution have been different if Watt had not found a business partner?**

Study the facts. Determine what facts and information the text states.

Summarize information. Confirm your understanding of the text by briefly summarizing it.

Ask questions. Use *who, what, when, where, why,* and *how* questions to analyze the text and learn more. For example, you might compare and contrast, or look for causes or effects.

Add your own knowledge. Consider what you know about the topic. Use this knowledge to evaluate the information.

Draw inferences and conclusions. Use what you learned from the text and your own knowledge to draw inferences and conclusions about the topic.

Practice and Apply the Skill

Use the biography above to answer these questions.

1. Who is discussed in the biography? When did he live?

2. Briefly summarize the text.

3. How do Watt's accomplishments still have an impact on our lives today?

4. Why do you think Watt wanted to improve a technology that already existed?

Use the Internet for Research

The Internet is a valuable research tool that provides links to millions of sources of information created by businesses, governments, schools, organizations, and individuals all over the world. Follow the steps to learn how you could use the Internet to research the European Renaissance.

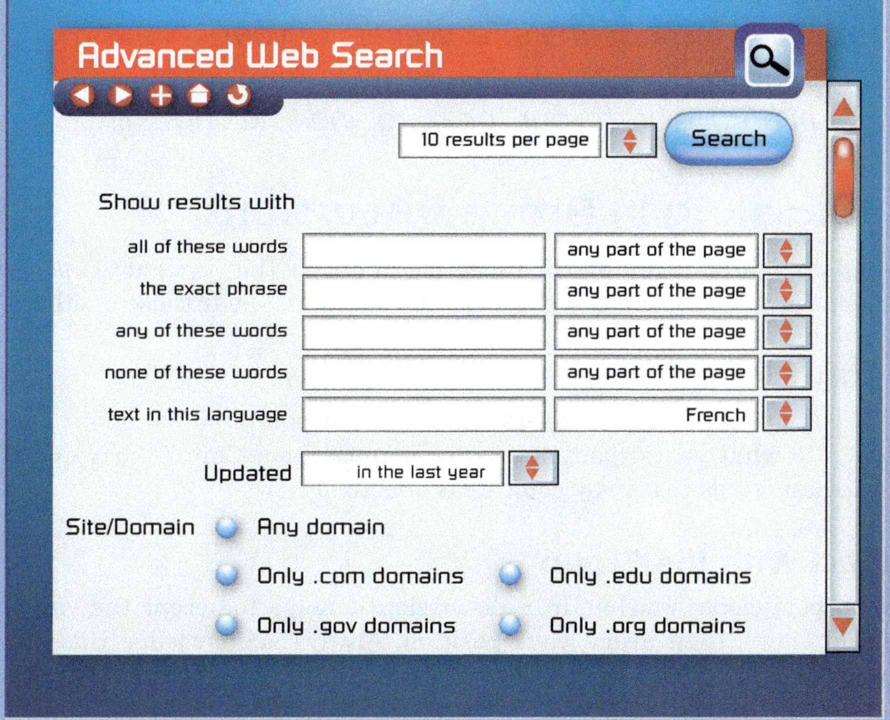

Sample search engine

Begin a search. Use search engines on the Internet to help you find useful Web sites. Type in key words that briefly summarize your topic. Use *and* between words to find documents containing all your keywords. Use *or* between words to find documents containing any one of several keywords.

Find reliable information. Universities, museums, libraries, and government agencies are usually the most reliable and useful for social studies research. The URLs for education sites end in *.edu,* government sites in *.gov,* and not-for-profit organization sites in *.org.* Read each site summary and choose those most likely to be reliable. Click on links to access individual sites.

Evaluate Web sites. Explore each Web site. Note its sponsor and when it was last updated.

Use advanced searches. Try advanced search options. Limit by date or type of site, such as educational institutions. Try new or different key words if you still don't get what you need.

Practice and Apply the Skill

Use a computer connected to the Internet to answer the following questions:

1. What key words might you use to learn about the European Renaissance? Type them into a search engine Web site and see what results you get.

2. Which of the first ten sites that came up in your search is most likely to be reliable? Why?

3. Who is the sponsor of the site you chose? What does this suggest about its quality or its possible bias?

Speaking and listening are forms of communication you use every day. In certain situations, however, specific skills and strategies can increase the effectiveness of your communication. The strategies offered in this section will help you improve both your speaking and listening skills.

Participating in Group Discussions

A group discussion is an informal meeting of people that is used to openly discuss ideas and topics. You can express your views and hear those of others.

Identify Issues

Before you speak, identify the issues and main points you want to address. Incorporate what you already know about these issues into your views. Then find the best words to convey your ideas effectively.

Interact With the Group

As with persuasive writing, in a discussion it helps to accept the validity of opposing views, then argue your position. Always acknowledge the views of others respectfully, but ask questions that challenge the accuracy, logic, or relevance of those views.

Debating

A debate is a formal argument about a specific issue. Explicit rules govern the procedure of a debate, with each debater or team given an allotted time to make arguments and respond to opposing positions. You may also find yourself arguing a position you don't personally hold.

Prepare Your Arguments

If you support a position, use your existing knowledge of it to direct your research. If you personally oppose an assigned position, use that knowledge to identify likely opposing arguments. Generate an outline and then number note cards to highlight key information for each of your main points.

Avoid Common Pitfalls

Stay focused on your arguments. Be aware of words that may reveal bias, such as *unpatriotic*. Speak assertively, but avoid getting overly emotional. Vary the pitch and tone of your voice to keep listeners engaged. Try to speak actively, rather than just reading aloud, and use eye contact and gestures to emphasize your message.

Giving an Oral or Multimedia Presentation

An oral or multimedia presentation provides an audience with information through a variety of media.

Choose Media

If you are limited to speaking only, focus your time on developing a presentation that engages listeners. If you can include other media, consider what kind of information each form of media conveys most effectively.

Maps	Graphs/charts	Pictures	Diagrams	Audio/video
Clarify historical or geographical information	Show complicated information in an accessible format	Illustrate objects, scenes, or other details	Show link between parts and a whole or a process	Brings the subject to life and engages audience

Generate Text

Gather information using library and online sources. Develop your most important ideas in the body of your presentation. Back up assertions with solid facts and use multimedia examples to illustrate key points.

Present With Authority

Practice your presentation to gain comfort with the text and the presentation sequence. Experiment with the timing of how to include multimedia elements. Make sure you have the necessary equipment and know how to use it.

Active Listening

Active listening is a key component of the communication process. Like all communication, it requires your engaged participation.

Focus Your Attention on Ideas

Look at and listen to the speaker. Think about what you hear and see. Which ideas are emphasized or repeated? What gestures or expressions suggest strong feelings? Can you connect the speaker's ideas to your own experiences?

Listen to Fit the Situation

Active listening involves matching your listening to the situation. Listen critically to a speech given by a candidate for office. Listen empathetically to the feelings of a friend. Listen appreciatively to a musical performance.

Ask Questions

Try to think of questions while you're listening. Look at these examples:

Open-ended	Closed	Fact
Why do you think it is so important for young people to vote?	Do you support the current voting age of 18?	How many people aged 18–25 voted in the most recent election?

"

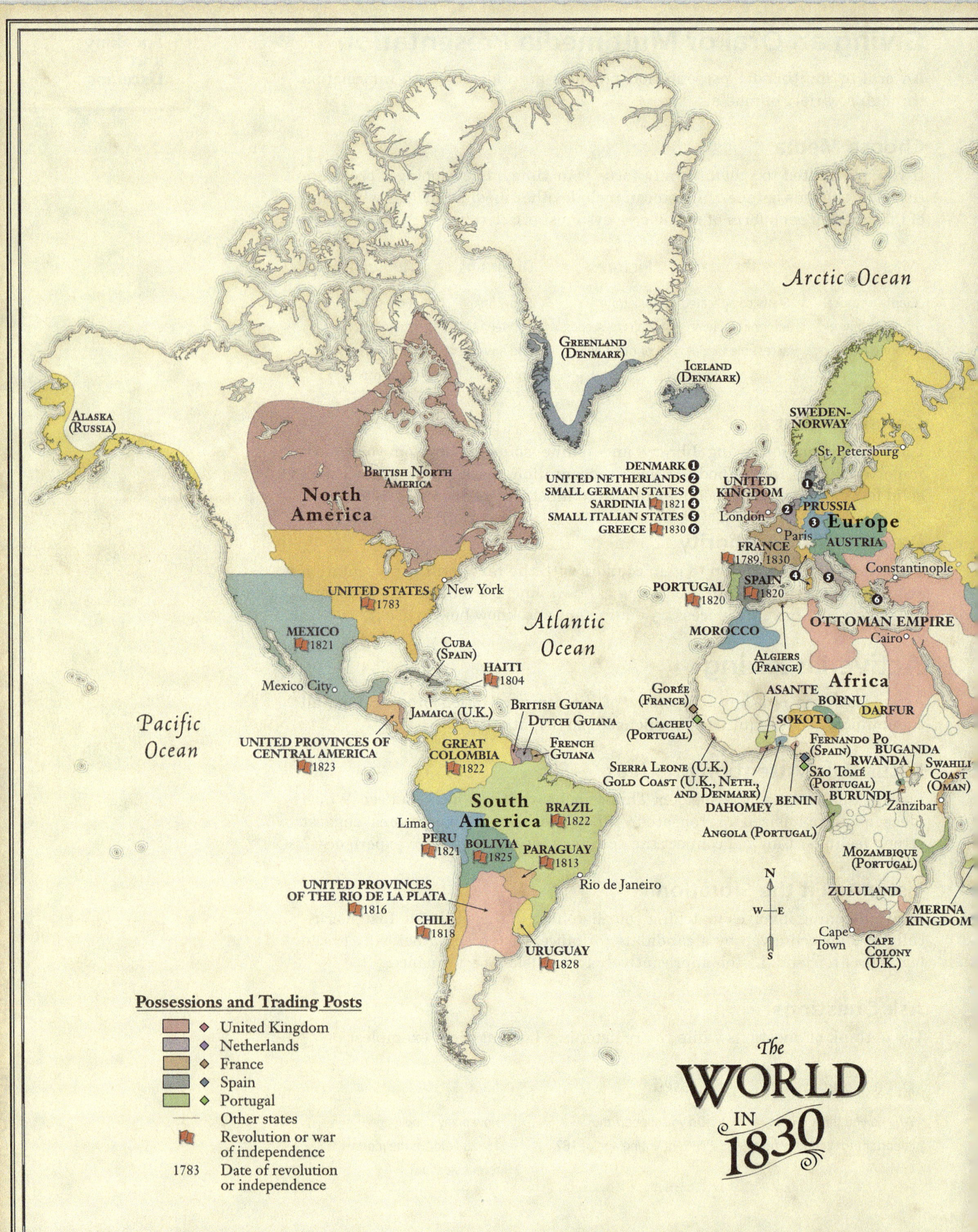

Arctic Ocean
GREENLAND (DENMARK)
ICELAND (DENMARK)
SWEDEN-NORWAY
St. Petersburg
ALASKA (RUSSIA)
BRITISH NORTH AMERICA
North America
DENMARK ❶
UNITED NETHERLANDS ❷
SMALL GERMAN STATES ❸
SARDINIA 1821 ❹
SMALL ITALIAN STATES ❺
GREECE 1830 ❻
UNITED KINGDOM
London
❶
❷ PRUSSIA
❸ Europe
FRANCE AUSTRIA
1789, 1830
Paris
❹ ❺ Constantinople
PORTUGAL 1820
SPAIN 1820
❻
UNITED STATES 1783
New York
Atlantic Ocean
MEXICO 1821
Mexico City
CUBA (SPAIN)
HAITI 1804
MOROCCO
ALGIERS (FRANCE)
OTTOMAN EMPIRE
Cairo
Africa
Pacific Ocean
JAMAICA (U.K.)
BRITISH GUIANA
DUTCH GUIANA
FRENCH GUIANA
UNITED PROVINCES OF CENTRAL AMERICA 1823
GREAT COLOMBIA 1822
South America
BRAZIL 1822
Lima
PERU 1821
BOLIVIA 1825
PARAGUAY 1813
Rio de Janeiro
UNITED PROVINCES OF THE RIO DE LA PLATA 1816
CHILE 1818
URUGUAY 1828
GORÉE (FRANCE)
CACHEU (PORTUGAL)
ASANTE
BORNU
DARFUR
SOKOTO
FERNANDO PO (SPAIN)
BUGANDA
RWANDA
SWAHILI COAST (OMAN)
SÃO TOMÉ (PORTUGAL)
SIERRA LEONE (U.K.)
GOLD COAST (U.K., NETH., AND DENMARK)
DAHOMEY
BENIN
BURUNDI
Zanzibar
ANGOLA (PORTUGAL)
MOZAMBIQUE (PORTUGAL)
N
W E
S
ZULULAND
MERINA KINGDOM
Cape Town
CAPE COLONY (U.K.)
Possessions and Trading Posts
◆ United Kingdom
◆ Netherlands
◆ France
◆ Spain
◆ Portugal
Other states
Revolution or war of independence
1783 Date of revolution or independence
The WORLD IN 1830

UNIT

4

Enlightenment and Revolution

1700–1850

17

The Enlightenment and the American Revolution

1700–1800

Pens to Inspire Revolution

Enlightenment thinker Denis Diderot compiled a 28-volume work called the *Encyclopedia,* published between 1751 and 1772. This work was a forum for Enlightenment thinkers who believed that with the power of reason, they could fix the problems of society. The *Encyclopedia* was banned in many places and censored in others. Yet it would prove to be a major influence in the years to come. It contains the passage below on freedom. Listen to the Witness History audio to hear more about this work.

66 No man has received from nature the right to give orders to others. Freedom is a gift from heaven, and every individual of the same species has the right to enjoy it as soon as he is in enjoyment of his reason. 99
—Denis Diderot

Denis Diderot bust

Rococo fan

◀ Madame Geoffrin (far right in blue), in her famous salon where Enlightenment thinkers gathered to share ideas.

Chapter Preview

Chapter Focus Question How did Enlightenment thinkers inspire revolutionaries to push for radical changes in government and society?

Section 1
Philosophy in the Age of Reason

Section 2
Enlightenment Ideas Spread

Section 3
Birth of the American Republic

Use the  ✓ **Quick Study Timeline** at the end of this chapter to preview chapter events.

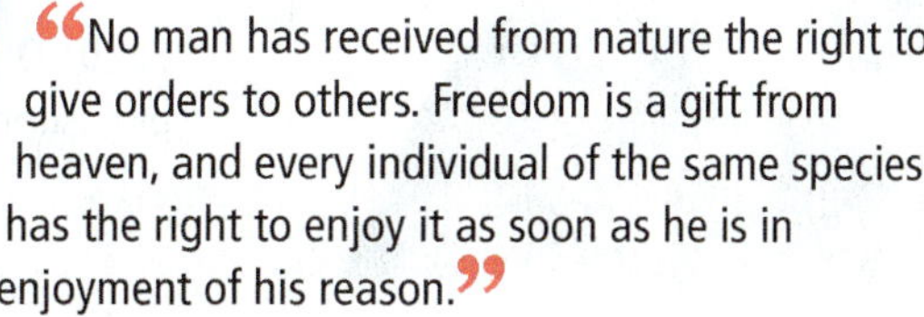

British tax stamp used in the American colonies

 **Concept Connector ONLINE**

To explore Essential Questions related to this chapter, go to PHSchool.com
Web Code: nad-1707

Jean-Jacques Rousseau
and quill pen

Rousseau Stirs Things Up

In Jean-Jacques Rousseau's most important work, *The Social Contract,* he argued that in order to be free, people should do what is best for their community. Rousseau had many supporters who were inspired by his passionate writings. European monarchs, on the other hand, were angry that Rousseau was questioning authority. As a result, Rousseau worried about persecution for much of his life. The "chains" below represent the social institutions that confined society.

> 66 Man is born free, and everywhere he is in chains. 99
> —Rousseau, *The Social Contract*

Focus Question What effects did Enlightenment philosophers have on government and society?

Philosophy in the Age of Reason

Objectives

- Explain how science led to the Enlightenment.
- Compare the ideas of Hobbes and Locke.
- Identify the beliefs and contributions of the *philosophes.*
- Summarize how economic thinking changed during this time.

Terms, People, and Places

natural law	Montesquieu
Thomas Hobbes	Voltaire
John Locke	Diderot
social contract	Rousseau
natural right	laissez faire
philosophe	Adam Smith

Note Taking

Reading Skill: Summarize Draw a table like the one shown here. As you read the section, summarize each thinker's works and ideas.

Thinkers' Works and Ideas	
Hobbes	*Leviathan,* social contract
Locke	
Montesquieu	

By the early 1700s, European thinkers felt that nothing was beyond the reach of the human mind. Through the use of reason, insisted these thinkers, people and governments could solve every social, political, and economic problem. In essence, these writers, scholars, and philosophers felt they could change the world.

Scientific Revolution Sparks the Enlightenment

The Scientific Revolution of the 1500s and 1600s had transformed the way people in Europe looked at the world. In the 1700s, other scientists expanded European knowledge. For example, Edward Jenner developed a vaccine against smallpox, a disease whose path of death spanned the centuries.

Scientific successes convinced educated Europeans of the power of human reason. **Natural law,** or rules discoverable by reason, govern scientific forces such as gravity and magnetism. Why not, then, use natural law to better understand social, economic, and political problems? Using the methods of the new science, reformers thus set out to study human behavior and solve the problems of society. In this way, the Scientific Revolution led to another revolution in thinking, known as the Enlightenment. Immanuel Kant, a German philosopher best known for his work *The Critique of Pure Reason,* was one of the first to describe this era with the word "Enlightenment." Despite Kant's skepticism about the power of reason, he was enthusiastic about the Enlightenment and believed, like many European philosophers, that natural law could help explain aspects of humanity.

✔ **Checkpoint** What convinced educated Europeans to accept the power of reason?

Hobbes and Locke Have Conflicting Views

Thomas Hobbes and **John Locke,** two seventeenth-century English thinkers, set forth ideas that were to become key to the Enlightenment. Both men lived through the upheavals of the English Civil War. Yet they came to very different conclusions about human nature and the role of government.

Hobbes Believes in Powerful Government Thomas Hobbes outlined his ideas in a work titled *Leviathan.* In it, he argued that people were naturally cruel, greedy, and selfish. If not strictly controlled, they would fight, rob, and oppress one another. Life in the "state of nature"—without laws or other control—would be "solitary, poor, nasty, brutish, and short."

To escape that "brutish" life, said Hobbes, people entered into a **social contract,** an agreement by which they gave up their freedom for an organized society. Hobbes believed that only a powerful government could ensure an orderly society. For him, such a government was an absolute monarchy, which could impose order and compel obedience.

Locke Advocates Natural Rights John Locke had a more optimistic view of human nature. He thought people were basically reasonable and moral. Further, they had certain **natural rights,** or rights that belonged to all humans from birth. These included the right to life, liberty, and property.

In *Two Treatises of Government,* Locke argued that people formed governments to protect their natural rights. The best kind of government, he said, had limited power and was accepted by all citizens. Thus, unlike Hobbes, Locke rejected absolute monarchy. England during this time experienced a shift in political power known as the Glorious Revolution. James II, an unpopular absolute monarch, left the throne and fled England in 1688. Locke later wrote that he thought James II deserved to be dethroned for violating the rights of the English.

Locke proposed a radical idea about this time. A government, he said, has an obligation to the people it governs. If a government fails its obligations or violates people's natural rights, the people have the right to overthrow that government. Locke's idea would one day influence leaders of the American Revolution, such as Benjamin Franklin, Thomas Jefferson, and James Madison. Locke's idea of the right of revolution would also echo across Europe and Latin America in the centuries that followed.

✔ **Checkpoint** How did Hobbes and Locke differ in their views on the role of government?

Hobbes Writes the *Leviathan*
The title page from *Leviathan* (1651) by Hobbes demonstrates his belief in a powerful ruler. The monarch here represents the Leviathan who rises above all of society.

Voltaire

François-Marie Arouet, known as Voltaire (1694–1778) was an impassioned poet, historian, essayist, and philosopher who wrote with cutting sarcasm and sharp wit. Voltaire was sent to the Bastille prison twice due to his criticism of French authorities and was eventually banned from Paris. When he was able to return to France, he wrote about political and religious freedom. Voltaire spent his life fighting enemies of freedom, such as ignorance, superstition, and intolerance. **What did Voltaire attack in his writings?**

Montesquieu

Born to wealth, Charles Louis de Secondat (1689–1755) inherited the title Baron de Montesquieu from his uncle. Like many other reformers, he did not let his privileged status keep him from becoming a voice for democracy. His first book titled *Persian Letters* ridiculed the French government and social classes. In his work published in 1748, *The Spirit of the Laws,* he advanced the idea of separation of powers—a foundation of modern democracy. **What did Montesquieu think was necessary to protect liberty?**

The *Philosophes*

In the 1700s, there was a flowering of Enlightenment thought. This was when a group of Enlightenment thinkers in France applied the methods of science to understand and improve society. They believed that the use of reason could lead to reforms of government, law, and society. These thinkers were called *philosophes* (fee loh ZOHFS), which means "philosophers." Their ideas soon spread beyond France and even beyond Europe.

Montesquieu Advances the Idea of Separation of Powers An early and influential thinker was Baron de Montesquieu (MAHN tus kyoo). Montesquieu studied the governments of Europe, from Italy to England. He read about ancient and medieval Europe, and learned about Chinese and Native American cultures. His sharp criticism of absolute monarchy would open doors for later debate.

In 1748, Montesquieu published *The Spirit of the Laws*, in which he discussed governments throughout history. Montesquieu felt that the best way to protect liberty was to divide the various functions and powers of government among three branches: the legislative, executive, and judicial. He also felt that each branch of government should be able to serve as a check on the other two, an idea that we call checks and balances. Montesquieu's beliefs would soon profoundly affect the Framers of the United States Constitution.

Voltaire Defends Freedom of Thought Probably the most famous of the *philosophes* was François-Marie Arouet, who took the name Voltaire. "My trade," said Voltaire, "is to say what I think," and he did so throughout his long, controversial life. Voltaire used biting wit as a weapon to expose the abuses of his day. He targeted corrupt officials and idle aristocrats. With his pen, he battled inequality, injustice, and superstition. He detested the slave trade and deplored religious prejudice.

Voltaire's outspoken attacks offended both the French government and the Catholic Church. He was imprisoned and forced into exile. Even as he saw his books outlawed and even burned, he continued to defend the principle of freedom of speech.

Diderot Edits the *Encyclopedia* Denis Diderot (DEE duh roh) worked for years to produce a 28-volume set of books called the *Encyclopedia*. As the editor, Diderot did more than just compile articles.

His purpose was "to change the general way of thinking" by explaining ideas on topics such as government, <u>philosophy</u>, and religion. Diderot's *Encyclopedia* included articles by leading thinkers of the day, including Montesquieu and Voltaire. In these articles, the *philosophes* denounced slavery, praised freedom of expression, and urged education for all. They attacked divine-right theory and traditional religions. Critics raised an outcry. The French government argued that the *Encyclopedia* was an attack on public morals, and the pope threatened to excommunicate Roman Catholics who bought or read the volumes.

Despite these and other efforts to ban the *Encyclopedia,* more than 4,000 copies were printed between 1751 and 1789. When translated into other languages, the *Encyclopedia* helped spread Enlightenment ideas throughout Europe and across the Atlantic Ocean to the Americas.

Rousseau Promotes *The Social Contract* Jean-Jacques Rousseau (roo SOH), believed that people in their natural state were basically good. This natural innocence, he felt, was corrupted by the evils of society, especially the unequal distribution of property. Many reformers and revolutionaries later adopted this view. Among them were Thomas Paine and Marquis de Lafayette, who were leading figures of the American and French Revolutions.

In 1762, Rousseau set forth his ideas about government and society in *The Social Contract.* Rousseau felt that society placed too many limitations on people's behavior. He believed that some controls were necessary, but that they should be minimal. Additionally, only governments that had been freely elected should impose these controls.

Rousseau put his faith in the "general will," or the best conscience of the people. The good of the community as a whole, he said, should be placed above individual interests. Rousseau has influenced political and social thinkers for more than 200 years. Woven through his work is a hatred of all forms of political and economic oppression. His bold ideas would help fan the flames of revolt in years to come.

Women Challenge the *Philosophes* The Enlightenment slogan "free and equal" did not apply to women. Though the *philosophes* said women had natural rights, their rights were limited to the areas of home and family.

By the mid- to late-1700s, a small but growing number of women protested this view. Germaine de Staël in France and Catharine Macaulay and Mary Wollstonecraft in Britain argued that women were being excluded from the social contract itself. Their arguments, however, were ridiculed and often sharply condemned.

Wollstonecraft was a well-known British social critic. She accepted that a woman's first duty was to be a good mother but felt that a woman should be able to decide what was in her own interest without depending on her husband. In 1792, Wollstonecraft published *A Vindication of the Rights of Woman.* In it, she called for equal education for girls and boys. Only education, she argued, could give women the tools they needed to participate equally with men in public life.

✔ **Checkpoint** What topics were addressed by the *philosophes* in their *Encyclopedia* articles?

Heated Debate
Rousseau (left) and Voltaire (right) are pictured here in the midst of an argument. Even though the *philosophes* were reform-minded, they disagreed about some issues. *Compare the beliefs of Rousseau and Voltaire.*

New Economic Thinking

French thinkers known as physiocrats focused on economic reforms. Like the *philosophes,* physiocrats based their thinking on natural laws. The physiocrats claimed that their rational economic system was based on the natural laws of economics.

Laissez Faire Replaces Mercantilism Physiocrats rejected mercantilism, which required government regulation of the economy to achieve a favorable balance of trade. Instead, they urged a policy of laissez faire (les ay FEHR), allowing business to operate with little or no government interference. Physiocrats also supported free trade and opposed tariffs.

Smith Argues for a Free Market Scottish economist Adam Smith greatly admired the physiocrats. In his influential work *The Wealth of Nations,* he argued that the free market should be allowed to regulate business activity. Smith tried to show how manufacturing, trade, wages, profits, and economic growth were all linked to the market forces of supply and demand. Wherever there was a demand for goods or services, he said, suppliers would seek to meet that demand in order to gain profits. Smith was a strong supporter of laissez faire. However, he felt that government had a duty to protect society, administer justice, and provide public works. Adam Smith's ideas would help to shape productive economies in the 1800s and 1900s.

✔ **Checkpoint** Why did Smith support laissez faire?

Investors in Paris, France, 1720

SECTION 1
Assessment

Terms, People, and Places

1. For each term, person, or place listed at the beginning of the section, write a sentence explaining its significance.

Note Taking

2. **Reading Skill: Summarize** Use your completed tables to answer the Focus Question: What effects did Enlightenment philosophers have on government and society?

Comprehension and Critical Thinking

3. **Summarize** How did the achievements of the Scientific Revolution contribute to the Enlightenment?
4. **Recognize Cause and Effect** What did the *philosophes* do to better understand and improve society?
5. **Synthesize Information** Explain the connection between the policy of laissez faire and natural economic laws.

● Writing About History

Quick Write: Explore a Topic On some essay tests, you may have a choice of topic. You should choose one that you feel most knowledgeable about. Choose from the following, and draft a single sentence that identifies the main idea:
(a) social contracts (b) freedom of speech (c) women in the mid-1700s

John Locke:
Two Treatises of Government

English philosopher John Locke (1632–1704) published *Two Treatises of Government* in 1690. Locke believed that all people had the same natural rights of life, liberty, and property. In this essay, Locke states that the primary purpose of government is to protect these natural rights. He also states that governments hold their power only with the consent of the people. Locke's ideas greatly influenced revolutions in America and France.

But though men, when they enter into society give up the equality, liberty, and executive power they had in the state of Nature into the hands of society . . . the power of the society or legislative constituted by them can never be supposed to extend farther than the common good. . . . Whoever has the legislative or supreme power of any commonwealth, is bound to govern by established standing laws, promulgated[1] and known to the people, and not by extemporary[2] decrees, by indifferent and upright judges, who are to decide controversies by those laws; and to employ the force of the community at home only in the execution of such laws, or abroad to prevent or redress foreign injuries and secure the community from inroads[3] and invasion. And all this to be directed to no other end but the peace, safety, and public good of the people. . . .

The reason why men enter into society is the preservation of their property; and the end while they choose and authorize a legislative is that there may be laws made, and rules set, as guards and fences to the properties of all the society, . . .

Whensoever, therefore, the legislative [power] shall transgress[4] this fundamental rule of society, and either by ambition, fear, folly, or corruption, endeavor to grasp themselves, or put into the hands of any other, an absolute power over the lives, liberties, and estates of the people, by this breach of trust they forfeit the power the people had put into their hands for quite contrary ends, and it devolves[5] to the people; who have a right to resume their original liberty, and by the establishment of a new legislative (such as they shall think fit), provide for their own safety and security. . . .

1. **promulgated** (PRAHM ul gayt id) *vt.* published or made known.
2. **extemporary** (ek STEM puh rehr ee) *adj.* without any preparation.
3. **inroads** (IN rohdz) *n.* advances at the expense of someone.
4. **transgress** (trans GRES) *vt.* go beyond; break.
5. **devolves** (dih VAHLVZ) *vt.* passes.

John Locke and a book of his writings

Thinking Critically

1. **Draw Inferences** According to Locke, how should a land be governed? Why do you think this is the case?
2. **Identify Central Issues** What does Locke say can happen if a government fails to protect the rights of its people?

Mozart and a sheet of his music

WITNESS HISTORY ◀)) AUDIO

Mozart, the Musical Genius

As a young boy, Wolfgang Amadeus Mozart astonished royalty with his musical talent. Although his life was relatively short, he composed more than 600 pieces of music. Many pieces embraced the spirit of the Enlightenment.

❝ Few have captured the spirit of the Enlightenment, its intellectual and social agenda, as has Mozart in his opera, *The Magic Flute*, . . . [It] is a series of variations on the triumph of light over darkness, of sun over moon, of day over night, of reason, tolerance, and love over passion, hate, and revenge. ❞
—Isaac Kramnick, historian

Focus Question As Enlightenment ideas spread across Europe, what cultural and political changes took place?

Enlightenment Ideas Spread

Objectives
- Identify the roles that censorship and salons played in the spread of new ideas.
- Describe how the Enlightenment affected the arts and literature.
- Understand how *philosophes* influenced enlightened despots.
- Explain why Enlightenment ideas were slow to reach most Europeans.

Terms, People, and Places

censorship	enlightened despot
salons	Frederick the Great
baroque	Catherine the Great
rococo	Joseph II

Note Taking

Reading Skill: Categorize On a sheet of paper, draw a concept web to help you record information from this section.

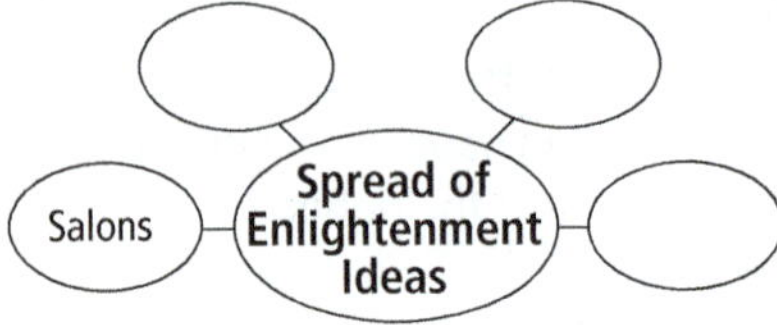

Paris, France, the heart of the Enlightenment, drew many intellectuals and others eager to debate new ideas. Reforms proposed one evening became the talk of the town the next day. Enlightenment ideas flowed from France, across Europe, and beyond. Everywhere, thinkers examined traditional beliefs and customs in the light of reason and found them flawed. Even some absolute monarchs experimented with Enlightenment ideas, although they drew back when changes threatened the established way of doing things.

New Ideas Challenge Society

Enlightenment ideas spread quickly through many levels of society. Educated people all over Europe eagerly read not only Diderot's *Encyclopedia* but also the small, inexpensive pamphlets that printers churned out on a broad range of issues. More and more, people saw that reform was necessary in order to achieve a just society.

During the Middle Ages, most Europeans had accepted without question a society based on divine-right rule, a strict class system, and a belief in heavenly reward for earthly suffering. In the Age of Reason, such ideas seemed unscientific and irrational. A just society, Enlightenment thinkers taught, should ensure social justice and happiness in this world. Not everyone agreed with this idea of replacing the values that existed, however.

Writers Face Censorship Most, but not all, government and church authorities felt they had a sacred duty to defend the old order. They believed that God had set up the old order. To protect against the attacks of the Enlightenment, they waged a war of **censorship,** or restricting access to ideas and information. They banned and burned books and imprisoned writers.

To avoid censorship, *philosophes* and writers like Montesquieu and Voltaire sometimes disguised their ideas in works of fiction. In the *Persian Letters,* Montesquieu used two fictional Persian travelers, named Usbék and Rica, to mock French society. The hero of Voltaire's satirical novel *Candide,* published in 1759, travels across Europe and even to the Americas and the Middle East in search of "the best of all possible worlds." Voltaire slyly uses the tale to expose the corruption and hypocrisy of European society.

Ideas Spread in Salons New literature, the arts, science, and philosophy were regular topics of discussion in **salons,** or informal social gatherings at which writers, artists, *philosophes,* and others exchanged ideas. The salon originated in the 1600s, when a group of noblewomen in Paris began inviting a few friends to their homes for poetry readings. By the 1700s, some middle-class women began holding salons. Here middle-class citizens could meet with the nobility on an equal footing to discuss and spread Enlightenment ideas.

Madame Geoffrin (zhoh FRAN) ran one of the most respected salons. In her home on the Rue St. Honoré (roo sant ahn ur AY), she brought together the brightest and most talented people of her day. The young musical genius Wolfgang Amadeus Mozart played for her guests, and Diderot was a regular at her weekly dinners for philosophers and poets.

 **Checkpoint** What did those opposed to Enlightenment ideas do to stop the spread of information?

Arts and Literature Reflect New Ideas

In the 1600s and 1700s, the arts <u>evolved</u> to meet changing tastes. As in earlier periods, artists and composers had to please their patrons, the men and women who commissioned works from them or gave them jobs.

From Grandeur to Charm In the age of Louis XIV, courtly art and architecture were either in the Greek and Roman tradition or in a grand, ornate style known as **baroque.** Baroque paintings were huge, colorful, and full of excitement. They glorified historic battles or the lives of saints. Such works matched the grandeur of European courts at that time.

Louis XV and his court led a much less formal lifestyle than Louis XIV. Architects and designers reflected this change by developing the **rococo** style. Rococo art moved away from religion and, unlike the heavy splendor of the baroque, was lighter, elegant, and charming. Rococo art in salons was believed to encourage the imagination. Furniture and tapestries featured delicate shells and flowers, and more pastel colors were used. Portrait painters showed noble subjects in charming rural settings, surrounded by happy servants and pets. Although this style was criticized by the *philosophes* for its superficiality, it had a vast audience in the upper class and with the growing middle class as well.

Satire by Swift
Jonathan Swift published the satirical *Gulliver's Travels* in 1726. Here, an illustration from the book depicts a bound Gulliver and the Lilliputians, who are six-inch-tall, bloodthirsty characters. Although *Gulliver's Travels* satirizes political life in eighteenth-century England, it is still a classic today. *Why did writers hide their feelings about society?*

Vocabulary Builder

<u>evolved</u>—(ee VAHLVD) *v.* developed gradually over time

The Enlightenment Inspires Composers The new Enlightenment ideals led composers and musicians to develop new forms of music. There was a transition in music, as well as art, from the baroque style to rococo. An elegant style of music known as "classical" followed. Ballets and opera—plays set to music—were performed at royal courts, and opera houses sprang up from Italy to England. Before this era, only the social elite could afford to commission musicians to play for them. In the early to mid-1700s, however, the growing middle class could afford to pay for concerts to be performed publicly.

Among the towering musical figures of the era was Johann Sebastian Bach. A devout German Lutheran, Bach wrote beautiful religious works for organ and choirs. He also wrote sonatas for violin and harpsichord. Another German-born composer, George Frideric Handel, spent much of his life in England. There, he wrote *Water Music* and other pieces for King George I, as well as more than 30 operas. His most celebrated work, the *Messiah,* combines instruments and voices and is often performed at Christmas and Easter.

Composer Franz Joseph Haydn was one of the most important figures in the development of classical music. He helped develop forms for the string quartet and the symphony. Haydn had a close friendship with another famous composer, Wolfgang Amadeus Mozart. Mozart was a child prodigy who gained instant celebrity status as a composer and performer. His brilliant operas, graceful symphonies, and moving religious music helped define the new style of composition. Although he died in poverty at age 35, he produced an enormous amount of music during his lifetime. Mozart's musical legacy thrives today.

Composers adopted the graceful rococo style in their works of music. They wrote pieces for an instrument called the harpsichord (above) that reflected this new style. AUDIO

ROCOCO REACTION

In the eighteenth century, France experienced an aesthetic shift in art, clothing, music, and architecture. Curving lines, pastel colors, elegant music, and paintings depicting delightful love scenes replaced the formal lines and dark colors of the baroque style. The rise of this new style, referred to as rococo, reflected changes in French society that were brought about by the Enlightenment. As the French elite became more involved in the salons of the day (numbering about 800 in Paris), they competed with each other for the most fashionable home in which to host their intellectual discussions.

The Novel Takes Shape By the 1700s, literature developed new forms and a wider audience. Middle-class readers, for example, liked stories about their own times told in straightforward prose. One result was an outpouring of novels, or long works of prose fiction. English novelists wrote many popular stories. Daniel Defoe wrote *Robinson Crusoe,* an exciting tale about a sailor shipwrecked on a tropical island. This novel is still well known today. In a novel called *Pamela,* Samuel Richardson used a series of letters to tell a story about a servant girl. This technique was adopted by other authors of the period.

✔ **Checkpoint** How did the arts and literature change as Enlightenment ideas spread?

Enlightened Despots Embrace New Ideas

The courts of Europe became enlivened as *philosophes* tried to persuade rulers to adopt their ideas. The *philosophes* hoped to convince the ruling classes that reform was necessary. Some monarchs did accept Enlightenment ideas. Others still practiced absolutism, a political doctrine in which a monarch had seemingly unlimited power. Those that did accept these new ideas became **enlightened despots,** or absolute rulers who used their power to bring about political and social change.

Frederick II Attempts Reform Frederick II, known as **Frederick the Great,** exerted extremely tight control over his subjects during his reign as king of Prussia from 1740 to 1786. Still, he saw himself as the "first servant of the state," with a duty to work for the common good.

Ornate Artifacts
In the examples of the rococo style shown here, notice the elegance of the delicate lace and floral patterns, as well as the charming paintings depicting the pleasures of everyday life.

Thinking Critically
1. **Make Generalizations** Based on what you see in the collection of images here, describe what you think it would have been like to live during this time period.
2. **Draw Inferences** Why might the *philosophes* have disliked the rococo style?

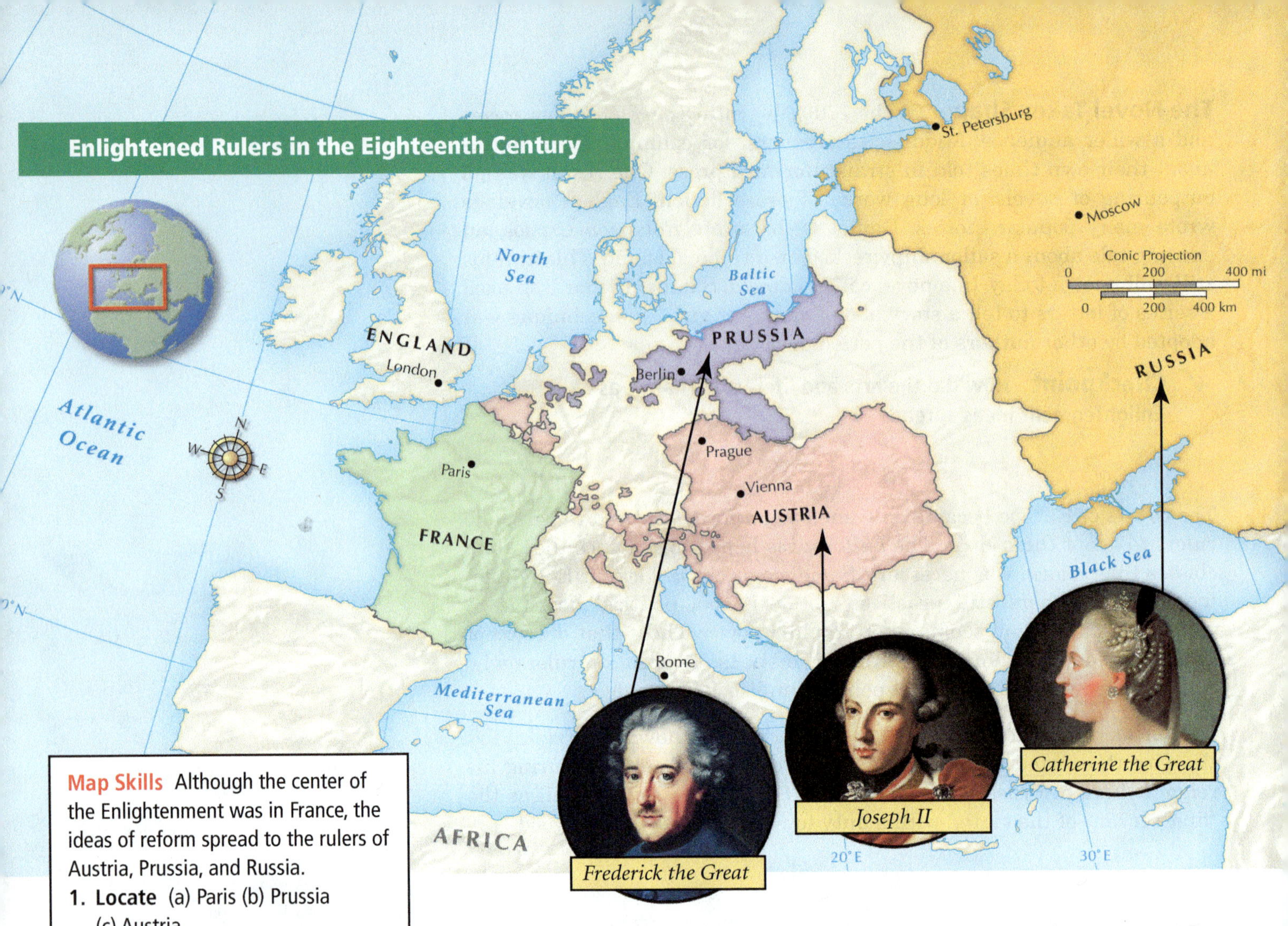

Map Skills Although the center of the Enlightenment was in France, the ideas of reform spread to the rulers of Austria, Prussia, and Russia.

1. **Locate** (a) Paris (b) Prussia (c) Austria
2. **Location** Which enlightened despot ruled farthest from Paris?
3. **Draw Conclusions** According to the map, what regions of Europe were affected by enlightened despots?

Geography *Interactive*
For: Audio guided tour
Web Code: nap-1721

Frederick openly praised Voltaire's work and invited several of the French intellectuals of the age to Prussia. Some of his first acts as king were to reduce the use of torture and allow a free press. Most of Frederick's reforms were directed at making the Prussian government more efficient. To do this, he reorganized the government's civil service and simplified laws. Frederick also tolerated religious differences, welcoming victims of religious persecution. "In my kingdom," he said, "everyone can go to heaven in his own fashion." His religious tolerance and also his disdain for torture showed Frederick's genuine belief in enlightened reform. In the end, however, Frederick desired a stronger monarchy and more power for himself.

Catherine the Great Studies *Philosophes'* Works

Catherine II, or **Catherine the Great,** empress of Russia, read the works of the *philosophes* and exchanged letters with Voltaire and Diderot. She praised Voltaire as someone who had "fought the united enemies of humankind: superstition, fanaticism, ignorance, trickery." Catherine believed in the Enlightenment ideas of equality and liberty.

Catherine, who became empress in 1762, toyed with implementing Enlightenment ideas. Early in her reign, she made some limited reforms in law and government. Catherine abolished torture and established religious tolerance in her lands. She granted nobles a charter of rights and criticized the institution of serfdom. Still, like Frederick in Prussia, Catherine did not intend to give up power. In the end, her main political contribution to Russia proved to be an expanded empire.

Joseph II Continues Reform In Austria, Hapsburg empress Maria Theresa ruled as an absolute monarch. Although she did not push for reforms, she is considered to be an enlightened despot by some historians because she worked to improve peasants' way of life. The most radical of the enlightened despots was her son and successor, Joseph II. Joseph was an eager student of the Enlightenment, and he traveled in disguise among his subjects to learn of their problems.

Joseph continued the work of Maria Theresa, who had begun to modernize Austria's government. Despite opposition, Joseph supported religious equality for Protestants and Jews in his Catholic empire. He ended censorship by allowing a free press and attempted to bring the Catholic Church under royal control. He sold the property of many monasteries that were not involved in education or care of the sick and used the proceeds to support those that were. Joseph even abolished serfdom. Like many of his other reforms, however, this measure was canceled after his death.

 **Checkpoint** Why were the *philosophes* interested in sharing their beliefs with European rulers?

Lives of the Majority Change Slowly

Most Europeans were untouched by either courtly or middle-class culture. They remained what they had always been—peasants living in small rural villages. Echoes of serfdom still remained throughout Europe despite advances in Western Europe. Their culture, based on centuries-old traditions, changed slowly.

By the late 1700s, however, radical ideas about equality and social justice finally seeped into peasant villages. While some peasants eagerly sought to topple the old order, others resisted efforts to bring about change. In the 1800s, war and political upheaval, as well as changing economic conditions, would transform peasant life in Europe.

 **Checkpoint** During this time, why did change occur slowly for most Europeans?

Terms, People, and Places

1. For each term, person, or place listed at the beginning of the section, write a sentence explaining its significance.

Note Taking

2. **Reading Skill: Categorize** Use your completed concept webs to answer the Focus Question: As Enlightenment ideas spread across Europe, what cultural and political changes took place?

Comprehension and Critical Thinking

3. **Draw Conclusions** How did ideas of a "just society" change during the Age of Reason?

4. **Summarize** Explain the differences between baroque and rococo, and how these styles were reflected in art.

5. **Analyze Information** What did Frederick the Great mean when he said, "In my kingdom, everyone can go to heaven in his own fashion"?

6. **Predict Consequences** What actions might peasants take as they learn more about ideas such as equality?

● **Writing About History**

Quick Write: Narrowing Your Response In the essay prompt below, identify and list the key words. Then write a brief outline of the main ideas to help you form the best response. In your own words, explain what is being asked of you in the instructions.

- Think of the various effects of the Enlightenment. Identify which effect you think most contributed to society, both short-term and long-term. Explain your response.

Reading Skill: Summarize Fill in a concept web like the one below with information about the enlightened despots and their contributions.

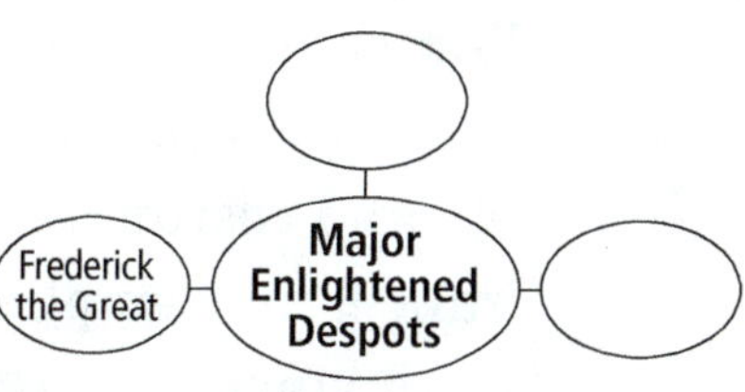

View of La Scala in Milan, mid-1800s ▼

Opera

Operas originated in Florence, Italy, in the seventeenth century. First called *drama per musica*, or drama through music, these musical performances typically involve large casts and elaborate sets and costumes. When Italian operas were performed in France, they emphasized glory and love, and included ballet and lavish stage settings to please the French court. Handel, Mozart, Verdi, Wagner, and Puccini composed some of the world's most famous operas. ◄)) AUDIO

◄ Empress Maria Theresa of Austria, whose country ruled Italy by the early 1700s, founded Milan's La Scala (background image), one of Europe's oldest and most celebrated opera houses. Built in 1776, this opera house still showcases the great operas of the nineteenth century, including composer Giuseppe Verdi's masterpieces, *Aida* and *La Traviata*. Verdi's first opera, *Oberto*, was performed at La Scala, and he was the beloved house composer for many years. After years of care and renovation, the interior of La Scala retains its elegance as operatic performances continue to entertain audiences today.

◄ The "Three Tenors" (from left), Placido Domingo, José Carreras, and Luciano Pavarotti, are some of the best-known opera singers of the modern era. In the hierarchy of the opera stage, the tenor is the highest male voice and usually plays the part of the hero. The female lead is typically sung by a soprano, which is the highest female voice. Singers in the lower ranges (mezzo-soprano and alto for women, baritone and bass for men) generally play villainous or comic roles.

Thinking Critically

1. **Draw Inferences** How do you think composing an opera is different from composing a symphony?
2. **Determine Relevance** Why did operas appeal to composers and musicians during the Enlightenment?

556

Thomas Paine

WITNESS HISTORY 🔊 AUDIO

Paine's *Common Sense*

Early in 1776, English colonists in North America eagerly read the newly published *Common Sense,* by Thomas Paine. This pamphlet called on them to declare their independence from Britain and echoed the themes of the Enlightenment.

> ❝'Tis repugnant to reason, to the universal order of things, to all examples from former ages, to suppose that this Continent can long remain subject to any external power.❞
>
> —Thomas Paine, *Common Sense*

Focus Question How did ideas of the Enlightenment lead to the independence and founding of the United States of America?

Birth of the American Republic

Objectives

- Describe characteristics of Britain and its American colonies in the mid-1700s.
- Outline the events that led to the American Revolution.
- Summarize the events and significance of the American Revolution.
- Analyze how the new Constitution reflected the ideas of the Enlightenment.

Terms, People, and Places

George III	Yorktown, Virginia
Stamp Act	Treaty of Paris
George Washington	James Madison
Thomas Jefferson	Benjamin Franklin
popular sovereignty	federal republic

Note Taking

Reading Skill: Recognize Sequence As you read, complete a timeline like the one below with important dates that led up to the formation of the United States government.

French and Indian War ends.

1763

On the eve of the American Revolution, Britain was a formidable foe whose power stretched throughout the world. In addition, an ambitious new ruler sought to expand the powers of the monarchy.

Britain Becomes a Global Power

There are several key reasons for Britain's rise to global prominence:

- Location placed England in a position to control trade. In the 1500s and 1600s, English merchants sent ships across the world's oceans and planted outposts in the West Indies, North America, and India. From these tiny settlements, England would build a global empire.
- England offered a climate favorable to business and commerce and put fewer restrictions on trade than some of its neighbors.
- In the 1700s, Britain was generally on the winning side in European conflicts. With the Treaty of Utrecht, France gave Nova Scotia and Newfoundland to Britain. In 1763, the end of the French and Indian War and the Seven Years' War brought Britain all of French Canada. The British also monopolized the slave trade in Spanish America, which brought enormous wealth to British merchants.
- England's territory expanded closer to home as well. In 1707, England and Wales were united with Scotland to become the United Kingdom of Great Britain. Free trade with Scotland created a larger market for farmers and manufacturers. Ireland had come under English control during the 1600s. It was formally united with Great Britain in 1801.

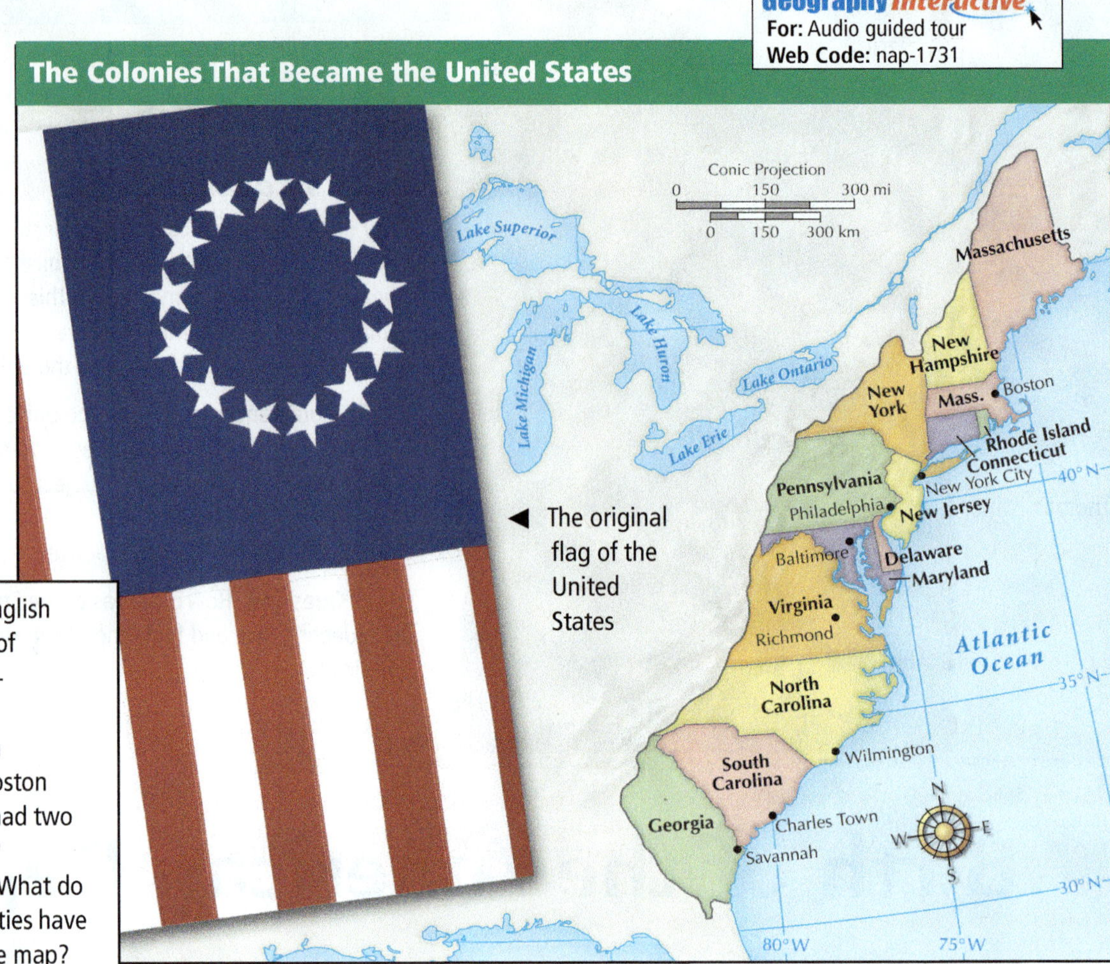

◀ The original flag of the United States

Map Skills Cities in the English colonies were busy centers of trade and important to Britain's economy.

1. **Locate** (a) Philadelphia (b) Massachusetts (c) Boston
2. **Region** Which colony had two separate pieces of land?
3. **Analyze Information** What do almost all the colonial cities have in common based on the map? Why was this important?

Vocabulary Builder

<u>assert</u>—(uh SURT) *vt.* to insist on being recognized

In 1760, George III began a 60-year reign. Unlike his father and grandfather, the new king was born in England. He spoke English and loved Britain. But George was eager to recover the powers the crown had lost. Following his mother's advice, "George, be a king!" he set out to reassert royal power. He wanted to end Whig domination, choose his own ministers, dissolve the cabinet system, and make Parliament follow his will. Gradually, George found seats in Parliament for "the king's friends." Then, with their help, he began to <u>assert</u> his leadership. Many of his policies, however, would prove disastrous.

✔ **Checkpoint**   What led to Britain's rise to global prominence in the mid-1700s?

The Colonies in the Mid-1700s

By 1750, a string of prosperous colonies stretched along the eastern coast of North America. They were part of Britain's growing empire. Colonial cities such as Boston, New York, and Philadelphia were busy commercial centers that linked North America to the West Indies, Africa, and Europe. Colonial shipyards produced many vessels for this trade.

Britain applied mercantilist policies to its colonies in an attempt to strengthen its own economy by exporting more than it imported. To this end, in the 1600s, Parliament had passed the Navigation Acts to regulate colonial trade and manufacturing. For the most part, however, these acts were not rigorously enforced. Therefore, activities like smuggling were common and not considered crimes by the colonists.

By the mid-1700s, the colonies were home to diverse religious and ethnic groups. Social distinctions were more blurred than in Europe, although wealthy landowners and merchants dominated government and society. In politics, as in much else, there was a good deal of free discussion. Colonists felt entitled to the rights of English citizens, and their colonial assemblies exercised much control over local affairs. Many also had an increasing sense of their own destiny separate from Britain.

✔ **Checkpoint** In what ways were the colonies already developing independence from Britain?

Colonists Express Discontent

The Seven Years' War and the French and Indian War in North America had drained the British treasury. King George III and his advisors thought that the colonists should help pay for these wars. To increase taxes paid by colonists, Parliament passed the Sugar Act in 1764, which imposed import taxes, and the **Stamp Act** in 1765, which imposed taxes on items such as newspapers and pamphlets. "No taxation without representation," the colonists protested. They believed that because they had no representatives in Parliament, they should not be taxed. Parliament repealed the Stamp Act in 1766, but then passed a Declaratory Act that said it had complete authority over the colonists.

Colonists Rebel Against Britain A series of violent clashes intensified the colonists' anger. In March 1770, British soldiers in Boston opened fire on a crowd that was pelting them with stones and snowballs. Colonists called the death of five protesters the Boston Massacre. Then in December 1773, a handful of colonists hurled a cargo of recently arrived British tea into the harbor to protest a tax on tea. The incident became known as the Boston Tea Party. When Parliament passed harsh laws to punish Massachusetts for the destruction of the tea, other colonies rallied to oppose the British response.

As tensions increased, fighting spread. Finally, representatives from each colony gathered in Philadelphia and met in a Continental Congress to decide what action to take. Among the participants were the radical yet fair-minded Massachusetts lawyer John Adams, who had defended the British soldiers involved in the Boston Massacre in their trial; Virginia planter and soldier **George Washington;** and political and social leaders from other colonies.

Colonists Declare Independence In April 1775, the ongoing tension between the colonists and the British exploded into war in Lexington and Concord, Massachusetts. This war is known as the Revolutionary War, or the American Revolution. The Congress met soon after and set up a Continental Army, with George Washington in command. Although many battles ended in British victories, the colonists were determined to fight at any cost. In 1776, the

Drafting the Declaration
Benjamin Franklin, John Adams, and Thomas Jefferson (from left to right)

The Declaration of Independence stands as one of the most important documents in all of history. It still serves as inspiration for people around the world. Where did some of the ideas of the Declaration originate?

66 We hold these truths to be self-evident, that all men are created equal, that they are endowed by their Creator with certain unalienable Rights, that among these are Life, Liberty and the pursuit of Happiness. That to secure these rights, Governments are instituted among Men, deriving their just powers from the consent of the governed; That whenever any Form of Government becomes destructive of these ends it is the Right of the People to alter or to abolish it, and to institute new Government, laying its foundation on such principles and organizing its powers in such form, as to them shall seem most likely to effect their Safety and Happiness. 99
—*Declaration of Independence*, July 4, 1776 ◀)) AUDIO

George Washington

When George Washington (1732–1799) was chosen to lead the American army, the British thought he would be a failure. Washington indeed faced many challenges, including an army that did not have weapons, uniforms, or bedding. He struggled to incorporate order and discipline and to instill pride and loyalty in his soldiers. Washington persevered to American victory. His success as a leader continued when he became the nation's first President. **How did Washington hold the army together through difficult times?**

James Madison

James Madison (1751–1836) arrived at the Constitutional Convention in Philadelphia in May 1787 with his thick notebooks on history and government. Madison chose a seat in front of the president's chair and kept detailed notes of the debates. Madison was greatly respected and quickly became the Convention's floor leader. His notebooks remained unpublished for more than 50 years, but they are now our main source of information about the birth of the Constitution. **What did the Framers of the Constitution have in common?**

Benjamin Franklin

Benjamin Franklin (1706–1790) was a philosopher, scientist, publisher, legislator, and diplomat. Sent by Congress to France in 1776 to seek financial and military support for the war, he soon became popular in France because of his intellect and wit. Those who admired America's goal of attaining freedom also admired Franklin. When Franklin returned to America after nine years, he served as a delegate to the Constitutional Convention as the eldest of the delegates. **Why was Franklin admired in France?**

Second Continental Congress took a momentous step, voting to declare independence from Britain. **Thomas Jefferson** of Virginia was the principal author of the Declaration of Independence, a document that reflects John Locke's ideas of the government's obligation to protect the people's natural rights to "life, liberty, and property."

The Declaration included another of Locke's ideas: people had the right "to alter or to abolish" unjust governments—a right to revolt. The principle of **popular sovereignty,** which states that all government power comes from the people, is also an important point in the Declaration. Jefferson carefully detailed the colonists' grievances against Britain. Because the king had trampled colonists' natural rights, he argued, the colonists had the right to rebel and set up a new government that would protect them. Aware of the risks involved, on July 4, 1776, American leaders adopted the Declaration, pledging "our lives, our fortunes, and our sacred honor" to creating and protecting the new United States of America.

 **Checkpoint** What Enlightenment ideas are reflected in the Declaration of Independence?

The American Revolution Continues

At first, the American cause looked bleak. The British had a large number of trained soldiers, a huge fleet, and greater resources. About one third of the American colonists were Loyalists, or those who supported Britain. Many others refused to fight for either side. The Americans lacked military resources, had little money to pay soldiers, and did not have a strategic plan.

Still, colonists had some advantages. One was the geography of the diverse continent. Since colonists were fighting on their own soil, they were familiar with its thick woods and inadequate roads. Other advantages were their strong leader, George Washington, and their fierce determination to fight for their ideals of liberty.

To counteract these advantages, the British worked to create alliances within the colonies. A number of Native American groups sided with the British, while others saw potential advantages in supporting the colonists' cause. Additionally, the British offered freedom to any enslaved people who were willing to fight the colonists.

France Provides Support The first turning point in the war came in 1777, when the Americans triumphed over the British at the Battle of Saratoga. This victory persuaded France to join the Americans against its old rival, Britain. The alliance brought the Americans desperately needed supplies, trained soldiers, and French warships. Spurred by the French example, the Netherlands and Spain added their support.

Hard times continued, however. In the brutal winter of 1777–1778, Continental troops at Valley Forge suffered from cold, hunger, and disease. Throughout this crisis and others, Washington was patient, courageous, and determined. He held the ragged army together.

Fearless Leader
George Washington directs his troops on the battlefield. *What traits did Washington possess that helped lead Americans to victory?*

The Roots of American Democracy

The Framers of the United States Constitution were well educated and widely read. They were familiar with governments of ancient Greece and Rome and those of contemporary Great Britain and Europe. Political writings such as Montesquieu's *The Spirit of the Laws*, Rousseau's *Social Contract*, and Locke's *Two Treatises of Government* contained principles that greatly influenced the Framers in the development of the Constitution. Centuries later, these fundamental democratic principles of American government—popular sovereignty, limited government, separation of powers, and checks and balances—are still in place. The diagram here shows checks and balances, one of Montesquieu's ideas, which ensures that one branch does not accumulate too much power.

Checks and Balances

Judicial Branch

Legislative Branch

Executive Branch

Congress may impeach judges; Senate may reject appointment of judges.

Courts may declare acts of Congress unconstitutional.

Courts may declare executive actions unconstitutional.

President appoints judges.

President may veto legislation.

Congress may impeach the President and may override veto; Senate approves or rejects treaties and appointments.

History Interactive
For: Interactive diagram
Web Code: nap-1732

Thinking Critically

1. **Draw Conclusions** What additional ideas might the Framers have learned from the political writings of the Enlightenment thinkers?
2. **Summarize** Explain how the basic principle of checks and balances works.

Treaty of Paris Ends the War In 1781, the French fleet blockaded the Chesapeake Bay, which enabled Washington to force the surrender of a British army at **Yorktown, Virginia.** With that defeat, the British war effort crumbled. Two years later, American, British, and French diplomats signed the **Treaty of Paris,** ending the war. In that treaty, Britain recognized the independence of the United States of America. The Americans' victory can be attributed to their resilient dedication to attaining independence.

✔ **Checkpoint** What advantages did the colonists have in battling Britain for their independence?

A New Constitution

The Articles of Confederation was the nation's first constitution. It proved to be too weak to rule the new United States effectively. To address this problem, the nation's leaders gathered once more in Philadelphia. Among them were George Washington, **James Madison,** and **Benjamin Franklin.**

During the hot summer of 1787, they met in secret to redraft the articles of the new constitution. The result was a document that established a government run by the people, for the people.

Enlightenment Ideas Have Great Impact The Framers of the Constitution had studied history and absorbed the ideas of Locke, Montesquieu, and Rousseau. They saw government in terms of a social contract into which "We the People of the United States" entered. They provided not only for an elective legislature but also for an elected president rather than a hereditary monarch. For the first President, voters would choose George Washington.

The Constitution created a **federal republic,** with power divided between the federal, or national, government and the states. A central feature of the new federal government was the separation of powers among the legislative, executive, and judicial branches, an idea borrowed directly from Montesquieu. Within that structure, each branch of government was provided with checks and balances on the other branches.

The Bill of Rights, the first ten amendments to the Constitution, was important to the passage of the Constitution. It recognized the idea that people had basic rights that the government must protect, such as freedom of religion, speech, and the press. The Bill of Rights, like the Constitution, put the *philosophes'* Enlightenment ideas into practice. In 1789, the Constitution became the supreme law of the land, which means it became the nation's fundamental law. This remarkable document has endured for more than 200 years.

Symbol of Freedom The Constitution of the United States created the most progressive government of its day. From the start, the new republic was a symbol of freedom to European countries and reformers in Latin America. Its constitution would be copied or adapted by many lands throughout the world. The Enlightenment ideals that had inspired American colonists brought changes in Europe too. In 1789, a revolution in France toppled the monarchy in the name of liberty and equality. Before long, other Europeans would take up the cry for freedom as well.

✔ **Checkpoint** Explain the influence of Enlightenment ideas on the United States Constitution and Bill of Rights.

The U.S. Bill of Rights

1st: Guarantees freedom of religion, speech, press, assembly, and petition

2nd: Right to bear arms

3rd: Prohibits quartering of troops in private homes

4th: Protects from unreasonable searches and seizures

5th: No punishment without due process of law

6th: Right to a speedy and public trial in the state where the offense was committed

7th: Right to jury trial for civil cases if over $20

8th: Prohibits excessive bail and cruel and unusual punishments

9th: Civil rights are not restricted to those specified by these amendments.

10th: Powers not granted to the national government belong to the states and to the people.

Chart Skills The first ten amendments to the United States Constitution are known as the Bill of Rights. *What is the significance of the 10th Amendment?*

SECTION 3 Assessment

Progress Monitoring Online
For: Self-quiz with vocabulary practice
Web Code: naa-1731

Terms, People, and Places

1. For each term, person, or place listed at the beginning of the section, write a sentence explaining its significance.

Note Taking

2. **Reading Skill: Recognize Sequence** Use your completed timeline to answer the Focus Question: How did ideas of the Enlightenment lead to the independence and founding of the United States of America?

Comprehension and Critical Thinking

3. **Make Generalizations** Describe society and politics in the 13 English colonies during the mid-1700s.
4. **Express Problems Clearly** Explain why conflict between the colonists and Britain increased after 1763.
5. **Identify Point of View** What reasons might a Loyalist have for opposing the American Revolution?
6. **Determine Relevance** Give two examples of why the Bill of Rights is important to you.

● Writing About History

Quick Write: Providing Elaboration To prove that you fully understand a subject, you need to include specific details. You should use facts, dates, names, examples, explanations, or quotes to support your answer. Write a paragraph to describe the events that led to the American Revolution. Then read through your response and add specific details where you can.

SPREADING THE WORD OF REVOLUTION

While Enlightenment thinkers had a profound impact on the leaders of the American Revolution, newspapers made a great impact on the colonists. Colonists depended on newspapers for information about the war and the economy. News about the war was the first great news event to report in America. Would the colonists be free? Or would English control continue? As demand increased, newspapers began publishing several times a week instead of weekly. The number of newspapers increased from 29 to 48 from 1770 to 1775. During this time, the American newspaper changed from a weak form of communication to a propaganda machine that included controversial political cartoons and essays.

Trouble for newspapers came in 1765 when the British government passed the Stamp Act. Newspapers were forced to pay the tax imposed by the Stamp Act or face heavy penalties. Colonists already felt they had no representation so they became even more discontented. Many newspapers strongly opposed the Stamp Act and showed their resentment in their pages with cartoons, editorial content, and typographical devices. The *Maryland Gazette*, for example, set a skull and crossbones on its front page where the tax stamp belonged (facing page). Others ceased publication. The strength of the press was evident when the British government was forced to repeal the Stamp Act. Newspapers had voiced protest effectively and would continue to be a powerful medium of communication for years to come.

▲ Engraving by Paul Revere of the 1770 Boston Massacre. Revere exaggerated the event to incite anger among the colonists against the British.

▼ Engraving of the Battle of Lexington, the first battle of the American Revolution. Demand for exciting news of the war led to the creation of more newspapers.

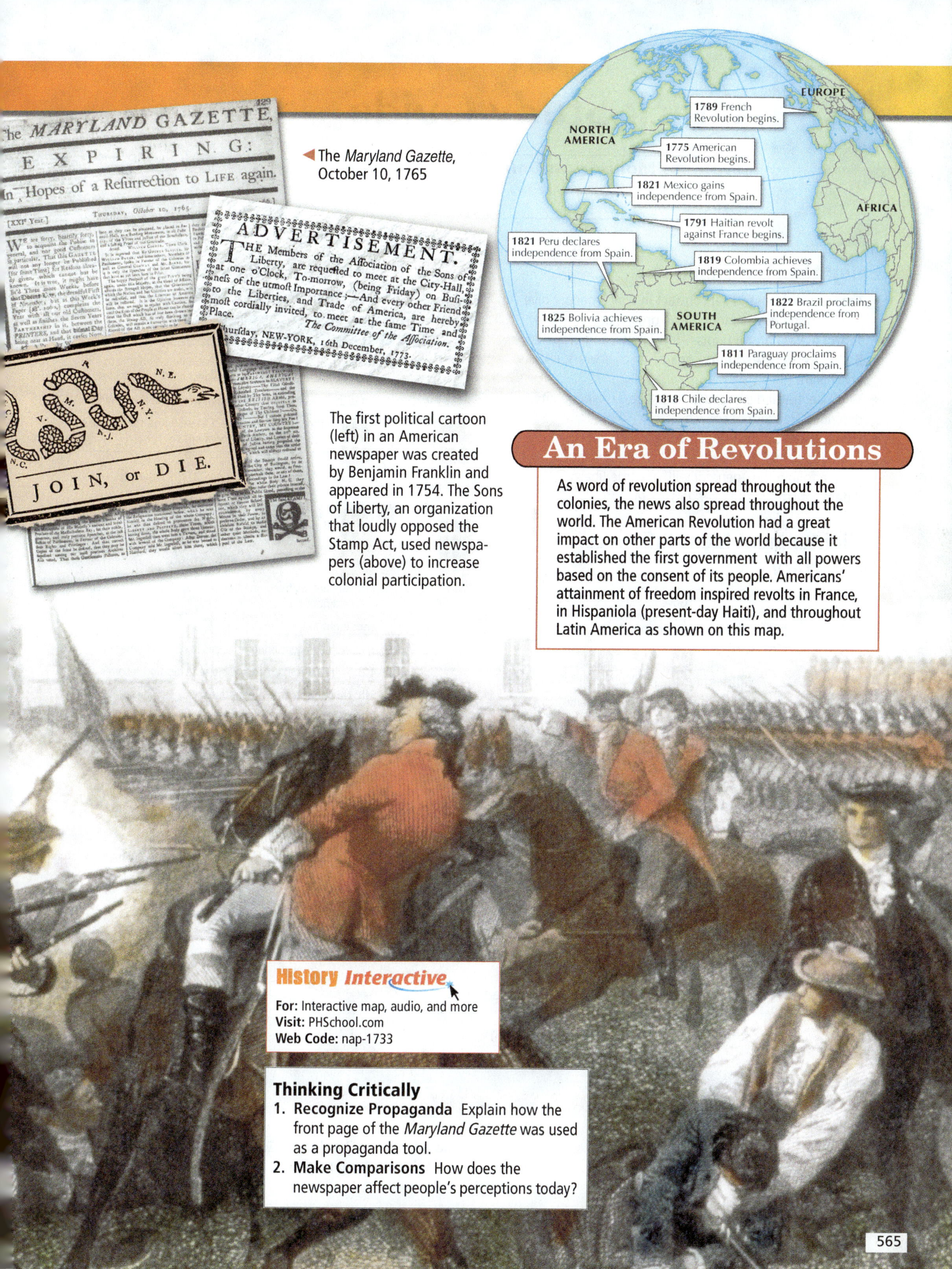

◀ The *Maryland Gazette*, October 10, 1765

The first political cartoon (left) in an American newspaper was created by Benjamin Franklin and appeared in 1754. The Sons of Liberty, an organization that loudly opposed the Stamp Act, used newspapers (above) to increase colonial participation.

An Era of Revolutions

As word of revolution spread throughout the colonies, the news also spread throughout the world. The American Revolution had a great impact on other parts of the world because it established the first government with all powers based on the consent of its people. Americans' attainment of freedom inspired revolts in France, in Hispaniola (present-day Haiti), and throughout Latin America as shown on this map.

History Interactive

For: Interactive map, audio, and more
Visit: PHSchool.com
Web Code: nap-1733

Thinking Critically

1. **Recognize Propaganda** Explain how the front page of the *Maryland Gazette* was used as a propaganda tool.
2. **Make Comparisons** How does the newspaper affect people's perceptions today?

Quick Study Guide

Progress Monitoring *Online*
For: Self-test with vocabulary practice
Web Code: naa-1741

Enlightenment Thinkers

- **Thomas Hobbes:** social contract in which people give power to the government for an organized society
- **John Locke:** natural rights—life, liberty, and property
- **Baron de Montesquieu:** separation of powers; checks and balances
- **Voltaire:** battled corruption, injustice, and inequality; defended freedom of speech
- **Denis Diderot:** *Encyclopedia*
- **Jean-Jacques Rousseau:** social contract in which people follow the "general will" for true liberty
- **Adam Smith:** free market; laissez faire

Enlightenment Ideas Influence Democracy

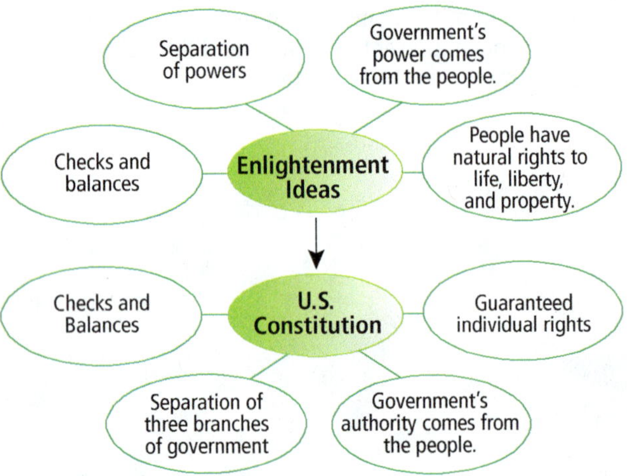

American Declaration of Independence: Main Ideas

Declaration of Independence: Main Ideas
• All men are created equal and have natural rights to life, liberty, and the pursuit of happiness.
• It is the government's obligation to protect these rights.
• If a government fails to protect these rights, the people can revolt and set up a new government.

The U.S. Bill of Rights

The U.S. Bill of Rights
1st: Guarantees freedom of religion, speech, press, assembly, and petition
2nd: Right to bear arms
3rd: Prohibits quartering of troops in private homes
4th: Protects from unreasonable searches and seizures
5th: No punishment without due process of law
6th: Right to a speedy and public trial in the state where the offense was committed
7th: Right to jury trial for civil cases if over $20
8th: Prohibits excessive bail and cruel and unusual punishments
9th: Civil rights are not restricted to those specified by these amendments.
10th: Powers not granted to the national government belong to the states and to the people.

Key Events From 1700–1789

1700s France sees flowering of Enlightenment thought.

1721 Johann Sebastian Bach publishes his Brandenburg Concertos.

1740 Frederick II begins his reign in Prussia.

Chapter Events
Global Events

1720   1730   1740

1735 China's Emperor Qianlong begins his long reign.

Concept Connector

Essential Question Review

To connect prior knowledge with what you have learned in this chapter, answer the questions below in your Concept Connector journal. Use the journal in the Reading and Note Taking Study Guide to record your answers (or go to www.phschool.com **Web Code: nad-1707**). In addition, record information about the following concepts:

- Cultural Diffusion: Roots of American Democracy
- Political Systems: federal government
- Democracy: The American Declaration of Independence
- Impact of the Individual: John Locke

1. **Cooperation** During the American Revolution economic and military aid from France helped the American colonists defeat the British. Suggest at least one reason why France would have helped the American colonists. What role did Benjamin Franklin play in the alliance forged between the two nations? What French military tactic made the colonists' defeat of the British army possible?

2. **Conflict** Inspired by the American Revolution, colonists in Central and South America fought for freedom from their colonial rulers. In addition, many revolutionary leaders in Central and South America were influenced by the ideas of the Enlightenment. Review the concept web "Enlightenment Ideas Influence Democracy" in the Quick Study Guide in this chapter. Which Enlightenment ideas would be most likely to cause conflict between colonists and their rulers? Why?

3. **Impact of the Individual** Many individuals contributed to the success of the American Revolution. Review Section 4 in this chapter and choose one individual who you believe made the most significant impact. Describe this individual's contribution and explain its importance to winning the American Revolution.

■ Connections to Today

1. **Democracy: Still Strong Today** As you have read, the Framers of the United States Constitution were inspired by Montesquieu, Rousseau, and Locke. Democratic revolutions around the world were inspired by the same Enlightenment ideas that had inspired American colonists. Even today, nations seeking a model for democratic government often turn to the Constitution of the United States. Research and write a newspaper article about one of these nations.

2. **Culture: Modern Salons** Salons provided a way for people to gather and share ideas, especially during the Enlightenment. Today, we know that many people do this without ever meeting in person—through the Internet. People are able to join chat rooms and newsgroups to share their thoughts. Many discussions on the Internet lack the serious-minded tone of a salon conversation and the benefit of face-to-face conversation. The Internet does, however, provide a sense of community, where people can gather to discuss ideas, even if it is a "virtual" living room. Compare salons of the Enlightenment and Internet chat rooms. Explain which you think is the better forum for sharing ideas, and why.

1751	1759	1762	1776
Diderot publishes *Encyclopedia*.	Voltaire publishes *Candide*.	Rousseau publishes *The Social Contract*.	American leaders sign the Declaration of Independence.

History *Interactive*
For: Interactive timeline
Web Code: nap-1701

1750 **1760** **1770** **1780**

1754	1763	1789
French and Indian War begins.	Treaty of Paris gives Britain control of Canada.	The French Revolution begins.

Chapter Assessment

Terms, People, and Places

Complete each sentence by choosing the correct answer from the list of terms below. You will not use all of the terms.

natural rights
John Locke
laissez faire
rococo
baroque
Joseph II

Montesquieu
federal republic
Yorktown, Virginia
Frederick the Great
Treaty of Paris
Rousseau

1. In a ______, power is divided between the federal government and the states.
2. ______ advanced the idea of separation of powers.
3. The ______ style influenced by the Enlightenment was personal, elegant, and charming.
4. The enlightened despot who ended censorship was ______.
5. The American Revolution ended when George Washington forced the surrender of the British at ______.
6. ______ believed in ______, which are the rights to life, liberty, and property.

Main Ideas

Section 1 (pp. 544–549)
7. What idea did John Locke advocate for the role of a government?
8. Explain the economic policy of laissez faire.

Section 2 (pp. 550–556)
9. How did the Enlightenment affect some rulers in Europe, and what are these rulers known as?

Section 3 (pp. 557–565)
10. How did taxation create tensions between the American colonies and the British government?

11. How does the Bill of Rights reflect a key Enlightenment idea?

Chapter Focus Question
12. How did Enlightenment thinkers inspire revolutionaries to push for radical changes in government and society?

Critical Thinking

13. **Synthesize Information** Choose one *philosophe* from this chapter and describe how he or she might respond to a human rights issue that has been in the news recently.
14. **Predict Consequences** Given the impact the Enlightenment thinkers had on the American Revolution, what can you predict will happen in other areas of the world? Explain why you predicted what you did.
15. **Analyzing Visuals** Identify the style of this painting and describe its characteristics.

16. **Make Comparisons** Compare Britain and its North American colonies in the mid-1700s.
17. **Analyze Information** What ideas about government do you think English settlers brought with them to the Americas?

● Writing About History

In this chapter's three Section Assessments, you developed skills for writing for assessment.

Writing for Assessment Select either a philosopher from the Enlightenment or an important figure from the American Revolution. Explain how his or her actions, beliefs, and/or works contributed to improving society.

Prewriting
- Consider what you know about the people in this chapter and choose one who interests you.
- Develop a focus or main idea. Write a single sentence identifying the main idea you will develop.
- As you prepare to write your essay, make sure you understand the instructions. Circle verbs, nouns, or important phrases in the question.

Drafting
- Develop a thesis statement that identifies the focus of your essay.
- Make an outline for your essay and fill in facts and examples.
- Write an introduction to explain your thesis, a body to provide evidence for your thesis, and a conclusion.

Revising
- Even though time is limited on essay tests, you should still leave time to check your writing for accuracy and clarity.
- Use the guidelines for revising your essay on page SH22 of the Writing Handbook.

Document-Based Assessment

Enlightenment Thought

Enlightenment thinkers believed in the possibility of social, political, and economic change. Often critical of society during this time, they were driven by the power of human reason and progress.

Document A

"Common sense is not so common."

—From ***Philosophical Dictionary*** by Voltaire

Document B

"A prince ought not to deem it beneath his dignity to state that he considers it his duty not to dictate anything to his subjects in religious matters, but to leave them complete freedom."

—From ***What Is Enlightenment?*** by Immanuel Kant

Document C

"A strange consequence that necessarily follows from the use of torture is that the innocent person is placed in a condition worse than that of the guilty, for if both are tortured, the circumstances are all against the former. Either he confesses the crime and is condemned, or he is declared innocent and has suffered a punishment he did not deserve."

—From ***On Crimes and Punishments*** by Marchese di Beccaria

Document D

Diderot and Catherine the Great

Document E

Selected Enlightenment Thinkers			
Thinker	**Lifespan**	**Nationality**	**Key Work**
Jean D'Alembert	1717–1783	French	*Encyclopedia*
Jeremy Bentham	1748–1832	English	*The Principles of Morals and Legislation*
Cesare Beccaria	1738–1794	Italian	*Crimes and Punishment*
Denis Diderot	1713–1784	French	*Encyclopedia*
David Hume	1711–1776	Scottish	*Treatise of Human Nature*
Immanuel Kant	1724–1804	E. Prussian	*Critique of Pure Reason*
John Locke	1632–1704	English	*Essay Concerning Human Understanding*
Charles Montesquieu	1689–1755	French	*The Spirit of the Laws*
Jean-Jacques Rousseau	1712–1778	French	*The Social Contract*
Adam Smith	1723–1790	English	*The Wealth of Nations*
Voltaire	1694–1778	French	*Philosophical Dictionary*

Analyzing Documents

Use your knowledge of the Enlightenment and Documents A, B, C, D, and E to answer the questions below.

1. Kant believes in _______ based on Document B.
    A freedom of religion
    B freedom of speech
    C the government making a religious choice for its people
    D dignity

2. In Document C, the author condemned
    A capital punishment.
    B religion of any kind.
    C torture.
    D the Inquisition.

3. Catherine the Great and Diderot pictured in Document D are most likely
    A sharing war stories.
    B sharing Enlightenment ideas.
    C planning the American Revolution.
    D discussing population growth in France.

4. **Writing Task** Which of the above documents do you think best exemplifies the spirit of the Enlightenment? Why? Use your knowledge of the Enlightenment and specific information from the documents to support your opinion.

18

The French Revolution and Napoleon

1789–1815

The Loss of Blood Begins

On July 14, 1789, after a daylong hunting expedition, King Louis XVI returned to his palace in Versailles. Hours earlier, armed Parisians had attacked the Bastille. They had cut the chains of the prison drawbridge, crushing a member of the crowd, and poured into the courtyard. Chaos ensued as shots rang out, blood was spattered, and heads were paraded down the streets on spikes. When Louis heard the news, he exclaimed, "Then it's a revolt?" "No, sire," replied the duke bearing the news, "it's a revolution!" The French Revolution had begun. Listen to the Witness History audio to hear more about the fall of the Bastille.

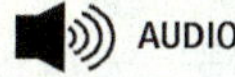
Plate declaring "Live Free or Die"

◄ *The Conquerors of the Bastille before the Hotel de Ville,* painted by Paul Delaroche.

Drum from the French revolutionary period

Chapter Preview

Chapter Focus Question What were the causes and effects of the French Revolution, and how did the revolution lead to the Napoleonic era?

Section 1
On the Eve of Revolution

Section 2
The French Revolution Unfolds

Section 3
Radical Days of the Revolution

Section 4
The Age of Napoleon

Bust of Napoleon Bonaparte

Use the ✓ **Quick Study Timeline** at the end of this chapter to preview chapter events.

Concept Connector ONLINE

To explore Essential Questions related to this chapter, go to PHSchool.com
Web Code: nad-1807

Inciting Revolution

Camille Desmoulins was a French revolutionary leader and journalist who wrote pamphlets and journals to express his views on the revolution. He also spoke to Parisian crowds and his stirring speeches in 1789 were a cause of the storming of the Bastille prison on July 14, 1789. This excerpt is from one of his speeches, "Better to Die than not Live Free":

> 66 In a democracy, tho the people may be deceived, yet they at least love virtue. It is merit which they believe they put in power as substitutes for the rascals who are the very essence of monarchies. The vices, conceal-ments, and crimes which are the diseases of republics are the very health and existence of monarchies. 99

Focus Question What led to the storming of the Bastille, and therefore, to the start of the French Revolution?

Camille Desmoulins and French Revolution banner

On the Eve of Revolution

Objectives

- Describe the social divisions of France's old order.
- List reasons for France's economic troubles in 1789.
- Explain why Louis XVI called the Estates-General and summarize what resulted.
- Understand why Parisians stormed the Bastille.

Terms, People, and Places

ancien régime	Jacques Necker
estate	Estates-General
bourgeoisie	cahier
deficit spending	Tennis Court Oath
Louis XVI	Bastille

Note Taking

Reading Skill: Recognize Multiple Causes Create a chart to identify causes of the French Revolution. Add as many boxes as you need.

Causes of the French Revolution

Inequalities among classes

On April 28, 1789, unrest exploded at a Paris wallpaper factory. A rumor had spread that the factory owner was planning to cut wages even though bread prices were soaring. Enraged workers vandalized the owner's home.

Riots like these did not worry most nobles. They knew that France faced a severe economic crisis but thought financial reforms would ease the problem. The nobles were wrong. The crisis went deeper than government finances. Reform would not be enough. By July, the hungry, unemployed, and poorly paid people of Paris had taken up arms. Their actions would push events further and faster than anyone could have foreseen.

French Society Divided

In 1789, France, like the rest of Europe, still clung to an outdated social system that had emerged in the Middle Ages. Under this **ancien régime,** or old order, everyone in France was divided into one of three social classes, or **estates.** The First Estate was made up of the clergy; the Second Estate was made up of the nobility; and the Third Estate comprised the vast majority of the population.

The Clergy Enjoy Wealth During the Middle Ages, the Church had exerted great influence throughout Christian Europe. In 1789, the French clergy still enjoyed enormous wealth and privilege. The Church owned about 10 percent of the land, collected tithes, and paid no direct taxes to the state. High Church leaders such as bishops and abbots were usually nobles who lived very well. Parish priests, however, often came from humble origins and might be as poor as their peasant congregations.

The First Estate did provide some social services. Nuns, monks, and priests ran schools, hospitals, and orphanages. But during the Enlightenment, *philosophes* targeted the Church for reform. They criticized the idleness of some clergy, the Church's interference in politics, and its intolerance of dissent. In response, many clergy condemned the Enlightenment for undermining religion and moral order.

Nobles Hold Top Government Jobs The Second Estate was the titled nobility of French society. In the Middle Ages, noble knights had defended the land. In the 1600s, Richelieu and Louis XIV had crushed the nobles' military power but had given them other rights—under strict royal control. Those rights included top jobs in government, the army, the courts, and the Church.

At Versailles, ambitious nobles competed for royal appointments while idle courtiers enjoyed endless entertainments. Many nobles, however, lived far from the center of power. Though they owned land, they received little financial income. As a result, they felt the pinch of trying to maintain their status in a period of rising prices.

Many nobles hated absolutism and resented the royal bureaucracy that employed middle-class men in positions that once had been reserved for them. They feared losing their traditional privileges, especially their freedom from paying taxes.

Third Estate Is Vastly Diverse The Third Estate was the most diverse social class. At the top sat the **bourgeoisie** (boor zhwah ZEE), or middle class. The bourgeoisie included prosperous bankers, merchants, and manufacturers, as well as lawyers, doctors, journalists, and professors. The bulk of the Third Estate, however, consisted of rural peasants.

The Old Regime This cartoon represents the social order in France before the French Revolution. While a member of the Third Estate is beginning to express anger and rise up, a nobleman representing the Second Estate and a priest, representing the First Estate, recoil in surprise and fear.

1. How does the cartoonist portray the Third Estate? Explain why.
2. What were the differences among the social classes in pre-revolutionary France?

Some were prosperous landowners who hired laborers to work for them. Others were tenant farmers or day laborers.

Among the poorest members of the Third Estate were urban workers. They included apprentices, journeymen, and others who worked in industries such as printing or cloth making. Many women and men earned a meager living as servants, construction workers, or street sellers of everything from food to pots and pans. A large number of the urban poor were unemployed. To survive, some turned to begging or crime.

From rich to poor, members of the Third Estate resented the privileges enjoyed by their social "betters." Wealthy bourgeois families in the Third Estate could buy political office and even titles, but the best jobs were still reserved for nobles. Urban workers earned miserable wages. Even the smallest rise in the price of bread, their main food, brought the threat of greater hunger or even starvation.

Because of traditional privileges, the First and Second Estates paid almost no taxes. Peasants were burdened by taxes on everything from land to soap to salt. Though they were technically free, many owed fees and services that dated back to medieval times, such as the corvée (kawr VAY), which was unpaid labor to repair roads and bridges. Peasants were

● INFOGRAPHIC

What Is the Third Estate?

"1. What is the Third Estate? *Everything.*
2. What has it been until now in the political order? *Nothing.*
3. What does it want to be? *Something.*"
—Abbé Emmanuel Sieyès

Sieyès, a clergyman before the revolution, captured the spirit of the Third Estate with these words in a pamphlet published in January 1789. The vast Third Estate—peasants, dentists, laborers, and more—comprising more than 95 percent of France, was ready to fight for equality.

▲ Ceramic bottle depicting dentist and patient

▲ *Woman of the French Revolution*, painting of a peasant woman by Jacques-Louis David

▼ Eighteenth-century French street traders

Thinking Critically
1. **Identify Point of View** According to the quote by Sieyès, why was the Third Estate ready to revolt?
2. **Make Generalizations** Why did Sieyès say the Third Estate was "nothing"?

also incensed when nobles, hurt by rising prices, tried to reimpose old manor dues.

In towns and cities, Enlightenment ideas led people to question the inequalities of the old regime. Why, people demanded, should the first two estates have such great privileges at the expense of the majority? Throughout France, the Third Estate called for the privileged classes to pay their share.

✓ **Checkpoint** What was the social structure of the old regime in France?

Financial Troubles

Economic woes in France added to the social unrest and heightened tensions. One of the causes of the economic troubles was a mushrooming financial crisis that was due in part to years of **deficit spending.** This occurs when a government spends more money than it takes in.

National Debt Soars Louis XIV had left France deeply in debt. The Seven Years' War and the American Revolution strained the treasury even further. Costs generally had risen in the 1700s, and the lavish court soaked up millions. To bridge the gap between income and expenses, the government borrowed more and more money. By 1789, half of the government's income from taxes went to paying the interest on this enormous debt. Also, in the late 1780s, bad harvests sent food prices soaring and brought hunger to poorer peasants and city dwellers.

To solve the financial crisis, the government would have to increase taxes, reduce expenses, or both. However, the nobles and clergy fiercely resisted any attempt to end their exemption from taxes.

Economic Reform Fails The heirs of Louis XIV were not the right men to solve the economic crisis that afflicted France. Louis XV, who ruled from 1715 to 1774, pursued pleasure before serious business and ran up more debts. **Louis XVI** was well-meaning but weak and indecisive. He did, however, wisely choose **Jacques Necker,** a financial expert, as an advisor. Necker urged the king to reduce extravagant court spending, reform government, and abolish burdensome tariffs on internal trade. When Necker proposed taxing the First and Second Estates, however, the nobles and high clergy forced the king to dismiss him.

As the crisis deepened, the pressure for reform mounted. The wealthy and powerful classes demanded, however, that the king summon the **Estates-General,** the legislative body consisting of representatives of the three estates, before making any changes. A French king had not called the Estates-General for 175 years, fearing that nobles would use it to recover the feudal powers they had lost under absolute rule. To reform-minded nobles, the Estates-General seemed to offer a chance of carrying out changes like those that had come with the Glorious Revolution in England. They hoped that they could bring the absolute monarch under the control of the nobles and guarantee their own privileges.

✓ **Checkpoint** What economic troubles did France face in 1789, and how did they lead to further unrest?

Poorer peasants and city dwellers in France were faced with great hunger as bad harvests sent food prices soaring. People began to riot to demand bread. In the countryside, peasants began to attack the manor houses of the nobles. Arthur Young, an English visitor to France, witnessed these riots and disturbances. Why did the poor attack the nobles' homes?

Primary Source

66 Everything conspires to render the present period in France critical: the [lack] of bread is terrible: accounts arrive every moment from the provinces of riots and disturbances, and calling in the military, to preserve the peace of the markets. 99
—Arthur Young, *Travels in France During the Years 1787–1789*

Louis XVI Calls the Estates-General

As 1788 came to a close, France tottered on the verge of bankruptcy. Bread riots were spreading, and nobles, fearful of taxes, were denouncing royal tyranny. A baffled Louis XVI finally summoned the Estates-General to meet at Versailles the following year.

Estates Prepare Grievance Notebooks In preparation, Louis had all three estates prepare **cahiers** (kah YAYZ), or notebooks, listing their grievances. Many cahiers called for reforms such as fairer taxes, freedom of the press, or regular meetings of the Estates-General. In one town, shoemakers denounced regulations that made leather so expensive they could not afford to make shoes. Servant girls in the city of Toulouse demanded the right to leave service when they wanted and that "after a girl has served her master for many years, she receive some reward for her service."

The cahiers testified to boiling class resentments. One called tax collectors "bloodsuckers of the nation who drink the tears of the unfortunate from goblets of gold." Another one of the cahiers condemned the courts of nobles as "vampires pumping the last drop of blood" from the people. Another complained that "20 million must live on half the wealth of France while the clergy . . . devour the other half."

Delegates Take the Tennis Court Oath Delegates to the Estates-General from the Third Estate were elected, though only propertied men could vote. Thus, the delegates were mostly lawyers, middle-class officials, and writers. They were familiar with the writings of Voltaire, Rousseau, and other *philosophes*. They went to Versailles not only to solve the financial crisis but also to insist on reform.

The Estates-General convened in May 1789. From the start, the delegates were deadlocked over the issue of voting. Traditionally, each estate had met and voted separately. Each group had one vote. Under this system, the First and Second Estates always outvoted the Third Estate two to one. This time, the Third Estate wanted all three estates to meet in a single body, with votes counted "by head."

After weeks of stalemate, delegates of the Third Estate took a daring step. In June 1789, claiming to represent the people of France, they declared themselves to be the National Assembly. A few days later, the National Assembly found its meeting hall locked and guarded. Fearing that the king planned to dismiss them, the delegates moved to a nearby indoor tennis court. As curious spectators looked on, the delegates took their famous **Tennis Court Oath.** They swore "never to separate

The Oath Is Taken
Delegates of the Third Estate declare themselves to be the National Assembly, representing the people of France. They take the Tennis Court Oath (bottom), vowing to create a constitution. The National Assembly later issues the assignat (top) as currency to help pay the government's debts. *What was the significance of the Tennis Court Oath?*

and to meet wherever the circumstances might require until we have established a sound and just constitution."

When reform-minded clergy and nobles joined the Assembly, Louis XVI grudgingly accepted it. But royal troops gathered around Paris, and rumors spread that the king planned to dissolve the Assembly.

✔ **Checkpoint** What actions did delegates of the Third Estate take when the Estates-General met in 1789?

Parisians Storm the Bastille

On July 14, 1789, the city of Paris seized the spotlight from the National Assembly meeting in Versailles. The streets buzzed with rumors that royal troops were going to occupy the capital. More than 800 Parisians assembled outside the Bastille, a grim medieval fortress used as a prison for political and other prisoners. The crowd demanded weapons and gunpowder believed to be stored there.

The commander of the Bastille refused to open the gates and opened fire on the crowd. In the battle that followed, many people were killed. Finally, the enraged mob broke through the defenses. They killed the commander and five guards and released the handful of prisoners who were being held there, but found no weapons.

The Bastille was a symbol to the people of France representing years of abuse by the monarchy. The storming of and subsequent fall of the Bastille was a wake-up call to Louis XVI. Unlike any other riot or short-lived protest, this event posed a challenge to the sheer existence of the regime. Since 1880, the French have celebrated Bastille Day annually as their national independence day.

✔ **Checkpoint** What was the significance of the storming of the Bastille?

Parisians storm the Bastille on July 14, 1789.

Terms, People, and Places

1. What do many of the key terms, people, and places listed at the beginning of the section have in common? Explain.

Note Taking

2. **Reading Skill: Recognize Multiple Causes** Use your completed chart to answer the Focus Question: What led to the storming of the Bastille, and therefore, to the start of the French Revolution?

Comprehension and Critical Thinking

3. **Compare Point of View** How did the views of society differ between the nobles and peasants in 1789 France?
4. **Identify Point of View** Suppose that you are Jacques Necker. Write a paragraph that explains how your economic reform program will benefit France.
5. **Express Problems Clearly** What issues arose when Louis XVI called the Estates-General in 1789?

● Writing About History

Quick Write: Make a Cause-and-Effect Organizer Choose a specific event from this section and write it in the center of a piece of paper. List causes above it and effects below it. This will give you the details to include in your cause-and-effect essay. You may need to do additional research to gather more details.

The French Revolution Unfolds

Objectives

- Explain how the political crisis of 1789 led to
  popular revolts.
- Summarize the moderate reforms enacted by
  the National Assembly in August 1789.
- Identify additional actions taken by the National
  Assembly as it pressed onward.
- Analyze why there was a mixed reaction around
  Europe to the events unfolding in France.

Terms, People, and Places

faction	émigré
Marquis de Lafayette	sans-culotte
Olympe de Gouges	republic
Marie Antoinette	Jacobins

Note Taking

Reading Skill: Identify Supporting Details As
you read this section, prepare an outline like the
one shown below. Remember to use numbers for
supporting details.

```
I. Political crisis leads to revolt
  A. The Great Fear
    1. Inflamed by famine and rumors
    2.
  B.
```

Excitement, wonder, and fear engulfed France as the revolution
unfolded at home and spread abroad. Historians divide this revolutionary era into different phases. The moderate phase of the
National Assembly (1789–1791) turned France into a constitutional monarchy. A radical phase (1792–1794) of escalating violence led to the end of the monarchy and a Reign of Terror. There
followed a period of reaction against extremism, known as the
Directory (1795–1799). Finally, the Age of Napoleon (1799–1815)
consolidated many revolutionary changes. In this section, you will
read about the moderate phase of the French Revolution.

Political Crisis Leads to Revolt

The political crisis of 1789 coincided with the worst famine in
memory. Starving peasants roamed the countryside or flocked to
towns, where they swelled the ranks of the unemployed. As grain
prices soared, even people with jobs had to spend as much as 80 percent of their income on bread.

Rumors Create the "Great Fear" In such desperate times,
rumors ran wild and set off what was later called the "Great Fear."
Tales of attacks on villages and towns spread panic. Other rumors
asserted that government troops were seizing peasant crops.

Inflamed by famine and fear, peasants unleashed their fury on
nobles who were trying to reimpose medieval dues. Defiant peasants set fire to old manor records and stole grain from storehouses.
The attacks died down after a period of time, but they clearly demonstrated peasant anger with an unjust regime.

Paris Commune Comes to Power Paris, too, was in turmoil. As the capital and chief city of France, it was the revolutionary center. A variety of **factions,** or dissenting groups of people, competed to gain power. Moderates looked to the **Marquis de Lafayette,** the aristocratic "hero of two worlds" who fought alongside George Washington in the American Revolution. Lafayette headed the National Guard, a largely middle-class militia organized in response to the arrival of royal troops in Paris. The Guard was the first group to don the tricolor—a red, white, and blue badge that was eventually adopted as the national flag of France.

A more radical group, the Paris Commune, replaced the royalist government of the city. It could mobilize whole neighborhoods for protests or violent action to further the revolution. Newspapers and political clubs—many even more radical than the Commune—blossomed everywhere. Some demanded an end to the monarchy and spread scandalous stories about the royal family and members of the court.

 **Checkpoint** What caused French peasants to revolt against nobles?

The National Assembly Acts

Peasant uprisings and the storming of the Bastille stampeded the National Assembly into action. On August 4, in a combative all-night meeting, nobles in the National Assembly voted to end their own privileges. They agreed to give up their old manorial dues, exclusive hunting rights, special legal status, and exemption from taxes.

Special Privilege Ends "Feudalism is abolished," announced the proud and weary delegates at 2 A.M. As the president of the Assembly later observed, "We may view this moment as the dawn of a new revolution, when all the burdens weighing on the people were abolished, and France was truly reborn."

Were nobles sacrificing much with their votes on the night of August 4? Both contemporary observers and modern historians note that the nobles gave up nothing that they had not already lost. Nevertheless, in the months ahead, the National Assembly turned the reforms of August 4 into law, meeting a key Enlightenment goal—the equality of all male citizens before the law.

Declaration of the Rights of Man In late August, as a first step toward writing a constitution, the Assembly issued the Declaration of the Rights of Man and the Citizen. The document was modeled in part on the American Declaration of Independence, written 13 years earlier. All men, the French declaration announced, were "born and remain free and equal in rights." They enjoyed natural rights to "liberty, property, security, and resistance to oppression." Like the writings of Locke and the *philosophes,* the constitution insisted that governments exist to protect the natural rights of citizens.

The declaration further <u>proclaimed</u> that all male citizens were equal before the law. Every Frenchman had an equal right to hold public office "with no distinction other than that of their virtues and talents." In addition, the declaration asserted freedom of religion and called for taxes to

The Marquis de Lafayette (honored on ribbon at right) and Thomas Paine were leading figures in both the American and French revolutions. Lafayette, a French nobleman and military commander, helped the Americans defeat the British at Yorktown. He admired the American Declaration of Independence and American democratic ideals. With these in mind, Lafayette wrote the first draft of the French Declaration of the Rights of Man and the Citizen.

Thomas Paine was a famous American patriot and writer whose ideas in *Common Sense* had a great influence on the American Revolution. During the French Revolution, Paine moved to France. There, he defended the ideals of the revolution and was elected to serve in the revolutionary government.

Identify Central Issues How did the American Revolution influence the French Revolution?

Vocabulary Builder

<u>proclaimed</u>—(proh KLAYMD) *vt.* announced officially

be levied according to ability to pay. Its principles were captured in the enduring slogan of the French Revolution, "Liberty, Equality, Fraternity."

Many women were disappointed that the Declaration of the Rights of Man did not grant equal citizenship to them. In 1791, **Olympe de Gouges** (oh LAMP duh GOOZH), a journalist, demanded equal rights in her Declaration of the Rights of Woman and the Female Citizen. "Woman is born free," she proclaimed, "and her rights are the same as those of man." Therefore, Gouges reasoned, "all citizens, be they men or women, being equal in the state's eyes, must be equally eligible for all public offices, positions, and jobs." Later in the revolution, women met resistance for expressing their views in public, and many, including Gouges, were imprisoned and executed.

The Declaration of the Rights of Man met resistance as well. Uncertain and hesitant, Louis XVI did not want to accept the reforms of the National Assembly. Nobles continued to enjoy gala banquets while people were starving. By autumn, anger again turned to action.

Women March on Versailles On October 5, about six thousand women marched 13 miles in the pouring rain from Paris to Versailles. "Bread!" they shouted. They demanded to see the king.

Much of the crowd's anger was directed at the Austrian-born queen, **Marie Antoinette** (daughter of Maria Theresa and brother of Joseph II). The queen lived a life of great pleasure and extravagance, and this led to further public unrest. Although compassionate to the poor, her small acts went largely unnoticed because her lifestyle overshadowed them. She was against reforms and bored with the French court. She often retreated to the Petit Trianon, a small chateau on the palace grounds at Versailles where she lived her own life of amusement.

The women refused to leave Versailles until the king met their most important demand—to return to Paris. Not too happily, the king agreed. The next morning, the crowd, with the king and his family in tow, set out for the city. At the head of the procession rode women perched on the barrels of seized cannons. They told bewildered spectators that they were bringing Louis XVI, Marie Antoinette, and their son back to Paris. "Now

Playing Dress-Up
Marie Antoinette spent millions on her clothing and jewels and set fashion trends throughout France and Europe. This painting (top) was painted by her friend and portraitist, Elisabeth Vigée-Lebrun. Queens traditionally did not own property, but Marie Antoinette had her own small royal mansion and amusement village, or hamlet (bottom), where she played as milkmaid and shepherdess. *Why did the French common people resent Marie Antoinette?*

we won't have to go so far when we want to see our king," they sang. Crowds along the way cheered the king, who now wore the tricolor. In Paris, the royal family moved into the Tuileries (TWEE luh reez) palace. For the next three years, Louis was a virtual prisoner.

 **Checkpoint** How did the National Assembly react to peasant uprisings?

The National Assembly Presses Onward

The National Assembly soon followed the king to Paris. Its largely bourgeois members worked to draft a constitution and to solve the continuing financial crisis. To pay off the huge government debt—much of it owed to the bourgeoisie—the Assembly voted to take over and sell Church lands.

The Church Is Placed Under State Control In an even more radical move, the National Assembly put the French Catholic Church under state control. Under the Civil Constitution of the Clergy, issued in 1790, bishops and priests became elected, salaried officials. The Civil Constitution ended papal authority over the French Church and dissolved convents and monasteries.

Reaction was swift and angry. Many bishops and priests refused to accept the Civil Constitution. The pope condemned it. Large numbers of French peasants, who were conservative concerning religion, also rejected the changes. When the government punished clergy who refused to support the Civil Constitution, a huge gulf opened between revolutionaries in Paris and the peasantry in the provinces.

The Constitution of 1791 Establishes a New Government The National Assembly completed its main task by producing a constitution. The Constitution of 1791 set up a limited monarchy in place of the absolute monarchy that had ruled France for centuries. A new Legislative Assembly had the power to make laws, collect taxes, and decide on issues of war and peace. Lawmakers would be elected by tax-paying male citizens over age 25.

To make government more efficient, the constitution replaced the old provinces with 83 departments of roughly equal size. It abolished the old provincial courts, and it reformed laws.

To moderate reformers, the Constitution of 1791 seemed to complete the revolution. Reflecting Enlightenment goals, it ensured equality before the law for all male citizens and ended Church interference in government. At the same time, it put power in the hands of men with the means and leisure to serve in government.

Louis's Escape Fails Meanwhile, Marie Antoinette and others had been urging the king to escape their humiliating situation. Louis finally gave in. One night in June 1791, a coach rolled north from Paris toward the border. Inside sat the king disguised as a servant, the queen dressed as a governess, and the royal children.

The attempted escape failed. In a town along the way, Louis's disguise was uncovered by someone who held up a piece of currency with the king's face on it. A company of soldiers escorted the royal family back to Paris, as onlooking crowds hurled insults at the king. To many, Louis's dash to the border showed that he was a traitor to the revolution.

✓ **Checkpoint** **What were the provisions of the Constitution of 1791?**

Radicals Take Over

Events in France stirred debate all over Europe. Supporters of the Enlightenment applauded the reforms of the National Assembly. They saw the French experiment as the dawn of a new age for justice and equality. European rulers and nobles, however, denounced the French Revolution.

Analyzing Political Cartoons

The French Plague European rulers, nobles, and clergy (such as, from left, Catherine the Great of Russia, the Pope, Emperor Leopold II of Prussia, and George III of England) feared the revolution in France would spread to their countries. Many émigrés fueled the flames with their tales of attacks by the revolutionary government.

1. Why were European rulers against revolutionary ideas coming into their countries?
2. How does the cartoonist portray the "plague?"

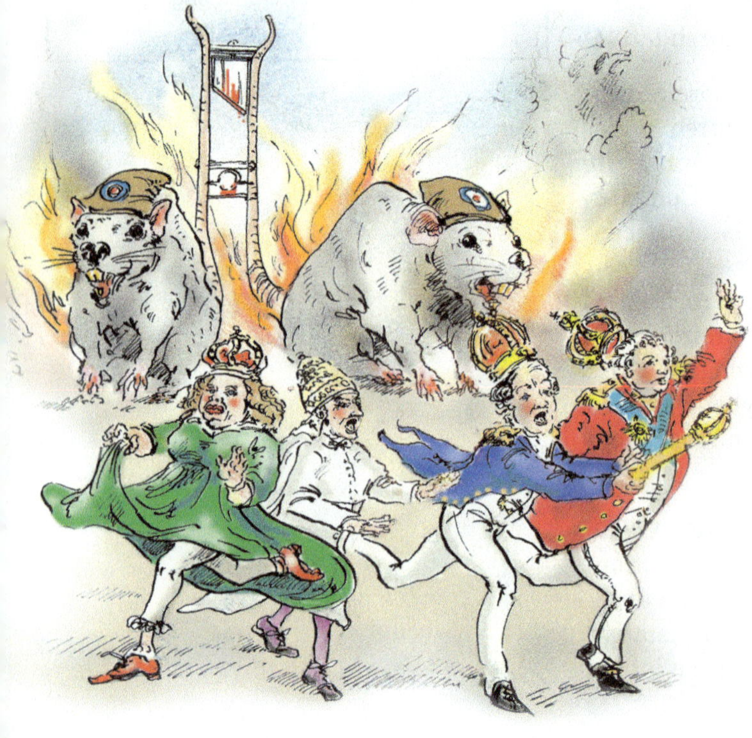

Rulers Fear Spread of Revolution European rulers increased border patrols to stop the spread of the "French plague." Fueling those fears were the horror stories that were told by **émigrés** (EM ih grayz)—nobles, clergy, and others who had fled France and its revolutionary forces. Émigrés reported attacks on their privileges, their property, their religion, and even their lives. Even "enlightened" rulers turned against France. Catherine the Great of Russia burned Voltaire's letters and locked up her critics.

Edmund Burke, a British writer and statesman who earlier had defended the American Revolution, bitterly condemned revolutionaries in Paris. He predicted all too accurately that the revolution would become more violent. "Plots and assassinations," he wrote, "will be anticipated by preventive murder and preventive confiscation." Burke warned: "When ancient opinions and rules of life are taken away . . . we have no compass to govern us."

Threats Come From Abroad The failed escape of Louis XVI brought further hostile rumblings from abroad. In August 1791, the king of Prussia and the emperor of Austria—who was Marie Antoinette's brother—issued the Declaration of Pilnitz. In this document, the two monarchs threatened to intervene to protect the French monarchy. The declaration may have been mostly a bluff, but revolutionaries in France took the threat seriously and prepared for war. The revolution was about to enter a new, more radical phase of change and conflict.

Radicals Fight for Power and Declare War In October 1791, the newly elected Legislative Assembly took office. Faced with crises at home and abroad, it survived for less than a year. Economic problems fed renewed turmoil. Assignats (AS ig nats), the revolutionary currency, dropped in value, causing prices to rise rapidly. Uncertainty about prices led to hoarding and caused additional food shortages.

In Paris and other cities, working-class men and women, called **sans-culottes** (sanz koo LAHTS), pushed the revolution into more radical action. They were called sans-culottes, which means "without breeches," because they wore long trousers instead of the fancy knee breeches that upper-class men wore. By 1791, many sans-culottes demanded a **republic,** or government ruled by elected representatives instead of a monarch.

Within the Legislative Assembly, several hostile factions competed for power. The sans-culottes found support among radicals in the Legislative Assembly, especially the Jacobins. A revolutionary political club, the **Jacobins** were mostly middle-class lawyers or intellectuals. They used pamphleteers and sympathetic newspaper editors to advance the republican cause. Opposing the radicals were moderate reformers and political officials who wanted no more reforms at all.

The National Assembly Declares War on Tyranny The radicals soon held the upper hand in the Legislative Assembly. In April 1792, the war of words between French revolutionaries and European monarchs moved onto the battlefield. Eager to spread the revolution and destroy tyranny abroad, the Legislative Assembly declared war first on Austria and then on Prussia, Britain, and other states. The great powers expected to win an easy victory against France, a land divided by revolution. In fact, however, the fighting that began in 1792 lasted on and off until 1815.

Sans-culotte, 1792

 **Checkpoint** How did the rest of Europe react to the French Revolution?

Terms, People, and Places

1. For each term, person, or place listed at the beginning of the section, write a sentence explaining its significance.

Note Taking

2. **Reading Skill: Identify Supporting Details** Use your completed outline to answer the Focus Question: What political and social reforms did the National Assembly institute in the first stage of the French Revolution?

Comprehension and Critical Thinking

3. **Make Comparisons** How was the French Declaration of the Rights of Man and the Citizen similar to the American Declaration of Independence?

4. **Summarize** What did the Constitution of 1791 do, and how did it reflect Enlightenment ideas?

5. **Draw Inferences** Describe what happened to France's constitutional monarchy because of the French Revolution.

● **Writing About History**

Quick Write: Create a Flowchart As you prepare to write a cause-and-effect essay, you need to decide how to organize it. To do this, create a flowchart that shows the effects of the French Revolution on other countries. Do you want to write about the events in chronological order? By the importance of each event?

Declaration of the Rights of Man and the Citizen

Painting of the declaration

The National Assembly issued this document in 1789 after having overthrown the established government in the early stages of the French Revolution. The document was modeled in part on the English Bill of Rights and on the American Declaration of Independence. The basic principles of the French declaration were those that inspired the revolution, such as the freedom and equality of all male citizens before the law. The Articles below identify additional principles.

Therefore the National Assembly recognizes and proclaims, in the presence and under the auspices[1] of the Supreme Being, the following rights of man and of the citizen:

1. Men are born and remain free and equal in rights. Social distinctions may be founded only upon the general good.
2. The aim of all political association is the preservation of the natural and imprescriptible[2] rights of man. These rights are liberty, property, security, and resistance to oppression. . . .
4. Liberty consists in the freedom to do everything which injures no one else. . . .
5. Law can only prohibit such actions as are hurtful to society. . . .
6. Law is the expression of the general will. Every citizen has a right to participate personally, or through his representative, in its formation. It must be the same for all, whether it protects or punishes. All citizens, being equal in the eyes of the law, are equally eligible to all dignities and to all public positions and occupations, according to their abilities, and without distinction except that of their virtues and talents.
7. No person shall be accused, arrested, or imprisoned except in the cases and according to the forms prescribed by law. . . .
11. The free communication of ideas and opinions is one of the most precious of the rights of man. Every citizen may, accordingly, speak, write, and print with freedom. . . .
13. A common contribution is essential for the maintenance of the public [military] forces and for the cost of administration. This should be equitably distributed among all the citizens in proportion to their means.

Thinking Critically

1. **Summarize** Summarize article 6. Why is this article especially significant?
2. **Identify Central Issues** What central idea does this declaration share with the American Declaration of Independence?

1. **auspices** (AWS puh siz) *n.* approval and support
2. **imprescriptible** (im prih SKRIP tuh bul) *adj.* that which cannot be rightfully taken away

Marie Antoinette transported by cart to the guillotine

The Engine of Terror

A new execution device called the guillotine was introduced during this phase of the revolution. With its large, diagonal blade that came crashing down from a great height, it cut off heads swiftly and accurately. Thousands of people were sent to the guillotine and executed without trial. In his novel *A Tale of Two Cities*, Charles Dickens describes daily life during the Reign of Terror:

> **66** Along the Paris streets, the death-carts rumble, hollow and harsh. Six tumbrils [carts that carried condemned persons to the guillotine] carry the day's wine to La Guillotine. **99**

Focus Question What events occurred during the radical phase of the French Revolution?

Radical Days of the Revolution

Objectives

- Understand how and why radicals abolished the monarchy.
- Explain why the Committee of Public Safety was created and why the Reign of Terror resulted.
- Summarize how the excesses of the Convention led to the formation of the Directory.
- Analyze how the French people were affected by the changes brought about by the revolution.

Terms, People, and Places

suffrage	Napoleon
Robespierre	nationalism
Reign of Terror	Marseilles
guillotine	

Note Taking

Reading Skill: Recognize Sequence Make a timeline like the one shown here. Add dates and important events as you read this section.

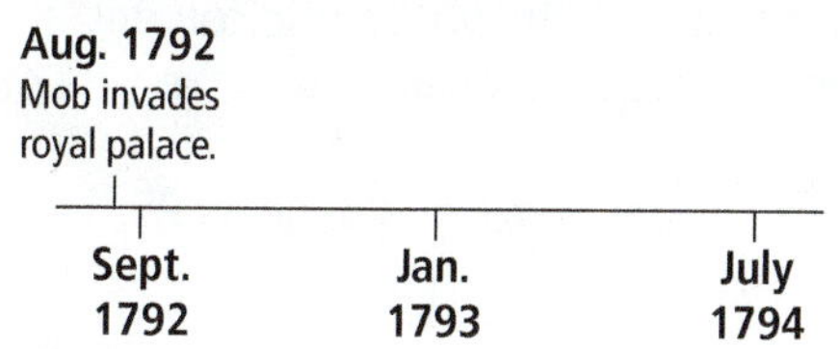

In 1793, the revolution entered a radical phase. For a year, France experienced one of the bloodiest regimes in its long history as determined leaders sought to extend and preserve the revolution.

The Monarchy Is Abolished

As the revolution continued, dismal news about the war abroad heightened tensions. Well-trained Prussian forces were cutting down raw French recruits. In addition, royalist officers were deserting the French army, joining émigrés and others hoping to restore the king's power.

Tensions Lead to Violence Battle disasters quickly inflamed revolutionaries who thought the king was in league with the enemies. On August 10, 1792, a crowd of Parisians stormed the royal palace of the Tuileries and slaughtered the king's guards. The royal family fled to the Legislative Assembly, escaping before the mob arrived.

A month later, citizens attacked prisons that held nobles and priests accused of political offenses. About 1,200 prisoners were killed; among them were many ordinary criminals. Historians disagree about the people who carried out the "September massacres." Some call them bloodthirsty mobs. Others describe them as patriots defending France from its enemies. In fact, most were ordinary citizens fired to fury by real and imagined grievances.

Radicals Take Control and Execute the King Backed by Paris crowds, radicals then took control of the Assembly. Radicals called for the election of a new legislative body called the National Convention. **Suffrage,** the right to vote, was to be extended to all male citizens, not just to property owners.

The Convention that met in September 1792 was a more <u>radical</u> body than earlier assemblies. It voted to abolish the monarchy and establish a republic—the French Republic. Deputies then drew up a new constitution for France. The Jacobins, who controlled the Convention, set out to erase all traces of the old order. They seized lands of nobles and abolished titles of nobility.

During the early months of the Republic, the Convention also put Louis XVI on trial as a traitor to France. The king was convicted by a single vote and sentenced to death. On a foggy morning in January 1793, Louis mounted a scaffold in a public square in Paris. He started to speak, "Frenchmen, I die innocent. I pardon the authors of my death. I pray God that the blood about to be spilt will never fall upon the head of France. . . ." Then a roll of drums drowned out his words. Moments later, the king was beheaded. The executioner lifted the king's head by its hair and held it before the crowd.

In October, Marie Antoinette was also executed. The popular press celebrated her death. The queen, however, showed great dignity as she went to her death.

✔ **Checkpoint** What occurred after radicals took control of the Assembly?

On the Execution of a King

On January 21, 1793, King Louis XVI of France was executed by order of the National Convention. Reaction to this event was both loud and varied throughout Europe. The excerpts below present two different views on this event. **Critical Thinking** *Which of the two viewpoints makes a better case for or against the execution of King Louis XVI? Cite examples from both statements to support your argument.*

For the Execution

The crimes of Louis XVI are unhappily all too real; they are consistent; they are notorious. Do we even have to ask the question of whether a nation has the right to judge, and execute, its highest ranking public official . . . when, to more securely plot against the nation, he concealed himself behind a mask of hypocrisy? Or when, instead of using the authority confided to him to protect his countrymen, he used it to oppress them? Or when he turned the laws into an instrument of violence to crush the supporters of the Revolution? Or when he robbed the citizens of their gold in order to subsidize their foes, and robbed them of their subsistence in order to feed the barbarian hordes who came to slaughter them? Or when he created monopolies in order to create famine by drying up the sources of abundance so that the people might die in misery and hunger? . . .

—Jean-Paul Marat

Against the Execution

The Republican tyrants of France have now carried their bloody purposes to the uttermost diabolical stretch of savage cruelty. They have murdered their King without even the shadow of justice, and of course they cannot expect friendship nor intercourse with any civilized part of the world. The vengeance of Europe will now rapidly fall on them; and, in process of time, make them the veriest wretches on the face of the earth. The name of Frenchman will be considered as the appellation of savage, and their presence shunned as a poison, deadly destructive to the peace and happiness of Mankind. It appears evident, that the majority of the National Convention, and the Executive Government of that truly despotic country, are comprised of the most execrable villains upon the face of the earth. . . .

—*London Times*, January 25, 1793

Terror and Danger Grip France

By early 1793, danger threatened France on all sides. The country was at war with much of Europe, including Britain, the Netherlands, Spain, and Prussia. In the Vendée (vahn DAY) region of France, royalists and priests led peasants in rebellion against the government. In Paris, the sans-culottes demanded relief from food shortages and inflation. The Convention itself was bitterly divided between Jacobins and a rival group, the Girondins.

The Convention Creates a New Committee To deal with the threats to France, the Convention created the Committee of Public Safety. The 12-member committee had almost absolute power as it battled to save the revolution. The Committee prepared France for all-out war, issuing a *levée en masse,* or mass levy (tax) that required all citizens to contribute to the war effort. In addition, the 12 members of the Committee were in charge of trials and executions.

Spurred by revolutionary fervor, French recruits marched off to defend the republic. Young officers developed effective new tactics to win battles with masses of ill-trained but patriotic forces. Soon, French armies overran the Netherlands. They later invaded Italy. At home, they crushed peasant revolts. European monarchs shuddered as the revolutionaries carried "freedom fever" into conquered lands.

Robespierre "the Incorruptible" At home, the government battled counterrevolutionaries under the guiding hand of Maximilien Robespierre (ROHBZ pyehr). Robespierre, a shrewd lawyer and politician, quickly rose to the leadership of the Committee of Public Safety. Among Jacobins, his selfless dedication to the revolution earned him the nickname "the incorruptible." The enemies of Robespierre called him a tyrant.

Robespierre had embraced Rousseau's idea of the general will as the source of all legitimate law. He promoted religious toleration and wanted to abolish slavery. Though cold and humorless, he was popular with the sans-culottes, who hated the old regime as much as he did. He believed that France could achieve a "republic of virtue" only through the use of terror, which he coolly defined as nothing more than "prompt, severe, inflexible justice." "Liberty cannot be secured," Robespierre cried, "unless criminals lose their heads."

The Guillotine Defines the Reign of Terror Robespierre was one of the chief architects of the Reign of Terror, which lasted from September 1793 to July 1794. Revolutionary courts conducted hasty trials. Spectators greeted death sentences with cries of "Hail the Republic!" or "Death to the traitors!"

In a speech given on February 5, 1794, Robespierre explained why the terror was necessary to achieve the goals of the revolution:

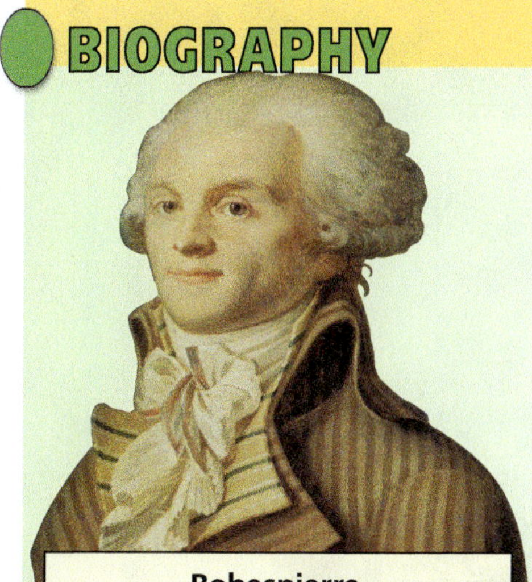

Robespierre

Maximilien Robespierre (1758–1794) did not have an easy childhood. His mother died when he was only 6 years old. Two years later, his father abandoned him and his three siblings. The children's aunts and grandfather then raised them. Because of this, Robespierre assumed responsibilities at an early age. Eventually, he went to study law at the University of Paris. His performance was so noteworthy that he was chosen to deliver a speech to Louis XVI on the occasion of the king's coronation. But young Robespierre was snubbed. After listening to the address in a pouring rainstorm, the king and queen left without acknowledging Robespierre in any way. Years later, in 1789, Robespierre was elected to the Estates-General, where his career as a revolutionary began. **How do you think Robespierre's early life might have influenced his political ideas?**

> 66 It is necessary to stifle the domestic and foreign enemies of the Republic or perish with them. . . . The first maxim of our politics ought to be to lead the people by means of reason and the enemies of the people by terror. . . . If the basis of popular government in time of peace is virtue, the basis of popular government in time of revolution is both virtue and terror. 99
> —Maximilien Robespierre, quoted in *Pageant of Europe* (Stearns)

Suspect were those who resisted the revolution. About 300,000 were arrested during the Reign of Terror. Seventeen thousand were executed. Many were victims of mistaken identity or were falsely accused by their neighbors. Many more were packed into hideous prisons, where deaths from disease were common.

The engine of the Terror was the **guillotine** (GIL uh teen). Its fast-falling blade extinguished life instantly. A member of the legislature, Dr. Joseph Guillotin (gee oh TAN), had introduced it as a more humane method of beheading than the uncertain ax. But the guillotine quickly became a symbol of horror.

Within a year, the Terror consumed those who initiated it. Weary of bloodshed and fearing for their own lives, members of the Convention turned on the Committee of Public Safety. On the night of July 27, 1794, Robespierre was arrested. The next day he was executed. After the heads of Robespierre and other radicals fell, executions slowed dramatically.

✔ **Checkpoint** Why did Robespierre think the Terror was necessary to achieve the goals of the revolution?

The Revolution Enters Its Third Stage

In reaction to the Terror, the revolution entered a third stage. Moving away from the excesses of the Convention, moderates produced another constitution, the third since 1789. The Constitution of 1795 set up a five-

● **INFOGRAPHIC**

THE REIGN OF TERROR

From autumn 1793 to midsummer 1794, the revolution in France was overshadowed by a time of terror as the Committee of Public Safety rounded up "suspected persons" all over France. Only about 15 percent of those sentenced to death by guillotine (model at left) were of the nobility and clergy. Most were artisans and peasants of the Third Estate. Prisons in Paris—which included places such as former mansions and palaces, religious premises, and colleges—became more and more crowded as the number of suspects increased. Once sentenced to death, the condemned might travel an hour to the guillotine by cart as onlookers threw mud at them.

Thieves stole ▲ items such as silver as émigrés fled the country due to the Terror.

◄ Interrogation of aristocratic prisoners at L'Abbaye prison man Directory and a two-house legislature elected by male citizens of property. The middle class and professional people of the bourgeoisie were the dominant force during this stage of the French Revolution. The Directory held power from 1795 to 1799.

Weak but dictatorial, the Directory faced growing discontent. Peace was made with Prussia and Spain, but war with Austria and Great Britain continued. Corrupt leaders lined their own pockets but failed to solve pressing problems. When rising bread prices stirred hungry sans-culottes to riot, the Directory quickly suppressed them. Another threat to the Directory was the revival of royalist feeling. Many émigrés were returning to France, and devout Catholics, who resented measures that had been taken against the Church, were welcoming them. In the election of 1797, supporters of a constitutional monarchy won the majority of seats in the legislature.

As chaos threatened, politicians turned to **Napoleon** Bonaparte, a popular military hero who had won a series of brilliant victories against the Austrians in Italy. The politicians planned to use him to advance their own goals. To their dismay, however, before long Napoleon would outwit them all to become ruler of France.

✔ **Checkpoint** What changes occurred after the Reign of Terror came to an end?

◄ People never knew if friends or family might appear on a list of guillotine victims. There is some debate on the humaneness of death by guillotine. Some authorities claim that even after the head has been severed, the victim could remain conscious for up to 30 seconds.

Georges Danton, ► a Revolutionary leader, challenged the Terror and was guillotined.

◄ This engraving depicts Robespierre's execution by guillotine. His was not the last. "Twenty minutes later, [those condemned for the day] were in front of the scaffold…. Pale, tense, shivering… several of them lowered their heads or shut their eyes…. The third [victim] was…the Princess of Monaco…. On the platform, her youthful beauty shone in the dazzling July light." The executioners then tossed the bodies and heads into large baskets near the scaffold.

Thinking Critically
1. **Identify Point of View** What were the goals of the Committee of Public Safety?
2. **Predict Consequences** How do you think life in France changed after the Terror came to an end?

French Nationalism
"La Marseillaise" (top) and a revolutionary-period drum (bottom) helped rally the French people.

Revolution Brings Change

By 1799, the 10-year-old French Revolution had dramatically changed France. It had dislodged the old social order, overthrown the monarchy, and brought the Church under state control.

New symbols such as the red "liberty caps" and the tricolor confirmed the liberty and equality of all male citizens. The new title "citizen" applied to people of all social classes. All other titles were eliminated. Before he was executed, Louis XVI was called Citizen Capet, from the name of the dynasty that had ruled France in the Middle Ages. Elaborate fashions and powdered wigs gave way to the practical clothes and simple haircuts of the sans-culottes.

Nationalism Spreads Revolution and war gave the French people a strong sense of national identity. In earlier times, people had felt loyalty to local authorities. As monarchs centralized power, loyalty shifted to the king or queen. Now, the government rallied sons and daughters of the revolution to defend the nation itself. **Nationalism,** a strong feeling of pride in and devotion to one's country, spread throughout France. The French people attended civic festivals that celebrated the nation and the revolution. A variety of dances and songs on themes of the revolution became immensely popular.

By 1793, France was a nation in arms. From the port city of **Marseilles** (mahr say), troops marched to a rousing new song. It urged the "children of the fatherland" to march against the "bloody banner of tyranny." This song, "La Marseillaise" (mahr say ez), would later become the French national anthem.

Revolutionaries Push For Social Reform Revolutionaries pushed for social reform and religious toleration. They set up state schools to replace religious ones and organized systems to help the poor, old soldiers, and war widows. With a major slave revolt raging in the colony of St. Domingue (Haiti), the government also abolished slavery in France's Caribbean colonies.

 **Checkpoint** What changes occurred in France because of the French Revolution?

Assessment

Terms, People, and Places

1. Place each of the key terms at the beginning of the section into one of the following categories: politics, culture, geography, or technology. Write a sentence for each term explaining your choice.

Note Taking

2. **Reading Skill: Recognize Sequence** Use your completed timeline to answer the Focus Question: What events occurred during the radical phase of the French Revolution?

Comprehension and Critical Thinking

3. **Summarize** Summarize the goals and actions of the Jacobins.
4. **Identify Central Issues** Why was the Committee of Public Safety created?
5. **Recognize Cause and Effect** How did the Reign of Terror cause the National Convention to be replaced by the Directory?
6. **Predict Consequences** How do you think French nationalism affected the war between France and the powers of Europe?

● Writing About History

Quick Write: Provide Elaboration To illustrate each cause and effect of your essay, you should have supporting details, facts, and examples. Choose one of the events below and list as many specific details as possible. Then write a paragraph using the details you listed to explain what caused the event.

- Reign of Terror
- Execution of King Louis XVI
- Creation of the Committee of Public Safety

Art of Revolution

Revolutions have visual chronicles as well as written ones, and in the days before photography, these depictions were often rendered with paint. The French artist Jacques-Louis David (ZHAHK loo EE dah VEED) and the Spanish artist Francisco Goya both portrayed aspects of revolution on canvas, but they had differing viewpoints. David supported the early French Revolution and embraced the revolutionary spirit in his work. Goya, however, was a realist who showed human suffering and the horrors of war in his paintings.

▲ *Napoleon Crossing Mont Saint Bernard,* **Jacques-Louis David, 1801**
Imprisoned after moderates turned against the Reign of Terror, David barely escaped with his life. When Napoleon rose to power, David deftly switched his political allegiance to the new Emperor of France and became one of Bonaparte's chief portraitists. Notice the names carved into the rocks. David included these names of great past rulers to show Napoleon's level of greatness. David's depictions of Napoleon helped cement him as a strong and heroic leader.

▲ *The Third of May, 1808,* **Francisco José de Goya y Lucientes, 1814**
One of the consequences of the French Revolution and Napoleon's rise was that France soon found itself at war with the rest of Europe. Francisco Goya saw firsthand the impact of these wars. Born in northern Spain, he rose to become the official painter of the Spanish court. When Napoleon invaded Spain and deposed its king, Goya chronicled the horrors of the resulting guerrilla warfare.

Thinking Critically
1. **Compare Points of View** What elements in each painting express the viewpoint of the artist? How are the elements different?
2. **Recognize Ideologies** How do you think the ideology of the French Revolution led to the scene Goya portrays here?

Unfinished portrait of Napoleon by Jacques-Louis David and Napoleon's signature

Enter Napoleon Bonaparte

After the execution of King Louis XVI, France entered a state of confusion and chaos without a single leader. Meanwhile, Napoleon Bonaparte, a brilliant and ambitious captain in the French army, was rapidly rising in the military ranks. Soon enough, Napoleon would come to rule almost all of Europe. One of his earliest victories in Lodi, Italy, convinced him that he was only just beginning his successful rise to power:

66 From that moment, I foresaw what I might be. Already I felt the earth flee from beneath me, as if I were being carried into the sky. 99
—Napoleon Bonaparte

Focus Question Explain Napoleon's rise to power in Europe, his subsequent defeat, and how the outcome still affects Europe today.

The Age of Napoleon

Objectives

- Understand Napoleon's rise to power and why the French strongly supported him.
- Explain how Napoleon built an empire and what challenges the empire faced.
- Analyze the events that led to Napoleon's downfall.
- Outline how the Congress of Vienna tried to create a lasting peace.

Terms, People, and Places

plebiscite	scorched-earth policy
Napoleonic Code	abdicate
annex	Congress of Vienna
Continental System	legitimacy
guerrilla warfare	Concert of Europe

Note Taking

Reading Skill: Identify Main Ideas As you read the section, use a flowchart to list the important events that led from Napoleon's rise to power to his defeat. Add boxes as you need them.

Napoleon quickly advances through military ranks.

From 1799 to 1815, Napoleon Bonaparte would dominate France and Europe. A hero to some, an evil force to others, he gave his name to the final phase of the revolution—the Age of Napoleon.

Napoleon Rises to Power

Napoleon was born in Corsica, a French-ruled island in the Mediterranean. At age nine, he was sent to France to be trained for a military career. When the revolution broke out, he was an ambitious 20-year-old lieutenant, eager to make a name for himself.

Napoleon favored the Jacobins and republican rule. However, he found the conflicting ideas and personalities of the French Revolution confusing. He wrote to his brother in 1793: "Since one must take sides, one might as well choose the side that is victorious, the side which devastates, loots, and burns. Considering the alternative, it is better to eat than be eaten."

Victories Cloud Losses During the turmoil of the revolution, Napoleon rose quickly in the army. In December 1793, he drove British forces out of the French port of Toulon (too LOHN). He then went on to win several dazzling victories against the Austrians, capturing most of northern Italy and forcing the Hapsburg emperor to make peace. Hoping to disrupt British trade with India, he led an expedition to Egypt in 1798. The Egyptian campaign proved to be a disaster, but Napoleon managed to hide stories of the worst losses from his admirers in France. He did so by establishing a network of spies and censoring the press.

Success fueled Napoleon's ambition. By 1799, he moved from victorious general to political leader. That year, he helped overthrow the weak Directory and set up a three-man governing board known as the Consulate. Another constitution was drawn up, but Napoleon soon took the title First Consul. In 1800, he forced Spain to return Louisiana Territory to France. In 1802, Napoleon had himself named consul for life.

Napoleon Crowns Himself Emperor Two years later, Napoleon had acquired enough power to assume the title Emperor of the French. He invited the pope to preside over his coronation in Paris. During the ceremony, however, Napoleon took the crown from the pope's hands and placed it on his own head. By this action, Napoleon meant to show that he owed his throne to no one but himself.

At each step on his rise to power, Napoleon had held a **plebiscite** (PLEB uh syt), or popular vote by ballot. Each time, the French strongly supported him. As you will read, although the people theoretically had a say in government through their votes, Napoleon still held absolute power. This is sometimes called democratic despotism. To understand why people supported him, we must look at his policies.

 **Checkpoint** How did Napoleon rise to power so quickly in France?

Napoleon Reforms France

Napoleon consolidated his power by strengthening the central government. Order, security, and efficiency replaced liberty, equality, and fraternity as the slogans of the new regime.

To restore economic prosperity, Napoleon controlled prices, encouraged new industry, and built roads and canals. He set up a system of public schools under strict government control to ensure well-trained officials and military officers. At the same time, Napoleon backed off from some of the revolution's social reforms. He made peace with the Catholic Church in the Concordat of 1801. The Concordat kept the Church under state control but recognized religious freedom for Catholics. Revolutionaries who opposed the Church denounced the agreement, but Catholics welcomed it.

Napoleon won support across class lines. He encouraged émigrés to return, provided they take an oath of loyalty. Peasants were relieved when he recognized their right to lands they had bought from the Church and nobles during the revolution. The middle class, who had benefited most from the revolution, approved of Napoleon's economic reforms and the restoration of order after years of chaos. Napoleon also opened jobs to all, based on talent, a popular policy among those who remembered the old aristocratic monopoly of power.

Among Napoleon's most lasting reforms was a new code of laws, popularly called the **Napoleonic Code.** It embodied Enlightenment principles such as the equality of all citizens before the law, religious toleration, and the abolition of feudalism.

The Egyptian Campaign
The Battle of the Pyramids, July 21, 1798, painted by Louis-Francois Lejeune. *How did Napoleon hide the fact that the Egyptian campaign was a disaster?*

But the Napoleonic Code undid some reforms of the French Revolution. Women, for example, lost most of their newly gained rights and could not exercise the rights of citizenship. Male heads of households regained complete authority over their wives and children. Again, Napoleon valued order and authority over individual rights.

 **Checkpoint**   What reforms did Napoleon introduce during his rise to power?

Napoleon Builds an Empire

From 1804 to 1812, Napoleon furthered his reputation on the battlefield. He successfully battled the combined forces of the greatest European powers. He took great risks and even suffered huge losses. "I grew up on the field of battle," he once said, "and a man such as I am cares little for the life of a million men." By 1812, his Grand Empire reached its greatest extent.

As a military leader, Napoleon valued rapid movements and made effective use of his large armies. He developed a new plan for each battle so opposing generals could never <u>anticipate</u> what he would do next. His enemies paid tribute to his leadership. Napoleon's presence on the battlefield, said one, was "worth 40,000 troops."

The Map of Europe Is Redrawn   As Napoleon created a vast French empire, he redrew the map of Europe. He **annexed,** or incorporated into his empire, the Netherlands, Belgium, and parts of Italy and Germany. He also abolished the tottering Holy Roman Empire and created a 38-member Confederation of the Rhine under French protection. He cut Prussian territory in half, turning part of old Poland into the Grand Duchy of Warsaw.

Napoleon controlled much of Europe through forceful diplomacy. One tactic was placing friends and relatives on the thrones of Europe. For example, after unseating the king of Spain, he placed his own brother, Joseph Bonaparte, on the throne. He also forced alliances on European powers from Madrid to Moscow. At various times, the rulers of Austria, Prussia, and Russia reluctantly signed treaties with the "Corsican ogre," as the monarchs he overthrew called him.

In France, Napoleon's successes boosted the spirit of nationalism. Great victory parades filled the streets of Paris with cheering crowds. The people celebrated the glory and grandeur that Napoleon had gained for France.

Napoleon Strikes Britain   Britain alone, of all the major European powers, remained outside Napoleon's European empire. With only a small army, Britain relied on its sea power to stop Napoleon's drive to rule the continent. In 1805, Napoleon prepared to invade England. But at the Battle of Trafalgar, fought off the southwest coast of Spain, British Admiral Horatio Nelson smashed the French fleet.

With an invasion ruled out, Napoleon struck at Britain's lifeblood, its commerce. He waged economic warfare through the **Continental System,** which closed European ports to British goods. Britain responded with its own blockade of European ports. A blockade involves shutting off ports to keep people or supplies from moving in or out. During their long struggle, both Britain and France seized neutral ships suspected of trading with the other side. British attacks on American ships sparked anger in the United States and eventually triggered the War of 1812.

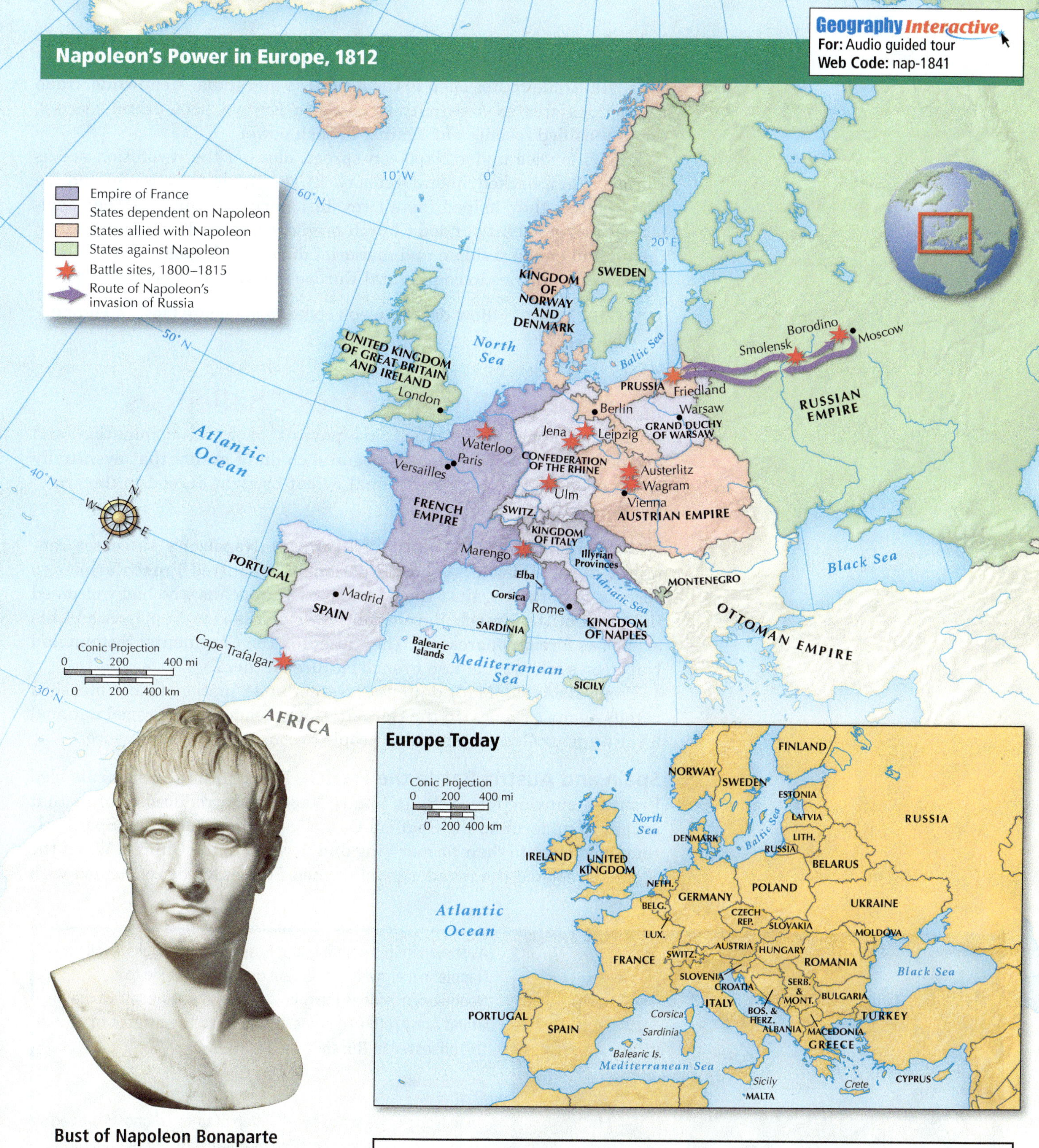

Bust of Napoleon Bonaparte

Map Skills Napoleon's empire reached its greatest extent in 1812. Most of the countries in Europe today have different names and borders.

1. **Locate:** (a) French empire, (b) Russian empire, (c) Germany
2. **Region** Locate the Confederation of the Rhine. What is this area called today?
3. **Make Comparisons** Compare Europe of Napoleon's empire to Europe of today on the maps above. How has Europe changed?

In the end, Napoleon's Continental System failed to bring Britain to its knees. Although British exports declined, Britain's powerful navy kept vital trade routes open to the Americas and India. Meanwhile, trade restrictions created a scarcity of goods in Europe, sent prices soaring, and intensified resentment against French power.

French armies under Napoleon spread ideas of the revolution across Europe. They backed liberal reforms in the lands they conquered. In some places, they helped install revolutionary governments that abolished titles of nobility, ended Church privileges, opened careers to men of talent, and ended serfdom and manorial dues. The Napoleonic Code, too, influenced countries in continental Europe and Latin America.

✔ **Checkpoint** How did Napoleon come to dominate most of Europe by 1812?

Napoleon's Empire Faces Challenges

In 1812, Napoleon continued his pursuit of world domination and invaded Russia. This campaign began a chain of events that eventually led to his downfall. Napoleon's final defeat brought an end to the era of the French Revolution.

Nationalism Works Against Napoleon Napoleon's successes contained seeds of defeat. Although nationalism spurred French armies to success, it worked against them too. Many Europeans who had welcomed the ideas of the French Revolution nevertheless saw Napoleon and his armies as foreign oppressors. They resented the Continental System and Napoleon's effort to impose French culture on them.

From Rome to Madrid to the Netherlands, nationalism unleashed revolts against France. In the German states, leaders encouraged national loyalty among German-speaking people to counter French influence.

Spain and Austria Battle the French Resistance to foreign rule bled French-occupying forces dry in Spain. Napoleon introduced reforms that sought to undermine the Spanish Catholic Church. But many Spaniards remained loyal to their former king and devoted to the Church. When the Spanish resisted the invaders, well-armed French forces responded with

As shown in this painting, the Russian winter took its toll on Napoleon's army. Philippe Paul de Ségur, an aide to Napoleon, describes the grim scene as the remnants of the Grand Army returned home. **What were the effects of this disaster in Russia?**

Primary Source

“ In Napoleon's wake [was] a mob of tattered ghosts draped in . . . odd pieces of carpet, or greatcoats burned full of holes, their feet wrapped in all sorts of rags. . . . [We] stared in horror as those skeletons of soldiers went by, their gaunt, gray faces covered with disfiguring beards, without weapons . . . with lowered heads, eyes on the ground, in absolute silence.”
—*Memoirs of Philippe Paul de Ségur*

brutal repression. Far from crushing resistance, however, the French response further inflamed Spanish nationalism. Efforts to drive out the French intensified.

Spanish patriots conducted a campaign of **guerrilla warfare,** or hit-and-run raids, against the French. (In Spanish, *guerrilla* means "little war.") Small bands of guerrillas ambushed French supply trains or troops before retreating into the countryside. These attacks kept large numbers of French soldiers tied down in Spain when Napoleon needed them elsewhere.

Spanish resistance encouraged Austria to resume hostilities against the French. In 1805, at the Battle of Austerlitz, Napoleon had won a crushing victory against an Austro-Russian army of superior numbers. Now, in 1809, the Austrians sought revenge. But once again, Napoleon triumphed—this time at the Battle of Wagram. By the peace agreement that followed, Austria surrendered lands populated by more than three million subjects.

The Russian Winter Stops the Grand Army

Tsar Alexander I of Russia was once an ally of Napoleon. The tsar and Napoleon planned to divide Europe if Alexander helped Napoleon in his Continental System. Many countries objected to this system, and Russia became unhappy with the economic effects of the system as well. Yet another cause for concern was that Napoleon had enlarged the Grand Duchy of Warsaw that bordered Russia on the west. These and other issues led the tsar to withdraw his support from the Continental System. Napoleon responded to the tsar's action by assembling an army with soldiers from 20 nations, known as the Grand Army.

In 1812, with about 600,000 soldiers and 50,000 horses, Napoleon invaded Russia. To avoid battles with Napoleon, the Russians retreated eastward, burning crops and villages as they went. This **scorched-earth policy** left the French hungry and cold as winter came. Napoleon entered Moscow in September. He realized, though, that he would not be able to feed and supply his army through the long Russian winter. In October, he turned homeward.

The 1,000-mile retreat from Moscow turned into a desperate battle for survival. Russian attacks and the brutal Russian winter took a terrible toll. Fewer than 20,000 soldiers of the once-proud Grand Army survived. Many died. Others deserted. French general Michel Ney sadly concluded: "General Famine and General Winter, rather than Russian bullets, have conquered the Grand Army." Napoleon rushed to Paris to raise a new force to defend France. His reputation for success had been shattered.

✔ **Checkpoint** What challenges threatened Napoleon's empire and what led to the disaster in Russia?

Napoleon Falls From Power
A defeated Napoleon after his abdication on April 6, 1814, in a painting by Paul Delaroche

Napoleon Falls From Power

The disaster in Russia brought a new alliance of Russia, Britain, Austria, and Prussia against a weakened France. In 1813, they defeated Napoleon in the Battle of the Nations at Leipzig.

Napoleon Abdicates Briefly The next year, Napoleon **abdicated,** or stepped down from power. The victors exiled him to Elba, an island in the Mediterranean. They then recognized Louis XVIII, brother of Louis XVI, as king of France.

The restoration of Louis XVIII did not go smoothly. He agreed to accept the Napoleonic Code and honor the land settlements made during the revolution. However, many émigrés rushed back to France bent on revenge. An economic depression and the fear of a return to the old regime helped rekindle loyalty to Napoleon.

As the victorious allies gathered in Vienna for a general peace conference, Napoleon escaped his island exile and returned to France. Soldiers flocked to his banner. As citizens cheered Napoleon's advance, Louis XVIII fled. In March 1815, Napoleon entered Paris in triumph.

Crushed at the Battle of Waterloo Napoleon's triumph was short-lived. His star soared for only 100 days, while the allies reassembled their forces. On June 18, 1815, the opposing armies met near the town of Waterloo in Belgium. British forces under the Duke of Wellington and a Prussian army commanded by General Blücher crushed the French in an agonizing day-long battle. Once again, Napoleon was forced to abdicate and to go into exile on St. Helena, a lonely island in the South Atlantic. This time, he would not return.

Napoleon's Legacy Napoleon died in 1821, but his legend lived on in France and around the world. His contemporaries as well as historians today have long debated his legacy. Was he "the revolution on horseback," as he claimed? Or was he a traitor to the revolution?

No one, however, questions Napoleon's impact on France and on Europe. The Napoleonic Code consolidated many changes of the revolution. The France of Napoleon was a centralized state with a constitution. Elections were held with expanded, though limited, suffrage. Many more citizens had rights to property and access to education than under the old regime. Still, French citizens lost many rights promised so fervently by republicans during the Convention.

On the world stage, Napoleon's conquests spread the ideas of the revolution. He failed to make Europe into a French empire. Instead, he sparked nationalist feelings across Europe. The abolition of the Holy Roman Empire would eventually help in creating a new Germany. Napoleon's impact also reached across the

Prince Clemens von Metternich

As Austria's foreign minister, Metternich (1773–1859) used a variety of means to achieve his goals. In 1809, when Napoleon seemed vulnerable, Metternich favored war against France. In 1810, after France had crushed Austria, he supported alliance with France. When the French army was in desperate retreat from Russia, Metternich became the "prime minister of the coalition" that defeated Napoleon. At the Congress of Vienna, Metternich helped create a new European order and made sure that Austria had a key role in it. He would skillfully defend that new order for more than 30 years. **Why did Metternich's policies toward France change?**

Europe After the Congress of Vienna, 1815

Map Skills At the Congress of Vienna, European leaders redrew the map of Europe in order to contain France and keep a balance of power.

1. **Locate** (a) German Confederation, (b) Netherlands, (c) Vienna
2. **Region** Name three states that were in the German Confederation.
3. **Recognize Cause and Effect** Why did the Congress enlarge some of the countries around France?

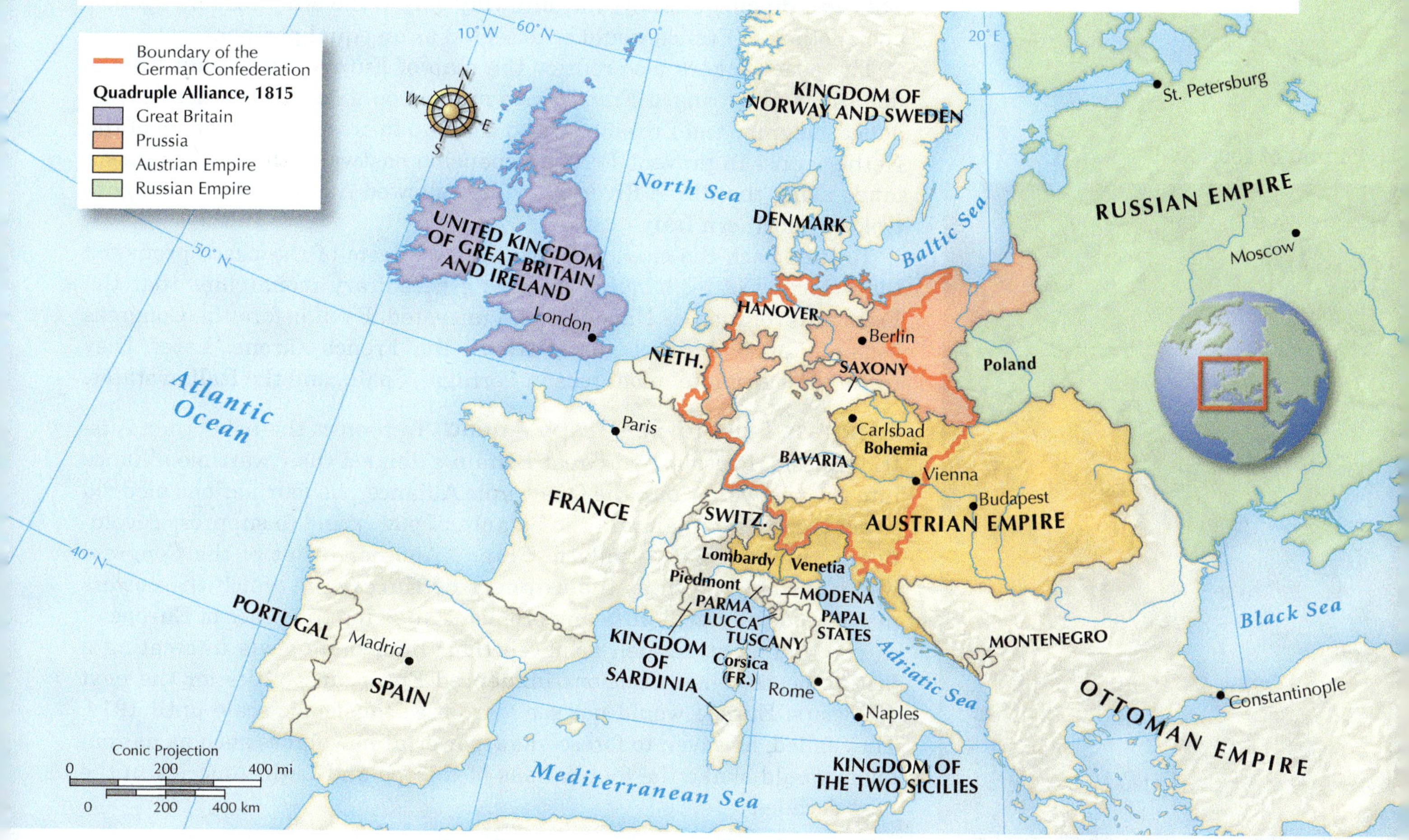

Atlantic. In 1803, his decision to sell France's vast Louisiana Territory to the American government doubled the size of the United States and ushered in an age of American expansion.

 **Checkpoint** How did Napoleon impact Europe and the rest of the world?

Leaders Meet at the Congress of Vienna

After Waterloo, diplomats and heads of state again sat down at the **Congress of Vienna.** They faced the monumental task of restoring stability and order in Europe after years of war. The Congress met for 10 months, from September 1814 to June 1815. It was a brilliant gathering of European leaders. Diplomats and royalty dined and danced, attended concerts and ballets, and enjoyed parties arranged by their host, Emperor Francis I of Austria. The work fell to Prince Clemens von Metternich of Austria, Tsar Alexander I of Russia, and Lord Robert Castlereagh of Britain. Defeated France was represented by Prince Charles Maurice de Talleyrand.

Portrait of Louis XVIII

Congress Strives For Peace The chief goal of the Vienna decision makers was to create a lasting peace by establishing a balance of power and protecting the system of monarchy. Each of the leaders also pursued his own goals. Metternich, the dominant figure at the Congress, wanted to restore things the way they were in 1792. Alexander I urged a "holy alliance" of Christian monarchs to suppress future revolutions. Lord Castlereagh was determined to prevent a revival of French military power. The aged diplomat Talleyrand shrewdly played the other leaders against one another so France would be accepted as an equal partner.

The peacemakers also redrew the map of Europe. To contain French ambitions, they ringed France with strong countries. In the north, they added Belgium and Luxembourg to Holland to create the kingdom of the Netherlands. To prevent French expansion eastward, they gave Prussia lands along the Rhine River. They also allowed Austria to reassert control over northern Italy.

To turn back the clock to 1792, the architects of the peace promoted the principle of **legitimacy,** restoring hereditary monarchies that the French Revolution or Napoleon had unseated. Even before the Congress began, they had put Louis XVIII on the French throne. Later, they restored "legitimate" monarchs in Portugal, Spain, and the Italian states.

Congress Fails to See Traps Ahead To protect the new order, Austria, Russia, Prussia, and Great Britain extended their wartime alliance into the postwar era. In the Quadruple Alliance, the four nations pledged to act together to maintain the balance of power and to suppress revolutionary uprisings, especially in France. Another result of the Congress was a system known as the **Concert of Europe,** in which the powers met periodically to discuss any problems affecting the peace of Europe.

The Vienna statesmen achieved their immediate goals in creating a lasting peace. Their decisions influenced European politics for the next 100 years. Europe would not see war on a Napoleonic scale until 1914. They failed, however, to foresee how powerful new forces such as nationalism would shake the foundations of Europe and Latin America in the next decades.

✔ **Checkpoint** Explain the chief goal and outcome of the Congress of Vienna.

4 Assessment

Terms, People, and Places

1. For each term, person, or place listed at the beginning of the section, write a sentence explaining its significance.

Note Taking

2. **Reading Skill: Identify Main Ideas** Use your completed flowchart to answer the Focus Question: Explain Napoleon's rise to power in Europe, his subsequent defeat, and how the outcome still affects Europe today.

Comprehension and Critical Thinking

3. **Demonstrate Reasoned Judgment** If you were a French voter in 1803, how would you have voted on the plebiscite to make Napoleon emperor? Explain.
4. **Synthesize Information** Describe the resistance Napoleon encountered as countries grew to resent him.
5. **Make Comparisons** How does the peacekeeping solution adopted by the Congress of Vienna compare to today's peacekeeping missions?

● **Writing About History**

Quick Write: Clarify When you write a rough draft of a cause-and-effect essay, you should highlight the causes and effects. Use two highlighters, one to show causes, and the other to show effects. Eliminate causes or effects that do not support your main point, and add transitional phrases as needed. Write a paragraph about Napoleon's downfall. Highlight the causes and effects to evaluate the effectiveness of your paragraph.

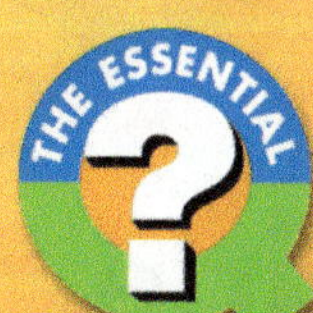

IMPACT OF THE INDIVIDUAL

How can an individual change the world?

In This Chapter

Some people have such an effect on history that historians name entire eras after them. During the Napoleonic Era, Napoleon Bonaparte's conquests changed the map of Europe. At the same time, his decision to sell the Louisiana Territory to the United States forever altered the course of American history.

Throughout History

1700s B.C. Hammurabi sets up the first known code of laws.

500–400s B.C. The teachings of Confucius shape Chinese values.

1400s A.D. Brunelleschi revolutionizes art by finding a way to show perspective.

1517 Luther posts the 95 Theses and ignites the Protestant Reformation.

1558 Elizabeth I of England calms religious turmoil and expands international power.

1920s–1940s Gandhi urges nonviolent protest to win Indian independence from Britain.

Continuing Today

No one knows whose contributions will have the most impact in the years to come. Will it be a political leader? A person of great moral integrity? Or a brilliant scientist? Could it be you?

TRANSFER Activities

1. Analyze How have individual people made lasting impacts on history?

2. Evaluate How could the small contributions of many individuals have as big an impact as the major contribution of one? Give an example.

3. Transfer Complete a Web quest in which you evaluate the impact of an individual; record your thoughts in the Concept Connector Journal; and learn to make a video. Web Code nah-1808

Quick Study Guide

Progress Monitoring *Online*
For: Self-test with vocabulary practice
Web Code: naa-1851

■ What Inspired the French Revolution?

- **Social:** Enlightenment ideas such as equality and justice
- **Political:** Ideas from the American Revolution
- **Economic:** Inequalities among classes; unrest due to extravagant monarchy

■ Reforms of the National Assembly

Political
• Proclaimed all male citizens equal before the law.
• Limited the power of the monarchy.
• Established the Legislative Assembly to make laws.
• Granted all tax-paying male citizens the right to elect members of the Legislative Assembly.

Social and Economic
• Abolished special privileges of the nobility.
• Announced an end to feudalism.
• Called for taxes to be levied according to ability to pay.
• Abolished guilds and forbade labor unions.
• Compensated nobles for lands seized by peasants.

Religious
• Declared freedom of religion.
• Took over and sold Church lands.
• Placed the French Catholic Church under control of the state.
• Provided that bishops and priests be elected and receive government salaries.

■ Causes and Effects of the French Revolution

Cause and Effect

Long-Term Causes	Immediate Causes
• Corrupt and inconsistent leadership	• Huge government debt
• Prosperous members of Third Estate resent privileges of First and Second Estates.	• Poor harvests and rising price of bread
• Spread of Enlightenment ideas	• Failure of Louis XVI to accept financial reforms
	• Formation of National Assembly
	• Storming of Bastille

The French Revolution

Immediate Effects	Long-Term Effects
• Declaration of the Rights of Man and the Citizen adopted.	• Napoleon gains power.
• France adopts its first written constitution.	• Napoleonic Code established.
• Revolutionary France fights coalition of European powers.	• French public schools set up.
• Monarchy abolished; execution of king and queen.	• French conquests spread nationalism.
• Reign of Terror	• Congress of Vienna convenes to restore stability to Europe.
	• Revolutions occur elsewhere in Europe and in Latin America.

Connections to Today

- French law reflects Napoleonic Code.
- France eventually became a democratic republic.

■ Key Events From 1789–1815

1789
Parisians storm the Bastille on July 14, starting the French Revolution.

1793
Radicals execute the king and queen, which leads to the Reign of Terror.

1799
Napoleon overthrows the Directory.

Chapter Events
Global Events

| 1790 | 1795 | 1800 |

1789
The United States Constitution is ratified.

1793
China rejects British trade offer.

Essential Question Review

To connect prior knowledge with what you have learned in this chapter, answer the questions below in your Concept Connector journal. Use the journal in the Reading and Note Taking Study Guide to record your answers (or go to www.phschool.com **Web Code: nad-1807**). In addition, record information about the following concept:

- Cooperation: Coalitions against Napoleon

1. **Nationalism** During the French Revolution, the people were inspired to rally to the cause of freedom. How did the leaders of the revolution motivate people? Consider the following.
   - songs
   - symbols
   - slogans

2. **Revolution** In 1524, German peasants rose up against the nobility in an effort to end serfdom. They hoped for but did not get the support of Martin Luther. The German nobility put down the rebellion and killed thousands of people. In the French Revolution, the Third Estate revolted against the Old Regime. Describe how the circumstances around the French Revolution were similar to and different from the Peasants' Revolt in Germany.

3. **Democracy** According to the text, "Napoleon's successes contained seeds of defeat." His conquests unleashed feelings of nationalism that led conquered countries to revolt against France. How did Napoleon strengthen democracy in France? How did he weaken democratic gains made during earlier phases of the Revolution? Focus on the following:
   - economic reforms
   - legal reforms
   - natural rights

■ Connections to Today

1. **Geography's Impact: Wars in the Middle East** Geography played an important role in Napoleon's defeat in Russia. Napoleon's Grand Army, once nearly 500,000 soldiers strong, shrank to about 20,000 due to the brutal Russian winter. Research newspaper and magazine articles to find how geography has impacted wars in the Middle East. Compile your research and write a script for your local newscast. Consider the following:
   - location
   - landforms
   - climate

Burning oil pipeline, September 14, 2004, caused by sabotage in the Middle East

2. **Cooperation: United Nations** Diplomats and heads of states from the powers that defeated Napoleon—Austria, Russia, Prussia, and Great Britain—gathered at the Congress of Vienna in 1814. Their main goal was to restore peace after the French Revolution and Napoleonic era. Today, U.N. peace-keeping operations take place around the globe with the same goal of keeping or restoring peace. Research to find more information on the Congress of Vienna and U.N. peace-keeping operations. Draw a table to write facts about each in individual columns. Think about the following:
   - history and purpose of the organizations
   - definitions of "peacekeeping"

1804
Napoleon crowns himself emperor of France.

1812
Napoleon invades Russia.

1814
Congress of Vienna meets.

1815
Napoleon is defeated at Waterloo.

1805   **1810**   **1815**

1804
Haiti declares independence from France.

1812
The United States declares war on Britain.

History Interactive
For: Interactive timeline
Web Code: nap-1801

Chapter Assessment

Terms, People, and Places

Match the following terms with the definitions below.

sans-culotte
bourgeoisie
Napoleonic Code
abdicate
Estates-General

Olympe de Gouges
plebiscite
deficit spending
Maximilien Robespierre
nationalism

1. a meeting of the representatives of the three estates
2. situation in which a government spends more money than it takes in
3. strong feeling of devotion to one's country
4. the middle class
5. journalist who demanded equal rights for women
6. leader of the Committee of Public Safety
7. ballot in which voters have a direct say on an issue
8. working-class men and women in France; means "without breeches"
9. law code that embodied Enlightenment principles such as equality
10. step down from power

Main Ideas

Section 1 (pp. 572–577)
11. What caused discontent in the old French regime?
12. When the Estates-General convened in May 1789, what actions did members of the Third Estate take and why?

Section 2 (pp. 578–584)
13. Describe one reform that the National Assembly enacted through each of the following documents: **(a)** the Declaration of the Rights of Man and the Citizen, **(b)** the Civil Constitution of the Clergy, **(c)** the Constitution of 1791.

Section 3 (pp. 585–591)
14. What was the Reign of Terror?

Section 4 (pp. 592–601)
15. List the reforms that Napoleon made as leader of France.
16. How did the Congress of Vienna try to restore the balance of power in Europe?

Chapter Focus Question
17. What were the causes and effects of the French Revolution, and how did the revolution lead to the Napoleonic era?

Critical Thinking

18. **Draw Conclusions** What impact did Enlightenment ideas have on the French Revolution?
19. **Recognize Cause and Effect** Explain the events that led to the end of the monarchy.
20. **Geography and History** How did the geography of the Russian empire work against Napoleon's Grand Army?
21. **Analyzing Cartoons** In the cartoon shown here, the figure on the left represents the British, and the other figure represents Napoleon. What are the figures carving, and why?

● Writing About History

In this chapter's four Section Assessments, you developed skills for writing an expository essay.

Expository Essay: Cause and Effect There were many key events in the French Revolution and Napoleonic era that affected France and the rest of the world. Write an essay that explains the causes of one of the following events and discuss what resulted: Parisians storming the Bastille; Women marching on Versailles; Napoleon crowning himself emperor of the French. Consult page SH10 of the Writing Handbook for additional help.

Prewriting
• Consider what you know about these events and choose one that you think best shows cause and effect.
• Take time to research facts, descriptions, and examples, to clearly illustrate the causes and effects in your essay.

Drafting
• Choose one of the following to organize the causes and effects in your essay: show the chronological order of events, or order the events from the least important to the most important.
• As you draft your essay, illustrate each cause and effect with supporting facts and details.

Revising
• Review your entire draft to ensure you show a clear relationship between the causes and effects.
• Analyze each paragraph to check that you have provided a thorough set of facts and details.

Document-Based Assessment

Storming the Bastille

One of the most famous and dramatic moments of the French Revolution was the storming of the Bastille. This prison fortress with 90-foot-high walls symbolized the injustices of absolute monarchy. The following documents describe the event from different viewpoints.

Document A

"Shouts of 'Give us the Bastille' were heard, and nine hundred had pressed into the undefended outer courtyard, becoming angrier by the minute. . . . At about half past three in the afternoon the crowd was reinforced by companies of *gardes françaises* [French guards] and by defecting soldiers, including a number who were veterans of the American campaign. Two in particular, Second-Lieutenant Jacob Elie, the standard-bearer of the Infantry of the Queen, and Pierre-Augustin Hulin, the director of the Queen's laundry, were crucial in turning the incoherent assault into an organized siege."

—From ***Citizens: A Chronicle of the French Revolution,*** (1989) by Simon Schama

Document B

"How much the greatest event it is that ever happened in the world! and how much the best!"

—**Letter, July 30, 1789,** by Charles James Fox (1749–1806), British politician, on the fall of the Bastille

Document C

"The mob came closer and the governor declared his willingness to capitulate [give up]. . . The streets and houses, even the roofs were filled with people abusing and cursing me. Daggers, bayonets, pistols were constantly pointed at me. I did not know how I would be killed but was sure my last hour had come. Those who had no arms were throwing stones at me, the women wrenched their teeth and threatened me with their fists. Two soldiers behind me had already been killed by the furious mob and I am convinced I could not have reached City Hall had not one officer . . . escorted me."

—**"Reports of the Taking of the Bastille, July 14, 1789, by One of Its Defenders"** (1834) by Ludwig von der Fluhe (Swiss officer)

Document D

▼ *Demolition of the Bastille, 1789*

Analyzing Documents

Use your knowledge of the storming of the Bastille and Documents A, B, C, and D to answer questions 1–4.

1. In Document B, Charles James Fox was mostly likely enthusiastic about the fall of the Bastille because
   A he had a personal grudge against prison guards.
   B the people stood up to authority.
   C he supported King Louis XVI.
   D he was anxious to see what the people of France would do next.

2. Which document attempts to give an objective view of the storming of the Bastille?
   A Document B
   B Document A
   C Document C
   D Document D

3. In Document C, which words best indicate which side the author is on?
   A the governor declared his willingness to capitulate
   B daggers, bayonets, pistols
   C even the roofs were filled with people
   D furious mob

4. **Writing Task** Compare the four documents. Which lasting document best conveys the significance of the event? Use your knowledge of this event and specific evidence from the documents to support your opinion.

19 The Industrial Revolution Begins

1750–1850

A Different Kind of Revolution

While the American Revolution and the French Revolution were being fought in the late 1700s, another kind of revolution took hold in Britain. Though not political, this revolution—known as the Industrial Revolution—brought about just as many changes to society. Paul Johnson, historian, describes this time period as "the age, above all in history, of matchless opportunities for penniless men with powerful brains and imaginations." Listen to the Witness History audio to hear more about the start of the Industrial Revolution.

Train ticket, 1830

◀ On September 27, 1825, the Stockton and Darlington Railway in England became the world's first steam railway to offer passenger and freight service.

James Watt

Chapter Preview

Chapter Focus Question What technological, social, economic, and cultural changes occurred as the Industrial Revolution took hold?

Section 1
Dawn of the Industrial Age

Section 2
Britain Leads the Way

Section 3
Social Impact of the Industrial Revolution

Section 4
New Ways of Thinking

Socialist leaflet

Use the ✓ **Quick Study Timeline** at the end of this chapter to preview chapter events.

 **Concept Connector ONLINE**

To explore Essential Questions related to this chapter, go to PHSchool.com
Web Code: nad-1907

Matthew
Boulton

From Hand Power to Steam Power

For centuries, people used their own energy to provide the power for their work. While the idea of using steam power came about in the seventeenth century, it was not until engineer James Watt improved the steam engine that it could be applied to machinery. His financial partner Matthew Boulton, a successful manufacturer, proclaimed:

66 I have at my disposal what the whole world demands, something which will uplift civilization more than ever by relieving man of all undignified drudgery. I have *steam power.* **99**

Focus Question What events helped bring about the Industrial Revolution?

Dawn of the Industrial Age

Objectives
- Analyze why life changed as industry spread.
- Summarize how an agricultural revolution led to the growth of industry.
- Outline the new technologies that helped trigger the Industrial Revolution.

Terms, People, and Places

anesthetic
enclosure
James Watt
smelt

Note Taking

Reading Skill: Recognize Multiple Causes
Several key events led to the Industrial Revolution. As you read the section, create a flowchart of these causes. Add categories as needed.

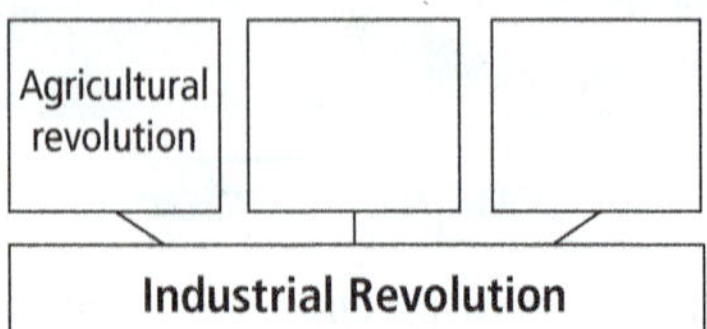

For thousands of years following the rise of civilization, most people lived and worked in small farming villages. However, a chain of events set in motion in the mid-1700s changed that way of life for all time. Today, we call this period of change the Industrial Revolution.

The Industrial Revolution started in Britain. The economic changes that Britain experienced affected people's lives as much as previous political changes and revolutions had. In contrast with most political revolutions, it was neither sudden nor swift. Instead, it was a long, slow, uneven process in which production shifted from simple hand tools to complex machines. From its beginnings in Britain, the Industrial Revolution has spread to the rest of Europe, North America, and around the globe.

Life Changes as Industry Spreads

In 1750, most people worked the land, using handmade tools. They lived in simple cottages lit by firelight and candles. They made their own clothing and grew their own food. In nearby towns, they might exchange goods at a weekly outdoor market.

Like their ancestors, these people knew little of the world that existed beyond their village. The few who left home traveled only as far as their feet or a horse-drawn cart could take them. Those bold adventurers who dared to cross the seas were at the mercy of the winds and tides.

With the onset of the Industrial Revolution, the rural way of life began to disappear. By the 1850s, many country villages had grown into industrial towns and cities. Those who lived there were able to buy clothing and food that someone else produced.

Industrial-age travelers moved rapidly between countries and continents by train or steamship. Urgent messages flew along telegraph wires. New inventions and scientific "firsts" poured out each year. Between 1830 and 1855, for example, an American dentist first used an **anesthetic,** or drug that prevents pain during surgery; an American inventor patented the first sewing machine; a French physicist measured the speed of light; and a Hungarian doctor introduced antiseptic methods to reduce the risk of women dying in childbirth.

Still more stunning changes occurred in the next century, which created our familiar world of skyscraper cities and carefully tended suburbs. How and why did these great changes occur? Historians point to a series of interrelated causes that helped trigger the industrialization of the West. The "West" referred originally to the industrialized countries in Europe but today includes many more.

 **Checkpoint** Why was the Industrial Revolution a turning point in world history?

Agriculture Spurs Industry

Oddly enough, the Industrial Revolution was made possible in part by a change in the farming fields of Western Europe. From the first agricultural revolution some 11,000 years ago, when people learned to farm and domesticate animals, until about 300 years ago, farming had remained pretty much the same. Then, a second agricultural revolution took place that greatly improved the quality and quantity of farm products.

Farming Methods Improve The Dutch led the way in this new agricultural revolution. They built earthen walls known as dikes to reclaim land from the sea. They also combined smaller fields into larger ones to make better use of the land and used fertilizer from livestock to renew the soil.

In the 1700s, British farmers expanded on Dutch agricultural experiments. Educated farmers exchanged news of experiments through farm journals. Some farmers mixed different kinds of soils to get higher crop yields. Others tried out new methods of crop rotation. Lord Charles Townshend urged farmers to grow turnips, which restored exhausted soil. Jethro Tull invented a new mechanical device, the seed drill, to aid farmers. It deposited seeds in rows rather than scattering them wastefully over the land.

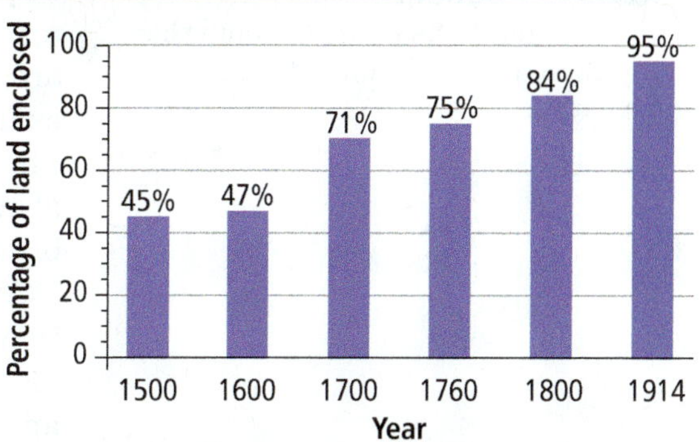

Graph Skills According to the graph, between which years was the largest percentage of land enclosed? What was the result of these land enclosures?

SOURCE: *Oxford Atlas of World History,* 1999

Jethro Tull's seed drill

Enclosure Increases Output but Causes Migration Meanwhile, rich landowners pushed ahead with **enclosure,** the process of taking over and consolidating land formerly shared by peasant farmers. In the 1500s, landowners had enclosed land to gain more pastures for sheep to increase wool output. By the 1700s, they wanted to create larger fields that could be cultivated more efficiently. The British Parliament facilitated enclosures through legislation.

As millions of acres were enclosed, farm output rose. Profits also rose because large fields needed fewer workers. But such progress had a large human cost. Many farm laborers were thrown out of work, and small farmers were forced off their land because they could not compete with large landholders. Villages shrank as cottagers left in search of work. In time, jobless farm workers migrated to towns and cities. There, they formed a growing labor force that would soon tend the machines of the Industrial Revolution.

Population Multiplies The agricultural revolution contributed to a rapid growth of population. Precise population <u>statistics</u> for the 1700s are rare, but those that do exist are striking. Britain's population, for example, soared from about 5 million in 1700 to almost 9 million in 1800. The population of Europe as a whole shot up from roughly 120 million to about 180 million during the same period. Such growth had never before been seen.

Why did this population increase occur? First, the agricultural revolution reduced the risk of death from famine because it created a surplus of food. Since people ate better, they were healthier. Also, better hygiene and sanitation, along with improved medical care, further slowed deaths from disease.

✔ **Checkpoint** How did an agricultural revolution contribute to population growth?

BIOGRAPHY

James Watt

How did a clever Scottish engineer become the "Father of the Industrial Revolution"? After repairing a Newcomen steam engine, James Watt (1736–1819) became fascinated with the idea of improving the device. Within a few months, he knew he had a product that would sell. Still, Watt lacked the money needed to produce and market it.

Fortunately, he was able to form a partnership with the shrewd manufacturer Matthew Boulton. They then founded Soho Engineering Works in Birmingham, England, to manufacture steam engines. Watt's version of the steam engine shown here had a separate condensing chamber and was patented in 1769. Eventually, a measure of mechanical and electrical power, the watt, would be named for James Watt. **How might the Industrial Revolution have been different if Watt had not found a business partner?**

New Technology Becomes Key

Another factor that helped trigger the Industrial Revolution was the development of new technology. Aided by new sources of energy and new materials, these new technologies enabled business owners to change the ways work was done.

An Energy Revolution During the 1700s, people began to harness new sources of energy. One vital power source was coal, used to develop the steam engine. In 1712, British inventor Thomas Newcomen had developed a steam engine powered by coal to pump water out of mines. Scottish engineer James Watt looked at Newcomen's invention in 1764 and set out to make improvements on the engine in order to make it more efficient. Watt's engine, after several years of work, would become a key power source of the Industrial Revolution. The steam engine opened the door not only to operating machinery but eventually to powering locomotives and steamships.

The Quality of Iron Improves Coal was also a vital source of fuel in the production of iron, a material needed for the construction of machines and steam engines. The Darby family of Coalbrookdale pioneered new methods of producing iron. In 1709, Abraham Darby used coal instead of charcoal to smelt iron, or separate iron from its ore.

Darby's experiments led him to produce less expensive and better-quality iron, which was used to produce parts for the steam engines. Both his son and grandson continued to improve on his methods. In fact, Abraham Darby III built the world's first iron bridge. In the decades that followed, high-quality iron was used more and more widely, especially after the world turned to building railroads.

Abraham Darby III completed the world's first iron bridge in 1779. The bridge still stands today.

 **Checkpoint** What new technologies helped trigger the Industrial Revolution?

Terms, People, and Places

1. For each term, person, or place listed at the beginning of the section, write a sentence explaining its significance.

Note Taking

2. **Reading Skill: Recognize Multiple Causes** Use your completed flowchart to answer the Focus Question: What events helped bring about the Industrial Revolution?

Comprehension and Critical Thinking

3. **Recognize Cause and Effect** What were the immediate and long-term effects of the agricultural revolution that occurred in the 1700s?

4. **Predict Consequences** How do you think population growth contributed to the Industrial Revolution?

5. **Summarize** Explain how new sources of energy, specifically coal, contributed to the Industrial Revolution.

● **Writing About History**

Quick Write: Give Background To explain a historical process, you should first orient the reader to time and place. Ask yourself when and where the process occurred. Practice by explaining in one or two sentences how an agricultural revolution led to the Industrial Revolution.

SECTION **2**

Train passengers in Britain

WITNESS HISTORY 🔊 AUDIO

Riding the Railway

One of the most important developments of the Industrial Revolution was the creation of a countrywide railway network. The world's first major rail line went from Liverpool to Manchester in England. Fanny Kemble, the most famous actress of the day, was one of the first passengers:

> **❝** We were introduced to the little engine which was to drag us along the rails. . . This snorting little animal, . . . started at about ten miles an hour. . . . You can't imagine how strange it seemed to be journeying on thus, without any visible cause of progress other than the magical machine . . . **❞**

Focus Question What key factors allowed Britain to lead the way in the Industrial Revolution?

Britain Leads the Way

Objectives
- Understand why Britain was the starting point for the Industrial Revolution.
- Describe the changes that transformed the textile industry.
- Explain the significance of the transportation revolution.

Terms, People, and Places

capital	Eli Whitney
enterprise	turnpike
entrepreneur	Liverpool
putting-out system	Manchester

Note Taking

Reading Skill: Identify Causes and Effects Fill in the circles of a concept web like the one below with the key factors that helped Britain take an early lead in industrialization. In a separate concept web, fill in the effects of Britain's early lead.

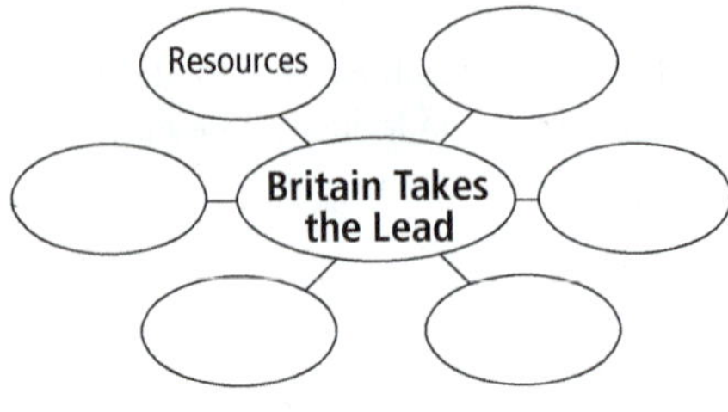

When agricultural practices changed in the eighteenth century, more food was able to be produced, which in turn fueled population growth in Britain. The agricultural changes also left many farmers homeless and jobless. These two factors led to a population boom in the cities as people migrated from rural England into towns and cities. This population increase, in turn, created a ready supply of labor to mine the coal, build the factories, and run the machines. The start of the Industrial Revolution in Britain can be attributed to many factors. Population growth was just one of them.

Why Britain?

What characteristics of eighteenth-century Britain made it ripe for industrialization? Historians cite several reasons for Britain's lead.

Natural Resources Abound Britain had the advantage of plentiful natural resources such as natural ports and navigable rivers. Rivers supplied water power and allowed for the construction of canals. These canals increased accessibility for trade and were instrumental in bringing goods to market. In addition, Britain was able to establish communications and transport relatively cheaply due to its easy accessibility to the sea from all points. Britain's plentiful supply of coal was fundamental to its industrialization and was used to power steam engines. Vast supplies of iron were available to be used to build the new machines.

The Effects of Demand and Capital In the 1700s, Britain had plenty of skilled mechanics who were eager to meet the growing demand for new, practical inventions. This ready workforce, along with the population explosion, boosted demand for goods. In order to increase the production of goods to meet the demand, however, another key ingredient was needed. Money was necessary to start businesses.

From the mid-1600s to 1700s, trade from a growing overseas empire helped the British economy prosper. Beginning with the slave trade, the business class accumulated **capital,** or money used to invest in enterprises. An **enterprise** is a business organization in an area such as shipping, mining, railroads, or factories. Many businessmen were ready to risk their capital in new ventures due to the healthy economy.

In addition to the advantages already cited, Britain had a stable government that supported economic growth. While other countries in Europe faced river tolls and other barriers, Britain did not. The government built a strong navy that protected its empire, shipping, and overseas trade. Although the upper class tended to look down on business people, it did not reject the wealth produced by the new entrepreneurs. These **entrepreneurs** were those who managed and assumed the financial risks of starting new businesses.

✓ **Checkpoint** What conditions in Britain paved the way for the Industrial Revolution?

Shuttle used to speed up weaving process

Geography *Interactive*
For: Audio guided tour
Web Code: nap-1921

Resources and Industries in England, 1750

Map Skills Plentiful supplies of coal, advancements in the textile industry, iron smelting, and the manufacturing of iron goods contributed to Britain's position as the world's leading industrial nation in the late eighteenth century.

1. **Locate** (a) London (b) Manchester (c) Thames River
2. **Region** Identify the centers of woolen industry in England.
3. **Draw Inferences** What were the industrial advantages of the rivers during this time?

These textile machines were constructed to increase cotton production. The flying shuttle sped up weaving, while the spinning jenny and the water frame increased the speed of spinning thread. How did these inventions change the textile industry?

John Kay's flying shuttle, 1733 ▶

◀ James Hargreaves' spinning jenny, 1764

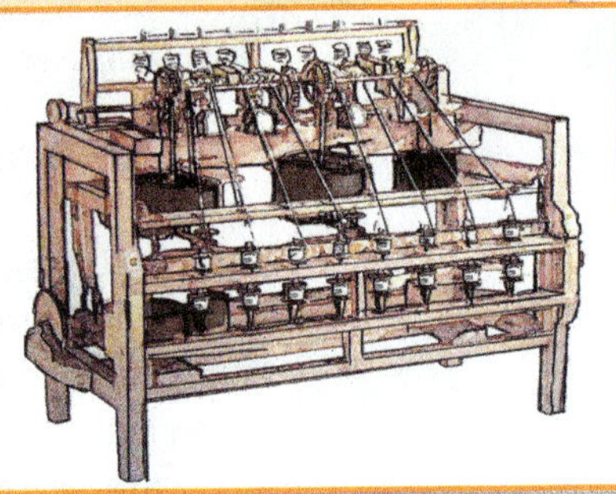
Richard Arkwright's water frame, 1769 ▶

The Textile Industry Advances

The Industrial Revolution first took hold in Britain's largest industry—textiles. In the 1600s, cotton cloth imported from India had become popular. British merchants tried to organize a cotton cloth industry at home. They developed the **putting-out system,** also known as cottage industry, in which raw cotton was distributed to peasant families who spun it into thread and then wove the thread into cloth in their own homes. Skilled artisans in the towns then finished and dyed the cloth.

Inventions Speed Production Under the putting-out system, production was slow. As the demand for cloth grew, inventors came up with a string of remarkable devices that revolutionized the British textile industry. For example, John Kay's flying shuttle enabled weavers to work so fast that they soon outpaced spinners. James Hargreaves solved that problem by producing the spinning jenny in 1764, which spun many threads at the same time. A few years later, in 1769, Richard Arkwright patented the water frame, which was a spinning machine that could be powered by water.

Meanwhile, in America, these faster spinning and weaving machines presented a challenge—how to produce enough cotton to keep up with England. Raw cotton grown in the South had to be cleaned of dirt and seeds by hand, a time-consuming task. To solve this, **Eli Whitney** invented a machine called the cotton gin that separated the seeds from the raw cotton at a fast rate. He finished the cotton gin in 1793, and cotton production increased exponentially.

Factories Are Born in Britain The new machines doomed the putting-out system. They were too large and expensive to be operated at home. Instead, manufacturers built long sheds to house the machines. At first, they located the sheds near rapidly moving streams, harnessing the water power to run the machines. Later, machines were powered by steam engines.

Spinners and weavers now came each day to work in these first factories, which brought together workers and machines to produce large quantities of goods. Early observers were awed at the size and output of these establishments. One onlooker noted: "The same [amount] of labor is now performed in one of these structures which formerly occupied the industry of an entire district."

 **Checkpoint** What led to the advancement of the British textile industry?

The Transportation Revolution

As production increased, entrepreneurs needed faster and cheaper methods of moving goods from place to place. Some capitalists invested in **turnpikes,** private roads built by entrepreneurs who charged travelers a toll, or fee, to use them. Goods traveled faster as a result, and turnpikes soon linked every part of Britain. Other entrepreneurs had canals dug to connect rivers together or to connect inland towns with coastal ports. Engineers also built stronger bridges and upgraded harbors to help the expanding overseas trade.

Canals Boom During the late 1700s and early 1800s, factories needed an efficient, inexpensive way to receive coal and raw materials and then to ship finished goods to market. In 1763, when the Bridgewater canal opened, it not only made a profit from tolls, but it cut in half the price of coal in Manchester. The success of this canal set off a canal-building frenzy. Entrepreneurs formed companies to construct canals for profit. Not all the canals that were built had enough traffic to support them, however, and bankruptcy often resulted. Then, beginning in the 1830s, canals lost their importance as steam locomotives made railroads the new preferred form of transportation.

Welcome the Steam Locomotive It was the invention of the steam locomotive that made the growth of railroads possible. In the early 1800s, pioneers like George Stephenson developed steam-powered locomotives to pull carriages along iron rails. The railroad did not have to follow the course of a river. This meant that tracks could go places where rivers did not, allowing factory owners and merchants to ship goods swiftly and cheaply over land. The world's first major rail line, from Liverpool to Manchester, opened in England in 1830. In the following decades, railroad travel became faster and railroad building boomed. By 1870, rail lines crisscrossed Britain, Europe, and North America.

Vocabulary Builder

decades—(DEK aydz) *n.* ten-year periods

One Thing Leads to Another As the Industrial Revolution got under way, it triggered a chain reaction. Once inventors developed machines that could produce large quantities of goods more efficiently, prices fell. Lower prices made goods more affordable and thus created more consumers who further fed the demand for goods. This new cycle caused a wave of economic and social changes that dramatically affected the way people lived.

 **Checkpoint** Why was the development of railroads important to industrialization?

Terms, People, and Places

1. For each term, person, or place listed at the beginning of the section, write a sentence explaining its significance.

Note Taking

2. **Reading Skill: Identify Causes and Effects** Use your completed concept webs to answer the Focus Question: What key factors allowed Britain to lead the way in the Industrial Revolution?

Comprehension and Critical Thinking

3. **Analyze Information** Explain how each of the following helped contribute to demand for consumer goods in Britain: **(a)** population explosion, **(b)** general economic prosperity.

4. **Determine Relevance** What was the significance of new machines to the textile industry?

5. **Summarize** Explain how advances in transportation contributed to Britain's global trade.

● **Writing About History**

Quick Write: Create a Flowchart Flowcharts are useful tools to help you write an explanatory essay. Create a flowchart to show the changes that occurred in the textile industry. Be sure that the sequence of events is clear.

Monmouth
Street, London

Stench and Sickness

As more and more people moved to the cities to work, they had little choice about where to live. There was no public water supply, waste lined the unpaved streets, and disease spread rapidly in these unsanitary conditions. Dr. Southwood-Smith worked in two districts of London and wrote:

66 Uncovered sewers, stagnant ditches and ponds, gutters always full of putrefying matter . . . It is not possible for any language to convey an adequate conception of the poisonous condition in which large portions of both these districts always remain, . . . from the masses of putrefying matter which are allowed to accumulate. 99

Focus Question What were the social effects of the Industrial Revolution?

Social Impact of the Industrial Revolution

Objectives

- Explain what caused urbanization and what life was like in the new industrial cities.
- Compare and contrast the industrial working class and the new middle class.
- Understand how the factory system and mines changed the way people worked.
- Analyze the benefits and challenges of industrialization.

Terms, People, and Places

urbanization
tenement
labor union

Note Taking

Reading Skill: Understand Effects As you read the section, complete a table that lists benefits and challenges of industrialization.

Industrialization	
Benefits	**Challenges**
• Created jobs	• Crowded cities
•	•

The Industrial Revolution brought great riches to most of the entrepreneurs who helped set it in motion. For the millions of workers who crowded into the new factories, however, the industrial age brought poverty and harsh living conditions.

In time, reforms would curb many of the worst abuses of the early industrial age in Europe and the Americas. As standards of living increased, people at all levels of society would benefit from industrialization. Until then, working people would suffer with dangerous working conditions; unsafe, unsanitary, and overcrowded housing; and unrelenting poverty.

People Move to New Industrial Cities

The Industrial Revolution brought rapid **urbanization,** or the movement of people to cities. Changes in farming, soaring population growth, and an ever-increasing demand for workers led masses of people to migrate from farms to cities. Almost overnight, small towns around coal or iron mines mushroomed into cities. Other cities grew up around the factories that entrepreneurs built in once-quiet market towns.

The British market town of Manchester numbered 17,000 people in the 1750s. Within a few years, it exploded into a center of the textile industry. Its population soared to 40,000 by 1780 and 70,000 by 1801. Visitors described the "cloud of coal vapor" that polluted

the air, the pounding noise of steam engines, and the filthy stench of its river. This growth of industry and rapid population growth dramatically changed the location and distribution of two resources—labor and people.

✔ **Checkpoint** What led to the massive migration of people from farms to cities?

Population Growth in London, c. 1750–1900

Graph Skills Population increased dramatically as factories sprung up in cities such as London (pictured here). How many more people were in London in 1900 than in 1750 according to the line graph?

SOURCE: *International Historical Statistics, Europe 1750–1993*, 1998

New Social Classes Emerge

The Industrial Revolution created a new middle class along with the working class. Those in the middle class owned and operated the new factories, mines, and railroads, among other industries. Their lifestyle was much more comfortable than that of the industrial working class.

When farm families moved to the new industrial cities, they became workers in mines or factories. Many felt lost and bewildered. They faced tough working conditions in uncomfortable environments. In time, though, factory and mine workers developed their own sense of community despite the terrible working conditions.

The Industrial Middle Class Those who benefited most from the Industrial Revolution were the entrepreneurs who set it in motion. The Industrial Revolution created this new middle class, or bourgeoisie (boor zhwah ZEE), whose members came from a variety of backgrounds. Some were merchants who invested their growing profits in factories. Others were inventors or skilled artisans who developed new technologies. Some rose from "rags to riches," a pattern that the age greatly admired.

Middle-class families lived in well-furnished, spacious homes on paved streets and had a ready supply of water. They wore fancy clothing and ate well. The new middle class took pride in their hard work and their determination to "get ahead." Only a few had sympathy for the poor. Women of the middle class did not leave the home to work but instead focused their energy on raising their children. This contrasted with the wealthy, who had maidservants to look after their children, and the working class, whose children were a part of the workforce.

The Industrial Working Class While the wealthy and the middle class lived in pleasant neighborhoods, vast numbers of poor struggled to survive in foul-smelling slums. They packed into tiny rooms in **tenements,** or multistory buildings divided into apartments. These tenements had no running water, only community pumps. There was no sewage or sanitation system, so wastes and garbage rotted in the streets. Sewage was also dumped into rivers, which created an overwhelming stench and <u>contaminated</u> drinking water. This led to the spread of diseases such as cholera.

Workers Stage Futile Protests Although **labor unions,** or workers' organizations, were illegal at this time, secret unions did exist among frustrated British workers. They wished to initiate worker reforms, such as increases in pay, but had no political power to effect change. Sometimes their frustration led to violence. The first instances of industrial riots occurred in England from 1811 to 1813. Groups of textile workers known as the Luddites (LUD yts) resisted the labor-saving machines that were costing them their jobs. Some of them smashed textile machines with sledgehammers and burned factories. They usually wore masks and operated at night. There was widespread support among the working class for these Luddite groups.

Workers Find Comfort in Religion Many working-class people found comfort in a religious movement called Methodism. This movement was influenced by the Industrial Revolution as people moved to cities and lost connections with their old churches. John Wesley had founded the Methodist movement in the mid-1700s. Wesley <u>stressed</u> the need for a personal sense of faith. He encouraged his followers to improve themselves by adopting sober, moral ways.

Methodist meetings featured hymns and sermons promising forgiveness of sin and a better life to come. Methodist preachers took this message of salvation into the slums. There, they tried to rekindle hope among the working poor. They set up Sunday schools where followers not only studied the Bible but also learned to read and write. Methodists helped channel workers' anger away from revolution and toward reform.

 **Checkpoint** How did members of the working class react to their new experiences in industrial cities?

Life in the Factories and Mines

The heart of the new industrial city was the factory. There, the technology of the machine age and the rapid pace of industrialization imposed a harsh new way of life on workers.

Factory Workers Face Harsh Conditions Working in a factory system differed greatly from working on a farm. In rural villages, people worked hard, but their work varied according to the season. Life was also hard for poor rural workers who were part of the putting-out system, but at least they worked at their own pace. In the grim factories of industrial towns, workers faced a rigid schedule set by the factory whistle.

Working hours were long, with shifts lasting from 12 to 16 hours, six or seven days a week. Workers could only take breaks when the factory owners gave permission. Exhausted workers suffered accidents from machines that had no safety devices. They might lose a finger, a limb, or even their lives. In textile mills, workers constantly breathed air filled with lint, which damaged their lungs. Those workers who became sick or injured lost their jobs.

The majority of early factory workers were women rather than men. Employers often preferred to hire women workers because they thought women could adapt more easily to machines and were easier to manage. In addition, employers generally paid women half what they paid men.

Factory work created a double burden for women. Their new jobs took them out of their homes for 12 hours or more a day. They then returned to their tenements, which might consist of one damp room with a single bed. They had to feed and clothe their families, clean, and cope with such problems as sickness and injury.

Miners Face Worse Conditions The Industrial Revolution increased the demand for iron and coal, which in turn increased the need for miners. Although miners were paid more, working conditions in the mines were even worse than in the factories. They worked in darkness, and the coal dust destroyed their lungs. There were always the dangers of explosions, flooding, and collapsing tunnels. Women and children carted heavy loads of coal, sometimes on all fours in low passages. They also climbed ladders carrying heavy baskets of coal several times a day.

Children Have Dangerous Jobs Factories and mines also hired many boys and girls. These children often started working at age seven or eight, a few as young as five. Nimble-fingered and quick-moving, they changed spools in the hot and humid textile mills where sometimes they could not see because of all the dust. They also crawled under machinery to repair broken threads in the mills. Conditions were even worse for children who worked in the mines. Some sat all day in the dark, opening

Even children as young as five years old worked in the mines. James Kay-Shuttleworth worked as a physician among the different classes of the Industrial Revolution in Manchester. His profession allowed him to see the working conditions of poor in the cities. How was work in factories and mines different from work on the farm?

Whilst the engine runs, people must work—men, women, and children are yoked together with iron and steam. The animal machine is chained fast to the iron machine, which knows no suffering and weariness.
—James Kay-Shuttleworth, 1832

and closing air vents. Others hauled coal carts in the extreme heat. Because children had helped with work on the farm, parents accepted the idea of child labor. The wages the children earned were needed to keep their families from starving.

Child labor reform laws called "factory acts" were passed in the early 1800s. These laws were passed to reduce a child's workday to twelve hours and also to remove children under the age of eight or nine from the cotton mills. Because the laws were generally not enforced, British lawmakers formed teams of inspectors to ensure that factories and mines obeyed the laws in the 1830s and 1840s. More laws were then passed to shorten the workday for women and require that child workers be educated.

 **Checkpoint** How did the Industrial Revolution affect the lives of men, women, and children?

The Results of Industrialization

Since the 1800s, people have debated whether the Industrial Revolution was a blessing or a curse. The early industrial age brought terrible hardships. In time, however, reformers pressed for laws to improve working conditions. Labor unions won the right to bargain with employers for better wages, hours, and working conditions. Eventually working-class men gained the right to vote, which gave them political power.

Despite the social problems created by the Industrial Revolution—low pay, dismal living conditions—the Industrial Age did have some positive effects. As demand for mass-produced goods grew, new factories opened, which in turn created more jobs. Wages rose so that workers had enough left after paying rent and buying food to buy a newspaper or visit a music hall. As the cost of railroad travel fell, people could visit family in other towns. Horizons widened and opportunities increased.

Families could afford to take trips to such places as the zoo as wages increased.

 **Checkpoint** Why was the Industrial Revolution seen as both a blessing and a curse?

Progress Monitoring *Online*
For: Self-quiz with vocabulary practice
Web Code: naa-1931

Terms, People, and Places

1. What do each of the key terms listed at the beginning of the section have in common? Explain.

Note Taking

2. **Reading Skill: Understand Effects** Use your completed table to answer the Focus Question: What were the social effects of the Industrial Revolution?

Comprehension and Critical Thinking

3. **Analyze Information** How did the Industrial Revolution affect **(a)** cities and **(b)** population distribution?
4. **Synthesize Information** Explain how the Industrial Revolution changed the living conditions for both the middle class and the working class.
5. **Demonstrate Reasoned Judgment** Do you think increases in wages justify harsh working conditions? Why or why not?

● Writing About History

Quick Write: Gather Details When writing an explanatory essay, you should include facts, examples, and descriptions that help explain your topic. Make a list of details to help explain what life was like when people moved from rural areas to the new industrial cities.

Friedrich Engels: *The Condition of the Working Class in England in 1844*

In *The Condition of the Working Class in England in 1844*, Friedrich Engels recorded his observations of the wretched living conditions in poor areas of nineteenth-century England. In this excerpt, Engels describes working-class districts in Manchester. He depicts the misery and filth typical of the living areas of industrial workers.

Friedrich Engels, 1845

The houses are packed very closely together and since the bank of the river is very steep it is possible to see a part of every house. All of them have been blackened by soot, all of them are crumbling with age and all have broken window-panes and window-frames. In the background there are old factory buildings which look like barracks. On the opposite, low-lying bank of the river, one sees a long row of houses and factories. The second house is a roofless ruin, filled with refuse, and the third is built in such a low situation that the ground floor is uninhabitable and has neither doors nor windows. In the background one sees the paupers'[1] cemetery, and the stations of the railways to Liverpool and Leeds. . . .

The recently constructed extension of the Leeds railway which crosses the Irk at this point has swept away some of these courts and alleys, but it has thrown open to public gaze some of the others. So it comes about that there is to be found immediately under the railway bridge a court which is even filthier and more revolting than all the others. This is simply because it was formerly so hidden and secluded that it could only be reached with considerable difficulty [but is now exposed to the human eye]. I thought I knew this district well, but even I would never have found it had not the railway viaduct [elevated roadway] made a breach[2] in the slums at this point. One walks along a very rough path on the river bank, in between clothesposts and washing lines, to reach a chaotic group of little, one-storied, one-roomed cabins. Most of them have earth floors, and working, living and sleeping all take place in the one room. In such a hole, barely six feet long and five feet wide, I saw two beds—and what beds and bedding!—which filled the room, except for the fireplace and the doorstep. Several of these huts, as far as I could see, were completely empty, although the door was open and the inhabitants were leaning against the door posts. In front of the doors filth and garbage abounded. I could not see the pavement, but from time to time I felt it was there because my feet scraped it. . . .

---

1. **pauper** (PAW pur) *n.* poor person
2. **breach** (breech) *n.* break

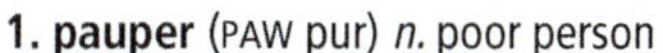

Thinking Critically

1. **Draw Inferences** (a) How did the development of the railways affect the working-class districts? (b) How does Engels feel about the living conditions he observes?
2. **Make Generalizations** What seems to be Engels' general attitude toward the Industrial Revolution?

Workers on
break, London

The Struggle of the Working Class

Karl Marx and Friedrich Engels give their view on how
the Industrial Revolution affected workers:

> 66 Owing to the extensive use of machinery and to
> division of labor, the work of the proletarians
> has lost all individual character, and, conse-
> quently, all charm for the workman. He
> becomes [a limb] of the machine, and it is
> only the most simple, most monotonous,
> and most easily acquired knack, that is
> required of him. . . . 99
> —From *The Communist Manifesto*

Focus Question What new ideas about
economics and society were fostered as a result
of the Industrial Revolution?

New Ways of Thinking

Objectives

- Understand laissez-faire economics and the
  beliefs of those who supported it.
- Describe the doctrine of utilitarianism.
- Summarize the theories of socialism.
- Explain Marx's views of the working class and
  the response to Marxism.

Terms, People, and Places

Thomas Malthus	Robert Owen
Jeremy Bentham	Karl Marx
utilitarianism	communism
socialism	proletariat
means of production	social democracy

Note Taking

Reading Skill: Identify Main Ideas Write an
outline like the one here to show the new
economic and social theories.

> I. Laissez-faire economics
>   A. Adam Smith and free enterprise
>   1.
>   2.
> II. Malthus on population
>   A.

Everywhere in Britain, British economist Thomas Malthus saw
the effects of the population explosion—crowded slums, hungry families, unemployment, and widespread misery. After careful study, in
1798 he published *An Essay on the Principle of Population*. He concluded that poverty was unavoidable because the population was
increasing faster than the food supply. Malthus wrote: "The power of
population is [far] greater than the power of the Earth to produce
subsistence for man."

Malthus was one of many thinkers who tried to understand the
staggering changes taking place in the early Industrial Age. As
heirs to the Enlightenment, these thinkers looked for natural laws
that governed the world of business and economics.

Laissez-Faire Economics

During the Enlightenment, physiocrats argued that natural laws
should be allowed to operate without interference. As part of this philosophy, they believed that government should not interfere in the
free operation of the economy. In the early 1800s, middle-class
business leaders embraced this laissez-faire, or "hands-off," approach.

As you have learned, the main proponent of laissez-faire economics was Adam Smith, author of bestseller *The Wealth of
Nations*. Smith asserted that a free market—the unregulated
exchange of goods and services—would come to help everyone, not
just the rich. The free market, Smith said, would produce more
goods at lower prices, making them affordable to everyone. A
growing economy would also encourage capitalists to reinvest

profits in new ventures. Supporters of this free-enterprise capitalism pointed to the successes of the Industrial Age, in which government had played no part.

Malthus Holds Bleak View Also a laissez-faire economist, Thomas Malthus predicted that population would outpace the food supply. The only checks on population growth, he said, were nature's "natural" methods of war, disease, and famine. As long as population kept increasing, he went on, the poor would suffer. He thus urged families to have fewer children and discouraged charitable handouts and vaccinations.

During the early 1800s, many people accepted Malthus's bleak view as the factory system changed people's lifestyles for the worse. His view was proved wrong, however. Although the population boom did continue, the food supply grew even faster. As the century progressed, living conditions for the Western world slowly improved—and then people began having fewer children. By the 1900s, population growth was no longer a problem in the West, but it did continue to afflict many nations elsewhere.

Ricardo Shares View Another influential British laissez-faire economist, David Ricardo, dedicated himself to economic studies after reading Smith's *The Wealth of Nations*. Like Malthus, Ricardo did not hold out hope for the working class to escape poverty. Because of such gloomy predictions, economics became known as the "dismal science." In his "Iron Law of Wages," Ricardo pointed out that wage increases were futile because increases would only cover the cost of necessities. This was because when wages were high, families often had more children instead of raising the family's current standard of living.

Both Malthus and Ricardo opposed any government help for the poor. In their view, the best cure for poverty was not government relief but the unrestricted "laws of the free market." They felt that individuals should be left to improve their lot through thrift, hard work, and limiting the size of their families.

 **Checkpoint** Explain the response to laissez-faire economics during the nineteenth century.

Population Theory
Thomas Malthus believed poor families should have fewer children to preserve the food supply. *What were the advantages of families with many children?*

Utilitarians For Limited Government

Other thinkers sought to modify laissez-faire doctrines to justify some government intervention. By 1800, British philosopher and economist Jeremy Bentham was advocating utilitarianism, or the idea that the goal of society should be "the greatest happiness for the greatest number" of its citizens. To Bentham, all laws or actions should be judged by their "utility." In other words, did they provide more pleasure or happiness than pain? Bentham strongly supported individual freedom, which he believed guaranteed happiness. Still, he saw the need for government to become involved under certain circumstances.

Bentham's ideas influenced the British philosopher and economist John Stuart Mill. Although he believed strongly in individual freedom, Mill wanted the government to step in to improve the hard lives of the working class. "The only purpose for which power can be rightfully exercised over any member of a civilized community, against his will," Mill wrote, "is to prevent harm to others." Therefore, while middle-class business and factory owners were entitled to increase their own happiness, the government should prevent them from doing so in a manner that would harm workers.

Mill further called for giving the vote to workers and women. These groups could then use their political power to win reforms. Most middle-class people rejected Mill's ideas. Only in the later 1800s were his views

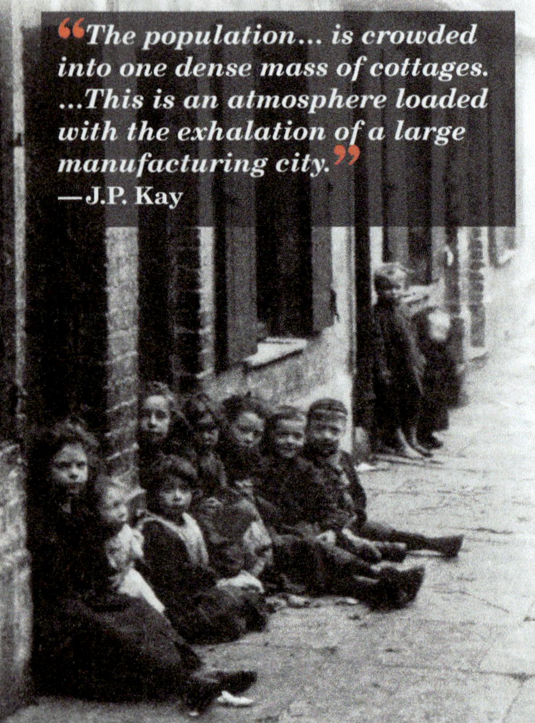

▲ The Industrial Age brought harsh living conditions and poverty as people crowded into cities.

Thinking Critically

1. **Make Generalizations** Based on the images, how did life for children at New Lanark differ from those who lived in industrial cities?
2. **Recognize Ideologies** Do you think Utopianism was an effective solution for the challenges of the Industrial Age? Why or why not?

Owen's Utopia

The poverty and filth of the Industrial Age did not sit well with Robert Owen, a British social reformer. Like other Utopians, he believed there was a way he could change society for the better. To prove his point, he set up his cotton mill in New Lanark, Scotland, as a model village. He insisted that the conditions in which people lived shaped their character. Owen reduced working hours, built homes for workers, started a school for children, and opened a company store where workers could buy food and clothes. He showed that an employer could offer decent living and working conditions and still run a profitable business. Between 1815 and 1825, about 20,000 people visited New Lanark to study Owen's reforms. The complex eventually fell into decline but visitors can still wander the village today.

▲ Children attended geography classes and dance lessons at the school in New Lanark.

History *Interactive*

For: Interactive Village
Web Code: nap-1941

slowly accepted. Today's democratic governments, however, have absorbed many ideas from Mill and the other utilitarians.

 **Checkpoint** What did John Stuart Mill see as the proper role of government?

Socialist Thought Emerges

While the champions of laissez-faire economics praised individual rights, other thinkers focused on the good of society in general. They condemned the evils of industrial capitalism, which they believed had created a gulf between rich and poor. To end poverty and injustice, they offered a radical solution—socialism. Under socialism, the people as a whole rather than private individuals would own and operate the means of production— the farms, factories, railways, and other large businesses that produced and distributed goods. Socialism grew out of the Enlightenment faith in progress and human nature and its concern for social justice.

Are Utopians Dreamers? A number of early socialists established communities in which all work was shared and all property was owned in common. When there was no difference between rich and poor, they said, fighting between people would disappear. These early socialists were called Utopians. The name implied that they were impractical dreamers. The Utopian Robert Owen set up a model community in New Lanark, Scotland, to put his own ideas into practice.

Owen Establishes a Utopia A poor Welsh boy, Owen became a successful mill owner. Unlike most industrialists at the time, he refused to use child labor. He campaigned vigorously for laws that limited child labor and encouraged the organization of labor unions.

 **Checkpoint** What did early socialists believe?

Karl Marx Calls for Worker Control

In the 1840s, Karl Marx, a German philosopher, condemned the ideas of the Utopians as unrealistic idealism. He <u>formulated</u> a new theory, "scientific socialism," which he claimed was based on a scientific study of history. He teamed up with another German socialist, Friedrich Engels, whose father owned a textile factory in England.

Marx and Engels wrote a pamphlet, *The Communist Manifesto*, which they published in 1848. "A spectre [ghost] is haunting Europe," it began, "the spectre of communism." Marx predicted a struggle between social classes that would lead to a classless society where all means of production would be owned by the community. In practice, however, communism later came to refer to a system in which governments led by a small elite controlled all economic and political life.

In *The Communist Manifesto*, Marx theorized that economics was the driving force in history. He argued that there was "the history of class struggles" between the "haves" and the "have-nots." The "haves" had always owned the means of production and thus controlled society and all its wealth. In industrialized Europe, Marx said, the "haves" were the bourgeoisie. The "have-nots" were the proletariat, or working class.

According to Marx, the modern class struggle pitted the bourgeoisie against the proletariat. In the end, he predicted, the proletariat would be

Vocabulary Builder

<u>formulated</u>—(FAWR myoo layt id) *vt.* devised or developed, as in a theory or plan

triumphant. Workers would then take control of the means of production and set up a classless, communist society. Such a society would mark the end of the struggles people had endured throughout history, because wealth and power would be equally shared. Marx despised capitalism. He believed it created prosperity for only a few and poverty for many. He called for an international struggle to bring about its downfall. "Workers of all countries," he urged, "unite!"

 **Checkpoint** What did Marx predict was the future of the proletariat?

Marxism in the Future

At first, Marxism gained popularity with many people around the world. Leaders of a number of reform movements adopted the idea that power should be held by workers rather than by business owners. Marx's ideas, however, would never be practiced exactly as he imagined.

Marxism Briefly Flourishes In the 1860s, German socialists adapted Marx's beliefs to form **social democracy,** a political ideology in which there is a gradual transition from capitalism to socialism instead of a sudden violent overthrow of the system. In the late 1800s, Russian socialists embraced Marxism, and the Russian Revolution of 1917 set up a communist-inspired government. For much of the 1900s, revolutionaries around the world would adapt Marxist ideas to their own situations and needs. Independence leaders in Asia, Latin America, and Africa would turn to Marxism.

Marxism Loses Appeal As time passed, however, the failures of Marxist governments would illustrate the flaws in Marx's arguments. He predicted that workers would unite across national borders to wage class warfare. Instead, nationalism won out over working-class loyalty. In general, people felt stronger ties to their own countries than to the international communist movement. By the end of the twentieth century, few nations remained with communist governments, while nearly every economy included elements of free-market capitalism.

 **Checkpoint** How accurate did Marx's predictions about social classes prove to be?

Workers of the World
An 1895 leaflet urges that "Workers of the World Unite," the slogan of the socialist movement of Marx (above) and Engels.

SECTION 4 Assessment

Terms, People, and Places

1. For each term, person, or place listed at the beginning of the section, write a sentence explaining its significance.

Note Taking

2. **Reading Skill: Identify Main Ideas** Use your completed outline to answer the Focus Question: What new ideas about economics and society were fostered as a result of the Industrial Revolution?

Comprehension and Critical Thinking

3. **Identify Points of View** What were the views of laissez-faire economists **(a)** Adam Smith, **(b)** Thomas Malthus, and **(c)** David Ricardo?

4. **Compare Points of View** Contrast the approaches of utilitarians and socialists to solving economic problems.

5. **Synthesize Information** How might workplace reforms have altered Marxist predictions of world revolution?

Writing About History

Quick Write: Write a Thesis Statement As in other types of essays, it is important to clearly state your thesis, or main idea, when writing an explanatory essay. Write a thesis statement followed by a short paragraph on one of the theories discussed in this section.

ECONOMIC SYSTEMS

How should resources and wealth be distributed?

In This Chapter

In the United States and Europe, industry began to replace traditional agriculture by the mid-1800s. New ways of thinking emerged about how to answer these three key economic questions: (1) What will be produced? (2) How will it be produced? (3) Who will get the product? In the illustration from Oliver Twist (right), a young orphan asks for more food.

Throughout History

- **Prehistory** Hunters and gatherers live off the land.

- **900s A.D.** The self-sufficient manor is at the heart of the feudal economy.

- **1500s–1700s** Under mercantalism, colonies exist to enrich European powers.

- **1800s** In the free market system, individual businesses operate without government control.

- **1800s** Industrial workers struggle to gain better wages and living conditions.

- **1900s** Under communism, the Soviet government owns most businesses and property.

Continuing Today

The World Trade Organization (WTO) negotiates the rules of trade between nations. At an annual WTO meeting, protestors express their view that the rights of developing nations are insufficiently protected.

TRANSFER Activities

1. **Analyze** Throughout history, how have answers to the key economic questions differed?

2. **Evaluate** Why does it matter who controls the economy?

3. **Transfer** Complete a Web quest in which you analyze how different economics systems allocate resources and wealth; record your thoughts in the Concept Connector Journal; and learn to make a video. Web Code nah-1908

Quick Study Guide

Progress Monitoring *Online*
For: Self-test with vocabulary practice
Web Code: naa-1951

■ New Inventions and Ideas

Inventors and Thinkers	Inventions and Ideas
Jethro Tull	Seed drill
Thomas Newcomen	Steam engine
James Watt	Improved steam engine
John Kay	Flying shuttle
James Hargreaves	Spinning jenny
Richard Arkwright	Water frame
Eli Whitney	Cotton gin
George Stephenson	Steam-powered locomotive
John Wesley	Methodism
Adam Smith	Laissez-faire economics
Thomas Malthus	Population growth could outpace food supply.
Jeremy Bentham	Utilitarianism
Robert Owen	Utopian communities
Karl Marx	Communism, Marxism

■ Effects of the Industrial Revolution

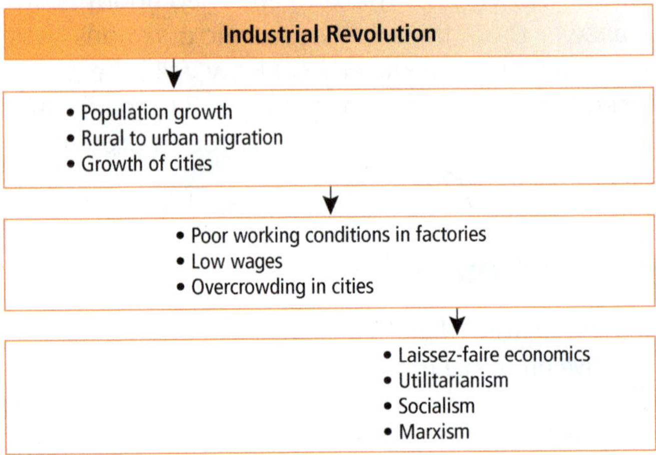

■ Why Britain Industrialized First

Industrial Revolution in Britain
Plentiful natural resources
Ready workforce
Prosperous economy
Availability of capital and demand
Stable government

■ Responses to the Industrial Revolution

- Bentham/Mill: utilitarianism
- Socialism
- Owen: utopianism
- Marx/Engels: communism

■ Key Events From 1750–1850

Early Industrial Revolution Events
Global Events

1760s
Watt improves the steam engine.

1764
The spinning jenny is invented.

1750

1775

1762
Catherine the Great comes to power in Russia.

1770
Cook claims Australia for Britain.

1788
Futa Toro outlaws slave trade.

Essential Question Review

To connect prior knowledge with what you have learned in this chapter, answer the questions below in your Concept Connector journal. Use the journal in the Reading and Note Taking Study Guide to record your answers (or go to www.phschool.com **Web Code: nad-1907**). In addition, record information about the following concepts:

- Economic Systems: market economy
- Economic Systems: centrally planned economy
- Economic Systems: mixed economy

1. **Economic Systems** The Commercial Revolution in the 1500s gave rise to capitalism and mercantalism. The Industrial Revolution gave rise to new economic theories: laissez-faire economics, utilitarianism, and socialism. Compare capitalism and socialism. Think about how wealth is gained and distributed in each economic system.

2. **Technology** Once James Watt made improvements to Thomas Newcomen's steam engine, it became a key power source of the Industrial Revolution. In a similar way, hundreds of years earlier, the printing press had dramatically changed how people communicated and shared information. Compare the impact of the two developments. Consider the following:
   - who benefited from the use of the invention
   - how the work was done before the invention
   - why the invention was important

Connections to Today

1. **Migration: Twentieth Century Global Migrations** During the Industrial Revolution, rural workers migrated to urban areas to live and work. Today, people still migrate in various parts of the world. Do online and library research to find information on rural-to-urban migration in a country located in Asia or Africa. Write a brief newspaper article in which you compare the experiences of those who migrated then and now.

Strawberry pickers at work, South Africa

2. **Geography's Impact** The population growth that occurred during the Industrial Revolution often created filth and unsanitary conditions as people crowded into tenements. The growth also caused an increase in the demand for products, which led to the opening of more factories. Do online and library research to find the history of population growth in the town or state in which you live. What are the patterns and results?

1800 Owen begins social reforms at New Lanark.

1807 Fulton develops the first successful steamboat, the *Clermont*.

1830 The Liverpool-Manchester Railroad opens.

1848 Marx and Engels publish *The Communist Manifesto*.

History Interactive
For: Interactive timeline
Web Code: nap-1901

1800   1825   1850

1804 Napoleon becomes the emperor of France.

1814 Congress of Vienna meets to restore stability in Europe.

1819 Bolívar captures Bogotá.

1848 Revolutions sweep Europe.

Chapter Assessment

Terms, People, and Places

Complete each sentence by choosing the correct answer from the list of terms below. You will not use all of the terms.

smelt	James Watt
urbanization	Manchester
Thomas Malthus	tenement
proletariat	socialism
enterprise	utilitarianism

1. _______ predicted that population would outpace the food supply.
2. A member of the _______ most likely lived in a small, crowded building called a _______.
3. Investors in Britain were ready to risk their capital to invest in _______.
4. Those who advocated _______ believed that the goal of society was to bring about the greatest happiness for the greatest number.
5. To _______ involves separating iron from its ore.
6. _______ improved the efficiency and design of Newcomen's steam engine.

Main Ideas

Section 1 (pp. 608–611)
7. How did the enclosure movement affect farmers?
8. Identify three causes of the population explosion that occurred in the 1700s.

Section 2 (pp. 612–615)
9. Describe four factors that helped bring about the Industrial Revolution in England.

10. How did the Industrial Revolution transform the textile industry?

Section 3 (pp. 616–621)
11. **(a)** What were the main characteristics of factory work? **(b)** What challenges did factory work create for women?

Section 4 (pp. 622–627)
12. List the government reforms sought by John Stuart Mill.
13. **(a)** Describe Karl Marx's view of history. **(b)** How have events challenged that view?

Chapter Focus Question
14. What technological, social, economic, and cultural changes occurred as the Industrial Revolution took hold?

Critical Thinking

15. **Synthesize Information** What were the impacts of each of the following technologies: **(a)** steam power, **(b)** improved methods for smelting iron, **(c)** railroad?
16. **Geography and History** Explain the link between Britain's natural resources and its rise as an industrial nation.
17. **Analyze Information** Describe how the Industrial Revolution affected each of the following: **(a)** size of population, **(b)** cities, **(c)** working and living conditions, **(d)** women and children.
18. **Predict Consequences** If more people had supported utilitarianism, how do you think it would have influenced society?
19. **Recognize Ideologies** Explain the major differences between Adam Smith's free market ideas and Karl Marx's socialist ideas.

● Writing About History

In this chapter's four Section Assessments, you developed skills for writing an explanatory essay.

Expository: Explanatory Essay During the late 1700s, the Industrial Revolution began to transform Britain. An agricultural revolution triggered a chain of events, and Britain sped ahead of the rest of the world to become the first industrial nation. But why is the Industrial Revolution considered to be a "revolution"? Write an explanatory essay to answer this question.

Prewriting
- Ask yourself what you need to know in order to write an effective explanation. Think about what you already know about revolutions.

- Do research to gather facts, descriptions, examples, and other details to clearly illustrate your point.

Drafting
- Create a Venn diagram to compare aspects of the Industrial Revolution to another revolution you have learned about, such as the American Revolution or the French Revolution.
- Write a thesis statement once you have a focus for your essay. Begin your introduction with an interesting lead-in to get your reader's attention.
- Be sure to include comparisons, analogies, and facts in your essay to support your explanation.

Revising
- Use the guidelines for revising your essay on page SH12 of the Writing Handbook.

Document-Based Assessment

New Economic and Social Theories

Various thinkers of the day attempted to understand and interpret the dramatic changes brought about by the Industrial Revolution. They responded with a wide range of explanations and solutions, as the documents below illustrate.

Document A

"As every individual, therefore, endeavours as much as he can both to employ his capital in the support of domestic industry, and so to direct that industry that its produce may be of the greatest value; every individual necessarily labours to render the annual revenue of the society as great as he can. . . . By preferring the support of domestic to that of foreign industry, he intends only his own security; and by directing that industry in such a manner as its produce may be of the greatest value, he intends only his own gain, and he is in this, as in many other cases, led by an invisible hand to promote an end which was no part of his intention. . . . every individual it is evident, can, in his local situation, judge much better than any statesman or lawgiver can do for him."

—From ***The Wealth of Nations*** by Adam Smith, 1776

Document B

"In those characters which now exhibit crime, the fault is obviously not in the individual, but the defects proceed from the system in which the individual was trained. Withdraw those circumstances which tend to create crime in the human character, and crime will not be created. Replace them with such as are calculated to form habits of order, regularity, temperance, industry; and these qualities will be formed. . . . Proceed systematically on principles of undeviating persevering kindness, yet retaining and using, with the least possible severity, the means of restraining crime from immediately injuring society, and by degrees even the crimes now existing in adults will also gradually disappear. . . ."

—From ***A New View of Society*** by Robert Owen, 1816

Document C
New Lanark Mills, Scotland

Document D

". . . the power of population is indefinitely greater than the power in the earth to produce subsistence for man. Population, when unchecked, increased in a geometrical ratio. Subsistence increases only in an arithmetical ratio. A slight acquaintance with numbers will show the immensity of the first power in comparison of the second. . . . No fancied equality, no agrarian regulations in their utmost extent, could remove the pressure of it even for a single century. And it appears, therefore, to be decisive against the possible existence of a society, all the members of which should live in ease, happiness, and comparative leisure; and feel no anxiety about providing the means of subsistence for themselves and families. Consequently, if the premises are just, the argument is conclusive against the perfectibility of the mass of mankind."

—From ***An Essay on the Principle of Population 1798***
by Thomas Malthus

Analyzing Documents

Use your knowledge of the new economic and social theories and Documents A, B, C, and D to answer the questions below.

1. According to Adam Smith in Document A, individuals promote the good of society because of
   A high ideals.
   B self-interest.
   C government pressure.
   D religion.

2. How did Robert Owen explain the fact that some people become criminals?
   A the invisible hand of fate
   B struggles between the ruling class and the oppressed
   C the influence of problems in society
   D the power of population over production

3. Thomas Malthus argued that a society where all individuals enjoy happiness, comfort, and pleasure is
   A only possible with increased agricultural output.
   B impossible because of the base nature of human greed.
   C impossible because of the pressures of population.
   D possible when people are treated decently and fairly.

4. **Writing Task** Suppose you were working in Britain in the year 1840. Which of the above economic philosophies would you support? Remember to identify your occupation and social class. Use your knowledge of the Industrial Revolution and the documents above to support your opinion.

Revolutions in Europe and Latin America

1790–1848

Freedom From Tyranny

Several revolutions erupted in Europe between 1815 and 1829, and the spread of revolutionary ideals would ignite new uprisings in 1830 and 1848. Also occurring during this time were the wars of independence in Latin America. These revolts began in the late 1700s and early 1800s and were inspired by the success of the American Revolution and the ideals of the French Revolution. Simón Bolívar was one of the great heroes in the fight for independence in Spanish South America. He helped win independence for Bolivia, Colombia, Ecuador, Peru, and Venezuela. Listen to the Witness History audio to learn more about revolutions in Europe and Latin America.

66 A state too extensive in itself, or by virtue of its dependencies, ultimately falls into decay; its free government is transformed into a tyranny; it disregards the principles which it should preserve, and finally degenerates into despotism. The distinguishing characteristic of small republics is stability. . . . 99
—Simón Bolívar

◄ Bolívar fights Spanish troops in his endeavor to free South America.

Simón Bolívar's crown

French military hat

José de San Martín

Chapter Preview

Chapter Focus Question How did revolutionary ideals in Europe and Latin America ignite uprisings in the first half of the nineteenth century?

Section 1
An Age of Ideologies

Section 2
Revolutions of 1830 and 1848

Section 3
Revolts in Latin America

Use the ☑ **Quick Study Timeline** at the end of this chapter to preview chapter events.

 Concept Connector ONLINE

To explore Essential Questions related to this chapter, go to PHSchool.com
Web Code: nad-2007

Hungarian revolutionary
Lajos Kossuth

WITNESS HISTORY ◀)) AUDIO

A "Revolutionary Seed"

Prince Clemens von Metternich warned that a seed had been planted in Europe that threatened Europe's monarchs and undermined its basic social values. This seed was nourished with the ideas spread by the French Revolution and Napoleon Bonaparte.

66 Passions are let loose . . . to overthrow everything that society respects as the basis of its existence: religion, public morality, laws, customs, rights, and duties, all are attacked, confounded [defeated], overthrown, or called in question. 99

Focus Question What events proved that Metternich was correct in his fears?

An Age of Ideologies

Objectives
- Understand the goals of the conservatives.
- Explain how liberals and nationalists challenged the old order.
- Summarize the early challenges to the old order in Europe.

Terms, People, and Places

ideology
universal manhood suffrage
autonomy

Note Taking

Reading Skill: Identify Main Ideas As you read the section, fill in a table like the one below with main ideas about conservatism, liberalism, and nationalism.

Conservatism	Liberalism	Nationalism
•	•	•
•	•	•

At the Congress of Vienna, the powers of Europe tried to uproot the "revolutionary seed" and suppress nationalist fervor. Others, however, challenged the order imposed in 1815. The clash of people with opposing **ideologies,** or systems of thought and belief, plunged Europe into more than 30 years of turmoil.

Conservatives Prefer the Old Order

The Congress of Vienna was a victory for the conservative forces, which included monarchs and their officials, noble landowners, and church leaders. Conservatives agreed to work together—in an agreement called the Concert of Europe—to support the political and social order that had existed before Napoleon and the French Revolution. Conservative ideas also appealed to peasants, who wanted to preserve traditional ways.

Conservatives of the early 1800s wanted to return to the way things had been before 1789. After all, they had benefited under the old order. They wanted to restore royal families to the thrones they had lost when Napoleon swept across Europe. They supported a social hierarchy in which lower classes respected and obeyed their social superiors. Conservatives also backed an established church—Catholic in Austria and southern Europe, Protestant in northern Europe, and Eastern Orthodox in eastern Europe.

Conservatives believed that talk about natural rights and constitutional government could lead only to chaos, as in France in 1789. If change had to come, they argued, it must come slowly. Conservatives felt that they benefited all people by defending peace and stability. Conservative leaders like Metternich sought to suppress revolutionary ideas. Metternich urged monarchs to oppose freedom of the press, crush protests in their own countries, and send troops to douse the flames of rebellion in neighboring lands.

 **Checkpoint** What was the goal of the conservatives in the Concert of Europe?

Liberals and Nationalists Seek Change

Inspired by the Enlightenment and the French Revolution, liberals and nationalists challenged the conservatives at every turn. Liberalism and nationalism ignited a number of revolts against established rule.

Liberals Promise Freedom Because liberals spoke mostly for the bourgeoisie, or middle class, their ideas are sometimes called "bourgeois liberalism." Liberals included business owners, bankers, and lawyers, as well as politicians, newspaper editors, writers, and others who helped to shape public opinion.

Liberals wanted governments to be based on written constitutions and separation of powers. Liberals spoke out against divine-right monarchy, the old aristocracy, and established churches. They defended the natural rights of individuals to liberty, equality, and property. They called for rulers elected by the people and responsible to them. Thus, most liberals favored a republican form of government over a monarchy, or at least wanted the monarch to be limited by a constitution.

The liberals of the early 1800s saw the role of government as limited to protecting basic rights such as freedom of thought, speech, and religion. They believed that only male property owners or others with a financial stake in society should have the right to vote. Only later in the century did liberals support the principle of **universal manhood suffrage,** giving all adult men the right to vote.

Liberals also strongly supported the laissez-faire economics of Adam Smith and David Ricardo. They saw the free market as an opportunity for capitalist entrepreneurs to succeed. As capitalists (and often employers), liberals had different goals from those of workers laboring in factories, mines, and other enterprises of the early Industrial Revolution.

Nationalists Strive for Unity For centuries, European rulers had gained or lost lands through wars, marriages, and treaties. They exchanged territories and the people in them like pieces in a game. As a result, by 1815 Europe had several empires that included many nationalities. The Austrian, Russian, and Ottoman empires, for example, each included diverse peoples.

Conflicting Ideologies This cartoon shows Prince Metternich standing resolute against the angry crowd behind him who are pushing for reform. Metternich represented the conservative order and opposed revolutionary ideals such as freedom and progress.

1. How does the cartoonist portray those in the crowd? What does the crowd support?
2. What did Metternich do to suppress revolutionary ideas?

In the 1800s, national groups who shared a common heritage set out to win their own states. Within the diverse Austrian empire, for example, various nationalist leaders tried to unite and win independence for each particular group. Nationalism gave people with a common heritage a sense of identity and the goal of creating their own homeland. At the same time, however, nationalism often bred intolerance and led to persecution of other ethnic or national groups.

✔ **Checkpoint** **How did the liberalism of the early 1800s reflect Enlightenment ideals?**

Central Europe Challenges the Old Order

Spurred by the ideas of liberalism and nationalism, revolutionaries fought against the old order. During the early 1800s, rebellions erupted in the Balkan Peninsula and elsewhere along the southern fringe of Europe. The Balkans, in southeastern Europe, were inhabited by people of various religions and ethnic groups. These peoples had lived under Ottoman rule for more than 300 years.

Serbia Seeks Independence The first Balkan people to revolt were the Serbs. From 1804 to 1813, the Serb leader Karageorge (ka rah JAWR juh) led a guerrilla war against the Ottomans. The intense struggle was unsuccessful, but it fostered a sense of Serbian identity. A revival of Serbian literature and culture added to the sense of nationhood.

In 1815, Milos Obrenovic (oh BRAY noh vich) led the Serbs in a second, more successful rebellion. One reason for the success was that Obrenovic turned to Russia for assistance. Like the Serbs, the Russian people were Slavic in language and Christian Orthodox in religion. By 1830, Russian support helped the Serbs win **autonomy,** or self-rule, within the

Serbs in Battle
Serb leader Karageorge (below left) led the Serbs in major battles against the Ottomans in the quest for independence. *(a) Why would this battle and others like it help lead to a sense of Serbian national identity? (b) Why was this sense of nationalism important for the Serbs?*

Ottoman empire. The Ottoman sultan later agreed to formal independence. In the future, Russia would continue to defend Serbian interests and affect events in the Balkans.

Greece Revolts to End Ottoman Rule

In 1821, the Greeks revolted, seeking to end centuries of Ottoman rule. At first, the Greeks were badly divided. But years of suffering in long, bloody wars of independence helped shape a national identity. Leaders of the rebellion justified their struggle as "a national war, a holy war, a war the object of which is to reconquer the rights of individual liberty." The Greeks had the support of romantic writers such as English poet Lord Byron, who went to Greece to aid the fight for independence.

Admirers of Greece in Europe backed the Greek rebels. In the late 1820s, Britain, France, and Russia forced the Ottomans to grant independence to some Greek provinces. By 1830, Greece was independent. The European powers, however, pressured the Greeks to accept a German king, a move meant to show that they did not support the nationalism that brought about the revolution.

More Challenges Erupt

Several other challenges to the Vienna peace settlement erupted in the 1820s. Revolts occurred along the southern fringe of Europe. In Spain, Portugal, and various states in the Italian peninsula, rebels struggled to gain constitutional governments.

Metternich urged conservative rulers to act decisively and crush the dangerous uprisings. In response, a French army marched over the Pyrenees to suppress a revolt in Spain. Austrian forces crossed the Alps to smash rebellious outbreaks in Italy.

Troops dampened the fires of liberalism and nationalism, but could not smother them. In the next decades, sparks would flare anew. Added to liberal and nationalist demands were the goals of the new industrial working class. By the mid-1800s, social reformers and <u>agitators</u> were urging workers to support socialism or other ways of reorganizing property ownership.

 **Checkpoint** Why would a monarch order his army to suppress an uprising in another country?

Reading Skill: Identify Supporting Details As you read, fill in a table like the one below with supporting details about revolts in Serbia, Greece, and other countries during the early 1800s.

Serbia	Greece	Other Revolts
•	•	•
•	•	•

Vocabulary Builder

agitator—(AJ ih tayt ur) *n.* someone who attempts to arouse feeling for or against something, especially a political cause

---

SECTION 1 Assessment

Progress Monitoring *Online*
For: Self-quiz with vocabulary practice
Web Code: naa-2011

Terms, People, and Places

1. For each term, person, or place listed at the beginning of the section, write a sentence explaining its significance.

Note Taking

2. **Reading Skill: Identify Main Ideas** Use your completed charts to answer the Focus Question: What events proved that Metternich was correct in his fears?

Comprehension and Critical Thinking

3. **Identify Point of View** What were the goals of conservative leaders?
4. **Compare Points of View** (a) How did the political goals of liberals differ from those of conservatives? (b) How did nationalists threaten the borders set up by European monarchs?
5. **Recognize Cause and Effect** (a) Why did the Serbs and Greeks revolt? (b) Why were there uprisings in Spain, Portugal, and the Italian states?

Writing About History

Quick Write: Choose a Topic To write an effective persuasive essay, you should begin with a clearly stated opinion or argument on an issue that has more than one side. Look back over Section 1, jotting down issues that have two or more sides. Then choose an issue and write a well-constructed sentence that states your opinion or argument against it.

Alexis de Tocqueville

French military hat

More Revolution in the Wind

Alexis de Tocqueville was a liberal French leader who closely observed the widespread support for revolutionary ideas. He knew that the revolutions of the 1820s were not over.

> We are sleeping on a volcano . . . Do you not see that the Earth trembles anew? A wind of revolution blows, the storm is on the horizon.
> —Alexis de Tocqueville

Focus Question What were the causes and effects of the revolutions in Europe in 1830 and 1848?

Revolutions of 1830 and 1848

Objectives

- Describe how French rebels won some reforms in 1830.
- Analyze how the spirit of reform spread in 1830.
- Explain the revolutions that surged through France and throughout the rest of Europe in 1848.

Terms, People, and Places

radicals	Napoleon III
Louis Philippe	Louis Kossuth
recession	

Note Taking

Reading Skill: Identify Main Ideas As you read the section, fill in a table like the one below with a country, date, and a main idea about the revolutions of 1830 and 1848. Add rows as needed.

Revolutions of 1830 and 1848		
France	1830	Radicals force king to abdicate.

The quick suppression of liberal and nationalist uprisings in the 1820s did not end Europe's age of revolutions. In 1830 and 1848, Europeans saw street protests explode into full-scale revolts. As in 1789, the upheavals began in Paris and radiated out across the continent.

French Rebels Win in 1830

When the Congress of Vienna restored Louis XVIII to the French throne, he wisely issued a constitution, the Charter of French Liberties. It created a two-house legislature and allowed limited freedom of the press. Still, the king retained much power.

Citizens Lead the July Revolution When Louis XVIII died in 1824, his younger brother, Charles X, inherited the throne. Charles, a strong believer in absolutism, rejected the very idea of the charter. In July 1830, he suspended the legislature, limited the right to vote, and restricted the press.

Liberals and **radicals**—those who favor extreme change— responded forcefully to the king's challenge. In Paris, angry citizens threw up barricades across the narrow streets. From behind them, they fired on the soldiers and pelted them with stones and roof tiles. Within days, rebels controlled Paris. The revolutionary tricolor flew from the towers of Notre Dame cathedral. A frightened Charles X abdicated and fled to England.

The "Citizen King" Rules France With the king gone, radicals wanted to set up a republic. Moderate liberals, however, insisted on a constitutional monarchy and chose Louis Philippe as king. Louis Philippe was a cousin of Charles X and in his youth had supported the revolution of 1789.

The French called Louis Philippe the "citizen king" because he owed his throne to the people. Louis got along well with the liberal bourgeoisie. He dressed like them in a frock coat and top hat. Sometimes he strolled the streets, shaking hands with well-wishers. Liberal politicians filled his government.

Under Louis Philippe, the upper bourgeoisie prospered. Louis extended suffrage, but only to France's wealthier citizens. The vast majority of the people still could not vote. The king's other policies also favored the middle class at the expense of the workers.

 **Checkpoint** What actions did Charles X take in 1830, and how did French rebels respond?

The Spirit of Reform Spreads

The revolts in Paris inspired the outbreak of uprisings elsewhere in Europe. As Metternich said, "When France sneezes, Europe catches cold." Most of the uprisings were suppressed by military force. But some rebels did win changes. Even when they failed, revolutions frightened rulers badly enough to encourage reform.

Belgium Wins Independence The one notable success in 1830 took place in Belgium. In 1815, the Congress of Vienna had united the Austrian Netherlands (present-day Belgium) and the Kingdom of Holland under the Dutch king. The Congress had wanted to create a strong barrier to help prevent French expansion in the future.

The French-speaking Belgian bourgeoisie resented the new arrangement. They and the Dutch had different languages. The Belgians were Catholic, while the Dutch king was Protestant. The Belgians relied on manufacturing; the Dutch, on trade.

In 1830, news of the Paris uprising ignited a revolutionary spark in Belgium. Citizens took up arms against the Dutch troops in Brussels, the

To the Barricades!

In 1830 and again in 1848, French rebels erected barricades in the streets using mattresses, wagons, furniture, and whatever else they could find that might offer protection during the fighting with government soldiers. *How does Hugo describe the barricades in his famous novel* Les Misérables?

❝You saw there, in a chaos full of despair, rafters from roofs, patches from garrets with their wall paper, window sashes with all their glass planted in the rubbish, awaiting artillery, chimneys torn down, wardrobes, tables, benches, a howling topsy-turvy, . . . which contain at once fury and nothingness.❞
—Victor Hugo

capital. Britain and France believed thay they would benefit from the separation of Belgium and Holland and supported Belgian demands for independence. As a result, in 1831, Belgium became an independent state with a liberal constitution.

Rebels Fail in Poland Nationalists in Poland also staged an uprising in 1830. But, unlike the Belgians, the Poles failed to win independence for their country.

In the late 1700s, Russia, Austria, and Prussia had divided up Poland. Poles had hoped that the Congress of Vienna would restore their homeland in 1815. Instead, the great powers handed most of Poland to Russia.

In 1830, Polish students, army officers, and landowners rose in revolt. The rebels failed to gain widespread support, however, and were brutally crushed by Russian forces. Some survivors fled to Western Europe and the United States, where they kept alive the dream of freedom.

✔ **Checkpoint** How did the Belgian and Polish revolutions in 1830 end differently?

The French Revolt Again in 1848

In the 1840s, discontent began to grow in France once again. Radicals formed secret societies to work for a French republic. Utopian socialists called for an end to private ownership of property. Even liberals <u>denounced</u> Louis Philippe's government for corruption and called for expanded suffrage.

Near the end of the decade, discontent was heightened by a **recession,** or period of reduced economic activity. Factories shut down and people lost their jobs. Poor harvests caused bread prices to rise. Newspapers blamed government officials for some of the problems. With conditions much like those in 1789, Paris was again ripe for revolution.

Vocabulary Builder

<u>denounce</u>—(dee NOWNS) *vt.* to express harsh criticism of something or somebody, usually in public

1848: The Year of Hope and Despair

Revolution in Europe spread like wildfire in the days and months of 1848. Although an outbreak in January occurred in Italy, France's successful February Revolution was the spark for other revolts throughout Europe. As shown on the map here, revolutions were not confined to one city or country. They engulfed the continent of Europe and numbered almost fifty in the first four months of the year alone. Despite the failures of the revolutions, Europe was transformed as governments and the rising middle class began to cooperate with one another.

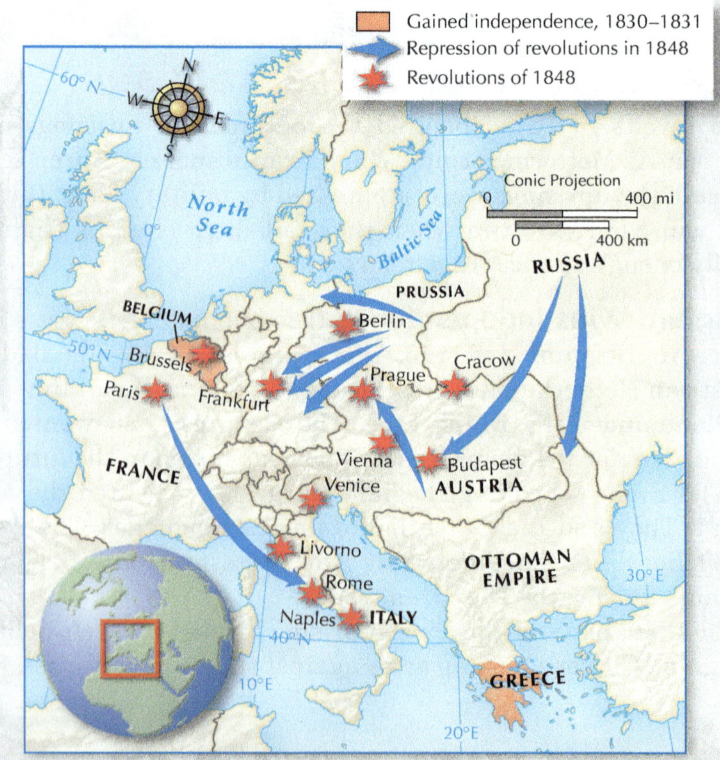

Turmoil Spreads During "February Days" In February 1848, when the government took steps to silence critics and prevent public meetings, angry crowds took to the streets. During the "February Days," overturned carts, paving stones, and toppled trees again blocked the streets of Paris. Church bells rang alarms, while women and men on the barricades sang the revolutionary anthem "La Marseillaise." A number of demonstrators clashed with royal troops and were killed.

As the turmoil spread, Louis Philippe abdicated. A group of liberal, radical, and socialist leaders proclaimed the Second Republic. (The First Republic had lasted from 1792 until 1804, when Napoleon became emperor.)

From the start, deep differences divided the new government. Middle-class liberals wanted moderate political reforms. Socialists wanted far-reaching social and economic change and forced the government to set up national workshops to provide jobs for the unemployed.

The Working Class Loses Out During "June Days" By June, however, upper- and middle-class interests had won control of the government. They saw the national workshops as a waste of money and shut them down.

Furious, workers again took to the streets of Paris. This time, however, bourgeois liberals turned violently against the protesters. Peasants, who feared that socialists might take their land, also attacked the rioting workers. At least 1,500 people were killed before the government crushed the rebellion.

The fighting of the "June Days" left a bitter legacy. The middle class both feared and distrusted the socialists, while the working class harbored a deep hatred for the bourgeoisie.

A New Napoleon Comes to Power By the end of 1848, the National Assembly, now dominated by members who wanted to restore order,

FEBRUARY

| | FEBRUARY | |
| S M T W T F S | | |

Opposition grew as Louis Philippe refused to listen to the middle class, workers, or peasants. In February, crowds revolted in the streets. As the turmoil of the "February Days" spread, Louis Philippe abdicated and a group of liberal, radical, and socialist leaders proclaimed the Second Republic.

MARCH

News of France's successful February revolution spread throughout the German states. In March, demonstrations broke out in the streets of Berlin, and the king agreed to an all-German constitution. When troops randomly fired two shots into the crowd, the demonstrations turned into eight hours of bitter violence.

JUNE

"June Days" in France again saw Paris streets crowded with angry protestors when the workshops for the unemployed were closed. Before this worker revolt ended, about 1,500 died in the first two days, while as many as 3,000 more were executed for their participation in the uprising.

Thinking Critically

1. **Make Comparisons** How were the "February Days" and the "June Days" similar and different?
2. **Recognize Ideologies** What ideals survived despite how quickly most rebellions throughout Europe were crushed?

Cause and Effect

Long-Term Causes
- Spread of Enlightenment ideas
- Growth of nationalism and liberalism
- Poverty caused by the Industrial Revolution

Immediate Causes
- Uprisings in Paris
- Economic recession
- Poor harvests
- Corrupt governments

The Revolutions of 1848

Immediate Effects
- A new republic in France
- Fall of Metternich
- Promises of reform in Austria, Italy, and Prussia

Long-Term Effects
- A new empire in France
- Successes for liberalism, nationalism, and socialism
- Germany and Italy united
- Labor unions
- Increased voting rights for men

Connections to Today

- Ongoing efforts to ensure basic rights for all citizens
- Ongoing efforts to ensure limited government and popular sovereignty worldwide

Analyze Cause and Effect The revolutions of 1848 were the result of new ways of thinking and hard times for workers. *Could one of these factors by itself have caused such widespread rebellion? Why or Why not?*

Italian revolutionary flag

issued a constitution for the Second Republic. It created a strong president and a one-house legislature. But it also gave the vote to all adult men, the widest suffrage in the world at the time. Nine million Frenchmen now could vote, compared with only 200,000 who had that right before.

When elections for president were held, the overwhelming winner was Louis Napoleon, nephew of Napoleon Bonaparte. The "new" Napoleon attracted the working classes by presenting himself as a man who cared about social issues such as poverty. At the same time, his famous name, linked with order and past French glory, helped him with conservatives.

Once in office, Louis Napoleon used his position as a stepping-stone to greater power. By 1852, he had proclaimed himself emperor, taking the title **Napoleon III.** Thus ended the short-lived Second Republic.

Like his celebrated uncle, Napoleon III used a plebiscite to win public approval for his seizure of power. A stunning 90 percent of voters supported his move to set up the Second Empire. Many thought that a monarchy was more stable than a republic or hoped that Napoleon III would restore the glory days of Napoleon Bonaparte.

Napoleon III, like Louis Philippe, ruled at a time of rapid economic growth. For the bourgeoisie, the early days of the Second Empire brought prosperity and contentment. In time, however, Napoleon III would embark on foreign adventures that would bring down his empire and end French leadership in Europe.

 **Checkpoint** How did the French revolutions of 1830 and 1848 differ?

Revolution Surges Through Europe

In 1848, revolts in Paris again unleashed a tidal wave of revolution across Europe. For opponents of the old order, it was a time of such hope that they called it the "springtime of the peoples." Although events in France touched off the revolts, grievances had been piling up for years. Middle-class liberals wanted a greater share of political power for themselves, as well as protections for the basic rights of all male citizens. Workers demanded relief from the miseries of the Industrial Revolution. And nationalists of all classes ached to throw off foreign rule.

Change in the Austrian Empire In the Austrian empire, revolts broke out in the major cities. Even though Metternich censored the press, books were smuggled to universities throughout the empire. Students demanded change. When workers joined the students on the streets of Vienna, Metternich resigned and fled in disguise.

Revolution continued to spread. In Budapest, Hungarian nationalists led by journalist **Louis Kossuth** demanded an independent government, an end to serfdom, and a written constitution to protect basic rights. In Prague, the Czechs made similar demands. Overwhelmed by events, the Austrian government agreed to the reforms. The gains were temporary, however.

Austrian troops soon regained control of Vienna and Prague and smashed the rebels in Budapest.

Revolts in Italy Uprisings also erupted in the Italian states. Nationalists wanted to end Hapsburg domination and set up a constitutional government. From Venice in the north to Naples in the south, Italians set up independent republics. Revolutionaries even expelled the pope from Rome and installed a nationalist government. Before long, the forces of reaction surged back here, too. Austrian troops ousted the new governments in northern Italy. A French army restored the pope to power in Rome. In Naples, local rulers canceled the reforms they had reluctantly accepted.

Rebellion in the German States In the German states, university students demanded national unity and liberal reforms. Economic hard times and a potato famine brought peasants and workers into the struggle. In Prussia, liberals forced King Frederick William IV to agree to a constitution written by an elected assembly. Within a year, though, he dissolved the assembly.

Throughout 1848, delegates from German states met in the Frankfurt Assembly. Divisions soon <u>emerged</u> over whether Germany should be a republic or a monarchy and whether to include Austria in a united German state. Finally, the assembly offered Prussia's Frederick William IV the crown of a united Germany. To their dismay, the conservative king rejected the offer because it came not from the German princes but from the people—"from the gutter," as he described it.

By 1850, rebellion faded, ending the age of liberal revolution that had begun in 1789. Why did the uprisings fail? The rulers' use of military force was just one reason. Another was that revolutionaries did not have mass support, and in many instances, constitutions that represented their principles were withdrawn or replaced. In the decades ahead, liberalism, nationalism, and socialism would win successes not through revolution, but through political activity.

✔ **Checkpoint** What was the outcome of most of the revolutions outside France in 1848?

Vocabulary Builder

<u>emerge</u>—(ee MURJ) *v.* to arise, appear, or come out of

SECTION 2 Assessment

Terms, People, and Places

1. For each term, person, or place listed at the beginning of the section, write a sentence explaining its significance.

Note Taking

2. **Reading Skill: Identify Causes and Effects** Use your completed chart to answer the Focus Question: What were the causes and effects of revolutions in Europe in 1830 and 1848?

Comprehension and Critical Thinking

3. **Draw Conclusions** What were the conditions under which the people of France lived that led to revolution rather than peace?
4. **Analyze Information** **(a)** Where did revolution spread in 1830? **(b)** Were these revolutions successful? Explain.
5. **Make Generalizations** Why did most of the revolutions of 1848 fail to achieve their goals?

● **Writing About History**

Quick Write: Gather and Organize Evidence In order to write a well-organized persuasive essay, you need to gather evidence to support your position. Gather evidence from the section to support an essay on whether workers were justified in taking to the streets in 1830 and 1848. Then create a chart that lists both sides of the issue.

Concept Connector

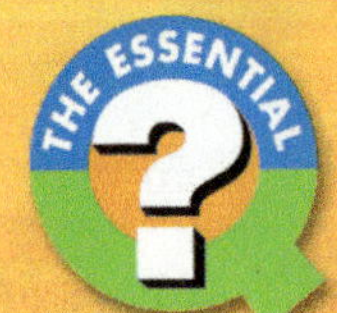

REVOLUTION
Why do political revolutions occur?

In This Chapter

The wave of revolution that swept Europe in the early 1800s mainly involved a clash between liberal and conservative political ideas. Conservatives wanted to keep the power in the hands of established institutions; liberals wanted to distribute power more widely, especially to the middle class. In Germany (right), the military clashed with revolutionaries.

Throughout History

200s A.D. Han empire is overthrown when it burdens peasants with heavy taxes.

1524 German peasants revolt against nobles to end serfdom.

1688 The Glorious Revolution replaces the Catholic King of England James II with his Protestant daughter Mary.

1789 Unequal distribution of wealth and power sparks the French Revolution.

1867 Social and economic unrest lead to the overthrow of the Japanese shogun.

1917 Bolsheviks seize power in Russia and overthrow the tsar.

Continuing Today

An election in Ukraine, seen by many to be fraudulent, sparked a series of nonviolent protests. The government was forced to call for a revote, which led to a change of leadership.

21st Century Skills

TRANSFER Activities

1. Analyze Throughout history, why have people revolted?

2. Draw Conclusions Why do you think every age in history has witnessed revolution?

3. Transfer Complete a Web quest in which you analyze the influence of revolution on a specific country; record your thoughts in the Concept Connector Journal; and learn to make a video. Web Code nah-2008

Simón Bolívar

Crown awarded to Bolívar

A Revolutionary Is Born

Like many wealthy Latin Americans, young Simón Bolívar was sent to Europe to complete his education. In Europe he became a strong admirer of the ideals of the Enlightenment and the French Revolution. One day while speaking with his Italian tutor about freedom and individual rights, he fell on his knees and swore an oath:

66 I swear before God and by my honor never to allow my hands to be idle nor my soul to rest until I have broken the chains that bind us to Spain. **99**

Focus Question Who were the key revolutionaries that led the movements for independence in Latin America, and what were their accomplishments?

Revolts in Latin America

Objectives

- Explain the causes of discontent in Latin America.
- Describe Haiti's fight for freedom.
- Summarize the revolts in Mexico and Central America.
- Understand how revolutions ignited South America.

Terms, People, and Places

peninsular	Toussaint L'Ouverture
creole	Father Miguel Hidalgo
mestizo	Father José Morelos
mulatto	José de San Martín
Simón Bolívar	Dom Pedro

Note Taking

Reading Skill: Identify Main Ideas As you read the section, fill in a table like the one below with a country, a date, and a main idea about revolts in Latin America. Add rows as needed.

Revolts in Latin America		
Haiti	1791	Toussaint L'Ouverture

Liberal ideas were spreading to Latin America with explosive results. From Mexico to the tip of South America, revolutionary movements arose to overthrow the reigning European powers. By 1825, most of Latin America was freed from colonial rule.

Discontent Fans the Fires

By the late 1700s, the revolutionary fever that gripped Western Europe had spread to Latin America. There, discontent was rooted in the social, racial, and political system that had emerged during 300 years of Spanish rule.

Social and Ethnic Structures Cause Resentment Spanish-born **peninsulares,** members of the highest social class, dominated Latin American political and social life. Only they could hold top jobs in government and the Church. Many **creoles**—the European-descended Latin Americans who owned the haciendas, ranches, and mines—bitterly resented their second-class status. Merchants fretted under mercantilist policies that tied the colonies to Spain.

Meanwhile, a growing population of **mestizos,** people of Native American and European descent, and **mulattoes,** people of African and European descent, were angry at being denied the status, wealth, and power that were available to whites. Native Americans suffered economic misery under the Spanish, who had conquered the lands of their ancestors. In the Caribbean region and parts of South America, masses of enslaved Africans who worked on plantations longed for freedom.

Portrait of Joseph Bonaparte,
King of Spain, 1808

The Enlightenment Inspires Latin Americans In the 1700s, educated creoles read the works of Enlightenment thinkers. They watched colonists in North America throw off British rule. Translations of the Declaration of Independence and the Constitution of the United States circulated among the creole elite.

During the French Revolution, young creoles like **Simón Bolívar** (boh LEE vahr) traveled in Europe and were inspired by the ideals of "liberty, equality, and fraternity." Yet despite their admiration for Enlightenment ideas and revolutions in other lands, most creoles were reluctant to act.

Napoleon Invades Spain The spark that finally ignited widespread rebellion in Latin America was Napoleon's invasion of Spain in 1808. Napoleon ousted the Spanish king and placed his brother Joseph on the Spanish throne. In Latin America, leaders saw Spain's weakness as an opportunity to reject foreign domination and demand independence from colonial rule.

 **Checkpoint** Where did creoles get many of their revolutionary ideas?

Slaves Win Freedom for Haiti

Even before Spanish colonists hoisted the flag of freedom, revolution had erupted in a French-ruled colony on the island of Hispaniola. In Haiti, as the island is now called, French planters owned very profitable sugar plantations worked by nearly a half million enslaved Africans. Sugar plantations were labor-intensive. The slaves were overworked and underfed.

Toussaint L'Ouverture Leads a Slave Revolt Embittered by suffering and inspired by the talk of liberty and equality, the island's slaves rose up in revolt in 1791. The rebels were fortunate to find an intelligent and skillful leader in **Toussaint L'Ouverture** (too SAN loo vehr TOOR), a self-educated former slave. Although untrained, Toussaint was a brilliant general and inspiring commander.

Toussaint's army of former slaves faced many enemies. Some mulattoes joined French planters against the rebels. France, Spain, and Britain all sent armies against them. The fighting took more lives than any other revolution in the Americas. But by 1798, the rebels had achieved their goal: slavery was abolished, and Toussaint's forces controlled most of the island.

Haiti Wins Independence In 1802, Napoleon Bonaparte sent a large army to reconquer the former colony. Toussaint urged his countrymen to take up arms once again to resist the invaders. In April 1802 the French agreed to a truce, but then they captured Toussaint and carried him in chains to France. He died there in a cold mountain prison a year later.

The struggle for freedom continued, however, and late in 1803, with yellow fever destroying their army, the French surrendered. In January 1804, the island declared itself an independent country under the name Haiti. In the following years, rival Haitian leaders fought for power. Finally, in 1820, Haiti became a republic.

 **Checkpoint** How were slaves instrumental in achieving Haiti's independence?

Liberty!
Toussaint L'Ouverture and his army of former slaves battle for independence from France and an end to slavery. Although Toussaint achieved his goal of ending slavery, Haiti (see inset) did not become independent until after his death. *Why do you think Toussaint and his army were willing to risk death to achieve their goals?*

Mexico and Central America Revolt

The slave revolt in Haiti frightened creoles in Spanish America. Although they wanted power themselves, most had no desire for economic or social changes that might threaten their way of life. In 1810, however, a creole priest in Mexico, **Father Miguel Hidalgo** (hee DAL goh), raised his voice for freedom.

Father Hidalgo Cries Out for Freedom Father Hidalgo presided over the poor rural parish of Dolores. On September 15, 1810, he rang the church bells summoning the people to prayer. When they gathered, he startled them with an urgent appeal, "My children, will you be free?" Father Hidalgo's speech became known as "el Grito de Dolores"—the cry of Dolores. It called Mexicans to fight for independence.

A ragged army of poor mestizos and Native Americans rallied to Father Hidalgo and marched to the outskirts of Mexico City. At first, some creoles supported the revolt. However, they soon rejected Hidalgo's call for an end to slavery and his plea for reforms to improve conditions for Native Americans. They felt that these policies would cost them power.

After some early successes, the rebels faced growing opposition. Less than a year after he issued the "Grito," Hidalgo was captured and executed, and his followers scattered.

José Morelos Continues the Fight Another priest picked up the banner of revolution. **Father José Morelos** was a mestizo who called for wide-ranging social and political reform. He wanted to improve conditions for the majority of Mexicans, abolish slavery, and give the vote to all men. For four years, Morelos led rebel forces before he, too, was captured and shot in 1815.

Spanish forces, backed by conservative creoles, hunted down the surviving guerrillas. They had almost succeeded in ending the rebel movement when events in Spain had unexpected effects.

Mexico Wins Independence In Spain in 1820, liberals forced the king to issue a constitution. This move alarmed Agustín de Iturbide (ee toor BEE day), a conservative creole in Mexico. He feared that the new Spanish government might impose liberal reforms on the colonies as well.

Iturbide had spent years fighting Mexican revolutionaries. Suddenly, in 1821, he reached out to them. Backed by creoles, mestizos, and Native Americans, he overthrew the Spanish viceroy. Mexico was independent at last. Iturbide took the title Emperor Agustín I. Soon, however, liberal Mexicans toppled the would-be monarch and set up the Republic of Mexico.

New Republics Emerge in Central America Spanish-ruled lands in Central America declared independence in the early 1820s. Iturbide tried to add these areas to his Mexican empire. After his overthrow, local leaders set up a republic called the United Provinces of Central America. The union soon fragmented into the separate republics of Guatemala, Nicaragua, Honduras, El Salvador, and Costa Rica.

 **Checkpoint** How did events in Spain affect the fight for Mexican independence?

Revolution Ignites South America

In South America, Native Americans had rebelled against Spanish rule as early as the 1700s, though with limited results. It was not until the 1800s that discontent among the creoles sparked a widespread drive for independence.

Bolívar Begins the Fight In the early 1800s, discontent spread across South America. Educated creoles like Simón Bolívar admired the French and American revolutions. They dreamed of winning their own independence from Spain.

In 1808, when Napoleon Bonaparte occupied Spain, Bolívar and his friends saw the occupation as a signal to act. In 1810, Bolívar led an uprising that established a republic in his native Venezuela. Bolívar's new republic was quickly toppled by conservative forces, however. For years, civil war raged in Venezuela. The revolutionaries suffered many setbacks. Twice Bolívar was forced into exile on the island of Haiti.

Then, Bolívar conceived a daring plan. He would march his army across the Andes and attack the Spanish at Bogotá, the capital of the viceroyalty of New Granada (present-day Colombia). First, he cemented an alliance with the hard-riding llañeros, or Venezuelan cowboys. Then, in a grueling campaign, he led an army through swampy lowlands and over the snowcapped Andes. Finally, in August 1819, he swooped down to take Bogotá from the surprised Spanish.

Other victories followed. By 1821, Bolívar had succeeded in freeing Caracas, Venezuela. "The Liberator," as he was now called, then moved south into Ecuador, Peru, and Bolivia. There, he joined forces with another great leader, **José de San Martín.**

LATIN AMERICAN INDEPENDENCE

Because Father Miguel Hidalgo rang the church bells calling people to revolt against the Spanish, his name became the symbol of Mexican independence.

Once Toussaint L'Ouverture, who was born a slave, was legally freed, he devoted himself to freeing slaves in St-Domingue (now Haiti), which led to Haiti's independence.

José de San Martín fought against Napoleon's army for years before helping Bolívar liberate Argentina, Chile, and Peru.

Simón Bolívar freed Venezuela, Colombia, Panama, Ecuador, Peru, and Bolivia from Spanish rule.

Geography Interactive

For: Interactive maps and biographies
Web Code: nap-2031

Thinking Critically

1. **Synthesize Information** Why did so many Latin American nations gain independence by 1830?
2. **Recognize Cause and Effect** What influenced the leaders of Latin American independence?

Dom Pedro, Emperor of Brazil

Vocabulary Builder

proclaim—(proh KLAYM) *vt.* to announce publicly or formally

San Martín Joins the Fight Like Bolívar, San Martín was a creole. He was born in Argentina but went to Europe for military training. In 1816, this gifted general helped Argentina win freedom from Spain. He then joined the independence struggle in other areas. He, too, led an army across the Andes, from Argentina into Chile. He defeated the Spanish in Chile before moving into Peru to strike further blows against colonial rule. San Martín turned his command over to Bolívar in 1822, allowing Bolívar's forces to win the final victories against Spain.

Freedom Leads to Power Struggles The wars of independence ended by 1824. Bolívar then worked tirelessly to unite the lands he had liberated into a single nation, called Gran Colombia. Bitter rivalries, however, made that dream impossible. Before long, Gran Colombia split into four independent countries: Colombia, Panama, Venezuela, and Ecuador.

Bolívar faced another disappointment as power struggles among rival leaders triggered destructive civil wars. Before his death in 1830, a discouraged Bolívar wrote, "We have achieved our independence at the expense of everything else." Contrary to his dreams, South America's common people had simply changed one set of masters for another.

Brazil Gains Independence When Napoleon's armies conquered Portugal, the Portuguese royal family fled to Brazil. When the king returned to Portugal, he left his son **Dom Pedro** to rule Brazil. "If Brazil demands independence," the king advised Pedro, "<u>proclaim</u> it yourself and put the crown on your own head."

In 1822, Pedro followed his father's advice. A revolution had brought new leaders to Portugal who planned to abolish reforms and demanded that Dom Pedro return. Dom Pedro refused to leave Brazil. Instead, he became emperor of an independent Brazil. He accepted a constitution that provided for freedom of the press, freedom of religion, and an elected legislature. Brazil remained a monarchy until 1889, when social and political turmoil led it to become a republic.

 **Checkpoint** How were the goals of the South American revolutions different from their results?

Terms, People, and Places

1. What do many of the key terms listed at the beginning of the section have in common? Explain.

Note Taking

2. **Reading Skill: Identify Supporting Details** Use your completed chart to answer the Focus Question: Who were the key revolutionaries that led the movements for independence in Latin America, and what were their accomplishments?

Comprehension and Critical Thinking

3. **Draw Conclusions** How did social structure contribute to discontent in Latin America?

4. **Analyze Information** (a) What was the first step on Haiti's road to independence? (b) Why did creoles refuse to support Hidalgo or Morelos?

5. **Identify Central Issues** Why did Bolívar admire the American and French revolutions?

● **Writing About History**

Quick Write: Use Effective Language Most effective persuasive essays contain memorable and convincing details and vivid, persuasive language. Suppose you were one of the revolutionary leaders mentioned in the section. Write notes for a speech in which you persuade others to join your cause. Include at least three compelling reasons why people should follow you.

Simón Bolívar: *Address to the Congress of Venezuela*

Encouraged by the revolutions in British North America and France, colonists in Spanish South America soon began to create a force for independence. Simón Bolívar was one of the leaders of this movement. The excerpt below is from Bolívar's Address to the Second National Congress of Venezuela, given in 1819. In this speech, Bolívar offers advice on what type of government to set up in Venezuela.

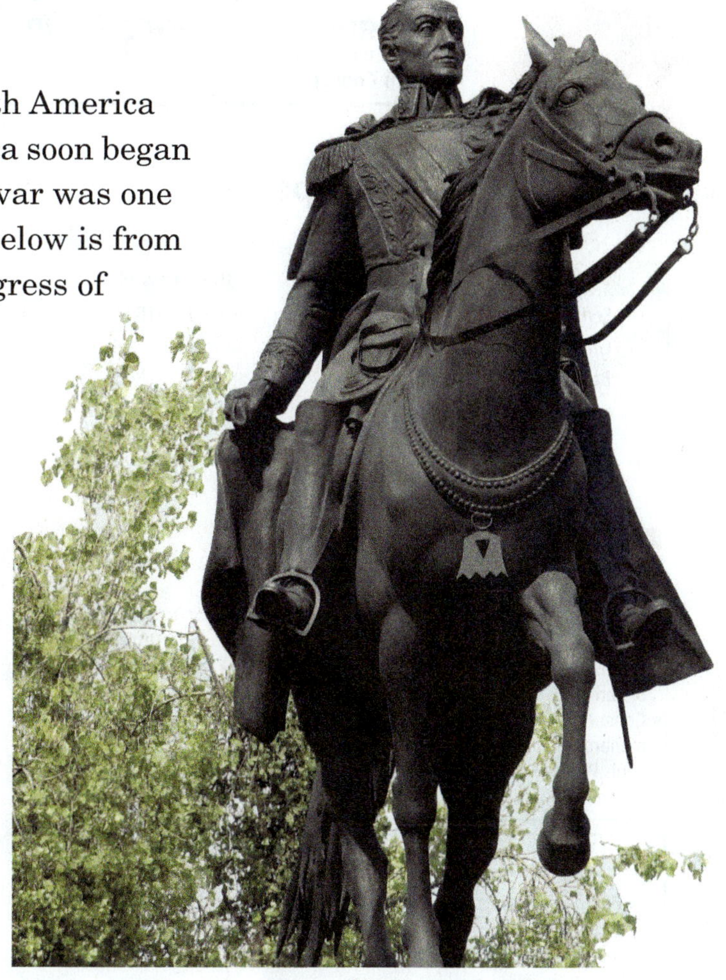

Statue of Bolívar as the Liberator, Mexico City

Subject to the threefold yoke of ignorance, tyranny, and vice, the American people have been unable to acquire knowledge, power, or [civic] virtue. The lessons we received and the models we studied, as pupils of such pernicious[1] teachers, were most destructive. . . .

If a people, perverted by their training, succeed in achieving their liberty, they will soon lose it, for it would be of no avail to endeavor to explain to them that happiness consists in the practice of virtue; that the rule of law is more powerful than the rule of tyrants, because, as the laws are more inflexible everyone should submit to their beneficent austerity; that proper morals, and not force, are the bases of law; and that to practice justice is to practice liberty.

Therefore, Legislators, your work is so much the more arduous[2], inasmuch as you have to reeducate men who have been corrupted by erroneous[3] illusions and false incentives[4]. Liberty, says Rousseau, is a succulent[5] morsel, but one difficult to digest. . . .

Legislators, meditate well before you choose. Forget not that you are to lay the political foundation for a newly born nation which can rise to the heights of greatness that Nature has marked out for it if you but proportion this foundation in keeping with the high plane that it aspires to attain. Unless your choice is based upon the peculiar . . . experience of Venezuelan people—a factor that should guide you in determining the nature and form of government you are about to adopt for the well-being of the people . . . the result of our reforms will again be slavery.

1. **pernicious** (pur NISH us) *adj.* harmful, injurious
2. **arduous** (AHR joo us) *adj.* difficult
3. **erroneous** (eh ROH nee us) *adj.* mistaken, wrong
4. **incentive** (in SEN tiv) *n.* reason for doing something
5. **succulent** (SUK yoo lunt) *adj.* juicy, tasty

Thinking Critically

1. **Analyze Literature** How did Bolívar feel the people of Latin America were prepared for new government?
2. **Draw Inferences** Do you think Bolívar was practical or idealistic? Use examples from the excerpt to defend your opinion.

Quick Study Guide

Progress Monitoring *Online*
For: Self-test with vocabulary practice
Web Code: naa-2041

■ Revolutions in Europe

Successful	Unsuccessful
Serbia (autonomy 1830)	Poland (1830)
Greece (1830)	Austria (1848)
Belgium (1830)	Italy (1848)
	Germany (1848)

■ Events in France

July 1830
- Rebels take control of Paris.
- Constitutional monarchy proclaimed.
- Louis Philippe becomes king.

1840
- Recession heightens discontent.

February 1848
- Rebels take to the streets.
- Second Republic is proclaimed.
- Louis Philippe abdicates.

June 1848
- Bourgeois liberals crush workers' rebellion.

1850
- Louis Napoleon is voted president of the Second Republic.

1852
- Louis Napoleon becomes emperor of the Second Empire.

■ Independence Movements in Latin America

Cause and Effect

Long-Term Causes	Immediate Causes
• European domination • Spread of Enlightenment ideas • American and French Revolutions • Growth of nationalism	• Social injustices • Revolutionary leaders emerge. • Napoleon invades Spain.

Independence Movements

Immediate Effects	Long-Term Effects
• Toussaint L'Ouverture leads slave revolt in Haiti. • Bolívar, San Martin, and others lead successful revolts. • Colonial rule ends in much of Latin America.	• Numerous independent nations in Latin America • Continuing efforts to achieve stable democratic governments and to gain economic independence

■ Age of Revolution

1804
Haiti declares independence from France.

1810
Father Miguel Hidalgo urges Mexicans to fight for independence from Spain.

1819
Simón Bolívar seizes Bogotá from the Spanish.

1821
Simón Bolívar liberates Caracas, Venezuela.

Chapter Events | **1800** | **1810** | **1820**
Global Events

1803
United States buys Louisiana from France.

1814
Napoleon is banished to Elba.

1819
The United States acquires Spanish Florida.

1823
U.S. President James Monroe issues the Monroe Doctrine.

Concept Connector

 Essential Question Review

To connect prior knowledge with what you have learned in this chapter, answer the questions below in your Concept Connector journal. Use the journal in the Reading and Note Taking Study Guide to record your answers (or go to www.phschool.com **Web Code:** nad-2007). In addition, record information about the following concepts:

• Conflict: European revolutionaries in 1830 and 1848
• Revolution: Latin American revolutions against European rulers

1. **Conflict** The early 1800s saw a clash of opposing ideologies. Conservatives favored monarchies as a political system. Liberals supported a republican form of government. How did conservatives benefit from the status quo, or existing state of affairs? Why did liberals and nationalists oppose the status quo? What steps did Prince Clemens von Metternich urge monarchs to take to maintain their power?

2. **Democracy** Before his death in 1830, Simón Bolívar wrote, "We have achieved our independence at the expense of everything else." What did he mean? How were the outcomes of Latin American revolutions similar to, and different from, the American Revolution? Think about the following:
   - social classes
   - constitutions
   - cooperation between the colonies

■ Connections to Today

1. **Nationalism: Mexican Independence Day** Today, the people of Mexico remember Father Hidalgo's speech as "el Grito de Dolores." Every September 15, the anniversary of the speech, the president of Mexico rings a bell—suggestive of the church bell in Dolores. The president then honors the Grito de Dolores by repeating the speech. The next day, September 16, marks the anniversary of the beginning of the fight against the Spanish. It is celebrated as Mexican Independence Day, a national holiday. Schools and businesses shut down, and people throw huge parties. Fireworks light the night sky. Why is the ringing of bells an important custom of Mexican Independence Day?

2. **Conflict: Chechnya and Russia** There are many struggles for independence in the world today. Certain Basques in Spain, Tibetans in China, and Chechens in Russia are all seeking their independence. In some cases, such as in Chechnya, revolutionaries resort to terrorism to fight for their goals. Conduct research and write a one-page report about Chechnya and why its revolutionaries seek independence from Russia.

1830
French revolutionaries battle the king's troops in the streets of Paris.

1848
Revolutions break out across much of Europe.

History Interactive
For: Interactive timeline
Web Code: nap-2001

1830 **1840** **1850**

1839
China and Britain clash in the Opium War.

1850
Taiping Rebellion begins in China.

Chapter Assessment

Terms, People, and Places

Match the following terms with the definitions below.

creole
autonomy
Louis Philippe
recession

peninsular
ideology
mestizo
José de San Martín

1. system of thought and belief
2. self-rule
3. person in Spain's colonies in the Americas who was an American-born descendant of Spanish settlers
4. period of reduced economic activity
5. person in Spain's colonies in the Americas who was of Native American and European descent
6. known as the "citizen king"
7. fought for freedom in South America
8. member of the highest class in Spain's colonies in the Americas

Main Ideas

Section 1 (pp. 634–637)

9. In the early 1800s, what were the main goals of (a) conservatives, (b) liberals, and (c) nationalists?

Section 2 (pp. 638–644)

10. What were the causes of the French revolution of 1830?
11. Describe the outcomes of the 1848 rebellions in Europe.

Section 3 (pp. 645–651)

12. (a) How did Mexico gain independence from Spain? (b) How did Mexico's independence change the lives of its people?
13. Why is Simón Bolívar known as "The Liberator"?

Chapter Focus Question

14. How did revolutionary ideals in Europe and Latin America ignite uprisings in the first half of the nineteenth century?

Critical Thinking

15. **Recognize Cause and Effect** How did the clash of conservatism, liberalism, and nationalism contribute to unrest in Europe in the 1800s?
16. **Draw Conclusions** Why do you think liberals of the early 1800s supported limited voting rights?
17. **Synthesize Information** In the 1820s, Britain, France, and Russia supported the Greek struggle for independence. (a) Why did these European powers support the Greeks? (b) Did the European powers usually respond to revolution in this way? Explain.
18. **Analyze Information** You have read Metternich's comment: "When France sneezes, Europe catches cold." (a) What did he mean by these words? (b) Was Metternich correct?
19. **Geography and History** Review the map in Section 3. How does the map show that Bolívar failed to achieve one of his dreams?
20. **Analyzing Visuals** The scene below is part of a famous mural by José Clemente Orozco. How do you think Orozco feels about Father Hidalgo?

21. **Geography and History** (a) How did climatic conditions help Haitians defeat the French? (b) Do you think the distance between Europe and Latin America affected the Latin American wars for independence? Explain.

● Writing About History

In this Chapter's three Section Assessments, you developed skills for writing a persuasive essay.

Writing a Persuasive Essay The early 1800s were a time of revolution across Europe. Liberals and nationalists attempted to organize revolts that might overthrow Europe's colonial rule. Write a persuasive essay that a liberal or nationalist might have published in an attempt to persuade people to join a revolution.

Prewriting

- Take notes about the ideas that motivated revolutionaries in the early 1800s.

- Generate arguments that a liberal or nationalist might make.

Drafting

- Using a convincing thesis, or main argument, make an outline that organizes the essay.
- Write an attention-grabbing introduction, a body, and a conclusion.
- Open and close with your strongest argument.

Revising

- Use the guidelines for revising your essay on page SH17 of the Writing Handbook.

Document-Based Assessment

The Revolutions of 1848: The Aftermath

The revolutions of 1848 began spontaneously in February 1848 on the streets of Paris. Reformers won short-lived success with the abdication of Louis Philippe. Uprisings spread across Europe to Austria, Hungary, Germany, and Italy, among others. These rebellions were quelled in short order, as the documents below illustrate, but some reverberations were more lasting.

Document A

"[O]n June 23rd, 1848 . . . the proletarians of Paris were defeated, decimated [killed off so that a large part of the population was removed], crushed with such an effect that even now they have not yet recovered from the blow. And immediately, all over Europe, the new and old Conservatives and Counter-Revolutionists raised their heads with an effrontery [boldness] that showed how well they understood the importance of the event. The Press was everywhere attacked, the rights of meeting and association were interfered with, every little event in every small provincial town was taken profit of to disarm the people to declare a state of siege, to drill the troops in the new maneuvers and artifices [clever tricks] that Cavaignac [French general known for his harsh treatment of Parisian rebels] had taught them."

—From ***The Paris Rising—Frankfort Assembly***
by Frederich Engels (February, 1852)

Document B

"[German] factory workers failed to win any lasting class advantages in 1848–1849 . . . Many artisans exerted themselves for the revolution; in October 1849 the magazine of the cigar workers estimated that three hundred in this industry alone had been forced to flee to Switzerland. . . . For German democrats— whether workers or from the middle class—the revolution left little immediate consolation. In a few states democrats retained large representation in the parliaments, but reactionary changes in the suffrage systems soon ended that. . . . But the long-range results of the revolution were not altogether negative. To be sure, those who worked for democracy after 1849 knew better than to try to create a republic. They also knew the futility of resorting to revolutionary violence. But their effort did not cease."

—From ***The Democratic Movement in Germany, 1789–1914***
by John L. Snell

Document C

Metternich Flees Austria

Document D

"The rising of 1848 was a spontaneous expression of national feeling but completely uncoordinated and therefore defeated in detail. After it, once more patrolled by Austria, Italy sank back into inaction. . . . From the wreck of Italian political institutions in 1849 there was only one survival, the constitution granted by [King] Charles Albert in Piedmont [kingdom in northwestern Italy]. It provided for a Premier or President of the Council, who, like the Senate, was nominated by the King, and a Chamber of Deputies numbering two hundred and four, elected on a narrow franchise [vote]."

—From ***The Evolution of Modern Italy***
by Arthur James Whyte

Analyzing Documents

Use your knowledge of the revolutions of 1848 and Documents A, B, C, and D to answer questions 1–4.

1. Which words describe the attitude of the author of Document A toward the counter-revolutionaries?
   A admiration and pride
   B understanding and sympathy
   C hatred and disapproval
   D respect and sympathy

2. According to Document B, what strategies did the democrats of Germany follow after the revolution was put down?
   A revolutionary plots
   B voter-registration drives
   C underground efforts
   D parliamentary politics

3. In Document C, Prince Clemens von Metternich is
   A proud to resign.
   B continuing Austrian governance.
   C expressing nationalism.
   D unpopular and defeated.

4. **Writing Task** Describe the aftermath of the revolutions of 1848. If you had lived in 1849, would you have seen causes for optimism or pessimism? How would your answer be different from the viewpoint of the twenty-first century?

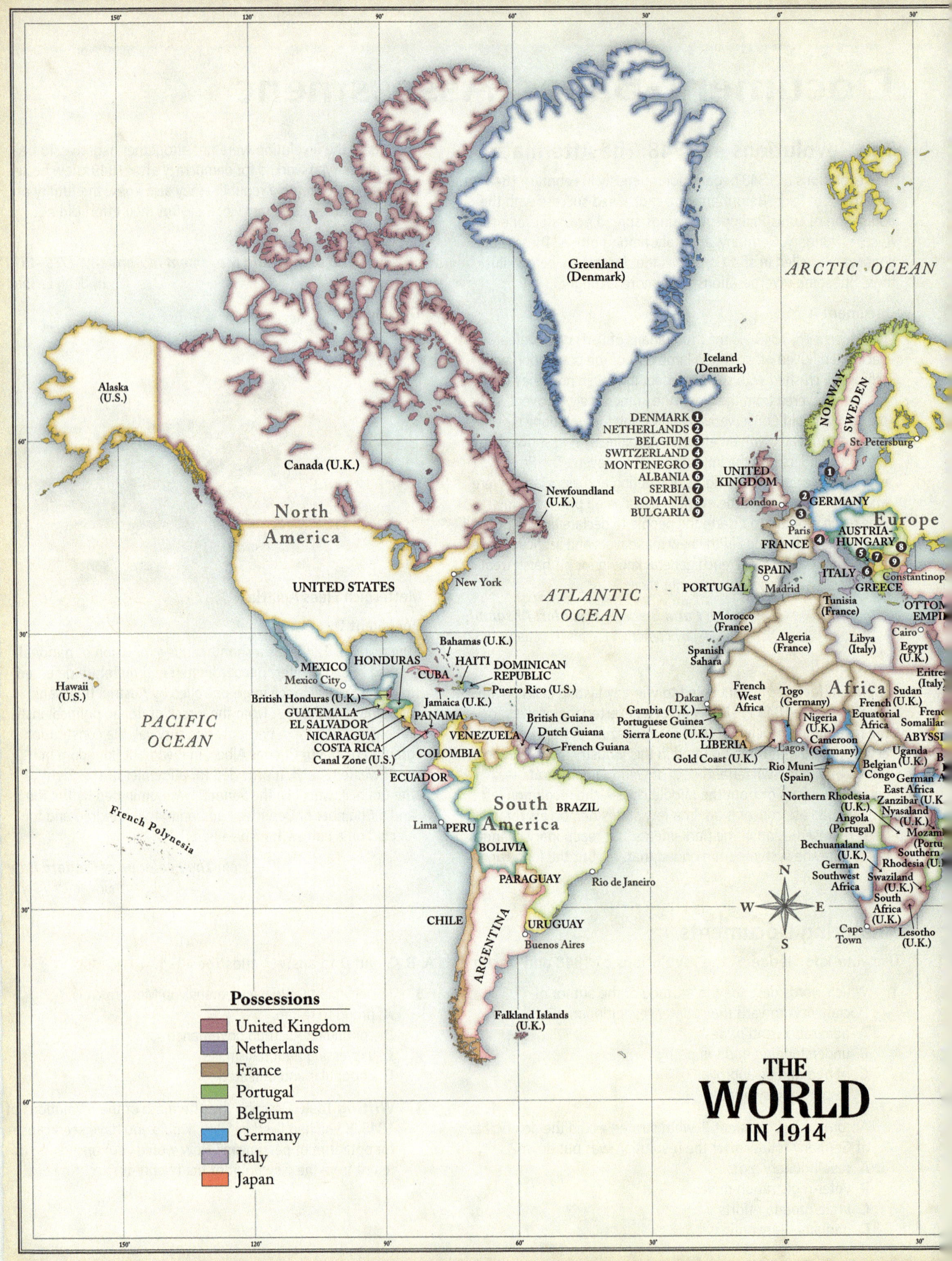

ARCTIC·OCEAN
Greenland
(Denmark)
Iceland
(Denmark)
Alaska
(U.S.)
DENMARK 1
NETHERLANDS 2
BELGIUM 3
SWITZERLAND 4
MONTENEGRO 5
ALBANIA 6
SERBIA 7
ROMANIA 8
BULGARIA 9
NORWAY
SWEDEN
St. Petersburg
Canada (U.K.)
UNITED
KINGDOM
GERMANY
Newfoundland
(U.K.)
London
Europe
North
America
Paris
FRANCE
AUSTRIA-
HUNGARY
UNITED STATES
New York
ATLANTIC
OCEAN
SPAIN
ITALY
PORTUGAL
Madrid
GREECE
Constantinop
OTTOM
EMPI
Morocco
(France)
Tunisia
(France)
Hawaii
(U.S.)
Bahamas (U.K.)
MEXICO
HONDURAS
HAITI
DOMINICAN
REPUBLIC
Algeria
(France)
Libya
(Italy)
Cairo
Egypt
(U.K.)
Eritre
(Italy)
Mexico City
CUBA
Puerto Rico (U.S.)
Spanish
Sahara
British Honduras (U.K.)
Jamaica (U.K.)
GUATEMALA
EL SALVADOR
NICARAGUA
COSTA RICA
Canal Zone (U.S.)
PANAMA
Dakar
French
West
Africa
Togo
(Germany)
Africa
Sudan
(U.K.)
Frenc
Somalilar
PACIFIC
OCEAN
VENEZUELA
British Guiana
Dutch Guiana
French Guiana
Gambia (U.K.)
Portuguese Guinea
Sierra Leone (U.K.)
Nigeria
(U.K.)
French
Equatorial
Africa
ABYSSI
COLOMBIA
LIBERIA
Gold Coast (U.K.)
Lagos
Cameroon
(Germany)
Uganda
(U.K.)
ECUADOR
Rio Muni
(Spain)
Belgian
Congo
German
East
Africa
Zanzibar (U.K
French Polynesia
South
America
BRAZIL
Northern Rhodesia
(U.K.)
Nyasaland
(U.K.)
Mozam
(Portu
Lima
PERU
BOLIVIA
Angola
(Portugal)
Southern
Rhodesia (U.
PARAGUAY
Rio de Janeiro
Bechuanaland
(U.K.)
German
Southwest
Africa
Swaziland
(U.K.)
N
CHILE
URUGUAY
South
Africa
(U.K.)
Lesotho
(U.K.)
ARGENTINA
Buenos Aires
W
E
Cape
Town
S
Falkland Islands
(U.K.)
Possessions
United Kingdom
Netherlands
France
Portugal
Belgium
Germany
Italy
Japan
THE
WORLD
IN 1914

656

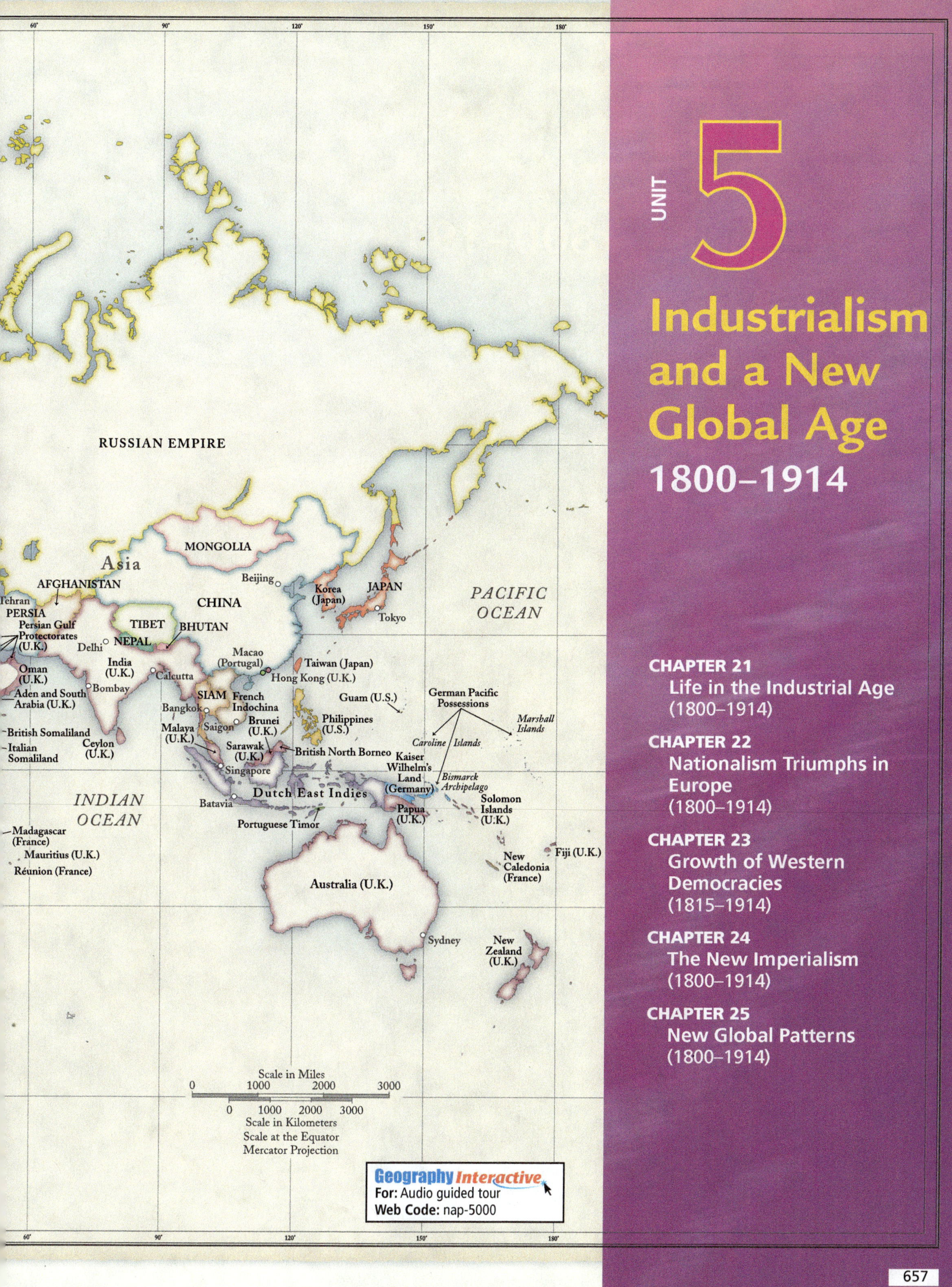

5

Industrialism and a New Global Age

1800–1914

Life in the Industrial Age

1800–1914

Factory Life

In 1888, Nell Cusack, a reporter for the Chicago *Times,* worked undercover to write a series of newspaper articles about the conditions under which factory girls worked:

❝ . . . The place was noisy with flying shuttles, clicking needles, and the whizzing wheels of the roaring machinery. . . . The clatter of the machines was deafening. . . . The room was low . . . and clouds of lint seemed floating about in space. Add to that poor light, bad ventilation, the exhalations of so many people, [and] the smell of dye from the cloth . . . and you have material for the make-up of [the] shop. All afternoon we sewed; sewed incessantly without uttering a syllable or resting a moment.**❞**

Listen to the Witness History audio to learn more about factory life.

◄ Spinner at a cotton mill in Whitnel, North Carolina, 1908

Chapter Preview

Chapter Focus Question What were the technological, social, and economic effects of the Industrial Revolution?

Section 1
The Industrial Revolution Spreads

Section 2
The Rise of the Cities

Section 3
Changing Attitudes and Values

Section 4
Arts in the Industrial Age

Use the ☑ **Quick Study Timeline** at the end of this chapter to preview chapter events.

German labor union poster

Banner from the National Union of Women's Suffrage Societies

The first commercially successful typewriter, 1875

 Concept **Connector** ONLINE

To explore Essential Questions related to this chapter, go to PHSchool.com
Web Code: nad-2107

Painting of a nineteenth-century steel mill

The Steelmaking Process

By the 1880s, steel had replaced steam as the great symbol of the Industrial Revolution. In huge steel mills, visitors watched with awe as tons of molten metal were poured into giant mixers:

> 66 At night the scene is indescribably wild and beautiful. The flashing fireworks, the terrific gusts of heat, the gaping, glowing mouth of the giant chest, the quivering light from the liquid iron, the roar of a near-by converter . . . combine to produce an effect on the mind that no words can translate. 99
>
> —J. H. Bridge, *The Inside History of the Carnegie Steel Company*

Focus Question How did science, technology, and big business promote industrial growth?

The Industrial Revolution Spreads

Objectives

- List the industrial powers that emerged in the 1800s.
- Describe the impact of new technology on industry, transportation, and communication.
- Understand how big business emerged in the late 1800s.

Terms, People, and Places

Henry Bessemer	assembly line
Alfred Nobel	Orville and Wilbur Wright
Michael Faraday	Guglielmo Marconi
dynamo	stock
Thomas Edison	corporation
interchangeable parts	cartel

Note Taking

Reading Skill: Identify Main Ideas Fill in a chart like this one with the major developments of the Industrial Revolution.

The Second Industrial Revolution		
New Powers	**Industry/Business**	**Transportation/ Communication**
•	•	•
•	•	•

The first phase of industrialization had largely been forged from iron, powered by steam engines, and driven by the British textile industry. By the mid-1800s, the Industrial Revolution entered a second phase. New industrial powers emerged. Factories powered by electricity used innovative processes to turn out new products. Changes in business organization contributed to the rise of giant companies. As the twentieth century dawned, this second Industrial Revolution transformed the economies of the Western world.

New Industrial Powers Emerge

During the early Industrial Revolution, Britain stood alone as the world's industrial giant. To protect its head start, Britain tried to enforce strict rules against exporting inventions.

For a while, the rules worked. Then, in 1807, British mechanic William Cockerill opened factories in Belgium to manufacture spinning and weaving machines. Belgium became the first European nation after Britain to industrialize. By the mid-1800s, other nations had joined the race, and several newcomers were challenging Britain's industrial supremacy.

Nations Race to Industrialize How were other nations able to catch up with Britain so quickly? First, nations such as Germany, France, and the United States had more abundant supplies of coal, iron, and other resources than did Britain. Also, they had the advantage of being able to follow Britain's lead. Like Belgium,

Centers of Industry, 1871

Geography *Interactive*
For: Audio guided tour
Web Code: nap-2111

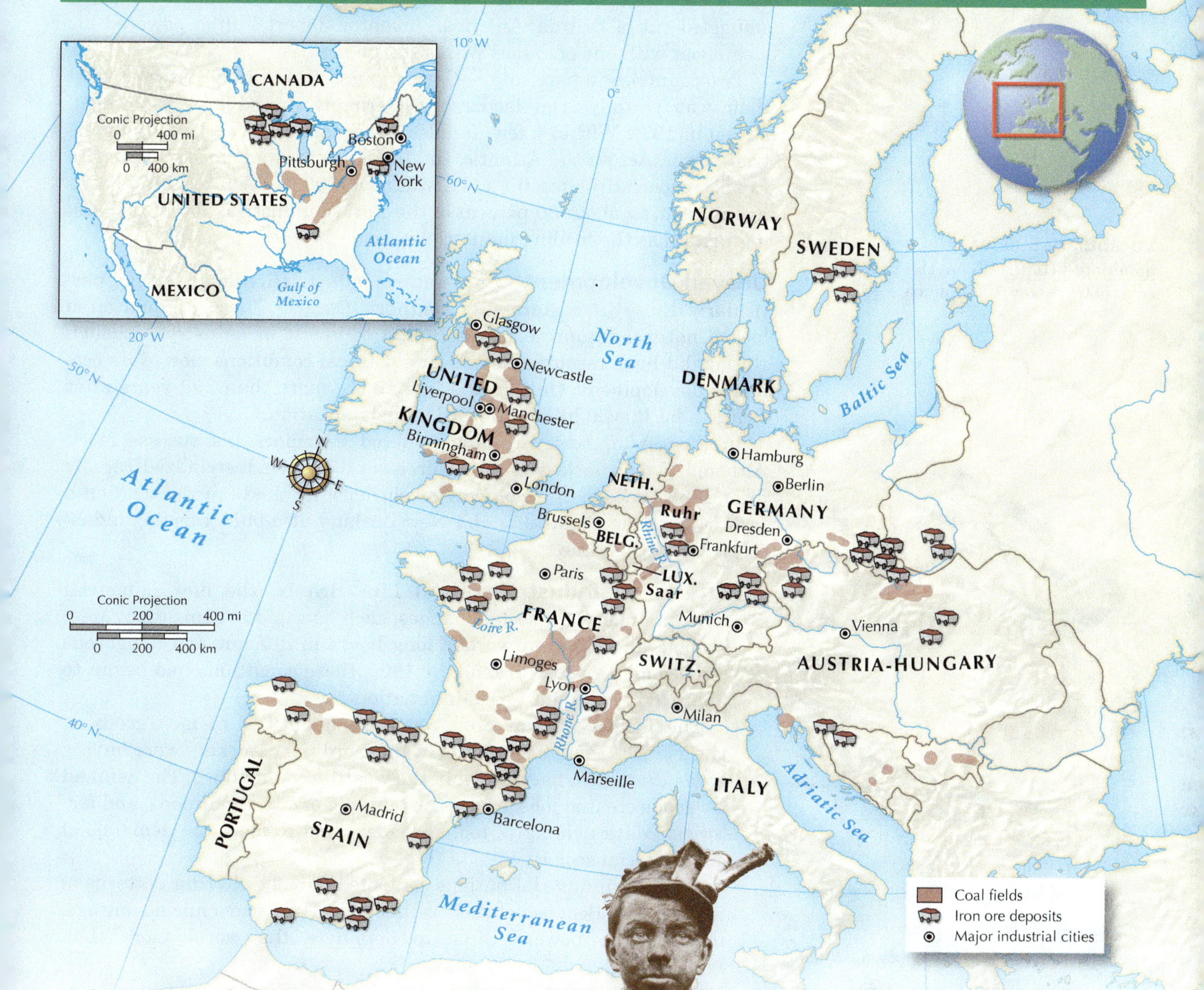

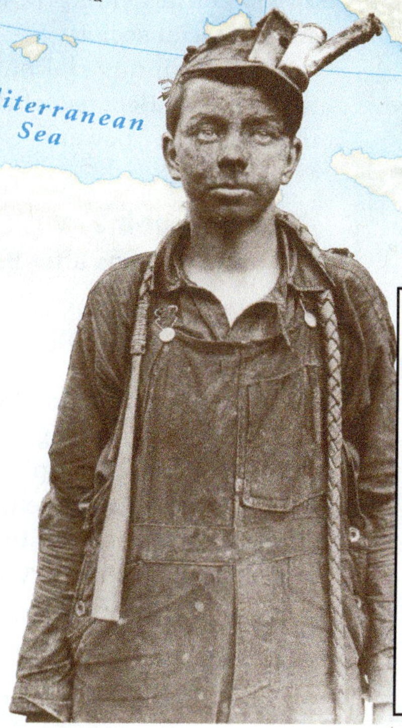

An increase in manufacturing created a demand for workers. Children began running machines and mining coal (right).

Primary Source

"Shut in from everything that is pleasant, with no chance to learn . . . grinding their little lives away in this dusty room, they are no more than the wire screens that separate the great lumps of coal from the small. They had no games; when their day's work is done, they are too tired for that. They know nothing but the difference between slate and coal."

—"The Labor Standard," 1877

Map Skills Deposits of raw materials such as iron and coal were essential to a nation's industrial success.

1. **Locate** (a) Belgium (b) Germany (c) Saar (d) Ruhr
2. **Region** Which American city probably grew because of its location near coal fields?
3. **Draw Inferences** Why would you expect Lyon, France, to become a major industrial city?

latecomers often borrowed British experts or technology. The first American textile factory was built in Pawtucket, Rhode Island, with plans smuggled out of Britain. American inventor Robert Fulton powered his steamboat with one of James Watt's steam engines.

Two countries in particular—Germany and the United States—thrust their way to industrial leadership. Germany united into a powerful nation in 1871. Within a few decades, it became Europe's leading industrial power. Across the Atlantic, the United States advanced even more rapidly, especially after the Civil War. By 1900, the United States was manufacturing about 30 percent of the world's industrial goods, surpassing Britain as the leading industrial nation.

Uneven Development Other nations industrialized more slowly, particularly those in eastern and southern Europe. These nations often lacked natural resources or the capital to invest in industry. Although Russia did have resources, social and political conditions slowed its economic development. Only in the late 1800s, more than 100 years after Britain, did Russia lumber toward industrialization.

In East Asia, however, Japan offered a remarkable success story. Although Japan lacked many basic resources, it industrialized rapidly after 1868 because of a political revolution that made modernization a priority. Canada, Australia, and New Zealand also built thriving industries during this time.

Effects of Industrialization Like Britain, the new industrial nations underwent social changes, such as rapid urbanization. Men, women, and children worked long hours in difficult and dangerous conditions. As you will read, by 1900, these conditions had begun to improve in many industrialized nations.

The factory system produced huge quantities of new goods at lower prices than ever before. In time, ordinary workers were buying goods that in earlier days only the wealthy could afford. The demand for goods created jobs, as did the building of cities, railroads, and factories. Politics changed, too, as leaders had to meet the demands of an industrial society.

Globally, industrial nations competed fiercely, altering patterns of world trade. Because of their technological and economic advantage, the Western powers came to <u>dominate</u> the world more than ever before.

✔ **Checkpoint** What factors led to the industrialization of other nations after Britain?

Technology Sparks Industrial Growth

During the early Industrial Revolution, inventions such as the steam engine were generally the work of gifted tinkerers. They experimented with simple machines to make them better. By the 1880s, the pace of change quickened as companies hired professional chemists and engineers to create new products and machinery. The union of science, technology, and industry spurred economic growth.

Steel Production and the Bessemer Process American inventor William Kelly and British engineer Henry Bessemer independently developed a new process for making steel from iron. In 1856, Bessemer

Graph Skills By the late 1800s, steel was the major material used in manufacturing tools, such as the sheep shears (above). The graph shows the amount of steel produced by the United States, Germany, and Great Britain. *Between 1890 and 1910, which nation had the greatest increase in steel production? The smallest?*

SOURCES: *European Historical Statistics, 1750–1970; Historical Statistics of the United States* patented this process. Steel was lighter, harder, and more durable than iron, so it could be produced very cheaply. Steel quickly became the major material used in tools, bridges, and railroads.

As steel production soared, industrialized countries measured their success in steel output. In 1880, for example, the average German steel mill produced less than 5 million metric tons of steel a year. By 1910, that figure reached nearly 15 million metric tons.

Innovations in Chemistry Chemists created hundreds of new products, from medicines such as aspirin to perfumes and soaps. Newly developed chemical fertilizers played a key role in increasing food production.

In 1866, the Swedish chemist **Alfred Nobel** invented dynamite, an explosive much safer than others used at the time. It was widely used in construction and, to Nobel's dismay, in warfare. Dynamite earned Nobel a huge fortune, which he willed to fund the famous Nobel prizes that are still awarded today.

Electric Power Replaces Steam In the late 1800s, a new power source—electricity—replaced steam as the dominant source of industrial power. Scientists like Benjamin Franklin had tinkered with electricity a century earlier. The Italian scientist Alessandro Volta developed the first battery around 1800. Later, the English chemist **Michael Faraday** created the first simple electric motor and the first **dynamo,** a machine that generates electricity. Today, all electrical generators and transformers work on the principle of Faraday's dynamo.

In the 1870s, the American inventor **Thomas Edison** made the first electric light bulb. Soon, Edison's "incandescent lamps" illuminated whole cities. The pace of city life quickened, and factories could continue to operate after dark. By the 1890s, cables carried electrical power from dynamos to factories.

New Methods of Production The basic features of the factory system remained the same during the 1800s. Factories still used large numbers of workers and power-driven machines to mass-produce goods. To improve efficiency, however, manufacturers designed products with **interchangeable parts,** identical components that could be used in place of one another. Interchangeable parts simplified both the assembly and repair of products.

By the early 1900s, manufacturers had introduced another new method of production, the **assembly line.** Workers on an assembly line add parts to a product that moves along a belt from one work station to the next. A different person performs each task along the assembly line. This division of labor in an assembly line, like interchangeable parts, made production faster and cheaper, lowering the price of goods. Although dividing labor into separate tasks proved to be more efficient, it took much of the joy out of the work itself.

Electricity Lights Up Cities
This early dynamo (above) generated enough electricity to power lights in factories. Electricity changed life outdoors as well. *Judging from this print, how did electricity make life easier for people in the city?*

 **Checkpoint** What was the dynamo's impact on the Industrial Revolution?

The Modern Office

The Bessemer process prepared the way for the use of steel in building construction. Before steel, frameworks consisted of heavy iron. Steel provided a much lighter framework and enabled the construction of taller buildings. The first skyscrapers were between 10 and 20 stories high. They were built in the United States in the 1880s to house large corporations.

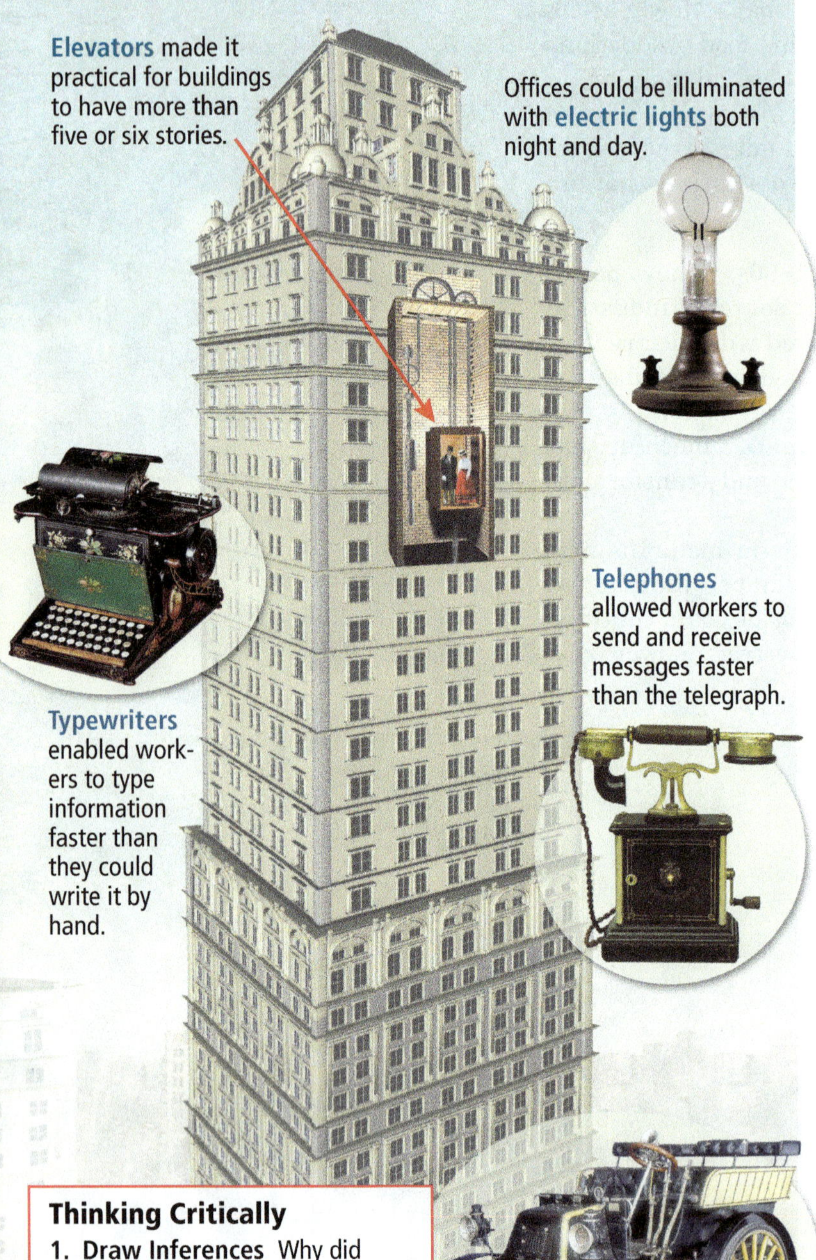

Thinking Critically

1. **Draw Inferences** Why did industrialization create a need for skyscrapers?
2. **Synthesize Information** What invention do you think had the most impact on offices? Explain.

Transportation and Communication Advances

During the Industrial Revolution, transportation and communications were transformed by technology. Steamships replaced sailing ships, and railroad building took off. In Europe and North America, rail lines connected inland cities and seaports, mining regions and industrial centers. In the United States, a transcontinental railroad provided rail service from the Atlantic to the Pacific. In the same way, Russians built the Trans-Siberian Railroad, linking Moscow in European Russia to Vladivostok on the Pacific. Railroad tunnels and bridges crossed the Alps in Europe and the Andes in South America. Passengers and goods rode on rails in India, China, Egypt, and South Africa.

The Automobile Age Begins The transportation revolution took a new turn when a German engineer, Nikolaus Otto, invented a gasoline-powered internal combustion engine. In 1886, Karl Benz received a patent for the first automobile, which had three wheels. A year later, Gottlieb Daimler (DYM lur) introduced the first four-wheeled automobile. People laughed at the "horseless carriages," but they quickly transformed transportation.

The French nosed out the Germans as early automakers. Then the American Henry Ford started making models that reached the breathtaking speed of 25 miles per hour. In the early 1900s, Ford began using the assembly line to mass-produce cars, making the United States a leader in the automobile industry.

Airplanes Take Flight The internal combustion engine powered more than cars. Motorized threshers and reapers boosted farm production. Even more dramatically, the internal combustion engine made possible sustained, pilot-controlled flight. In 1903, American bicycle makers Orville and Wilbur Wright designed and flew a flimsy airplane at Kitty Hawk, North Carolina. Although their flying machine stayed aloft for only a few seconds, it ushered in the air age.

Soon, daredevil pilots were flying airplanes across the English Channel and over the Alps. Commercial passenger travel, however, would not begin until the 1920s.

Rapid Communication A revolution in communications also made the world smaller. An American inventor, Samuel F. B. Morse, developed

One View of Big Business To some critics, the growth of monopolies had a dangerous effect on society. This 1899 American cartoon shows a monopoly as an octopus-like monster. *Do you think this cartoonist favored or opposed government regulation of business? Explain.*

In their pursuit of profit, ruthless business leaders destroyed competing companies. With the competition gone, they were free to raise prices. Sometimes, a group of corporations would join forces and form a **cartel,** an association to fix prices, set production quotas, or control markets. In Germany, a single cartel fixed prices for 170 coal mines.

Move Toward Regulation The rise of big business and the creation of such great wealth sparked a stormy debate. Some people saw the Krupps and Rockefellers as "captains of industry" and praised their vision and skills. They pointed out that capitalists invested their wealth in worldwide ventures, such as railroad building, that employed thousands of workers and added to the general prosperity.

To others, the aggressive magnates were "robber barons." Destroying competition, critics argued, damaged the free-enterprise system, or the laissez-faire economy. Reformers called for laws to prevent monopolies and regulate large corporations. Despite questionable business practices, big business found support from many government leaders. By the early 1900s, some governments did move against monopolies. However, the political and economic power of business leaders often hindered efforts at regulation.

✓ **Checkpoint** Why were big business leaders "captains of industry" to some, but "robber barons" to others?

Assessment

Terms, People, and Places

1. For each term, person, or place listed at the beginning of the section, write a sentence explaining its significance.

Note Taking

2. **Reading Skill: Identify Main Ideas** Use your completed chart to answer the Focus Question: How did science, technology, and big business promote industrial growth?

Comprehension and Critical Thinking

3. **Summarize** How did the Industrial Revolution spread in the 1800s?
4. **Draw Conclusions** How did technology help industry expand?
5. **Recognize Cause and Effect** How did the need for capital lead to new business organizations and methods?
6. **Predict** How might government change as a result of industrialization?

● **Writing About History**

Quick Write: Define a Problem Choose one topic from this section that you could use to write a problem-and-solution essay. For example, you could write about the impact of powerful monopolies. Make a list of details, facts, and examples that define the problems that monopolies pose to a free market.

Charles Dickens with an illustration from one of his serialized novels

London Fog

Between 1850 and 1900, London's population more than doubled, rising from about 2.6 million people to more than 6.5 million people. With the rapid population growth came increased pollution and health problems:

> It was a foggy day in London, and the fog was heavy and dark. Animate [living] London, with smarting eyes and irritated lungs, was blinking, wheezing, and choking; inanimate [nonliving] London was a sooty spectre, divided in purpose between being visible and invisible, and so being wholly neither.
> —Charles Dickens, *Our Mutual Friend*

Focus Question How did the Industrial Revolution change life in the cities?

The Rise of the Cities

Objectives
- Summarize the impact of medical advances in the late 1800s.
- Describe how cities had changed by 1900.
- Explain how working-class struggles led to improved conditions for workers.

Terms, People, and Places

germ theory	Joseph Lister
Louis Pasteur	urban renewal
Robert Koch	mutual-aid society
Florence Nightingale	standard of living

Note Taking

Reading Skill: Identify Supporting Details As you read, look for the main ideas and supporting details and how they relate to each other. Use the format below to create an outline of the section.

```
I. Medicine and the population explosion
   A. The fight against disease
      1.
      2.
   B.
II.
```

The population explosion that had begun during the 1700s continued through the 1800s. Cities grew as rural people streamed into urban areas. By the end of the century, European and American cities had begun to take on many of the features of cities today.

Medicine Contributes to the Population Explosion

Between 1800 and 1900, the population of Europe more than doubled. This rapid growth was not due to larger families. In fact, families in most industrializing countries had fewer children. Instead, populations soared because the death rate fell. Nutrition improved, thanks in part to improved methods of farming, food storage, and distribution. Medical advances and improvements in public sanitation also slowed death rates.

The Fight Against Disease Since the 1600s, scientists had known of microscopic organisms, or microbes. Some scientists speculated that certain microbes might cause specific infectious diseases. Yet most doctors scoffed at this **germ theory.** Not until 1870 did French chemist **Louis Pasteur** (pas TUR) clearly show the link between microbes and disease. Pasteur went on to make other major contributions to medicine, including the development of vaccines against rabies and anthrax. He also discovered a process called pasteurization that killed disease-carrying microbes in milk.

Florence Nightingale

When Florence Nightingale (1820–1910) arrived at a British military hospital in the Crimea in 1854, she was horrified by what she saw. The sick and wounded lay on bare ground. With no sanitation and a shortage of food, some 60 percent of all patients died. But Nightingale was a fighter. Bullying the military and medical staff, she soon had every available person cleaning barracks, digging latrines, doing laundry, and caring for the wounded. Six months later, the death rate had dropped to 2 percent.

Back in England, Nightingale was hailed as a saint. Ballads were even written about her. She took advantage of her popularity and connections to pressure the government for reforms.

How did Nightingale achieve reforms in British army hospitals?

In the 1880s, the German doctor **Robert Koch** identified the bacterium that caused tuberculosis, a respiratory disease that claimed about 30 million human lives in the 1800s. The search for a tuberculosis cure, however, took half a century. By 1914, yellow fever and malaria had been traced to microbes carried by mosquitoes.

As people understood how germs caused disease, they bathed and changed their clothes more often. In European cities, better hygiene helped decrease the rate of disease.

Hospital Care Improves In the early 1840s, anesthesia was first used to relieve pain during surgery. The use of anesthetics allowed doctors to experiment with operations that had never before been possible.

Yet, throughout the century, hospitals could be dangerous places. Surgery was performed with dirty instruments in dank rooms. Often, a patient would survive an operation, only to die days later of infection. For the poor, being admitted to a hospital was often a death sentence. Wealthy or middle-class patients insisted on treatment in their own homes.

"The very first requirement in a hospital," said British nurse **Florence Nightingale,** "is that it should do the sick no harm." As an army nurse during the Crimean War, Nightingale insisted on better hygiene in field hospitals. After the war, she worked to introduce sanitary measures in British hospitals. She also founded the world's first school of nursing.

The English surgeon **Joseph Lister** discovered how antiseptics prevented infection. He insisted that surgeons sterilize their instruments and wash their hands before operating. Eventually, the use of antiseptics drastically reduced deaths from infection.

 **Checkpoint** Which factors caused population rates to soar between 1800 and 1900?

City Life Changes

As industrialization progressed, cities came to dominate the West. City life, as old as civilization itself, underwent dramatic changes in Europe and the United States.

City Landscapes Change Growing wealth and industrialization altered the basic layout of European cities. City planners created spacious new squares and boulevards. They lined these avenues with government buildings, offices, department stores, and theaters.

The most extensive **urban renewal,** or rebuilding of the poor areas of a city, took place in Paris in the 1850s. Georges Haussmann, chief planner for Napoleon III, destroyed many tangled medieval streets full of tenement housing. In their place, he built wide boulevards and splendid public buildings. The project put many people to work, decreasing the threat of social unrest. The wide boulevards also made it harder for rebels to put up barricades and easier for troops to reach any part of the city.

Gradually, settlement patterns shifted. In most American cities, the rich lived in pleasant neighborhoods on the outskirts of the city. The poor crowded into slums near the city center, within reach of factories. Trolley lines made it possible to live in one part of the city and work in another.

Sidewalks, Sewers, and Skyscrapers Paved streets made urban areas much more livable. First gas lamps, and then electric street lights <u>illuminated</u> the night, increasing safety. Cities organized police forces and expanded fire protection.

Beneath the streets, sewage systems made cities much healthier places to live. City planners knew that clean water supplies and better sanitation methods were needed to combat epidemics of cholera and tuberculosis. In Paris, sewer lines expanded from 87 miles (139 kilometers) in 1852 to more than 750 miles (1200 kilometers) by 1911. The massive new sewer systems of London and Paris were costly, but they cut death rates dramatically.

By 1900, architects were using steel to construct soaring buildings. American architects like Louis Sullivan pioneered a new structure, the skyscraper. In large cities, single-family middle-class homes gave way to multistory apartment buildings.

Slum Conditions Despite efforts to improve cities, urban life remained harsh for the poor. Some working-class families could afford better clothing, newspapers, or tickets to a music hall. But they went home to small, cramped row houses or tenements in overcrowded neighborhoods.

In the worst tenements, whole families were often crammed into a single room. Unemployment or illness meant lost wages that could ruin a family. High rates of crime and alcoholism were a constant curse. Conditions had improved somewhat from the early Industrial Revolution, but slums remained a fact of city life.

Jacob Riis, a police reporter, photographer, and social activist in New York City published *How the Other Half Lives* in 1890 in an effort to expose the horrible living conditions of the city slums and tenements. Conditions among the urban working class in Britain (right) were similar to those in New York described by Riis:

Primary Source

“ Look into any of these houses, everywhere the same . . . . Here is a "flat" or "parlor" and two pitch-dark coops called bedrooms. . . . One, two, three beds are there, if the old boxes and heaps of foul straw can be called by that name; a broken stove with crazy pipe from which the smoke leaks at every joint, a table of rough boards propped up on boxes, piles of rubbish in the corner. The closeness and smell are appalling. How many people sleep here? The woman with the red bandanna shakes her head sullenly, but the bare-legged girl with the bright face counts on her fingers. . . "Six, sir!" ”

Analyze Cause and Effect The long-term effects of the Industrial Revolution touched nearly every aspect of life. *Identify two social and two economic effects of the Industrial Revolution.*

The Lure of the City Despite their drawbacks, cities attracted millions. New residents were drawn as much by the excitement as by the promise of work. For tourists, too, cities were centers of action.

Music halls, opera houses, and theaters provided entertainment for every taste. Museums and libraries offered educational opportunities. Sports, from tennis to bare-knuckle boxing, drew citizens of all classes. Few of these enjoyments were available in country villages.

 **Checkpoint** How did industrialization change the face of cities?

The Working Class Advances

Workers tried to improve the harsh conditions of industrial life. They protested low wages, long hours, unsafe conditions, and the constant threat of unemployment. At first, business owners and governments tried to silence protesters. By midcentury, however, workers began to make progress.

Labor Unions Begin to Grow Workers formed **mutual-aid societies,** self-help groups to aid sick or injured workers. Men and women joined socialist parties or organized unions. The revolutions of 1830 and 1848 left vivid images of worker discontent, which governments could not ignore.

By the late 1800s, most Western countries had granted all men the vote. Workers also won the right to organize unions to bargain on their behalf. Germany legalized labor unions in 1869. Britain, Austria, and France followed. By 1900, Britain had about three million union members, and Germany had about two million. In France, membership grew from 140,000 in 1890 to over a million in 1912.

The main tactic of unions was the strike, or work stoppage. Workers used strikes to demand better working conditions, wage increases, or other benefits from their employers. Violence was often a result of strikes, particularly if employers tried to continue operating their businesses without the striking workers. Employers often called in the police to stop strikes.

Pressured by unions, reformers, and working-class voters, governments passed laws to regulate working conditions. Early laws forbade employers to hire children under the age of ten. Later, laws were passed outlawing child labor entirely and banning the employment of women in mines. Other laws limited work hours and improved safety. By 1909, British coal miners had won an eight-hour day, setting a standard for workers in other countries. In Germany, and then elsewhere, Western governments established old-age pensions, as well as disability insurance for workers who were hurt or became ill. These programs protected workers from poverty once they were no longer able to work.

Family Life and Leisure
With standards of living rising, families could pursue activities such as going to the movies. This 1896 French poster (left) advertises the Cinématographe Lumière (loom YEHR), the most successful motion-picture camera and projector of its day. *What does the clothing of the people in the poster suggest about their social rank?*

Standards of Living Rise Wages varied throughout the industrialized world, with unskilled laborers earning less than skilled workers. Women received less than half the pay of men doing the same work. Farm laborers barely scraped by during the economic slump of the late 1800s. Periods of unemployment brought desperate hardships to industrial workers and helped boost union membership.

Overall, though, standards of living for workers did rise. The **standard of living** measures the quality and availability of necessities and comforts in a society. Families ate more varied diets, lived in better homes, and dressed in inexpensive, mass-produced clothing. Advances in medicine improved health. Some workers moved to the suburbs, traveling to work on subways and trolleys. Still, the gap between workers and the middle class widened.

✔ **Checkpoint** How did workers try to improve their living and working conditions?

2 Assessment

Terms, People, and Places

1. For each term, person, or place listed at the beginning of the section, write a sentence explaining its significance.

Note Taking

2. **Reading Skill: Identify Supporting Details** Use your completed outline to answer the Focus Question: How did the Industrial Revolution change life in the cities?

Comprehension and Critical Thinking

3. **Recognize Cause and Effect** Why did the rate of population growth increase in the late 1800s?

4. **Summarize** What are three ways that city life changed in the 1800s?

5. **Analyze Information** What laws helped workers in the late 1800s?

6. **Synthesize Information** How did the rise of the cities challenge the economic and social order of the time?

● **Writing About History**

Quick Write: Brainstorm Possible Solutions Choose one topic from this section, such as the hardships of city life, about which you could write a problem-solution essay. Use the text and your own knowledge to create a list of possible solutions to the problem that you've chosen to write about. Next, organize your list to rank the solutions from most effective to least effective.

Electricity's Impact on Daily Life

Few technologies have transformed daily life as dramatically as electrification. Electric power lit up city streets, helped to improve workplace productivity, revolutionized life at home, and modernized rural farms and businesses. Although electrification began in urban areas of Europe and the United States in the 1880s, it took several decades to spread to rural areas. Electrification remains an ongoing process in developing nations today.

Installing insulators on an electric pole in 1940

Electricity Customers in England and Wales

Year	Customers in Millions
1920	0.9
1930	3.5
1940	9.6
1950	12.0
1960	15.5
1970	18.3
1980	20.3

SOURCE: Department of Trade and Industry, United Kingdom

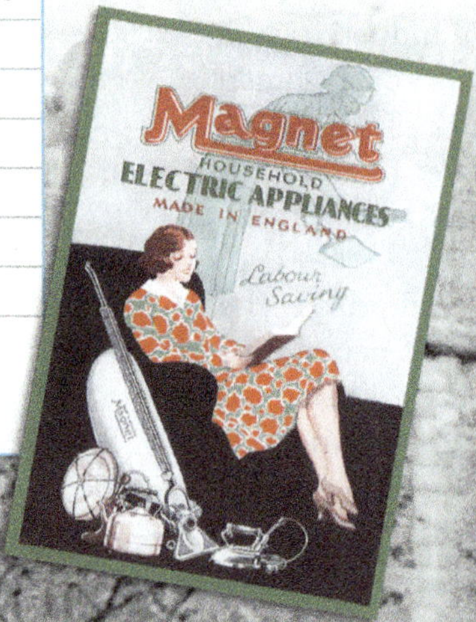

Advertisement for household electrical appliances

An electric streetcar in England, around 1900

Poster celebrating the use of hydroelectric power in the former Soviet Union

Although only two percent of Japanese homes had electric power in 1907, nearly 90% had electric lighting by 1927. Above, the first electric streetlight in Tokyo's Ginza district draws a crowd.

Electric Generation Stations

Country	Year	Number of Stations
Russia	1913	220
Germany	1913	4,040
Great Britain	1912	568
Sweden	NA*	440
United States	1912	5,221

*NA Not available
SOURCE: *The Electrification of Russia, 1880–1926*

American electric mixer

The 1931 horror film *Frankenstein* exploited people's fear of electricity.

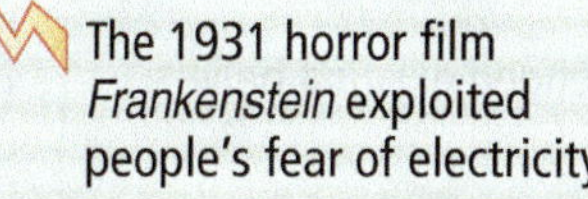

History Interactive

For: interactive map, audio, and more
Visit: PHSchool.com
Web Code: nap-2101

Thinking Critically

1. **Chart Skills** Which country had the fewest number of electric generation stations by 1913? Which country had the largest number? Why was there such a large difference between the two countries?
2. **Draw Conclusions** How did electricity change daily life?

Women's suffrage banner

Suffragette arrested in London, 1914

Votes for Women

After years of peacefully protesting the British government's refusal to allow women to vote, some activists turned to confrontation:

66 We have been driven to the conclusion that only through legislation can any improvement be effected, and that that legislation can never be effected until we have the same power as men have to bring pressure to bear upon our representatives and upon Governments to give us the necessary legislation. . . . We are here not because we are law-breakers; we are here in our efforts to become law-makers. 99
—Emmeline Pankhurst, October 21, 1908

Focus Question How did the Industrial Revolution change the old social order and long-held traditions in the Western world?

Changing Attitudes and Values

Objectives
- Explain what values shaped the new social order.
- Understand how women and educators sought change.
- Learn how science challenged existing beliefs.

Terms, People, and Places

cult of domesticity	John Dalton
temperance movement	Charles Darwin
Elizabeth Cady Stanton	racism
women's suffrage	social gospel
Sojourner Truth	

Note Taking

Reading Skill: Identify Supporting Details As you read, create a table listing new attitudes and values in the left-hand column. List the supporting details in the right-hand column.

Changes in Social Order and Values	
Issue	**Change**
• New social order	•
• Rights for women	•
•	•

Demand for women's rights was one of many issues that challenged the traditional social order in the late 1800s. By then, in many countries, the middle class—aspiring to upper-class wealth and privilege—increasingly came to dominate society.

A New Social Order Arises

The Industrial Revolution slowly changed the social order in the Western world. For centuries, the two main classes were nobles and peasants. Their roles were defined by their relationship to the land. While middle-class merchants, artisans, and lawyers played important roles, they still had a secondary position in society. With the spread of industry, a more complex social structure emerged.

Three Social Classes Emerge By the late 1800s, Western Europe's new upper class included very rich business families. Wealthy entrepreneurs married into aristocratic families, gaining the status of noble titles. Nobles needed the money brought by the industrial rich to support their lands and lifestyle.

Below this tiny elite, a growing middle class was pushing its way up the social ladder. Its highest rungs were filled with mid-level business people and professionals such as doctors and scientists. With comfortable incomes, they enjoyed a wide range of material goods. Next came the lower middle class, which included teachers and office workers. They struggled to keep up with their "betters,"

Workers and peasants were at the base of the social ladder. In highly industrialized Britain, workers made up more than 30 percent of the population in 1900. In Western Europe and the United States, the number of farmworkers dropped, but many families still worked the land. The rural population was higher in eastern and southern Europe, where industrialization was more limited.

Middle-Class Tastes and Values By midcentury, the modern middle class had developed its own way of life. A strict code of etiquette governed social behavior. Rules dictated how to dress for every occasion, how to give a dinner party, how to pay a social call, when to write letters, and how long to mourn for dead relatives.

Parents strictly supervised their children, who were expected to be "seen but not heard." A child who misbehaved was considered to reflect badly on the entire family. Servants, too, were seen as a reflection of their employers. Even a small middle-class household was expected to have at least a cook and a housemaid.

The Ideal Home Within the family, the division of labor between wife and husband changed. Earlier, middle-class women had helped run family businesses out of the home. By the later 1800s, most middle-class husbands went to work in an office or shop. A successful husband was one who earned enough to keep his wife at home. Women spent their time raising children, directing servants, and doing religious or charitable service.

Books, magazines, and popular songs supported a **cult of domesticity** that idealized women and the home. Sayings like "home, sweet home" were stitched into needlework and hung on parlor walls. The ideal woman was seen as a tender, self-sacrificing caregiver who provided a nest for her children and a peaceful refuge for her husband to escape from the hardships of the working world.

This ideal rarely applied to the lower classes. Working-class women labored for low pay in garment factories or worked as domestic servants. Young women might leave domestic service after they married, but often had to seek other employment. Despite long days working for wages, they were still expected to take full responsibility for child care and homemaking.

✔ **Checkpoint** How had the social order changed by the late 1800s?

Tin toys (at right and below), about 1890

Domestic Life in the 1800s

During the Industrial Age, the middle-class nuclear family lived in a large house with a parlor like the one above, or perhaps in one of the new apartment houses. Rooms were crammed with large overstuffed furniture, and paintings and photographs lined the walls. Clothing reflected middle-class tastes for luxury and respectability. For the first time, women began spending more time buying household items than producing them. Women shopped at stores and through mail-order catalogs (below) that were geared toward attracting their business.

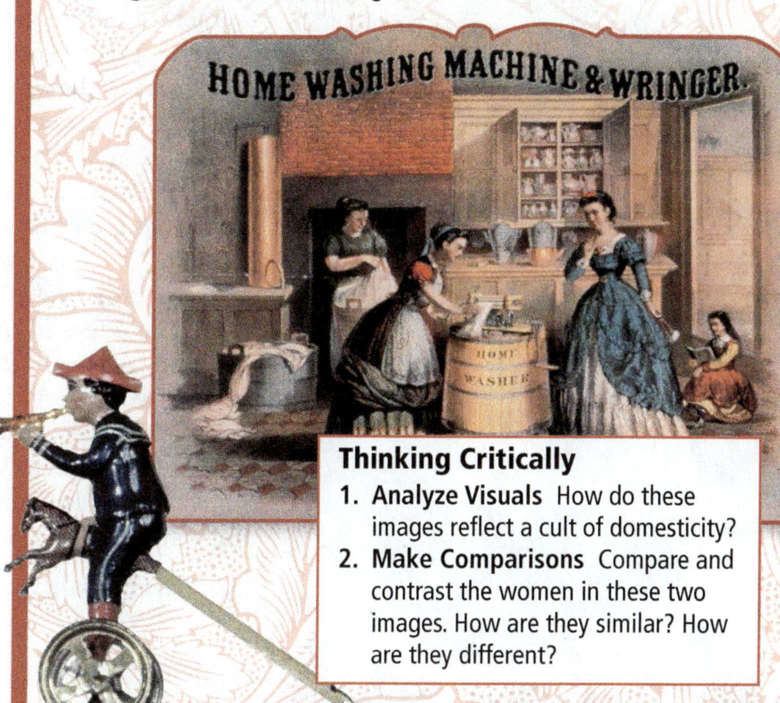

Thinking Critically
1. **Analyze Visuals** How do these images reflect a cult of domesticity?
2. **Make Comparisons** Compare and contrast the women in these two images. How are they similar? How are they different?

Women Work for Rights

Some individual women and women's groups protested restrictions on women. They sought a broad range of rights. Across Europe and the United States, politically active women campaigned for fairness in marriage, divorce, and property laws. Women's groups also supported the **temperance movement,** a campaign to limit or ban the use of alcoholic beverages. Temperance leaders argued not only that drinking threatened family life, but that banning it was important for a productive and efficient workforce.

These reformers faced many obstacles. In Europe and the United States, women could not vote. They were barred from most schools and had little, if any, protection under the law. A woman's husband or father controlled all of her property.

Early Voices Before 1850, some women—mostly from the middle class—had campaigned for the abolition of slavery. In the process, they realized the severe restrictions on their own lives. In the United States, Lucretia Mott, **Elizabeth Cady Stanton,** and Susan B. Anthony crusaded against slavery before organizing a movement for women's rights.

Many women broke the barriers that kept them out of universities and professions. By the late 1800s, a few women trained as doctors or lawyers. Others became explorers, researchers, or inventors, often without recognition. For example, Julia Brainerd Hall worked with her brother to develop an aluminum-producing process. Their company became hugely successful, but Charles Hall received almost all of the credit.

The Suffrage Struggle By the late 1800s, married women in some countries had won the right to control their own property. The struggle for political rights proved far more difficult. In the United States, the Seneca Falls Convention of 1848 demanded that women be granted the right to vote. In Europe, groups dedicated to **women's suffrage,** or women's right to vote, emerged in the later 1800s.

Among men, some liberals and socialists supported women's suffrage. In general, though, suffragists faced intense opposition. Some critics claimed that women were too emotional to be allowed to vote. Others argued that women needed to be "protected" from grubby politics or that a woman's place was in the home, not in government. To such claims, **Sojourner Truth,** an African American suffragist, is believed to have replied, "Nobody ever helps me into carriages, or over mudpuddles, or gives me any best place! And ain't I a woman?"

On the edges of the Western world, women made faster strides. In New Zealand, Australia, and some western territories of the United States, women won the vote by the early 1900s. There, women who had "tamed the frontier" alongside men were not dismissed as weak and helpless. In the United States, Wyoming became the first state to grant women the right to vote. In Europe and most of the United States, however, the suffrage struggle succeeded only after World War I.

✓ **Checkpoint** What were the arguments against women's suffrage?

African American suffragist Sojourner Truth

Growth of Public Education

By the late 1800s, reformers persuaded many governments to set up public schools and require basic education for all children. Teaching "the three Rs"—reading, writing, and 'rithmetic—was thought to produce better citizens. In addition, industrialized societies recognized the need for a literate workforce. Schools taught punctuality, obedience to authority, disciplined work habits, and patriotism. In European schools, children also received basic religious education.

Public Education Improves At first, elementary schools were primitive. Many teachers had little schooling themselves. In rural areas, students attended class only during the times when they were not needed on the farm or in their parents' shops.

By the late 1800s, more and more children were in school, and the quality of elementary education improved. Teachers received training at Normal Schools, where the latest "norms and standards" of educational practices were taught. Beginning in 1879, schools to train teachers were established in France. In England, schooling girls and boys between the ages of five and ten became compulsory after 1881. Also, governments began to expand secondary schools, known as high schools in the United States. In secondary schools, students learned the "classical languages," Latin and Greek, along with history and mathematics.

In general, only middle-class families could afford to have their sons attend these schools, which trained students for more serious study or for government jobs. Middle-class girls were sent to school primarily in the hope that they might marry well and become better wives and mothers. Education for girls did not include subjects such as science, mathematics, or physical education because they were not seen as necessary subjects for girls to learn.

Higher Education Expands Colleges and universities expanded in this period, too. Most university students were the sons of middle- or upper-class families. The university curriculum emphasized ancient history and languages, philosophy, religion, and law. By the late 1800s, universities added courses in the sciences, especially in chemistry and physics. At the same time, engineering schools trained students who would have the knowledge and skills to build the new industrial society.

Some women sought greater educational opportunities. By the 1840s, a few small colleges for women opened, including Bedford College in England and Mount Holyoke in the United States. In 1863, the British reformer Emily Davies campaigned for female students to be allowed to take the entrance examinations for Cambridge University. She succeeded, but as late as 1897, male Cambridge students rioted against granting degrees to women.

✔ **Checkpoint** Why did more children attend school in the late 1800s than before?

Public Education
Before 1870, the only formal education available for British children was in religious schools or "ragged schools," which taught poor children basic skills, such as reading. The Industrial Revolution changed that as it created a growing need for people to be better educated. *How does this 1908 photo of a science class in London illustrate the changes that had taken place in the British educational system?*

Science Takes New Directions

Science in the service of industry brought great changes in the later 1800s. At the same time, researchers advanced startling theories about the natural world. Their new ideas challenged long-held beliefs.

Atomic Theory Develops A crucial breakthrough in chemistry came in the early 1800s when the English Quaker schoolteacher **John Dalton** developed modern atomic theory. The ancient Greeks had <u>speculated</u> that all matter was made of tiny particles called atoms. Dalton showed that each element has its own kind of atoms. Earlier theories put forth the idea that all atoms were basically alike. Dalton also showed how different kinds of atoms combine to make all chemical substances. In 1869, the Russian chemist Dmitri Mendeleyev (men duh LAY ef) drew up a table that grouped elements according to their atomic weights. His table became the basis for the periodic table of elements used today.

Debating the Earth's Age The new science of geology opened avenues of debate. In *Principles of Geology*, Charles Lyell offered evidence to

Vocabulary Builder

<u>speculate</u>—(SPEK yuh layt) *v.* to think about

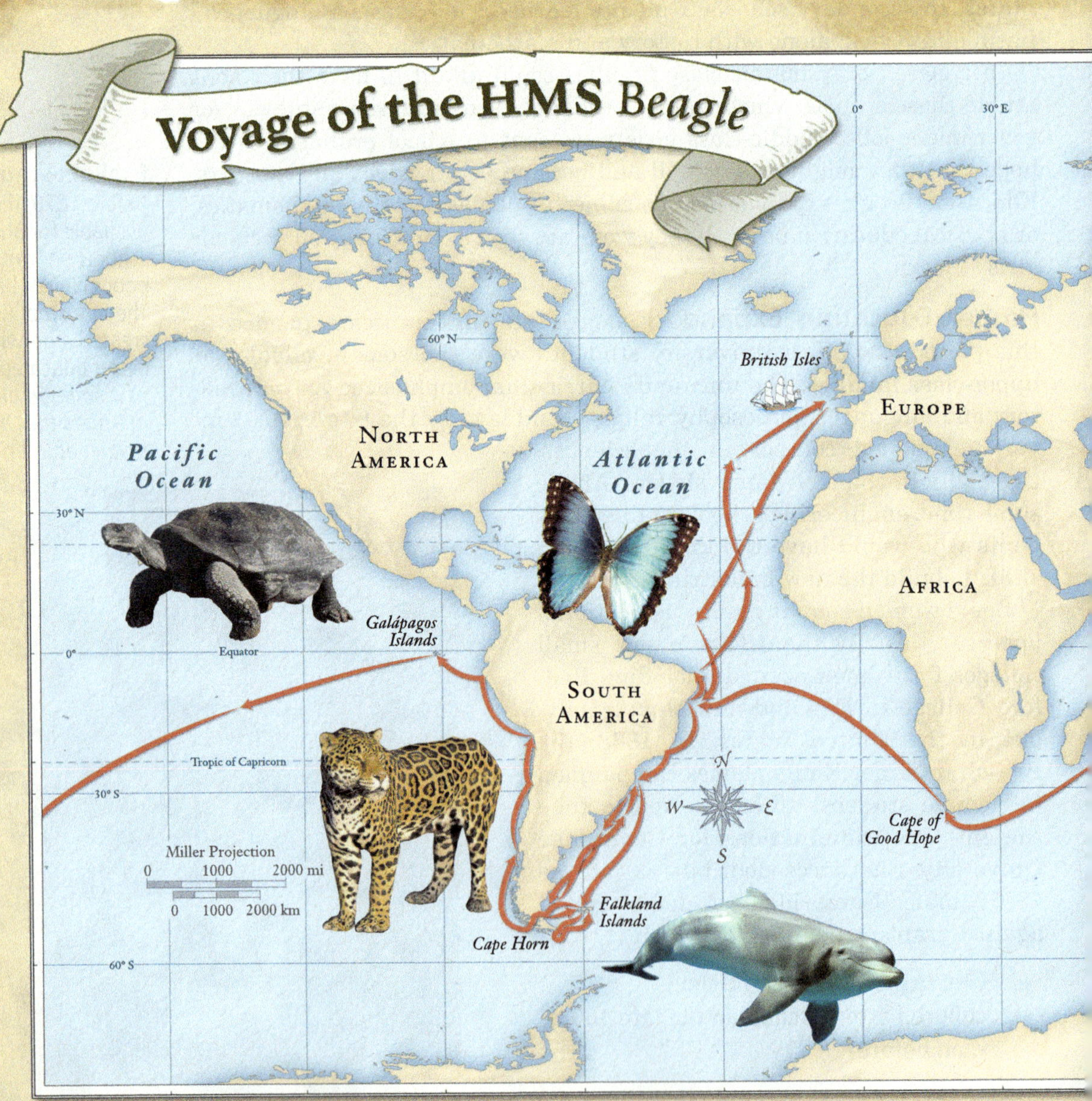

show that Earth had formed over millions of years. His successors concluded that Earth was at least two billion years old and that life had not appeared until long after Earth was formed. These ideas did not seem to agree with biblical accounts of creation.

Archaeology added other pieces to an emerging debate about the origins of life on Earth. In 1856, workers in Germany accidentally uncovered fossilized Neanderthal bones. Later scholars found fossils of other early modern humans. These archaeologists had limited evidence and often drew mistaken conclusions. But as more discoveries were made, scholars developed new ideas about early humans and their ancestors.

Darwin's Theory of Natural Selection The most <u>controversial</u> new idea came from the British naturalist **Charles Darwin.** In 1859, after years of research, he published *On the Origin of Species.* Darwin argued that all forms of life, including human beings, had evolved into their present state over millions of years. To explain the long, slow process of evolution, he put forward his theory of natural selection.

Darwin adopted Thomas Malthus's idea that all plants and animals produced more offspring than the food supply could support. As a result,

Vocabulary Builder

<u>controversial</u>—(kahn truh VUR shul) *adj.* that is or can be argued about or debated

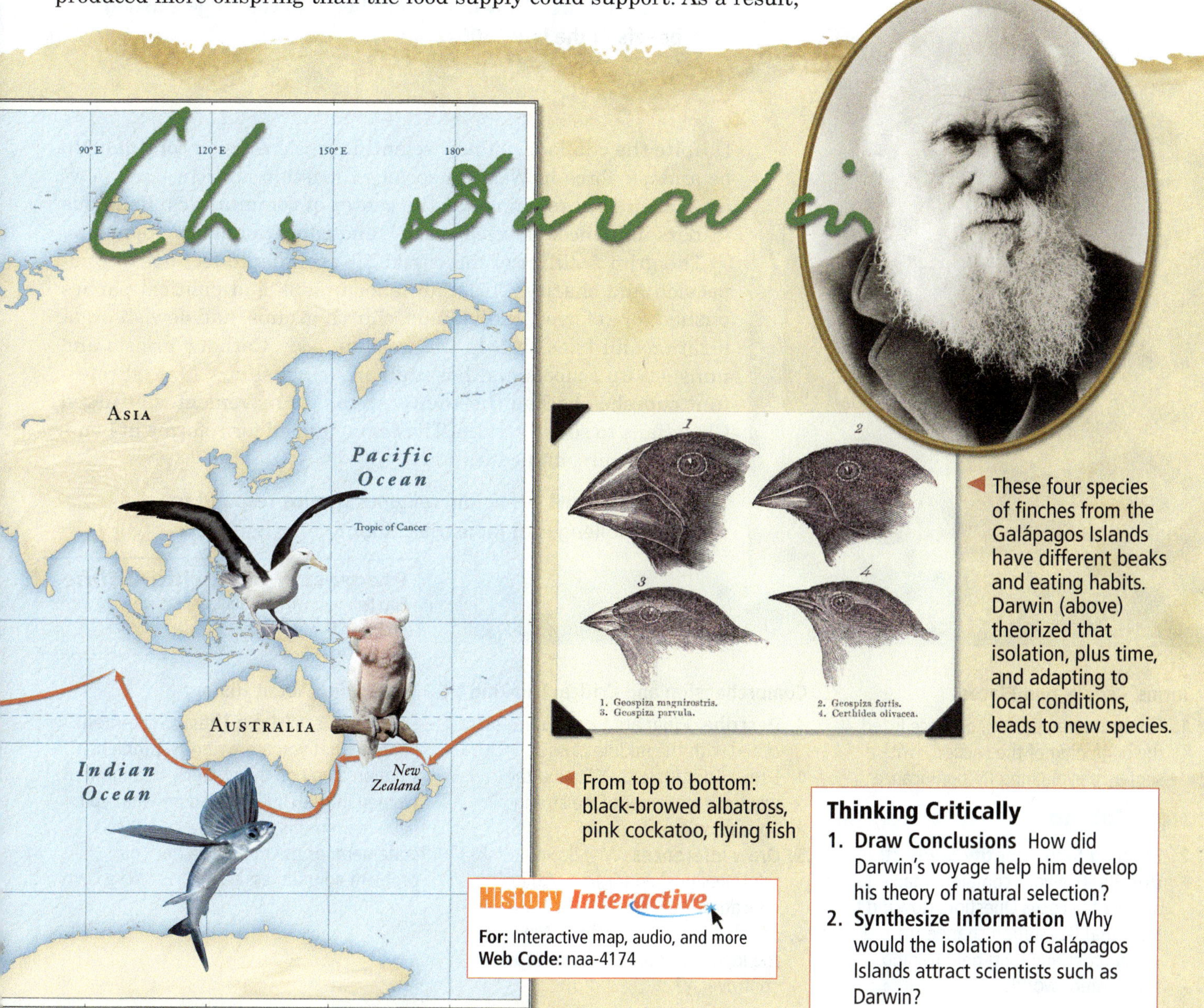

These four species of finches from the Galápagos Islands have different beaks and eating habits. Darwin (above) theorized that isolation, plus time, and adapting to local conditions, leads to new species.

From top to bottom: black-browed albatross, pink cockatoo, flying fish

History *Interactive*

For: Interactive map, audio, and more
Web Code: naa-4174

Thinking Critically
1. **Draw Conclusions** How did Darwin's voyage help him develop his theory of natural selection?
2. **Synthesize Information** Why would the isolation of Galápagos Islands attract scientists such as Darwin?

he said, members of each species constantly competed to survive. Natural forces "selected" those with physical traits best adapted to their environment to survive and to pass the trait on to their offspring. This process of natural selection came to be known as "survival of the fittest."

Social Darwinism and Racism Although Darwin himself never promoted any social ideas, some thinkers used his theories to support their own beliefs about society. Applying the idea of survival of the fittest to war and economic competition came to be known as Social Darwinism. Industrial tycoons, argued Social Darwinists, were more "fit" than those they put out of business. War brought progress by weeding out weak nations. Victory was seen as proof of superiority.

Social Darwinism encouraged racism, the unscientific belief that one racial group is superior to another. By the late 1800s, many Europeans and Americans claimed that the success of Western civilization was due to the supremacy of the white race. As you will read, such powerful ideas would have a long-lasting impact on world history.

✔ **Checkpoint** How did science begin to challenge existing beliefs in the late 1800s?

Religion in an Urban Age

Despite the challenge of new scientific ideas, religion continued to be a major force in Western society. Christian churches and Jewish synagogues remained at the center of communities. Religious leaders influenced political, social, and educational developments.

The grim realities of industrial life stimulated feelings of compassion and charity. Christian labor unions and political parties pushed for reforms. Individuals, church groups, and Jewish organizations all tried to help the working poor. Catholic priests and nuns set up schools and hospitals in urban slums. Many Protestant churches backed the social gospel, a movement that urged Christians to social service. They campaigned for reforms in housing, healthcare, and education.

✔ **Checkpoint** How did religious groups respond to the challenges of industrialization?

The Salvation Army
By 1878, William and Catherine Booth had set up the Salvation Army in London to spread Christian teachings and provide social services. Their daughter, Evangeline (below), stands in front of one the kettles used to gather funds for the needy. *What services did religious organizations provide?*

Progress Monitoring *Online*
For: Self-quiz with vocabulary practice
Web Code: naa-2131

Terms, People, and Places

1. For each term, person, or place listed at the beginning of the section, write a sentence explaining its significance.

Note Taking

2. **Reading Skill: Identify Supporting Details** Use your completed table to answer the Focus Question: How did the Industrial Revolution change the old social order and long-held traditions in the Western world?

Comprehension and Critical Thinking

3. **Describe** What are three values associated with the middle class?
4. **Draw Conclusions** Why did the women's movement face strong opposition?
5. **Draw Inferences** Why do you think reformers pushed for free public education?
6. **Synthesize Information** Why did the ideas of Charles Darwin cause controversy?

Writing About History

Quick Write: Write a Thesis Statement Imagine that you are writing a problem-solution essay on the unequal treatment of women in the 1800s. Based on what you have read in this section, write a thesis statement, or the main idea, for your problem-solution essay.

Albert Bierstadt, *Hetch Hetchy Canyon,* 1875

Arts in the Industrial Age

Objectives

- Understand what themes shaped romantic art, literature, and music.
- Explain how realists responded to the industrialized, urban world.
- Describe how the visual arts changed.

Terms, People, and Places

William Wordsworth	realism
William Blake	Charles Dickens
romanticism	Gustave Courbet
Lord Byron	Louis Daguerre
Victor Hugo	impressionism
Ludwig van Beethoven	Claude Monet
	Vincent van Gogh

Note Taking

Reading Skill: Identify Supporting Details Fill in a table like the one below with details about the artistic movements in the 1800s.

Major Artistic Movements of the 1800s		
Movement	**Goals/ Characteristics**	**Major Figures**
Romanticism	• Rebellion against reason	• Wordsworth
Realism	•	•
Impressionism	•	•

William Wordsworth, along with **William Blake,** Samuel Taylor Coleridge, and Percy Bysshe Shelley among others, was part of a cultural movement called romanticism. From about 1750 to 1850, romanticism shaped Western literature and arts.

The Romantic Revolt Against Reason

Romanticism does not refer to romance in the sense of an affectionate relationship, but rather to an artistic style emphasizing imagination, freedom, and emotion. Romanticism was a reaction to the neoclassical writers of the Enlightenment, who had turned to classical Greek and Roman literature and ideals that stressed order, harmony, reason, and emotional restraint. In contrast to Enlightenment literature, the works of romantic writers included simple, direct language, intense feelings, and a glorification of nature. Artists, composers, and architects were also followers of the movement.

The Romantic Hero Romantic writers created a new kind of hero—a mysterious, melancholy figure who felt out of step with society. "My joys, my grief, my passions, and my powers, / Made me a stranger," wrote Britain's George Gordon, **Lord Byron.** He himself was a larger-than-life figure equal to those he created. After a rebellious, wandering life, he joined Greek forces battling for freedom. When he died of a fever there, his legend bloomed. In fact, public interest in his poetry and adventures was so great that moody, isolated romantic heroes came to be described as "Byronic."

Ludwig van Beethoven

An accomplished musician by age 12, composer Ludwig van Beethoven (1770–1827) agonized over every note of every composition. The result was stunning music that expresses intense emotion. The famous opening of his Fifth Symphony conveys the sense of fate knocking at the door. His Sixth Symphony captures a joyful day in the countryside, interrupted by a violent thunderstorm.

Beethoven's career was haunted by perhaps the greatest tragedy a musician can face. In 1798, he began to lose his hearing. Still, he continued to compose music he could hear only in his mind. **How did Beethoven's music reflect romanticism?**

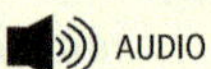 AUDIO

The romantic hero often hid a guilty secret and faced a grim destiny. German writer Johann Wolfgang von Goethe (GUR tuh) wrote the dramatic poem *Faust.* The aging scholar Faust makes a pact with the devil, exchanging his soul for youth. After much agony, Faust wins salvation by accepting his duty to help others. In *Jane Eyre,* British novelist Charlotte Brontë weaves a tale about a quiet governess and her brooding, Byronic employer, whose large mansion conceals a terrifying secret.

Inspired by the Past Romantic writers combined history, legend, and folklore. Sir Walter Scott's novels and ballads evoked the turbulent history of Scottish clans or medieval knights. Alexandre Dumas (doo MAH) and Victor Hugo re-created France's past in novels like *The Three Musketeers* and *The Hunchback of Notre Dame.*

Architects, too, were inspired by old styles and forms. Churches and other buildings, including the British Parliament, were modeled on medieval Gothic styles. To people living in the 1800s, medieval towers and lacy stonework conjured up images of a glorious past.

Music Stirs Emotions Romantic composers also tried to stir deep emotions. Audiences were moved to laughter or tears at Hungarian Franz Liszt's piano playing. The passionate music of German composer Ludwig van Beethoven combined classical forms with a stirring range of sound. He was the first composer to take full advantage of the broad range of instruments in the modern orchestra. In all, Beethoven produced nine symphonies, five piano concertos, a violin concerto, an opera, two masses, and dozens of shorter pieces. To many, he is considered the greatest composer of his day.

Other romantic composers wove traditional folk melodies into their works to glorify their nations' pasts. In his piano works, Frederic Chopin (shoh PAN) used Polish peasant dances to convey the sorrows and joys of people living under foreign occupation.

Romanticism in Art Painters, too, broke free from the discipline and strict rules of the Enlightenment. Landscape painters like J.M.W. Turner sought to capture the beauty and power of nature. Using bold brush strokes and colors, Turner often showed tiny human figures struggling against sea and storm.

Romantics painted many subjects, from simple peasant life to medieval knights to current events. Bright colors conveyed violent energy and emotion. The French painter Eugène Delacroix (deh luh KRWAH) filled his canvases with dramatic action. In *Liberty Leading the People,* the Goddess of Liberty carries the revolutionary tricolor as French citizens rally to the cause.

 **Checkpoint** How did romantic writers, musicians, and artists respond to the Enlightenment?

The Call to Realism

By the mid-1800s, a new artistic movement, realism, took hold in the West. Realism was an attempt to represent the world as it was, without the sentiment associated with romanticism. Realists often focused their work on the harsh side of life in cities or villages. Many writers and artists were committed to improving the lot of the unfortunates whose lives they depicted.

Novels Depict Grim Reality The English novelist **Charles Dickens** vividly portrayed the lives of slum dwellers and factory workers, including children. In *Oliver Twist,* Dickens tells the story of a nine-year-old orphan raised in a grim poorhouse. In response to a request for more food, Oliver is smacked on the head and sent away to work. Later, he runs away to London. There he is taken in by Fagin, a villain who trains homeless children to become pickpockets. The book shocked many middle-class readers with its picture of poverty, mistreatment of children, and urban crime. Yet Dickens' humor and colorful characters made him one of the most popular novelists in the world.

French novelists also portrayed the ills of their time. Victor Hugo, who moved from romantic to realistic novels, revealed how hunger drove a good man to crime and how the law hounded him ever after in *Les Misérables* (lay miz ehr AHB). The novels of Émile Zola painted an even grimmer picture. In *Germinal*, Zola exposed class warfare in the French mining industry. To Zola's characters, neither the Enlightenment's faith in reason nor the romantic movement's feelings mattered at all.

Realism in Drama Norwegian dramatist Henrik Ibsen brought realism to the stage. His plays attacked the hypocrisy he observed around him. *A Doll's House* shows a woman caught in a straitjacket of social rules. In *An Enemy of the People,* a doctor discovers that the water in a local spa is polluted. Because the town's economy depends on its spa, the citizens denounce the doctor and suppress the truth. Ibsen's realistic dramas had a wide influence in Europe and the United States.

Arts Reject Romantic Ideas Painters also represented the realities of their time. Rejecting the romantic <u>emphasis</u> on imagination, they focused on ordinary subjects, especially working-class men and women. "I cannot paint an angel," said the French realist **Gustave Courbet** (koor BAY) "because I have never seen one." Instead, he painted works such as *The Stone Breakers,* which shows two rough laborers on a country road. Later in the century, *The Gross Clinic,* by American painter Thomas Eakins, shocked viewers with its realistic depiction of an autopsy conducted in a medical classroom.

✔ **Checkpoint** How did the realism movement differ from the romantic movement?

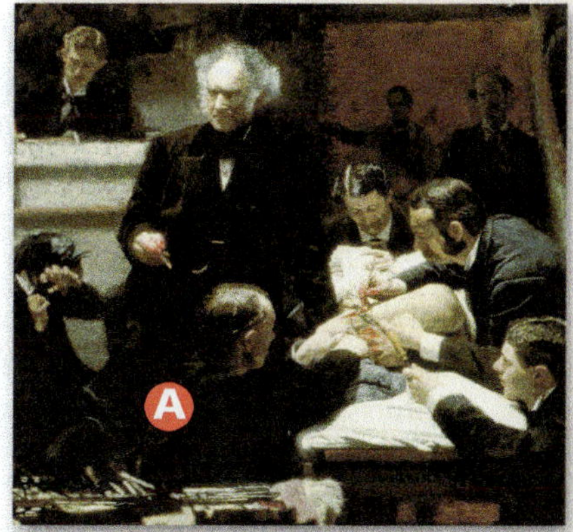

A Thomas Eakins's 1875 painting *The Gross Clinic* depicts the realism of medical school where students learn by performing autopsies. The artist included many realistic elements such as the surgical tools in the foreground and the reaction of the spectator at the far left.

B Edvard Munch's 1898 painting shows an impression of Henrik Ibsen filled with psychological realism, similar to that found in Ibsen's plays.

C This 1896 portrait of Ibsen shows photographic realism in the playwright's appearance and expression.

D Victor Hugo's 1862 novel *Les Misérables* describes the reality of poverty, hunger, and corruption among the poor in Paris. This 1886 poster depicts the novel's main characters: the convict Jean Valjean at the center, and Cosette, the girl he adopts, at the right.

Vocabulary Builder

<u>emphasis</u>—(EM fuh sis) *n.* special attention given to something to make it stand out

The Visual Arts Take New Directions

By the 1840s, a new art form, photography, was emerging. **Louis Daguerre** (dah GEHR) in France and William Fox Talbot in England had improved on earlier technologies to produce successful photographs. At first, many photos were stiff, posed portraits of middle-class families or prominent people. Other photographs reflected the romantics' fascination with faraway places.

In time, photographers used the camera to present the grim realities of life. During the American Civil War, Mathew B. Brady preserved a vivid, realistic record of the corpse-strewn battlefields. Other photographers showed the harsh conditions in industrial factories or slums.

The Impressionists Photography posed a challenge to painters. Why try for realism, some artists asked, when a camera could do the same thing better? By the 1870s, a group of painters took art in a new direction, seeking to capture the first fleeting impression made by a scene or object on the viewer's eye. The new movement, known as **impressionism,** took root in Paris, capital of the Western art world.

Since the Renaissance, painters had carefully finished their paintings so that no brush strokes showed. But impressionists like **Claude Monet** (moh NAY) and Edgar Degas (day GAH) brushed strokes of color side by side without any blending. According to new scientific studies of optics, the human eye would mix these patches of color.

By concentrating on visual impressions rather than realism, artists achieved a fresh view of familiar subjects. Monet, for example, painted the cathedral at Rouen (roo AHN), France, dozens of times from the same angle, capturing how it looked in different lights at different times of day.

The Postimpressionists Later painters, called postimpressionists, developed a variety of styles. Georges Seurat (suh RAH) arranged small dots of color to define the shapes of objects. **Vincent van Gogh** experimented with sharp brush lines and bright colors. His unique brushwork lent a dreamlike quality to everyday subjects. Paul Gauguin (goh GAN) also developed a bold, personal style. In his paintings, people look flat, as in "primitive" folk art. But his brooding colors and black outlining of shapes convey _intense_ feelings and images.

 **Checkpoint** How did photography influence the development of painting?

Postimpressionism
This self-portrait of Dutch painter Vincent van Gogh shows his bandaged ear, which he cut off in a state of depression. *What postimpressionist features are demonstrated in Van Gogh's self-portrait?*

Vocabulary Builder

intense—(in TENS) *adj.* very strong or deep

Terms, People, and Places

1. For each term, person, or place listed at the beginning of the section, write a sentence explaining its significance.

Note Taking

2. **Reading Skill: Identify Supporting Details** Use your completed table to answer the Focus Question: What artistic movements emerged in reaction to the Industrial Revolution?

Comprehension and Critical Thinking

3. **Summarize** What are three subjects romantics favored?

4. **Draw Conclusions** What did Courbet mean when he said, "I cannot paint an angel because I have never seen one"? Do you agree with his attitude? Explain.

5. **Recognize Cause and Effect** In what ways were the new artistic styles of the 1800s a reaction to changes in society?

● **Writing About History**

Quick Write: Support a Solution Based on what you've read, list supporting information, such as details, data, and facts, for the following thesis statement of a problem-solution essay: Artists in the 1800s portrayed subjects realistically to make the public more aware of some of the grim problems of life in industrialized nations.

Impressionism

Impressionism was one of the most important art movements of the 1800s. It marked a departure from tradition, both in subject matter and painting technique. Artists sought to depict the human eye's first perception of a scene. Characterized by the use of unmixed primary colors and small, visible brush strokes, impressionism attempted to show the effects of direct or reflected light. Impressionist artists often painted outdoors for maximum effect.

▲ **Claude Monet,** *Impression: Sunrise,* **1872**
In the 1800s, "The Salon," an annual exhibition that accepted only traditional paintings, dominated the Parisian art scene. In 1874, a group of artists held their own exhibition at a local photographer's studio. Claude Monet's *Impression: Sunrise* was one of the works displayed. Monet's painting demonstrates several characteristics of impressionist work, including short, visible brush strokes and an idealized depiction of a landscape.

▲ **Edgar Degas,** *The Dancing Class,* *c.* **1873–1875**
This painting by Edgar Degas shows the influence of the newly invented camera. Impressionists' paintings moved away from the traditional placement of subjects in favor of off-center compositions. Figures were also painted on the outermost parts of the canvas. Much like photographs, impressionist paintings were often snapshots of life rather than elaborate portraits.

▲ **Berthe Morisot,** *Eugène Manet and His Daughter at Bougival, c.* **1881**
French impressionist painter Berthe Morisot also participated in the first impressionist exhibit in 1874. Morisot's delicate, subtle paintings often portrayed her family and friends—as this one of her husband and daughter.

Thinking Critically
1. **Summarize** How did impressionism depart from tradition?
2. **Draw Conclusions** What are the advantages and disadvantages of painting outdoors?

Quick Study Guide

Progress Monitoring *Online*
For: Self-test with vocabulary practice
Web Code: naa-2151

■ Key People

Inventors/Developers

Henry Bessemer—steel processing
Michael Faraday—dynamo
Thomas Edison—electric light bulb
Gottlieb Daimler—automobile
Samuel F.B. Morse—telegraph
Alexander Graham Bell—telephone
Guglielmo Marconi—radio

Scientists

Louis Pasteur—vaccinations, pasteurization
Joseph Lister—antiseptics
John Dalton—modern atomic theory
Charles Darwin—theory of natural selection

Reformers

Florence Nightingale—sanitary measures in hospitals
Elizabeth Cady Stanton—womenís rights
Susan B. Anthony—women's rights
William and Catherine Booth—Salvation Army

Artists, Writers, and Composers

William Wordsworth—romantic writer
Lord Byron—romantic writer
Ludwig van Beethoven—romantic composer
Charles Dickens—realist writer
Émile Zola—realist writer
Gustave Courbet—realist painter
Claude Monet—impressionist painter
Edgar Degas—impressionist painter
Vincent van Gogh—postimpressionist painter

■ Life Expectancy in the Industrial Age

Average Life Expectancy in Selected Industrial Areas, 1850–1910		
Year	Male	Female
1850	40.3 years	42.8 years
1870	42.3 years	44.7 years
1890	45.8 years	48.5 years
1910	52.7 years	56.0 years

SOURCE: E.A. Wrigley, *Population and History* (based on data for parts of Western Europe and the United States)

■ Impact of the Industrial Revolution

Key Effects of the Industrial Revolution

Industrialization
- Germany, France, and the U.S. join Great Britain as industrial powers.
- Rise of factories; new production methods
- Advances in transportation and communication
- Rise of big business
- Growth of labor unions

Urbanization
- Advances in medicine and science
- Population growth due to falling death rates
- Higher standard of living

Social Structure
- Three social classes emerge
- Middle class expands
- Rise of urban working class
- Reform movements grow
- Public education expands

■ Key Events of the Industrial Revolution

Early 1800s
Romanticism begins to shape Western art and literature.

1807
First factories open in Belgium, setting off the Industrial Revolution on the European continent.

1839
French inventor Louis Daguerre perfects an effective method of photography.

Chapter Events
Global Events

1800	1815	1830	1845

1819
Simón Bolívar establishes Gran Colombia.

1842
The Treaty of Nanjing gives Britain trading rights in China.

Essential Question Review

To connect prior knowledge with what you have learned in this chapter, answer the questions below in your Concept Connector journal. Use the journal in the Reading and Note Taking Study Guide to record your answers (or go to www.phschool.com **Web Code:** nad-2107).

1. **Science** Major shifts in how scientists thought about the world in the 1500s and 1600s led to a period called the Scientific Revolution. During this time, advances in mathematics, astronomy, medicine, chemistry, and other fields led to many new discoveries. In this chapter, you read about how scientific advances during the Industrial Revolution changed the way in which people lived and worked. Choose one scientific discovery or advance from the Scientific Revolution and one from the Industrial Revolution. In a few sentences, explain how these discoveries changed peoples' lives.

2. **Technology** During the High Middle Ages, an agricultural revolution brought about great change. Compare the technological changes that took place from about 1000 to 1300 to the changes that took place during the Industrial Revolution. Think about the following:
   - how a new invention or method may have solved a problem
   - how a new technology or method sparked economic growth
   - how the invention or method changed people's lives

3. **Economic Systems** The revival of trade during the High Middle Ages resulted in a commercial revolution. Hundreds of years later, the Industrial Revolution brought about changes in business. In what ways were the changes during the two periods similar? Think about the following:
   - new business practices
   - role of guilds and labor unions

Connections to Today

1. **Technology: Power Outage** In August 2003, people in Canada and the northeastern part of the United States found out just how much their lives depend on electricity. When an energy plant unexpectedly shut down, it led to the largest power outage in North America's history—more than 50 million people were left in the dark.

   Lights and elevators stopped working in skyscrapers, and workers had to carefully make their way down darkened stairways. Others were trapped on trains or stuck in traffic jams caused by inoperable traffic lights. Airports experienced extended delays. Business slowed because Internet servers were not functioning properly, phone systems crashed, computerized cash registers could not ring up sales, and ATMs went down. With today's linked power grids, the possibility of more massive blackouts that disrupt the lives of millions of people across county, state, and international lines is very real. What economic effects might a power outage have?

2. **Belief Systems: Social Darwinism** British philosopher and Social Darwinist Herbert Spencer coined the phrase "survival of the fittest," meaning that the strong grow in power and influence over the weaker members of society. Social Darwinists promoted the beliefs that the group was more important than the individual, and that privileged, powerful people had the right to make decisions about those whom they believed were inferior.

   These ideas had horrific consequences for people throughout the world. For example, they led to unethical medical experimentation on people of color, abuse of the mentally ill, and countless acts of violence toward people of "different" religions, races, and ethnicities. To what degree do you think Social Darwinism is still a part of our culture today?

1859
Charles Darwin publishes *On the Origin of Species*. Many religious leaders denounce his theory of evolution.

1869
Germany legalizes labor unions.

1903
Wilbur and Orville Wright conduct tests of their airplane at Kitty Hawk, North Carolina.

History Interactive
For: Interactive timeline
Web Code: nap-2151

1860 · **1875** · **1890** · **1905**

1861
Tsar Alexander II emancipates Russian serfs.

1884
European nations carve up Africa at the Berlin Conference.

1898
Spanish-American War is fought.

1914
The Panama Canal opens.

Chapter Assessment

Terms, People, and Places

Choose the italicized term in parentheses that best completes each sentence.

1. A *(dynamo/cartel)* is a machine that generates electricity.
2. Business owners sell *(corporations/stock)*, or shares in their companies, to investors.
3. *(Racism/Germ theory)* is the belief that one racial group is superior to another.
4. The *(cult of domesticity/standard of living)* measures the quality and availability of necessities and comforts in a society.
5. A self-help group to aid sick or injured workers is called a *(social gospel/mutual-aid society)*.
6. *(Impressionism/Realism)* attempted to represent the world as it was.

Main Ideas

Section 1 (pp. 660–666)
7. Describe the impact of new technology on industry, transportation, and communication.
8. Why did big businesses emerge during the Industrial Revolution?

Section 2 (pp. 667–673)
9. How did the Industrial Revolution improve city life? How did it make city life worse?

Section 3 (pp. 674–680)
10. How did the Industrial Revolution influence the class structure of Western Europe?
11. What existing beliefs did new scientific theories challenge?

Section 4 (pp. 681–685)
12. How did artists, composers, writers, and others respond to industrialization?

Chapter Focus Question
13. What were the technological, social, and economic effects of the Industrial Revolution?

Critical Thinking

14. **Geography and History** How did technology affect the movement of people and goods in the 1800s and in the early 1900s?
15. **Identify Point of View** How might each of the following have viewed the Industrial Revolution: (a) an inventor, (b) an entrepreneur, (c) a worker?
16. **Draw Conclusions** Do you think women's lives improved as a result of the Industrial Revolution? Why or why not?
17. **Draw Inferences** Referring to *Oliver Twist*, Dickens wrote that "to show [criminals] as they really are, for ever skulking uneasily through the dirtiest paths of life . . . would be a service to society." How does his claim reflect the goals of realism?
18. **Summarize** How would you describe Victorian middle-class values?
19. **Demonstrate Reasoned Judgment** Some historians have suggested that we are now in a third phase of the Industrial Revolution, characterized by information technology and computers. Do you agree or disagree? Explain the reasons for your answer.
20. **Analyzing Visuals** Which artistic movement of the 1800s does *Cathedral of Rouen, Afternoon* (right) by Claude Monet reflect: romanticism, realism, or impressionism? Explain your reasoning.

● Writing About History

In this chapter's four Section Assessments, you developed skills for writing a problem-solution essay.

Writing a Problem-Solution Essay The second Industrial Revolution ushered in a period of great change to the modern world. But it brought with it problems that people had not experienced before. Write a problem-solution essay about one of these topics or choose your own topic relating to the content in this chapter.

Prewriting
- Choose the topic that interests you most.
- Narrow your topic.
- Make a list of details, facts, and examples that proves there is a problem. Then, identify the specific parts of your solution.

Drafting
- Develop a working thesis and choose information to support it.
- Organize the paragraphs in a logical order so that readers can understand the solution you propose.

Revising
- Use the guidelines for revising your essay on page SH12 of the Writing Handbook.

Document-Based Assessment

Birth of the Modern City

The birth of the modern city helped to define the Industrial Age. The documents below show that the modern city represented progress, but not without costs.

Document A

"The first shock of a great earthquake had, just at that period, rent the whole neighborhood to its center. Traces of its course were visible on every side. Houses were knocked down; streets broken through and stopped; deep pits and trenches dug in the ground; enormous heaps of earth and clay thrown up; buildings that were undermined and shaking, propped by great beams of wood. . . . In short, the yet unfinished and unopened Railroad was in progress; and, from the very core of all this dire disorder, trailed smoothly away, upon its mighty course of civilization and improvement."

—from ***Dombey and Son*** by Charles Dickens

Document B

Selected Inventions, 1824–1911	
Cement	1824
Locomotive	1830
Dynamite	1866
Telephone	1876
Cash register	1879
Electric trolley car	1884–1887
Steel alloy	1891
Self-starting auto	1911

SOURCE: *The World Almanac*, 2004

Document C

Population of Major Cities		
City	1850	1900
Berlin, Germany	419,000	1,889,000
London, England	2,685,000	6,586,000
Moscow, Russia	365,000	989,000
New York, United States	696,000	3,437,000
Paris, France	1,053,000	2,714,000

SOURCE: *International Historical Statistics*

Document D

Brooklyn Bridge, 1883

Analyzing Documents

Use your knowledge of the industrial age and Documents A, B, C, and D to answer questions 1–4.

1. The cause of the earthquake described in Document A was
   A an underground fault in London.
   B poorly constructed tall buildings.
   C construction of a railroad.
   D deep pits and trenches in the ground.

2. Which inventions from Document B had the most impact on New York City at the time Document D was created?
   A trolley cars, steel alloy, cash registers
   B dynamite, telephones, cash registers
   C cement, locomotives, telephones
   D cement, locomotives, dynamite

3. Which trend does Document C illustrate?
   A the shift in population from Europe to the United States
   B the shift in population from East Coast to West Coast
   C the increase in population of cities
   D the decrease in rural population

4. **Writing Task** What were the most significant features of the modern city? Why? Use the information from Documents A through D, as well as what you've learned in this chapter, to support your opinion.

22 Nationalism Triumphs in Europe
1800–1914

The Price of Nationalism

The last half of the 1800s can be called the Age of Nationalism. By harnessing national feeling, European leaders fought ruthlessly to create strong, unified nations. Under Otto von Bismarck, Germany emerged as Europe's most powerful empire—but at a considerable cost. In his 1870 diary, Crown Prince Friedrich wrote:

66[Germany had once been admired as a] nation of thinkers and philosophers, poets and artists, idealists and enthusiasts . . . [but now the world saw Germany as] a nation of conquerors and destroyers, to which no pledged word, no treaty, is sacred. . . . We are neither loved nor respected, but only feared.99

Listen to the Witness History audio to learn more about nationalism.

◄ Otto von Bismarck (center), chancellor of Germany, meets with European and Turkish leaders at the Congress of Berlin.

Helmet from the Franco-Prussian war era

Chapter Preview

Chapter Focus Question What effects did nationalism and the demand for reform have in Europe?

Austria-Hungary empire flag

Soviet stamp commemorating the Decembrist Revolt

Use the  **Quick Study Timeline** at the end of this chapter to preview chapter events.

Concept Connector ONLINE

To explore Essential Questions related to this chapter, go to PHSchool.com
Web Code: nad-2207

Otto von Bismarck

Helmet from the Franco-Prussian war era

WITNESS HISTORY ◀)) AUDIO

Blood and Iron

Prussian legislators waited restlessly for Otto von Bismarck to speak. He wanted them to vote for more money to build up the army. Liberal members opposed the move. Bismarck rose and dismissed their concerns:

> 66 Germany does not look to Prussia's liberalism, but to her power. . . . The great questions of the day are not to be decided by speeches and majority resolutions—that was the mistake of 1848 and 1849— but by blood and iron! 99
> —Otto von Bismarck, 1862

Focus Question How did Otto von Bismarck, the chancellor of Prussia, lead the drive for German unity?

Building a German Nation

Objectives

- Identify several events that promoted German unity during the early 1800s.
- Explain how Bismarck unified Germany.
- Analyze the basic political organization of the new German empire.

Terms, People, and Places

Otto von Bismarck
chancellor
Realpolitik
annex
kaiser
Reich

Note Taking

Reading Skill: Recognize Sequence Keep track of the sequence of events that led to German unification by completing a chart like the one below. Add more boxes as needed.

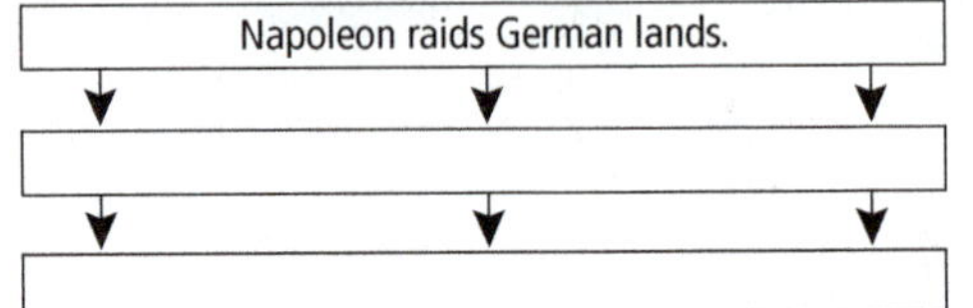

Otto von Bismarck delivered his "blood and iron" speech in 1862. It set the tone for his future policies. Bismarck was determined to build a strong, unified German state, with Prussia at its head.

Taking Initial Steps Toward Unity

In the early 1800s, German-speaking people lived in a number of small and medium-sized states as well as in Prussia and the Austrian Hapsburg empire. Napoleon's invasions unleashed new forces in these territories.

Napoleon Raids German Lands Between 1806 and 1812, Napoleon made important territorial changes in German-speaking lands. He annexed lands along the Rhine River for France. He dissolved the Holy Roman Empire by forcing the emperor of Austria to agree to the lesser title of king. He also organized a number of German states into the Rhine Confederation.

At first, some Germans welcomed the French emperor as a hero with enlightened, modern policies. He encouraged freeing the serfs, made trade easier, and abolished laws against Jews. However, not all Germans appreciated Napoleon and his changes. As people fought to free their lands from French rule, they began to demand a unified German state.

Napoleon's defeat did not resolve the issue. At the Congress of Vienna, Metternich pointed out that a united Germany would require dismantling the government of each German state. Instead, the peacemakers created the German Confederation, a weak alliance headed by Austria.

Economic Changes Promote Unity In the 1830s, Prussia created an economic union called the *Zollverein* (TSAWL fur yn). It dismantled tariff barriers between many German states. Still, Germany remained politically fragmented.

In 1848, liberals meeting in the Frankfurt Assembly again demanded German political unity. They offered the throne of a united German state to Frederick William IV of Prussia. The Prussian ruler, however, rejected the notion of a throne offered by "the people."

 **Checkpoint** What was the German Confederation?

Bismarck Unites Germany

Otto von Bismarck succeeded where others had failed. Bismarck came from Prussia's Junker (YOONG kur) class, made up of conservative landowning nobles. Bismarck first served Prussia as a diplomat in Russia and France. In 1862, King William I made him prime minister. Within a decade, the new prime minister had become **chancellor,** or the highest official of a monarch, and had used his policy of "blood and iron" to unite the German states under Prussian rule.

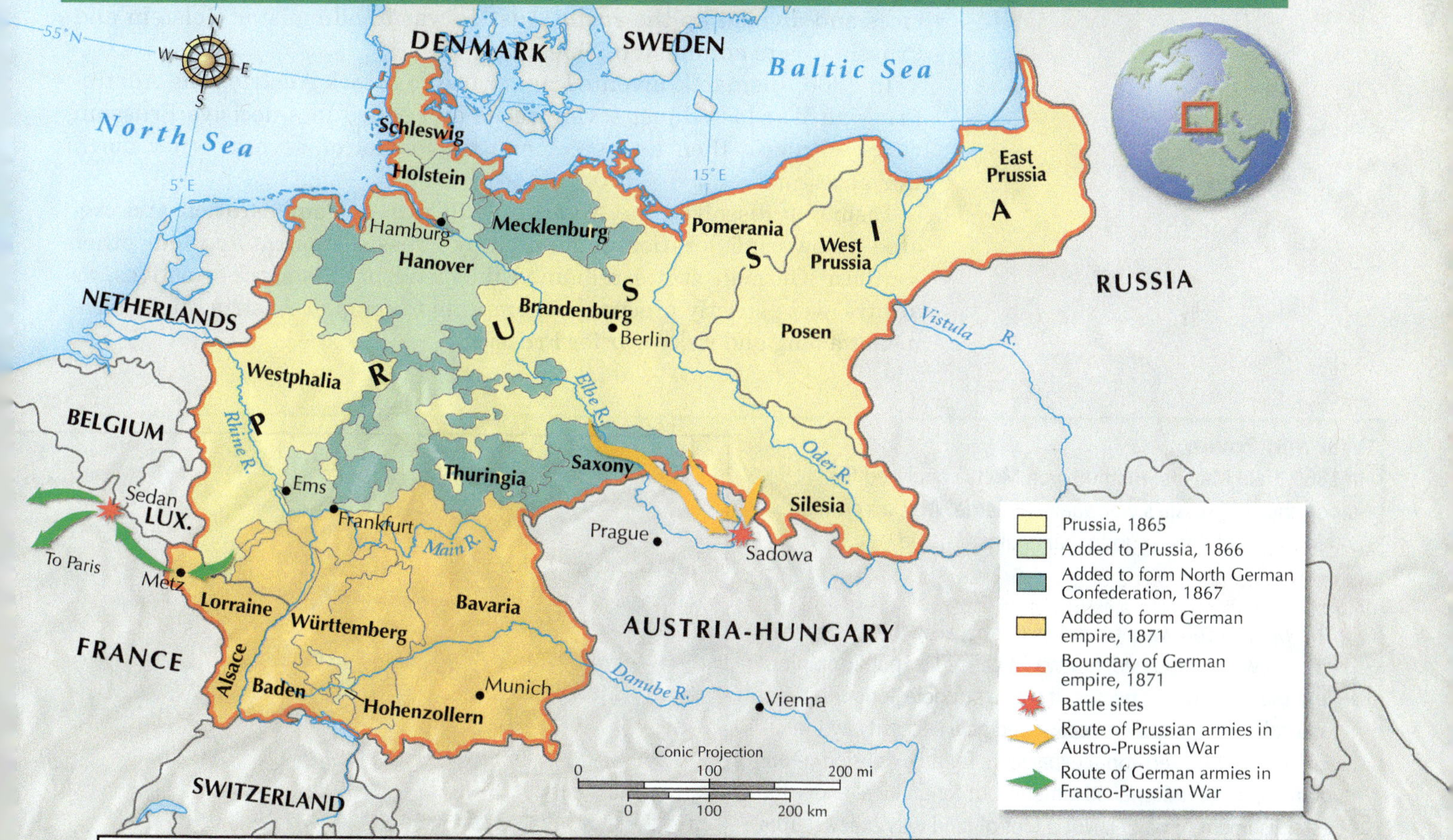

Map Skills In the early 1800s, people living in German-speaking states had local loyalties. By the mid-1800s, however, they were developing a national identity.

1. **Locate:** (a) Prussia (b) Silesia (c) Bavaria (d) Schleswig
2. **Region** What area did Prussia add to its territory in 1866?
3. **Analyzing Information** Why do you think Austrian influence was greater among the southern German states than among the northern ones?

Master of Realpolitik Bismarck's success was due in part to his strong will. He was a master of **Realpolitik** (ray AHL poh lee teek), or realistic politics based on the needs of the state. In the case of Realpolitik, power was more important than principles.

Although Bismarck was the architect of German unity, he was not really a German nationalist. His primary loyalty was to the Hohenzollerns (hoh un TSAWL urnz), the ruling dynasty of Prussia, who represented a powerful, traditional monarchy. Through unification, he hoped to bring more power to the Hohenzollerns.

Strengthening the Army As Prussia's prime minister, Bismarck first moved to build up the Prussian army. Despite his "blood and iron" speech, the liberal legislature refused to vote for funds for the military. In response, Bismarck strengthened the army with money that had been collected for other purposes. With a powerful, well-equipped military, he was then ready to pursue an aggressive foreign policy. Over the next decade, Bismarck led Prussia into three wars. Each war increased Prussian prestige and power and paved the way for German unity.

Prussia Declares War With Denmark and Austria Bismarck's first maneuver was to form an alliance in 1864 with Austria. Prussia and Austria then seized the provinces of Schleswig and Holstein from Denmark. After a brief war, Prussia and Austria "liberated" the two provinces and divided up the spoils. Austria was to administer Holstein and Prussia was to administer Schleswig.

In 1866, Bismarck invented an excuse to attack Austria. The Austro-Prussian War lasted just seven weeks and ended in a decisive Prussian victory. Prussia then **annexed,** or took control of, several other north German states.

Bismarck dissolved the Austrian-led German Confederation and created a new confederation dominated by Prussia. Austria and four other southern German states remained independent. Bismarck's motives, as always, were strictly practical. Attempting to conquer Austria might have meant a long and risky war for Prussia.

War and Power

In 1866, Field Marshal Helmuth von Moltke analyzed the importance of Prussia's war against Austria. Why, according to von Moltke, did Prussia go to war against Austria?

Primary Source

66 The war of 1866 was entered on not because the existence of Prussia was threatened, nor was it caused by public opinion and the voice of the people; it was a struggle, long foreseen and calmly prepared for, recognized as a necessity by the Cabinet, not for territorial expansion, for an extension of our domain, or for material advantage, but for an ideal end—the establishment of power. Not a foot of land was exacted from Austria. . . . Its center of gravity lay out of Germany; Prussia's lay within it. Prussia felt itself called upon and strong enough to assume the leadership of the German races. 99

Austro-Prussian War painting (above) and a medal of victory (left)

France Declares War on Prussia In France, the Prussian victory over Austria angered Napoleon III. A growing rivalry between the two nations led to the Franco-Prussian War of 1870.

Germans recalled only too well the invasions of Napoleon I some 60 years earlier. Bismarck played up the image of the French menace to spur German nationalism. For his part, Napoleon III did little to avoid war, hoping to mask problems at home with military glory.

Bismarck furthered the crisis by rewriting and then releasing to the press a telegram that reported on a meeting between King William I and the French ambassador. Bismarck's editing of the "Ems dispatch" made it seem that William I had insulted the Frenchman. Furious, Napoleon III declared war on Prussia, as Bismarck had hoped.

A superior Prussian force, supported by troops from other German states, smashed the badly organized and poorly supplied French soldiers. Napoleon III, old and ill, surrendered within a few weeks. France had to accept a humiliating peace.

 **Checkpoint** What techniques did Bismarck use to unify the German states?

Birth of the German Empire

Delighted by the victory over France, princes from the southern German states and the North German Confederation persuaded William I of Prussia to take the title **kaiser** (KY zur), or emperor. In January 1871, German nationalists celebrated the birth of the second **Reich,** or empire. They called it that because they considered it heir to the Holy Roman Empire.

A constitution drafted by Bismarck set up a two-house legislature. The Bundesrat (BOON dus raht), or upper house, was appointed by the rulers of the German states. The Reichstag (RYKS tahg), or lower house, was elected by universal male suffrage. Because the Bundesrat could veto any decisions of the Reichstag, real power remained in the hands of the emperor and his chancellor.

 **Checkpoint** How was the new German government, drafted by Bismarck, structured?

Vocabulary Builder

edit—(ED it) *v.* to make additions, deletions, or other changes to a piece of writing

---

Assessment

Terms, People, and Places

1. For each term, person, or place listed at the beginning of the section, write a sentence explaining its significance.

Note Taking

2. **Reading Skill: Recognize Sequence** Use your completed chart to answer the Focus Question: How did Otto von Bismarck, the chancellor of Prussia, lead the drive for German unity?

Comprehension and Critical Thinking

3. **Summarize** What territorial and economic changes promoted German unity?

4. **Analyze Information** Identify three examples of Bismarck's use of Realpolitik.

5. **Draw Conclusions** How did the emperor and his chancellor retain power in the new German government?

● **Writing About History**

Quick Write: Generate Arguments Choose one topic from this section that you could use to write a persuasive essay. For example, you could write about whether Germany's war against Austria was justifiable. Make sure that the topic you choose to write about has at least two sides that could provoke an argument.

French bayonet

Prussian soldiers at Versailles

The New German Empire

In 1870, German historian Heinrich von Treitschke (vawn TRYCH kuh) wrote a newspaper article demanding the annexation of Alsace and Lorraine from France. A year later, annexation became a condition of the peace settlement in the Franco-Prussian War:

> **66** The sense of justice to Germany demands the lessening of France. . . . These territories are ours by the right of the sword, and . . . [by] virtue of a higher right—the right of the German nation, which will not permit its lost children to remain strangers to the German Empire. **99**

Focus Question How did Germany increase its power after unifying in 1871?

Germany Strengthens

Objectives
- Describe how Germany became an industrial giant.
- Explain why Bismarck was called the Iron Chancellor.
- List the policies of Kaiser William II.

Terms, People, and Places
Kulturkampf
William II
social welfare

Note Taking

Reading Skill: Recognize Sequence Keep track of the sequence of events described in this section by completing a chart like the one below. List the causes that led to a strong German nation.

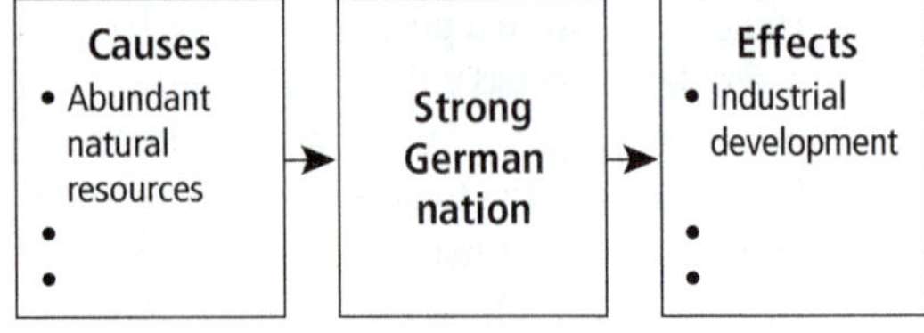

In January 1871, German princes gathered in the glittering Hall of Mirrors at the French palace of Versailles. They had just defeated Napoleon III in the Franco-Prussian War. Once home to French kings, the palace seemed the perfect place to proclaim the new German empire. To the winners as well as to the losers, the symbolism was clear: French domination of Europe had ended. Germany was now the dominant power in Europe.

Germany Becomes an Industrial Giant

In the aftermath of unification, the German empire emerged as the industrial giant of the European continent. By the late 1800s, German chemical and electrical industries were setting the standard worldwide. Among the European powers, German shipping was second only to Britain's.

Making Economic Progress Germany, like Great Britain, possessed several of the factors that made industrialization possible. Germany's spectacular growth was due in part to ample iron and coal resources, the basic ingredients for industrial development. A disciplined and educated workforce also helped the economy. The German middle class and educated professionals helped to create a productive and efficient society that prided itself on its sense of responsibility and deference to authority. Germany's rapidly growing population—from 41 million in 1871 to 67 million by 1914—also provided a huge home market along with a larger supply of industrial workers.

The new nation also benefited from earlier progress. During the 1850s and 1860s, Germans had founded large companies and built many railroads. The house of Krupp (kroop) boomed after 1871, becoming an enormous industrial complex that produced steel and weapons for a world market. Between 1871 and 1914, the business tycoon August Thyssen (TEES un) built a small steel factory of 70 workers into a giant empire with 50,000 employees. Optics was another important industry. German industrialist and inventor Carl Zeiss built a company that became known for its telescopes, microscopes, and other optical equipment.

Promoting Scientific and Economic Development German industrialists were the first to see the value of applied science in developing new products such as <u>synthetic</u> chemicals and dyes. Industrialists, as well as the government, supported research and development in the universities and hired trained scientists to solve technological problems in their factories.

The German government also promoted economic development. After 1871, it issued a single currency for Germany, reorganized the banking system, and <u>coordinated</u> railroads built by the various German states. When a worldwide depression hit in the late 1800s, Germany raised tariffs to protect home industries from foreign competition. The leaders of the new German empire were determined to maintain economic strength as well as military power.

✔ **Checkpoint** What factors did Germany possess that made industrialization possible there?

The Iron Chancellor

As chancellor of the new German empire, Bismarck pursued several foreign-policy goals. He wanted to keep France weak and isolated while building strong links with Austria and Russia. He respected British naval power but did not seek to compete in that arena. "Water rats," he said, "do not fight with land rats." Later, however, he would take a more aggressive stand against Britain as the two nations competed for overseas colonies.

BIOGRAPHY

Otto von Bismarck

Otto von Bismarck (1815–1898) spent his early years on his father's country estate. He worked briefly as a civil servant, but found the work boring. At 24, Bismarck resigned his post as a bureaucrat. "My ambition strives more to command than to obey," the independent-minded young man explained.

The resignation did not end his career in government. While he was a delegate to a United Diet that was called by Prussian King Frederick William IV, Bismarck's conservative views and passionate speeches in defense of government policies won him the support of the king. He then served as a diplomat to the German Federation. He became chancellor of the German empire in 1871, a position he held for 19 years. **What path did Bismarck take to win political power?**

Analyzing Political Cartoons

A Political Game of Chess This political cartoon shows Otto von Bismarck and Pope Pius IX trying to checkmate each other in a game of chess.

1. How does this cartoon reflect the relationship between Bismarck and the Catholic Church?
2. How did the conflict between church and state affect German politics in the 1870s?

On the domestic front, Bismarck applied the same ruthless methods he had used to achieve unification. The Iron Chancellor, as he was called, sought to erase local loyalties and crush all opposition to the imperial state. He targeted two groups—the Catholic Church and the Socialists. In his view, both posed a threat to the new German state.

Campaign Against the Church After unification, Catholics made up about a third of the German population. Bismarck, who was Lutheran, distrusted Catholics—especially the clergy—whose first loyalty, he believed, was to the pope instead of to Germany.

In response to what he saw as the Catholic threat, Bismarck launched the *Kulturkampf* (kool TOOR kahmpf), or "battle for civilization," which lasted from 1871 to 1878. His goal was to make Catholics put loyalty to the state above allegiance to the Church. The chancellor had laws passed that gave the state the right to supervise Catholic education and approve the appointment of priests. Other laws closed some religious orders, expelled the Jesuits from Prussia, and made it compulsory for couples to be married by civil authority.

Bismarck's moves against the Catholic Church backfired. The faithful rallied behind the Church, and the Catholic Center party gained strength in the Reichstag. A realist, Bismarck saw his mistake and worked to make peace with the Church.

Campaign Against the Socialists Bismarck also saw a threat to the new German empire in the growing power of socialism. By the late 1870s, German Marxists had organized the Social Democratic party, which called for parliamentary democracy and laws to improve conditions for the working class. Bismarck feared that socialists would undermine the loyalty of German workers and turn them toward revolution. Following a failed assassination plot against the kaiser, Bismarck had laws passed that dissolved socialist groups, shut down their newspapers, and banned their meetings. Once again, repression backfired. Workers were unified in support of the socialist cause.

Bismarck then changed course. He set out to woo workers away from socialism by sponsoring laws to protect them. By the 1890s, Germans had health and accident insurance as well as old-age insurance to provide retirement benefits. Thus, under Bismarck, Germany was a pioneer in social reform. Its system of economic safeguards became the model for other European nations.

Although workers benefited from Bismarck's plan, they did not abandon socialism. In fact, the Social Democratic party continued to grow in strength. By 1912, it held more seats in the Reichstag than any other party. Yet Bismarck's program showed that conditions for workers could be improved without the upheaval of a revolution. Later, Germany and other European nations would build on Bismarck's social policies, greatly increasing government's role in providing for the needs of its citizens.

✔ **Checkpoint** Why did Bismarck try to crush the Catholic Church and the Socialists?

Kaiser William II

In 1888, **William II** succeeded his grandfather as kaiser. The new emperor was supremely confident in his abilities and wished to put his own stamp on Germany. In 1890, he shocked Europe by asking the dominating Bismarck to resign. "There is only one master in the Reich," he said, "and that is I."

William II seriously believed that his right to rule came from God. He expressed this view when he said:

> ❝My grandfather considered that the office of king was a task that God had assigned to him. . . . That which he thought I also think. . . . Those who wish to aid me in that task . . . I welcome with all my heart; those who oppose me in this work I shall crush.❞
> —William II

Not surprisingly, William resisted efforts to introduce democratic reforms. At the same time, however, his government provided programs for **social welfare,** or programs to help certain groups of people. His government also provided services such as cheap transportation and electricity. An excellent system of public schools, which had flourished under Bismarck, taught students obedience to the emperor along with reading, writing, and mathematics.

Like his grandfather, William II lavished funds on the German military machine, already the most powerful in Europe. He also launched an ambitious campaign to expand the German navy and win an overseas empire to rival those of Britain and France. William's nationalism and aggressive military stance helped increase tensions on the eve of World War I.

✔ **Checkpoint** Why did William II ask Bismarck to resign in 1890?

Social Reform

Under Bismarck's leadership, Germany pioneered social reform. By 1884, Germans had health and accident insurance. By 1889, they had disability and old-age insurance. *Why did Bismarck introduce these social reforms?*

SECTION 2 Assessment

Terms, People, and Places

1. For each term, person, or place listed at the beginning of the section, write a sentence explaining its significance.

Note Taking

2. **Reading Skill: Recognize Sequence** Use your completed chart to answer the Focus Question: How did Germany increase its power after unifying in 1871?

Comprehension and Critical Thinking

3. **Summarize** How did Germany become an industrial giant in the late 1800s?
4. **Demonstrate Reasoned Judgment** Do you think Bismarck's methods were justified by his social reforms? Explain.
5. **Draw Conclusions** Do you think the supporters of a democratic government in Germany in the late 1800s had hope of success? Explain.

● Writing About History

Quick Write: Answer Opposing Arguments To write a strong persuasive essay, you need to address arguments that can be used to contradict your position. Choose a topic from the section. For example, think about whether a government should guarantee that its citizens have adequate healthcare. List the arguments for and against your position on a piece of paper.

Giuseppe Mazzini,
around 1865

Stirrings of Nationalism

After a failed revolution against Austrian rule in northern Italy, many rebels, fearing retribution, begged for funds to pay for safe passage to Spain. Giuseppe Mazzini (mat SEE nee), still a boy, described his reaction to the situation:

66 He (a rebel) held out a white handkerchief, merely saying, 'For the refugees of Italy.' My mother . . . dropped some money into the handkerchief. . . . That day was the first in which a confused idea presented itself to my mind . . . an idea that we Italians could and therefore ought to struggle for the liberty of our country. . . . 99
—Giuseppe Mazzini, *Life and Writings*

Focus Question How did influential leaders help to create a unified Italy?

Unifying Italy

Objectives

- List the key obstacles to Italian unity.
- Understand what roles Count Camillo Cavour and Giuseppe Garibaldi played in the struggle for Italy.
- Describe the challenges that faced the new nation of Italy.

Terms, People, and Places

Camillo Cavour
Giuseppe Garibaldi
anarchist
emigration

Note Taking

Reading Skill: Recognize Sequence As you read, create a timeline showing the sequence of events from 1831 to 1871 that led to Italian unification.

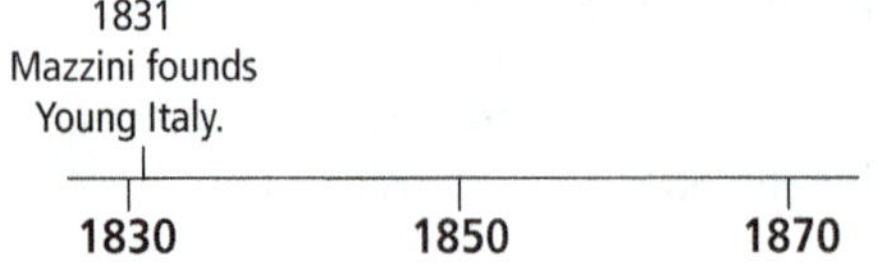

Although the people of the Italian peninsula spoke the same language, they had not experienced political unity since Roman times. By the early 1800s, though, Italian patriots—including Mazzini, who would become a revolutionary—were determined to build a new, united Italy. As in Germany, unification was brought about by the efforts of a strong state and furthered by a shrewd, ruthless politician—Count **Camillo Cavour** (kah VOOR).

Obstacles to Italian Unity

For centuries, Italy had been a battleground for ambitious foreign and local princes. Frequent warfare and foreign rule had led people to identify with local regions. The people of Florence considered themselves Tuscans, those of Venice Venetians, those of Naples Neapolitans, and so on. But as in Germany, the invasions of Napoleon had sparked dreams of national unity.

The Congress of Vienna, however, ignored the nationalists who hoped to end centuries of foreign rule and achieve unity. To Prince Metternich of Austria, the idea of a unified Italy was laughable. At Vienna, Austria took control of much of northern Italy, while Hapsburg monarchs ruled various other Italian states. In the south, a French Bourbon ruler was put in charge of Naples and Sicily.

In response, nationalists organized secret patriotic societies and focused their efforts on expelling Austrian forces from northern Italy. Between 1820 and 1848, nationalist revolts exploded across the region. Each time, Austria sent in troops to crush the rebels.

Mazzini Establishes Young Italy In the 1830s, the nationalist leader Giuseppe Mazzini founded Young Italy. The goal of this secret society was "to <u>constitute</u> Italy, one, free, independent, republican nation." In 1849, Mazzini helped set up a revolutionary republic in Rome, but French forces soon toppled it. Like many other nationalists, Mazzini spent much of his life in exile, plotting and dreaming of a united Italy.

Nationalism Takes Root "Ideas grow quickly," Mazzini once said, "when watered by the blood of martyrs." Although revolution had failed, nationalist agitation had planted seeds for future harvests.

To nationalists like Mazzini, a united Italy made sense not only because of geography, but also because of a common language and history. Nationalists reminded Italians of the glories of ancient Rome and the medieval papacy. To others, unity made practical economic sense. It would end trade barriers among the Italian states and stimulate industry.

 **Checkpoint** What forces hindered Italian unity?

The Struggle for Italy

After 1848, leadership of the Risorgimento (ree sawr jee MEN toh), or Italian nationalist movement, passed to the kingdom of Sardinia, which included Piedmont, Nice, and Savoy as well as the island of Sardinia. Its constitutional monarch, Victor Emmanuel II, hoped to join other states to his own, thereby increasing his power.

Cavour Becomes Prime Minister In 1852, Victor Emmanuel made Count Camillo Cavour his prime minister. Cavour came from a noble family but favored liberal goals. He was a flexible, practical, crafty politician, willing to use almost any means to achieve his goals. Like Bismarck in Prussia, Cavour was a monarchist who believed in Realpolitik.

Once in office, Cavour moved first to reform Sardinia's economy. He improved agriculture, had railroads built, and encouraged commerce by supporting free trade. Cavour's long-term goal, however, was to end Austrian power in Italy and annex the provinces of Lombardy and Venetia.

Opposing Austrian Rule
In March 1848, nationalists in Venice took over the city's arsenal and declared the establishment of the Republic of Venice. Their success was short lived, however, as the republic was soon disbanded and Venice again fell under the rule of Austria in 1849.

Intrigue With France In 1855, Sardinia, led by Cavour, joined Britain and France against Russia in the Crimean War. Sardinia did not win territory, but it did have a voice at the peace conference. Sardinia also gained the attention of Napoleon III.

In 1858, Cavour negotiated a secret deal with Napoleon, who promised to aid Sardinia in case it faced a war with Austria. A year later, the shrewd Cavour provoked that war. With help from France, Sardinia defeated Austria and annexed Lombardy. Meanwhile, nationalist groups overthrew Austrian-backed rulers in several other northern Italian states. These states then joined with Sardinia.

Garibaldi's "Red Shirts" Next, attention shifted to the Kingdom of the Two Sicilies in southern Italy. There, Giuseppe Garibaldi (gah ree BAHL dee), a longtime nationalist and an ally of Mazzini, was ready for action. Like Mazzini, Garibaldi wanted to create an Italian republic. He did not hesitate, however, to accept aid from the monarchist Cavour. By 1860, Garibaldi had recruited a force of 1,000 red-shirted volunteers. Cavour provided weapons and allowed two ships to take Garibaldi and his "Red Shirts" south to Sicily. With surprising speed, Garibaldi's forces won control of Sicily, crossed to the mainland, and marched triumphantly north to Naples.

Unity at Last Garibaldi's success alarmed Cavour, who feared that the nationalist hero would set up his own republic in the south. To prevent this, Cavour urged Victor Emmanuel to send Sardinian troops to deal with Garibaldi. Instead, the Sardinians overran the Papal States and linked up with Garibaldi and his forces in Naples.

In a patriotic move, Garibaldi turned over Naples and Sicily to Victor Emmanuel. Shortly afterward, southern Italy voted to approve the move, and in 1861, Victor Emmanuel II was crowned king of Italy.

Two areas remained outside the new Italian nation: Rome and Venetia. Cavour died in 1861, but his <u>successors</u> completed his dream. Italy formed an alliance with Prussia in the Austro-Prussian War and won the province of Venetia. Then, during the Franco-Prussian War in 1870, France was forced to withdraw its troops from Rome. For the first time since the fall of the Roman empire, Italy was a united land.

✔ **Checkpoint** What steps did Camillo Cavour take to promote Italian unity?

Vocabulary Builder
<u>successor</u>—(suk SES ur) *n.* a person who succeeds another to an office or rank

Challenges Facing the New Nation

Italy faced a host of problems. Like the German empire that Bismarck cemented together out of many states, Italy had no tradition of unity. Few Italians felt ties to the new nation. Strong regional rivalries left Italy unable to solve critical national issues.

Divisions The greatest regional differences were between the north and the south. The north was richer and had more cities than the south. For centuries, northern Italian cities had flourished as centers of business and culture. The south, on the other hand, was rural and poor. Its population was booming, but illiterate peasants could extract only a meager existence from the exhausted farmland.

Hostility between Italy and the Roman Catholic Church further divided the nation. Popes bitterly resented the seizure of the Papal

Unifying Italy

The Italian peninsula had been divided into small independent states since the fall of the Roman empire in 476. Political unification seemed impossible. However, rebellion, nationalism, and unity slowly took hold with the help of four individuals: a revolutionary, a statesman, a soldier, and a king.

① Giuseppe Mazzini
Giuseppe Mazzini, founder of Young Italy, helps set up a revolutionary republic in Rome in 1849. French troops soon topple it.

② Camillo Cavour
In 1859, prime minister Camillo Cavour provokes a war with Austria after secret negotiations with Napoleon III, who promised aid to Sardinia.

③ Nationalist Revolts
Italian nationalists overthrow Austrian-backed rulers in several northern states.

④ Giuseppe Garibaldi
In 1860, Cavour provides weapons to Giuseppe Garibaldi, who invades Sicily with 1,000 Red Shirt volunteers (below). Garibaldi then captures Naples.

⑤ Victor Emmanuel II
In a patriotic move, Garibaldi turns over Naples and Sicily to Victor Emmanuel, who is crowned king. In 1870, Italians conquer Rome, which becomes the capital city of a unified Italy.

Thinking Critically

1. **Map Skills** What route did Garibaldi's expedition take?
2. **Draw Conclusions** Why was Italian unification difficult to achieve?

History Interactive
For: Interactive timeline
Web Code: nap-2232

703

States and of Rome. The government granted the papacy limited rights and control over church properties. Popes, however, saw themselves as "prisoners" and urged Italian Catholics—almost all Italians—not to cooperate with their new government.

Turmoil Under Victor Emmanuel, Italy was a constitutional monarchy with a two-house legislature. The king appointed members to the upper house, which could veto bills passed by the lower house. Although the lower house consisted of elected representatives, only a small number of men had the right to vote.

In the late 1800s, unrest increased as radicals on the left struggled against a conservative government. Socialists organized strikes while **anarchists,** people who want to abolish all government, turned to sabotage and violence. Slowly, the government extended suffrage to more men and passed laws to improve social conditions. Still, the turmoil continued. To distract attention from troubles at home, the government set out to win an overseas empire in Ethiopia.

Economic Progress Despite its problems, Italy did develop economically, especially after 1900. Although the nation lacked important natural resources such as coal, industries did sprout up in northern regions. Industrialization, of course, brought urbanization as peasants flocked to the cities to find jobs in factories. As in other countries, reformers campaigned to improve education and working conditions.

The population explosion of this period created tensions. One important safety valve for many people was **emigration,** or movement away from their homeland. Many Italians left for the United States, Canada, and Latin American nations. By 1914, the country was significantly better off than it had been in 1861. But, it was hardly prepared for the great war that broke out in that year.

✔ **Checkpoint** What problems did Italians experience after unification?

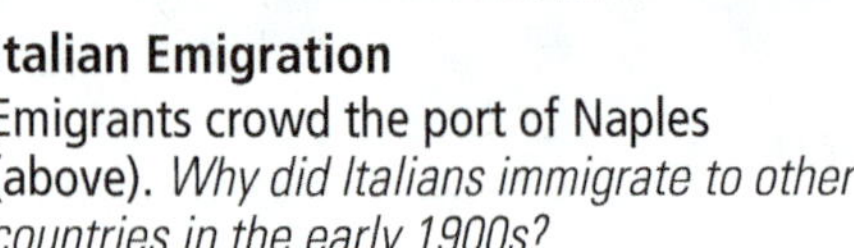

Italian Emigration
Emigrants crowd the port of Naples (above). *Why did Italians immigrate to other countries in the early 1900s?*

SECTION 3 Assessment

Terms, People, and Places

1. For each term, person, or place listed at the beginning of the section, write a sentence explaining its significance.

Note Taking

2. **Reading Skill: Recognize Sequence** Use your completed timeline to answer the Focus Question: How did influential leaders help to create a unified Italy?

Comprehension and Critical Thinking

3. **Summarize** (a) What obstacles to unity did Italian nationalists face? (b) What conditions favored unity?

4. **Analyze Information** (a) What was the source of conflict between Garibaldi and Cavour? (b) How was the conflict resolved?

5. **Express Problems Clearly** What challenges did Italians face after unification?

● **Writing About History**

Quick Write: Decide on an Organizational Strategy Using clear organization to present a logical argument is a good way to keep the reader's attention in a persuasive essay. Choose an issue from the section about which you could make an argument. Then write an outline showing how you would organize a persuasive essay.

Hungarian parliament passes legislation funding an army to fight against the Hapsburg empire, 1848

Austria-Hungarian empire flag

Balkan Nationalism

> 66 How is it that they [European powers] cannot understand that less and less is it possible . . . to direct the destinies of the Balkans from the outside? We are growing up, gaining confidence, and becoming independent . . . 99
> —Bulgarian statesman on the first Balkan War and the European powers

Focus Question How did the desire for national independence among ethnic groups weaken and ultimately destroy the Austrian and Ottoman empires?

Nationalism Threatens Old Empires

Objectives

- Describe how nationalism contributed to the decline of the Hapsburg empire.
- List the main characteristics of the Dual Monarchy.
- Understand how the growth of nationalism affected the Ottoman empire.

Terms, People, and Places

Francis Joseph
Ferenc Deák
Dual Monarchy

Note Taking

Reading Skill: Recognize Sequence Complete a table like the one below to keep track of the sequence of events that led Austria into the Dual Monarchy. Look for dates and other clues to sequence in the text.

Events in Austrian History	
1840	
1848	
1859	
1866	
1867	

Napoleon had dissolved the Holy Roman Empire, which the Hapsburgs had led for nearly 400 years. Austria's center of power had shifted to Central Europe. Additional wars resulted in continued loss of territory to Germany and Italy. Why did nationalism bring new strength to some countries and weaken others?

In Eastern and Central Europe, the Austrian Hapsburgs and the Ottoman Turks ruled lands that included diverse ethnic groups. Nationalist feelings among these subject peoples contributed to tensions building across Europe.

The Hapsburg Empire Declines

In 1800, the Hapsburgs were the oldest ruling house in Europe. In addition to their homeland of Austria, over the centuries they had acquired the territories of Bohemia and Hungary, as well as parts of Romania, Poland, Ukraine, and northern Italy.

Austria Faces Change Since the Congress of Vienna, the Austrian emperor Francis I and his foreign minister Metternich had upheld conservative goals against liberal forces. "Rule and change nothing," the emperor told his son. Under Francis and Metternich, newspapers could not even use the word *constitution*, much less discuss this key demand of liberals. The government also tried to limit industrial development, which would threaten traditional ways of life.

Austria, however, could not hold back the changes that were engulfing the rest of Europe. By the 1840s, factories were springing up. Soon, the Hapsburgs found themselves facing the problems of industrial life that had long been familiar in Britain—the growth of cities, worker discontent, and the stirrings of socialism.

A Multinational Empire Equally disturbing to the old order were the urgent demands of nationalists. The Hapsburgs presided over a multinational empire. Of its 50 million people at mid-century, fewer than a quarter were German-speaking Austrians. Almost half belonged to different Slavic groups, including Czechs, Slovaks, Poles, Ukrainians, Serbs, Croats, and Slovenes. Often, rival groups shared the same region. The empire also included large numbers of Hungarians and Italians. The Hapsburgs ignored nationalist demands as long as they could. When nationalist revolts broke out in 1848, the government crushed them.

Francis Joseph Grants Limited Reforms Amid the turmoil, 18-year-old Francis Joseph inherited the Hapsburg throne. He would rule until 1916, presiding over the empire during its fading days into World War I.

An early challenge came when Austria suffered its humiliating defeat at the hands of France and Sardinia in 1859. Francis Joseph realized he needed to strengthen the empire at home. Accordingly, he made some limited reforms. He granted a new constitution that set up a legislature. This body, however, was dominated by German-speaking Austrians. The reforms thus satisfied none of the other national groups that populated the empire. The Hungarians, especially, were determined to settle for nothing less than total self-government.

 **Checkpoint** What actions did Francis Joseph take to maintain power?

Formation of the Dual Monarchy

Austria's disastrous defeat in the 1866 war with Prussia brought renewed pressure for change from Hungarians within the empire. One year later, Ferenc Deák (DEH ahk), a moderate Hungarian leader, helped work out a compromise that created a new political power known as the Dual Monarchy of Austria-Hungary.

The Austria-Hungary Government Under the agreement, Austria and Hungary were separate states. Each had its own constitution and parliament. Francis Joseph ruled both, as emperor of Austria and king of Hungary. The two states also shared ministries of finance, defense, and foreign affairs, but were independent of each other in all other areas.

Nationalist Unrest Increases Although Hungarians welcomed the compromise, other subject peoples resented it. Restlessness increased among various Slavic groups, especially the Czechs in Bohemia. Some nationalist leaders called on Slavs to unite, insisting that "only through liberty, equality, and fraternal solidarity" could Slavic peoples fulfill their "great mission in the history of mankind." By the early 1900s, nationalist unrest often left the government paralyzed in the face of pressing political and social problems.

 **Checkpoint** How did Hungarians and Slavic groups respond to the Dual Monarchy?

Colors reflect the major languages spoken in Eastern Europe, 1800 to 1914.

Map Skills In the late 1800s, the Balkans had become a center of conflict, as various peoples and empires competed for power.

1. **Locate** (a) Black Sea (b) Ottoman empire (c) Serbia (d) Greece (e) Austria-Hungary
2. **Place** Which four large seas border the Balkan Peninsula?
3. **Identify Central Issues** Why do you think competing interests in the Balkans led the region to be called a powder keg?

The Ottoman Empire Collapses

Like the Hapsburgs, the Ottomans ruled a multinational empire. It stretched from Eastern Europe and the Balkans to North Africa and the Middle East. There, as in Austria, nationalist demands tore at the fabric of the empire.

Balkan Nationalism Erupts In the Balkans, Serbia won autonomy in 1830, and southern Greece won independence during the 1830s. But many Serbs and Greeks still lived in the Balkans under Ottoman rule. The Ottoman empire was also home to other national groups, such as Bulgarians and Romanians. During the 1800s, various subject peoples staged revolts against the Ottomans, hoping to set up their own independent states.

European Powers Divide Up the Ottoman Empire Such nationalist stirrings became mixed up with the ambitions of the great European powers. In the mid-1800s, Europeans came to see the Ottoman empire as "the sick man of Europe." Eagerly, they scrambled to divide up Ottoman lands. Russia pushed south toward the Black Sea and Istanbul, which Russians still called Constantinople. Austria-Hungary took control of the provinces of Bosnia and Herzegovina. This action angered the Serbs, who also had hoped to expand into that area. Meanwhile, Britain and France set their sights on other Ottoman lands in the Middle East and North Africa.

War in the Balkans In the end, a complex web of competing interests contributed to a series of crises and wars in the Balkans. Russia fought several wars against the Ottomans. France and Britain sometimes joined the Russians and sometimes the Ottomans. Germany supported Austrian authority over the discontented national groups. But Germany also encouraged the Ottomans because of their strategic location in the eastern Mediterranean. In between, the subject peoples revolted and then fought among themselves. By the early 1900s, observers were referring to the region as the "Balkan powder keg." The explosion that came in 1914 helped set off World War I.

 **Checkpoint** How did the European powers divide up Ottoman lands?

"The Sick Man of Europe"
Turkey's Abdul Hamid II (right) reacts to Bulgarian and Austrian rulers claiming parts of the Ottoman empire. *How does this cartoon show the Ottoman empire as "the sick man of Europe"?*

Terms, People, and Places

1. For each term, person, or place listed at the beginning of the section, write a sentence explaining its significance.

Note Taking

2. **Reading Skill: Recognize Sequence** Use your completed table to answer the Focus Question: How did the desire for national independence among ethnic groups weaken and ultimately destroy the Austrian and Ottoman empires?

Comprehension and Critical Thinking

3. **Identify Alternatives** What alternatives did Francis Joseph have in responding to nationalist demands? How might Austrian history have been different if he had chosen a different course of action?

4. **Draw Conclusions** Why did the Dual Monarchy fail to end nationalist demands?

5. **Identify Central Issues** How did Balkan nationalism contribute to the decline of the Ottoman empire?

● **Writing About History**

Quick Write: Draft an Opening Paragraph In a persuasive essay, you want to grab the reader's attention by opening with a strong example, and then convincingly stating your views. Choose a topic from the section, such as whether the Hapsburgs or the Ottoman Turks could have built a modern, unified nation from their multinational empires. Then draft an opening paragraph.

NATIONALISM

How can nationalism be a unifying and a divisive force?

In This Chapter

Nationalism is a powerful force characterized by strong feelings of pride in and devotion to one's nation. In the 1800s, nationalism forged new nations and tore old empires apart. For example, nationalists who believed that all Italian-speaking people on the Italian peninsula should be united created the nation of Italy (right).

Throughout History

1776 Americans declare independence from Great Britain.

1800s Latin America colonies rise up in rebellion against Spain.

1800s The Ottoman Empire is weakened by nationalist movements.

1900s After World War II, African nations gain independence from colonial rulers.

1990s Nationalist feelings among diverse ethnic groups leads to war in Yugoslavia.

Continuing Today

People will fight to establish or preserve their national identity, defend their own land, or even aggressively grab the territory of others. In Canada, the English-speaking majority has sought to maintain national unity in the face of a movement by French Canadians to establish an independent Quebec.

21st Century Skills

TRANSFER Activities

1. **Analyze** How has nationalism changed the course of history?

2. **Evaluate** Why do people respond to nationalism?

3. **Transfer** Complete a Web quest in which you decide if you would or would not support a nationalist movement; record your thoughts in the Concept Connector Journal; and learn to make a video. Web Code nah-2208

Russian peasant women clearing stones from a field

Plight of the Serfs

Although serfdom had almost disappeared in Western Europe by the 1700s, it survived in Russia. Masters exercised almost total power over their serfs. A noble turned revolutionary described the treatment of the serfs:

> **❝** I heard . . . stories of men and women torn from their families and their villages, and sold, or lost in gambling, or exchanged for a couple of hunting dogs, and then transported to some remote part of Russia to create a [master's] new estate; of children taken from their parents and sold to cruel . . . masters. **❞**
> —Peter Kropotkin, *Memoirs of a Revolutionist*

Focus Question Why did industrialization and reform come more slowly to Russia than to Western Europe?

Russia: Reform and Reaction

Objectives

- Describe major obstacles to progress in Russia.
- Explain why tsars followed a cycle of absolutism, reform, and reaction.
- Understand why the problems of industrialization contributed to the outbreak of revolution.

Terms, People, and Places

colossus	pogrom
Alexander II	refugees
Crimean War	Duma
emancipation	Peter Stolypin
zemstvo	

Note Taking

Reading Skill: Recognize Sequence Create a timeline of Russian events like the one below to keep track of the sequence of events that led to the revolution of 1905. Look for dates and other clues to sequence in the text.

1801
Alexander I
inherits throne.

1800   1850   1900   1950

Reformers hoped to free Russia from autocratic rule, economic backwardness, and social injustice. But efforts to modernize Russia had little success, as tsars imprisoned critics or sent them into exile.

Conditions in Russia

By 1815, Russia was not only the largest, most populous nation in Europe but also a great world power. Since the 1600s, explorers, soldiers, and traders seeking furs had expanded Russia's empire eastward across Siberia to the Pacific. Seeking ports, Peter the Great and Catherine the Great had added lands on the Baltic and Black seas. Seeking to contain the Ottoman and British empires, tsars in the 1800s expanded into the Caucasus and Central Asia. Russia thus acquired a huge multinational empire, part European and part Asian.

Other European nations looked on the Russian **colossus,** or giant, anxiously. Russia had immense natural resources. Its vast size gave it global influence. But many Europeans disliked its autocratic government and feared its expansion. At the same time, Russia remained economically undeveloped. By the 1800s, tsars saw the need to modernize but resisted reforms that would undermine their absolute rule.

Russia's Social Structure A great obstacle to progress was the rigid social structure. Landowning nobles dominated society and rejected any change that would threaten their power. The middle class was small and weak. Most Russians were serfs, or laborers bound to the land and to the landowners who controlled them.

Most serfs were peasants. Others were servants, artisans, or soldiers forced into the tsar's army. As industry expanded, some masters sent serfs to work in factories but took much of their pay.

Many enlightened Russians knew that serfdom was inefficient. As long as most people had to serve the whim of their masters, Russia's economy would remain backward. However, landowning nobles had no reason to improve agriculture and took little interest in industry.

Ruling With Absolute Power For centuries, tsars had ruled with absolute power, imposing their will on their subjects. On occasion, the tsars made limited attempts at liberal reform, such as easing censorship or making legal and economic reforms to improve the lives of serfs. However, in each instance the tsars drew back from their reforms when they began to fear losing the support of nobles. In short, the liberal and nationalist changes brought about by the Enlightenment and the French Revolution had almost no effect on Russian autocracy.

 **Checkpoint** Describe the social structure that existed in Russia during the 1800s.

Emancipation and Stirrings of Revolution

Alexander II came to the throne in 1855 during the **Crimean War.** His reign represents the pattern of reform and repression used by his father and grandfather, Alexander I and Nicholas I. The Crimean War had broken out after Russia tried to seize Ottoman lands along the Danube River. Britain and France stepped in to help the Ottoman Turks, invading the Crimean peninsula that juts into the Black Sea. The war, which ended in a Russian defeat, revealed the country's backwardness. Russia had only a few miles of railroads, and the military bureaucracy was hopelessly inefficient. Many felt that dramatic changes were needed.

Freeing the Serfs A widespread popular reaction followed. Liberals demanded changes, and students demonstrated, seeking reform. Pressed from all sides, Alexander II finally agreed to reforms. In 1861, he issued a royal decree that required **emancipation,** or freeing of the serfs.

Freedom brought problems. Former serfs had to buy the land they had worked, but many were too poor to do so. Also, the lands allotted to peasants were often too small to farm efficiently or to support a family. Peasants remained poor, and discontent festered.

Still, emancipation was a turning point. Many peasants moved to the cities, taking jobs in factories and building Russian industries. Equally important, freeing the serfs boosted the drive for further reform.

Introducing Other Reforms Along with emancipation, Alexander II set up a system of local government. Elected assemblies, called **zemstvos,** were made responsible for matters such as road repair, schools, and agriculture. Through this system, Russians gained some experience of self-government at the local level.

The Decembrist Revolt
In 1825, army officers led an uprising known as the Decembrist Revolt (below). They had picked up liberal ideas while fighting in Western Europe and demanded reforms and a constitution. Tsar Nicholas I repressed the revolt. This stamp (inset) commemorates the 125th anniversary of the revolt. *How did the revolt symbolize Russia in the 1800s?*

The tsar also introduced legal reforms based on ideas like trial by jury, and he eased censorship. Military service terms were reduced, and brutal discipline was limited. Alexander also encouraged the growth of industry in Russia, which still relied heavily on agriculture.

Revolutionary Currents Alexander's reforms failed to satisfy many Russians. Peasants had freedom but not land. Liberals wanted a constitution and an elected legislature. Radicals, who had adopted socialist ideas from the West, demanded even more revolutionary changes. The tsar, meantime, moved away from reform and toward repression.

In the 1870s, some socialists went to live and work among peasants, preaching reform and rebellion. They had little success. The peasants scarcely understood them and sometimes turned them over to the police. The failure of this movement, combined with renewed government repression, sparked anger among radicals. Some turned to terrorism. On March 13, 1881, terrorists assassinated Alexander II.

Crackdown Alexander III responded to his father's assassination by reviving the harsh methods of Nicholas I. To wipe out liberals and revolutionaries, he increased the power of the secret police, restored strict censorship, and exiled critics to Siberia. The tsar also launched a program of Russification aimed at suppressing the cultures of non-Russian peoples within the empire. Alexander insisted on one language, Russian,

Vocabulary Builder

radical—(RAD ih kul) *n.* a person who favors great changes or reforms

Tug of War: Reform and Repression by the Russian Tsars

The five tsars that ruled Russia from 1801 to 1917 all followed a similar pattern of autocratic rule: at times they appeared open to liberal ideas and enacted reforms to satisfy the groups demanding change. In every case, however, the tsars pulled back on these reforms and launched a battery of repressive measures designed to preserve their absolute power and the support of the nobles.

The Tsars Resist: Repression and Crackdown
- Secret police, arrests, executions
- Strict censorship of liberal ideas
- Exiling liberals
- Bolstering Russian Orthodox Church
- Insisting on the absolute power of the state
- Persecuting non-Russian groups within empire

◀ **Tsars**
Alexander I,
Nicholas I, Alexander II,
Alexander III, Nicholas II

▲ Jewish men survey damage done to sacred Torah scrolls during an 1881 pogrom in Russia.

and one church, the Russian Orthodox Church. Poles, Ukrainians, Finns, Armenians, Muslims, Jews, and many others suffered persecution.

Persecution and Pogroms Russia had acquired a large Jewish population when it carved up Poland and expanded into Ukraine. Under Alexander III, persecution of Jewish people in Russia increased. The tsar limited the number of Jewish people who were allowed to study in universities and practice certain professions. He also forced them to live in restricted areas.

Official persecution encouraged **pogroms,** or violent mob attacks on Jewish people. Gangs beat and killed Jewish people and looted and burned their homes and stores. Faced with savage persecution, many left Russia. They became **refugees,** or people who flee their homeland to seek safety elsewhere. Large numbers of Russian Jews went to the United States.

 **Checkpoint** How did Alexander III respond to the murder of his father?

The Drive to Industrialize

Russia finally entered the industrial age under Alexander III and his son Nicholas II. In the 1890s, Nicholas' government

Russian peasants in a rural village around 1900

The Tsars Give In:
Concessions and Reforms
- Easing censorship
- Revising law code
- Limiting the power of landowners
- Freeing serfs (1861)
- Creating local self-government, or zemstovs
- Creating national legislature, or Duma
- Land reforms

Opposing the Tsars ▶
Liberals, socialists, nationalists, army officers, workers

Thinking Critically
1. **Identify Main Ideas** What factors brought about so much opposition to the tsars?
2. **Draw Conclusions** Why do you think the tsars swung back and forth between repression and reform?

focused on economic development. It encouraged the building of railroads to connect iron and coal mines with factories and to transport goods across Russia. It also secured foreign capital to invest in industry and transportation systems, such as the Trans-Siberian Railroad, which linked European Russia to the Pacific Ocean.

Political and social problems increased as a result of industrialization. Government officials and business leaders applauded economic growth. Nobles and peasants opposed it, fearing the changes it brought. Industrialization also created new social ills as peasants flocked to cities to work in factories. Instead of a better life, they found long hours and low pay in dangerous conditions. In the slums around the factories, poverty, disease, and discontent multiplied. Radicals sought supporters among the new industrial workers. At factory gates, Socialists often handed out pamphlets that preached the revolutionary ideas of Karl Marx.

✔ **Checkpoint** How did Russia industrialize?

Turning Point: Crisis and Revolution

When war broke out between Russia and Japan in 1904, Nicholas II called on his people to fight for "the Faith, the Tsar, and the Fatherland." Despite all of their efforts, the Russians suffered one humiliating defeat after another.

Bloody Sunday News of the military disasters unleashed pent-up discontent created by years of oppression. Protesters poured into the streets. Workers went on strike, demanding shorter hours and better wages. Liberals called for a constitution and reforms to overhaul the government.

As the crisis deepened, a young Orthodox priest organized a peaceful march for Sunday, January 22, 1905. Marchers flowed through the streets of St. Petersburg toward the tsar's Winter Palace. Chanting prayers and singing hymns, workers carried holy icons and pictures of the tsar. They also brought a petition for justice and freedom.

Bloody Sunday

An artist's depiction shows the execution of workers in front of the Winter Palace in Saint Petersburg, January 9, 1905 (below). The magazine cover (inset) shows "Le Tzar Rouge," or "The Red Tsar." *Compare and contrast these images of Bloody Sunday.*

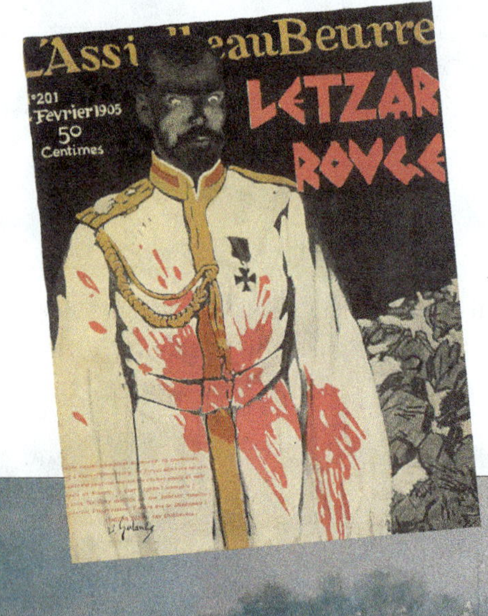

Fearing the marchers, the tsar had fled the palace and called in soldiers. As the people approached, they saw troops lined up across the square. Suddenly, gunfire rang out. Hundreds of men and women fell dead or wounded in the snow. One woman stumbling away from the scene moaned: "The tsar has deserted us! They shot away the orthodox faith." Indeed, the slaughter marked a turning point for Russians. "Bloody Sunday" killed the people's faith and trust in the tsar.

The Revolution of 1905 In the months that followed Bloody Sunday, discontent exploded across Russia. Strikes multiplied. In some cities, workers took over local government. In the countryside, peasants revolted and demanded land. Minority nationalities called for autonomy from Russia. Terrorists targeted officials, and some assassins were cheered as heroes by discontented Russians.

At last, the clamor grew so great that Nicholas was forced to announce sweeping reforms. In the October Manifesto, he promised "freedom of person, conscience, speech, assembly, and union." He agreed to summon a **Duma,** or elected national legislature. No law, he declared, would go into effect without approval by the Duma.

Results of the Revolution The manifesto won over moderates, leaving Socialists isolated. These divisions helped the tsar, who had no intention of letting strikers, revolutionaries, and rebellious peasants challenge him.

In 1906, the first Duma met, but the tsar quickly dissolved it when leaders criticized the government. Nicholas then appointed a new prime minister, **Peter Stolypin** (stuh LIP yin). Arrests, pogroms, and executions followed as the conservative Stolypin sought to restore order.

Stolypin soon realized that Russia needed reform, not just repression. To regain peasant support, he introduced moderate land reforms. He strengthened the zemstvos and improved education. Unfortunately, these reforms were too limited to meet the broad needs of most Russians, and dissatisfaction still simmered. Stolypin was assassinated in 1911. Several more Dumas met during this period, but new voting laws made sure they were conservative. By 1914, Russia was still an autocracy, but one simmering with unrest.

 **Checkpoint** Why was Bloody Sunday a turning point for the Russians?

Terms, People, and Places

1. For each term, person, or place listed at the beginning of the section, write a sentence explaining its significance.

Note Taking

2. **Reading Skill: Recognize Sequence** Use your completed timeline to answer the Focus Question: Why did industrialization and reform come more slowly to Russia than to Western Europe?

Comprehension and Critical Thinking

3. **Summarize** What conditions in Russia challenged progress during the early 1800s?

4. **Draw Conclusions** How did Russian tsars typically react to change?

5. **Draw Inferences** What does Bloody Sunday suggest about the relationship between the tsar and the Russian people?

● **Writing About History**

Quick Write: Gather Evidence to Support Thesis Statement Choose a topic from the section, such as whether you think emancipation helped or hurt Russian serfs. Make a list of evidence from the section that supports your view.

Quick Study Guide

Progress Monitoring *Online*
For: Self-test with vocabulary practice
Web Code: naa-2266

■ Effects of Nationalism

Nationalism by Region				
Germany	**Italy**	**Austria**	**Balkans**	**Russia**
• German states unite under William I. • Empire takes leading role in Europe. • Bismarck becomes known as the Iron Chancellor.	• Mazzini founds Young Italy. • Garibaldi leads Red Shirts. • Victor Emmanuel II makes Cavour prime minister of Sardinia. • Italian states become unified by 1871.	• Francis I and Metternich uphold conservative goals. • Dual Monarchy with Hungary is set up. • Nationalist groups grow restless. • Empire becomes weakened.	• Serbians achieve autonomy in 1830. • Greeks achieve independence in the 1830s. • European nations divide up Ottoman lands. • "Balkan powder keg" helps set off World War I.	• Serfs are freed in 1861. • Alexander III encourages persecution and pogroms. • Russia enters the industrial age late. • Bloody Sunday leads to revolution in 1905. • Duma has limited power.

■ Unification in Europe, 1873

As the map below shows, nationalist movements led to the creation of several new nations across Europe.

■ Key Leaders

Germany
Otto von Bismarck, *chancellor*
William I, *Prussian king, German kaiser*
William II, *kaiser*

Italy
Giuseppe Mazzini, *founder of Young Italy*
Victor Emmanuel II, *king*
Count Camillo Cavour, *prime minister*
Giuseppe Garibaldi, *leader of Red Shirts*

Austria-Hungary
Ferenc Deák, *Hungarian politician*
Francis Joseph, *Austrian emperor, Hungarian king*

Russia
Alexander II, *tsar of Russia*
Alexander III, *tsar of Russia*
Nicholas II, *tsar of Russia*

■ Key Events of Nationalism

Early 1800s
Nationalism rises in Germany.

1814
The Congress of Vienna redraws the map of Europe after Napoleon's defeat.

1830s
Giuseppe Mazzini founds Young Italy to encourage Italian unification.

Chapter Events
Global Events

1800   **1825**   **1850**

1804
Haiti declares independence from France.

1848
Revolutions take place throughout Europe.

Concept Connector

Essential Question Review

To connect prior knowledge with what you have learned in this chapter, answer the questions below in your Concept Connector journal. Use the journal in the Reading and Note Taking Study Guide to record your answers (or go to www.phschool.com Web Code: nad-2207).

1. **Empire** In 1864, the Prussian prime minister, Otto von Bismarck, formed an alliance with Austria. Prussia and Austria then seized and "liberated" two provinces from Denmark. By 1871, German nationalists were celebrating the birth of the second Reich. Describe two actions that von Bismarck took between 1864 and 1871 that show why he was considered a master of Realpolitik. What was von Bismarck's ultimate goal? How did these events result in the formation of the second Reich?

2. **Nationalism** During the early1800s, nationalist rebellions erupted in the Balkans. Many of the ethnic groups in the region hoped to overthrow Austrian and Ottoman rule and set up independent states of their own. Re-read Section 4 in this chapter. Take notes on the situation in the Balkans between 1800 and the early 1900s. Using your notes, create a timeline of the events in the Balkans leading up to 1914.

3. **Revolution** Many revolutions involve a conflict between tradition and progress. How did the conditions in Russia leading to the Revolution of 1905 demonstrate this conflict? Consider the actions of the tsar, the liberals, and the peasants. How did industrialization intensify the struggle between opposing factions?

■ Connections to Today

1. **Nationalism: The State of Nationalism Today** You've read how nationalism was a strong enough force in the 1800s to help unify nations, such as Italy and Germany, but threatened to destroy the Austrian and Ottoman empires. Do you think that nationalism is still a force in the world today? Conduct research to learn more about current nationalist issues. You may want to focus your research on Kurdistan, Northern Ireland, the former Yugoslavia, or Russia. Write two paragraphs on nationalism today, citing examples from current events to support your answer.

2. **Economic Systems: Social Welfare Programs** Under Otto von Bismarck, Germany was a pioneer in social reform, providing several social welfare programs to its citizens. By the 1890s, Germans had health and accident insurance as well as retirement benefits. Social welfare programs soon spread to other European nations. Conduct research to learn more about social welfare programs today. Compare social welfare programs in one country in Europe with those in the United States. How are they similar? How are they different?

1861
Tsar Alexander II frees the serfs.

1870
Bismarck provokes Franco-Prussian War to create a unified German empire.

1905
Revolution breaks out in St. Petersburg after Bloody Sunday massacre.

1875

1900

1925

1861
The Civil War begins in the United States.

1898
The Philippines declares independence from Spain.

1914
World War I begins.

Chapter Assessment

Terms, People, and Places

Match the following definitions with the terms listed below.

chancellor
Realpolitik
kaiser
social welfare
anarchist

emigration
emancipation
pogrom
Duma

1. someone who wants to abolish all government
2. elected national legislature in Russia
3. emperor of Germany
4. granting of freedom to serfs
5. the highest official of a monarch
6. violent attack on a Jewish community
7. movement away from one's homeland
8. realistic politics based on the needs of the state
9. programs to help people in need

Main Ideas

Section 1 (pp. 692–695)

10. What was Chancellor Otto von Bismarck's main goal? What policies did he follow to meet that goal?

Section 2 (pp. 696–699)

11. How did Germany increase its power in the late 1800s?

Section 3 (pp. 700–704)

12. Summarize the process by which Italy unified. Include information on the leaders who helped unify Italy.

Section 4 (pp. 705–709)

13. How did nationalism contribute to the decline of the Hapsburg and Ottoman empires?

Section 5 (pp. 710–715)

14. Why was Russia slow to industrialize?

Chapter Focus Question

15. What effects did nationalism and the demand for reform have in Europe?

Critical Thinking

16. **Make Comparisons** How did the nationalism represented by Bismarck differ from that embraced by liberals in the early 1800s?
17. **Make Comparisons** Compare and contrast the goals and methods of Cavour in Italy and Bismarck in Germany.
18. **Analyze Information** Tsar Alexander II declared that it is "better to abolish serfdom from above than to wait until it will be abolished by a movement from below." Explain his statement.
19. **Geography and History** How did regional differences contribute to continued divisions in Italy after unification?
20. **Analyzing Cartoons** How does this French cartoonist view Bismarck? Explain.
21. **Predict Consequences** Based on your reading of the chapter, predict the consequences of the following: (a) defeat of France in the Franco-Prussian War, (b) growth of German nationalism and militarism in the late 1800s, (c) failure to satisfy nationalist ambitions in Austria-Hungary, and (d) weakening of the Ottoman empire.

● Writing About History

In this chapter's five Section Assessments, you developed skills to write a pursuasive essay.

Writing a Persuasive Essay Some people define nationalism as excessive, narrow, or jingoist patriotism. A nationalist might be described as someone who boasts of his patriotism and favors aggressive or warlike policies. The rise of nationalism in Europe led to both division and unification. For example, it unified Germany, but it led Russian tsars to suppress the cultures of national minorities within the country. Nationalism remains a powerful force to this day for unifying countries and for sparking rivalries, conflicts, and bloodshed. Write a persuasive essay in which you support or oppose the idea that nationalism is an excessive form of patriotism.

Prewriting

- Collect the examples and evidence that you need to support your position convincingly.
- Use a graphic organizer to list points on both sides of the issue.

Drafting

- Focus on a thesis statement. Clearly state the position that you will prove. Use the rest of your introduction to provide readers with the necessary context about the issue.
- Acknowledge the opposition by stating, and then refuting, opposing arguments.

Revising

- Use the guidelines for revising your essay on page SH17 of the Writing Handbook.

Document-Based Assessment

On the Crimean Front

In 1853, the British, the French, and their allies took on the vast Russian empire in the Crimean War. Called a "perfectly useless modern war," it was fought in the Black Sea region, although major campaigns took place well beyond that area. Like all wars, it was grim. More than 500,000 people died during the conflict.

Document A

"[The Crimean War] was one of the last times that the massed formations of cavalry and infantry were employed—the thin red line was to disappear forever. Henceforward, armies would rely on open, flexible formations and on trench warfare. For the British, it was the end of an era: never again would their soldiers fight in full-dress uniform. Never again would the colors be carried into the fray and the infantry would no longer march into battle to the stirring tunes of regimental bands. The Crimean War ushered in the age of the percussion cap rifle. The new Minie rifle was the decisive weapon, replacing the clumsy . . . musket. The weapon fired a cartridge, not a ball, with accuracy far superior to the old firelocks. . . ."

—From ***The Road to Balaklava,*** by Alexis S. Troubetzkoy

Document B

"I see men in hundreds rushing from the Mamelon [bastion] to the Malakoff [tower]. . . . with all its bristling guns. Under what a storm of fire they advance, supported by that impenetrable red line, which marks our own infantry! The fire from the Malakoff is tremendous—terrible. . . . Presently the twilight deepens, and the light of rocket, mortar, and shell falls over the town."

—From ***Journal kept during the Russian War: From the Departure of the Army from England in April 1854, to the Fall of Sebastopol,*** by Mrs. Henry Duberly, an army wife

Document C

"Men sent in there [French hospital] with fevers and other disorders were frequently attacked with the cholera in its worst form, and died with unusual rapidity, in spite of all that could be done to save them. I visited the hospital, and observed that a long train of . . . carts, filled with sick soldiers, were drawn up by the walls. . . . the quiet that prevailed was only broken now and then by the moans and cries of pain of the poor sufferers in the carts."

—From ***The British Expedition to the Crimea*** by W. H. Russell, ***Times*** correspondent

Document D

Treating Cholera

Analyzing Documents

Use your knowledge of the Crimean War and Documents A, B, C, and D to answer questions 1–4.

1. According to Document A, the Crimean War marked the end of
   A private soldiers in war.
   B most small wars in Europe.
   C old ways of fighting.
   D soldiers dying of diseases in military hospitals.

2. With what purpose did the author write Document B?
   A to help people understand the dangers of fighting with new weapons
   B to criticize inadequate technology
   C to describe the state of mind of the soldiers
   D to make the British public understand how quickly the war was progressing

3. With what purpose did the artist create Document D?
   A to help the British public understand the dangers of fighting with new weapons
   B to criticize the inadequate state of army hospitals
   C to describe the dangers of soldiering and soldiers' valor
   D to make the British public understand the toll that disease was taking on soldiers

4. **Writing Task** Suppose you are a surgeon working near the war front. Write a brief letter home describing your impressions. Use the four documents along with information from the chapter to write your letter.

23

Growth of Western Democracies

1815–1914

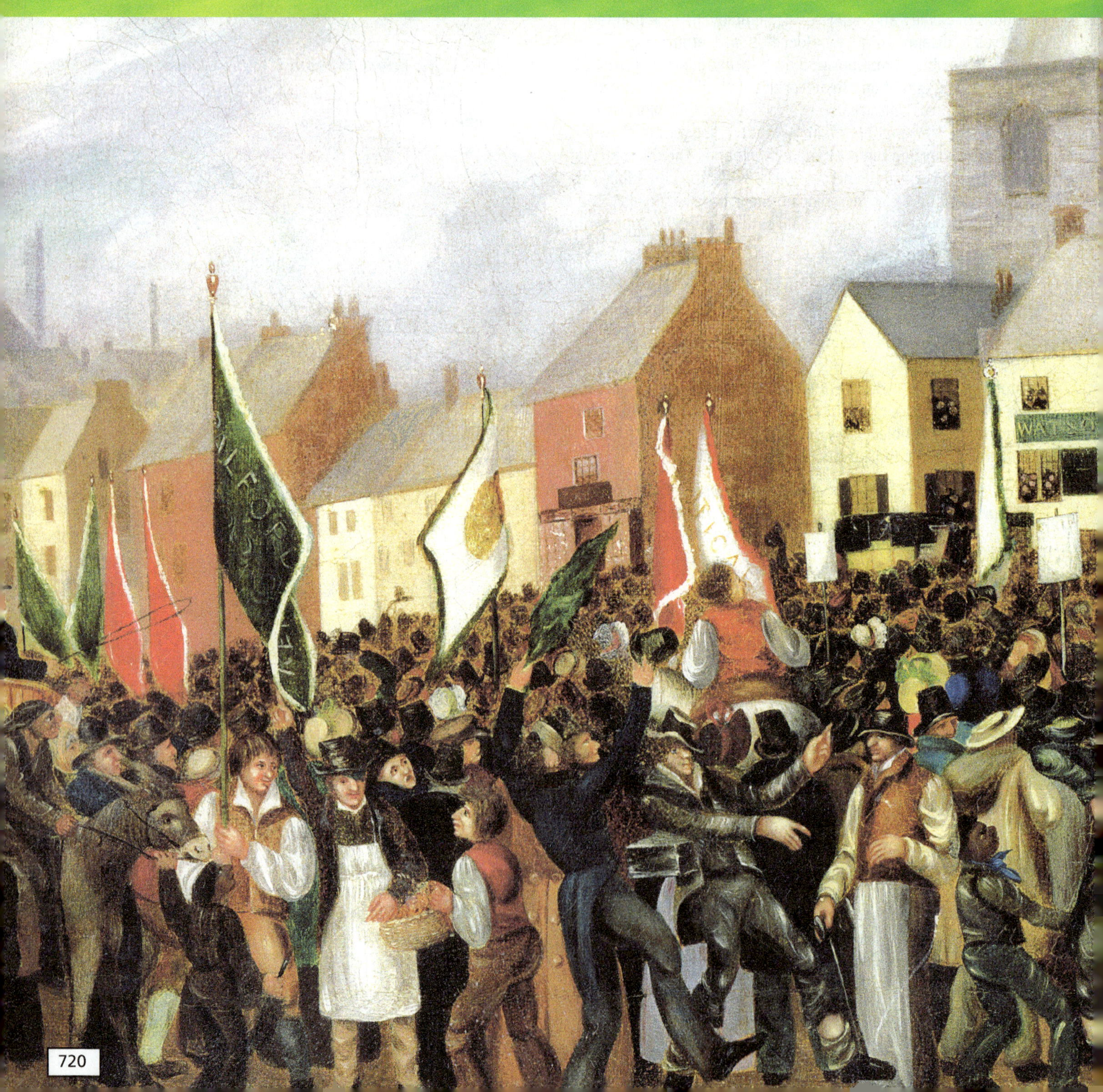

The People Demand Reform

A series of political reforms during the 1800s and early 1900s transformed Great Britain from a monarchy and aristocracy into a democracy. While some British politicians opposed the reforms, most sided in favor of reforming Parliament.

66No doubt, at that very early period, the House of Commons did represent the people of England but. . . . the House of Commons, as it presently subsists, does not represent the people of England. . . . The people called loudly for reform, saying that whatever good existed in the constitution of this House—whatever confidence was placed in it by the people, was completely gone. 99
—Lord John Russell, March 1, 1831

Listen to the Witness History audio to learn more about democratic developments in Britain.

◀ **Parliamentary Election of 1836**
Though most were unable to vote, many townspeople gathered in the marketplace to cheer or harass the candidates.

Queen Victoria of Great Britain and Ireland

A Liberal Party poster from 1911

Chapter Preview

Chapter Focus Question How did Britain, France, and the United States slowly extend democratic rights during the 1800s and early 1900s?

Section 1
Democratic Reform in Britain

Section 2
Social and Economic Reform in Britain

Section 3
Division and Democracy in France

Section 4
Expansion of the United States

Use the ✔ **Quick Study Timeline** at the end of this chapter to preview chapter events.

Advertisement for transportation to California during the Gold Rush

 Concept Connector ONLINE

To explore Essential Questions related to this chapter, go to PHSchool.com
Web Code: nad-2307

Fashions of the rich (above right), and poverty on the streets of London, circa 1877 (above)

WITNESS HISTORY AUDIO

Two Nations

One day a wealthy Englishman named Charles Egremont boasted to strangers that Victoria, the queen of England, "reigns over the greatest nation that ever existed."

"Which nation?" asks one of the strangers, "for she reigns over two. . . . Two nations; between whom there is no [communication] and no sympathy; who are as ignorant of each other's habits, thoughts, and feelings, as if they were . . . inhabitants of different planets."

What are these "two nations," Egremont asks. "THE RICH AND THE POOR," the stranger replies.

—Benjamin Disraeli, *Sybil*

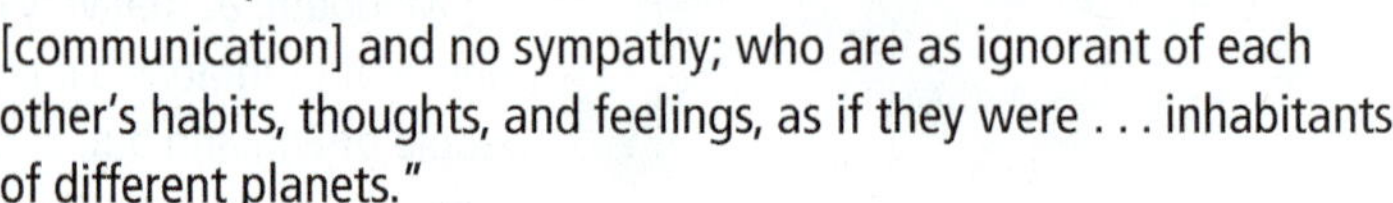

Focus Question How did political reform gradually expand suffrage and make the British Parliament more democratic during the 1800s?

Democratic Reform in Britain

Objectives

- Describe how reformers worked to change Parliament in the 1800s.
- Understand the values that Queen Victoria represented.
- Summarize how the Liberal and Conservative parties helped bring a new era to British politics.

Terms, People, and Places

rotten borough
electorate
secret ballot
Queen Victoria

Benjamin Disraeli
William Gladstone
parliamentary democracy

Note Taking

Reading Skill: Identify Main Ideas As you read this section, complete an outline of the contents.

I. Reforming Parliament
  A. Reformers press for change
    1.
    2.

In the 1800s, Benjamin Disraeli and other political leaders slowly worked to bridge Britain's "two nations" and extend democratic rights. Unlike some of its neighbors in Europe, Britain generally achieved change through reform rather than revolution.

Reforming Parliament

In 1815, Britain was a constitutional monarchy with a parliament and two political parties. Still, it was far from democratic. Although members of the House of Commons were elected, less than five percent of the people had the right to vote. Wealthy nobles and squires, or country landowners, dominated politics and heavily influenced voters. In addition, the House of Lords—made up of hereditary nobles and high-ranking clergy—could veto any bill passed by the House of Commons.

Reformers Press for Change Long-standing laws kept many people from voting. Catholics and non-Anglican Protestants, for example, could not vote or serve in Parliament. In the 1820s, reformers pushed to end religious restrictions. After fierce debate, Parliament finally granted Catholics and non-Anglican Protestants equal political rights.

An even greater battle soon erupted over making Parliament more representative. During the Industrial Revolution, centers of population shifted. Some rural towns lost so many people that they had few or no voters. Yet local landowners in these **rotten boroughs** still sent members to Parliament. At the same time, populous new industrial cities like Manchester and Birmingham had no seats <u>allocated</u> in Parliament because they had not existed as population centers in earlier times.

Reform Act of 1832 By 1830, Whigs and Tories were battling over a bill to reform Parliament. The Whig Party largely represented middle-class and business interests. The Tory Party spoke for nobles, landowners, and others whose interests and income were rooted in agriculture. In the streets, supporters of reform chanted, "The Bill, the whole Bill, and nothing but the Bill!" Their shouts seemed to echo the cries of revolutionaries on the continent.

Parliament finally passed the Great Reform Act in 1832. It redistributed seats in the House of Commons, giving representation to large towns and cities and eliminating rotten boroughs. It also enlarged the **electorate,** the body of people allowed to vote, by granting suffrage to more men. The Act did, however, keep a property requirement for voting.

The Reform Act of 1832 did not bring full democracy, but it did give a greater political voice to middle-class men. Landowning nobles, however, remained a powerful force in the government and in the economy.

The Chartist Movement The reform bill did not help rural or urban workers. Some of them demanded more radical change. In the 1830s, protesters known as Chartists drew up the People's Charter. This petition demanded universal male suffrage, annual parliamentary elections, and salaries for members of Parliament. Another key demand was for a **secret ballot,** which would allow people to cast their votes without announcing them publicly.

Twice the Chartists presented petitions with over a million signatures to Parliament. Both petitions were ignored. In 1848, as revolutions swept Europe, the Chartists prepared a third petition and organized a march on Parliament. Fearing violence, the government moved to suppress the march. Soon after, the unsuccessful Chartist movement declined. In time, however, Parliament would pass most of the major reforms proposed by the Chartists.

 **Checkpoint** How was the British Parliament reformed during the early 1800s?

The Victorian Age

From 1837 to 1901, the great symbol in British life was **Queen Victoria.** Her reign was the longest in British history. Although she exercised little real political power, she set the tone for what is now called the Victorian age.

Symbol of a Nation's Values As queen, Victoria came to embody the values of her age. These Victorian ideals included duty, thrift, honesty, hard work, and above all respectability. Victoria herself embraced a strict code of morals and manners. As a young woman, she married a German prince, Albert, and they raised a large family.

A Confident Age Under Victoria, the British middle class—and growing numbers of the working class—felt great confidence in the future. That confidence grew as Britain expanded its already huge empire.

Meeting of the Unions on Newhall Hill, Birmingham
The Birmingham Political Union's enormous rallies (above) and calls for reform are credited with the final passage of the Great Reform Bill of 1832. As one politician said of the BPU, "To this body, more than to any other, is confessedly due the triumph (such as it was) of the Reform Bill. Its well-ordered proceedings, extended organisation, and immense assemblages of people, at critical periods of its progress, rendered the measure irresistible."

From Monarchy to Democracy in Britain

In the early 1800s, Britain's government was a monarchy and an aristocracy under the rule of Queen Victoria ① and the aristocrats and landowners in the House of Lords. ② A series of reforms during the 1800s and early 1900s transformed Britain's government into a democracy. The first of these reforms was the Great Reform Act of 1832, by which seats in the Parliament were redistributed to give more representation to growing industrial areas. The act also expanded the vote to include about one in five adult men. The Second Reform Act in 1867 was spearheaded by Benjamin Disraeli, ④ a Conservative leader who hoped to defeat his liberal rival William Gladstone ③ and

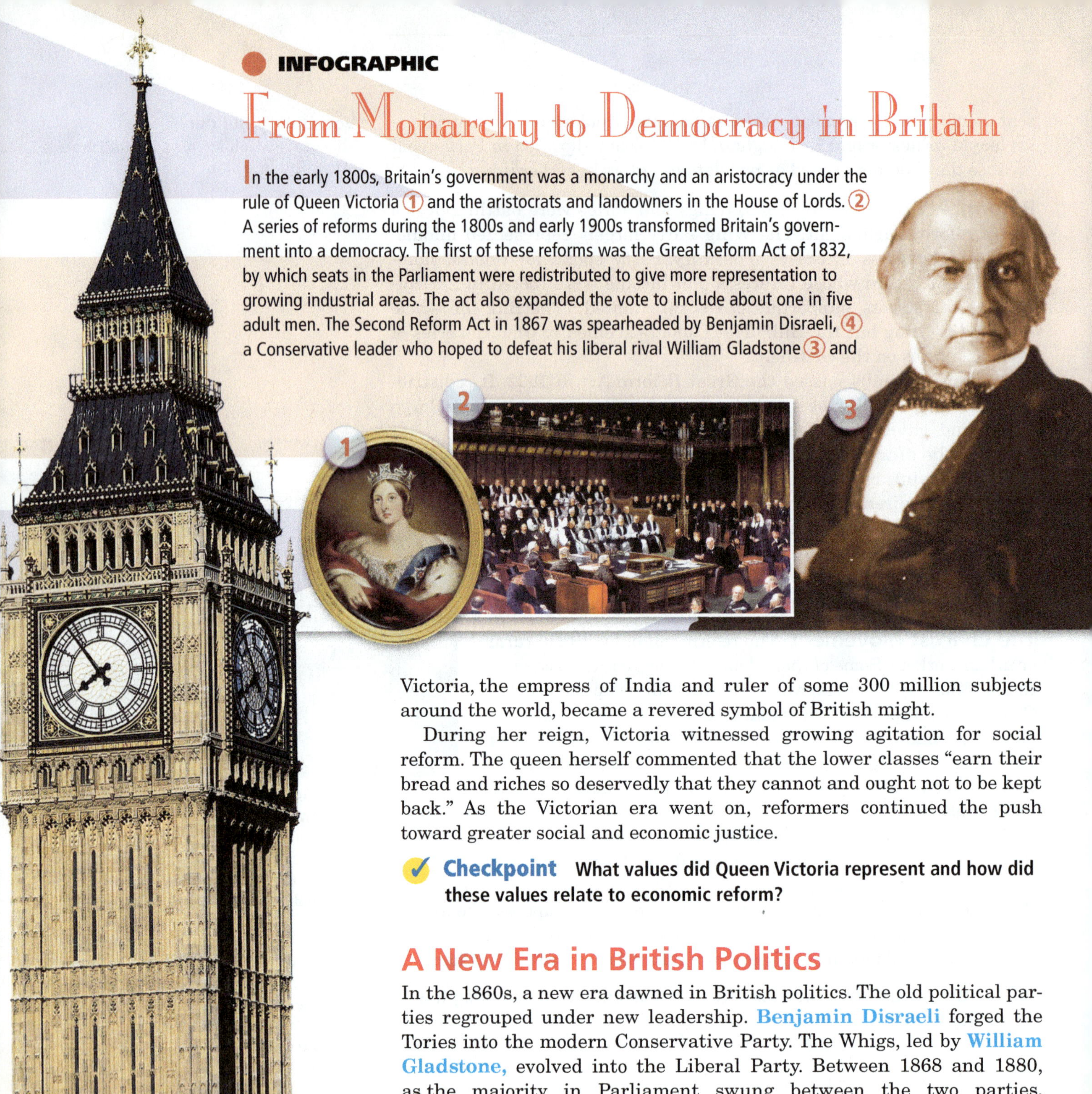

Victoria, the empress of India and ruler of some 300 million subjects around the world, became a revered symbol of British might.

During her reign, Victoria witnessed growing agitation for social reform. The queen herself commented that the lower classes "earn their bread and riches so deservedly that they cannot and ought not to be kept back." As the Victorian era went on, reformers continued the push toward greater social and economic justice.

✔ **Checkpoint**   What values did Queen Victoria represent and how did these values relate to economic reform?

A New Era in British Politics

In the 1860s, a new era dawned in British politics. The old political parties regrouped under new leadership. **Benjamin Disraeli** forged the Tories into the modern Conservative Party. The Whigs, led by **William Gladstone,** evolved into the Liberal Party. Between 1868 and 1880, as the majority in Parliament swung between the two parties, Gladstone and Disraeli alternated as prime minister. Both fought for important reforms.

Expanding Suffrage Disraeli and the Conservative Party pushed through the Reform Bill of 1867. By giving the vote to many working-class men, the new law almost doubled the size of the electorate.

In the 1880s, it was the turn of Gladstone and the Liberal Party to extend suffrage. Their reforms gave the vote to farmworkers and most other men. By century's end, almost-universal male suffrage, the secret ballot, and other Chartist ambitions had been achieved. Britain had truly transformed itself from a constitutional monarchy to a **parliamentary democracy,** a form of government in which the executive leaders (usually

give the vote to people who might vote for his Conservative party. As a result of the act, about one in three adult men could vote, including many working-class men. 
The Third Reform Act in 1884–1885 further extended the vote to two out of three adult males and redistributed seats in Parliament to more accurately reflect the distribution of the population. The outbreak of World War I brought about the Fourth Reform Act of 1918, which extended suffrage to all men over 21, and those aged 19 and over who were fighting the war. Women over 30 were also given the vote.
Meanwhile, a power struggle between the House of Lords and the House of Commons resulted in the Parliament Bill of 1911 which gave the House of Commons  supremacy over the House of Lords.

a prime minister and cabinet) are chosen by and responsible to the legislature (parliament), and are also members of it.

Limiting the Lords In the early 1900s, many bills passed by the House of Commons met defeat in the House of Lords. In 1911, a Liberal government passed measures to restrict the power of the Lords, including their power to veto tax bills. The Lords resisted. Finally, the government threatened to create enough new lords to approve the law, and the Lords backed down. People hailed the change as a victory for democracy. In time, the House of Lords would become a largely ceremonial body with little power. The elected House of Commons would reign supreme.

✔ **Checkpoint** How was Parliament reformed during the late 1800s and early 1900s?

Thinking Critically

1. **Recognize Ideologies** Which group in the early 1800s do you think most feared the "democratization" of Britain? Why?
2. **Identify Central Issues** How did the Parliament Bill in 1911 reflect the same trends occurring as a result of the reform acts?

Assessment

Progress Monitoring *Online*
For: Self-quiz with vocabulary practice
Web Code: naa-2312

Terms, People, and Places

1. What do each of the key terms listed at the beginning of the section have in common? Explain.

Note Taking

2. **Reading Skill: Identify Main Ideas** Use your completed outline to answer the Focus Question: How did political reform gradually expand suffrage and make the British Parliament more democratic during the 1800s?

Comprehension and Critical Thinking

3. **Summarize** How did the Reform Act of 1832 change Parliament?
4. **Categorize** What middle-class values are associated with the Victorian age?
5. **Identify Central Issues** What reforms did the Liberal and Conservative parties achieve?
6. **Draw Conclusions** Why do you think the Chartists demanded (a) a secret ballot, (b) salaries for members of Parliament?

● **Writing About History**

Quick Write: Gather Information If you were assigned to write a biographical essay on Queen Victoria, Benjamin Disraeli, or William Gladstone, what questions about these individuals would you want to answer in your essay? Choose one of these people and create a list of such questions about that person.

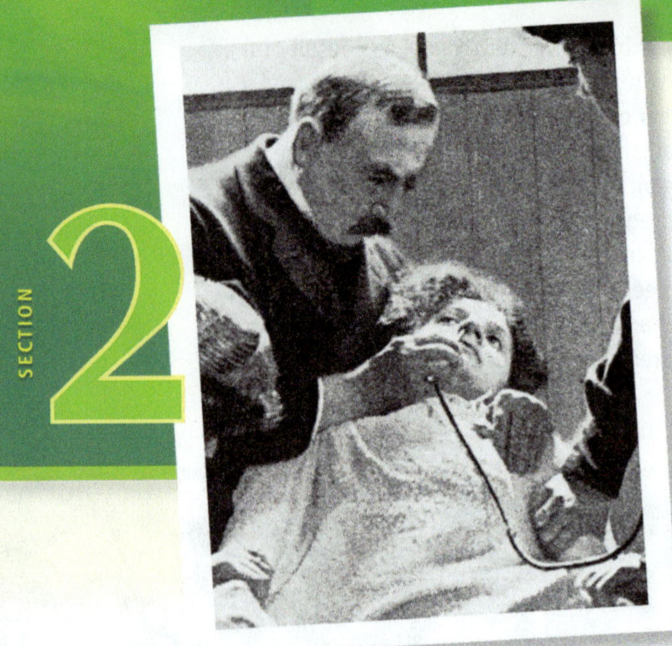

Forced feeding of English suffragist, 1912

No Surrender

Lady Constance Lytton had been arrested for taking part in a women's suffrage protest. Once arrested, she refused to eat. Her hunger strike, she vowed, would go on until the British government granted the vote to women. Lytton later recalled:

> **❝**I was visited again by the Senior Medical Officer, who asked me how long I had been without food. I said I had eaten . . . on Friday at about midnight. He said, 'Oh, then, this is the fourth day; that is too long, I shall feed you, I must feed you at once.'**❞**
> —Constance Lytton, *Prisons and Prisoners*

In the end, the doctor force-fed Lytton through a tube. Yet the painful ordeal failed to weaken her resolve. "No surrender," she whispered. "No surrender."

Focus Question What social and economic reforms were passed by the British Parliament during the 1800s and early 1900s?

Social and Economic Reform in Britain

Objectives
- Identify the social and economic reforms benefiting British workers and others.
- Describe how British women worked to win the right to vote.
- Understand the causes of conflict between the British and the Irish nationalists.

Terms, People, and Places

free trade   penal colony
repeal   absentee landlord
abolition movement   home rule
capital offense

Note Taking

Reading Skill: Categorize Complete a chart like this one listing the reforms in Britain during the 1800s and early 1900s.

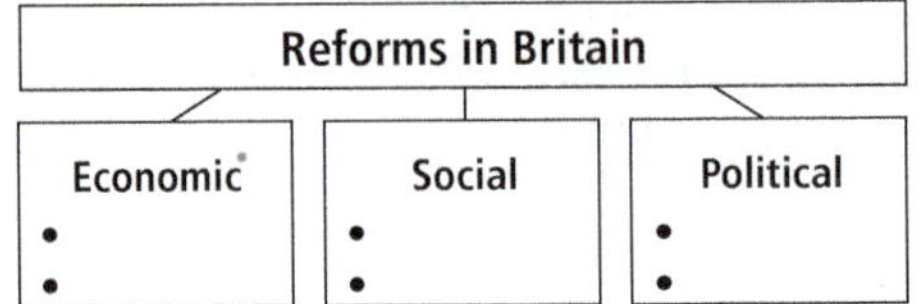

Lytton's 1910 hunger strike was part of the long struggle for women's suffrage in Britain. Suffragists were not the only people to fight for change. Between 1815 and 1914, Parliament responded to widespread discontent with a series of social and economic reforms. At the same time, the question of British control over Ireland was becoming a dominant and divisive political issue.

A Series of Reforms

During the early and mid-1800s, Parliament passed a wide variety of important new laws. One of the most controversial measures involved the issue of **free trade,** or trade between countries without quotas, tariffs, or other restrictions.

Free Trade and the Corn Laws In the early 1800s, Britain, like other European nations, taxed foreign imports in order to protect local economies. But supporters of free trade demanded an end to such protective tariffs. Free traders, usually middle-class business leaders, agreed with Adam Smith that a policy of laissez faire would increase prosperity for all. If tariffs were abolished, merchants everywhere would have larger markets in which to sell their goods, and consumers would benefit from open competition.

Some British tariffs were repealed in the 1820s. However, fierce debate erupted over the Corn Laws, which imposed high tariffs on imported grain. (In Britain, "corn" refers to all cereal grains, such as wheat, barley, and oats.) Farmers and wealthy landowners supported the Corn Laws because they kept the price of British grain high. Free traders, however, wanted Parliament to **repeal,** or cancel, the Corn Laws. They argued that repeal of these laws would lower the price of grain, make bread cheaper for workers, and open up trade in general.

Parliament finally repealed the Corn Laws in 1846, after widespread crop failures swept many parts of Europe. Liberals hailed the repeal as a victory for free trade and laissez-faire capitalism. However, in the late 1800s, economic hard times led Britain and other European countries to impose protective tariffs on many goods again.

Campaign Against Slavery During the 1700s, Enlightenment thinkers had turned the spotlight on the evils of the slave trade. At the time, British ships were carrying more Africans to the Americas than any other European country. Under pressure from middle-class reformers in Britain, France, and the United States, the **abolition movement,** or the campaign against slavery and the slave trade, slowly took off. In 1807, Britain became the first European power to abolish the slave trade.

Banning the slave trade did not end slavery. Although the Congress of Vienna had condemned slavery, it had taken no action. In Britain, liberals preached the immorality of slavery. Finally, in 1833, Parliament passed a law banning slavery in all British colonies.

Crime and Punishment Other reforms were aimed at the criminal justice system. In the early 1800s, more than 200 crimes were punishable by death. Such **capital offenses** included not only murder but also shoplifting, sheep stealing, and impersonating an army veteran. In practice, some juries refused to convict criminals, because the punishments were so harsh. Executions were public occasions, and the hanging of a well-known murderer might attract thousands of curious spectators. Afterward, instead of receiving a proper burial, the criminal's body might be given to a medical college for dissection.

Reformers began to reduce the number of capital offenses. By 1850, the death penalty was reserved for murder, piracy, treason, and arson. Many petty criminals were instead transported to **penal colonies,** or settlements for convicts, in the new British territory of Australia. In 1868, Parliament ended public hangings. Additional reforms improved prison conditions and outlawed imprisonment due to debt.

 **Checkpoint** How did abolition and criminal justice reform reflect Victorian values?

Victories for the Working Class

"Four [ghosts] haunt the Poor: Old Age, Accident, Sickness and Unemployment," declared Liberal politician David Lloyd George in 1905. "We are going to [expel] them." Parliament had begun passing laws aimed at improving social conditions as early as the 1840s. During the early 1900s, it passed a series of additional reforms designed to help the men, women, and children whose labor supported the new industrial society.

Improving Working Conditions As you have read, working conditions in the early industrial age were grim and often dangerous. Gradually, Parliament passed laws to regulate conditions in factories and mines. In 1842, for example, mineowners were forbidden to employ

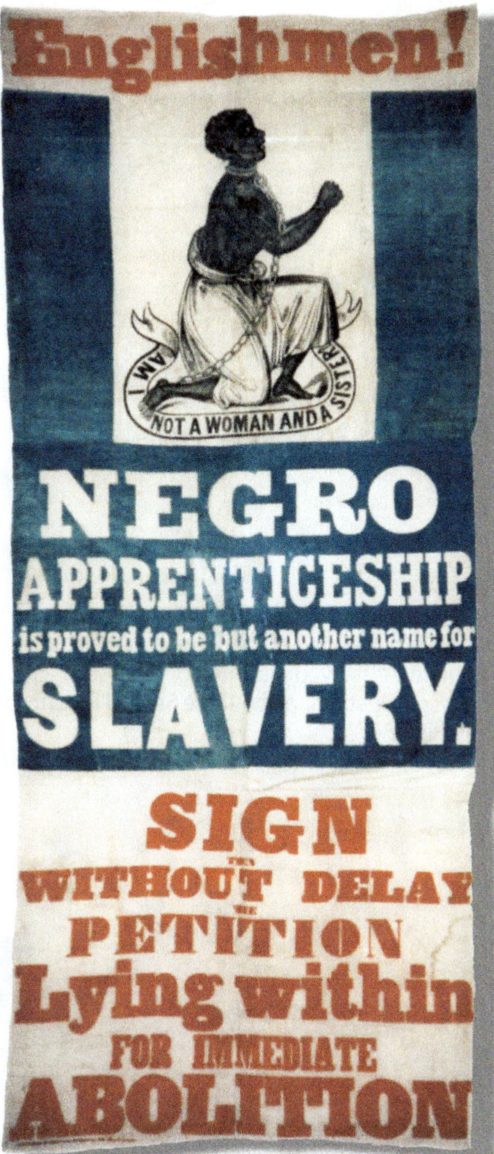

Abolitionist Poster
Abolitionists hoped that ending the slave trade would also bring about the end of slavery. As this poster shows, even ending slavery did not end the economic mistreatment of people of African descent.

women or children under age 10. An 1847 law limited women and children to a 10-hour day. Later in the 1800s, the government regulated many safety conditions in factories and mines—and sent inspectors to see that the laws were enforced. Other laws set minimum wages and maximum hours of work.

The Growth of Labor Unions Early in the Industrial Revolution, labor unions were outlawed. Under pressure, government and business leaders slowly accepted worker organizations. Trade unions were made legal in 1825 but it remained illegal to go on strike until later in the century.

Despite restrictions, unions spread, and gradually they won additional rights. Between 1890 and 1914, union membership soared. Besides winning higher wages and shorter hours for workers, unions pressed for other laws to improve the lives of the working class.

Later Reforms During the late 1800s and early 1900s, both political parties enacted social reforms to benefit the working class. Disraeli sponsored laws to improve public health and housing for workers in cities. Under Gladstone, an education act called for free elementary education for all children. Gladstone also pushed to open up government jobs based on merit rather than on birth or wealth.

Another force for reform was the Fabian Society, a socialist organization founded in 1883. The Fabians promoted gradual change through legal means rather than by violence. Though small in number, the Fabians had a strong influence on British politics.

In 1900, socialists and union members backed the formation of a new political party, which became the Labour Party. ("Labour" is the British spelling of "labor.") The Labour Party would quickly grow in power and membership until, by the 1920s, it surpassed the Liberal Party and became one of Britain's two major parties.

▼ **Riots in Hyde Park, London**
An 1866 meeting of the Reform League in London dissolved into rioting. Riots such as these helped bring about the Second Reform Bill in 1867.

In the early 1900s, Britain began to pass social welfare laws to protect the well-being of the poor and disadvantaged. These laws were modeled on those Bismarck had introduced in Germany. They protected workers with accident, health, and unemployment insurance as well as old-age pensions. One result of such reforms was that Marxism gained only limited support among the British working class. The middle class hailed reforms as proof that democracy was working.

 **Checkpoint** Describe several social welfare reforms during the 1800s and early 1900s.

▲ A Liberal Party poster from 1911

The Struggle to Win Votes for Women

In Britain, as elsewhere, women struggled against strong opposition for the right to vote. Women themselves were divided on the issue. Some women opposed suffrage altogether. Queen Victoria, for example, called the suffrage struggle "mad, wicked folly." Even women in favor of suffrage disagreed about how best to achieve it.

Suffragists Revolt By the early 1900s, Emmeline Pankhurst, a leading suffragist, had become convinced that only aggressive tactics would bring victory. Pankhurst and other radical suffragists interrupted speakers in Parliament, shouting, "Votes for women!" until they were carried away. They collected petitions and organized huge public demonstrations. When mass meetings and other peaceful efforts brought no results, some women turned to more <u>drastic</u>, violent protest. They smashed windows or even burned buildings. Pankhurst justified such tactics as necessary to achieve victory. "There is something that governments care far more for than human life," she declared, "and that is the security of property, so it is through property that we shall strike the enemy." As you have read, some suffragists went on hunger strikes, risking their lives to achieve their goals.

Victory at Last Even middle-class women who disapproved of such radical and violent actions increasingly demanded votes for women. Still, Parliament refused to grant women's suffrage. Not until 1918 did Parliament finally grant suffrage to women over age 30. Younger women did not win the right to vote for another decade.

Checkpoint Why do you think women disagreed about how best to gain suffrage?

Instability in Ireland

Throughout the 1800s, Britain faced the ever-present "Irish question." The English had begun conquering Ireland in the 1100s. In the 1600s, English and Scottish settlers colonized Ireland, taking possession of much of the best farmland.

The Irish never accepted English rule. They bitterly resented settlers, especially **absentee landlords** who owned large estates but did not live on them. Many Irish peasants lived in desperate poverty, while paying high rents to landlords living in England. In addition, the Irish, most of whom were Catholic, had to pay tithes to support the Church of England. Under these conditions, resistance and rebellion were common.

Vocabulary Builder

<u>drastic</u>—(DRAS tik) *adj.* severe, harsh, extreme

The Irish Potato Famine

Under British rule, three quarters of Irish farmland was used to grow crops that were exported. The potato was the main source of food for most of the Irish people. In 1845, disaster struck. A blight, or disease, destroyed the potato crop. Other crops, such as wheat and oats, were not affected. Yet British landowners continued to ship these crops outside Ireland, leaving little for the Irish except the blighted potatoes. The result was a terrible famine that the Irish called the "Great Hunger." In four years, about one million Irish men, women, and children died of starvation or disease. Many more emigrated to the United States and Canada. The Great Hunger left a legacy of Irish bitterness toward the English.

"Tumbled" Houses and Eviction ▶

Unable to grow potatoes to sell or eat, thousands of penniless tenants were evicted from their homes by landlords who needed the rent to pay their taxes. The roofs of the peasants' homes were "tumbled," or removed, to prevent the tenants from returning.

Number of Overseas Emigrants from Ireland, 1851–1921*	
1851–1860	1,216,219
1861–1870	818,582
1871–1880	542,703
1881–1890	734,475
1891–1900	461,282
1901–1910	485,461
1911–1921	355,295
Total 1851–1921	**4,614,017**

*Primarily to the United States, Canada, Australia, and New Zealand

SOURCE: Commission on Emigration and Other Population Problems, Dublin, 1954

Human Suffering ▼

One official told of entering what he thought was a deserted village. In one home, he saw "six famished and ghastly skeletons, to all appearances dead…" huddled in a corner on some filthy straw. "I approached with horror and found by a low moaning they were alive—they were in a fever, four children, a woman and what had once been a man…."

Limited Relief Measures ▲

Charles Trevelyan, the senior British official in charge of Irish relief efforts, held ruthless views of the Irish, insisting that they learn to "depend upon themselves…instead of…the assistance of the Government on every occasion."

Thinking Critically

1. **Graph Skills** Which decade saw the greatest number of emigrants from Ireland?
2. **Draw Conclusions** Do you think the Irish famine was more accurately described as a natural disaster or a human-made disaster? Why?

Irish Nationalism   Like the national minorities in the Austrian empire, Irish nationalists campaigned vigorously for freedom and justice in the 1800s. Nationalist leader Daniel O'Connell, nicknamed "the Liberator," organized an Irish Catholic League and held mass meetings to demand repeal of unfair laws. "My first object," declared O'Connell, "is to get Ireland for the Irish."

Under pressure from O'Connell and other Irish nationalists, Britain slowly moved to improve conditions in Ireland. In 1829, Parliament passed the Catholic Emancipation Act, which allowed Irish Catholics to vote and hold political office. Yet many injustices remained. Absentee landlords could evict tenants almost at will. Other British laws forbade the teaching and speaking of the Irish language.

Struggle for Home Rule   The famine in Ireland (see facing page) left the Irish with a legacy of bitterness and distrust toward Britain. In the 1850s, some Irish militants organized the Fenian Brotherhood. Its goal was to liberate Ireland from British rule by force. In the 1870s, moderate Irish nationalists found a rousing leader in Charles Stewart Parnell. He rallied Irish members of Parliament to press for **home rule**, or local self-government. The debate dragged on for decades.

The "Irish question" disrupted English politics. At times, political parties were so deeply split over the Irish question that they could not take care of other business. As prime minister, Gladstone pushed for reforms in Ireland. He ended the use of Irish tithe money to support the Anglican church and tried to ease the hardships of Irish tenant farmers. New laws prevented landlords from charging unfair rents and protected the rights of tenants to the land they worked.

Finally, in 1914, Parliament passed a home rule bill. But it delayed putting the new law into effect when World War I broke out that year. As you will read, the southern counties of Ireland finally became independent in 1921.

 **Checkpoint**   How did English policies toward Ireland affect the cause of Irish Nationalism?

SECTION **2**

Assessment

Terms, People, and Places

1. Place each of the key terms at the beginning of the section into these two categories: economic or political. Write a sentence for each term explaining your choice.

Note Taking

2. **Reading Skill: Categorize**   Use your chart to answer the Focus Question: What social and economic reforms were passed by the British Parliament during the 1800s and early 1900s?

Comprehension and Critical Thinking

3. **Summarize**   Describe three reforms that helped the British working class.
4. **Compare Points of View**   What actions did women suffragists take to achieve their goals? How did the views of women differ regarding tactics?
5. **Identify Central Issues**   (a) Why did Irish nationalists oppose British rule? (b) Describe two reforms that improved conditions in Ireland.

 **Writing About History**

Quick Write: Write a Thesis Statement   Write the thesis statement for an editorial written by an Irish nationalist of the late 1800s or early 1900s. First, decide whether your main goal is to win support for your cause from the Irish or to persuade members of the British Parliament.

Concept Connector

MIGRATION

Under what circumstances do people migrate?

In This Chapter

In the 1800s, famine drove more than a million Irish to leave their homeland for distant shores (right). In later years, millions more Europeans would migrate to North and South America, mainly seeking economic opportunity. Like most emigrants, they left home for a future that was uncertain at best.

Throughout History

200s–400s A.D. Mongol invasions ultimately drive the Vandals into the western Roman empire.

900s Nomadic Magyars settle in what is now Hungary.

1500s–1800s In a forced migration, millions of enslaved Africans are transported to the Americas.

1930s Stalin forces millions of peasants and political opponents into labor camps in Siberia.

1947 Muslims flee to India and Hindus flee to Pakistan to escape religious persecution after the partition of India.

Continuing Today

While the circumstances surrounding migration change over time, the motives remain very constant. The migration to Europe of Muslims from the Middle East and North Africa began in the 1960s with Turkish guest workers. Many of these "guests" have become permanent residents.

21st Century Skills

? TRANSFER Activities

1. **Analyze** Throughout history, what has motivated people to move?

2. **Evaluate** How do the factors for voluntary migration differ from those for involuntary migration?

3. **Transfer** Complete a Web quest analyzing the paths and motives of migrants; record your thoughts in the Concept Connector Journal; and learn to make a video. Web Code nah-2308

Following Napoleon III's surrender (above), Georges Clemenceau (above right) rallied the people of Paris to defend their city.

Vive la France!

The news sent shock waves through Paris. Napoleon III had surrendered to the Prussians and Prussian forces were now about to advance on Paris. Could the city survive? Georges Clemenceau (kleh mahn soh), a young French politician, rallied the people of Paris to defend their homeland:

> **66** Citizens, must France destroy herself and disappear, or shall she resume her old place in the vanguard of nations? . . . Each of us knows his duty. We are children of the Revolution. Let us seek inspiration in the example of our forefathers in 1792, and like them we shall conquer. *Vive la France!* (Long Live France!) **99**

Focus Question What democratic reforms were made in France during the Third Republic?

Division and Democracy in France

Objectives

- List the domestic and foreign policies of Napoleon III.
- Analyze the impact of the Dreyfus affair and other challenges of the Third Republic.
- Describe the French government's steps toward reform in the early 1900s.

Terms, People, and Places

Napoleon III	coalition
Suez Canal	Dreyfus affair
provisional	libel
premier	Zionism

Note Taking

Reading Skill: Recognize Sequence Draw a timeline and label the main events described in this section.

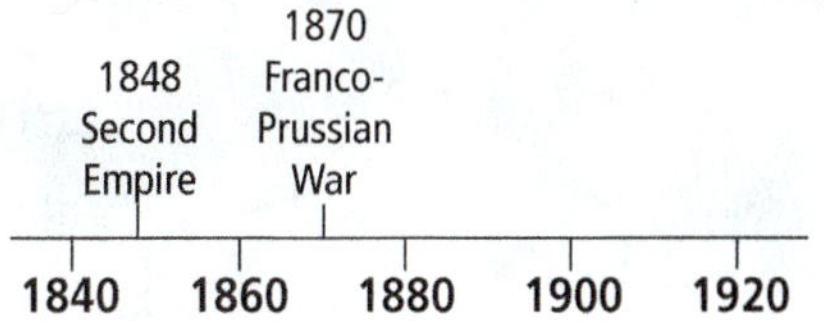

For four months, Paris resisted the German onslaught. But finally, in January 1871, the French government at Versailles was forced to accept Prussian surrender terms.

The Franco-Prussian War ended a long period of French domination of Europe that had begun under Louis XIV. Yet a Third Republic rose from the ashes of the Second Empire of Napoleon III. Economic growth, democratic reforms, and the fierce nationalism expressed by Clemenceau all played a part in shaping modern France.

France Under Napoleon III

After the revolution of 1848, **Napoleon III,** nephew of Napoleon Bonaparte, rose to power and set up the Second Empire. His appeal cut across lines of class and ideology. The bourgeoisie saw him as a strong leader who would restore order. His promise to end poverty gave hope to the lower classes. People of all classes were attracted by his name, a reminder of the days when France had towered over Europe. Unlike his famous uncle, however, Napoleon III would bring France neither glory nor an empire.

Limits on Liberty On the surface, the Second Empire looked like a constitutional monarchy. In fact, Napoleon III ruled almost as a dictator, with the power to appoint his cabinet, the upper house of the legislature, and many officials. Although the assembly was elected by universal male suffrage, appointed officials "managed" elections so that supporters of the emperor would win. Debate was limited, and newspapers faced strict censorship.

In the 1860s, the emperor began to ease controls. He lifted some censorship and gave the legislature more power. On the eve of his disastrous war with Prussia, Napoleon III even issued a new constitution that extended democratic rights.

Promoting Economic Growth Like much of Europe, France prospered at mid-century. Napoleon III promoted investment in industry and large-scale ventures such as railroad building and the urban renewal of Paris. During this period, a French entrepreneur, Ferdinand de Lesseps (LAY seps), organized the building of the **Suez Canal** in Egypt to link the Mediterranean with the Red Sea and the Indian Ocean.

Workers enjoyed some benefits of economic growth. Napoleon legalized labor unions, extended public education to girls, and created a small public health program. Still, in France, as in other industrial nations, many people lived in great poverty.

Foreign Adventures Napoleon's worst failures were in foreign affairs. In the 1860s, he tried to place Maximilian, an Austrian Hapsburg prince, on the throne of Mexico. Through Maximilian, Napoleon hoped to turn Mexico into a French satellite. But after a large commitment of troops and money, the adventure failed. Mexican patriots resisted fiercely, and the United States protested. After four years, France withdrew its troops. Maximilian was overthrown and shot by Mexican patriots.

Napoleon's successes were almost as costly as his failures. He helped Italian nationalists defeat Austria, and in return, the regions of Nice (nees) and Savoy were ceded to France. But this victory soon backfired when a united Italy emerged as a rival on France's border. And, though

The Siege of Paris

For over four months beginning in September 1870, Prussian troops surrounded Paris. The city was almost completely cut off from the rest of the country except for messages that could be carried out on perilous balloon flights (far right top), by carrier pigeon, or by small capsules floated down the Seine River (far right bottom). Despite the large amounts of food that had been amassed prior to the siege, food was in short supply. Parisians searched for horses, rats (right), and even zoo and circus animals were consumed in the face of hunger. In the end, the French surrendered and agreed to disband their army and pay a war indemnity. Nearly 2,000 French troops were killed and thousands of Parisians died of diseases worsened by malnutrition and the cold weather.

Victorious Prussian troops pose in front of the ruins of the French Fort Issy near Paris.

France and Britain won the Crimean War, France had little to show for its terrible losses except a small foothold in the Middle East.

A Disastrous War With Prussia At this same time, France was growing increasingly concerned about the rise of a great rival, Prussia. The Prussian leader Otto von Bismarck shrewdly manipulated the French and lured Napoleon into war in 1870.

As you have read, the Franco-Prussian War was a disaster for France. Following the capture of Napoleon III, German forces advanced toward Paris and encircled the city. After four months of siege by Prussian troops, starving Parisians were reduced to catching rats and killing circus animals for food.

 **Checkpoint** What were some of the successes and failures of Napoleon III's Second Empire?

Challenges of the Third Republic

At the news of Napoleon's capture, republicans in Paris declared an end to the Second Empire. They set up a **provisional,** or temporary, government that shortly evolved into France's Third Republic. In 1871, the newly elected National Assembly accepted a harsh peace with Germany. France had to surrender the provinces of Alsace and Lorraine and pay a huge sum to Germany. The French were eager to avenge their loss.

The Paris Commune In 1871, an uprising broke out in Paris. Rebels set up the Paris Commune. Like the radical government during the French Revolution, its goal was to save the Republic from royalists. Communards,

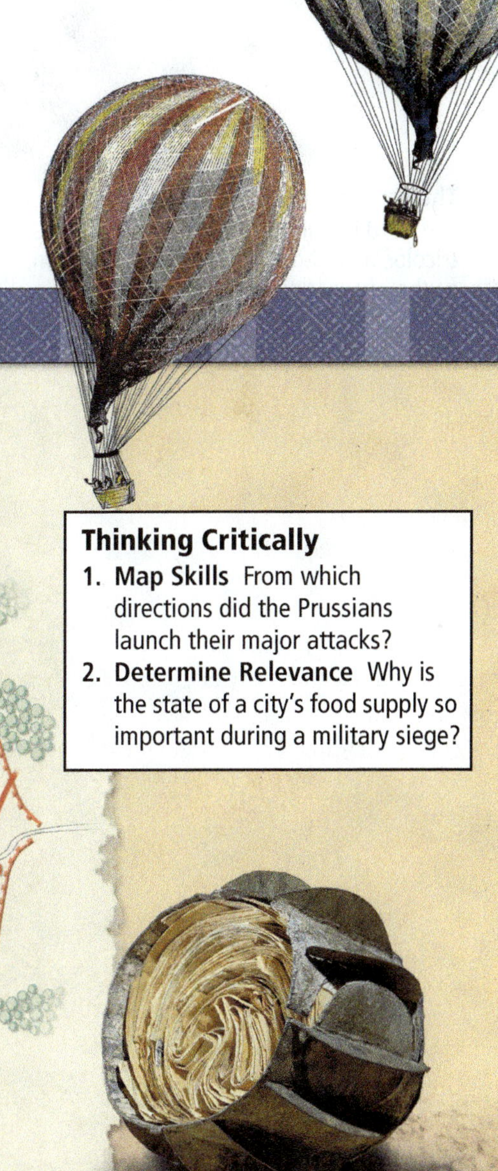

Paris Under Seige

Thinking Critically
1. **Map Skills** From which directions did the Prussians launch their major attacks?
2. **Determine Relevance** Why is the state of a city's food supply so important during a military siege?

as the rebels were called, included workers and socialists as well as bourgeois republicans. As patriots, they rejected the harsh peace that the National Assembly had signed with Germany. Radicals dreamed of creating a new socialist order.

The National Assembly ordered the Paris Commune to disband. When the Communards refused, the government sent troops to retake Paris. For weeks, civil war raged. As government troops advanced, the rebels set fire to several government buildings, toppled a monument commemorating Napoleon I, and slaughtered a number of hostages. Finally, government forces butchered some 20,000 Communards. The suppression of the Paris Commune left bitter memories that deepened social divisions within France.

Government Structure Despite its shaky beginnings, the Third Republic remained in place for 70 years. The new republic had a two-house legislature. The powerful lower house, or Chamber of Deputies, was elected by universal male suffrage. Together with the Senate, it elected the president of the republic. However, he had little power and served mostly as a figurehead. Real power was in the hands of the **premier** (prih MIR), or prime minister.

Unlike Britain, with its two-party system, France had many parties, reflecting the wide splits within the country. Among them were royalists, constitutional monarchists, moderate republicans, and radicals. With so many parties, no single party could win a majority in the legislature. In order to govern, politicians had to form **coalitions,** or alliances of various parties. Once a coalition controlled enough votes, it could then name a premier and form a cabinet.

Multiparty systems and coalition governments are common in Europe. Such alliances allow citizens to vote for a party that most nearly matches their own beliefs. Coalition governments, however, are often unstable. If one party deserts a coalition, the government might lose its majority in the legislature. The government then falls, and new elections must be held. In the first 10 years of the Third Republic, 50 different coalition governments were formed and fell.

Political Scandals Despite frequent changes of governments, France made economic progress. It paid Germany the huge sum required by the peace treaty and expanded its overseas empire. But in the 1880s and 1890s, a series of political scandals shook public trust in the government.

One crisis erupted when a popular minister of war, General Georges Boulanger (boo lahn zhay), rallied royalists and ultranationalists eager for revenge on Germany. Accused of plotting to overthrow the republic, Boulanger fled to Belgium. In another scandal, a nephew of the president was caught selling nominations for the Legion of Honor, France's highest award. The president was forced to resign.

✓ **Checkpoint** What challenges did the Third Republic face during its 70 years in power?

Anti-Semitism and the Dreyfus Affair

The most serious and divisive scandal began in 1894. A high-ranking army officer, Alfred Dreyfus, was accused of spying for Germany. However, at his military trial, neither Dreyfus nor his lawyer was allowed to

The French Tricolor
The Third Republic eventually adopted the tricolor, a symbol of the French Revolution, as the official flag of France.

see the evidence against him. The injustice was rooted in anti-Semitism. The military elite detested Dreyfus, the first Jewish person to reach such a high position in the army. Although Dreyfus proclaimed his innocence, he was convicted and condemned to life imprisonment on Devil's Island, a desolate penal colony off the coast of South America. By 1896, new evidence pointed to another officer, Ferdinand Esterhazy, as the spy. Still, the army refused to grant Dreyfus a new trial.

Deep Divisions The Dreyfus affair, as it was called, scarred French politics and society for decades. Royalists, ultranationalists, and Church officials charged Dreyfus supporters, or "Dreyfusards," with undermining France. Paris echoed with cries of "Long live the army!" and "Death to traitors!" Dreyfusards, mostly liberals and republicans, upheld ideals of justice and equality in the face of massive public anger. In 1898, French novelist Émile Zola joined the battle. In an article headlined *J'Accuse!* (I Accuse!), he charged the army and government with suppressing the truth. As a result, Zola was convicted of libel, or the knowing publication of false and damaging statements. He fled into exile.

Slowly, though, the Dreyfusards made progress and eventually the evidence against Dreyfus was shown to be forged. In 1906, a French court finally cleared Dreyfus of all charges and restored his honors. That was a victory for justice, but the political scars of the Dreyfus affair took longer to heal.

Calls for a Jewish State The Dreyfus case reflected the rise of anti-Semitism in Europe. The Enlightenment and the French Revolution had spread ideas about religious toleration. In Western Europe, some Jews had gained jobs in government, universities, and other areas of life. Others had achieved success in banking and business, but most struggled to survive in the ghettos of Eastern Europe or the slums of Western Europe.

By the late 1800s, however, anti-Semitism was again on the rise. Anti-Semites were often members of the lower middle class who felt insecure in their social and economic position. Steeped in the new nationalist fervor, they adopted an aggressive intolerance for outsiders and a violent hatred of Jews.

The Dreyfus case and the pogroms in Russia stirred Theodor Herzl (HURT sul), a Hungarian Jewish journalist living in France. He called for Jews to form their own separate state, where they would have rights that were otherwise denied to them in European countries. Herzl helped launch Zionism, a movement devoted to rebuilding a Jewish state in the ancient homeland. Many Jews had kept this dream alive since the destruction of the temple in Jerusalem by the Romans. In 1897, Herzl organized the First Zionist Congress in Basel, Switzerland.

✔ **Checkpoint** In what ways was the Zionist movement a reaction to the Dreyfus case?

Reforms in France

Although shaken by the Dreyfus affair, France achieved serious reforms in the early 1900s. Like Britain, France passed laws regulating wages, hours, and safety conditions for workers. It set up a system of free public elementary schools. Creating public

Dreyfus Affair Caricature
This 1899 caricature, *The Traitor*, portrays Alfred Dreyfus as a lindworm, a mythical dragon with no wings in many German legends. In protest of Dreyfus's conviction, French novelist Émile Zola published a letter in 1898 in which he accused the army and government of suppressing the truth in the Dreyfus trial. "The truth is on the march, and nothing shall stop it," Zola wrote.

schools was also part of a campaign to reduce the power of the Roman Catholic Church, which controlled education.

Separating Church and State Like Germany, France tried to <u>repress</u> Church involvement in government. Republicans viewed the Church as a conservative force that opposed progressive policies. In the Dreyfus affair, it had backed the army and ultranationalists.

The government closed Church schools, along with many convents and monasteries. In 1905, it passed a law to separate church and state and stopped paying the salaries of the clergy. Catholics, Protestants, and Jews were all to enjoy freedom of worship, but none would have any special treatment from the government.

Women's Rights Under the Napoleonic Code, French women had few rights. By the 1890s, a growing women's rights movement sought legal reforms. It made some gains, such as an 1896 law giving married women the right to their own earnings. In 1909, Jeanne-Elizabeth Schmahl founded the French Union for Women's Suffrage. Rejecting the radical tactics used in Britain, Schmahl favored legal protests. Yet even liberal men were reluctant to grant women suffrage. They feared that women would vote for Church and conservative causes. In the end, French women did not win the vote until after World War II.

✔ **Checkpoint** Describe two social reforms during the late 1800s and early 1900s in France.

Looking Ahead

By 1914, France was the largest democratic country in Europe, with a constitution that protected basic rights. France's economy was generally prosperous, and its overseas empire was second only to that of Britain.

Yet the outlook was not all smooth. Coalition governments rose and fell at the slightest pressure. To the east loomed the industrial might of Germany. Many French citizens were itching for a chance to avenge the defeat in the Franco-Prussian War and liberate the "lost provinces" of Alsace and Lorraine. That chance came in 1914, when all of Europe exploded into World War I.

Penmanship Lesson
One of the many reforms of the early 1900s in France was the establishment of free public elementary schools.

Vocabulary Builder
<u>repress</u>—(ree PRES) *vt.* to put down, subdue

SECTION **3** Assessment

Terms, People, and Places

1. For each term, person, or place listed at the beginning of the section, write a sentence explaining its significance.

Note Taking

2. **Reading Skill: Recognize Sequence** Use your completed timeline to answer the Focus Question: What democratic reforms were made in France during the Third Republic?

Comprehension and Critical Thinking

3. **Summarize** Describe the government of France during the Second Empire.
4. **Draw Inferences** How did the Paris Commune and the Dreyfus affair heighten divisions in France?
5. **Summarize** Describe two reforms enacted in France in the early 1900s.
6. **Express Problems Clearly** (a) What solution did Zionists propose for the problem of widespread anti-Semitism? (b) Why do you think they felt it was the best solution?

● **Writing About History**

Quick Write: Write a Conclusion Do additional research to learn more about Ferdinand de Lesseps, the Frenchman who orchestrated the construction of the Suez Canal. Write a one-paragraph conclusion that could be used at the end of a biographical essay on de Lesseps.

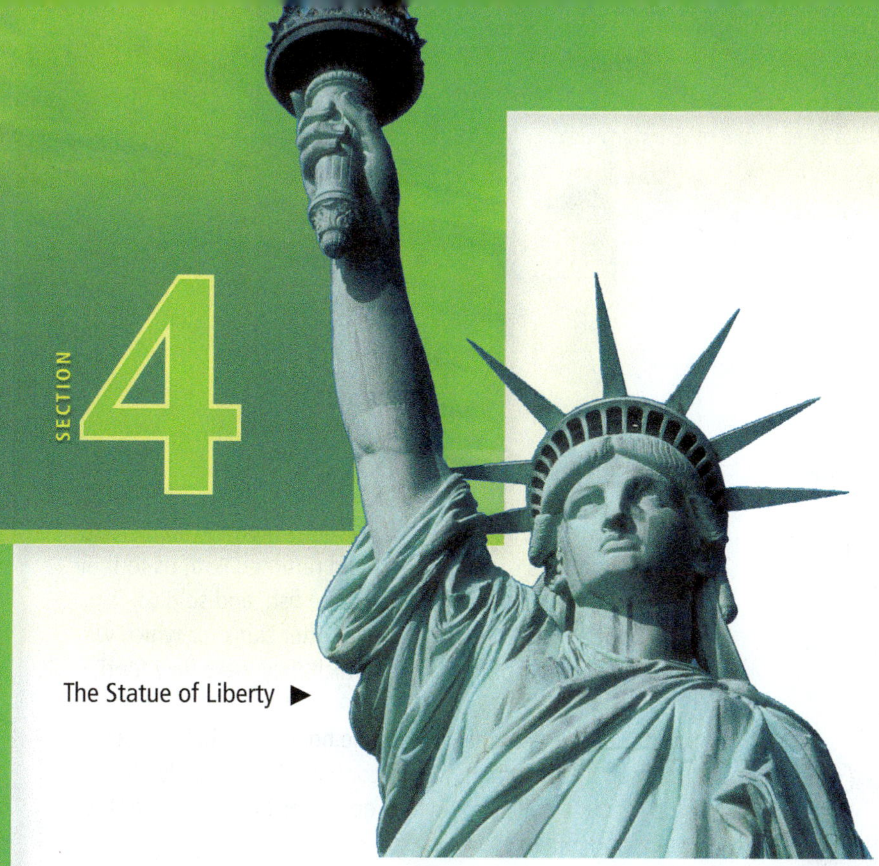
The Statue of Liberty ▶

Focus Question How did the United States develop during the 1800s?

Expansion of the United States

Objectives
- Describe how the territory of the United States changed during the 1800s.
- Summarize how American democracy grew before and after the Civil War.
- Analyze the impact of economic growth and social reform on the United States.

Terms, People, and Places

expansionism
Louisiana Purchase
Manifest Destiny
secede
segregation

Note Taking

Reading Skill: Categorize Create a chart like the one below. As you read this section, list key events under the appropriate columns.

Civil War	
Before	**After**
• Western expansion	• Fifteenth Amendment
•	•
•	•

In the 1800s, the United States was a beacon of hope for many people. The American economy was growing rapidly, offering jobs to newcomers. The Constitution and Bill of Rights held out the hope of political and religious freedom. Not everyone shared in the prosperity or the ideals of democracy. Still, by the turn of the nineteenth century, important reforms were being made.

Territorial Expansion

From the earliest years of its history, the United States followed a policy of **expansionism,** or extending the nation's boundaries. At first, the United States stretched only from the Atlantic coast to the Mississippi River. In 1803, President Thomas Jefferson bought the Louisiana territory from France. In one stroke, the **Louisiana Purchase** virtually doubled the size of the nation.

By 1846, the United States had expanded to include Florida, Oregon, and the Republic of Texas. The Mexican War (1846–1848) added California and the Southwest. With growing pride and confidence, Americans claimed that their nation was destined to spread across the entire continent, from sea to sea. This idea became known as **Manifest Destiny.** Some expansionists even hoped to absorb Canada and Mexico. In fact, the United States did go far afield. In 1867, it bought Alaska from Russia and in 1898 annexed the Hawaiian Islands.

 **Checkpoint** Describe the United States' physical expansion during the 1800s.

Lewis and Clark Reach the Pacific Ocean

In 1803, Thomas Jefferson appointed Meriwether Lewis to lead an expedition from the Missouri River to the Pacific Ocean. Lewis invited William Clark to share the leadership. The expedition set out from St. Louis in May 1804 and returned in September 1806. Along the way, both Lewis and Clark kept extensive journals (background), which included detailed maps, drawings (below), and descriptions of the land, people, and animals they encountered. The entry here describes the events surrounding what he believed was the group's first view of the Pacific Ocean (above).

> November 7th, 1805—A cloudy foggy morning some rain. …Two canoes of Indians met and returned with us to their village…. They gave us to eat some fish, and sold us, fish, wappato roots, three dogs, and 2 otter skins for which we gave fishhooks principally, of which they were very fond….
>
> After delaying at this village one hour and a half we set out piloted by an Indian…. Rain continued moderately all day…our small canoe which got separated in the fog this morning joined us this evening….
>
> Great joy in camp we are in view of the Ocean, …this great Pacific Ocean which we [have] been so long anxious to see. And the roaring or noise made by the waves breaking on the rocky shores (as I suppose) may be heard distinctly.

—Captain William Clark,
from *The Journals of the Lewis and Clark Expedition*

Thinking Critically

1. **Summarize** According to Clark's entry, what was the land like in this area?
2. **Draw Conclusions** What conclusions can you draw about William Clark's character from this journal entry?

Expanding Democracy

In 1800, the United States had the most liberal suffrage in the world, but still only white men who owned property could vote. States slowly chipped away at requirements. By the 1830s, most white men had the right to vote. Democracy was still far from complete, however.

By mid-century, reformers were campaigning for many changes. Some demanded a ban on the sale of alcoholic beverages. Others called for better treatment of the mentally ill or pushed for free elementary schools. But two crusades stood out above all others because they highlighted the limits of American democracy—the abolition movement and the women's rights movement.

Calls for Abolition In the early 1800s, a few Americans began to call for an immediate and complete end to slavery. One of these abolitionists was William Lloyd Garrison, who pressed the antislavery cause through his newspaper, the *Liberator*. Another was Frederick Douglass. He had been born into slavery and escaped, and he spoke eloquently in the North about the evils of the system.

By the 1850s, the battle over slavery had intensified. As each new state entered the union, proslavery and antislavery forces met in violent confrontations to decide whether slavery would be legal in the new state. Harriet Beecher Stowe's novel *Uncle Tom's Cabin* helped convince many northerners that slavery was a great social evil.

Women's Rights Movement Women worked hard in the antislavery movement. Lucretia Mott and Elizabeth Cady Stanton traveled to London for the World Antislavery Convention—only to find they were forbidden to speak because they were women. Gradually, American women began to protest the laws and customs that limited their lives.

In 1848, in Seneca Falls, New York, Mott and Stanton organized the first women's rights convention. The convention passed a resolution, based on the Declaration of Independence. It began, "We hold these truths to be self evident: that all men and women are created equal." The women's rights movement set as its goal equality before the law, in the workplace, and in education. Some women also demanded the vote.

✔ **Checkpoint** How did the abolition movement and the women's rights movement highlight the limits of American democracy?

The Civil War and Its Aftermath

Economic differences, as well as the slavery issue, drove the Northern and Southern regions of the United States apart. The division reached a crisis in 1860 when Abraham Lincoln was elected president. Lincoln opposed extending slavery into new territories. Southerners feared that he would eventually abolish slavery altogether and that the federal government would infringe on their states' rights.

North Versus South Soon after Lincoln's election, most southern states **seceded,** or withdrew, from the Union and formed the Confederate States of America. This action sparked the Civil War, which lasted from 1861 to 1865.

The South had fewer resources, fewer people, and less industry than the North. Still, Southerners fought fiercely to defend their cause. The Confederacy finally surrendered in 1865. The struggle cost more than 600,000 lives—the largest casualty figures of any American war.

Challenges for African Americans During the war, Lincoln issued the Emancipation Proclamation, by which enslaved African Americans in the South were declared free. After the war, three amendments to the Constitution banned slavery throughout the country and granted political rights to African Americans. Under the Fifteenth Amendment, African American men won the right to vote.

Still, African Americans faced many restrictions. In the South, state laws imposed **segregation,** or legal separation of the races, in hospitals, schools, and other public places. Other state laws imposed conditions for voter eligibility that, despite the Fifteenth Amendment, prevented African Americans from voting.

✔ **Checkpoint** What changes did the Civil War bring about for African Americans?

The American Civil War, 1861–1865
During the American Civil War, Union forces from the North fought against the Confederate Army of the South. This scene shows the black 54th Massachusetts Regiment of the Union army attacking Fort Wagner in South Carolina.

Expansion of the United States, 1783–1898

Geography *Interactive*
For: Interactive map
Web Code: nap-2345

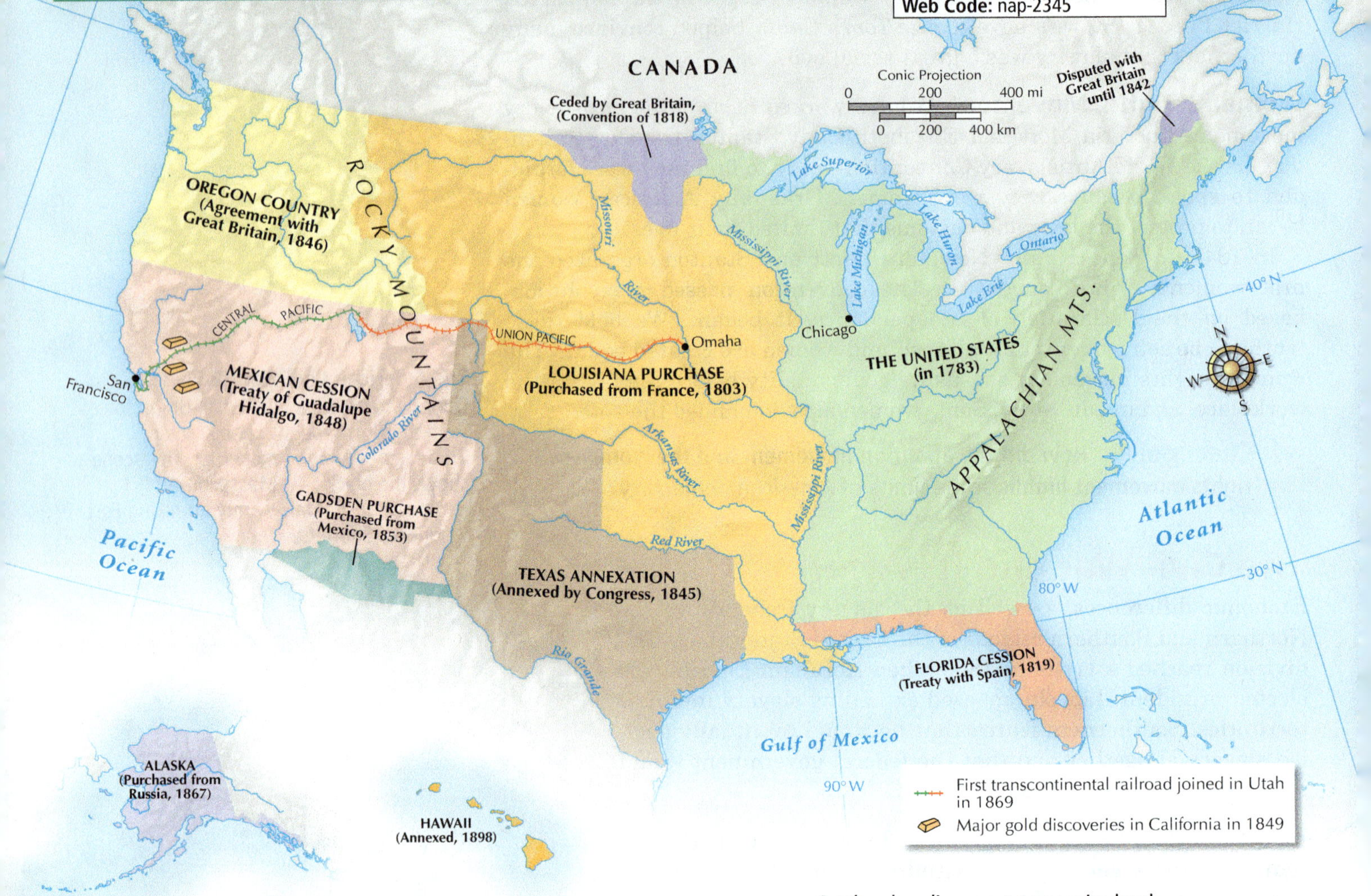

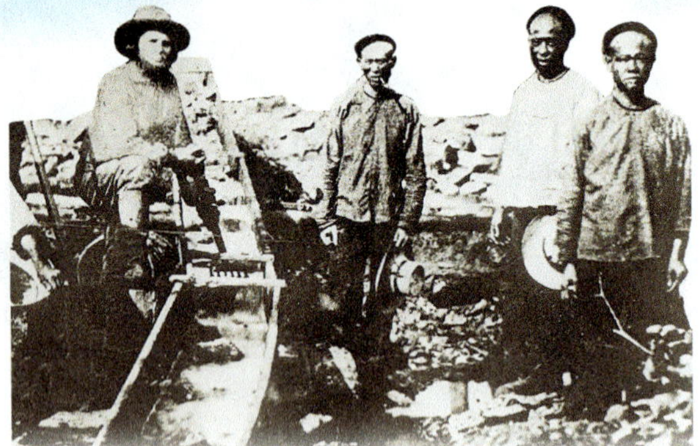

Chinese laborers helped build the railroads.

Settlers heading west to acquire land

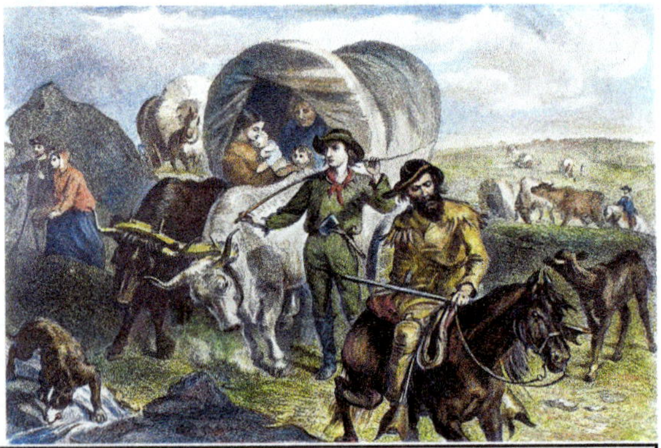

Map Skills Through wars and treaties, the United States expanded its borders to its present size. During the 1800s, settlers flocked to newly acquired lands. The discovery of gold in California drew a flood of easterners. Other people, like the Mormons, sought a place to practice their religion freely. Still others headed west in the spirit of adventure. Some Native American nations resisted the invaders, but they were outgunned and outnumbered. By the 1890s, most surviving Native Americans had been driven onto reservations.

1. **Locate** (a) Louisiana Purchase (b) Florida (c) Texas (d) Alaska (e) Hawaii
2. **Place** Identify three countries that sold territories to the United States.
3. **Make Comparisons** Compare this map to a map of the present-day United States. How did the area where you live become part of the United States?

Economic Growth and Social Reform

After the Civil War, the United States grew to lead the world in industrial and agricultural production. A special combination of factors made this possible including political stability, private property rights, a free enterprise system, and an inexpensive supply of land and labor—supplied mostly by immigrants. Finally, a growing network of transportation and communications technologies aided businesses in transporting resources and finished products.

Business and Labor By 1900, giant monopolies controlled whole industries. Scottish-born Andrew Carnegie built the nation's largest steel company, while John D. Rockefeller's Standard Oil Company <u>dominated</u> the world's petroleum industry. Big business enjoyed tremendous profits.

But the growing prosperity was not shared by all. In factories, wages were low and conditions were often brutal. To defend their interests, American workers organized labor unions such as the American Federation of Labor. Unions sought better wages, hours, and working conditions. Struggles with management sometimes erupted into violent confrontations. Slowly, however, workers made gains.

Populists and Progressives In the economic hard times of the late 1800s, farmers also organized themselves to defend their interests. In the 1890s, they joined city workers to support the new Populist party. The Populists never became a major party, but their platform of reforms, such as an eight-hour workday, eventually became law.

By 1900, reformers known as Progressives also pressed for change. They sought laws to ban child labor, limit working hours, regulate monopolies, and give voters more power. Another major goal of the Progressives was obtaining voting rights for women. After a long struggle, American suffragists finally won the vote in 1920, when the Nineteenth Amendment went into effect.

 **Checkpoint** Describe the factors that helped the United States become an industrial and agricultural leader.

SECTION 4 Assessment

Terms, People, and Places

1. Place each of the key terms at the beginning of the section into one of these two categories: geography or politics. Explain your choices.

Note Taking

2. **Reading Skill: Categorize** Use your completed chart to answer the Focus Question: How did the United States develop during the 1800s?

Comprehension and Critical Thinking

3. **Summarize** Describe how the United States grew in each of these areas in the 1800s: (a) territory, (b) population, (c) economy.

4. **Identify Central Issues** Describe two ways that democracy expanded.

5. **Draw Conclusions** (a) How did immigrants benefit from economic growth in the United States after the Civil War? (b) What problems did workers face?

● **Writing About History**

Quick Write: Write a Thesis Statement Conduct research to learn more about American entrepreneur, Andrew Carnegie. While some historians have portrayed Carnegie and others like him as philanthropists and captains of industry, others have portrayed him as a "robber baron." Write a thesis statement for a biographical essay on Carnegie in which you summarize your views of the man and his achievements.

Quick Study Guide

Progress Monitoring *Online*
For: Self-test with vocabulary practice
Web Code: naa-2307

■ Democratic Reforms in Britain 1800s–Early 1900s

- Redistribution of seats in the House of Commons from rural towns to growing cities (1832)
- Expansion of suffrage for men with property (1832)
- Expansion of suffrage for many working-class men (1867)
- Expansion of suffrage to farm workers and most men
- Introduction of secret ballot
- Power of the House of Lords restricted (1911)

■ Social and Economic Reforms in Britain 1800s–Early 1900s

- Slave trade prohibited (1807)
- Slavery in all British colonies abolished (1833)
- Repeal of high tariffs on grains (1846)
- Women and children under ten forbidden to work in mines (1842)
- Women and children limited to 10-hour workday (1847)
- Improvements in public health and housing
- Free elementary education
- Accident, health, and unemployment insurance
- Old-age pensions
- Suffrage extended to women over 30 (1918)

■ Key Events in France, 1800s–Early 1900s

1852 Napoleon III sets up Second Empire.
1856 France and Britain defeat Russia in Crimean War.
1863 Napoleon III sends troops and Archduke Maximilian to Mexico.
1860 France gains Nice and Savoy by helping Italian nationalists defeat Austria.
1870 Napoleon III captured in Franco-Prussian war; Four-month siege of Paris by Prussians; France defeated and Alsace Lorraine ceded to Germany; Republicans in Paris establish the Third Republic.
1871 Paris Commune uprising
1894 Dreyfus affair
1905 Separation of church and state established by law.

■ Key Events in the United States 1800s–Early 1900s

1803	Louisiana Purchase
1846–1848	Mexican War
1849	California Gold Rush
1861–1865	Civil War
1867	Purchase of Alaska
1869	Completion of Transcontinental Railroad
1882	Formation of Standard Oil Trust
1898	Spanish-American War; Hawaiian islands annexed
1908	Development of Henry Ford's Model T

■ Key Events in the Growth of Western Democracies

1832 Great Reform Act gives more British men suffrage and redistributes seats in House of Commons.

1845 Potato famine in Ireland begins.

1861–1865 American Civil War ends slavery in the United States.

Europe and North America World Events

1815

1835

1855

1821 Mexico wins independence from Spain.

1858 Britain begins rule of India.

Concept Connector

Essential Question Review

To connect prior knowledge with what you have learned in this chapter, answer the questions below in your Concept Connector journal. Use the journal in the Reading and Note Taking Study Guide to record your answers (or go to www.phschool.com **Web Code: nad-2307). In addition, record information about the following concept:**

• **Migration:** Westward Movement in the United States

1. **Cooperation** During France's Third Republic, political parties had to form coalitions—alliances of various parties—in order to form a government. In other countries, different groups often formed coalitions or alliances to achieve common goals. Identify and explain the goals of alliances that were formed in
   • Britain in the 1830s
   • France during the Dreyfus affair
   • the United States in the 1860s and 1890s

2. **Migration** By the mid-1800s, the United States had expanded its borders through wars and treaties. Americans believed that their nation was destined to spread across the entire continent. How did American migration to the West in the late 1800s differ from Irish migration to the United States during the same period? How did migration to the West affect the Native American population?

3. **Democracy** Democratic reforms swept through Britain, France, and the United States during the 1800s. Identify specific reforms that each country achieved during this period. Focus on the following:
   • suffrage
   • natural rights
   • government
   • workers' rights

Connections to Today

1. **Trade: Free Trade and Tariffs** The British Corn laws imposed high, protective tariffs on imported grains and kept the price of British grown grain high. Do library research to learn more about a current protective tariff that is opposed by those who favor free trade. Which country has imposed this tariff on imports? What goods are affected? Which groups oppose the tariff and why?

2. **Conflict: Northern Ireland** The southern counties of Ireland gained independence from Britain in 1922, but Northern Ireland remained under British rule. Conflict ensued between minority Catholics in Northern Ireland, who demanded the reunification of Ireland, and majority Protestants, who favored a continued union with Britain. In 1998, the main political parties signed a peace accord that would eventually bring self-rule to Northern Ireland. Do research to learn more about the status of peace in Northern Ireland.

3. **Conflict: Native Americans** The expansion of the United States proved to be devastating for most Native American groups in North America. By the 1890s, most surviving Native Americans had been driven onto reservations. Conduct library research to learn more about the status of Native Americans living in the United States today. Write a paragraph summarizing the information you find.

History Interactive
For: Interactive timeline
Web Code: nap-2308

1870	1897	1900s
France defeated in the Franco-Prussian War; Third Republic established.	Theodor Herzl organizes the First Zionist Congress for the purpose of founding a Jewish state.	The women's suffrage movement grows in Britain and the United States.

1875	**1895**	**1915**

1869	1889	1893	1910
The French-built Suez Canal opens in Egypt.	Brazil becomes a republic.	New Zealand is the first nation to give women the vote.	The Union of South Africa is formed.

Chapter Assessment

Terms, People, and Places

1. How did the Great Reform Act of 1832 correct the problem of **rotten boroughs?**
2. What group of people was added to the British **electorate** in 1918?
3. Why did members of the Chartist movement demand the use of **secret ballots?**
4. Why did the opponents of the Corn Laws in Britain favor **free trade?**
5. Why did French politicians need to form **coalitions?**
6. Where did Britain establish **penal colonies?**
7. What is **segregation?**
8. What is a **provisional** government?

Main Ideas

Section 1 (pp. 722–725)

9. What were the effects of the Great Reform Act of 1832?

Section 2 (pp. 726–732)

10. How did British policy toward slavery change in 1833?

Section 3 (pp. 733–738)

11. How did the party system in France's Third Republic differ from the British party system?
12. What was the main goal of the Zionist movement?

Section 4 (pp. 739–743)

13. List two goals of the Progressives in the United States in the early 1900s.

Chapter Focus Question

14. How did Britain, France, and the United States slowly extend democratic rights during the 1800s and early 1900s?

Critical Thinking

15. **Analyzing Cartoons** What views of suffrage does this cartoon reflect?

16. **Draw Conclusions** Britain and France faced many similar political and social problems in the 1800s. Why do you think Britain was able to avoid the upheavals that plagued France?
17. **Recognize Cause and Effect** (a) List two long-term causes and two immediate causes of the Great Hunger; (b) list two immediate effects. (c) Why do you think the famine sparked lasting feelings of bitterness against Britain?
18. **Synthesize Information** Describe how each of the following was related to nationalism: (a) the prestige of Queen Victoria, (b) the revolt of the Paris Commune, (c) the rise of Zionism.
19. **Geography and History** How did the geography of the United States encourage the American government to achieve its goal of Manifest Destiny?

● Writing About History

In this chapter's four Section Assessments, you developed skills for writing a compare and contrast essay.

Writing a Compare and Contrast Expository Essay
Conduct research and write a compare and contrast essay on the careers and accomplishments of Benjamin Disraeli and William Gladstone (left).

Prewriting
- Identify points of comparison and contrast for your essay. For example, you may want to compare and contrast the two men in terms of their background, political views, specific accomplishments, and impact on British politics. These categories will help you organize details in your essay.
- Create a Venn Diagram showing differences between the two men in the outside circles and similarities in the overlapping center.
- Collect the facts you need to write your essay.

Drafting
- Start with an engaging opening that defines the comparison/contrast and grabs readers' interest. This could be a quotation, surprising detail or statistic, or a question.
- Give details about each point of comparison to make it more accessible to readers. For example, you might give the years during which each man served as prime minister.
- Discuss the points about each man in the same order. You might even use similar sentence structure to emphasize this.

Revising
- Use the guidelines for revising your essay on page SH12 of the Writing Handbook.

Document-Based Assessment

The Dreyfus Affair

On December 22, 1894, a French military court convicted an innocent Jewish man, Captain Alfred Dreyfus, of selling state secrets to Germany. Dreyfus was imprisoned on Devil's Island off of South America and his conviction was reversed only after nearly twelve years. The Dreyfus affair caused a great division between conservatives, who still disliked the outcome of the French Revolution and held strong anti-Semitic beliefs, and liberals, who viewed the case as a gross abuse of individual rights.

Document A

"... if my voice ceased to be heard, it would mean that it had been extinguished forever, for if I have survived, it has been in order to insist on my honor—my property and the patrimony of our children—and in order to do my duty, as I have done it everywhere and always, and as it must always be done, when right and justice are on one's side, without ever fearing anything or anyone."

—From a letter to his wife Lucie, by Alfred Dreyfus, September 1898, published in ***Cinq Années***

Document B

"I accuse the offices of War of having conducted in the press, particularly in L'Eclair and in L'Echo de Paris, an abominable campaign designed to mislead public opinion and to conceal their wrongdoing."

"Finally, I accuse the first Court Martial of having violated the law in convicting a defendant on the basis of a document kept secret, and I accuse the second Court Martial of having covered up . . . [and] knowingly acquitting a guilty man."

—From ***"J'Accuse"*** a letter to the President of the Republic by Émile Zola

Document C

"Un Diner En Famille"

Translation: "It is agreed that there should be no talk of the affair! But they did talk about it . . ."

—From ***Le Figaro*** by Caran d'Ache, February, 1898

Analyzing Documents

Use your knowledge of the Dreyfus affair and Documents A, B, and C to answer questions 1–4.

1. In Document A, Dreyfus suggests that his wish to prove his innocence helped to—
    A keep him close to his family.
    B keep him alive.
    C make the Army take illegal actions.
    D make anti-Semitic groups angry.

2. Which statement best summarizes Zola's letter in Document B?
    A Although the French military convicted the wrong man, they attempted to carry out a fair trial.
    B The French military was fooled by handwriting experts, who tried to convict the wrong man.
    C The French military knowingly and illegally convicted an innocent man.
    D The French military showed that the army was anti-Semitic at the highest levels.

3. Document C illustrates—
    A why many French families believed Dreyfus was guilty.
    B why Dreyfus was convicted unfairly of treason.
    C how the Dreyfus case divided France.
    D how anti-Semitism was a factor in the Dreyfus case.

4. **Writing Task** On July 21, 1906, a French general knighted Alfred Dreyfus a member of the Legion of Honor. Well wishers attended the ceremony in the courtyard of the École Militaire. Some shouted "Long live Dreyfus." Suppose you were reporting on the event for an American newspaper. Write a news story, using the documents on this page along with information from the chapter.

24

The New Imperialism

1800–1914

Empire Builders

Lord Frederick Lugard, a British empire builder, tried to justify imperialism in Africa with these words:

> **“**There are some who say we have no *right* to Africa at all, that 'it belongs to the natives.' I hold that our right is the necessity that is upon us to provide for our ever-growing population—either by opening new fields for emigration, or by providing work and employment . . . and to stimulate trade by finding new markets.**”**

Listen to the Witness History audio to learn more about imperialism.

◀ **One of several journalists in South Africa, British writer Rudyard Kipling (bottom right) considered imperialism to be beneficial to Africans.**

British East India Company coat of arms

Ivory carving of Africans carrying a European

Chapter Preview

Chapter Focus Question How did Western industrial powers gain global empires?

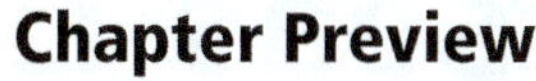

Section 1
Building Overseas Empires

Section 2
The Partition of Africa

Section 3
European Claims in Muslim Regions

Section 4
The British Take Over India

Lamp from a mosque

Section 5
China and the New Imperialism

Use the ☑ **Quick Study Timeline** at the end of this chapter to preview chapter events.

 **Concept Connector ONLINE**

To explore Essential Questions related to this chapter, go to PHSchool.com
Web Code: nad-2407

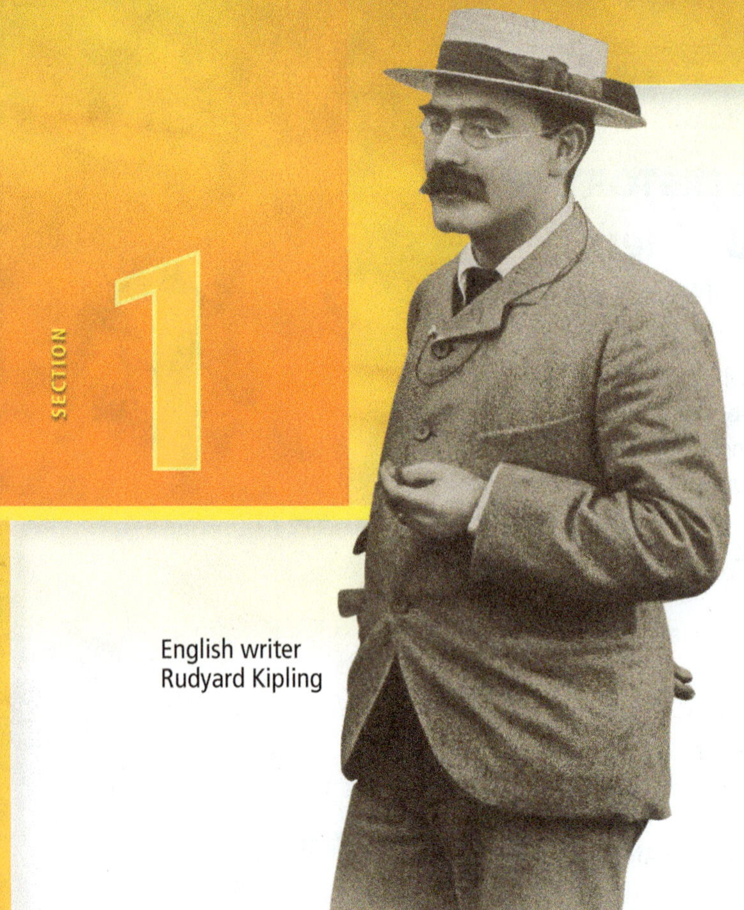

English writer
Rudyard Kipling

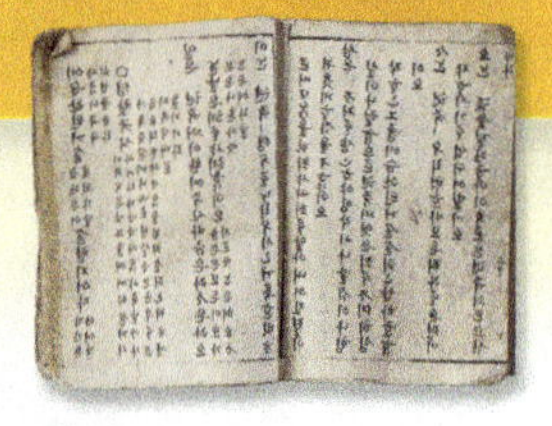

Missionary prayer
book in Korean

The White Man's Burden

Born in India, English writer Rudyard Kipling witnessed British imperialism firsthand. His 1899 poem "The White Man's Burden" summarizes his view of the duties of imperial nations:

> **66** Take up the White Man's burden—
>   In patience to abide,
> To veil the threat of terror
>   And check the show of pride;
> By open speech and simple,
>   An hundred times made plain,
> To seek another's profit,
>   And work another's gain. **99**

Focus Question How did Western nations come to dominate much of the world in the late 1800s?

Building Overseas Empires

Objectives

- Analyze the causes of the "new imperialism."
- Explain why Western imperialism spread so rapidly.
- Describe how imperial governments ruled their empires.

Terms, People, and Places

imperialism
protectorate
sphere of influence

Note Taking

Reading Skill: Recognize Multiple Causes As you read the section, make a chart like the one below showing the multiple causes of imperialism in the 1800s.

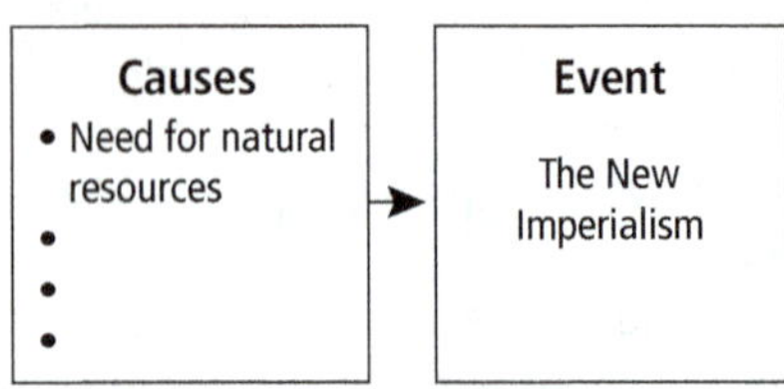

Like Great Britain, other Western countries built overseas empires in the late 1800s. The Industrial Revolution had transformed the West. Advances in science and technology, industry, transportation, and communication provided Western nations with many advantages. Armed with new economic and political power, Western nations set out to dominate the world.

Motives Driving the New Imperialism

European imperialism did not begin in the 1800s. **Imperialism** is the domination by one country of the political, economic, or cultural life of another country or region. As you have learned, European states won empires in the Americas after 1492, established colonies in South Asia, and gained toeholds on the coasts of Africa and China. Despite these gains, between 1500 and 1800, Europe had little influence on the lives of the peoples of China, India, or Africa.

By the 1800s, however, Europe had gained considerable power. Strong, centrally governed nation-states had emerged, and the Industrial Revolution had greatly enriched European economies. Encouraged by their new economic and military strength, Europeans embarked on a path of aggressive expansion that today's historians call the "new imperialism." In just a few decades, beginning in the 1870s, Europeans brought much of the world under their influence and control. Like other key developments in world history, the new imperialism exploded out of a combination of causes.

Economic Interests Spur Expansion The Industrial Revolution created needs and desires that spurred overseas expansion. Manufacturers wanted access to natural resources such as rubber, petroleum, manganese for steel, and palm oil for machinery. They also hoped for new markets of consumers to whom they could sell their factory goods. Bankers sought ventures to invest their profits. In addition, colonies offered a valuable outlet for Europe's growing population.

Political and Military Motives Political and military issues were closely linked to economic motives. Steam-powered merchant ships and naval vessels needed bases around the world to take on coal and supplies. Industrial powers seized islands or harbors to satisfy these needs.

Nationalism played an important role, too. When France, for example, moved into West Africa, rival nations like Britain and Germany seized lands nearby to halt further French expansion. Western leaders claimed that colonies were needed for national security. They also felt that ruling a global empire increased a nation's <u>prestige</u> around the world.

Humanitarian and Religious Goals Many Westerners felt a genuine concern for their "little brothers" beyond the seas. Missionaries, doctors, and colonial officials believed they had a duty to spread what they saw as the blessings of Western civilization, including its medicine, law, and Christian religion.

Applying Social Darwinism Behind the idea of the West's civilizing mission was a growing sense of racial superiority. Many Westerners had embraced the ideas of Social Darwinism. They applied Darwin's ideas about natural selection and survival of the fittest to human societies. European races, they argued, were superior to all others, and imperial domination of weaker races was simply nature's way of improving the human species. As a result, millions of non-Westerners were robbed of their cultural heritage.

 **Checkpoint** What factors contributed to European imperialism in the 1800s?

A Market for Goods
A driving force behind imperialism was the desire for access to new markets in which to sell goods. This British propaganda poster boasts that Africa would become a gold mine for British-made products. Britain's sense of national pride and aggressive foreign policy during this period came to be known as jingoism. *What does this poster show about the British attitude toward Africa?*

European Conquest of Africa

The excerpts below present two different views on the partition of Africa by European nations in the 1800s. **Critical Thinking** *What is Cecil Rhodes's argument for imperialism? What is Chief Kabongo's argument against it?*

Favoring Imperialism

"I contend that we are the first race in the world and that the more of the world we inhabit the better it is for the human race. I contend that every acre added to our territory provides for the birth of more of the English race, who otherwise would not be brought into existence . . . . I believe it to be my duty to God, my Queen and my country to paint the whole map of Africa red, red from the Cape to Cairo. That is my creed, my dream and my mission."

—*Cecil Rhodes*

Opposing Imperialism

"A Pink Cheek man came one day to our Council . . . and he told us of the King of the Pink Cheek who . . . lived in a land over the seas. 'This great king is now your king,' he said. This was strange news. For this land was ours. . . . We had no king, we elected our Councils and they made our laws. With patience, our leading Elders tried to tell this to the Pink Cheek. . . . But at the end he said, 'This we know, but in spite of this what I have told you is a fact. You have now a king . . . and his laws are your laws.'"

—*Chief Kabongo of the Kikuyu in Kenya*

The Rapid Spread of Western Imperialism

From about 1870 to 1914, imperialist nations gained control over much of the world. Leading the way were soldiers, merchants, settlers, missionaries, and explorers. In Europe, imperial expansion found favor with all classes, from bankers and manufacturers to workers. Western imperialism expanded rapidly for a number of reasons.

Weakness of Non-Western States While European nations had grown stronger in the 1800s, several older civilizations were in decline, especially the Ottoman Middle East, Mughal (MOO gul) India, and Qing (ching) China. In West Africa, wars among African peoples and the damaging effect of the slave trade had undermined established empires, kingdoms, and city-states. Newer African states were not strong enough to resist the Western onslaught.

Western Advantages European powers had the advantages of strong economies, well-organized governments, and powerful armies and navies. Superior technology, including riverboats and the telegraph, as well as improved medical knowledge also played a role. Quinine and other new medicines helped Europeans survive deadly tropical diseases. And, of course, advances such as Maxim machine guns, repeating rifles, and steam-driven warships were very strong arguments in persuading Africans and Asians to accept Western control.

Resisting Imperialism Africans and Asians strongly resisted Western expansion into their lands. Some people fought the invaders, even though they had no weapons to equal the Maxim gun. Ruling groups in certain areas tried to strengthen their societies against outsiders by reforming their own Muslim, Hindu, or Confucian traditions. Finally, many

The Maxim Gun
Sir Hiram Maxim with his invention, the Maxim machine gun. *Why were European armies often able to defeat African or Asian forces?*

Western-educated Africans and Asians organized nationalist movements to expel the imperialists from their lands.

Facing Criticism at Home In the West itself, a small group of anti-imperialists emerged. Some argued that colonialism was a tool of the rich. Others said it was immoral. Westerners, they pointed out, were moving toward greater democracy at home but were imposing undemocratic rule on other peoples.

✔ **Checkpoint** How did Western imperialism spread through Africa and Asia so quickly?

Forms of Imperial Rule

The leading imperial powers developed several kinds of colonial rule. The French practiced direct rule, sending officials and soldiers from France to administer their colonies. Their goal was to impose French culture on their colonies and turn them into French provinces.

The British, by contrast, often used a system of indirect rule. To govern their colonies, they used sultans, chiefs, or other local rulers. They then encouraged the children of the local ruling class to get an education in Britain. In that way, they groomed a new "Westernized" generation of leaders to continue indirect imperial rule and to spread British civilization. Like France and other imperialist nations, however, Britain could still resort to military force if its control over a colony was threatened.

In a **protectorate,** local rulers were left in place but were expected to follow the advice of European advisors on issues such as trade or missionary activity. A protectorate cost less to run than a colony did, and usually did not require a large commitment of military forces.

A third form of Western control was the **sphere of influence,** an area in which an outside power claimed exclusive investment or trading privileges. Europeans carved out these spheres in China and elsewhere to prevent conflicts among themselves.

✔ **Checkpoint** Compare and contrast how Britain and France ruled their colonies.

Indian princes and British army officers play polo in 1880.

SECTION 1 Assessment

Terms, People, and Places

1. What do each of the key terms listed at the beginning of the section have in common? Explain.

Note Taking

2. **Reading Skill: Recognize Multiple Causes** Use your completed chart to answer the Focus Question: How did Western nations come to dominate much of the world in the late 1800s?

Comprehension and Critical Thinking

3. **Explain** (a) What were three reasons for the rapid spread of Western imperialism? (b) How did people oppose it?

4. **Recognize Bias** Western colonial officials and missionaries thought that they had a duty to spread the "blessings of Western civilization" to their African and Asian "little brothers." How was this a biased viewpoint?

● **Writing About History**

Quick Write: Write a Thesis Statement Suppose that you are writing a persuasive essay using the point of view of an anti-imperialist from a Western nation trying to persuade the public that imperialism is wrong. Based on what you have read in this section, write a thesis statement for your essay.

African soldiers in German uniforms

Resisting Imperialism

In 1890, Chief Machemba (mah CHEM bah) of the Yao (YAH oh) people in East Africa wrote in Swahili to a German officer:

> If it be friendship that you desire, then I am ready for it . . . but to be your subject, that I cannot be. . . . I do not fall at your feet, for you are God's creature just as I am.
> —Chief Machemba, Letter to Herman von Wissman

Focus Question How did imperialist European powers claim control over most of Africa by the end of the 1800s?

The Partition of Africa

Objectives

- Analyze the forces that shaped Africa.
- Explain why European contact with Africa increased during the 1800s.
- Understand how Leopold II started a scramble for colonies.
- Describe how Africans resisted imperialism.

Terms, People, and Places

Usman dan Fodio	Boer War
Shaka	Samori Touré
paternalistic	Yaa Asantewaa
David Livingstone	Nehanda
Henry Stanley	Menelik II
King Leopold II	elite

Note Taking

Reading Skill: Identify Causes and Effects As you read the section, fill in the chart with information about the causes and effects of the partition of Africa by European nations.

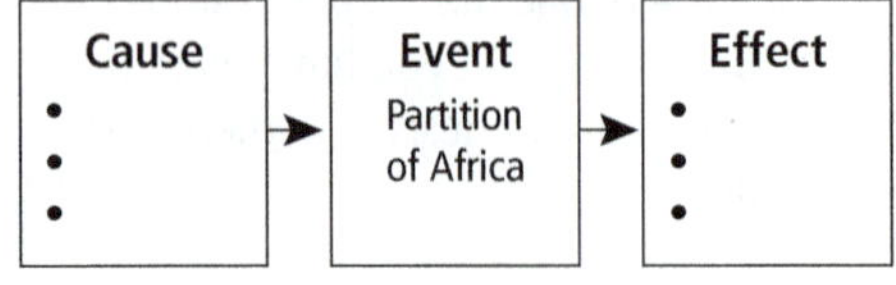

In the late 1800s, Britain, France, Germany, and other European powers began a scramble for African territories. Within about 20 years, the Europeans had carved up the continent and dominated millions of Africans. Although the Yao and others resisted, they could not prevent European conquest.

Africa in the Early 1800s

To understand the impact of European domination, we must look at Africa in the early 1800s, before the scramble for colonies began. Africa is a huge continent, nearly three times the size of Europe. Across its many regions, people spoke hundreds of languages and had developed varied governments. Some people lived in large centralized states, while others lived in village communities.

North Africa North Africa includes the enormous Sahara and the fertile land along the Mediterranean. Since long before 1800, the region was a part of the Muslim world. In the early 1800s, much of North Africa remained under the rule of the declining Ottoman empire.

Islamic Crusades in West Africa By the early 1800s, an Islamic revival spread across West Africa. It began among the Fulani people in northern Nigeria. The scholar and preacher **Usman dan Fodio** (oo SMAHN dahn foh DEE oh) denounced the corruption of the local Hausa rulers. He called for social and religious reforms based on the sharia, or Islamic law. Usman inspired Fulani herders and Hausa townspeople to rise up against their European rulers.

Usman and his successors set up a powerful Islamic state in northern Nigeria. Under their rule, literacy increased, local wars quieted, and trade improved. Their success inspired other Muslim reform movements in West Africa. Between about 1780 and 1880, more than a dozen Islamic leaders rose to power, replacing old rulers or founding new states in the western Sudan.

In the forest regions, strong states like the Asante (uh SAHN teh) kingdom had arisen. The Asante traded with Europeans and Muslims and controlled several smaller states. However, these tributary states were ready to turn to Europeans or others who might help them defeat their Asante rulers.

East Africa Islam had long influenced the east coast of Africa, where port cities like Mombasa (mahm BAH suh) and Kilwa (KEEL wah) carried on profitable trade. The cargoes were often slaves. Captives were marched from the interior to the coast to be shipped as slaves to the Middle East. Ivory and copper from Central Africa were also exchanged for goods such as cloth and firearms from India.

Southern Africa In the early 1800s, the Zulus emerged as a major force in southern Africa under a ruthless and brilliant leader, **Shaka.** Between 1818 and 1828, Shaka waged relentless war and conquered many nearby peoples. He absorbed their young men and women into Zulu regiments. By encouraging rival groups to forget their differences, he cemented a growing pride in the Zulu kingdom.

His conquests, however, set off mass migrations and wars, creating chaos across much of the region. Groups driven from their homelands by the Zulus then migrated north, conquering still other peoples and creating their own powerful states. By the 1830s, the Zulus faced a new threat, the arrival of well-armed, mounted Boers, descendants of Dutch farmers who were migrating north from the Cape Colony. In 1814, the Cape Colony had passed from the Dutch to the British. Many Boers resented British laws that abolished slavery and otherwise interfered with their way of life. To escape British rule, they loaded their goods into covered wagons and started north. Several thousand Boer families joined this "Great Trek."

As the migrating Boers came into contact with Zulus, fighting quickly broke out. At first, Zulu regiments held their own. But in the end, Zulu spears could not defeat Boer guns. The struggle for control of the land would rage until the end of the century.

Impact of the Slave Trade In the early 1800s, European nations began to outlaw the transatlantic slave trade, though it took years to end. Meanwhile, the East African slave trade continued to Asia.

Some people helped freed slaves resettle in Africa. In 1787, the British organized Sierra Leone in West Africa as a colony for former slaves. Later, some free blacks from the United States settled in nearby Liberia. By 1847, Liberia had become an independent republic.

✔ **Checkpoint** What factors shaped each of the main regions of Africa during the early 1800s?

Zulu King Cetshwayo
A nephew of Shaka, Cetshwayo (kech WY oh) was the last of the great Zulu kings. He ruled a disciplined army of about 40,000 men until the British defeated him in 1879. *Why was Cetshwayo considered a threat to British colonial interests?*

European Contact Increases

From the 1500s through the 1700s, Europeans traded along the African coast. Africans wanted trade with Europeans but did not want to "house them." Resistance by Africans, difficult geography, and diseases all kept Europeans from moving into the interior regions of the continent. Medical advances and river steamships changed all that in the 1800s.

Explorers Advance Into Africa's Interior

In the early 1800s, European explorers began pushing into the interior of Africa. Explorers like Mungo Park and Richard Burton set out to map the course and sources of the great African rivers such as the Niger, the Nile, and the Congo. They were fascinated by African geography, but they had little understanding of the peoples they met. All, however, endured great hardships while exploring Africa.

Missionaries Follow Explorers

Catholic and Protestant missionaries followed the explorers. All across Africa, they sought to win people to Christianity. The missionaries were sincere in their desire to help Africans. They built schools and medical clinics alongside churches. They also focused attention on the evils of the slave trade. Still, missionaries, like most Westerners, took a **paternalistic** view of Africans, meaning they saw them as children in need of guidance. To them, African cultures and religions were "degraded." They urged Africans to reject their own traditions in favor of Western civilization.

Livingstone Blazes a Trail

The best-known explorer and missionary was **Dr. David Livingstone.** For 30 years, he crisscrossed Africa. He wrote about the many peoples he met with more sympathy and less bias than did most Europeans. He relentlessly opposed the slave trade, which remained a profitable business for some African rulers and foreign traders. The only way to end this cruel traffic, he believed, was to open up the interior of Africa to Christianity and trade.

Livingstone blazed a trail that others soon followed. In 1869, the journalist **Henry Stanley** trekked into Central Africa to find Livingstone, who had not been heard from for years. He finally tracked him down in 1871 in what is today Tanzania, greeting him with the now-legendary phrase "Dr. Livingstone, I presume?"

 **Checkpoint** How did European contact with Africa increase in the late 1800s?

Missionaries at Work
Missionaries conduct a baptism ceremony in the Lower Congo in 1907. Others performed communion with chalices and patens, or ceremonial plates, like those above. *Why did missionaries seek to convert people to Christianity?*

A Scramble for Colonies

Shortly afterward, **King Leopold II** of Belgium hired Stanley to explore the Congo River basin and arrange trade treaties with African leaders. Publicly, Leopold spoke of a civilizing mission to carry the light "that for millions of men still plunged in barbarism will be the dawn of a better era." Privately, he dreamed of conquest and profit. Leopold's activities in the Congo set off a scramble by other nations. Before long, Britain, France, and Germany were pressing rival claims to the region.

Berlin Conference

To avoid bloodshed, European powers met at an international conference in 1884. It took place not in Africa but in Berlin, Germany. No Africans were invited to the conference.

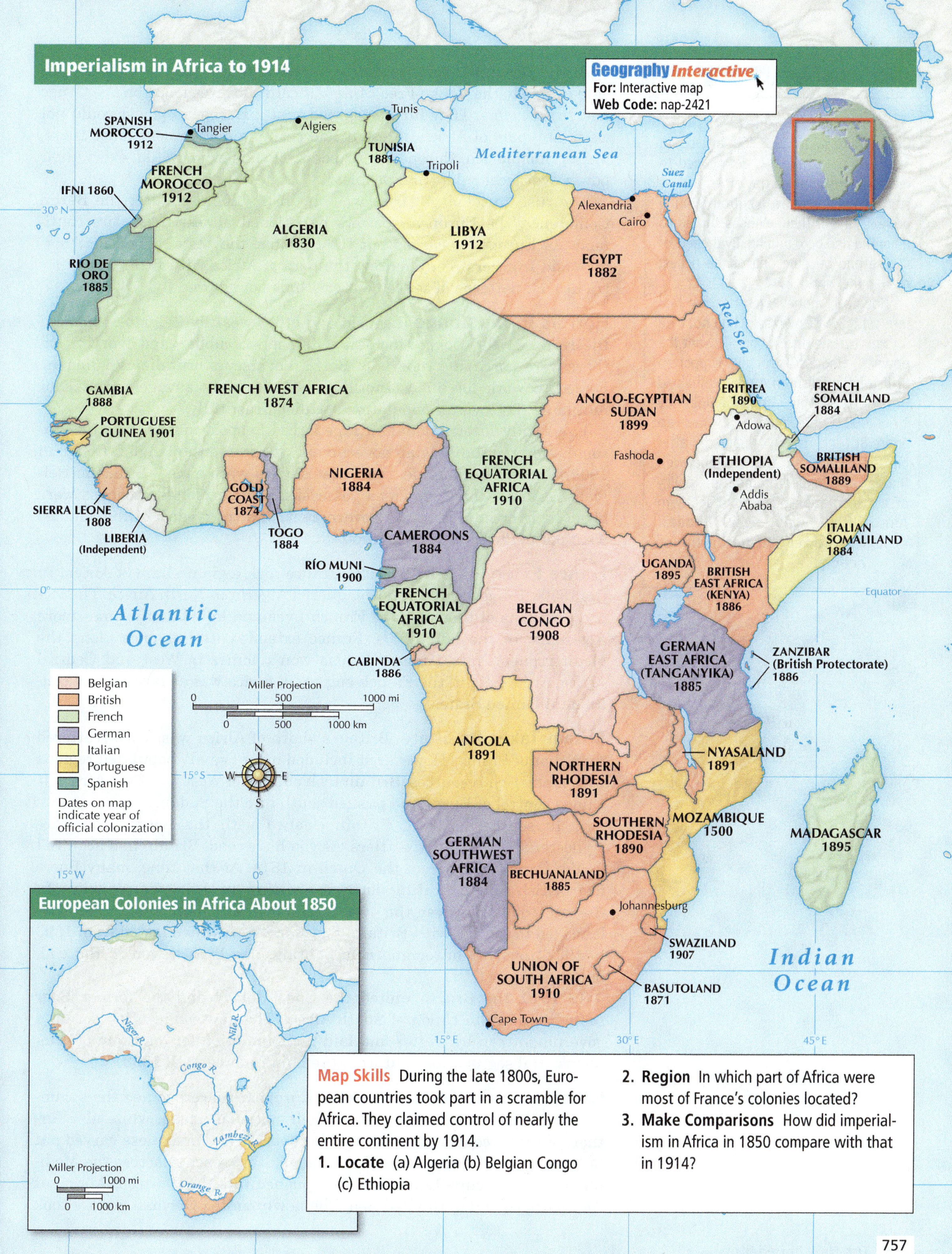

Map Skills During the late 1800s, European countries took part in a scramble for Africa. They claimed control of nearly the entire continent by 1914.

1. **Locate** (a) Algeria (b) Belgian Congo (c) Ethiopia

2. **Region** In which part of Africa were most of France's colonies located?

3. **Make Comparisons** How did imperialism in Africa in 1850 compare with that in 1914?

Cecil Rhodes

Cecil Rhodes (1853–1902) arrived in South Africa at age 17, determined to make his fortune. He got off to a slow start. His first venture, a cotton-farming project, failed. Then, Rhodes turned to diamond and gold mining. By the age of 40, he had become one of the richest men in the world.

However, money was not his real interest. "For its own sake I do not care for money," he once wrote. "I want the power." Rhodes strongly supported British imperialism in Africa. He helped Britain extend its African empire by 1,000,000 square miles and had an entire British colony named after himself—Rhodesia (now Zimbabwe). Rhodes also helped promote the policy of the separation of races in southern Africa. **How was Cecil Rhodes' desire for power illustrated by his actions?**

At the Berlin Conference, European powers recognized Leopold's private claims to the Congo Free State but called for free trade on the Congo and Niger rivers. They further agreed that a European power could not claim any part of Africa unless it had set up a government office there. This principle led Europeans to send officials who would exert their power over local rulers and peoples.

The rush to colonize Africa was on. In the 20 years after the Berlin Conference, the European powers partitioned almost the entire continent. As Europeans carved out their claims, they established new borders and frontiers. They redrew the map of Africa with little regard for traditional patterns of settlement or ethnic boundaries.

Horrors in the Congo Leopold and other wealthy Belgians exploited the riches of the Congo, including its copper, rubber, and ivory. Soon, there were horrifying reports of Belgian overseers brutalizing villagers. Forced to work for almost nothing, laborers were savagely beaten or mutilated. The overall population declined drastically.

Eventually, international outrage forced Leopold to turn over his personal colony to the Belgian government. It became the Belgian Congo in 1908. Under Belgian rule, the worst abuses were ended. Still, the Belgians regarded the Congo as a possession to be exploited. Africans were given little or no role in the government, and the wealth of their mines went out of the country to Europe.

France Extends Its Influence France took a giant share of Africa. In the 1830s, it had invaded and conquered Algeria in North Africa. The victory cost tens of thousands of French lives and killed many times more Algerians. In the late 1800s, France extended its influence along the Mediterranean into Tunisia. It also won colonies in West and Central Africa. At its height, the French empire in Africa was as large as the continental United States.

Britain Takes Its Share Britain's share of Africa was more scattered than that of France. However, it included more heavily populated regions with many rich resources. Britain took chunks of West and East Africa. It gained control of Egypt and pushed south into the Sudan.

In southern Africa, Britain clashed with the Boers, who were descendants of Dutch settlers. As you have read, Britain had acquired the Cape Colony from the Dutch in 1814. At that time, many Boers fled British rule, migrating north and setting up their own republics. In the late 1800s, however, the discovery of gold and diamonds in the Boer lands led to conflict with Britain. The **Boer War,** which lasted from 1899 to 1902, involved bitter guerrilla fighting. The British won in the end, but at great cost.

In 1910, the British united the Cape Colony and the former Boer republics into the Union of South Africa. The new constitution set up a government run by whites and laid the foundation for a system of complete racial segregation that would remain in force until 1993.

Others Join the Scramble Other European powers joined the scramble for colonies, in part to bolster their national image, while also furthering their economic growth and influence. The Portuguese carved out large colonies in Angola and Mozambique. Italy reached across the Mediterranean to occupy Libya and then pushed into the "horn" of Africa, at the southern end of the Red Sea. The newly united German empire took lands in eastern and southwestern Africa, including Cameroons and Togo. A German politician, trying to ease the worries of European rivals, explained, "We do not want to put anyone in the shade, but we also demand our place in the sun."

✓ **Checkpoint** How did King Leopold II set off a scramble for colonies in Africa?

Africans Resist Imperialism

Europeans met armed resistance across the continent. The Algerians battled the French for years. Samori Touré (sah MAWR ee too RAY) fought French forces in West Africa, where he was building his own empire. The British battled the Zulus in southern Africa and the Asante in West Africa. When their king was exiled, the Asante put themselves under the command of their queen, Yaa Asantewaa (YA uh ah sahn TAY wuh). She led the fight against the British in the last Asante war. Another woman who became a military leader was Nehanda (neh HAHN duh), of the Shona in Zimbabwe. Although a clever tactician, Nehanda was captured and executed. However, the memory of her achievements inspired later generations to fight for freedom.

In East Africa, the Germans fought wars against the Yao and Herero (huh REHR oh). Fighting was especially fierce in the Maji-Maji Rebellion of 1905. The Germans triumphed only after burning acres and acres of farmland, leaving thousands of local people to die of starvation.

Ethiopia Survives One ancient Christian kingdom in East Africa, Ethiopia, managed to resist European colonization and maintain its independence. Like feudal Europe, Ethiopia had been divided up among a number of rival princes who ruled their own <u>domains</u>. In the late 1800s, however, a reforming ruler, Menelik II, began to modernize his country. He hired European experts to plan modern roads and bridges and set up a Western school system. He imported the latest weapons and European officers to help train his army. Thus, when Italy invaded Ethiopia in 1896, Menelik was prepared. At the battle of Adowa (AH duh wuh), the Ethiopians smashed the Italian invaders. Ethiopia was the only African nation, aside from Liberia, to preserve its independence.

Vocabulary Builder

<u>domain</u>—(doh MAYN) *n.* territory over which rule or control is exercised

BIOGRAPHY

Menelik II

Before becoming emperor of Ethiopia, Menelik II (1844–1913) ruled the Shoa region in central Ethiopia. He ensured that he would succeed John IV as emperor by marrying his daughter to John's son. After John died in 1889, Menelik took the throne.

Menelik used profits from ivory sales to buy modern weapons. He then hired European advisors to teach his soldiers how to use the new guns. Menelik's army conquered neighboring lands and won a stunning victory over the Italians at Adowa. European nations rushed to establish diplomatic ties with Ethiopia. Around the world, people of African descent hailed Menelik's victory over European imperialism. **How did Menelik preserve Ethiopian independence?**

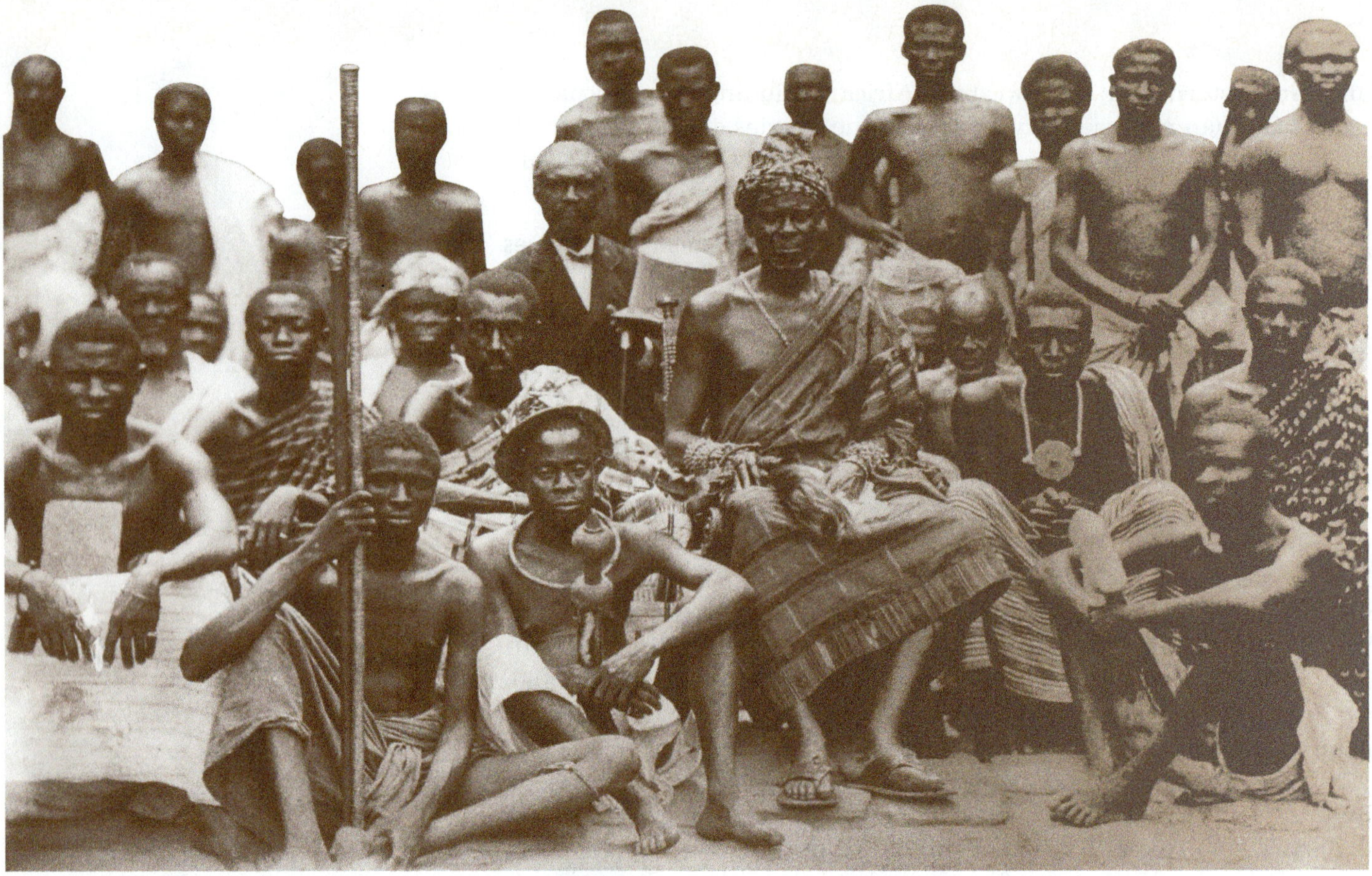

An Asante King
A king of the Asante people in Ghana (center) sits surrounded by his people. *What do the clothes of the man to the left of the king suggest about his social rank?*

A New African Elite Emerges During the Age of Imperialism, a Western-educated African **elite,** or upper class, emerged. Some middle-class Africans admired Western ways and rejected their own culture. Others valued their African traditions and condemned Western societies that upheld liberty and equality for whites only. By the early 1900s, African leaders were forging nationalist movements to pursue self-determination and independence.

✓ **Checkpoint** **How did Ethiopians resist imperialism?**

SECTION 2 Assessment

Progress Monitoring *Online*
For: Self-quiz with vocabulary practice
Web Code: naa-2421

Terms, People, and Places

1. For each term, person, or place listed at the beginning of the section, write a sentence explaining its significance.

Note Taking

2. **Reading Skill: Identify Causes and Effects** Use your completed chart to answer the Focus Question: How did imperialist European powers claim control over most of Africa by the end of the 1800s?

Comprehension and Critical Thinking

3. **Describe** Name one development in each region of Africa in the early 1800s.
4. **Analyze Information** What impact did explorers and missionaries have on Africa?
5. **Draw Inferences** (a) Why do you think the Europeans did not invite Africans to the Berlin Conference? (b) What might be the effect of this exclusion upon later African leaders?
6. **Summarize** How did Africans resist European imperialism?

Writing About History

Quick Write: Generate Arguments One way to approach a persuasive essay is to create a list of arguments that you can include to persuade your audience. For practice, create a list of three arguments that could be used in a persuasive essay either in favor of or opposed to the European colonization of Africa.

On Trial for My Country
by Stanlake Samkange

European imperialists gained control over much of Africa by signing treaties with local rulers. In most cases, the chiefs did not understand what rights they were signing away. Cecil Rhodes used this tactic with King Lobengula, who thought that he was allowing the British only to dig on his land. Rhodes, however, took control of the kingdom, eventually naming it Rhodesia. The novel *On Trial for My Country* is a fictional account of a conversation between King Lobengula and his father.

"Why did you not stand up to Rhodes and prevent him from taking your country by strength? Why did you not fight?"

"I thought that if I appealed to the white men's sense of justice and fair play, reminding them how good I had been to them since I had never killed or ill-treated a white man, they might hear my word and return to their homes. . . ."

"I . . . told them that I had not given them the road to Mashonaland."

"Yes, and they replied and told you that they had been given the road by their Queen and would only return on the orders of their Queen. What did you do then?"

"I mobilized[1] the army and told them to wait for my word."

"Did you give that word?"

"No."

"Were the soldiers keen to fight?"

"Yes, they were dying to fight."

"Why did you not let them fight?"

"I wanted to avoid bloodshed and war. . . ."

"And you allowed them to flout[2] your word as king of the Amandebele? You let them have their way. . . . Is that right?. . . .Why did you not . . . seek their protection and declare your country a British protectorate?"

". . . I knew that if I fought the white men I would be beaten. If I sought the white man's friendship and protection, there would be opposition to me or civil war. So I decided to pretend to the white men that if they came into the country I would fight, and hoped that they would be afraid and not come. . . . [T]hey called my bluff and came . . ."

"Was there no other way out of your dilemma?"

"I did consider marrying the Queen, but even though I hinted at this several times no one followed it up."

"I see!"

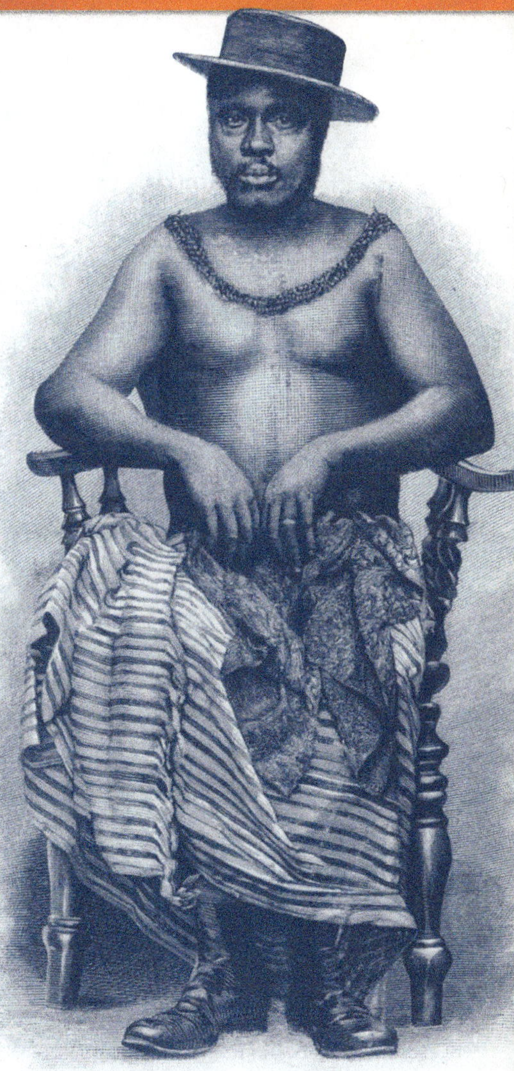

▲ King Lobengula of the Matabele nation in present-day Zimbabwe

1. **mobilize** (MOH buh lyz) *v.* to assemble for war
2. **flout** (flowt) *v.* to mock

Thinking Critically

1. **Synthesize Information** Why did King Lobengula want to avoid fighting the British?
2. **Analyze Literature** How does Samkange show that Lobengula's father disagreed with his son's decision?

Poster of Napoleon in Egypt

The Egyptian Campaign

By 1797, Napoleon Bonaparte felt that Europe offered too few chances for glory. Setting his sights toward Africa in 1798, he invaded Egypt, a province of the Ottoman empire.

> **66** Europe is a molehill. . . . We must go to the East. . . . All great glory has been acquired there.**99**

Focus Question How did European nations extend their power into Muslim regions of the world?

Lamp from a mosque

European Claims in Muslim Regions

Objectives
- Analyze the sources of stress in Muslim regions.
- Explain the problems the Ottoman empire faced.
- Describe how Egypt sought to modernize.
- Understand European interest in Persia.

Terms, People, and Places

Muhammad Ahmad
Mahdi
pasha
sultan
genocide
Muhammad Ali
concession

Note Taking

Reading Skill: Understand Effects As you read, fill in a concept web like the one below with the effects of European imperialism in Muslim regions of the world.

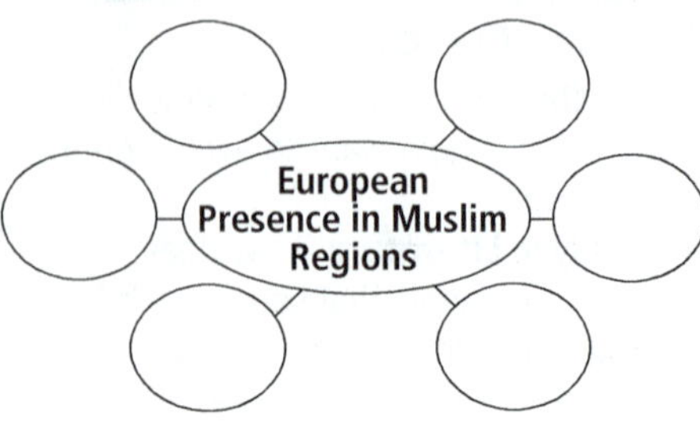

Napoleon's Egyptian campaign highlighted Ottoman decline and opened a new era of European contact with Muslim regions of the world. European countries were just nibbling at the edges of Muslim countries. Before long, they would strike at their heartland.

Stresses in Muslim Regions

Muslim lands extended from western Africa to Southeast Asia. In the 1500s, three giant Muslim empires ruled much of this world—the Ottomans in the Middle East, the Safavids (sah FAH vidz) in Persia, and the Mughals in India.

Empires in Decline By the 1700s, all three Muslim empires were in decline. The decay had many causes. Central governments had lost control over powerful groups such as landowning nobles, military elites, and urban craft guilds. Corruption was widespread. In some places, Muslim scholars and religious leaders were allied with the state. In other areas, they helped to stir discontent against the government.

Rise of Muslim Reform Movements In the 1700s and 1800s, reform movements sprang up across various Muslim regions of Africa and Asia. Most stressed religious piety and strict rules of behavior. Usman dan Fodio led the struggle to reform Muslim practices in northern Africa. In the Sudan, **Muhammad Ahmad** (AHK mud) announced that he was the **Mahdi** (mahk DEE), the long-awaited savior of the faith. The Mahdi and his followers fiercely resisted British expansion into the region.

Another Islamic reform movement, the Wahhabi (wah HAHB ee) movement in Arabia, rejected the schools of theology and law that had emerged in the Ottoman empire. In their place, they wanted to recapture the purity and simplicity of Muhammad's original teachings. Although the revolt was put down, the Wahhabi movement survived. Its teachings remain influential in the kingdom of Saudi Arabia today.

European Imperialism In addition to internal decay and stress, the three Muslim empires faced powerful threats from Western imperialists. Through diplomacy and military threats, European powers won treaties giving them favorable trading terms. They then demanded special rights for Europeans residing in Muslim lands. At times, European powers protected those rights by intervening in local affairs.

 **Checkpoint** How was Western imperialism a source of stress in Muslim regions of the world?

Problems for the Ottoman Empire

At its height, the Ottoman empire had extended across North Africa, Southeastern Europe, and the Middle East. By the early 1800s, however, it faced serious challenges. Ambitious **pashas,** or provincial rulers, had increased their power. Economic problems and corruption added to Ottoman decay.

Nationalist Revolts Break Out As ideas of nationalism spread from Western Europe, internal revolts weakened the multiethnic Ottoman empire. Subject peoples in North Africa, Eastern Europe, and the Middle East threatened to break away. In the Balkans, Greeks, Serbs, Bulgarians, and Romanians gained their independence. Revolts against Ottoman rule also erupted in Arabia, Lebanon, and Armenia. The Ottomans suppressed these uprisings, but Egypt slipped out of their control.

European Pressure Increases European states sought to benefit from the slow crumbling of the Ottoman empire. After seizing Algeria in the 1830s, France hoped to gain more Ottoman territory. Russia schemed to gain control of the Bosporus (BAHS puh rus) and the Dardanelles. Control of these straits would give the Russians access to the Mediterranean Sea. Britain tried to thwart Russia's ambitions, which it saw as a threat to its own power in the Mediterranean and beyond to India. And in 1898, the new German empire hoped to increase its influence in the region by building a Berlin-to-Baghdad railway.

Efforts to Westernize Since the late 1700s, several Ottoman rulers had seen the need for reform and looked to the West for ideas. They reorganized the bureaucracy and system of tax collection. They built railroads, improved education, and hired Europeans to train a modern military. Young men were sent to the West to study science and technology. Many returned with Western political ideas about democracy and equality.

The reforms also brought improved medical care and revitalized farming. These improvements,

General Ismail Pasha (center) fought for the British army in the Crimean War.

however, created a different set of problems. Better healthcare resulted in a population explosion that increased the already intense competition for the best land and led to unrest.

The adoption of Western ideas also increased tension. Many officials objected to changes that were inspired by a foreign culture. For their part, repressive **sultans,** rulers of the Ottoman Turkish empire, rejected reform and tried to rebuild the autocratic power enjoyed by earlier rulers.

Young Turks Demand Reform In the 1890s, a group of liberals formed a movement called the Young Turks. They insisted that reform was the only way to save the empire. In 1908, the Young Turks overthrew the sultan. Before they could achieve their planned reforms, however, the Ottoman empire was plunged into the world war that erupted in 1914.

Armenian Genocide Traditionally, the Ottomans had let minority nationalities live in their own communities and practice their own religions. By the 1890s, however, nationalism was igniting new tensions, especially between Turkish nationalists and minority peoples who sought their own states. These tensions triggered a brutal genocide of the Armenians, a Christian people concentrated in the eastern mountains of the empire. **Genocide** is a deliberate attempt to destroy a racial, political, or cultural group.

The Muslim Turks accused Christian Armenians of supporting Russian plans against the Ottoman empire. When Armenians protested repressive Ottoman policies, the sultan had tens of thousands of them slaughtered. Over the next 25 years, between 600,000 and 1.5 million Armenians were killed or died from disease and starvation.

 **Checkpoint** How were efforts to Westernize problematic for the Ottoman empire?

Egypt Seeks to Modernize

In the early 1800s, Egypt was a semi-independent province of the Ottoman empire, making great strides toward reform. Its success was due to **Muhammad Ali,** an ambitious soldier appointed governor of Egypt by the Ottomans. Ali used the opportunity created by Napoleon's invasion and the civil war that followed to seize power in 1805.

Muhammad Ali Introduces Reforms Muhammad Ali is sometimes called the "father of modern Egypt." He introduced a number of political and economic reforms, including improving tax collection, reorganizing the landholding system, and backing large irrigation projects to increase farm output. By expanding cotton production and encouraging the development of many local industries, Ali increased Egyptian participation in world trade.

Muhammad Ali also brought Western military experts to Egypt to help him build a well-trained, modern army. He conquered the neighboring lands of Arabia, Syria, and Sudan. Before he died in 1849, he had set Egypt on the road to becoming a major Middle Eastern power.

Building the Suez Canal Muhammad Ali's successors lacked his skills, and Egypt came increasingly under foreign control. In 1858, a French entrepreneur, Ferdinand de Lesseps (LAY seps), organized a company to build the Suez Canal. European nations gained power over the Ottomans by extending loans at high interest rates. In 1875, the ruler of

INFOGRAPHIC

Suez Canal

The Suez Canal is a waterway in Egypt that stretches for more than 100 miles (160 kilometers). It connects the Mediterranean and Red seas, shortening the travel distance from Western Europe to ports in East Africa and Asia. After it opened in 1869, European ships no longer had to sail around the southern tip of Africa. The canal reduced the trip from London, England, to Bombay, India, by 5,150 miles (8,280 kilometers). The canal averaged between one and two ships per day (below) in its first year of operation and travel time averaged about 40 hours. Today, oil tankers and cargo ships make up most of the canal's traffic with a travel time of about 14 hours.

Geography Interactive
For: Audio guided tour
Web Code: nap-2431

Route Through the Suez Canal

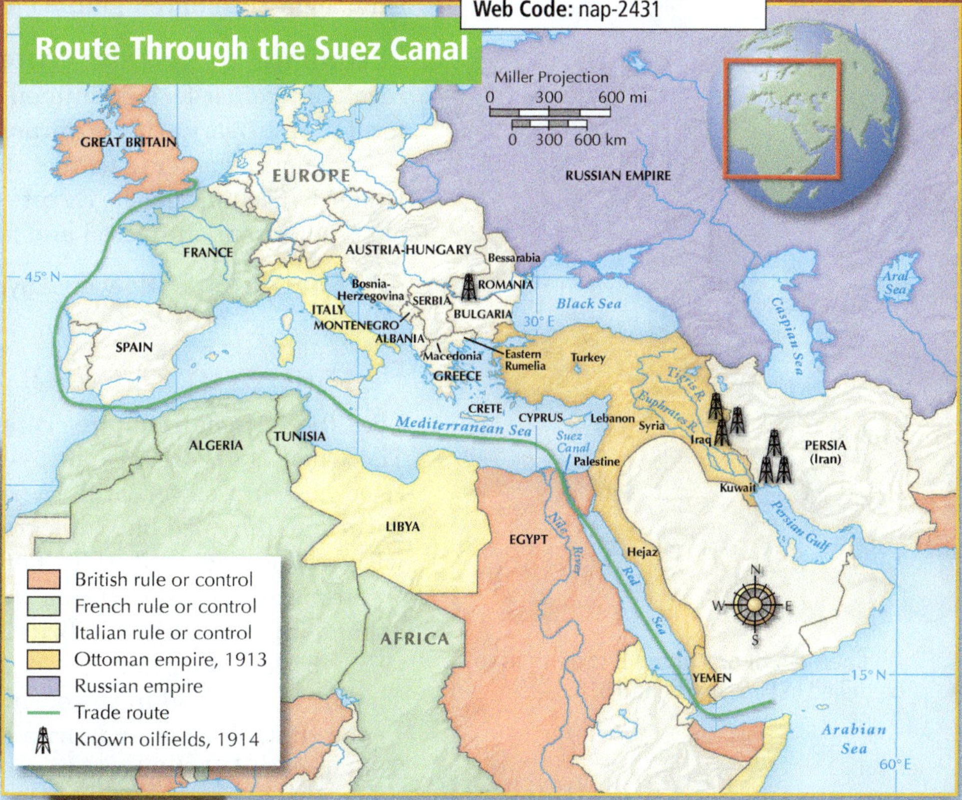

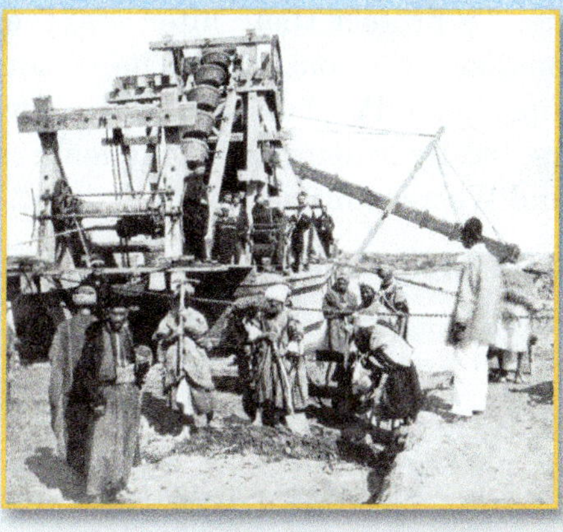

▲ Construction of the Suez Canal began in 1859 and took workers 10 years to complete. Although digging was first done by hand, laborers later used dredgers and steam shovels to remove sediment.

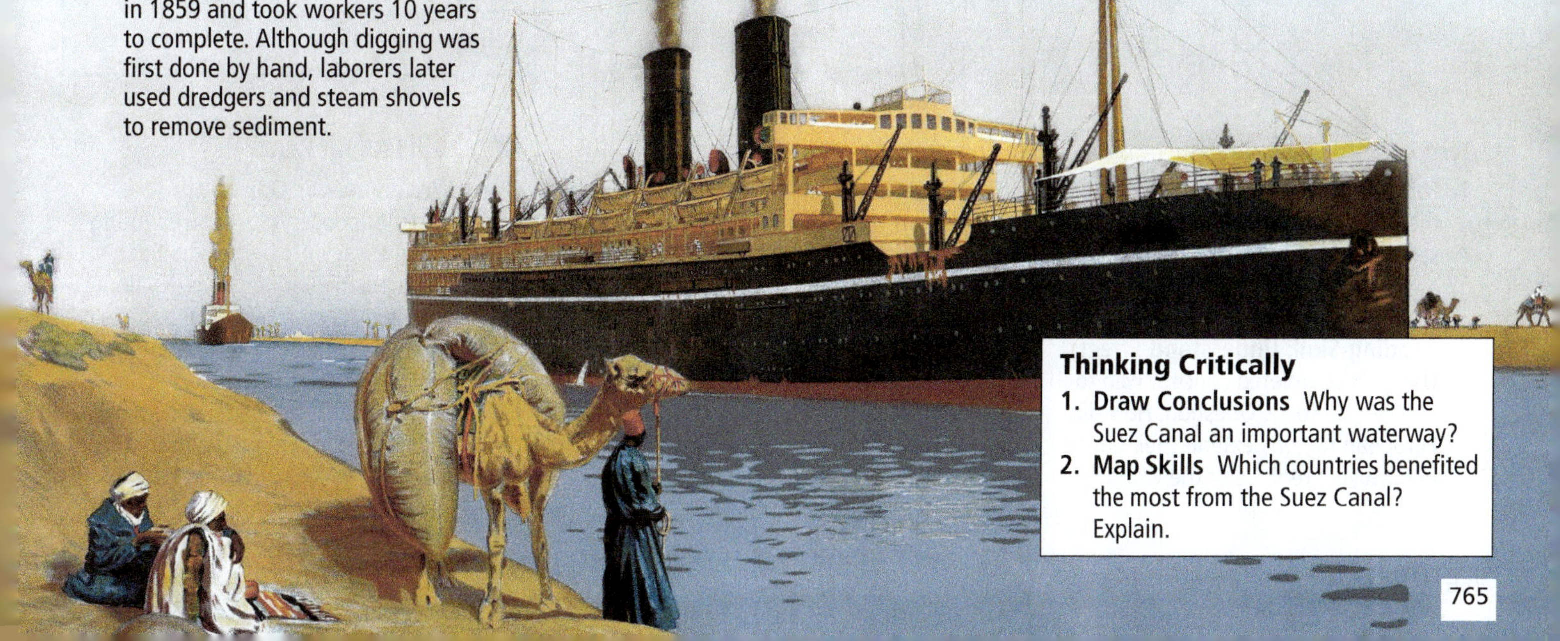

Thinking Critically

1. **Draw Conclusions** Why was the Suez Canal an important waterway?
2. **Map Skills** Which countries benefited the most from the Suez Canal? Explain.

Oil flows out of one of the first oil wells to be drilled in Persia, around 1910.

Egypt was unable to repay loans he had contracted for the canal and other projects. To pay his debts, he sold his shares in the canal. The British bought the shares, gaining a controlling interest in the canal.

Becoming a British Protectorate When Egyptian nationalists revolted against foreign influence in 1882, Britain made Egypt a protectorate. In theory, the governor of Egypt was still an official of the Ottoman government. In fact, he followed policies dictated by Britain. Under British influence, Egypt continued to modernize. However, nationalist discontent simmered and flared into protests and riots.

✔ **Checkpoint**   How did Egypt fall under British control?

Persia and the European Powers

Like the Ottoman empire, Persia faced major challenges in the 1800s. The Qajar (kah JAHR) shahs, who ruled Persia from 1794 to 1925, exercised absolute power. Still, they did take steps to introduce reforms. The government helped build telegraph lines and railroads and experimented with a liberal constitution. Reform, however, did not save Persia from Western imperialism. Russia wanted to protect its southern frontier and expand into Central Asia. Britain wanted to protect its interests in India.

For a time, each nation set up its own sphere of influence in Persia. The discovery of oil in the early 1900s heightened foreign interest in the region. Both Russia and Britain plotted for control of Persian oil fields. They persuaded the Persian government to grant them **concessions,** or special rights given to foreign powers. To protect their interests, they sent troops into Persia. Persian nationalists were outraged. The nationalists included two very different groups. Some Persians wanted to move swiftly to adopt Western ways. Others, led by Muslim religious leaders, condemned the Persian government and Western influences.

✔ **Checkpoint**   How did Persia attract foreign interest in the early 1900s?

SECTION 3 Assessment

Terms, People, and Places

1. For each term, person, or place listed at the beginning of the section, write a sentence explaining its significance.

Note Taking

2. **Reading Skill: Understand Effects** Use your completed concept web to answer the Focus Question: How did European nations extend their power into Muslim regions of the world?

Comprehension and Critical Thinking

3. **Draw Conclusions** How did European nations take advantage of stresses in the Muslim world?

4. **Summarize** Describe two problems that contributed to Ottoman decline.

5. **Synthesize Information** How did Muhammad Ali modernize Egypt?

6. **Identify Central Issues** Why did Russia and Britain compete for power in Persia?

● Writing About History

Quick Write: Answer Opposing Arguments Suppose that you are writing a persuasive essay on whether the Suez Canal was a positive or negative development for Egypt. An effective way to make your arguments convincing is to address both sides of the topic. Create a chart noting facts and ideas that support your position on one side and arguments that might be used against your position on the other.

SECTION 4

WITNESS HISTORY AUDIO

Critical of British Rule

In 1871, Indian nationalist Dadabhai Naoroji (DAH dah by now ROH jee) criticized British rule in India:

> “[Indians] call the British system ‘Sakar ki Churi’ (SA kur kee CHOO ree), the knife of sugar. That is to say, there is no oppression, it is all smooth and sweet, but it is the knife notwithstanding.”

Focus Question How did Britain gradually extend its control over most of India, despite opposition?

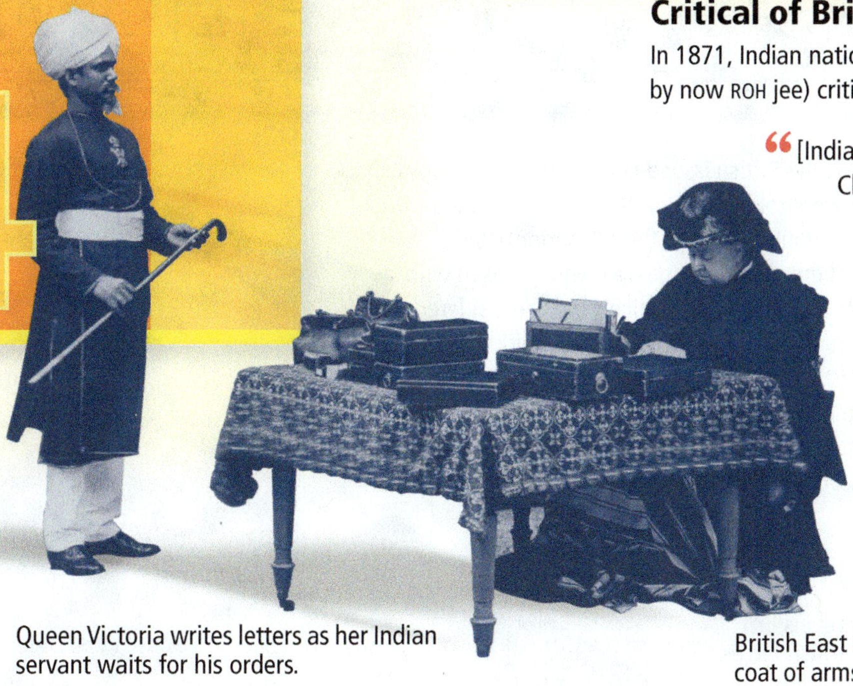

Queen Victoria writes letters as her Indian servant waits for his orders.

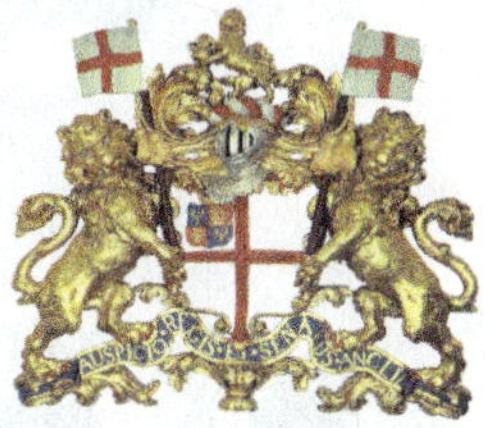

British East India Company's coat of arms

The British Take Over India

Objectives

- Understand the causes and effects of the Sepoy Rebellion.
- Explain how British rule affected India.
- Describe how Indians viewed Western culture.
- Identify the origins of Indian nationalism.

Terms, People, and Places

sati
sepoy
viceroy
deforestation
Ram Mohun Roy
purdah

Note Taking

Reading Skill: Identify Causes and Effects As you read this section, make a flowchart to show the causes and effects of British rule in India.

Cause	→	Event	→	Effect
• • •	→	British colonial rule in India	→	• • •

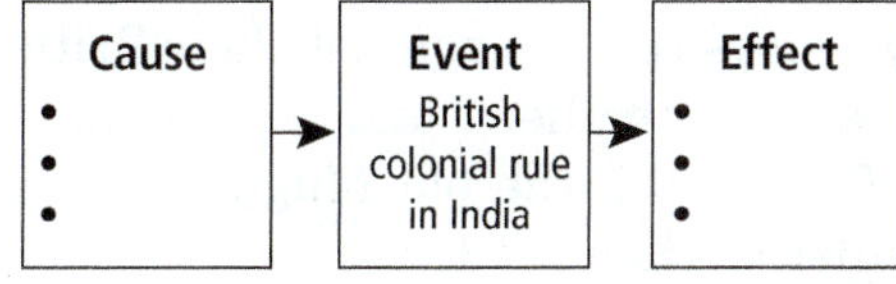

For more than 200 years, Mughal rulers governed a powerful empire in India. By the mid-1700s, however, the Mughal empire was collapsing from a lack of strong rulers. Britain then turned its commercial interests in the region into political ones.

East India Company and Rebellion

In the early 1600s, the British East India Company won trading rights on the fringe of the Mughal empire. As Mughal power declined, the company's influence grew. By the mid-1800s, it controlled three fifths of India.

Exploiting Indian Diversity The British were able to conquer India by exploiting its diversity. Even when Mughal power was at its height, India was home to many people and cultures. As Mughal power crumbled, India became fragmented. Indians with different traditions and dozens of different languages were not able to unite against the newcomers. The British took advantage of Indian divisions by encouraging competition and disunity among rival princes. Where diplomacy or intrigue did not work, the British used their superior weapons to overpower local rulers.

Implementing British Policies The East India Company's main goal in India was to make money, and leading officials often grew rich. At the same time, the company did work to improve roads, preserve peace, and reduce banditry.

THE SEPOY REBELLION

In 1857, the British issued new rifles to the sepoys. Troops were told to bite off the tips of cartridges before loading them into the rifles (right). Sepoys believed the cartridges (below) were greased with animal fat—from cows, which Hindus considered sacred, and from pigs, which were forbidden to Muslims. When sepoys (right) refused to load the guns, they were imprisoned. Angry sepoys rebelled against British officers, sparking a massacre of British troops, as well as women and children.

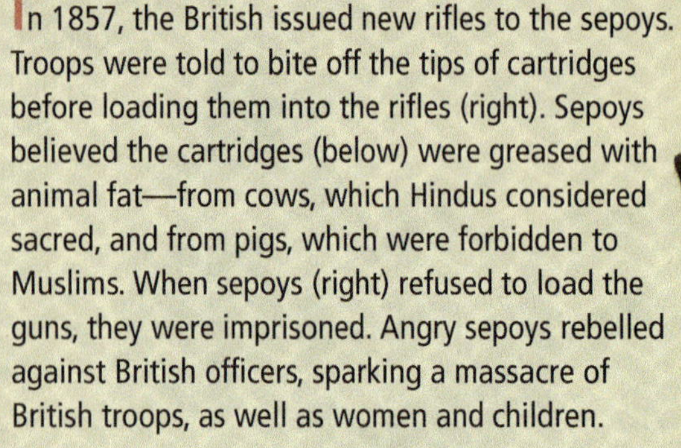

◄ A Sepoy rebels against British forces.

By the early 1800s, British officials introduced Western education and legal procedures. Missionaries tried to convert Indians to Christianity, which they felt was superior to Indian religions. The British also pressed for social change. They worked to end slavery and the caste system and to improve the position of women within the family. One law banned **sati** (SUH tee), a Hindu custom practiced mainly by the upper classes. It called for a widow to join her husband in death by throwing herself on his funeral fire.

Growing Discontent In the 1850s, the East India Company made several unpopular moves. First, it required **sepoys** (SEE poyz), or Indian soldiers in its service, to serve anywhere, either in India or overseas. For high-caste Hindus, however, overseas travel was an offense against their religion. Second, the East India Company passed a law that allowed Hindu widows to remarry. Hindus viewed both moves as a Christian conspiracy to undermine their beliefs.

Then, in 1857, the British issued new rifles to the sepoys. Troops were told to bite off the tips of cartridges before loading them into the rifles. The cartridges, however, were greased with animal fat—either from cows, which Hindus considered sacred, or from pigs, which were forbidden to Muslims. When the troops refused the order to "load rifles," they were imprisoned.

Rebellion and Aftermath Angry sepoys rose up against their British officers. The Sepoy Rebellion swept across northern and central India. Several sepoy regiments marched off to Delhi, the old Mughal capital. There, they hailed the last Mughal ruler as their leader.

In some places, the sepoys brutally massacred British men, women, and children. But the British soon rallied and crushed the revolt. They then took terrible revenge for their earlier losses, torching villages and slaughtering thousands of unarmed Indians.

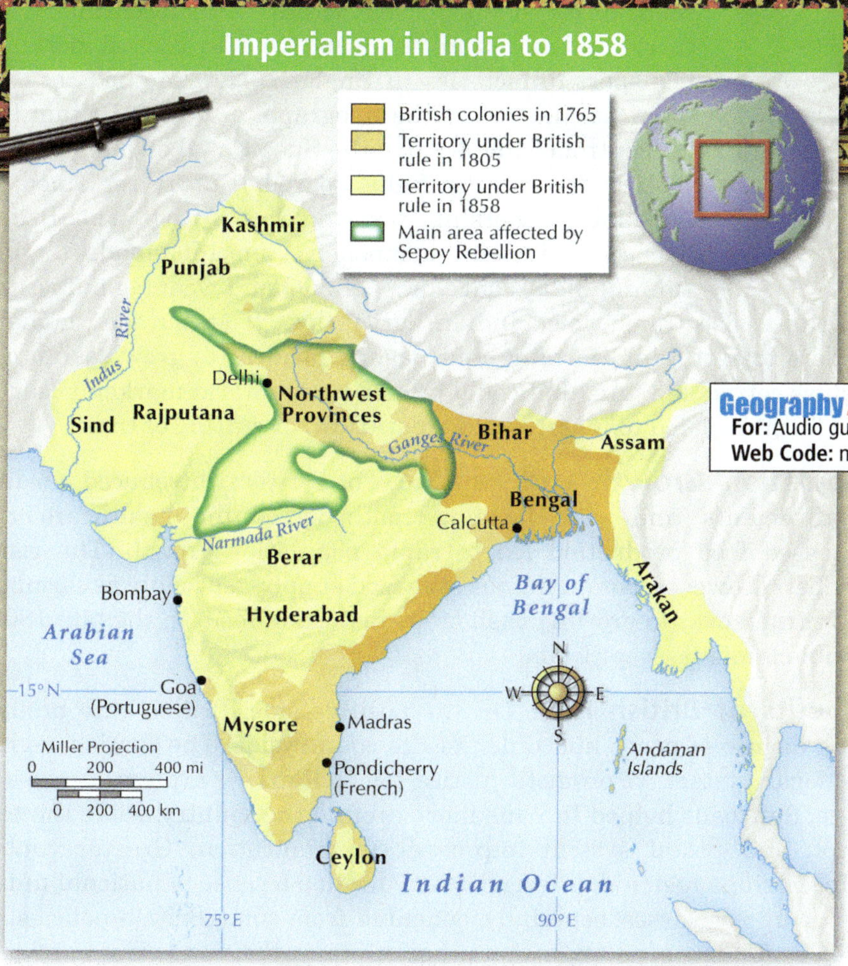

Geography Interactive
For: Audio guided tour
Web Code: nap-2441

A British officer ▶ fights sepoys near Delhi.

Thinking Critically

1. **Draw Conclusions** How was the Sepoy Rebellion a clash of cultures?
2. **Map Skills** Which regions were most affected by the Sepoy Rebellion?

The Sepoy Rebellion left a bitter legacy of fear, hatred, and mistrust on both sides. It also brought major changes in British policy. In 1858, Parliament ended the rule of the East India Company and put India directly under the British crown. It sent more troops to India, taxing Indians to pay the cost of these occupying forces. While it slowed the "reforms" that had angered Hindus and Muslims, it continued to develop India for Britain's own economic benefit.

✓ **Checkpoint** **What were the causes of the Sepoy Rebellion in northern and central India?**

Impact of British Colonial Rule

After 1858, Parliament set up a system of colonial rule in India called the British Raj. A British **viceroy** in India governed in the name of the queen, and British officials held the top positions in the civil service and army. Indians filled most other jobs. With their cooperation, the British made India the "brightest jewel" in the crown of their empire.

British policies were designed to incorporate India into the overall British economy. At the same time, British officials felt they were helping India to modernize. In their terms, modernizing meant adopting not only Western technology but also Western culture.

Vocabulary Builder
overall—(OH vur awl) *adj.* total

An Unequal Partnership Britain saw India both as a market and as a source of raw materials. To this end, the British built roads and an impressive railroad network. Improved transportation let the British sell

their factory-made goods across the subcontinent and carry Indian cotton, jute, and coal to coastal ports for transport to factories in England. New methods of communication, such as the telegraph, also gave Britain better control of India. After the Suez Canal opened in 1869, British trade with India soared. But it remained an unequal partnership, favoring the British. The British flooded India with inexpensive, machine-made textiles, ruining India's once-prosperous hand-weaving industry.

Britain also transformed Indian agriculture. It encouraged nomadic herders to settle into farming and pushed farmers to grow cash crops, such as cotton and jute, that could be sold on the world market. Clearing new farmlands led to massive **deforestation,** or cutting of trees.

Population Growth and Famine The British introduced medical improvements and new farming methods. Better healthcare and increased food production led to rapid population growth. The rising numbers, however, put a strain on the food supply, especially as farmland was turned over to growing cash crops instead of food. In the late 1800s, terrible famines swept India.

Benefits of British Rule On the positive side, British rule brought some degree of peace and order to the countryside. The British revised the legal system to promote justice for Indians regardless of class or caste. Railroads helped Indians move around the country, while the telegraph and postal system improved communication. Greater contact helped bridge regional differences and develop a sense of national unity.

The upper classes, especially, benefited from some British policies. They sent their sons to British schools, where they were trained for posts in the civil service and military. Indian landowners and princes, who still ruled their own territories, grew rich from exporting cash crops.

✔ **Checkpoint** How did British colonial rule affect Indian agriculture?

Different Views on Culture

Some educated Indians were impressed by British power and technology and urged India to follow a Western model of progress. These mostly upper-class Indians learned English and adopted Western ways. Other Indians felt that the answer to change lay with their own Hindu or Muslim cultures.

Indian Attitudes In the early 1800s, **Ram Mohun Roy** combined both views. A great scholar, he knew Sanskrit, Persian, and Arabic classics, as well as English, Greek, and Latin works. Roy felt that India could learn from the West. He was a founder of Hindu College in Calcutta, which provided an English-style education to Indians. Many of its graduates went on to establish English schools all over the region. While Roy saw the value of Western education, he also wanted to reform traditional Indian culture.

Roy condemned some traditions, such as rigid caste distinctions, child marriage, sati, and **purdah** (PUR duh), the isolation of women in separate quarters. But he also set up educational societies that helped revive pride in Indian culture. Because of his influence on later leaders, he is often hailed today as the founder of Indian nationalism.

Railroads and Trade
By building thousands of miles of railroads, the British opened up India's vast interior to trade. The British also encouraged Indians to grow tea (top photo) and jute (bottom photo). Today, tea is one of India's biggest crops. *What were some of the benefits of British rule?*

Western Attitudes The British disagreed among themselves about India. A few admired Indian theology and philosophy. As Western scholars translated Indian classics, they acquired respect for India's ancient heritage. Western writers and philosophers borrowed ideas from Hinduism and Buddhism.

However, most British people knew little about Indian achievements and dismissed Indian culture with contempt. In an essay on whether Indians should be taught in English or their own languages, British historian Thomas Macaulay arrogantly wrote that "a single shelf of a good European library is worth the whole native literature of India and Arabia."

✔ **Checkpoint** How did Indians and British view each other's culture in the 1800s?

Indian Nationalism Grows

During the years of British rule, a class of Western-educated Indians emerged. In the view of Macaulay and others, this elite class would bolster British power. As it turned out, exposure to European ideas had the opposite effect. By the late 1800s, Western-educated Indians were spearheading a nationalist movement. Schooled in Western ideals such as democracy and equality, they dreamed of ending imperial rule.

Indian National Congress In 1885, nationalist leaders organized the Indian National Congress, which became known as the Congress party. Its members believed in peaceful protest to gain their ends. They called for greater democracy, which they felt would bring more power to Indians like themselves. The Indian National Congress looked forward to eventual self-rule, but supported Western-style modernization.

Muslim League At first, Muslims and Hindus worked together for self-rule. In time, however, Muslims grew to resent Hindu domination of the Congress party. They also worried that a Hindu-run government would oppress Muslims. In 1906, Muslims formed the Muslim League to pursue their own goals. Soon, they were talking of a separate Muslim state.

✔ **Checkpoint** How are the origins of Indian nationalism linked to British rule?

SECTION 4 Assessment

Terms, People, and Places

1. What do the key terms listed at the beginning of the section have in common?

 **Note Taking**

2. **Reading Skill: Identify Causes and Effects** Use your completed flowchart to answer the Focus Question: How did Britain gradually extend its control over most of India, despite opposition?

Comprehension and Critical Thinking

3. **Recognize Cause and Effect** What were the causes and effects of the Sepoy Rebellion?

4. **Draw Conclusions** What were the positive and negative effects of British rule on Indians?

5. **Analyze Information** How did British rule lead to growing Indian nationalism?

● **Writing About History**

Quick Write: Draft an Opening Paragraph Write an opening paragraph for a persuasive essay on whether the British were right to pass laws that tried to reform the caste system. Remember that the first few sentences of your draft are your chance to build interest in your topic. Add details that will help grab the reader's attention.

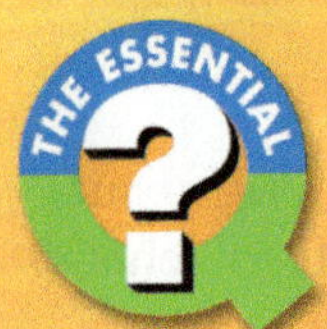

EMPIRE

How does a state gain or lose power over others?

In This Chapter

Britain brought much of the globe under its control in the 1800s because of its industrial strength and powerful navy. The "jewel in the crown" of the British Empire was India (right). India supplied British factories with raw materials and served as a huge market for British manufactured goods. But in the twentieth century, independence movements in India and elsewhere broke the British Empire apart.

Throughout History

522 B.C.–486 B.C. Darius I unifies the Persian empire by setting up a strong bureaucracy and building hundreds of miles of roads

31 B.C.–A.D. 14 Emperor Augustus encourages loyalty by allowing Roman provinces a large measure of self-government.

1500s Spain used wealth from its empire in the Americas to wage wars in Europe, neglecting its own economic development.

1800s The French Empire rises and falls with the rise and fall of Napoleon I.

1990s Economic weakness and involvement in a long war in Afghanistan leads to the breakup of the Soviet Union.

Continuing Today

Although the Soviet Union has broken apart, Russia maintains its interest in the affairs of former Soviet states. Russia will flex its military muscle to keep them in line. Here Russian tanks roll into neighboring Georgia to support South Ossetia.

21st Century Skills

TRANSFER Activities

1. **Analyze** Throughout history, how have different empires been strengthened or weakened?

2. **Evaluate** Why do you think no empire has even been able to maintain its influence forever?

3. **Transfer** Complete a Web quest, record your thoughts in the Concept Connector Journal, and learn to make a video. Web Code nah-2408

Lin Zexu,
Chinese official

Trading Opium for Tea

By the 1830s, British merchant ships were arriving in China loaded with opium to trade with the Chinese for tea. In 1839, Chinese government official Lin Zexu (lin DZUH shoo) wrote a letter to Britain's Queen Victoria condemning the practice:

> ❝ We have heard that in your own country opium is prohibited with the utmost strictness and severity—this is strong proof that you know full well how hurtful it is. . . . Since . . . you do not permit it to injure your own country, you ought not to have the injurious drug transferred to another country. ❞

Britain's Union Jack

Focus Question How did Western powers use diplomacy and war to gain power in Qing China?

China and the New Imperialism

Objectives

- Describe what trade rights Westerners sought in China.
- Explain the internal problems Chinese reformers tried to solve.
- Understand how the Qing dynasty fell.

Terms, People, and Places

balance of trade	Taiping Rebellion
trade surplus	Sino-Japanese War
trade deficit	Open Door Policy
Opium War	Guang Xu
indemnity	Boxer Uprising
extraterritoriality	Sun Yixian

Note Taking

Reading Skill: Recognize Multiple Causes As you read, create a flowchart like the one below in which you can record key events and developments that led to the decline of Qing China.

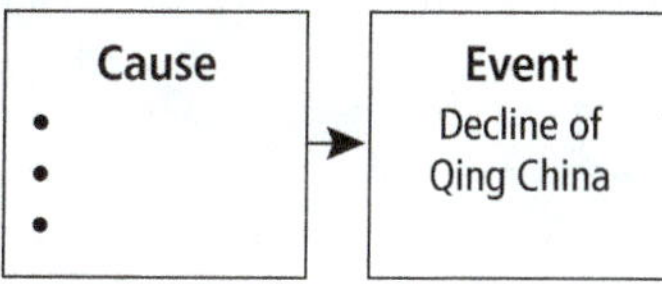

For centuries, Chinese regulations had ensured that China had a favorable **balance of trade** with other nations. A nation's balance of trade refers to the difference between how much a country imports and how much it exports. By the 1800s, however, Western nations were using their growing power to tilt the balance of trade with East Asia in their favor.

Trade Between Britain and China

Prior to the 1800s, Chinese rulers placed strict limits on foreign traders. European merchants were restricted to a small area in southern China. China sold them silk, porcelain, and tea in exchange for gold and silver. Under this arrangement, China enjoyed a **trade surplus,** or exported more than it imported. Westerners, on the other hand, had a **trade deficit** with China, buying more from the Chinese than they sold to them.

By the late 1700s, two developments were underway that would transform China's relations with the Western world. First, China entered a period of decline. Second, the Industrial Revolution created a need for expanded markets for European goods. At the same time, it gave the West superior military power.

The Opium War During the late 1700s, British merchants began making huge profits by trading opium grown in India for Chinese tea, which was popular in Britain. Soon, many Chinese had become addicted to the drug. Silver flowed out of China in payment for the drug, disrupting the economy.

The Chinese government outlawed opium and executed Chinese drug dealers. They called on Britain to stop the trade. The British refused, insisting on the right of free trade.

In 1839, Chinese warships clashed with British merchants, triggering the **Opium War.** British gunboats, equipped with the latest in firepower, bombarded Chinese coastal and river ports. With outdated weapons and fighting methods, the Chinese were easily defeated.

Unequal Treaties In 1842, Britain made China accept the Treaty of Nanjing (NAHN jing). Britain received a huge **indemnity,** or payment for losses in the war. The British also gained the island of Hong Kong. China had to open five ports to foreign trade and grant British citizens in China **extraterritoriality,** the right to live under their own laws and be tried in their own courts.

The treaty was the first of a series of "unequal treaties" that forced China to make concessions to Western powers. A second war, lasting from 1856 to 1858, ended with France, Russia, and the United States pressuring China to sign treaties <u>stipulating</u> the opening of more ports to foreign trade and letting Christian missionaries preach in China.

✔ **Checkpoint**   **How did British trade with China trigger the Opium Wars?**

The Taiping Rebellion Weakens China

By the 1800s, the Qing dynasty was in decline. Irrigation systems and canals were poorly maintained, leading to massive flooding of the Huang valley. The population explosion that had begun a century earlier created hardship

Vocabulary Builder
stipulate—(STIP yuh layt) *v.* to specifically demand something in an agreement

● **INFOGRAPHIC**

Taiping Rebellion

Taiping Rebellion leader Hong Xiuquan (at right), was a village schoolteacher. Inspired by religious visions and Christian missionaries, he wanted to establish a "Heavenly Kingdom of Peace"—the Taiping. Hong endorsed ideas that Chinese leaders considered radical, including community ownership of property and the equality of women and men.

◀ Chinese coins *c.*1850

for China's peasants. An extravagant imperial court, tax evasion by the rich, and widespread official corruption added to the peasants' burden. As poverty and misery increased, peasants rebelled. The **Taiping Rebellion** (TY ping), which lasted from 1850 to 1864, was probably the most devastating peasant revolt in history. The leader, Hong Xiuquan (hong shyoo CHWAHN), called for an end to the hated Qing dynasty. The Taiping rebels won control of large parts of China and held out for 14 years. However, with the help of loyal regional governors and generals, the government crushed the rebellion.

The Taiping Rebellion almost toppled the Qing dynasty. It is estimated to have caused the deaths of between 20 million and 30 million Chinese. The Qing government survived, but it had to share power with regional commanders. During the rebellion, Europeans kept up pressure on China, and Russia seized lands in the north.

✔ **Checkpoint** How did the Taiping Rebellion and other internal problems weaken the Qing dynasty?

Launching Reform Efforts

By the mid-1800s, educated Chinese were divided over the need to adopt Western ways. Most saw no reason for new industries because China's wealth and taxes came from land. Although Chinese merchants were allowed to do business, they were not seen as a source of prosperity.

Scholar-officials also disapproved of the ideas of Western missionaries, whose emphasis on individual choice challenged the Confucian order. They saw Western technology as dangerous, too, because it threatened Confucian ways that had served China successfully for so long.

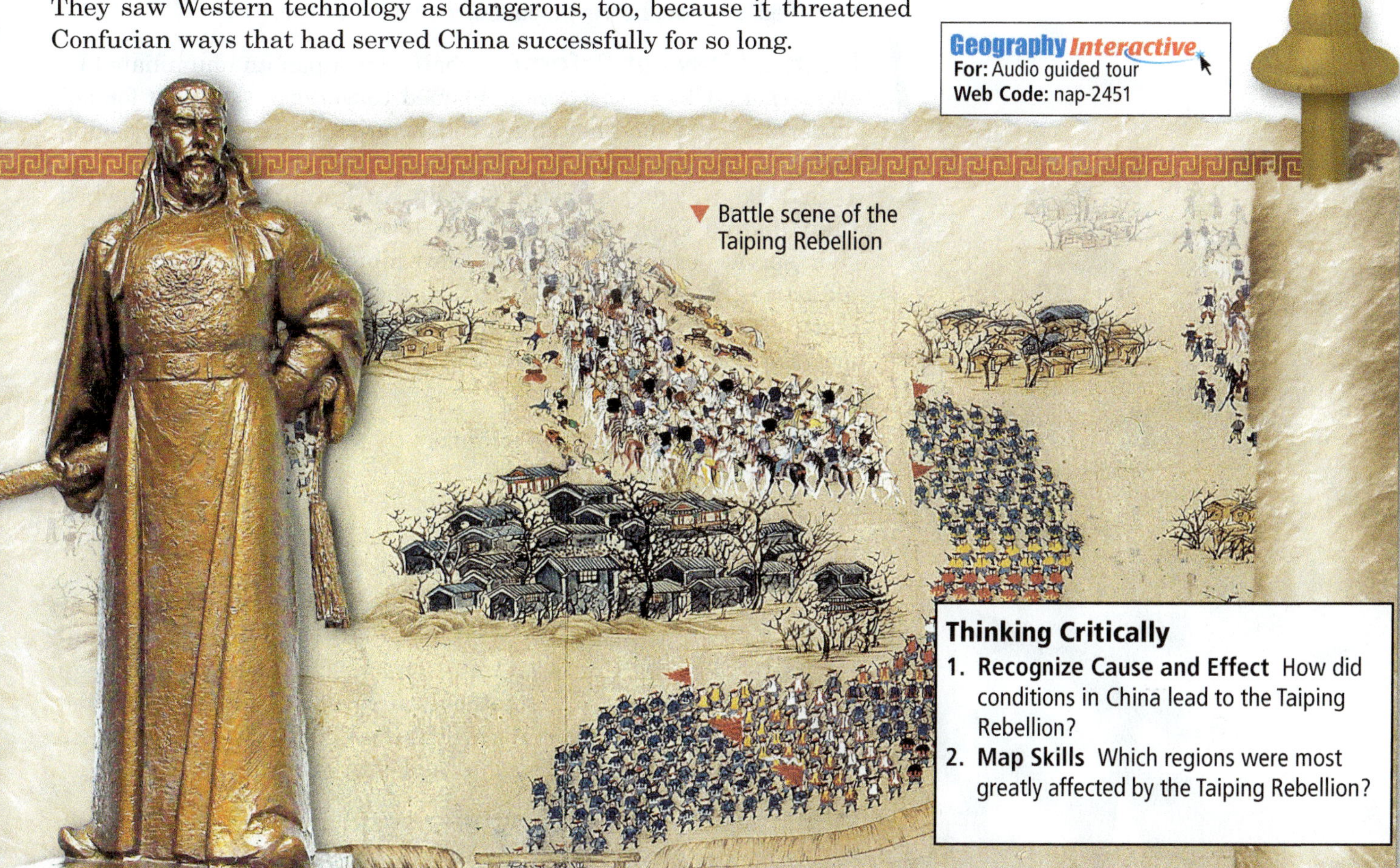

Thinking Critically
1. **Recognize Cause and Effect** How did conditions in China lead to the Taiping Rebellion?
2. **Map Skills** Which regions were most greatly affected by the Taiping Rebellion?

By the late 1800s, the empress Ci Xi (tsih shih) had gained power. A strong-willed ruler, she surrounded herself with advisors who were deeply committed to Confucian traditions.

Self-Strengthening Movement In the 1860s, reformers launched the "self-strengthening movement." They imported Western technology, setting up factories to make modern weapons. They developed shipyards, railroads, mining, and light industry. The Chinese translated Western works on science, government, and the economy. However, the movement made limited progress because the government did not rally behind it.

War With Japan Meanwhile, the Western powers and nearby Japan moved rapidly ahead. Japan began to modernize after 1868. It then joined the Western imperialists in the competition for a global empire.

In 1894, Japanese pressure on China led to the **Sino-Japanese War.** It ended in disaster for China, with Japan gaining the island of Taiwan.

Carving Spheres of Influence The crushing defeat revealed China's weakness. Western powers moved swiftly to carve out spheres of influence along the Chinese coast. The British took the Chang River valley. The French acquired the territory near their colony of Indochina. Germany and Russia gained territory in northern China.

The United States, a longtime trader with the Chinese, did not take part in the carving up of China. It feared that European powers might shut out American merchants. A few years later, in 1899, it called for a policy to keep Chinese trade open to everyone on an equal basis. The imperial powers accepted the idea of an **Open Door Policy,** as it came to be called. No one, however, consulted the Chinese.

Hundred Days of Reform Defeated by Japan and humiliated by Westerners, Chinese reformers blamed conservative officials for not modernizing China. They urged conservative leaders to stop looking back at China's past and to modernize as Japan had.

In 1898, a young emperor, **Guang Xu** (gwahng shoo), launched the Hundred Days of Reform. New laws set out to modernize the civil service exams, streamline government, and encourage new industries. Reforms affected schools, the military, and the bureaucracy. Conservatives soon rallied against the reform effort. The emperor was imprisoned, and the aging empress Ci Xi reasserted control. Reformers fled for their lives.

✔ **Checkpoint** How did reformers try to solve China's internal problems?

The Qing Dynasty Falls

As the century ended, China was in turmoil. Anger grew against Christian missionaries who threatened traditional Chinese Confucianism. The presence of foreign troops was another source of discontent. Protected by extraterritoriality, foreigners ignored Chinese laws and lived in their own communities.

Boxer Uprising Anti-foreign feeling finally exploded in the **Boxer Uprising.** In 1899, a group of Chinese had formed a secret society, the Righteous Harmonious Fists. Westerners watching them

The Boxer Rebellion
Suffering from the effects of floods and famine, poverty, and foreign aggression, Boxers (below) participated in an antiforeign movement. In 1900, some 140,000 Boxers attempted to drive Westerners out of China. An international force eventually put down the uprising. *Why were Westerners and Western influences a source of discontent for the Boxers?*

train in the martial arts dubbed them Boxers. Their goal was to drive out the "foreign devils" who were polluting the land with their un-Chinese ways, strange buildings, machines, and telegraph lines.

In 1900, the Boxers attacked foreigners across China. In response, the Western powers and Japan organized a multinational force. This force crushed the Boxers and rescued foreigners besieged in Beijing. The empress Ci Xi had at first supported the Boxers but reversed her policy as they retreated.

Aftermath of the Uprising China once again had to make concessions to foreigners. The defeat, however, forced even Chinese conservatives to support Westernization. In a rush of reforms, China admitted women to schools and stressed science and mathematics in place of Confucian thought. More students were sent abroad to study.

China also expanded economically. Mining, shipping, railroads, banking, and exports of cash crops grew. Small-scale Chinese industry developed with the help of foreign capital. A Chinese business class emerged, and a new urban working class began to press for rights.

Three Principles of the People Although the Boxer Uprising failed, the flames of Chinese nationalism spread. Reformers wanted to strengthen China's government. By the early 1900s, they had introduced a constitutional monarchy. Some reformers called for a republic.

A passionate spokesman for a Chinese republic was Sun Yixian (soon yee SHYAHN), also known as Sun Yat-sen. In the early 1900s, he organized the Revolutionary Alliance to rebuild China on "Three Principles of the People." The first principle was nationalism, or freeing China from foreign domination. The second was democracy, or representative government. The third was livelihood, or economic security for all Chinese.

Birth of a Republic When Ci Xi died in 1908 and a two-year-old boy inherited the throne, China slipped into chaos. In 1911, uprisings in the provinces swiftly spread. Peasants, students, local warlords, and even court politicians helped topple the Qing dynasty.

In December 1911, Sun Yixian was named president of the new Chinese republic. The republic faced overwhelming problems and was almost constantly at war with itself or foreign invaders.

✔ **Checkpoint** What caused the Qing dynasty to fall?

Sun Yixian

Sun Yixian (1866–1925) was not born to power. His parents were poor farmers. Sun's preparation for leadership came from his travels, education, and personal ambitions. In his teen years, he lived with his brother in Hawaii and attended British and American schools. Later on, he earned a medical degree.

Sun left his career in medicine to struggle against the Qing government. After a failed uprising in 1895, he went into exile. Sun visited many nations, seeking support against the Qing dynasty. When revolution erupted in China, Sun was in Denver, Colorado. He returned to China to begin his leading role in the new republic. **How did Sun's background prepare him to lead?**

Assessment

SECTION 5

Terms, People, and Places

1. For each term, person, or place listed at the beginning of the section, write a sentence explaining its significance.

Note Taking

2. **Reading Skill: Recognize Multiple Causes** Use your completed flowchart to answer the Focus Question: How did Western powers use diplomacy and war to gain power in Qing China?

Comprehension and Critical Thinking

3. **Draw Conclusions** How did Western powers gain greater trading rights in China?

4. **Summarize** (a) What internal problems threatened the Qing dynasty? (b) What were the goals of Chinese reformers?

5. **Synthesize Information** How was the Qing dynasty replaced by a republic?

● **Writing About History**

Quick Write: Write a Conclusion Before writing a persuasive essay, make a list of your arguments. In organizing the essay, it's often a good idea to save your strongest argument for last. For practice, write a concluding paragraph for a persuasive essay that either supports or opposes internal reform efforts to Westernize China in the 1800s.

Quick Study Guide

Progress Monitoring *Online*
For: Self-test with vocabulary practice
Web Code: naa-2461

■ Western Imperialism

Africa	Muslim Regions	India	China
• Berlin Conference • Raw materials exploited • Boer War • Racial segregation in South Africa • Western-educated African elite • Nationalism grows	• Islamic reform movements • Internal revolts • Armenian genocide • Egypt modernizes	• British East India Company • Changes to legal and caste systems • Sepoy Rebellion • Indians forced to raise cash crops • Population growth and famine • Indian National Congress • Muslim League	• Opium War • Unequal trade treaties • Self-strengthening movement • Sino-Japanese War • Boxer Uprising

■ Imports from Africa and Asia about 1870

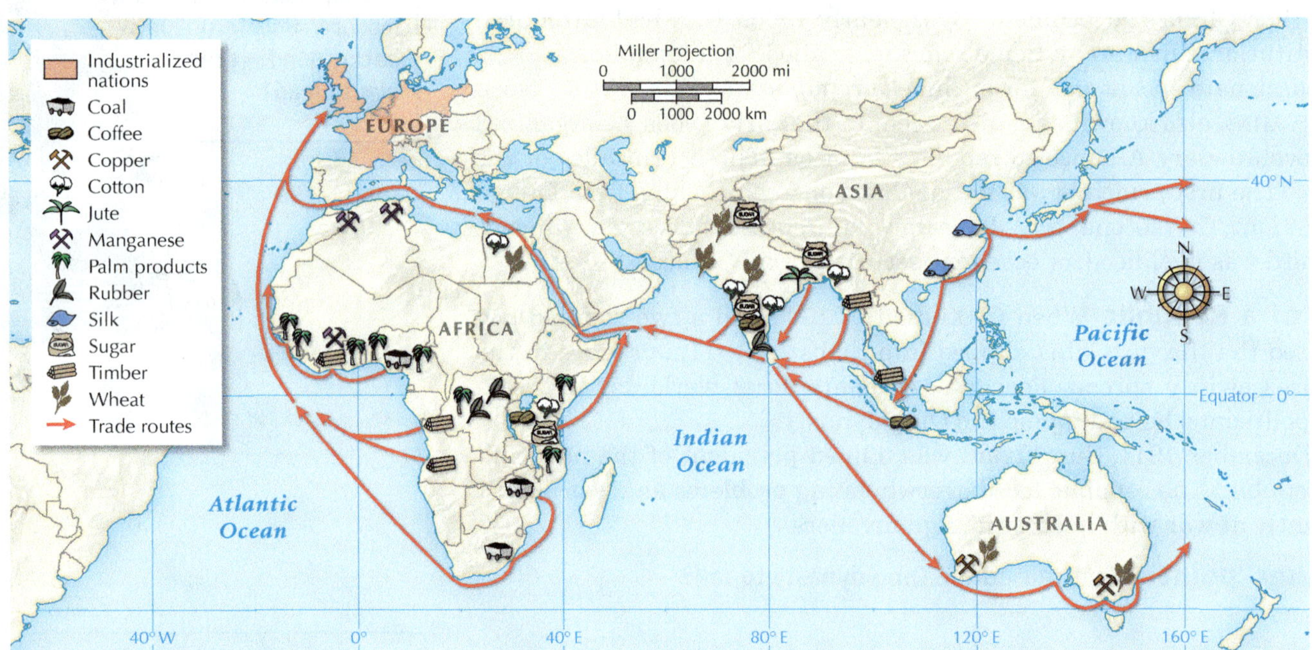

■ Key Events of the New Imperialism

1805
Muhammad Ali is named governor of Egypt.

1830
France begins efforts to conquer Algeria in North Africa.

1857
The Sepoy Rebellion breaks out in India.

Chapter Events
Global Events

1800

1825

1850

1807
In the United States, Robert Fulton uses a steam engine to power a ship.

1848
Revolutions break out throughout much of Europe.

Essential Question Review

To connect prior knowledge with what you have learned in this chapter, answer the questions below in your Concept Connector journal. Use the journal in the Reading and Note Taking Study Guide to record your answers (or go to www.phschool.com **Web Code:** nad-2407). In addition, record information about the following concepts:

- Nationalism: English nationalism
- Nationalism: American nationalism

1. **Belief Systems** Both foreign and Chinese belief systems influenced China during the 1800s. Some Chinese wanted to adopt Western ways, while others wanted to maintain Confucian ways. How did the choices China made influence its future relationship with Western nations? Do you think China's history would have been different if it had made the same choices as Japan? Why or why not?

2. **Genocide** In the 1890s, tensions between Muslim Turkish nationalists and Christian Armenians triggered a brutal genocide of the minority Armenians. It is estimated that more than one million Armenians were killed or died as a result. Review what you learned about Social Darwinism. How might a Social Darwinist explain the Armenian genocide?

3. **Empire** Powerful armies and navies, advanced weapons, and superior technologies were the tools of the "new imperialism." But the European powers also employed other strategies to gain and keep control over colonies. For example, in South Africa, the British set up a government run by whites and imposed a system of complete racial segregation. What were some of the other strategies Europeans used to control colonies or spheres of influence? Think about the following:

- indirect rule
- exploitation
- trade
- treaties

■ Connections to Today

1. **Economics: Trade and the Suez Canal** Reread the information in Section 3 on the Suez Canal. How did the opening of the Suez Canal in 1869 transform world trade? Then, find a recent newspaper or magazine article on the Suez Canal today. Do you think the canal is more or less important today than it was in 1869? Write two paragraphs on trade and the Suez Canal today, citing examples from current events to support your answer.

Suez Canal Traffic

Year	Number of Ships	Net Tons
1975	5,579	50,441,000
1985	19,791	352,579,000
1995	15,051	360,372,000
2003	15,667	549,381,000

SOURCE: Leth Suez Transit Online, 2004

2. **Geography's Impact: Famine** You have read how disaster struck Ireland in October 1845 when a deadly plant disease ruined the potato crop. In the late 1800s, famines also swept through India. What were the major causes of these famines? What was the effect of growing cash crops instead of food? Conduct research to learn more about the causes of hunger and malnutrition in the world today.

1884
European officials meet at the Berlin Conference to settle rival land claims in Africa.

1899
Boer War erupts in South Africa.

1911
Sun Yixian becomes president of Chinese republic.

History Interactive
For: Interactive timeline
Web Code: nap-2462

1875　　1900　　1925

Mid-1880s
German engineers develop the first automobile.

1914
World War I begins in Europe.

Chapter Assessment

Terms, People, and Places

Match the following definitions with the terms listed below. You will not use all of the terms.

genocide	trade surplus
imperialism	trade deficit
indemnity	Menelik II
Sino-Japanese War	Muhammad Ali
pasha	Taiping Rebellion
viceroy	Boxer Uprising

1. the domination by one country of the political, economic, or cultural life of another country or region
2. war between China and Japan where Japan gained Taiwan
3. provincial ruler in the Ottoman empire
4. situation in which a country imports more than it exports
5. governor of Egypt, sometimes called the "father of modern Egypt"
6. peasant revolt in China from 1850–1864
7. a deliberate attempt to destroy an entire religious or ethnic group
8. payment for losses in war

Main Ideas

Section 1 (pp. 750–753)
9. Describe the four main motives of the new imperialists.
10. Why did Western imperialism spread so rapidly?

Section 2 (pp. 754–761)
11. How did European contact with Africa increase during the 1800s?
12. How did the scramble for African colonies begin?

Section 3 (pp. 762–766)
13. What problems faced the Ottoman empire in the 1800s?
14. How did the modernization of Egypt lead to British rule?

Section 4 (pp. 767–772)
15. Explain the impact of British colonial rule on India.
16. Describe the origins of Indian nationalism.

Section 5 (pp. 773–777)
17. How did westerners gain trading rights in China during the 1800s?
18. Why did the Qing dynasty come to an end?

Chapter Focus Question
19. How did Western industrial powers gain global empires?

Critical Thinking

20. **Geography and History** Why were the natural resources of Africa and Asia important to Europeans in the 1800s?
21. **Analyzing Cartoons** The political cartoon below shows a French soldier (left) and a British soldier (right) ripping apart a map. How do you think the situation depicted in the cartoon affected relations between Britain and France?

22. **Summarize** How did the Ottoman empire try to westernize?
23. **Predict Consequences** How do you think rivalries between religious groups affected anti-imperialism efforts in India? Explain your answer.
24. **Analyze Information** Why did Western industrial nations establish spheres of influence in China rather than colonies as they did in Africa and India?

● Writing About History

In this chapter's five Section Assessments, you developed skills for writing a persuasive essay.

Writing a Persuasive Essay During the 1800s, European powers embarked on a period of expansion known as the Age of Imperialism. Despite resistance, these powers brought much of the world under their control between 1870 and 1914. Write a persuasive essay from the point of view of a Chinese government official in which the official tries to persuade the British that the Treaty of Nanjing is too harsh and will lead to dangerous anti-foreign feelings. Consult page SH16 of the Writing Handbook for additional help.

Prewriting
- Make a list of what you believe to be the strongest arguments of the Chinese official.
- Organize the arguments from weakest to strongest.

Drafting
- Clearly state the position that you will prove in the thesis statement.
- Sequence your arguments so that you open or close with your strongest one.
- Write a conclusion that restates your thesis and closes with a strong argument.

Revising
- Review your arguments to make sure that you have explained them logically and clearly.

Document-Based Assessment

The Forgotten Genocide

The Armenian massacre has been called the "forgotten geno-cide." It refers to the destruction, between 1895 and 1923, of the Christian Armenians of Turkey under the Muslim Ottoman government. More than 2 million Armenians lived in Turkey before the genocide. Estimates of those killed vary from 600,000 to 1.5 million. The rest were driven from their ancestral home. Most perpetrators were freed, despite pledges by the Allies to punish them after World War I.

Document A

"As it got worse, all of us, and all the people, began gathering in our school. The word came around that the Turks were going on the streets and killing all the Armenians and leaving them on the streets. I, myself, was in school already, so I simply stayed there. Then orders came from the school that we, too, should run away. But where? All the buildings were on fire! The Turks were burning everything. There was a whole group of us running away from the school."

—Annalin, a survivor from Smyrna on events of 1922

Document B

"The massacre of Armenian subjects in the Ottoman Empire in 1896 . . . was amateur and ineffective compared with the largely successful attempt to exterminate [them] during the First World War in 1915. . . . [This] genocide was carried out under the cloak of legality by cold-blooded governmental action. These were not mass-murders committed spontaneously by mobs of private people. . . ."

—Arnold Toynbee, British historian, cited in **Experiences**

Document C

"The 1,000 Armenian houses are being emptied of furniture by the police one after the other. The furniture, bedding and everything of value is being stored in large buildings about the city. . . . The goods are piled in without any attempt at labeling or systematic storage. A crowd of Turkish women and children follow the police about like a lot of vultures and seize anything they can lay their hands on and when the more valuable things are carried out of the house by the police they rush in and take the balance. . . . I suppose it will take several weeks to empty all the houses and then the Armenian shops and stores will be cleared out."

—From a report to the American embassy by Oscar S. Heizer, American consul in Tebizond, July 1915

Document D

"The proportion of Armenians killed by the Turks in World War I out of the general number of Armenians in the Ottoman Empire was no less than that of the Jewish victims [during the Holocaust] out of the total Jewish population in Europe. Nor are the methods of killing unique. . . . The type of murder committed by the Germans in the USSR—mass machine-gunning—was the traditional method of mass murder in our century, and the death marches of Jews in the closing stages of the war had their precedent in the Armenian case as well. Nor is the fact that in the case of the Holocaust it was a state machine and a bureaucracy that was responsible for the murder unique, because there, too, the Young Turks had preceded the German Nazis in planning the execution of a population with such means as were modern at the time."

—From **Remembrance and Denial** by Richard G. Hovannisian

Analyzing Documents

Use your knowledge of the Armenian massacre and Documents A, B, C, and D to answer questions 1–4.

1. According to Document B, the 1915 massacre of Armenians
   A went unpunished.
   B was ineffective and unsuccessful.
   C was not as well documented as the 1896 massacre.
   D was committed with the knowledge of the Turkish government.

2. Document C shows that the Turkish police
   A tried to protect the property of Armenian citizens, despite their government's orders.
   B tried to help Armenian citizens as best they could.
   C took part in stealing the property of Armenian citizens.
   D protested to the American embassy to try to help their friends.

3. According to Document D, the Armenian Massacre and the Holocaust
   A were committed by the same people.
   B were carried out in a similar way.
   C had very few similarities, except for the large number of murders.
   D both took place in Germany.

4. **Writing Task** Ismayale Kemal Pasha, a governor in Marash, was described by one survivor as kind and justice-loving. He tried saving Armenian citizens, despite orders from his superiors to carry out the genocide without remorse. Suppose Ismayale Kemal Pasha explained his decision to help in a memoir. Write a brief explanation from his point of view. Use these documents along with information from the chapter in your writing.

25 New Global Patterns
1800–1914

A New Pattern

Japan's response to the threat of Western imperialism was different from that of many other countries. In 1871, a delegation of Japanese officials journeyed to the United States with the goal of learning as much as possible about Western culture and technology.

> We expect and intend to reform and improve so as to stand upon a similar footing with the most enlightened nations. . . . It is our purpose to select from the various institutions prevailing among enlightened nations such as are the best suited to our present condition and adopt them, in gradual reforms and improvements of our policy and customs. . . .
>
> —Japanese emperor Meiji in a letter to the American president introducing the delegation

Listen to the Witness History audio to hear more about Japan's drive to modernize.

◄ **Japanese women mingle with Europeans in Yokohama's trading compound in this woodcut print created by a Japanese artist in 1861.**

Chapter Preview

Chapter Focus Question How did political and economic imperialism influence nations around the world?

Section 1
Japan Modernizes

Section 2
Imperialism in Southeast Asia and the Pacific

Section 3
Self-Rule for Canada, Australia, and New Zealand

Section 4
Economic Imperialism in Latin America

Use the ✓ **Quick Study Timeline** at the end of this chapter to preview chapter events.

A New Zealand postage stamp featuring the British empire's Queen Victoria

An Australian Aborigine boomerang

A bottle of quinine, which was used to fight malaria in Panama

Concept Connector ONLINE
To explore Essential Questions related to this chapter, go to PHSchool.com
Web Code: nad-2507

Emperor Meiji

A traditional Japanese fan

Changes for Japan

The emperor Meiji wrote a poem to provide inspiration for Japan's efforts to become a modern country in the late 1800s:

" May our country,
Taking what is good,
and rejecting what is bad,
Be not inferior
To any other. **"**

Focus Question How did Japan become a modern industrial power, and what did it do with its new strength?

Japan Modernizes

Objectives

- Explain how problems in Japanese society and the opening of Japan to other countries led to the Meiji Restoration.
- Describe the main reforms under the Meiji government.
- Analyze the factors contributing to Japan's drive for empire.

Terms, People, and Places

Matthew Perry
Tokyo
Meiji Restoration
Diet
zaibatsu
homogeneous society
First Sino-Japanese War
Russo-Japanese War

Note Taking

Reading Skill: Identify Causes and Effects As you read this section, identify the causes and effects of the Meiji Restoration in a chart like the one below.

Causes		Meiji Restoration		Effects

In 1853, the United States displayed its new military might, sending a naval force to make Japan open its ports to trade. Japanese leaders debated how to respond. While some resisted giving up their 215-year-old policy of seclusion, others felt that it would be wiser for Japan to learn from the foreigners.

In the end, Japan chose to abandon its centuries of isolation. The country swiftly transformed itself into a modern industrial power and then set out on its own imperialist path.

Discontent in Tokugawa Japan

In the early 1600s, Japan was still ruled by shoguns, or supreme military dictators. Although emperors still lived in the ceremonial capital of Kyoto, the shoguns held the real power in Edo. Daimyo, or landholding warrior lords, helped the shoguns control Japan. In 1603, a new family, the Tokugawas, seized power. The Tokugawa shoguns reimposed centralized feudalism, closed Japan to foreigners, and forbade Japanese people to travel overseas. The nation's only window on the world was through Nagasaki, where the Dutch were allowed very limited trade.

For more than 200 years, Japan developed in isolation. Internal commerce expanded, agricultural production grew, and bustling cities sprang up. However, these economic changes strained Japanese society. Many daimyo suffered financial hardship. They needed money in a commercial economy, but a daimyo's wealth was in land rather than cash. Lesser samurai were unhappy, too, because they lacked the money to live as well as urban merchants.

Merchants in turn resented their place at the bottom of the social ladder. No matter how rich they were, they had no political power. Peasants, meanwhile, suffered under heavy taxes.

The government responded by trying to revive old ways, <u>emphasizing</u> farming over commerce and praising traditional values. These efforts had scant success. By the 1800s, shoguns were no longer strong leaders, and corruption was common. Discontent simmered throughout Japan.

✔ **Checkpoint** **By the mid-1800s, why did so many groups of people in Japan feel discontented?**

Vocabulary Builder

emphasizing—(EM fuh syz ing) *vt.* stressing

Japan Opens Up

While the shoguns faced troubles at home, disturbing news of the British victory over China in the Opium War and the way in which imperialists had forced China to sign unequal treaties reached Japan. Surely, Japanese officials reasoned, it would not be long before Western powers turned towards Japan.

External Pressure and Internal Revolt The officials' fears were correct. In July 1853, a fleet of well-armed American ships commanded by Commodore **Matthew Perry** sailed into lower Tokyo Bay. Perry carried a letter from Millard Fillmore, the President of the United States. The letter demanded that Japan open its ports to diplomatic and commercial exchange.

The shogun's advisors debated what to do. Japan did not have the ability to defend itself against the powerful United States Navy. In the Treaty of Kanagawa in 1854, the shogun Iesada agreed to open two Japanese ports to American ships, though not for trade.

The United States soon won trading and other rights, including extraterritoriality and low taxes on American imports. European nations demanded and won similar rights. Like the Chinese, the Japanese felt humiliated by the terms of these unequal treaties. Some bitterly criticized the shogun for not taking a strong stand against the foreigners.

In the Japanese woodblock print below, Japanese boats go out to meet one of Commodore Matthew Perry's ships in Tokyo Bay. In response to Perry's expedition, the Japanese statesman Lord Ii considered Japan's strategy toward contact with foreign powers:

Primary Source

❝There is a saying that when one is besieged in a castle, to raise the drawbridge is to imprison oneself. . . . Even though the Shogun's ancestors set up seclusion laws, they left the Dutch and Chinese to act as a bridge. . . . Might this bridge not now be of advantage to us in handling foreign affairs, providing us with the means whereby we may for a time avert the outbreak of hostilities and then, after some time has elapsed, gain a complete victory?❞

Japanese Diplomat
Fukuzawa Yukichi Visits America

In 1860, writer and educator Fukuzawa Yukichi (1835–1901) joined the first Japanese diplomatic mission to the United States. When he returned home, he wrote articles and books explaining Western customs and practices to the Japanese. In this selection from his autobiography, Fukuzawa recalls his early impressions of San Francisco and discusses some of the differences between American and Japanese cultures and attitudes.

Foreign pressure deepened the social and economic unrest. In 1867, discontented daimyo and samurai led a revolt that unseated the shogun and "restored" the 15-year-old emperor Mutsuhito to power. When he was crowned emperor, Mutsuhito took the name Meiji (MAY jee), which means "enlightened rule." He moved from the old imperial capital in Kyoto to the shogun's palace in Edo, which was renamed **Tokyo,** or "eastern capital."

The Meiji Restoration The young emperor began a long reign known as the **Meiji Restoration.** This period, which lasted from 1868 to 1912, was a major turning point in Japanese history. The Meiji reformers, who ruled in the emperor's name, were determined to strengthen Japan. Their goal was summarized in their motto, "A rich country, a strong military." The emperor supported and embodied the reforms.

The new leaders set out to study Western ways, adapt them to Japanese needs, and <u>thereby</u> keep Japan from having to give in to Western demands. In 1871, members of the government traveled overseas to learn about Western governments, economies, technology, and customs. The government brought experts from Western countries to Japan and sent young samurai to study abroad, furthering Japan's knowledge of Western industrial techniques.

Vocabulary Builder
<u>thereby</u>—(THEHR by) *adv.* by that means, because of that

✔ **Checkpoint** How did Japan react when it was forced to accept unequal treaties?

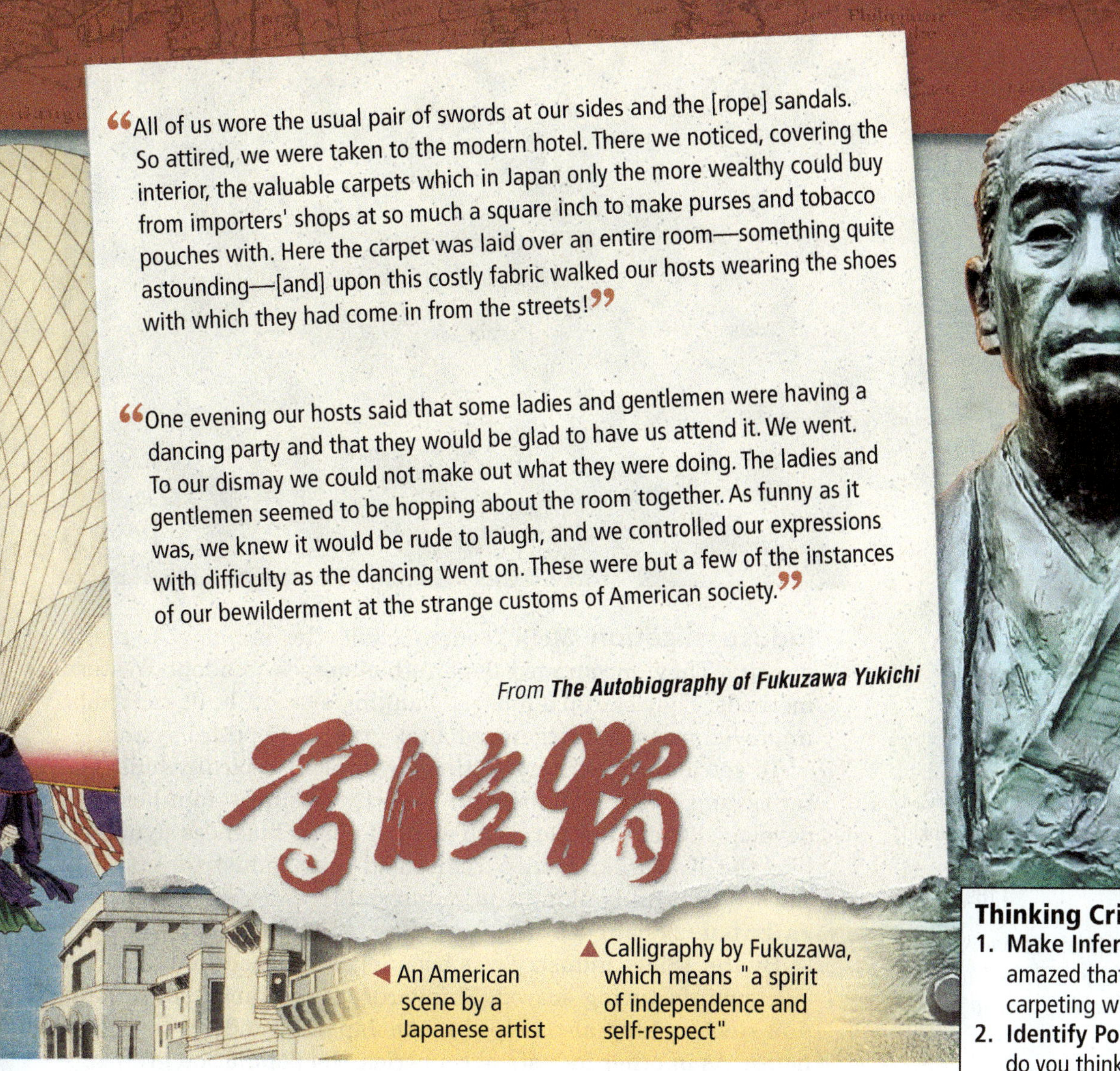

◀ Fukuzawa Yukichi

◀ An American scene by a Japanese artist

▲ Calligraphy by Fukuzawa, which means "a spirit of independence and self-respect"

Thinking Critically
1. **Make Inferences** Why is Fukuzawa amazed that people in America walk on carpeting with their shoes on?
2. **Identify Point of View** What opinion do you think Fukuzawa has of American culture?

The Meiji Transformation

The Meiji reformers faced an enormous task. They were committed to replacing the rigid feudal order with a completely new political and social system and to building a modern industrial economy. Change did not come easily. In the end, however, Japan adapted foreign ideas with great speed and success.

A Modern Government The reformers wanted to create a strong central government, equal to those of Western powers. After studying various European governments, they adapted the German model. In 1889, the emperor issued the Meiji constitution. It set forth the principle that all citizens were equal before the law. Like the German system, however, it gave the emperor autocratic, or absolute, power. A legislature, or **Diet,** was formed, made up of one elected house and one house appointed by the emperor. Additionally, voting rights were sharply limited.

Japan then established a Western-style bureaucracy with separate departments to supervise finance, the army, the navy, and education. To strengthen the military, it turned to Western technology and ended the special privilege of samurai. In the past, samurai alone were warriors. In modern Japan, as in the West, all men were subject to military service.

Investment in Meiji Japan

Chart Skills Japanese women (above) work in a silk manufacturing factory in the 1890s. *How does the graph reflect the Meiji reformers' drive to industrialize Japan?*

SOURCE: S. Uyehara, *The Industry and Trade of Japan*

Industrialization Meiji leaders made the economy a major priority. They encouraged Japan's businesses to adopt Western methods. They set up a modern banking system, built railroads, improved ports, and organized a telegraph and postal system.

To get industries started, the government typically built factories and then sold them to wealthy business families who developed them further. With such support, business dynasties like the Kawasaki family soon ruled over industrial empires. These powerful banking and industrial families were known as **zaibatsu** (zy baht soo).

By the 1890s, industry was booming. With modern machines, silk manufacturing soared. Shipyards, copper and coal mining, and steel making also helped make Japan an industrial powerhouse. As in other industrial countries, the population grew rapidly, and many peasants flocked to the growing cities for work.

Changes in Society The constitution ended legal distinctions between classes, thus allowing more people to become involved in nation building. The government set up schools and a university. It hired Westerners to teach the new generation how to use modern technology.

Despite the reforms, class distinctions survived in Japan as they did in the West. Also, although literacy increased and some women gained an education, women in general were still assigned a secondary role in society. The reform of the Japanese family system, and women's position in it, became the topic of major debates in the 1870s. Although the government agreed to some increases in education for women, it dealt harshly with other attempts at change. After 1898, Japanese women were forbidden any political participation and legally were lumped together with minors.

An Amazing Success Japan modernized with amazing speed during the Meiji period. Its success was due to a number of causes. Japan had a strong sense of identity, partly because it had a **homogeneous society**—that is, its people shared a common culture and language. Economic growth during Tokugawa times had set Japan on the road to development. Japan also had experience in learning and adapting ideas from foreign nations, such as China.

The Japanese were determined to resist foreign rule. By the 1890s, Japan was strong enough to force Western powers to revise the unequal treaties. By then, it was already acquiring its own overseas empire.

✔ **Checkpoint** What changes did the reforms of the Meiji Restoration bring about in Japan?

Japan's Growing Military Strength

As in Western industrial nations, Japan's economic needs fed its imperialist desires. As a small island nation, Japan lacked many basic resources that were essential for industrial growth. It depended on other countries to obtain raw materials. Spurred by this dependency and a strong ambition to equal the West, Japan sought to build an empire. With its modern army and navy, it maneuvered for power in East Asia.

Korea in the Middle Imperialist rivalries put the spotlight on Korea. Located at a crossroads of East Asia, the Korean peninsula was a focus of competition among Russia, China, and Japan. Korea had been a tributary state to China for many years. A tributary state is a state that is independent but acknowledges the supremacy of a stronger state. Although influenced by China, Korea had its own traditions and government. Korea had also shut its doors to foreigners. It did, however, maintain relations with China and sometimes with Japan.

By the 1800s, Korea faced pressure from outsiders. As Chinese power declined, Russia expanded into East Asia. Then, as Japan industrialized, it too eyed Korea. In 1876, Japan used its superior power to force Korea to open its ports to Japanese trade. Faced with similar demands from Western powers, Korea had to accept unequal treaties.

Japan Gains Power As Japan extended its influence in Korea, it came into conflict with China. In 1894, competition between Japan and China in Korea led to the **First Sino-Japanese War.** ("Sino" means "Chinese.") Although China had greater resources, Japan had benefited from modernization. To the surprise of China and the West, Japan won easily. It used its victory to gain treaty ports in China and control over the island of Taiwan, thus joining the West in the race for empire.

Japan Rising
In this political cartoon, Japan is depicted marching over Korea on its way to Russia. *Why would Russia feel threatened by Japan's aggression in Korea?*

■ **COMPARING VIEWPOINTS**

Colonization in Korea

The excerpts below present two different views of the effect of Japan's control of Korea in the early 1900s. **Critical Thinking** *How do the two views on the results of colonization in Korea differ?*

Positive Effects	Negative Effects
Mining, fishery, and manufacturing have advanced. The bald mountains have been covered with young trees. Trade has increased by leaps and bounds.... Study what we are doing in Korea.... Japan is a steward on whom devolves [falls] the gigantic task of uplifting the Far East.	The result of annexation, brought about without any conference with the Korean people, is that the Japanese ... by a false set of figures show a profit and loss account between us two peoples most untrue, digging a trench of everlasting resentment deeper and deeper....
—*Japanese academic Nitobe Inazo*	—*From the Declaration of Korean Independence, 1919*

Ten years later, Japan successfully challenged Russia, its other rival for power in Korea and Manchuria. During the **Russo-Japanese War,** Japan's armies defeated Russian troops in Manchuria, and its navy destroyed almost an entire Russian fleet. For the first time in modern history, an Asian power humbled a European nation. In the 1905 Treaty of Portsmouth, Japan gained control of Korea as well as rights in parts of Manchuria.

The Japanese in Korea
In this illustration, Japanese soldiers march into Seoul, Korea's capital city. Japan controlled Korea from 1905 until 1945.

Japan Rules Korea Japan made Korea a protectorate. In 1910, it annexed Korea outright, absorbing the kingdom into the Japanese empire. Japan ruled Korea for 35 years. Like Western imperialists, the Japanese set out to modernize their newly acquired territory. They built factories, railroads, and communications systems. Development, however, generally benefited Japan. Under Japanese rule, Koreans produced more rice than ever before, but most of it went to Japan.

The Japanese were as unpopular in Korea as Western imperialists were elsewhere. They imposed harsh rule on their colony and deliberately set out to erase the Korean language and identity. Repression bred resentment. And resentment, in turn, nourished a Korean nationalist movement.

Nine years after annexation, a nonviolent protest against the Japanese began on March 1, 1919, and soon spread throughout Korea. The Japanese crushed the uprising and massacred many Koreans. The violence did not discourage people who worked to end Japanese rule. Instead, the March First Movement became a rallying symbol for Korean nationalists.

The Koreans would have to wait many years for freedom. Japan continued to expand in East Asia during the years that followed, seeking natural resources and territory. By the early 1900s, Japan was the strongest power in Asia.

✔ **Checkpoint** How did industrialization help start Japan on an imperialist course?

Assessment

Progress Monitoring *Online*
For: Self-quiz with vocabulary practice
Web Code: naa-2511

Terms, People, and Places

1. Place each of the terms listed at the beginning of the section into one of the following categories: politics, culture, or economics. Write a sentence for each term explaining your choice.

Note Taking

2. **Reading Strategy: Identify Causes and Effects** Use your completed chart to answer the section Focus Question: How did Japan become a modern industrial power, and what did it do with its new strength?

Comprehension and Critical Thinking

3. **Identify Central Issues** What problems weakened shogun rule in Japan in the mid-1800s?

4. **Recognize Causes** What caused Japan to end over 200 years of seclusion?

5. **Draw Conclusions** List three ways in which Japan modernized. Explain how each of these actions helped strengthen Japan so it could resist Western pressure.

6. **Connect to Geography** Why was control of Korea desirable to both China and Japan?

● Writing About History

Quick Write: Choose a Topic When you write for assessment, you may occasionally be given a choice of topics. In that case, quickly jot down notes you could use to answer each prompt. Then, choose the prompt you know the most about. Practice this process using the two sample prompts below. Jot down notes about each prompt, choose one, and then write a sentence explaining why you chose that prompt.

• Explain how Japan modernized under the Meiji reformers.
• Summarize how and why Korea became a Japanese colony.

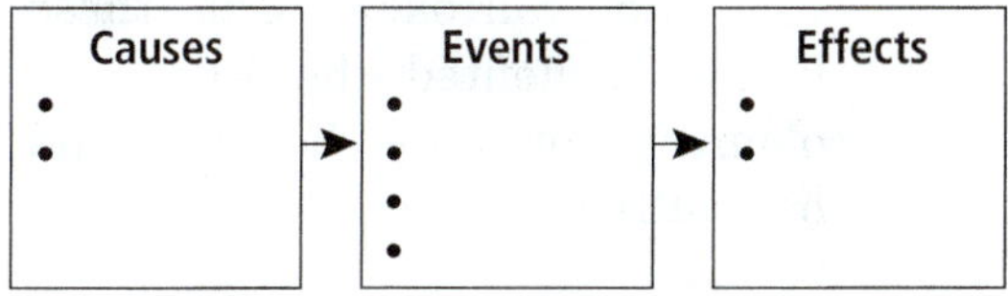
Currency from a British colony in Malaya

A European woman being transported in a rickshaw in French Indochina

WITNESS HISTORY  AUDIO

A Patriot's Dilemma

In 1867, Phan Thanh Gian, a Vietnamese official, faced a dilemma. The French were threatening to invade. As a patriot, Phan Thanh Gian wanted to resist. But as a devoted follower of Confucius, he was obliged "to live in obedience to reason." And based on the power of the French military, he concluded that the only reasonable course was to surrender:

❝ The French have immense warships, filled with soldiers and armed with huge cannons. No one can resist them. They go where they want, the strongest [walls] fall before them. ❞

Focus Question How did industrialized powers divide up Southeast Asia and the Pacific, and how did the colonized peoples react?

Imperialism in Southeast Asia and the Pacific

Objectives

- Outline how Europeans colonized Southeast Asia and how Siam avoided colonial rule.
- Explain how the United States gained control over the Philippines.
- Describe how imperialism spread to the Pacific islands.

Terms, People, and Places

French Indochina   Spanish-American War
Mongkut   Liliuokalani

Note Taking

Reading Skill: Identify Causes and Effects As you read, fill in a flowchart similar to the one below to record the causes, events, and effects of imperialism in Southeast Asia and the Pacific.

Causes	Events	Effects
• •	• • • •	• •

Leaders throughout Southeast Asia faced the same dilemma as Phan Thanh Gian did in 1867. As they had in Africa, Western industrial powers divided up the region in search of raw materials, new markets, and Christian converts.

Europeans Colonize Southeast Asia

Southeast Asia commands the sea lanes between India and China. The region had been influenced by both civilizations. From the 1500s through the 1700s, European merchants gained footholds in Southeast Asia, but most of the area remained independent. This changed in the 1800s. Westerners—notably the Dutch, British, and French—manipulated local rivalries and used modern armies and technology to colonize much of Southeast Asia.

The Dutch East Indies Established During the early 1600s, the Dutch East India Company established bases on the island of Java and in the Moluccas, or Spice Islands. From there, the Dutch slowly expanded to dominate the rest of the Dutch East Indies (now Indonesia). The Dutch expected their Southeast Asian colonies to produce profitable crops of coffee, indigo, and spices.

The British in Burma and Malaya In the early 1800s, rulers of Burma (present-day Myanmar) clashed with the British, who were expanding eastward from India. The Burmese suffered disastrous defeats in several wars. They continued to resist British rule, however, even after Britain annexed Burma in 1886.

At the same time, the British expanded their influence in Malaya. The busy port of Singapore grew up at the southern tip of the peninsula. Soon, natural resources and profits from Asian trade flowed through Singapore to enrich Britain.

French Indochina Seized The French, meanwhile, were building an empire on the Southeast Asian mainland. In the 1500s, Portuguese traders had set up a trading center in what today is Vietnam. Christian missionaries from France and other European countries moved into Vietnam and won some converts. Threatened by growing Western influence, Vietnamese officials tried to suppress Christianity by killing converts and missionary priests. Partly in response, France invaded Vietnam in 1858. The French also wanted more influence and markets in Southeast Asia.

The Vietnamese fought fiercely but could not withstand superior European firepower. By the early 1860s, France had seized a portion of southern Vietnam. Over the next decades, the French took over the rest of Vietnam and all of Laos and Cambodia. The French and other Westerners referred to these holdings as **French Indochina.** (Mainland Southeast Asia was known during this period as "Indochina.")

Siam Survives The kingdom of Siam (present-day Thailand) lay between British-ruled Burma and French Indochina. The king of Siam, **Mongkut** (mahng KOOT), who ruled from 1851 to 1868, did not underestimate Western power. He studied foreign languages and read widely on modern science and mathematics. He used this knowledge to negotiate with the Western powers and satisfy their goals in Siam by making agreements in unequal treaties. In this way, Siam escaped becoming a European colony.

Mongkut and his son, Chulalongkorn, (CHOO lah lawng kawrn) set Siam on the road to modernization. They reformed the government, modernized the army, and hired Western experts to teach Thais how to use the new technology. They abolished slavery and gave women some choice in marriage. As Siam modernized, Chulalongkorn bargained to remove the unequal treaties.

Colonial Southeast Asia During this period, many Chinese people migrated to Southeast Asia to take advantage of the economic opportunities there. They left China to escape hardship and turmoil. Despite local resentment, these communities formed vital networks in trade, banking, and other economic activities.

By the 1890s, Europeans controlled most of Southeast Asia. They introduced modern technology and expanded commerce and industry. Europeans directed the mining of tin, the harvesting of rubber, and the building of harbors and railroads. But these changes benefited the European colonizers far more than they did the Southeast Asians.

✔ **Checkpoint** How did the Burmese and the Vietnamese respond to attempts to colonize them?

Two Paths in Southeast Asia
King Mongkut of Siam managed to keep his kingdom out of European control. In other parts of Southeast Asia, colonized peoples labored to produce export crops for their colonial rulers. Below, workers process sugar cane in the Philippines in the early 1900s.

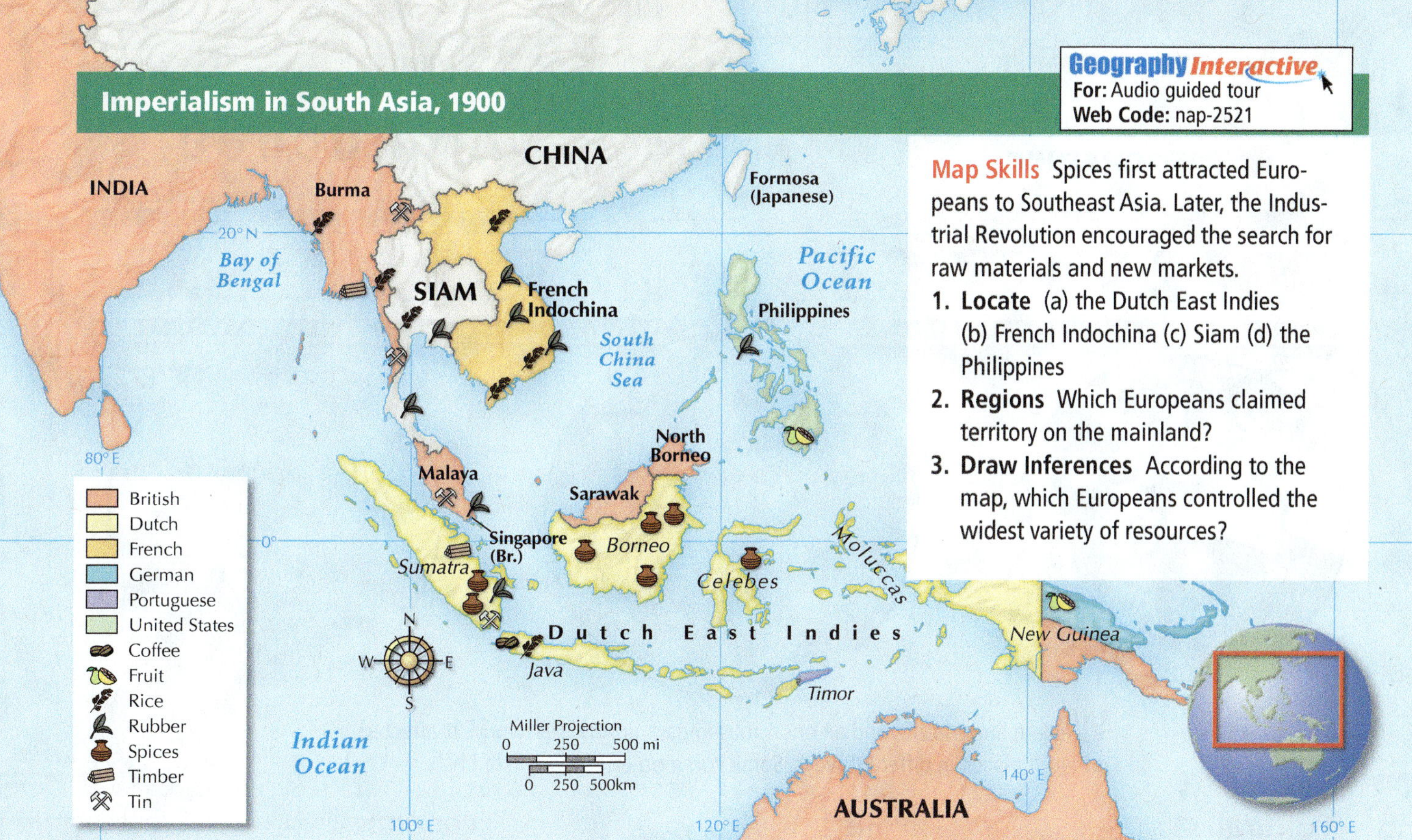

Map Skills Spices first attracted Europeans to Southeast Asia. Later, the Industrial Revolution encouraged the search for raw materials and new markets.

1. **Locate** (a) the Dutch East Indies (b) French Indochina (c) Siam (d) the Philippines
2. **Regions** Which Europeans claimed territory on the mainland?
3. **Draw Inferences** According to the map, which Europeans controlled the widest variety of resources?

The United States and the Philippines

In the 1500s, Spain had seized the Philippines. Catholic missionaries spread Christianity among the Filipinos. As the Catholic Church gained enormous power and wealth, many Filipinos accused the Church of abusing its position. By the late 1800s, their anger fueled strong resistance to Spanish rule.

The opening of the Suez Canal in 1860 helped the economy of the Philippines by making trade with European countries easier. Some upper class Filipinos gained access to better education. Leaders such as José Rizal inspired Filipinos to work to gain better treatment from Spain.

The **Spanish-American War** broke out in 1898 between Spain and the United States over Cuba's attempts to win independence from Spain. During the war, American battleships destroyed the Spanish fleet, which was stationed in the Philippines. Encouraged by American naval officers, Filipino rebel leaders declared independence from Spain. Rebel soldiers threw their support into the fight against Spanish troops.

In return for their help, the Filipino rebels expected the Americans to recognize their independence. Instead, in the treaty that ended the war with Spain, the United States agreed to give Spain $20 million in return for control of the Philippines. Within the United States, debate raged over the treaty's ratification. American imperialists wanted to join the European competition for territory. Anti-imperialists wanted the United States to steer clear of foreign entanglements. The United States Senate ratified the treaty by only one vote over the required two-thirds majority.

Bitterly disappointed, Filipino nationalists renewed their struggle. From 1899 to 1901, Filipinos led by Emilio Aguinaldo (ah gee NAHL doh) battled American forces. Thousands of Americans and hundreds of thousands of Filipinos died. In the end, the Americans crushed the rebellion.

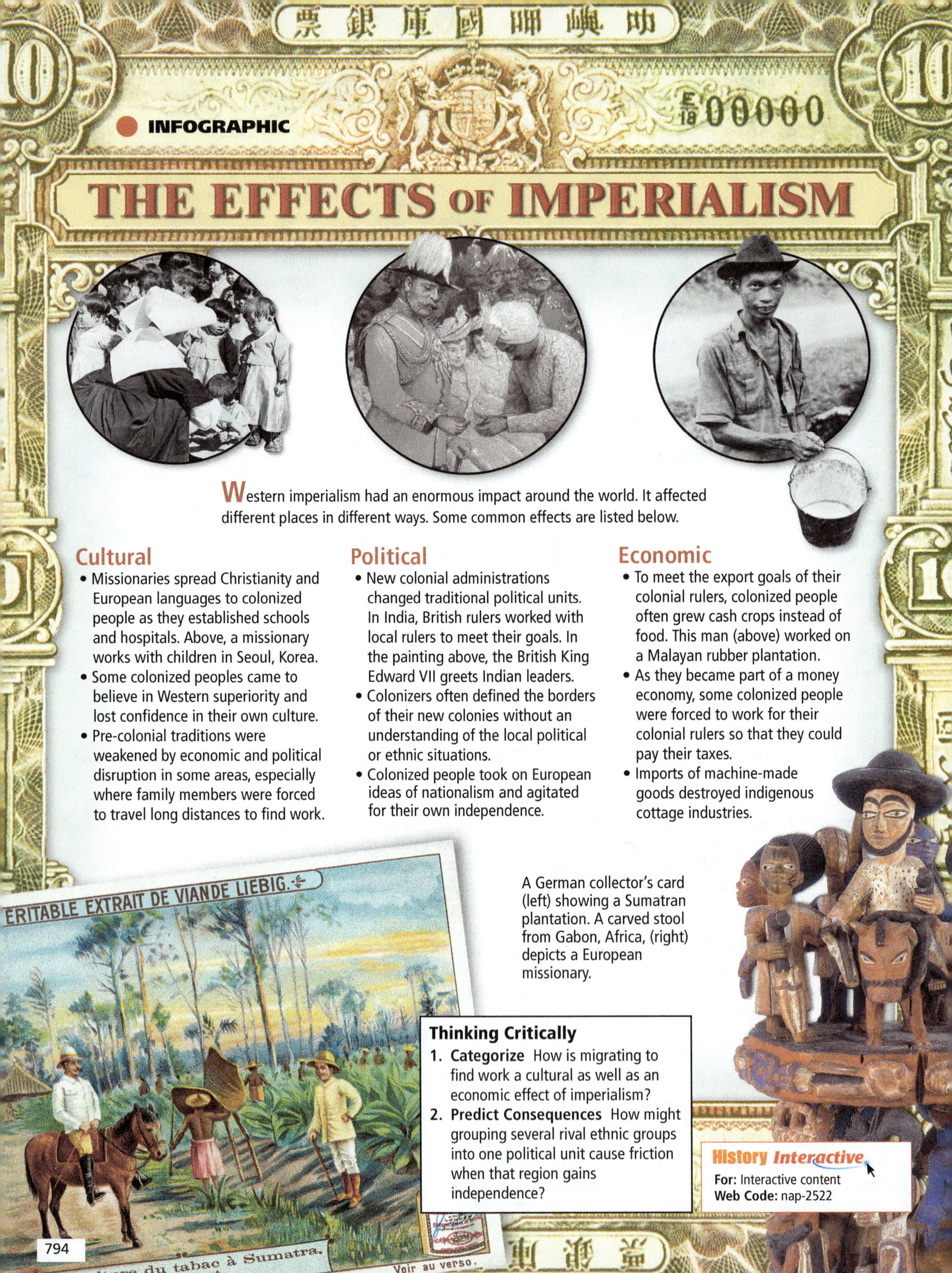

● **INFOGRAPHIC**

THE EFFECTS OF IMPERIALISM

Western imperialism had an enormous impact around the world. It affected different places in different ways. Some common effects are listed below.

Cultural
- Missionaries spread Christianity and European languages to colonized people as they established schools and hospitals. Above, a missionary works with children in Seoul, Korea.
- Some colonized peoples came to believe in Western superiority and lost confidence in their own culture.
- Pre-colonial traditions were weakened by economic and political disruption in some areas, especially where family members were forced to travel long distances to find work.

Political
- New colonial administrations changed traditional political units. In India, British rulers worked with local rulers to meet their goals. In the painting above, the British King Edward VII greets Indian leaders.
- Colonizers often defined the borders of their new colonies without an understanding of the local political or ethnic situations.
- Colonized people took on European ideas of nationalism and agitated for their own independence.

Economic
- To meet the export goals of their colonial rulers, colonized people often grew cash crops instead of food. This man (above) worked on a Malayan rubber plantation.
- As they became part of a money economy, some colonized people were forced to work for their colonial rulers so that they could pay their taxes.
- Imports of machine-made goods destroyed indigenous cottage industries.

A German collector's card (left) showing a Sumatran plantation. A carved stool from Gabon, Africa, (right) depicts a European missionary.

Thinking Critically
1. **Categorize** How is migrating to find work a cultural as well as an economic effect of imperialism?
2. **Predict Consequences** How might grouping several rival ethnic groups into one political unit cause friction when that region gains independence?

History Interactive
For: Interactive content
Web Code: nap-2522

The United States set out to modernize the Philippines through education, improved health care, and economic reforms. The United States also built dams, roads, railways, and ports. In addition, the United States promised Filipinos a gradual <u>transition</u> to self-rule some time in the future.

✓ **Checkpoint** How did the United States gain control of the Philippines?

Western Powers Seize the Pacific Islands

In the 1800s, the industrialized powers also began to take an interest in the islands of the Pacific. The thousands of islands splashed across the Pacific include the three regions of Melanesia, Micronesia, and Polynesia.

At first, American, French, and British whaling and sealing ships looked for bases to take on supplies in the Pacific. Missionaries, too, moved into the region and opened the way for political involvement.

In 1878, the United States secured an unequal treaty from Samoa, a group of islands in the South Pacific. The United States gained rights such as extraterritoriality and a naval station. Other nations gained similar agreements. As their rivalry increased, the United States, Germany, and Britain agreed to a triple protectorate over Samoa.

Beginning in the mid-1800s, American sugar growers pressed for power in the Hawaiian Islands. When the Hawaiian queen **Liliuokalani** (lih lee uh oh kuh LAH nee) tried to reduce foreign influence, American planters overthrew her in 1893. They then asked the United States to annex Hawaii, which it finally did in 1898. Supporters of annexation argued that if the United States did not take Hawaii, Britain or Japan might do so. By 1900, the United States, Britain, France, and Germany had claimed nearly every island in the Pacific.

✓ **Checkpoint** Why did some Americans think the United States should control Hawaii?

SECTION **2** Assessment

Terms, People, and Places

1. For each term, person, or place listed at the beginning of the section, write a sentence explaining its significance.

Note Taking

2. **Reading Strategy: Identify Causes and Effects** Use your completed chart to answer the Focus Question: How did industrialized powers divide up Southeast Asia and the Pacific, and how did the colonized peoples react?

Comprehension and Critical Thinking

3. **Summarize** What steps did Siam take to preserve its independence?
4. **Draw Conclusions** Why were Filipino rebels disappointed when the United States took control of the Philippines?
5. **Synthesize Information** How did Hawaii become part of the United States?
6. **Make Comparisons** Compare the partition of Southeast Asia to the partition of Africa. How was it similar? How was it different?

● **Writing About History**

Quick Write: Examine the Question To answer a short answer or extended-response question effectively, first examine the question. Look for key words like *explain, compare,* or *persuade,* which will tell you what type of answer to provide. Then look for words that signal the topic. Identifying key words will help you focus and organize your response. Copy the prompt below and underline its key words.

• Compare Siam's relationship with imperial powers to that of Vietnam.

Settler's Log House (above) was painted in 1856 by a Dutch immigrant to Canada, Cornelius Krieghoff. The maple leaf (above right) is an emblem of Canada.

O Canada!

In the early 1860s, the separate colonies of British North America considered whether they should join together to create one powerful confederation—Canada. George Brown, an influential politician who helped bring about the confederation, shared his dream for Canada:

> **66** Sir, it may be that some among us will live to see the day when, as the result of [the confederation], a great and powerful people may have grown up in these lands—when the boundless forests all around us shall have given way to smiling fields and thriving towns—and when one united government, under the British flag, shall extend from shore to shore. **99**

Focus Question How were the British colonies of Canada, Australia, and New Zealand settled, and how did they win self-rule?

Self-Rule for Canada, Australia, and New Zealand

Objectives

- Describe how Canada achieved self-rule.
- Analyze how European settlement changed the course of Australian history.
- Summarize how New Zealand was settled and how it emerged as an independent nation.

Terms, People, and Places

confederation	indigenous
dominion	penal colony
métis	Maori

Note Taking

Reading Skill: Identify Cause and Effects As you read, record the causes and effects of the events you read about in a chart like this one.

Cause	Event	Effect
Loyalist Americans flee to Canada.	Up to 30,000 loyalists settle in Canada.	Ethnic tensions arise between English- and French-speaking Canadians.

Canada, Australia, and New Zealand won independence faster and easier than other British colonies in Africa or Asia. The language and cultural roots they shared with Britain helped. Racial attitudes also played a part. Imperialists in nations like Britain felt that whites, unlike non-whites, were capable of governing themselves.

Canada Achieves Self-Rule

When France lost Canada to Britain in 1763, thousands of French-speaking Catholic settlers remained. After the American Revolution, about 30,000 British loyalists fled to Canada. They were English-speaking Protestants. In addition, in the 1790s, several groups of Native American peoples still lived in eastern Canada. Others, in the west and the north, had not yet come into contact with European settlers.

Unrest in the Two Canadas To ease ethnic tensions, Britain passed the Constitutional Act of 1791. The act created two provinces: English-speaking Upper Canada (now Ontario) and French-speaking Lower Canada (now Quebec). French traditions and the Catholic Church were protected in Lower Canada. English traditions and laws guided Upper Canada.

During the early 1800s, unrest grew in both colonies. The people of Upper Canada resented the power held by a small group of elites who controlled the government. Lower Canada had similar problems. In 1837, discontent flared into rebellion in both places. Louis Joseph Papineau, the head of the French Canadian Reform party, led the rebellion in Lower Canada. William Lyon Mackenzie led the revolt in Upper Canada, crying, "Put down the villains who oppress and enslave our country!"

Britain Responds The British had learned from the American Revolution. While they hurried to put down the disorder, they sent an able politician, Lord Durham, to <u>compile</u> a report on the causes of the unrest. In 1840, Parliament acted on some of Durham's recommendations by passing the Act of Union. The act joined the two Canadas into one province. It also gave them an elected legislature that determined some domestic policies. Britain still controlled foreign policy and trade.

Canada Becomes a Dominion In the mid-1800s, thousands of English, Scottish, and Irish people immigrated to Canada. As the country grew, two Canadians, John Macdonald and George Étienne Cartier, urged **confederation,** or unification, of Britain's North American colonies. These colonies included Nova Scotia, New Brunswick, Prince Edward Island, and British Columbia, as well as the united Upper and Lower Canadas. The two leaders felt that confederation would strengthen the new nation against American ambitions and help its economic development.

Britain finally agreed, passing the British North America Act of 1867. The act created the Dominion of Canada. A **dominion** is a self-governing nation. As a dominion, Canada had its own parliament, modeled on that

Canada, 1867–1914

Map Skills Canada grew throughout the latter half of the 1800s.

1. **Locate:** (a) Quebec (b) Ontario (c) British Columbia (d) Saskatchewan

2. **Movement** Why did British Columbia become a part of Canada before Alberta and Saskatchewan?

3. **Make Comparisons** Compare Nova Scotia's natural resources to those of Manitoba.

of Britain. By 1900, Canada also had some control over its own foreign policy. Still, Canada maintained close ties with Britain.

Canada Grows Like the United States, Canada expanded westward in the 1800s. In 1885, the Canadian Pacific Railway opened, linking eastern and western Canada. Wherever the railroad went, settlers followed. It moved people and products, such as timber and manufactured goods across the country. In the late 1800s and early 1900s, more immigrants flooded into Canada from Germany, Italy, Poland, Russia, Ukraine, China, and Japan. They enriched Canada's economy and culture.

As in the United States, westward expansion destroyed the way of life of Native Americans in Canada. Most were forced to sign treaties giving up their lands. Some resisted. In central Canada, Louis Riel led a revolt of the **métis,** people of mixed Native American and French Canadian descent, in 1869 and again in 1885. Many métis were French-speaking Catholics who believed that the government was trying to take their land and destroy their language and religion. Government troops put down both uprisings. Riel was executed in 1885.

By 1914, Canada was a flourishing nation. Still, French-speaking Canadians were determined to preserve their separate heritage, making it hard for Canadians to create a single national identity. Also, the cultural and economic influence of the United States threatened to dominate Canada. Both issues continue to affect Canada today.

✔ **Checkpoint** How did the British respond to the Canadians' desire for self-rule?

Europeans in Australia

The Dutch in the 1600s were the first Europeans to reach Australia. In 1770, Captain James Cook claimed Australia for Britain. For a time, however, Australia remained too distant to attract European settlers.

The First Settlers Like most regions claimed by imperialist powers, Australia had long been inhabited by other people. The first settlers had reached Australia perhaps 40,000 years earlier, probably from Southeast Asia, and spread across the continent. These **indigenous,** or original, people were called Aborigines, a word used by Europeans to denote the earliest people to live in a place. Today, many Australian Aborigines call themselves Kooris. Isolated from the larger world, the Aborigines lived in small hunting and food-gathering bands, much as their Stone Age ancestors had. Aboriginal groups spoke as many as 250 distinct languages. When white settlers arrived in Australia, the indigenous population suffered disastrously.

A Penal Colony During the 1700s, Britain had sent convicts to its North American colonies, especially to Georgia. The American Revolution closed that outlet. Prisons in London and other cities were jammed.

To fill the need for prisons, Britain made Australia into a **penal colony,** or a place where convicted

Life in Australia
Australian Aborigines used boomerangs, like this one decorated with traditional motifs, to hunt and in battles. The first British settlers in Australia were convicted criminals. The convicts in the illustration below are being forced to carry heavy loads of shingles as part of their hard labor. *What happened to Aborigines as British settlement spread?*

Map Skills British settlement in Australia started with penal settlements on both coasts and slowly spread into the interior of the continent.

1. **Locate** (a) Simpson Desert (b) Great Sandy Desert (c) Sydney (d) Perth
2. **Regions** What physical features probably slowed British settlement of Australia's interior?
3. **Draw Inferences** What types of economic activity do you think took place in the area of Australia that was settled by Europeans between 1831 and 1875?

criminals are sent to be punished. The first British ships, carrying about 700 convicts, arrived in Botany Bay, Australia, in 1788. The people who survived the grueling eight-month voyage faced more hardships on shore. Many were city dwellers with no farming skills. Under the brutal discipline of soldiers, work gangs cleared land for settlement.

The Colonies Grow In the early 1800s, Britain encouraged free citizens to emigrate to Australia by offering them land and tools. A prosperous wool industry grew up as settlers found that the land and climate suited sheepherding. In 1851, a gold rush in eastern Australia brought a population boom. Many gold hunters stayed on to become ranchers and farmers. They pushed into the rugged interior known as the Outback, carving out huge sheep ranches and wheat farms. As the newcomers settled in, they thrust aside or killed the Aborigines.

Achieving Self-Government Like Canada, Australia was made up of separate colonies scattered around the continent. Britain worried about interference from other European powers. To counter this threat and to boost development, it responded to Australian demands for self-rule. In 1901, Britain helped the colonies unite into the independent Commonwealth of Australia. The new country kept its ties to Britain by recognizing the British monarch as its head of state.

The Australian constitution drew on both British and American models. Unlike Britain and the United States, Australia quickly granted women the right to vote. In 1856, it also became the first nation to introduce the secret ballot.

✔ **Checkpoint** What effect did colonization have on Australia's indigenous population?

New Zealand's Story

To the southeast of Australia lies New Zealand. In 1769, Captain Cook claimed its islands for Britain. Missionaries landed there in 1814 to convert the indigenous people, the **Maori** (MAH oh ree), to Christianity.

The Maori Struggle Unlike Australia, where the Aborigines were spread thinly across a large continent, the Maori were concentrated in a smaller area. They were descended from seafaring people who had reached New Zealand from Polynesia in the 1200s. The Maori were settled farmers. They were also determined to defend their land.

White settlers, who were attracted by New Zealand's mild climate and good soil, followed the missionaries. These settlers introduced sheep and cattle and were soon exporting wool, mutton, and beef. In 1840, Britain annexed New Zealand.

As colonists poured in, they took over more and more of the land, leading to fierce wars with the Maori. Many Maori died in the struggle. Still more perished from disease, alcoholism, and other misfortunes that followed European colonization. By the 1870s, resistance crumbled. The Maori population had fallen drastically, from about 200,000 to less than 45,000 in 1896. Only recently has the Maori population started to grow once more.

Settlers Win Self-Government Like settlers in Australia and Canada, white New Zealanders sought self-rule. In 1907, they won independence, with their own parliament, prime minister, and elected legislature. They, too, preserved close ties to the British empire.

✔ **Checkpoint** Compare and contrast the European settlement of Australia and New Zealand.

Maori Traditions
The portrait below shows a Maori leader in 1882. Many Maori men of high social standing commissioned tattoos on their faces. Maori war canoes, like the one below, often carried distinctive carving.

SECTION 3
Assessment

Terms, People, and Places

1. For each term, person, or place listed at the beginning of the section, write a sentence explaining its significance.

Note Taking

2. **Reading Skill: Identify Causes and Effects** Use your completed chart to answer the Focus Question: How were the British colonies of Canada, Australia, and New Zealand settled, and how did they win self-rule?

Comprehension and Critical Thinking

3. **Sequence** What steps led to Canadian self-rule?
4. **Compare** Compare the European settlement of Australia with that of Canada.
5. **Identify Causes** Why did the Maori fight colonists in New Zealand?
6. **Synthesize Information** What ethnic tensions did Australia, Canada, and New Zealand face?

● **Writing About History**

Quick Write: Focus Your Time To stay focused as you respond to a short answer or extended-response question on a test, plan to spend a quarter of the allotted time on prewriting, half on drafting, and the remaining quarter on revising. Write a short answer response to the following prompt using a 20-minute time limit. Time yourself to practice staying within the appropriate time limit during each stage.

• Compare how Canada and Australia gained self-rule.

Benito Juárez, Mexican president and national hero, stands firm against foreign intervention in this fresco by artist Gonzales Orozco.

Sugar cane, a Latin American cash crop

La Reforma

The Mexican reformer Benito Juárez criticized the continuing inequality in Mexico:

❝ The constitution of 1824 was a compromise between progress and reaction, and [that compromise was a] seedbed of the incessant convulsions [disorders] that the Republic has suffered, and that it will still suffer while society does not recover its balance by making effective the equality of rights and duties of all citizens and of all persons who inhabit the national territory, without privileges, without exemptions [exceptions], without monopolies, and without odious distinctions . . . . ❞

Focus Question How did Latin American nations struggle for stability, and how did industrialized nations affect them?

Economic Imperialism in Latin America

Objectives

- Describe the political problems faced by Mexico and other new Latin American nations.
- List the ways industrialized nations effected Latin America.

Terms, People, and Places

regionalism
caudillo
Benito Juárez
La Reforma

peonage
Monroe Doctrine
Panama Canal

Note Taking

Reading Skill: Recognize Multiple Causes As you read, record the causes of instability in Latin America in a chart similar to this one. Then give an example of how each cause affected Mexico.

Instability in Latin America	
Causes	Mexican Example

Despite bright hopes, democracy failed to take root in most of the newly independent nations of Latin America in the 1800s. Instead, wealth and power remained in the hands of the few. At the same time, new technology such as refrigerated ships helped to intertwine the economies of nations that were thousands of miles apart. Latin American economies became increasingly dependent upon those of more developed countries. Britain, and later the United States, invested heavily in Latin America.

Lingering Political Problems

Simón Bolívar had hoped to create strong ties among the nations of Latin America. But feuds among leaders, geographic barriers, and local nationalism shattered that dream of unity. In the end, 20 separate nations emerged.

These new nations wrote constitutions modeled on that of the United States. They set up republics with elected legislatures. However, true democracy failed to take hold. During the 1800s, many succumbed to revolts, civil war, and dictatorships.

The Colonial Legacy Many of the problems in the new nations had their origins in colonial rule. The existing social and political hierarchy barely changed. Creoles simply replaced *peninsulares* as the ruling class. The Roman Catholic Church kept its privileged position and still controlled huge amounts of land.

For most people—mestizos, mulattoes, blacks, and Indians—life did not improve after independence. The new constitutions guaranteed equality before the law, but deep-rooted inequalities remained. Voting rights were limited. Many people felt the effects of racial prejudice. Small groups of people held most of the land. Owners of haciendas ruled their great estates, and the peasants who worked them, like medieval European lords.

The Search for Stability With few roads and no tradition of unity, **regionalism,** or loyalty to a local area, weakened the new nations. Local strongmen, called *caudillos* (kow THEE yohs), assembled private armies to resist the central government. At times, popular caudillos, occasionally former military leaders, gained national power. They looted the treasury and ruled as dictators. Power struggles led to frequent revolts that changed little except the name of the leader. In the long run, power remained in the hands of a privileged few who had no desire to share it.

As in Europe, the ruling elite in Latin America were divided between conservatives and liberals. Conservatives defended the traditional social order, favored press censorship, and strongly supported the Catholic Church. Liberals backed laissez-faire economics, religious toleration, greater access to education, and freedom of the press. Liberals saw themselves as <u>enlightened</u> supporters of progress but often showed little concern for the needs of the majority of the people.

✔ **Checkpoint** What factors undermined democracy in post-independence Latin America?

Mexico's Struggle for Stability

During the 1800s, each Latin American nation followed its own course. Mexico provides an example of the challenges facing many Latin American nations. Large landowners, army leaders, and the Catholic Church dominated Mexican politics. However, bitter battles between conservatives and liberals led to revolts and the rise of dictators. Deep social divisions separated wealthy creoles from mestizos and Indians who lived in poverty.

Santa Anna and War With the United States Between 1833 and 1855, an ambitious and cunning *caudillo,* Antonio López de Santa Anna, gained and lost power many times. At first, he posed as a liberal reformer.

Life on a Hacienda
Peasant women process a crop grown on a hacienda in Mexico in the 1800s.

Soon, however, he reversed his stand and crushed efforts at reform.

In Mexico's northern territory of Texas, discontent grew. In 1835, settlers who had moved to Texas from the United States and other places revolted. After a brief struggle with Santa Anna's forces, the settlers gained independence from Mexico. They quickly set up an independent republic. Then in 1845 the United States annexed Texas. Mexicans saw this act as a declaration of war. In the fighting that followed, the United States invaded and defeated Mexico. In the Treaty of Guadalupe-Hidalgo, which ended the war, Mexico lost almost half its territory. The embarrassing defeat triggered new violence between conservatives and liberals.

La Reforma Changes Mexico In 1855, Benito Juárez (WAHR ez), a liberal reformer of Zapotec Indian heritage, and other liberals gained power and opened an era of reform known as La Reforma. Juárez offered hope to the oppressed people of Mexico. He and his fellow reformers revised the Mexican constitution to strip the military of power and end the special privileges of the Church. They ordered the Church to sell unused lands to peasants.

Conservatives resisted La Reforma and began a civil war. Still, Juárez was elected president in 1861 and expanded his reforms. His opponents turned to Europe for help. In 1863, Napoleon III sent troops to Mexico and set up Austrian archduke Maximilian as emperor.

For four years, Juárez's forces battled the combined conservative and French forces. When France withdrew its troops, Maximilian was captured and shot. In 1867, Juárez returned to power and tried to renew reform, but opponents resisted. Juárez died in office in 1872, never achieving all the reforms he envisioned. He did, however, help unite Mexico, bring mestizos into politics, and separate church and state.

Growth and Oppression Under Díaz After Juárez died, General Porfirio Díaz, a hero of the war against the French, staged a military coup and gained power. From 1876 to 1880 and 1884 to 1911, he ruled as a dictator. In the name of "Order and Progress," he strengthened the army, local police, and central government. He crushed opposition.

Under his harsh rule, Mexico made <u>tangible</u> economic advances. Railroads were built, foreign trade increased, some industry developed, and mining expanded. Growth, however, had a high cost. Capital for development came from foreign investors, to whom Díaz granted special rights. He also let wealthy landowners buy up Indian lands.

The rich prospered, but most Mexicans remained poor. Many Indians and mestizos fell into peonage to their employers. In the peonage system, hacienda owners would give workers advances on their wages and require them to stay on the hacienda until they had paid back what they owed. Wages remained low, and workers were rarely able to repay the hacienda owner. Many children died in infancy. Other children worked 12-hour days and never learned to read or write.

✔ **Checkpoint** What struggles did Mexico go through as it tried to find stability in the 1800s?

Remember the Alamo!
Mexican President Antonio López de Santa Anna (above) is well-known for his ruthless decision to give no quarter to the Texan defenders of the Alamo, a fort in San Antonio, Texas, during the Texas Revolution. The illustration above shows Texan defenders of the Alamo bravely fighting against overwhelming odds. *In what light does this illustration present the defenders of the Alamo?*

Vocabulary Builder
tangible—(TAN juh bul) *adj.* real or concrete

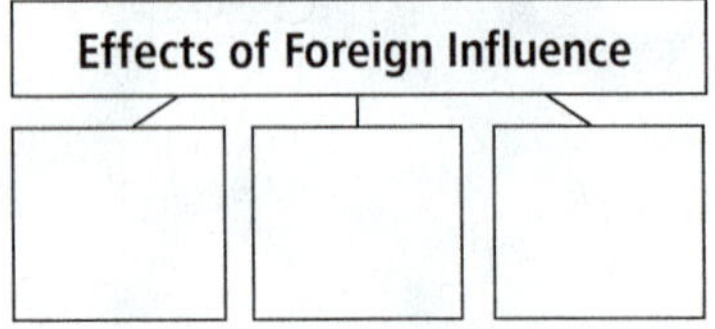

The Economics of Dependence

Under colonial rule, mercantilist policies made Latin America economically dependent on Spain and Portugal. Colonies sent raw materials such as cash crops or precious metals to the parent country and had to buy manufactured goods from them. Strict laws kept colonists from trading with other countries and possibly obtaining goods at a lower price. In addition, laws prohibited the building of local industries that would have competed with the parent country. In short, the policies prevented the colonies from developing their own economies.

The Cycle of Economic Dependence After independence, this pattern changed very little. The new Latin American republics did adopt free trade, welcoming all comers. Britain and the United States rushed into the new markets, replacing Spain as Latin America's chief trading partners. But the region remained as economically dependent as before.

Foreign Influence Mounts In the 1800s, foreign goods flooded Latin America, creating large profits for foreigners and for a handful of local business people. Foreign investment, which could yield enormous profits, was often accompanied by local interference. Investors from Britain, the United States, and other nations pressured their own governments to take action if political events or reform movements in a Latin American country seemed to threaten their interests.

Some Economic Growth After 1850, some Latin American economies did grow. With foreign capital, they were able to develop mining and agriculture. Chile exported copper and nitrates, and Argentina expanded

Geography Interactive
For: Audio guided tour
Web Code: nap-2541

Imperialism in Latin America, 1898–1917

Map Skills In the early 1900s, European powers held possessions in Latin America. The United States often intervened to protect business interests there.

1. **Locate** (a) Cuba (b) Canal Zone (c) British Guiana (d) Honduras
2. **Location** Why did the United States have a particularly strong interest in Latin American affairs?
3. **Identify Point of View** What natural resources did the Dutch exploit in Dutch Guiana?

its livestock and wheat production. Brazil exported the cash crops coffee and sugar, as well as rubber. By the early 1900s, both Venezuela and Mexico were developing important and lucrative oil industries.

Throughout the region, foreigners invested in modern ports and railroads to carry goods from the interior to coastal cities. European immigrants poured into Latin America. The newcomers helped to promote economic activity, and a small middle class emerged.

Thanks to trade, investment, technology, and migration, Latin American nations moved into the world economy. Yet internal development was limited. The tiny elite at the top benefited from the economic upturn, but very little trickled down to the masses of people at the bottom. The poor earned too little to buy consumer goods. Without a strong demand, many industries failed to develop.

 **Checkpoint** How did foreign influence and investment affect Latin America?

Uncle Sam Takes Off This cartoon represents the entry of the United States into competition with European powers over new territory in the Eastern Hemisphere in the early 1900s.

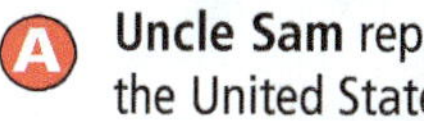

A **Uncle Sam** represents the United States.

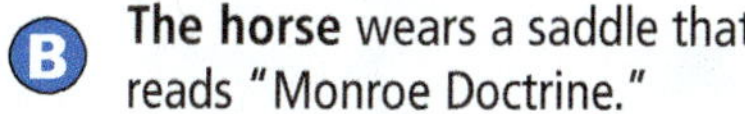

B **The horse** wears a saddle that reads "Monroe Doctrine."

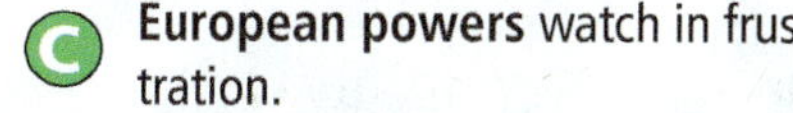

C **European powers** watch in frustration.

1. What do the wheels on Uncle Sam's bicycle represent?
2. Why are the European powers shouting at Uncle Sam?

The Influence of the United States

As nations like Mexico tried to build stable governments, a neighboring republic, the United States, expanded across North America. Latin American nations began to feel threatened by the "Colossus of the North," the giant power that cast its shadow over the entire hemisphere.

The Monroe Doctrine In the 1820s, Spain plotted to recover its American colonies. Britain opposed any move that might close the door to trade with Latin America. British leaders asked American President James Monroe to join them in a statement opposing any new colonization of the Americas.

Monroe, however, wanted to avoid any "entangling alliance" with Britain. Acting alone, he issued the Monroe Doctrine in 1823. "The American continents," it declared, "are henceforth not to be considered as subjects for future colonization by any European powers." The United States lacked the military power to enforce the doctrine. But with the support of Britain's strong navy, the doctrine discouraged European interference. For more than a century, the Monroe Doctrine would be the key to United States policy in the Americas.

The United States Expands Into Latin America As a result of the war with Mexico, in 1848 the United States acquired the thinly populated regions of northern Mexico, gaining all or part of the present-day states of California, Arizona, New Mexico, Nevada, Utah, and Colorado. The victory fed dreams of future expansion. Before the century had ended, the United States controlled much of North America and was becoming involved in overseas conflicts.

For decades, Cuban patriots had battled to free their island from Spanish rule. As they began to make headway, the United States joined their cause, declaring war on Spain in 1898. The brief Spanish-American War ended in a crushing defeat for Spain. At the war's end, Cuba was granted independence. But in 1901, the United States forced Cubans to add the Platt Amendment to their constitution. The amendment gave the United States naval bases in Cuba and the right to intervene in Cuban affairs.

AN EPIC UNDERTAKING:
PANAMA CANAL

The Panama Canal was a massive undertaking. The sheer scale of the project astounded engineers, politicians, and tourists. Building the canal cost the American government $352 million (about $7 billion in today's money). Workers excavated about 232 million cubic yards of dirt, rocks, and debris from the Canal Zone—enough debris to create a pyramid seven times the height of the Washington Monument, as one newspaper writer noted. Nearly six thousand workers died from industrial accidents or disease in the ten years it took to build the canal.

Despite many challenges, the builders would not give up. They completed the canal in 1914. The beginning of World War I in the summer of 1914, however, overshadowed what was to be its grand opening.

▲ Playing cards featuring scenes from the canal's construction (above) helped to feed Americans' fascination with the canal.

◄ Two men (below) stand inside one of the canal lock's enormous gates. The gates allow water to flow in and out of the lock, raising or lowering ships to different levels.

▼ The tropical diseases malaria and yellow fever killed many workers. Quinine (below right) was used to treat some cases of malaria. The canal builders' massive efforts to kill disease-carrying mosquitoes, using methods, such as spraying swampy areas with oil (below left), were more effective.

Thinking Critically
1. **Draw Conclusions** Based on the map, why did Americans want to build a canal in Panama?
2. **Draw Inferences** Why was it important to control disease during the building of the canal?

The United States Interferes American investments in Latin America grew in the early 1900s. Citing the need to protect those investments, in 1904 the United States issued the Roosevelt Corollary to the Monroe Doctrine. Under this policy, the United States claimed "international police power" in the Western Hemisphere. When the Dominican Republic failed to pay its foreign debts, the United States sent in troops. Americans collected customs duties, paid off the debts, and remained for years.

Under the Roosevelt Corollary and then President William Howard Taft's policy of Dollar Diplomacy, American companies continued to invest in the countries of Latin America. To protect those investments, the United States sent troops to Cuba, Haiti, Mexico, Honduras, Nicaragua, and other countries in Central America and the Caribbean. As a result, like European powers in Africa and Asia, the United States became the target of increasing resentment and rebellion.

Building the Panama Canal From the late 1800s, the United States had wanted to build a canal across Central America. Panama was a proposed site. However, Panama belonged to Colombia, which refused to sell the United States land for the canal. In 1903, the United States backed a revolt by Panamanians against Colombia. The Panamanians quickly won independence and gave the United States control of the land to build the canal.

Construction began in 1904. Engineers solved many difficult problems in the course of building the canal. The Panama Canal opened in 1914. The canal cut the distance of a sea journey between such cities as New York and San Francisco by thousands of miles. It was an engineering marvel that boosted trade and shipping worldwide.

To people in Latin America, however, the canal was another example of "Yankee imperialism." Nationalist feeling in the hemisphere was often expressed as anti-Americanism. Panama did not gain complete control over the canal until 2000. It now forms a vital part of the Panamanian economy.

✔ Checkpoint How did the United States act as an imperialist power in Latin America?

SECTION 4 Assessment

Terms, People, and Places

1. For each term, person, or place listed at the beginning of the section, write a sentence explaining its significance.

Note Taking

2. **Reading Skill: Recognize Multiple Causes** Use your completed charts to answer the Focus Question: How did Latin American nations struggle for stability, and how did industrialized nations affect them?

Critical Thinking and Comprehension

3. **Express Problems Clearly** What problems faced new nations in Latin America?
4. **Recognize Cause and Effect** How did the cycle of economic dependence continue after independence?
5. **Synthesize Information** Describe two ways the United States influenced Latin America.
6. **Draw Conclusions** Why might developing nations encourage foreign investment? Do you think foreign investors should have the right to intervene in another nation's affairs to protect their investments? Explain.

● **Writing About History**

Quick Write: Support Your Ideas As you respond to a short-answer or extended-response question on a test, keep in mind that each sentence or paragraph should support your main idea. Omit information, no matter how interesting, that is not central to your argument. To practice, write an outline of an argument responding to the following extended-response prompt.

- Explain how American interference led to the building of the Panama Canal.

Quick Study Guide

Progress Monitoring *Online*
For: Self-test with vocabulary practice
Web Code: naa-2551

◼ Imperialism in Japan and Southeast Asia and the Pacific

Japan	Southeast Asia and the Pacific
• United States opens by show of force. • Meiji restoration begins modernization. • Japan becomes an imperialist power itself.	• European powers expand footholds. • Some countries resist, but succumb to European force. • Europeans gain resources and trade networks at expense of indigenous people.

◼ Three British Colonies: Canada, Australia, and New Zealand

British Colony	Settled by	Impact on Indigenous People	Gained Self-Rule From Britain
Canada	First France, then Britain	Native Americans forced to give up lands	1867
Australia	Britain, as penal colony	Aborigines suffered disastrously	1901
New Zealand	Britain, attracted by climate	Maori fought against settlers, population reduced drastically	1907

◼ The Cycle of Economic Dependence in Latin America

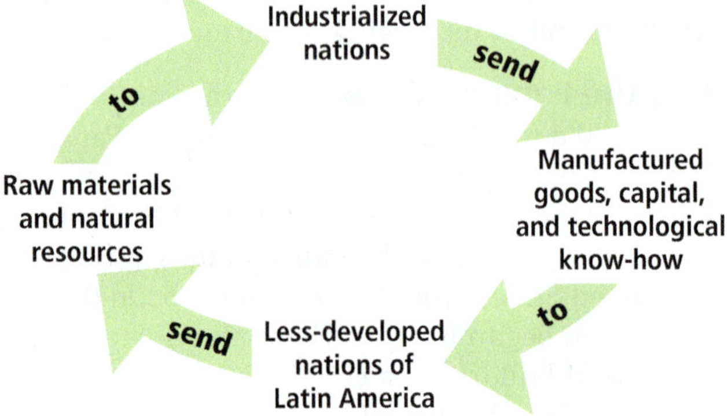

The relationship is unequal because the stronger, more developed nations control prices and terms of trade.

◼ Key Events in Worldwide Imperialism

Southeast Asia, the Pacific, and Japan
British Colonies and Latin America

1835 — **1850** — **1865**

- **1840** Britain annexes New Zealand.
- **1853** American ships commanded by Commodore Perry arrive in Japan.
- **1855** La Reforma begins in Mexico.
- **1858** France invades Vietnam.
- **1867** Britain grants Canada self-rule.
- **1868** Meiji Restoration begins in Japan.

Concept Connector

Essential Question Review

To connect prior knowledge with what you have learned in this chapter, answer the questions below in your Concept Connector journal. Use the journal in the Reading and Note Taking Study Guide to record your answers (or go to www.phschool.com **Web Code:** nad-2507).

1. **Cooperation** In response to Commodore Perry's demands, Japanese statesman Lord Ii suggested a strategy for dealing with the Americans:

    > "Even though the Shogun's ancestors set up seclusion laws, they left the Dutch and the Chinese to act as a bridge…. Might this bridge not now be of advantage to us in handling foreign affairs, providing us with the means whereby we may for a time avert the outbreak of hostilities and then, after some time has elapsed, gain a complete victory?"

    Why did Lord Ii want to cooperate with the Americans? What steps did the Japanese take to "gain a complete victory?" Did this prove to be a good strategy for Japan? Why or why not?

2. **Geography's Impact** Location links the fate of Latin America with that of the United States. In the 1800s, ideas about independence springing from the American Revolution inspired independence leaders in Latin America, such as Simón Bolívar. However, in the late 1800s, the United States began to interfere more aggressively in the affairs of Latin American countries. Create a timeline tracking the relationship between the United States and Latin America from 1800 through 1914. Include a brief description of the significance of each event on the timeline.

3. **Migration** Native Americans made up the original population of Canada, Kooris inhabited Australia, and Maoris lived in New Zealand. Today, along with descendents of these early people, more of the inhabitants of these countries are of British ancestry. Explain the role migration played in changing the population of these lands.

Connections to Today

1. **Conflict: Unrest in Quebec** Although French-Canadian leaders agreed to confederation with the rest of Canada in 1867, the French-English question was never truly put to rest. Many French-Canadians continued to feel that the English-speaking majority in Canada threatened their unique French culture. In the late 1900s, a movement for an independent Quebec arose. Research the path of this movement and create a bulleted list of significant events that occurred within the last fifty years.

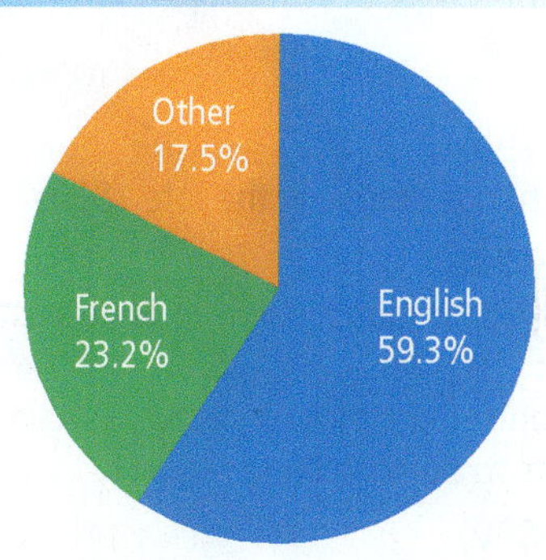

Languages Spoken in Canada Today

SOURCE: The World Factbook Online

2. **Cooperation: Japan as a World Power** After its rapid modernization in the late 1800s, Japan took its place among the leading powers of the world. It asserted that power throughout the 1900s, with varying results. Today, Japan's economy is second in size only to that of the United States. Conduct research on Japan and write a paragraph describing its role in international affairs today.

1886
Britain annexes Burma.

1898
The Philippines declares independence from Spain.

1910
Japan annexes Korea.

History Interactive
For: Interactive timeline
Web Code: nap-2551

| 1880 | 1895 | 1910 | 1925 |

1885
The Canadian Pacific Railway opens.

1904
The United States issues the Roosevelt Corollary.

1914
The Panama Canal opens.

Chapter Assessment

Terms, People, and Places

1. In what ways did **Matthew Perry's** opening of Japan lead to the **Meiji Restoration?**
2. How did the **Sino-Japanese** and **Russo-Japanese wars** spring out of Japan's new strength as a modernized nation?
3. What steps did **King Mongkut** take to help Siam avoid the fate of **French Indochina?**
4. How did Canada become a **dominion?**
5. Describe how the **Spanish-American War** affected both the Philippines and Cuba.
6. How did **regionalism** and *caudillos* weaken the stability of Latin American countries in the 1800s?

Main Ideas

Section 1 (pp. 784–790)

7. How did Japan change course in the late 1800s?

Section 2 (pp. 791–795)

8. Why were imperialist nations drawn to Southeast Asia and the Pacific?
9. How did the colonized peoples of Southeast Asia react to Western attempts to dominate the region?

Section 3 (pp. 796–800)

10. Describe settlement in Canada, Australia, and New Zealand.
11. How did these colonies gain independence?

Section 4 (pp. 801–807)

12. What factors caused instability in Latin America after independence?
13. How did the United States influence Latin America?

Chapter Focus question:

14. How did political and economic imperialism influence nations around the world?

Critical Thinking

15. **Compare** Compare Japan's response to Western imperialism to that of China. How were the two responses similar? How were they different?
16. **Identify Causes** In the image below, a Japanese woman wears Western clothing. What role did westernization play in helping both Japan and Siam avoid colonization by European nations?

17. **Connect to Geography** How did the creation of the Dominion of Canada encourage expansion?
18. **Synthesize Information** What principle did the United States express in the Monroe Doctrine? How did the Roosevelt Corollary alter the Monroe Doctrine?
19. **Draw Conclusions** List the benefits and disadvantages brought about by colonial rule. Do you think subject people were better or worse off as a result of the Age of Imperialism? Explain.

● Writing About History

In this chapter's four Section Assessments, you learned how to write for assessment.

Writing for Assessment Write an answer to one of the following extended response essay prompts. Spend only 40 minutes on the writing process. Consult page SH20 of the Writing Handbook for additional help.

- Analyze the effects of Japanese imperialism in Korea.
- Analyze the effects of American intervention in Latin America.

Prewriting

- Read both prompts and determine what you know about each. Choose the one whose topic you recall the most information about.
- Look for key words that will tell you what kind of answer to provide, such as *"explain."*

Drafting

- Focus your time by allowing 10 minutes for prewriting, 20 minutes for drafting, and 10 minutes for revising your response.
- Develop a thesis for your essay and make sure each piece of information supports it.

Revising

- Check that you open and close your response strongly, that each point supports your main idea, and that you've answered all aspects of the question.

Document-Based Assessment

The Imperialism Debate and the Philippines

After defeating Spain in Manila Bay in May 1898, American forces remained in the Philippines. In February 1899, the United States Senate voted to annex the Philippines. The Philippines were one aspect of the United States' efforts to compete with Europe in the scramble for new foreign markets, investment opportunities and raw materials. A great debate took place in the United States over the issue of imperialism, as the documents below show.

Document A

"I have been criticized a good deal about the Philippines, but don't deserve it. The truth is I didn't want the Philippines, and when they came to us, as a gift from the gods, I did not know what to do with them. . . . And one night late it came to me this way—I don't know how it was, but it came: (1) That we could not give them back to Spain—that would be cowardly and dishonorable; (2) that we could not turn them over to France and Germany—our commercial rivals in the Orient—that would be bad business and discreditable; (3) that we could not leave them to themselves—they were unfit for self-government—and they would soon have anarchy and misrule over there worse than Spain's was; and (4) that there was nothing left for us to do but to take them all, and to educate the Filipinos, and uplift and civilize and Christianize them . . ."

—From remarks to a visiting delegation of Methodist church leaders made by President William McKinley on November 21, 1899

Document B

"We hold that the policy known as imperialism is hostile to liberty and tends toward militarism, an evil from which it has been our glory to be free. . . . We maintain that governments derive their just powers from the consent of the governed. We insist that the subjugation of any people is "criminal aggression" and open disloyalty to the distinctive principles of our government.

We earnestly condemn the policy of the present National Administration in the Philippines. It seeks to extinguish the spirit of 1776 in those islands. . . . We denounce the slaughter of the Filipinos as a needless horror."

—From the Platform of the American Anti-Imperialist League, 1899

Document C

"Isn't Every American proud of the part that American soldiers bore in the relief of Pekin [i.e., Beijing, where some U.S. citizens were held hostage by the Boxers]? But that would have been impossible if our flag had not been in the Philippines.

Gen. Chaffee led two infantry regiments, the Ninth and the Fourteen, and one battery of the Fifth Artillery to Pekin. They did not come direct from the United States; there was not time. . . . But for these men and the marines from Manilla barracks, Minister Conger and his American comrades in the besieged legation would not have seen their country's flag, and would OWE THEIR RELIEF TO BRITISH, JAPANESE AND RUSSIANS.

When Mr. Bryan [Democratic candidate for president] tells you that the Philippines are worth nothing to America, you tell him to 'REMEMBER PEKIN!'"

—From a leaflet of the Republican Club of Massachusetts, 1900

Analyzing Documents

Use your knowledge of this chapter and Documents A, B, and C to answer questions 1–4.

1. In Document A, which of McKinley's four reasons for the takeover of the Philippines explained that important business interests were at stake?
   A 1
   B 2
   C 3
   D 4

2. In Document B, what is the meaning of "It seeks to extinguish the spirit of 1776 in those islands"?
   A The U.S. vowed never to give the Philippines its freedom.
   B The U.S. is undermining an independence movement that is like the American Revolution.
   C Self-government in the Philippines is inevitable.
   D The U.S. has the ability and the duty to educate Filipinos about self-government.

3. According to Document C, the Philippines are necessary to the United States as a(n)
   A source for raw materials.
   B outpost for Christian missionaries.
   C base for military actions.
   D market for U.S. goods.

4. William Jennings Bryan considered imperialism which he opposed, to be the top issue in the 1900 presidential campaign. Who would have received your vote, the Democratic candidate, Bryan, or the Republican, William McKinley? Give your reasons, using these documents and information from the chapter.

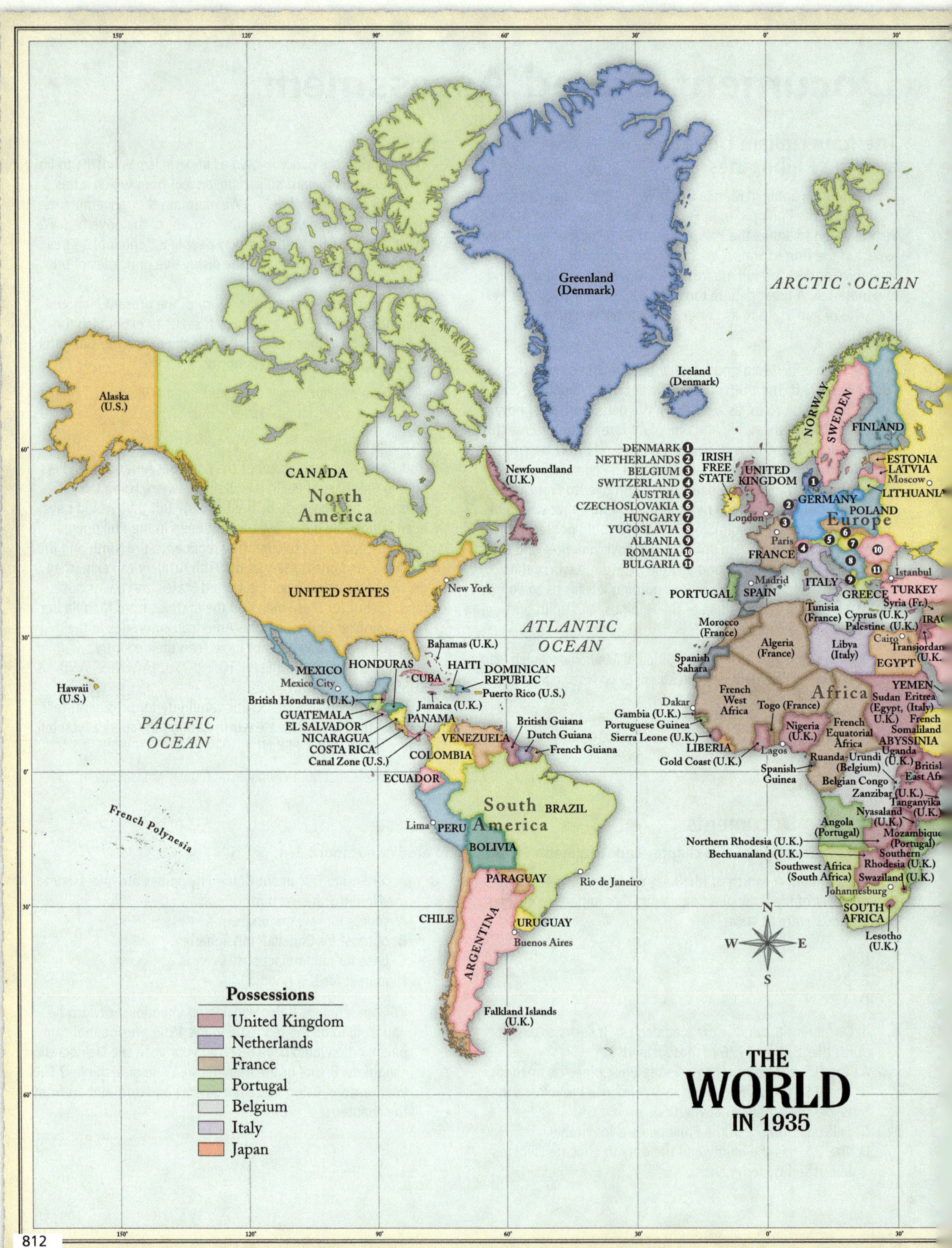
THE
WORLD
IN 1935

ARCTIC OCEAN
ATLANTIC OCEAN
PACIFIC OCEAN

North America
South America
Europe
Africa

Greenland (Denmark)
Iceland (Denmark)
Alaska (U.S.)
CANADA
UNITED STATES
Hawaii (U.S.)
New York
Newfoundland (U.K.)
MEXICO
Mexico City
HONDURAS
British Honduras (U.K.)
GUATEMALA
EL SALVADOR
NICARAGUA
COSTA RICA
Canal Zone (U.S.)
PANAMA
CUBA
Jamaica (U.K.)
Bahamas (U.K.)
HAITI
DOMINICAN REPUBLIC
Puerto Rico (U.S.)
VENEZUELA
COLOMBIA
ECUADOR
PERU
Lima
BOLIVIA
BRAZIL
Rio de Janeiro
PARAGUAY
CHILE
ARGENTINA
URUGUAY
Buenos Aires
Falkland Islands (U.K.)
British Guiana
Dutch Guiana
French Guiana
French Polynesia

NORWAY
SWEDEN
FINLAND
ESTONIA
LATVIA
LITHUANIA
Moscow
GERMANY
POLAND
UNITED KINGDOM
London
Paris
FRANCE
IRISH FREE STATE
PORTUGAL
SPAIN
Madrid
ITALY
GREECE
TURKEY
Istanbul

DENMARK 1
NETHERLANDS 2
BELGIUM 3
SWITZERLAND 4
AUSTRIA 5
CZECHOSLOVAKIA 6
HUNGARY 7
YUGOSLAVIA 8
ALBANIA 9
ROMANIA 10
BULGARIA 11

Morocco (France)
Tunisia (France)
Algeria (France)
Libya (Italy)
Spanish Sahara
French West Africa
Togo (France)
Gambia (U.K.)
Portuguese Guinea
Sierra Leone (U.K.)
LIBERIA
Gold Coast (U.K.)
Nigeria (U.K.)
French Equatorial Africa
Spanish Guinea
Belgian Congo
Dakar
Lagos
Cyprus (U.K.)
Syria (Fr.)
Palestine (U.K.)
Transjordan (U.K.)
EGYPT
Cairo
Sudan (Egypt, U.K.)
Eritrea (Italy)
YEMEN
ABYSSINIA
French Somaliland
Uganda (U.K.)
British East Afr.
Ruanda-Urundi (Belgium)
Zanzibar (U.K.)
Tanganyika (U.K.)
Nyasaland (U.K.)
Angola (Portugal)
Mozambique (Portugal)
Northern Rhodesia (U.K.)
Bechuanaland (U.K.)
Southwest Africa (South Africa)
Southern Rhodesia (U.K.)
Swaziland (U.K.)
SOUTH AFRICA
Johannesburg
Lesotho (U.K.)
IRAQ

N
S
E
W

Possessions
United Kingdom
Netherlands
France
Portugal
Belgium
Italy
Japan

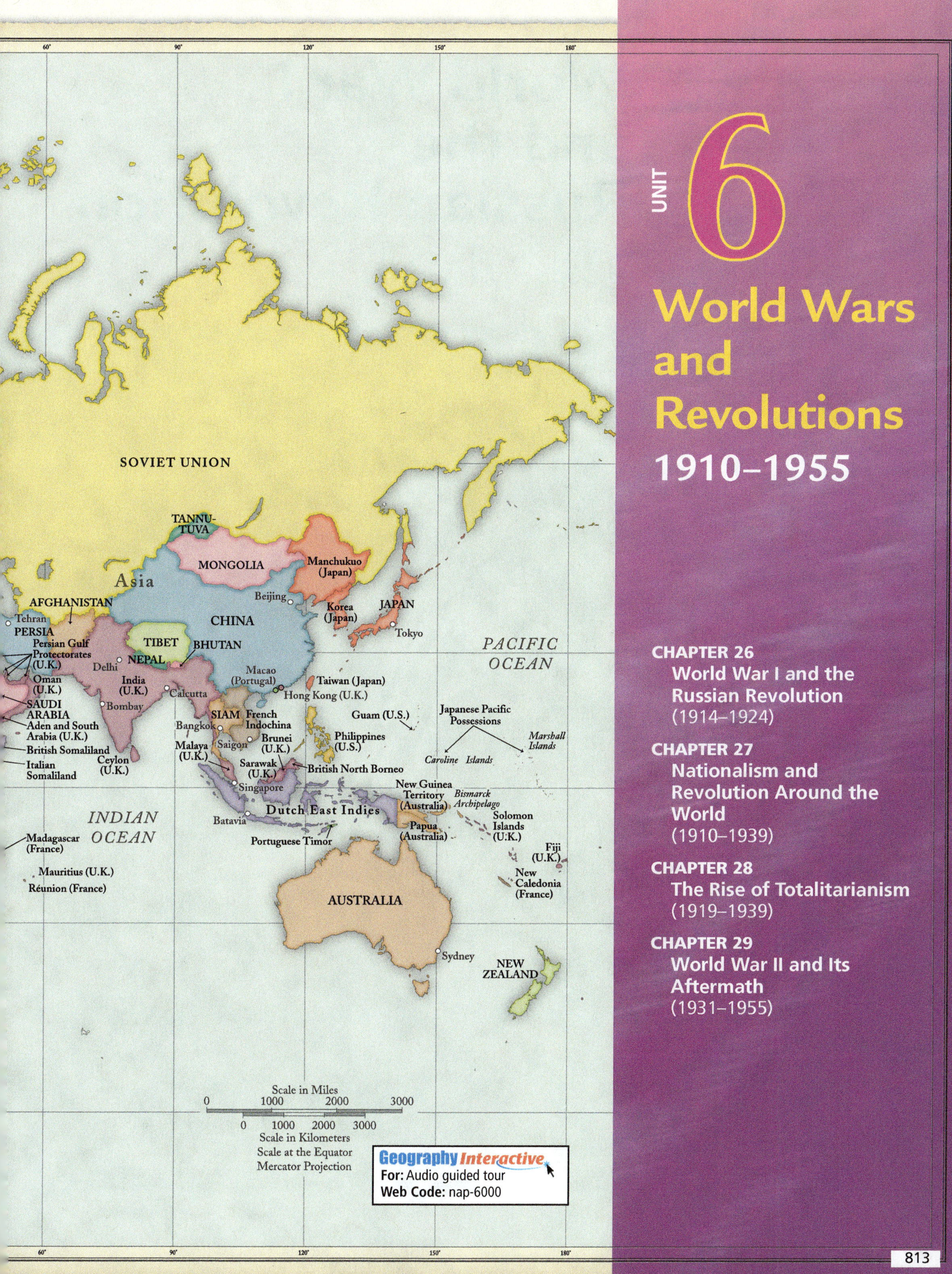

6

World Wars and Revolutions

1910–1955

CHAPTER 26
World War I and the Russian Revolution
(1914–1924)

CHAPTER 27
Nationalism and Revolution Around the World
(1910–1939)

CHAPTER 28
The Rise of Totalitarianism
(1919–1939)

CHAPTER 29
World War II and Its Aftermath
(1931–1955)

Geography *Interactive*
For: Audio guided tour
Web Code: nap-6000

26 World War I and the Russian Revolution

1914–1924

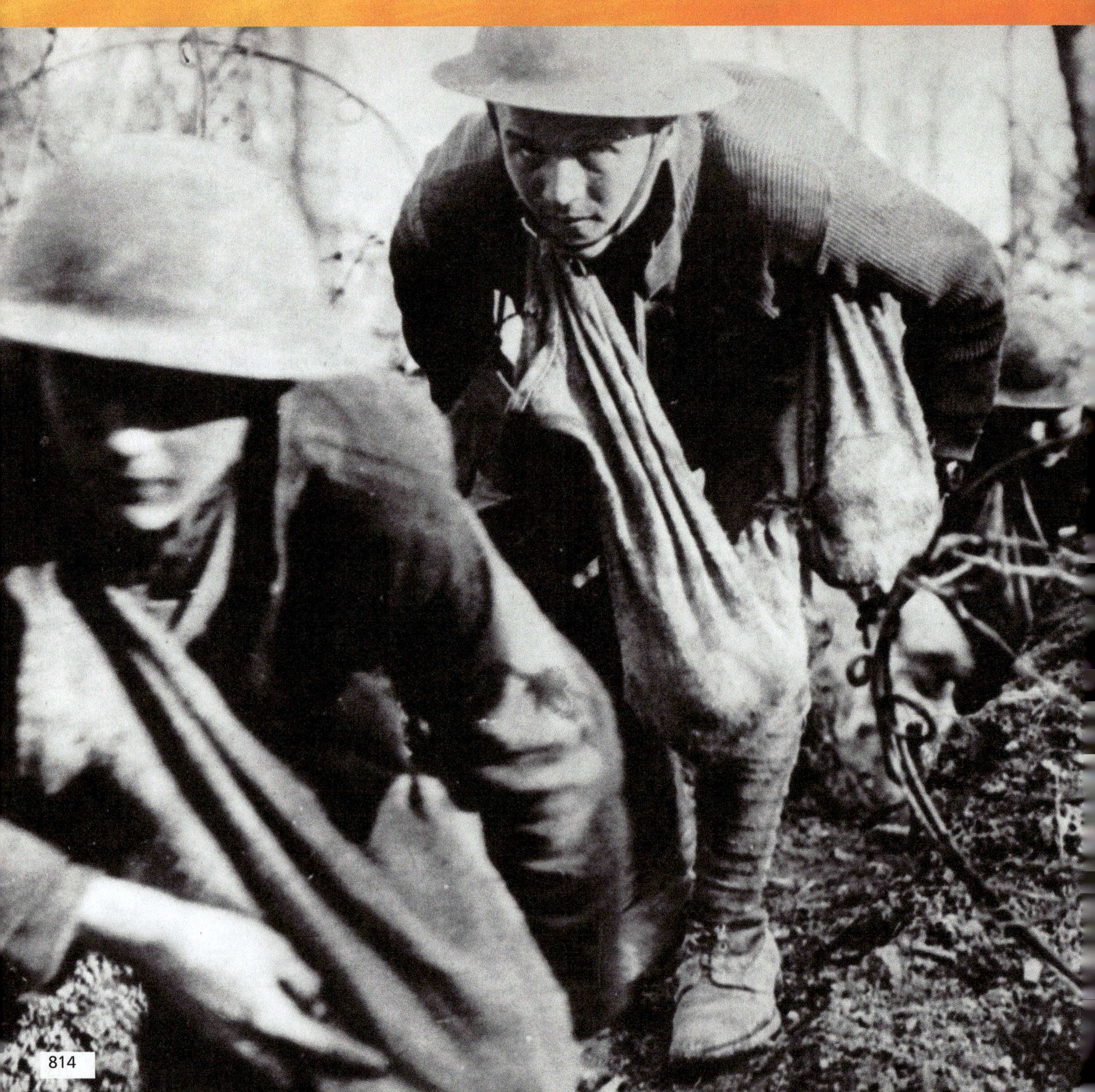

In Flanders Fields

Canadian John McCrae served as a military doctor on the Western Front in World War I. In 1915, McCrae wrote the following poem in the voice of those he had watched die.

"In Flanders fields the poppies blow
Between the crosses, row on row
That mark our place; and in the sky
The larks, still bravely singing, fly
Scarce heard amid the guns below.

We are the Dead. Short days ago
We lived, felt dawn, saw sunset glow,
Loved and were loved, and now we lie
In Flanders fields.**"**

—Dr. John McCrae, 1915

Listen to the Witness History audio to hear more about McCrae's experience during World War I.

◄ **American soldiers on a trench raid during World War I**

The poppy became a symbol of remembrance for veterans after World War I.

Chapter Preview

Chapter Focus Question What caused World War I and the Russian Revolution, and what effect did they have on world events?

The sickle and hammer on this pin symbolize the Russian Revolution.

Section 1
The Great War Begins

Section 2
A New Kind of War

Section 3
Winning the War

Section 4
Making the Peace

Section 5
Revolution and Civil War in Russia

Poison gas was widely used for the first time during World War I.

Use the  **Quick Study Timeline** at the end of this chapter to preview chapter events.

 **Concept Connector** ONLINE

To explore Essential Questions related to this chapter, go to PHSchool.com
Web Code: nad-2607

▲ The assassin, Gavrilo Princip

◄ Austrian Archduke Francis Ferdinand and his wife Sophie

The Spark

On June 28, 1914, Gavrilo Princip, a member of a Serbian terrorist group, killed Austrian Archduke Francis Ferdinand and his wife Sophie.

66 The first [bullet] struck the wife of the Archduke, the Archduchess Sofia, in the abdomen. . . . She died instantly.

The second bullet struck the Archduke close to the heart. He uttered only one word, 'Sofia'—a call to his stricken wife. Then his head fell back and he collapsed. He died almost instantly. 99

—Borijove Jevtic, co-conspirator

The assassinations triggered World War I, called "The Great War" by people at the time.

Focus Question Why and how did World War I begin in 1914?

The Great War Begins

Objectives

- Describe how international rivalries and nationalism pushed Europe toward war.
- Explain how the assassination in Sarajevo led to the start of World War I.
- Analyze the causes and effects of the European alliance system.

Terms, People, and Places

entente	ultimatum
militarism	mobilize
Alsace and Lorraine	neutrality

Note Taking

Reading Skill: Summarize As you read, use a chart to summarize the events that led up to the outbreak of World War I.

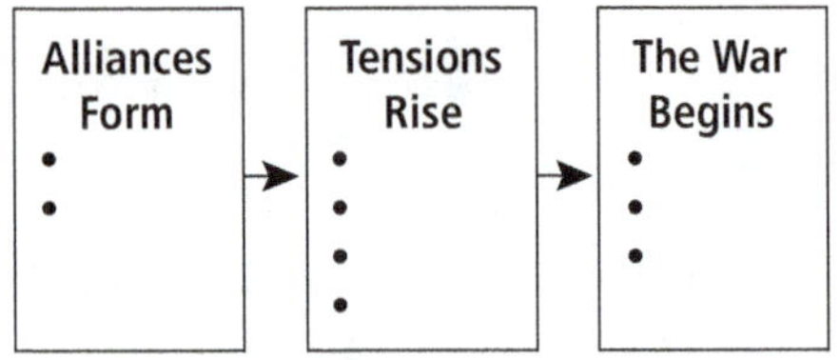

By 1914, Europe had enjoyed a century of relative peace. Idealists hoped for a permanent end to the scourge of war. International events, such as the first modern Olympic games in 1896 and the First Universal Peace Conference in 1899, were steps toward keeping the peace. "The future belongs to peace," said French economist Frédéric Passy (pa SEE).

Not everyone was so hopeful. "I shall not live to see the Great War," warned German Chancellor Otto von Bismarck, "but you will see it, and it will start in the east." It was Bismarck's prediction, rather than Passy's, that came true.

Alliances Draw Lines

While peace efforts were under way, powerful forces were pushing Europe towards war. Spurred by distrust of one another, the great powers of Europe—Germany, Austria-Hungary, Italy, Britain, France, and Russia—signed treaties pledging to defend one another. These alliances were intended to promote peace by creating powerful combinations that no one would dare attack. In the end, they had the opposite effect. Two huge alliances emerged.

The Triple Alliance The first of these alliances had its origins in Bismarck's day. He knew that France longed to avenge its defeat in the Franco-Prussian War. Sure that France would not attack Germany without help, Bismarck signed treaties with other powers. In 1882, he formed the Triple Alliance with Italy and Austria-Hungary. In 1914, when war did erupt, Germany and Austria-Hungary fought on the same side. They became known as the Central Powers.

Map Skills By 1914, most of Europe was divided into two armed camps, the Allies and the Central Powers. Millions of troops stood ready for war.

1. **Locate** (a) Germany (b) Alsace-Lorraine (c) the Balkans (d) Serbia
2. **Regions** Why would Germans worry about the alliance between France and Russia?
3. **Synthesize Information** Based on the information on the map, which alliance do you think had the greater military advantage in 1914?

The Triple Entente A rival bloc took shape in 1893, when France and Russia formed an alliance. In 1904, France and Britain signed an **entente** (ahn TAHNT), a nonbinding agreement to follow common policies. Though not as formal as a treaty, the entente led to close military and diplomatic ties. Britain later signed a similar agreement with Russia. When war began, these powers became known as the Allies.

Other alliances also formed. Germany signed a treaty with the Ottoman empire. Britain drew close to Japan.

 **Checkpoint** What two large alliances took shape before the beginning of World War I?

Rivalries and Nationalism Increase Tension

The European powers jealously guarded their <u>status</u>. They competed for position in many areas. Two old empires, Austria-Hungary and Ottoman Turkey, struggled to survive in an age of nationalism.

Vocabulary Builder

<u>status</u>—(STAT us) *n.* high standing, rank, or prestige

Competition Economic rivalries helped sour the international atmosphere. Germany, the newest of the great powers, was growing into an economic and military powerhouse. Britain felt threatened by its rapid economic growth. Germany, in turn, thought the other great powers did not give it enough respect. Germany also feared that when Russia caught up to other industrialized nations, its huge population and vast supply of natural resources would make it an unbeatable competitor.

Overseas rivalries also divided European nations. In 1905 and again in 1911, competition for colonies brought France and Germany to the brink of war in Morocco, then under France's influence. Although diplomats kept the peace, Germany did gain some territory in central Africa. As a result of the two Moroccan crises, Britain and France strengthened their ties against Germany.

With international tensions on the rise, the great powers began to build up their armies and navies. The fiercest competition was the naval rivalry between Britain and Germany. To protect its vast overseas empire, Britain had built the world's most respected navy. As Germany began acquiring overseas colonies, it began to build up its own navy. Suspicious of Germany's motives, Britain in turn increased naval spending. Sensational journalism dramatized the arms race and stirred national public opinion against rival countries.

The rise of **militarism,** or the glorification of the military, also helped to feed the arms race. The militarist tradition painted war in romantic colors. Young men dreamed of blaring trumpets and dashing cavalry charges—not at all the sort of conflict they would soon face.

Nationalism Aggressive nationalism also caused tension. Nationalism was strong in both Germany and France. Germans were proud of their new empire's military power and industrial leadership. The French were bitter about their 1871 defeat in the Franco-Prussian War and yearned to recover the lost border province of **Alsace and Lorraine.**

In Eastern Europe, Russia sponsored a powerful form of nationalism called Pan-Slavism. It held that all Slavic peoples shared a common nationality. As the largest Slavic country, Russia felt that it had a duty to lead and defend all Slavs. By 1914, it stood ready to support Serbia, a proud young nation that dreamed of creating a South Slav state.

Germany's Glorious Military
Eager crowds watch a cavalry regiment, or group of troops serving on horseback, ride through Berlin in August 1914. Germany's army was known to be highly trained and well disciplined, making it a formidable fighting force. *How are the people pictured showing pride in their military?*

Two old multinational empires particularly feared rising nationalism. Austria-Hungary worried that nationalism might foster rebellion among the many minority populations within its empire. Ottoman Turkey felt threatened by nearby new nations, such as Serbia. If realized, Serbia's dream of a South Slav state could take territory away from both Austria-Hungary and Turkey.

In 1912, several Balkan states attacked Turkey and succeeded in taking a large area of land away from Turkish control. The next year, the Balkan states fought among themselves over the spoils of war. These brief but bloody Balkan wars raised tensions to a fever pitch. By 1914, the Balkans were called the "powder keg of Europe"—a barrel of gunpowder that a tiny spark might cause to explode.

 **Checkpoint** How did international competition and nationalism increase tensions in Europe?

The Powder Keg Ignites

As Bismarck had predicted, the Great War began in Eastern Europe. A regional conflict between tiny Serbia and the huge empire of Austria-Hungary grew rapidly into a general war.

Assassination in Sarajevo The crisis began when Archduke Francis Ferdinand of Austria-Hungary announced that he would visit Sarajevo (sa ruh YAY voh), the capital of Bosnia. Francis Ferdinand was the nephew and heir of the aging Austrian emperor, Francis Joseph. At the time of his visit, Bosnia was under the rule of Austria-Hungary. But it was also the home of many Serbs and other Slavs. News of the royal visit angered many Serbian nationalists. They viewed the Austrians as foreign oppressors. Some members of Unity or Death, a Serbian terrorist group commonly known as the Black Hand, vowed to take action.

The archduke ignored warnings of anti-Austrian unrest in Sarajevo. On June 28, 1914, he and his wife, Sophie, rode through Sarajevo in an open car. As the car passed by, a conspirator named Gavrilo Princip (GAV ree loh PREEN tseep) seized his chance and fired twice into the car. Moments later, the archduke and his wife were dead.

Austria Strikes Back The news of the assassination shocked Francis Joseph. Still, he was reluctant to go to war. The government in Vienna, however, saw the incident as an excuse to crush Serbia. In Berlin, Kaiser William II was horrified at the assassination of his ally's heir. He wrote to Francis Joseph, advising him to take a firm stand toward Serbia. Instead of urging restraint, Germany gave Austria a "blank check," or a promise of unconditional support no matter what the cost.

Austria sent Serbia a sweeping **ultimatum,** or final set of demands. To avoid war, said the ultimatum, Serbia must end all anti-Austrian agitation and punish any Serbian official involved in the murder plot. It must even let Austria join in the investigation. Serbia agreed to most, but not all, of the terms of Austria's ultimatum. This partial refusal gave Austria the opportunity it was seeking. On July 28, 1914, Austria declared war on Serbia.

 **Checkpoint** What happened because of the assassination of Francis Ferdinand and his wife?

Chart Skills Who started the war? During the war, each side blamed the other. Afterward, the victorious Allies placed all blame on Germany, because it invaded Belgium. Today, historians still debate who should bear the blame for a catastrophe nobody wanted. **Using information from the chart, describe why Russians might feel that Germany started the war.**

Alliances Kick In

The war between Austria and Serbia might have been another "summer war," like most European wars of the previous century. However, the carefully planned alliances soon drew the great powers deeper into conflict.

Russia and France Back Serbia After Austria's declaration of war, Serbia turned to its ally, Russia, the champion of Slavic nations. From St. Petersburg, Nicholas II telegraphed William II. The tsar asked the kaiser to urge Austria to soften its demands. When this plea failed, Russia began to **mobilize,** or prepare its military forces for war. On August 1, Germany responded by declaring war on Russia.

Russia, in turn, appealed to its ally France. In Paris, nationalists saw a chance to avenge France's defeat in the Franco-Prussian War. Though French leaders had some doubts, they gave Russia the same kind of backing Germany offered to Austria. When Germany demanded that France keep out of the conflict, France refused. Germany then declared war on France.

Germany Invades Belgium By early August, the battle lines were hardening. Italy and Britain still remained uncommitted. Italy chose to stay neutral for the time being. **Neutrality** is a policy of supporting neither side in a war. Britain had to decide quickly whether or not to support its ally France. Then, Germany's war plans suddenly made the decision for Britain.

A cornerstone of Germany's military policy was a plan developed years earlier by General Alfred von Schlieffen (SHLEE fun). Germany's location presented the possibility of a two-front war—against France in the west and Russia to the east. The Schlieffen Plan was designed to avoid this problem. Schlieffen reasoned that Germany should move against France first because Russia's lumbering military would be slow to mobilize.

However, Germany had to defeat France quickly so that its armies could then turn around and fight Russia.

To ensure a swift victory in the west, the Schlieffen Plan required German armies to march through neutral Belgium and then swing south behind French lines. The goal was to encircle and crush France's army. The Germans embarked on the plan by invading Belgium on August 3. However, Britain and other European powers had signed a treaty guaranteeing Belgian neutrality. Outraged by the invasion of Belgium, Britain declared war on Germany on August 4.

Once the machinery of war was set in motion, it seemed impossible to stop. Military leaders insisted that they must mobilize their forces immediately to accomplish their military goals. These military timetables made it impossible for political leaders to negotiate instead of fight.

✔ **Checkpoint** How did the alliance system deepen the original conflict between Austria-Hungary and Serbia into a general war?

Reaction to the War

Before the war, many countries were troubled by domestic problems. For example, Britain struggled with labor unrest and the issue of home rule in Ireland. Russia wrestled with problems stirred up by the Revolution of 1905. The outbreak of war brought a temporary relief from these internal divisions. A renewed sense of patriotism united countries. Governments on both sides emphasized that their countries were fighting for justice and a better world. Young men rushed to enlist, cheered on by women and their elders. Now that war had come at last, it seemed an exciting adventure.

British diplomat Edward Grey was less optimistic. As armies began to move, he predicted, "The lamps are going out all over Europe. We shall not see them lit again in our lifetime."

✔ **Checkpoint** Why were young men on both sides eager to fight when World War I started?

War Enthusiasm
People cheered as soldiers marched off to war. In this photograph, a woman is giving a soldier an apple to eat on his journey.

Terms, People, and Places

1. For each term or place listed at the beginning of the section, write a sentence explaining its significance.

 **Note Taking**

2. **Reading Skill: Summarize** Use your completed chart to answer the Focus Question: Why and how did World War I begin in 1914?

Comprehension and Critical Thinking

3. **Analyze Information** Why did European nations form alliances?

4. **Identify Central Issues** Why might the Balkans be called the "powder keg of Europe"?

5. **Recognize Causes** How did Austria's government react to the assassination of Archduke Francis Ferdinand?

6. **Determine Relevance** What role did geography play in the outbreak of World War I?

● **Writing About History**

Quick Write: Identify Causes and Effects Choose a specific event from the section and identify one cause and one effect of the event. Ask yourself the following questions:

- Why did this event happen? (cause)
- What happened as a result of this event? (effect)

Record your ideas in a chart that shows their cause-and-effect relationships.

▼ A wounded German soldier in 1915

A Soldier on the Western Front

❝The blue French cloth mingled with the German grey upon the ground, and in some places the bodies were piled so high that one could take cover from shell-fire behind them. The noise was so terrific that orders had to be shouted by each man into the ear of the next. And whenever there was a momentary lull in the tumult of battle and the groans of the wounded, one heard, high up in the blue sky, the joyful song of birds! Birds singing just as they do at home in spring-time! It was enough to tear the heart out of one's body!❞
—German soldier Richard Schmieder, writing from the trenches in France

Focus Question How and where was World War I fought?

World War I artillery shell ▶

A New Kind of War

Objectives

- Understand why a stalemate developed on the Western Front.
- Describe how technology made World War I different from earlier wars.
- Outline the course of the war on the Eastern Front, in other parts of Europe, in Turkey, and in the Middle East.
- Summarize how colonies fought in the war.

Terms, People, and Places

stalemate
zeppelin
U-boat
convoy
Dardanelles
T. E. Lawrence

Note Taking

Reading Skill: Identify Supporting Details Record important details about the various battlefronts of World War I in a flowchart.

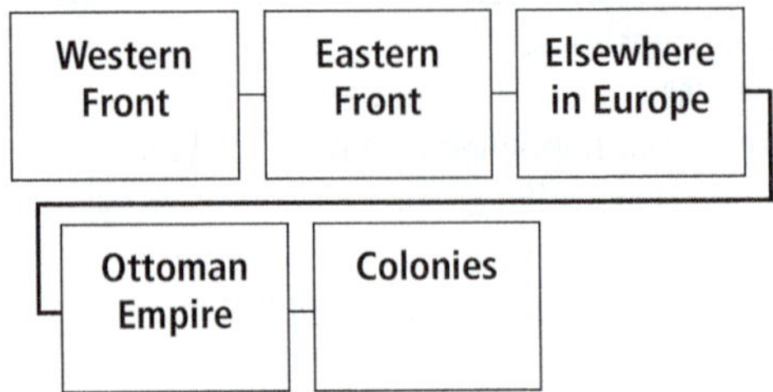

The Great War was the largest conflict in history up to that time. The French mobilized almost 8.5 million men, the British nearly 9 million, the Russians 12 million, and the Germans 11 million. "One out of every four men who went out to the World War did not come back again," recalled a survivor, "and of those who came back, many are maimed and blind and some are mad."

Stalemate on the Western Front

As the war began, German forces fought their way through Belgium toward Paris. The Belgians resisted more than German generals had expected, but the German forces prevailed. However, Germany's plans for a quick defeat of France soon faltered.

The Germans' Schlieffen Plan failed for several reasons. First, Russia mobilized more quickly than expected. After a few small Russian victories, German generals hastily shifted some troops to the east, weakening their forces in the west. Then, in September 1914, British and French troops pushed back the German drive along the Marne River. The first battle of the Marne ended Germany's hopes for a quick victory on the Western Front.

Both sides then began to dig deep trenches to protect their armies from fierce enemy fire. They did not know that the conflict would turn into a long, deadly **stalemate,** a deadlock in which neither side is able to defeat the other. Battle lines in France would remain almost unchanged for four years.

✔ **Checkpoint** How did the Allies stop the Germans from executing the Schlieffen Plan?

Map Skills World War I was fought on several fronts in Europe. Despite huge loss of life and property, the two sides came to a stalemate on the Western and Eastern fronts in 1915 and 1916.

1. **Locate** (a) Paris (b) Battle of the Marne (c) Verdun (d) Tannenberg
2. **Movement** Using the scale, describe how the battle lines moved on the Western Front from 1914 to 1918.
3. **Draw Inferences** Based on this map, why do you think many Russians were demoralized by the progress of the war?

▲ Wounded soldiers on stretchers in Verdun in 1916

The Human Cost To break the stalemate on the Western Front, both the Allies and the Central Powers launched massive offensives in 1916. German forces tried to overwhelm the French at Verdun (vur DUN). The French defenders held firm, sending up the battle cry "They shall not pass." The 11-month struggle cost more than a half a million casualties, or soldiers killed, wounded, or missing, on both sides.

An Allied offensive at the Somme River (sum) was even more costly. In a single grisly day, nearly 60,000 British soldiers were killed or wounded. In the five-month battle, more than one million soldiers were killed, without either side winning an advantage.

Note Taking

Reading Skill: Summarize Review the information under the heading "Technology of Modern Warfare." Summarize key points using a concept web like the one below. Add circles as needed.

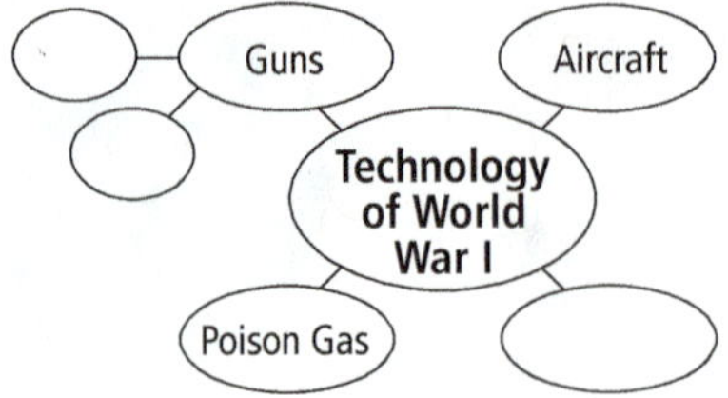

Technology of Modern Warfare

The enormous casualties suffered on the Western Front proved the destructive power of modern weapons. Two significant new or improved weapons were the rapid-fire machine gun and the long-range artillery gun. Machine guns mowed down waves of soldiers. The shrapnel, or flying debris from artillery shells, killed or wounded even more soldiers than the guns. Artillery allowed troops to shell the enemy from more than 10 miles away.

Poison Gas In 1915, first Germany and then the Allies began using another new weapon—poison gas. Poison gas blinded or choked its victims or caused agonizing burns and blisters. It could be fatal. Though soldiers were eventually given gas masks, poison gas remained one of the most dreaded hazards of the war. One British soldier recalled the effects of being gassed:

Primary Source

> "I suppose I resembled a kind of fish with my mouth open gasping for air. It seemed as if my lungs were gradually shutting up and my heart pounded away in my ears like the beat of a drum. . . . To get air into my lungs was real agony."
>
> —William Pressey, quoted in *People at War 1914–1918*

Poison gas was an uncertain weapon. Shifting winds could blow the gas back on the soldiers who launched it.

INFOGRAPHIC

Trench Warfare

From the end of 1914 through 1918, the warring armies on the Western Front faced each other from a vast system of deep trenches. There, millions of soldiers lived out in the open, sharing their food with rats and their beds with lice. Between the opposing trench lines lay "no man's land." In this tract of land pocked with shell holes, every house and tree had long since been destroyed. Sooner or later, soldiers would go "over the top," charging into this manmade desert. With luck, the attackers might overrun a few enemy trenches. In time, the enemy would launch a counterattack, with similar results. The struggle continued, back and forth, over a few hundred yards of territory.

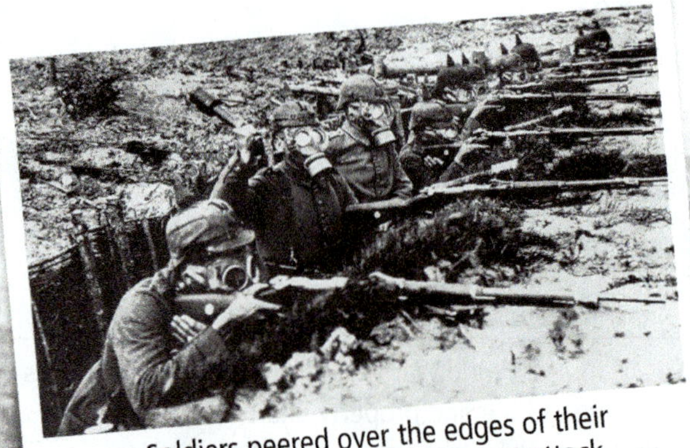

Soldiers peered over the edges of their trenches, watching for the next attack.

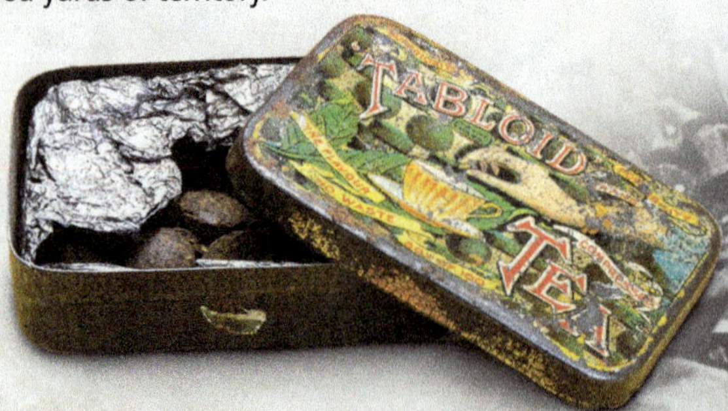

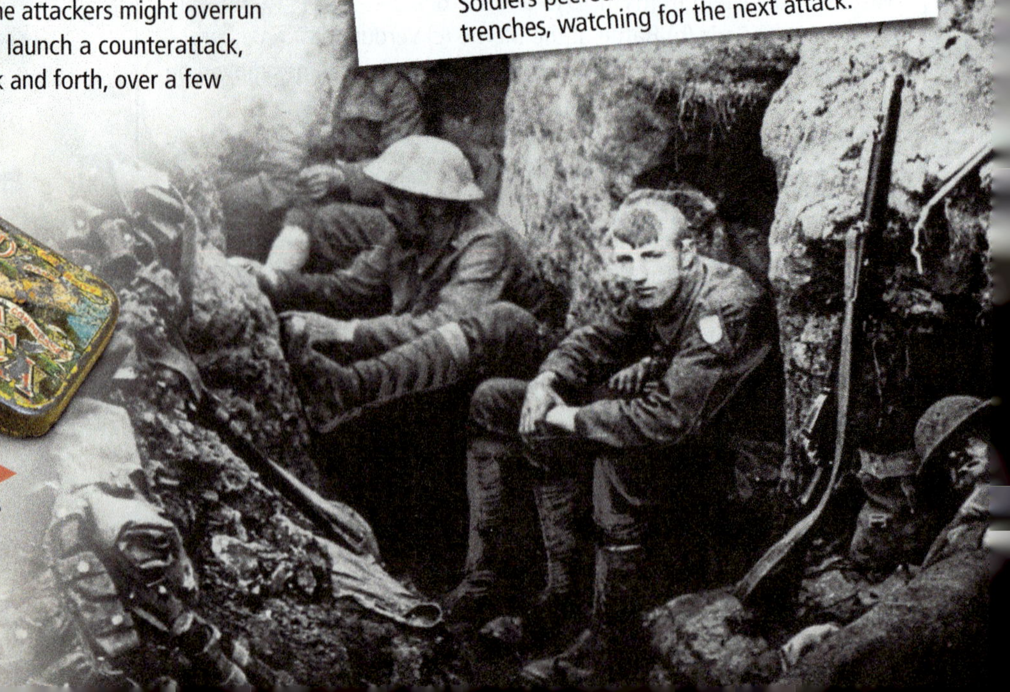

Soldiers ate, slept, and fought in trenches. ▶ Tea tins (above) supplied to British soldiers in World War I, contained 200 tablets of compressed tea.

Tanks, Airplanes, and Submarines During World War I, advances in technology, such as the gasoline-powered engine, led the opposing forces to use tanks, airplanes, and submarines against each other. In 1916, Britain introduced the first armored tank. Mounted with machine guns, the tanks were designed to move across no man's land. Still, the first tanks broke down often. They failed to break the stalemate.

Both sides also used aircraft. At first, planes were <u>utilized</u> simply to observe enemy troop movements. In 1915, Germany used **zeppelins** (ZEP uh linz), large gas-filled balloons, to bomb the English coast. Later, both sides equipped airplanes with machine guns. Pilots known as "flying aces" <u>confronted</u> each other in the skies. These "dogfights" were spectacular, but had little effect on the course of the war on the ground.

Submarines proved much more important. German **U-boats,** nicknamed from the German word for submarine, *Unterseeboot,* did tremendous damage to the Allied side, sinking merchant ships carrying vital supplies to Britain. To defend against the submarines, the Allies organized **convoys,** or groups of merchant ships protected by warships.

✔ **Checkpoint** What made World War I much more deadly than previous wars?

Battle on Other European Fronts

On Europe's Eastern Front, battle lines shifted back and forth, sometimes over large areas. Even though the armies were not mired in trench warfare, casualties rose even higher than on the Western Front. The results were just as indecisive.

Messenger dogs, trained to leap over barbed wire, carried vital information to the front lines. ▼

◄ **Trench Design**

Front line trenches were dug in a zigzag pattern to prevent the enemy from firing down the line.

Communications trenches, perpendicular to the front line trenches, served as routes for mail, food, supplies, reinforcements, and the transport of wounded soldiers.

Tanks, developed during the ► war, rolled on sturdy tracks, which allowed them to navigate through barbed wire and over the rough terrain of no man's land.

Thinking Critically

1. **Determine Relevance** How did technological advances in machine guns and tanks affect soldiers in the trenches?
2. **Make Inferences** What effect do you think that trench warfare had on soldiers' morale?

Russian Losses on the Eastern Front In August 1914, Russian armies pushed into eastern Germany. Then, the Russians suffered a disastrous defeat at Tannenberg, causing them to retreat back into Russia. As the least industrialized of the great powers, Russia was poorly equipped to fight a modern war. Some troops even lacked rifles. Still, Russian commanders continued to send masses of soldiers into combat.

New Combatants in the Balkans and Southern Europe The Balkans were another battleground. In 1915, Bulgaria joined the Central Powers and helped defeat its old Balkan rival Serbia. Romania, hoping to gain some land in Hungary, joined the Allies in 1916, only to be crushed by the Central Powers.

Also in 1915, Italy declared war on Austria-Hungary and later on Germany. The Allies had agreed in a secret treaty to give Italy some Austrian-ruled lands inhabited by Italians. Over the next two years, the Italians and Austrians fought eleven battles along the Isonzo river, with few major breakthroughs. In October 1917, the Austrians and Germans launched a major offensive against the Italian position at Caporetto, also on the Isonzo. The Italians retreated in disarray. British and French forces later helped stop the Central Powers' advance into Italy. Still, Caporetto proved as disastrous for Italy as Tannenberg had been for Russia.

✔ **Checkpoint** In what way was the Eastern Front different from the Western Front?

Map Skills From 1914 to 1918, the Ottoman empire struggled against enemies on multiple fronts.

Location Given that Britain controlled Egypt at this time, describe how the Ottoman empire's location affected what happened to it during World War I.

War Around the World

Though most of the fighting took place in Europe, World War I was a global conflict. Japan, allied with Britain, used the war as an excuse to seize German outposts in China and islands in the Pacific.

The Ottoman Empire Joins the Central Powers Because of its strategic location, the Ottoman empire was a desirable ally. If the Ottoman Turks had joined the Allies, the Central Powers would have been almost completely encircled. However, the Turks joined the Central Powers in late October 1914. The Turks then cut off crucial Allied supply lines to Russia through the **Dardanelles,** a vital strait connecting the Black Sea and the Mediterranean.

In 1915, the Allies sent a massive force of British, Indian, Australian, and New Zealander troops to attempt to open up the strait. At the battle of Gallipoli (guh LIP uh lee), Turkish troops trapped the Allies on the beaches of the Gallipoli peninsula. In January 1916, after 10 months and more than 200,000 casualties, the Allies finally withdrew from the Dardanelles.

Meanwhile, Turkey was fighting Russia in the Caucasus mountains on Turkey's northern border. This region was home to ethnic Armenians, some of whom lived under Ottoman rule and some of whom lived under Russian rule. As Christians, the Armenians were a minority in the Ottoman empire and did not have the same rights as Muslims. As the Russians advanced in 1914, some

Turkish Armenians joined or helped the Russian army against the Turks. The Ottoman government used this cooperation as a reason to deport the entire Armenian population south to Syria and Mesopotamia. During the deportation, between 600,000 and 1.5 million Armenians died. Many were killed by planned massacres; others starved as they were forced to march with no food. Many Armenians fled to other countries, including the United States, leaving almost no Armenians in the historic Armenian homeland in Turkey.

On a third front, the Turks were hard hit in the Middle East. The Ottoman empire included vast areas of Arab land. In 1916, Arab nationalists led by Husayn ibn Ali (HOO sayn IB un AH lee) declared a revolt against Ottoman rule. The British government sent Colonel **T. E. Lawrence**—later known as Lawrence of Arabia—to support the Arab revolt. Lawrence led guerrilla raids against the Turks, dynamiting bridges and supply trains. Eventually, the Ottoman empire lost a great deal of territory to the Arabs, including the key city of Baghdad.

War and the Colonies European colonies were also drawn into the struggle. The Allies overran scattered German colonies in Africa and Asia. They also turned to their own colonies and dominions for troops, laborers, and supplies. Colonial recruits from British India and French West Africa fought on European battlefields. Canada, Australia, and New Zealand sent troops to Britain's aid.

People in the colonies had mixed feelings about serving. Some were reluctant to serve rulers who did not treat them fairly. Other colonial troops volunteered eagerly. They expected that their service would be a step toward citizenship or independence. As you will read, such hopes would be dashed after the war.

Armenian Refugees
A group of Armenian refugees wait for their daily rations from Near East Relief, an American organization founded to help the surviving Turkish Armenians. Public opinion, especially in the United States, was sympathetic to the Armenians during and after World War I. However, the Allies' attempts to protect the Armenians through the treaty that ended the war with Turkey ultimately failed.

✓ **Checkpoint** How did World War I affect the Ottoman empire and European colonies and dominions?

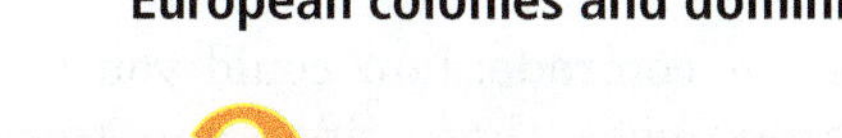

SECTION 2 Assessment

Progress Monitoring Online
For: Self-quiz with vocabulary practice
Web Code: naa-2621

Terms, People, and Places

1. For each term, person, or place listed at the beginning of the section, write a sentence explaining its significance.

Note Taking

2. **Reading Skill: Identify Supporting Details** Use your chart and concept web to answer the Focus Question: How and where was World War I fought?

Comprehension and Critical Thinking

3. **Draw Conclusions** Why did a stalemate develop on the Western Front?

4. **Synthesize Information** Describe three ways in which technology affected the war.

5. **Predict Consequences** Governments on both sides of World War I tried to keep full casualty figures and other bad news from reaching the public. What effect do you think news about disastrous defeats such as Tannenberg and Caporetto would have had on the attitudes of people back home?

6. **Recognize Causes** How did nationalism within the Ottoman Empire come into play during the war?

● Writing About History

Quick Write: Write a Thesis Statement Suppose that you are writing an essay on the effects of Ottoman Turkey's decision to join the Central Powers during World War I. Answer the questions below. Use your answers to create a thesis statement for the essay.

- Why were the Dardanelles important to the Allies?
- Who won the Battle of Gallipoli?
- What impact do you think Gallipoli had on the Russian war effort?

Erich Maria Remarque: *All Quiet on the Western Front*

Erich Maria Remarque (1898–1970) was wounded five times while serving in the German army during World War I. In 1929, he published *All Quiet on the Western Front,* which is often considered the greatest novel about World War I.

It follows the narrator, Paul Baumer, from eager recruit to disillusioned veteran. In this passage, Paul is trapped for hours in a foxhole with a French soldier he has just killed.

In the afternoon, about three, he is dead.

I breathe freely again. But only for a short time. Soon the silence is more unbearable than the groans. I wish the gurgling were there again, gasping hoarse, now whistling softly and again hoarse and loud.

It is mad, what I do. But I must do something. I prop the dead man up again so that he lies comfortably, although he feels nothing any more. I close his eyes. They are brown, his hair is black and a bit curly at the sides. . . .

The silence spreads. I talk and must talk. So I speak to him and say to him: "Comrade, I did not want to kill you. If you jumped in here again, I would not do it, if you would be sensible too. But you were only an idea to me before, an abstraction[1] that lived in my mind and called forth its appropriate response. It was that abstraction I stabbed. But now, for the first time, I see you are a man like me. I thought of your hand-grenades, of your bayonet[2], of your rifle; now I see your wife and your face and our fellowship. Forgive me, comrade. We always see it too late. Why do they never tell us that you are poor devils like us, that your mothers are just as anxious as ours, and that we have the same fear of death, and the same dying and the same agony—Forgive me, comrade; how could you be my enemy? If we threw away these rifles and this uniform you could be my brother just like Kat and Albert. Take twenty years of my life, comrade, and stand up—take more, for I do not know what I can even attempt to do with it now."

It is quiet, the front is still except for the crackle of rifle fire. The bullets rain over, they are not fired haphazard, but shrewdly aimed from all sides. I cannot get out.

▲ This painting is titled *Notre-Dame de Lorette—A Soldier Walks Through the Flooded Trenches.* It was painted by François Flameng, a French artist who was given access to the front lines by the French government.

---

1. abstraction (ab STRAK shun) *n.* an idea or term that is developed from a concrete reality

2. bayonet (bay oh NET) *n.* a blade attached to an end of a rifle for stabbing in hand-to-hand combat

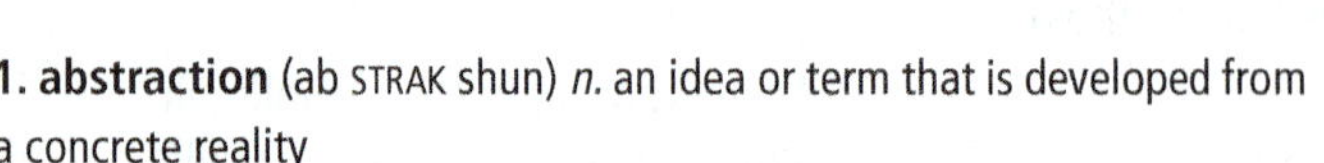

Thinking Critically
1. **Recognize Point of View** Why does Paul speak to the dead French soldier?
2. **Synthesize Information** What does Paul mean by "We always see it too late"?

An American soldier bids goodbye to his sweetheart.

An American War Song

❝Over there, over there,
Send the word, send the word over there,
That the Yanks are coming,
The Yanks are coming…
We'll be over, we're coming over,
And we won't come back till it's over
Over there.❞
—George M. Cohan, from the song "Over There," written in 1917

On April 6, 1917, the United States declared war on Germany.

Focus Question How did the Allies win World War I?

Sheet music for the patriotic song "Over There"

Winning the War

Objectives
- Describe how World War I became a total war.
- Explain the effect that years of warfare had on morale.
- Analyze the causes and effects of American entry into the war.
- Summarize events that led to the end of the war.

Terms, People, and Places

total war
conscription
contraband
Lusitania
propaganda
atrocity
Fourteen Points
self-determination
armistice

Note Taking

Reading Skill: Summarize As you read, use an outline to summarize the events in this section.

> I. Waging total war
>   A. Economies committed to war production
>   1. Conscription
>   2. Rationing
>   3. Price controls
>   B. Economic warfare

By 1917, European societies were cracking under the strain of war. Casualties on the fronts and shortages at home sapped morale. The stalemate dragged on, seemingly without end. Soon, however, the departure of one country from the war and the entry of another would tip the balance and end the stalemate.

Waging Total War

As the struggle wore on, nations realized that a modern, mechanized war required the channeling of a nation's entire resources into the war effort, or **total war.** To achieve total war, governments began to take a stronger role in directing the economic and cultural lives of their people.

Economies Committed to War Production Early on, both sides set up systems to recruit, arm, transport, and supply armies that numbered in the millions. All of the warring nations except Britain immediately imposed universal military **conscription,** or "the draft," which required all young men to be ready for military or other service. Britain, too, instituted conscription in 1916. Germany set up a system of forced civilian labor as well.

Governments raised taxes and borrowed huge amounts of money to pay the costs of war. They rationed food and other products, from boots to gasoline. In addition, they introduced other economic controls, such as setting prices and forbidding strikes.

Economic Warfare At the start of the war, Britain's navy formed a blockade in the North Sea to keep ships from carrying supplies in and out of Germany. International law allowed wartime blockades

to confiscate **contraband,** or military supplies and raw materials needed
to make military supplies, but not items such as food and clothing. In spite
of international law, the British blockade stopped both types of goods from
reaching Germany. As the war progressed, it became harder and harder to
feed the German and Austrian people. In Germany, the winter of 1916 and
1917 was remembered as "the turnip winter," because the potato crop
failed and people ate turnips instead.

To retaliate, Germany used U-boats to create its own blockade. In
1915, Germany declared that it would sink all ships carrying goods to
Britain. In May 1915, a German submarine torpedoed the British liner
Lusitania off the coast of Ireland. Almost 1,200 passengers were killed,
including 128 Americans. Germany justified the attack, arguing that the
Lusitania was carrying weapons. When American President Woodrow
Wilson threatened to cut off diplomatic relations with Germany, though,
Germany agreed to restrict its submarine campaign. Before attacking
any ship, U-boats would surface and give warning, allowing neutral pas-
sengers to escape to lifeboats. Unrestricted submarine warfare stopped—
for the moment.

Propaganda War Total war also meant controlling public opinion. Even
in democratic countries, special boards censored the press. Their aim was
to keep complete casualty figures and other discouraging news from reaching the public. Government censors also restricted popular literature, historical writings, motion pictures, and the arts.

Both sides waged a propaganda war. **Propaganda** is the spreading of
ideas to promote a cause or to damage an opposing cause. Governments
used propaganda to motivate military mobilization, especially in Britain
before conscription started in 1916. In France and Germany, propaganda
urged civilians to loan money to the government. Later in the war, Allied
propaganda played up the brutality of Germany's invasion of Belgium. The
British and French press circulated tales of **atrocities,** horrible acts

**A German Submarine Sinks
the *Lusitania***
The sinking of the British line *Lusitania* in
1915, illustrated below, was part of
Germany's policy of unrestricted submarine
warfare. The incident was featured in
propaganda posters as evidence of German
brutality. *How does the poster below use
emotion to encourage men to enlist?*

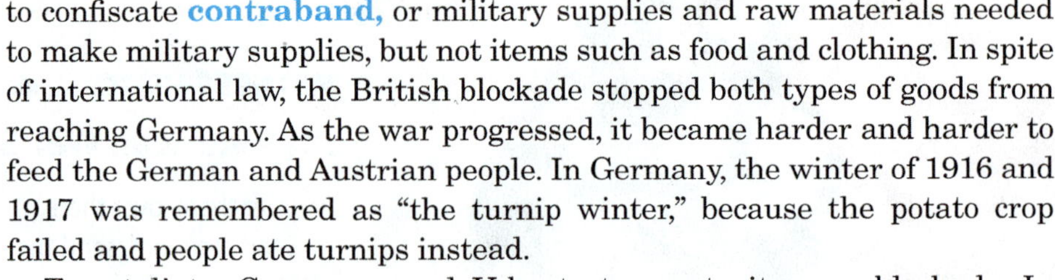

committed against innocent people. Although some atrocities did occur, often the stories were distorted by exaggerations or completely made up.

Women Join the War Effort Women played a critical role in total war. As millions of men left to fight, women took over their jobs and kept national economies going. Many women worked in war industries, manufacturing weapons and supplies. Others joined women's branches of the armed forces. When food shortages threatened Britain, volunteers in the Women's Land Army went to the fields to grow their nation's food.

Nurses shared the dangers of the men whose wounds they tended. At aid stations close to the front lines, nurses often worked around the clock, especially after a big "push" brought a flood of casualties. In her diary, English nurse Vera Brittain describes sweating through 90-degree days in France, "stopping hemorrhages, replacing intestines, and draining and reinserting innumerable rubber tubes" with "gruesome human remnants heaped on the floor."

War work gave women a new sense of pride and confidence. After the war, most women had to give up their jobs to men returning home. Still, they had challenged the idea that women could not handle demanding and dangerous jobs. In many countries, including Britain, Germany, and the United States, women's support for the war effort helped them finally win the right to vote, after decades of struggle.

 **Checkpoint** Why was it important for both sides to keep civilian morale high during the war?

Morale Collapses

Despite inspiring propaganda, by 1917 the morale of troops and civilians had plunged. Germany was sending 15-year-old recruits to the front. Britain was on the brink of bankruptcy.

War Fatigue Long casualty lists, food shortages, and the failure of generals to win promised victories led to calls for peace. Instead of praising the glorious deeds of heroes, war poets began denouncing the leaders whose errors wasted so many lives. British poet and soldier Siegfried Sassoon captured the bitter mood:

66 You smug-faced crowds with kindling eye
Who cheer when soldier lads march by,
Sneak home and pray you'll never know
The hell where youth and laughter go. 99
—Siegfried Sassoon, "Suicide in the Trenches"

As morale collapsed, troops in some French units mutinied. In Italy, many soldiers deserted during the retreat at Caporetto. In Russia, soldiers left the front to join in a full-scale revolution back home.

Revolution in Russia Three years of war had hit Russia especially hard. Stories of incompetent generals and corruption eroded public confidence. In March 1917, bread riots in St. Petersburg erupted into a revolution that brought down the Russian monarchy. (You'll read more about the causes and effects of the Russian Revolution in Section 5.)

At first, the Allies welcomed the overthrow of the tsar. They hoped Russia would institute a democratic government and become a stronger

Vocabulary Builder

eroded (ee ROHD id)—*vt.* ate into or wore away

American Troops "Over There"
The arrival of fresh American troops in Europe throughout 1918 helped turn the tide of the war in favor of the Allies. Recruitment posters, like the one above, inspired soldiers to enlist. *How was the experience of American soldiers different from that of other Allied soldiers?*

ally. But later that year V. I. Lenin came to power with a promise to pull Russian troops out of the war. Early in 1918, Lenin signed the Treaty of Brest-Litovsk (brest lih TAWFSK) with Germany. The treaty ended Russian participation in World War I.

Russia's withdrawal had an immediate impact on the war. With Russia out of the struggle, Germany could concentrate its forces on the Western Front. In the spring of 1918, the Central Powers stood ready to achieve the great breakthrough they had sought for so long.

✔ **Checkpoint** How did Russia's loss of morale affect the strategic position of the Allies in World War I?

The United States Declares War

Soon after the Russian Revolution began, however, another event altered the balance of forces. The United States declared war on Germany. Many factors contributed to the decision of the United States to exchange neutrality for war in 1917.

Why Join the Allies? Many Americans supported the Allies because of cultural ties. The United States shared a cultural history and language with Britain and sympathized with France as another democracy. On the other hand, some German Americans favored the Central Powers. So did many Irish Americans, who resented British rule of Ireland, and Russian Jewish immigrants, who did not want to be allied with the tsar.

Germany had ceased submarine attacks in 1915 after pressure from President Wilson. However, in early 1917, Germany was desperate to break the stalemate. On February 1, the German government announced that it would resume unrestricted submarine warfare. Wilson angrily denounced Germany.

Also, in early 1917, the British intercepted a message from the German foreign minister, Arthur Zimmermann, to his ambassador in Mexico. In the note, Zimmermann authorized his ambassador to propose that Germany would help Mexico "to reconquer the lost territory in New Mexico, Texas, and Arizona" in return for Mexican support against the United States. Britain revealed the Zimmermann note to the American government. When the note became public, anti-German feeling intensified in the United States.

Declaring War In April 1917, Wilson asked Congress to declare war on Germany. "We have no selfish ends to serve," he stated. Instead, he painted the conflict idealistically as a war "to make the world safe for democracy" and later as a "war to end war."

The United States needed months to recruit, train, supply, and transport a modern army across the Atlantic. But by 1918, about two million American soldiers had joined the war-weary Allied troops fighting on the Western Front. Although relatively few American troops engaged in combat, their arrival gave Allied troops a much-needed morale boost. Just as important to the debt-ridden Allies was American financial aid.

The Fourteen Points Though he had failed to maintain American neutrality, Wilson still hoped to be a peacemaker. In January 1918, he issued the Fourteen Points, a list of his terms for resolving this and future wars. He called for freedom of the seas, free trade, large-scale reductions of arms, and an end to secret treaties. For Eastern Europe, Wilson favored self-determination, the right of people to choose their own form of government. Finally, Wilson urged the creation of a "general association of nations" to keep the peace in the future.

✔ **Checkpoint** What are three factors that led the United States to enter the war?

Victory at Last

A final showdown on the Western Front began in early 1918. The Germans badly wanted to achieve a major victory before eager American troops arrived in Europe. In March, the Germans launched a huge offensive that by July had pushed the Allies back 40 miles. These efforts exhausted the Germans, however, and by then American troops were arriving by the thousands. The Allies then launched a counterattack, slowly driving German forces back across France and Belgium. In September, German generals told the kaiser that the war could not be won.

Uprisings exploded among hungry city dwellers across Germany. German commanders advised the kaiser to step down. William II did so in early November, fleeing into exile in the Netherlands.

By autumn, Austria-Hungary was also reeling toward collapse. As the government in Vienna tottered, the subject nationalities revolted, splintering the empire of the Hapsburgs. Bulgaria and the Ottoman empire also asked for peace.

The new German government sought an armistice, or agreement to end fighting, with the Allies. At 11 A.M. on November 11, 1918, the Great War at last came to an end.

✔ **Checkpoint** Why did Germany ask the Allies for an armistice in November 1918?

Celebrating the Armistice
Around the globe, crowds celebrated the end of the war. Here, British and American soldiers and civilians wave the American and French flags in relief and jubilation.

SECTION 3 Assessment

Progress Monitoring Online
For: Self-quiz with vocabulary practice
Web Code: naa-2631

Terms, People, and Places

1. For each term, person, or place listed at the beginning of the section, write a sentence explaining its significance.

Note Taking

2. **Reading Skill: Summarize** Use your completed outline to answer the Focus Question: How did the Allies win World War I?

Comprehension and Critical Thinking

3. **Summarize** What measures did wartime governments take to control national economies and public opinion?
4. **Recognize Effects** What impact did wartime failures have on Russia?
5. **Draw Conclusions** Describe how the entry of United States into the war was a turning point.
6. **Analyze Information** Reread the poem by Siegfried Sassoon. What does it suggest about the effects of trench warfare?

● **Writing About History**

Quick Write: Gather Evidence to Support Thesis Statement Suppose you are writing an essay with the following thesis statement "Women played a critical role in World War I." Write three questions like the two below that would help you gather evidence to support this thesis.

- What types of things did women do during the war?
- Why was this work important?

Lloyd George, Clemenceau, and Wilson (left to right) at the Paris Peace Conference. Above right, a medal sold to raise funds for wounded soldiers.

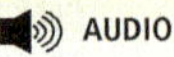

Worth the Cost?

Vera Brittain, a British nurse, lost her brother Edward and her fiancé Roland on the battlefield.

❝ Although they would no doubt have welcomed the idea of a League of Nations, Roland and Edward certainly had not died in order that Clemenceau should outwit Lloyd George, and both of them bamboozle President Wilson, and all three combine to make the beaten, block-aded enemy pay the cost of the War. ❞
—Vera Brittain, *Testament of Youth*

Focus Question What factors influenced the peace treaties that ended World War I, and how did people react to the treaties?

Making the Peace

Objectives

- Analyze the costs of World War I.
- Describe the issues faced by the delegates to the Paris Peace Conference.
- Explain why many people were dissatisfied with the Treaty of Versailles and other peace settlements.

Terms, People, and Places

pandemic	radicals
reparations	collective security
	mandate

Note Taking

Reading Skill: Summarize As you read, summarize the main points of the text under the heading "The Costs of War" in a concept web like the one below.

Just weeks after the war ended, President Wilson boarded a steamship bound for France. He had decided to go in person to Paris, where Allied leaders would make the peace. Wilson was certain that he could solve the problems of old Europe. "Tell me what is right," Wilson urged his advisors, "and I'll fight for it." Sadly, it would not be that easy. Europe was a shattered continent. Its problems, and those of the world, would not be solved at the Paris Peace Conference, or for many years afterward.

The Costs of War

The human and material costs of the war were staggering. Millions of soldiers were dead, and even more wounded. The devastation was made even worse in 1918 by a deadly **pandemic** of influenza. A pandemic is the spread of a disease across a large area—in this case, the whole world. In just a few months, the flu killed more than 20 million people worldwide.

The Financial Toll In battle zones from France to Russia, homes, farms, factories, roads, and churches had been shelled into rubble. People had fled these areas as refugees. Now they had to return and start to rebuild. The costs of reconstruction and paying off huge war debts would burden an already battered world.

Shaken and disillusioned, people everywhere felt bitter about the war. The Allies blamed the conflict on their defeated foes and insisted that the losers make **reparations,** or payments for war damage. The stunned Central Powers, who had viewed the armistice as a cease-fire rather than a surrender, looked for scapegoats on whom they could blame their defeat.

Political Turmoil Under the stress of war, governments had collapsed in Russia, Germany, Austria-Hungary, and the Ottoman empire. Political radicals, or people who wanted to make extreme changes, dreamed of building a new social order from the chaos. Conservatives warned against the spread of bolshevism, or communism, as it was soon called.

Unrest also swept through Europe's colonial empires. African and Asian soldiers had discovered that the imperial powers were not as invincible as they seemed. Colonial troops returned home with a more cynical view of Europeans and renewed hopes for independence.

✔ **Checkpoint** What were some of the human, economic, and political costs of the war?

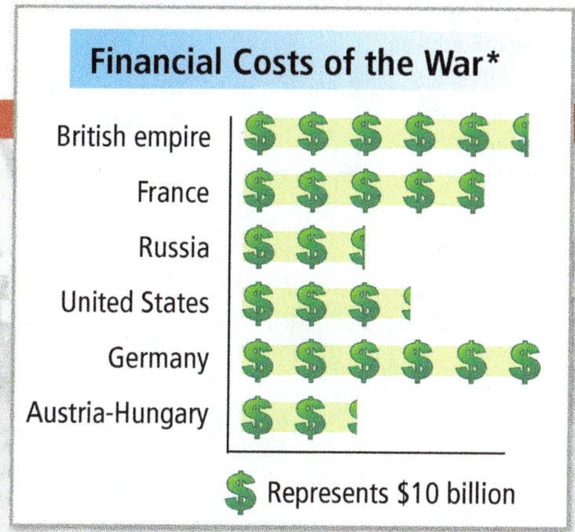

SOURCE: *The Harper Encyclopedia of Military History,* R. Ernest Dupuy and Trevor N. Dupuy
* Includes war expenditures, property losses, and shipping losses

● **INFOGRAPHIC**

The Costs of World War I

The war ended in 1918, but its effects would be felt for decades to come. More than 8.5 million men had died in battle. Twice that number had been wounded, many of them disabled for life. Historians estimate that from 6 to 13 million civilians also lost their lives as a result of the war. Many of the combatant nations had thrown all of their resources into the fight, leaving them little with which to rebuild. Below an American nurse tends to soldiers in France in 1918.

Casualties of Mobilized Soldiers

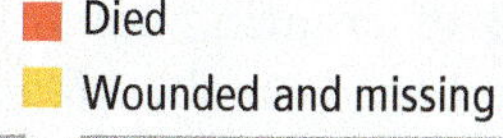

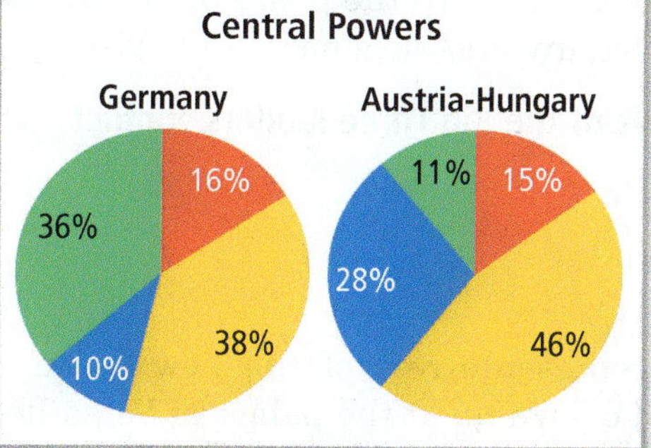

SOURCE: *Encyclopædia Britannica,* 2004

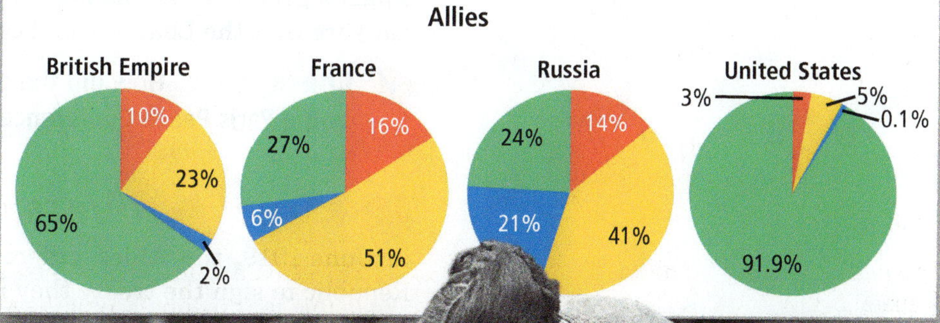

Thinking Critically

1. **Draw Conclusions** Which two nations suffered the highest proportion of soldier deaths? Why were American casualties relatively low?
2. **Predict Consequences** What long-term impact might the number of casualties have on a country like France?

The Paris Peace Conference

The victorious Allies met at the Paris Peace Conference to discuss the fate of Europe, the former Ottoman empire, and various colonies around the world. The Central Powers and Russia were not allowed to take part in the negotiations.

Conflicting Goals Wilson was one of three strong leaders who dominated the Paris Peace Conference. He was a dedicated reformer and at times was so stubbornly convinced that he was right that he could be hard to work with. Wilson urged for "peace without victory" based on the Fourteen Points.

Two other Allied leaders at the peace conference had different aims. British prime minister David Lloyd George had promised to build a postwar Britain "fit for heroes"—a goal that would cost money. The chief goal of the French leader, Georges Clemenceau (KLEM un soh), was to weaken Germany so that it could never again threaten France. "Mr. Wilson bores me with his Fourteen Points," complained Clemenceau. "Why, God Almighty has only ten!"

Problems With the Peace Crowds of other representatives circled around the "Big Three" with their own demands and interests. The Italian prime minister, Vittorio Orlando (awr LAN doh), insisted that the Allies honor their secret agreement to give former Austro-Hungarian lands to Italy. Such secret agreements violated the principle of self-determination.

Self-determination posed other problems. Many people who had been ruled by Russia, Austria-Hungary, or the Ottoman empire now demanded national states of their own. The territories claimed by these peoples often overlapped, so it was impossible to satisfy them all. Some ethnic groups became unwanted minorities in newly created states.

Wilson had to compromise on his Fourteen Points. However, he stood firm on his goal of creating an international League of Nations. The League would be based on the idea of **collective security,** a system in which a group of nations acts as one to preserve the peace of all. Wilson felt sure that the League could correct any mistakes made in Paris.

 **Checkpoint** How did the goals of the Big Three leaders conflict at the Paris Peace Conference?

The Treaty of Versailles

In June 1919, the Allies ordered representatives of the new German Republic to sign the treaty they had drawn up at the palace of Versailles (vur SY) outside Paris. The German delegates were horrified. The treaty forced Germany to assume full blame for causing the war. It also imposed huge reparations that would burden an already damaged German economy. The reparations covered not only the destruction caused by the war, but also pensions for millions of Allied soldiers or their widows and families. The total cost of German reparations would later be calculated at $30 billion (the equivalent of about $2.7 trillion today).

Other parts of the treaty were aimed at weakening Germany. The treaty severely limited the size of the once-feared German military. It returned Alsace and Lorraine to France, removed hundreds of square miles of territory from western and eastern Germany, and stripped Germany of its overseas colonies. The treaty compelled many Germans to

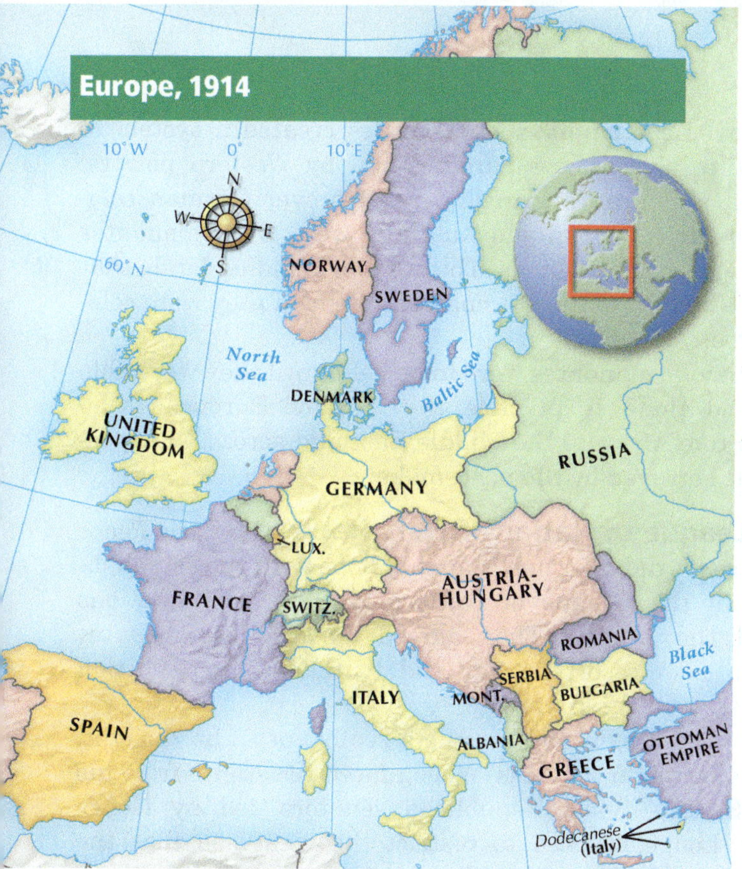

leave the homes they had made in Russia, Poland, Alsace-Lorraine, and the German colonies to return to Germany or Austria.

The Germans signed because they had no choice. However, German resentment of the Treaty of Versailles would poison the international climate for 20 years. It would help spark an even deadlier world war in the years to come.

 **Checkpoint** **Why were the German delegates surprised when they read the treaty?**

Outcome of the Peace Settlements

The Allies drew up separate treaties with the other Central Powers. Like the Treaty of Versailles, these treaties left <u>widespread</u> dissatisfaction. Discontented nations waited for a chance to revise the peace settlements in their favor.

Self-Determination in Eastern Europe Where the German, Austrian, and Russian empires had once ruled, a band of new nations emerged. Poland became an independent nation after more than 100 years of foreign rule. The Baltic states of Latvia, Lithuania, and Estonia fought for and achieved independence.

Three new republics—Czechoslovakia, Austria, and Hungary—rose in the old Hapsburg heartland. In the Balkans, the peacemakers created a new South Slav state, Yugoslavia, dominated by Serbia.

The Mandate System European colonies in Africa, Asia, and the Pacific had looked to the Paris Peace Conference with high hopes. Colonial leaders expected that the peace would bring new respect and an end to imperial rule. However, the leaders at Paris applied self-determination only to parts of Europe. Outside Europe, the victorious Allies added to

Map Skills The peace treaties that ended World War I redrew the map of Europe.
1. **Locate** (a) Lithuania (b) Czechoslovakia (c) Yugoslavia (c) Poland (d) Danzig
2. **Regions** Which countries lost territory in Eastern Europe?
3. **Draw Conclusions** Why might the distribution of territory after World War I leave behind widespread dissatisfaction?

Vocabulary Builder

<u>widespread</u>—(wyd SPRED) *adj.* occurring in many places

Analyzing Political Cartoons

This cartoon portrays one view of the peace treaties that ended World War I.

A The turkey symbolizes Germany.

B Britain holds a carving knife and fork, ready to carve the turkey.

C Other Allies await the feast.

1. What does carving up the turkey symbolize?
2. What attitude do you think that the cartoonist has towards the treaties?

their overseas empires. The treaties created a system of **mandates,** territories administered by Western powers. Britain and France gained mandates over German colonies in Africa. Japan and Australia were given mandates over some Pacific islands. The treaties handled lands that used to be part of the Ottoman empire as if they were colonies, too.

In theory, mandates were to be held until they were able to stand alone. In practice, they became European colonies. From Africa to the Middle East and across Asia, people felt betrayed by the peacemakers.

The League of Nations Offers Hope The Paris Peace Conference did offer one beacon of hope with the establishment of the League of Nations. More than 40 nations joined the League. They agreed to negotiate disputes rather than resort to war and to take common action against any aggressor state.

Wilson's dream had become a reality, or so he thought. On his return from Paris, Wilson faced resistance from his own Senate. Some Republican senators, led by Henry Cabot Lodge, wanted to restrict the treaty so that the United States would not be obligated to fight in future wars. Lodge's reservations echoed the feelings of many Americans. Wilson would not accept Lodge's compromises. In the end, the Senate refused to ratify the treaty, and the United States never joined the League.

The loss of the United States weakened the League's power. In addition, the League had no power outside of its member states. As time soon revealed, the League could not prevent war. Still, it was a first step toward something genuinely new—an international organization dedicated to maintaining peace and advancing the interests of all peoples.

✔ **Checkpoint** Why did the League of Nations fail to accomplish Wilson's dreams?

SECTION 4 Assessment

Progress Monitoring _Online_
For: Self-quiz with vocabulary practice
Web Code: naa-2641

Terms, People, and Places

1. For each term, person, or place listed at the beginning of the section, write a sentence explaining its significance.

Note Taking

2. **Reading Skill: Summarize** Use your completed concept web and table to answer the Focus Question: What factors influenced the peace treaties that ended World War I, and how did people react to the treaties?

Comprehension and Critical Thinking

3. **Make Generalizations** Describe conditions in Europe after World War I.

4. **Draw Conclusions** How did the peace treaties both follow and violate the principle of self-determination?

5. **Draw Inferences** Wilson's closest advisor wrote of the Paris Peace Conference, "there is much to approve and much to regret." What do you think he might have approved? What might he have regretted?

● **Writing About History**

Quick Write: Choose an Organization Use an organizational strategy that suits the topic of your essay. For instance, if you are writing about one event with many causes, you might write one paragraph about each cause, followed by a paragraph that sums up the effects. If you are writing about a series of events, you might order your paragraphs chronologically.

Choose two topics from this section, one that suits the first type of organization and on that suits the second. Then write a brief outline for an essay about each.

A pin showing the Soviet hammer and sickle (left). A propaganda poster asks Russians to choose sides in the Russian Civil War (right).

Voices From the Front

❝ Mr. War Minister!
We, soldiers from various regiments,. . . ask you to end the war and its bloodshed at any cost.... If this is not done, then believe us when we say that we will take our weapons and head out for our own hearths to save our fathers, mothers, wives, and children from death by starvation (which is nigh). And if we cannot save them, then we'd rather die with them in our native lands than be killed, poisoned, or frozen to death somewhere and cast into the earth like a dog. ❞
—Letter from the front, 1917

The voices from the front joined voices at home, calling for change in Russia.

Focus Question How did two revolutions and a civil war bring about Communist control of Russia?

Revolution and Civil War in Russia

Objectives
- Explain the causes of the March Revolution.
- Describe the goals of Lenin and the Bolsheviks in the November Revolution.
- Outline how the Communists defeated their opponents in Russia's civil war.
- Analyze how the Communist state developed under Lenin.

Terms, People, and Places

proletariat	Cheka
soviet	commissar

Note Taking

Reading Skill: Summarize Copy the timeline below and fill it in as you read this section. When you finish, write two sentences that summarize the information in your timeline.

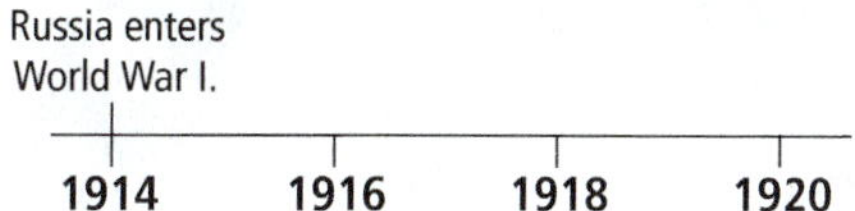

The year 1913 marked the 300th anniversary of the Romanov dynasty. Everywhere, Russians honored the tsar and his family. Tsarina Alexandra felt confident that the people loved Nicholas too much to ever threaten him. "They are constantly frightening the emperor with threats of revolution," she told a friend, "and here,—you see it yourself—we need merely to show ourselves and at once their hearts are ours."

Appearances were deceiving. In March 1917, the first of two revolutions would topple the Romanov dynasty and pave the way for even more radical changes.

The March Revolution Ends Tsarism

In 1914, the huge Russian empire stretched from Eastern Europe east to the Pacific Ocean. Unlike Western Europe, Russia was slow to industrialize despite its huge potential. Landowning nobles, priests, and an autocratic tsar controlled the government and economy. Much of the majority peasant population endured stark poverty. As Russia began to industrialize, a small middle class and an urban working class emerged.

Unrest Deepens After the Revolution of 1905, Nicholas had failed to solve Russia's basic political, economic, and social problems. The elected Duma set up after the revolution had no real power. Moderates pressed for a constitution and social change. But Nicholas II, a weak and ineffective leader, blocked attempts to limit his authority. Like past tsars, he relied on his secret police and other enforcers to impose his will. A corrupt bureaucracy and an overburdened court system added to the government's problems.

Revolutionaries hatched radical plots. Some hoped to lead discontented peasants to overthrow the tsarist regime. Marxists tried to ignite revolution among the **proletariat**—the growing class of factory and railroad workers, miners, and urban wage earners. A revolution, they believed, would occur when the time was ripe.

Impact of World War I The outbreak of war in 1914 fueled national pride and united Russians. Armies dashed to battle with enthusiasm. But like the Crimean and Russo-Japanese wars, World War I quickly strained Russian resources. Factories could not turn out enough supplies. The transportation system broke down, delivering only a trickle of crucial materials to the front. By 1915, many soldiers had no rifles and no ammunition. Badly equipped and poorly led, they died in staggering numbers. In 1915 alone, Russian casualties reached two million.

In a patriotic gesture, Nicholas II went to the front to take personal charge. The decision proved a disastrous blunder. The tsar was no more competent than many of his generals. Worse, he left domestic affairs to the tsarina, Alexandra. In Nicholas' absence, Alexandra relied on the advice of Gregory Rasputin, an illiterate peasant and self-proclaimed "holy man." The tsarina came to believe that Rasputin had miraculous powers after he helped her son, who suffered from hemophilia, a disorder in which any injury can result in uncontrollable bleeding.

By 1916, Rasputin's influence over Alexandra had reached new heights and weakened confidence in the government. Fearing for the monarchy, a group of Russian nobles killed Rasputin on December 29, 1916.

The Tsar Steps Down By March 1917, disasters on the battlefield, combined with food and fuel shortages on the home front, brought the monarchy to collapse. In St. Petersburg (renamed Petrograd during the war), workers were going on strike. Marchers, mostly women, surged through the streets, shouting, "Bread! Bread!" Troops refused to fire on the demonstrators, leaving the government helpless. Finally, on the advice of military and political leaders, the tsar abdicated.

Duma politicians then set up a provisional, or temporary, government. Middle-class liberals in the government began preparing a constitution for a new Russian republic. At the same time, they continued the war against Germany.

Outside the provisional government, revolutionary socialists plotted their own course. In Petrograd and other cities, they set up **soviets,** or councils of workers and soldiers. At first, the soviets worked democratically within the government. Before long, though, the Bolsheviks, a radical socialist group, took charge. The leader of the Bolsheviks was a determined revolutionary, V. I. Lenin.

The revolutions of March and November 1917 are known to Russians as the February and October revolutions. In 1917, Russia still used an old calendar, which was 13 days behind the one used in Western Europe. Russia adopted the Western calendar in 1918.

✔ **Checkpoint** What provoked the March Revolution?

The Tsar's Downfall
Tsarina Alexandra's reliance on the "mad monk" Gregory Rasputin (below left) to help her govern proved fatal for Rasputin, and ultimately for Alexandra. A lavish Fabergé egg (below right) details three centuries of Romanov tsars. *How do both images show the gulf between Russia's rulers and its people?*

Lenin and the Bolsheviks

Vladimir Ilyich Ulyanov (ool YAHN uf) was born in 1870 to a middle-class family. He adopted the name Lenin when he became a revolutionary. When he was 17, his older brother was arrested and hanged for plotting to kill the tsar. The execution branded his family as a threat to the state and made the young Vladimir hate the tsarist government.

A Brilliant Revolutionary As a young man, Lenin read the works of Karl Marx and participated in student demonstrations. He spread Marxist ideas among factory workers along with other socialists, including Nadezhda Krupskaya (nah DYEZ duh kroop SKY uh), the daughter of a poor noble family. In 1895, Lenin and Krupskaya were arrested and sent to Siberia. During their imprisonment, they were married. After their release, they went into exile in Switzerland. There they worked tirelessly to spread revolutionary ideas.

Lenin's View of Marx Lenin adapted Marxist ideas to fit Russian conditions. Marx had predicted that the industrial working class would rise spontaneously to overthrow capitalism. But Russia did not have a large urban proletariat. Instead, Lenin called for an elite group to lead the revolution and set up a "dictatorship of the proletariat." Though this elite revolutionary party represented a small percentage of socialists, Lenin gave them the name Bolsheviks, meaning "majority."

In Western Europe, many leading socialists had come to think that socialism could be achieved through gradual and moderate reforms such as higher wages, increased suffrage, and social welfare programs. A group of socialists in Russia, the Mensheviks, favored this approach. The Bolsheviks rejected it. To Lenin, reforms of this nature were merely capitalist tricks to repress the masses. Only revolution, he said, could bring about needed changes.

In March 1917, Lenin was still in exile. As Russia stumbled into revolution, Germany saw a chance to weaken its enemy by helping Lenin return home. Lenin rushed across Germany to the Russian frontier in a special train. He greeted a crowd of fellow exiles and activists with this cry: "Long live the worldwide Socialist revolution!"

✔ **Checkpoint** Why did Germany want Lenin to return to Russia in 1917?

The November Revolution Brings the Bolsheviks to Power

Lenin threw himself into the work of furthering the revolution. Another dynamic Marxist revolutionary, Leon Trotsky, helped lead the fight. To the hungry, war-weary Russian people, Lenin and the Bolsheviks promised "Peace, Land, and Bread."

The Provisional Government's Mistakes Meanwhile, the provisional government, led by Alexander Kerensky, continued the war effort and failed to deal with land reform. Those decisions proved fatal. Most Russians were tired of war. Troops at the front were deserting in droves. Peasants wanted land, while city workers demanded an end to the desperate shortages.

In July 1917, the government launched the disastrous Kerensky offensive against Germany. By November, according to one official report, the army was "a huge crowd of tired, poorly clad, poorly fed, embittered men." Growing numbers of troops mutinied. Peasants seized land and drove off fearful landlords.

The Bolshevik Takeover Conditions were ripe for the Bolsheviks to make their move. In November 1917, squads of Red Guards—armed factory workers—joined mutinous sailors from the Russian fleet in attacking the provisional government. In just a matter of days, Lenin's forces overthrew the provisional government without a struggle.

The Bolsheviks quickly seized power in other cities. In Moscow, it took a week of fighting to blast the local government out of the walled Kremlin, the former tsarist center of government. Moscow became the Bolsheviks' capital, and the Kremlin their headquarters.

"We shall now occupy ourselves in Russia in building up a proletarian socialist state," declared Lenin. The Bolsheviks ended private ownership of land and distributed land to peasants. Workers were given control of the factories and mines. A new red flag with an entwined hammer and sickle symbolized union between workers and peasants. Throughout the land, millions thought they had at last gained control over their own lives. In fact, the Bolsheviks—renamed Communists—would soon become their new masters.

✔ **Checkpoint**　How were the Bolsheviks able to seize power from the provisional government?

Tsar Nicholas II (left), preoccupied by war, neglected unrest at home. Revolts erupted in March 1917 in response to poor leadership and equipment on the front and lack of food at home. ▶

Russia Plunges Into Civil War

After the Bolshevik Revolution, Lenin quickly sought peace with Germany. Russia signed the Treaty of Brest-Litovsk in March 1918, giving up a huge chunk of its territory and its population. The cost of peace was extremely high, but the Communist leaders knew that they needed all their energy to defeat a collection of enemies at home. Russia's <u>withdrawal</u> affected the hopes of both the Allies and the Central Powers, as you read in Section 3.

Opposing Forces For three years, civil war raged between the "Reds," as the Communists were known, and the counterrevolutionary "Whites." The "White" armies were made up of tsarist imperial officers, Mensheviks, democrats, and others, all of whom were united only by their desire to defeat the Bolsheviks. Nationalist groups from many of the former empire's non-Russian regions joined them in their fight. Poland, Estonia, Latvia, and Lithuania broke free, but nationalists in Ukraine, the Caucasus, and Central Asia were eventually subdued.

The Allies intervened in the civil war. They hoped that the Whites might overthrow the Communists and support the fight against Germany. Britain, France, and the United States sent forces to help the Whites. Japan seized land in East Asia that tsarist Russia had once claimed. The Allied presence, however, did little to help the Whites. The Reds appealed to nationalism and urged Russians to drive out the foreigners. In the long run, the Allied invasion fed Communist distrust of the West.

▲ The victorious Reds' symbol of worker and farmer unity—the hammer and sickle—comes to represent the new regime.

Thinking Critically
1. **Identify Central Issues** Describe Russia's performance in World War I.
2. **Draw Conclusions** How did involvement in World War I affect events within Russia?

Brutality was common in the civil war. Counterrevolutionary forces slaughtered captured Communists and tried to assassinate Lenin. The Communists shot the former tsar and tsarina and their five children in July 1918 to keep them from becoming a rallying symbol for counterrevolutionary forces.

War Under Communism The Communists used terror not only against the Whites, but also to control their own people. They organized the **Cheka,** a secret police force much like the tsar's. The Cheka executed ordinary citizens, even if they were only suspected of taking action against the revolution. The Communists also set up a network of forced-labor camps in 1919—which grew under Stalin into the dreaded Gulag.

The Communists adopted a policy known as "war communism." They took over banks, mines, factories, and railroads. Peasants in the countryside were forced to deliver almost all of their crops to feed the army and hungry people in the cities. Peasant laborers were drafted into the military or forced to work in factories.

Meanwhile, Trotsky turned the Red Army into an effective fighting force. He used former tsarist officers under the close watch of **commissars,** Communist party officials assigned to the army to teach party principles and ensure party loyalty. Trotsky's passionate speeches roused soldiers to fight. So did the order to shoot every tenth man if a unit performed poorly.

The Reds' position in the center of Russia gave them a strategic advantage. The White armies were forced to attack separately from all sides. They were never able to cooperate effectively with one another. By 1921, the Communists had managed to defeat their scattered foes.

 **Checkpoint** How did the Red army defeat the White army to end the civil war?

Building the Communist Soviet Union

Russia was in chaos. Millions of people had died since the beginning of World War I. Millions more perished from famine and disease. Lenin faced the enormous problem of rebuilding a shattered state and economy.

New Government, Same Problems In 1922, Lenin's Communist government united much of the old Russian empire into the Union of Soviet Socialist Republics (USSR), or Soviet Union. The Communists produced a constitution that seemed both democratic and socialist. It set up an elected legislature, later called the Supreme Soviet, and gave all citizens over 18 the right to vote. All political power, resources, and means of production would belong to workers and peasants. The Soviet Union was a multinational state made up of European and Asian peoples. In theory, all the member republics shared certain equal rights.

Reality, however, differed greatly from theory. The Communist party, not the people, reigned supreme. Just as the Russian tsars had, the party used the army and secret police to enforce its will. Russia, which was the largest republic, dominated the other republics.

Lenin's New Economic Policy On the economic front, Lenin retreated from his policy of "war communism," which had brought the economy to near collapse. Under party control, factory and mine output had fallen. Peasants stopped producing grain, knowing the government would only seize it.

In 1921, Lenin adopted the New Economic Policy, or NEP. It allowed some capitalist ventures. Although the state kept control of banks, foreign trade, and large industries, small businesses were allowed to reopen for private profit. The government also stopped squeezing peasants for grain. Under the NEP, peasants held on to small plots of land and freely sold their surplus crops.

Lenin's compromise with capitalism helped the Soviet economy recover and ended armed resistance to the new government. By 1928, food and industrial production climbed back to prewar levels. The standard of living improved, too. But Lenin always saw the NEP as just a temporary retreat from communism. His successor would soon return the Soviet Union to "pure" communism.

Stalin Takes Over Lenin died in 1924 at the age of 54. His death set off a power struggle among Communist leaders. The chief contenders were Trotsky and Joseph Stalin. Trotsky was a brilliant Marxist thinker, a skillful speaker, and an architect of the Bolshevik Revolution. Stalin, by contrast, was neither a scholar nor an orator. He was, however, a shrewd political operator and behind-the-scenes organizer. Trotsky and Stalin differed on the future of communism. Trotsky urged support for a worldwide revolution against capitalism. Stalin, more cautious, wanted to concentrate on building socialism at home first.

Eventually, Stalin isolated Trotsky within the party and stripped him of party membership. Trotsky fled the country in 1929, but continued to criticize Stalin. In 1940, a Stalinist agent murdered Trotsky in Mexico.

In 1922, Lenin had expressed grave doubts about Stalin's ambitious nature: "Comrade Stalin . . . has concentrated an enormous power in his hands; and I am not sure that he always knows how to use that power with sufficient caution." Just as Lenin had warned, in the years that followed, Stalin used ruthless measures to win dictatorial power.

✔ **Checkpoint** How did the government and the economy under Lenin differ from "pure" communism?

Famine in Russia
Years of war took its toll on Russian people, like these starving families in the Volga region. An American journalist, accompanying an international relief team in Russia, described the horrible desolation. In village after village, he noted, "no one stirred from the little wooden house…where Russian families were hibernating and waiting for death."

Assessment

Terms, People, and Places

1. For each term, person, or place listed at the beginning of the section, write a sentence explaining its significance.

Note Taking

2. **Reading Skill: Summarize** Use your completed timeline to answer the Focus Question: How did two revolutions and a civil war bring about Communist control of Russia?

Comprehension and Critical Thinking

3. **Draw Conclusions** What were the causes of the March Revolution?
4. **Recognize Ideologies** How did Lenin adapt Marxism to conditions in Russia?
5. **Recognize Cause and Effect** What were the causes and effects of the civil war in Russia?
6. **Recognize Effects** Why did Lenin compromise between the ideas of capitalism and communism in creating the NEP?

Writing About History

Quick Write: Clarify Cause-and-Effect Transitions Writing clear transitions can help strengthen your points in a cause-and-effect essay. Connecting words like *since, as soon as, because* and *until* introduce causes. *Therefore, consequently, as a result,* and *then* introduce effects. Rewrite the sentence below to include a clear transition.

- Tsar Nicholas' government collapsed. He did not solve key problems.

Quick Study Guide

Progress Monitoring *Online*
For: Self-test with vocabulary practice
Web Code: naa-2611

■ Causes and Effects of World War I

Cause and Effect

Long-Term Causes	Immediate Causes
• Rivalries among European powers • European alliance system • Militarism and arms race • Nationalist tensions in the Balkans	• Austria-Hungaryís annexation of Bosnia and Herzegovina • Fighting in the Balkans • Assassination of Archduke Francis Ferdinand • Russian mobilization • German invasion of Belgium

World War I

Immediate Effects	Long-Term Effects
• Enormous cost in lives and property • Revolution in Russia • Creation of new nations in Eastern Europe • German reparations • German loss of overseas colonies • Balfour Declaration • League of Nations	• Economic impact of war debts on Europe • Stronger central governments • Emergence of United States and Japan as important powers • Growth of nationalism in colonies • Rise of fascism • Increased anti-Semitism in Germany • World War II

■ The Allies Fight the Central Powers

■ Key Events in the Russian Revolution

1914–1917 World War I pressures Russia.
March 1917 March Revolution causes tsar to abdicate; the provisional government takes power.
November 1917 Bolsheviks under Lenin topple provisional government (November Revolution).

■ Key Events of World War I

June 1914
Archduke Francis Ferdinand and his wife are assassinated in Sarajevo.

1916
More than two million soldiers are killed in the battle of Verdun and the battle of the Somme.

Chapter Events
Global Events

1914   **1915**   **1916**

August 1914
The Panama Canal opens.

January 1915
Japan tries to establish a protectorate over China with the Twenty-One Demands.

Concept Connector

Essential Question Review

To connect prior knowledge with what you have learned in this chapter, answer the questions below in your Concept Connector journal. Use the journal in the Reading and Note Taking Study Guide to record your answers (or go to www.phschool.com **Web Code:** nad-2607).

1. **Conflict** By 1914, the Balkans were known as the "powder keg of Europe." That same year, a Serbian terrorist assassinated Austrian Archduke Francis Ferdinand and his wife. Write a paragraph explaining why, in addition to avenging the assassination, Austria-Hungary and Germany went to war against Serbia. Think about the following:
   - nationalism
   - international rivalries
   - militarism

2. **Revolution** Compare the Russian Revolution and the French Revolution. How were they similar and different? Create a chart comparing the two revolutions in the following categories:
   - causes
   - duration/phases
   - leaders
   - world reaction
   - results

3. **Cooperation** In his farewell address, President George Washington warned against "entangling alliances." Prewar treaties between European powers were intended to promote peace by creating alliances that no country would dare attack. Identify other reasons for the formation of these prewar European alliances. Do you think the true cause of World War I was entangling alliances? Why or why not?

Connections To Today

1. **Conflict: The Balkan Powder Keg** The formation of Yugoslavia after World War I fulfilled the dream of a South Slav state in the Balkans. Yet unrest continued, erupting as recently as 2008. Conduct research and create a timeline of major events in the Balkans from 1918 to the present.

2. **Genocide: Memory and the Armenian Genocide** The Republic of Turkey still maintains that the deportation of the Turkish Armenian population during World War I was a result of civil unrest, not a genocide. Armenian advocacy groups disagree and wage an ongoing campaign for recognition of the Armenians' experience as a planned genocide. Find out where the campaign stands now. Summarize your findings in an essay.

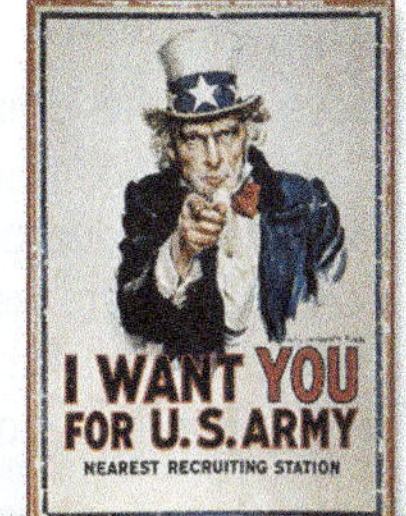

April 1917
The United States joins the Allies.

November 1918
Armistice with Germany ends the war.

April–May 1919
Delegates to the Paris Peace Conference draft the Treaty of Versailles.

1917   **1918**   **1919**

1918–1919
A deadly influenza pandemic sweeps across the world, killing more than 20 million people.

February 1919
The first Pan-African Congress meets in Paris.

History Interactive
For: Interactive timeline
Web Code: nap-2662

Chapter Assessment

Terms, People, and Places

Choose the italicized term in parentheses that best completes each sentence.

1. The Allies tried to regain access to (*Alsace and Lorraine/the Dardanelles*) in the Battle of Gallipoli.
2. After the first battle of the Marne, the war on the Western Front turned into a/an (*entente/stalemate*) until 1918.
3. The British blockade kept both (*contraband/conscription*) and goods like food and clothing from reaching Germany.
4. Both sides used (*reparations/propaganda*) to influence public opinion as a part of total war.
5. After World War I, parts of the Middle East became (*soviets/mandates*) of Britain and France.
6. Lenin wanted to set up a "dictatorship of the (*Fourteen Points/proletariat*)" in Russia.

Main Ideas

Section 1 (pp. 816–821)

7. How did the alliance system that developed in the early 1900s help cause World War I?

Section 2 (pp. 822–828)

8. Describe trench warfare.
9. How did technology affect the way the war was fought?

Section 3 (pp. 829–833)

10. What nation joined the Allied war effort in 1917? What nation dropped out of the war in 1918? How did these two changes affect the war?

Section 4 (pp. 834–838)

11. How did the Treaty of Versailles punish Germany?

Section 5 (pp. 839–845)

12. How did World War I contribute to the collapse of the Russian monarchy?
13. How did the Bolsheviks take power in Russia?

Chapter Focus Question

14. What caused World War I and the Russian Revolution, and what effect did they have on world events?

Critical Thinking

15. **Geography and History** What role did geography play in Germany's war plans?
16. **Synthesize Information** Describe how World War I was a global war.

17. **Analyze Visuals** How did the poster above appeal to the emotions of its intended audience?
18. **Draw Inferences** What do you think Woodrow Wilson meant by "peace without victory"? Why do you think the European Allies were unwilling to accept this idea?
19. **Make Comparisons** In what ways did Soviet communism conform to the teachings of Marx? In what ways did it differ?

● Writing About History

In this chapter's five Section Assessments, you developed skills for writing a Cause-and-Effect Essay.

Writing a Cause-and-Effect Essay World War I was a definitive event of the 1900s. Write an essay in which you analyze the causes and effects of an event that took place during the World War I era. Consider using one of the following topics: Archduke Francis Ferdinand's assassination or Russia's March Revolution.

Prewriting
- Choose the topic listed above that interests you most, or choose another topic that appeals to you.
- Consider multiple causes and immediate and long-term effects of the event you've chosen. Create a cause-and-effect chart to identify your essay's most important points.

Drafting
- Develop a thesis and find information to support it.
- Choose an organizational structure for your essay.
- Write an introduction, several body paragraphs, and a conclusion. State the cause-and-effect relationship you are focusing on clearly in your introduction, and follow up your points in the conclusion.

Revising
- As you review your essay, make sure that each body paragraph supports or develops the cause-and-effect relationship you laid out in your thesis statement.
- Use the guidelines for revising your essay on page SH12 of the Writing Handbook.

Document-Based Assessment

The United States Enters the War

The entry of the United States into the war in April 1917 was a turning point in World War I. The documents below describe different ways that the United States affected the war.

Document A

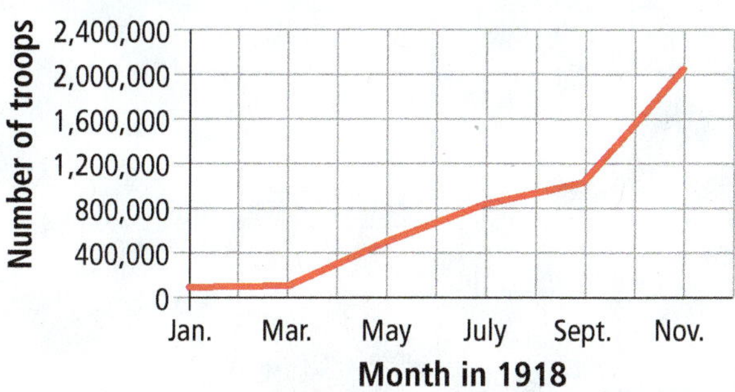

SOURCE: *The First World War: An Eyewitness History*, Joe H. Kirchberger

Document B

"British shipping losses, especially since the declaration of unrestricted submarine warfare, had risen dangerously. . . . But the entry of the United States into the war made the German submarine warfare an evident failure, because thereafter the number of ships convoyed and the number of ships protecting the convoys was increased steadily. Convoys of ships transporting food, war materials, and troops arrived safely in Britain, and the rate of shipping construction soon exceeded the rate of loss."

—From ***The End of the European Era, 1890 to the Present,***
by Felix Gilbert and David Clay Large

Document C

Winston Churchill, who served in Britain's navy and army during World War I, wrote about the effect American troops had on their tired Allies.

"The impression made upon the hard-pressed French by this seemingly inexhaustible flood of gleaming youth in its first maturity of health and vigour was prodigious [amazing]. None were under twenty, and few were over thirty . . . the French Headquarters were thrilled with the impulse of new life. . . . Half trained, half organized, with only their courage, their numbers and their magnificent youth behind their weapons, they were to buy their experience at a bitter price. But this they were quite ready to do."

Document D

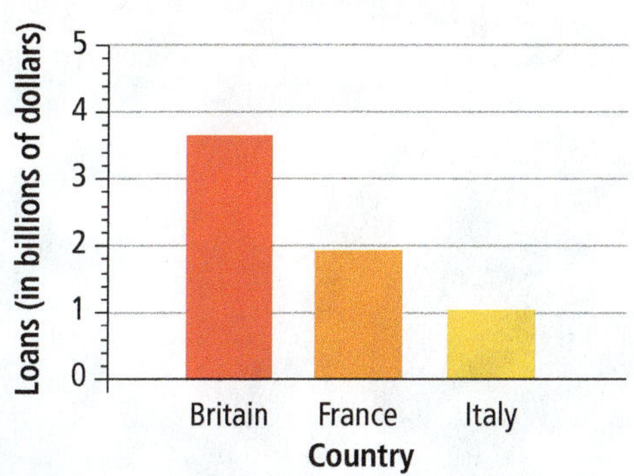

SOURCE: *The End of the European Era, 1890 to the Present*, Felix Gilbert and David Clay Large

Analyzing Documents

Use your knowledge of World War I and Documents A, B, C, and D to answer questions 1–4.

1. How would you describe the arrival of American troops in Europe in 1918?
   A slow at first, but rapid after March
   B steady throughout the year
   C rapid at first, but slow after March
   D No American troops arrived in Europe in 1918.

2. How did the United States navy help break Germany's submarine blockade of Britain?
   A by completely destroying the German submarine fleet
   B by finding new routes around the German submarine fleet
   C by strengthening the convoys
   D by sending supplies to France rather than Britain

3. Based on Document C, how did Churchill feel about American soldiers?
   A They were experienced, but had a poor attitude towards the war.
   B They were energetic and willing to fight, although not experienced.
   C They were well-trained and energetic.
   D They were neither energetic nor experienced.

4. **Writing Task** How did the United States help bring about the Allied victory in 1918? Use your knowledge of World War I and specific evidence from the documents to support your points.

27 Nationalism and Revolution Around the World

1910–1939

Revolution in Mexico

This Mexican peasants' song from the early 1900s reflected many Mexican's desire for change under the rule of the dictator Porfirio Díaz:

> **“**Our homes and humble dwellings
> always full of sadness
> living like animals
> in the midst of riches.
> On the other hand, the haciendados,
> owners of lives and lands,
> appear disinterested
> and don't listen to our complaints.**”**

Listen to the Witness History audio to learn more about the Mexican Revolution.

◀ General Carranza with some of his rebel forces during the Mexican Revolution

Chapter Preview

Chapter Focus Question How did nationalism and the desire for change shape world events in the early 1900s?

Section 1
Struggle in Latin America

Section 2
Nationalism in Africa and the Middle East

Section 3
India Seeks Self-Rule

Section 4
Upheavals in China

Section 5
Conflicting Forces in Japan

Use the  **Quick Study Timeline** at the end of this chapter to preview chapter events.

Mexico's Coat of Arms

Beaded elephant mask from Africa

Japan's naval flag

 **Concept Connector** ONLINE

To explore Essential Questions related to this chapter, go to PHSchool.com
Web Code: nad-2707

Mexican peasant revolutionaries

Coffee beans, one of Latin America's major export crops

Fighting for an Ideal

Zeferino Diego Ferreira, a peasant soldier at the time of the Mexican Revolution, describes his feelings on fighting with the rebel leaders Pancho Villa and Emiliano Zapata:

> 66 I am glad to have fought in the same cause with Zapata . . . and so many of my dear revolutionary friends who were left behind in the hills, their bones eaten by animals. I wasn't afraid. Just the opposite, I was *glad*. It's a *beautiful* thing to fight to realize an ideal. 99

Mexico's revolution was a dramatic fight for reform, with mixed results.

Focus Question How did Latin Americans struggle for change in the early 1900s?

Struggle in Latin America

Objectives

- Identify the causes and effects of the Mexican Revolution.
- Describe the Institutional Revolutionary Party (PRI) and the reforms it introduced in Mexico after the revolution.
- Analyze the effects of nationalism in Latin America in the 1920s and 1930s.

Terms, People, and Places

haciendas	cultural nationalism
nationalization	Good Neighbor Policy
economic nationalism	

Note Taking

Reading Skill: Identify Causes and Effects
As you read, note the causes and effects of the Mexican Revolution in a chart like the one below.

In the early 1900s, Latin America's economy was booming because of exports. Latin Americans sold their plentiful natural resources and cash crops to industrialized countries. In return, they bought products made in those countries. Meanwhile, foreign investors controlled many of Latin America's natural resources.

Stable governments helped to keep the region's economy on a good footing. Some Latin American nations, such as Argentina and Uruguay, had democratic constitutions. However, military dictators or small groups of wealthy landowners held the real power. The tiny ruling class kept the economic benefits of the booming economy for themselves. The growing middle class and the lower classes—workers and peasants—had no say in their own government. These inequalities troubled many Latin American countries, but in Mexico the situation led to an explosive revolution.

The Mexican Revolution

By 1910, the dictator Porfirio Díaz had ruled Mexico for almost 35 years, winning reelection as president again and again. On the surface, Mexico enjoyed peace and economic growth. Díaz welcomed foreign investors who developed mines, built railroads, and drilled for oil. However, underneath the surface, discontent rippled through Mexico. The country's prosperity benefited only a small group. Most Mexicans were mestizos or Indian peasants who lived in desperate poverty. Most of these peasants worked on **haciendas,** or large plantations, controlled by the landowning elite. Some peasants earned meager wages in factories and mines in Mexico's cities. Meanwhile, the growing urban middle class wanted democracy and the elite resented the power of foreign companies. All of these groups opposed the Diáz dictatorship.

The unrest boiled over in 1910 when Francisco Madero, a liberal reformer from an elite family, demanded free elections. Faced with rebellion in several parts of the country, Díaz resigned in 1911. Soon a bloody, complex struggle engulfed Mexico. (See below.)

✓ **Checkpoint** **What political and economic factors helped to cause the Mexican Revolution?**

INFOGRAPHIC

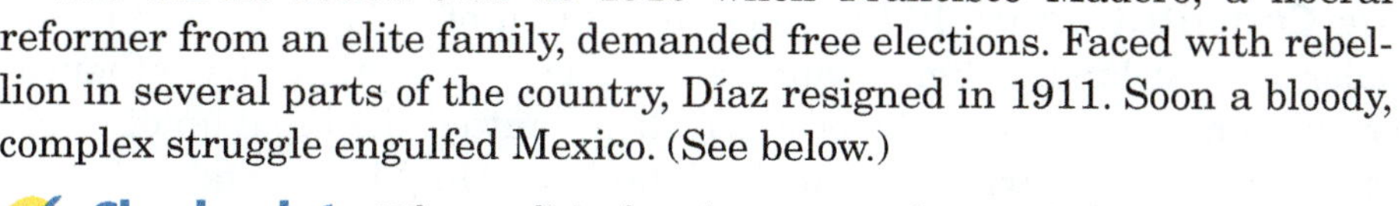

THE MEXICAN REVOLUTION

Fighting raged across Mexico for over a decade. Peasants, small farmers, ranchers, and urban workers were drawn into the violent struggle. Women soldiers called *soldaderas* cooked, tended the wounded, and fought alongside the men. The struggle took a terrible toll. When it ended, the Mexican economy was in shambles and more than one million people were dead.

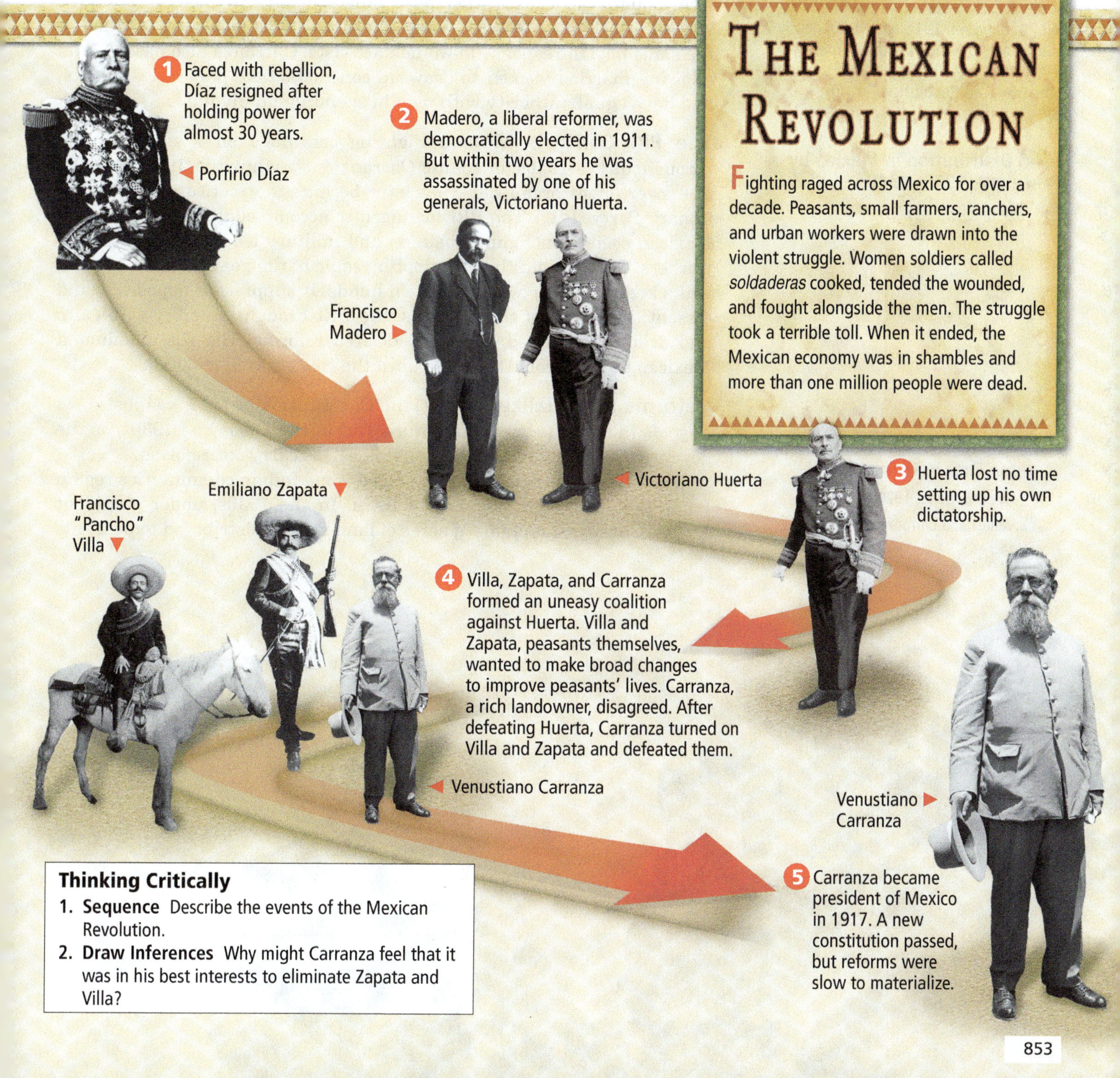

Thinking Critically

1. **Sequence** Describe the events of the Mexican Revolution.
2. **Draw Inferences** Why might Carranza feel that it was in his best interests to eliminate Zapata and Villa?

Revolution Leads to Change

In 1917, voters elected Venustiano Carranza president of Mexico. That year, Carranza reluctantly approved a new constitution that included land and labor reform. With amendments, it is still in force today.

The Constitution of 1917 The Constitution of 1917 addressed three major issues: land, religion, and labor. The constitution strengthened government control over the economy. It permitted the breakup of large estates, placed restrictions on foreigners owning land, and allowed **nationalization,** or government takeover, of natural resources. Church land was made "the property of the nation." The constitution set a minimum wage and protected workers' right to strike.

Although the constitution gave suffrage only to men, it did give women some rights. Women doing the same job as men were entitled to the same pay. In response to women activists, Carranza also passed laws allowing married women to draw up contracts, take part in legal suits, and have equal authority with men in spending family funds.

The PRI Controls Mexico Fighting continued on a smaller scale throughout the 1920s, including Carranza's overthrow in 1920. In 1929, the government organized what later became the Institutional Revolutionary Party (PRI). The PRI managed to accommodate many groups in Mexican society, including business and military leaders, peasants, and workers. The PRI did this by adopting some of the goals of these groups, while keeping real power in its own hands. It suppressed opposition and dissent. Using all of these tactics, the PRI brought stability to Mexico and over time carried out many desired reforms. The PRI dominated Mexican politics from the 1930s until the free election of 2000.

Reforms Materialize At first, the Constitution of 1917 was just a set of goals to be achieved in the future. But in the 1920s and 1930s, as the government finally restored order, it began to carry out reforms.

In the 1920s, the government helped some Indian communities regain lands that had been taken from them. In the 1930s, under President Lázaro Cárdenas, millions of acres of land were redistributed to peasants

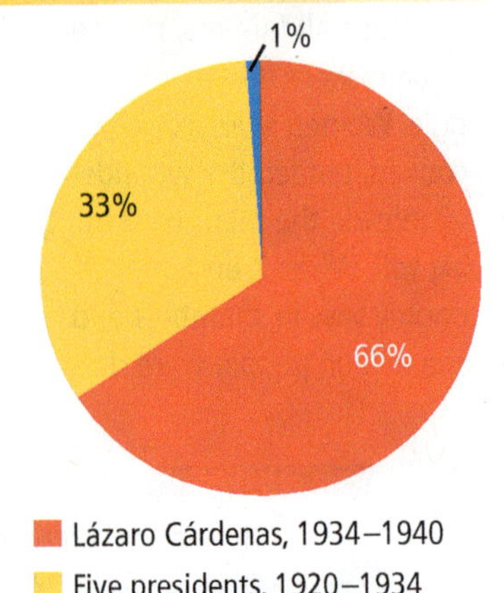

A President of the People

Mexican President Lázaro Cárdenas greets people at a train station in the 1930s (below). Between 1915 and 1940, nearly 75 million acres of land was distributed to Mexico's people, fulfilling one of the goals of the Mexican Revolution. *Which president distributed the most land?*

Land Distribution in Mexico by President, 1915–1940

- ■ Lázaro Cárdenas, 1934–1940
- ■ Five presidents, 1920–1934
- ■ Venustiano Carranza, 1915–1920

SOURCE: Michael C. Meyer and William L. Sherman, *The Course of Mexican History*

under a communal land program. The government supported labor unions and launched a massive effort to combat illiteracy. Schools and libraries were set up. Dedicated teachers, often young women, worked for low pay. While they taught basic skills, they spread ideas of nationalism that began to bridge the gulf between the regions and the central government. As the revolutionary era ended, Mexico became the first Latin American nation to pursue real social and economic reforms for the majority of its people.

The government also took a strong role in directing the economy. In 1938, labor disputes broke out between Mexican workers and the management of some foreign-owned petroleum companies. In response, President Cárdenas decreed that the Mexican government would nationalize Mexico's oil resources. American and British oil companies resisted Cárdenas's decision, but eventually accepted compensation for their losses. Mexicans felt that they had at last gained economic independence from foreign influence.

 **Checkpoint** How did the Constitution of 1917 try to resolve some of the problems that started the revolution?

Nationalism at Work in Latin America

Mexico's move to reclaim its oil fields from foreign investors reflected a growing spirit of nationalism throughout Latin America. This spirit focused in part on ending economic dependence on the industrial powers, especially the United States, but it echoed throughout political and cultural life as well.

Economic Nationalism During the 1920s and 1930s, world events affected Latin American economies. After World War I, trade with Europe fell off. The Great Depression that struck the United States in 1929 spread around the world in the 1930s. Prices for Latin American exports plunged as demand dried up. At the same time, the cost of imported consumer goods rose. Latin America's economies, dependent on export trade, declined rapidly.

A tide of economic nationalism, or emphasis on home control of the economy, swept Latin American countries. They were determined to develop their own industries so they would not have to buy so many products from other countries. Local entrepreneurs set up factories to produce goods. Governments raised tariffs, or taxes on imports, to protect the new industries. Governments also invested directly in new businesses. Following Mexico's lead, some nations took over foreign-owned assets. The drive to create domestic industries was not wholly successful. Unequal distribution of wealth held back economic development.

Political Nationalism The Great Depression also triggered political changes in Latin America. The economic crisis caused people to lose faith in the ruling oligarchies and the ideas of liberal government. Liberalism, a belief in the individual and in limited government, was a European theory. People began to feel that it did not work in Latin America. However, ideas about what form a new type of government should take varied.

In the midst of economic crisis, stronger, authoritarian governments of different types rose in Latin American countries. People hoped that these governments could control, direct, and protect each country's economy more effectively.

Vocabulary Builder

assets—(AS ets) *n.* things of value

Note Taking

Identify Effects As you read, identify the effects of nationalism in Latin America and record them a chart like the one below.

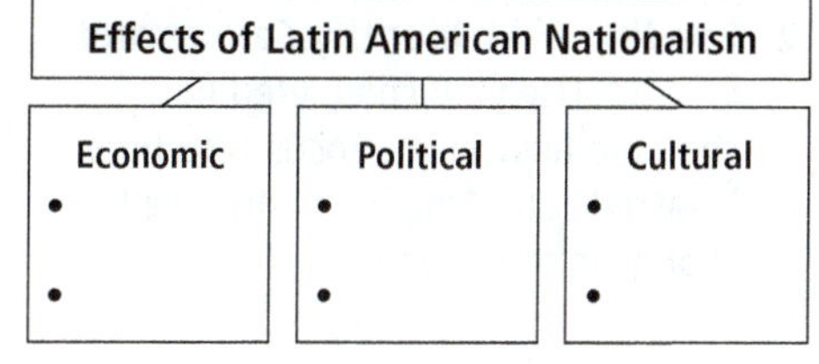

Effects of Latin American Nationalism		
Economic	Political	Cultural

Mexico's Heritage
This stained glass image shows one variation of the Mexican coat of arms that appears on Mexico's flag today. An ancient prophecy dictated that the Aztec capital should be founded where scouts saw an eagle perched on a cactus growing out of a rock surrounded by water, holding a snake in its beak. Accordingly, the founders of Tenochtitlán were believed to have seen this sign in 1325 at the site of present-day Mexico City. The symbol is an emblem of Mexican nationalism. *Why do you think that an Aztec symbol is included on the Mexican flag?*

Vocabulary Builder
intervening—(in tur VEEN ing) *vi.*
coming between two arguing factions

Cultural Nationalism By the 1920s, Latin American writers, artists, and thinkers began to reject European influences in culture as well. Instead, they took pride in their own culture, with its blend of Western and native traditions.

In Mexico, cultural nationalism, or pride in one's own culture, was reflected in the revival of mural painting, a major art form of the Aztecs and Maya. In the 1920s and 1930s, Diego Rivera, José Clemente Orozco (oh ROHS koh), David Alfaro Siqueiros (see KEH rohs), and other muralists created magnificent works. On the walls of public buildings, they portrayed the struggles of the Mexican people for liberty. The murals have been a great source of national pride ever since.

The Good Neighbor Policy During and after World War I, investments by the United States in the nations of Latin America soared. British influence declined. The United States continued to play the role of international policeman, intervening to restore order when it felt its interests were threatened.

During the Mexican Revolution, the United States stepped in to support the leaders who favored American interests. In 1914, the United States attacked the port of Veracruz to punish Mexico for imprisoning several American sailors. In 1916, the U.S. army invaded Mexico after Pancho Villa killed more than a dozen Americans in New Mexico. This interference stirred up anti-American feelings, which increased throughout Latin America during the 1920s. For example, in Nicaragua, Augusto César Sandino led a guerrilla movement against United States forces occupying his country.

In the 1930s, President Franklin Roosevelt took a new approach to Latin America and pledged to follow "the policy of the good neighbor." Under the Good Neighbor Policy, the United States pledged to lessen its interference in the affairs of Latin American nations. The United States withdrew troops stationed in Haiti and Nicaragua. It lifted the Platt Amendment, which had limited Cuban independence. Roosevelt also supported Mexico's nationalization of its oil companies. The Good Neighbor policy strengthened Latin American nationalism and improved relations between Latin America and the United States.

 **Checkpoint** Describe how economic and political nationalism in Latin America were related.

Progress Monitoring *Online*
For: Self-quiz with vocabulary practice
Web Code: naa-2711

Terms, People, and Places

1. What do each of the key terms listed at the beginning of the section, except "haciendas," have in common? Explain.

Note Taking

2. **Reading Skill: Identify Causes and Effects** Use your completed flow-charts to answer the Focus Question: How did Latin Americans struggle for change in the early 1900s?

Comprehension and Critical Thinking

3. **Recognize Causes** Describe three causes of the Mexican Revolution.

4. **Analyze Credibility** How did the PRI fulfill some goals of the revolution but not others?

5. **Identify Central Issues** How did nationalism affect Latin America?

6. **Summarize** How did Franklin Roosevelt change the policy of the United States toward Latin America?

● **Writing About History**

Quick Write: Write a Thesis Statement
A persuasive essay seeks to convince its reader to accept the writer's position on a topic. To be effective, the thesis statement must state a position that provokes valid arguments. Write an effective thesis statement on the topic of economic nationalism in Latin America.

Mexican Murals

Diego Rivera ▶

During the 1920s and 1930s, the Mexican government commissioned artists to paint beautiful murals about revolutionary themes on the walls of public buildings. The murals were meant to help all Mexicans, even those who couldn't read, learn about the ideals of the Revolution.

The most famous Mexican muralist was Diego Rivera. The panel to the right is part of a huge work on Mexican history that Rivera painted on the stairway of the National Palace in Mexico City.

Zapata, Villa, and other revolutionaries appear at the top of the panel, holding a banner that reads "Tierra y Libertad" ("Land and Liberty")—Zapata's slogan.

The center of the composition shows an eagle sitting on a cactus. The eagle is part of a national symbol of Mexico. A variation of it appears on the current Mexican flag. However, here, the eagle holds the Aztec war symbol in its beak rather than the traditional serpent.

The bottom segment shows the conquest of Mexico by Hernán Cortés. Cortés's armies battle the native Aztecs.

Thinking Critically

1. **Make Inferences** Why do you think Diego Rivera has the Mexican eagle holding the Aztec war symbol rather than the serpent?
2. **Draw Conclusions** What do Rivera's murals reveal about how he viewed Mexican history?

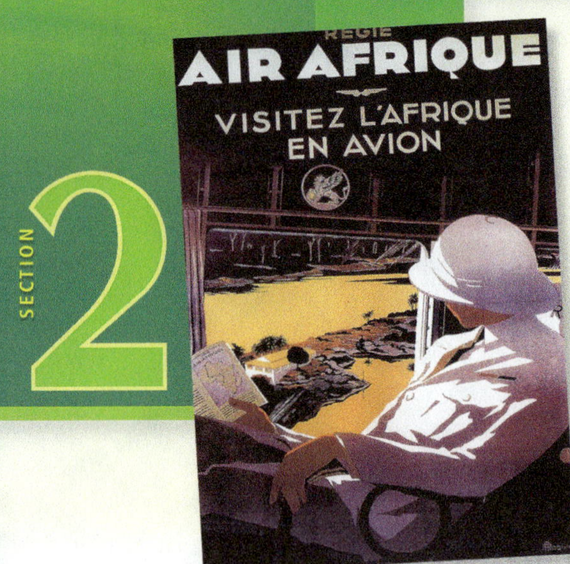

A French poster urges Europeans to visit Africa.

An African Protests Colonialism

❝If you woke up one morning and found that somebody had come to your house, and had declared that house belonged to him, you would naturally be surprised, and you would like to know by what arrangement. Many Africans at that time found that, on land that had been in the possession of their ancestors from time immemorial, they were now working as squatters or as laborers.**❞**

—Jomo Kenyatta, Kenyan independence leader

Focus Question How did nationalism contribute to changes in Africa and the Middle East following World War I?

Nationalism in Africa and the Middle East

Objectives
- Describe how Africans resisted colonial rule.
- Analyze how nationalism grew in Africa.
- Explain how Turkey and Persia modernized.
- Summarize how European mandates contributed to the growth of Arab nationalism.
- Understand the roots of conflict between Jews and Arabs in the Palestinian mandate.

Terms, People, and Places

apartheid	Asia Minor
Pan-Africanism	Pan-Arabism
négritude movement	Balfour Declaration

Note Taking

Reading Skill: Identify Causes and Effects Record reasons for the rise of nationalism in Africa and the Middle East and its effects in a chart like the one below.

Rise of Nationalism		
Region	**Reasons for Rise**	**Effects**
Africa		
Turkey and Persia		
Middle East		

Jomo Kenyatta, quoted above, was a leader in Kenya's struggle for independence from British rule. During the 1920s and 1930s, a new generation of leaders, proud of their unique heritage, struggled to stop imperialism and restore Africa for Africans.

Africans Resist Colonial Rule

During the early 1900s, almost every part of Africa was a European colony. Agricultural improvements in some areas caused a boom in export crops. However, the colonizers exploited the boom solely for their own benefit.

Some Africans were forced to work on plantations or in mines run by Europeans. The money they earned went to pay taxes to the colonial government. In Kenya and Rhodesia, white settlers forced Africans off the best land. The few who kept their land were forbidden to grow the most profitable crops. Only Europeans could grow these. Also in Kenya, the British made all Africans carry identification cards, imposed a tax, and restricted where they could live or travel. In other parts of Africa, farmers kept their land but had to grow cash crops, like cotton, instead of food. This led to famines in some regions.

During World War I, more than one million Africans had fought on behalf of their colonial rulers. Many had hoped that their service would lead to more rights and opportunities. Instead, the situation remained mostly the same or even worsened.

Opposing Imperialism Many Western-educated Africans criticized the injustice of imperial rule. Although they had trained for professional careers, the best jobs went to Europeans. Inspired by President Woodrow Wilson's call for self-determination, Africans condemned the colonial system. In Africa, as in other regions around the world, socialism found a growing audience. Protests and opposition to imperialism multiplied.

Racial Segregation and Nationalism in South Africa Between 1910 and 1940, whites strengthened their grip on South Africa. They imposed a system of racial segregation. Their goal was to ensure white economic, political, and social supremacy. New laws, for example, restricted better-paying jobs in mines to whites only. Blacks were pushed into low-paid, less-skilled work. As in Kenya, South African blacks had to carry passes at all times. They were evicted from the best land, which was set aside for whites, and forced to live on crowded "reserves," which were located in dry, infertile areas.

Other laws chipped away at the rights of blacks. In one South African province, educated blacks who owned property had been allowed to vote in local elections. In 1936, the government abolished that right. The system of segregation set up at this time would become even stricter after 1948, when **apartheid** (uh PAHR tayt), a policy of rigid segregation, became law.

Yet South Africa was also home to a vital nationalist movement. African Christian churches and African-run newspapers demanded rights for black South Africans. They formed a political party, later known as the African National Congress (ANC), to protest unfair laws. Their efforts, however, had no effect on South Africa's white government. Still, the ANC did build a framework for political action in later years.

✔ **Checkpoint** In what ways did colonial powers try to control African life?

Nationalism and an "Africa for Africans"

In the 1920s, a movement known as **Pan-Africanism** began to nourish the nationalist spirit and strengthen resistance. Pan-Africanism emphasized the unity of Africans and people of African descent worldwide. Among its most inspiring leaders was Jamaica-born Marcus Garvey. He preached a forceful, appealing message of "Africa for Africans" and

Segregation in South Africa
In the early 1900s, white people in South Africa began to force urban Africans to move to camps outside of the larger cities, such as this settlement outside of Cape Town. *Why do you think that the white people have forced the African people behind a barbed wire fence?*

African Resistance

Opposition to imperialism grew among Africans in the 1920s and 1930s. Resistance took many forms. Those who had lost their lands to Europeans sometimes squatted, or settled illegally, on European-owned plantations. In cities, workers began to form labor unions, even though they were illegal under colonial law codes. Africans formed associations and political parties to express their opposition to the colonial system. Although large-scale revolts were rare, protests were common.

Nigeria

In 1929, Ibo market women in Nigeria denounced British policies. They demanded a voice in decisions that affected their markets (below). The "Women's War," as it was called, soon became a full-fledged revolt.

South Africa

In 1912, Pixley Ka Isaka Seme organized a political party that later became the African National Congress (ANC). Its members worked through legal means, protesting laws that restricted the freedom of black Africans.

demanded an end to colonial rule. Garvey's ideas influenced a new generation of African leaders.

Pan-African Congress Forges Ties African American scholar and activist W.E.B. DuBois (doo BOYS) organized the first Pan-African Congress in 1919. It met in Paris, where the Allies were holding their peace conference. Delegates from African colonies, the West Indies, and the United States called on the Paris peacemakers to approve a charter of rights for Africans. Although the Western powers ignored their demands, the Pan-African Congress established cooperation among African and African American leaders.

The Négritude Movement Shows Pride French-speaking writers in West Africa and the Caribbean further awakened self-confidence among Africans through the **négritude movement.** In the négritude movement, writers expressed pride in their African roots and protested colonial rule. Best known among them was the Senegalese poet Léopold Senghor, who celebrated Africa's rich cultural heritage. He fostered African pride by rejecting the negative views of Africa spread by colonial rulers. Later, Senghor would take an active role in Senegal's drive to independence, and he would serve as its first president.

Egypt Gains Independence African nationalism brought little political change, except to Egypt. Egyptians had suffered during World War I. After the war, protests, strikes, and riots forced Britain to grant Egypt independence in 1922. However, Britain still controlled Egypt's monarchy.

Egypt

Simmering resistance to British rule in Egypt flared as World War I ended. Peasants, landowners, Christians, Muslims and Western-educated officials united behind the Wafd party, which launched strikes and protests (right). In 1922, the British finally agreed to declare Egypt independent. In fact, however, British troops stayed in Egypt to guard the Suez Canal, and Britain remained the real power behind Egypt's King Faud.

Kenya

Members of the Kikuyu ethnic group formed the Kikuyu Central Association in 1924. The Association protested the Kikuyu's loss of land, forced labor, heavy taxes, and the hated identification cards. The British jailed Harry Thuku (right) and other Kikuyu leaders, but protests continued.

Thinking Critically

1. **Make Comparisons** How did the methods of the ANC in South Africa differ from the Wafd party in Egypt?
2. **Determine Relevance** Why is it important to learn about early protest movements in Africa, despite the fact that most colonies did not gain independence until after World War II?

Displeased with this state of affairs, during the 1930s many young Egyptians joined an organization called the Muslim Brotherhood. This group fostered a broad Islamic nationalism that rejected Western culture and denounced corruption in the Egyptian government.

 **Checkpoint** What significance does the phrase "Africa for Africans" have?

Turkey and Persia Modernize

Nationalist movements brought immense changes to the Middle East in the aftermath of World War I. The defeated Ottoman empire was near collapse in 1918. Its Arab lands, as you have read, were divided between Britain and France. However, in **Asia Minor,** the Turkish peninsula between the Black Sea and the Mediterranean Sea, Turks resisted Western control and fought to build a modern nation.

Atatürk Sets Goals In 1920, the Ottoman sultan reluctantly signed the Treaty of Sèvres, in which the empire lost its Arab and North African lands. The sultan also had to give up some land in Asia Minor to a number of Allied countries, including Greece. A Greek force landed in the city of Smyrna (now Izmir) to <u>assert</u> Greece's claims. Turkish nationalists, led by the determined and energetic Mustafa Kemal, overthrew the sultan, defeated the Greeks, and declared Turkey a republic. Kemal negotiated a new treaty. Among other provisions, the treaty called for about 1.3 million Greeks to leave Turkey, while some 400,000 Turks left Greece.

Vocabulary Builder

<u>assert</u>—(uh SURT) *vt.* maintain or defend

Atatürk (1881–1938)

"Atatürk" is the name that Mustafa Kemal gave himself when he ordered all Turkish people to take on surnames, or last names. It means "Father of the Turks." In 1920, he led Turkish nationalists in the fight against Greek forces trying to enforce the Treaty of Sèvres, establishing the borders of the modern Republic of Turkey. Once in power, he passed many reforms to modernize, Westernize, and secularize Turkey. Atatürk is still honored throughout Turkey today—his portrait appears on postage and all currency. **Why is Atatürk considered the "Father of the Turks"?**

Atatürk's Reforms in Turkey

- Replaced Islamic law with European model
- Replaced Muslim calendar with Western (Christian) calendar
- Moved day of rest from Friday to Sunday
- Closed religious schools and opened state schools
- Forced people to wear Western-style clothes
- Replaced Arabic alphabet with Latin alphabet
- Gave women the right to vote and to work outside the home.

Kemal later took the name Atatürk (ah tah TURK), meaning "father of the Turks." Between 1923 and his death in 1938, Atatürk forced through an ambitious program of radical reforms. His goals were to modernize Turkey along Western lines and to separate religion from government. To achieve these goals, Atatürk mandated that Islamic traditions in several fields be replaced with Western alternatives (see Biography).

Westernization Transforms Turkey Atatürk's government encouraged industrial expansion. The government built railroads, set up factories, and hired westerners to advise on how to make Turkey economically independent.

To achieve his reforms, Atatürk ruled with an iron hand. To many Turks, he was a hero who was transforming Turkey into a strong, modern power. Others questioned Atatürk's dictatorial powers and complete rejection of religion in laws and government. They believed that Islam could play a constructive role in a modern, civil state.

Nationalism and Reform at Work in Persia The success of Atatürk's reforms inspired nationalists in neighboring Persia (present-day Iran). Persian nationalists greatly resented the British and Russians, who had won spheres of influence over Persia in 1907. In 1925, an ambitious army officer, Reza Khan, overthrew the shah. He set up his own dynasty, with himself as shah.

Like Atatürk, Reza Khan rushed to modernize Persia and make it fully independent. He built factories, roads, and railroads and strengthened the army. He forced Persians to wear Western clothing and set up modern, secular schools. In addition, he moved to replace Islamic law with secular law and encouraged women to take part in public life. Muslim religious leaders fiercely condemned Reza Khan's efforts to introduce Western ways to the nation.

Reza Khan also persuaded the British company that controlled Persia's oil industry to give Persia a larger share of the profits and insisted that Persian workers be hired at all levels of the company. In the decades ahead, oil would become a major factor in Persia's economy and foreign policy.

✔ **Checkpoint** What did the reforms of Atatürk and Reza Khan have in common?

Arab Nationalism in the Middle East

Oil became a major factor throughout the Middle East during this period. The use of gasoline-powered engines in various vehicles during World War I showed that oil was the fuel of the future. Foreign companies began to move into the Middle East to exploit its large oil reserves.

Pan-Arabism Grows Partly in response to foreign influence, Arab nationalism grew after World War I and gave rise to **Pan-Arabism.** This nationalist movement was built on the shared heritage of Arabs who lived in lands from the Arabian Peninsula to North Africa. Today, this

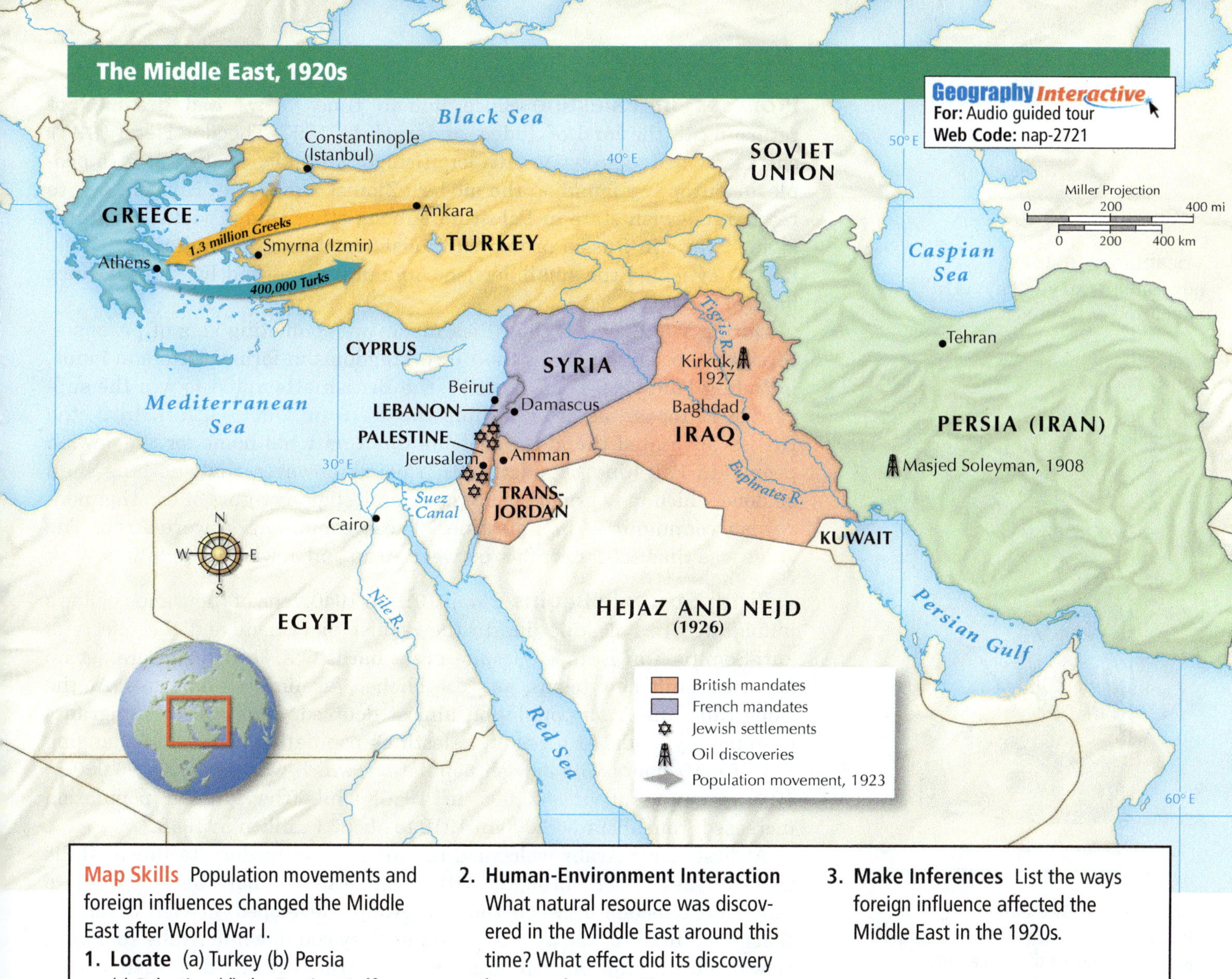

area includes Syria, Jordan, Iraq, Egypt, Algeria, and Morocco. Pan-Arabism emphasized the common history and language of Arabs and recalled the golden age of Arab civilization. The movement sought to free Arabs from foreign domination and unite them in their own state.

Betrayal at the Peace Conference Arabs were outraged by the European-controlled mandates set up at the Paris Peace Conference. During World War I, Arabs had helped the Allies against the Central Powers, especially the Ottoman empire. In return for their help, the Allies led the Arabs to believe that they would gain independence after the war. Instead, the Allies carved up the Ottoman lands, giving France mandates in Syria and Lebanon and Britain mandates in Palestine and Iraq. Later, Britain gave a large part of the Palestinian mandate, Trans-Jordan, to Abdullah for a kingdom.

Arabs felt betrayed by the West—a feeling that has endured to this day. During the 1920s and 1930s, their anger erupted in frequent protests and revolts against Western imperialism. A major center of turmoil was the British mandate of Palestine. There, Arab nationalists and Jewish nationalists, known as Zionists, increasingly clashed.

Promises in Palestine Since Roman times, Jews had dreamed of returning to the land of Judea, or Israel. In 1897, Theodor Herzl (HURT sul) responded to growing anti-Semitism, or prejudice against Jewish people, in Europe by founding the modern Zionist movement. His goal was to rebuild a Jewish state in Palestine. Among other things, violent pogroms against Jews in Russia prompted thousands of them to migrate to Palestine. They joined the small Jewish community that had lived there since biblical times.

During World War I, the Allies made two conflicting sets of promises. First, they promised Arabs their own kingdoms in former Ottoman lands, including Palestine. Then, in 1917, the British attempted to win the support of European Jews by issuing the **Balfour Declaration.** In it, the British advocated the idea of setting up "a national home for the Jewish people" in Palestine. The declaration noted, however, that "nothing shall be done which may prejudice the civil and religious rights of existing non-Jewish communities in Palestine." Those communities were Arab. The stage was thus set for conflict between Arab and Jewish nationalists.

A Bitter Struggle Begins From 1919 to 1940, tens of thousands of Jews immigrated to Palestine due to the Zionist movement and the effects of anti-Semitism in Europe. Despite great hardships, Jewish settlers set up factories, built new towns, and established farming communities. At the same time, the Arab population almost doubled. Some were immigrants from nearby lands. As a result, Palestine's population included a changing mix of newcomers. The Jewish population, which was less than 60,000 in 1919, grew to about 400,000 in 1936, while the Muslim population increased from about 568,000 in 1919 to about 1 million in 1940.

At first, some Arabs welcomed the money and modern technical skills that the newcomers brought with them. But as more Jews moved to Palestine, tensions between the two groups developed. Jewish organizations tried to purchase as much land as they could, while Arabs sought to slow down or stop Jewish immigration. Arabs attacked Jewish settlements, hoping to discourage settlers. The Jewish settlers established their own military defense force. For the rest of the century, Arabs and Jews fought over the land that Arabs called Palestine and Jews called Israel.

✔ **Checkpoint** Why did Palestine become a center of conflict after World War I?

Vocabulary Builder

advocated—(AD vuh kayt id) *v.* supported or favored

Two Views of One Place
Posters encouraged visitors and settlers to go to Palestine. At the same time, Palestinian Arabs tried to limit Jewish settlement in the area.

SECTION 2 Assessment

Progress Monitoring Online
For: Self-quiz with vocabulary practice
Web Code: naa-2721

Terms, People, and Places

1. For each term, person, or place listed at the beginning of the section, write a sentence explaining its significance.

Note Taking

2. **Reading Skill: Identify Causes and Effects** Use your completed chart to answer the Focus Question: How did nationalism contribute to changes in Africa and the Middle East following World War I?

Comprehension and Critical Thinking

3. **Identify Central Issues** How did Africans resist colonial rule?
4. **Summarize** What are three examples of the rise of nationalism in Africa?
5. **Identify Central Issues** Why might Muslim religious leaders object to reforms in Turkey and Persia?
6. **Draw Conclusions** How did the Balfour Declaration affect the Middle East?

● Writing About History

Quick Write: Generate Arguments
When you write a persuasive essay, you want to support your thesis statement with valid, convincing arguments. You'll need to read about your topic in order to formulate your list of arguments. Write down ideas for three arguments supporting the following thesis: The ANC was a valuable political party even though it did not affect the white-run government of South Africa for many years.

A Hindu servant serves tea to his mistress in colonial India.

Indian Frustration

In the early 1900s, many Indians were dissatisfied with British rule. An early leader of the Indian National Congress party expressed his frustration with an unpopular policy to divide the province of Bengal into smaller sections:

> 66 The scheme [to divide Bengal] . . . will always stand as a complete illustration of the worst features of the present system of bureaucratic rule—its utter contempt for public opinion, its arrogant pretensions to superior wisdom, its reckless disregard of the most cherished feelings of the people, the mockery of an appeal to its sense of justice, [and] its cool preference of [British civil service workers'] interests to those of the governed. 99
> —Gopal Krishna Gokhale, 1905

Focus Question How did Gandhi and the Congress party work for independence in India?

India Seeks Self-Rule

Objectives
- Explain what motivated the Indian independence movement after World War I.
- Analyze how Mohandas Gandhi influenced the independence movement.
- Describe the impact of the Salt March on the course of the Indian independence movement.

Terms, People, and Places

Amritsar massacre   untouchables
ahimsa   boycott
civil disobedience

Note Taking

Reading Skill: Identify Causes and Effects
Recognizing causes and effects can help you understand the significance of certain events. In a chart like the one below, record the causes and effects of Gandhi's leadership of India's independence movement.

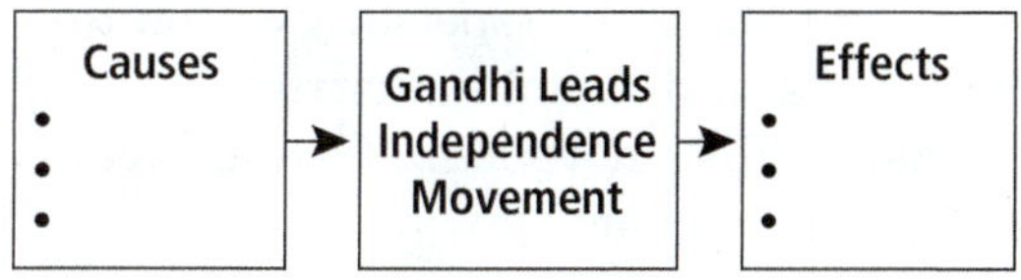

Tensions were running high in Amritsar, a city in northern India. Protests against British rule had sparked riots and attacks on British residents. On April 13, 1919, a large but peaceful crowd of Indians jammed into an enclosed field. The British commander, General Reginald Dyer, had banned public meetings, but the crowd either ignored or had not heard the order. As Indian leaders spoke, Dyer and 50 soldiers opened fire on the unarmed crowd, killing nearly 400 people and wounding more than 1,100. The **Amritsar massacre** was a turning point for many Indians. It convinced them that India needed to govern itself.

Calls for Independence

The tragedy at Amritsar was linked to broader Indian frustrations after World War I. During the war, more than a million Indians had served overseas. Under pressure from Indian nationalists, the British promised Indians greater self-government. But when the fighting ended, Britain proposed only a few minor reforms.

Since 1885, the Indian National Congress party, called the Congress party, had pressed for self-rule within the British empire. After Amritsar, it began to call for full independence. But party members were mostly middle-class, Western-educated elite who had little in common with the masses of Indian peasants. In the 1920s, a new leader named Mohandas Gandhi emerged and united Indians across class lines.

Gandhi came from a middle-class Hindu family. At age 19, he went to England to study law. Then, like many Indians, Gandhi

The Salt March

Gandhi's march to the sea to collect forbidden salt started out with Gandhi and 78 followers, but gathered strength as it progressed. As he picked up the first lump of salt, he declared, "With this, I am shaking the foundations of the British empire." *How do you think people in other countries would have reacted to British authorities using violence against this group?*

Vocabulary Builder

discriminated—(dih SKRIM ih nayt ed) *vi.* treated differently because of a prejudice

went to South Africa. For 20 years, Gandhi fought laws that <u>discriminated</u> against Indians in South Africa. In 1914, Gandhi returned to India. Soon, he became the leader of the Congress party.

 **Checkpoint**   Why did Indians call for independence after World War I?

The Power of Nonviolence

Gandhi's ideas inspired Indians of all religious and ethnic backgrounds. His nonviolent protests caught the attention of the British government and the world.

Gandhi's Ideas Gandhi's theories embraced Hindu traditions. He preached the ancient doctrine of **ahimsa** (uh HIM sah), or nonviolence and reverence for all life. By using the power of love, he believed, people could convert even the worst wrongdoer to the right course of action. To fight against injustice, he advocated the use of nonviolent resistance.

Gandhi's philosophy reflected Western as well as Indian influences. He admired Christian teachings about love. He believed in the American philosopher Henry David Thoreau's ideas about **civil disobedience,** the refusal to obey unjust laws. Gandhi was also influenced by Western ideas of democracy and nationalism. He urged equal rights for all Indians, women as well as men. He fought hard to end the harsh treatment of **untouchables,** who were members of the lowest caste, or class.

Gandhi Sets an Example During the 1920s and 1930s, Gandhi launched a series of nonviolent actions against British rule. He called for Indians to **boycott,** or refuse to buy, British goods, especially cotton textiles. He worked to restore pride in India's traditional industries, making the spinning wheel a symbol of the nationalist movement. Gandhi's campaigns of civil disobedience attracted wide support.

Checkpoint   What methods did Indians under Gandhi use to resist British rule?

Gandhi Takes a Stand: The Salt March

To mobilize mass support, Gandhi decided to take a stand against the British salt monopoly, which he saw as a symbol of British oppression. Natural salt was available in the sea, but the British government required Indians to buy only salt sold by the monopoly.

Breaking the Law On March 12, 1930, Gandhi set out with 78 followers on a 240-mile march to the sea. As the tiny band passed through villages, crowds responded to Gandhi's message. By the time they reached the sea, the marchers numbered in the thousands. On April 6, Gandhi waded into the surf and picked up a lump of sea salt. He was soon arrested and jailed. Still, Indians followed his lead. Coastal villages started collecting salt. Indians sold salt on city streets. As Gandhi's campaign gained force, tens of thousands of Indians were imprisoned.

Steps Toward Freedom All around the world, newspapers criticized Britain's harsh reaction to the protests. Stories revealed how police brutally clubbed peaceful marchers who tried to occupy a government saltworks. Slowly, Gandhi's campaign forced Britain to hand over some power to Indians. Britain also agreed to meet other demands of the Congress party.

 **Checkpoint** What did the Salt March symbolize?

Looking Ahead

In 1939, a new world war exploded. Britain outraged Indian leaders by postponing independence and bringing Indians into the war without consulting them. Angry nationalists launched a campaign of noncooperation and were jailed. Millions of Indians, however, did help Britain during World War II.

When the war ended in 1945, India's independence could no longer be delayed. As it neared, Muslim fears of the Hindu majority increased. Conflict between Hindus and Muslims would trouble the new nation in the years to come.

Progress Monitoring *Online*
For: Self-quiz with vocabulary practice
Web Code: naa-2731

Terms, People, and Places

1. Place each of the key terms listed at the beginning of the section into one of the following categories: politics, culture, or economy. Write a sentence for each term explaining your choice.

Note Taking

2. **Reading Skill: Identify Causes and Effects** Use your completed chart to answer the Focus Question: How did Gandhi and the Congress party work for independence in India?

Comprehension and Critical Thinking

3. **Identify Point of View** How did the Amritsar massacre affect the movement for Indian independence?
4. **Recognize Cause and Effect** Why do you think Gandhi was able to unite Indians when earlier attempts had not succeeded?
5. **Analyze Information** How did the Salt March force Britain to respond to Indian demands?

Writing About History

Quick Write: Use Valid Logic In a persuasive essay, you must back up your conclusions with valid logic. One common pattern of weak logic is circular reasoning, where a writer simply restates ideas instead of defending them. Bring in an example of weak logic from recent editorials in your local paper. Include a paragraph explaining the problems with the author's logic.

Mohandas Gandhi: *Hind Swaraj*

Mohandas Gandhi led a successful, peaceful revolution in India against British rule. In the following excerpt from his book *Hind Swaraj (Indian Home Rule),* Gandhi explains the ideas behind his nonviolent method of passive resistance in the form of an imaginary conversation between an editor and a reader. *Hind Swaraj* was first published in 1909 in South Africa, but was banned in India.

Mohandas Gandhi 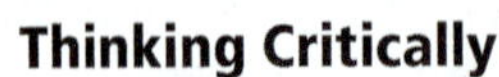

Editor: Passive resistance is a method of securing rights by personal suffering; it is the reverse of resistance by arms. When I refuse to do a thing that is repugnant [offensive] to my conscience, I use soul-force. For instance, the government of the day has passed a law which is applicable to me. I do not like it. If by using violence, I force the government to repeal the law, I am employing what may be termed body-force. If I do not obey the law, and accept the penalty for its breach, I use soul-force. It involves sacrifice of self.

Everybody admits that sacrifice of self is infinitely superior to sacrifice of others. Moreover, if this kind of force is used in a cause that is unjust, only the person using it suffers. He does not make others suffer for his mistakes. Men have before now done many things which were subsequently found to have been wrong. No man can claim that he is absolutely in the right, or that a particular thing is wrong, because he thinks so, but it is wrong for him so long as that is his deliberate judgment. It is therefore meet [proper] that he should not do that which he knows to be wrong, and suffer the consequence whatever it may be. This is the key to the use of soul-force.

Reader: You would then disregard laws—this is rank disloyalty. We have always been considered a law-abiding nation. You seem to be going even beyond the extremists. They say that we must obey the laws that have been passed, but that, if the laws be bad, we must drive out the lawgivers even by force.

Editor: Whether I go beyond them or whether I do not is a matter of no consequence to either of us. We simply want to find out what is right, and to act accordingly. The real meaning of the statement that we are a law-abiding nation is that we are passive resisters. When we do not like certain laws, we do not break the heads of law-givers, but we suffer and do not submit to the laws.

Thinking Critically

1. **Identify Central Issues** What is the goal of passive resistance?
2. **Draw Conclusions** According to Gandhi, could soul-force ever be used to support an unjust cause? What does Gandhi mean when he says that a person using soul-force "does not make others suffer for his mistakes"?

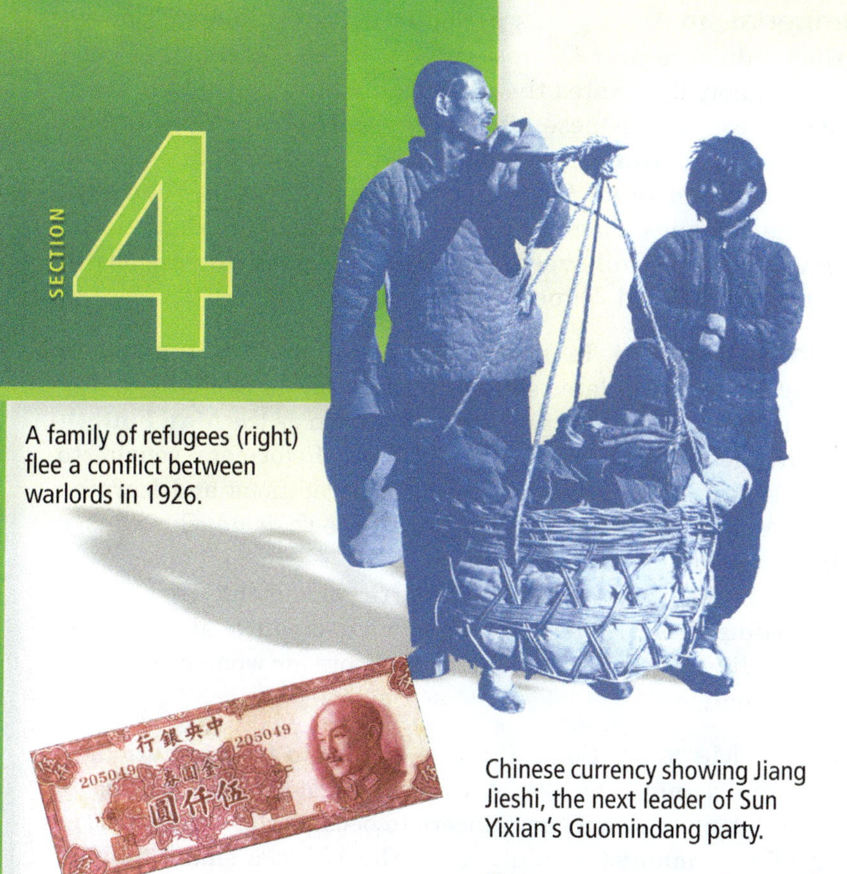

A family of refugees (right) flee a conflict between warlords in 1926.

Chinese currency showing Jiang Jieshi, the next leader of Sun Yixian's Guomindang party.

Change in China

Sun Yixian, "father" of modern China, painted a grim picture of China after the end of the Qing dynasty.

“ But the Chinese people have only family and clan solidarity; they do not have national spirit. There-fore, even though we have four hundred million people gathered together in one China, in reality they are just a heap of loose sand. Today we are the poorest and weakest nation in the world and occupy the lowest position in international affairs. Other men are the carving knife and serving dish, we are the fish and the meat.**”**

As Sun emphasized, China needed to change, but how and in what direction?

Focus Question How did China cope with internal division and foreign invasion in the early 1900s?

Upheavals in China

Objectives
- Explain the key challenges faced by the Chinese republic in the early 1900s.
- Analyze the struggle between two rival parties as they fought to control China.
- Describe how invasion by Japan affected China.

Terms, People, and Places

Twenty-One Demands Guomindang
May Fourth Movement Long March
vanguard

Note Taking

Reading Skill: Recognize Multiple Causes
Use a chart like the one below to record the causes of upheaval in the Chinese Republic.

Causes of Upheaval

As the new Chinese republic took shape, nationalists like Sun Yixian (soon yee SHYAHN) set the goal of "catching up and surpassing the powers, east and west." But that goal would remain a distant dream as China suffered the turmoil of civil war and foreign invasion.

The Chinese Republic in Trouble

As you have read, China's Qing dynasty collapsed in 1911. The president of China's new republic, Sun Yixian (also called Sun Yat-sen) hoped to rebuild China on the Three Principles of the People—nationalism, democracy, and economic security for everyone. But he made little progress. China quickly fell into chaos in the face of the "twin evils" of warlord uprisings and foreign imperialism.

The Warlord Problem In 1912, Sun Yixian stepped down as president in favor of Yuan Shikai (yoo AHN shih KY), a powerful general. Sun hoped that Yuan would create a strong central government, but instead, the ambitious general tried to set up a new dynasty. The military, however, did not support Yuan, and opposition divided the nation. When Yuan died in 1916, China plunged into still greater disorder.

In the provinces, local warlords seized power. As rival armies battled for control, the economy collapsed and millions of peasants suffered terrible hardships. Famine and attacks by bandits added to their misery.

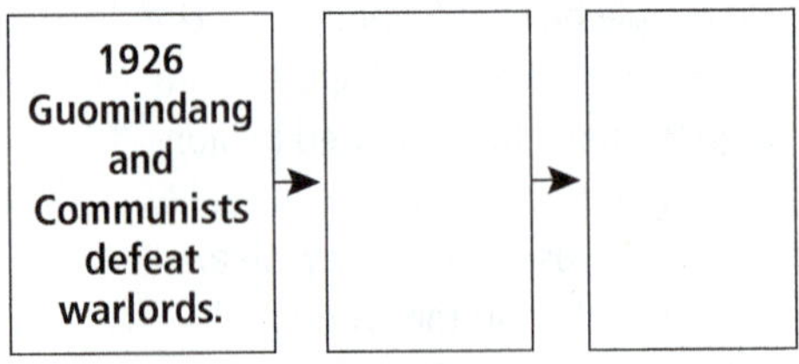

Foreign Imperialism During this period of upheaval, foreign powers increased their influence over Chinese affairs. Foreign merchants, missionaries, and soldiers dominated the ports China had opened to trade.

During World War I, Japanese officials presented Yuan Shikai with the **Twenty-One Demands,** a list of demands that sought to make China a Japanese protectorate. With China too weak to resist, Yuan gave in to some of the demands. Then, in 1919, at the Paris Peace Conference, the Allies gave Japan control over some former German possessions in China. That news infuriated Chinese Nationalists.

May Fourth Movement In response, student protests erupted in Beijing on May 4, 1919, and later spread to cities across China. The protests set off a cultural and <u>intellectual</u> ferment known as the **May Fourth Movement.** Its goal was to strengthen China. Reformers sought to improve China's position by rejecting Confucian traditions and learning from the West. As in Meiji Japan, they hoped to use their new knowledge to end foreign domination.

Women played a key role in the May Fourth Movement. They joined marches and campaigned to end a number of traditional practices, including footbinding. Their work helped open doors for women in education and the economy.

The Appeal of Marxism Some Chinese turned to the revolutionary ideas of Marx and Lenin. The Soviet Union was more than willing to train Chinese students and military officers to become the **vanguard,** or elite leaders, of a communist revolution. By the 1920s, a small group of Chinese Communists had formed their own political party.

 **Checkpoint** How did warlord uprisings and foreign imperialism lead to the May Fourth movement?

Struggle for a New China

In 1921, Sun Yixian and his **Guomindang** (gwoh meen DAWNG) or Nationalist party, established a government in south China. Sun planned to raise an army, defeat the warlords, and spread his government's rule over all of China. When Western democracies refused to help, Sun accepted aid from the Soviet Union and joined forces with the small group of Chinese Communists. However, he still believed that China's future should be based on his Three Principles of the People.

Jiang Jieshi Leads the Nationalists After Sun's death in 1925, an energetic young army officer, Jiang Jieshi (jahng jeh shur), took over the Guomindang. Jiang Jieshi (also called Chiang Kai-Shek) was determined to smash the power of the warlords and reunite China, but he had little interest in either democracy or communism.

In 1926, Jiang Jieshi began the Northern Expedition in cooperation with the Chinese Communists. In the Northern Expedition, Jiang led the combined forces into northern China, crushing or winning over local warlords as he advanced and capturing Beijing. Jiang would go on to take control of a new government led by the Guomindang—but without the Communists.

Jiang Jieshi, Leader of the Guomindang
Jiang Jieshi headed the Guomindang (Nationalist) government in China from the late 1920s until 1949.

Who Should Lead the New China?

The excerpts below present the views of China's two most influential leaders on who should direct the future of China. **Critical Thinking** *Who does each person think should lead China?*

One Strong Leader	Peasant Masses
The most important point of fascism is absolute trust in a sagely able leader. Aside from complete trust in one person, there is no other leader or ism. Therefore, with the organization, although there are cadre, council members, and executives, there is no conflict among them, there is only the trust in the one leader. The leader has final decision in all matters. —Jiang Jieshi, 1933	The broad peasant masses have risen to fulfill their historic mission … the democratic forces in the rural areas have risen to overthrow the rural feudal power. . . . To overthrow this feudal power is the real objective of the national revolution. What Dr. Sun Yat-sen [Yixian] wanted to do . . . but failed to accomplish, the peasants have accomplished in a few months. —Mao Zedong, 1927

In mid-campaign, Jiang seized the chance to strike at the Chinese Communist Party, which he saw as a threat to his power. The Communists were winning converts among the small proletariat in cities like Shanghai. Early in 1927, on orders from Jiang, Guomindang troops slaughtered Communist Party members and the workers who supported them. In Shanghai and elsewhere, thousands of people were killed. This massacre marked the beginning of a bitter civil war between the Communists and the Guomindang that lasted for 22 years.

Mao Zedong and the Communists Among the Communists who escaped Jiang's attack was a young revolutionary of peasant origins, Mao Zedong (mow dzuh doong) (also called Mao Tse-tung). Unlike earlier Chinese Communists, Mao believed that the Communists should seek support not among the small urban working class but among the large peasant masses.

Although the Communists were pursued at every turn by Guomindang forces, Mao was optimistic about eventual success. In southeastern China, Mao and the Communists redistributed land to peasants and promised other reforms.

Mao Zedong, Leader of the Communists
Mao Zedong led the Chinese Communists through some of their darkest times, including the Long March.

The Long March Jiang Jieshi, however, was determined to destroy the "Red bandits," as he called the Communists. He led the Guomindang in a series of "extermination campaigns" against them. The Guomindang harassed Mao's retreating army throughout the Long March from 1934 to 1935. Mao's forces used guerrilla, or irregular hit-and-run, tactics to fight back. At the end of the Long March, the Communists set up a new base in a remote region of northern China. There, Mao rebuilt his forces and plotted new strategies for fighting the Guomindang.

During the march, the Communists enforced strict discipline. Soldiers were told to treat peasants politely, pay for goods they wanted, and avoid damaging crops. Such behavior made Mao's forces welcome among peasants, many of whom had suffered greatly at the hands of the Guomindang.

✔ **Checkpoint** How did the Communists manage to survive Jiang's "extermination campaigns"?

The Communists scale a mountain pass during the Long March.

Map Skills The Guomindang and the Communists waged a long and bitter war for control of China.

1. **Locate:** (a) Beijing (b) Shanghai (c) Jiangxi (d) Yan'an
2. **Movement** What natural features made the Long March difficult?
3. **Synthesize Information** Based on the map and timeline, describe the relationship between the Guomindang and the Communists.

One of the most dramatic events in the conflict between the Guomindang and the Communists was the epic retreat known as the Long March. During the Long March, Mao and about 100,000 of his followers fled the Guomindang. In the next year, they trekked more than 6,000 miles, facing daily attacks as they crossed rugged mountains and mighty rivers. Only about 8,000 marchers survived the ordeal. For decades, the Long March stood as a symbol of communist heroism and inspired new recruits to follow Mao. He claimed the great retreat as a victory. As he observed:

Primary Source

❝The Long March is also a seeding-machine. It has sown many seeds in eleven provinces, which will sprout, grow leaves, blossom into flowers, bear fruit, and yield a crop.❞
—Mao Zedong, "On the Tactics of Fighting Japanese Imperialism"

Japanese Invasion

While Jiang was pursuing the Communists across China, the country faced another danger. In 1931, Japan invaded Manchuria in northeastern China, adding it to the growing Japanese empire. As Japanese aggression increased, a <u>faction</u> within the Guomindang forced Jiang to form a united front with the Communists against Japan.

In 1937, the Japanese struck again, starting what became the Second Sino-Japanese War. Airplanes bombed Chinese cities, and Japanese troops overran eastern China, including Beijing and Guangzhou. Jiang Jieshi and his government retreated to the interior and set up a new capital at Chongqing (chawng CHING).

After a lengthy siege, Japanese troops marched into the city of Nanjing (nahn jing) on December 13. Nanjing was an important cultural center and had been the Guomindang capital before Chongqing. After the city's surrender, the Japanese killed hundreds of thousands of soldiers and civilians and brutalized still more. The cruelty and destruction became known around the world as the "rape of Nanjing."

The united Chinese fought back against the Japanese. The Soviet Union sent advisors and equipment to help. Great Britain, France, and the United States gave economic aid. The Guomindang and the Communists still clashed occasionally, but the united front stayed intact until the end of the war with Japan.

 **Checkpoint** How did the Japanese invasion help unify the Chinese temporarily?

Vocabulary Builder

<u>faction</u>—(FAK shun) *n.* a group within a larger group

Looking Ahead

The bombing of Pearl Harbor in 1941 brought the United States into the war against Japan and into an alliance with the Chinese. By the end of World War II, Jiang and the Guomindang controlled China's central government, but Mao's Communist Party controlled much of northern and central China. The Communists had organized hundreds of thousands of Chinese peasants at the village level, spreading their political ideas. Meanwhile, corruption grew in Jiang's government. Soon, the Communists would triumph, and Mao would impose revolutionary change on China.

SECTION 4 Assessment

Progress Monitoring *Online*
For: Self-quiz with vocabulary practice
Web Code: naa-2741

Terms, People, and Places

1. What do many of the key terms listed at the beginning of the section have in common? Explain.

Note Taking

2. **Reading Skill: Recognize Multiple Causes** Use your completed charts to answer the Focus Question: How did China cope with internal division and foreign invasion in the early 1900s?

Comprehension and Critical Thinking

3. **Identify Central Issues** Why did the new republic of China fall into chaos after 1912?

4. **Identify Point of View** Do you think that the retreating Communists' policy to pay for goods they wanted during the Long March was a good idea? Why or why not?

5. **Predict Consequences** How do you think the "rape of Nanjing" affected Japan's reputation around the world?

● Writing About History

Quick Write: Answer Opposing Arguments Every persuasive essay should present arguments that support the thesis *and* refute arguments that oppose the thesis. Your thesis for a persuasive essay is "The Long March ultimately helped Chinese Communists' cause." Think of the strongest argument against this thesis, and then write a paragraph to refute that argument.

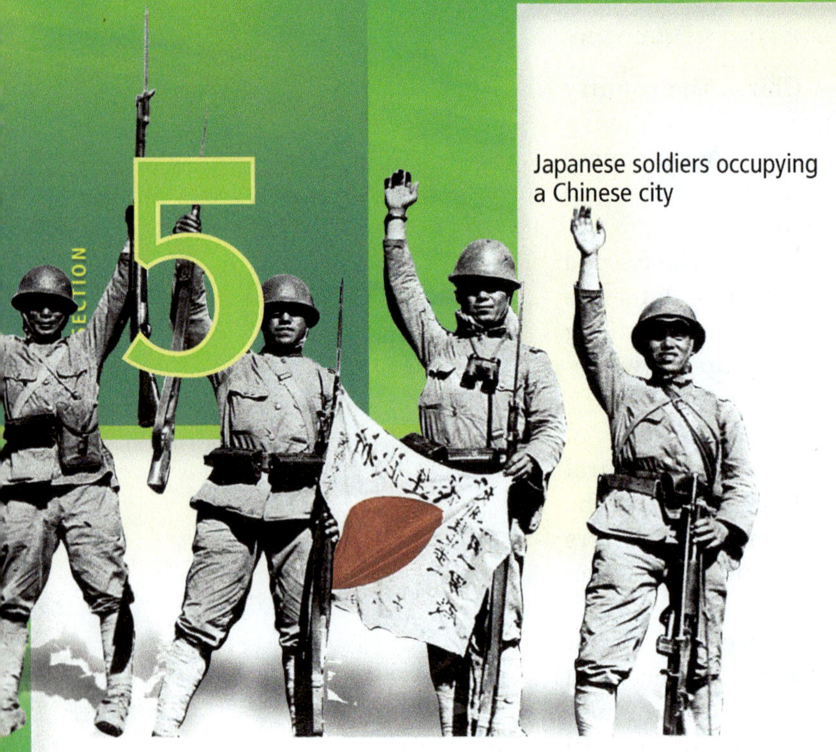
Japanese soldiers occupying a Chinese city

Japan in the Midst of Change

Groups with conflicting ideologies fought for control of Japan in the 1930s.

❝ Look straight at the present state of your fatherland, Japan! Where, we dare ask, can you find the genuine manifestation of the godliness of the Imperial Country of Japan? Political parties are blind in their pursuit of power and egoistic gains. Large enterprises are firmly in collusion with politicians as they suck the sweat and blood of the common people . . . Diplomacy is weak-kneed. Education is rotten to the core. Now is the time to carry out drastic, revolutionary change. Rise, and take action now! ❞
—A Japanese ultranationalist criticizing the government, 1932

Focus Question How did Japan change in the 1920s and 1930s?

Conflicting Forces in Japan

Objectives

- Explain the effects of liberal changes in Japan during the 1920s.
- Analyze how nationalists reacted to Japan's problems during the Great Depression.
- Describe how the militarists used their power in the 1930s.

Terms, People, and Places

Hirohito
ultranationalist
Manchuria

Note Taking

Reading Skill: Understand Effects As you read this section, fill in the effects of two opposing outlooks in Japan in the 1920s and 1930s in a table like the one below.

Conflicting Forces in Japan	
Liberalism in the 1920s	Militarism in the 1930s
•	•
•	•
•	•

Solemn ceremonies marked the start of Emperor Hirohito's reign. In the Secret Purple Hall, the new emperor sat on the ancient throne of Japan. Beside him was his wife, the empress Nagako. Calling on the spirits of his ancestors, he pledged "to preserve world peace and benefit the welfare of the human race."

In fact, **Hirohito** reigned from 1926 to 1989—an astonishing 63 years. During those decades, Japan experienced remarkable successes and appalling tragedies. In this section, we will focus on the 1920s and 1930s, when the pressures of extreme nationalism and economic upheaval set Japan on a militaristic and expansionist path that would engulf all of Asia.

Japan on the Rise in the 1920s

In the 1920s, Japan moved toward greater prosperity and democracy. To strengthen its relationship with other countries, Japan drew back from some of its imperial goals in the 1920s. The country grew in international prestige. However, conflicts lurked beneath the surface. The economic crisis of the Great Depression in the 1930s would bring them to light.

Growth and Expansion After World War I During World War I, the Japanese economy enjoyed remarkable growth. Its exports to Allied nations soared. Heavy industrial production grew, making Japan a true industrial power.

While Western powers battled in Europe, Japan expanded its influence throughout East Asia. Japan had already annexed Korea as a colony in 1910. During the war, Japan also sought further rights in China with the Twenty-One Demands. After the war, Japan took over former German possessions in East Asia, including the Shandong province in China.

Liberal Changes in the 1920s During the 1920s, Japan moved toward more widespread democracy. Political parties grew stronger. Elected members of the Diet—the Japanese parliament—exercised their power. In 1925, all adult men, regardless of class, won the right to vote. In addition, Western ideas about women's rights brought some changes. Overall, however, the status of Japanese women remained below that of men. They would not win suffrage, or the right to vote, until 1945.

Despite leaning toward greater democracy, political parties were manipulated by the zaibatsu (zy baht soo), Japan's powerful business leaders. The zaibatsu influenced the government through donations to political parties. They pushed for policies that favored international trade and their own interests.

Japan's aggressive expansion began to affect its economic relationship with the Western powers. To protect relations, moderate Japanese politicians decided to slow down foreign expansion. In 1922, Japan signed an agreement to limit the size of its navy with the United States, Britain, and France. It also agreed to leave Shandong. The government reduced military spending.

Problems Below the Surface Behind this well-being, Japan faced some grave problems. Rural peasants did not share in the nation's prosperity. They were still very poor. In the cities, factory workers earned low wages. Their poverty drew them to the socialist ideas of Marx and Lenin.

In the cities, members of the younger generation were also in revolt against tradition. They adopted Western fads and fashions. Also, they rejected family authority for the Western ideal of individual freedom, shocking their elders.

During the 1920s, tensions between the government and the military simmered not far below the surface. Conservatives, especially military officers, blasted government corruption, including payoffs by powerful zaibatsu. They also condemned Western influences for undermining basic Japanese values of obedience and respect for authority.

Although the economy grew throughout the 1920s, it experienced many highs and lows. One low point occurred when a devastating earthquake, one of the most destructive quakes in history, struck the Tokyo area in 1923. The earthquake and the widespread fires it caused resulted in the deaths of over 100,000 people and damaged more than 650,000 buildings. As many as 45 percent of surviving workers lost their jobs because so many businesses were destroyed. With help from the government, the Tokyo area gradually recovered—just as Japan faced a worldwide economic crisis.

✔ **Checkpoint** How did democratic participation in Japan both grow and stagnate in the 1920s?

Vocabulary Builder

manipulated—(muh NIP yoo layt id) vt. influenced skillfully, often unfairly

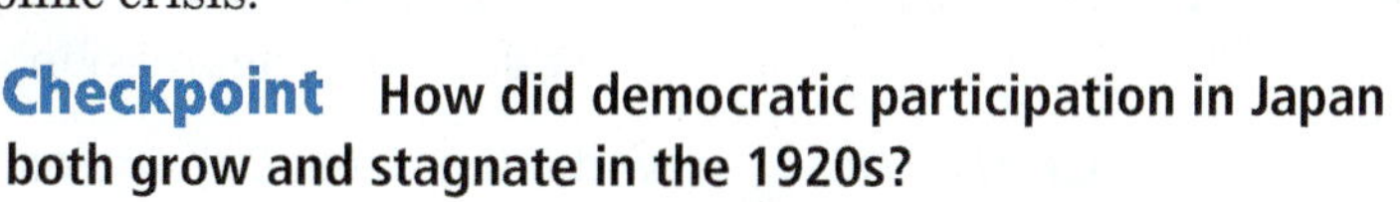

A Combination of the Old and the New In this lithograph (above), Japanese people in traditional clothing walk with others in Western clothing in one of Tokyo's parks. A woman protests low wages at a Japanese factory in 1920 (left).

Map Skills Japan expanded its territory in Asia between 1918 and 1934. From their conquered lands, the Japanese acquired natural resources to fuel their industries.

1. **Locate:** (a) Japan (b) Korea (c) Manchuria (d) Taiwan
2. **Region** Where were Japan's main manufacturing areas located?
3. **Draw Conclusions** What natural resource does Korea lack but Manchuria have?

The Nationalist Reaction

In 1929, the Great Depression rippled across the Pacific, striking Japan with devastating force. Trade suffered as foreign buyers could no longer afford to purchase Japanese silks and other exports. Unemployment in the cities soared, while rural peasants were only a mouthful from starvation.

Unrest Grows Economic disaster fed the discontent of the leading military officials and extreme nationalists, or **ultranationalists.** They condemned politicians for agreeing to Western demands to stop overseas expansion. Western industrial powers, they pointed out, had long ago grabbed huge empires. By comparison, Japan's empire was tiny.

Japanese nationalists were further outraged by racial policies in the United States, Canada, and Australia that shut out Japanese immigrants. The Japanese took great pride in their industrial achievements. They bitterly resented being treated as second-class citizens in other parts of the world.

As the economic crisis worsened, nationalists demanded renewed expansion. An empire in Asia, they argued, would provide much-needed raw materials as well as an outlet for Japan's rapidly growing population. They set their sights on the northern Chinese province of **Manchuria.** This region was rich in natural resources, and Japanese businesses had already invested heavily there.

The Manchurian Incident In 1931, a group of Japanese army officers provoked an incident that provided an excuse to seize Manchuria. They set explosives and blew up tracks on a Japanese-owned railroad line. Then, they claimed that the Chinese had committed the act. Claiming self-defense, the army attacked Chinese forces. Without consulting their own government, the Japanese military forces conquered all of Manchuria and set up a puppet state there that they called Manzhouguo (man choo KWOO). They brought in Puyi, the last Chinese emperor, to head the puppet state. When politicians in Tokyo objected to the army's highhanded actions, public opinion sided with the military.

When the League of Nations condemned Japanese aggression against China, Japan simply withdrew itself from the League. Soon, the Japanese government nullified the agreements limiting naval armament that it had signed with the Western democracies in the 1920s. The League's member states failed to take military action against Japanese aggression.

 **Checkpoint** How did the Great Depression lead to calls for renewed expansion?

Militarists in Power

In the early 1930s, ultranationalists were winning support from the people for foreign conquests and a tough stand against the Western powers. Members of extreme nationalist societies assassinated a number of politicians and business leaders who opposed expansion. Military leaders plotted to overthrow the government and, in 1936, briefly occupied the center of Tokyo.

Traditional Values Revived Civilian government survived, but the unrest forced the government to accept military domination in 1937. To please the ultranationalists, the government cracked down on socialists and suppressed most democratic freedoms. It revived ancient warrior values and built a cult around Emperor Hirohito, whom many believed was descended from the sun goddess. To spread its nationalist message, the government used schools to teach students absolute obedience to the emperor and service to the state.

More Expansion in China During the 1930s, Japan took advantage of China's civil war to increase its influence there. Japan expected to complete its conquest of China within a few years. But in 1939, while the two nations were locked in deadly combat, World War II broke out in Europe. That conflict swiftly spread to Asia.

In 1936, Japan allied with two aggressive European powers, Germany and Italy. These three powers signed the Tripartite Pact in September 1940, cementing the alliance known as the Axis Powers. That alliance, combined with renewed Japanese conquests, would turn World War II into a brutal, wide-ranging conflict waged not only across the continent of Europe but across Asia and the islands of the Pacific as well.

✔ **Checkpoint** What changes did militarists make when they came to power?

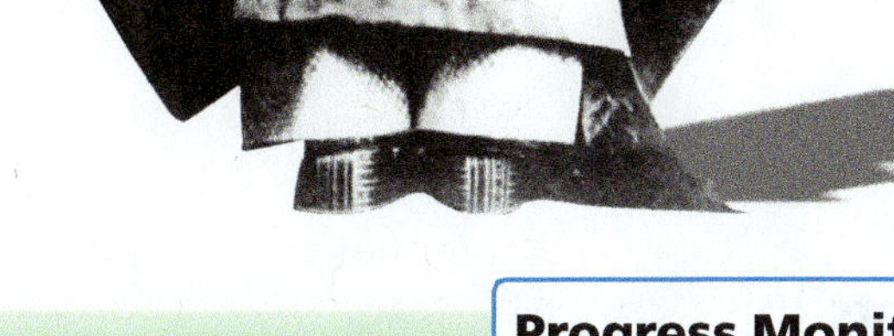

Hirohito

Hirohito (1901–1989) became emperor of Japan in 1926. As emperor, according to Japanese tradition, he was the nation's supreme authority and a living god—no one could look at his face or even mention his name. In practice, however, he merely approved the policies that his ministers formulated.

Hirohito was a private man who preferred marine biology to power politics. As a result, his role in Japan's move toward aggression is unclear. Some historians believe that Hirohito did not encourage Japanese military leaders. Others assert that he was actively involved in expansionist policies. **Why was Hirohito given great respect?**

SECTION **5** Assessment

Terms, People, and Places

1. For each term, person, or place listed at the beginning of the section, write a sentence explaining its significance.

Note Taking

2. **Reading Skill: Understand Effects** Use your completed chart to answer the Focus Question: How did Japan change in the 1920s and 1930s?

Comprehension and Critical Thinking

3. **Summarize** What changes occurred in Japan in the 1920s?
4. **Recognize Effects** How did nationalists respond to the Great Depression?
5. **Geography and History** What role did geography play in Japan's desire to expand its empire?
6. **Predict Consequences** Why might a nation turn to military leaders and extreme nationalists during a crisis?

● **Writing About History**

Quick Write: Decide on an Organizational Strategy Most persuasive essays follow this organization:
   I. Introduction, including thesis statement
  II. Second-strongest argument
 III. Answer to opposing arguments
 IV. Strongest argument
  V. Conclusion
Write a thesis statement based on the content of this section, and write an outline showing how you would organize your arguments.

Quick Study Guide

Progress Monitoring *Online*
For: Self-test with vocabulary practice
Web Code: naa-2761

■ Nationalism Around the World 1910–1939

Location	Goals	Expression
Mexico	To reject foreign influence	Nationalizing foreign companies; emphasizing Latin American culture
Africa	To fight for rights under colonial system	Organizing resistance, including protests, boycotts, strikes, squatting; founding of associations and political parties
Turkey and Persia	To strengthen countries by modernizing and westernizing	Secularizing daily life; adopting Western ways; building industry
The Middle East	To create a Pan-Arab state	Resisting mandate system; ongoing friction between Jewish settlers and Palestinians
India	To gain independence from British	Protesting British rule using nonviolent methods, under Gandhiís leadership
China	To lessen foreign domination of China	Resisting Japanese encroachment; attempting to strengthen China
Japan	To build an empire	Issuing the Twenty-One Demands; invading China multiple times

■ Key Leaders

Emiliano Zapata—Mexican land reformer
Venustiano Carranza—conservative Mexican president
Atatürk—father of modern Turkey
Reza Khan—modernizing Shah of Persia
Gandhi—Congress Party leader (led self-rule protest movement)
Jiang Jieshi—leader of Guomindang (Chinese Nationalists)
Mao Zedong—leader of Chinese Communist Party

■ Effects of World War I on World Events

Effects of World War I				
Trade fell off in Latin America after war.	Resistance to colonial rule grew when war service failed to improve treatment of African and Indian colonies.	Atatürk united Turkey and fought to renegotiate the Treaty of Sévres.	The Allies broke promises in the Middle East, fostering bitterness.	Japan expanded its influence in China.

■ Key Events in Latin America, Africa, and Asia

Latin America and Africa

Asia

1910
Mexican Revolution begins.

1912
Black South Africans form a political party, which later becomes the African National Congress (ANC).

1917
A new Mexican constitution is passed, but fighting continues.

1910 — **1915** — **1920**

1911
Sun Yixian and the Guomindang establish the Republic of China.

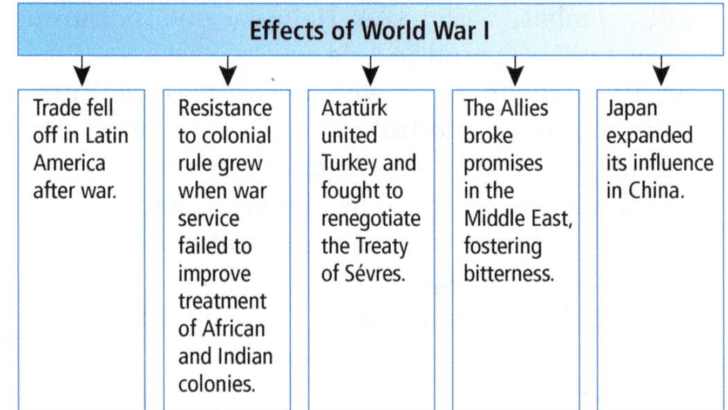

1923
Atatürk founds modern Turkey.

Concept Connector

 Essential Question Review

To connect prior knowledge with what you have learned in this chapter, answer the questions below in your Concept Connector journal. Use the journal in the Reading and Note Taking Study Guide to record your answers (or go to www.phschool.com **Web Code:** nad-2707).

1. **Democracy** Mohandas Gandhi used the power of nonviolence to protest British rule and achieve democratic reforms in India. Create a flowchart to describe how Gandhi's protests launched a democratic movement in India. Focus on the following:
   - the class system
   - civil disobedience
   - boycotts
   - the Salt March

2. **Impact of the Individual** In this chapter, you read about the influence of Jiang Jieshi and Mao Zedong in China. How were the goals of Jiang and Mao similar? How were their goals different? How did each of these leaders influence events in China?

3. **Nationalism** As you have read, During the 1920s and the 1930s, economic, political, and cultural nationalism in Latin American nations were triggered by world events. Do you think nationalism unified or divided the nations of Latin America? Write a paragraph that explains your point of view. Focus on the following:
   - the world economy
   - influence of the United States on Latin America
   - the types of governments that developed in Latin America

■ Connections to Today

1. **Conflict: The Zapatista Army of National Liberation** Although Emiliano Zapata was assassinated in 1919, the spirit of his movement has lived on. In the early 1990s, poverty-stricken Indian peasants in the southern state of Chiapas formed a revolutionary group named the Zapatista Army of National Liberation, after Zapata. Conduct research on the issues behind the Zapatista movement, and then create a chart comparing issues from the Mexican Revolution era to those of the Zapatistas today.

2. **Conflict: Soweto, Then and Now** Soweto, a poor suburb of Johannesburg, South Africa, was a harsh symbol of apartheid. Soweto has changed since apartheid began to end in 1990, but poverty is still widespread. Conduct research and write two paragraphs about life in Soweto today.

1929
Ibo women protest British policies in Nigeria.

1938
Mexico nationalizes foreign-owned oil companies.

History Interactive
For: Interactive timeline
Web Code: nap-2762

1925 1930 1935 1940

1925
Jiang Jieshi becomes the leader of the Guomindang in China.

1930
Thousands of Indians join Gandhi in the Salt March.

1937
The Japanese army captures Nanjing.

Chapter Assessment

Terms, People, and Places

1. Define **economic nationalism.** How did this movement bring change to Latin America in the early 1900s?
2. What was the **Balfour Declaration**? Did it further or hinder the aims of **Pan-Arabism**? Explain.
3. Define **ahimsa** and **civil disobedience**. How did Gandhi use both in his campaign for self-rule in India?
4. What were the **Twenty-One Demands?** How were they an example of foreign imperialism in China?
5. Define **Manchuria** and **ultranationalist**. Describe how what happened in Manchuria was a result of ultranationalist aims in Japan.

Main Ideas

Section 1 (pp. 852–857)
6. What caused the Mexican Revolution?
7. How did nationalism affect Latin America in the early 1900s?

Section 2 (pp. 858–864)
8. How did African nationalism grow in the early 1900s?
9. What changes took place in the Middle East?

Section 3 (pp. 865–868)
10. How did Mohandas Gandhi help Indians work to gain self-rule?

Section 4 (pp. 869–873)
11. Describe the two phases of civil war in China.
12. How did Japan interfere in China in the 1930s?

Section 5 (pp. 874–877)
13. Describe how ultranationalists in Japan sought to solve Japan's economic problems during the Great Depression.

Chapter Focus Question
14. How did nationalism and the desire for change shape world events in the early 1900s?

Critical Thinking

15. **Draw Conclusions** How did the Good Neighbor Policy change the relationship between the United States and Latin America?
16. **Draw Inferences** How did Pan-Africanism affect people around the world?
17. **Recognize Cause and Effect** How did World War I affect relations between India and Britain?

18. **Analyzing Visuals** In the photo above, Mexican *soldaderas* stand with some male soldiers. How does this image embody some of the goals of the Mexican Revolution?
19. **Identify Central Issues** What three-sided struggle took place in China from 1937 to 1945?
20. **Predict Consequences** How were liberal changes in 1920s Japan reversed by ultranationalists in the 1930s?

● Writing About History

In this chapter's five Section Assessments, you developed skills for writing a persuasive essay.

Writing a Persuasive Essay In this chapter, you learned about how people in many different regions of the world struggled to change their lives in the early 1900s. Pick a major issue from one of these regions, choose a stance on it, and then write an essay that persuades the reader to believe in your point of view.

Prewriting
• Choose a topic that provokes a valid argument, not a topic on which most people would agree or disagree.
• Gather information about your topic to help you generate arguments.

Drafting
• Develop a thesis and arguments that support your position.
• Use an organizational structure to help build your argument.
• Write an introduction outlining your position and arguments on the topic, a body, and a conclusion.

Revising
• As you review your essay, look for and eliminate weak logic.
• Use the guidelines for revising your essay on page SH17 of the Writing Handbook.

Document-Based Assessment

A Fistful of Salt

Mohandas Gandhi's campaign of nonviolent resistance was a potent weapon in the Indian struggle for independence from Britain. The documents below describe one hard-fought battle: the Salt March of 1930.

Document A

"Wherever possible, civil disobedience of the salt laws should be started. These laws can be violated in three ways. It is an offense to manufacture salt wherever there are facilities for doing so. The possession and sale of contraband salt, which includes natural salt or salt earth, [is] also an offense. The purchasers of such salt will be equally guilty. To carry away the natural salt deposits on the seashore is likewise violation of the law. So is the hawking of such salt. In short, you may choose any one or all of these devices to break the salt monopoly."

—Gandhi on the Salt March

Document B

"The Salt Satyagraha started with a dramatic long march by Gandhi and a group of picked companions from Sabarmati to the coast at Dandi, 240 miles away, where he proceeded to make salt illegally by boiling sea water. The march was a publicity enterprise of great power as the press followed the party's progress . . . As he journeyed . . ., deliberately challenging established authority, village headmen began to resign in large numbers . . . in April, [India's Viceroy, Lord] Irwin reported to London that in Gujarat 'the personal influence of Gandhi threatens to create a position of real embarrassment to the administration . . . as in some areas he has already achieved a considerable measure of success in undermining the authority of Government.'"

—From ***Modern India: The Origins of Asian Democracy***
by Judith M. Brown

Document C

"Suddenly, at a word of command, scores of native policemen rushed upon the advancing marchers and rained blows on their heads with their steel-shod *lathis.* Not one of the marchers even raised an arm to fend off the blows. They went down like ten-pins. . . . The survivors, without breaking ranks, silently and doggedly marched on until struck down."

—Webb Miller, a British journalist reporting on a march to the salt deposits at Dharsana

Document D

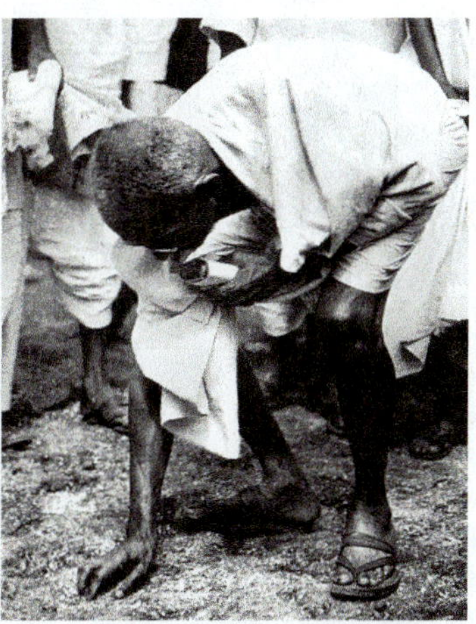

Gandhi picking up salt at the coastal village of Dandi in India, April 6, 1930

Analyzing Documents

Use your knowledge of India's struggle for self-rule and Documents A, B, C, and D to answer questions 1–4.

1. In Document A, Gandhi was mainly addressing
   A British authorities.
   B journalists around the world.
   C the British people.
   D the Indian people.

2. In Document B, the historian describes the effect of the Salt March on
   A the supply of salt.
   B the authority of the British government.
   C protesters in other countries.
   D Gandhi's health.

3. Which words from Document C reflect the attitude of the reporter toward the marchers?
   A suddenly, command
   B steel-shod *lathis,* ten-pins
   C fend, blows
   D silently, doggedly

4. **Writing Task** How was the Salt March a turning point in India's struggle for independence? Use what you have learned from these documents and the chapter in your response.

28

The Rise of Totalitarianism

1919–1939

 🔊 AUDIO

Nazi Germany

Martin Niemöller, a Lutheran minister, preached against ruthless Nazi policies and was ultimately jailed. He later observed:

> 66[The Nazis] came first for the Communists, and I didn't speak up because I wasn't a Communist. Then they came for the Jews, and I didn't speak up because I wasn't a Jew. Then they came for the Catholics, and I didn't speak up because I was a Protestant. Then they came for me, and by that time there was no one left to speak up.99
> —Martin Niemöller, quoted in *Time* magazine

Listen to the Witness History audio to learn more about totalitarian states in Europe.

◄ Adolf Hitler surrounded by supporters at a Nazi party rally in 1934

A toy replica of a Nazi storm trooper

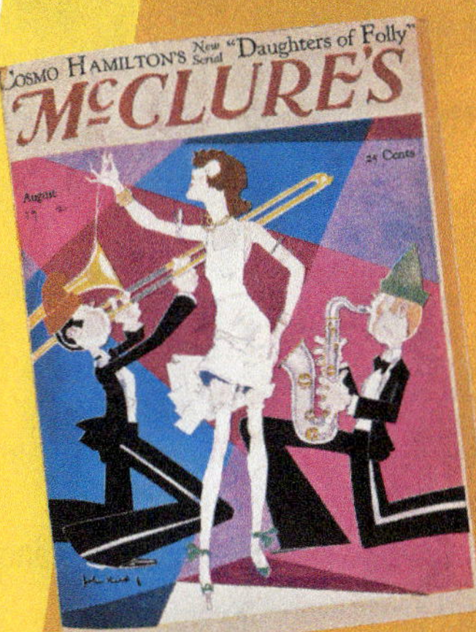

A magazine cover showing a Jazz Age flapper

A mug shot from a Soviet secret police file

Chapter Preview

Chapter Focus Question What political and economic challenges did the Western world face in the 1920s and 1930s, and how did various countries react to these challenges?

Use the ☑ **Quick Study Timeline** at the end of this chapter to preview chapter events.

 **Concept Connector** ONLINE

To explore Essential Questions related to this chapter, go to PHSchool.com Web Code: nad-2807

Jazz musician
Louis Armstrong

The Jazz Age

Many young people reacted to the trauma of World War I by rejecting the values of their parents. During the Jazz Age, this rebellion was exemplified by a new type of young woman—the flapper.

❝ The Flapper awoke from her lethargy [tiredness] . . . bobbed her hair, put on her choicest pair of earrings and a great deal of audacity [boldness] and rouge, and went into the battle. She flirted because it was fun to flirt and . . . refused to be bored chiefly because she wasn't boring. . . . Mothers disapproved of their sons taking the Flapper to dances, to teas, to swim, and most of all to heart. ❞
—Zelda Fitzgerald, flapper and wife of author F. Scott Fitzgerald

Focus Question What changes did Western society and culture experience after World War I?

Postwar Social Changes

Objectives
- Analyze how Western society changed after World War I.
- Describe the literary and artistic trends that emerged in the 1920s.
- List several advances in modern scientific thought.

Terms, People, and Places

flapper	psychoanalysis
Prohibition	abstract
speakeasies	dada
Harlem Renaissance	surrealism

Note Taking

Reading Skill: Identify Supporting Details Use a concept web like the one below to record details related to the main ideas of this section.

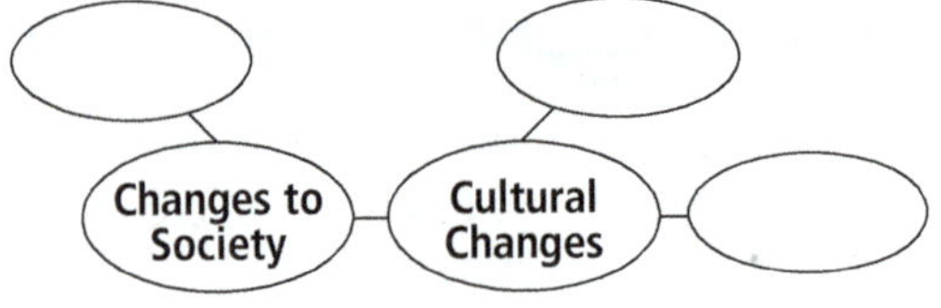

The catastrophe of World War I shattered the sense of optimism that had grown in the West since the Enlightenment. Despair gripped survivors on both sides as they added up the staggering costs of the war. It seemed as though a whole generation of young men had been lost on the battlefields. In reaction, the society and culture of Europe, the United States, and many other parts of the world experienced rapid changes.

Changes in Society After World War I

During the 1920s, new technologies helped create a mass culture shared by millions in the world's developed countries. Affordable cars, improved telephones, and new forms of media such as motion pictures and radio brought people around the world closer together than ever before.

The Roaring Twenties In the 1920s, many radios tuned into the new sounds of jazz. In fact, the 1920s are often called the Jazz Age. African American musicians combined Western harmonies with African rhythms to create jazz. Jazz musicians, like trumpeter Louis Armstrong and pianist Duke Ellington, took simple melodies and improvised endless subtle variations in rhythm and beat. They produced original music, and people loved it. Much of today's popular music has been influenced by jazz.

While Europe recovered from the war, the United States experienced a boom time. Europeans embraced American popular culture, with its greater freedom and willingness to experiment. The nightclub and the sounds of jazz were symbols of that freedom.

After the war, rebellious young people, disillusioned by the war, rejected the moral values and rules of the Victorian Age and chased after excitement. One symbol of rebellious Jazz Age youth was the liberated young woman called the **flapper.** The first flappers were American, but their European sisters soon adopted the fashion. Flappers rejected old ways in favor of new, exciting freedom.

Women's Lives Flappers were highly visible, but they were a small minority. Most women saw limited progress in the postwar period. During the war, women had held a wide range of jobs. Although most women left those jobs when the war ended, their war work helped them win the vote in many Western countries. A few women were elected to public office, such as Texas governor Miriam Ferguson or Lady Nancy Astor, the first woman to serve in the British Parliament.

By the 1920s, labor-saving devices had become common in middle-class homes. Washing machines, vacuum cleaners, and canned foods lightened the burden of household chores. Some women then sought work outside the home or did volunteer work to help the less fortunate.

In the new atmosphere of <u>emancipation</u>, women pursued careers in many areas—from sports to the arts. Women golfers, tennis players, swimmers, and pilots set new records. Women worked as newspaper reporters, published bestselling novels, and won recognition as artists. Most professions, though, were still dominated by men.

Reactions to the Jazz Age Not everyone approved of the freewheeling lifestyle of the Jazz Age. For example, many Americans supported **Prohibition,** a ban on the manufacture and sale of alcoholic beverages. For almost 90 years, social activists had waged an intense campaign against the abuse of alcohol. Finally, they gained enough support to get the Eighteenth, or Prohibition, Amendment ratified in 1919. Prohibition was meant to keep people from the negative effects of drinking. Instead, it caused an explosion of organized crime and **speakeasies,** or illegal bars. The Amendment was repealed in 1933.

In the United States in the early 1900s, a Christian fundamentalist movement swept rural areas. Fundamentalists support traditional Christian ideas about Jesus and believe that all of the events described in the Bible are literally true. Popular fundamentalist preachers traveled around the country holding inspirational revival meetings. Some used the new technology of radio to spread their message.

In 1925, a biology teacher in Tennessee named John T. Scopes was tried for teaching evolution in his classroom. His action broke a law that barred any teaching that went against the Bible's version of creation. The teacher was found guilty in the well-publicized Scopes trial, but many fundamentalists believed that the proceedings had hurt their cause.

✔ **Checkpoint** Describe the Jazz Age and some of the reactions to it.

Vocabulary Builder
<u>emancipation</u>—(ee man suh PAY shun) *n.* freedom from restrictions

Life Under Prohibition
A well-dressed couple waits to enter an illicit speakeasy (below right). Members of the United States Prohibition Service wore badges (below left) when they raided speakeasies and breweries and fought bootleggers such as Al Capone. *What does the clothing the couple is wearing tell you about who could afford to go to speakeasies?*

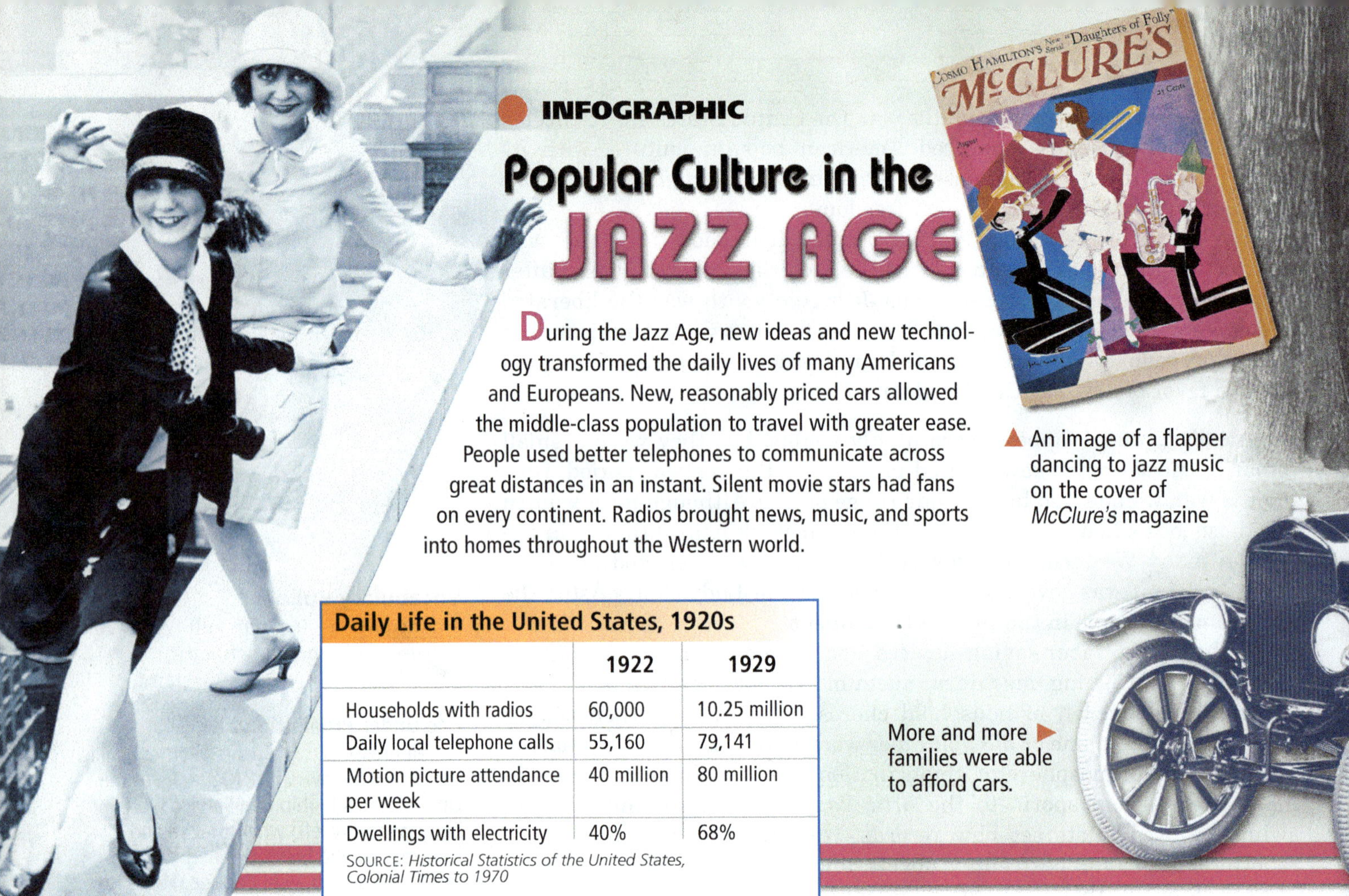

Popular Culture in the
JAZZ AGE

During the Jazz Age, new ideas and new technology transformed the daily lives of many Americans and Europeans. New, reasonably priced cars allowed the middle-class population to travel with greater ease. People used better telephones to communicate across great distances in an instant. Silent movie stars had fans on every continent. Radios brought news, music, and sports into homes throughout the Western world.

▲ An image of a flapper dancing to jazz music on the cover of *McClure's* magazine

Daily Life in the United States, 1920s

	1922	1929
Households with radios	60,000	10.25 million
Daily local telephone calls	55,160	79,141
Motion picture attendance per week	40 million	80 million
Dwellings with electricity	40%	68%

SOURCE: *Historical Statistics of the United States, Colonial Times to 1970*

More and more ▶ families were able to afford cars.

▲ Jazz Age flappers shocked their elders by bobbing, or cutting short, their hair and wearing skirts far shorter than those of prewar fashions. They went out on dates unchaperoned, enjoyed wild new dance fads such as the Charleston, smoked cigarettes, and drank in nightclubs.

The New Literature

In the 1920s, war novels, poetry, plays, and memoirs flowed off the presses. *All Quiet on the Western Front* by German novelist Erich Remarque, and other works like it, exposed the grim horrors of modern warfare. These works reflected a powerful disgust with war.

A Loss of Faith To many postwar writers, the war symbolized the moral breakdown of Western civilization. In 1922, the English poet T. S. Eliot published *The Waste Land*. This long poem portrays the modern world as spiritually empty and barren. In *The Sun Also Rises,* the American novelist Ernest Hemingway shows the rootless wanderings of young people who lack deep convictions. "I did not care what it was all about," says the narrator. "All I wanted to know was how to live in it." Many of these authors, including Hemingway and F. Scott Fitzgerald, left the United States and moved to Paris. Gertrude Stein, an American writer living in Paris, called them the "lost generation." Her label caught on. It referred to Stein's literary friends, and their generation as a whole.

Literature of the Inner Mind Some writers experimented with stream of consciousness. In this technique, a writer appears to present a character's random thoughts and feelings without imposing any logic or order. In the novel *Mrs. Dalloway,* British novelist Virginia Woolf used stream of consciousness to explore the thoughts of people going through the

In 1921, the Irish poet William Butler Yeats summed up the mood of many in postwar Europe and the United States:

❝ Things fall apart; the centre cannot hold;
Mere anarchy is loosed upon the world,
The blood-dimmed tide is loosed, and everywhere
The ceremony of innocence is drowned.❞
—William Butler Yeats, "The Second Coming"

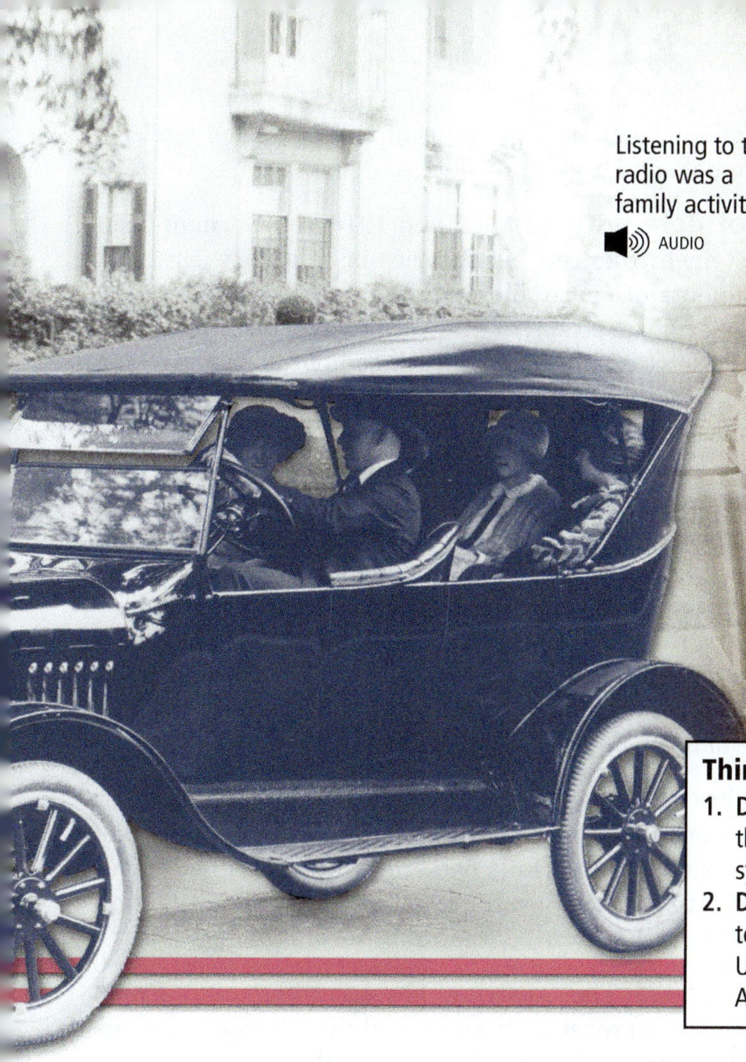

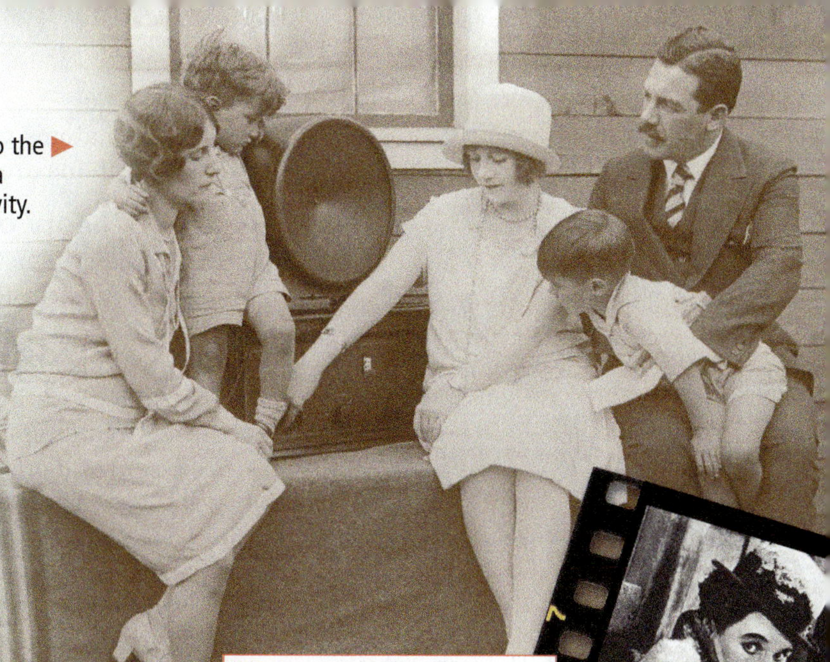

Listening to the radio was a family activity.

AUDIO

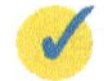

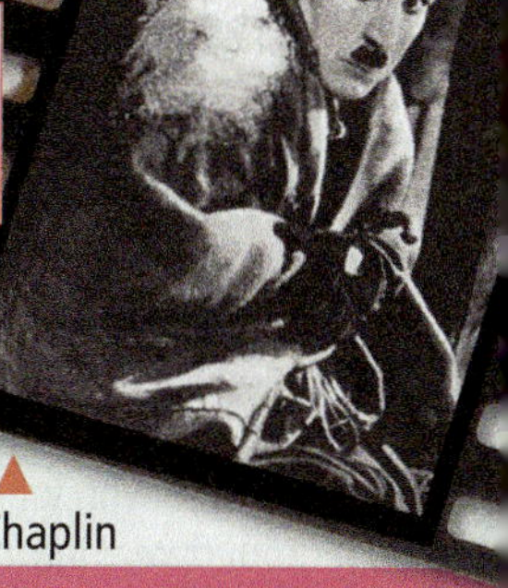

Silent movie star Charlie Chaplin

History Interactive

For: Interactive audio and visuals
Web Code: nap-2811

Thinking Critically

1. **Draw Inferences** Why do you think the flapper is considered the symbol of the Jazz Age?
2. **Draw Conclusions** How did technology affect daily life in the United States during the Jazz Age?

ordinary actions of their everyday lives. In *Finnegans Wake,* the Irish novelist James Joyce explored the inner mind of a hero who remains sound asleep throughout the novel.

The Harlem Renaissance Also during the 1920s, an African American cultural awakening called the **Harlem Renaissance** began in Harlem, a neighborhood in New York City that was home to many African Americans. African American writers and artists expressed their pride in their unique culture. James Weldon Johnson, Jean Toomer, and Zora Neale Hurston explored the African American experience in their novels and essays. The poets Claude McKay and Langston Hughes experimented with new styles, while Countee Cullen adapted traditional poetic forms to new content.

Checkpoint **How did postwar authors show disillusionment with prewar institutions?**

New Scientific Theories

It was not only the war that fostered a sense of uncertainty. New scientific discoveries challenged long-held ideas about the nature of the world. Discoveries made in the late 1800s and early 1900s showed that the atom was more complex than anyone suspected.

Marie Curie and Radioactivity In the early 1900s, the Polish-born French scientist Marie Curie and others found that the atoms of certain elements, such as radium and uranium, spontaneously release charged particles. As scientists studied radioactivity further, they discovered that

Vocabulary Builder
spontaneously—(spahn TAY nee us lee) *adv.* caused by inner forces, self-generated

Marie Curie

Marie Curie (1867–1934) won two Nobel prizes, one in physics and one in chemistry. Still, like many other women, she struggled to balance her work with home duties. "I have a great deal of work," she said, "what with the housekeeping, the children, the teaching, and the laboratory, and I don't know how I shall manage it all."

Curie won worldwide fame for her groundbreaking research on radioactivity. But she paid a high price for knowledge. Although she shrugged off the health dangers, she died from radiation poisoning. **Why do you think Marie Curie's achievements were unique for her time?**

it can change atoms of one element into atoms of another. Such findings proved that atoms are not solid and indivisible.

Einstein's Theory of Relativity In 1905 and 1916, the German-born physicist Albert Einstein introduced his theories of relativity. Einstein argued that measurements of space and time are not absolute but are determined by the relative position of the observer. Einstein's ideas raised questions about Newtonian science, which compared the universe to a machine operating according to absolute laws.

In 1934, building on Curie's and Einstein's theories, Italian physicist Enrico Fermi and other scientists around the world discovered atomic fission, or the splitting of the nuclei of atoms in two. This splitting produces a huge burst of energy. In the 1940s, Fermi (now an American), along with fellow American physicists J. Robert Oppenheimer and Edward Teller, would use this discovery to create the devastating atomic bomb.

In the postwar years, many scientists came to accept the theories of relativity. To the general public, however, Einstein's ideas were difficult to understand. They seemed to further reinforce the unsettling sense of a universe whirling beyond the understanding of human reason.

Fleming Discovers Penicillin In 1928, the Scottish scientist Alexander Fleming made a different type of scientific discovery. He accidentally discovered a type of nontoxic mold that kills bacteria, which he called "penicillin." Later, other scientists used Fleming's work to develop antibiotics, which are now used all over the world to treat infections.

Freud Probes the Mind The Austrian physician Sigmund Freud (froyd) also challenged faith in reason. He suggested that the subconscious mind drives much of human behavior. Freud said that learned social values such as morality and reason help people to repress, or check, powerful urges. But an individual feels constant tension between repressed drives and social training. This tension, argued Freud, may cause psychological or physical illness. Freud pioneered **psychoanalysis,** a method of studying how the mind works and treating mental disorders. Although many of his theories have been discredited, Freud's ideas have had an extraordinary impact far beyond medicine.

 **Checkpoint** How did scientific discoveries in the 1920s change people's views of the world?

Modern Art and Architecture

In the early 1900s, many Western artists rejected traditional styles. Instead of trying to reproduce the real world, they explored other dimensions of color, line, and shape. Painters like Henri Matisse (ma TEES) utilized bold, wild strokes of color and odd distortions to produce works of strong emotion. He and fellow artists outraged the public and were dubbed *fauves* (fohv), or wild beasts, by critics.

New Directions in Painting While Matisse continued in the fauvist style, other artists explored styles based on new ideas. Before World War I, the Spanish artist Pablo Picasso and the French artist Georges Braque (brak) created a revolutionary new style called cubism. Cubists painted three-dimensional objects as complex patterns of angles and planes, as if they were composed of fragmented parts.

Later, the Russian Vasily Kandinsky and the Swiss Paul Klee moved even further away from representing reality. Their artwork was **abstract,** composed only of lines, colors, and shapes, sometimes with no recognizable subject matter at all.

During and after the war, the **dada** movement burst onto the art world. Dadaists rejected all traditional conventions and believed that there was no sense or truth in the world. Paintings and sculptures by Jean Arp and Max Ernst were intended to shock and disturb viewers. Other dadaist artists created collages, photomontages, or sculptures made of objects they found abandoned or thrown away.

Cubism and dada both helped to inspire **surrealism,** a movement that attempted to portray the workings of the unconscious mind. Surrealism rejected rational thought, which had produced the horrors of World War I, in favor of irrational or unconscious ideas. The Spanish surrealist Salvador Dali used images of melting clocks and burning giraffes to suggest the chaotic dream state described by Freud.

New Styles of Architecture Architects, too, rejected classical traditions and developed new styles to match a new world. The famous Bauhaus school in Germany influenced architecture by blending science and technology with design. Bauhaus buildings feature glass, steel, and concrete but have little ornamentation. The American architect Frank Lloyd Wright held that the function of a building should determine its form. He used materials and forms that fit a building's environment.

✔ **Checkpoint** What effect did World War I have on art movements in the 1920s?

Looking Ahead

Stunned by the trauma of World War I, many people sought to change the way they thought and acted during the turbulent 1920s. As nations recovered from the war, people began to feel hope rising out of their disillusionment. But soon, the "lost generation" would face a new crisis—this one economic—that would revive many old problems and spark new conflicts.

Abstract Art
Vasily Kandinsky painted *Swinging* (above) in 1925. He used geometrical shapes to convey the feeling of movement that the title suggests. **Analyzing Art** *How does* Swinging *show the abstract style of art that Kandinsky pioneered?*

Progress Monitoring *Online*
For: Self-quiz with vocabulary practice
Web Code: naa-2811

Terms, People, and Places

1. What do many of the key terms listed at the beginning of the section have in common? Explain.

Note Taking

2. **Reading Skill: Identify Supporting Details** Use your completed concept web to answer the Focus Question: What changes did Western society and culture experience after World War I?

Comprehension and Critical Thinking

3. **Determine Relevance** How did flappers symbolize changes in Western society during the 1920s?

4. **Identify Point of View** How did the ideas of Einstein and Freud contribute to a sense of uncertainty?

5. **Synthesize Information** Choose one postwar writer and one postwar artist. Explain how the work of each reflected a new view of the world.

● **Writing About History**

Quick Write: Choose a Topic The topic of a compare-and-contrast essay must involve two things that are neither nearly identical nor extremely different. Think of a topic from this section that would be a good candidate for a compare-and-contrast essay. Show why it would be a good topic by listing categories in which the two items could be compared and contrasted.

Pablo Picasso

The painter Pablo Picasso was one of the most important artists of the last century. Picasso and his friend Georges Braque together developed the art movement known as Cubism. The movement began around 1907 and continued through the First World War into the 1920s. Picasso's work continued to develop until his death in 1973 at the age of 91. Here are some of his best known artworks.

Picasso in his studio working on a sculpture

Still Life With Violin, 1912. In this Cubist still life, the objects, which include a violin, are fragmented into so many views that they are barely distinguishable.

Mother and Child, 1901. The years 1901 to 1904 are known as Picasso's Blue Period. Following the death of a close friend, Picasso used the color blue in many paintings to express his sadness.

Hands With Flowers, 1958. This lithograph, done after Picasso's Cubist period, is a simple image of a hand holding flowers.

Thinking Critically

1. **Compare** Describe the differences between *Mother and Child* and *Still Life With Violin.*
2. **Synthesize Information** Describe how Picasso's style changed over time, based on the artworks shown here.

Men eating at a soup kitchen during the Great Depression

WITNESS HISTORY 🔊 AUDIO

Brother, Can You Spare a Dime?

In the early 1930s, a worldwide economic depression threw thousands out of work and into lives of poverty. The song below summed up the mood of the time:

> **❝** They used to tell me I was building a dream
> With peace and glory ahead—
> Why should I be standing in line,
> Just waiting for bread?
>
> Once I built a railroad, I made it run,
> Made it race against time.
> Once I built a railroad, now it's done—
> Brother, can you spare a dime? **❞**

— from the song "Brother, Can You Spare a Dime?," lyrics by E.Y. "Yip" Harburg & Jay Gorney. Published by Glocca Morra Music (ASCAP) & Gorney Music (ASCAP). Administered by Next Decade Entertainment, Inc. All rights reserved. Used by permission.

Focus Question What political and economic challenges did the leading democracies face in the 1920s and 1930s?

The Western Democracies Stumble

Objectives

- Summarize the domestic and foreign policy issues Europe faced after World War I.
- Compare the postwar economic situations in Britain, France, and the United States.
- Describe how the Great Depression began and spread and how Britain, France, and the United States tried to address it.

Terms, People, and Places

Maginot Line	finance
Kellogg-Briand Pact	Federal Reserve
disarmament	Great Depression
general strike	Franklin D. Roosevelt
overproduction	New Deal

Note Taking

Reading Skill: Identify Main Ideas Record main ideas from the first part of this section in a table like the one below.

Postwar Issues			
Country	Politics	Foreign Policy	Economics

In 1919, the three Western democracies—Britain, France, and the United States—appeared powerful. They had ruled the Paris Peace Conference and boosted hopes for democracy among the new nations of Eastern Europe. Beneath the surface, however, postwar Europe faced grave problems. To make matters worse, many members of the younger generation who might have become the next great leaders had been killed in the war.

Politics in the Postwar World

At first, the most pressing issues were finding jobs for returning veterans and rebuilding war-ravaged lands. Economic problems fed social unrest and made radical ideas more popular.

Party Struggles in Britain In Britain during the 1920s, the Labour party surpassed the Liberal party in strength. The Labour party gained support among workers by promoting a gradual move toward socialism. The Liberal party passed some social legislation, but it traditionally represented middle-class business interests. As the Liberal party faltered, the middle class began to back the Conservative party, joining the upper class, professionals, and farmers. With this support, the Conservative party held power during much of 1920s. After a massive strike of over three million workers in 1926, Conservatives passed legislation limiting the power of workers to strike.

The Irish Resist

Members of the Irish Republican Army prepare to resist the British occupation of Dublin in 1921 by erecting a barbed wire barricade. The Irish Free State, established in 1922, was a compromise between the opposing sides, but peace was short-lived.

Vocabulary Builder

suppressed—(suh PRESD) *vt.* put down by force, subdued

Irish Independence at Last Britain still faced the "Irish question." In 1914, Parliament passed a home-rule bill that was shelved when the war began. On Easter 1916, a small group of militant Irish nationalists launched a revolt against British rule. Although the Easter Rising was quickly <u>suppressed</u>, it stirred wider support for the Irish cause. When Parliament again failed to grant home rule in 1919, members of the Irish Republican Army (IRA) began a guerrilla war against British forces and their supporters. In 1922, moderates in Ireland and Britain reached an agreement. Most of Ireland became the self-governing Irish Free State. The largely Protestant northern counties remained under British rule. However, the IRA and others fought for decades against the division.

France's Troubled Peace Like Britain, France emerged from World War I both a victor and a loser. Political divisions and financial scandals plagued the government of the Third Republic. Several parties—from conservatives to communists—competed for power. The parties differed on many issues, including how to get reparations payments from Germany. A series of quickly changing coalition governments ruled France.

"The Red Scare" and Isolationism in the United States In contrast, the United States emerged from World War I in good shape. A late entrant into the war, it had suffered relatively few casualties and little loss of property. However, the United States did experience some domestic unrest. Fear of radicals and the Bolshevik Revolution in Russia set off a "Red Scare" in 1919 and 1920. Police rounded up suspected foreign-born radicals, and a number were expelled from the United States.

The "Red Scare" fed growing demands to limit immigration. Millions of immigrants from southern and eastern Europe had poured into the United States between 1890 and 1914. Some native-born Americans sought to exclude these newcomers, whose cultures differed from those of earlier settlers from northern Europe. In response, Congress passed laws limiting immigration from Europe. Earlier laws had already excluded or limited Chinese and Japanese immigration.

✔ **Checkpoint** What political issues did each of the three democracies face after World War I?

Postwar Foreign Policy

In addition to problems at home, the three democracies faced a difficult international situation. The peace settlements caused friction, especially in Germany and among some ethnic groups in Eastern Europe.

Arguing Allies France's chief concern after the war was securing its borders against Germany. The French remembered the German invasions of 1870 and 1914. To prevent a third invasion, France built massive fortifications called the **Maginot Line** (ma zhee NOH) along its border with Germany. However, the line would not be enough to stop another German invasion in 1940.

In its quest for security, France also strengthened its military and sought alliances with other countries, including the Soviet Union. It insisted on strict enforcement of the Versailles treaty and complete payment of reparations. France's goal was to keep the German economy weak.

Britain disagreed with this aim. Almost from the signing of the Treaty of Versailles, British leaders wanted to relax the treaty's harsh treatment of Germany. They feared that if Germany became too weak, the Soviet Union and France would become too powerful.

The Search for Peace Despite disagreements, many people worked for peace in the 1920s. Hopes soared in 1925 when representatives from seven European nations signed a series of treaties at Locarno, Switzerland. These treaties settled Germany's disputed borders with France, Belgium, Czechoslovakia, and Poland. The Locarno treaties became the symbol of a new era of peace.

The **Kellogg-Briand Pact,** which was sponsored by the United States in 1928, echoed the hopeful "spirit of Locarno." Almost every independent nation signed this agreement, promising to "renounce war as an instrument of national policy." In this optimistic spirit, the great powers pursued **disarmament,** the reduction of armed forces and weapons. The United States, Britain, France, Japan, and other nations signed treaties to reduce the size of their navies. However, they failed to agree on limiting the size of their armies.

From its headquarters in Geneva, Switzerland, the League of Nations encouraged cooperation and tried to get members to make a commitment to stop aggression. In 1926, after signing the Locarno agreements, Germany joined the League. Later, the Soviet Union was also admitted.

The League's Weakness The peace was fragile. Although the Kellogg-Briand Pact outlawed war, it provided no way of enforcing the ban. The League of Nations, too, was powerless to stop aggression. In 1931, the League vigorously condemned Japan's invasion of Manchuria, but did not take military action to stop it. Ambitious dictators in Europe noted the League's weakness and began to pursue aggressive foreign policies.

✔ **Checkpoint** How did the Treaty of Versailles affect the relationship between France and Britain?

HAVING AN INSURANCE POLICY DOESN'T MEAN YOU CAN DO WITHOUT FIRE PREVENTION

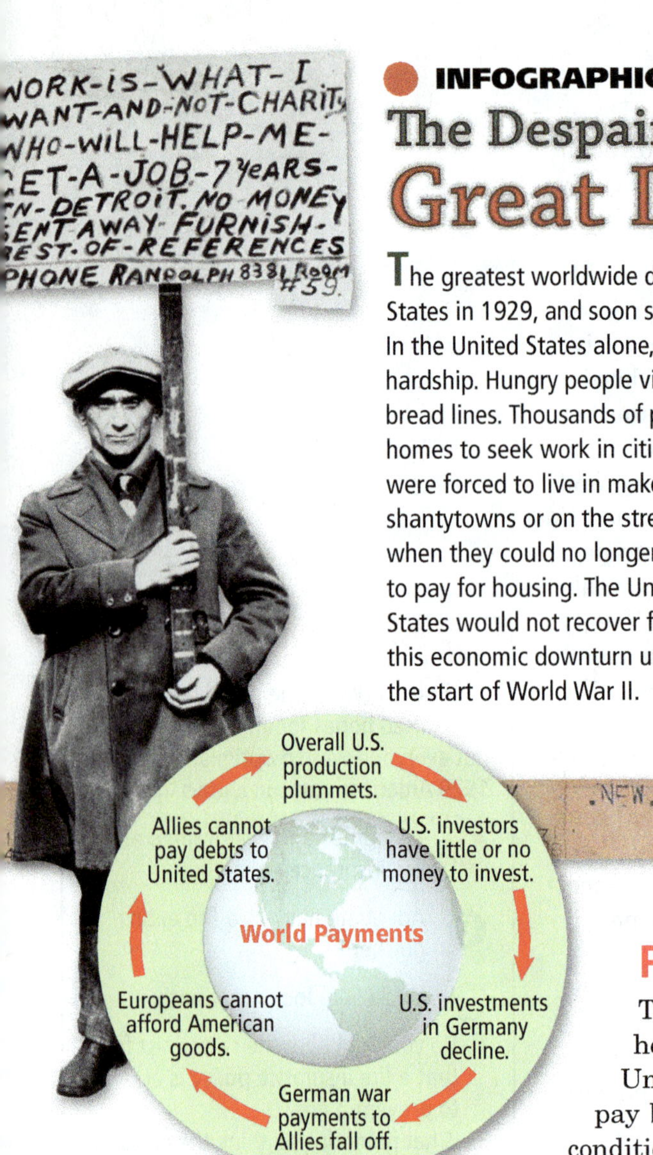

▲ A man tries to find work (above). The cycle of war payments helped spread the Great Depression to Europe.

● **INFOGRAPHIC**

The Despair of the
Great Depression

The greatest worldwide depression in history began in the United States in 1929, and soon spread to touch most parts of the world. In the United States alone, millions lost their jobs and endured great hardship. Hungry people visited soup kitchens or waited in long bread lines. Thousands of people left their homes to seek work in cities. Some were forced to live in makeshift shantytowns or on the streets when they could no longer afford to pay for housing. The United States would not recover from this economic downturn until the start of World War II.

Unemployment led people to visit soup kitchens like the one below in Berlin. In New York and other cities, bread lines spanned multiple city blocks (below right), and many people became homeless (far right).

Postwar Economics

The war affected economies all over the world, hurting some and helping others. Britain and France both owed huge war debts to the United States. Both relied on reparation payments from Germany to pay back their loans. Meanwhile, the crushing reparations and other conditions hurt Germany's economy.

Britain and France Recover Britain faced serious economic problems in the 1920s. It was deeply in debt, and its factories were out of date. Unemployment was severe. Wages remained low, leading to worker unrest and frequent strikes. In 1926, a **general strike,** or strike by workers in many different industries at the same time, lasted nine days and involved some three million workers.

In comparison, the French economy recovered fairly rapidly. Financial reparations and territories gained from Germany helped. Still, economic swings did occur, adding to an unstable political scene.

Despite these problems, Europe made a shaky recovery during the 1920s. Economies returned to peacetime manufacturing and trade. Veterans gradually found jobs, although unemployment never ceased to be a problem. Middle-class families enjoyed a rising standard of living.

The United States Booms In contrast, the United States emerged from the war as the world's leading economic power. In the affluent 1920s, middle-class Americans enjoyed the benefits of capitalism. American loans and investments backed the recovery in Europe. As long as the American economy prospered, the global economy remained stable.

✔ **Checkpoint** How did the war and its peace treaties affect the international economy?

The Great Depression

This prosperity did not last. At the end of the 1920s, an economic crisis began in the United States and spread to the rest of the world, leaving almost no corner untouched.

Falling Demand and Overproduction The wealth created during the 1920s in the United States was not shared evenly. Farmers and unskilled workers were on the losing end. Though demand for raw materials and agricultural products had skyrocketed during the war, demand dwindled and prices fell after the war. Farmers, miners and other suppliers of raw materials suffered. Because they earned less, they bought less. At the same time, better technology allowed factories to make more products faster. This led to **overproduction,** a condition in which the production of goods exceeds the demand for them. As demand slowed, factories cut back on production and workers lost their jobs.

Crash and Collapse Meanwhile, a crisis in **finance**—the management of money matters, including the circulation of money, loans, investments, and banking—was brewing. Few saw the danger. Prices on the New York Stock Exchange were at an all-time high. Eager investors acquired stocks through risky methods. To slow the run on the stock market, the **Federal Reserve,** the central banking system of the United States, which regulates banks, raised interest rates in 1928 and again 1929. It didn't work. Instead, the higher interest rates made people nervous about borrowing money and investing, thereby hurting demand.

In the autumn of 1929, jitters about the economy caused many people to sell their stocks at once. Financial panic set in. Stock prices crashed, wiping out the fortunes of many investors. The **Great Depression,** a painful time of global economic collapse, had begun quietly in the

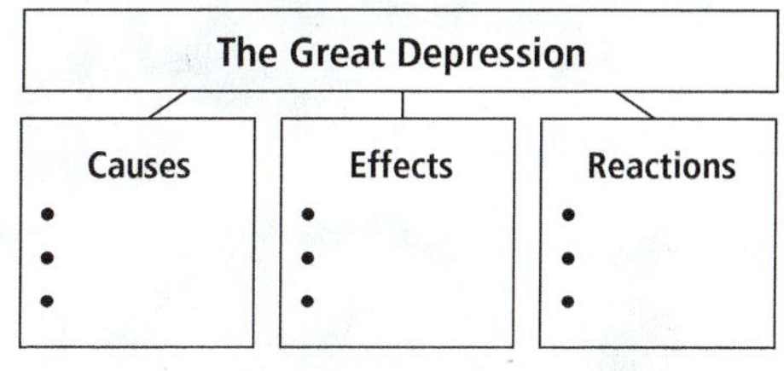

summer of 1929 with decreasing production. The October stock market crash aggravated the economic decline.

In 1931, the Federal Reserve again increased the interest rate, with an even more disastrous effect. As people bought and invested less, businesses closed and banks failed, throwing millions out of work. The cycle spiraled steadily downward. The jobless could not afford to buy goods, so more factories had to close, which in turn increased unemployment. People slept on park benches and lined up to eat in soup kitchens.

The Depression Spreads The economic problems quickly spread around the world. American banks stopped making loans abroad and demanded repayment of foreign loans. Without support from the United States, Germany suffered. It could not make its reparations payments. France and Britain were not able to make their loan payments.

Desperate governments tried to protect their economies from foreign competition. The United States imposed the highest tariffs in its history. The policy backfired when other nations retaliated by raising their tariffs. In 1932 and 1933, global world trade sank to its 1900 level. As you have read, the Great Depression spread misery from the industrial world to Latin America, Africa, and Asia.

 **Checkpoint** How did the Federal Reserve's policies affect the Great Depression?

The Democracies React to the Depression

The governments of Britain, France, and the United States, like others around the world, tried to find ways to lift the Depression. None of their methods provided a quick fix, but they did alleviate some of the suffering.

Britain and France Search for Solutions In response to the Depression, Britain set up a coalition government made up of leaders from all three of its major political parties. The government provided some unemployment benefits but failed to take decisive action to improve the economy. By 1931, one in every four workers was unemployed.

The Great Depression took longer to hurt France than some other countries. However, by the mid-1930s, France was feeling the pinch of decreased production and unemployment. In response, several leftist parties united behind the socialist leader Leon Blum. His Popular Front government tried to solve labor problems and passed some social legislation. But it could not satisfy more radical leftists. Strikes soon brought down Blum's government. Democracy survived, but the country lacked strong leadership able to respond to the clamor for change.

The Dust Bowl
In Dorothea Lange's famous 1936 photo *Migrant Mother, Nipomo, California,* a mother looks into the future with despair. She migrated to escape scenes like the one below, where huge dust storms buried farm equipment in Dallas, Texas. *How did geography help aggravate the depression in the United States?*

Roosevelt Offers the United States a New Deal Meanwhile, in the United States, President Herbert Hoover firmly believed that the government should not intervene in private business matters. Even so, he did try a variety of limited measures to solve the crisis. Nothing seemed to work. In 1932, Americans elected a new President, **Franklin D. Roosevelt.** "FDR" argued that the government had to take an active role in combating the Great Depression. He introduced the **New Deal,** a massive package of economic and social programs.

Under the New Deal, the federal government became more directly involved in people's everyday lives than ever before. New laws regulated the stock market and protected bank deposits. Government programs created jobs and gave aid to farmers. A new Social Security system provided pensions for the elderly and other benefits.

As the New Deal programs were being put into effect, a natural disaster in 1934 hit several central states. After years of drought and over-farming, huge winds blew across the plains. The winds picked up and carried away the topsoil exposed by erosion, creating the Dust Bowl. The storms destroyed crops, land, and equipment. Thousands of farmers lost their land. Many migrated to the cities of the West Coast in search of work and a new life.

The New Deal failed to end the Great Depression, although it did ease the suffering for many. Still, some critics fiercely condemned FDR's expansion of the role of government. The debate about the size and role of the federal government continues to this day.

Loss of Faith in Democracy As the Depression wore on, many people lost faith in the ability of democratic governments to solve the problems of the modern world. Postwar disillusionment, soothed by the few good years of the 1920s, turned into despair in Europe. Misery and hopelessness created fertile ground for extremists who promised radical solutions.

 **Checkpoint** How did the government of the United States react to the Depression?

Economic Theories and the Great Depression

According to classical economists, free market economies naturally regulate their own highs and lows. The government should interfere as little as possible. The economist John Maynard Keynes argued that during a depression, the government should step in and spend more to bring the economy back up to its full productive capacity.

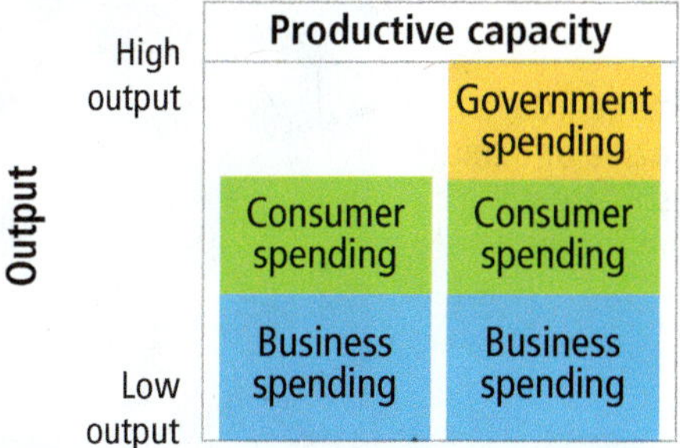

Diagram Skills *What role did Keynes envision for government in the economy?*

SECTION **2 Assessment**

Progress Monitoring *Online*
For: Self-quiz with vocabulary practice
Web Code: naa-2821

Terms, People, and Places

1. For each term, person, or place listed at the beginning of the section, write a sentence explaining its significance.

Note Taking

2. **Reading Skill: Identify Main Ideas** Use your completed table and chart to answer the Focus Question: What political and economic challenges did the leading democracies face in the 1920s and 1930s?

Comprehension and Critical Thinking

3. **Synthesize Information** How did Britain and France emerge from World War I as both victors and losers?

4. **Predict Consequences** What steps did the major powers take to protect the peace? Why did these moves have limited effects?

5. **Recognize Cause and Effect** Explain how each of the following contributed to the outbreak or spread of the Great Depression: (a) falling demand, (b) Federal Reserve Board, and (c) financial crisis.

6. **Identify Central Issues** How did the Great Depression affect political developments in the United States?

● **Writing About History**

Quick Write: Make a Venn Diagram A useful way to gather details for a compare-and-contrast essay is to use a Venn diagram. Place similarities between two ideas in the overlapping part of the circles; place differences in the parts that don't overlap. Create a Venn diagram for an essay on the following thesis statement: The United States was in better shape than Britain and France after World War I.

A New Leader: Mussolini

In the early 1920s, a new leader named Benito Mussolini arose in Italy. The Italian people were inspired by Mussolini's promises to bring stability and glory to Italy.

❝ [Only joy at finding such a leader] can explain the enthusiasm [Mussolini] evoked at gathering after gathering, where his mere presence drew the people from all sides to greet him with frenzied acclamations. Even the men who at first came out of mere curiosity and with indifferent or even hostile feelings gradually felt themselves fired by his personal magnetic influence. . . .❞
—Margherita G. Sarfatti, *The Life of Benito Mussolini* (tr. Frederic Whyte)

Focus Question How and why did fascism rise in Italy?

An image from a magazine of Benito Mussolini leading his nation to war ▶

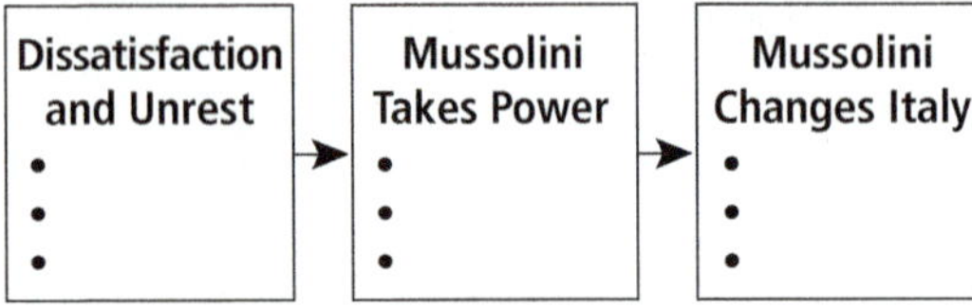
◀ Italian national flag during Mussolini's rule

Fascism in Italy

Objectives

- Describe how conditions in Italy favored the rise of Mussolini.
- Summarize how Mussolini changed Italy.
- Understand the values and goals of fascist ideology.
- Compare and contrast fascism and communism.

Terms, People, and Places

Benito Mussolini	totalitarian state
Black Shirts	fascism
March on Rome	

Note Taking

Reading Skill: Identify Main Ideas Find the main points of the text under the first two headings and record them in a flowchart like the one below.

Dissatisfaction and Unrest	→	Mussolini Takes Power	→	Mussolini Changes Italy
• • •		• • •		• • •

"I hated politics and politicians," said Italo Balbo. Like many Italian veterans of World War I, he had come home to a land of economic chaos and political corruption. Italy's constitutional government, he felt, "had betrayed the hopes of soldiers, reducing Italy to a shameful peace." Disgusted and angry, Balbo rallied behind a fiercely nationalist leader, Benito Mussolini. Mussolini's rise to power in the 1920s served as a model for ambitious strongmen elsewhere in Europe.

Mussolini's Rise to Power

When Italy agreed to join the Allies in 1915, France and Britain secretly promised to give Italy certain Austro-Hungarian territories. When the Allies won, Italy received some of the promised territories, but others became part of the new Yugoslavia. The broken promises outraged Italian nationalists.

Disorders within Italy multiplied. Inspired in part by the revolution in Russia, peasants seized land, and workers went on strike or seized factories. Amid the chaos, returning veterans faced unemployment. Trade declined and taxes rose. The government, split into feuding factions, seemed powerless to end the crisis.

A Leader Emerges Into this turmoil stepped **Benito Mussolini.** The son of a socialist blacksmith and a teacher, Mussolini had been a socialist in his youth. During the war, however, he rejected socialism for intense nationalism. In 1919, he organized veterans and other discontented Italians into the Fascist party. They took the name from the Latin *fasces,* a bundle of sticks wrapped around an ax. In ancient Rome, the fasces symbolized unity and authority.

Mussolini was a fiery and charismatic speaker. He promised to end corruption and replace turmoil with order. He also spoke of reviving Roman greatness, pledging to turn the Mediterranean into a "Roman lake" once again.

Mussolini Gains Control Mussolini organized his supporters into "combat squads." The squads wore black shirts to emulate an earlier nationalist revolt. These **Black Shirts,** or party militants, rejected the democratic process in favor of violent action. They broke up socialist rallies, smashed leftist presses, and attacked farmers' cooperatives. Fascist gangs used intimidation and terror to oust elected officials in northern Italy. Many Italians accepted these actions because they, too, had lost faith in constitutional government.

In 1922, the Fascists made a bid for power. At a rally in Naples, they announced their intention to go to Rome to demand that the government make changes. In the **March on Rome,** tens of thousands of Fascists swarmed towards the capital. Fearing civil war, King Victor Emmanuel III asked Mussolini to form a government as prime minister. Mussolini entered the city triumphantly on October 30, 1922. He thus obtained a nominally legal, constitutional appointment from the king to lead Italy.

 **Checkpoint** How did postwar disillusionment contribute to Mussolini's rise?

Mussolini's Rule

At first, Fascists held only a few cabinet posts in the new government. By 1925, though, Mussolini had assumed more power and taken the title Il Duce (eel DOO chay), "The Leader." He suppressed rival parties, muzzled the press, rigged elections, and replaced elected officials with Fascist supporters. In 1929, Mussolini received support from Pope Pius XI in return for recognizing Vatican City as an independent state, although the pope continued to disagree with some of Mussolini's goals. In theory, Italy remained a parliamentary monarchy. In fact, it was a dictatorship upheld by terror. Critics were thrown into prison, forced into exile, or murdered. Secret police and propaganda bolstered the regime.

State Control of the Economy To spur economic growth and end conflicts between owners and workers, Mussolini brought the economy under state control. However, he preserved capitalism. Under Mussolini's corporate state, representatives of business, labor, government, and the Fascist

Mussolini and the People
An excited crowd of women and children greets the Italian leader in 1940.

party controlled industry, agriculture, and trade. Mussolini's system favored the upper classes and industrial leaders. Although production increased, success came at the expense of workers. They were forbidden to strike, and their wages were kept low.

The Individual and the State In Mussolini's new system, loyalty to the state replaced conflicting individual goals. To Fascists, the glorious state was all-important, and the individual was unimportant except as a member of the state. Men, women, and children were bombarded with slogans glorifying the state and Mussolini. "Believe! Obey! Fight!" loudspeakers blared and posters proclaimed. Men were urged to be ruthless, selfless warriors fighting for the glory of Italy. Women were pushed out of paying jobs. Instead, Mussolini called on women to "win the battle of motherhood." Those who bore more than 14 children were given a medal by Il Duce himself.

Shaping the young was a major Fascist goal. Fascist youth groups toughened children and taught them to obey strict military discipline. Boys and girls learned about the glories of ancient Rome. Young Fascists marched in torchlight parades, singing patriotic hymns and chanting, "Mussolini is always right." By the 1930s, a generation of young soldiers stood ready to back Il Duce's drive to expand Italian power.

✔ **Checkpoint** How did the Fascist party transform Italy's government and economy?

● **INFOGRAPHIC**

The Makings of a *Totalitarian* State

As part of a propaganda drive, German mothers received medals for bearing several children. ▶

In totalitarian Italy, Mussolini's government tried to dominate every part of the lives of Italians. Mussolini's totalitarian state became a model for others, although his rule in Italy was not as absolute as that of Stalin in the Soviet Union or Adolf Hitler in Germany. Still, all three governments shared the following basic features: (1) a single-party dictatorship with blind obedience to a single leader, (2) state control of the economy, (3) use of police spies and terror to enforce the will of the state, (4) government control of the media to indoctrinate and mobilize citizens through propaganda, (5) use of schools and youth organizations to spread ideology to children, and (6) strict censorship of artists and intellectuals with dissenting opinions.

◀ The dictators built cults of personality around themselves. At left, a statue of Stalin in a heroic pose, and (inset) Mussolini depicted working alongside Italian builders.

A photo from the Soviet secret police file on author Alexander Solzhenitsyn, who was sent to the Gulag for criticizing Stalin. ▶

The Nature of Fascism

Mussolini built the first **totalitarian state.** In this form of government, a one-party dictatorship attempts to regulate every aspect of the lives of its citizens. Other dictators, notably Stalin and Hitler, followed Mussolini's lead. Mussolini's rule was fascist in nature, as was Hitler's, but totalitarian governments rise under other kinds of ideology as well, such as communism in Stalin's Soviet Union.

What Is Fascism? Historians still debate the real nature of Mussolini's fascist <u>ideology</u>. Mussolini coined the term, but fascists had no unifying theory as Marxists did. Today, we generally use the term **fascism** to describe any centralized, authoritarian government that is not communist whose policies glorify the state over the individual and are destructive to basic human rights. In the 1920s and 1930s, though, fascism meant different things in different countries.

All forms of fascism, however, shared some basic features. They were rooted in extreme nationalism. Fascists glorified action, violence, discipline, and, above all, blind loyalty to the state. Fascists also pursued aggressive foreign expansion. Echoing the idea of "survival of the fittest," Fascist leaders glorified warfare as a noble struggle for survival.

Fascists were also antidemocratic. They rejected faith in reason and the concepts of equality and liberty. To them, democracy led to corruption and weakness and put individual or class interests above national goals. Instead, fascists emphasized emotion and the supremacy of the state.

Reading Skill: Identify Main Ideas Use a table like the one below to record information about fascism.

What Is Fascism?	
Values	
Characteristics	
Differences From Communism	
Similarities to Communism	

Vocabulary Builder

<u>ideology</u>—(ih dee AHL uh jee) *n.* a system of ideas that guides an individual, movement, or political program

Thinking Critically

1. **Draw Inferences** Why did totalitarian governments try to win the loyalty of their nations' young people?
2. **Recognize Ideologies** Why did leaders honor women for having many children?

A Fascist Childhood
Children were required to use notebooks that featured fascist drawings and quotes from Mussolini.

The Appeal of Fascism Given its restrictions on individual freedom, why did fascism appeal to many Italians? First, it promised a strong, stable government and an end to the political feuding that had paralyzed democracy in Italy. Mussolini projected a sense of power and confidence at a time of disorder and despair. Mussolini's intense nationalism also revived national pride.

At first, newspapers in Britain, France, and North America applauded the discipline and order of Mussolini's government. "He got the trains running on time," admirers said. Only later, when Mussolini embarked on a course of foreign conquest, did Western democracies protest.

Fascism Compared to Communism Fascists were the sworn enemies of socialists and communists. While communists worked for international change, fascists pursued nationalist goals. Fascists supported a society with defined classes. They found allies among business leaders, wealthy landowners, and the lower middle class. Communists touted a classless society. They won support among both urban and agricultural workers.

Despite such differences, the products of these two ideologies had much in common. Both drew their power by inspiring a blind devotion to the state, or a charismatic leader as the embodiment of the state. Both used terror to guard their power. Both flourished during economic hard times by promoting extreme programs of social change. In both, a party elite claimed to rule in the name of the national interest.

✔ **Checkpoint** Describe the similarities between fascism and communism.

Looking Ahead

Three systems of government competed for influence in postwar Europe. Democracy endured in Britain and France but faced an uphill struggle in hard times. Communism emerged in Russia and won support elsewhere. In Italy, fascism offered a different option. As the Great Depression spread, other nations—most notably Germany—looked to fascist leaders.

SECTION **3** Assessment

Terms, People, and Places

1. For each term listed at the beginning of the section, write a sentence explaining its significance.

Note Taking

2. **Reading Skill: Identify Main Ideas** Use your completed flowchart and table to answer the section Focus Question: How and why did fascism rise in Italy?

Comprehension and Critical Thinking

3. **Recognize Cause and Effect** What problems did Italy face after World War I? How did these problems help Mussolini win power?

4. **Summarize** Describe one of Mussolini's economic or social goals, and explain the actions he took to achieve it.

5. **Compare and Contrast** List two similarities and two differences between fascism and communism.

6. **Identify Point of View** Mussolini said, "Machines and women are the two main causes of unemployment." (a) What do you think he meant? (b) How did Mussolini's policies reflect his attitude toward women?

● **Writing About History**

Quick Write: Write a Thesis Statement
A compare-and-contrast thesis statement should introduce the items you are comparing and the point you intend to make. Which of the following thesis statements would work best for a compare-and-contrast essay?

- Fascism and communism are very different ideologies, but they both led to the imposition of totalitarian governments.
- Fascism led to a totalitarian government in Italy.

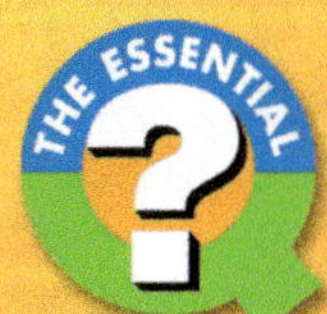

DICTATORSHIP
Why do people sometimes support dictators?

In This Chapter

Following World War I, European countries experienced economic and political turmoil. In Germany, money was worth so little that people used it as fuel for cooking (right). As society seemed to unravel, desperate people looked to strong leaders to create stability. In some countries, people were willing to give up individual freedoms to gain security and order.

Throughout History

48 B.C.– 44 B.C. Julius Caesar forces the Roman Senate to grant him absolute power and initiates reforms.

1547–1580 A.D. Ivan the Terrible, the Russian tsar, organizes agents of terror to enforce his will.

1920s Mussolini promises to restore order to Italy and revive its Roman greatness.

1930s Stalin uses terror and censorship to strengthen his power over the Soviet people.

1934 Hitler's extreme nationalism, racism, and economic goals appeal to many German people.

1950s–1970s Military leaders in Brazil, Argentina, and Chile use force to seize and maintain power.

Continuing Today

To maintain power, dictators like Kim Jong-Il of North Korea (below) create a cult of personality. They present themselves as heroic figures and people are encouraged to view them as an objects of worship.

21st Century Skills

 **TRANSFER Activities**

1. Analyze Throughout history, how have dictators maintained control?

2. Evaluate What are the dangers of giving up rights in order to gain stability and order?

3. Transfer Complete a Web quest in which you speak out against a modern dictator; record your thoughts in the Concept Connector Journal; and learn to make a video. Web Code nah-2808

In this propaganda image, people offer Stalin flowers.

The Heart of the Party

On the occasion of Stalin's sixtieth birthday, the Communist party newspaper, *Pravda*, or "Truth," printed this praise of Stalin:

> **66** There is no similar name on the planet like the name of Stalin. It shines like a bright torch of freedom, it flies like a battle standard for millions of laborers around the world. . . . Stalin is today's Lenin! Stalin is the brain and heart of the party! Stalin is the banner of millions of people in their fight for a better life. **99**

Far from helping people fight for a better life, Stalin's ruthless policies brought suffering and death to millions of Soviets.

Focus Question How did Stalin transform the Soviet Union into a totalitarian state?

The Soviet Union Under Stalin

Objectives
- Describe the effects of Stalin's five-year plans.
- Explain how Stalin tried to control how people thought in the Soviet Union.
- List communist changes to Soviet society.
- Outline Soviet foreign policy under Stalin.

Terms, People, and Places

command economy · russification
collectives · atheism
kulaks · Comintern
Gulag
socialist realism

Note Taking

Reading Strategy: Identify Main Ideas Summarize the main points of the section in a chart like the one below.

The Soviet Union Under Stalin		
Five-Year Plans	Methods of Control	Daily Life

In January 1924, tens of thousands of people lined up in Moscow's historic Red Square. They had come to view the body of Lenin, who had died a few days earlier. Lenin's widow, Nadezhda Krupskaya, wanted to bury him simply next to his mother. Communist party officials—including Joseph Stalin—wanted to preserve Lenin's body and put it on permanent display. In the end, Lenin's body was displayed in Red Square for more than 65 years. By preserving Lenin's body, Stalin wanted to show that he would carry on the goals of the revolution. However, in the years that followed, he used ruthless measures to control the Soviet Union and its people.

A Totalitarian State

Karl Marx had predicted that under communism the state would eventually wither away. Under Stalin, the opposite occurred. He turned the Soviet Union into a totalitarian state controlled by a powerful and complex bureaucracy.

Stalin's Five-Year Plans Once in power, Stalin imposed government control over the Soviet Union's economy. In the past, said Stalin, Russia had suffered because of its economic backwardness. In 1928, he proposed the first of several "five-year plans" aimed at building heavy industry, improving transportation, and increasing farm output. He brought all economic activity under government control. The government owned all businesses and distributed all resources. The Soviet Union developed a **command economy,** in which government officials made all basic economic decisions. By contrast, in a capitalist system, the free market determine most economic decisions. Privately owned businesses compete to win the consumer's choice. This competition regulates the price and quality of goods.

Mixed Results in Industry Stalin's five-year plans set high production goals, especially for heavy industry and transportation. The government pushed workers and managers to meet these goals by giving bonuses to those who succeeded—and by punishing those who did not. Between 1928 and 1939, large factories, hydroelectric power stations, and huge industrial complexes rose across the Soviet Union. Oil, coal, and steel production grew. Mining expanded, and new railroads were built.

Despite the impressive progress in some areas, Soviet workers had little to show for their efforts. Some former peasants did become skilled factory workers or managers. Overall, though, the standard of living remained low. Central planning was often inefficient, causing shortages in some areas and surpluses in others. Many managers, concerned only with meeting production quotas, turned out large quantities of low-quality goods. Consumer products such as clothing, cars, and refrigerators were scarce. Wages were low and workers were forbidden to strike. The party restricted workers' movements.

Forced Collectivization in Agriculture Stalin also brought agriculture under government control, but at a horrendous cost. The government wanted farmers to produce more grain to feed workers in the cities. It also hoped to sell grain abroad to earn money.

As you have read, under Lenin's New Economic Plan (NEP), peasants had held on to small plots of land. Many had prospered. Stalin saw that system as being inefficient and a threat to state power. Stalin wanted all peasants to farm on either state-owned farms or **collectives,** large farms owned and operated by peasants as a group. On collectives, the government would provide tractors, fertilizers, and better seed, and peasants would learn modern farm methods. Peasants would be permitted to keep their houses and personal belongings, but all farm animals and implements were to be turned over to the collective. The state set all prices and controlled access to farm supplies.

Some peasants did not want to give up their land and sell their crops at the state's low prices. They resisted collectivization by killing farm animals, destroying tools, and burning crops. Stalin was furious. He believed that **kulaks,** or wealthy farmers, were behind the resistance. He responded with brutal force. In 1929, Stalin declared his intention to "liquidate the kulaks as a class." To this end, the government confiscated kulaks' land and sent them to labor camps. Thousands were killed or died from overwork.

Even after the "de-kulakization," angry peasants resisted by growing just enough to feed themselves. In response, the government seized all of their grain to meet industrial goals, purposely leaving the peasants to starve. In 1932, this ruthless policy, combined with poor harvests, led to a terrible

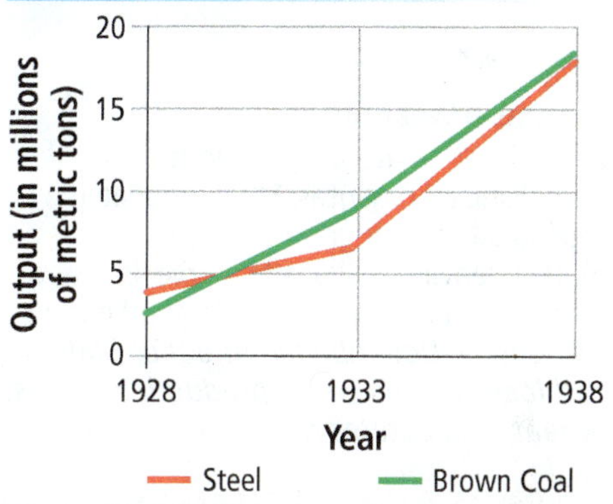

Effects of the Five-Year Plans on Soviet Industry

SOURCE: B.R. Mitchell, *European Historical Statistics, 1750–1970*

This 1931 propaganda poster supports the Five Year Plan for industry. Stalin's government saw rapid industrialization as the key to the success of the Soviet Union. *Using the line graph, describe the effect of the Five-Year Plans on steel and brown coal output.*

famine. Later called the Terror Famine, it caused between five and eight million people to die of starvation in the Ukraine alone.

Although collectivization increased Stalin's control of the peasantry, it did not improve farm output. During the 1930s, grain production inched upward, but meat, vegetables, and fruits remained in short supply. Feeding the population would remain a major problem in the Soviet Union.

✔ **Checkpoint** How did Stalin take control of the Soviet Union's economic life?

Stalin's Terror Tactics

In addition to tactics like the Terror Famine, Stalin's Communist party used secret police, torture, and violent purges to ensure obedience. Stalin tightened his grasp on every aspect of Soviet life, even stamping out any signs of dissent within the Communist elites.

Terror as a Weapon Stalin ruthlessly used terror as a weapon against his own people. He perpetrated crimes against humanity and systematically violated his people's individual rights. Police spies did not hesitate to open private letters or plant listening devices. Nothing appeared in print without official approval. There was no free press, and no safe method of voicing protest. Grumblers or critics were rounded up and sent to the **Gulag,** a system of brutal labor camps, where many died.

The Great Purge Even though Stalin's power was absolute, he still feared that rival party leaders were plotting against him. In 1934, he launched the Great Purge. During this reign of terror, Stalin and his secret police cracked down especially on Old Bolsheviks, or party activists from the early days of the revolution. His net soon widened to target army heroes, industrial managers, writers, and ordinary citizens. They were charged with a wide range of crimes, from counterrevolutionary plots to failure to meet production quotas.

Between 1936 and 1938, Stalin staged a series of spectacular public "show trials" in Moscow. Former Communist leaders confessed to all kinds of crimes after officials tortured them or threatened their families or friends. Many of the purged party members were never tried but were sent straight to the Gulag. Secret police files reveal that at least four million people were purged during the Stalin years. Some historians estimate the toll to be much greater.

Results of the Purge The purges increased Stalin's power. All Soviet citizens were now well aware of the consequences of disloyalty. However, Stalin's government also paid a price. Among the purged were experts in industry, economics, and engineering, and many of the Soviet Union's most talented

Food as a Weapon
In 1932, when peasants failed to meet unrealistic crop quotas, Stalin retaliated by seizing all of their grain to sell on the market, leaving millions to starve. Below, a woman and her son search for food during the famine. *Describe the effect of Stalin's ruthless policies on the production of oats, wheat, and potatoes.*

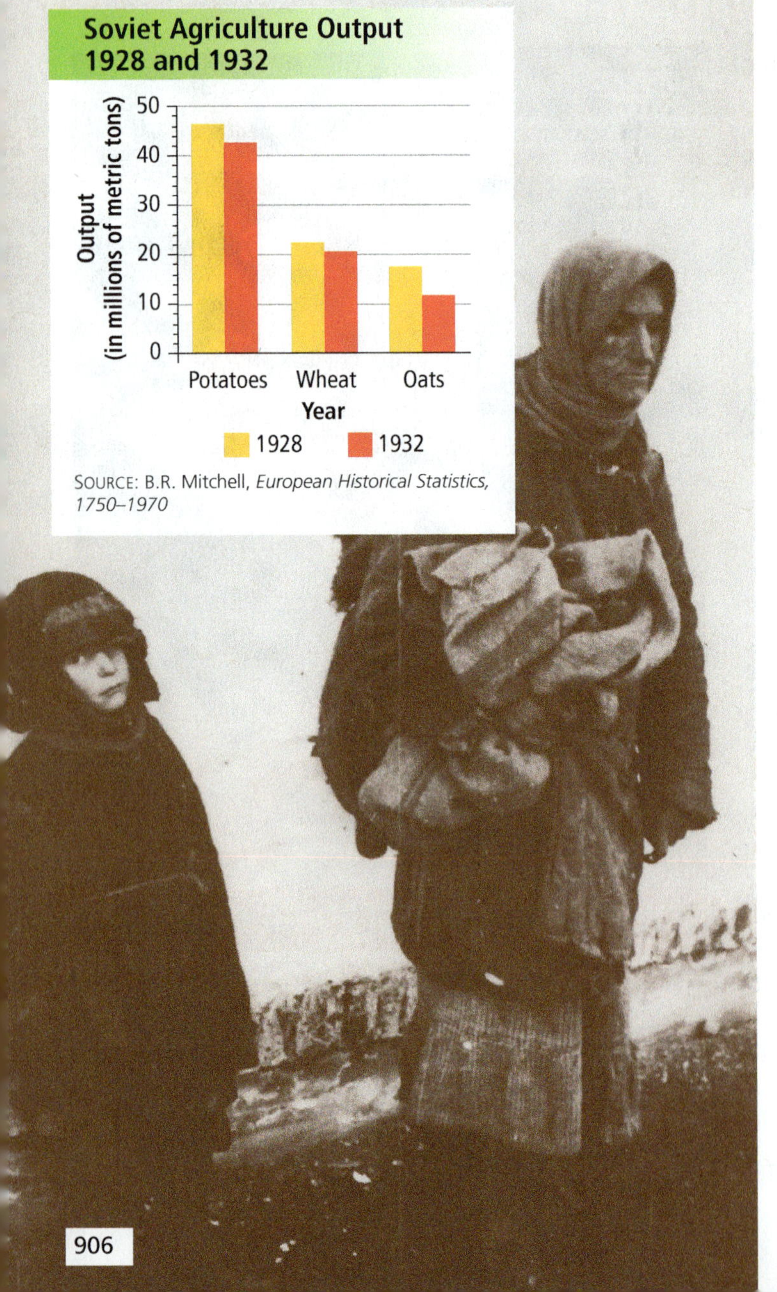

SOURCE: B.R. Mitchell, *European Historical Statistics, 1750–1970*

Map of the Soviet Union, 1928–1941

Map Skills Stalin used terror and Gulag labor camps to control the huge, multinational Soviet Union.

1. **Locate** (a) Ukrainian S.S.R. (b) Russian Soviet Federated Socialist Republic (c) forced labor camp region

2. **Regions** How does the map help explain why Russia was the most influential republic in the Soviet Union?

3. **Make Inferences** What does the number of labor camps in the Soviet Union indicate about Stalin's rule?

A Gulag labor camp in 1934

writers and thinkers. The victims included most of the nation's military leaders and about half of its military officers, a loss that would weigh heavily on Stalin in 1941, when Germany invaded the Soviet Union.

 **Checkpoint** In what ways did Stalin's terror tactics harm the Soviet Union?

Communist Attempts to Control Thought

At the same time that he was purging any elements of resistance in Soviet society, Stalin also sought to control the hearts and minds of Soviet citizens. He tried to do this by tirelessly distributing propaganda, censoring opposing ideas, imposing Russian culture on minorities, and replacing religion with communist ideology.

Propaganda Stalin tried to boost morale and faith in the communist system by making himself a godlike figure. He used propaganda as a tool to build up a "cult of personality" around himself. Using modern technology, the party bombarded the public with relentless propaganda. Radios and loudspeakers blared into factories and villages. In movies, theaters, and schools, citizens heard about communist successes and the evils of capitalism. Billboards and posters urged workers to meet or exceed production quotas. Headlines in the Communist party newspaper *Pravda,* or "Truth," linked enemies at home to foreign agents seeking to overthrow the Communist regime.

Censorship and the Arts At first, the Bolshevik Revolution had meant greater freedom for Soviet artists and writers. Under Stalin, however, the heavy hand of state control also gripped the arts. The government controlled what books were published, what music was heard, and which works of art were displayed. Stalin required artists and writers to create their works in a style called **socialist realism.** Its goal was to show Soviet life in a positive light and promote hope in the communist future.

In theory, socialist realism followed in the footstep of Russian greats Tolstoy and Chekhov; in practice it was rarely allowed to be realistic. Socialist realist novels usually featured a positive hero, often an engineer or scientist, battling against the odds to accomplish a goal. Popular themes for socialist-realist visual artists were peasants, workers, heroes of the revolution, and—of course—Stalin.

If they refused to <u>conform</u> to government expectations, writers, artists, and composers faced government persecution. The Jewish poet Osip Mandelstam, for example, was imprisoned, tortured, and exiled for composing a satirical verse that was critical of Stalin. Out of fear for his wife's safety, Mandelstam finally submitted to threats and wrote an "Ode to Stalin." Boris Pasternak, who would later win fame for his novel *Doctor Zhivago,* was afraid to publish anything at all during the Stalin years. Rather than write in the favored style of socialist realism, he translated foreign literary works instead.

Despite restrictions, some Soviet writers produced magnificent works. Yevgeny Zamyatin's classic anti-Utopian novel *We* became well known outside of the Soviet Union, but was not published in his home country until 1989. The novel depicts a nightmare future in which people go by numbers, not names, and the "One State" controls people's thoughts. *And Quiet Flows the Don,* by Mikhail Sholokhov, passed the censor. The novel tells the story of a man who spends years fighting in World War I, the Russian Revolution, and the civil war. Sholokhov later won the Nobel Prize for literature.

Russification Yet another way Stalin controlled the cultural life of the Soviet Union was by promoting a policy of **russification,** or making a nationality's culture more Russian. By 1936, the U.S.S.R. was made up of 11 Soviet Socialist Republics. The Russian Soviet Federated Socialist Republic consisted of the old Russian heartland and was the largest and dominant republic. The other

AUDIO

SSRs, such as Uzbek and the Ukraine, were the homelands of other nationalities and had their own languages, historical traditions, and cultures. At first, Stalin encouraged the autonomy, or independence, of these cultures. However, in the late 1920s, Stalin turned this policy on its head and systematically tried to make the cultures of the non-Russian SSRs more Russian. He appointed Russians to high-ranking positions in non-Russian SSRs and required the Russian language to be used in schools and businesses.

War on Religion The Communist party also tried to strengthen its hold on the minds of the people by destroying their religious faith. In accordance with the ideas of Marx, **atheism,** or the belief that there is no god, became an official state policy. Early on, the Communists targeted the Russian Orthodox Church, which had strongly supported the tsars. Many priests and other religious leaders were among those killed in the purges or sent to die in prison camps. Other religions were persecuted as well. At one show trial, 15 Roman Catholic priests were charged with teaching religion to the young, a counterrevolutionary activity. The state seized Jewish synagogues and banned the use of Hebrew. Islam was also officially discouraged.

The Communists tried to replace religion with their own ideology. Like a religion, communist ideology had its own "sacred" texts—the writings of Marx and Lenin—and its own shrines, such as the tomb of Lenin. Portraits of Stalin replaced religious icons in Russian homes. However, millions of Soviets continued to worship, in private and sometimes in public, in defiance of the government's prohibitions.

 **Checkpoint** How did Stalin use censorship and propaganda to support his rule?

The Party Versus the Church
To weaken the power of the Russian Orthodox Church, the party seized church property and converted churches into offices and museums. Here, Red Army soldiers carry off religious relics from a Russian church. *How might the policy of destroying churches in such a public way have backfired on the party?*

Soviet Society Under Stalin

The terror and cultural coercion of Stalin's rule made a mockery of the original theories and promises of communism. The lives of most Russians did change. But, while the changes had some benefits, they were often outweighed by continuous shortages and restricted freedoms.

The New Elite Takes Control The Communists destroyed the old social order of landowning nobles at the top and peasants at the bottom. But instead of creating a society of equals as they promised, they created a society where a few elite groups emerged as a new ruling class. At the head of society were members of the Communist party. Only a small fraction of Soviet citizens could join the party. Many who did so were motivated by a desire to get ahead, rather than a belief in communism.

The Soviet elite also included industrial managers, military leaders, scientists, and some artists and writers. The elite enjoyed benefits denied to most people. They lived in the best apartments in the cities and rested at the best vacation homes in the country. They could shop at special stores for scarce consumer goods. On the other hand, Stalin's purges often fell on the elite.

Benefits and Drawbacks Although excluded from party membership, most people did enjoy several new benefits. The party required all children to attend free Communist-built schools. The state supported technical schools and universities as well. Schools served many important goals. Educated workers were needed to build a modern industrial state. The Communist party also set up programs for students outside school. These programs included sports, cultural activities, and political classes to train teenagers for party membership. However, in addition to important basic skills, schools also taught communist values, such as atheism, the glory of collective farming, and love of Stalin.

The state also provided free medical care, day care for children, inexpensive housing, and public recreation. While these benefits were real, many people still lacked vital necessities. Although the state built massive apartment complexes, housing was scarce. Entire families might be packed into a single room. Bread was plentiful, but meat, fresh fruit, and other foods remained in short supply.

Women in the Soviet Union Long before 1917, women such as Nadezhda Krupskaya and Alexandra Kollontai worked for the revolution, spreading radical ideas among peasants and workers. Under the Communists, women won equality under the law. They gained <u>access</u> to education and a wide range of jobs. By the 1930s, many Soviet women were working in medicine, engineering, or the sciences. By their labor, women contributed to Soviet economic growth. They worked in factories, in construction, and on collectives. Within the family, their wages were needed because men and women earned the same low salaries.

✔ **Checkpoint** How did Communist schools benefit the state and the Communist party?

Women at Work
Soviet women, such as these concrete workers, were able to take jobs alongside men as equals, doing the same work and earning the same party. *What role did women play in the Soviet Union?*

Soviet Foreign Policy

Between 1917 and 1939, the Soviet Union pursued two very different goals in foreign policy. As Communists, both Lenin and Stalin wanted to bring about the worldwide revolution that Marx had predicted. But as Soviets, they wanted to guarantee their nation's security by winning the support of other countries. The result of pursuing these two different goals was a contradictory and generally unsuccessful foreign policy.

In 1919, Lenin formed the Communist International, or **Comintern.** The purpose of the Comintern was to encourage world-wide revolution. To this end, it aided revolutionary groups around the world and urged colonial peoples to rise up against imperialist powers.

The Comintern's support of revolutionary groups outside the Soviet Union and its propaganda against capitalism made Western powers highly suspicious of the Soviet Union. In the United States, fear of Bolshevik plots led to the "Red Scare" in the early 1920s. Britain broke off relations with the Soviet Union when evidence revealed Soviet schemes to turn a 1926 strike into a revolution. Even so, the Soviet Union slowly won recognition from Western powers and increased trade with capitalist countries. It also joined the League of Nations. However, mistrust still poisoned relations, especially after the Great Purge.

 **Checkpoint** How did the Soviet Union's foreign policy goals contradict one another?

Looking Ahead

By the time Stalin died in 1953, the Soviet Union had become a military superpower and a world leader in heavy industry. Yet Stalin's efforts exacted a brutal toll. The Soviet people were dominated by a totalitarian system based on terror. The reality of communism fell far short of Lenin's promises. Most people in the Soviet Union lived meager lives compared with people in the West.

SECTION 4 Assessment

Terms, People, and Places

1. What do many of the key terms listed at the beginning of the section have in common? Explain.

Note Taking

2. **Reading Skill: Identify Main Ideas** Use your completed chart to answer the section Focus Question: How did Stalin transform the Soviet Union into a totalitarian state?

Comprehension and Critical Thinking

3. **Identify Effects** What were the goals and results of Stalin's five-year plans? How did the effects differ between industry and agriculture?

4. **Contrast** How did the command economy under Stalin differ from a capitalist economy?

5. **Synthesize Information** What methods did Stalin use to create a totalitarian state?

6. **Synthesize Information** One historian has said that socialist realism was "communism with a smiling face." What do you think he meant?

7. **Compare** Compare life under Stalin's rule with life under the Russian tsars.

● **Writing About History**
Quick Write: Choose an Organization Compare-and-contrast essays are often organized either point by point or by block. The first organization involves a discussion of one idea first, followed by the discussion of another, and emphasizes the two ideas. The second discusses all of the similarities, followed by all the differences, and emphasizes the comparison or contrast itself. Write an outline for each type for an essay comparing and contrasting the results of the Five-Year Plans in industry and agriculture.

Adolf Hitler with a member of a
Nazi youth organization

The Nazis in Control of Germany

In the 1930s, Adolf Hitler and the Nazi party brought hope to Germans suffering from the Great Depression. On the dark side of Hitler's promises was a message of hate, aimed particularly at Jews. A German Jewish woman recalls an attack on her family during *Kristallnacht,* a night in early November 1938 when Nazi mobs attacked Jewish homes and businesses.

> 66 They broke our windowpanes, and the house became very cold. . . . We were standing there, outside in the cold, still in our night clothes, with only a coat thrown over. . . . Then they made everyone lie face down on the ground . . . 'Now, they will shoot us,' we thought. We were very afraid. 99

Focus Question How did Hitler and the Nazi party establish and maintain a totalitarian government in Germany?

Hitler and the Rise of Nazi Germany

Objectives

- Analyze the problems faced by the Weimar Republic.
- Describe the Nazi party's political, social, economic, and cultural policies.
- Summarize the rise of authoritarian rule in Eastern Europe in the 1920s and 1930s.

Terms, People, and Places

chancellor	Gestapo
Ruhr Valley	Nuremberg Laws
Third Reich	

Note Taking

Reading Skill: Identify Main Ideas As you read, summarize the section's main ideas in a flowchart like the one below.

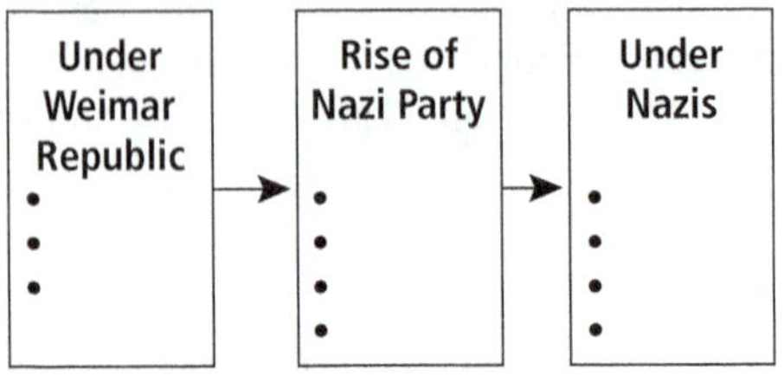

Under Weimar Republic	→	Rise of Nazi Party	→	Under Nazis
• • •		• • •		• • •

In November 1923, a German army veteran and leader of an extremist party, Adolf Hitler, tried to follow Mussolini's example by staging a small-scale coup in Munich. The coup failed, and Hitler was soon behind bars. But Hitler proved to be a force that could not be ignored. Within a decade, he made a new bid for power. This time, he succeeded by legal means.

Hitler's rise to power raises disturbing questions that we still debate today. Why did Germany, which had a democratic government in the 1920s, become a totalitarian state in the 1930s? How could a ruthless, hate-filled dictator gain the enthusiastic support of many Germans?

The Weimar Republic's Rise and Fall

As World War I drew to a close, Germany tottered on the brink of chaos. Under the threat of a socialist revolution, the kaiser abdicated. Moderate leaders signed the armistice and later, under protest, the Versailles treaty.

In 1919, German leaders drafted a constitution in the city of Weimar (VY mahr). It created a democratic government known as the Weimar Republic. The constitution set up a parliamentary system led by a **chancellor,** or prime minister. It gave women the vote and included a bill of rights.

Political Struggles The republic faced severe problems from the start. Politically, it was weak because Germany, like France, had many small parties. The chancellor had to form coalitions that easily fell apart.

The government, led by moderate democratic socialists, came under constant fire from both the left and right. Communists demanded radical changes like those Lenin had brought to Russia. Conservatives—including the old Junker nobility, military officers, and wealthy bourgeoisie—attacked the government as too liberal and weak. They longed for another strong leader like Bismarck. Germans of all classes blamed the Weimar Republic for the hated Versailles treaty. Bitter, they looked for scapegoats. Many blamed German Jews for economic and political problems.

Runaway Inflation Economic disaster fed unrest. In 1923, when Germany fell behind in reparations payments, France occupied the coal-rich Ruhr Valley (roor). Germans workers in the Ruhr protested using <u>passive</u> resistance and refused to work. To support the workers, the government continued to pay them, and printed huge quantities of paper money to do so. Inflation soon spiraled out of control, spreading misery and despair. The German mark became almost worthless. An item that cost 100 marks in July 1922 cost 944,000 marks by August 1923. Salaries rose by billions of marks, but they still could not keep up with skyrocketing prices. Many middle-class families saw their savings wiped out.

Recovery and Collapse With help from the Western powers, the government did bring inflation under control. In 1924, the United States gained British and French approval for a plan to reduce German reparations payments. Under the Dawes Plan, France withdrew its forces from the Ruhr, and American loans helped the German economy recover. Germany began to prosper. Then, the Great Depression hit, reviving memories of the miseries of 1923. Germans turned to an energetic leader, Adolf Hitler, who promised to solve the economic crisis and restore Germany's former greatness.

Weimar Culture Culture flourished in the Weimar Republic even as the government struggled through crisis after crisis. The tumultuous times helped to stimulate new cultural movements, such as dadaist art and Bauhaus architecture. Berlin attracted writers and artists from around the world, just as Paris did. The German playwright Bertolt Brecht sharply criticized middle-class values with *The Three-Penny Opera*. The artist George Grosz, through scathing drawings and paintings, blasted the failings of the Weimar Republic. However, many believed that this modern culture and the Weimar Republic itself were not in keeping with Germany's illustrious past.

✔ **Checkpoint** What political and economic problems did the Weimar Republic face?

The Nazi Party's Rise to Power

Adolf Hitler was born in Austria in 1889. When he was 18, he went to Vienna, then the capital of the multinational Hapsburg empire. German Austrians

Inflation Rocks Germany
A man uses German marks to paper his wall because it costs less than buying wallpaper. At the height of the inflation, it would have taken 84,000 fifty-million mark notes like the one below, to equal a single American dollar. *Why would inflation hit middle class people with modest savings hard?*

Adolf Hitler

As a boy, Adolf Hitler (1889–1945) became obsessed with Germany's 1871 victory in the Franco–Prussian War. "The great historic struggle would become my greatest spiritual experience," he later wrote. "I became more and more enthusiastic about everything . . . connected with war."

In school, young Hitler was known as a ringleader. One of his teachers recalled, "He demanded of his fellow pupils their unqualified obedience." He failed to finish high school and was later crushed when he was rejected by art school.

After Hitler came to power, he used his elite guard of storm troopers to terrorize his opponents. But when he felt his power threatened, Hitler had leaders of the storm troopers murdered during the "Night of the Long Knives" on June 30, 1934. **Why do you think historians study Hitler's upbringing?**

made up just one of many ethnic groups in Vienna. Yet they felt superior to Jews, Serbs, Poles, and other groups. While living in Vienna, Hitler developed the fanatical anti-Semitism, or prejudice against Jewish people, that would later play a major role in his rise to power.

Hitler went to Germany and fought in the German army during World War I. In 1919, he joined a small group of right-wing extremists. Like many ex-soldiers, he despised the Weimar government, which he saw as weak. Within a year, he was the unquestioned leader of the National Socialist German Workers, or Nazi, party. Like Mussolini, Hitler organized his supporters into fighting squads. Nazi "storm troopers" fought in the streets against their political enemies.

Hitler's Manifesto In 1923, as you have read, Hitler made a failed attempt to seize power in Munich. He was arrested and found guilty of treason. While in prison, Hitler wrote *Mein Kampf ("My Struggle")*. It would later become the basic book of Nazi goals and ideology.

Mein Kampf reflected Hitler's obsessions—extreme nationalism, racism, and anti-Semitism. Germans, he said, belonged to a superior "master race" of Aryans, or light-skinned Europeans, whose greatest enemies were the Jews. Hitler's ideas were rooted in a long tradition of anti-Semitism. In the Middle Ages, Christians persecuted Jews because of their different beliefs. The rise of nationalism in the 1800s caused people to identify Jews as ethnic outsiders. Hitler viewed Jews not as members of a religion but as a separate race. (He defined a Jew as anyone with one Jewish grandparent.) Echoing a familiar right-wing theme, he blamed Germany's defeat in World War I on a conspiracy of Marxists, Jews, corrupt politicians, and business leaders.

In his recipe for revival, Hitler urged Germans everywhere to unite into one great nation. Germany must expand, he said, to gain *Lebensraum* (LAY buns rowm), or living space, for its people. Slavs and other inferior races must bow to Aryan needs. To achieve its greatness, Germany needed a strong leader, or Führer (FYOO rur). Hitler was determined to become that leader.

Hitler Comes to Power After less than a year, Hitler was released from prison. He soon renewed his table-thumping speeches. The Great Depression played into Hitler's hands. As unemployment rose, Nazi membership grew to almost a million. Hitler's program appealed to veterans, workers, the lower middle classes, small-town Germans, and business people alike. He promised to end reparations, create jobs, and defy the Versailles treaty by rearming Germany.

With the government paralyzed by divisions, both Nazis and Communists won more seats in the Reichstag, or lower house of the legislature. Fearing the growth of communist political power, conservative politicians turned to Hitler. Although they despised him, they believed they could control him. Thus, with conservative support, Hitler was appointed chancellor in 1933 through legal means under the Weimar constitution.

Within a year, Hitler was dictator of Germany. He and his supporters suspended civil rights, destroyed the socialists and Communists, and disbanded other political parties. Germany became a one-party state. Like Stalin in Russia, Hitler purged his own party, brutally executing Nazis he felt were disloyal. Nazis learned that Hitler demanded unquestioning obedience.

 **Checkpoint** Describe the Nazi party's ideology and Hitler's plans for ruling Germany.

The Third Reich Controls Germany

Once in power, Hitler and the Nazis moved to build a new Germany. Like Mussolini, Hitler appealed to nationalism by recalling past glories. Germany's First Reich, or empire, was the medieval Holy Roman Empire. The Second Reich was the empire forged by Bismarck in 1871. Under Hitler's new **Third Reich,** he boasted, the German master race would dominate Europe for a thousand years.

To combat the Great Depression, Hitler launched large public works programs (as did Britain and the United States). Tens of thousands of people were put to work building highways and housing or replanting forests. Hitler also began a crash program to rearm Germany and schemed to unite Germany and Austria. Both measures were a strong repudiation, or rejection, of the hated Versailles treaty.

Germany Becomes a Totalitarian State To achieve his goals, Hitler organized an efficient but brutal system of totalitarian rule. Nazis controlled all areas of German life—from government to religion to education. Elite, black-uniformed troops, called the SS, enforced the Führer's will. His secret police, the **Gestapo** (guh STAH poh), rooted out opposition. The masses, relieved by belief in the Nazis' promises, cheered Hitler's accomplishments in ending unemployment and reviving German power. Those who worried about Hitler's terror apparatus quickly became its victims or were cowed into silence in fear for their own safety.

The Campaign Against the Jews Begins In his fanatical anti-Semitism, Hitler set out to drive Jews from Germany. In 1935, the Nazis passed the **Nuremberg Laws,** which deprived Jews of German citizenship and placed severe restrictions on them. They were prohibited from marrying non-Jews, attending or teaching at German schools or universities, holding government jobs, practicing law or medicine, or publishing

"Night of Broken Glass"
On the night of November 9, 1938, and into the next day, German mobs smashed the windows of Jewish homes and businesses, looted Jewish shops, and burned synagogues. Many Jewish people were dragged from their homes and beaten in the streets. Not only did the Nazi government authorize these attacks, it made the Jewish victims pay for the damage.

books. Nazis beat and robbed Jews and roused mobs to do the same. Many German Jews fled, seeking refuge in other countries.

Night of Broken Glass On November 7, 1938, a young Jew whose parents had been mistreated in Germany shot and wounded a German diplomat in Paris. Hitler used the incident as an excuse to stage an attack on all Jews. *Kristallnacht* (krih STAHL nahkt), or the "Night of Broken Glass," took place on November 9 and 10. Nazi-led mobs attacked Jewish communities all over Germany, Austria, and the annexed portions of Czechoslovakia. Before long, Hitler and his henchmen were making even more sinister plans for what they called the "Final Solution"—the extermination of all Jews.

Nazi Youth To build for the future, the Nazis indoctrinated young people with their ideology. In passionate speeches, the Führer spewed his message of racism. He urged young Germans to destroy their so-called enemies without mercy. On hikes and in camps, the "Hitler Youth" pledged absolute loyalty to Germany and undertook physical fitness programs to prepare for war. School courses and textbooks were rewritten to reflect Nazi racial views.

Like Fascists in Italy, Nazis sought to limit women's roles. Women were dismissed from upper-level jobs and turned away from universities. To raise the birthrate, Nazis offered "pure-blooded Aryan" women rewards for having more children. Still, Hitler's goal to keep women in the home and out of the workforce applied mainly to the privileged. As German industry expanded, women factory workers were needed.

Purging German Culture The Nazis also sought to purge, or purify, German culture. They denounced modern art, saying that it was corrupted by Jewish influences. They condemned jazz because of its African roots. Instead, the Nazis glorified old German myths such as those re-created in the operas of Richard Wagner (VAHG nur).

Hitler despised Christianity as "weak" and "flabby." He sought to replace religion with his racial creed. To control the churches, the Nazis combined all Protestant sects into a single state church. They closed Catholic schools and muzzled the Catholic clergy. Although many clergy either supported the new <u>regime</u> or remained silent, some courageously spoke out against Hitler.

✔ **Checkpoint** How did the Nazi party maintain its control of Germany?

Authoritarian Rule in Eastern Europe

Like Germany, most new nations in Eastern Europe slid from democratic to authoritarian rule in the postwar era. In 1919, a dozen countries were carved out of the old Russian, Austro-Hungarian, Ottoman and German empires. Although they differed from one another in important ways, they faced some common problems. They were small countries whose rural agricultural economies lacked capital to develop industry. Social and economic inequalities separated

Nazi Book Burnings
Nazis burned books of which they disapproved, such as *All Quiet on the Western Front,* in huge, organized public bonfires. The Nazis viewed Remarque's novel as an insult to the German military.

poor peasants from wealthy landlords. None had much experience with the democratic process. Further complicating the situation, tensions leftover from World War I hindered economic cooperation between countries. Each country in the region tried to be independent of its neighbors, which hurt all of them. The region was hit hard by the Great Depression.

Ethnic Conflict Old rivalries between ethnic and religious groups created severe tensions. In Czechoslovakia, Czechs and Slovaks were unwilling partners. Serbs dominated the new state of Yugoslavia, but restless Slovenes and Croats living there pressed for independence. In Poland, Hungary, and Romania, conflict flared among various ethnic groups.

Democracy Retreats Economic problems and ethnic tensions contributed to instability, which in turn helped fascist rulers gain power. In Hungary, military strongman Nicholas Horthy (HAWR tay) overthrew a Communist-led government in 1919. By 1926, the military hero Joseph Pilsudski (peel SOOT skee) had taken control over Poland. Eventually, right-wing dictators emerged in every Eastern European country except Czechoslovakia and Finland. Like Hitler, these dictators promised order and won the backing of the military and wealthy. They also turned to anti-Semitism, using Jewish people as scapegoats for many national problems. Meanwhile, strong, aggressive neighbors eyed these small, weak states of Eastern Europe as tempting targets.

✔ **Checkpoint** Why did authoritarian states rise in Eastern Europe after World War I?

Notable Jewish Figures of Europe, Early 1900s	
Person	**Achievements**
Marc Chagall	Forerunner of Surrealism
Gustav Mahler	Composed symphonies and conducted many major orchestras
Arnold Schoenberg	Pioneered new styles of music
Franz Kafka	Influential style of surrealist writing
Albert Einstein	Important scientist
Sigmund Freud	Founder of psychoanalysis
Edmund Husserl	Founder of phenomenology movement
Rudolph Lipschitz	Worked on number theory and potential theory

The table above lists a few of the notable Jewish people whose exceptional talents flew in the face of Hitler's claims of Aryan superiority. Some of these people fled Europe in the face of the Nazi regime. **Chart Skills** *Describe how losing some of its leading thinkers might have hurt Nazi Germany.*

SECTION 5 Assessment

Progress Monitoring *Online*
For: Self-quiz with vocabulary practice
Web Code: naa-2851

Terms, People, and Places

1. Place each of the terms listed at the beginning of the section into one of the following categories: politics, culture, or economy. Write a sentence explaining your choice.

 **Note Taking**

2. **Reading Skill: Identify Main Ideas** Use your completed flowchart to answer the section Focus Question: How did Hitler and the Nazi Party establish and maintain a totalitarian government in Germany?

Comprehension and Critical Thinking

3. **Express Problems Clearly** List three problems faced by the Weimar Republic.

4. **Recognize Ideologies** What racial and nationalistic ideas did Nazis promote?

5. **Summarize** What were some of the restrictions that Hitler placed on German Jews?

6. **Demonstrate Reasoned Judgment** Do you think that there are any reasons why a government would be justified in banning books or censoring ideas? Explain.

7. **Identify Effects** Why did dictators gain power in much of Eastern Europe?

8. **Draw Conclusions** Both Stalin and Hitler instituted ruthless campaigns against supposed enemies of the state. Why do you think dictators need to find scapegoats for their nation's ills?

● **Writing About History**

Quick Write: Use Compare-and-Contrast Transitions Use strong transitions to help readers navigate your compare-and-contrast essays. Words such as *however, but, nevertheless, yet, likewise, similarly,* and *instead* signal comparison-and-contrast relationships. Add one of these words to the statements below to clarify their meanings.

- Hitler's rise was based on hate. He was a popular leader.
- Germany became a fascist state. Many of the countries of Eastern Europe became fascist states.

Quick Study Guide

■ Causes and Effects of the Great Depression

Cause and Effect

Long-Term Causes	Immediate Causes
• Worldwide interrelationship of governments and economies • Gold standard • Overproduction of goods • Agricultural slump • Uneven distribution of wealth	• Falling demand • Financial crisis kicked off by New York stock market crash • Banks demand repayment of loans • American loans to other countries dry up • Without capital, businesses and factories fail

↓

Worldwide Economic Depression

↓

Immediate Effects	Long-Term Effects
• Vast unemployment and misery • Protective tariffs imposed • Countries abandon gold standard • Loss of faith in capitalism and democracy • Authoritarian leaders emerge	• Rise of fascism and Nazism • Governments experiment with social programs • People blame scapegoats • World War II begins

■ Three Totalitarian States: Italy, the Soviet Union, and Germany

Country	Dictator in Power	Ideology	Example of Terror Tactics
Italy	Benito Mussolini in power in 1922	Fascist; Fanatic nationalism	Black Shirts suppressed dissent.
Soviet Union	Joseph Stalin in power in 1924	Communist	Stalin sent millions to Gulag labor camps.
Germany	Adolf Hitler in power in 1933	Fascist; Racial policies of hatred, aimed particularly at Jews	Nazis began to restrict and terrorize German Jews.

■ Some Cultural Figures of the Post World War I Era

Literature
Ernest Hemingway
Virginia Woolf
Langston Hughes
Mikhail Sholokhov

Music and Theater
Louis Armstrong
Bertolt Brecht

Visual Arts
Pablo Picasso
Jean Arp
Salvador Dali
Frank Lloyd Wright
George Grosz
Vasily Kandinsky

■ Key Events in Europe and the United States, 1919–1939

Britain, France, and the United States

Germany, Italy, and the Soviet Union

1919–1920 Red Scare sweeps the United States.

1925 Seven European nations sign the Locarno treaties, raising hopes for world peace.

1926 More than three million workers in several different industries strike in Britain.

1920

1925

1919 The Weimar Republic is established in Germany.

1922 Benito Mussolini comes to power after the March on Rome.

Concept Connector

Essential Question Review

To connect prior knowledge with what you have learned in this chapter, answer the questions below in your Concept Connector journal. Use the journal in the Reading and Note Taking Study Guide to record your answers (or go to www.phschool.com **Web Code:** nad-2807). In addition, record information about the following concept:

- Dictatorship: Mussolini and Hitler

1. **Dictatorship** As the Western democracies stumbled after World War I, totalitarian governments gained power in Italy, Germany, and the Soviet Union. Summarize social, political, and economic conditions in postwar Europe. Then create a list of reasons that explain why an average citizen living in postwar Europe in the 1920s or early 1930s might support a dictator.

2. **Human Rights** Mussolini, Hitler, and Stalin were brutal dictators. In disregard for human rights, political opponents were murdered, imprisoned, or exiled. But terror was not the dictator's only weapon. Give examples of other methods they used to maintain power, strengthen their totalitarian states, and strip people of their human rights. Focus on the following:
   - culture
   - education
   - propaganda

3. **Science and Technology** In the 1940s, scientists built on Marie Curie's research on radioactivity and Albert Einstein's theories of relativity to develop atomic energy. How do these discoveries demonstrate the benefits and costs of technology?

Connections To Today

1. **Dictatorship: North Korea's Kim Jong Il** Dictatorship as a form of government still exists today. Kim Jong Il (below), head of a communist totalitarian regime in North Korea, is considered among the most dangerous of the present-day dictators. In fact, Kim has been described as "Stalinist." Kim took over as dictator from his father, Kim Il-Sung, in 1994. Since then, he has violated the civil liberties of his own people, and he has destabilized international relations in the region with claims that North Korea possesses nuclear weapons. Research Kim Jong Il's record in North Korea and write two paragraphs comparing his regime to Stalin's in Russia.

2. **Political Systems: The Former Soviet Union** The Soviet Union came to an end in 1991. Its collapse produced 14 new republics, besides the Russian Federation, as each of the former SSRs became independent. The transition was not easy. Choose one of the following countries and then research and write a brief report on its transition from SSR to independent republic: Armenia, Azerbaijan, Belarus, Estonia, Georgia, Kazakhstan, Kyrgyzstan, Latvia, Lithuania, Moldova, Tajikistan, Turkmenistan, Ukraine, Uzbekistan.

1929
The Great Depression begins in the United States.

1930
Construction on the Maginot Line begins on the border of France and Germany.

1933
Prohibition is repealed in the United States.

History Interactive
For: Interactive timeline
Web Code: nap-2862

1930

1935

1928
Joseph Stalin launches the first of his Five-Year Plans in the Soviet Union.

1932
Stalin's ruthless policies, combined with failed crops, cause mass starvation in the Soviet Union.

1933
Adolf Hitler becomes chancellor of Germany.

1935
The Nazi Party in Germany passes the Nuremberg Laws, limiting the rights of Jews.

Chapter Assessment

Terms, People, and Places

Match the following terms with the definitions below.

flapper
Harlem Renaissance
Franklin Delano Roosevelt
disarmament
totalitarian state

Benito Mussolini
command economy
Gulag
Ruhr Valley
Third Reich

1. rebellious young woman of the 1920s
2. leader of the first modern fascist state
3. reduction of armed forces and weapons
4. government in which a one-party dictatorship regulates every aspect of citizens' lives
5. president of the United States who established the New Deal to help Americans during the Great Depression
6. African American cultural movement in the 1920s and 1930s
7. coal-rich industrial region of Germany

Main Ideas

Section 1 (pp. 884–890)
8. How did Western culture and society change in reaction to World War I?

Section 2 (pp. 891–897)
9. Describe the search for peace in the 1920s and its results.
10. What were the effects of the Great Depression?

Section 3 (pp. 898–903)
11. What is fascism?
12. How did Mussolini's fascist regime rule Italy?

Section 4 (pp. 904–911)
13. Summarize conditions in the Soviet Union under Stalin.

Section 5 (pp. 912–917)
14. How did Hitler establish a totalitarian state in Germany?

Chapter Focus Question
15. What political and economic challenges did the Western world face in the 1920s and 1930s, and how did various countries react to these challenges?

Critical Thinking

16. **Synthesize Information** How did the literature and art of the 1920s reflect the influence of World War I?
17. **Identify Causes** What imbalances helped cause the Great Depression of the 1930s?
18. **Recognize Ideologies** Why did the ideology of fascism appeal to many Italians?
19. **Compare Points of View** Describe the similarities and differences between fascism and communism.
20. **Recognize Propaganda** Why was propaganda an important tool of totalitarian dictators?
21. **Make Comparisons** Both Germany under Hitler and the Nazis and the Soviet Union under Stalin and the Communists were totalitarian states. How was totalitarian rule similar in these two countries? How did Nazi totalitarianism differ from that of the Communist Soviet Union?

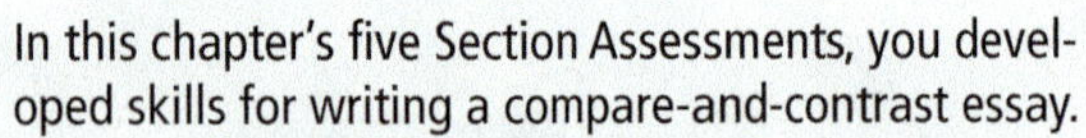

● Writing About History

In this chapter's five Section Assessments, you developed skills for writing a compare-and-contrast essay.

Writing a Compare-and-Contrast Essay The period between World War I and World War II was a time of rapid change with some serious crises of its own. Write a compare-and-contrast essay on one of the following pairs of ideas: society before and after World War I, solutions to alleviate the Great Depression in the United States and in Germany, fascism compared to democracy in the 1920s and 1930s, or a topic of your own choosing.

Prewriting
- Choose a valid topic for your essay by choosing two things that are neither too similar nor wildly different.
- Choose categories in which the two items could be compared and contrasted.
- Use a Venn diagram to gather and record details for your essay.

Drafting
- Develop a thesis that introduces the items you are comparing and the point you intend to make by the comparison.
- Outline how you will organize your arguments and the details that will support them.
- Write an introduction explaining what you are comparing and contrasting, a body, and a conclusion that restates your main points.

Revising
- Use the guidelines for revising your essay on page SH12 of the Writing Handbook.

Document-Based Assessment

Hitler's Rise to Power

In 1919, Hitler joined the National Socialist German Workers Party, later known as the Nazi party. It was a marginal party that only received one million votes in 1924. By 1932, however, the Nazi party, with Hitler at its helm, was Germany's largest party. Many factors contributed to Hitler's surprising rise to power, as the documents below illustrate.

Document A

This poster, displayed in Berlin in 1932, tells voters: "We want work and bread! Elect Hitler!"

Document B

"The National Socialist movement must strive to eliminate the disproportion between our population and our area—viewing this latter as a source of food as well as a basis for power politics. . . . We must hold unflinchingly to our aim . . . to secure for the German people the land and soil to which they are entitled. . . ."

—From ***Mein Kampf*** by Adolf Hitler

Document C

". . . [T]hough the Fuehrer's anti-Semitic programme furnished the National Socialist party in the first instance with a nucleus and a rallying-cry, it was swept into office by two things with which the "Jewish Problem" did not have the slightest connexion. On the one side was economic distress and the revulsion against Versailles; on the other, chicanery and intrigue. . . . Hitler and his party had promised the unhappy Germans a new heaven and a new earth, coupled with the persecution of the Jews. Unfortunately, a new heaven and earth cannot be manufactured to order. But a persecution of the Jews can. . . ."

—From ***The Jewish Problem*** by Louis Golding, 1939

Document D

"The Versailles settlement was seen as a means by which Germany's enemies aimed to keep the Reich prostrate forever and had to be overturned not merely to restore the status quo ante, but to allow Germany to expand and seize the "living space" that it allegedly needed in the east. And violence was viewed as the means by which to achieve a Third Reich and a German-dominated Europe—by smashing the democratic Weimar "system," destroying Marxism, solving the "Jewish question," breaking the "chains of Versailles," and building up the armed forces so that Germany again could go to war."

—From ***Nazism and War*** by historian Richard Bessel

Analyzing Documents

Use your knowledge of the rise of Nazism in Germany and Documents A, B, C, and D to answer questions 1–4.

1. Document A focuses on which factor that aided Hitler's rise to power?
   A anger over World War I
   B social considerations
   C the economy
   D racial and religious prejudice

2. According to Document C, the Nazis persecuted the Jews, because
   A most Germans hated them.
   B they wanted to keep attention from other problems.
   C they had already achieved their other goals.
   D their opponents were all Jews.

3. According to Document D, the Nazis' main goal was to
   A dominate Europe.
   B get revenge for the Treaty of Versailles.
   C stop communism.
   D end democracy.

4. Explain why Germany was fertile soil for the Nazis following World War I. Give your reasons, using these documents and information from the chapter.

A City Lies in Ruins

March 6, 1944—The Allies' mission to bomb Berlin, Germany, includes 810 bombers plus 800 fighter escorts. The stream of aircraft stretches a mile wide and a half-mile deep and takes more than half an hour to pass over any given point. Approaching the city, the bombers press on through flak—anti-aircraft fire from the ground—"so thick you can walk on it." Then, bomb bay doors open, and their payloads rain down on the city.

Listen to the Witness History audio to hear more about the Allied bombing efforts.

◄ Cologne, Germany, in ruins, 1944

Japanese pilot's goggles recovered from Pearl Harbor

"Cricket" noisemakers used by Allied para-troopers to locate each other after landing

Chapter Preview

Chapter Focus Question How did aggressive world powers emerge, and what did it take to defeat them during World War II?

Section 1
From Appeasement to War

Section 2
The Axis Advances

Section 3
The Allies Turn the Tide

Section 4
Victory in Europe and the Pacific

Section 5
The End of World War II

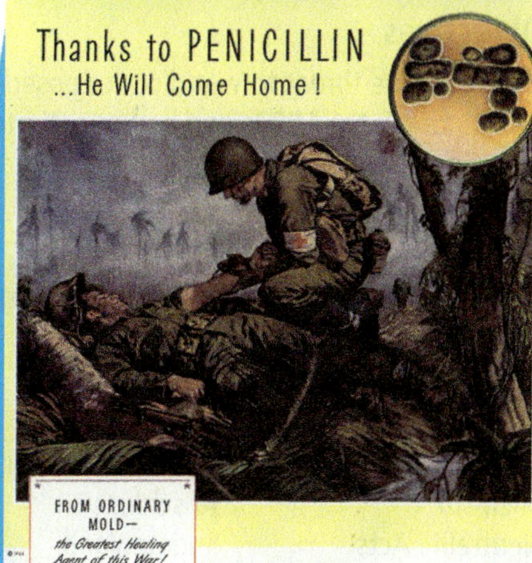

An advertisement praising the benefits of penicillin

 Concept Connector ONLINE

To explore Essential Questions related to this chapter, go to PHSchool.com Web Code: nad-2907

Use the ✓ **Quick Study Timeline** at the end of this chapter to preview chapter events.

Neville Chamberlain and headlines announcing the Munich Pact

A Desperate Peace

British Prime Minister Neville Chamberlain spoke to a jubilant crowd upon returning to London from a conference with Adolf Hitler in Munich, Germany, in September 1938:

> **66** For the second time in our history, a British Prime Minister has returned from Germany bringing peace with honor. I believe it is peace for our time . . . Go home and get a nice quiet sleep. **99**

Focus Question What events unfolded between Chamberlain's declaration of "peace for our time" and the outbreak of a world war?

From Appeasement to War

Objectives

- Analyze the threat to world peace posed by dictators in the 1930s and how the Western democracies responded.
- Describe how the Spanish Civil War was a "dress rehearsal" for World War II.
- Summarize the ways in which continuing Nazi aggression led Europe to war.

Terms, People, and Places

appeasement	Francisco Franco
pacifism	Anschluss
Neutrality Acts	Sudetenland
Axis powers	Nazi-Soviet Pact

Note Taking

Reading Skill: Recognize Sequence As you read, keep track of the sequence of events that led to the outbreak of World War II by completing a table like the one below.

Acts of Aggression	
Japan	
Italy	
Germany	
Spain	

After the horrors of World War I, Western democracies desperately tried to preserve peace during the 1930s while ignoring signs that the rulers of Germany, Italy, and Japan were preparing to build new empires. Despite the best efforts of Neville Chamberlain and other Western leaders, the world was headed to war again.

Aggression Goes Unchecked

Throughout the 1930s, challenges to peace followed a pattern. Dictators took aggressive action but met only verbal protests and pleas for peace from the democracies. Mussolini, Hitler, and the leaders of Japan viewed that desire for peace as weakness and responded with new acts of aggression. With hindsight, we can see the shortcomings of the democracies' policies. These policies, however, were the product of long and careful deliberation. At the time, some people believed they would work.

Japan Overruns Manchuria and Eastern China One of the earliest tests had been posed by Japan. Japanese military leaders and ultranationalists thought that Japan should have an empire equal to those of the Western powers. In pursuit of this goal, Japan seized Manchuria in 1931. When the League of Nations condemned the aggression, Japan simply withdrew from the organization. Japan's easy success strengthened the militarist faction in Japan. In 1937, Japanese armies overran much of eastern China, starting the Second Sino-Japanese War. Once again, Western protests did not stop Japan.

Hitler Remilitarizes Germany
Hitler rebuilt the German military during the 1930s in defiance of the Treaty of Versailles. The government's investment in armaments also helped pull Germany out of the Great Depression. Here, German police march in goose step as Hitler salutes in the background. *How did rearmament affect the rest of Germany?*

Italy Invades Ethiopia In Italy, Mussolini decided to act on his own imperialist ambitions. Italy's defeat by the Ethiopians at the battle of Adowa in 1896 still rankled. In 1935, Italy invaded Ethiopia, located in northeastern Africa. Although the Ethiopians resisted bravely, their outdated weapons were no match for Mussolini's tanks, machine guns, poison gas, and airplanes. The Ethiopian king Haile Selassie (HY luh suh lah SEE) appealed to the League of Nations for help. The League voted <u>sanctions</u> against Italy for violating international law. But the League had no power to enforce the sanctions, and by early 1936, Italy had conquered Ethiopia.

Vocabulary Builder
<u>sanctions</u>—(SANGK shunz) *n.* penalties

Hitler Goes Against the Treaty of Versailles By then, Hitler, too, had tested the will of the Western democracies and found it weak. First, he built up the German military in defiance of the treaty that had ended World War I. Then, in 1936, he sent troops into the "demilitarized" Rhineland bordering France—another treaty violation.

Germans hated the Versailles treaty, and Hitler's successful challenge made him more popular at home. The Western democracies denounced his moves but took no real action. Instead, they adopted a policy of **appeasement,** or giving in to the demands of an aggressor in order to keep the peace.

Keeping the Peace The Western policy of appeasement developed for a number of reasons. France was demoralized, suffering from political divisions at home. It could not take on Hitler without British support. The British, however, had no desire to confront the German dictator. Some even thought that Hitler's actions constituted a justifiable response to the terms of the Treaty of Versailles, which they believed had been too harsh on Germany.

In both Britain and France, many saw Hitler and fascism as a defense against a worse evil—the spread of Soviet communism. Additionally, the Great Depression sapped the energies of the Western democracies. Finally, widespread **pacifism,** or opposition to all war, and disgust with the destruction from the previous war pushed many governments to seek peace at any price.

Three leaders in Europe and one in Japan launched ambitious plans to increase their power.

● Benito Mussolini—Italy

● Adolf Hitler—Germany

● Tojo Hideki—Japan

● Francisco Franco—Spain

As war clouds gathered in Europe in the mid-1930s, the United States Congress passed a series of **Neutrality Acts.** One law forbade the sale of arms to any nation at war. Others outlawed loans to warring nations and prohibited Americans from traveling on ships of warring powers. The fundamental goal of American policy, however, was to avoid involvement in a European war, not to prevent such a conflict.

Rome-Berlin-Tokyo Axis In the face of the apparent weakness of Britain, France, and the United States, Germany, Italy, and Japan formed what became known as the Rome-Berlin-Tokyo Axis. Known as the **Axis powers,** the three nations agreed to fight Soviet communism. They also agreed not to interfere with one another's plans for territorial expansion. The agreement cleared the way for these anti-democratic, aggressor powers to take even bolder steps.

 **Checkpoint** Describe the German, Italian, and Japanese drives for empire.

Spain Collapses Into Civil War

In 1936, a local struggle in Spain polarized public opinion throughout Europe. Trouble in Spain started in 1931, when popular unrest against the old order forced the king to leave Spain. A republic was set up with a new, more liberal constitution. The government passed a series of controversial reforms, taking land and privileges away from the Church and old ruling classes. Still, leftists demanded more radical reforms. Conservatives, backed by the military, rejected change.

In 1936, a conservative general named **Francisco Franco** led a revolt that touched off a bloody civil war. Fascists and supporters of right-wing policies, called Nationalists, rallied to back Franco. Supporters of the republic, known as Loyalists, included Communists, Socialists, and those who wanted democracy.

People from other nations soon jumped in to support both sides. Hitler and Mussolini sent arms and forces to help Franco. The Soviet Union sent soldiers to fight against fascism alongside the Spanish Loyalists. Although the governments of Britain, France, and the United States remained neutral, individuals from those countries, as well as other countries, also fought with the Loyalists. Anti-Nazi Germans and anti-Fascist Italians joined the Loyalist cause as well.

Both sides committed horrible atrocities. The ruinous struggle took more than 500,000 lives. One of the worst horrors was a German air raid on Guernica, a small Spanish market town, in April 1937. German planes dropped their load of bombs, and then swooped low to machine-gun anyone who had survived the bombs. Nearly 1,000 innocent civilians were killed. To Nazi leaders, the attack on Guernica was an experiment to identify what their new planes could do. To the rest of the world, it was a grim warning of the destructive power of modern warfare.

By 1939, Franco had triumphed. Once in power, he created a fascist dictatorship similar to the dictatorships of Hitler and Mussolini. He rolled back earlier reforms, killed or jailed enemies, and used terror to promote order.

Checkpoint How did the Spanish Civil War involve combatants from other countries?

German Aggression Continues

In the meantime, Hitler pursued his goal of bringing all German-speaking people into the Third Reich. He also took steps to gain "living space" for Germans in Eastern Europe. Hitler, who believed in the superiority of the German people, thought that Germany had a right to conquer the Slavs to the east. Hitler claimed, "I have the right to remove millions of an inferior race that breeds like vermin."

Hitler's aggressive plans also served economic purposes. Production of military equipment would benefit German industry, which would also gain new raw materials and markets in the east.

Austria Annexed By March, 1938, Hitler was ready to engineer the **Anschluss** (AHN shloos), or union of Austria and Germany. When Austria's chancellor refused to agree to Hitler's demands, Hitler sent in the German army to "preserve order." To indicate his new role as ruler of Austria, Hitler made a speech from the Hofburg Palace, the former residence of the Hapsburg emperors.

The Anschluss violated the Versailles treaty and created a brief war scare. Some Austrians favored annexation. Hitler quickly silenced any Austrians who opposed it. And since the Western democracies took no action, Hitler easily had his way.

The Czech Crisis Germany turned next to Czechoslovakia. At first, Hitler insisted that the three million Germans in the **Sudetenland** (soo DAY tun land)—a region of western Czechoslovakia—be given autonomy. Czechoslovakia was one of only two remaining democracies in Eastern Europe. (Finland was the other.) Still, Britain and France were not willing to go to war to save it. As British and French leaders searched for a peaceful solution, Hitler increased his demands. The Sudetenland, he said, must be annexed to Germany.

Reading Skill: Recognize Sequence
Complete this timetable of German aggression as you read.

German Aggression	
March 1938	
September 1938	
March 1939	
September 1939	

Germany in Czechoslovakia
A Sudeten woman grieves while dutifully saluting Hitler's troops (below). German tanks roll through Wenceslas Square in Prague (left).

At the Munich Conference in September 1938, British and French leaders again chose appeasement. They caved in to Hitler's demands and then persuaded the Czechs to surrender the Sudetenland without a fight. In exchange, Hitler assured Britain and France that he had no further plans to expand his territory.

"Peace for Our Time" Returning from Munich, British Prime Minister Neville Chamberlain told cheering crowds that he had achieved "peace for our time." He told Parliament that the Munich Pact had "saved Czechoslovakia from destruction and Europe from Armageddon." French leader Edouard Daladier (dah lahd yay) reacted differently to the joyous crowds that greeted him in Paris. "The fools, why are they cheering?" he asked. British politician Winston Churchill, who had long warned of the Nazi threat, judged the diplomats harshly: "They had to choose between war and dishonor. They chose dishonor; they will have war."

✓ **Checkpoint** **Why did Hitler feel justified in taking over Austria and the Sudetenland?**

Geography *Interactive*
For: Audio guided tour
Web Code: nap-2911

Aggression in Europe and Africa to September, 1939

Map Skills Between 1936 and 1939, Germany and Italy repeatedly threatened peace in Europe.

1. **Locate** (a) Austria (b) Rhineland (c) Poland
2. **Regions** The strip of land between East Prussia and the rest of Germany is called the Polish Corridor. Why is that an appropriate name for the region?
3. **Predict Consequences** Which countries in 1939 were probably the most likely targets for future acts of German or Italian aggression? Explain.

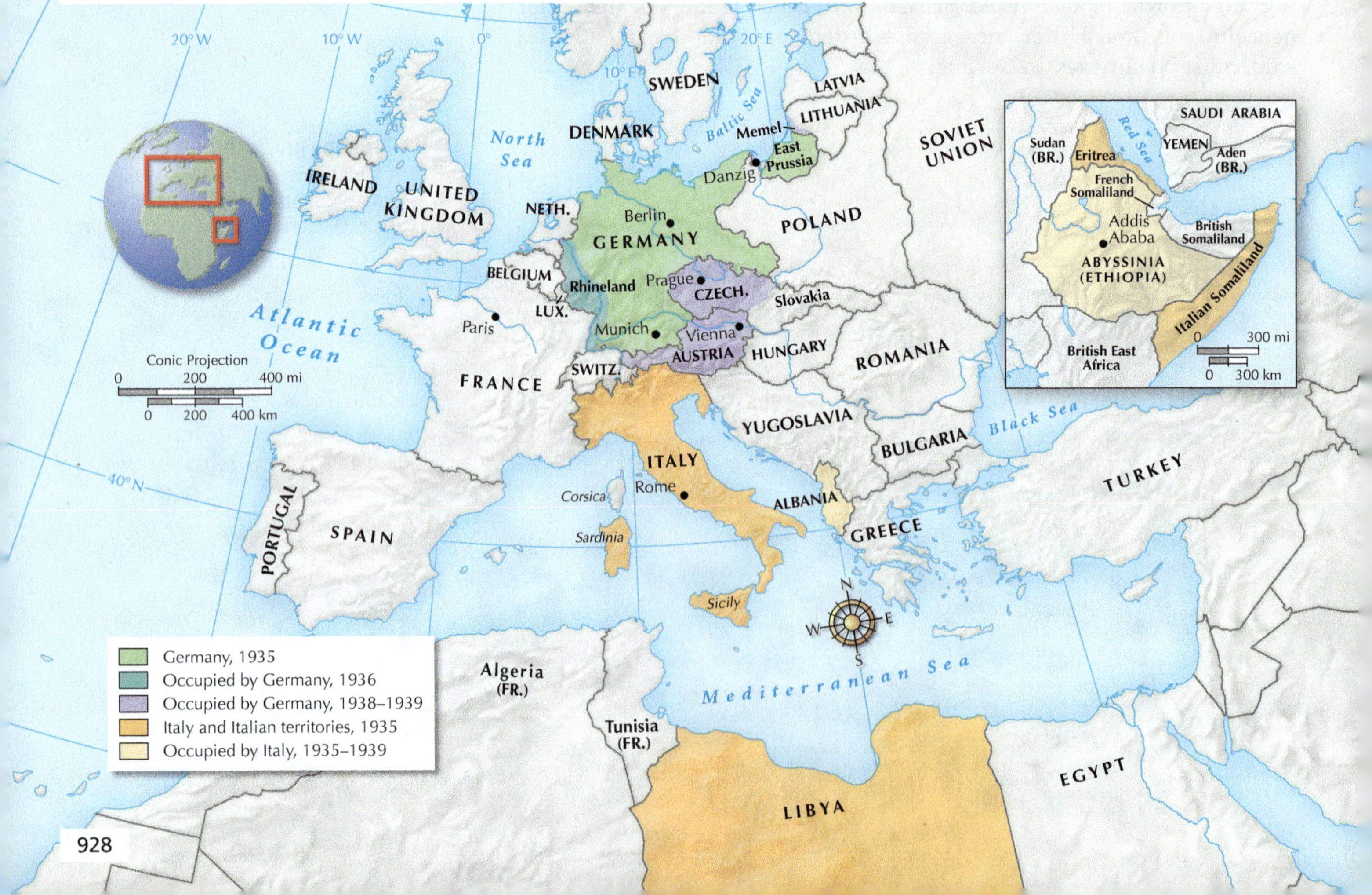

Europe Plunges Toward War

Just as Churchill predicted, Europe plunged rapidly toward war. In March 1939, Hitler broke his promises and gobbled up the rest of Czechoslovakia. The democracies finally accepted the fact that appeasement had failed. At last thoroughly alarmed, they promised to protect Poland, most likely the next target of Hitler's expansion.

Nazi-Soviet Pact In August 1939, Hitler stunned the world by announcing a nonaggression pact with his great enemy—Joseph Stalin, the Soviet dictator. Publicly, the Nazi-Soviet Pact bound Hitler and Stalin to peaceful relations. Secretly, the two agreed not to fight if the other went to war and to divide up Poland and other parts of Eastern Europe between them.

The pact was based not on friendship or respect but on mutual need. Hitler feared communism as Stalin feared fascism. But Hitler wanted a free hand in Poland. Also, he did not want to fight a war with the Western democracies and the Soviet Union at the same time. For his part, Stalin had sought allies among the Western democracies against the Nazi menace. Mutual suspicions, however, kept them apart. By joining with Hitler, Stalin tried to protect the Soviet Union from the threat of war with Germany and grabbed a chance to gain land in Eastern Europe.

Invasion of Poland On September 1, 1939, a week after the Nazi-Soviet Pact, German forces invaded Poland. Two days later, Britain and France declared war on Germany. World War II had begun.

The devastation of World War I and the awareness of the destructive power of modern <u>technology</u> made the idea of more fighting unbearable. Unfortunately, the war proved to be even more horrendous than anyone had imagined.

 **Checkpoint** What convinced Britain and France to end their policy of appeasement? Why?

Why the West Appeased Hitler

- Fear of the destructive power of modern technology
- Widespread pacifism following World War I
- Hitler's actions seen as a justifiable response to the harsh Treaty of Versailles
- Widespread economic depression
- Hitler's fascism seen as a defense against Soviet communism
- Faith in diplomacy and compromise
- Misreading of Hitler's intentions

Chart Skills Agree or disagree with the following statement: "World War II was in large part a continuation of World War I." Provide evidence from the chart and your knowledge of history to support your view.

Vocabulary Builder

technology—(tek NAHL uh jee) *n.* scientific advances applied to practical purposes

Assessment

Progress Monitoring *Online*
For: Self-quiz with vocabulary practice
Web Code: naa-2911

Terms, People, and Places

1. For each term, person, or place listed at the beginning of the section, write a sentence explaining its significance.

Note Taking

2. **Reading Skill: Recognize Sequence** Use your completed tables to answer the Focus Question: What events unfolded between Chamberlain's declaration of "peace for our time" and the outbreak of a world war?

Comprehension and Critical Thinking

3. **Identify Central Issues** How did the Western democracies respond to the aggression of the Axis powers during the 1930s?
4. **Synthesize Information** Why did Germany and Italy become involved in the Spanish Civil War?
5. **Recognize Cause and Effect** How was the Munich Conference a turning point in the road toward world war?
6. **Analyze Information** Why do you think some historians call the period between 1919 and 1939 the 20-year truce?

 **Writing About History**

Quick Write: Explore a Topic Choose one specific event from this section and write a series of questions that you could use to direct research on the topic. For example, on the formation of the Rome-Berlin-Tokyo Axis you could ask

- How did the Axis benefit each of the member countries?
- How did the Axis clear the way for the members to take even bolder aggressive actions?

▶ Janina Sulkowska
in the early 1930s

▶ German fighter plane

Janina's War Story

❝It was 10:30 in the morning and I was helping my mother and a servant girl with bags and baskets as they set out for the market. . . . Suddenly the high-pitch scream of diving planes caused everyone to freeze. . . . Countless explosions shook our house followed by the *rat-tat-tat* of strafing machine guns. We could only stare at each other in horror. Later reports would confirm that several German Stukas had screamed out of a blue sky and . . . dropped several bombs along the main street— and then returned to strafe the market. The carnage was terrible.❞
—Janina Sulkowska, Krzemieniec, Poland, September 12, 1939

Focus Question Which regions were attacked and occupied by the Axis powers, and what was life like under their occupation?

The Axis Advances

Objectives

- Describe how the Axis powers came to control much of Europe, but failed to conquer Britain.
- Summarize Germany's invasion of the Soviet Union.
- Understand the horror of the genocide the Nazis committed.
- Describe the role of the United States before and after joining World War II.

Terms, People, and Places

blitzkrieg	General Erwin Rommel
Luftwaffe	concentration camps
Dunkirk	Holocaust
Vichy	Lend-Lease Act

Note Taking

Reading Skill: Recognize Sequence Sequence events as you read in a flowchart.

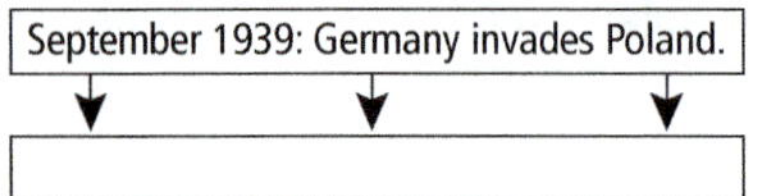

Diplomacy and compromise had not satisfied the Axis powers' hunger for empire. Western democracies had hoped that appeasement would help establish a peaceful world order. But Nazi Germany, Fascist Italy, and imperial Japan plunged ahead with their plans for conquest.

The Axis Attacks

On September 1, 1939, Nazi forces stormed into Poland, revealing the enormous power of Hitler's **blitzkrieg,** or "lightning war." The blitzkrieg utilized improved tank and airpower technology to strike a devastating blow against the enemy. First, the **Luftwaffe,** or German air force, bombed airfields, factories, towns, and cities, and screaming dive bombers fired on troops and civilians. Then, fast-moving tanks and troop transports pushed their way into the defending Polish army, encircling whole divisions of troops and forcing them to surrender.

While Germany attacked from the west, Stalin's forces invaded from the east, grabbing lands promised to them under the Nazi-Soviet Pact. Within a month, Poland ceased to exist. Because of Poland's location and the speed of the attacks, Britain and France could do nothing to help beyond declaring war on Germany.

Hitler passed the winter without much further action. Stalin's armies, however, forced the Baltic states of Estonia, Latvia, and

Lithuania to agree to host bases for the Soviet military. Soviet forces also seized part of Finland, which put up stiff but unsuccessful resistance.

The Miracle of Dunkirk During that first winter, the French hunkered down behind the Maginot Line. Britain sent troops to wait with them. Some reporters referred to this quiet time as the "phony war." Then, in April 1940, Hitler launched a blitzkrieg against Norway and Denmark, both of which soon fell. Next, his forces slammed into the Netherlands and Belgium.

In May, German forces surprised the French and British by attacking through the Ardennes Forest in Belgium, an area that was considered invasion proof. Bypassing the Maginot Line, German troops poured into France. Retreating British forces were soon trapped between the Nazi army and the English Channel. In a desperate gamble, the British sent all <u>available</u> naval vessels, merchant ships, and even fishing and pleasure boats across the channel to pluck stranded troops off the beach of **Dunkirk.** Despite German air attacks, the improvised armada ferried more than 300,000 troops to safety in Britain. This heroic rescue raised British morale.

France Falls Meanwhile, German forces headed south toward Paris. Italy declared war on France and attacked from the south. Overrun and demoralized, France surrendered. On June 22, 1940, Hitler forced the French to sign the surrender documents in the same railroad car in which Germany had signed the armistice ending World War I. Following the surrender, Germany occupied northern France. In the south, the Germans set up a "puppet state," with its capital at **Vichy** (VEE shee).

Some French officers escaped to England and set up a government-in-exile. Led by Charles de Gaulle, these "free French" worked to liberate their homeland. Within France, resistance fighters used guerrilla tactics against German forces.

Operation Sea Lion With the fall of France, Britain stood alone in Western Europe. Hitler was sure that the British would sue for peace. But Winston Churchill, who had replaced Neville Chamberlain as prime minister, had other plans. Faced with this defiance, Hitler made plans for Operation Sea Lion—the invasion of Britain. In preparation for the invasion, he launched massive air strikes against the island nation.

Beginning in August 1940, German bombers began a daily bombardment of England's southern coast. For a month, Britain's Royal Air Force valiantly battled the Luftwaffe. Then, the Germans changed their tactics. Instead of bombing military targets in the south, they began to bomb London and other cities.

Germany Launches the Blitz German bombers first appeared over London late on September 7, 1940. All through the night, relays of aircraft showered high explosives and firebombs on the sprawling capital. The bombing continued for 57 nights in a row and then sporadically until the next May. These bombing attacks are known as "the blitz." Much of London was destroyed, and thousands of people lost their lives.

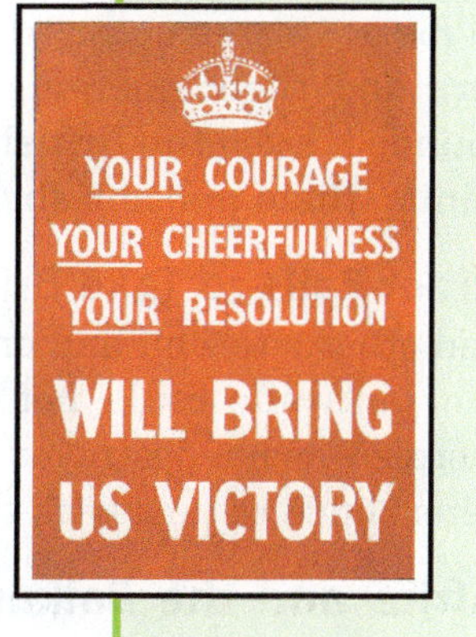

Winston Churchill's defiance gave voice to the determination of the British. *How did Churchill give weight to his speech?*

Primary Source

66 We shall defend our island, whatever the cost may be, we shall fight on the beaches, we shall fight on the landing grounds, we shall fight in the fields and in the streets, we shall fight in the hills; we shall never surrender. 99

—*Winston Churchill, June 4, 1940*   AUDIO

SURVIVING THE BLITZ

From 1940 to 1941, Germany tried to pummel Britain into submission during a months-long bombing campaign known as "the blitz." From September through May, German pilots targeted London with night after night of bombing, but other cities such as Liverpool, Glasgow, and Belfast became targets, too. These nighttime raids sent ordinary civilians scrambling for safety—in crowded public shelters, in homemade shelters, or even in the London Underground. During the blitz, German bombers killed more than 40,000 British civilians and damaged millions of homes. AUDIO 🔊

◀ Fearing poisonous gas attacks, the British government issued gas masks to its citizens. However, gas was never used against British civilians.

Small gestures of kindness helped Londoners deal with the effects of bombing raids. ▼

▲ Nearly three million people were evacuated from Britain's cities to the safer countryside.

London did not break under the blitz. Defiantly, Parliament continued to meet. Citizens carried on their daily lives, seeking protection in shelters and then emerging to resume their routines when the all-clear sounded. Even the British king and queen chose to support Londoners by joining them in bomb shelters rather than fleeing to the countryside.

Hitler Fails to Take Britain German planes continued to bomb London and other cities off and on until May 1941. But contrary to Hitler's hopes, the Luftwaffe could not gain air superiority over Britain, and British morale was not destroyed. In fact, the bombing only made the British more determined to turn back the enemy. Operation Sea Lion was a failure.

Africa and the Balkans Axis armies also pushed into North Africa and the Balkans. In September 1940, Mussolini ordered forces from Italy's North African colony of Libya into Egypt. When the British army repulsed these invaders, Hitler sent one of his most brilliant commanders, General Erwin Rommel, to North Africa. The "Desert Fox," as he was called, chalked up a string of successes in 1941 and 1942. He pushed the British back across the desert toward Cairo, Egypt.

In October 1940, Italian forces invaded Greece. They encountered stiff resistance, and in 1941 German troops once again provided reinforcements. Both Greece and Yugoslavia were added to the growing Axis empire. Even after the Axis triumph, however, Greek and Yugoslav

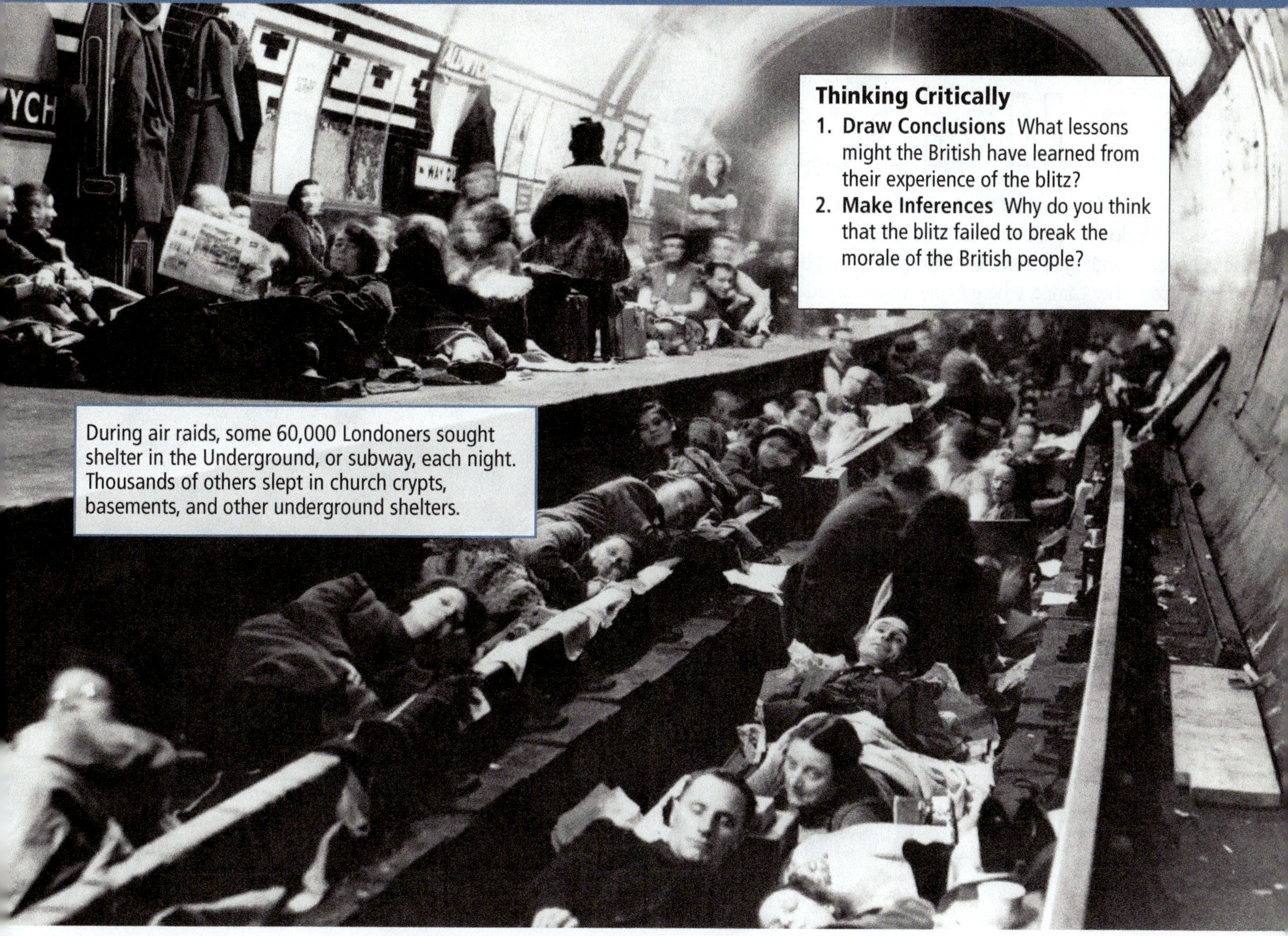

Thinking Critically

1. **Draw Conclusions** What lessons might the British have learned from their experience of the blitz?
2. **Make Inferences** Why do you think that the blitz failed to break the morale of the British people?

During air raids, some 60,000 Londoners sought shelter in the Underground, or subway, each night. Thousands of others slept in church crypts, basements, and other underground shelters.

guerrillas plagued the occupying forces. Meanwhile, both Bulgaria and Hungary had joined the Axis alliance. By 1941, the Axis powers or their allies controlled most of Europe.

✓ **Checkpoint** **Which regions fell under Axis rule between 1939 and 1941?**

Germany Invades the Soviet Union

After the failure in Britain, Hitler turned his military might to a new target—the Soviet Union. The decision to invade the Soviet Union helped relieve Britain. It also proved to be one of Hitler's costliest mistakes.

An Unstoppable German Army Stalls In June 1941, Hitler nullified the Nazi-Soviet Pact by invading the Soviet Union in Operation Barbarossa, a plan which took its name from the medieval Germanic leader, Frederick Barbarossa. Hitler made his motives clear. "If I had the Ural Mountains with their incalculable store of treasures in raw materials," he declared, "Siberia with its vast forests, and the Ukraine with its tremendous wheat fields, Germany under National Socialist leadership would swim in plenty." He also wanted to crush communism in Europe and defeat his powerful rival, Stalin.

Hitler unleashed a new blitzkrieg in the Soviet Union. About three million German soldiers invaded. The Germans caught Stalin unprepared.

Vocabulary Builder
nullified—(NUL uh fyd) *vt.* made invalid

The Holocaust

When Hitler's forces invaded the Soviet Union in 1941, Hilter began implementing what he called the "Final Solution"—the organized murder of all European Jews under his control. At first, Nazi troops began rounding up Jews, executing them and burying them in mass graves. Other Jews were sent to forced labor camps, where many were worked to death. But the Nazis were not satisfied with the pace of these ruthless murders. Beginning in 1942, they began to force Jews from Nazi-occupied Europe into specially designed death camps. By 1945, the Nazis had mercilessly killed some six million Jews—nearly two thirds of all European Jews.

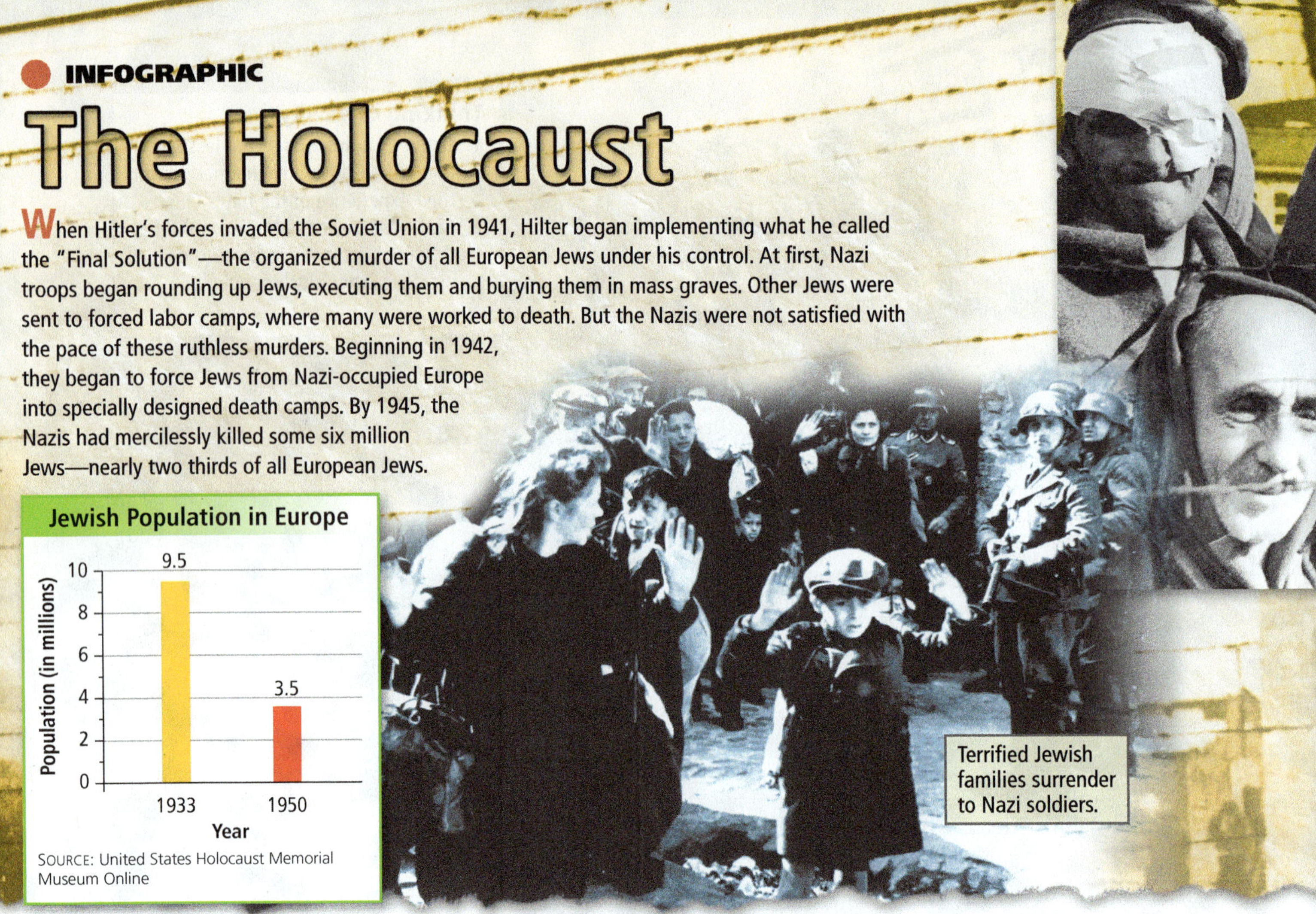

Terrified Jewish families surrender to Nazi soldiers.

His army was still suffering from the purges that had wiped out many of its top officers.

The Soviets lost two and a half million soldiers trying to fend off the invaders. As they were forced back, Soviet troops destroyed factories and farm equipment and burned crops to keep them out of enemy hands. But they could not stop the German war machine. By autumn, the Nazis had smashed deep into the Soviet Union and were poised to take Moscow and Leningrad (present-day St. Petersburg).

There, however, the German advance stalled. Like Napoleon's Grand Army in 1812, Hitler's forces were not prepared for the fury of "General Winter." By early December, temperatures plunged to −40°F (−4°C). Thousands of German soldiers froze to death.

Germany's Siege of Leningrad The Soviets, meanwhile, suffered appalling hardships. In September 1941, the two-and-a-half-year siege of Leningrad began. Food was rationed to two pieces of bread a day. Desperate Leningraders ate almost anything. For example, they boiled wallpaper scraped off walls because its paste was said to contain potato flour.

Although more than a million Leningraders died during the siege, the city did not fall to the Germans. Hoping to gain some relief for his exhausted people, Stalin urged Britain to open a second front in Western Europe. Although Churchill could not offer much real help, the two powers did agree to work together.

✔ **Checkpoint** What caused Hitler's invasion of the Soviet Union to stall?

▲ Survivors of the Holocaust at the Auschwitz death camp in Poland

Thinking Critically

1. **Map Skills** Where were the death camps located? How did this location reflect the goal of the "Final Solution"?
2. **Graph Skills** How does the graph show the horror of the Holocaust?

Life Under Nazi and Japanese Occupation

While Nazi forces rampaged across Europe, the Japanese military conquered an empire in Asia and the Pacific. Each set out to build a "new order" in the occupied lands.

Hitler's "New Order" Hitler's new order grew out of his racial obsessions. As his forces conquered most of Europe, Hitler set up puppet governments in Western European countries that were peopled by Aryans, or light-skinned Europeans, whom Hitler and his followers believed to be a "master race." The Slavs of Eastern Europe were considered to be an inferior "race." They were shoved aside to provide more "living space" for Germans, the strongest of the Aryans.

To the Nazis, occupied lands were an economic resource to be plundered and looted. The Nazis systematically stripped conquered nations of their works of art, factories, and other resources. To counter resistance movements that emerged in occupied countries, the Nazis took savage revenge, shooting hostages and torturing prisoners.

But the Nazis' most sinister plans centered on the people of the occupied countries. During the 1930s, the Nazis had sent thousands of Jewish people and political opponents to concentration camps, detention centers for civilians considered enemies of the state. Over the course of the war, the Nazis forced these people, along with millions of Polish and Soviet Slavs and people from other parts of Europe, to work as slave laborers. Prisoners were poorly fed and often worked to death.

Reading Skill: Identify Supporting Details In a concept web like the one below, fill in details about how the Nazis and Japanese military treated people under their power during World War II. Add circles as necessary.

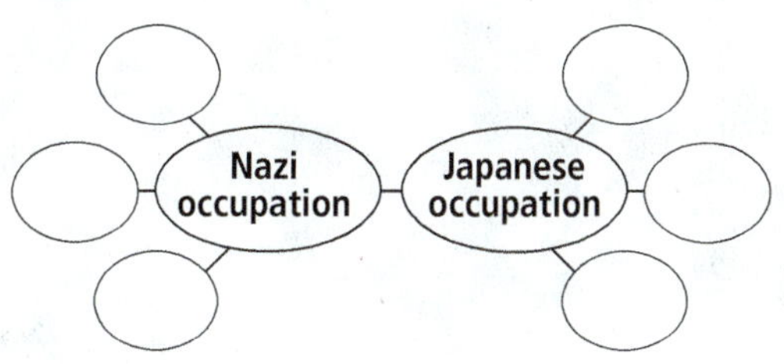

The Nazis Commit Genocide At the same time, Hitler pursued a vicious program to kill all people he judged "racially inferior," particularly Europe's Jews. The Nazis also targeted other groups who did not meet the Aryan racial ideal, including Slavs, Romas (Gypsies), homosexuals, and the disabled. Political and religious leaders who spoke out against Nazism also suffered abuse. Starting in 1939, the Nazis forced Jews in Poland and other countries to live in ghettos, or sections of cities where Jewish people were confined. Many died from starvation, disease, overwork, and the harsh elements. By 1941, however, German leaders had devised plans for the "Final Solution of the Jewish problem"—the genocide of all European Jews.

To accomplish this goal, Hitler had six special "death camps" built in Poland. The Nazis shipped "undesirables" from all over occupied Europe to the camps. There, Nazi engineers designed the most efficient means of killing millions of men, women, and children.

As the prisoners reached the camps, they were stripped of their clothes and valuables. Their heads were shaved. Guards separated men from women and children from their parents. The young, elderly, and sick were targeted for immediate killing. Within a few days, they were herded into "shower rooms" and gassed. The Nazis worked others to death or used them for perverse "medical" experiments. By 1945, the Nazis had massacred some six million Jews in what became known as the Holocaust. Nearly six million other people were killed as well.

Jewish people resisted the Nazis even though they knew their efforts could not succeed. In July 1942, the Nazis began sending Polish Jews from the Warsaw ghetto to the Treblinka death camp at a rate of about 5,000 per day. In the spring of 1943, knowing that their situation was hopeless, the Jews took over the ghetto and used a small collection of guns and homemade bombs to damage the Nazi forces as much as possible. On May 16, the Nazis regained control of the ghetto and eliminated the remaining Warsaw Jews. Still, their courage has inspired many over the years.

In some cases, friends, neighbors, or strangers protected Jews. Italian peasants hid Jews in their villages. Denmark and Bulgaria saved almost

all their Jewish populations. Many people, however, pretended not to notice what was happening. Some even became collaborators and cooperated with the Nazis. In France, the Vichy government helped ship thousands of Jewish people to their deaths. Strict immigration policies in many Western countries as well as conscious efforts to block Jewish immigration prevented many Jews from gaining refuge elsewhere.

The scale and savagery of the Holocaust are unequaled in history. The Nazis deliberately set out to destroy the Jews for no reason other than their religious and ethnic heritage. Today, the record of that slaughter is a vivid reminder of the monstrous results of racism and intolerance.

Japan's Brutal Conquest Japanese forces took control across Asia and the Pacific. Their self-proclaimed mission was to help Asians escape Western colonial rule. In fact, the real goal was a Japanese empire in Asia. The Japanese invaders treated the Chinese, Filipinos, Malaysians, and other conquered people with great brutality, killing and torturing civilians throughout East and Southeast Asia. The occupiers seized food crops, destroyed cities and towns, and made local people into slave laborers. Whatever welcome the Japanese had first met as "liberators" was soon turned to hatred. In the Philippines, Indochina, and elsewhere, nationalist groups waged guerrilla warfare against the Japanese invaders.

✔ **Checkpoint** How did Hitler's views about race lead to the murder of six million Jewish people and millions of Slavs, Gypsies, and others?

Japan Attacks the United States

When the war began in 1939, the United States declared its neutrality. Still, although isolationist feeling remained strong, many Americans sympathized with those who battled the Axis powers. As one of those sympathizers, President Franklin Delano Roosevelt (FDR) looked for ways around the Neutrality Acts to provide warships and other aid to Britain as it stood alone against Hitler.

American Involvement Grows In March 1941, FDR persuaded Congress to pass the **Lend-Lease Act.** It allowed him to sell or lend war materials to "any country whose defense the President deems vital to the defense of the United States." The United States, said Roosevelt, would not be drawn into the war, but it would become "the arsenal of democracy," supplying arms to those who were fighting for freedom.

To show further support, Roosevelt met secretly with Churchill on a warship in the Atlantic in August 1941. The two leaders issued the Atlantic Charter, which set goals for the war—"the final destruction of the Nazi tyranny"—and for the postwar world. They pledged to support "the right of all peoples to choose the form of government under which they will live" and called for a "permanent system of general security."

Japan and the United States Face Off When war broke out in Europe in 1939, the Japanese saw a chance to grab European possessions in Southeast Asia. The rich resources of the region, including oil, rubber, and tin, would be of immense value in fighting its war against the Chinese.

In 1940, Japan advanced into French Indochina and the Dutch East Indies. In response, the United States banned the sale of war materials, such as iron, steel, and oil, to Japan. Japanese leaders saw this move as a threat to Japan's economy and its Asian sphere of influence.

Meeting at Sea
President Roosevelt and Prime Minister Churchill issued the Atlantic Charter in August 1941.

Damage at Pearl Harbor	
U.S. ships sunk or damaged	19
U.S. aircraft destroyed	188
Americans killed	2,348
Americans injured	1,109

SOURCE: *Columbia Encyclopedia, Sixth Edition*

December 7, 1941

On the sleepy Sunday morning of December 7, 1941, the military complex at Pearl Harbor was suddenly jolted awake by a surprise attack. Planes screamed down from the sky, dropping bombs and torpedoes. Americans were shocked and horrified by the attacks. *How did Pearl Harbor change the isolationist policies of the United States?*

Japan and the United States held talks to ease the growing tension. But extreme militarists, such as General Tojo Hideki, hoped to expand Japan's empire, and the United States was interfering with their plans.

Attack on Pearl Harbor With talks at a standstill, General Tojo ordered a surprise attack. Early on December 7, 1941, Japanese airplanes bombed the American fleet at Pearl Harbor in Hawaii. The attack took the lives of about 2,400 people and destroyed battleships and aircraft. The next day, a grim-faced President Roosevelt told the nation that December 7 was "a date which will live in infamy." He asked Congress to declare war on Japan. On December 11, Germany and Italy, as Japan's allies, declared war on the United States.

Japanese Victories In the long run, the Japanese attack on Pearl Harbor would be as serious a mistake as Hitler's invasion of the Soviet Union. But in the months after Pearl Harbor, possessions in the Pacific fell to the Japanese one by one. The Japanese captured the Philippines and other islands held by the United States. They overran the British colonies of Hong Kong, Burma, and Malaya, and advanced deeper into the Dutch East Indies and French Indochina. By 1942, the Japanese empire stretched from Southeast Asia to the western Pacific Ocean.

 **Checkpoint** Why did Japanese leaders view the United States as an enemy?

<hr>

Terms, People, and Places

1. For each term, person, or place listed at the beginning of the section, write a sentence explaining its significance.

Note Taking

2. **Reading Skill: Recognize Sequence** Use your completed flowchart and concept web to answer the Focus Question: Which regions were attacked and occupied by the Axis powers, and what was life like under their occupation?

Comprehension and Critical Thinking

3. **Summarize** Describe Hitler's blitzkrieg tactics.
4. **Recognize Effects** Referring to the Battle of Britain in 1940, Winston Churchill said "Never in the field of human conflict was so much owed by so many to so few." What did he mean?
5. **Recognize Ideologies** Hitler translated his hatred into a program of genocide. How do ethnic, racial, and religious hatreds weaken society?

● Writing About History

Quick Write: Gather Information Use the library and reliable Internet sources to find information about Pearl Harbor. Create a source card for each book or Web site you use. Then create note cards to record and organize at least three pieces of information.

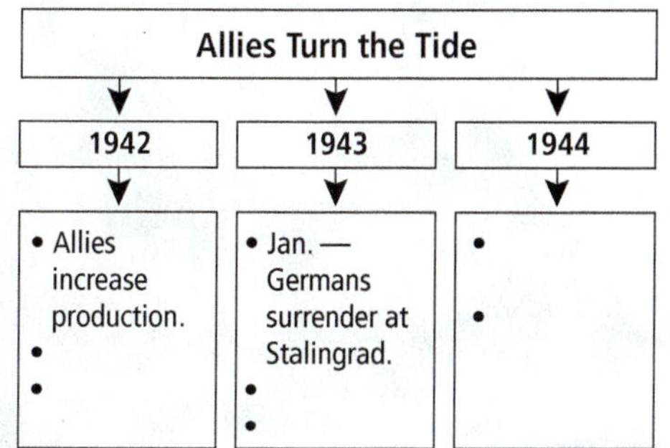

British poster encouraging women to work in factories to increase production

SECTION 3

WITNESS HISTORY ◀)) AUDIO

Support the War!

For the Allies to succeed against the relentless Axis war machine, everyone—on the home front as well as on the battlefield—had to work tirelessly. Ships needed to be built in a matter of days, not months. Airplanes, tanks, and ammunition had to be mass-produced. As factories converted to war production, the production of consumer goods such as automobiles ceased. All efforts were focused on the massive production of the materials of war.

Focus Question How did the Allies begin to push back the Axis powers?

The Allies Turn the Tide

Objectives

- Understand how nations devoted all of their resources to fighting World War II.
- Explain how Allied victories began to push back the Axis powers.
- Describe D-Day and the Allied advance toward Germany.

Terms, People, and Places

Rosie the Riveter	Stalingrad
aircraft carrier	D-Day
Dwight Eisenhower	Yalta Conference

Note Taking

Recognize Sequence In a flowchart like the one below, sequence the events that turned the tide of the war towards the Allies.

Allies Turn the Tide		
1942	1943	1944
• Allies increase production. • •	• Jan. — Germans surrender at Stalingrad. • •	• •

As 1942 began, the Allies were in trouble. German bombers flew unrelenting raids over Britain, and the German army advanced deep into the Soviet Union. In the Pacific, the Japanese onslaught seemed unstoppable. But helped by extraordinary efforts on the home front and a series of military victories, the tide was about to turn.

All-Out War

To defeat the Axis war machine, the Allies had to commit themselves to total war. Total war means nations devote all of their resources to the war effort.

Governments Increase Power To achieve maximum war production, democratic governments in the United States and Great Britain increased their political power. They directed economic resources into the war effort, ordering factories to stop making cars or refrigerators and to turn out airplanes or tanks instead. Governments implemented programs to ration or control the amount of food and other vital goods consumers could buy. They raised money by holding war bond drives, in which citizens lent their government certain sums of money that would be returned with interest later. Prices and wages were also regulated. While the war brought some shortages and hardships, the increase in production ended the unemployment of the depression era.

Under the pressures of war, even democratic governments limited the rights of citizens, censored the press, and used propaganda to win public support for the war. In the United States and Canada, many citizens of Japanese descent lost their jobs, property, and civil rights. Many Japanese Americans and Japanese Canadians were even interned in camps after their governments decided that they were a security risk. The British took similar action against German refugees. Some 40 years later, both the United States and Canada provided former internees with reparations, or payment for damages, but for many the compensation came too late.

Women Help Win the War As men joined the military, millions of women around the world replaced them in essential war industry jobs. Women, symbolized by the character **"Rosie the Riveter"** in the United States, built ships and planes and produced munitions.

British and American women served in the armed forces in many auxiliary roles—driving ambulances, delivering airplanes, and decoding messages. In occupied Europe, women fought in the resistance. Marie Fourcade, a French woman, helped downed Allied pilots escape to safety. Soviet women served in combat roles. Soviet pilot Lily Litvak, for example, shot down 12 German planes before she herself was killed.

✔ **Checkpoint** How did the Allies mobilize all of their resources for the war effort?

The Allies Forge Ahead

The years 1942–1943 marked the turning point of the war. The Allies won victories on four fronts—the Pacific, North Africa and Italy, the Soviet Union, and France—to push back the Axis tide.

Japanese Navy Battered In the Pacific, the Japanese suffered their first serious setback at the Battle of the Coral Sea. The battle lasted for five days in May 1942. For the first time in naval history, the enemy ships never even saw each other. Attacks were carried out by planes launched from **aircraft carriers,** or ships that transport aircraft and accommodate the take-off and landing of airplanes. The Japanese were prevented from seizing several important islands. More importantly, the Americans sank one Japanese aircraft carrier and several cruisers and destroyers.

This Allied victory was followed by an even more impressive win at the Battle of Midway in June 1942, which was also fought entirely from the air. The Americans destroyed four Japanese carriers and more than 250 planes. The battle was a devastating blow to the Japanese. After Midway, Japan was unable to launch any more offensive operations.

The Big Three Plot Their Strategy After the United States entered the war, the Allied leaders met periodically to hammer out their strategy.

Air War in the Pacific
Allied forces won decisive victories in the Coral Sea and at Midway Island. The Japanese pilots below may have taken part in these battles, which were fought from planes launched from aircraft carriers. *How do you think aircraft carriers changed naval warfare?*

Technology That Helped Win the War

Deadlier bombs, machines that broke secret codes, dive-bombers—all of these technologies gave those who used them a military advantage. Scientists and engineers on both sides of World War II created and improved technologies at a fast and furious pace in a desperate effort to win the war.

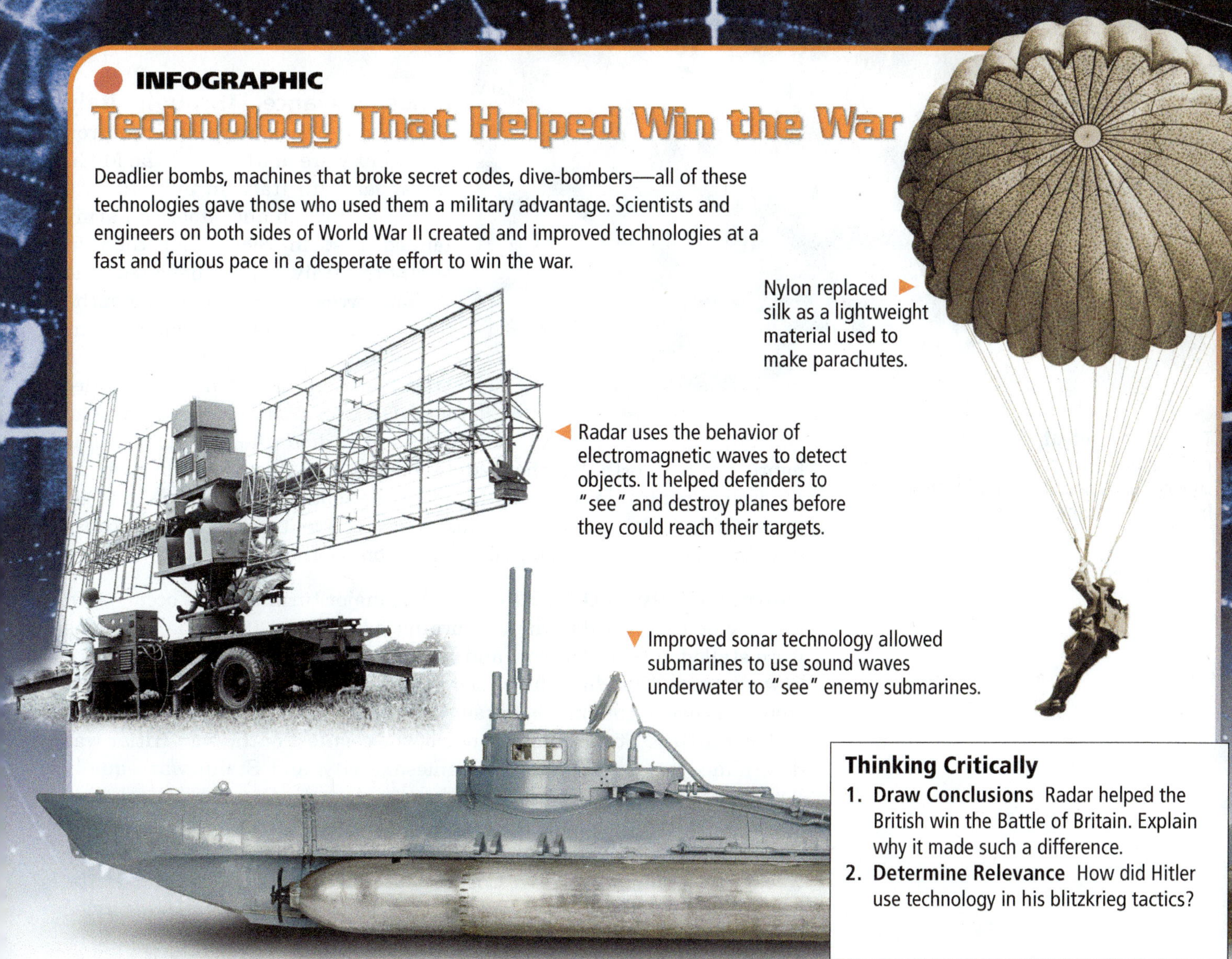

Thinking Critically

1. **Draw Conclusions** Radar helped the British win the Battle of Britain. Explain why it made such a difference.
2. **Determine Relevance** How did Hitler use technology in his blitzkrieg tactics?

In 1942, the "Big Three"—Roosevelt, Churchill, and Stalin—agreed to focus on finishing the war in Europe before trying to end the war in Asia.

From the outset, the Allies distrusted one another. Churchill and Roosevelt feared that Stalin wanted to dominate Europe. Stalin believed the West wanted to destroy communism. None of the new Allies wanted to risk a breakdown in their alliance, however. At a conference in Tehran, Iran, in late 1943, Churchill and Roosevelt yielded to Stalin by agreeing to let the borders outlined in the Nazi-Soviet Pact stand, against the wishes of Poland's government-in-exile. However, Stalin also wanted Roosevelt and Churchill to open a second front against Germany in Western Europe to relieve the pressure on the Soviet Union. Roosevelt and Churchill replied that they did not yet have the resources. Stalin saw the delay as a deliberate policy to weaken the Soviet Union.

Allied Victory in North Africa In North Africa, the British led by General Bernard Montgomery fought Rommel. After the fierce Battle of El Alamein in November 1942, the Allies finally halted the Desert Fox's advance. Allied tanks drove the Axis back across Libya into Tunisia.

Later in 1942, American General **Dwight Eisenhower** took command of a joint British and American force in Morocco and Algeria. Advancing on Tunisia from the west, the Allies trapped Rommel's army, which surrendered in May 1943.

The Pain of Defeat
German prisoners are marched through the snowy streets of Stalingrad after their defeat by the Soviet army.

Allies Advance Through Italy

With North Africa under their control, the Allies were able to cross the Mediterranean into Italy. In July 1943, a combined British and American army landed first in Sicily and then in southern Italy. They defeated the Italian forces there in about a month.

After the defeats, the Italians overthrew Mussolini and signed an armistice, but fighting did not end. Hitler sent German troops to rescue Mussolini and stiffen the will of Italians fighting in the north. For the next 18 months, the Allies pushed slowly up the Italian peninsula, suffering heavy losses against strong German resistance. Still, the Italian invasion was a decisive event for the Allies because it weakened Hitler by forcing him to fight on another front.

Germans Defeated at Stalingrad A major turning point occurred in the Soviet Union. After their lightning advance in 1941, the Germans were stalled outside Moscow and Leningrad. In 1942, Hitler launched a new offensive. This time, he aimed for the rich oil fields of the south. His troops, however, got only as far as **Stalingrad.**

The Battle of Stalingrad was one of the costliest of the war. Hitler was determined to capture Stalin's namesake city, and Stalin was equally determined to defend it. The battle began when the Germans surrounded the city. As winter closed in, a bitter street-by-street, house-by-house struggle raged. A German officer wrote that soldiers fought for two weeks for a single building. Corpses "are strewn in the cellars, on the landings and the staircases," he said. In November, the Soviets encircled their attackers. Trapped, without food or ammunition and with no hope of rescue, the German commander finally surrendered in January 1943.

After the Battle of Stalingrad, the Red Army took the offensive and drove the invaders out of the Soviet Union entirely. Hitler's forces suffered irreplaceable losses of both troops and equipment. By early 1944, Soviet troops were advancing into Eastern Europe.

 **Checkpoint** How did the Allies push back the Axis powers on four fronts?

The Allies Push Toward Germany

By 1944, the Western Allies were at last ready to open a second front in Europe by invading France. Allied leaders under Eisenhower faced the enormous task of planning the operation and assembling troops and supplies. To prepare the way for the invasion, Allied bombers flew constant missions over Germany. They targeted factories and destroyed aircraft that might be used against the invasion force. They also bombed railroads and bridges in France.

The D-Day Assault The Allies chose June 6, 1944—known as **D-Day**—for the invasion of France. Just before midnight on June 5, Allied planes dropped paratroopers behind enemy lines. Then, at dawn, thousands of ships ferried 156,000 Allied troops across the English Channel. The troops

World War II in Europe and North Africa, 1942–1945

Geography Interactive
For: Interactive map and timeline
Web Code: nap-2931

Map Skills Axis power reached its height in Europe in 1942. Then the tide began to turn.
1. Locate (a) Vichy France (b) Soviet Union (c) El Alamein (d) Normandy (e) Berlin
2. Place Describe the extent of Axis control in 1942.
3. Make Inferences How did geography both help and hinder Allied advances?

Europe Axis powers, 1942
Maximum Axis control, 1942
Neutral nations, 1942
Allied territory, 1942
Allied advances
Major battles

SWEDEN
FINLAND
NORWAY
Leningrad
Moscow
SOVIET UNION
DENMARK
North Sea
Baltic Sea
Danzig
1945
1944
1943
Stalingrad
Kursk
1943
1944
1943
UNITED KINGDOM
IRELAND
London
Dunkirk
NETH.
Berlin
Warsaw
1945
1944
1945
Elbe R.
BELGIUM
LUX.
1945
GERMANY
Rhine R.
1945
SLOVAKIA
Normandy
1944
Atlantic Ocean
FRANCE
Paris
Vichy
Vichy France
SWITZ.
1944
HUNGARY Budapest
1945
1944
ROMANIA
Danube R.
Yalta
Black Sea
CROATIA SERBIA
MONT.
BULGARIA
TURKEY
1942
PORTUGAL
SPAIN
ITALY
1944
Rome
Anzio
Salerno
ALB.
GREECE
SYRIA
1944
1943
Palermo
Sicily
Lebanon (FR.)
IRAQ
Algiers
Tunis
1943
Transjordan (FR.)
Spanish Morocco
Oran
Algeria (FR.)
1942
Casablanca
1942
Tobruk
El Alamein
Cairo
Palestine (BR.)
SAUDI ARABIA
MOROCCO
Tripoli
Mediterranean Sea
1942
Conic Projection
0 200 400 mi
0 200 400 km
Tunisia (FR.)
1943
LIBYA
EGYPT

Jan 1943
Germans surrender at Stalingrad
Jul 1943
Allied forces land in Sicily
Jan 1945
Soviets enter Warsaw
May 7, 1945
Germany surrenders

1942   1943   1944   1945   1946

Nov 1942
British defeat Germans at El Alamein
Sep 1943
Italians surrender to Allies
Jun 6, 1944
D-Day invasion at Normandy
Mar 1945
British and American forces cross Rhine

Churchill

Winston Churchill (1874–1965) was a staunch antisocialist and defender of the British Empire. As a member of Parliament, he loudly warned the British of the threat posed by Nazi Germany. After Neville Chamberlain's government failed to defend Norway from Hitler, Churchill replaced him as prime minister on May 10, 1940. Within seven weeks, France had surrendered, and Nazi forces threatened Britain. Churchill's courage and defiance steeled British resolve in the darkest days of the war when Britain stood alone against the Nazis. **How did Churchill inspire the British people?**

Roosevelt

In 1933, Franklin Delano Roosevelt (1882–1945) started his first term as president, promising to bring the United States out of the Great Depression. During his second term, FDR lent, and then gave, millions of dollars in war supplies to the struggling British. Japan's attack on Pearl Harbor quickly brought the United States into the war. From the start of American involvement, Roosevelt took the lead in establishing alliances among all countries fighting the Axis powers—including the Soviet Union. **How did Roosevelt influence World War II before Pearl Harbor?**

Stalin

Joseph Stalin (1879–1953) was born Joseph Dzhugashvili (joo gush VYEE lyee). He changed his name to Stalin, meaning "man of steel," after he joined the Bolshevik underground in the early 1900s. Stalin emerged as the sole ruler of the Soviet Union in the 1920s, and he maintained an iron grasp on the nation until his death in 1953. When Hitler's army invaded the Soviet Union and threatened Moscow in 1941, Stalin refused to leave the capital city. He eventually forced the Germans into retreat. **Why would Churchill and Roosevelt have distrusted Stalin?**

---

fought their way to shore amid underwater mines and raking machine-gun fire. As one soldier who landed in the first wave of D-Day assault recalled,

> "It all seemed unreal, a sort of dreaming while awake, men were screaming and dying all around me. . . I honestly could have walked the full length of the beach without touching the ground, they were that thickly strewn about."
> —Melvin B. Farrell, *War Memories*

Still, the Allied troops clawed their way inland through the tangled hedges of Normandy. In early August, a massive armored division under American General George S. Patton helped the joint British and American forces break through German defenses and advance toward Paris. Meanwhile, other Allied forces sailed from Italy to land in southern France. In Paris, French resistance forces rose up against the occupying Germans. Under pressure from all sides, the Germans retreated. On August 25, the Allies entered Paris. Within a month, all of France was free.

Allies Continue to Advance By this time, Germany was reeling under <u>incessant</u>, round-the-clock bombing. For two years, Allied bombers had hammered military bases, factories, railroads, oil depots, and cities.

Vocabulary Builder

<u>incessant</u>—(in SES unt) *adj.* uninterrupted, ceaseless

The goal of this kind of bombing was to cripple Germany's industries and destroy the morale of its civilians. In one 10-day period, bombing almost erased the huge industrial city of Hamburg, killing 40,000 civilians and forcing one million to flee their homes. In February 1945, Allied raids on Dresden, not an industrial target, but considered one of the most beautiful cities in Europe, killed as many as 135,000 people.

After freeing France, Allied forces battled toward Germany. As their armies advanced into Belgium in December, Germany launched a massive counterattack. At the bloody Battle of the Bulge, which lasted more than a month, both sides took terrible losses. The Germans were unable to break through. The battle delayed the Allied advance from the west, but only for six weeks. Meanwhile, the Soviet army battled through Germany and advanced on Berlin from the east. Hitler's support within Germany was declining, and he had already survived one assassination attempt by senior officers in the German military. By early 1945, the defeat of Germany seemed <u>inevitable</u>.

Uneasy Agreement at Yalta In February 1945, Roosevelt, Churchill, and Stalin met again at Yalta, in the southern Soviet Union. Once again, the Big Three planned strategy in an atmosphere of distrust. Stalin insisted that the Soviet Union needed to maintain control of Eastern Europe to be able to protect itself from future aggression. Churchill and Roosevelt favored self-determination for Eastern Europe, which would give people the right to choose their own form of government. However, Churchill and Roosevelt needed Stalin's help to win the war.

At the Yalta Conference, the three leaders agreed that the Soviet Union would enter the war against Japan within three months of Germany's surrender. In return, Churchill and Roosevelt promised Stalin that the Soviets would take possession of southern Sakhalin Island, the Kuril Islands, and an occupation zone in Korea. They also agreed that Germany would be temporarily divided into four zones, to be governed by American, French, British, and Soviet forces. Stalin agreed to hold free elections in Eastern Europe. However, as you will read later, growing mistrust would later cause a split between the Allies.

 **Checkpoint** What agreements did Churchill, Roosevelt, and Stalin come to at Yalta?

Vocabulary Builder
inevitable—(in EV ih tuh bul) *adj.* unavoidable, inescapable

SECTION 3 Assessment

Terms, People, and Places

1. For each term, person, or place listed at the beginning of the section, write a sentence explaining its significance.

Note Taking

2. **Reading Skill: Recognize Sequence** Use your completed timeline to answer the Focus Question: How did the Allies begin to push back the Axis powers?

Comprehension and Critical Thinking

3. **Analyze Information** How did democratic governments mobilize their economies for war?

4. **Determine Relevance** Explain why the battles of Midway, El Alamein, and Stalingrad were important turning points in the war.

5. **Predict Consequences** Why didn't the Yalta Conference lead to lasting unity among the Big Three leaders?

Writing About History

Quick Write: Develop a Thesis A thesis statement summarizes the main idea of your research paper. The thesis statement should express an idea that can be defended or refuted. It should also be narrow enough to be addressed clearly in your writing.

Based on what you have read, write a thesis statement for an essay explaining the importance of the Battle of Stalingrad.

D-DAY

In the earliest hours of June 6, 1944, the Allies launched a surprise invasion of Normandy in France—the largest amphibious, or land and water, invasion in history. More than 156,000 Allied troops crossed the English Channel. Thousands of these troops landed on the beaches, fighting and clawing their way up the steep cliffs under heavy German fire. Paratroopers dropped from the sky. By the end of the day, about 2,500 men had given their lives. But by August, the Allies had made their way to Paris and freed it from German control.

Overcoming Hitler's Defenses at Normandy

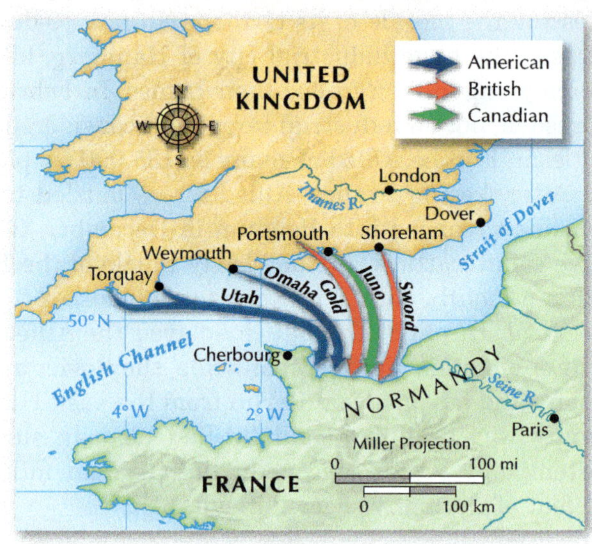

▲ Allied troops landed at five Normandy beaches, code-named Utah, Omaha, Gold, Juno, and Sword.

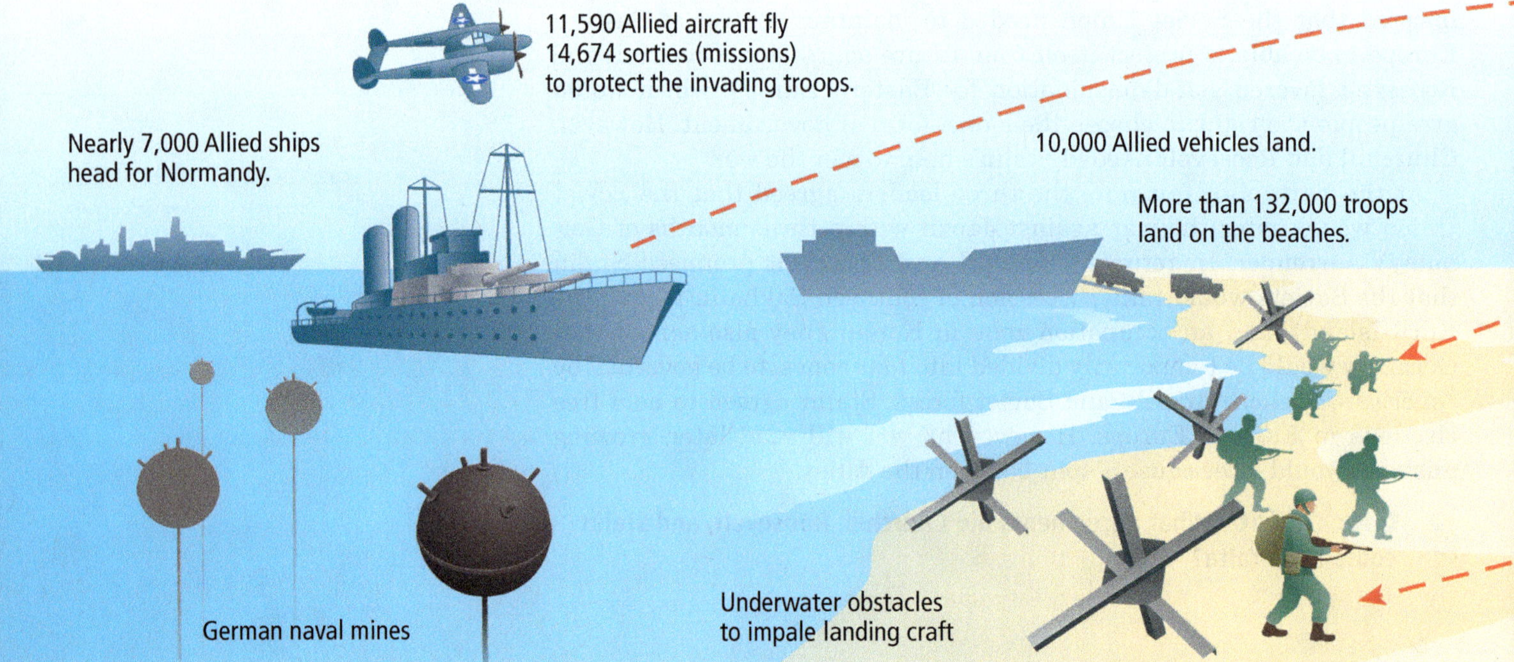

Allied troops faced daunting obstacles on D-Day. Naval mines threatened ships trying to land. Steel obstacles on the beaches could rip the bottoms out of landing craft at high tide. The Germans waited atop the steep cliffs.

▼ British special forces storm the beach.

Allied Troop Strengths and Casualties on D-Day		
Country	Troops	Estimated Casualties*
United States	73,000	6,603
Britain	61,715	2,700
Canada	21,400	946
Allied Total	**156,115**	**10,249**

*includes those killed, wounded, missing, and captured
SOURCE: The D-Day Museum Online

▲ Wounded Allied soldiers after the battle

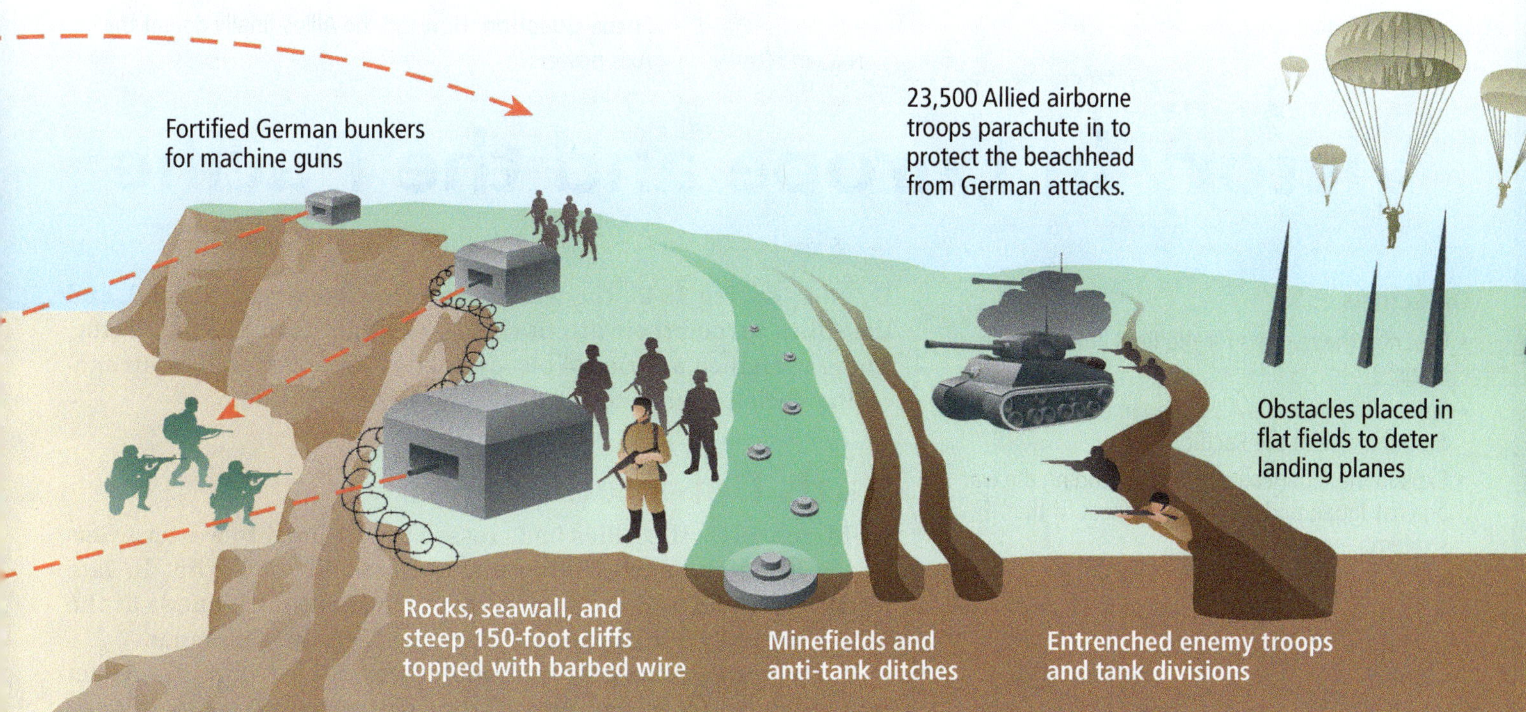

▼ Omaha Beach at the end of D-Day

Thinking Critically

1. **Chart Skills** Which of the Allies suffered the greatest losses on D-Day?
2. **Draw Conclusions** Why do you think the D-Day landings were made on beaches instead of at established harbors?
3. **Diagram Skills** What do you think was the greatest obstacle the Allies had to overcome on D-Day? Explain.

History Interactive

For: interactive map, audio, and more
Visit: PHSchool.com
Web Code: nap-2932

Allied soldier
in the Pacific

A Soldier Remembers

A defeated General Douglas MacArthur left the Philippines in 1942. As he departed, he pledged his determination to free the islands with the words "I shall return." In October 1944, that pledge became a reality when MacArthur landed on the Philippine island of Leyte. As one soldier recalled,

> **"**When I heard that he had returned, I finally had the feeling that I might have a chance of living through the war. . . . [O]nce they landed in Leyte, I knew it was only a question of hanging on for a few more months and I would be able to live through it.**"**
> —Edwin Ramsey

Focus Question How did the Allies finally defeat the Axis powers?

Victory in Europe and the Pacific

Objectives

- Describe the reasons for the final defeat of the Nazis.
- Summarize how the Allies began to push back the Japanese in the Pacific.
- Explain the American strategy for ending the war against Japan and the consequences of that strategy.

Terms, People, and Places

V-E Day	kamikaze
Bataan Death March	Manhattan Project
Douglas MacArthur	Hiroshima
island-hopping	Nagasaki

Note Taking

Reading Skill: Recognize Sequence Use a timeline like the one below to sequence the events that led to the defeat of the Axis powers.

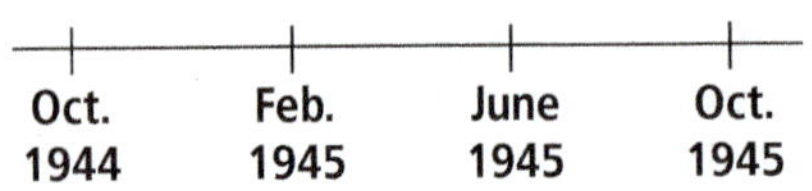

By early spring 1945, the war in Europe was nearing its end, and the Allies turned their attention to winning the war in the Pacific. There remained a series of bloody battles ahead, as well as an agonizing decision for American President Harry Truman.

Nazis Defeated

By March 1945, the Allies had crossed the Rhine into western Germany. From the east, Soviet troops closed in on Berlin. In late April, American and Russian soldiers met and shook hands at the Elbe River. All over Europe, Axis armies began to surrender.

In Italy, guerrillas captured and executed Mussolini. As Soviet troops fought their way into Berlin, Hitler committed suicide in his underground bunker. On May 7, Germany surrendered. Officially, the war in Europe ended the next day, May 8, 1945, which was proclaimed **V-E Day** (Victory in Europe). After just 12 years, Hitler's "thousand-year Reich" was bomb-ravaged and in ruins.

The Allies were able to defeat the Axis powers in Europe for a number of reasons. Because of the location of Germany and its allies, they had to fight on several fronts simultaneously. Hitler, who took almost complete control over military decisions, made some poor ones. He underestimated the ability of the Soviet Union to fight his armies.

The enormous productive capacity of the United States was another factor. By 1944, the United States was producing twice as much as all of the Axis powers combined. Meanwhile, Allied bombing hindered German production. Oil became so scarce because of

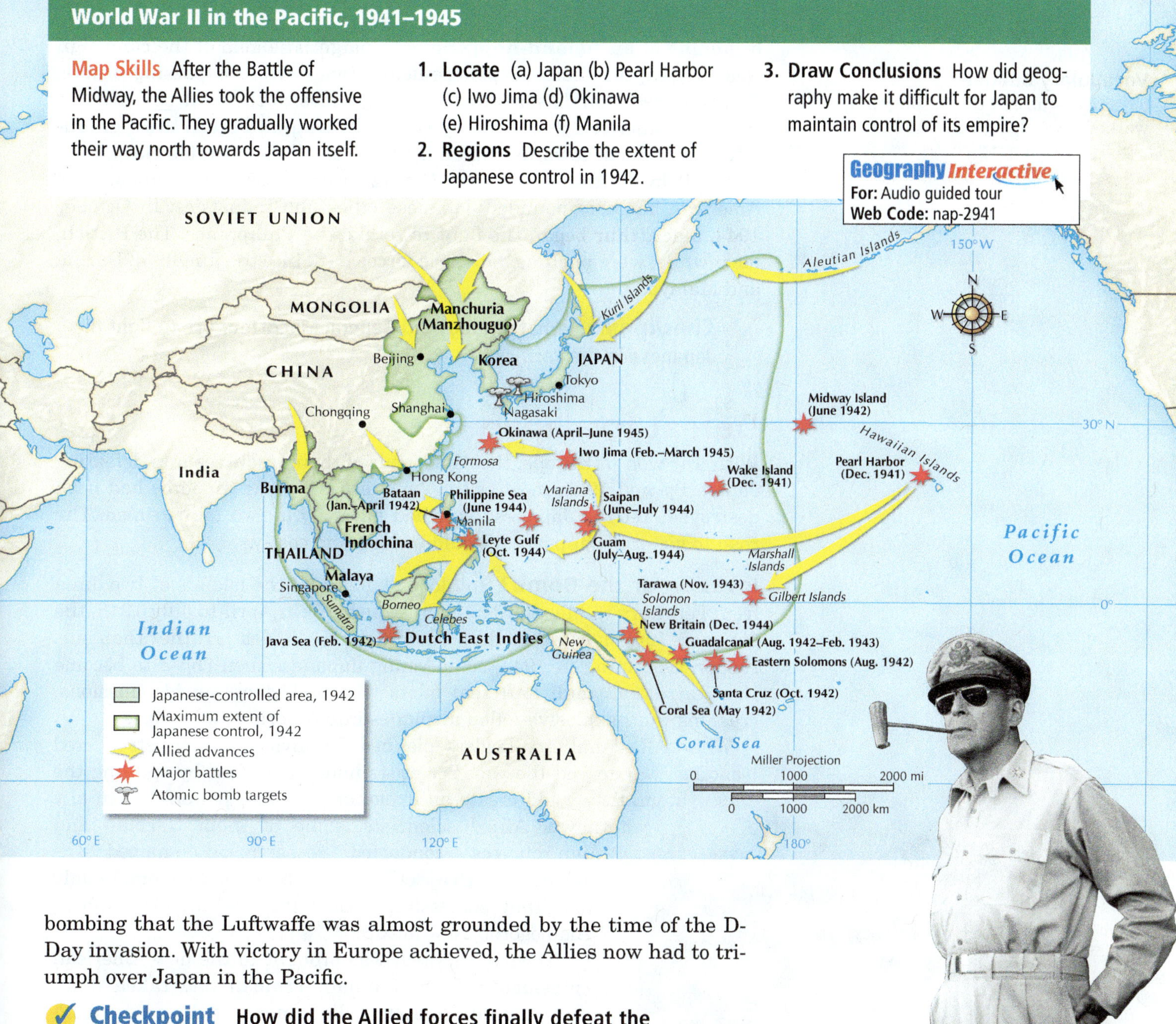

bombing that the Luftwaffe was almost grounded by the time of the D-Day invasion. With victory in Europe achieved, the Allies now had to triumph over Japan in the Pacific.

✔ **Checkpoint** How did the Allied forces finally defeat the Germans?

General Douglas MacArthur

Struggle for the Pacific

Until mid-1942, the Japanese had won an uninterrupted series of victories. They controlled much of Southeast Asia and many Pacific islands. By May 1942, the Japanese had gained control of the Philippines, killing several hundred American soldiers and as many as 10,000 Filipino soldiers during the 65-mile **Bataan Death March.** One survivor described the ordeal as "a macabre litany of heat, dust, starvation, thirst, flies, filth, stench, murder, torture, corpses, and wholesale brutality that numbs the memory." Many Filipino civilians risked—and sometimes lost—their lives to give food and water to captives on the march.

After the battles of Midway and the Coral Sea, however, the United States took the offensive. That summer, United States Marines landed at Guadalcanal in the Solomon Islands. Victory at Guadalcanal marked the beginning of an **"island-hopping"** campaign. The goal of the campaign was to recapture some Japanese-held islands while bypassing others. The captured islands served as steppingstones to the next <u>objective</u>. In this way, American forces, led by General **Douglas MacArthur,** gradually moved north towards Japan. By 1944, the United States Navy, commanded by Admiral Chester Nimitz, was blockading Japan, and American bombers pounded Japanese cities and industries. In October 1944, MacArthur began the fight to retake the Philippines. The British, meanwhile, were pushing Japanese forces back into the jungles of Burma and Malaya.

✔ **Checkpoint** What strategy did General MacArthur use to fight the Japanese in the Pacific?

Defeat for Japan

With war won in Europe, the Allies poured their resources into defeating Japan. By mid-1945, most of the Japanese navy and air force had been destroyed. Yet the Japanese still had an army of two million men. The road to victory, it appeared, would be long and costly.

Invasion or the Bomb? In bloody battles on the islands of Iwo Jima from February to March 1945 and Okinawa from April to July 1945, the Japanese had shown that they would fight to the death rather than surrender. Beginning in 1944, some young Japanese men chose to become **kamikaze** (kah muh KAH zee) pilots who undertook suicide missions, crashing their explosive-laden airplanes into American warships.

While Allied military leaders planned for invasion, scientists offered another way to end the war. Scientists understood that by splitting the atom, they could create an explosion far more powerful than any yet known. Allied scientists, some of them German and Italian refugees, conducted research, code-named the **Manhattan Project,** racing to harness the atom. In July 1945, they successfully tested the first atomic bomb at Alamogordo, New Mexico.

News of this test was brought to the new American president, Harry Truman. Truman had taken office after Franklin Roosevelt died unexpectedly on April 12. He realized that the atomic bomb was a terrible new force for destruction. Still, after consulting with his advisors, and

Nuclear Blast
The world's first nuclear explosion instantly vaporized the tower from which it was launched. Seconds later an enormous blast sent searing heat across the desert and knocked observers to the ground. Shown here is an atomic bomb's characteristic mushroom cloud. *Why might the scientists who created the bomb have counseled leaders not to use it?*

determining that it would save American lives, he decided to use the new weapon against Japan.

At the time, Truman was meeting with other Allied leaders in the city of Potsdam, Germany. They issued a warning to Japan to surrender or face "complete destruction" and "utter devastation." When the Japanese ignored the warning, the United States took action.

Utter Devastation On August 6, 1945, an American plane dropped an atomic bomb over the city of **Hiroshima.** The bomb flattened four square miles and instantly killed more than 70,000 people. In the months that followed, many more would die from radiation sickness, a deadly after-effect of exposure to radioactive materials.

On August 8, the Soviet Union declared war on Japan and invaded Manchuria. Again, Japanese leaders did not respond. The next day, the United States dropped a second atomic bomb, this time on the city of **Nagasaki.** More than 40,000 people were killed in this second explosion.

Finally, on August 10, Emperor Hirohito intervened, an action unheard of for a Japanese emperor, and forced the government to surrender. On September 2, 1945, the formal peace treaty was signed on board the American battleship *Missouri,* anchored in Tokyo Bay.

Hiroshima in Ruins
The atomic bomb reduced the center of Hiroshima to smoldering ruins (top left), but the full effect of the bomb would take years to materialize. A woman (above) pays respects to the victims of the atomic bomb at the Memorial Cenotaph in Peace Memorial Park in Hiroshima. A cenotaph is a monument that honors people who are buried elsewhere.

✔ **Checkpoint** What strategies did the Allies use to end the war with Japan?

Assessment

Terms, People, and Places

1. For each term, person, or place listed at the beginning of the section, write a sentence explaining its significance.

Note Taking 

2. **Reading Skill: Recognize Sequence** Use your completed flowchart to answer the Focus Question: How did the Allies finally defeat the Axis powers?

Comprehension and Critical Thinking

3. **Determine Relevance** How did the location of the Axis powers in Europe contribute to their defeat?

4. **Draw Inferences** What factors besides ending the war in the Pacific might have contributed to President Harry Truman's decision to drop the atomic bomb?

● Writing About History

Quick Write: Make an Outline Once you have a thesis and have gathered research on your topics, you must choose an organization. Some choices are compare and contrast, order of importance, chronological, and cause and effect. Using one of these organizations, create an outline for the following thesis statement: The atomic bomb was a decisive weapon in World War II.

▲ Newspaper headline on the day Japan surrendered

▶ A sailor embraces a nurse when the end of the war is announced.

WITNESS HISTORY 🔊 AUDIO

The War Is Over!

American President Harry Truman made these remarks on the day the Japanese surrendered:

❝ Our first thoughts, of course—thoughts of gratefulness and deep obligation—go out to those of our loved ones who have been killed or maimed in this terrible war. On land and sea and in the air, American men and women have given their lives so that this day of ultimate victory might come and assure the survival of a civilized world . . . ❞

Focus Question What issues arose in the aftermath of World War II and how did new tensions develop?

The End of World War II

Objectives

- Describe the issues faced by the Allies after World War II ended.
- Summarize the organization of the United Nations.
- Analyze how new conflicts developed among the former Allies after World War II.

Terms, People, and Places

Nuremberg	Marshall Plan
United Nations (UN)	North Atlantic Treaty
Cold War	Organization (NATO)
Truman Doctrine	Warsaw Pact

Note Taking

Reading Skill: Recognize Sequence Sequence the events following World War II by creating an outline of this section. Use the outline below as a starting point.

> I. The War's Aftermath
>   A. Devastation
>   1. As many as 50 million dead
>   2.

Even as the Allies celebrated victory, the appalling costs of the war began to emerge. The war had killed as many as 50 million people around the world. In Europe alone, over 30 million people had lost their lives, more than half of them civilians. The Soviet Union suffered the worst casualties, with over 20 million dead. As they had after World War I, the Allies faced difficult decisions about the future.

The War's Aftermath

"Give me ten years and you will not be able to recognize Germany," said Hitler in 1933. Indeed, Germany in 1945 was an unrecognizable ruin. Parts of Poland, the Soviet Union, Japan, China, and other countries also lay in ruins. Total war had gutted cities, factories, harbors, bridges, railroads, farms, and homes. Over twenty million refugees wandered Europe. Amid the devastation, hunger, disease, and mental illness took their toll for years after the fighting ended. As they had after World War I, the Allies faced difficult decisions about the future.

Horrors of the Holocaust Numbers alone did not tell the story of the Nazi nightmare in Europe or the Japanese brutality in Asia. During the war, the Allies were aware of the existence of Nazi concentration camps and death camps. But only at war's end did they learn the full extent of the inhumanity of the Holocaust. American General Dwight Eisenhower, who visited the camps, was stunned to come "face to face with indisputable evidence of Nazi brutality and ruthless disregard of every sense of decency."

War Crimes Trials At wartime meetings, the Allies had agreed that Axis leaders should be tried for "crimes against humanity." In Germany, the Allies held war crimes trials in Nuremberg, where Hitler had staged mass rallies in the 1930s. Nearly 200 Germans and Austrians were tried, and most were found guilty. A handful of top Nazis received death sentences. Others were imprisoned. Similar war crimes trials were held in Japan. Many of those accused of war crimes were never captured or brought to trial. However, the trials showed that political and military leaders could be held accountable for actions in wartime.

Occupying Allies The war crimes trials further discredited the totalitarian ideologies that had led to the war. Yet disturbing questions remained. Why had ordinary people in Germany, Poland, France, and elsewhere accepted—and even collaborated in—Hitler's "Final Solution"?

The United States felt that strengthening democracy would ensure tolerance and peace. The Western Allies built new governments in occupied Germany and Japan with democratic constitutions to protect the rights of all citizens. In Japan, the occupying forces under General MacArthur helped Japanese politicians to create a new constitution that gave power to the Japanese people, rather than the emperor.

 **Checkpoint** Why did the Allies hold war crimes trials for Axis leaders?

Establishing the United Nations

In April 1945, delegates from 50 nations <u>convened</u> in San Francisco to draft a charter for the United Nations (UN). The UN would play a greater role in world affairs than did its predecessor, the League of Nations.

Under the UN Charter, each of the member nations has one vote in the General Assembly. A much smaller body called the Security Council has greater power. Each of its five permanent members—the United States, the Soviet Union (today Russia), Britain, France, and China—has the right to veto any council decision. The goal was to give these great powers the authority to ensure the peace. The Security Council has the power to apply economic sanctions or send a peace-keeping military force to try to resolve disputes. Differences among the nations on the Security Council, most notably the United States and the Soviet Union, have often kept the UN from taking action. Since the fall of the Soviet Union in 1991, more peacekeeping delegations have been approved.

The UN's work would go far beyond peacekeeping. The organization would take on many world problems—from preventing the outbreak of disease and improving education to protecting refugees and helping nations to develop economically. UN agencies like the World Health Organization and the Food and Agricultural Organization have provided aid for millions of people around the world.

 **Checkpoint** Compare and contrast the United Nations and the League of Nations.

Casualties of World War II

	Military Dead*	Military Wounded*	Civilian Dead*
Allies			
Britain	264,000	277,000	93,000
France	213,000	400,000	350,000
China	1,310,000	1,753,000	1,000,000
Soviet Union	7,500,000	14,012,000	15,000,000
United States	292,000	672,000	6,000
Axis Powers			
Germany	3,500,000	5,000,000	780,000
Italy	242,000	66,000	153,000
Japan	1,300,000	4,000,000	672,000

World War II resulted in enormous casualties and disruption. Afterwards, millions of displaced Europeans, like the Germans above, searched for relatives they had been separated from during the war. **Chart Skills** *Which nation suffered the greatest number of both civilian and military casualties?*

* All figures are estimates.

SOURCE: *Encyclopædia Britannica; The Harper Encyclopedia of Military History*, R. Ernest Dupuy and Trevor N. Dupuy

Vocabulary Builder

convened—(kun VEEND) *vi.* met; assembled

The Alliance Breaks Apart

Amid the rubble of war, a new power structure emerged. In Europe, Germany was defeated. France and Britain were exhausted. Two other powers, the United States and the Soviet Union, emerged as the new world leaders. The United States abandoned its traditional policy of isolationism to counter what President Truman saw as the communist threat.

Differences Grow Between the Allies During the war, the Soviet Union and the nations of the West had cooperated to defeat Nazi Germany. After the war's end, the Allies set up councils made up of foreign ministers from Britain, France, China, the United States, and the Soviet Union to iron out the peace agreements discussed at various conferences during the war. The councils concluded peace agreements with several Axis nations in 1947. However, reparations in Germany and the nature of the governments of Eastern Europe caused divisions to deepen between the former Allies. Conflicting ideologies and mutual distrust soon led to the conflict known as the Cold War. The **Cold War** was a state of tension and hostility between nations aligned with the United States on one side and the Soviet Union on the other, without armed conflict between the major rivals.

The Cold War Begins Stalin had two goals in Eastern Europe. First, he wanted to spread communism in the area. Second, he wanted to create a buffer zone of friendly governments as a defense against Germany, which had invaded Russia during World War I and again in 1941.

As the Red Army had pushed German forces out of Eastern Europe, it had left behind occupying forces. At wartime conferences, Stalin tried to persuade the West to accept Soviet influence in Eastern Europe. The Soviet dictator pointed out that the United States was not consulting the Soviet Union about peace terms for Italy or Japan, both of which were defeated and occupied by American and British troops. In the same way, the Soviet Union would determine the fate of the Eastern European lands that it occupied.

Roosevelt and Churchill rejected Stalin's view, making him promise "free elections" in Eastern Europe. Stalin ignored that pledge. Most Eastern European countries had existing Communist parties, many of which had actively resisted the Nazis during the war. Backed by the Red Army, these local Communists in Poland, Czechoslovakia, and elsewhere destroyed rival political parties and even assassinated democratic leaders. By 1948, pro-Soviet communist governments were in place throughout Eastern Europe.

✓ **Checkpoint** What post-war issues caused the Western Allies and the Soviet Union to disagree?

New Conflicts Develop

Stalin soon showed his aggressive intentions outside of Eastern Europe. In Greece, Stalin backed communist rebels who were fighting to overturn a right-wing monarchy supported by Britain. By 1947, however, Britain could no longer afford to defend Greece. Stalin was also menacing Turkey in the Dardanelles.

A Widening Gulf
Although Stalin and Truman were friendly at the Potsdam Conference (above), this Soviet propaganda poster from 1949 shows that relations between the two nations were becoming strained. The poster urges support "For a stable peace! Against those who would ignite a new war." The small caricatures of Churchill and Uncle Sam in the lower corner indicate who "those" people are.

The Truman Doctrine Truman took action. On March 12, 1947, Truman outlined a new policy to Congress: "I believe that it must be the policy of the United States to support free peoples who are resisting attempted subjugation by armed minorities or by outside pressures." This policy, known as the **Truman Doctrine,** was rooted in the idea of containment, limiting communism to the areas already under Soviet control.

The Truman Doctrine would guide the United States for decades. It made clear that Americans would resist Soviet expansion in Europe or elsewhere in the world. Truman soon sent military and economic aid and advisors to Greece and Turkey so that they could withstand the communist threat.

The Marshall Plan Postwar hunger and poverty made Western European lands fertile ground for communist ideas. To strengthen democratic governments, the United States offered a massive aid package, called the **Marshall Plan.** Under it, the United States funneled food and economic assistance to Europe to help countries rebuild. Billions of dollars in American aid helped war-shattered Europe recover rapidly.

President Truman also offered aid to the Soviet Union and its satellites, or dependent states, in Eastern Europe. However, Stalin declined and forbade Eastern European countries to accept American aid. Instead, he promised help from the Soviet Union in its place.

Germany Stays Divided Defeated Germany became another focus of the Cold War. The Soviet Union took reparations for its massive war losses by dismantling and moving factories and other resources in its occupation zone to help rebuild the Soviet Union. France, Britain, and the United States also took some reparations out of their portions of Germany. However, Western leaders wanted the German economy to recover in order to restore political stability to the region. The Western Allies decided to unite their zones of occupation. Then, they extended the Marshall Plan to western Germany. The Soviets were furious at Western moves to rebuild the German economy and deny them further reparations. They strengthened their hold on eastern Germany.

The Berlin Airlift

After World War II, Germany, and Berlin within it, was divided into communist and noncommunist zones. In the photo below, children in West Berlin greet a plane delivering supplies during the Berlin Airlift.

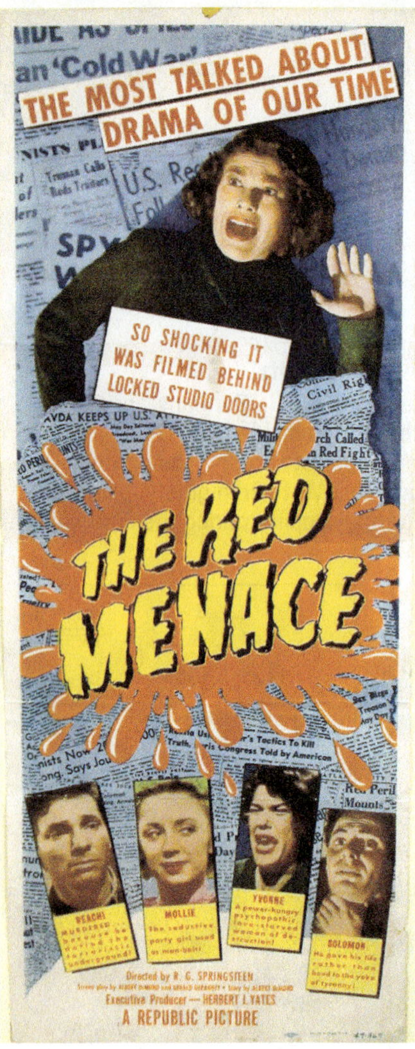

The Red Menace
Films like *The Red Menace* (1949) dramatized the threat of communism in the United States and formed a vital part of the propaganda war.

Vocabulary Builder

<u>invoked</u>—(in VOKED) *vt.* resorted to; called upon

Germany thus became a divided nation. In West Germany, the democratic nations allowed the people to write their own constitution and regain self-government. In East Germany, the Soviet Union installed a socialist dictatorship under Stalin's control.

The Berlin Airlift Stalin's resentment at Western moves to rebuild Germany triggered a crisis over Berlin. Even though it lay deep within the Soviet zone, the former German capital was occupied by all four victorious Allies. In June 1948, Stalin tried to force the Western Allies out of Berlin by sealing off every railroad and highway into the Western sectors of the city. The Western powers responded to the blockade by mounting a round-the-clock airlift. For more than a year, cargo planes supplied West Berliners with food and fuel. Their success forced the Soviets to end the blockade. Although the West had won, the crisis deepened.

Opposing Alliances Tensions continued to grow. In 1949, the United States, Canada, and ten other countries formed a new military alliance called the **North Atlantic Treaty Organization (NATO).** Members pledged to help one another if any one of them were attacked.

In 1955, the Soviet Union responded by forming its own military alliance, the **Warsaw Pact.** It included the Soviet Union and seven satellites in Eastern Europe. Unlike NATO, however, the Warsaw Pact was often <u>invoked</u> by the Soviets to keep its satellites in order. The Warsaw Pact cemented the division of Europe into "eastern" and "western" blocs. In the East were the Soviet-dominated countries of Eastern Europe. These countries were communist in name but dictatorships in practice, like the Soviet Union itself. In the West were the Western democracies, led by the United States.

The Propaganda War Both sides participated in a propaganda war. The United States spoke of defending capitalism and democracy against communism and totalitarianism. The Soviet Union claimed the moral high ground in the struggle against Western imperialism. Yet linked to those stands, both sides sought world power.

 **Checkpoint** What foreign policy pattern did the United States establish with the Truman Doctrine?

Assessment

Terms, People, and Places

1. What do many of the key terms listed at the beginning of the section have in common? Explain.

Note Taking

2. **Reading Skill: Recognize Sequence** Use your completed outline to answer the Focus Question: What issues arose in the aftermath of World War II and how did new tensions develop?

Comprehension and Critical Thinking

3. **Compare and Contrast** How did the peace made after World War II differ from that made after World War I?

4. **Identify Central Issues** What was the main purpose of the UN when it was founded?

5. **Recognize Causes** List two causes of the Cold War.

6. **Draw Conclusions** Why is it important to remember the inhumanity of the Holocaust?

● Writing About History

Quick Write: Credit Sources When you use quotes or ideas from your sources in your paper, you must give proper credit. One way to do this is to list the author and page number of the material you have used in parentheses following the statement. Then, include a bibliography at the end of your paper. Research a topic from this section and write a paragraph using two sources. Credit the sources where appropriate and list them at the end.

GENOCIDE

Why do people sometimes commit the crime of genocide?

In This Chapter

Hitler's Final Solution involved rounding up all the Jews in German-held territory (right). Millions were then brutally killed in death camps. British Prime Minister Winston Churchill called this well-organized plan of mass murder "a crime that has no name." After the war, the United Nations gave the crime a name: genocide. Genocide is any act committed with the intention of destroying an entire national, ethnic, racial or religious group.

Throughout History

1500s European guns and disease kill millions of Native Americans in the Americas.

1915–1916 Muslim Turks slaughter members of the Armenian Christian minority in the Ottoman Empire.

1938 Nazis urge mobs to attack and rob German Jews during Kristallnacht.

1994 Ethnic conflict in Rwanda leads to the murder of 800,000 Tutsis and moderate Hutus.

2004 Arab militias in Sudan unleash violence against non-Arab Muslim villagers in Darfur.

Continuing Today

In recent times, countries on the Balkan peninsula and in Africa have witnessed widespread violence against ethnic or religious minorities. The struggle in Darfur has driven thousands of refugees into refugee camps (below), where they depend on international relief agencies for food and medical help.

TRANSFER Activities

1. Analyze Throughout history, what motives have led people to commit genocide?

2. Infer Under what conditions is genocide more likely to occur?

3. Transfer Complete a Web quest in which you document the motives for genocide; record your thoughts in the Concept Connector Journal; and learn to make a video. Web Code nah-2908

Quick Study Guide

Progress Monitoring *Online*
For: Self-test with vocabulary practice
Web Code: naa-2961

■ Key Causes of World War II

- Failure of World War I peace settlement, Treaty of Versailles
- Global economic depression
- Fascism, militarism, and imperialism in Germany, Italy, and Japan
- Weakness of the League of Nations
- British and French appeasement

■ The Allies vs. the Axis

As the map below shows, most of the world was divided into areas controlled by the Allies or the Axis powers during the war.

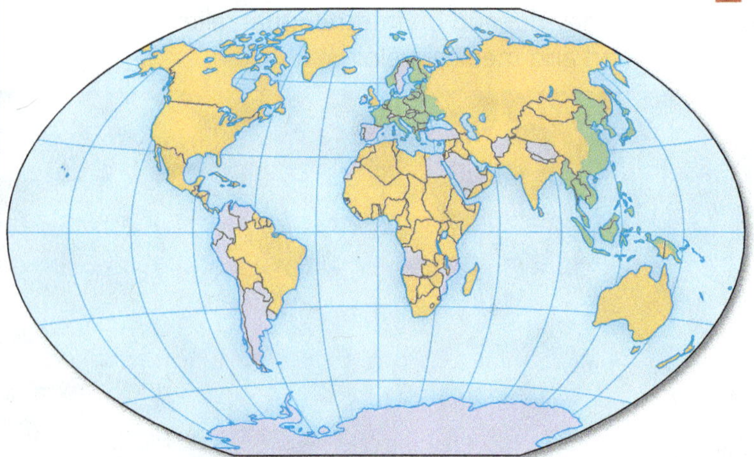

■ Key Political Leaders

Allies
Franklin Delano Roosevelt, *U.S. president*
Harry S Truman, *U.S. president*
Neville Chamberlain, *British prime minister*
Winston Churchill, *British prime minister*
Joseph Stalin, *Soviet dictator*
Charles de Gaulle, *leader of Free French*

Axis Powers
Adolf Hitler, *German dictator*
Benito Mussolini, *Italian dictator*
Hirohito, *Japanese emperor*
Tojo Hideki, *Japanese prime minister*

■ Reasons for Allied Victory

Location of Germany—surrounded by enemies
Location of Japan—dependent on imported goods
Poor military decisions by Axis leaders
Huge productive capability of the United States
Better technology developed and used by Allies

■ Key Events of World War II

Sept. 1939
Germany invades Poland. France and Britain declare war on Germany.

June–July 1940
France falls to Germany. Germany begins Battle of Britain.

June 1941
Germany invades the Soviet Union.

Europe and Africa
The Pacific

1939 **1940** **1941**

Sept. 1940
Japan signs Tripartite Pact with Germany and Italy.

Dec. 1941
Japan attacks Pearl Harbor.

Concept Connector

Essential Question Review

To connect prior knowledge with what you have learned in this chapter, answer the questions below in your Concept Connector journal. Use the journal in the Reading and Note Taking Study Guide to record your answers (or go to www.phschool.com **Web Code:** nad-2907). In addition, record information about the following concepts:

- Cooperation: United Nations
- Conflict: World War II
- Technology: Nuclear Power

1. **Democracy** During World War II, the United States government interned Japanese Americans in camps, citing security concerns. This was a curtailment of American citizens' individual rights. Do you think such actions are ever justified by a democratic government? Why or why not?

2. **Genocide** In *Mein Kampf,* Hitler said that Germans were a "master race" whose greatest enemies were the Jews. In 1935, the Nazis passed the Nuremberg Laws, which deprived Jews of German citizenship. The Nazis massacred six million Jews in the Holocaust. Read the Witness History at the beginning of Chapter 28. Then suggest reasons why ordinary Germans and other Europeans accepted, or even collaborated in, Hitler's "Final Solution." Focus on the following:
   - conditions in Depression-era Europe
   - anti-Semitism
   - propaganda
   - Nazi occupation

▪ Connections to Today

1. **Conflict: The Arab-Israeli Conflict** Partly in response to the horrors of the Holocaust, the United Nations created a plan to divide Palestine into two states—one Arab and one Jewish. Jews accepted the plan, but Arabs rejected it. When the Jewish state of Israel was born in 1948, the surrounding Arab countries invaded Israel. Between 1956 and 1973, three more wars erupted between Israel and Arab states. Conflict between Arabs and Israelis continued into the 2000s despite many attempts at peace. What historical reasons did the United Nations have for creating a Jewish state in Palestine?

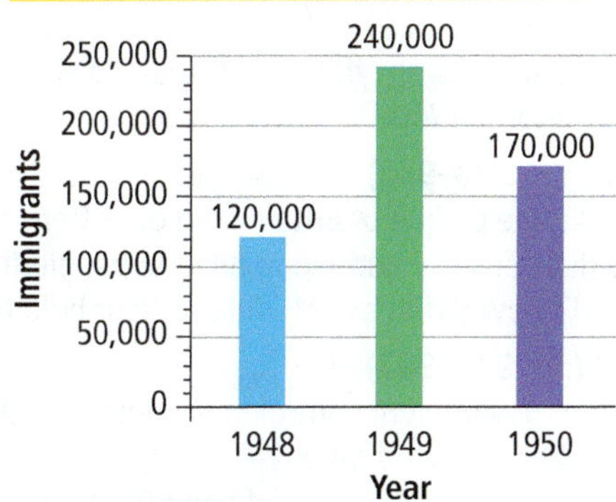

SOURCE: United States Holocaust Memorial Museum Online

2. **Cooperation: The United Nations Is Established** Fifty nations met in April 1945 to draft a charter for the United Nations. Today, the UN's work goes far beyond peacekeeping to include economic development, disease prevention, and refugee protection. Conduct research and write two paragraphs about a program sponsored by the UN in the last five years.

History Interactive
For: Interactive timeline
Web Code: nap-2962

Nov. 1942
The Allies push Rommel back in North Africa.

Jan. 1943
Germans surrender at Stalingrad.

June 1944
D-Day invasion of Normandy

May 1945
Germany surrenders.

1942   **1943**   **1944**   **1945**

June 1942
Japan defeated at Battle of Midway.

Feb. 1943
Japan defeated at Guadalcanal.

Oct. 1944
Japan defeated at Battle of Leyte Gulf.

Aug–Sept. 1945
U.S. drops atomic bombs on Hiroshima and Nagasaki, Japan. Japan surrenders.

Chapter Assessment

Terms, People, and Places

1. Define **appeasement** and **Anschluss.** How was Hitler's Anschluss an example of British and French appeasement?
2. Define **blitzkrieg.** What were the advantages of this war tactic?
3. Where did the **D-Day** invasion take place? What was its significance?
4. What happened at the **Yalta Conference**? How did it foreshadow later events?
5. What technological advantage did the **Manhattan Project** give the Allies? How was it used?
6. Describe how the **Marshall Plan** was part of the **Truman Doctrine.**

Main Ideas

Section 1 (pp. 924–929)
7. Summarize the steps that Axis powers took to achieve world power prior to World War II.

Section 2 (pp. 930–938)
8. How did the people of Britain fend off a German invasion?
9. How did Germany and Japan rule the people they conquered? How did this contribute to their hold on power?

Section 3 (pp. 939–947)
10. How did government control of economic production help defeat Germany and Japan?
11. Summarize how the Allies defeated Germany.

Section 4 (pp. 948–951)
12. What strategy did the Allies use to defeat Japan?

Section 5 (pp. 952–957)
13. What conflicts emerged between the former Allies after the end of World War II?

Chapter Focus Question
14. How did aggressive world powers emerge, and what did it take to defeat them during World War II?

Critical Thinking

15. **Recognize Cause and Effect** How did the World War I peace settlement help cause World War II?
16. **Analyze Information** What lessons does the Holocaust have for people today?

17. **Analyzing Cartoons** How does this cartoon reflect the cause of Hitler's defeat?
18. **Predict Consequences** The Atlantic Charter called for the establishment of a "permanent system of general security." What form did this "system" take when it was established following the war?
19. **Synthesize Information** Was participation by the United States crucial to winning the war? Explain.
20. **Draw Conclusions** Which battle was most important in the war in Europe? In the war in the Pacific? Explain.

● Writing About History

In this chapter's five Section Assessments, you developed skills to write a research report.

Writing a Research Report The history of World War II includes many stories of great courage and personal sacrifice. Write a research report on one of the following topics in which you describe the actions of the person or group: the Kindertransport, Oskar Schindler, Miep Gies, Raoul Wallenberg, Dietrich Bonhoeffer. Consult pages SH13–SH15 of the Writing Handbook for additional help.

Prewriting
- Do some preliminary research on each of the topics listed above.
- Choose the topic that interests you most and take notes about the people involved and the personal risks they took.
- Create a set of questions about the topic and gather additional resources.

Drafting
- Develop a working thesis and choose information to support the thesis.
- Make an outline organizing the report.
- Write an introduction in which you explain why the topic is interesting, a body, and a conclusion.

Revising
- Use the guidelines for revising your report on page SH15 of the Writing Handbook.

Document-Based Assessment

The Decision to Use the Atomic Bomb

Perhaps no decision in American history has been more hotly debated than Harry S. Truman's decision to drop atomic bombs on Hiroshima and Nagasaki, Japan, in August 1945. Documents A and B are two historians' views on Truman's decision.

Document A

"It was believed with deep apprehension that many thousands, probably tens of thousands, of lives of Allied combatants would have been spent in the continuation of our air and sea bombardment and blockade. . . . But the people who would have suffered most, had the war gone on much longer and their country invaded, were the Japanese. One American incendiary air raid on the Tokyo area in March 1945 did more damage and killed and injured more Japanese than the bomb on Hiroshima."

—From ***The Atomic Bomb and the End of World War II*** by Herbert Feis

Document B

"Even without the use of the atomic bombs, the war would probably have ended before an American invasion of Kyushu [one of the four main islands of Japan] became necessary. Conditions in Japan were steadily deteriorating . . . The destruction of cities from B-29 raids, diminishing food supplies, [and] decreased public morale fostered enough discontent to worry the emperor and his advisors. . . . Even without the atomic attacks, it seems likely that the emperor at some point would have acted in the same way that he did in the aftermath of Hiroshima to end the war."

—From ***Prompt and Utter Destruction: Truman and the Use of Atomic Bombs Against Japan*** by J. Samuel Walker

Document C

In the spring of 1945, the Allies' island-hopping campaign in the Pacific brought them closer to the heart of Japan. When American troops invaded first the island of Iwo Jima, then the island of Okinawa, the Japanese fought fiercely, but unsuccessfully, to keep them from gaining control. They knew that the Allies planned to use the islands as a base for an invasion of Japan itself.

Troops Killed at Iwo Jima and Okinawa, 1945		
Battle	Japanese troops killed	American troops killed
Iwo Jima	21,000	6,800
Okinawa	100,000	12,000

SOURCE: Encyclopaedia Brittannica

Document D

Analyzing Documents

Use your knowledge of World War II and Documents A, B, C, and D to answer questions 1–4.

1. Which of the following cities experienced the most damage from the American bombing raids?
   A Tokyo
   B Yokohama
   C Hiroshima
   D Osaka

2. Which of the following statements BEST summarizes Herbert Feis's explanation for Truman's use of the atomic bomb?
   A Use of the atomic bombs would cause more destruction.
   B Use of the atomic bombs would save lives.
   C Use of the atomic bombs would ensure surrender.
   D Use of the atomic bombs would make it more difficult for Japan to rebuild its military.

3. J. Samuel Walker's main argument against the use of atomic bombs is that
   A atomic bombs were more destructive than conventional bombs.
   B an American invasion would not have been as destructive as the bombs.
   C the war would have ended anyway.
   D the Japanese emperor opposed the use of atomic bombs.

4. **Writing Task** Which of the historians quoted in Documents A and B do you agree with most strongly? Why? Use your knowledge of World War II and specific evidence from the documents to support your opinion.

Arctic Ocean
Greenland (Denmark)
ICELAND
Alaska (U.S.)
CANADA
NORTH AMERICA
UNITED STATES
New York
Los Angeles
Hawaii (U.S.)
Pacific Ocean
MEXICO
Mexico City
BAHAMAS
HONDURAS
CUBA
HAITI
DOMINICAN REPUBLIC
BELIZE
JAMAICA
Puerto Rico (U.S.)
GUATEMALA
EL SALVADOR
NICARAGUA
COSTA RICA
PANAMA
GUYANA
VENEZUELA
SURINAME
French Guiana (France)
COLOMBIA
Atlantic Ocean
ECUADOR
French Polynesia (France)
Lima
PERU
SOUTH AMERICA
BRAZIL
São Paulo
BOLIVIA
PARAGUAY
CHILE
ARGENTINA
URUGUAY
Buenos Aires
Falkland Islands (U.K.)
NETHERLANDS 1
BELGIUM 2
GERMANY 3
SWITZERLAND 4
ITALY 5
SLOVENIA 6
AUSTRIA 7
CZECH REPUBLIC 8
SLOVAKIA 9
HUNGARY 10
CROATIA 11
BOSNIA & HERZEGOVINA 12
SERBIA 13
MONTENEGRO 14
ALBANIA 15
MACEDONIA 16
BULGARIA 17
ROMANIA 18
MOLDOVA 19
ARMENIA 20
AZERBAIJAN 21
NORWAY
SWEDEN
FINLAND
ESTONIA
LATVIA
LITHUANIA
Moscow
DENMARK
UNITED KINGDOM
IRELAND
London
Berlin
POLAND
BELARUS
EUROPE
UKRAINE
Paris
FRANCE
GEORGIA
PORTUGAL
Madrid
SPAIN
Rome
Istanbul
TURKEY
GREECE
CYPRUS
SYRIA
IRAQ
LEBANON
ISRAEL
KUWAIT
JORDAN
SAUDI ARABIA
MOROCCO
TUNISIA
Cairo
EGYPT
ALGERIA
LIBYA
MAURITANIA
MALI
NIGER
CHAD
SUDAN
ERITREA
YEMEN
SENEGAL
GAMBIA
BURKINA FASO
DJIBOUTI
GUINEA-BISSAU
GUINEA
NIGERIA
AFRICA
CENTRAL AFRICAN REP.
ETHIOPIA
SIERRA LEONE
Lagos
SOMALIA
LIBERIA
CAMEROON
CÔTE D'IVOIRE
GHANA
TOGO
BENIN
CONGO
UGANDA
KENYA
EQUATORIAL GUINEA
GABON
DEM. REP. OF CONGO
RWANDA
BURUNDI
TANZANIA
MALAWI
ANGOLA
ZAMBIA
MOZAMBIQUE
NAMIBIA
ZIMBABWE
BOTSWANA
Johannesburg
SWAZILAND
MADAGASCAR
SOUTH AFRICA
LESOTHO
Dakar
N
W E
S
THE WORLD TODAY

7

The World Since 1945

1945–Present

The Cold War

1945–1991

WITNESS HISTORY

Berlin Is Walled In

On August 13, 1961, the first morning after the Berlin Wall was built, thousands of East Berliners arrived at the main border crossing hoping to travel to West Berlin. Transportation Police, or Trapos, blocked the way. Robert Lochner recalls, "A timid old woman . . . asked one of the Trapos when the next train would go to West Berlin. Sneeringly he answered: 'None of that anymore, grandma. You are all now caught in a mousetrap.'" Listen to the Witness History audio to hear more about the Berlin Wall.

◀ East German guards watch the newly built Berlin Wall.

U.S. President Ronald Reagan

Pin promoting the Soviet reforms that helped to end the Cold War

Chapter Preview

Chapter Focus Question How did the Cold War develop, how did it shape political and economic life in individual nations, and how did it end?

Section 1
The Cold War Unfolds

Section 2
The Industrialized Democracies

Section 3
Communism Spreads in East Asia

Section 4
War in Southeast Asia

Section 5
The End of the Cold War

Use the ☑ **Quick Study Timeline** at the end of this chapter to preview chapter events.

U.S. military helicopter over Vietnam

Concept Connector ONLINE

To explore Essential Questions related to this chapter, go to PHSchool.com
Web Code: nad-3007

Nuclear fallout shelter sign

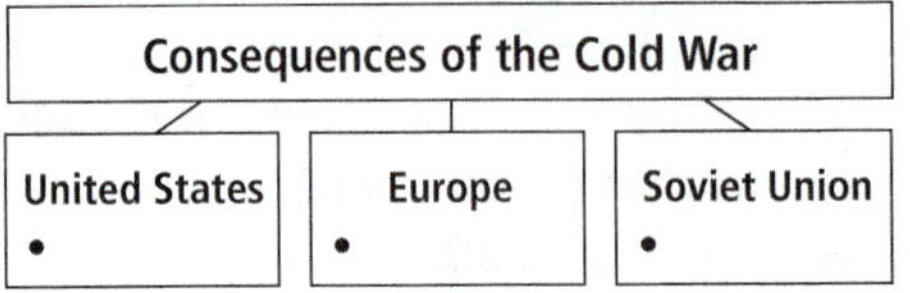
Winston Churchill

An Iron Curtain

In 1946, Winston Churchill, former prime minister of Britain, spoke of an "iron curtain" sealing off the countries in Eastern Europe that the Soviet Union had occupied at the end of World War II:

> **❝**[A]n iron curtain has descended [fallen] across the Continent. Behind that line lie all the capitals of the ancient states of Central and Eastern Europe. . . . [A]ll these famous cities . . . lie in what I must call the Soviet sphere, and are all subject . . . to a very high . . . measure of control from Moscow.**❞**

Focus Question What were the military and political consequences of the Cold War in the Soviet Union, Europe, and the United States?

The Cold War Unfolds

Objectives
- Understand how two sides faced off in Europe during the Cold War.
- Learn how nuclear weapons threatened the world.
- Understand how the Cold War spread globally.
- Compare and contrast the Soviet Union and the United States in the Cold War.

Terms, People, and Places

superpowers
anti-ballistic missiles (ABMs)
Ronald Reagan
détente
Fidel Castro

John F. Kennedy
ideology
Nikita Khrushchev
Leonid Brezhnev
containment

Note Taking

Reading Skill: Summarize Sum up the consequences of the Cold War in the United States, Europe, and the Soviet Union in a chart like the one below.

Consequences of the Cold War		
United States	Europe	Soviet Union
•	•	•

After World War II devastated Europe and Japan, two great powers remained: the United States and the Soviet Union. These two nations were known as **superpowers,** or nations stronger than other powerful nations. The Cold War between these superpowers cast a shadow over the world for more than 40 years.

Two Sides Face Off in Europe

Cold War confrontation began in Europe, where the two superpowers' armies confronted each other after World War II. Each superpower formed a European military alliance made up of the nations that it occupied or protected. The United States led the North Atlantic Treaty Organization, or NATO, in Western Europe. The Soviet Union led the Warsaw Pact in Eastern Europe. The two alliances in Europe faced each other along the Iron Curtain, the tense line between the democratic West and the communist East.

A Wall Divides Berlin Berlin was a key focus of Cold War tensions. The city was split into democratic West Berlin and communist East Berlin. In the 1950s, West Berlin became a showcase for West German prosperity. A massive exodus of low-paid East Germans, unhappy with communism, fled into West Berlin. To stop the flight, East Germany built a wall in 1961 that sealed off West Berlin. When completed, the Berlin Wall was a massive concrete barrier, topped with barbed wire and patrolled by guards. The wall showed that workers, far from enjoying a communist paradise, had to be forcibly kept from fleeing.

Eastern Europe Resists Other explosions of Cold War tension included revolts against Soviet domination in East Germany, Poland, Hungary, and Czechoslovakia. One of the earliest revolts occurred in East Berlin. In 1953, some 50,000 workers confronted the Soviet army in the streets of the German capital. The uprising spread to other East German cities, but the demonstrators could not stand up to Russian tanks.

In 1956, Eastern Europeans challenged Soviet authority in the name of economic reform in both Poland and Hungary. Poles were responding in part to Soviet-backed mass arrests of noncommunist leaders and government seizures of private lands and industry. Hungarian leader Imre Nagy (nahj) went furthest, ending one-party rule and seeking to pull his country out of the Warsaw Pact. In response, Soviet troops launched a massive assault that overwhelmed resistance. Nagy was later executed.

In early 1968, Czechoslovak leader Alexander Dubček introduced greater freedom of expression and limited democracy. This blossoming of freedom came to be known as the "Prague Spring." Soviet leaders feared that democracy would threaten communist power and Soviet domination. Warsaw Pact troops launched a massive invasion of Czechoslovakia in August of that year to put an end to these freedoms.

 **Checkpoint** How was Europe divided, and what were three consequences of its division?

Nuclear Weapons Threaten the World

One of the most terrifying aspects of the Cold War was the arms race that began right after World War II. At first, the United States was the only nuclear power. By 1949, however, the Soviet Union had also developed nuclear weapons. By 1953, both sides had developed hydrogen bombs, which are much more destructive than atomic bombs.

Critics argued that a nuclear war would destroy both sides. Yet each superpower wanted to be able to deter the other from launching its nuclear weapons. Both sides engaged in a race to match each other's new weapons. The result was a "balance of terror." Mutually assured destruction—in which each side knew that the other side would itself be

Soviet Nuclear Missiles
Every year on May 1, the Soviet Union demonstrated its military and nuclear strength in a parade through Moscow's Red Square. *Why might the Soviet Union have wanted to show off its nuclear might?*

Arms Control Agreements		
Date	Agreement	Effect
1963	Nuclear Test Ban Treaty	Banned testing of nuclear weapons in the atmosphere
1972	SALT I Interim Agreement	Froze existing number of weapons held by each side
1972	SALT I Anti-Ballistic Missile Treaty	Set strict limits on missiles that could shoot down missiles from the other side
1979	SALT II Treaty	Set absolute limit on number of weapons each side could hold
1991	START Treaty	Required both sides to reduce the number of weapons each held

Chart Skills Compare the Nuclear Test Ban Treaty, the SALT II Treaty, and the START Treaty. *How did each of the later treaties advance beyond the treaty that came before it?*

destroyed if it launched its weapons—discouraged nuclear war. Still, the world's people lived in constant fear of nuclear doom.

Limiting Nuclear Weapons To reduce the threat of nuclear war, the two sides met at disarmament talks. Although mutual distrust slowed progress, the rival powers did reach some agreements. In 1969, the United States and the Soviet Union began Strategic Arms Limitation Talks (SALT) to limit the number of nuclear weapons held by each side. In 1972 and 1979, both sides signed agreements setting these limits.

One of these agreements limited **anti-ballistic missiles (ABMs),** or missiles that could shoot down other missiles from hostile countries. ABMs were seen as a particular threat to the balance of terror because, by giving one side some protection against the other, they might encourage the protected side to attack. They were also seen as a technology that could provoke a renewed arms race. During the 1980s, U.S. President **Ronald Reagan** launched a program to build a "Star Wars" missile defense against nuclear attack. Critics objected that this program would violate the ABM treaty. Nonetheless, the two sides signed the Strategic Arms Reduction Treaty (START) in 1991.

Building Détente American and Soviet arms control agreements led to an era of **détente** (day TAHNT), or relaxation of tensions, during the 1970s. The American strategy under détente was to restrain the Soviet Union through diplomatic agreements rather than by military means. The era of détente ended in 1979, when the Soviet Union invaded Afghanistan.

Stopping the Spread of Nuclear Weapons By the late 1960s, Britain, France, and China had developed their own nuclear weapons. However, many world leaders worked to keep the arms race from spreading any further. In 1968, many nations signed the Nuclear Non-Proliferation Treaty (NPT). These nations agreed not to develop nuclear weapons or to stop the proliferation, or spread, of nuclear weapons.

 **Checkpoint** What factors discouraged the use of nuclear weapons during the Cold War?

The Cold War Goes Global

Although the Cold War began in Central Europe, it quickly spread around the world. When World War II ended, the Soviets were assisting communist forces in China and Korea. American leaders saw that the United States faced a conflict as global as the two world wars that had preceded it. They therefore developed policies to respond to challenges anywhere in the world.

Building Alliances and Bases As part of its strategy to contain Soviet power, the United States reached out to the rest of the world both diplomatically and militarily. The NATO alliance with Europe's democracies was only one of several regional alliances.

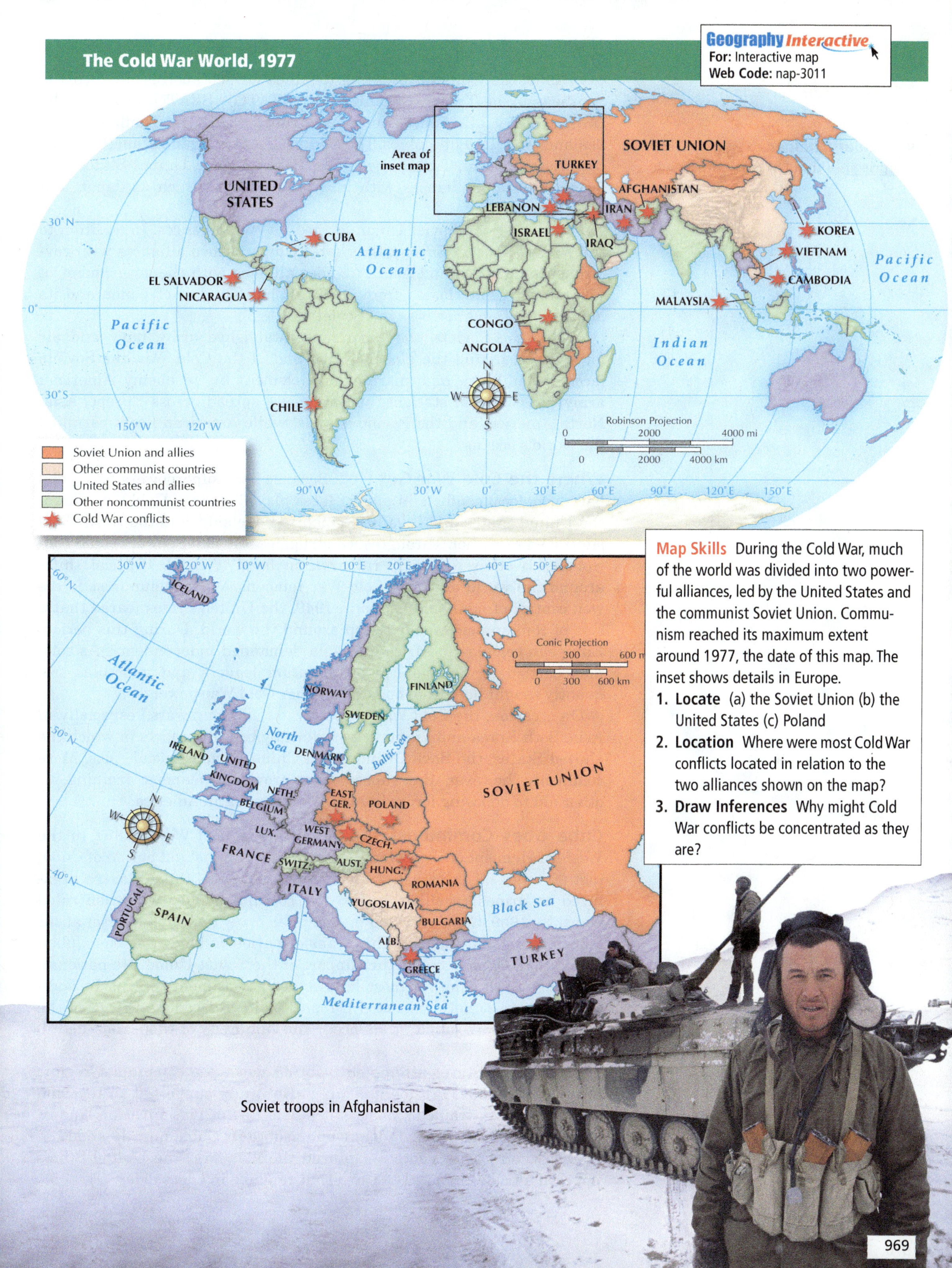

Map Skills During the Cold War, much of the world was divided into two powerful alliances, led by the United States and the communist Soviet Union. Communism reached its maximum extent around 1977, the date of this map. The inset shows details in Europe.

1. **Locate** (a) the Soviet Union (b) the United States (c) Poland
2. **Location** Where were most Cold War conflicts located in relation to the two alliances shown on the map?
3. **Draw Inferences** Why might Cold War conflicts be concentrated as they are?

Soviet troops in Afghanistan ▶

In 1955, the United States and its allies formed another alliance, the Southeast-Asia Treaty Organization (SEATO). SEATO included the United States, Britain, France, Australia, Pakistan, Thailand, New Zealand, and the Philippines. The Central Treaty Organization (CENTO) <u>comprised</u> Britain, Turkey, Iran, and Pakistan. The United States also formed military alliances with individual nations, such as Japan and South Korea.

Meanwhile, the Soviet Union formed its own alliances. In addition to the Warsaw Pact in Europe, the Soviet Union formed alliances with governments in Africa and Asia. A Soviet alliance with the government of Communist China lasted from 1949 to 1960. The Soviet Union and its allies were often known as the Soviet bloc.

Unlike the Soviets, the Americans established army, navy, and air force bases around the globe. By the end of the Cold War, the Soviets faced the military nightmare of encirclement by an enemy. American army camps, naval stations, and air bases spread across Europe, Asia, North America, and the Pacific islands, while American fleets patrolled the world's oceans.

Where the Cold War Got Hot Because both superpowers had a global reach, local conflicts in many places played into the Cold War. Often, the United States and its allies supported one side, and the Soviet bloc supported the other. Through such struggles, the superpowers could confront each other indirectly rather than head to head. Political shifts around the world added to Cold War tensions. When communist forces won control of mainland China in 1949, the United States feared that a tide of communism would sweep around the world. During this period, European colonies in Africa and Asia demanded independence. As colonies battled for independence, liberation leaders and guerrillas frequently sought help from one or the other Cold War power.

On occasion, the Cold War erupted into "shooting wars," especially in Asia. Both Korea and Vietnam were torn by brutal conflicts in which the United States, the Soviet Union, and China played crucial roles. More commonly, however, the superpowers provided weapons, training, or other aid to opposing forces in Asia, Africa, or Latin America.

Cuba Goes Communist The most serious Cold War conflict in the Western Hemisphere involved the Latin American island nation of Cuba, just 90 miles off the coast of Florida. In the 1950s, **Fidel Castro** organized an armed rebellion against the corrupt dictator who then ruled Cuba. By 1959, Castro had led his guerrilla army to victory and set about transforming the country. This transformation is known as the Cuban Revolution. Castro sought the support of the Soviet Union. He nationalized businesses and put most land under government control. In addition, Castro severely restricted Cubans' political freedom. Critics of the new regime were jailed or silenced, and hundreds of thousands fled to Florida.

The United States attempted to bring down the communist regime next door. In 1961, President **John F. Kennedy** supported an invasion attempt by U.S.-trained Cuban exiles. The Bay of Pigs Invasion, known for the bay where the invaders came ashore in Cuba, quickly ended in failure when Castro's forces captured the invaders. The United States imposed a trade embargo on Cuba that remains in effect today.

Cuban Missiles Spark a Crisis In 1962, the Soviet Union sent nuclear missiles to Cuba. President Kennedy responded by imposing a naval blockade that prevented further Soviet shipments. Kennedy demanded that the Soviet Union remove its nuclear missiles from Cuba, and for a few tense days, the world faced a risk of nuclear war over the issue. Finally, however, Soviet Premier Nikita Khrushchev agreed to remove the Soviet missiles, and war was averted.

✔ **Checkpoint** How did the U.S. and the Soviet Union confront each other around the world during the Cold War?

● **INFOGRAPHIC**

THE CUBAN MISSILE *CRISIS*

In the summer of 1962, the United States learned that the Soviet Union was shipping nuclear missiles to Cuba, less than 100 miles off the coast of Florida. President John F. Kennedy demanded that the Soviet Union remove the missiles from Cuba. In October 1962, the United States imposed a naval blockade on Cuba. For one week, a tense confrontation brought the world to the brink of nuclear war. Finally, on October 28, Khrushchev agreed to remove the Soviet missiles.

◀ U.S. President John F. Kennedy

▲ Soviet Premier Nikita Khrushchev

▲ This aerial photo shows Soviet missiles being unloaded at a Cuban port.

▶During the U.S. naval blockade, the U.S. Navy surrounded Cuba with ships. (See the map below). In this photo, the USS *Barry* inspects the cargo of a Soviet freighter returning from Cuba.

Thinking Critically

1. **Map Skills** Considering Cuba's location on the map, why did Soviet nuclear missiles on the island pose a threat to the United States?
2. **Draw Conclusions** Why might Khrushchev have agreed to withdraw the missiles from Cuba?

Communist Countries	Democratic Capitalist Countries
The Communist Party makes all political decisions.	The people and their elected representatives make decisions.
Command economy (The government makes most economic decisions and owns most property.)	Market economy (Private consumers and producers make most economic decisions and own most property.)
The political leadership values obedience, discipline, and economic security.	The political leadership values freedom and prosperity.

Chart Skills The communist system often offered few choices for consumers, such as for the Russian woman above. By contrast, capitalist societies provided a wealth of choices for consumers, such as for the American girl at the right. *What facts in the chart above help to explain the different experiences of consumers under these contrasting systems?*

The Soviet Union in the Cold War

Victory in World War II brought few rewards to the Soviet people. Stalin continued his ruthless policies. He filled labor camps with "enemies of the state" and seemed ready to launch new purges when he died in 1953.

Soviet Communism In the Soviet Union, the government controlled most aspects of public life. Communists valued obedience, discipline, and economic security. They sought to spread their communist **ideology,** or value system and beliefs, around the globe. The Soviet Union also aimed to spread its communist command economy to other countries. In command economies, government bureaus make most economic decisions. They often make decisions for political reasons that do not make much economic sense. The government owns most property.

Stalin's Successors Hold the Line After Stalin's death in 1953, **Nikita Khrushchev** (KROOSH chawf) emerged as the new Soviet leader. In 1956, he shocked top Communist Party members when he publicly denounced Stalin's abuse of power. Khrushchev maintained the Communist Party's political control, but he closed prison camps and eased censorship. He called for a "peaceful coexistence" with the West.

Khrushchev's successor, **Leonid Brezhnev** (BREZH nef) held power from the mid-1960s until he died in 1982. Under Brezhnev, critics faced arrest and imprisonment.

Some Soviets Bravely Resist Despite the risk of punishment, some courageous people dared to criticize the government. Andrey Sakharov (SAH kuh rawf), a distinguished Soviet scientist, spoke out for civil liberties. Brezhnev's government silenced him. As a Soviet soldier during World War II, Aleksandr Solzhenitsyn (sohl zhuh NEET sin) wrote a letter to a friend criticizing Stalin. He was sent to a prison camp. Under Khrushchev, he was released and wrote fiction that drew on his experience as a prisoner. His writing was banned in the Soviet Union, and in 1974 he was exiled. Despite the government's actions, Sakharov and Solzhenitsyn inspired others to resist communist policies.

✔ **Checkpoint** How did the Soviet government handle critics of its policies?

The United States in the Cold War

The Cold War was not just a military rivalry. It was also a competition between two contrasting economic and political value systems. Unlike the communist countries, the democratic, capitalist countries, led by the United States, gave citizens the freedom to make economic and political choices. These nations valued freedom and prosperity.

Free Markets While communist countries had command economies, capitalist countries had market economies. In market economies, producers and consumers make economic decisions. Prices are based on supply and demand in a free market. Property is privately owned. Producers compete to offer the best products for the lowest prices. By deciding what to buy, consumers ultimately decide which products are produced. Producers who win consumers' business make profits and grow.

The United States economy is basically a market economy. However, the United States and Western Europe have what can be called mixed economies, because their governments have an economic role.

Containing the Soviet Union America's basic policy toward communist countries was known as **containment.** This was a strategy of containing communism, or keeping it within its existing boundaries and preventing further expansion. This strategy meant supporting any government facing invasion or internal rebellion by communists.

Living With Nuclear Dangers The nuclear threat led many people in the United States and other countries to build fallout shelters. Fallout shelters

Preparing for a Nuclear Attack
"Duck and cover" air-raid drills were common during the Cold War, even though it is doubtful that ducking and covering would offer much protection in an actual nuclear attack. *What does this photo suggest about Americans' fears during the Cold War?*

Red Scare Culture
Pop culture during the "red scare" of the 1940s and 1950s reflected the fears of the times. "I Was a Communist for the FBI" thrilled movie-goers in 1951.

were structures, often underground, designed to protect people from fallout, or radioactive particles from a nuclear explosion. In 1961, the U.S. government launched a community fallout shelter program to create fallout shelters in public and commercial buildings, stocked with a two-week supply of food for the surrounding population. The fear of nuclear attack reached a peak in the United States during the Cuban missile crisis of 1962. Thousands of Americans built private fallout shelters underneath their backyards.

From the 1950s into the 1970s, American schools conducted air-raid drills in anticipation of a nuclear attack. These drills were nearly as common as fire drills. Children were trained to duck underneath desks and crouch with their hands over their heads. Although this would not have protected them from an actual nuclear explosion, the drills reflected the widespread fear of nuclear war.

Seeking Enemies Within Cold War fears led to a "red scare" within the United States. During the late 1940s and early 1950s, many Americans feared that communists inside the United States might try to undermine the U.S. government. Around 1950, Senator Joseph McCarthy led a hunt for suspected American communists. McCarthy became notorious for unproven charges. Accusing innocent people of communism, and the fear that this created, became known as McCarthyism. McCarthy's influence, however, faded after he attacked the patriotism of the United States Army.

During the same period, the House Un-American Activities Committee (HUAC) led a similar campaign to identify supposed communist sympathizers. HUAC was made up of members of the U.S. House of Representatives. In 1947, the Committee sought to expose communist sympathizers in Hollywood's movie industry. People who had flirted with communist ideas in their youth and later rejected them were labeled as communists. Many who were labeled in this way were no longer able to get decent jobs.

 **Checkpoint** How did America respond to the threat of communism at home and overseas?

Assessment

Terms, People, and Places

1. For each term, person, or place listed at the beginning of the section, write a sentence explaining its significance.

Note Taking

2. **Reading Skill: Summarize** Use your completed chart to answer the Focus Question: What were the military and political consequences of the Cold War in the Soviet Union, Europe, and the United States?

Comprehension and Critical Thinking

3. **Make Generalizations** What kinds of conflicts resulted from the global confrontation between the two superpowers?

4. **Draw Inferences** How did the buildup of nuclear weapons discourage their use?

5. **Make Comparisons** Identify similarities and differences between the Soviet Union and the United States during the Cold War.

Writing About History

Quick Write: Understand the Purpose
To write a problem-solution essay, you first need to understand the purpose of this type of essay. In this section, you learned that the superpowers' possession of nuclear weapons posed a risk of nuclear war. Write sentences answering each of the following questions: What makes this issue a problem? What benefit comes from solving this problem?

THE ESSENTIAL **?**

COOPERATION

With whom should we cooperate and why?

In This Chapter

Cooperation between the United States and the Soviet Union broke down as soon as Germany was defeated. Each superpower developed its own network of allies, NATO and the Warsaw Pact, and built large nuclear arsenals. Faced with the possibility of devastating war, American and Soviet leaders (right) negotiated treaties that gradually reduced the number of nuclear weapons.

Throughout History

400s B.C. Greek city-states unite to defeat the Persians.

1200s A.D. Hanseatic League promotes trade in northern Europe.

Late 1500s Five Iroquois groups form the Iroquois League to keep peace among themselves.

Late 1800s European and American workers form unions to improve pay and working conditions.

2000s The Kyoto Protocol to reduce greenhouse gas emissions is signed by 140 countries.

Continuing Today

Despite political differences, many nations come together every four years to take part in the Olympic Games. Athletes compete in individual and team events.

21st Century Skills

TRANSFER Activities

1. Analyze What goals have motivated people to cooperate throughout history?

2. Evaluate Why is it sometimes necessary to cooperate with an enemy?

3. Transfer Complete a Web quest in which you, as an advisor to the President, consider whether or not to cooperate with a new regime; record your thoughts in the Concept Connector Journal; and learn to make a video. Web Code nah-3008

Marshall Plan poster

Marshall Plan food aid being distributed in France

The Marshall Plan

In a speech at Harvard University in June 1947, U.S. Secretary of State George Marshall made the case for the Marshall Plan, a United States assistance program for Western Europe.

❝ Our policy is directed not against any country or doctrine but against hunger, poverty, desperation, and chaos. Its purpose should be the revival of a working economy in the world so as to permit the emergence of . . . conditions in which free institutions can exist. ❞

Focus Question How did the United States, Western Europe, and Japan achieve economic prosperity and strengthen democracy during the Cold War years?

The Industrialized Democracies

Objectives

- Understand how the United States prospered and expanded opportunities.
- Explain how Western Europe rebuilt its economy after World War II.
- Describe how Japan was transformed.

Terms, People, and Places

recession
suburbanization
segregation
discrimination
Dr. Martin Luther King, Jr.

Konrad Adenauer
welfare state
European Community
gross domestic product (GDP)

Note Taking

Reading Skill: Categorize Keep track of changes in the industrialized democracies with a chart like the one below.

Economic and Political Changes in the Industrialized Democracies		
United States	Western Europe	Japan
•	•	•
•	•	•
•	•	•

The industrialized democracies of North America, Western Europe, and Japan grew in prosperity and went through social change during the Cold War. Throughout this period, the United States was the world's wealthiest and most powerful country. By the end of the Cold War, however, Western Europe and Japan rivaled the United States economically.

America Prospers and Changes

In the postwar decades, American businesses expanded into markets around the globe. The dollar was the world's strongest currency. Foreigners flocked to invest in American industry and to buy U.S. government bonds. America's wealth was a model for other democracies and a challenge to the stagnant economies of the communist world.

America Plays a Central Role During the Cold War, the United States was a global political leader. The headquarters of the League of Nations had been symbolically located in neutral Switzerland. The headquarters of the newly formed United Nations was built in New York City.

The United States also played a leading economic role. America had emerged untouched from the horrendous destruction of the Second World War. Other nations needed American goods and services, and foreign trade helped the United States achieve a long postwar boom. The long postwar peace among democratic nations helped to spread this boom worldwide. The World Bank, an international agency that finances world economic development, was headquartered in Washington, D.C. The International Monetary Fund (IMF), which oversees the finances of the world's nations, was based there as well.

The Postwar American Boom America's economic strength transformed life in the United States itself. During the 1950s and 1960s, boom times prevailed. **Recessions,** or periods when the economy shrinks, were brief and mild. Although segments of the population were left behind, many Americans prospered in the world's wealthiest economy. As Americans grew more affluent, many moved from the cities to the suburbs. The movement to communities outside an urban core is known as **suburbanization.** Suburbanites typically lived in single-family houses with lawns and access to good schools. Suburban highways allowed residents to commute to work by car.

During the postwar decades, many Americans also moved to the Sunbelt, or the states in the South and Southwest of the United States. Jobs in these states were becoming more plentiful than in the industrialized North, and the warmer climate was an added bonus. The growing availability of air conditioning and water for irrigation in states such as Arizona helped make the movement to the Sunbelt possible.

The wide popularity of American culture abroad vividly illustrated the global influence of the United States. The world embraced twentieth-century art forms such as American movies, television, and rock-and-roll music. American originals such as Elvis Presley, musical comedies, Hollywood romances, and action movies had a worldwide following.

The federal government contributed to the economic boom. Under President Truman, Congress created programs that helped veterans, the elderly, and the poor. Truman's successor, Dwight Eisenhower, approved government funding to build a vast interstate highway system. Government programs also made it easier for people to buy homes.

Moving to the Suburbs
This image shows a family watching the progress as their new, suburban home is built. The photo below shows a suburb in New York in 1954. *Why might suburbs such as this attract families from cities?*

The Oil Shock of the 1970s
In 1973 and 1974, a reduction in the supply of oil led to shortages and higher prices for gasoline. In the photos above, motorists wait on line to fill up with scarce gasoline.

An Oil Shock Brings Recession However, America's growing dependence on the world economy brought problems. In the early 1970s, a political crisis in the Middle East led to decreased oil exports. Oil prices soared worldwide. Waiting in long lines for scarce and expensive gasoline, Americans became aware of their dependence on imported oil and on global economic forces.

In America and in the other industrialized democracies, which were even more dependent on imported oil, higher prices for oil left businesses and consumers with less to spend on other products. The decades of postwar prosperity ended with a serious recession in 1974. During the 1970s and 1980s, the world's economies suffered a series of recessions alternating with years of renewed prosperity.

 **Checkpoint** How was the U.S. economy linked to the broader global economy during the Cold War?

Vocabulary Builder
prospered—(PRAHS purd) *vi.* succeeded, thrived, did well

Democracy Expands Opportunities

Although America prospered after World War II, the American promise of equality and opportunity had not yet been fulfilled for ethnic minorities and women. In the postwar decades, these groups demanded equality. In American politics, liberals and conservatives offered contrasting programs to increase opportunities for the American people.

Segregation and Discrimination The prosperity of the postwar years failed to benefit all Americans equally. Although slavery had been abolished a century before, many states denied equality to African Americans and other minority groups. These groups faced legal **segregation,** or forced separation, in education and housing. Minorities also suffered **discrimination**—unequal treatment or barriers—in jobs and voting. After World War II, President Harry Truman desegregated the armed forces. Then, in 1954, the U.S. Supreme Court made a landmark ruling, *Brown* v. *Board of Education of Topeka,* declaring that segregated schools were unconstitutional.

Americans Demand Civil Rights By 1956, a gifted preacher, **Dr. Martin Luther King, Jr.,** had emerged as a leader of the civil rights movement. This movement aimed to extend equal rights to all Americans, and particularly African Americans. King organized boycotts and led peaceful marches to end segregation in the United States. In 1963, King made a stirring speech. "I have a dream," he proclaimed, "that one day this nation will rise up and live out the true meaning of its creed: 'We hold these truths to be self-evident, that all men are created equal.'"

Americans of all races joined the civil rights movement. Their courage in the face of sometimes brutal attacks stirred the nation's conscience. Asians, Latinos, Native Americans, and other groups joined African Americans in demanding equality. The U.S. Congress outlawed public segregation, protected voting rights, and required equal access to housing and jobs. Poverty, unemployment, and discrimination still plagued many African Americans. However, some were elected to political office or gained top jobs in business and the military.

Women Demand Equality Women too faced discrimination in employment and other areas. Inspired by the civil rights movement, women fought gender-based discrimination during the 1960s and 1970s. The women's rights movement won laws banning discrimination against women. More women also gained higher salaries and positions in politics and business.

The Government's Role Grows During the 1960s, the government further expanded social programs to help the poor and disadvantaged. Under Presidents John F. Kennedy and Lyndon Johnson, both Democrats,

BIOGRAPHY

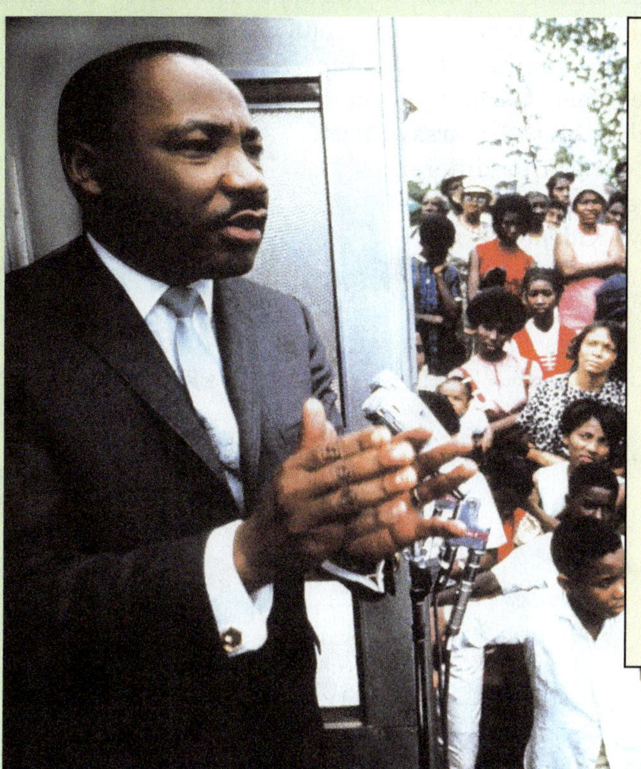

MARTIN LUTHER KING, Jr.

Dr. Martin Luther King, Jr. (1929–1968) was born in Atlanta, Georgia, and grew up in the segregated American South. He earned a doctorate in divinity in 1955 and became a minister at a church in Montgomery, Alabama. Beginning that year, King helped lead the Montgomery Bus Boycott to protest segregation on the city's buses. In the years that followed, King emerged as the most respected leader of the American civil rights movement. He was repeatedly attacked and jailed for his beliefs. He helped organize the massive March on Washington, D.C., for civil rights in 1963. He gave his famous "I Have a Dream" speech at this event. King lived to see the passage of the Civil Rights Act of 1965 that outlawed segregation. However, he was killed in 1968 by an assassin. **How did King's actions show courage?**

Congress funded Medicare, providing health care for the elderly. Other programs offered housing for the poor.

Republicans Respond In the 1980s, President Reagan and the Republican Party called for cutbacks in taxes and government spending. They argued that cutting taxes was the best way to improve opportunities for Americans. Congress ended some social programs, reduced government regulation of the economy, and cut taxes. At the same time, however, military spending increased.

The combination of increased spending and tax cuts greatly increased the national budget deficit, or the shortfall between what the government spends and what it receives in taxes and other income. To deal with the deficit, Republicans pushed for deeper cuts in social and economic programs, including education, welfare, and environmental protection.

✔ **Checkpoint** Over time, how did the U.S. government expand opportunities for Americans?

Western Europe Rebuilds

Americans arriving in Europe as liberators or occupiers in 1945 were astonished at the damage that the war had inflicted. Germany in particular lay in ruins. Many Europeans had suffered grievously. However, Western Europe recovered economically more rapidly than anyone had expected—and then moved on to even higher standards of living.

Germany Divided and Reunited At the end of World War II, the United States, Britain, and France—all democracies—occupied the western portion of Germany. The Soviet Union occupied eastern Germany. The goal had been to hold elections throughout Germany for a single German government, but disputes between the Soviet Union and the Western powers led to Germany's division into two separate countries by 1949. West Germany became a member of NATO, while East Germany became a member of the Warsaw Pact. For 40 years, differences between the two Germanys widened.

66 There are no homes, no shops, no transportation, no government buildings. Only a few walls. . . . Berlin can now be regarded only as a geographical location heaped with mountainous mounds of debris. 99
—*New York Herald Tribune*, May 3, 1945

Wartime Destruction in Germany
Many German cities suffered serious wartime damage. In this photo, civilians walk through the rubble left by wartime bombing in Nuremberg, Germany, in 1945. *What challenges would residents of a city face after such heavy destruction?*

While West Germany had a democratic government, East Germany was a communist state. While West Germany enjoyed an economic boom, East Germany's command economy stagnated. Before the Berlin Wall was built, millions of East Germans fled to the freedom and prosperity of West Germany. After the wall was built, some East Germans still managed to escape, but others were shot as they tried to cross the border.

In 1989, as Soviet communism declined, Germany moved toward reunification. Without Soviet backing, East German communist leaders were unable to maintain control. They were forced to reopen their western borders. Quickly, East Germans demanded reunification with the West. In 1990, German voters approved reunification.

West Germany's "Economic Miracle" Early in the Cold War, the United States rushed aid to its former enemy through the Marshall Plan and other programs. It wanted to strengthen West Germany against communist Eastern Europe. From 1949 to 1963, Konrad Adenauer (AHD uh now ur) was West Germany's chancellor, or prime minister. He guided the rebuilding of cities, factories, and trade. Because many of its old factories had been destroyed, Germany built a modern and highly productive industrial base. Despite high taxes to pay for the recovery, West Germans created a booming industrial economy.

Britain's Narrowed Horizons Britain's economy was slow to recover after the war. Despite U.S. assistance through the Marshall Plan, Britain could no longer afford a large military presence overseas. Therefore, Britain abandoned its colonial empire in the face of demands for independence. After several years of economic hardship, however, Britain's economy recovered during the 1950s and 1960s. Although Britain did not enjoy a boom like Germany's, its living standard did improve.

Other European Nations Prosper Most European nations emerged from World War II greatly weakened. Like Britain, European colonial powers such as Belgium and the Netherlands gave in to demands for independence from former colonies. France was forced to abandon its

The Iron Curtain Divides Germany
While the Berlin Wall divided the city of Berlin, a much longer series of concrete walls, barbed wire, and watchtowers ran along the border between East and West Germany, forming part of the Iron Curtain. *Why might East Germany have built a fortified border such as this?*

empire after bloody colonial wars in Vietnam and Algeria drained and demoralized the country.

Most Western European countries had suffered serious wartime damage. Like West Germany, they received U.S. assistance through the Marshall Plan. As in West Germany, this helped them to build more modern and productive facilities. During the 1950s and 1960s, most of Europe enjoyed an economic boom. Living standards improved greatly for most Dutch, Belgians, French, and Italians. Poorer European countries, such as Spain and Ireland, were able to attract outside investment that led to economic growth.

Building the Welfare State In the postwar decades, Europeans worked to secure their economic prosperity. From the 1950s through the 1970s, European nations expanded social benefits to their citizens. During this time, many European nations also moved toward greater economic cooperation.

Many European political parties, and particularly those representing workers, wanted to extend the **welfare state.** A welfare state is a country with a market economy but with increased government responsibility for the social and economic needs of its people. The welfare state had its roots in the late 1800s. During that period, Germany, Britain, and other nations had set up basic old-age pensions and unemployment insurance.

After 1945, European governments expanded these social programs. Both the middle class and the poor enjoyed increased benefits from national healthcare, unemployment insurance, and old-age pensions. Other programs gave aid to the poor and created an economic cushion to help people get through difficult times.

However, the welfare state brought high taxes and greater government regulation of private enterprise. In Britain, France, and elsewhere, governments took over basic industries such as railroads, airlines, and steel. Conservatives, or people who favor free markets and a limited role for government, condemned this drift from the free enterprise system toward socialism.

Limiting the Welfare State In 1979, British voters turned to the Conservative Party, which denounced the welfare state as costly and inefficient. The Conservatives were led by Margaret Thatcher. Thatcher's government reduced social welfare programs and returned government-owned industries to private control. Faced with soaring costs, other European nations also moved to limit social welfare benefits and to privatize state-owned businesses during the 1980s and 1990s.

Toward European Unity Greater economic cooperation helped fuel Europe's economic boom during the 1950s and 1960s. In 1952, six nations—West Germany, the Netherlands, Belgium, Luxembourg, France, and Italy—set up the European Coal and Steel Community. This agency established free trade in coal and steel among member states by eliminating tariffs, or fees, and other barriers that limited trade. This small start spurred economic growth across Western Europe and led to further regional cooperation.

In 1957, the same six European nations signed a treaty to form the European Economic Community, later known simply as the **European Community.** This was an organization dedicated to establishing free trade among member nations for all products. The European Community

Building Britain's Welfare State
Britain's Labour Party won support after World War II by expanding social programs and the government's role in the economy.

gradually ended tariffs and allowed workers and capital to move freely across national borders. In later years, the European Community expanded to include Britain and other European countries.

✔ **Checkpoint** What were some advantages and disadvantages of the welfare state in Europe?

Japan Is Transformed

In 1945, Japan, like Germany, lay in ruins. It had suffered perhaps the most devastating damage of any nation involved in World War II. Tens of thousands of Japanese were homeless and hungry.

American Occupiers Bring Changes Under General Douglas MacArthur, the Japanese emperor lost all political power. Japan's new constitution established a parliamentary democracy. Occupation forces also introduced social reforms. They opened the education system to all people, with legal equality for women. A land-reform program bought out large landowners and gave land to landless farmers. The United States also provided funds to rebuild Japan's cities and economy.

In 1952, the United States ended the occupation and signed a peace treaty with Japan. Still, the two nations kept close ties. American military forces maintained bases in Japan, which in turn was protected by American nuclear weapons. The two countries were also trading partners, eventually competing with each other in the global economy.

Japan Develops a Democracy Over the years, democracy took root in Japan. The Liberal Democratic Party (LDP) dominated the government from the 1950s to the 1990s. The LDP, however, differs from political parties in the United States. The LDP is a coalition, or alliance, of factions that compete for government positions.

Peace Comes to Japan
A 1945 poster printed by a Japanese bank encourages people to "make a bright future for Japan."

Land Reform Benefits Japanese Farmers
Japan's postwar land reform redistributed land from wealthy landlords to small farmers such as the ones in this photo. *How would ownership of land benefit farmers?*

Japan's Economic Miracle
By the 1970s and 1980s, Japan prospered by manufacturing products to be sold overseas, such as the televisions being assembled in this photo.

An Economic Miracle Relies on Exports Like Western Europe, Japan achieved an economic miracle between 1950 and 1970. Its **gross domestic product (GDP)** soared year after year. GDP is the total value of all goods and services produced in a nation within a particular year.

Japan's success was built on producing goods for export. At first, Japan sold textiles. Later, it shifted to selling steel and machinery. By the 1970s, Japanese cars, cameras, and televisions found eager buyers on the world market. Soon, a wide range of Japanese electronic goods were competing with Western, and especially American, products.

How did Japan enjoy such success? After World War II, Japan, like Germany, had to rebuild from scratch. Also like Germany, it had successfully industrialized in the past, so it quickly built efficient, modern factories that outproduced older industries in the West. With American military protection, Japan spent little money on its own military and could invest more in its economy. In addition, Japan benefited from an educated and skilled workforce. Finally, the government protected home industries by imposing tariffs and regulations that limited imports.

These policies, along with the high quality of Japanese exports, resulted in a trade surplus for Japan. That is, Japan sold more goods overseas than it bought from other countries. By the 1980s, United States manufacturers were angered by what they saw as unfair competition, and the United States pushed Japan to open its economy to more imports. However, Japan's trade surplus persisted.

 **Checkpoint** What factors explain Japan's economic success in the decades after World War II?

Assessment

Terms, People, and Places

1. Place each of the key terms at the beginning of the section into one of the following categories: politics, culture, or the economy. Write a sentence for each term explaining your choice.

Note Taking

2. **Reading Skill: Categorize** Use your completed chart to answer the Focus Question: How did the United States, Western Europe, and Japan achieve economic prosperity and strengthen democracy during the Cold War years?

Comprehension and Critical Thinking

3. **Compare Points of View** How did Democrats and Republicans differ on the best ways to improve opportunity for Americans?

4. **Make Comparisons** How was the economic development of Western Europe during the Cold War years similar to or different from that of Japan?

5. **Make Generalizations** How was trade important to the economic development of Western Europe, the United States, and Japan during the postwar decades?

● Writing About History

Quick Write: Brainstorm Possible Solutions To write a problem-solution essay, you first need to brainstorm possible solutions to a problem you have defined. In this section, you learned that European welfare states offered social benefits but that these benefits were very costly. List possible solutions to this problem, and explain the advantages and disadvantages of each.

Chinese communist soldier marching into Beijing, 1949

The "little red book" of quotations from Mao Zedong

Communist Victory in China

On September 21, 1949, at a rally in the Chinese capital, Beijing, the victorious communist leader Mao Zedong said:

> 66 We have closed our ranks and defeated both domestic and foreign oppressors through the People's War of Liberation and the great people's revolution, and now we are proclaiming the founding of the People's Republic of China. 99

Focus Question What did the communist victory mean for China and the rest of East Asia?

Communism Spreads in East Asia

Objectives

- Analyze China's Communist Revolution.
- Describe China's role as a "wild card" in the Cold War.
- Explain how war came to Korea and how the two Koreas followed different paths.

Terms, People, and Places

collectivization	Kim Il Sung
Great Leap Forward	Syngman Rhee
Cultural Revolution	Pusan Perimeter
38th parallel	demilitarized zone

Note Taking

Reading Skill: Summarize Complete this chart to summarize the effects of the Communist Revolution on China and the impact of the Cold War on China and Korea.

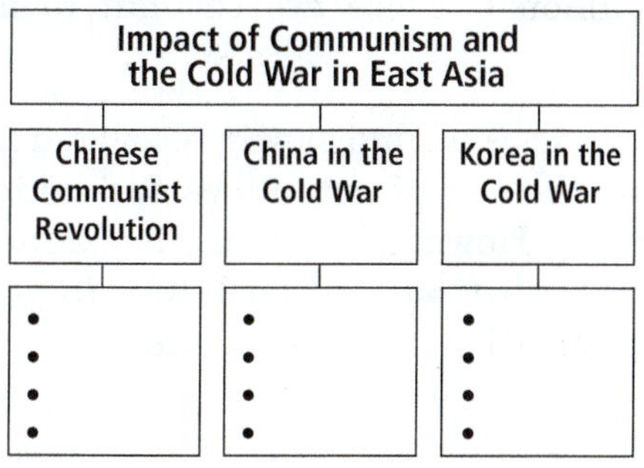

In the late 1940s, communism made advances in East Asia. With their victory in China in 1949, the Communists gained control of one fifth of the world's people.

China's Communist Revolution

By the end of World War II, the Chinese Communists had gained control of much of northern China. After Japan's defeat, Communist forces led by Mao Zedong (Mao Tse-tung) fought a civil war against Nationalists headed by Jiang Jieshi (jahng jeh shur). Battles raged until Mao's forces swept to victory and set up the People's Republic of China. The defeated Nationalists fled to the island of Taiwan, off the Chinese coast. After decades of struggle, China was finally under Communist control.

How the Communists Won Mao's Communists triumphed for several reasons. Mao had won the support of China's huge peasant population. Peasants had long suffered from brutal landlords and crushing taxes. The Communists redistributed land to poor peasants and ended oppression by landlords.

While support for the Communists grew, the Nationalists lost popularity. Nationalist policies had led to widespread economic hardship. Many Chinese people also resented corruption in Jiang's government and the government's reliance on support from Western "imperialist" powers. They hoped that the Communists would build a new China and end foreign domination.

Widespread support for the Communists in the countryside helped them to capture rail lines and surround Nationalist-held cities. One after another, these cities fell, and Mao's People's Liberation Army

Mao Zedong

During the mid-1950s, divisions arose within the Communist Party in China. In response, Mao Zedong (1893–1976) launched a campaign under the slogan "Let a hundred flowers bloom, let a hundred thoughts contend." Mao hoped that by offering people the opportunity to openly express their views he would gain more support. When people began to criticize the Communist Party, however, Mao ended the campaign. Of the nearly 550,000 Chinese who had spoken out, thousands were executed and hundreds of thousands were exiled to the countryside to "rectify their thinking through labor." **What methods did Mao use to keep power for himself?**

Vocabulary Builder

<u>communes</u>—(KAHM yoonz) *n.* commonly owned and operated farms or communities

emerged victorious. After their victory against the Nationalists, the Communists conquered Tibet in 1950. In 1959, Tibet's most revered religious leader, the Dalai Lama, was forced to flee the country.

Changing Chinese Society Mao Zedong built a Communist one-party totalitarian state in the People's Republic of China. Communist ideology guided the government's efforts to reshape the economy and society that China had inherited from the dynastic period. The Communist government discouraged the practice of Buddhism, Confucianism, and other traditional Chinese beliefs. Meanwhile, the government seized the property of rural landlords and urban business owners throughout China.

Opponents of the Communists were put down as "counterrevolutionaries." Many thousands of people who had belonged to the propertied middle class, or "bourgeoisie," were accused of counterrevolutionary beliefs. They were then beaten, sent to labor camps, or killed.

With Soviet help, the Chinese built dams and factories. To boost agriculture, Mao at first distributed land to peasants. Soon, however, he called for **collectivization,** or the forced pooling of peasant land and labor, in an attempt to increase productivity.

The Great Leap Forward Fails From 1958 to 1960, Mao led a program known as the **Great Leap Forward.** He urged people to make a superhuman effort to increase farm and industrial output. In an attempt to make agriculture more efficient, he created <u>communes</u>. A typical commune brought together several villages, thousands of acres of land, and up to 25,000 people. Rural communes set up small-scale "backyard" industries to produce steel and other products.

The Great Leap Forward, however, proved to be a dismal failure. Backyard industries turned out low-quality, useless goods. The commune system cut food output partly by removing incentives for individual farmers and families, leading to neglect of farmland and food shortages. Bad weather added to the problems and led to a terrible famine. Between 1959 and 1961, as many as 55 million Chinese are thought to have starved to death.

The Cultural Revolution Disrupts Life China slowly recovered from the Great Leap Forward by reducing the size of communes and taking a more practical approach to the economy. However, in 1966, Mao launched the Great Proletarian **Cultural Revolution.** Its goal was to purge China of "bourgeois" tendencies. He urged young Chinese to experience revolution firsthand, as his generation had.

In response, teenagers formed bands of Red Guards. Waving copies of the "little red book," *Quotations From Chairman Mao Tse-tung* [Zedong], Red Guards attacked those they considered bourgeois. The accused were publicly humiliated or beaten, and sometimes even killed. Skilled workers and managers were forced to leave their jobs and do manual labor on rural farms or in forced labor camps. Schools and factories closed. The economy slowed, and civil war threatened. Finally, Mao had the army restore order.

✔ **Checkpoint**   What were the main successes and failures of the Chinese Communist Revolution?

China, the Cold War's "Wild Card"

In 1949, the triumph of the Communists in China had seemed like a gain for the Soviet Union and a loss for the United States and its democratic allies. The number of people under communist rule had more than tripled. China's role in the Cold War, however, proved to be more complex than a simple expansion of communist power.

Split With the Soviet Union   The People's Republic of China and the Soviet Union were uneasy allies in the 1950s. Stalin sent economic aid and technical experts to help China modernize, but distrust between the two countries created tensions. Some of these tensions dated back to territorial disputes between tsarist Russia and dynastic China. By 1960, border clashes and disputes over ideology led the Soviets to withdraw all aid and advisors from China. Western fears of a strong alliance between the Soviet Union and China had proved unfounded.

Promoting the Cultural Revolution
The Cultural Revolution poster above shows soldiers holding "little red books" and urges them to "destroy all enemies." The photo to the left shows Chinese soldiers waving their "little red books" during this same period. *What do these images suggest about freedom of speech and freedom of thought during the Cultural Revolution in China?*

Washington Plays the China Card Relations between China and the United States were even more complex. After Jiang Jieshi (Chiang Kai-shek) fled to Taiwan, the United States supported his Nationalist government as the rightful representative of China. Washington refused diplomatic recognition of the mainland People's Republic of China, which American leaders saw as a communist threat to all of Asia.

As the Cold War dragged on, however, the United States took a second look at the People's Republic. From the American point of view, there were strategic advantages to improving relations with Communist China after its split with the Soviet Union. By "playing the China card," as this strategy was sometimes called, the United States might isolate the Soviets between NATO in the west and a hostile China in the east.

The United States allowed the People's Republic to replace Taiwan in the United Nations in 1971. A year later, U.S. President Richard Nixon visited Mao in Beijing. Finally, in 1979, the United States set up formal diplomatic relations with China.

Taiwan and the Nationalists Jiang Jieshi's government continued to rule Taiwan under martial law as a one-party dictatorship. Not until the late 1980s did Taiwan's government end martial law and allow opposition

▼ U.S. soldiers advance to fight North Koreans as South Korean civilians retreat from the front.

Korea Is Divided

Summer 1945
Korea is divided along the 38th parallel into a Soviet-occupied north and an American-occupied south.

North Korea Invades

Summer 1950
North Korea invades South Korea. U.S. and South Korean forces halt their retreat around Pusan.

parties. Mainland China saw Taiwan as a breakaway province and threatened military action when Taiwanese politicians proposed declaring the island's formal independence. In the long term, the mainland government insisted that Taiwan be rejoined with China. Taiwan's government resisted such pressure.

✔ **Checkpoint** How did China's relationships with the Soviet Union and the United States change during the Cold War?

War Comes to Korea

The nation of Korea occupies a peninsula on China's northeastern border. Like East and West Germany, Korea was split in two by rival forces after World War II. And like other divided lands, the two Koreas found themselves on opposite sides in the Cold War.

A Divided Nation Korea was an independent kingdom until Japan conquered it in the early twentieth century. After Japan's defeat in World War II, Soviet and American forces agreed to divide Korea temporarily along the **38th parallel** of latitude. However, North Korea, ruled by the

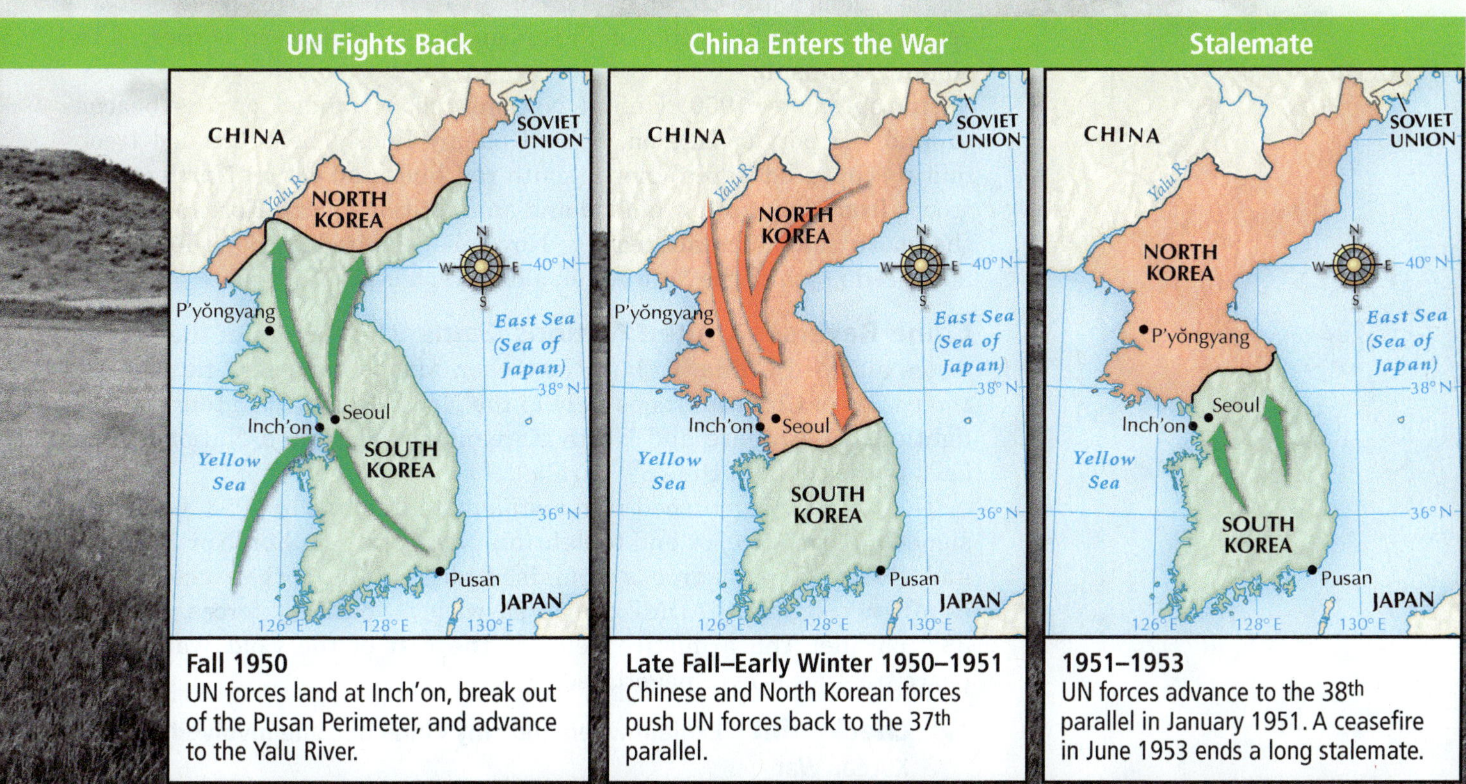

Fall 1950
UN forces land at Inch'on, break out of the Pusan Perimeter, and advance to the Yalu River.

Late Fall–Early Winter 1950–1951
Chinese and North Korean forces push UN forces back to the 37th parallel.

1951–1953
UN forces advance to the 38th parallel in January 1951. A ceasefire in June 1953 ends a long stalemate.

Winter Battle Scene in Korea
U.S. soldiers rest after winning a battle for a snowy hill in Korea, February 1951. *Based on the photograph, what advantage did these soldiers gain by winning control of this hill?*

dictator **Kim Il Sung,** became a communist ally of the Soviet Union. In South Korea, the United States backed the dictatorial—but noncommunist—leader, **Syngman Rhee.**

North Korean Attack Brings a United Nations Response

Both leaders wanted to rule the entire country. In early 1950, Kim Il Sung called for a "heroic struggle" to reunite Korea. North Korean troops attacked in June of that year and soon overran most of the south. The United Nations Security Council condemned the invasion. The United States then organized a United Nations force to help South Korea.

United Nations forces were made up mostly of Americans and South Koreans. Although U.S. troops arrived in early July, North Korean troops continued to advance until United Nations forces stopped them in August along a line known as the **Pusan Perimeter.** This perimeter was centered on the port city of Pusan, in the southeastern corner of the Korean peninsula.

In September 1950, United Nations troops landed on the beaches around the port of Inch'on, behind enemy lines. These U.S.-led troops quickly captured Korea's north-south rail lines and cut off North Korean troops from their supply of food and ammunition. North Korean forces in the south soon surrendered. By November, United Nations forces had advanced north to the Yalu River, along the border of China.

China Reverses United Nations Gains

The success of the U.S.-led forces alarmed China. In late November, Mao Zedong sent hundreds of thousands of Chinese troops to help the North Koreans. In tough winter fighting, the Chinese and North Koreans forced United Nations troops back to the south of the 38th parallel.

The Korean War turned into a stalemate. Finally, in 1953, both sides signed an armistice, or end to fighting. Nearly two million North Korean and South Korean troops remained dug in on either side of the **demilitarized zone** (DMZ), an area with no military forces, near the 38th parallel. The armistice held for the rest of the Cold War, but no peace treaty was ever negotiated.

✔ **Checkpoint** Explain when and why China became involved in the Korean War.

Two Koreas

Like the two Germanys, North and South Korea developed separately after the armistice—North Korea as a communist command economy, South Korea as a capitalist market economy. As in Germany, the capitalist portion of the country had an economic boom and rising standards of living, while the communist zone went through economic stagnation and decline. Also as in Germany, the United States gave economic and military aid to capitalist South Korea, while the Soviets helped the communist north.

Unlike democratic West Germany, however, South Korea was governed by a series of dictators and military rulers during much of the Cold War. Unlike East Germany, where a series of officials led the communist government, a single dictator controlled North Korea throughout the Cold War. Whereas Germany was reunited at the end of the Cold War, Korea remained divided.

South Korea Recovers After the war, South Korea slowly rebuilt its economy. By the mid-1960s, South Korea's economy had leapt ahead. After decades of dictatorship and military rule, a prosperous middle class and fierce student protests pushed the government to hold direct elections in 1987. These elections began a successful transition to democracy. Despite the bloody Korean War, most South Koreans during the Cold War years wanted to see their ancient nation reunited, as did many North Koreans. All Koreans shared the same history, language, and traditions. For many, this meant more than Cold War differences.

North Korea Digs In Under Kim Il Sung, the command economy increased output for a time in North Korea. However, in the late 1960s, economic growth slowed. Kim's emphasis on self-reliance kept North Korea isolated and poor. The government built a personality cult around Kim, who was constantly glorified as the "Great Leader" in propaganda. Even after its Soviet and Chinese allies undertook economic reforms in the 1980s, North Korea clung to hard-line communism.

 **Checkpoint** How did North Korea's economic performance compare to South Korea's?

Terms, People, and Places

1. For each term, person, or place listed at the beginning of the section, write a sentence explaining its significance.

Note Taking

2. **Reading Skill: Summarize** Use your completed chart to answer the Focus Question: What did the communist victory mean for China and the rest of East Asia?

Comprehension and Critical Thinking

3. **Recognize Ideologies** What ideologies did Mao's programs to transform China reflect?

4. **Draw Inferences** How did the United States use the changing relationship between China and the Soviet Union to its own advantage?

5. **Predict Consequences** How might the history of Korea have been different if United Nations forces had not stepped in to oppose the North Korean invasion in 1950?

● **Writing About History**

Quick Write: Write a Thesis Statement To write a problem-solution essay, you need to choose the best solution to a problem. In this section, you learned that both North and South Koreans wanted to reunify their country, but that Cold War differences got in the way. List possible solutions to Korea's Cold War division and write a thesis statement arguing for the best solution.

U.S. military helicopter in Vietnam

A family watches President Kennedy speak on television.

America's Role in Vietnam

In a television interview on September 2, 1963, U.S. President John F. Kennedy referred to U.S. support for the noncommunist government of South Vietnam. He did not foresee that five years later, more than 500,000 Americans would be fighting a bloody and divisive war there.

❝ I don't think that unless a greater effort is made by the Government to win popular support that the war can be won out there. . . . We can help them, we can give them equipment, we can send our men out there as advisors, but they have to win it, the people of Viet-nam, against the Communists.**❞**

Focus Question What were the causes and effects of war in Southeast Asia, and what was the American role in this region?

War in Southeast Asia

Objectives
- Describe events in Indochina after World War II.
- Learn how America entered the Vietnam War.
- Understand how the Vietnam War ended.
- Analyze Southeast Asia after the war.

Terms, People, and Places

guerrillas	Viet Cong
Ho Chi Minh	Tet Offensive
Dienbienphu	Khmer Rouge
domino theory	Pol Pot

Note Taking

Reading Skill: Summarize Complete a chart like the one below to summarize the events connected to the wars in Southeast Asia.

War in Southeast Asia		
Indochina After World War II	Vietnam War	Aftereffects of War
•	•	•

Southeast Asia's wars were, for many local participants, nationalist struggles against foreign domination. Like Korea, however, Southeast Asia eventually played a part in the global Cold War.

Indochina After World War II

In mainland Southeast Asia after World War II, an agonizing liberation struggle tore apart the region once known as French Indochina. The nearly 30-year conflict had two major phases. First was the war against the French, dating from 1946 to 1954. Second was the Cold War conflict that involved the United States and raged from 1955 to 1975.

Indochina Under Foreign Rule The eastern part of mainland Southeast Asia, or Indochina, was conquered by the French during the 1800s. The Japanese overran Indochina during World War II, but faced fierce resistance, especially in Vietnam, from local **guerrillas** (guh RIL uz), or small groups of loosely organized soldiers making surprise raids. The guerrillas, determined to be free of all foreign rule, turned their guns on the European colonialists who returned after the war. The guerrillas were strongly influenced by communist opposition to European colonial powers.

Ho Chi Minh Fights the French After the Japanese were defeated, the French set out in 1946 to re-establish their authority in Indochina. In Vietnam, they faced guerrilla forces led by

Ho Chi Minh (hoh chee min). Ho was a nationalist and communist who had fought the Japanese. He then fought the French in what is known as the First Indochina War. An unexpected Vietnamese victory at the bloody battle of Dienbienphu (dyen byen foo) in 1954 convinced the French to leave Vietnam. Cambodia and Laos had meanwhile gained their independence separately.

Vietnam Is Divided After 1954, however, the struggle for Vietnam became part of the Cold War. At an international conference that year, Western and communist powers agreed to a temporary division of Vietnam. Ho's communists controlled North Vietnam. A noncommunist government led by Ngo Dinh Diem (ngoh din dee EM), supported by the United States, ruled South Vietnam. The agreement called for elections to reunite the two Vietnams. These elections were never held, largely because the Americans and Ngo Dinh Diem feared that the Communists would win.

Ho Chi Minh

Ho Chi Minh (1890–1969) was born in central Vietnam at a time when Vietnam was under French colonial control. Ho discovered communism while working abroad and quickly adapted it to his struggle against French rule back in Vietnam. While Soviet communism gave a leading role to urban workers, Ho saw rural peasants as the driving force behind a successful revolution. Ho was more interested in national liberation than following a Soviet communist model. As president of North Vietnam, he led his people first against French control and later against the U.S-backed South Vietnamese government. **How did Ho Chi Minh's approach to communism differ from the Soviet model?**

Some South Vietnamese preferred Ho Chi Minh, a national hero, to the South Vietnamese government backed by the United States, a foreign power. But Ho's communist rule in the North alienated some Vietnamese. Many Catholic and pro-French Vietnamese fled to the south.

The United States supported Ngo Dinh Diem's regime against what American leaders saw as the communist threat from North Vietnam. Meanwhile, Ngo Dinh Diem's dictatorial regime alienated many Vietnamese with its corruption and brutal tactics against political opponents.

By the early 1960s, communist guerrilla fighters had appeared in the jungles of South Vietnam. Many of them were South Vietnamese, but they received strong support from the north. Many saw their fight as a nationalist struggle to liberate Vietnam from foreign domination.

✔ **Checkpoint** Why did Vietnamese guerrillas fight the French in Indochina?

America Enters the Vietnam War

American foreign policy planners saw the situation in Vietnam as part of the global Cold War. They developed the **domino theory**—the view that a communist victory in South Vietnam would cause noncommunist governments across Southeast Asia to fall to communism, like a row of dominoes. America's leaders wanted to prevent this from happening.

The War Intensifies Ho Chi Minh remained determined to unite Vietnam under communist rule. He continued to aid the National Liberation Front, or **Viet Cong,** the communist rebels trying to overthrow South Vietnam's government. At first, the United States sent only supplies and military advisors to South Vietnam. Later, it sent thousands of troops, turning a local struggle into a major Cold War conflict.

THE VIETNAM WAR

The Vietnam War thrust American soldiers into an alien and dangerous environment of jungles and swamps. The Viet Cong guerrillas were often local villagers, so it was hard for American soldiers to tell friend from foe. Local guerrillas' knowledge of the land allowed them to hide behind vegetation or behind the earthen banks of canals before a surprise ambush. The map at the right shows how North Vietnam delivered supplies to the Viet Cong in South Vietnam along the Ho Chi Minh Trail. These supply lines and the Viet Cong's knowledge of the land made the Viet Cong a deadly foe, even against the better-equipped American forces.

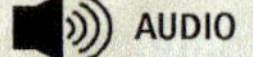 AUDIO

Viet Cong guerrillas train in a ditch for combat against American soldiers.

An American soldier sits on the bank of a canal during a skirmish with Viet Cong snipers. Vietnamese children are clinging to their mothers nearby, trying to stay low to avoid gunfire.

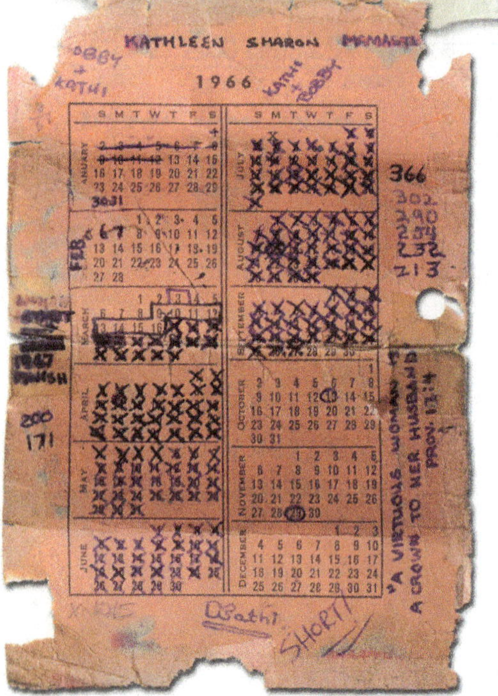

▲ This 1966 calendar may have belonged to one of the 58,000 American soldiers killed in the Vietnam War. It was left at the Vietnam Veterans Memorial in Washington, D.C., by a visitor.

On August 1, 1964, South Vietnamese commandos conducted raids on North Vietnamese islands in the Gulf of Tonkin. The following day, the North Vietnamese attacked a nearby U.S. Navy destroyer, the *Maddox,* which they mistakenly believed had assisted the South Vietnamese raids. Three days later, sailors on the *Maddox* thought that they had been attacked a second time, although it seems likely that their sonar and radar equipment were malfunctioning due to heavy seas.

U.S. President Johnson reported the attacks to Congress without mentioning the South Vietnamese raids or the doubts about the second attack. Believing that the attacks had been unprovoked, Congress passed the Gulf of Tonkin Resolution on August 7, 1964. The resolution authorized the President to take all necessary measures to prevent further aggression in Southeast Asia.

After the resolution passed, the United States began bombing targets in North Vietnam. Eventually, more than 500,000 American troops were committed to the war. At the same time, both the Soviet Union and China sent aid—but no troops—to help North Vietnam.

▲ This American soldier is patrolling a swamp in the Mekong Delta in the summer of 1969.

During the Vietnam era, young American men were required to register for the military draft. Men were then selected for the draft in a random lottery. Many saw fighting for their country as their patriotic duty. However, to avoid being drafted, some military-age American men left the country and sought refuge in other nations not involved in the war.

Guerrilla War. Like the French in Vietnam, America faced a guerrilla war. The rebels in South Vietnam tended to be local peasants. They thus knew the countryside much better than their American enemies. They also knew the local people. Villagers frequently offered them safe haven against foreign troops. The close connections between guerrilla fighters and the villagers turned the Vietnamese villages themselves into military targets. Supplies for the guerrillas came from the north, following trails that wound through the jungles of neighboring Cambodia and Laos. In response, American aircraft and ground troops crossed the borders of these nations, drawing them into the war.

The Tet Offensive Despite massive American support, South Vietnam failed to defeat the communist guerrillas and their North Vietnamese allies. In 1968, guerrilla forces came out of the jungles and attacked American and South Vietnamese forces in cities all across the south. The assault was unexpected because it took place during Tet, the Vietnamese New Year. The communists lost many of their best troops and did not hold any cities against American counterattacks. Nevertheless, the bloody Tet Offensive marked a turning point in public opinion in the United States.

 **Checkpoint** How did the domino theory lead the United States to send troops to Vietnam?

The Vietnam War Ends

As the fighting continued, civilian deaths caused by the bombing of North Vietnam and growing American casualties inflamed antiwar opinion in the United States. Growing numbers of American troops were prisoners of war (POWs) or missing in action (MIAs). Some Americans began to think that the Vietnam War was a quagmire, or swamp, in which the United States was becoming more and more bogged down.

More Americans Oppose the War As the war continued, the nation became deeply and bitterly divided over the ongoing struggle. Many Americans of all ages continued to support the war effort in Vietnam. Others wanted to end the loss of lives. More and more young people turned out for massive street demonstrations, all part of a growing antiwar movement. It was clear that an increasing number of Americans wanted no more "body bags" coming back or television footage of burned Vietnamese villages. At the same time, many agreed with a housewife who said, "I want to get out, but I don't want to give up."

America Withdraws In the end, American leaders decided that they had to get out of Vietnam. Faced with conflict at home and abroad, President Lyndon Johnson, who had presided over the massive expansion of the war in the 1960s, decided not to run for a second term. Johnson also opened peace talks with North Vietnam in Paris.

Although American troops had seldom lost a battle in the long struggle, they had not destroyed the Vietnamese Communists' determination to keep fighting. Johnson's successor, President Nixon, came under increasing pressure to <u>terminate</u> American involvement. Nixon finally negotiated the Paris Peace Accord in January 1973. This agreement established a cease-fire, or a halt in fighting. The United States agreed to withdraw its troops, and North Vietnam agreed not to send any more troops into the South. The accord left South Vietnam to determine its own future and set a goal of peaceful reunification with the North.

North Vietnam Wins the War Two years after American troops had withdrawn from the country, the North Vietnamese conquered South Vietnam. The South Vietnamese capital, Saigon, was renamed Ho Chi Minh City in 1976 in honor of the late leader. The North Vietnamese capital, Hanoi, became the capital of the reunited nation.

 **Checkpoint** Why did the United States withdraw its troops from Vietnam?

Southeast Asia After the War

After the American withdrawal from Vietnam, some dominos did fall. Both Cambodia and Laos ended up with governments dominated by Communist Vietnam. However, the falling dominos stopped at the

Peace Necklace
The peace sign on this necklace was a popular symbol of protest against the Vietnam War.

Vocabulary Builder
<u>terminate</u>—(TUR mih nayt) *vt.* finish, bring to an end

former borders of French Indochina. Other parts of Southeast Asia remained thoroughly capitalist, if less than democratic.

Tragedy in Cambodia During the Vietnam War, fighting had spilled over into neighboring Cambodia. In 1970, the United States bombed North Vietnamese supply routes in Cambodia and then briefly invaded the country. Afterwards, the **Khmer Rouge** (kuh MEHR roozh), a force of Cambodian communist guerrillas, gained ground in Cambodia. Finally, in 1975, the Khmer Rouge overthrew the Cambodian government.

Led by the brutal dictator **Pol Pot,** the Khmer Rouge unleashed a reign of terror. To destroy all Western influences, they drove people from the cities and forced them to work in the fields. They slaughtered, starved, or worked to death more than a million Cambodians, about a third of the population.

In the end, it took a Vietnamese invasion to drive Pol Pot and his Khmer Rouge back into the jungle. Vietnam imposed an authoritarian government on Cambodia, but they at least ended the genocide.

Vietnam Under the Communists In the newly reunited Vietnam, the communist victors imposed a harsh rule of their own on the south. Hundreds of thousands of Vietnamese fled their country, most in small boats. Many of these "boat people" drowned. Survivors landed in refugee camps in neighboring countries. Eventually, some settled in the United States. Meanwhile, Vietnam had to rebuild a land destroyed by war. Recovery was slow due to a lack of resources and an American-led embargo, or blockage of trade. For years, the country remained mired in poverty.

✔ **Checkpoint** How did communist Vietnam dominate parts of Southeast Asia after the Vietnam War?

Fleeing Communist Control
These South Vietnamese refugees are fleeing their country after communist forces took control in April 1975. Refugees who fled in small boats like this one were known as "boat people." *Why might people choose to flee across the open ocean in a small boat like this one?*

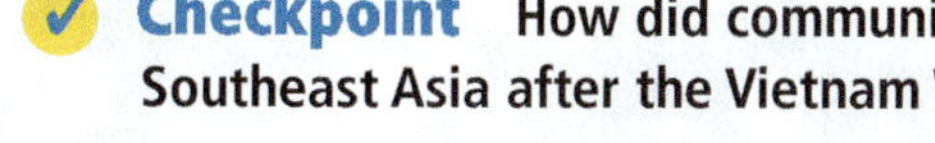

SECTION 4 Assessment

Progress Monitoring Online
For: Self-quiz with vocabulary practice
Web Code: naa-3041

Terms, People, and Places

1. For each term, person, or place listed at the beginning of the section, write a sentence explaining its significance.

Note Taking

2. **Reading Skill: Summarize** Use your completed chart to answer the Focus Question: What were the causes and effects of war in Southeast Asia, and what was the American role in this region?

Comprehension and Critical Thinking

3. **Draw Conclusions** Why did the French withdraw from Indochina in the 1950s?

4. **Summarize** How did a local struggle in Vietnam become a major Cold War conflict?

5. **Compare Points of View** What different opinions did Americans have about U.S. involvement in the Vietnam War?

6. **Synthesize Information** When the text states that "dominos fell" after the Vietnam War, what does this mean?

● Writing About History

Quick Write: Write a Supporting Paragraph To write a problem-solution essay, you need to provide arguments to support a proposed solution to a problem. In this section, an American was quoted as wanting to "get out" of South Vietnam without giving up on it. Write a thesis statement proposing a way to do this. Based on the text or your own ideas, write a paragraph with arguments supporting your thesis statement.

THE FALL OF THE SOVIET UNION

Soviet president Mikhail Gorbachev was due to sign a treaty that would reduce the power of the Soviet government. On August 18, 1991, two days before the signing, a committee of Communist hardliners detained Gorbachev at his summer home. The next day, the committee announced to the nation that Gorbachev had resigned and that they were taking control of the government. The committee sent columns of tanks and troops to take control of the capital, Moscow. (See photo at the right.) However, Boris Yeltsin, the president of Russia, the largest Soviet republic, defied the hardliners. Yeltsin called on thousands of Russians to resist the unlawful takeover. Finally, on August 21, the hardliners gave up their takeover and ordered Soviet troops to retreat from Moscow. Yeltsin's defeat of the hardliners led a few months later to the breakup of the Soviet Union.

◄ Soviet president Mikhail Gorbachev

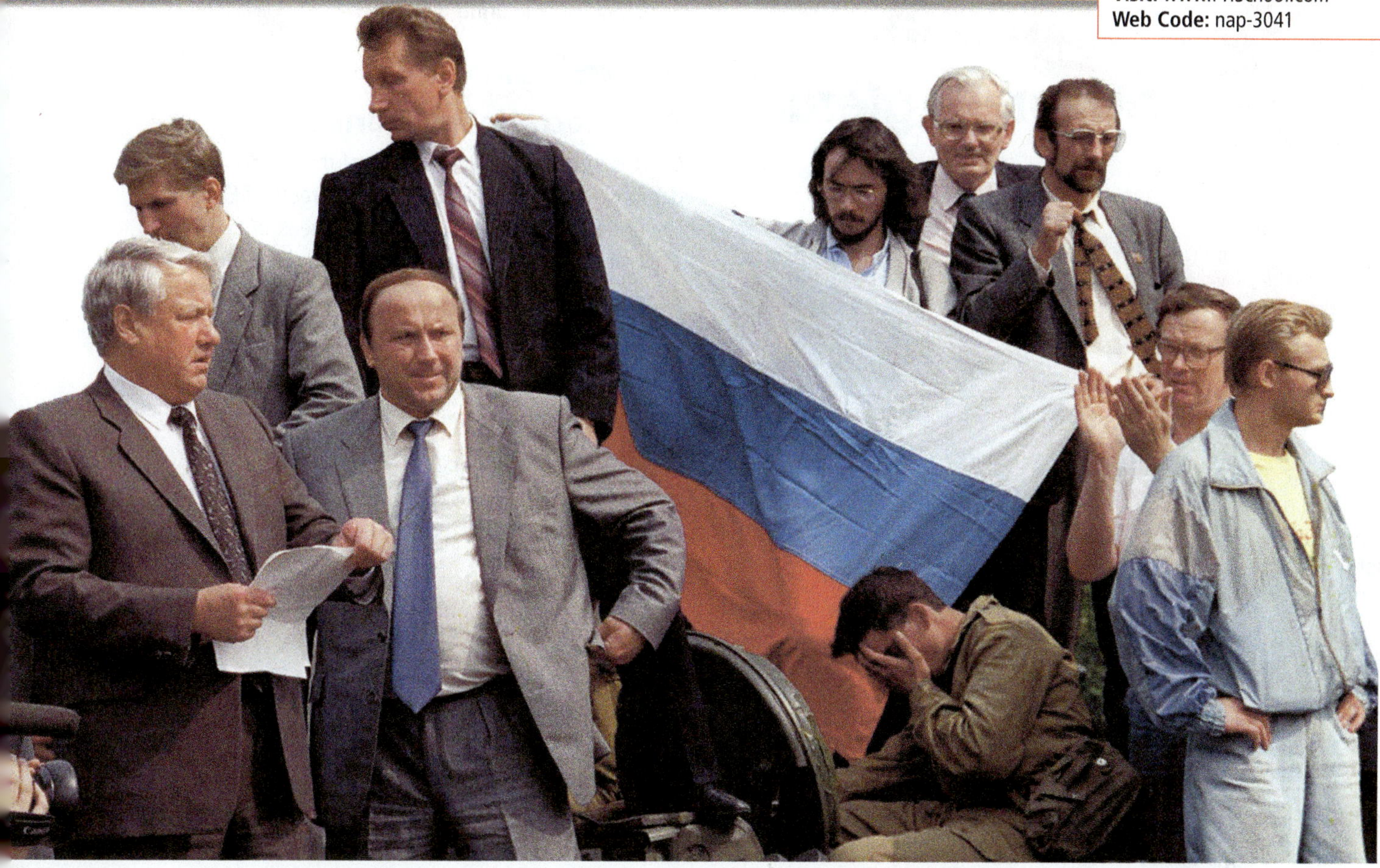

▲ Russian president Boris Yeltsin, holding a sheet of paper at left, stands atop a Soviet tank on August 19, 1991, and calls on Russians to resist the attempted takeover of the Soviet Union by hardliners. Behind him, a supporter holds a Russian flag. Yeltsin's success in defying the takeover broke the power of the central Soviet government and led to the independence of Russia and the other Soviet republics.

◀ Stanislav Shushkevich (left), president of Belarus; Boris Yeltsin (center), president of Russia; and Leonid Kravchuk (right), president of Ukraine, agreed on December 8, 1991, to dissolve the Soviet Union, effective at the end of 1991.

Thinking Critically

1. **Analyze Images** Why is it significant that Russian President Yeltsin is standing on top of a Soviet tank in the photo at the top of the page?
2. **Synthesize Information** How did the events of August 1991 cause the Soviet government to lose power to Russia?
3. **Map Skills** Based on the maps, why would Russia's wish for independence lead to the Soviet Union's breakup?

Independent Republics, 1992

Demonstrators
in East Berlin,
November 4, 1989

Soviet pin promoting
"openness, democracy,
and restructuring"

WITNESS HISTORY ◄)) AUDIO

A Democratic Transformation

On November 4, 1989, hundreds of thousands of people demonstrated for democracy in the streets of East Berlin. Never before had so many dared to speak out. Speaking to the crowd, author Stefan Heym captured the mood:

> **66** Dear friends, fellow citizens, it is as if someone had thrown open the window after all the years of stagnation. . . . What a transformation! **99**

Ultimately, the transformation in Eastern Europe led to the end of the Cold War.

Focus Question What were the causes and effects of the end of the Cold War?

The End of the Cold War

Objectives

- Understand how the Soviet Union declined.
- Analyze the changes that transformed Eastern Europe.
- Explain how communism declined worldwide and the United States became the sole superpower.

Terms, People, and Places

mujahedin	Lech Walesa
Mikhail Gorbachev	Solidarity
glasnost	Václav Havel
perestroika	Nicolae Ceausescu

Note Taking

Reading Skill: Categorize Complete a flowchart like the one below to categorize each event connected to the end of the Cold War.

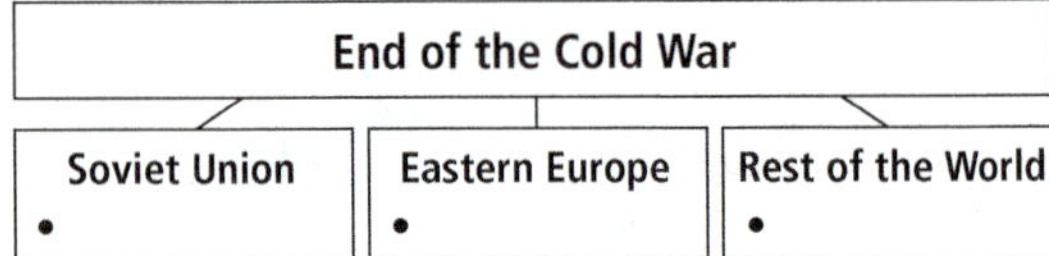

The global Cold War between two armed camps led by the United States and the Soviet Union lasted almost half a century. In the years around 1990, however, the struggle finally ended. The much-feared nuclear confrontation between the two superpowers never came about, but the end was as clear as any military victory.

The Soviet Union Declines

Western fears of growing Soviet power did not come true. In fact, Soviet communism was doomed. Signs of the weakness of the Soviet system had in fact been visible from the beginning.

A Hollow Victory Stalin's Soviet Union emerged from World War II as a superpower with an Eastern European sphere of influence stretching from the Baltic to the Balkans. Victory, however, brought few rewards to the Soviet people. Stalin continued to fill forced labor camps with "enemies of the state."

Reforms Give Way to Repression Under Stalin's successor, Nikita Khrushchev, Soviets enjoyed greater freedom of speech. Some government critics were freed from prisons and labor camps. Khrushchev oversaw a shift in economic priorities away from heavy industry and toward the production of consumer goods. But Khrushchev remained firmly committed to a command economy.

The thaw in Moscow inspired some East Europeans to move toward greater independence. However, Khrushchev himself remained a determined cold warrior. When Hungarians tried to break free of Soviet control in 1956, Khrushchev sent tanks in to enforce obedience, and his successor, Leonid Brezhnev, did the same thing when Czechs challenged the Soviets in the "Prague spring" of 1968.

The Command Economy Stagnates The Soviet Union rebuilt its shattered industries after World War II, using equipment stripped from Germany. The government poured resources into science and technology, launching *Sputnik I,* the first artificial satellite, in 1957.

Yet the Soviet economy faced severe problems. Collectivized agriculture remained so unproductive that Russia, a grain exporter in tsarist times, had to import grain to feed its people. The Soviet command economy could not match Western market economies in producing consumer goods. Soviet shoes and television sets were far inferior, while such luxuries as clothes washers or automobiles remained rare.

Central economic planning led to inefficiency and waste. A huge bureaucracy decided what and how much to produce. Government planners in Moscow, however, knew little about local needs. They chose to produce many unneeded goods. Consumers' needs often were not met. Although workers were paid low wages, lifetime job security gave them little <u>incentive</u> to produce better-quality goods.

Unlike the economies of Western Europe and the United States, which experienced booms during the Cold War, the economies of Eastern Europe and the Soviet Union stagnated. People saw little improvement in their standards of living and envied the prosperity of the West. Soviet economic inferiority made it impossible for the Soviet Union to keep up with the United States in the arms race and in military preparedness.

Cracking Under the Burden of Military Commitments As you have read, Soviet-American relations swung between confrontation and détente during the Cold War. Meanwhile, both sides maintained large military budgets and built expensive nuclear weapons.

Soviet Tanks Bring Repression
A boy watches Soviet tanks in the Hungarian capital, Budapest, in 1956. The Soviet Union sent tanks to stop Hungary's attempt to take an independent course. *What does this suggest about the independence of Eastern European countries such as Hungary during the Cold War?*

The arms race put a particular strain on the inefficient Soviet command economy. And when U.S. President Ronald Reagan launched a new round of missile development, it was clear that the Soviet economy could not afford to match it.

Soviets Have Their Own "Vietnam" in Afghanistan In 1979, the Soviet Union became involved in a long war in Afghanistan, an Islamic country just south of the Soviet Union. A Soviet-supported Afghan government had tried to modernize the nation. Its policies included social reforms and land redistribution that would reduce the power of regional landlords. Afghan landlords—who commanded armed men as warlords— and Muslim conservatives charged that both policies threatened Islamic tradition. When these warlords took up arms against the government, Soviet troops moved in.

Battling **mujahedin** (moo jah heh DEEN), or Muslim religious warriors, in the mountains of Afghanistan, however, proved as difficult as fighting guerrillas in the jungles of Vietnam had been for Americans. By the mid-1980s, the American government began to smuggle modern weaponry to the mujahedin. The Soviets had years of heavy casualties, high costs, and few successes. Like America's Vietnam War, the struggle in Afghanistan provoked a crisis in morale for the Soviets at home.

Gorbachev Tries Reform In 1985, an energetic new leader, **Mikhail Gorbachev** (GAWR buh chawf), came to power in the Soviet Union. With the economy in bad shape and the war dragging on in Afghanistan, Gorbachev was eager to bring about reforms. The changes he urged, however, soon spiraled out of control.

Gorbachev sought to avoid Cold-War confrontations. He signed arms control treaties with the United States and pulled Soviet troops out of Afghanistan.

At home, he called for **glasnost,** or openness. He ended censorship and encouraged people to discuss the country's problems openly. He also urged **perestroika** (pehr uh STROY kuh), or restructuring, of the government and economy. To improve efficiency, he reduced the size of the bureaucracy and backed limited private enterprise. His reforms made factory managers rather than central planners responsible for decisions. They also allowed farmers to sell produce on the free market.

The Crumbling Soviet Union This cartoon shows Soviet leader Mikhail Gorbachev with an egg-shaped head sitting on a wall marked with the national symbol of the Soviet Union. The cartoon draws on the nursery rhyme *Humpty Dumpty.*

1. What does the cartoon suggest about the state of the Soviet Union under Gorbachev?
2. What does it imply about Gorbachev's future?
3. How does this cartoon communicate ideas without using any words?

An Empire Crumbles Gorbachev's reforms, however, brought economic turmoil. Shortages grew worse and prices soared. Factories that could not survive without government help closed, leading to high unemployment. Those whose jobs were threatened denounced the reforms. Other critics demanded even more radical changes.

Gorbachev's policies also fed unrest across the Soviet empire. Eastern European countries from Poland to Bulgaria broke out of the Soviet orbit beginning in 1989. The Baltic States—Estonia, Latvia, and Lithuania—which the Soviet Union had seized in 1940, regained full independence in 1991. Russia's postwar empire seemed to many to be collapsing. Soviet hard-liners tried to overthrow Gorbachev that year and restore the old order. Their attempted coup failed, but it further weakened Gorbachev, who soon resigned as president.

At the end of 1991, the remaining Soviet republics separated to form 12 independent nations, in addition to the three Baltic States. The largest of these was Russia, which had most of the population and territory of the former Soviet Union. The next largest were Kazakhstan and Ukraine. Maps of Europe and Asia had to be redrawn to reflect the new political boundaries. After 69 years, the Soviet Union had ceased to exist.

 **Checkpoint** How did Gorbachev's policies lead to a new map of Europe and Asia?

Changes Transform Eastern Europe

The Soviet Union had maintained control over its Eastern European satellites by force. When Gorbachev introduced glasnost and perestroika in the Soviet Union, Eastern Europeans began to seek greater freedom in their own countries. As the Soviet Union crumbled, Eastern Europeans demanded an end to Soviet domination. This time they got it.

Demands for Freedom Increase As you have read, unrest had long simmered across the Soviet bloc. Many Eastern Europeans opposed communist rule. Nationalists resented Russian domination. Revolts had erupted in Poland, Hungary, Czechoslovakia, and elsewhere in the 1950s and 1960s. In the 1980s, demands for change mounted once again.

Hungary Quietly Reforms In 1968, when Czechoslovakia's defiance of Soviet control led to a Soviet invasion, Hungary quietly introduced modest economic reforms. Because Hungary remained loyal to the Warsaw Pact and maintained communist political control, it was allowed to go ahead with these reforms, which included elements of a market economy. During the 1970s, Hungary expanded its market economy. During the late 1980s, under the spirit of glasnost, Hungarians began to criticize the communist government more openly. Economic troubles led to greater discontent. Finally, in 1988 and 1989, under public pressure, the communist government allowed greater freedoms. New political parties were allowed to form, and the western border with Austria was opened.

Poland Embraces Solidarity Poland led the way in the new surge of resistance that shattered the Soviet satellite empire. In 1980, economic hardships ignited strikes by shipyard workers. Led by **Lech Walesa** (lek vah WEN suh), they organized **Solidarity,** an independent labor union. It won millions of members and demanded political as well as economic change.

Defending Lithuania's Independence
This woman, holding a Lithuanian flag, is guarding Lithuania's parliament building and TV tower from Soviet troops that tried and failed to regain control after Lithuania declared independence in January 1991.

Lech Walesa and Solidarity
Lech Walesa, at the left, speaks at a shipyard workers' strike in August 1980. The following month, he helped found the Polish national union known as Solidarity (Solidarnosc in Polish). At the right, Poles defy the government by holding a banner for the outlawed Solidarity union in 1983. *Why would a communist government ban a labor union?*

Under pressure from the Soviet Union, the Polish government outlawed the union and arrested its leaders, including Walesa. Still, unrest continued. Walesa became a national hero, and the Polish government eventually released him from prison. Pope John Paul II visited Poland, met with Solidarity leaders, and criticized communist policies. The pope was the former Karol Wojtyla, archbishop of the Polish city of Cracow.

East Germans Demand Change Unlike Poland or Hungary, East Germany resisted Gorbachev's calls for change. In 1988, the rigidly communist East German government banned Soviet publications, because it considered glasnost subversive. East Germany's communists blocked moves toward a market economy or greater political freedom. However, East Germans could watch television broadcasts from West Germany. They were thus intensely aware how much more prosperity and political freedom existed on the other side of the Berlin Wall. When Hungary opened its border with Austria in 1989, thousands of East Germans fled through Hungary and Austria to West Germany. Thousands more held demonstrations across East Germany demanding change.

Communist Governments Fall In the late 1980s, Gorbachev declared that he would not interfere with Eastern European reforms. Poland legalized Solidarity and, in 1989, held the first free elections in 50 years. A year later, Lech Walesa was elected president of Poland. The new government began a difficult, but peaceful, transition from a command economy to a market economy.

A flowering of opposition and reform movements spread across the Eastern European countries. By late 1989, a powerful democracy movement was sweeping throughout the region. Everywhere, people took to the streets, demanding reform. One by one, communist governments fell. In Czechoslovakia, **Václav Havel** (VAHTS lahv HAH vul), a dissident writer and human rights activist, was elected president. In East Germany, the gates of the Berlin Wall were opened, and the country started down the road to reunification with West Germany. Most changes came peacefully, but when Nicolae Ceausescu (chow SHES koo), Romania's longtime dictator, refused to step down, he was overthrown and executed.

For the first time since 1939, Eastern European countries were free. They dissolved the Warsaw Pact in 1991 and requested that Russian troops leave. By then, the Soviet Union itself had crumbled.

Czechoslovakia Splits Czechoslovakia was a relatively new nation, formed in 1918 at the breakup of the Austro-Hungarian Empire. Before 1918, the country's Czech and Slovak ethnic groups—each with its own language and traditions—had lived separately. After Czechoslovakia's founding, Czechs dominated the country's government. During World War II, Czechoslovakia was conquered and partitioned, or divided, by Nazi Germany. Czechoslovakia was reunified under communist control after the war. When the communists lost power in 1989, some Slovaks began to call for independence. In 1992, the Slovaks and Czechs peacefully agreed to divide Czechoslovakia into the new nations of Slovakia and the Czech Republic.

✔ **Checkpoint** How did glasnost in the Soviet Union lead to the end of communism in Eastern Europe?

Communism Declines Around the World

The collapse of communism in the Soviet bloc affected communist countries from China to Castro's Cuba. Many were already suffering economic decline by the 1980s as their command economies stagnated. Although political dictatorships still prevailed, rigid, government-run economies sometimes gave way to freer, more productive economic systems.

China Builds on Deng's Reforms Gorbachev had urged the leaders of other communist states to consider both political and economic changes. China's leaders, building on Deng Xiaoping's 1980s economic reforms, generated an amazing economic boom in the 1990s. China became a major producer of consumer goods and achieved double-digit growth rates.

China's government undertook no major political reforms. However, as the global economic crisis that began in 2008 led to factory closings, protests by unemployed workers increased. China's government responded with a $600 billion stimulus package to retrain workers and improve productivity.

Vietnam and North Korea Differ Communist Vietnam established diplomatic relations with the United States in the 1990s. Vietnam also began to change economically, encouraging tourism and becoming a leading exporter of coffee.

North Korea, on the other hand, hunkered down in grim isolation, rejecting all reforms. Its rigidly totalitarian regime often proved unable to feed its own

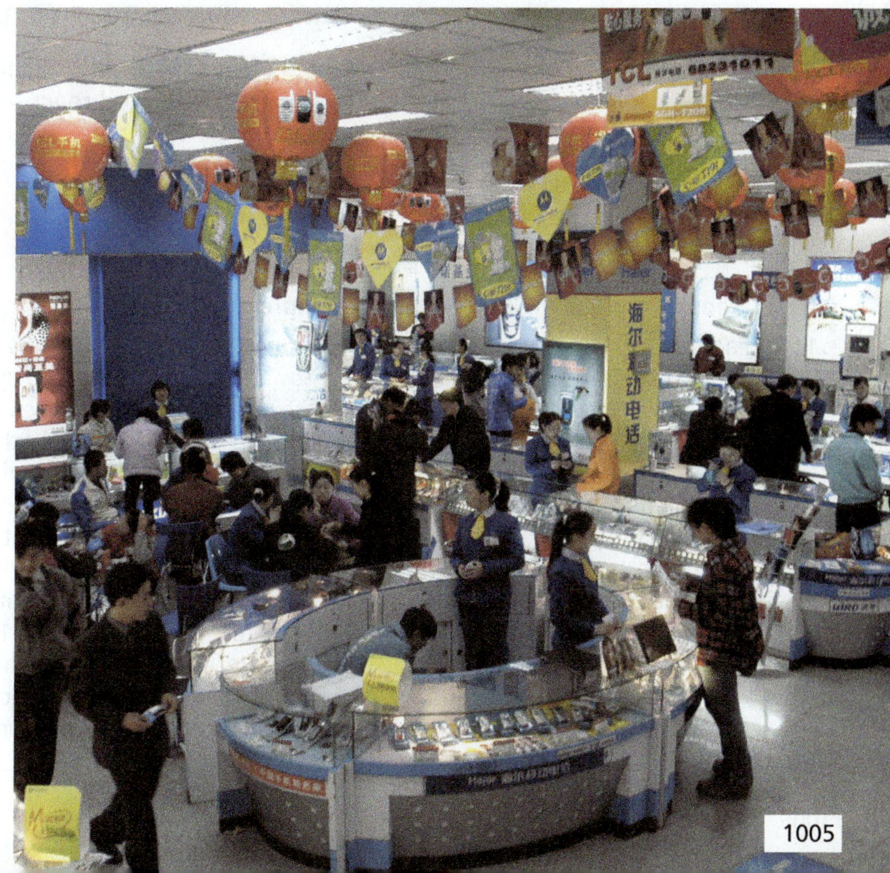

Capitalism Comes to China
Chinese consumers shop for mobile phones in this recent photo. *Do the activities in this photo reflect a command economy or a market economy? Explain why.*

people, leading to hundreds of thousands of deaths. A 2007 agreement to dismantle its nuclear weapons program in exchange for U.S. aid seemed to founder as the decade drew to a close.

Cuba Declines Cuba's economy, deprived of Soviet support and still crippled by American sanctions, deteriorated. Many felt that communism in Cuba would not outlive its leader, Fidel Castro. In 2006, the ailing Castro surrendered control of the government to his younger brother Raúl, who allowed some market reforms.

 **Checkpoint** How did communist countries react differently to the collapse of the Soviet bloc?

The United States as Sole Superpower

With the collapse of its great rival, the United States was widely recognized as the only remaining superpower. After years of thin budgets, Russia's armed forces seemed weak and ineffective. Only the United States could project its power around the world.

The United States thus emerged as the world's leading military power. From time to time, the United States exercised this power. Beginning in the 1990s, the United States staged several military missions around the world. You will learn more about these in upcoming chapters.

Americans seemed unsure of their proper role in the world. Some objected to the risk and expense of being "the world's policeman." Others, however, believed that the United States should play an even more aggressive part in world affairs.

America's unrivaled power produced mixed reactions around the world. When the Soviet threat had loomed, American power had been seen as a valuable counterweight. Some continued to see the United States as a protector of freedom. With no rival threat in sight, however, people in many parts of the world were less pleased to see any single nation as powerful as the United States had become.

 **Checkpoint** Why did America's position as the sole superpower produce mixed reactions?

SECTION **5** Assessment

Terms, People, and Places

1. For each term, person, or place listed at the beginning of the section, write a sentence explaining its significance.

Note Taking

2. **Reading Skill: Categorize** Use your completed chart to answer the Focus Question: What were the causes and effects of the end of the Cold War?

Comprehension and Critical Thinking

3. **Draw Conclusions** Why was the Soviet Union unable to keep up with the market economies of the West?

4. **Summarize** How did Gorbachev's reforms lead to the breakup of the Soviet empire?

5. **Recognize Cause and Effect** Why were Eastern Europeans able to break free of communist governments and Soviet domination in the late 1980s?

6. **Draw Inferences** How did the collapse of the Soviet Union affect the power of other countries around the world?

● Writing About History

Quick Write: Gather Evidence To write a problem-solution essay, you need to gather evidence to support a proposed solution to a problem. In this section, you learned that rigidly communist countries faced isolation and economic decline after the fall of the Soviet Union. Identify a solution to this problem and gather evidence to support your solution. Then write a paragraph with a thesis statement proposing a solution. Include the evidence you have gathered in support of your thesis statement.

Václav Havel: *New Year's Address*

Václav Havel was a leading dissident and human rights activist in communist Czechoslovakia. When the "democracy movement" swept through Eastern Europe in 1989, Havel was elected president. In the following speech delivered on January 1, 1990, Havel asks the citizens of Czechoslovakia to accept responsibility for their past and to move forward in building a democracy. Havel calls on Czechs and Slovaks to be active participants in their new democracy.

Václav Havel

Our country is not flourishing. The enormous creative and spiritual potential of our nations is not being used sensibly. Entire branches of industry are producing goods that are of no interest to anyone. . . . [W]e have today the most contaminated environment in Europe. . . .

But all this is still not the main problem. The worst thing is that we live in a contaminated moral environment. We fell morally ill because we became used to saying something different from what we thought. We learned not to believe in anything, to ignore each other, to care only about ourselves. Concepts such as love, friendship, compassion, humility, or forgiveness lost their depth and dimensions. . . . Only a few of us were able to cry out loud that the powers that be should not be all-powerful. . . .

We had all become used to the totalitarian system and accepted it as an unchangeable fact and thus helped to perpetuate it. In other words, we are all . . . responsible for the operation of the totalitarian machinery. . . .

Why do I say this? It would be very unreasonable to understand the sad legacy of the last forty years as something alien, which some distant relative bequeathed to us. On the contrary, we have to accept this legacy as a sin we committed against ourselves. If we accept it as such, we will understand that it is up to us all, and up to us only, to do something about it. We cannot blame the previous rulers for everything, not only because it would be untrue but also because it could blunt the duty that each of us faces today, namely, the obligation to act independently, freely, reasonably, and quickly. Let us not be mistaken: the best government in the world, the best parliament and the best president, cannot achieve much on their own. And it would also be wrong to expect a general remedy from them only. Freedom and democracy include participation and therefore responsibility from us all.

Czechoslovak democracy demonstrators

Thinking Critically
1. **Identify Point of View** Who does Havel hold responsible for Czechoslovakia's totalitarian past?
2. **Draw Conclusions** What does Havel see as the solution to his country's problems?

Quick Study Guide

Progress Monitoring *Online*
For: Self-test with vocabulary practice
Web Code: naa-3061

■ Cold War Contrasts

Communist Countries	Industrialized Democracies
Compete in arms race to maintain "balance of terror."	Compete in arms race to maintain "balance of terror."
Form Warsaw Pact. China follows separate path.	Form NATO and SEATO.
Seek to spread communism.	Seek to contain communism.
Command economies	Market economies
Economic stagnation, low standards of living	Economic "miracles," prosperity with scattered recessions
Repression of dissent, labor camps	Free expression, but fears lead to an episode of McCarthyism
Power is closely held by communist parties.	Democracy is established in Japan, civil rights movement extends democracy in the United States.
Lost arms race.	Won arms race.

■ Cold War Hot Spots

Korea	Vietnam
Divided into communist north and noncommunist, U.S.-supported south.	Divided into communist north and noncommunist, U.S.-supported south.
China provided troops to support North Korea.	China and the Soviet Union provided economic and military aid, but not troops, to North Vietnam.
The United States led United Nations troops supporting South Korea.	The United States and some allies provided troops to support South Vietnam.
Warfare mainly involved regular troops.	Viet Cong fighting in the south were mainly guerrillas.
United States troops remained in South Korea after war.	United States troops withdrew before the war ended.
Korean War ended in a stalemate between the two sides and a ceasefire.	Vietnam War ended when North Vietnam defeated South Vietnam and reunited the country.

■ Steps in the Collapse of the Soviet Empire

- The command economy could not create wealth or raise living standards as quickly as market economies.
- The Soviet Union could not afford the expense of maintaining a "balance of terror" in the arms race.
- East Europeans resisted communism and Soviet control.
- Soviet military failure in Afghanistan led to calls for change.
- Reforms in Russia included glasnost, or freedom of expression, and perestroika, or market reforms.
- East Germans forced their government to open the Berlin Wall.
- Eastern European nations rejected Soviet control and adopted market economies and democracy.
- Glasnost led to drive for independence by Soviet ethnic minorities and the breakup of the Soviet Union.
- Soviet Union was divided into 15 independent nations.
- The Warsaw Pact was dissolved.

■ Key Events of the Cold War

Americas, Europe, and Soviet Union

East and Southeast Asia

1945
World War II ends in Europe.

1949
Germany is divided.

1959
Fidel Castro leads communist revolution in Cuba.

1945

1955

1945
World War II ends in Asia.

1949
Mao Zedong leads communists to victory in China.

1950–1953
Korean War

Concept Connector

 Essential Question Review

To connect prior knowledge with what you have learned in this chapter, answer the questions below in your Concept Connector journal. Use the journal in the Reading and Note Taking Study Guide to record your answers (or go to www.phschool.com **Web Code:** nad-3007). In addition, record information about the following concepts:

• Cooperation: European Community

1. **Empire** During the 1950s and 1960s, Soviet military forces crushed democratic reforms in East Germany, Poland, Hungary, and Czechoslovakia. By the mid-1980s, the weakness of the Soviet system was becoming apparent. Compare the decline of the Soviet empire to the decline of the Ottoman empire. Identify any similarities. Then identify the single most important reason for the fall of communist governments in Eastern Europe.

2. **Dictatorship** Mao Zedong built a one-party totalitarian state in China. Critics and opponents were labeled "counter-revolutionaries" and beaten, exiled, or killed. How do you think adult Chinese might have viewed the Cultural Revolution? Did the Cultural Revolution strengthen Mao's hold on China? Focus on:
   • Red Guards
   • propaganda
   • forced labor camps
   • civil war

3. **Human Rights** After World War II, the American promise of equality and opportunity had not yet been fulfilled for minorities and women. African Americans and other minority groups faced segregation and discrimination. What tactics did these groups use to gain their civil rights? What were the results? Think about:
   • protests
   • spending power
   • legislation

▉ Connections to Today

1. **Conflict: India and Pakistan** The Cold War was a tense standoff between the United States and the Soviet Union, with only brief outbreaks of actual fighting. Since India and Pakistan gained independence in 1947, the two countries have engaged in a similar conflict. This conflict involves occasional fighting, often involving guerrillas in the disputed Kashmir region. Since 1998, both India and Pakistan have had nuclear weapons. Using recent news articles and the Internet, research the current state of this conflict. How is it similar to the Cold War? How is it different?

2. **Democracy: The Global Spread of Democracy** This chapter describes the spread of democracy to West Germany and Japan and later to Eastern Europe. Using an encyclopedia, research the move to democracy in an Eastern European country. Then research a move to democracy in a country in Latin America, East Asia, or Africa. How was the transition to democracy similar or different in these two countries?

1961
Berlin Wall is built.

1989
Eastern Europeans overthrow communist rulers.

1991
The Soviet Union breaks up and the Cold War ends.

1965   **1975**   **1985**   **1995**

1964
U.S. enters the Vietnam War.

1975
Vietnam War ends with North Vietnamese victory.

1976
Mao Zedong dies.

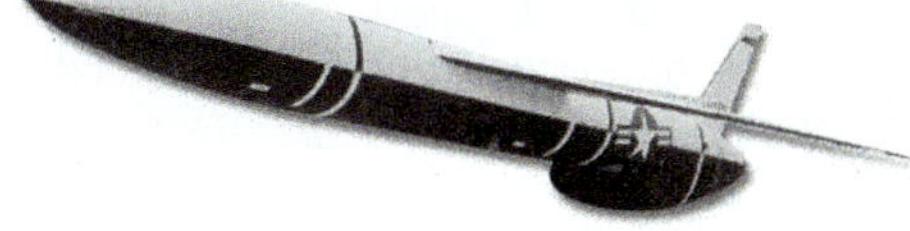

History Interactive
For: Interactive timeline
Web Code: nap-3061

Chapter Assessment

Terms, People, and Places

Choose the italicized term in parentheses that best completes each sentence.

1. The United States aimed to prevent the spread of communism through a policy of (*containment/glasnost*).
2. (*Ngo Dinh Diem/Ho Chi Minh*) was the leader of North Vietnam.
3. European nations eliminated barriers to trade by establishing the (*welfare state/European Community*).
4. At the end of the Korean War, a cease-fire line was established near the (*38th parallel/Pusan Perimeter*).
5. A period of economic decline is a (*budget deficit/recession*).
6. During the 1970s, the United States and the Soviet Union had a period of reduced Cold War tensions known as (*collectivization/détente*).

Main Ideas

Section 1 (pp. 966–975)

7. How did the Cold War develop in the Soviet Union, Europe, and the United States?
8. What were the main features of the nuclear arms race?

Section 2 (pp. 976–984)

9. How did political and economic life change during the Cold War years in the United States?
10. What was the relationship between economic growth and trade in Western Europe and Japan?

Section 3 (pp. 985–991)

11. How did the Korean War influence U.S. relations with Communist China? How did those relations change as a result of hostility between China and the Soviet Union?

Section 4 (pp. 992–999)

12. Why did the United States enter the Vietnam War?

Section 5 (pp. 1000–1007)

13. How did Gorbachev's reforms lead to the breakup of the Soviet Union?
14. What events marked the end of the Cold War?

Chapter Focus Question

15. How did the Cold War develop, how did it shape political and economic life in individual nations, and how did it end?

Critical Thinking

16. **Analyze Visuals** Turn to the photo of the Berlin Wall on the first page of this chapter. How do you think that the Berliners in this photo felt about the wall that had been built through their city?
17. **Make Comparisons** What factors contributed to economic booms after World War II in Western Europe, the United States and Japan? Why was the economic performance of Eastern Europe and the Soviet Union different?
18. **Draw Inferences** You have read that the leaders of the Soviet Union retained power in Poland and elsewhere in Eastern Europe for over forty years. How were they able to do so despite lacking the consent of the governed?
19. **Predict Consequences** During the Cold War, many nations formed alliances with one superpower for protection against the other. After the Cold War, the United States emerged as the sole superpower. How might this change the nature of alliances?
20. **Recognize Cause and Effect** Which factors allowed North Vietnam to achieve victory over South Vietnam? What were some consequences of North Vietnam's victory in Vietnam and other parts of Southeast Asia?

● Writing About History

In this chapter's five Section Assessments, you developed skills to write a problem-solving essay.

Writing a Problem-Solution Essay Write a problem-solution essay on one of the Cold War problems listed below. Problems to address include the military standoff on the Iron Curtain, the arms race, and the division of Germany, Korea, or Vietnam. Consult page SH10 of the Writing Handbook for additional help.

Prewriting

- Go online or do library research to find evidence on each of the problems listed above.
- Choose the problem that interests you most and take notes about the evidence you find.
- Decide on the best solution to this problem and gather the evidence that supports your solution.

Drafting

- Write a first paragraph stating the problem and explaining why it is important.
- Write a thesis statement arguing for your solution to the problem.
- Write a second paragraph beginning with your thesis statement, followed by supporting sentences.

Revising

- Use the guidelines for revising your report on page SH12 of the Writing Handbook.

Document-Based Assessment

Cold War Chills

The United States and the Soviet Union confronted each other in the Cold War—a global conflict that included a nuclear arms race. In Document A, Nikita Khrushchev discusses the border fortifications that prevented East Germans from entering West Germany. In Document B, U.S. Vice President Richard Nixon warns Khrushchev about restricting western access to Berlin.

Document A

"Seeing that their government had reasserted control over its own frontiers, the East Germans were heartened by the solidification and fortification of their state. . . .I know there are people who claim that the East Germans are imprisoned in paradise and that the gates of the Socialist paradise are guarded by armed troops. I'm aware that a defect exists, but I believe it's a necessary and only temporary defect."

—From ***Khrushchev Remembers*** by Nikita Khrushchev

Document B

". . . I hope the Prime Minister has understood all the implications of what I said," Nixon went on, with an oblique [indirect] reference to Berlin. "What I mean is that the moment we place either one of these powerful nations, through an ultimatum, in a position where it has no choice but to accept dictation or fight, then you are playing with the most destructive force in the world."

Khrushchev: (flushed, wagging a finger near Nixon's face): We too are giants. If you want to threaten, we will answer threat with threat.

Nixon: We never engage in threats.

Khrushchev: You wanted indirectly to threaten me. But we have means at our disposal that can have very bad consequences.

Nixon: We have too.

—From ***Time***, August 3, 1959

Document C

Document D

Fortifications that kept East Germans from crossing into West Germany

Analyzing Documents

Use your knowledge of the Cold War and Documents A, B, C, and D to answer questions 1–4.

1. The author's purpose in Document A was to
   A explain East German discipline.
   B offer a balanced perspective on the Cold War.
   C argue for a fortified barrier between East and West Germany.
   D explain the role of the Soviet Union in East Germany.

2. The tone of the exchange in Document B is
   A friendly and joking.
   B tense and hostile.
   C cautious.
   D businesslike.

3. Document C shows that
   A West Berlin was located inside West Germany.
   B the border between East and West Germany passed through Berlin.
   C East Germany surrounded West Germany.
   D two East German borders separated West Berlin from West Germany.

4. **Writing Task** How was the Cold War fought? Use what you have read in the chapter, along with these documents, to write a response.

31

New Nations Emerge
1945–Present

Independence in Eritrea

To escape the dangers of the war for independence in the African nation of Eritrea, Almaz Isaac fled to America as a refugee when she was a teenager. When Eritrea won its independence ten years later and peace returned, Almaz returned to Eritrea. She said, "This is the first time I've been able to come back, to see my family. We waited, our people fought, and now this is it. We have our freedom." As in Eritrea, independence brought a new sense of hope to many countries in Africa and elsewhere in recent decades. Listen to the Witness History audio to hear more about independence in Africa.

 Eritreans celebrate independence in 1993 at the end of their long war for freedom.

Chapter Preview

Chapter Focus Question How did former European colonies gain independence, and what challenges did they face after independence?

Section 1
Independent Nations of South Asia

Section 2
New Nations of Southeast Asia

Section 3
African Nations Gain Independence

Section 4
The Modern Middle East

Use the ✓ **Quick Study Timeline** at the end of this chapter to preview chapter events.

Monument showing the sandals worn by soldiers in Eritrea's war for independence

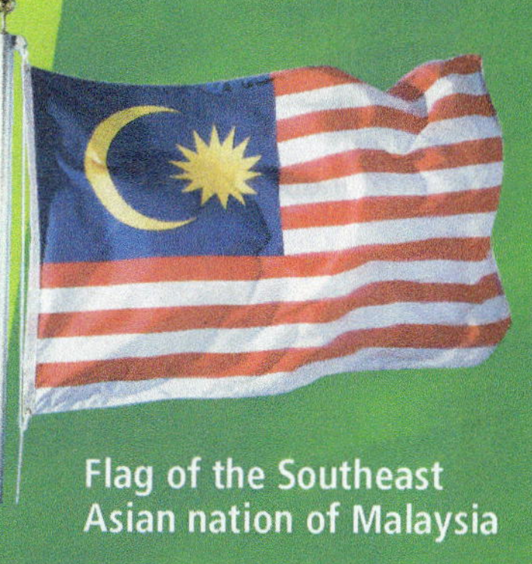

Flag of the Southeast Asian nation of Malaysia

Hat worn by border guards in India

Concept Connector ONLINE

To explore Essential Questions related to this chapter, go to PHSchool.com
Web Code: nad-3107

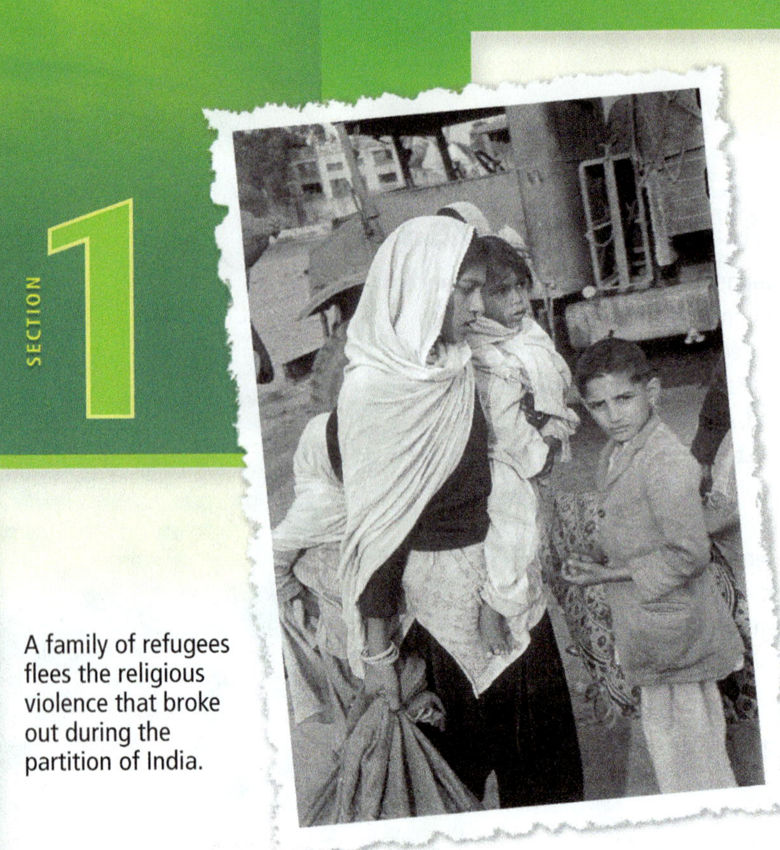

A family of refugees flees the religious violence that broke out during the partition of India.

Hat worn by Indian border guards along the border with Pakistan

Fleeing Religious Violence

At independence, India was partitioned, or divided, into India and Pakistan, a new, largely Muslim country. Damyanti Sahgal, a Hindu, describes fleeing from Hindu-Muslim violence during the partition.

> 66 When we came close to Amritsar, we found that they had started stopping trains, killing people in them, but we were lucky. Everyone said put your windows up, they are cutting down people. 99

While people in India and Pakistan welcomed independence, they had to live with the violence of partition and its legacy of distrust.

Focus Question How did nationalist demands for independence affect South Asia and the world?

Independent Nations of South Asia

Objectives

- Understand why independence brought partition to South Asia.
- Describe how Indian leaders built a new nation.
- Summarize how Pakistan and Bangladesh grew apart.
- Explain how India and Pakistan pursued independence from the superpowers in their foreign relations.

Terms, People, and Places

partition	Indira Gandhi
Sikhs	Punjab
Kashmir	Golden Temple
Jawaharlal Nehru	Bangladesh
dalits	nonalignment

Note Taking

Reading Skill: Identify Causes and Effects Fill in a concept web like this one to keep track of causes and effects of events in South Asia. Add ovals as needed for additional concepts.

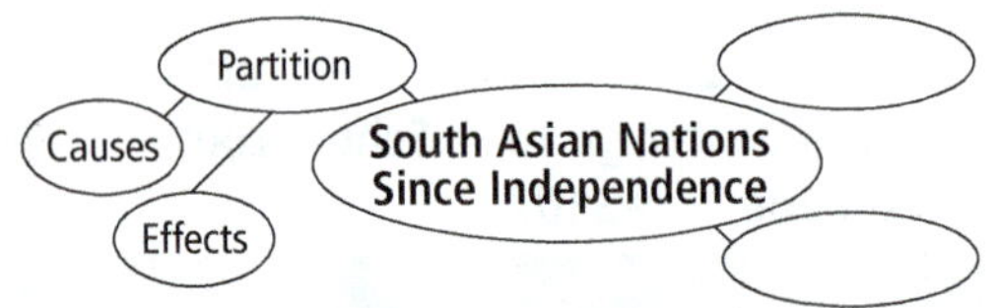

At the same time that the Cold War was unfolding, a global independence movement was reshaping the world. Among the first new nations to win independence were the former British colonies of South Asia.

Independence Brings Partition

Nationalists in British-ruled India had demanded self-rule since the late 1800s. As independence neared, however, a long-simmering issue surfaced. What would happen to the Muslim minority in a Hindu-dominated India?

Two New Nations Emerge Like Mohandas Gandhi, most of the leaders and members of the Congress Party were Hindus. However, the party wanted a unified India that would include both Muslims and Hindus. The Muslim League, led by Muhammad Ali Jinnah, had a different view of liberation. The Muslim League feared discrimination against the Muslim minority in a unified India. Therefore, the Muslim League demanded the creation of a separate nation, called Pakistan, that would include the parts of British India where Muslims formed a majority. In the 1940s, tensions between Muslims and the Hindu majority in British India led to increasing violence.

After World War II, the British government decided that it could no longer afford to resist Indian demands for independence.

As independence approached, violence between Hindus and Muslims accelerated. In response, Britain decided to accept the idea of **partition,** or dividing the subcontinent into two nations. Hindu-dominated India, and Pakistan, which had a Muslim majority, both won independence on August 13, 1947.

Refugees Flee Amid Violence However, Hindus and Muslims still lived side by side in many cities and rural areas. As soon as the new borders became known, millions of Hindus on the Pakistani side of the borders packed up their belongings and fled to the new India. At the same time, millions of Muslims fled into newly created Pakistan. An estimated 10 million people fled their homes, most of them on foot.

Muslims fleeing along the crowded roads into Pakistan were slaughtered by Hindus and **Sikhs** (seeks), members of an Indian religious minority. Muslims massacred Hindu and Sikh neighbors. Around one million people died in these massacres. Others died of starvation and exposure on the road.

Struggles Over Kashmir Since independence, India and Pakistan have fought a series of wars over **Kashmir,** a state in the Himalayas. In 1947, Kashmir's Hindu ruler tried to join India. However, Kashmir's Muslim majority wanted to be part of Pakistan. For decades, Kashmiri separatists, often supported by Pakistani militants, have fought Indian troops. Indian and Pakistani forces have also battled along Kashmir's mountainous border. Today, Kashmir remains a flashpoint in the tense relations between India and Pakistan.

A Nuclear Arms Race In the 1970s, first India and then Pakistan developed nuclear weapons programs. By 1998, both nations had successfully tested nuclear weapons. The emergence of these two nuclear powers alarmed neighbors in South Asia and the world, in part because of the ongoing hostility between India and Pakistan. Another concern was the danger that extremists might get access to nuclear technology or even nuclear weapons.

Conflict Divides Sri Lanka The island of Ceylon won freedom from Britain in 1948. Later, it took the name Sri (sree) Lanka. Most Sri Lankans are Buddhists who speak Sinhalese. However, a large Tamil-speaking Hindu minority lives in the north and east. The Sri Lankan government favored the Sinhalese majority, which angered many Tamils. In the late 1970s, Tamil rebels battled to set up their own separate nation. For three decades, terrorism and brutality fed a deadly conflict between government forces and Tamil rebels. By 2009, the government had regained control of Tamil-held towns, but peace was by no means assured.

✔ **Checkpoint** Why was Kashmir a source of conflict between India and Pakistan?

Building a Modern Nation

At independence, India established a parliamentary democracy. Although India remains the world's largest democracy, it has faced many challenges. Ethnic and religious tensions threatened its unity. Its people speak over 100 languages and many dialects. Hundreds of millions of Indians lived in desperate poverty. Despite unrest and diversity, India has emerged as a major world power.

Strong Leaders During its early decades, India benefited from strong leadership. The Congress Party, which had spearheaded the independence movement, worked to turn India into a modern nation. From 1947 to 1964, **Jawaharlal Nehru,** leader of the Congress Party, was India's prime minister. He promoted economic growth and social change. Under Nehru, food output rose, but so did India's population. The government encouraged family planning to reduce the birthrate, but with limited success.

Although India's 1947 constitution banned discrimination against **dalits,** or people in the lowest castes, discrimination based on caste continued. Nehru's government set aside jobs and places in universities for dalits and other lower-caste Indians. Still, higher-caste Hindus generally got better schooling and jobs.

Later, Nehru's daughter, **Indira Gandhi,** served as prime minister for most of the years between 1966 and 1984. She led India with a firm hand and challenged traditional discrimination against women.

Religious Conflicts India was a land of many religions. A majority of Indians were Hindu, but millions were Muslim, Sikh, Christian, or Buddhist. At times, religious divisions led to violence.

Some Sikhs wanted independence for **Punjab,** a prosperous, largely Sikh state in northern India. In 1984,

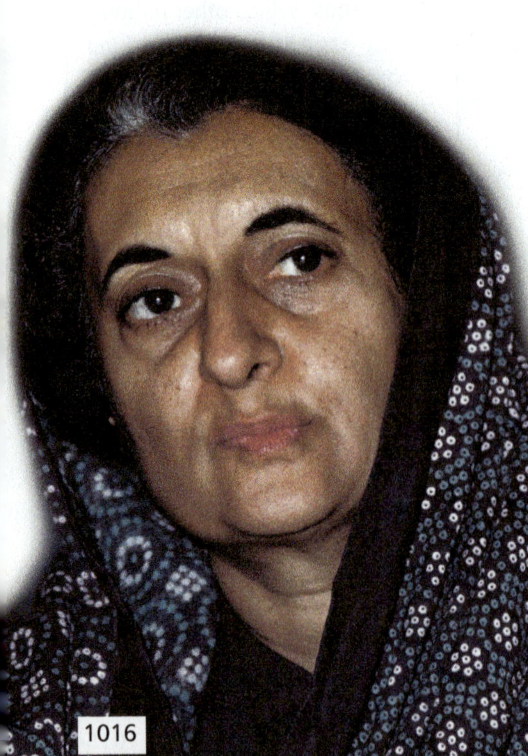

Indira Gandhi
Prime Minister Indira Gandhi led India from 1966 to 1977 and again from 1980 to 1984.

armed Sikh separatists took dramatic action. They occupied the Golden Temple, the holiest Sikh shrine. When Indira Gandhi sent troops to oust them, bloody fighting erupted. Soon after, Gandhi was assassinated by her Sikh bodyguards, igniting terrible violence.

In the late 1980s, the Hindu nationalist party, Bharatiya Janata Party (BJP) challenged the secular, or nonreligious, Congress Party. The BJP wanted a government based on Hindu traditions and some-times encouraged violence against Muslims.

 **Checkpoint** How did the Indian government try to improve conditions for lower castes?

Pakistan and Bangladesh Separate

Pakistan gained independence in 1947, at the same time as India. Geographically, it was a divided coun-try, with West Pakistan and East Pakistan located on either side of India. A thousand miles of Indian terri-tory separated the two regions, and India made trade and travel between the two Pakistans difficult.

Bangladesh Breaks Away From the start, West Pakistan dominated the government even though East Pakistan had a larger population. The government concentrated most economic development programs in West Pakistan, while East Pakistan remained deep in poverty. Most people in East Pakistan were Bengalis, while West Pakistan was home to other ethnic groups. Many Bengalis resented governmental neglect of East Pakistan.

In 1971, Bengalis in East Pakistan declared independence. They named their country Bangladesh, or "Bengali nation." When the Paki-stani army tried to crush the rebellion, India sent forces to help Bang-ladesh. Pakistan was then <u>compelled</u> to recognize the new country.

Pakistan's Shaky Government After independence, Pakistan strug-gled to build a stable government. Power shifted back and forth between elected civilian leaders and military rulers. Tensions among the country's diverse ethnic groups posed problems. The fiercely independent people in the northwestern "tribal areas" were left largely on their own and resisted government control. The activities of Islamic fundamentalists created tension. The fundamentalists wanted a government that fol-lowed strict Islamic principles, while other Pakistanis wanted greater separation between religion and state.

Ongoing Challenges In 2008, after nine years in power, General Pervez Musharraf allowed elections. Before the election, Islamic extrem-ists assassinated one of the candidates, Benazir Bhutto, a popular former prime minister. Pakistan's new civilian government faced tough challenges, including the global economic recession.

Religions of India			
Religion	**Population (millions)**	**Percentage**	**Regional Concentration**
Hinduism	828	80.5	Throughout India
Islam	138	13.4	Kashmir, Northern India, Southwest Coast
Christianity	24	2.3	Northeastern India, Southwest Coast
Sikhism	19	1.9	Northwestern India
Buddhism	8	0.8	Northeastern India, West Coast
Others	11	1.0	Throughout India

Chart Skills What is India's largest minority religion? Where do most of its followers live?

SOURCE: Census of India 2001

Vocabulary Builder

<u>compelled</u>—(kum PELD) *v.* made to or forced

Meanwhile, support for Islamic fundamentalist groups based in Pakistan grew, especially in the northwest. In November 2008, Islamic militants from Pakistan launched terror attacks on hotels and tourists in Mumbai, India, fueling tensions between the hostile neighbors.

Islamic traditions were strong in the rugged border area between Pakistan and Afghanistan. When the Soviet Union invaded Afghanistan in 1979, one million Afghan refugees fled into Pakistan. There, many joined Islamic fundamentalist groups to battle the invaders.

After Russia withdrew from Afghanistan, the Taliban, an extreme Islamist group, seized power with the support of Pakistan. The Taliban backed Al Qaeda, which launched terrorist attacks on the United States in 2001. When U.S. forces invaded Afghanistan and overthrew the Taliban, its supporters fled into Pakistan. They set up strongholds in northwestern Pakistan, where their influence spread. Pakistan's government had limited success fighting the terrorists. However, it was angered by American missile attacks on suspected terrorists within its borders.

Bangladesh Struggles Bangladesh ranks among the world's poorest, most crowded countries. Its population, more than half as large as that of the United States, lives in an area the size of Alabama. The flat Ganges Delta, just a few feet above sea level, covers much of the country. Bangladesh has suffered repeatedly from devastating tropical storms and floods.

Floods Ravage Bangladesh
Summer rains often flood much of low-lying Bangladesh. Here, aid workers bring supplies to a family trapped on the roof of their home. *How might frequent floods hurt efforts to improve conditions in Bangladesh?*

Geographic conditions made it hard for the government to ease the desperate poverty that most people endure. One hopeful program, however, came from the Grameen Bank, founded by Bangladeshi economist Muhammad Yunus. It gave tiny loans, or "microcredit" to poor people so they could open small businesses. Although microcredit helped only a few, it offered a model to poor nations around the world. In 2006, Yunus was awarded the Nobel Peace Prize for his efforts.

 **Checkpoint** How did geography pose challenges for Bangladesh?

Finding an Independent Path

India and Pakistan were among the first of more than 90 new nations to emerge after World War II. By the 1930s, nationalist movements had taken root in European colonies across Africa, Asia, and the Middle East. After World War II, nationalist leaders such as Ghandi and Nehru insisted on independence. After India and Pakistan gained independence, nationalist leaders in Africa and other regions demanded the same for their countries.

India, Pakistan, and other new nations condemned colonialism and rejected Cold War expansion and the divisions between the West and the Soviet Union. In response, they sought **nonalignment,** or political and diplomatic independence from the Cold War superpowers. In 1955, India and Pakistan helped organize a conference of newly independent nations in Bandung, Indonesia, which marked the birth of the nonaligned movement.

The nonaligned movement had its first formal meeting in 1961 in Yugoslavia. India was a leader of the nonaligned movement, which came to include more than 100 nations, mainly in Asia, Africa, and Latin America. Because they rejected both the Western allies, or the First World, and the Soviet alliance, or the Second World, the Nonaligned Movement was seen as the voice of a "Third World" of countries.

Checkpoint What global role did India and Pakistan play after independence?

Terms, People, and Places

1. For each term, person, or place in the beginning of the section, write a sentence explaining its significance.

Note Taking

2. **Reading Skill: Identify Causes and Effects** Use your completed concept web to answer the Focus Question: What were the consequences of independence in South Asia for the region and for the world?

Comprehension and Critical Thinking

3. **Recognize Cause and Effect** Why did the partition of British India cause refugees to flee?

4. **Express Problems Clearly** What problems did India's religious diversity pose?

5. **Summarize** Why did Bangladesh separate from Pakistan?

6. **Draw Conclusions** How did a policy of nonalignment influence the relations of India and Pakistan with the Cold War superpowers?

 **Writing About History**

Quick Write: Outline Your Topic To write a compare-and-contrast essay, you need to consider two subjects and find similarities and differences between them. In this section, you learned that India and Pakistan share a common history but were separated at independence. Write features of each country's history in three lists: a list of features specific to India, a list of features specific to Pakistan, and a list of features shared by both countries.

Sukarno, Indonesia's
first president

Indonesia's flag

All for All

Most Southeast Asian nations are home to
diverse people speaking many languages and
practicing different religions. Indonesia's
independence leader, Sukarno, stressed the
importance of unity for his nation:

> 66 [W]e are establishing an Indonesian state
> which all of us must support. All for all. Not
> the Christians for Indonesia, not the Islamic
> group for Indonesia . . . but the Indonesians
> for Indonesia—all for all! 99

Achieving unity was one of many challenges that
Indonesia faced after independence.

Focus Question What challenges did Southeast
Asian nations face after winning independence?

New Nations of Southeast Asia

Objectives

- Explain the political and economic contrasts in
  mainland Southeast Asia.
- Understand how Indonesia's size posed
  challenges.
- Summarize how the Philippines sought
  democracy.

Terms, People, and Places

autocratic	East Timor
Aung San Suu Kyi	Ferdinand Marcos
Sukarno	Benigno Aquino
Suharto	Corazon Aquino

Note Taking

Reading Skills: Understand Effects Fill in a
concept web like the one below to keep track of
the effects of recent historical processes in
Southeast Asia. Add to it as needed for additional
concepts in the section.

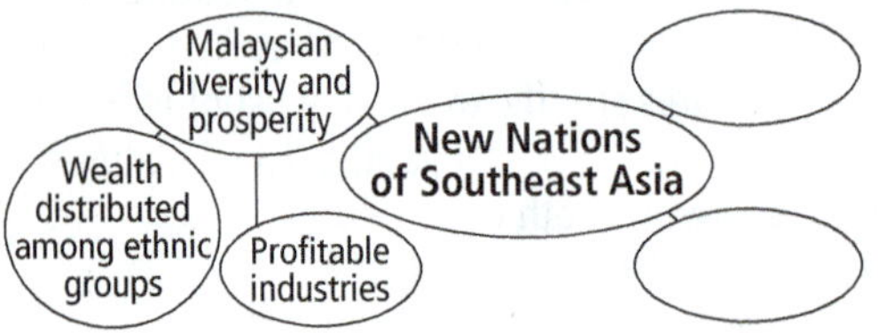

Southeast Asia includes part of the Asian mainland and thousands
of islands that stretch from the Indian Ocean to the South China
Sea. In 1939, most of the region was under colonial rule by European
nations or the United States. During World War II, Japan seized
the region. After the war, nationalist groups demanded independence
and resisted reoccupation by European nations.

Mainland Contrasts

Mainland Southeast Asia is a region of contrasts. Thailand and
Malaysia have mostly prospered as market economies, although they
have been affected by global financial crises. However, nearby Myanmar has suffered under a brutal **autocratic,** or repressive, government with unlimited power.

Malaysia Prospers British colonies on the Malay Peninsula and
the island of Borneo gained independence in the 1950s and joined
to form the nation of Malaysia. The oil-rich monarchy of Brunei,
on Borneo, and the prosperous city-state of Singapore gained independence as separate nations.

Malaysia has a very diverse population. People of Chinese and
Indian descent have long dominated business. They have made the
nation a Southeast Asian leader in profitable industries such as
rubber and electronics. The government, however, has tried to
include the Malay majority in the country's prosperity. The result
has been a more equal distribution of wealth in Malaysia than in
most countries in the region.

Myanmar Suffers Burma won independence from Britain in 1948 and took the name Myanmar in 1989. Ethnic tensions and a repressive government have plagued the country. The Burmese majority dominated other ethnic groups. The harsh military government limited foreign trade, and living standards remained low.

Under mounting pressure, the military held elections in1990. When an opposition party won the election, the military rejected the results. It put the opposition leader, **Aung San Suu Kyi,** (awn sahn soo chee) under house arrest, and jailed, killed, or exiled many opponents. In 1991, Suu Kyi won the Nobel Peace Prize for her "nonviolent struggle for democracy and human rights." For twenty years, the military has silenced demands for new elections and crushed peaceful demonstrations by Buddhist monks. It even prevented humanitarian aid from reaching areas of Myanmar that were devastated by a cyclone in 2008.

 **Checkpoint**   How did Malaysia's approach to ethnic diversity differ from Myanmar's?

Indonesia's Size Poses Challenges

After World War II, the Netherlands attempted to regain power in Indonesia, formerly the Dutch East Indies. The Dutch, however, were forced to give up their possessions when the Indonesian government declared independence in 1949 after the Japanese defeat.

Geography and diversity posed an obstacle to unity in Indonesia. Indonesia includes more than 13,000 islands, many very small but some as large as European nations. Javanese make up almost half of the population, but there are hundreds of other ethnic groups. About 90 percent of Indonesians are Muslims, but the population includes substantial Christian, Buddhist, and Hindu minorities.

Seeking Stability At independence, Indonesia formed a parliamentary government under its first president, **Sukarno.** But Sukarno shifted from democracy to authoritarian rule. In 1967, an army general, **Suharto,** seized power. Suharto claimed that communists were responsible for an earlier attempt by military officers to overthrow the government and ordered the slaughter of hundreds of thousands of communists and suspected communists. For decades, Suharto imposed his will on Indonesia. A financial crisis finally forced Suharto to resign from power in 1998.

Since then, elected governments have worked to build democracy, strengthen the economy, and fight corruption. Indonesia is home to the world's largest Muslim population. But Islamic extremists have challenged Indonesia's long tradition of religious tolerance. Islamic terrorist groups in Indonesia have targeted foreigners and non-Muslims and threatened the stability of the government.

East Timor Fights for Freedom Indonesia seized **East Timor** in 1975, just after it had been granted independence by Portugal. However, most East Timorese wanted independence. For years, the government battled the mostly Catholic East Timorese. East Timor finally won independence from Indonesia in 2002. This very poor new nation struggled to meet its people's need for jobs and decent living standards.

Brunei's Oil Wealth
A few Southeast Asian nations such as Indonesia have oil and gas reserves. This oil well produces revenues for Brunei (broo NY), a tiny kingdom located on the island of Borneo.

RELIGIOUS DIVERSITY IN SOUTHEAST ASIA

Southeast Asia is one of the world's most religiously diverse regions. This diversity is a result of its history as a crossroads between South and East Asia. In some countries, such as Indonesia and the Philippines, religious differences have played a part in civil conflicts. In others, such as Malaysia and Singapore, people of different religions live together in peace.

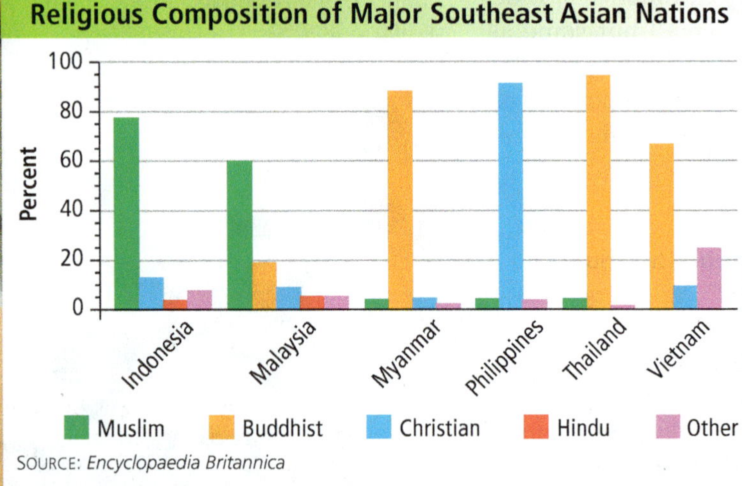

Islam links many Southeast Asians to other parts of the Muslim world. The Indonesian Muslim woman to the left is attending a prayer service.

Religions of Southeast Asia

Religious Composition of Major Southeast Asian Nations

SOURCE: *Encyclopaedia Britannica*

Buddhism plays an important role in the lives of many mainland Southeast Asians. In Thailand, all young Buddhist men are expected to live for at least a short time as monks, such as the ones in this photo.

Thinking Critically

1. **Graph Skills** Based on the graph, are the people in the two photos members of their country's majority or minority religion?
2. **Map Skills** Notice that some religious groups shown on the graph for Malaysia do not have distinct areas on the map. What might explain this?

Ethnic Conflicts and Natural Disasters Religious and ethnic conflicts fueled violence in parts of Indonesia. In the Moluccas, a group of eastern islands, fighting between Muslims and Christians killed thousands. Discrimination against Chinese people led to vicious attacks. Rebels in Papua, on the island of New Guinea, sought independence, as did Muslim separatists in Aceh (AH chay) in the northwest.

Natural disasters have added to Indonesia's troubles. In 2004, a tsunami (tsoo NAH mee), or giant wave, devastated the coast of Aceh and killed more than 100,000 people. The tsunami also ravaged Thailand, Sri Lanka, and other lands around the Indian Ocean. Following the disaster, rebels in Aceh and the Indonesian government signed a peace accord. Helped by international aid donors, they worked together to rebuild Aceh.

✓ **Checkpoint** How has diversity posed challenges to Indonesia?

The Philippines Seeks Democracy

Like Indonesia, the Philippines include thousands of islands with diverse ethnic and religious groups. Catholics are <u>predominant</u>, but many Muslims live in the south. In 1946, the Philippines gained independence after almost 50 years of American rule. American influence remained strong through military and economic aid.

Marcos Becomes a Dictator Although the Filipino constitution set up a democratic government, a wealthy elite controlled politics and the economy. The peasant majority was poor. For years, the government battled Huks (hooks), local communists with strong peasant support. **Ferdinand Marcos,** elected president in 1965, abandoned democracy. He became a dictator and cracked down on basic freedoms. He even had **Benigno Aquino** (beh NEE nyoh ah KEE noh), a popular rival, murdered.

Filipinos Demand Democracy When Marcos finally held elections in 1986, voters chose **Corazon Aquino** (kawr ah SOHN), the widow of the slain Benigno. Marcos tried to deny the results, but massive protests forced him to resign during the "people power" revolution. Under Aquino and her successors, this fragile democracy survived, despite many political scandals. Economic growth was limited, and poverty remained widespread. With the highest birth rate in Asia, the population continues to rise rapidly, straining already limited resources.

Clashes With Rebels Continue For decades, various rebel groups have waged guerrilla wars across the Philippines. Some rebels were communists. Others were Muslim separatists. Some Muslim rebels have links to international terrorist groups such as Al Qaeda. In the early 2000s, the Filipino government accepted aid from its ally, the United States, to fight rebels and pursue President George W. Bush's "war on terror."

 **Checkpoint** Why has the Philippines had trouble preserving its democracy?

Vocabulary Builder

<u>predominant</u>—(pree DAHM uh nunt) *adj.* most common or numerous

---

SECTION 2 Assessment

Progress Monitoring *Online*
For: Self-quiz with vocabulary practice
Web Code: naa-3121

Terms, People, and Places

1. For each term, person, or place listed at the beginning of the section, write a sentence explaining its significance.

Note Taking

2. **Reading Skill: Understand Effects** Use your completed concept web to answer the Focus Question: What challenges did Southeast Asian nations face after winning independence?

Comprehension and Critical Thinking

3. **Make Comparisons** Why did policies toward ethnic diversity lead to prosperity in Malaysia but to conflict in other parts of Southeast Asia?
4. **Synthesize Information** How have religious and ethnic diversity affected the recent history of Indonesia?
5. **Draw Inferences** What conclusions might separatist movements in Indonesia draw from East Timor's successful independence struggle?
6. **Recognize Cause and Effect** What causes explain the overthrow of Ferdinand Marcos?

● Writing About History

Quick Write: Evaluate Your Topic To write a compare-and-contrast essay, you can organize your ideas in a point-by-point comparison. In this section, you learned that Malaysia and Indonesia are both ethnically diverse. Draft two sentences for an essay. In each sentence, compare or contrast an aspect of ethnic diversity in one of these countries with a related aspect of ethnic diversity in the other.

Britain's Prince Philip and Queen Elizabeth II congratulate Jomo Kenyatta as his nation, Kenya, gains independence in 1963.

WITNESS HISTORY 🔊 AUDIO

Kenya Achieves Independence

A scene from a novel by Ngugi wa Thiong'o describes the moment of independence in Nairobi, Kenya's capital:

❝A minute before midnight, lights were put out. . . . In the dark, the Union Jack [British flag] was quickly lowered. When next the lights came on the new Kenya flag was . . . waving in the air.❞
—Ngugi wa Thiong'o, *A Grain of Wheat*

Kenya was one of more than 40 African nations that gained independence from European colonial powers in the decades after World War II.

Focus Question What challenges did new African nations face?

African Nations Gain Independence

Objectives
- Describe how Africa's colonies gained independence.
- Explain how Africans built new nations.
- Analyze the recent histories of five African nations.

Terms, People, and Places

savannas	Mobutu Sese Seko
Kwame Nkrumah	Islamist
Jomo Kenyatta	Katanga
coup d'état	Biafra

Note Taking

Reading Skill: Identify Causes and Effects Fill in a concept web like this one to keep track of the causes and effects of independence in Africa.

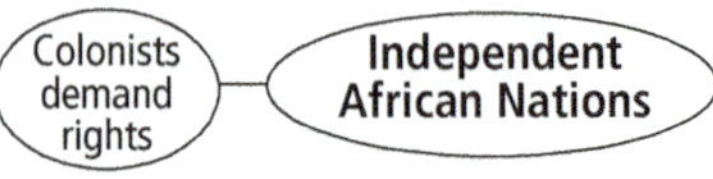

In new nations all across Africa, crowds celebrated their freedom, while bands played each country's new national anthem. However, even as independence celebrations took place, the new nations of Africa faced tough challenges.

New Nations Emerge in Africa

After World War II, European colonial powers could no longer afford to hold onto their colonies. As nationalist demands forced Britain to withdraw from India, African leaders, too, pressed for independence.

A Geographically Diverse Continent Africa is the world's second-largest continent, more than three times the size of the United States. Tropical rain forests cover central Africa's Congo Basin and coastal West Africa. Vast **savannas,** or grasslands with scattered trees, make up interior West Africa, East Africa, and much of central and southern Africa. Africa has the world's largest desert—the Sahara—in the north and the smaller Kalahari Desert in the south, as well as fertile coastal strips in North and South Africa.

Africa's people are concentrated in the most fertile areas, such as the savanna and forest regions of Nigeria and the moist highlands of East Africa. These regions produce enough food to support large populations. Like people in other parts of the world, however, millions of Africans were migrating, or moving, from rural areas to cities.

Africa has rich deposits of minerals such as gold ore, copper ore, and diamonds. Some African nations produce valuable cash crops, including coffee and cacao—used to make chocolate. Some regions also have large oil reserves. European powers had established colonies in Africa to tap into these natural resources.

Nationalist Leaders Demand Freedom By the 1950s, nationalist movements in Africa had grown stronger. Skilled organizers such as Kwame Nkrumah (KWAH may un KROO muh) in Gold Coast (later Ghana), Jomo Kenyatta in Kenya, and Léopold Senghor (sahn GAWR) in Senegal led independence movements in their own countries.

Most African nations won independence through largely peaceful means. Drained by World War II, European powers had few resources to resist the pressure to give up their colonial empires. The struggle for freedom turned violent, however, in a few colonies where large numbers of Europeans had settled, such as Kenya and Algeria.

 **Checkpoint** Why did some African countries have to fight for independence?

New Nations Build Governments

Some new nations enjoyed peace and had democratic governments. Others were plunged into crisis by civil war, military rule, or corrupt dictators. In recent decades, a number of African nations have taken steps toward democracy.

Challenges to Unity The new nations of Africa faced many difficulties, including the need to unify their people. European colonial powers had drawn boundaries around their colonies without regard to the many rival ethnic groups living in a particular region. At independence, most African nations included a patchwork of peoples with different languages, religions, and traditions. Within these new nations, people often felt their first loyalty was to their own ethnic group, not to a distant national government. As a result, conflict between different ethnic groups plagued many new nations..

Dictators Gain Power Many leaders of the new nations were heroes of the liberation struggle. Some chose to build one-party states. These leaders claimed that multiparty systems encouraged disunity. In time, these one-party governments became repressive, and some liberation leaders became dictators. Dictators often used their positions to enrich themselves and their supporters at the expense of the nation.

When bad or corrupt governments led to civil unrest, the military seized power in many countries. More than half of all African nations suffered military coups (kooz). A coup, or coup d'état (koo day TAH) is the forcible overthrow of a government. Some military rulers were brutal tyrants. Others tried to end corruption and improve conditions. Military leaders usually promised to restore civilian rule. But in many cases, they only surrendered power when they were toppled by another coup.

Moves Toward Democracy By the 1990s, some African nations were moving away from strongman rule. Western

Mineral Resources
A miner in the West African nation of Sierra Leone sifts gravel to find rough diamonds. Minerals are important to the economy of many African nations.

governments and lenders, such as the World Bank, demanded political reforms before granting loans. In response, some governments allowed opposition parties to emerge and expanded freedom of expression. In nations such as Nigeria, Tanzania, and Benin, multiparty elections were held, removing long-ruling leaders from office.

The Superpowers Compete for Influence Even after African nations won independence, colonial powers and foreign companies often retained control of businesses and resources in these former colonies. Many new nations remained dependent on their former colonial rulers for aid, trade, and investment.

The new nations were also buffeted by the Cold War. Both the United States and the Soviet Union competed for military and strategic advantage through alliances with several African countries. The United States, for example, backed **Mobutu Seso Seko,** the dictator of Zaire (now called the Democratic Republic of Congo). It wanted to counter Soviet influence in nearby Angola. During the 1970s, the United States backed Somalia, while the Soviet Union supported neighboring Ethiopia. Both African countries were important because they controlled access to the Red Sea, a vital world-shipping route.

 **Checkpoint** Why have some African nations taken steps toward democracy in recent years?

The Stories of Five African Nations

While the new nations of Africa faced many of the same challenges, each nation had a unique history. To gain a better understanding of the process of nation-building in Africa, we will examine the recent histories of five important nations.

Ghana In 1957, Ghana was the first African nation south of the Sahara to win independence. Britain had called this colony Gold Coast, for its rich mineral resources. Under independence leader Kwame Nkrumah, it took the name Ghana, after the ancient West African kingdom.

As president, Nkrumah supported socialism and government ownership of major industries. He backed the building of a huge dam to provide electric power, but the project left Ghana with massive debts. Nkrumah's government became increasingly corrupt and dictatorial. In 1966, Nkrumah was toppled by the first of several military coups.

This pattern repeated itself in many new African nations. Large costly projects, often poorly planned, left many countries in debt to foreign lenders. Coups and dictators became common.

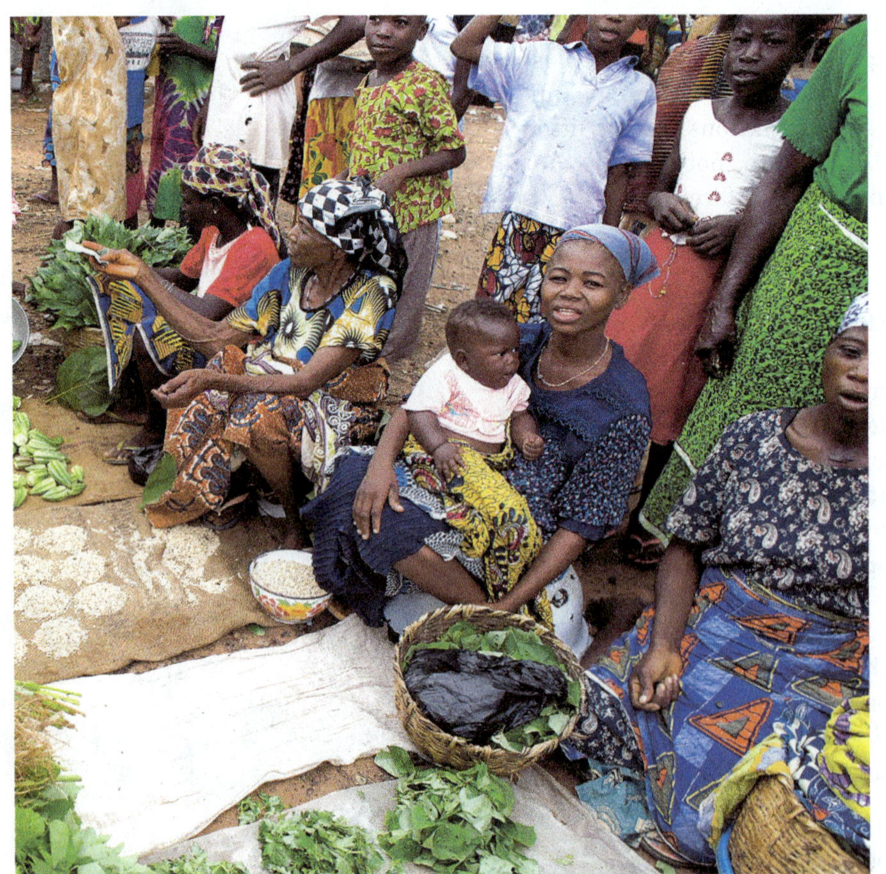

Market Women in Ghana
In West African countries such as Ghana, women have traditionally sold goods in the markets. These women wait for customers with a display of food and other goods. *Why might political candidates in Ghana and elsewhere seek support from local market women?*

Independence in Africa

Map Skills From the late 1800s until the 1950s and 1960s, most African countries were colonies of European powers, which drew their borders. Most African nations gained independence during the 1950s and 1960s.

1. **Locate** (a) Kenya (b) Democratic Republic of the Congo (c) Angola (d) Ghana

2. **Regions** Which was the last of the Democratic Republic of the Congo's neighbors to gain independence?

3. **Draw Conclusions** When must the Cold War conflict involving independent Angola have taken place?

In the 1980s, Jerry Rawlings, a military officer, took power in a coup. He strengthened the economy and moved Ghana toward democracy. In 1992, Rawlings allowed multiparty elections and was chosen president. Other elections followed. Although the economy suffered from falling prices for cocoa and gold, its main exports, Ghana made progress toward improving life for its people. The recent discovery of offshore oil raised hopes for more economic growth.

Kenya While Ghana made a peaceful transition to freedom, Kenya faced an armed struggle. A large number of white settlers had built successful plantations on the fertile highlands once occupied by the Kikuyu (kee KOO yoo), Kenya's largest ethnic group. White Kenyans had passed laws to <u>ensure</u> their domination over the black majority. Nationalist leader and Kikuyu spokesman Jomo Kenyatta had long sought justice for the black majority and called for nonviolent means to end oppressive laws.

In the 1950s, some black Kenyans turned to guerrilla warfare, attacking and killing white settlers. The British called them Mau Mau. Claiming that he was a secret leader of the Mau Mau, the British imprisoned Kenyatta. Both sides committed terrible atrocities during this period, and thousands of Kikuyu were killed. In 1963, the British finally withdrew, and Kenyatta became the first leader of an independent Kenya.

Kenyatta and his successor dominated the country for decades. They limited freedom of expression and resisted free elections. Since the 1990s, Kenya has held multiparty elections, but corruption remained widespread. In 2007, a disputed election sparked violence and ethnic unrest. The conflict hurt tourism—one of Kenya's largest industries.

Algeria Like Kenya, the French colony of Algeria had a large population of European settlers. Over one million French people called Algeria home and were determined to remain part of France. The French government, which had recently lost its Asian colony, Vietnam, also wanted to hold onto Algeria, especially after deposits of oil and natural gas were discovered there. As a result, the struggle for independence turned violent in the 1950s.

BIOGRAPHY

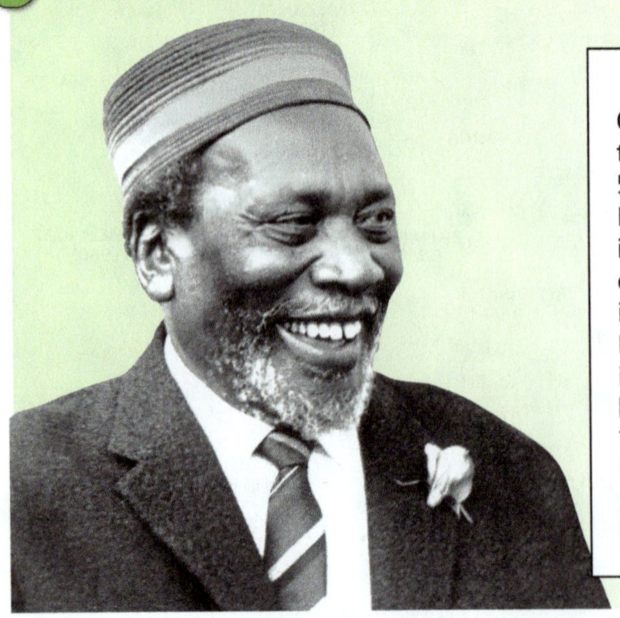

Jomo Kenyatta

On December 12, 1963, Jomo Kenyatta (c. 1894–1978) watched the flag of an independent Kenya rise above Nairobi. After 50 years, his dream of independence for Kenya had come true. Early in life, Kenyatta was drawn to the nationalist cause. "The land is ours," declared Kenyatta, who was a Kikuyu. "When Europeans came, they kept us back and took our land." Kenyatta spent time in England, where he met Mahatma Gandhi in 1932. Back in Kenya, he helped organize nonviolent protests against British injustices. Later, he led the drive for independence. When Kenya became a republic in 1964, Kenyatta was elected its first president. To black Kenyans, Kenyatta was known as "Mzee," or "Wise Elder." Kenyans celebrate October 20, the date of his arrest by the British, as Kenyatta Day. **What role do you think national heroes play in helping to form a nation's identity?**

Algerian nationalists set up the National Liberation Front, which turned to guerrilla warfare to win freedom. From 1954 to 1962, more than one million Algerians were killed in this bloody conflict. When public opinion in France finally turned against the war, Algeria won independence.

Algeria's oil and gas resources have helped it economically. Politically, it has suffered through periods of military rule and internal conflict. During the 1970s, the government nationalized, or took over, foreign-owned companies and created a command economy. Since the 1980s, Algeria has been moving toward a market economy.

By the 1990s, a growing struggle had erupted between the military and **Islamists,** people who want a government based on Islamic law and beliefs. In 1992, the Algerian government allowed free elections. When an Islamist party won, the military rejected the results. For seven years, civil war raged between Islamist militants and the military, leaving as many as 150,000 dead. The violence slowed after 1999, but tensions remained.

Democratic Republic of Congo The Democratic Republic of Congo (or Congo) covers a vast region of central Africa. It includes a million square miles of rain forest and savanna centered on the Congo River basin. Congo was a Belgian colony, and the Belgians were eager to keep control of Congo's rich resources, such as copper and diamonds.

When Congo gained independence in 1960, it was not prepared for self-government. The new nation included 14 million people from more than 200 separate groups. Competing economic interests and rival political leaders soon plunged Congo into civil war when the copper-rich **Katanga** province broke away. Belgian mining companies supported Katanga, hoping to control its mineral resources. The Cold War superpowers backed rival leaders, further complicating the fighting. The United Nations ended the Katanga rebellion in 1963.

An Election Celebration
Citizens of Mauritania, in West Africa, celebrate the reelection of the country's president in 2003. *Why did many nations have difficulty building democratic governments?*

In 1965, Colonel Joseph Mobutu, later known as Mobutu Sese Seko, seized power. For 32 years, Mobutu's harsh, corrupt rule brought poverty and unrest to Congo. Rebels finally forced Mobutu from power in 1997. But civil war again raged as rival military leaders battled to control Congo's mineral riches.

The country's first free elections in 41 years brought Joseph Kabila to power in 2006. As on and off violence continued in the eastern region, Kabila had to reduce corruption, calm ethnic tensions, protect Congo's mineral resources, and heal the scars caused by decades of war.

Nigeria Nigeria, on the coast of West Africa, includes diverse people and climates. Nigeria's huge population is the largest in Africa. Its people belong to more than 250 ethnic groups, speak many languages, and practice different religions. The dominant groups are the mainly Christian Ibo (EE boh) and Yoruba (YOH roo buh) in the south, and the Muslim Hausa (HOW suh) in the north.

Nigeria won independence peacefully from Britain in 1960. The next year, oil was discovered, raising hopes for the country's economic future. Instead, the country faced military coups, corruption, and economic crises. In 1966, the Ibo people in the oil-rich south rebelled and set up the independent Republic of **Biafra.** A brutal civil war led to famine, the death of an estimated half million people, and the end of Biafra's independence.

Between 1996 and 1999, the military was in and out of power in Nigeria. Military leaders ruled with an iron hand but failed to improve Nigeria's government or its economy. In 1999, Nigeria again held elections. A new civilian government introduced reforms to strengthen the economy and restore political freedom.

Because Nigeria relied heavily on oil exports, it was affected by the rise and fall of oil prices. Nigeria also faced ethnic and religious violence. In the north, Islamists wanted strict Sharia law. In the oil-producing Niger Delta region, local people were bitter about the environmental damage caused by oil drilling and the huge profits going to foreign companies. Armed groups attacked pipelines and held foreign oil workers for ransom.

✔ **Checkpoint** How did Katanga and Biafra reflect the challenges that new African nations faced after independence?

Nigeria's Oil Industry
This oil worker is drilling for oil in southeastern Nigeria. Nigeria's vital oil industry is threatened by conflict in this oil-producing region.

SECTION **3** Assessment

Terms, People, and Places

1. Place each of the key terms at the beginning of the section into one of the following categories: politics, economy, or geography. Write a sentence for each term explaining your choice.

Note Taking

2. **Reading Skill: Identify Causes and Effects** Use your completed concept web to answer the Focus Question: What challenges did new African nations face?

Comprehension and Critical Thinking

3. **Make Comparisons** Why did some countries gain independence peacefully, while others faced violent struggles?

4. **Identify Central Issues** Why did the Cold War superpowers seek alliances with African nations?

5. **Express Problems Clearly** Based on what you have read about Algeria, what problems caused the civil war in Algeria?

6. **Draw Conclusions** How have religious and ethnic divisions affected Nigeria's history?

● Writing About History

Quick Write: Provide Elaboration To write a compare-and-contrast essay, you need to provide examples that support the main point of the essay. Suppose that the point of your essay is to compare and contrast challenges faced by Algeria and Nigeria since independence. Draft two sentences for an essay. In each sentence, give examples that compare or contrast a challenge faced by these countries.

Kwame Nkrumah: *Autobiography*

Kwame Nkrumah led the people of Gold Coast in their quest for independence from Britain. After succeeding in 1957, Nkrumah became the first prime minister and renamed the country Ghana. In this excerpt from his *Autobiography,* Nkrumah speaks of the need to establish economic independence as a means of maintaining political independence. Nkrumah describes the difficult work of building an independent economy.

▲ Prime Minister Kwame Nkrumah of Ghana

Independence for the Gold Coast was my aim. It was a colony, and I have always regarded colonialism as the policy by which a foreign power binds territories to herself by political ties with the primary object of promoting her own economic advantage. No one need be surprised if this system has led to disturbances and political tension in many territories. There are few people who would not rid themselves of such domination if they could. . . .

I saw that the whole solution to [our] problem lay in political freedom for our people, for it is only when a people are politically free that other races can give them the respect that is due to them. It is impossible to talk of equality of races in any other terms. No people without a government of their own can expect to be treated on the same level as peoples of independent sovereign[1] states. It is far better to be free to govern or misgovern yourself than to be governed by anybody else. . . .

Once this freedom is gained, a greater task comes into view. All dependent[2] territories are backward in education, in science, in agriculture, and in industry. The economic independence that should follow and maintain political independence demands every effort from the people, a total mobilization of brain and manpower resources. What other countries have taken three hundred years or more to achieve, a once dependent territory must try to accomplish in a generation if it is to survive. . . .

▲ Ghana's leaders—including Kwame Nkrumah, at center—celebrate Ghana's independence in 1957.

Thinking Critically

1. **Identify Point of View** What does Nkrumah think the people of a dependent territory must do before they can achieve economic independence?
2. **Draw Inferences** Based on Nkrumah's remarks, what makes economic independence difficult for newly independent nations to achieve?

1. **sovereign** (SAHV run) *adj.* not subject to any other power
2. **dependent** (dee PEN dunt) *adj.* subject to the power of another

Islamic ornamental writing from a mosque in Iran

Egypt's leader, Gamal Abdel Nasser, greets children in 1956.

Remembering Nasser

As a young boy in Syria, Nasser Rabbat recalls seeing the Arab leader, Gamal Abdel Nasser.

66 One of my earliest memories dates back to the winter of 1960 when I was almost four years old. I remember . . . screaming with the crowd around us 'Nasser, Nasser.' . . . I had been taught . . . to be proud of . . . Nasser, 'the unifier of the Arabs' and 'the leader of our new renaissance.' 99
—Nasser Rabbat, "On being named Nasser"

In the decades after World War II, nationalism was a major force shaping Middle Eastern nations from Egypt and Israel to Turkey and Iran.

Focus Question What were some similarities and differences in the nations of the Middle East?

The Modern Middle East

Objectives

- Analyze the diversity of the Middle East and the political challenges it has faced.
- Explain the region's conflicts over resources and religion.
- Outline the history of nation-building in three Middle Eastern nations.

Terms, People, and Places

kibbutz
secular
hejab
Suez Canal
Gamal Abdel Nasser

Anwar Sadat
Mohammad Mosaddeq
Ruhollah Khomeini
theocracy

Note Taking

Reading Skill: Identify Causes and Effects Fill in a concept web like this one to keep track of events in the Middle East since 1945.

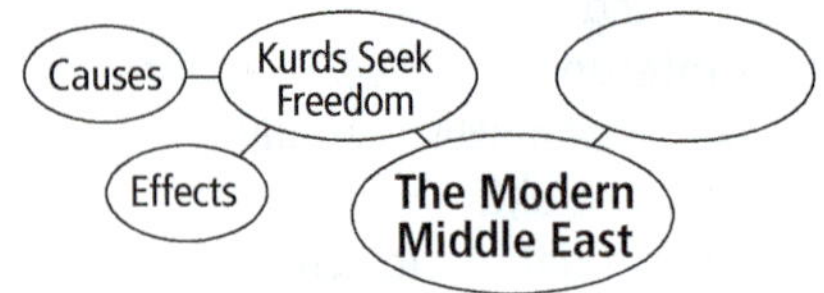

In the 1950s, leaders like Egypt's Gamal Abdel Nasser set out to build strong nations across the Middle East. Most Middle Eastern countries were poor—only a few had rich oil reserves. Autocratic governments and internal divisions hindered progress throughout the region.

Diversity Brings Challenges

The Middle East, as we use the term in this chapter, is the region stretching from Egypt in the west to Iran in the east and from Turkey in the north to the Arabian Peninsula in the south. Though most people in the region today are Muslims, there are also Christian communities and the predominantly Jewish nation of Israel. Most countries have large ethnic or religious minorities.

Mandates Gain Independence After World War I, Britain and France were given mandates over parts of the Middle East. During the 1930s and 1940s, nationalists demanded an end to European control, and the mandates became the independent states of Iraq, Syria, Lebanon, Jordan, and Israel.

Kurds Seek Rights In the Middle East, as elsewhere, new nations faced challenges from ethnic minorities that demanded self rule, or even independence. The Kurds are an ethnic group with their own language and culture, and are an important minority in Turkey, Iran, and Iraq.

Kurds faced discrimination and harsh treatment, especially in Iraq and Turkey. In Turkey, Kurdish rebels resisted government efforts to suppress their culture. Thousands died fighting the government. In Iraq, a Kurdish rebellion after the 1991 Gulf War was brutally suppressed. As you will read, Kurds form one of the three main groups sharing power in Iraq. However, some Kurds still want their own state.

Israel Is Founded As you have learned, Britain supported a Jewish national homeland in part of its Palestine Mandate. The horrific experience of Jews in the Holocaust added to worldwide support for a Jewish home-land. Jews, including many Holocaust survivors, sought to migrate there after World War II. In 1947, the UN drew up a plan to divide the Palestine Mandate into an Arab and a Jewish state. Jews accepted the plan, but Arabs rejected it. They felt that all of Palestine should belong to them.

After Britain withdrew from Palestine in 1948, Jews proclaimed the independent State of Israel. Arab states launched the first of several wars against Israel but were defeated. Israel developed rapidly. A skilled workforce built businesses. Kibbutzim produced crops for export. A **kibbutz** (kih BOOTS) is a collective farm. Israel attracted Jews from around the world, including Jews expelled from other Middle Eastern lands.

The conflicts of 1948 created enormous refugee problems. As a result of the war, hundreds of thousands of Palestinian Arabs fled their homes

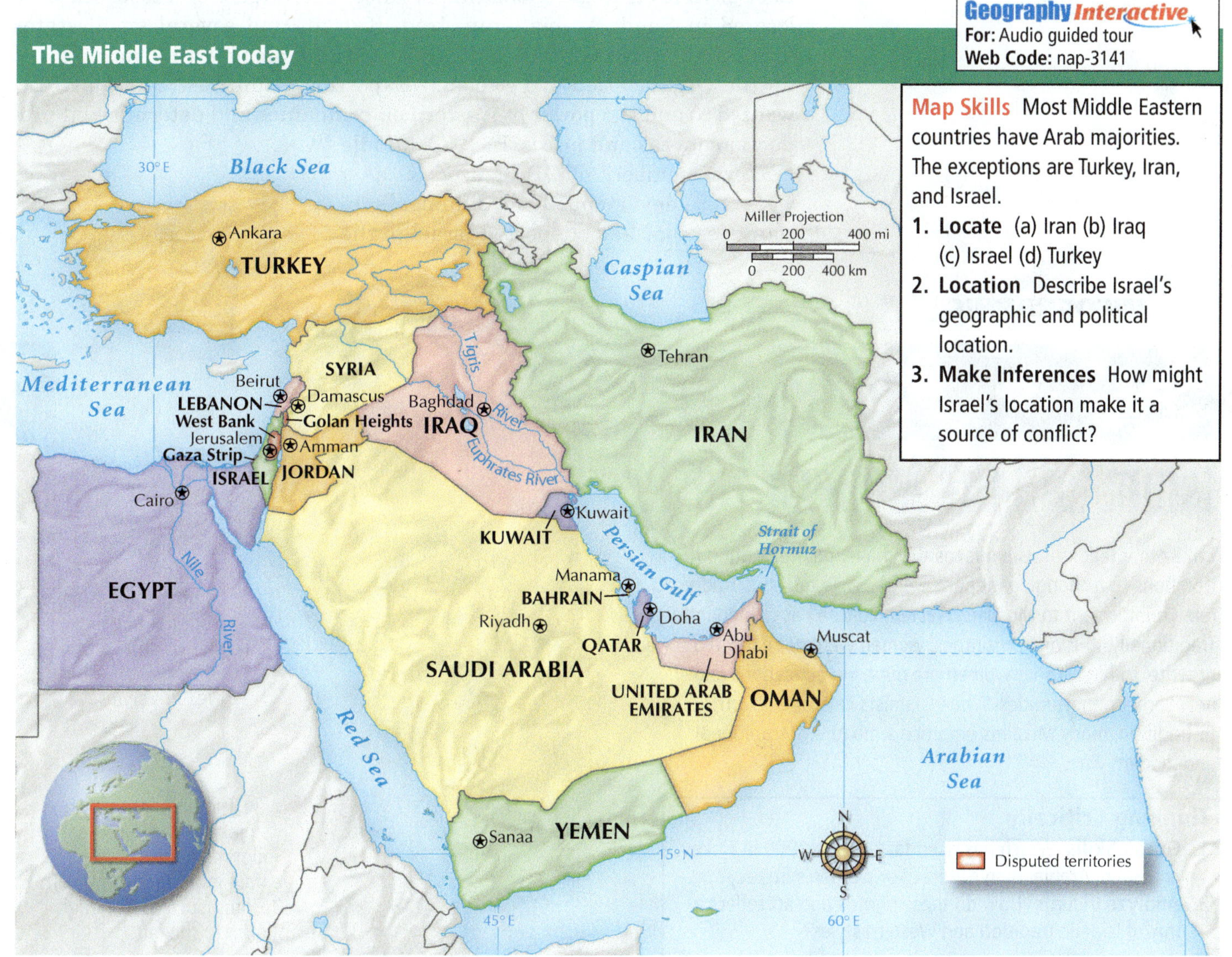

Geography *Interactive*
For: Audio guided tour
Web Code: nap-3141

Map Skills Most Middle Eastern countries have Arab majorities. The exceptions are Turkey, Iran, and Israel.
1. **Locate** (a) Iran (b) Iraq (c) Israel (d) Turkey
2. **Location** Describe Israel's geographic and political location.
3. **Make Inferences** How might Israel's location make it a source of conflict?

in Israeli territory. The UN set up camps in neighboring areas to house them. Hundreds of thousands of Jews from Arab lands were also driven from their homes. Both sides feel embittered by the displacements.

Political Systems Limit Freedom Most Middle Eastern nations have had autocratic governments. In some countries, nationalist military leaders seized power. In other countries, such as Jordan and Saudi Arabia, hereditary monarchs remained in power. Only Israel and Turkey had stable multiparty democratic systems by 2005.

✔ **Checkpoint** Why did many people around the world support a Jewish homeland in Palestine?

Sources of Conflict

Some Middle Eastern nations sit atop vast oil and gas reserves. These oil-rich nations have prospered. Although these countries have helped their less fortunate neighbors, many Middle Eastern nations struggled economically. Meanwhile, Muslims have disagreed over the role of Islam in a modern society.

Supplying the World With Oil The huge oil resources of the Middle East gave it strategic, global importance. The largest oil resources were located in Saudi Arabia, Iran, Iraq, Kuwait, and several small states along the Persian Gulf. In 1960, these nations, along with Venezuela, set up the Organization of Petroleum Exporting Countries (OPEC). OPEC wanted to end the power of Western oil companies and determine oil production quotas and prices. In 1973, Middle Eastern members of OPEC used oil as a weapon. They stopped oil shipments to countries that had supported Israel in the

Islam and the Modern World

Like other religions, Islam faces the challenge of adapting its traditions to a changing modern world. While religious traditions remain important to Muslims, Western culture has gained influence. Traditionally, in Islamic countries, women were not expected to read or write. Today, Muslim women are pursuing educations and new career opportunities. While Islamists call for a return to tradition, many Muslims embrace a mixture of traditional and modern ways.

The Iraqi artist ▲ Hassan Massoudy combines the Islamic tradition of calligraphy, or ornamental writing, with abstract Western styles.

◀ The basic principles of Islam, such as pilgrimage and prayer, remain important to modern Muslims, such as the Iraqi pilgrim to the left.

Thinking Critically
1. **Graph Skills** Which has risen faster since 1990 in Turkey and Saudi Arabia, men's literacy or women's literacy?
2. **Analyze Visuals** How do these photos and art reflect a mix of Islamic tradition and Western styles?

Yom Kippur War. This oil embargo triggered a worldwide recession. Since then, OPEC has focused on setting production quotas.

Islam in the Modern World After independence, some Middle Eastern countries adopted Western-style **secular,** or nonreligious, governments. At the same time, Western cultural influences grew. In cities, people bought imported goods from the West, wore Western fashions, and watched American television shows and movies.

Some Muslims claimed that secular Western culture was undermining Islamic society. They called for a return to Sharia, or Islamic law based on the Quran. These conservative reformers, known as Islamists, blamed social and economic ills on the West. Only a renewed commitment to Islamic doctrine, they declared, could improve conditions in the Muslim world. Many Muslims welcomed the Islamist movement as a way to cope with rapid social and economic changes. Although some people advocated violence to achieve their goals, most Muslims opposed Islamic extremists.

Changes Affect Women's Lives Conditions for women vary greatly across the Middle East. In most countries, women won equality before the law. Educated women entered professions such as law and medicine. In Turkey, Egypt, and Syria, many urban women gave up the **hejab,** or traditional Muslim headscarf, or wearing loose, ankle-length garments meant to conceal. Some women, however, embraced these traditions as a symbol of their Islamic faith.

In religiously conservative countries like Saudi Arabia and Iran, women must follow Islamic traditions, such as wearing the hejab. In many Middle Eastern countries, girls are less likely to attend school than boys, because of a traditional belief that girls do not need a formal education for their expected roles as wives and mothers. Women's rights movements, however, have challenged these traditions.

✓ **Checkpoint** Why did Islamists oppose secular government and culture in the Muslim world?

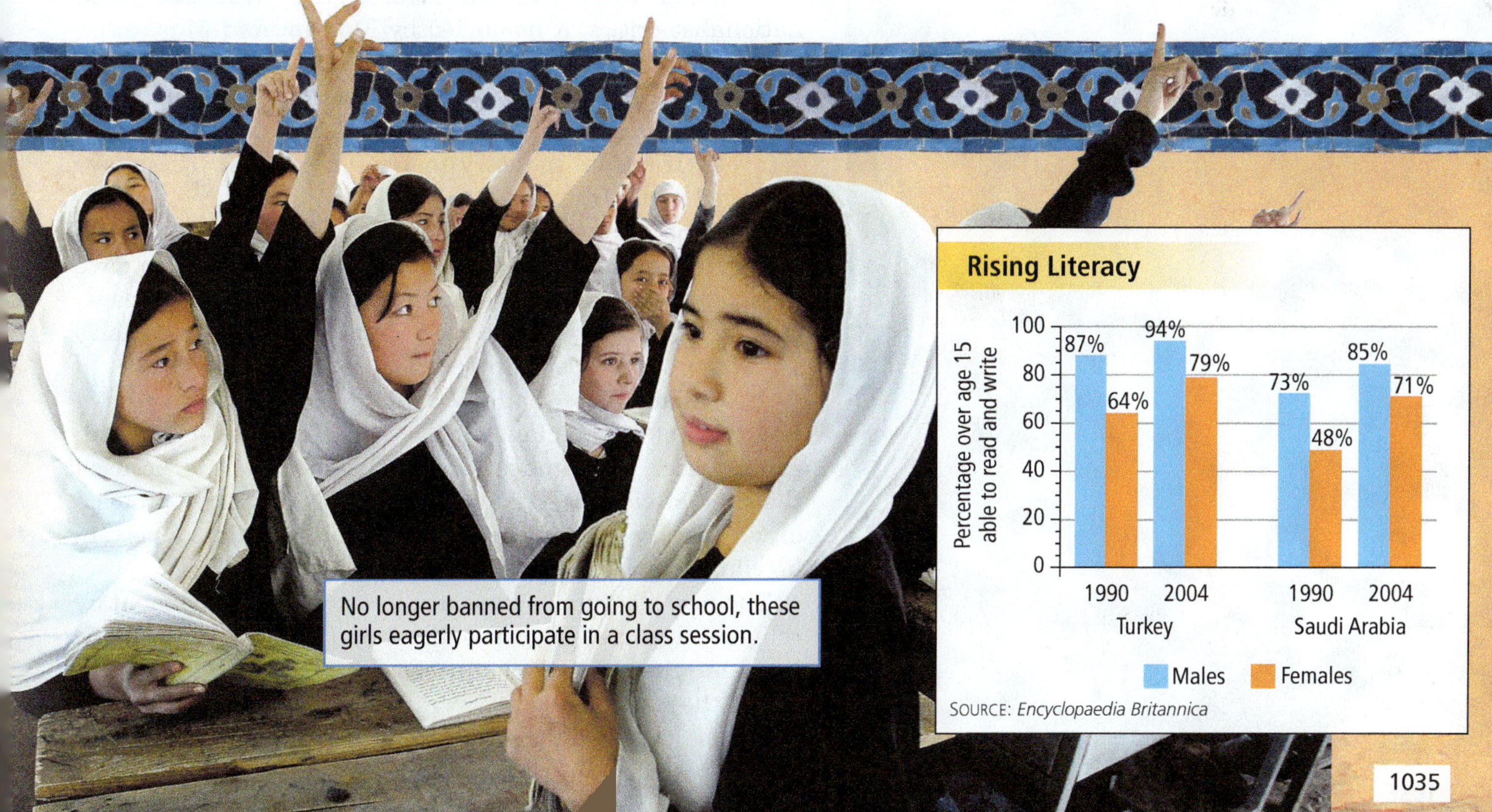

No longer banned from going to school, these girls eagerly participate in a class session.

Building Nations in the Middle East

Across the Middle East, leaders sought to build strong and prosperous nations. However, in the years since World War II, each nation has faced different challenges.

Egypt, a Leader in the Arab World Egypt has the largest population of the Arab nations. While most of Egypt is desert, its large population is crammed into the narrow Nile River valley. Egypt's location is strategically important, because it shares a long border with Israel and controls the Suez Canal, which links Europe with Asia and East Africa.

In 1952, Gamal Abdel Nasser seized power in Egypt. Determined to modernize Egypt and stop Western domination, Nasser nationalized the Suez Canal in 1956, ending British and French control. Although Britain and France responded militarily, the United States and the Soviet Union forced them to withdraw. Nasser's Arab nationalism made him popular throughout the Arab world. Nasser led two unsuccessful wars against Israel. To counter U.S. support for Israel, Egypt relied on Soviet aid. Egypt's foreign relations thus took on Cold War significance.

In 1979, Nasser's successor, Anwar Sadat, became the first Arab leader to make peace with Israel. Sadat also weakened ties with the Soviet Union and sought U.S. aid. However, Islamists denounced the undemocratic government's failure to end corruption and poverty. In 1981, Muslim fundamentalists assassinated Sadat. Under Sadat's appointed successor, Hosni Mubarak, extremists turned to terrorist attacks, and harsh government crackdowns tended to increase support for Islamists.

Iran's Islamic Revolution Because of its vast oil fields, Iran was a focus of Cold War interest. Iran's ruler, Shah Mohammad Reza Pahlavi, favored the West but faced nationalist critics at home, led by Mohammad Mosaddeq (MAW sah dek). When Mosaddeq was elected prime minister in 1951, he nationalized the foreign-owned oil industry. With American help, the shah ousted Mosaddeq and returned Iran's oil industry to Western control. This move outraged many Iranians.

Over the next decades, the shah used oil wealth to build industries and redistribute land to peasants. He also gave new rights to women. Opposition to the shah grew, especially among the Islamic clergy. In response, the shah's secret police terrorized critics.

The shah's foes rallied behind Ayatollah Ruhollah Khomeini (ROO hoh lah koh MAY nee). The ayatollah, a religious leader, condemned Western influences and accused the shah of violating Islamic law. In 1979, massive protests drove the shah from power. Khomeini and his supporters proclaimed an Islamic republic.

The new government was a theocracy, or government by religious leaders. They ran the country based on Islamic law. Like the shah, they silenced critics. In 1979, Islamists seized the American embassy in the capital and held 52 hostages for more than a year. The new Islamic republic soon

An Islamist Government
Iran's political leaders, who are Muslim clergymen, gather in 2003 to commemorate the death of Ayatollah Khomeini, a religious leader and the founder of Iran's Islamist government. The leaders are seated beneath a giant portrait of Khomeini. *How does promoting the memory of Khomeini help to justify rule by religious leaders?*

faced a long, bloody war with its neighbor, Iraq, and tense relations with the West. The United States imposed economic sanctions and accused Iran of backing terrorists. After the 2003 U.S. occupation of Iraq, American officials accused Iran of providing weapons to Iraqi fighters for use against U.S. forces. Iran was also accused of using nuclear research as a cover for developing nuclear weapons.

Oil, Religion, and Threats to Stability Saudi Arabia, a vast desert land, has the world's largest oil reserves. It also includes Islam's holy land. Since the 1920s, kings from the Sa'ud (sah OOD) family have ruled Saudi Arabia. They justify their rule by their commitment to the strict Wahhabi sect of Sunni Islam.

However, Saudi Arabia's economic development after World War II depended on massive oil exports to the Western world. In return, Saudi leaders relied on the military support of the United States. Although Saudi Arabia joined the OPEC oil embargo in 1973, the nation's rulers quickly returned to their cooperative relationship with the West.

To build support within the country, the royal family backed fundamentalist religious leaders. However, some of these leaders and their followers criticized the kingdom's close ties to the West. They also charged that Western influence in the kingdom violated Islamic principles.

Increasingly, opponents of the kingdom's Western ties adopted violent or terrorist tactics. Attacks on western targets included an attack on a U.S. military compound in 1996 and another on a U.S. consulate in 2004. These attacks threatened to disrupt the Saudi oil industry, which depends on Western expertise. Some feared that growing unrest could threaten the country's ability to supply oil vital to the world's economy.

Other oil-rich monarchies along the Persian Gulf, such as Kuwait, Bahrain, Qatar, and the United Arab Emirates, face similar threats. In Kuwait, Qatar, and the U.A.E., foreign citizens are a majority of the population. In Bahrain, there has been growing opposition among the majority of the people, who follow Shiite Islam, toward Bahrain's royal family, who follow the Sunni branch of Islam.

✔ **Checkpoint** What were Ayatollah Khomeini's reasons for opposing the shah?

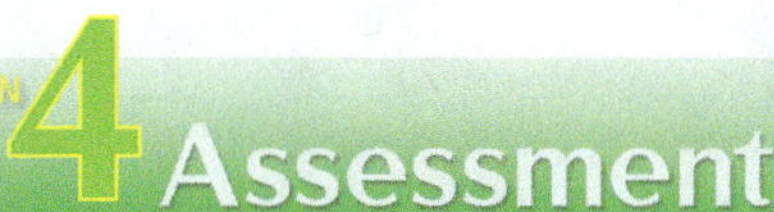

Terms, People, and Places

1. For each term, person, or place listed in the beginning of the section, write a sentence explaining its significance.

Note Taking

2. **Reading Skill: Identify Causes and Effects** Use your completed concept web to answer the Focus Question: What were some main similarities and differences in the nations of the Middle East?

Comprehension and Critical Thinking

3. **Summarize** How was the Holocaust connected to the birth of Israel?
4. **Identify Central Issues** What changes in government policies did the Islamists seek?
5. **Draw Conclusions** Why did Egypt attract the interest of the superpowers during the Cold War?
6. **Synthesize Information** How has the Saudi royal family's support for fundamentalism made their kingdom more unstable in recent years?

● Writing About History

Quick Write: Revise Your Writing When you write a compare-and-contrast essay, combining short sentences can improve your writing. Write a short sentence that states a fact about a Middle Eastern country. Write a second sentence stating a similar or different fact about another Middle Eastern country. Revise your sentences by joining them into a single sentence that compares or contrasts these facts, using conjunctions such as *while, whereas, yet, both, and,* or *also.*

Quick Study Guide

Progress Monitoring *Online*
For: Self-test with vocabulary practice
Web Code: naa-3151

■ Common Themes in New Nations

- Borders drawn by European colonial powers left nations with diverse religions and ethnic groups.
- Ethnic and religious diversity has brought conflict.
- Military coups, one-party systems, and dictatorships kept some countries from achieving democracy.
- Citizens and foreign lenders have forced former dictatorships to hold elections and transition to democracy.
- Natural resources such as oil have been a source of wealth for some nations but have fueled conflicts in others.
- During the Cold War, the United States and Soviet Union competed for influence, particularly in regions with natural resources such as oil, or locations near strategic waterways.

■ Leaders of New Nations

- Jawaharlal Nehru, *first prime minister of India*
- Indira Gandhi, *first female prime minister of India*
- Aung San Suu Kyi, *leader of Myanmar democracy movement*
- Sukarno, *founder and first president of Indonesia*
- Suharto, *military dictator of Indonesia*
- Corazon Aquino, *democratic president of the Philippines*
- Kwame Nkrumah, *founder and first president of Ghana*
- Jomo Kenyatta, *founder and first president of Kenya*
- David Ben-Gurion, *first prime minister of Israel*
- Gamal Abdel Nasser, *an Arab nationalist and first president of Egypt*
- Mohammad Reza Pahlavi, *shah of Iran*
- Ruhollah Khomeini, *leader of the religious government of Iran*

■ New Nations Emerge

■ Key Events in the Emergence of New Nations

Africa and the Middle East
South and Southeast Asia

1946
Syria and Jordan gain independence.

1948
Israel is founded.

1956–1966
More than 30 African nations win independence.

1940 **1950** **1960** **1970**

1947
India and Pakistan win independence after partition.

1966
Suharto establishes military dictatorship in Indonesia.

Concept Connector

Essential Question Review

To connect prior knowledge with what you have learned in this chapter, answer the questions below in your Concept Connector journal. Use the journal in the Reading and Note Taking Study Guide to record your answers (or go to www.phschool.com **Web Code**: nad-3107).

1. **Revolution** Between 1946 and 1970, European colonies around the world won independence. Choose one of these colonies and compare its struggle for independence with the American Revolution, which brought independence to the United States in the late 1700s. Consider the following:
   - the presence or the absence of military conflict
   - the challenge of forming stable governments after independence

2. **Nationalism** Although India has large religious minorities, the Bharatiya Janata Party (BJP) promoted Hindu nationalism, or the idea that India should favor the Hindu majority and the Hindu religion. How do you think the BJP's stand affected peace and stability in India?

3. **Dictatorship** In many African nations that gained independence after World War II, dictators seized power and established one-party political systems. These leaders claimed that multiparty systems encouraged disunity. Do you think the dictators' concerns were genuine? What appeal might the disunity argument have for citizens of a newly independent nation?

4. **Geography's Impact** The world's largest reserves of oil are located in the Middle East. What impact has the location of this valuable resource had on global politics and the economy?

■ Connections to Today

1. **Conflict: Struggles for Independence** Former European colonies such as Algeria had to fight deadly wars to win their independence. Today, in different parts of the world, people continue to fight for independence. Examples include Darfur, where rebels have fought against Sudan, and Papua, where rebels seek independence from Indonesia. Research one of these regions. Explain why this region is fighting for independence.

2. **Belief Systems: World Religions** In this chapter, you have seen that religions remain an important force in today's world. Turn to the Concept Connector Handbook on Culture at the back of your textbook. There you will find a list of world religions and their key beliefs. List the beliefs, traditions, customs, and sacred writings of Judaism, Christianity, Islam, Buddhism, and Hinduism. Then, using reliable sources from the Internet or a library, research and list the present-day geographic distribution of each of these religions.

1973
OPEC oil embargo

1979
Iranian revolution

1990–2002
African nations move toward democracy.

Mid-2000s
Tensions grow between Iran and the West.

1980   1990   2000   2010

1971
Bangladesh wins independence.

1986
"People power" revolution in the Philippines

1998
Indonesia returns to democracy.

History Interactive
For: Interactive timeline
Web Code: nap-3151

Chapter Assessment

Terms, People, and Places

Match the following definitions with the terms listed below.

Indira Gandhi	coup d'état
nonalignment	theocracy
Corazon Aquino	kibbutz

1. rule by religious leaders
2. a political leader in the Philippines
3. the first female prime minister of India
4. a collective farm
5. political and diplomatic independence
6. the forcible overthrow of a government

Main Ideas

Section 1 (pp. 1014–1019)
7. Why was British India divided into India and Pakistan?
8. How did religious and ethnic diversity pose challenges for South Asian nations after independence?

Section 2 (pp. 1020–1023)
9. Compare the nations of Southeast Asia in the progress that they have made toward democracy.

Section 3 (pp. 1024–1031)
10. How did African nations win their independence? How did this differ among nations?
11. What obstacles slowed progress toward democracy for some African nations?

Section 4 (pp. 1032–1037)
12. How has the Islamist movement affected politics in the Middle East?

Chapter Focus Question
13. How did former European colonies gain independence, and what challenges did they face after independence?

Critical Thinking

14. **Draw Conclusions** How did the Philippines and Indonesia achieve democracy?
15. **Synthesize Information** How has religion influenced the recent history of the Middle East?
16. **Analyzing Visuals** The photograph below shows refugees from the partition of India and Pakistan. What does it suggest about conditions for these refugees?

17. **Make Comparisons** Compare the impact of ethnic and religious diversity on the histories of India and Pakistan.
18. **Analyze Information** How have the natural resources of the Middle East affected its recent history?
19. **Draw Conclusions** How were African nations affected by military rule and dictatorships? Support your conclusions with examples.
20. **Recognize Cause and Effect** What have been some lasting effects of colonial rule on African nations?

● Writing About History

In this chapter's four Section Assessments, you learned how to write a compare-contrast essay.

Writing a Compare-Contrast Essay Write a compare-contrast essay on the post-independence histories of two countries covered in different sections of this chapter. Discuss similarities and differences in the histories of the two countries. Consult page SH10 of the Writing Handbook for additional help.

Prewriting
- Go online or do library research to find information about the post-independence histories of countries covered in this chapter.
- Choose two countries that interest you and take notes about the challenges these countries faced.
- Gather evidence that supports comparisons and contrasts between these countries.

Drafting
- Write a first paragraph with a thesis statement and details about similarities between the two countries.
- Write a second paragraph with a topic sentence and details about differences between the two countries.

Revising
- Use the guidelines for revising your report on page SH12 of the Writing Handbook.

Document-Based Assessment

The Kashmir Question

In 1947, British India was partitioned into Hindu-majority India and Muslim-majority Pakistan. Kashmir is claimed by both India and Pakistan and has been a battleground between the two countries. The documents below help to show why the "Kashmir problem" remains worrisome today.

Document A

Hum kya chahtey? Azaadi! (What do we want? Freedom!)

—Slogan in Kashmir Valley

Document B

"Mr. Jinnah and his colleagues in the Muslim League, the creators of Pakistan, had always considered that the Vale of Kashmir at least would form part of the new Islamic State . . . When in 1933 Choudhri Rahmat Ali coined the word Pakistan as a suitable name for the State, he intended the letter K in 'Pak' to stand for Kashmir. The geographical and historical links between the Panjab and the Vale of Kashmir were so close that it was inevitable that the two regions should find themselves combined in the thoughts of the protagonists of a separate Islamic State."

—From ***Crisis in Kashmir, 1947–1966*** by Alastair Lamb

Document C

Document D

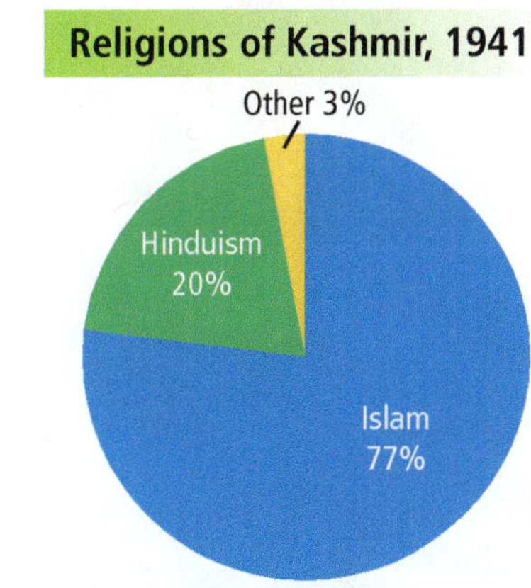

SOURCE: *Census of India, 1941*

Document E

Analyzing Documents

Use your knowledge of World War II and Documents A, B, C, D, and E to answer questions 1–4.

1. According to Document B, Kashmir and Pakistan share
   A the same heroes and poets.
   B a similar history and geography.
   C the same language and literature.
   D similar architecture and art.

2. What argument does the billboard in Document C support?
   A India is a diverse country, and the region of Kashmir is an important part of it.
   B India will never let go of Kashmir.
   C Kashmir is more beautiful than other parts of India.
   D Indians are tired of dealing with Kashmir and its thorny problems.

3. According to Document D, Kashmir's population
   A is evenly balanced among its different religions.
   B is about one-half Hindu and "Other."
   C only has two religious affiliations.
   D is more than three-quarters Muslim.

4. **Writing Task** Why has Kashmir continued to be a volatile spot for so long? What are the main causes of the conflict there? Use information from these documents along with information from the chapter to write your response.

32

Regional Conflicts
1945–Present

Life in a War Zone

For more than a year, hostile troops surrounded the city of Sarajevo in Bosnia and fired down on it from the hills above. Zlatko Dizdarevic, a journalist in Sarajevo, wrote this journal entry during the conflict:

“It's been a relentless morning. Shells are falling close by us, perhaps closer than ever before. The official alert remains in force; so does our private and personal alert. We evaluate our chances, run risks, and keep hoping.”

Listen to the Witness History audio to hear more about the war in Bosnia.

◀ **A boy dodging sniper fire to get water, Sarajevo, Bosnia, 1993**

Chapter Preview

Chapter Focus Question Why have deadly conflicts plagued some regions of the world?

Section 1
Conflicts Divide Nations

Section 2
Struggles in Africa

Section 3
Conflicts in the Middle East

Use the ✔ **Quick Study Timeline** at the end of this chapter to preview chapter events.

Zlata's Diary, a teenage girl's account of the conflict in Bosnia

Nelson Mandela, who led a struggle against racial discrimination and became president of South Africa

A fallen statue of Saddam Hussein, the dictator of Iraq, who was overthrown by American troops

 **Concept Connector ONLINE**

To explore Essential Questions related to this chapter, go to PHSchool.com
Web Code: nad-3207

Zlata Filipovic
in 1994

A Young Girl in Wartime

Zlata Filipovic (fee LEEP uh vich) was 11 years old in 1992 when she began a diary about her life in war-torn Sarajevo, the capital of Bosnia. Here is an excerpt:

66 Today a shell fell on the park in front of my house, the park where I used to play and sit with my girl-friends. A lot of people were hurt . . . AND NINA IS DEAD . . . She was such a sweet, nice little girl. **99**
—Zlata Filipovic, *Zlata's Diary*

Bosnia is just one of the nations that have faced ethnic, religious, or national conflicts in recent decades.

Focus Question Why have ethnic and religious conflicts divided some nations?

Conflicts Divide Nations

Objectives
- Explain the complex causes of ethnic and religious conflicts.
- Describe how war ravaged Chechnya.
- Understand how Yugoslavia broke apart.

Terms, People, and Places

Northern Ireland	Slobodan Milosevic
Good Friday Agreement	ethnic cleansing
Chechnya	Kosovo
multiethnic	

Note Taking

Reading Skill: Recognize Sequence Fill in a flowchart like the one below to keep track of the sequence of events in the conflicts in Northern Ireland, Chechnya, and Yugoslavia.

Sequence of Conflicts		
Northern Ireland	**Chechnya**	**Yugoslavia**
• **1922:** Six Irish counties vote to remain in the United Kingdom.	•	•
•	•	•

In recent decades, wars have raged in many parts of the world. These conflicts had complex causes. But rivalries between different ethnic, religious, and nationalist groups have often led to civil wars and regional conflicts.

Sources of Conflict

Nationalism led to the creation of many new nations after World War II. Many of these nations were former colonies or mandates. Their borders had been drawn by European powers with little concern for ethnic, religious, or regional differences. As a result, these new nations had culturally diverse populations. In some cases, minorities controlled the government and imposed their will on the majority. Often, the majority ethnic or religious group dominated the government and the economy and oppressed other groups.

War in Sri Lanka Discrimination, or unfair treatment, based on language, ethnicity, and culture has frequently set one group against another. In the island nation of Sri Lanka, discrimination and violence by majority Sinhalese Buddhists against Tamil-speaking Hindus led to rebellion. Since 1983, Tamil rebels, known as the Tamil Tigers, have fought to establish a separate Tamil homeland. The Tamil Tigers used terrorist tactics and guerrilla warfare. Peace talks held in 2002 led to a truce that slowed, but did not end the violence. However, by early 2009, government troops had toppled several Tamil rebel strongholds in a final push to end the 25-year-old civil war.

Divisions in Canada Some countries, such as Canada, have found peaceful ways to resolve internal conflicts. Although Canada is mostly English-speaking, the province of Quebec is mainly French-speaking. At times, many people in Quebec wanted to separate from Canada. While a few separatists turned to violence, most worked within Canada's democratic system to protect their language and culture.

Troubles in Northern Ireland Religious and economic discrimination fueled a long struggle in Northern Ireland. When Ireland won independence in 1922, Britain kept control of **Northern Ireland,** the six northern counties that had a Protestant majority. Faced with discrimination, minority Catholics demanded civil rights and unification with the rest of Ireland. Protestants wanted Northern Ireland to remain part of Britain.

In the 1960s, extremists on both sides turned to violence and terrorism. The mostly Catholic Irish Republican Army (IRA) attacked Protestants, while armed Protestant groups targeted Catholics. The violence, known as "the Troubles," raged for three decades. Finally, in 1998, both sides signed a peace accord, known as the **Good Friday Agreement.** Protestants and Catholics set up a power-sharing government in 2007. Although there have been isolated acts of violence, most people hoped that peace would last after years of conflict.

✔ **Checkpoint** Why did conflict break out in Northern Ireland?

Russia and Its Neighbors

Ethnic and religious tensions in Russia and in several former Soviet republics fueled conflicts within Russia. In 1994, separatists in **Chechnya** tried to break away from Russian rule. Chechnya was home to diverse ethnic and religious groups, including Muslim Chechens.

Russia crushed the Chechen revolt, killing many civilians. During two wars and nearly ten years of fighting, both sides committed atrocities. In the early 2000s, Chechen rebels launched terrorist attacks on Moscow, and killed school children in the city of Beslan. By 2009, a Russian-backed leader was rebuilding Chechnya, despite occasional violence.

In the oil-rich former Soviet republic of Azerbaijan, Azeris are the majority. In the region of Nagorno-Karabakh, however, ethnic Armenians outnumbered Azeris. When Armenians declared independence, fierce fighting raged. The Armenians gained control of the region, creating one million Azeri refugees.

In Georgia, another former Soviet republic, two provinces, South Ossetia and Abkhazia, wanted to break away. Russia backed the separatists. In 2008, after Georgia attacked separatists in South Ossetia, fighting erupted between Russian and Georgian troops. International pressure soon ended the conflict, but tensions remained high.

✔ **Checkpoint** What were the causes of the conflicts that erupted in the former Soviet Union?

<table>
<tr><td colspan="3">Contrasting Ethnic Relations</td></tr>
<tr><th>Nation</th><th>Political System</th><th>Ethnic Conflict</th></tr>
<tr><td>Sri Lanka</td><td>Limits rights of minority groups</td><td>Has led to violence</td></tr>
<tr><td>Canada</td><td>Protects minority groups</td><td>Resolved democratically</td></tr>
</table>

Chart Skills Based on the chart and the information in this section, explain why the response of the ethnic minority to discrimination in Sri Lanka differed from that in Canada.

Grozny in Ruins
Russian forces destroyed Grozny, the capital of Chechnya, during the fighting in 2000. The city was later rebuilt.

Yugoslavia Breaks Apart

Ethnic, nationalist, and religious tensions tore Yugoslavia apart during the 1990s. Before 1991, Yugoslavia was **multiethnic,** or made up of several ethnic groups. These groups included Serbs, Montenegrins, and Macedonians, who were Orthodox Christians; Croats and Slovenes, who were Roman Catholics; and the mostly Muslim Bosniaks and Albanians. A majority of Yugoslavians—including the Serbs, Montenegrins, Croats, and Bosniaks—all spoke the same language, Serbo-Croatian, but these groups had different religions. Albanians, Slovenes, and Macedonians spoke minority languages.

Yugoslavia was made up of six republics, similar to states in the United States. These were Slovenia, Croatia, Serbia, Bosnia and Herzegovina (often known as Bosnia for short), Montenegro, and Macedonia. Each republic had a dominant ethnic group but also was home to ethnic minorities. Serbs formed the majority in Serbia but were an important ethnic minority in several of the other republics. Serbs <u>dominated</u> Yugoslavia, which was held together and controlled by its Communist Party.

Republics Break Away The fall of communism fed nationalist unrest throughout Yugoslavia. The Serbian-dominated government tried to preserve the country. In 1991, however, Slovenia and Croatia declared independence. This move triggered fighting between Croats and the Serbian minority within Croatia. Macedonia and Bosnia soon broke away from Yugoslavia as well, leaving only Serbia and Montenegro. In 2006, Montenegro also went its own way, separate from Serbia.

Civil War Devastates Bosnia When Bosnia declared independence in 1992, civil war erupted among Bosniaks, Serbs, and Croats. Bosnian Serbs wanted to set up their own government. They received money and arms from Serbian president **Slobodan Milosevic** (mih LOH shuh vich), an extreme Serb nationalist. The largest group in Bosnia, the Muslim Bosniaks, lived scattered across Bosnia. They did not want the country divided into ethnic regions.

During the war, all sides committed atrocities. Bosnian Serbs conducted a vicious campaign of **ethnic cleansing.** This meant killing people from other ethnic groups or forcibly removing them from their homes to create ethnically "pure" areas, in this case for Serbs. Tens of thousands of Bosniaks and Croats were brutalized or killed, sometimes in mass executions. Croat and Bosnian fighters took revenge. Croats launched an ethnic cleansing campaign to drive ethnic Serbs from parts of Croatia.

Finally, NATO air strikes against the Bosnian Serb military forced the warring parties to the peace table. Guided by the United States, the rival groups signed the Dayton Accords, ending the war in 1995. An international force helped maintain a fragile peace in Bosnia.

Vocabulary Builder

<u>dominate</u>—(DAHM uh nayt) *v.* to control or have power over

Map Skills The former nation of Yugoslavia had broken apart into six new nations by 2006. In 2008, Kosovo declared its independence from Serbia.

1. **Locate** (a) Sarajevo (b) Serbia (c) Kosovo
2. **Location** Which new nation does not share a border with Serbia on any side?
3. **Make Inferences** How did the location of Bosnia and Herzegovina put it at risk of becoming involved in conflicts between Serbians and Croatians?

The Fight for Kosovo As Bosnia reached a tense peace, a crisis broke out in the Serbian province of Kosovo. Over the centuries, many Albanians, mostly Muslim, had settled in Kosovo. By the 1990s, they made up about 90 percent of Kosovo's population. The rest of the population was mostly Serb.

In 1989, Serbian leader Slobodan Milosevic began oppressing Kosovo Albanians. By the mid-1990s, a small guerrilla force of Kosovo Albanians had emerged. It attacked Serbian targets. Milosevic rejected international peace efforts and stepped up a campaign of ethnic cleansing against Kosovo Albanians. In response, NATO launched air attacks against Serbia in 1999.

The air strikes forced Milosevic to withdraw Serbian forces from Kosovo. UN and NATO forces then supervised a tense peace. After years of negotiation, Kosovo declared independence in 2008. While Kosovo Albanians celebrated, Serbs angrily protested. For them, Kosovo was a historic part of Serbia. A small NATO force remained in Kosovo to keep the peace between the majority Albanians and the minority Serbs.

Fighters in Kosovo
Kosovo Albanians claim an area after Serbian forces withdrew in 1999. *What does this photograph suggest about relations between Albanians and Serbs in Kosovo?*

✔ **Checkpoint** How did the breakup of Yugoslavia lead to ethnic cleansing in Bosnia and Herzegovina?

Progress Monitoring *Online*
For: Self-quiz with vocabulary practice
Web Code: naa-3211

Terms, People, and Places

1. What do many of the terms, people, and places listed at the beginning of the section have in common? Explain.

Note Taking

2. **Reading Skill: Recognize Sequence** Use your completed flowchart to answer the Focus Question: Why have ethnic and religious conflicts divided some nations?

Comprehension and Critical Thinking

3. **Synthesize Information** How might Malaysia and Singapore serve as examples of how to resolve ethnic conflict in the nations that make up the former Yugoslavia?

4. **Predict Consequences** Do you think Kosovo will be able to maintain its independence and resolve the conflict between Albanians and Serbs?

5. **Draw Conclusions** Why do you think Russia intervened in Georgia's conflict with its provinces?

● **Writing About History**

Quick Write: Explore a Topic To write a research report, you first need to frame questions that will help you to explore your topic. Choose one of the conflicts in this section and write a series of questions that you could try to answer through research. For example, if you choose the Northern Ireland conflict, you might ask why the IRA has been reluctant to turn over weapons, or who has been responsible for recent attacks in Northern Ireland.

Since 1994, peace has returned to Rwanda. This recent photo shows Rwandan boys running home after school.

Recovering From Genocide

Although other African nations suffered brutal ethnic conflicts and civil wars, Rwanda's 1994 genocide was one of the most deadly. However, as UN Secretary General Kofi Annan points out, Rwanda's recovery in the years since offers hope that the continent's conflicts can be resolved.

> 66 Rwanda has much to show the world about confronting the legacy of the past and is demonstrating that it is possible to reach beyond tragedy and rekindle hope. 99
> — Tribute by Kofi Annan on the tenth anniversary of genocide in Rwanda

This section explores the problems that have led to conflicts in Rwanda and in other African countries.

Focus Question Why have conflicts plagued some African countries?

Struggles in Africa

Objectives
- Understand South Africa's struggle for freedom.
- Describe how struggles for independence and Cold War rivalries brought decades of conflict to South Africa's neighbors.
- Analyze how ethnic conflicts killed millions in Rwanda and Sudan.

Terms, People, and Places

apartheid	Desmond Tutu
African National Congress (ANC)	F.W. de Klerk
	Hutus
Sharpeville	Tutsis
Nelson Mandela	Darfur

Note Taking

Reading Skill: Recognize Sequence Keep track of the sequence of events in the conflicts in South Africa and its neighbors. Add boxes as needed.

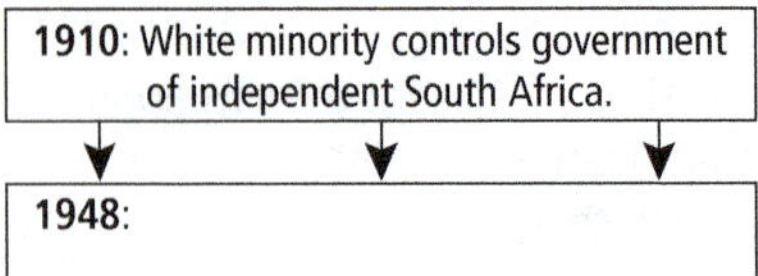

In the 1950s and 1960s, many new nations won independence in Africa. National unity, however, was hard to achieve. Most African nations were home to diverse ethnic groups. Often, people did not even share a common language. They spoke dozens of local languages. Religious differences and longstanding rivalries further divided people within a nation.

After independence, a single ethnic group often dominated a nation's government and economy at the expense of other groups. The Cold War further complicated matters, as you have read. As a result, several African nations suffered internal conflicts and civil war.

South Africa Struggles for Freedom

In South Africa, the struggle for freedom was different from that elsewhere in Africa. In 1910, South Africa achieved self-rule from Britain. Freedom, however, was limited to white settlers. The black majority was denied the right to vote. Whites made up less than 20 percent of the population but controlled the government and the economy. The white-minority government passed racial laws that severely restricted the black majority.

Apartheid Divides South Africa After 1948, the government expanded the existing system of racial segregation, creating what was known as **apartheid,** or the separation of the races. Under apartheid, all South Africans were registered by race: Black,

White, Colored (people of mixed ancestry), Asian. Supporters of apartheid claimed it would allow each race to protect its culture. In fact, the policy was designed to keep white control over South Africa.

Under apartheid, nonwhites faced many restrictions. Blacks were treated like foreigners in their own land. Under the pass laws, they had to get permission to travel. Other laws banned marriages between the races and <u>stipulated</u> segregated restaurants, beaches, and schools. Black workers were paid less than whites for the same job. Blacks could not own land in most areas. Low wages and inferior schooling condemned most blacks to poverty.

The Struggle for Majority Black Rule Black South Africans resisted apartheid. The **African National Congress (ANC)** emerged as the main party opposed to apartheid and led the struggle for majority rule. In the 1950s, the government imposed strict new rules to separate the races. The ANC organized marches, boycotts, and strikes. In 1960, police gunned down 69 men, women, and children during a peaceful protest in **Sharpeville,** a black township. The government then outlawed the ANC and cracked down on other groups that opposed apartheid.

The Sharpeville massacre led some ANC activists to shift from nonviolent protest to armed struggle. Some leaders, like **Nelson Mandela,** went underground. As an ANC leader, Mandela had first mobilized young South Africans to peacefully resist apartheid laws. As government oppression grew, Mandela joined ANC militants who called for armed struggle against the white-minority government. In the early 1960s, Mandela was arrested, tried, and condemned to life in prison for treason. Even in prison, he remained a powerful symbol of the struggle for freedom.

In the 1980s, demands for an end to apartheid and for Mandela's release increased. Many countries, including the United States, imposed economic sanctions on South Africa. In 1984, black South African bishop **Desmond Tutu** won the Nobel Peace Prize for his nonviolent opposition to apartheid.

Ending Apartheid Outside pressure and protests at home finally convinced South African president **F. W. de Klerk** to end apartheid. In 1990, he lifted the ban on the ANC and freed Mandela. In 1994, South Africans of every race were allowed to vote for the first time.

The Sharpeville Massacre
When South African police opened fire on peaceful demonstrators at Sharpeville in 1960, many demonstrators ran for their lives. *How might this police action lead anti-apartheid activists to give up on peaceful methods?*

For more than 40 years, apartheid shaped the lives of the black majority and of whites and other minorities in South Africa. Whites made up less than one fifth of South Africa's population, as you can see in the graph at the right. However, apartheid gave whites not only political power, but also control of South Africa's best lands and economic resources. This hurt blacks, Asians, and people of mixed backgrounds economically and socially. *Based on the information in the graph and elsewhere in this section, about what percentage of South Africa's population suffered from apartheid?*

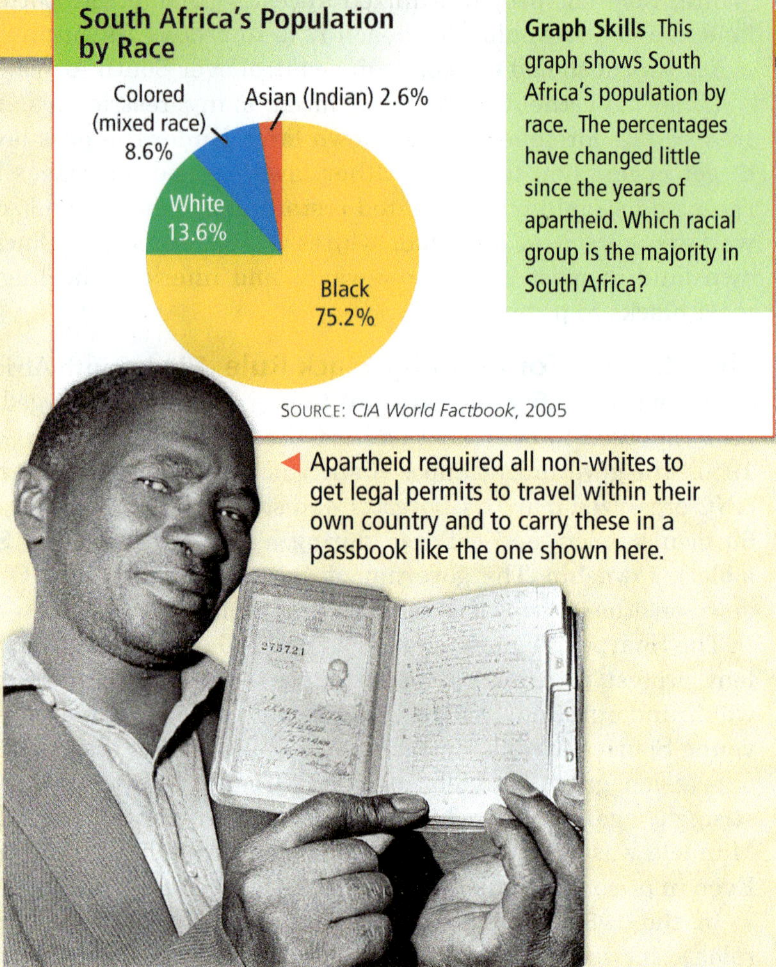

SOURCE: *CIA World Factbook*, 2005

Graph Skills This graph shows South Africa's population by race. The percentages have changed little since the years of apartheid. Which racial group is the majority in South Africa?

◀ Apartheid required all non-whites to get legal permits to travel within their own country and to carry these in a passbook like the one shown here.

▲ Apartheid gave many white South Africans a life of privilege.

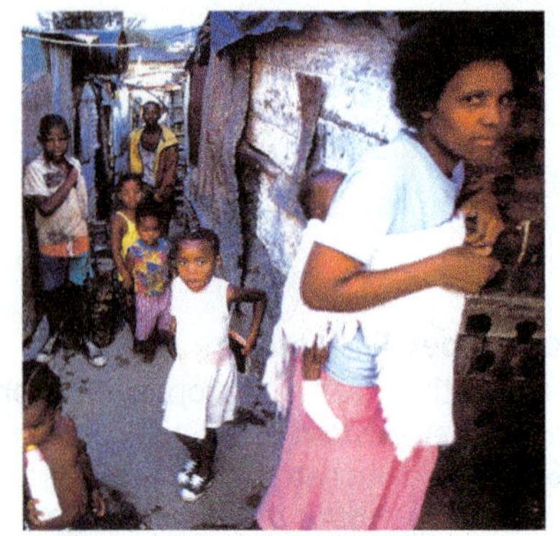

Deprived of opportunities, many black South Africans lived in poverty.

Voters chose Nelson Mandela as president in South Africa's first multiracial election. Mandela worked to heal the country's wounds. "Let us build together," he declared. He welcomed old foes into his government, including whites who had supported apartheid.

Since 1994, South Africa has faced huge challenges. With majority rule, black South Africans expected a better life. Although South Africa was a rich, industrial country, it had limited resources to spend on housing, education, and other programs. The income and education gap between blacks and whites remained large. Poverty and unemployment were high among blacks. The AIDS epidemic hit South Africa severely. As South Africa's government struggled with these problems, the global economic slowdown created new challenges.

✔ **Checkpoint** What factors finally brought an end to apartheid in South Africa?

Struggles in Southern Africa

Most African nations achieved independence through peaceful means during the 1950s and 1960s. In southern Africa, however, the road to freedom was marked by some long, violent struggles. For many years, the apartheid government of South Africa supported white minority rule in neighboring nations.

Zimbabwe As African nations won independence, whites in Southern Rhodesia refused to share power with the black majority. Conservative whites, led by Ian Smith, declared independence in 1965. For years, black guerrilla groups fought for majority rule. In 1980, after a ceasefire and elections, the country gained independence and was renamed Zimbabwe.

Robert Mugabe, a liberation leader, was elected president. Although popular at first, Mugabe grew increasingly dictatorial. He cracked down on opponents and was accused of electoral fraud. Despite international pressure and an economic crisis, the aging Mugabe held onto power.

Angola and Mozambique While Britain and France gave up their African possessions, Portugal clung fiercely to its colonies of Angola and Mozambique. In response, nationalist groups waged a long guerrilla war. In 1975, after Portugal finally agreed to withdraw, Angola and Mozambique celebrated independence.

Both countries then faced brutal civil wars fueled by Cold War rivalries. Because some liberation leaders had ties to the Soviet Union or the ANC, the United States and South Africa aided a rebel group in Angola. South Africa also supported a rebel group in Mozambique. The fighting continued until 1992 in Mozambique, and 2002 in Angola. Decades of war had ravaged both countries, which slowly began to rebuild.

 **Checkpoint** Why did fighting continue after Angola and Mozambique achieved independence?

Reading Skill: Identify Causes and Effects Fill in a concept web like the one below to keep track of the causes and effects of the conflicts in Rwanda and Sudan.

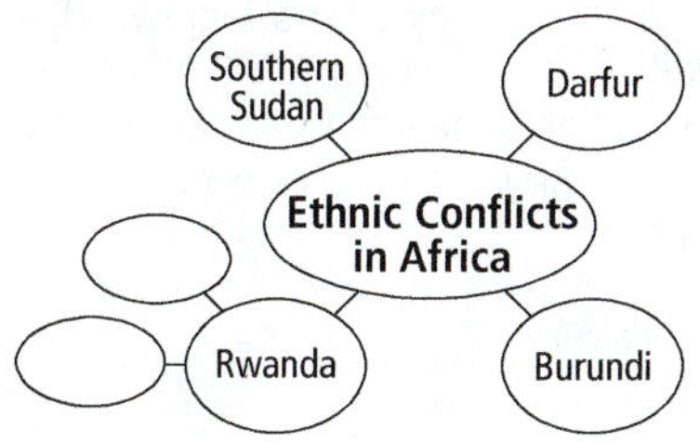

Ethnic Conflicts Fuel Power Struggles

After independence, ethnic conflicts plagued several African nations. The causes were complex. Historic resentments divided ethnically diverse nations. Unjust governments and regional rivalries fed ethnic violence.

Rwanda and Burundi Power struggles between ethnic groups led to a deadly genocide in Rwanda, a small central African nation. The country was home to two main ethnic groups. **Hutus** were the majority group, but **Tutsis** had long dominated Rwanda. Both groups spoke the same language, but they had different traditions. After independence, Hutu violence against Tutsis increased.

Tensions worsened in early 1994, after the presidents of Rwanda and neighboring Burundi were killed in a suspicious plane crash. Extremist Hutu officials urged civilians to turn on their Tutsi neighbors. At least 800,000 Tutsis and moderate Hutus were slaughtered. Millions of Rwandans lost their homes to destructive mobs. Even as the death toll rose, the world community was slow to act to stop the genocide.

In July 1994, a Tutsi exile army conquered Rwanda and set up a unity government. Those accused of genocide faced trials in an international court.

Nearby Burundi faced similar ethnic tensions between Hutus and Tutsis. In 1993, Tutsi military officers killed Burundi's Hutu president in a failed coup attempt. Violence erupted, but did not lead to genocide as in Rwanda. In 2005, voters approved a new constitution that guaranteed both groups participation in the government and military.

Strife in Sudan Genocide also took place in oil-rich Sudan. Since independence, Sudan's Arab Muslim north has dominated the non-Muslim, non-Arab south. Sudan's Muslim government even tried to impose

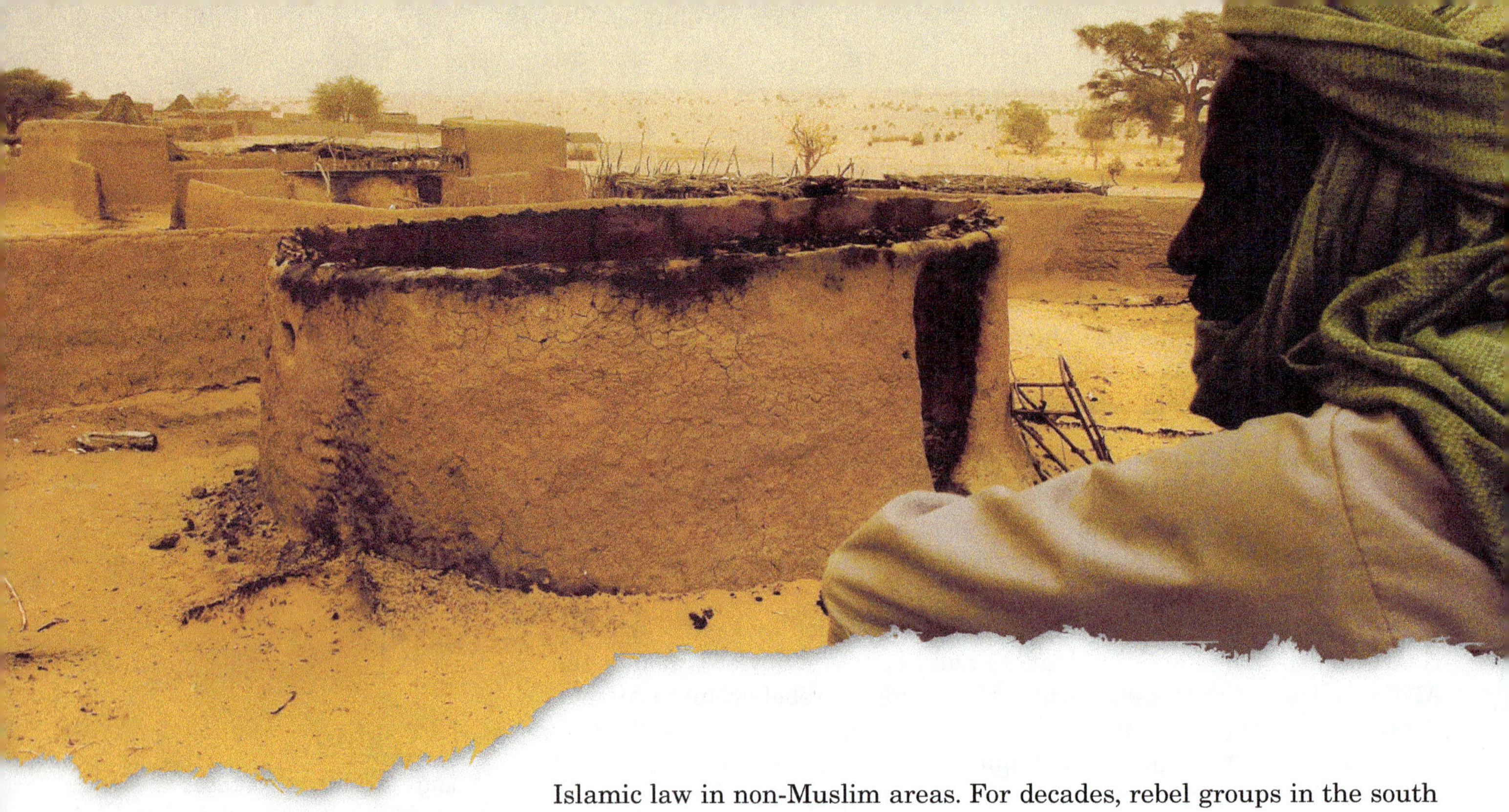

Terror in Darfur
Arab militias, known as *janjaweed* or "bandits," spread terror across the Darfur region of Sudan. Above is all that is left of the village of Tontobay after a Janjaweed attack killed 80 and forced 3,000 other residents to flee to nearby Chad. *How might an attack by the janjaweed affect unarmed villagers?*

Islamic law in non-Muslim areas. For decades, rebel groups in the south battled northern political domination. The fighting also spilled into neighboring Chad. Sudan's north-south conflict killed millions and displaced many more.

In 2005, the Sudanese government and rebels in the south agreed to a peace accord. However, in 2004, fighting worsened in the western region of **Darfur.** With government backing, Arab militias conducted widespread killings of civilians. They burned homes and drove farmers off the land.

The United States and other countries sent humanitarian aid to the refugees. Sudan allowed UN peacekeepers into the region, but they were unable to end the violence. In 2009, the International Criminal Court charged Sudan's president with crimes against humanity.

✓ **Checkpoint** **How was the conflict in Rwanda similar to the conflict in Darfur?**

SECTION 2 Assessment

Progress Monitoring *Online*
For: Self-quiz with vocabulary practice
Web Code: naa-3221

Terms, People, and Places

1. For each term, person, or place listed at the beginning of the section, write a sentence explaining its significance.

Note Taking

2. **Reading Skill: Recognize Sequence** Use your completed flowchart to answer the Focus Question: Why have conflicts plagued some African countries?

Comprehension and Critical Thinking

3. **Analyze Information** Was apartheid a product of a democratic system of government? Explain.
4. **Summarize** What was South Africa's role in the conflicts that plagued its neighbors from the 1960s to the 1990s?
5. **Make Comparisons** How was the ethnic conflict in Burundi similar to or different from the conflict in Rwanda?
6. **Synthesize Information** A newspaper headline read, "Looking at Darfur, Seeing Rwanda." Explain what that headline meant. How did the world community respond to genocide after the events in Rwanda?

Writing About History

Quick Write: Gather Information To write a research report, you need to gather information about your topic. Choose one of the conflicts in this section and gather facts about the topic from the library or reliable sources online. Make a list of facts about your topic.

Nelson Mandela: *Glory and Hope*

Nelson Mandela delivered this speech after having been elected president in South Africa's first multiracial election in 1994. Knowing that the injustices of apartheid would be hard to overcome, Mandela asked the people to work together for peace and justice.

Today, all of us do, by our presence here, and by our celebrations . . . confer glory and hope to newborn liberty.

Out of the experience of an extraordinary human disaster that lasted too long must be born a society of which all humanity will be proud.

Our daily deeds as ordinary South Africans must produce an actual South African reality that will reinforce humanity's belief in justice, strengthen its confidence in the nobility of the human soul and sustain all our hopes for a glorious life for all. . . .

The time for the healing of the wounds has come. . . .

The time to build is upon us.

We have, at last, achieved our political emancipation.[1] We pledge ourselves to liberate all our people from the continuing bondage of poverty, deprivation, suffering, gender and other discrimination. . . .

We have triumphed in the effort to implant hope in the breasts of the millions of our people. We enter into a covenant[2] that we shall build the society in which all South Africans, both black and white, will be able to walk tall, without any fear in their hearts, assured of their inalienable right to human dignity—a rainbow nation at peace with itself and the world. . . .

We understand it still that there is no easy road to freedom.

We know it well that none of us acting alone can achieve success.

We must therefore act together as a united people, for national reconciliation,[3] for nation building, for the birth of a new world.

Let there be justice for all. Let there be peace for all. Let there be work, bread, water, and salt for all. . . . The sun shall never set on so glorious a human achievement!

1. **emancipation** (ee man suh PAY shun) *n.* the gaining of freedom from bondage or control by others
2. **covenant** (KUV uh nunt) *n.* a binding and solemn pledge to do something
3. **reconciliation** (rek un sil ee AY shun) *n.* a settling of differences that results in harmony

Students in South Africa after the end of apartheid

Thinking Critically

1. **Identify Alternatives** When apartheid ended, there was a danger of a backlash by blacks against whites who supported apartheid. How does Mandela's speech respond to that danger?
2. **Draw Inferences** In addition to political freedom, what further freedoms does Mandela call for in his speech?

Nelson Mandela with supporters in 1994

An Israeli soldier and a Palestinian Arab pass each other in the street.

Two Peoples Claim the Same Land

Many Jewish Israelis believe that the quotation from the Bible, below, promises Israel to the Jewish people as descendants of Abraham (Abram). Many Muslims also believe that they are the spiritual heirs to Abraham, as stated in the Quran. They too feel entitled to the land as part of Abraham's legacy. Representatives of both peoples have lived in the land for centuries.

> On that day the LORD made a covenant with Abram, saying, 'To your descendants I give this land. . . .'
>
> —Genesis 15:18

> He [Allah] has chosen you and has placed no hardship on you in practicing your religion—the religion of your father Abraham.
>
> —Quran 22:78

Focus Question What are the causes of conflict in the Middle East?

Conflicts in the Middle East

Objectives
- Understand why Arabs and Israelis fought over land.
- Explain why civil war ravaged Lebanon.
- Outline Iraq's long history of conflict.

Terms, People, and Places

occupied territories
Yasir Arafat
intifada
Yitzhak Rabin
Jerusalem
militia

Saddam Hussein
no-fly zone
weapons of mass
  destruction (WMDs)
insurgent

Note Taking

Reading Skill: Recognize Sequence Keep track of the sequence of events in the conflicts in the Middle East with a flowchart like the one below.

Middle Eastern Conflicts		
Arab-Israeli Conflict	**Lebanon**	**Iraq**
• 1948: Israel is founded •	• •	• •

For decades, the Middle East has been the focus of conflicts that have had a global impact. The Middle East commands vast oil resources and key waterways such as the Persian Gulf. During the Cold War, both the United States and the Soviet Union wanted access to the oil and the waterways. Since the end of the Cold War, Western nations have acted to prevent regional powers from interfering with the region's oil supply. Meanwhile, the persistent dispute between Israelis and Palestinian Arabs has added to tensions.

Arabs and Israelis Fight Over Land

Modern Israel was established in 1948 in accordance with the United Nations Partition Plan. The Palestinian Arabs regarded the UN action as illegitimate and rejected the state offered to them. Conflicting claims to this land led to repeated violence. After the 1948 war that followed Israel's founding, Israel and its Arab neighbors fought three more wars, in 1956, 1967, and 1973. In these wars, Israel defeated Arab forces and gained more land. Between the wars, Israel faced guerrilla and terrorist attacks. Repeatedly, the United States tried to bring about peace.

Israel Controls the Occupied Territories In the 1967 war, in response to hostility by its neighbors, Israeli forces took control of territories occupied by Jordan and Egypt since 1948, including the West Bank, East Jerusalem, and the Gaza Strip. They also took control of the Sinai Peninsula from Egypt and the Golan Heights from Syria. In 1973, these nations attacked Israel on Yom Kippur, one of the holiest days of the Jewish year.

In the 1973 war, Arabs failed to regain the regions they had lost to Israel, known today as the **occupied territories.** Israel's government later helped Jewish settlers build homes in settlements in these territories, causing more bitterness among the Palestinians.

Palestinian Attacks Bring Israeli Response For decades, the Palestinian Liberation Organization (PLO) led the struggle against Israel. Headed by **Yasir Arafat,** the PLO had deep support among Palestinians. The PLO called for the destruction of Israel. It attacked Israelis at home and abroad. The PLO gained world attention with airplane hijackings and the killing of Israeli athletes at the 1972 Olympic games.

In 1987, Palestinians in the occupied territories started to resist Israel with **intifadas,** or uprisings. Demanding an end to Israeli occupation, young Palestinians stoned and fired on Israeli troops. Suicide bombers blew up buses, stores, and clubs in Israel, killing many civilians. Israel responded by sealing off and raiding Palestinian towns and targeting terrorist leaders. Many Palestinian civilians lost their lives in these raids.

Seeking Peace Despite the violence, the United States, the UN, and other nations pushed for peace. Golda Meir, Israel's first woman prime minister, was planning peace talks when Arab nations attacked in 1973. As you have read, Israel and Egypt signed a peace accord in 1979. Israel then returned the Sinai Peninsula to Egypt. In 1994, Jordan's King Hussein made peace with Israel. However, talks between Syria and Israel failed over various issues, including control of the Golan Heights.

In 1993, Yasir Arafat and Israeli Prime Minister **Yitzhak Rabin** (rah BEEN) signed the Oslo Accords. This plan gave Palestinians in Gaza and the West Bank limited self-rule under a Palestinian Authority. The PLO recognized Israel's right to exist and pledged to stop terrorist attacks on Israel. Arafat led the Palestinian Authority until his death in 2004.

A City Sacred to Many
Jerusalem is dotted with many places that are sacred to the Jewish people, Christians, and Muslims. This photograph shows the Western Wall, a Jewish holy place. In the background is the Dome of the Rock, an important Islamic shrine. *How might Jerusalem's sacred status make it harder to resolve competing Israeli and Palestinian Arab claims to the city?*

The Israeli-Palestinian Conflict

Conflict has dragged on for years in the region. Palestinian Arabs resent the Israeli occupation. Some have responded with suicide bombings targeting Israeli civilians. Israeli forces have responded with attacks on Palestinian militants that have also killed some civilians. Hopes for peace in the region center on ending this cycle of violence and retaliation.

◀ Palestinian suicide bombers have set off deadly explosions in public places that have killed Israeli civilians. The bus in this photo was torn apart by a bomb carried by a Palestinian terrorist.

Ongoing Violence Although Arafat's successor, Mahmoud Abbas (ah BAHS), pledged to stop Palestinian attacks on Israel, violence continued. Fierce divisions split the Palestinian Authority between Fatah, the party of Arafat and his successors, and Hamas, a radical Islamist group. Hamas was funded by Iran and rejected Israel's right to exist. After its impressive victory in the 2006 Palestinian parliamentary election, Hamas seized control of Gaza in 2007, ousting Fatah supporters.

In response, Israel imposed an economic blockade on Gaza, allowing only humanitarian aid to enter. Hamas used Gaza as a launching ground for rocket attacks on Israel. In early 2009, Israeli forces invaded the densely populated Gaza Strip to stop the attacks. A short destructive war resulted in high civilian casualties and ended in a shaky ceasefire.

Obstacles to Peace Decades of conflict and mistrust make peace hard to achieve. Many issues pose obstacles. One issue is land claims. Palestinians who were forced off their lands in earlier wars want the "right of return," or the right to resettle on their lands in Israel. Israelis oppose this right, which could overwhelm the Jewish state with large numbers of Palestinians.

A second obstacle to peace is the issue of Jewish settlements in the West Bank, an area claimed by Palestinians. In the early 2000s, the Israeli government forced Jewish settlers to leave Gaza. Palestinians also insist that Jewish settlers must leave the West Bank.

A third stumbling block is **Jerusalem,** a city sacred to Jews, Christians, and Muslims. Israel occupied Arab East Jerusalem in 1967. Later, it added East Jerusalem to Israel and made the city the capital of Israel. The government allowed Muslims and Christians to control their holy sites within the city. Palestinians, however, insist that East Jerusalem must be the capital of any Palestinian state.

Israeli counterattacks in the occupied territories have killed Palestinians, including some civilians. Some 20,000 people attended this funeral for Palestinians killed in an Israeli attack.

Some Israelis and Palestinians, such as the men in this photograph, have chosen peaceful dialogue rather than violence as a way to bridge their differences. Dialogue between the two sides offers the best hope for ending this regional conflict. ▼

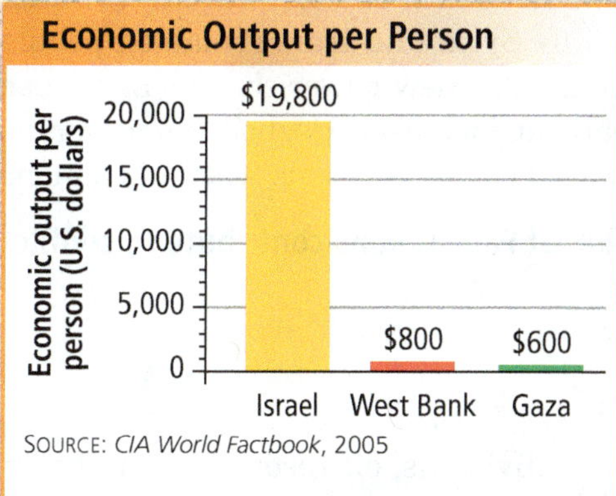

Lack of development, years of conflict, and corruption have crippled the economy of the West Bank and Gaza. Meanwhile, Palestinian attacks have forced Israel to limit Palestinians' access to jobs in Israel. Poverty in the West Bank and Gaza Strip has led to desperation among Palestinians.

Thinking Critically

1. **Graph Skills** How does economic output in the West Bank and Gaza Strip compare with that in Israel?
2. **Draw Conclusions** How might violence by both sides tend to prolong the Palestinian-Israeli conflict?

Over time, the Israeli-Palestinian conflict has fueled the anger of radical Islamist groups around the world. The growing popularity of Hamas and Hezbollah, a radical Islamist group based in Lebanon, created more conflict. These groups reject Israel's right to exist and condemn its ally, the United States, as well as moderate Arab governments involved in the peace process.

By the early 2000s, the United States, the European Union, Russia, and the UN supported a plan known as the "road map" to peace in the Middle East. It supports a two-state solution, with peaceful coexistence between Israel and a stable, democratic Palestinian state. To achieve this, it called for an end to violence and terrorism. Some Israeli and Palestinian leaders accepted the plan, while Iran and radical Islamist groups rejected it.

✔ **Checkpoint** What obstacles have prevented peace between Israel and the Palestinians?

Civil War Ravages Lebanon

Historically, Lebanon was a thriving center of commerce. Its population included <u>diverse</u> ethnic and religious groups. After Lebanon won independence, the government depended on a delicate balance among Arab Christian sects, Sunni and Shiite Muslims, and Druze, people with a religion related to Islam. Arab Christians held the most power, but local strongmen controlled their own districts with private armies.

Growing Tensions By the 1970s, the Arab-Israeli conflict was contributing to problems in nearby Lebanon. As Palestinian refugees fled into Lebanon after each new conflict with Israel, Lebanon's Muslim population grew to outnumber Christians. Tensions rose as PLO guerrillas disguised as refugees then crossed the border to attack Israel.

Vocabulary Builder

<u>diverse</u>—(dih VURS) *adj.* multiple, varied, different

Civil War and Conflict With Israel In 1975, Lebanon was plunged into civil war. Christian and Muslim **militias,** or armed groups of citizen soldiers, battled each other. In 1982, Israel invaded southern Lebanon to stop cross-border attacks. Syria occupied eastern Lebanon. UN peace-keepers tried to end the fighting but withdrew after hundreds were killed by suicide bombers. After 16 years, Lebanese leaders finally restored order. Beirut, the ruined capital, was slowly rebuilt.

Deep divisions remained in Lebanon. Rival militias controlled different regions. In 2006, Hezbollah attacked Israel from southern Lebanon, sparking a war that lasted just over a month. The war killed civilians in both Israel and Lebanon and caused widespread damage across Lebanon. Despite the costs, Hezbollah, backed by Syria and Iran, remained popular among Lebanon's Shiite Muslims. In 2008, a new power-sharing agreement was reached in Lebanon. The agreement increased Hezbollah's power, but contained a pledge that no faction would use its weapons within Lebanon.

✔ **Checkpoint** How did an influx of Palestinians contribute to conflict in Lebanon?

Iraq's History of Conflict

Since the 1950s, ethnic and religious divisions, oil resources, and border disputes have led to conflict in Iraq. During the Cold War, the United States and the Soviet Union competed for influence in Iraq, which had vast oil reserves and was strategically located on the Persian Gulf.

Iraq was carved out of the Ottoman Empire after World War I. Its population included Sunni and Shiite Arabs as well as Kurds. Although Shiites formed a majority in Iraq, Sunni Arabs controlled the government. Kurds, who lived in the north, distrusted the government and wanted self-rule. Divisions among these groups fed tensions in Iraq.

The Iran-Iraq War In 1980, Iraqi dictator, **Saddam Hussein,** took advantage of turmoil in neighboring Iran following its Islamic revolution by seizing a disputed border region. His action sparked a long, costly war.

Iraq used superior weapons and poison gas to stop waves of Iranian soldiers. After both sides attacked foreign oil tankers and oil fields in the Persian Gulf, the United States sent naval forces to protect shipping lanes. The war ended in a stalemate in 1988. For both Iran and Iraq, the human and economic toll was enormous.

During the war, Saddam Hussein brutally repressed a Kurdish revolt in the north. He also used chemical weapons on Kurdish civilians. His actions sparked outrage and charges of genocide.

The 1991 Gulf War In 1990, Iraq invaded its oil-rich neighbor, Kuwait. Saddam Hussein claimed that Kuwait was historically part of Iraq. In fact, he wanted control of Kuwait's vast oil fields and greater access to the Persian Gulf.

The United States saw Saddam's move not only as illegal, but also as a threat to its ally, Saudi Arabia, and to the oil resources of the region. It formed an international coalition to drive Iraq out of Kuwait. In the 1991 Gulf War, the U.S.-led coalition operated under the UN banner. It quickly crushed Iraqi forces and freed Kuwait.

Despite defeat, Saddam Hussein remained in power. He brutally crushed revolts by Shiite Muslims and the minority Kurds. He used torture and terror to impose his will.

Saddam Hussein's Dictatorship
Saddam Hussein, shown here in a propaganda poster in 1988, turned Iraq into a brutal police state, in which critics were tortured and killed.

Saddam Defies the UN To protect the Shiites and Kurds, the UN set up **no-fly zones,** or areas where Iraqi aircraft were banned. The UN also tried to discover if Saddam Hussein was building **weapons of mass destruction (WMDs),** or nuclear, biological, and chemical weapons. It imposed economic sanctions on Iraq to limit its oil sales and its use of oil profits. For years, Saddam Hussein defied the UN.

U.S. Forces Invade After the 2001 terrorist attacks, the United States claimed that Saddam Hussein had weapons of mass destruction and was supporting terrorists. It formed a coalition that invaded Iraq in 2003. Coalition forces toppled Saddam, who was later tried and executed for war crimes by a new Iraqi government.

Backed by U.S. and coalition forces, Shiite, Kurdish, and Sunni leaders wrote a constitution and held national elections in 2005. Efforts to rebuild Iraq were hampered by guerrilla attacks and suicide bombings. **Insurgents,** or rebels, from rival Shiite and Sunni groups targeted civilians and government workers.

Civil War Threatens Iraq By 2005, ethnic and religious divisions had pushed the country to the brink of civil war. The United States and Britain worked to train the Iraqi military and police. In 2007, the United States increased troop levels in a "surge" to end the fighting. The violence and death tolls declined.

Iraq's Shiite-led government faced many obstacles. It needed to promote reconciliation among bitterly divided factions. Sunnis claimed that the new government failed to represent their interests. Kurds in the north still sought autonomy. Much of the country's oil industry had been destroyed. An estimated 2 million Iraqi refugees remained outside the country.

Despite the troubles, Iraqi leaders grew more confident. They expanded their security forces and agreed to a withdrawal of all U.S. troops by 2011.

Urban Warfare in Iraq
Iraqi foot soldiers accompany a U.S. military vehicle. They are patrolling a war-torn neighborhood of Baghdad, Iraq's capital, in 2007. U.S. and Iraqi forces worked together to try to stop violence between Sunni and Shiite forces.

✔ **Checkpoint** Why has conflict persisted in Iraq since the defeat of Saddam Hussein?

SECTION **3** Assessment

Terms, People, and Places

1. What do each of the terms, people, and places listed at the beginning of the section have in common? Explain.

Note Taking

2. **Reading Skill: Recognize Sequence** Use your finished flowchart to answer the Focus Question: What are the causes of conflict in the Middle East?

Comprehension and Critical Thinking

3. **Draw Conclusions** Why has the Arab-Israeli conflict been difficult to resolve?
4. **Identify Central Issues** What were the causes of Lebanon's civil war?
5. **Synthesize Information** Why did the UN impose economic sanctions in Iraq after the 1991 Gulf War?

● Writing About History

Quick Write: Make an Outline To write a research report, you need to make an outline that organizes information that you have gathered. Suppose that you are writing a research report on the Arab-Israeli conflict. Make an outline that organizes the information in this section about that conflict.

Quick Study Guide

Progress Monitoring *Online*
For: Self-test with vocabulary practice
Web Code: naa-3241

■ Conflicts in Iraq

Conflict	Duration	Main Events
Iran-Iraq War	1980–1988	Saddam Hussein tried to seize an Iranian border region. Saddam used chemical weapons against Kurds.
Gulf War	1990–1991	Saddam Hussein invaded Kuwait. Coalition led by United States defeated Saddam's army and freed Kuwait.
Iraq War	2003–	Coalition led by the United States defeated Saddam Hussein's forces and occupied Iraq. Fighting with insurgents continued after Saddam's defeat in 2003.

■ Conflicts in Former Yugoslavia

Area of Conflict	Duration	Main Events
Croatia	1991–1995	Croatian forces fought with ethnic Serbs and the Yugoslav army over ethnic Serb areas. Serbs faced ethnic cleansing.
Bosnia	1992–1995	Ethnic Serbs, Croats, and Muslim Bosniaks fought each other. Muslims faced ethnic cleansing by Serbs.
Kosovo	1996–1999	Ethnic Albanians clashed with the Yugoslav army. Yugoslav forces attempted ethnic cleansing of Albanians.

■ Locations of Regional Conflicts

■ Key Events of Regional Conflicts

1948
South Africa expands apartheid system.

1960
Sharpeville massacre marks violent turn in anti-apartheid struggle.

Late 1960s
Conflict in Northern Ireland turns violent.

Africa and Europe
Middle East

| 1940 | 1950 | 1960 | 1970 |

1948
Israel's founding brings attack by Arab neighbors.

1967
Israel gains territory in the 1967 war, and Palestinians increase attacks on Israel.

 # Concept Connector

Essential Question Review

To connect prior knowledge with what you have learned in this chapter, answer the questions below in your Concept Connector journal. Use the journal in the Reading and Note Taking Study Guide to record your answers (or go to www.phschool.com **Web Code:** nad-3207). In addition, record information about the following concepts:

- Impact of the Individual: Nelson Mandela

1. **Dictatorship** Iraq was carved out of the old Ottoman empire after World War I, without regard for the ethnic and religious divisions of the population. Differences between Sunni Arabs, Shiite Arabs, and Kurds often led to conflicts. Given these differences, why might Iraqis support a dictator like Saddam Hussein? Identify at least one other reason for Iraqi support of Saddam Hussein.

2. **Genocide** During Bosnia's civil war, Bosnian Serbs conducted a campaign of ethnic cleansing—killing people from other ethnic groups or forcibly removing them from their homes to create ethnically "pure" areas. Croat and Bosnian fighters responded by launching ethnic cleansing campaigns against Serbs in Croatia. Suggest other possible motives for ethnic cleansing.

3. **Human Rights** After 1948, South Africa's government created apartheid, or the separation of the races. Because apartheid was designed to protect white control over South Africa, blacks were treated like foreigners in their own land. What restrictions did black South Africans face under apartheid? How did the ANC respond to apartheid? What factors caused South African president F.W. de Klerk to end apartheid?

■ Connections to Today

1. **Democracy** In this chapter, you read that Canada's democracy has allowed ethnic differences to be resolved peacefully, rather than through violent conflict. Through democratic means, the French-speaking majority in Quebec has secured rights for their language in Canada, even though French speakers are a minority in Canada (see the graphs below). Use the library and online research to identify another country where a democratic system has recently helped bring a peaceful resolution to ethnic differences. Compare your country's ethnic politics to those in Canada.

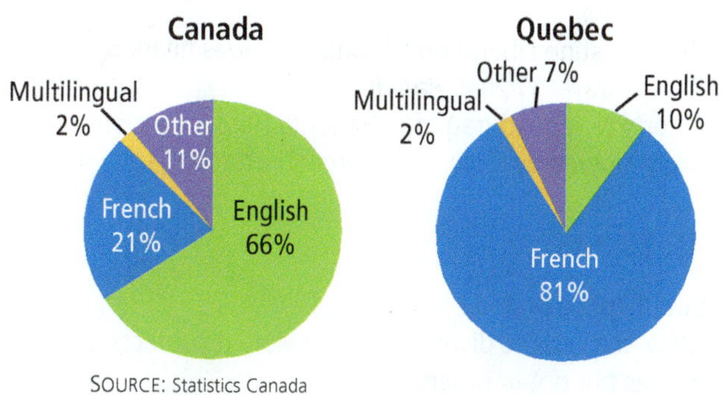

2. **Cooperation** In this chapter, you learned that members of the NATO military alliance cooperated to end ethnic cleansing and warfare in Kosovo in 1999. Use the library and online research to identify a more recent case in which cooperation among concerned nations has helped to bring peace to a country involved in a violent conflict. How does this recent case compare to what you learned about Kosovo?

History Interactive
For: Interactive timeline
Web Code: nap-3241

1992 Ethnic conflict erupts in Bosnia.

1994 Open elections bring end of apartheid in South Africa.

1999 Brutal ethnic conflict in Kosovo brings NATO intervention.

1980 **1990** **2000** **2010**

1975 Lebanon plunges into civil war.

1991 U.S.-led coalition defeats Iraq in Gulf War.

2003– U.S.-led coalition occupies Iraq and faces ongoing resistance.

Chapter Assessment

Terms, People, and Places

Choose the italicized term in parentheses that best completes each sentence.

1. Muslim nationalists in (*Kosovo/Chechnya*) have fought to free their homeland from Russian control.
2. There were hopes that (*the Good Friday Agreement/ethnic cleansing*) would provide for a peaceful resolution of the conflict in Northern Ireland.
3. (*Desmond Tutu/Nelson Mandela*) led the struggle against apartheid even when he was imprisoned for his role in the African National Congress.
4. In Rwanda, extremist (*Hutus/Tutsis*), the country's ethnic majority, slaughtered members of the country's ethnic minority in 1994.
5. Both Israel and the Palestinians claim (*Mecca / Jerusalem*) as their capital.
6. The Palestine Liberation Organization was headed by (*Yasir Arafat/Yitzhak Rabin*).
7. Efforts to rebuild Iraq after Saddam Hussein's overthrow were slowed by (*intifada/insurgent*) attacks.

Main Ideas

Section 1 (pp. 1044–1047)

8. Why does ethnic diversity lead to violent conflicts in some places but not in others?
9. How did Yugoslavia's breakup lead to ethnic conflicts?

Section 2 (pp. 1048–1053)

10. How did South Africa overcome apartheid?
11. What factors contributed to Africa's deadly ethnic conflicts?

Section 3 (pp. 1054–1059)

12. Explain the basic causes of the Israeli-Palestinian conflict.
13. Why did the removal of Saddam Hussein's regime fail to bring peace to Iraq?

Chapter Focus Question

14. Why have deadly conflicts plagued some regions of the world?

Critical Thinking

15. **Predict Consequences** Identify possible solutions to the ethnic conflicts in Bosnia and Kosovo and predict the consequences of these solutions.
16. **Draw Conclusions** Why was the idea of majority rule important to people in South Africa and in neighboring African countries?
17. **Express Problems Clearly** What are the main problems that have stood in the way of a peace settlement between Palestinians and Israelis?
18. **Recognize Cause and Effect** How did Saddam Hussein's policies cause suffering for Iraqis?
19. **Analyzing Visuals** What is the main message of the cartoon below? How might violence have been prevented in these countries?

● Writing About History

In this chapter's three Section Assessments, you developed skills for writing a research report.

Writing a Research Report This chapter discusses several ethnic and regional conflicts. Choose one of the conflicts covered or find another conflict that interests you. Write a research report on the causes of the conflict, how the conflict unfolded, and how it was resolved or might be resolved. Consult page SH13 of the Writing Handbook for additional help.

Prewriting

- Do online or library research to read background materials about your conflict.
- Take notes on relevant details, events, and the people involved in the conflict.
- Create a set of questions about your conflict and gather additional resources.

Drafting

- Develop a working thesis about the cause of this conflict—for example, is the main issue control of land, government policies, or some other issue?
- Make an outline to organize a report that supports your thesis. Find information from your research that supports each part of your outline.
- Write an introduction explaining your thesis, a body, and a conclusion.

Revising

- Use the guidelines for revising your report on page SH15 of the Writing Handbook.

Document-Based Assessment

The Palestinian Question

In 1947, the United Nations drew up a plan dividing the Palestine Mandate into two states, Jewish and Arab, which the Arabs rejected. The next year, Israel was established as an independent nation according to the United Nations guidelines. As a result of the 1967 war, Israel gained control of the West Bank and Gaza. Israeli troops and civilians withdrew from Gaza in 2005. Palestinians still do not have an independent state of their own. Despite ongoing conflict between Israelis and Palestinians, many on both sides still hope for peace.

Document A

UN Partition Plan, 1947

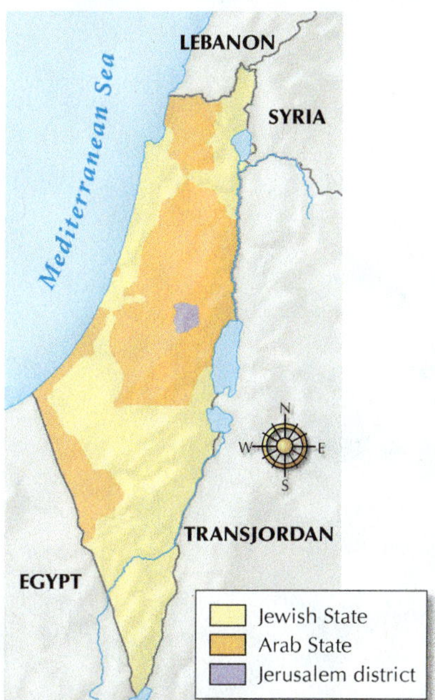

Document B

Israel and Occupied Territories, 2005

Document C

"As I have said, we came to Palestine to do away with the helplessness of the Jewish people through our own endeavors. Therefore, you will realize what it meant for us to watch from here millions of Jews being slaughtered during these years of war. . . . We Jews only want that which is given naturally to all peoples of the world to be masters of our own fate . . . . We are certain that given an opportunity of bringing in large masses of Jews into this country, of opening the doors of Palestine to all Jews who wish to come here, we can . . . create a free Jewish society built on the basis of cooperation, equality, and mutual aid."

—From **"The Zionist Case"** by Golda Meir (speech given March 25, 1946)

Document D

"Late at night when everything is quiet I think about how I will ever forgive the Israelis for what they did to me. I don't mean stealing my homeland, killing my people, turning me into a refugee, or depriving me from having a Palestinian state. I'm talking about myself—what they did to my personality.

I wish I had a normal life: no tension, no rage, no hatred, no hard feelings toward anybody. Even if they leave my country and give me back my rights, how will I overcome these feelings inside me?"

—From **"Children of a Tenth-Class God?"** by Nihaya Qawasmi (1998)

Analyzing Documents

Use your knowledge of the Palestinian-Israeli conflict and Documents A, B, C, and D to answer questions 1–4.

1. According to Documents A and B, what is the present status of the area outlined in the UN Partition Plan?
   A It is divided between Israel and neighboring countries.
   B Palestine is now an independent nation.
   C Part of it is the State of Israel, part is occupied by Israel, and part is ruled by the Palestinians.
   D It is divided among three independent nations.

2. In Document C, "helplessness" refers to
   A Israel's inability to help the Palestinians.
   B the inability of Jews in Palestine to help Jews in Nazi territory.
   C the inability of Palestinians to change their attitude toward Israel.
   D the inability of the Allies to do anything about Nazi atrocities.

3. Which words best describe the feelings of the author of Document D toward Israel?
   A acceptance and understanding
   B discouragement and fear
   C anger and resentment
   D trust and hope

4. **Writing Task** What are the prospects for a peaceful settlement of the Palestinian question? Use the documents on this page along with information from the chapter to write a short essay on this topic.

33

The Developing World

1945–Present

 ◉ AUDIO

A Sleeping Giant Awakes

In the past few decades, many nations in the developing world have experienced rapid social and economic change. One such nation is China. Fifty years ago, China was recovering from civil war and just starting to modernize. Today, China is an economic powerhouse. Robert Broadfoot, managing director of Hong Kong's Political and Economic Risk Consultancy, said,

66 . . . I have never seen so much hope in China. The Chinese will produce much cheaper items and export them. I think that will shape the course of commerce in the coming century. 99

Listen to the Witness History audio to hear more about China's economic development.

◀ China's rapid development is reflected in the city of Shenzhen, where modern glass buildings tower above old, shabby houses.

Chapter Preview

Chapter Focus Question What challenges have nations of the developing world faced, and what steps have they taken to meet those challenges?

Section 1
The Challenges of Development

Section 2
Africa Seeks a Better Future

Section 3
China and India: Two Giants of Asia

Section 4
Latin America Builds Democracy

Use the ✔ **Quick Study Timeline** at the end of this chapter to preview chapter events.

Concept Connector ONLINE

To explore Essential Questions related to this chapter, go to PHSchool.com
Web Code: nad-3307

A loan recipient poses with the cows she bought to help generate income.

Bangladesh's currency, the taka

Building a Better Life

Bangladeshi Laily Begum used to sleep in a cow shed and spend her days begging. Then she got a loan for $119 from Grameen Bank, a Bangladesh-based organization that lends money to the poor. She bought a cow and began to build her own business selling milk. Today she and her husband own several shops and a restaurant.

66 People now come to me for help . . . I can feed myself and my family, and now other people look at me and they treat me with respect. 99
—Laily Begum, February 12, 1998

Focus Question How have the nations of the developing world tried to build better lives for their people?

The Challenges of Development

Objectives

- Understand the paths that nations in Asia, Africa, and Latin America have taken in developing strong economies.
- Describe some obstacles to development in the global South.
- Explain how development is changing patterns of life in the developing world.

Terms, People, and Places

development	Green Revolution
developing world	fundamentalists
literacy	shantytowns
traditional economies	

Note Taking

Reading Skill: Identify Supporting Details
Expand this chart to record details about development as you read.

Development		
Economic Change	Obstacles	Changes in Patterns of Life
• •	• •	• •

Many new nations emerged in Africa and Asia in the decades after World War II. These new nations, along with countries in Latin America, focused on development. **Development** means building stable governments, improving agriculture and industry, and raising standards of living. The nations working toward development in Africa, Asia, and Latin America are known collectively as the **developing world.** From the beginning, nations in the developing world faced many challenges.

Goals of Development

At independence, new nations wrote constitutions that set up representative governments and protected the rights of citizens. Their leaders also pushed to build strong modern economies. Since a modern economy needs well-trained workers, developing nations built schools to increase **literacy,** or the ability to read and write.

The Global South The developing world is sometimes called the global South because it is located mostly south of the Tropic of Cancer. The global South holds 75 percent of the world's people and much of its natural resources. It was poor, however, compared to the global North, the rich industrial nations located mostly north of the Tropic of Cancer.

Transforming Economies Leaders of new nations in the developing world set ambitious economic goals. They wanted to increase food output, develop industry, construct roads, airports, and railroads, and build power plants.

Despite these goals, much of the developing world still lived and worked in traditional economies. **Traditional economies** are undeveloped economic systems that rely on custom and tradition, using simple tools and methods of production passed down from earlier generations. In traditional economies, most people are farmers or craftspeople who make or grow enough to meet their own needs. They trade any surplus, or extra, for goods they cannot make themselves.

Economic Policies Developing nations needed vast amounts of capital to finance projects to modernize their economies. After independence, some political leaders tried to speed development by replacing traditional and market economies with government-led command economies. This meant that governments owned most businesses and controlled farming.

To pay for development, many countries procured large loans from banks and governments in the global North. When poor economic conditions made it difficult for these countries to repay their loans, lenders insisted that developing countries sell government businesses, hold free elections, and establish market economies. Lenders required these changes so developing countries could pay off debts and be eligible for new loans.

Vocabulary Builder
procure—(proh KYOOR) *v.* obtain, make an effort to get

Geography Interactive
For: Audio guided tour
Web Code: nap-3311

The Global North and Global South

Map Skills The developed countries are also known as the global North, while the developing countries are known as the global South.

1. **Locate** (a) Brazil (b) India (c) Japan
2. **Regions** Which continents lie partly within both the global North and the global South?
3. **Make Comparisons** Based on the graph, how does the standard of living of nations in the global North compare with that in the global South?

Economic Output per Person

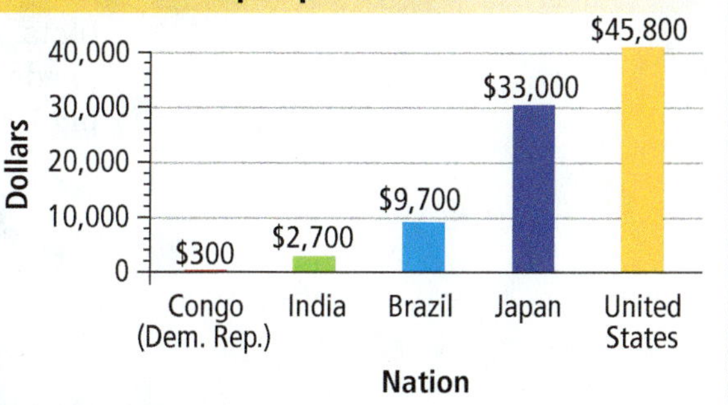

SOURCE: *CIA World Factbook*

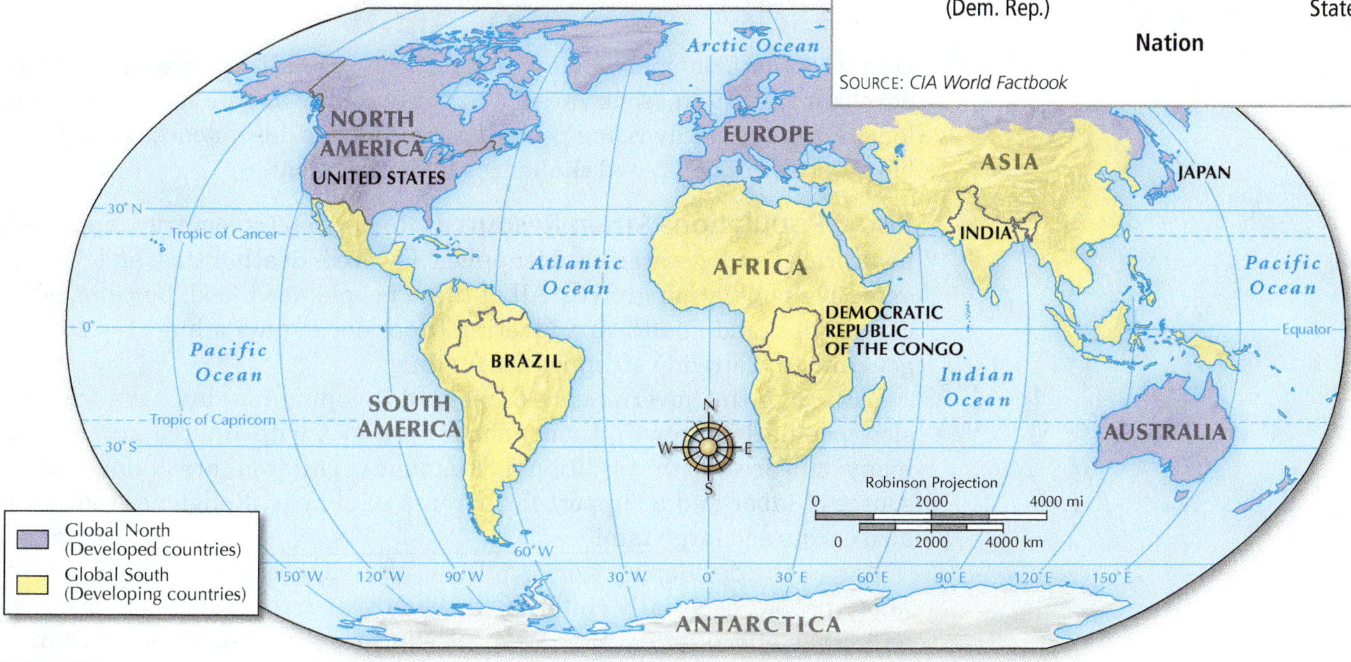

After developing countries shifted to market economies, companies and individuals from the global North invested in industries in these countries. Investors put money into businesses that produced income for them, but were not always best for the developing nation's economy.

The Green Revolution During the 1950s and 1960s, new high-yield seeds, fertilizers, and pesticides, along with mechanical equipment such as tractors, were introduced in many parts of the developing world. These new products, along with new methods of farming, are known as the Green Revolution. The Green Revolution raised farm output in developing countries. But it had unforeseen consequences. Only big landowners could afford these new tools and methods. Because they farmed more land, they could grow crops more cheaply than farmers with small plots. As a result, prices for crops dropped below what smaller farmers needed to make to earn a living. Many were forced to sell their farms to big landowners. They became farm workers or moved to cities.

 **Checkpoint**   How did the Green Revolution affect traditional economies?

Obstacles to Development

Despite ambitious goals, many new nations made little progress toward development. The reasons varied, but many countries shared similar problems. Poverty, rapidly rising populations, economic dependence, and unstable governments all posed challenges to development.

Rising Populations Strain Resources In developing countries, improved healthcare and greater food supplies lowered death rates and led to explosive population growth. All of these people need food, housing, education, jobs, and healthcare. Meeting these needs puts a huge burden on governments already strapped for funding.

Although the governments of many developing nations have tried to slow population growth, their efforts have met with limited success. In many cultures with traditional economies, children are valued as a source of labor and a support for parents in old age. Religious traditions also encourage large families.

Across the developing world, millions are trapped in a cycle of poverty. Many people, especially children, die each year from starvation, disease, and other effects of poverty. Without education and jobs, people cannot earn living wages and are unable to escape this tragic cycle.

Economic Dependence Despite their efforts to build industry, many developing nations remain economically dependent on their former colonial rulers. Western nations had used their colonies as sources of raw materials. They used the raw materials to produce manufactured goods that they sold to their colonies.

This pattern continued after colonies won their independence. Industrialized countries purchase agricultural goods and raw materials from the developing world. In turn, the industrial nations provide technology, investment, and manufactured goods to developing countries. However, in recent years, lower labor costs have led Western companies to relocate their manufacturing operations to the global South.

Some developing nations produce only a single export crop or commodity, such as sugar or cocoa. Their economies depend on global demand for the cash crop or commodity. If demand weakens and prices drop, their economies suffer.

Unstable Governments Civil wars and other conflicts hinder development in some countries. Poor leadership and corrupt governments also prevent growth. Dictators spend resources on weapons instead of on education or healthcare. Corrupt leaders loot their nations' treasuries and allow a culture of bribery to thrive.

✔ **Checkpoint** How did population growth affect developing nations?

Patterns of Life Change

Economic development has unleashed great changes across the developing world. Just as the Industrial Revolution disrupted traditional ways of life in Europe and North America, economic development is now transforming life in the global South.

Women's Lives Change In the developing world, the move away from traditional ways of life has brought new opportunities for women. New constitutions granted equality to women, at least on paper. In some countries, such as India, Argentina, and Liberia, women have served as heads of state. Although women still have less access to education than men, the gap has narrowed. Women are joining the work force in growing numbers and contributing their skills to their nations' wealth.

Child Labor In traditional economies, children worked alongside parents, farming or herding to meet the family's needs. When development forces people off their farms, they often move to cities and take low-paying

Different Kinds of Labor
A mechanical harvester cuts rice in South America, while women in West Africa prepare fields for planting. *How do traditional economies affect economic development?*

manufacturing jobs. Because these jobs do not pay enough to cover basic needs, parents depend on the low wages that children earn in factory jobs to survive. In India, around 44 million children work for pay. In Pakistan, children make up 10 percent of the workforce.

Religious Revivals In recent decades, religious revivals have swept many developing nations. Some religious leaders are called **fundamentalists,** because they call for a return to what they see as the fundamental, or basic values of their faiths. Many seek political power to oppose changes that undermine their valued religious traditions.

Rapid Growth of Cities Across the developing world, people have flooded into cities to escape rural poverty and find jobs. Besides economic opportunities, cities offer attractions such as entertainment and sports. With no money and few jobs, most newcomers settle in **shantytowns,** crowded, dangerous slums on the edges of cities. These crime-ridden slums lack basic services such as running water, electricity, or sewer systems.

✔ **Checkpoint** How did development change life for women?

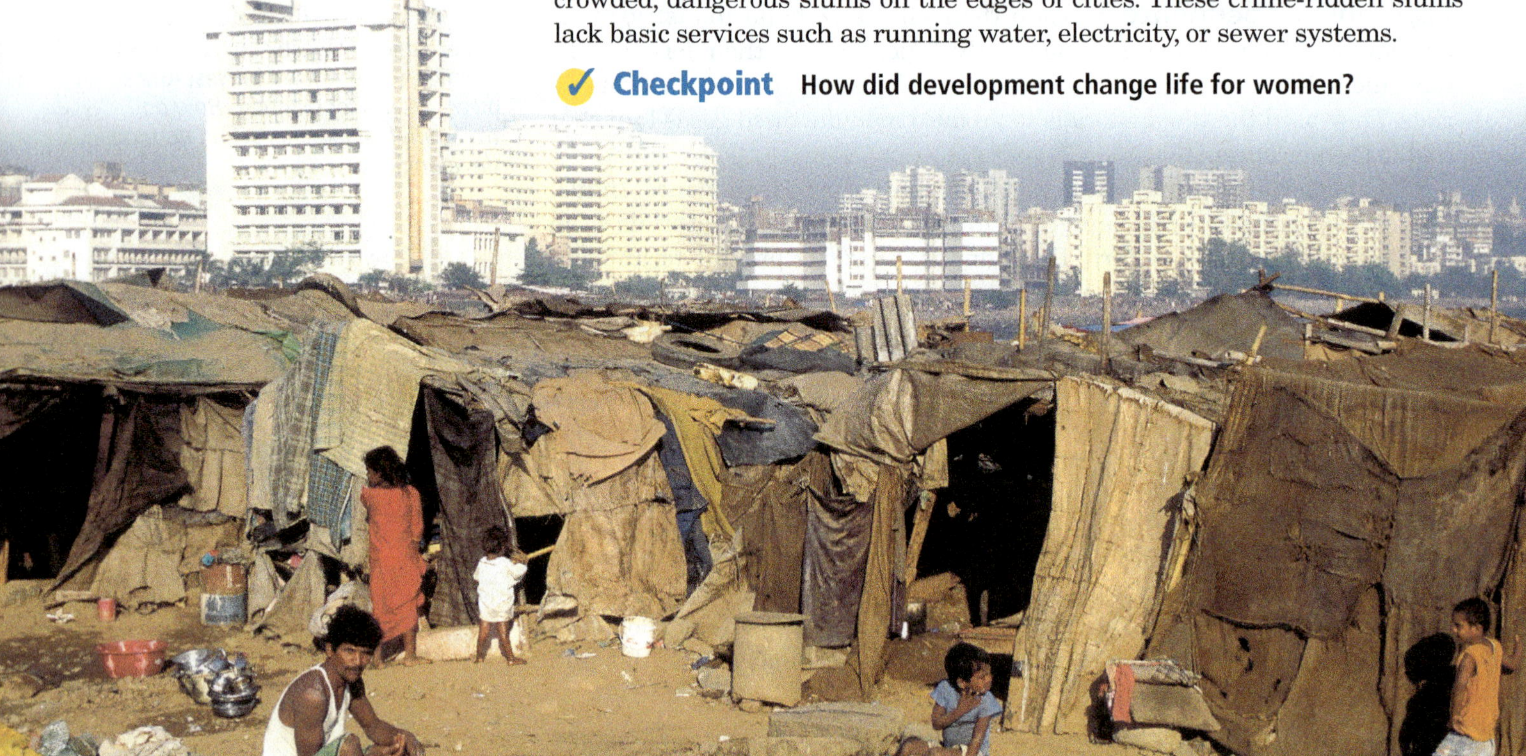

Mumbai: A Divided City
In Mumbai, India, the poverty of slums stands in stark contrast to the comfortable high-rise apartments of wealthier city dwellers. *How did rapid population growth create problems for cities?*

1 Assessment

Progress Monitoring _Online_
For: Self-quiz with vocabulary practice
Web Code: naa-3311

Terms, People, and Places

1. For each term, person, or place listed at the beginning of the section, write a sentence explaining its significance.

Note Taking

2. **Reading Skill: Identify Supporting Details** Use your completed chart to answer the Focus Question: How have the nations of the developing world tried to build better lives for their people?

Comprehension and Critical Thinking

3. **Summarize** In general, what are the economic goals of developing nations?
4. **Categorize** What are the differences between the global North and the global South?
5. **Identify Central Issues** Why do developing countries remain dependent on former colonial powers or other industrialized countries?
6. **Predict Consequences** How might modern products and technologies weaken traditional cultures?

● Writing About History

Quick Write: Explore a Topic Choose one challenge facing developing nations and write a series of questions you could use to direct research on the topic. For example, on the topic of industrialization in developing nations you could ask:
- Which five developing nations have the highest level of industrialization today?
- What industries do these nations engage in?

THE ESSENTIAL ?

DEMOCRACY

Under what conditions is democracy most likely to succeed?

In This Chapter

Developing countries have had to overcome many obstacles in order to establish democratic governments. Poverty, illiteracy, political corruption, and inequality among ethnic groups are among the factors that have stood in their way. The education of children like these (right) will be critical to the future of democratic government everywhere.

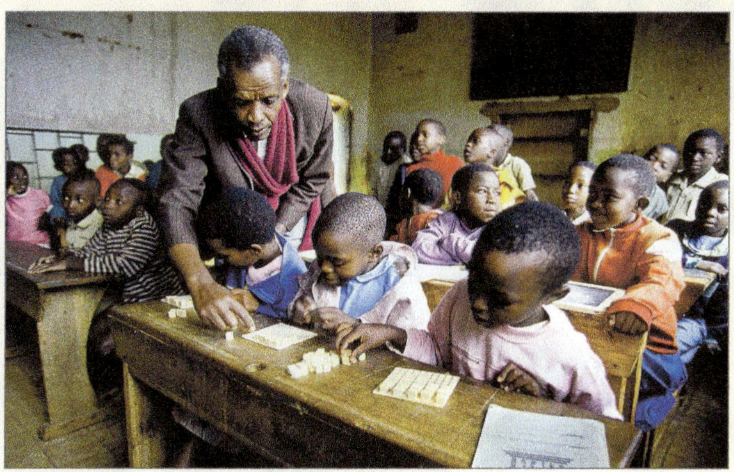

Throughout History

400s B.C. The Athenian leader, Pericles, believes all citizens should take part in government.

400s B.C. Plebeians in ancient Rome demand and get the right to elect their own officials.

1215 A.D. English nobles force King John to sign the Magna Carta, limiting the power of the king.

1776 The American colonies wage a war to gain independence and the right to rule themselves.

1930s Germany, facing economic and social problems, turns away from democracy.

Continuing Today

Zimbabwe went from being a model of development to one of the poorest nations in the world under the leadership of Robert Mugabe. Mugabe has ruthlessly held on to power, threatening anyone who has challenged him.

21st Century Skills

TRANSFER Activities

1. Analyze Throughout history, how have people gained the right to a say in government?

2. Explain How can democratic government be undermined?

3. Transfer Complete a Web quest in which you compare democratic countries; record your thoughts in the Concept Connector Journal; and learn to make a video. Web Code nah-3308

A Nigerian child stands in front of the massive trunk of a felled ironwood tree.

SECTION 2

Plundering Forests

Civil wars, economic development, and the demand for valuable woods have led to the destruction of ancient African forests. In Ivory Coast, also known as Côte d'Ivoire (koht dee VWAHR), rebels cut trees to sell for money to buy weapons. Illegal logging is devastating local economies. A village chief, Kouadio Yao (KWAH dyoh yow), told a UN worker of watching helplessly as valuable teak trees were chopped down:

> **66** If someone came with a gun, would you be able to stop them and demand that they pay for the trees? What I do know is that because of the conflict, we have lost everything. **99**
> —Integrated Regional Information Networks (IRIN), December 23, 2004

Focus Question What challenges have African nations faced in their effort to develop their economies?

Africa Seeks a Better Future

Objectives

- Describe the goals of developing nations in Africa.
- Understand the obstacles that African nations faced as they pursued development.
- Analyze the challenges faced by a developing nation by taking a closer look at Tanzania.

Terms, People, and Places

socialism	endangered species
desertification	Wangari Maathai
urbanization	sustainable development

Note Taking

Reading Skill: Identify Main Ideas As you read, use a concept web to record the main ideas in this section and to note details that support those main ideas.

More than fifty new nations emerged in Africa in the decades after World War II. African nations are a large part of the developing world. As they set out to build stable governments and modern economies, they faced serious challenges.

Making Economic Choices

In Africa, as elsewhere, development meant building productive economies and raising standards of living. To achieve these goals, African nations had to establish industries, build transportation systems, increase literacy, and reduce poverty. Many countries had little capital to invest in such projects. Each nation had to make difficult choices about how to achieve their goals.

Socialism or Capitalism Many newly independent nations were attracted to **socialism,** a system in which the people as a whole own all property and operate all businesses. Through socialism, the new nations hoped to reduce dependence on their former colonial rulers and end the inequalities between rich and poor. To regulate the economy, socialism relied on large, generally inefficient bureaucracies.

Some nations chose capitalism, or market economies with private ownership of property, as a path to development. To get the huge sums needed for development, they turned to foreign lenders to invest capital in new industries. These countries often had more efficient economies, but foreign lenders took more profits out of the country.

Cash Crops or Food Governments tried to raise development funds by producing raising cash crops for export, such as coffee or cotton. Some nations or exporting a commodity, such as copper or oil. However, dependence on a single crop or commodity is risky, because it puts economies at the mercy of sudden price changes in the market.

Because land used for cash crops could not be used to produce food, some countries had to buy costly imported food. To prevent unrest among the urban poor, many governments kept food prices artificially low. However, low prices discouraged local farmers from growing food crops. Governments then had to <u>subsidize</u> part of the cost of importing food.

✔ **Checkpoint**   **Why did governments promote cash crops?**

Obstacles to Progress

Developing African nations faced numerous problems. The challenges included deadly civil wars, rapid population growth, epidemics, and damage to the environment and wildlife.

Drought Brings Starvation From time to time, droughts struck parts of Africa, killing livestock and crops. The Sahel, a semi-desert region just south of the Sahara, was especially hard hit in the late 1960s. The drought, which lasted for decades, led to famine. Overgrazing and farming in this fragile area removed topsoil and led to **desertification,** or a change of semi-dry land into desert. International relief efforts eased the famine, but wars that raged in several countries in the Sahel added to the suffering.

The AIDS Epidemic Since the 1980s, the deadly disease AIDS (Acquired Immune Deficiency Syndrome), has spread across Africa. AIDS is caused by HIV, a virus that damages the body's ability to fight infections. In South Africa and Botswana, up to one third of adults were infected with HIV. More than 11 million children in Africa have been orphaned by the AIDS epidemic.

The loss of so many skilled and productive workers hurt the economies of African countries. A global effort to combat AIDS led to the development of drugs to treat people infected with HIV. African nations set up treatment programs and worked hard to stop the spread of AIDS.

People Move to Cities African nations experienced rapid **urbanization,** or the movement of people from rural areas to cities. The newcomers hoped to find a better life. Instead, millions faced unemployment, terrible living conditions, and crime. However, in much of West Africa, the growth of cities has provided increased opportunities for women, who have historically dominated urban markets as traders.

Urbanization also brought people from different ethnic groups together and helped replace ethnic loyalties with a larger national identity. But modern urban lifestyles weakened traditional cultures and undermined ethnic and kinship ties. Despite rapid urbanization, most people in Africa still lived in villages.

Displaced by Drought
A Sudanese mother and children escape famine caused by years of drought. *How can geography affect migration patterns?*

ENDANGERED SPECIES

The threats to Africa's endangered species include a loss of habitats and poaching, or illegal hunting. The map below shows that most of Africa's forests have been disturbed or cut down. However, Africans have taken steps to save their rich wildlife. Earnings from tourism have given local people a stake in saving these animals' lives.

▲ Foreign demand for leopard skins has encouraged illegal killing of leopards.

Elephants have been killed for their valuable tusks. ▶

▲ Africa's wildlife draw foreign tourists, who provide a steady income to local guides and tour operators. This gives Africans a stake in preventing poaching.

◀ African nations have set aside preserves to protect endangered species such as these mountain gorillas in Rwanda.

Thinking Critically

1. **Draw Conclusions** Based on the map at the right, how have changes in Africa's forest cover affected its forest species?
2. **Synthesize Information** How might wildlife tourism discourage poaching in Africa?

Development Hurts the Environment In Africa, as elsewhere, urbanization, population growth, farming, and logging led to the destruction of Africa's animal habitats. As habitats were destroyed, some animals became **endangered species,** or species threatened with extinction. Foreign demand for elephant tusks to make ivory, or for rare pelts or furs, has encouraged impoverished Africans to kill endangered animals, even when it is illegal.

In Kenya, **Wangari Maathai** (mah THY), an environmental activist, started the Green Belt Movement. She was inspired to plant trees with women to help them meet basic needs, such as energy, clean drinking water, and nutritious food. Maathai wanted to heal the land, empower women, and promote **sustainable development,** or development that meets the needs of the present without compromising the ability of future generations to meet their own needs.

✔ **Checkpoint** What are some advantages and disadvantages of urbanization in Africa?

Tanzania: A Closer Look

Tanganyika, a large country in East Africa, gained independence in the early 1960s and later merged with the island state of Zanzibar to form the republic of Tanzania. Julius Nyerere, the country's first president, wanted to raise the standard of living for Tanzania's impoverished, population.

African Socialism Tanzania had little capital or technology. Most people were farmers. The country's main exports were coffee, cotton, tea, and tobacco. To improve life for Tanzanians, Nyerere's government embraced what he called "African socialism." This was based on village traditions of cooperation and shared responsibility.

The government took over banks, businesses, and factories. In a program of rural development called *ujamaa* (pulling together), farmers were encouraged to move to large villages and work on collective farms. The goal was to increase output and produce surplus crops for export.

Nyerere's experiment failed, partly because farmers did not want to leave their own land for collective farms. Agricultural output did not rise. However, Tanzania did make important advances in education and healthcare during this period.

Debt Leads to Reforms The experiment created a huge and inefficient government bureaucracy. The expense of this huge bureaucracy, along with high oil prices, plunged Tanzania into debt. In 1985, President Nyerere resigned. Tanzania's new leaders introduced economic reforms, cutting the size of government and promoting a market economy. By 2003, Tanzania's debt was being reduced through participation in an IMF/World Bank program.

Outlook Today, Tanzania still has an overwhelmingly agricultural economy. Although Tanzania remains poor, its economy received a boost in the early 2000s from the opening of a huge new gold mine. The government planned to use gold mine profits along with foreign aid to reduce poverty and improve basic services.

✔ **Checkpoint** What was the result of Tanzania's experiment with socialism?

BIOGRAPHY

Wangari Maathai

While working with a women's rights group, Kenyan activist Wangari Maathai (born in 1940) came up with the idea of getting ordinary women involved in tree-planting projects. In 1977, she launched the Green Belt Movement (GBM). This grassroots organization promotes reforestation and controlled wood cutting to ensure a sustainable supply of wood fuel. The group also sought jobs for women in Kenya, Tanzania, and other East African countries. In 2004, Maathai became the first African woman to be awarded the Nobel Peace Prize. Today, Maathai continues to work with the GBM. She is also a member of Kenya's government. **In what ways might planting trees help improve women's lives?**

SECTION 2 Assessment

Terms, People, and Places

1. For each term or person listed at the beginning of the section, write a sentence explaining its significance.

Note Taking

2. **Reading Skill: Identify Main Ideas** Use your completed concept web to answer the Focus Question: What challenges have African nations faced in their effort to develop their economies?

Comprehension and Critical Thinking

3. **Summarize** What obstacles kept many African nations from developing strong economies?

4. **Synthesize Information** Why have African nations had trouble feeding their people?

5. **Draw Inferences** Urbanization is a problem for many developing nations. Why do you think this is?

6. **Summarize** Why did socialism in Tanzania fail?

● Writing About History

Quick Write: Gather Information Review the material in this section on social issues in Africa. For each problem, list the causes, the effects, and any actions that have been taken to solve that problem.

"

A man tries to stop a line of tanks heading into the crowd of protesters in Tiananmen Square (top). Protesters erect a statue of the goddess of democracy in front of a poster of Mao (right).

A Violent Crackdown

When students and other Chinese citizens protested to demand more political freedom in the 1980s, the government cracked down. Cheng Zhen, a student, describes what she saw in Beijing's Tiananmen (TYEN ahn mun) Square on the night of June 4, 1989.

66 [A]t about 2 A.M. we . . . could see that the troops were already in the square, and we quickly ran to the other side. . . . While I was running, I noticed a young man ahead of me. He picked up a bottle on the ground, and was about to throw it at the troops, angry because they were holding up their guns and firing. Suddenly, he fell to the ground. . . . He was shot. . . . 99
—BBC News Online, June 2, 2004

Focus Question What are the similarities and differences between the economies and governments of China and India?

China and India: Two Giants of Asia

Objectives
- Analyze how China has reformed its economy but limited freedom.
- Describe the continuing challenges that China faces.
- Understand how India has faced poverty but built a stronger economy.
- Explain important Indian social reforms.

Terms, People, and Places

Deng Xiaoping	Mumbai
Tiananmen Square	Mother Teresa
one-child policy	dalits
Kolkata	

Note Taking

Reading Skill: Identify Main Ideas As you read, make a table like this one to record the main ideas.

Reform and Change in China and India		
Type	China	India
Economic	• Free market •	
Political		

China and India dominate much of Asia. Together, they are home to about two-fifths of the world's population. China is a major industrial nation. Although India's economy is smaller, like China, it is a leading Asian and global power. Over the last 60 years, China and India have taken different paths toward development.

China Mixes Reform and Repression

Mao Zedong, China's communist revolutionary leader, died in 1976. After Mao's death, more moderate leaders took control of China. By 1981, **Deng Xiaoping** (dung show ping), had taken a new approach to China's economy. Deng was a practical reformer, more interested in improving economic output than in political purity. "I don't care if a cat is black or white," he declared, "as long as it catches mice."

Modernizing the Economy Deng's program, the Four Modernizations, emphasized agriculture, industry, science, and defense. The plan allowed some features of a free market, such as some private ownership of property. Communes, or collectively owned farms, were dismantled, and peasant families were allotted plots of farmland in what was called the "responsibility system." Farmers still did not own the land, and the government took a share of their crops. However, farmers could sell any surplus produce and keep their profits. Chinese entrepreneurs were allowed to set up businesses. Managers of state-run factories were given more freedom, but they had to make their plants more efficient. Deng also welcomed foreign capital and technology. Investors from Japan, Hong Kong, Taiwan, and Western nations invested heavily in Chinese firms.

Economic reforms brought a surge of growth. In coastal cities, foreign investment created an economic boom. Some Chinese enjoyed an improved standard of living. They bought refrigerators, televisions, and cars. On the other hand, crime and corruption increased and a growing economic and regional gap developed between poor rural farmers and wealthy city dwellers.

The Government Crushes Protests Economic reforms and increased contact with the West led some Chinese to demand greater political freedom. In the late 1980s, students, workers, and others created a democracy movement similar to those sweeping across Eastern Europe. However, Deng and other Chinese leaders refused to allow democratic reforms.

In 1989, thousands of protesters, many of them students, occupied Tiananmen (TYEN ahn mun) Square, a huge public plaza in Beijing. They raised banners calling for democracy. The government ordered the protesters to <u>disperse.</u> When they refused, the government sent in troops and tanks. Thousands of demonstrators were killed or wounded in the Tiananmen Square Massacre. Many others were imprisoned and tortured. The crackdown showed that the communist government was determined to keep control.

China Limits Population Growth China's population, at more than 1.3 billion, is the largest in the world. In the 1980s, the government imposed a one-child policy, which limited urban families to a single child, and rural families to two children. The goal was to keep population growth from hurting economic development. The government enforced the policy with fines and other penalties. Although the one-child policy was harshly condemned, it did slow population growth.

✔ **Checkpoint** How did economic reforms benefit China?

China Faces Ongoing Challenges

Economic reforms had more than quadrupled China's economic output by the early 2000s. China's industrial power made it a growing rival of the United States. China's achievements—symbolized by the newly built Beijing National Stadium—were displayed to the world when it hosted the 2008 summer Olympic games. But the country still faced serious internal challenges.

Growth Brings Problems Boom times led to rapid urbanization as millions of rural workers flooded into China's cities. Urban newcomers worked for low wages in manufacturing jobs. Although these workers lived in poverty, their needs strained local resources. Rapid development brought

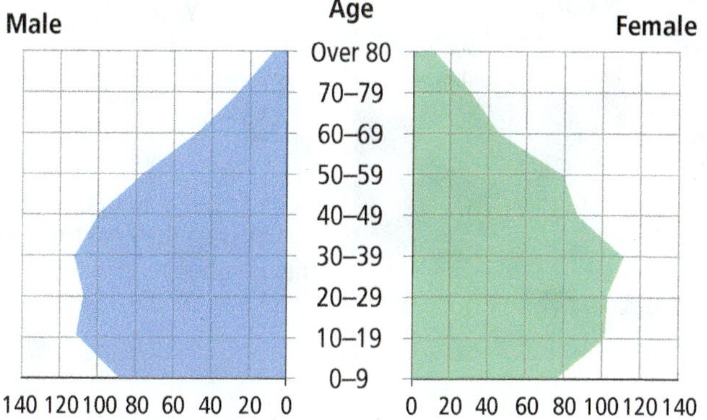
China, Estimated Population by Age and Gender, 2008

Graph Skills China's population growth has slowed in recent years due to government efforts like the one-child policy, encouraged in the billboard below. *According to the graph, in what age groups is most of China's population concentrated? What might this mean for China's future?*

SOURCE: U.S. Census Bureau, International Data Base

India and China are both huge Asian nations with rapidly growing populations. They have very different governments: India is a democracy, while China is communist. However, they have taken similar economic paths in recent years. Study the chart (right) and graph (left) below. *Which country has achieved a higher economic output in recent years? How might policies adopted by that nation help explain this success?*

Economic Growth in India and China, 1960–2007

Comparing India and China

China	India
Shift to free market economy in 1980s	Shift to free market economy in 1980s
Government policies limit population growth	Population growth remains a serious issue
Autocratic communist government	Democratic government

A man casts a vote in an election ▶ in Kashmir, India. Religious and political conflict has limited economic growth in that region.

◀ A pedestrian in Shanghai, China, walks past the construction of a new high-rise apartment building.

other problems. Industrial production led to dangerously polluted air and water. In 2007, China's Ministry of Health said that pollution caused hundreds of thousands of premature deaths each year. Increased travel and trade helped spread AIDS and other diseases across China.

The global economic recession that began in 2008 took its toll. Chinese factories closed as overseas orders fell. As the economy slowed and unemployment rose, many workers returned to family homes in rural areas. Protests by unemployed urban workers increased. To prevent social unrest, the government announced an economic stimulus package to improve productivity and retrain workers.

Human Rights Abuses Despite the global outcry after the Tiananmen Square massacre, China continued to jail critics and limit freedom. Human rights activists inside and outside China protested abuses such as the use of prison labor to produce cheap goods for export and the suppression of Tibetan culture and rights. China's trading partners called for an end to human rights abuses. Party leaders said that outsiders had no right to try to impose "Western-style" ideas of human rights on China. However, China's cabinet issued the country's first human rights action plan in 2009. It included the right to question government policies.

✓ **Checkpoint** How did the global economic recession affect China?

India Builds a Modern Economy

Like China, India is a big country with a large, diverse population and widespread poverty. After gaining independence in 1947, India set up a democratic government and planned to develop a modern economy.

Agriculture and Industry Expand Like other developing nations, India was determined to use modern technology to expand agriculture and industry. The government followed a socialist model, using five-year plans to set economic goals and manage resources. Development, however, was uneven. India built some industries, but it lacked oil and natural gas, key resources for economic growth. Instead, it had to rely on costly imported oil.

India benefited from the Green Revolution. High-yield crops, chemical fertilizers, and better irrigation systems increased output. Still, most farmers used traditional methods and relied on seasonal rains for water. They produced enough to survive, but little surplus.

By the 1980s, an economic slowdown and outside pressure pushed India toward a market economy. Some industries were privatized and limits on foreign investment were eased. During the 1990s, Indian textiles, technology, and other industries saw rapid expansion. By 2000, India was a leader in information technology, providing computer software services to the world. Although India's booming economy slowed after 2008 as a result of the global recession, it stood ready to move ahead when economic conditions improved.

Population Growth and Poverty In India, as in China, rapid population growth hurt efforts to improve living conditions. As food output rose, so did demand. More than one-third of Indians lived in poverty, unable to meet basic needs for food, clothing, and shelter. The growing population put added pressure on India's healthcare system, which faced additional challenges after 1990 from the spread of AIDS.

The population boom and the labor-saving methods of the Green Revolution led millions of rural families to migrate to cities. But overcrowded cities like Kolkata (or Calcutta) and Mumbai (or Bombay) could not provide jobs

Bangalore: A Customer Support Center
Workers in Bangalore, India, serve as customer service operators for American and European companies. To make callers feel more comfortable, the operators are trained in English and American slang. *How do you expect the customer service industry to change as more countries develop?*

Combating Poverty
Mother Teresa, shown with children in Calcutta, inspired others to help people living in poverty.

for everyone or even basic services, such as water or sewage systems. To help the urban poor, **Mother Teresa,** a Roman Catholic nun, founded the Missionaries of Charity in Calcutta. This group provided food and medical care to thousands. Still, millions more remained in desperate need.

The Indian government supported family planning but did not adopt the harsh policies that were used in China. Efforts to slow population growth had limited success. Poor families, especially in rural areas, saw children as an economic resource to work the land and care for parents in old age.

 **Checkpoint** How did market reforms affect India's economy during the 1990s?

Reforming Indian Society

In India, as elsewhere, urbanization, education, and the growth of a modern economy undermined traditional ways of life. These changes benefited India's lowest social castes and women. In the cities, many people adopted western-style clothing and bought modern consumer goods. Yet most Indians still lived in villages and followed traditional ways.

Caste Discrimination Persists India's constitution banned discrimination against **dalits,** or people of the lowest caste. To improve conditions, the government set aside jobs and places in universities for members of these groups. However, discrimination based on caste continued.

Women Make Progress India's constitution granted equal rights to women. In the cities, girls from well-to-do families were educated. Women entered many professions. Some, like Indira Gandhi, won political office. Girls from poor families, however, received little or no education. Although women in rural areas worked the land or contributed to household industries, few received wages. Across India, women organized self-help groups to start small businesses and improve their lives.

Checkpoint How did the Indian government try to improve the status of dalits?

Progress Monitoring *Online*
For: Self-quiz with vocabulary practice
Web Code: naa-3331

Terms, People, and Places

1. For each term, person, or place listed at the beginning of the section, write a sentence explaining its significance.

Note Taking

2. **Reading Skill: Identify Main Ideas** Use your completed table to answer the Focus Question: What are the similarities and differences between the economies and governments of China and India?

Comprehension and Critical Thinking

3. **Identify Central Issues** What obstacles to economic development does China still face?
4. **Draw Inferences** How did the Green Revolution contribute to urbanization in India?
5. **Summarize** What economic goals has the Indian government pursued and how has it met these goals?
6. **Predict Consequences** Do you think that China can continue to develop economically without making political reforms? Explain.

● Writing About History

Quick Write: Write a Conclusion
Choose one subheading from this section—for example "Reforming Indian Society." After rereading the text under that subheading, write a conclusion that summarizes the information.

Brotherhood by Octavio Paz

Mexican poet, essayist, and critic Octavio Paz (1914–1998) was one of Latin America's great modern writers. Besides enjoying enormous success as an author, he was also a diplomat. Paz held diplomatic positions in France and India, where he was exposed to different schools of literature. In France, he explored surrealism. This literary movement encouraged the expression of the irrational and freed Paz to write beyond the limits of literal meaning. In India, Paz studied Buddhism, which also influenced his work. However, even as he contributed to the global culture, Paz maintained his national identity. He thought and wrote much about Mexico, its past, and its place in the modern world. In 1990, Paz became the first Mexican writer to receive the Nobel Prize for Literature. The poem below is dedicated to the Greek scientist and geographer Ptolemy (TAHL uh mee), who wrote one of the most influential astronomy texts of the ancient world.

▲ Octavio Paz

Brotherhood
Homage to Claudius Ptolemy

I am a man: little do I last
and the night is enormous.
But I look up:
the stars write.
Unknowing I understand:
I too am written,
and at this very moment
someone spells me out.

Hermandad
Homenaje a Claudio Ptolomeo

Soy hombre: duro poco
y es enorme la noche.
Pero miro hacia arriba:
las estrellas escriben.
Sin entender comprendo:
también soy escritura
y en este mismo instante
alguien me deletrea.

Thinking Critically

1. **Analyze Literature** What do you think is the meaning of the lines "I am a man: little do I last / and the night is enormous"?
2. **Draw Conclusions** Why do you think Paz chose the title "Brotherhood" for this poem?

A woman at a municipal dump in Mexico collects garbage to sell.

A Daily Struggle

Carolina Maria de Jesus (day zhay ZOOS) faced a life of hardship in the slums of São Paulo (sow POW loh), Brazil. Like millions of other poor, rural people, she came to the city hoping to improve her life. Instead, to buy food, she spent her days combing through garbage for paper, cans, and other scraps to sell. In her diary, de Jesus described her daily struggle against poverty:

> 66 July 16 . . . I went to Senhor Manuel, carrying some cans to sell. . . . He gave me 13 [coins]. I kept thinking that I had to buy bread, soap, and milk. . . . The 13 [coins] wouldn't make it. I returned . . . to my shack, nervous and exhausted. I thought of the worrisome life that I led. Carrying paper, washing clothes for children, staying in the street all day long. 99
> —Carolina Maria de Jesus, *Child of the Dark*

Focus Question What challenges have Latin American nations faced in recent decades in their struggle for democracy and prosperity?

Latin America Builds Democracy

Objectives
- Analyze how Latin America grappled with poverty.
- Describe Latin America's difficult road to democracy.
- Understand the struggle for democracy in Argentina.

Terms, People, and Places

import substitution
agribusiness
liberation theology
Organization of
   American States
   (OAS)
Sandinista
contra
indigenous
Juan Perón
Mothers of the
   Plaza de Mayo

Note Taking

Reading Skill: Identify Main Ideas and Supporting Details As you read this section, make an outline like the one below.

I. Economic and Social Forces
   A. Society
      1.
      2.

Latin America comprises Mexico, Central America, the Caribbean, and South America. It includes 33 independent nations, ranging from small islands, such as Grenada, to giant Brazil.

For decades, Latin American nations have faced political, economic, and social challenges similar to those of other developing nations—rapid population growth, poverty, illiteracy, political instability, and authoritarian governments.

Latin America Grapples With Poverty

From the 1950s to the 1980s, economic development failed to change deep-rooted inequalities in many Latin American countries. Due to inequality and growing populations, most countries saw little improvement in living standards.

Promoting Industry and Agriculture In Latin America, as in other developing regions, nations often relied heavily on a single cash crop or commodity to earn money for needed imports. If harvests failed or if world demand fell, their economies were hard hit.

To reduce their dependence on imported goods, many Latin American governments adopted a policy of **import substitution,** or manufacturing goods locally to replace imports. This policy, pursued mainly in the 1950s and 1960s, was a mixed success. Many of the new industries needed government help or foreign capital to survive.

Latin America: Economic Activity

Map Skills Latin American nations have been diversifying their economies in recent decades.

1. **Locate** (a) Venezuela (b) Nicaragua (c) Brazil (d) Haiti

2. **Region** Which region is the least diversified? What factors might explain this?

3. **Synthesize Information** Locate the areas on the map with manufacturing and trade. Are those areas likely to be near cities or countryside? Explain.

▲ Mexican men harvest tangerines, carrying baskets weighing up to 200 pounds.

▲ A man works at an off-shore oil rig in Venezuela. Like many oil companies in Venezuela, the company he works for is foreign-owned.

Legend

- Forestry
- Livestock raising
- Mainly commercial farming
- Mainly subsistence farming
- Manufacturing and trade
- Little or no activity
- Petroleum (oil)

Equal Area Projection

0   500   1000 mi
0   500   1000 km

FIGHTING POVERTY IN BRAZIL

More than a quarter of Brazil's population lives on less than two dollars a day. A minority controls most of the country's wealth and income. In recent years, though, better jobs and education have provided more opportunities for many Brazilians. The country's steady economic growth, shown in the graph at right, has helped make these improvements possible.

◀ In Brazil's countryside, most land is owned by a wealthy few. In this photo, members of the Landless Peasants' Movement occupy a large privately owned ranch.

To escape rural poverty, many ▶ Brazilians seek better-paying urban employment, such as the factory job shown here.

In time, Latin American governments moved away from import substitution because of its high cost. Instead, they have tried to generate income by promoting exports. Specifically, they have focused on developing a variety of cash crops and encouraging industries that they hope will produce goods for export.

Governments also backed efforts to open more land to farming through irrigation and the clearing of forests. Much of the best farmland belongs to **agribusinesses,** or giant commercial farms owned by multinational corporations. In Central America and Brazil, developers continue to clear tropical rain forests for use as farmland. This practice has had environmental costs, as you will read in the next chapter.

A Growing Gap One major obstacle to progress in Latin America is the uneven distribution of wealth. In many countries, a tiny elite controls the land, businesses, and factories. These powerful groups oppose changes that might undermine their position. As a result, the gap between the rich and the poor has widened, fueling discontent.

Poverty Latin American nations, like the rest of the developing world, experienced a population explosion that contributed to poverty. Although population growth rates slowed somewhat in the 1990s, economies were hard-pressed to keep pace with growing populations. Overall, the population of Latin America was 570 million in 2008.

In rural areas, population pressures made life more difficult for peasant farmers. Even though a family might own a small plot to grow their own food, most farmers worked on the estates of large landowners for low wages. Their wages pay for needed essentials like clothing, tools, and the food they cannot grow themselves.

Harsh conditions and limited land drove millions of peasants to the cities. Today, more than half of all people in Latin America live in cities. Some newcomers found jobs in factories, offices, and stores. Many more, like Carolina de Jesus, survive by working odd jobs. They fill the shantytowns on the edges of Latin American cities such as Mexico City and Sao Paulo. The shantytowns in these cities are among the largest in the world.

Brazilians have also escaped from poverty through education, such as this adult literacy class. ▼

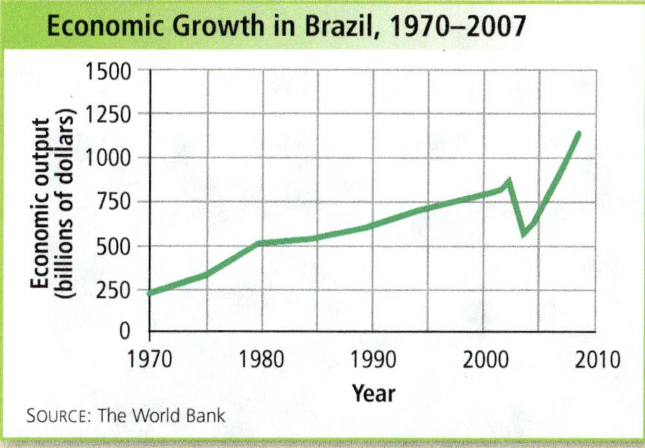

Economic Growth in Brazil, 1970–2007

SOURCE: The World Bank

Thinking Critically
1. **Make Generalizations** How did Brazil's economic output change from 1970 to 2002?
2. **Synthesize Information** How did this change help Brazilians to move out of poverty?

Churches Help the Poor The Catholic Church remained a powerful force across Latin America. Although it was often tied to the ruling class, some church leaders spoke up for the poor. During the 1960s and 1970s, many priests, nuns, and church workers crusaded for social justice and an end to poverty. This movement, known as **liberation theology,** urged the church to become a force for reform. Meanwhile, evangelical Protestant groups won converts among the poor in many countries.

 **Checkpoint** How did the gulf between the rich and the poor cause problems in Latin America?

Dictatorships and Democracy

Democracy was difficult to achieve in Latin American nations plagued by poverty and inequality. From the 1950s on, many groups pressed for reforms. They included liberals, socialists, urban workers, peasants, and Catholic priests and nuns. Although they differed over how to achieve their goals, all wanted to improve conditions for the poor. Conservatives, however, resisted reforms. Conflict between conservatives and reformers contributed to political unrest in many nations.

Military Leaders Seize Power Between the 1950s and 1970s, as social unrest grew, military leaders in Argentina, Brazil, Chile, and other nations seized power. Claiming the need for order, they imposed harsh, autocratic regimes. These military rulers outlawed political parties, censored the press, and closed universities. They also imprisoned and executed thousands. "Death squads" linked to the government murdered many more. Latin American writers, such as Pablo Neruda of Chile and Gabriel García Márquez of Colombia, went into exile after speaking out against repressive governments or social inequality.

Threats of Revolution Beginning in the 1950s, leftist guerrillas battled repressive governments across much of Latin America. They believed that only socialism could end inequalities. Others were nationalists who opposed economic and cultural domination by the United States.

Lula da Silva

As a child, Luíz Inácio Lula da Silva sold peanuts and shined shoes on the streets of Sao Paulo, Brazil. The son of poor peasants with eight children, the boy did not learn to read and write until he was 10 years old. From this humble background, Lula, as he is called, rose to become president of Brazil. Lula left school at age 14 to become a metal worker in a factory. Ambitious and bright, he worked his way up and took courses to improve his skills. Lula also became active in workers rights issues. A fierce union leader, he helped start the Workers' Party, which became a major political force in Brazil. Even though he vigorously supported workers' rights, Lula gradually moved the party platform from revolutionary idealism to practical goals. Lula ran three times for president before finally winning the office in 2002 on his fourth try. As president, he expanded social programs and tried to narrow the huge gap between rich and poor in Brazil. When he won a second term in 2006, Lula declared, "The foundation is in place and now we have to get to work." **How does Lula's life illustrate both the problems and successes of development in Brazil?**

Cold War fears about the spread of Marxism complicated moderate reform efforts. Many Latin American conservatives saw any call for reform as a communist threat. These groups were often supported by the United States.

Civil Wars Shake Central America Several Central American nations were torn by civil wars as revolutionaries battled authoritarian governments. In 1954, the United States helped the Guatemalan military overthrow an elected, leftist government. Leftists and others fought the military regime, which responded savagely. The military targeted Guatemala's **indigenous,** or native people, slaughtering tens of thousands. The fighting ended in the 1990s, after the government finally held elections and signed a peace accord with leftist guerillas.

In the 1970s and 1980s, reformers and revolutionaries challenged El Salvador's landowning and military elite. One reformer, Archbishop Oscar Romero, preached liberation theology until he was assassinated while celebrating mass in 1980. A brutal civil war shook El Salvador until the rebels and the military agreed to a UN-backed peace plan in 1991.

In 1979, the **Sandinistas,** socialist rebels in Nicaragua, toppled the ruling Somoza family. The Sandinistas introduced land reform and tried to redistribute wealth to the country's poor. Claiming that Nicaragua could become "another Cuba," United States President Ronald Reagan financed the **contras,** guerrillas who fought the Sandinistas. Fighting raged until a 1990 compromise brought peace and multiparty elections.

Progress Toward Democracy By the 1990s, pressure from democracy activists and foreign lenders led military rulers to restore civilian rule. Argentina, Brazil, Chile, and other countries held elections. In some countries, such as Brazil, Venezuela, and Bolivia, leftist leaders won office. These new leaders challenged U.S. economic and political dominance over the region.

In Mexico, which had escaped military rule, demands for reform grew. There, a single party–the Institutional Revolutionary Party (PRI)–had controlled the government for 70 years. It claimed to represent all groups in Mexican society. But in reality, PRI bosses moved forcefully against any serious opposition.

Under pressure, the PRI made some reforms in the 1990s. In 2000, Vicente Fox became the first candidate from an opposition party to be elected president. Fox and his successor, conservative Felipe Calderón, faced tough challenges, ranging from desperate rural poverty, to crime, corruption, and violent drug gangs.

 **Checkpoint** What conditions led to civil wars in many Latin American countries?

Latin America and the United States

Politically, a fact of life for Latin Americans has been the looming presence of the United States. An economic and military giant, the United

States has dominated the **Organization of American States (OAS),** a group formed in 1948 to promote democracy, economic cooperation, and peace in the Americas. Today, Latin America and the United States are still closely linked. The United States is the region's most important investor and trading partner.

Despite these links, the United States and Latin American nations view each other very differently. The United States sees itself as the defender of democracy and capitalism in the region. It also provides much-needed aid. While many Latin Americans admire the wealth of the United States, they resent what they see as its political, economic, and cultural domination. However, in 2000, when the United States honored its 1977 treaty and turned control of the Panama Canal over to Panama, many Latin American nations welcomed it as a sign of respect for Panama's independence.

The United States Intervenes During the Cold War, the United States backed anti-communist dictators in Latin America. On several occasions, it intervened militarily to stop the spread of communism. As you have read, in 1954, the United States helped overthrow Guatemala's leftist government. In 1961, President John F. Kennedy supported the Bay of Pigs invasion of Castro's Cuba. Since that failed invasion, the United States has imposed economic sanctions on Cuba. In 1973, the United States secretly backed the military coup that toppled Chile's democratically elected socialist president, Salvador Allende (ah YEN day), putting military dictator, Augusto Pinochet (pee noh SHAY), in power.

In 1994, a UN force led by the United States stepped into Haiti to restore its elected leader three years after a military coup. In 2004, the U.S. withdrew, leaving UN peacekeepers the job of restoring democracy to poverty-stricken, hurricane-ravaged Haiti.

The War on Drugs In the 1980s, illegal drug use grew in the United States, leading the U.S. government to declare a "war on drugs." The United States tried to stop illegal drugs from being smuggled into the country from Colombia, Peru, Bolivia, and elsewhere. It pressed Latin American governments to destroy drug crops and crush the drug cartels, or criminal gangs that ran the drug trade.

Governments cooperated, but critics in Latin America alleged that the main problem was growing demand for illegal drugs in the United States. Efforts to stop the drug trade led drug gangs to bribe government officials and hire assassins to kill judges, journalists, and others who worked against them. In 1989, U.S. forces invaded Panama and arrested its president, Manuel Noriega (noh ree AY guh), for drug trafficking. He was later tried and convicted.

Migration Poverty and unrest led many people to flee their homes in Latin America for the United States. Many entered the country legally. A large number were illegal immigrants. Their remittances, or the earnings they sent home, helped raise the standard of living for their families in Latin America. As the economic slowdown worsened after 2008, many newcomers lost their jobs and returned to their homelands.

✔ **Checkpoint** Why do people in Latin America have mixed reactions to the United States?

Democracy in Mexico
Mexican president Felipe Calderón waves after being sworn in on December 1, 2006. Although his opponent claimed that he was elected unfairly, international observers and Mexico's courts rejected these claims. *What does the free election of two presidents in a row suggest about the stability of Mexico's democracy?*

Argentina Survives Upheavals

Once the most prosperous country in Latin America, Argentina enjoyed a robust economy based on exports of beef and grain. It attracted millions of immigrants. But since the Great Depression of the 1930s, Argentina has experienced more than 60 years of political and economic upheavals.

Remembering the Disappeared
The Mothers of the Plaza de Mayo demanded to know the fate of family members who had disappeared under military rule.

Military Rule From 1946 to 1955, nationalist president **Juan Perón** enjoyed great support from workers. He increased the government's economic role, boosted wages, and backed labor unions. He also suppressed opposition.

When Perón's policies led to an economic crisis, he was ousted in a 1955 military coup. Although Perón was reelected in 1973, the military was in and out of power for two decades. In 1976, as a wave of political unrest swept Argentina, the military again seized control. As the military battled leftist guerrillas, it waged a "dirty war" of torture and murder against its own citizens. As many as 20,000 people were kidnapped by the government and disappeared. Every week, women, known as the **Mothers of the Plaza de Mayo,** marched in Buenos Aires, the capital of Argentina. They demanded to know what had happened to their missing sons and daughters.

Democracy Is Restored By 1983, failed policies and a lost war with Britain over the Falkland Islands forced the military to restore civilian rule and allow elections. A financial crisis in 2001 devastated Argentina's economy and brought widespread poverty. Argentina's democracy survived the economic crisis and its economy recovered after 2003. However, like other Latin American nations, Argentina's economic progress was undermined by the 2008 global recession.

✓ **Checkpoint** Why did the military restore civilian rule in Argentina?

Progress Monitoring *Online*
For: Self-quiz with vocabulary practice
Web Code: naa-3341

Terms, People, and Places

1. For each term or person listed at the beginning of the section, write a sentence explaining its significance.

Note Taking

2. **Reading Skill: Identify Main Ideas and Supporting Details** Use your completed outline to answer the Focus Question: What challenges have Latin American nations faced in recent decades in their struggle for democracy and prosperity?

Comprehension and Critical Thinking

3. **Draw Conclusions** How has U.S. involvement in Latin America affected the region?

4. **Analyze Information** Explain the impact of social inequality on politics in Argentina.

5. **Make Inferences** What do you think was the appeal of liberation theology to people in Latin American nations?

● **Writing About History**

Quick Write: Develop a Working Thesis and Choose Supporting Information
Reread the information in this section or review your outline. Then develop a thesis statement that expresses what you think is the main idea of this section. Locate details within the text that support your thesis statement. Evaluate your thesis to be sure that the details support it, and if not, revise it accordingly.

Mario Vargas Llosa:
Latin America—The Democratic Option

In this speech delivered in 1987, Peruvian novelist, playwright, and journalist Mario Vargas Llosa (BAHR gahs YOH sah) (born 1936) discussed the state of democracy in Latin America. He also described the changes that he believed were needed to maintain and extend that democracy.

The democratization of Latin America, even though it has today an unprecedented[1] popular base, is very fragile. To maintain and extend this popular base, governments will have to prove to their citizens that democracy means not only the end of political brutality but progress—concrete benefits in areas such as labor, health, and education, where so much remains to be done. But, given Latin America's current economic crisis, when the prices of its exports are hitting record lows and the weight of its foreign debt is crushing, those governments have virtually no alternative but to demand that their citizens—especially the poor—make even greater sacrifices than they've already made. . . .

A realistic and ethically sound approach that our creditors could take would be to demand that each debtor nation pay what it can without placing its stability in jeopardy. . . .

If we want democracy to take hold in our countries, our most urgent task is to broaden it, give it substance and truth. Democracy is fragile in so many countries because it is superficial[2], a mere framework within which institutions and political parties go about their business in their traditionally arbitrary, bullying way. . . .

Perhaps the hardest struggle we Latin Americans will have will be against ourselves. Centuries of intolerance, of absolute truths, of despotic governments, weigh us down—and it won't be easy to shake that burden off. The tradition of absolute power that began with our pre-Columbian empires, and the tradition that might makes right that the Spanish and Portuguese explorers practiced, were perpetuated in the nineteenth century, after our independence, by our *caudillos*[3] and our oligarchies[4], often with the blessing or direct intervention of foreign powers.

▲ Mario Vargas Llosa in 1997

1. **unprecedented** (un PRES uh den tid) *adj.* new; never having happened before
2. **superficial** (SOO pur FISH ul) *adj.* shallow; on the surface
3. *caudillos* (kow THEE yohs) *n. pl.* military dictators
4. **oligarchies** (AHL ih gahr keez) *n. pl.* governments run by a few powerful individuals or families

Thinking Critically
1. **Synthesize Information** According to Vargas Llosa, what currently threatens democracy in Latin America?
2. **Recognize Cause and Effect** How has Latin America's past led to the region's difficulty in maintaining democracy?

Quick Study Guide

Progress Monitoring *Online*
For: Self-test with vocabulary practice
Web Code: naa-3351

■ Key Problems Facing Developing Nations

- rapid population growth
- urbanization
- widespread poverty
- food shortages
- economic dependence on foreign lenders and on exports
- repressive, authoritarian governments
- diseases
- environmental damage
- poor education

■ Global North and Global South

■ Economic Output for Selected Developing Nations

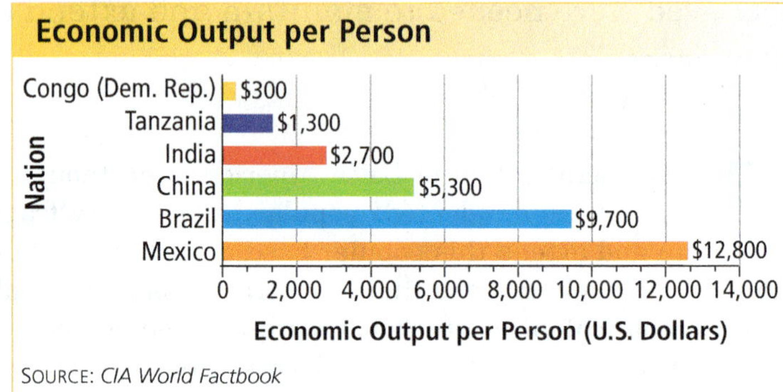

SOURCE: *CIA World Factbook*

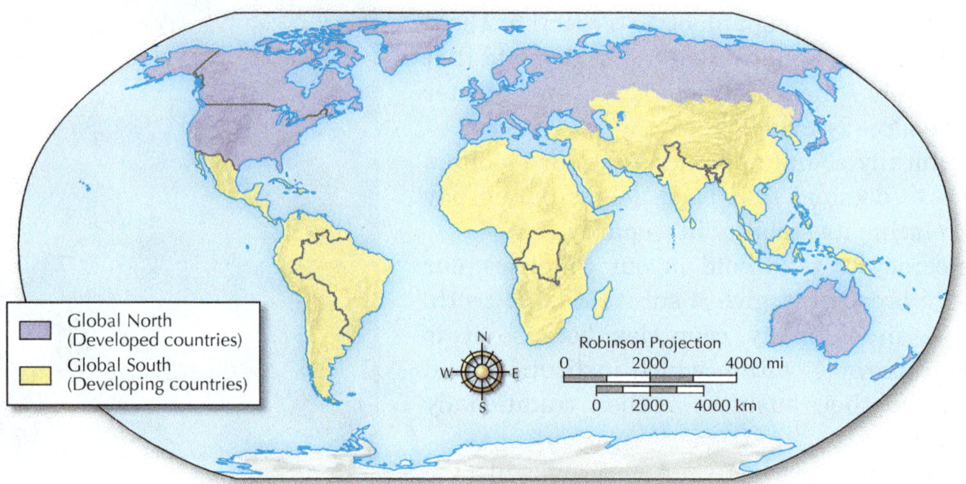

■ Key Events in the Developing World

1950s–1960s
Green Revolution transforms agriculture.

Africa and Asia
Latin America

| 1940 | 1950 | 1960 | 1970 |

1946
Juan Perón is elected president of Argentina.

1950s–1960s
Latin American countries pursue policy of import substitution.

 Essential Question Review

To connect prior knowledge with what you have learned in this chapter, answer the questions below in your Concept Connector journal. Use the journal in the Reading and Note Taking Study Guide to record your answers (or go to www.phschool.com Web Code: nad-3307).

1. **Economic Systems** Developing countries face economic challenges as they industrialize and urbanize. Choose one of the nations described in this chapter. Discuss how that nation's economic development created challenges for its people. Consider some of the following in your response:
   - poverty and the gap between the rich and poor
   - lack of resources for healthcare, education, and food
   - human rights

2. **Dictatorship** The United States sees itself as the defender of democracy and free markets in Latin America. However, from the 1950s to the 1980s, the United States helped overthrow democratically elected governments and install dictators in some Latin American countries. Provide a list of reasons that explain why the United States government would support dictators or repressive governments in Latin America. Think about the following:
   - Cold War
   - policy of containment
   - economy

3. **Revolution** During the French Revolution, the poor and the middle classes rebelled against privileged monarchs and aristocrats. During the Russian Revolution, the Communists mobilized working people to overthrow the privileged rulers of Russia. How do recent rebellions in Latin America, for example in Guatemala or Nicaragua, compare with earlier revolutions? Consider social and economic inequalities and ideologies or belief systems.

■ Connections to Today

1. **Cooperation** In this chapter, you read about cooperation between the United States and the nations of Latin America. In recent years, cooperation among Latin American nations and between the United States and Latin America has spread to include economic development. Mercosur is a trade alliance among South American nations. Meanwhile, the United States has proposed trade alliances with Chile and Central American nations. Refer to online news services or other sources to learn about Latin American trade alliances today. Investigate whether cooperation in the area of trade has spread in recent years within Latin America and between Latin America and the United States.

2. **Nationalism** In this chapter, you learned that during the 1950s and 1960s many developing nations tried to decrease their economic dependence on foreign investors by developing their own industries. Then, in the 1980s and 1990s, many of these nations put more emphasis on foreign trade and investment, often under pressure from foreign lenders. However, the pendulum has begun to swing back toward economic independence. After 2000, China, Argentina, and other nations put the economic concerns of their own people ahead of those of foreign investors. Why might a nation choose a course of economic independence? Consult news sources to find out how countries that resisted foreign economic pressure have fared in recent years.

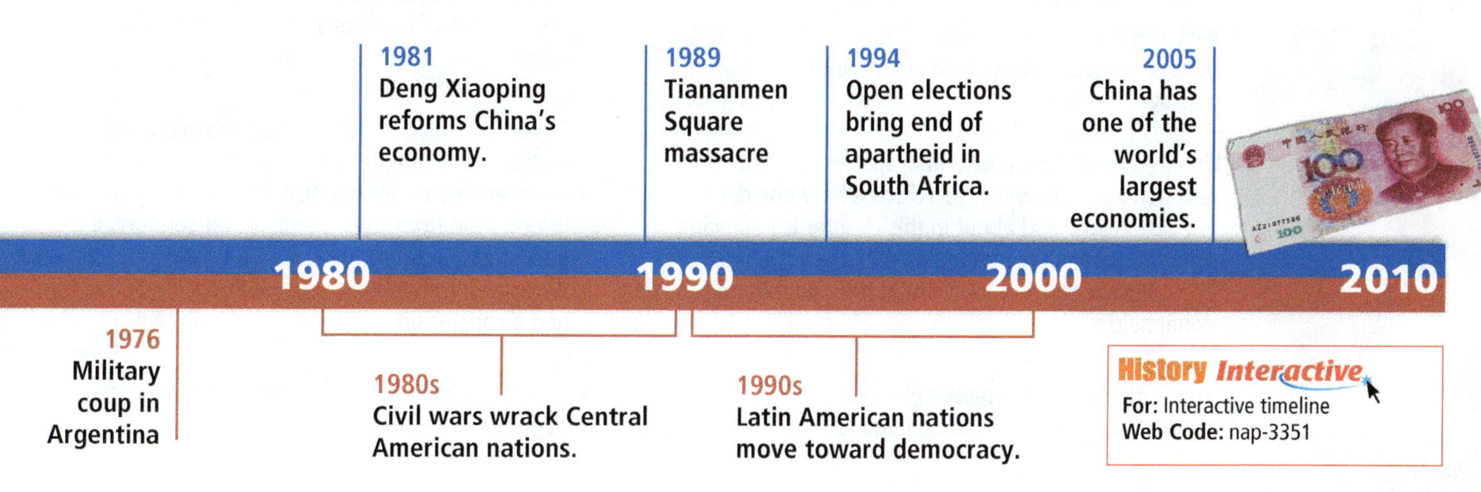

Chapter Assessment

Terms, People, and Places

Complete each sentence by choosing the correct answer from the list of terms below. You will not use all the terms.

desertification	sustainable development
developing world	Tiananmen Square
Green Revolution	urbanization
liberation theology	Mumbai

1. In parts of Africa, drought and over-farming have brought about the _______ of land that was previously farmable.
2. Many Catholic clergy were part of a movement known as _______ that called for social justice and an end to poverty.
3. New nations attempting to improve their economies and achieve higher living standards are known as the _______.
4. Many poorer nations have seen rapid _______, or the movement of rural people to the cities.
5. In 1989, troops had a deadly encounter with protesters in _______.
6. The use of new technologies in the mid-1900s for improving crop production was known as the _______.

Main Ideas

Section 1 (pp. 1066–1071)
7. Summarize the challenges faced by most developing nations.
8. Compare and contrast the global North with the global South.

Section 2 (pp. 1072–1075)
9. How successful were new African nations that tried to develop by creating command economies?
10. Who is Wangari Maathai and what was her role in sustainable development efforts in Africa?

Section 3 (pp. 1076–1081)
11. After Mao's death, what reforms did China's government make and what reforms did they block?
12. What were the main challenges to economic growth in India?

Section 4 (pp. 1082–1089)
13. What role did the military play in the governments of Latin America?
14. Describe the democratic progress that was made in Mexico in 2000.

Chapter Focus Question
15. What challenges have nations of the developing world faced and what steps have they taken to meet those challenges?

Critical Thinking

16. **Synthesize Information** How has rapid population growth affected developing nations?
17. **Draw Conclusions** Which problem facing developing nations do you think is the most important one to solve? Explain your answer.
18. **Analyze Images** How does the photo of Mumbai at the end of Section 1 reflect some of the challenges facing developing nations? Explain your answer.
19. **Make Inferences** Many developing nations are ruled by dictators or by one party, as in China. Does autocratic rule help or hurt economic progress? Explain.
20. **Cause and Effect** How did the Cold War affect the United States' relations with Latin American nations?

● Writing About History

In this chapter's four Section Assessments, you developed skills to write a research report.

Writing a Research Report As governments in the developing world struggle to grow their economies and improve the well being of their citizens, they may set policies that cause damage to the environment and threaten local plant and animal species. Write a research report in which you discuss how one developing nation you read about in this chapter is balancing economic development with environmental concerns. Consult page SH13 of the Writing Handbook for additional help.

Prewriting
- Do online or library research to read background materials about developing nations.
- Choose a developing nation and take notes on relevant details, events, and the people.
- Create a set of questions about your developing nation and gather additional resources.

Drafting
- Develop a thesis about this nation's economic status—for example, is it succeeding or failing?
- Make an outline to organize the report. Then choose information from your research that supports each part of your outline.
- Write an introduction explaining your thesis, a body, and a conclusion.

Revising
- Use the guidelines for revising your report on page SH15 of the Writing Handbook.

Document-Based Assessment

China's Economy

China has one of the fastest-growing economies in the world. Many who once thought of China as backward now see the country as a lively economic giant. Though China's economic gains are impressive, China's critics see a dark underside, as Documents C and D illustrate.

Document A

"China's annual GDP [gross domestic product, or economic output] growth has averaged more than 8 percent in the past 25 years, and in 2003, its GDP grew by a record-breaking 9.1 percent. . . . Noting these economic achievements as well as the complete success of China's first manned space flight in 2003, Premier Wen Jiabao in his annual address to the NPC [National People's Congress] in March 2004 pointed to a national strength that has reached new heights. . . ."

—From **China Internet Information Center**, May 4, 2005

Document B

Chinese workers assemble electronic parts.

Document C

". . . China has not changed in non-economic matters . . . [T]he leadership remains deaf to democracy and human rights. Religion is on a tight leash. . . . Basic legal safeguards are non-existent in the judicial system, and prison conditions are harsh. Privacy rights are routinely violated, and the government maintains tight restrictions on freedom of speech and the press. Increased control and monitoring of the Internet has led to arrest of dissidents, and most "Netizens" practice self-censorship, or face the long arm of the law. Freedom of association and assembly are virtually non-existent. . . ."

—From **"Only China's Economy Has Changed"** in *Taipei Times*, April 29, 2005, by Robert Bedeski

Document D

"China's grim 19th century style mines—many of them little more than holes in the ground—claimed yet more lives this week. A gas explosion ripped through the Sunjiawan coal mine in the northeastern province of Liaoning on Monday, killing at least 210. . . . They were just the latest casualties in a familiar story of mining accidents, which routinely claim the lives of dozens of young miners every month. . . . Many of those who die belong to China's growing underclass. They are desperately impoverished boys and men from rural villages."

—From **The Wall Street Journal**, February 18, 2005, by Sara Davis and Mickey Spiegel

Analyzing Documents

Use your knowledge of China's economic reforms and Documents A, B, C, and D to answer questions 1–4.

1. The author of Document A is best described as a
   A harsh critic of China's economic inequality.
   B strong supporter of China's economic policies.
   C shrewd observer of China's social system.
   D half-hearted supporter of the socialist market economy.

2. What is the main point of Document C?
   A China's social progress is equal to the country's economic gains.
   B China's human rights record is poor, despite economic progress.
   C China's economic progress outweighs any human rights problems.
   D China's economic success has led a commitment to human rights.

3. Some critics of China say that China's new wealth has not been evenly shared. According to Document D, one of the groups that has been left out is
   A people from the large cities.
   B young people.
   C women.
   D males from rural villages.

4. Do the current leaders of China deserve praise or criticism? Give your opinions based on the documents on this page and information from the chapter.

34 The World Today

A Changing World

In 2001, Mongolia's prime minister declared that "in order to survive we have to stop being nomads." His words—and his plans to settle 90% of Mongolia's people in cities by the year 2030—came as a shock to a people who have been nomadic herders for centuries. At the same time, his idea seemed inevitable. Listen to the Witness History audio to hear more about how Mongolians are struggling to modernize without losing their traditions.

◀ This nomadic family in Mongolia lives in a yurt, or tent, with a solar-powered satellite dish that picks up television broadcasts.

Chapter Preview

Chapter Focus Question What are the major issues facing the world today?

Section 1
Industrialized Nations After the Cold War

Section 2
Globalization

Section 3
Social and Environmental Challenges

Section 4
Security in a Dangerous World

Section 5
Advances in Science and Technology

Use the  **Quick Study Timeline** at the end of this chapter to preview chapter events.

Logo for the international aid organization CARE

Euro coin

NASA seal

 **Concept Connector ONLINE**

To explore Essential Questions related to this chapter, go to PHSchool.com
Web Code: nad-3407

A euro coin

Turks celebrate their country's efforts to join the European Union (EU).

The Nations of Europe Unite

❝Resolved to mark a new stage in the process of European integration . . . Recalling the historic importance of the ending of the division of the European continent and the need to create firm bases for the construction of the future Europe . . . Desiring to deepen the solidarity between their peoples while respecting their history, their culture, and their traditions . . . [We] have decided to establish a European Union . . .**❞**
—The Maastricht Treaty on the European Union, 1992

Focus Question How did the end of the Cold War affect industrialized nations and regions around the world?

Industrialized Nations After the Cold War

Objectives
- Examine social, political, and economic trends in Europe after the Cold War.
- Analyze how the United States' and Russia's shifting roles have affected the balance of global power.
- Understand how important economic changes have affected Asia since the end of the Cold War.

Terms, People, and Places

European Union	Vladimir Putin
euro	surplus
default	deficit
Barack Obama	Pacific Rim

Note Taking

Reading Skill: Compare and Contrast Create a chart to compare and contrast developments in industrialized nations after the Cold War.

Europe	Russia/ United States	Asia
• 1991 Germany reunified	•	•
•	•	•

The end of the Cold War created favorable conditions for the spread of democracy. It also marked the beginning of a new global economy. Growing economic ties and increased international trade would become a driving force shaping the world in the new millennium.

The New Face of Europe

The collapse of communism ended decades of division between communist Eastern Europe and democratic Western Europe. Trade, business, travel, and communications across the continent became easier. Yet, many European nations faced common problems such as large-scale immigration from the developing world, growing discrimination against foreigners, and rising unemployment.

Germany Reunifies After more than 45 years of division, East and West Germany were reunited in 1990. Germans welcomed reunification, but they paid a high price. East Germany's economy and infrastructure were weak and had to be modernized. Unemployment rose in the former East Germany when inefficient communist-era factories were closed. West Germans paid higher taxes to finance the rebuilding of the eastern part of the country.

Reunification brought social problems. Racist groups, such as neo-Nazis, a hate group modeled on the Nazi party, blamed immigrants for the country's problems and viciously attacked foreign workers. The vast majority of Germans condemned such actions. Twenty years after reunification, Germany remained an economic giant and a strong European leader.

NATO Evolves The collapse of the Soviet Union ended the Warsaw Pact. Many of the nations of Eastern Europe wanted to join NATO. Poland, Hungary, and the Czech Republic joined in 1999, soon followed by other countries. Russia disliked NATO's eastward expansion, but agreed to a NATO-Russia Council to consult on issues of common interest.

Europe was changing and NATO had to reassess its purpose. Many NATO officials believed that NATO's primary goal should be that of peacekeeper and protector of human rights. Following terrorist attacks in the United States, Europe, and elsewhere, the fight against terrorism has become a priority for the alliance.

The European Union Expands Like NATO, the European Economic Community expanded over the years to add nations from Eastern Europe. In 1993, the European Economic Community became the **European Union (EU),** a group of European nations that work together to promote a freer flow of capital, labor, services, and goods. Members also cooperate on security matters.

In 2002, the **euro** became the common currency for most of Western Europe. By then, EU passports had replaced national passports. Today, the expanded EU has the world's largest economy and competes with economic superpowers like the United States and Japan.

Some European leaders supported even greater economic and political unity for the region. However, many ordinary citizens felt greater loyalty to their own nations than to the EU. Also the economies of Eastern Europe were weaker than those in the West, causing worries about the EU's overall economic outlook.

Turkey, long a member of NATO, wants full membership in the EU. But Turkey's application faced opposition because of its poor record on human rights and other issues. Also, some Europeans are concerned about admitting countries with large Muslim populations into the EU. They worry that if the EU changes too quickly, it will be less stable.

✓ **Checkpoint** **What challenges did Germany face after reunification?**

The European Union

Geography Interactive
For: Audio guided tour
Web Code: nap-3411

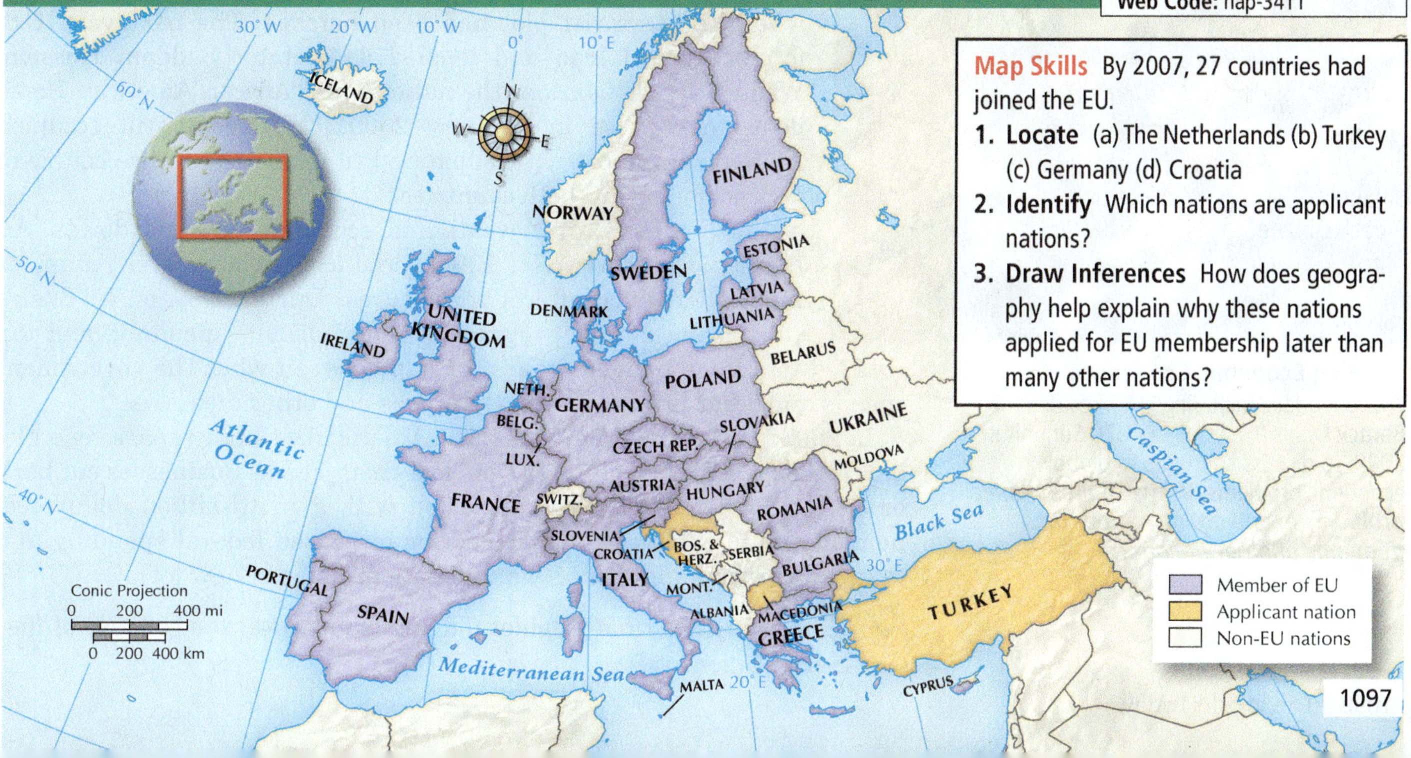

Map Skills By 2007, 27 countries had joined the EU.

1. **Locate** (a) The Netherlands (b) Turkey (c) Germany (d) Croatia
2. **Identify** Which nations are applicant nations?
3. **Draw Inferences** How does geography help explain why these nations applied for EU membership later than many other nations?

Global Power Shifts

After the Soviet Union collapsed and the Cold War ended, the balance of global power shifted. The United States became the world's sole superpower. Recently, though, Russia has reemerged as a powerful force.

Russia Rebuilds Russia faced hard times after the breakup of the Soviet Union. In an effort to shift to a market economy, Russia's president, Boris Yeltsin, privatized many state-run industries and collective farms. This change brought great hardships to many Russians as unemployment and prices soared.

In 1998, Russia barely avoided financial collapse. It defaulted, or failed to make payments, on much of its foreign debt. High inflation and the collapse of the ruble, Russia's currency, forced many banks and businesses to close. People lost their savings and jobs, although some Russians did prosper in the new economy.

In 2000, Vladimir Putin was elected president in Russia's second free election. Putin, who served two terms, helped rebuild Russia's economy. However, his government was plagued by corruption and Putin came under fire for increasing the power of the central government at the expense of peoples' civil liberties. Putin's handpicked successor, Dmitri Medvedev, was sworn in as president in May 2008. The next day, Putin was appointed prime minister by Russia's Parliament. While Russia benefited from rising prices for its oil and gas exports, the 2008 global economic slowdown posed challenges for Russia, as it did for other nations.

As Russia rebounded, it defended its interests, which sometimes caused tensions with the West. Despite UN sanctions against Iran, Russia assisted Iran with its nuclear energy program. In 2008, Russia sent troops into neighboring Georgia to help two breakaway regions gain independence.

The United States Faces New Challenges As the world's only superpower, the United States had a great deal of military and political influence. After the terrorist attacks on the United States in September 2001, President George W. Bush declared a "war on terror." In 2002, the United States sent forces to Afghanistan, where the terrorist plot had been hatched. The next year, U.S. forces invaded Iraq and toppled its dictator Saddam Hussein. When Barack Obama, the nation's first African American President, took office in January 2009, U.S. forces still occupied Afghanistan and Iraq. Obama had to decide the future course of U.S. policy toward both countries.

The United States weathered economic ups and downs. An economic boom in the 1990s produced a budget surplus, or money left over after expenditures. During George W. Bush's presidency, slower growth, massive military spending, and tax cuts led to a huge budget deficit, or gap between what the government spends and what it takes in through taxes and other measures.

In 2008, a financial crisis shook the American economy, sparking a global recession. Millions of Americans lost their jobs as businesses cut back or closed. President Obama responded with a multi-billion dollar economic stimulus package that called for increased federal spending and tax cuts to revive the economy and create millions of new jobs.

✔ **Checkpoint** What troubles did Russia face after the collapse of the Soviet Union?

Vocabulary Builder

inflation—(in FLAY shun) *n.* a rise in prices linked to an increase in the amount of money available

Meeting Economic Challenges
World leaders, including U.S. President Barack Obama, met at the G20 Summit in 2009, to discuss solutions to global economic problems. *Why might economic problems in one country affect the economy of other nations?*

Changes in Asia

As the Cold War ended, Asia experienced the successes and downturns of being part of the global economy.

The Pacific Rim A major force in the global economy is the Pacific Rim, the many Asian nations that border the Pacific Ocean. The Pacific Ocean first became a highway for world trade in the 1500s. By the mid-1900s, links across the Pacific had grown dramatically. By the 1990s, the volume of trade across the Pacific was greater than that across the Atlantic. Some analysts predict that the 2000s will be the "Pacific century" because of this region's potential for further growth.

Japan and China For decades, Japan dominated the Asian Pacific Rim. But in the 1990s, as Japan suffered a long economic downturn, China's economy boomed. However, the global recession that began in 2008 hurt China's export-based economy.

Pacific Powerhouse
The countries of the Pacific Rim have geographic, cultural, and economic ties. The region is a major center of ocean trade routes, shown on the map above.

The Asian Tigers Among the powerhouses of the Pacific Rim were Taiwan, Hong Kong, Singapore, and South Korea. Although they differed in important ways, all had quickly modernized and industrialized by the 1980s. All four were influenced to some degree by China, and Confucian traditions of loyalty, hard work, and consensus. Each stressed education as a way to increase worker productivity.

Because of their economic success, these countries were nicknamed the "Asian tigers" or "four tigers." The Asian tigers first focused on light industries, such as textiles. As their economies grew, they shifted to higher-priced exports, such as electronics. Their stunning growth was due in part to low wages, long hours, and other worker sacrifices. Like other export-driven economies, the Asian tigers were hurt by the 2008 global economic slowdown.

✓ **Checkpoint** Why did the Asian Tigers enjoy strong economic growth?

SECTION 1 Assessment

Progress Monitoring Online
For: Self-quiz with vocabulary practice
Web Code: naa-3411

Terms, People, and Places

1. For each term, person, or place listed at the beginning of the section, write a sentence explaining its significance.

Note Taking

2. **Reading Skill: Compare and Contrast** Use your completed chart to answer the Focus Question: How did the end of the Cold War affect industrialized nations and regions around the world?

Comprehension and Critical Thinking

3. **Determine Relevance** How did the collapse of the Soviet Union affect organizations such as NATO and the EU?

4. **Draw Conclusions** Do you think an American investor would choose to invest large sums of money in Russia? Why or why not?

5. **Analyze Information** Why is the Pacific Rim seen as an important link in the global economy?

● **Writing About History**

Quick Write: Write a Thesis Statement
To persuade someone in an essay, you must have a strong opinion on a subject and express it clearly in a thesis statement. Write a single sentence that expresses the main point you want to make about developments in the industrialized world after the Cold War.

Russian immigrants sell caviar at a kiosk in Brooklyn, New York.

A Connected World

❝ Few topics are as controversial as globalization. That is hardly surprising. It is the defining feature of our time. Bringing distant markets and people across the world together is a huge change that affects everyone, whether they are peasants in India, students in London, or bankers in New York. ❞
—Mike Moore, director-general of the WTO, 2000

Focus Question How is globalization affecting economies and societies around the world?

Globalization

Objectives

- Describe the ways in which countries around the world are interdependent.
- Understand how international treaties and organizations make global trade possible.
- Analyze the costs and benefits of global trade.

Terms, People, and Places

globalization	World Trade Organization
interdependence	(WTO)
outsourcing	protectionism
multinational	bloc
corporation	sustainability

Note Taking

Reading Skill: Compare and Contrast As you read, use the Venn diagram to track how globalization has affected developed and developing nations.

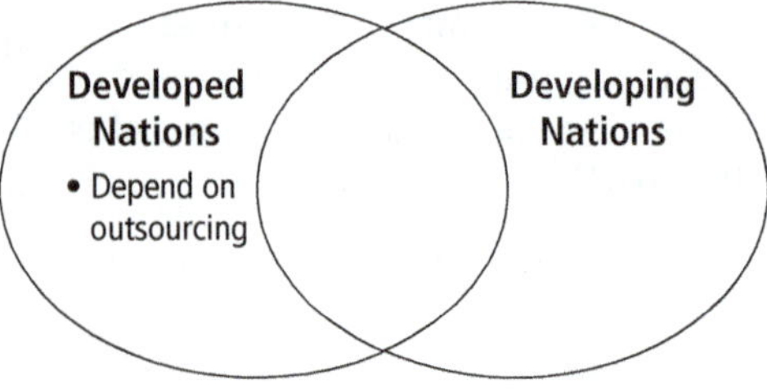

Globalization defines the world of the post-Cold War. **Globalization** refers to the process by which national economies, politics, cultures, and societies become integrated with those of other nations around the world. Globalization began on a small scale 500 years ago, with the European Age of Exploration. By the 2000s, globalization was occurring at a dramatic, unprecedented pace.

An Interdependent World

One major effect of globalization is economic interdependence. **Interdependence** is the dependence of countries on each other for goods, resources, knowledge, and labor from other parts of the world. Improvements in transportation and communication, the spread of democratic systems, and the rise of free trade—the buying and selling of goods by private individuals and corporations in a free market—have made the world increasingly interdependent. The spread of goods and ideas has even led to the development of a global culture. All of these links, from economic to cultural, have created both challenges and opportunities.

Doing the World's Work The world's rich and poor nations are linked. The nations of the developed world control much of the world's capital, trade, and technology. Yet they increasingly depend on largely low-paid workers in developing countries to produce manufactured goods cheaply. Companies in industrial nations also choose to outsource jobs. **Outsourcing** is the practice of sending work to the developing world in order to save money or increase efficiency. Many technological jobs have been outsourced to India, Russia, China, and the Philippines.

Multinational Corporations Grow Globalization has led to the growth of huge, powerful, multinational corporations. **Multinational corporations** have <u>assets</u> in many countries and sell their goods and services worldwide. These corporations have invested heavily in the developing world. They brought new technology to industries, built factories, improved transportation networks, and provided jobs. Critics, however, have blasted multinational corporations for taking large profits out of developing countries, causing environmental damage, and paying low wages.

Global Economic Crises Globalization led to financial interdependence in the world's markets. As a result, an economic crisis in one country or region can have a global impact. In 1997, a financial crisis struck Thailand and quickly spread across Asia. A 2008 banking crisis in the United States and Europe set off global shockwaves as world stock markets plunged. Wealthy nations shored up their economies with economic stimulus packages and costly bailout plans for banks and other troubled industries. Developing countries felt the impact as prices for their goods fell and international aid decreased.

Oil Prices Rise and Fall Energy resources play a huge role in the global economy. All nations, for example, need oil for transportation and to manufacture products ranging from plastics to fertilizers. Any change in the global oil supply can have a huge impact worldwide.

In 1973, OPEC limited oil exports and raised prices, creating shortages and hurting economies throughout the world. Since then, whenever oil prices have risen sharply, people have faced economic uncertainties. In 2008, oil prices shot up, partly because the growing economy in China, India, and elsewhere led to increased demand. When the global economic crisis slowed demand, prices fell. This sudden, rapid change in oil prices has led to renewed calls to develop alternative energy sources. Still, the world has remained largely dependent on oil.

World Oil Resources and Consumption

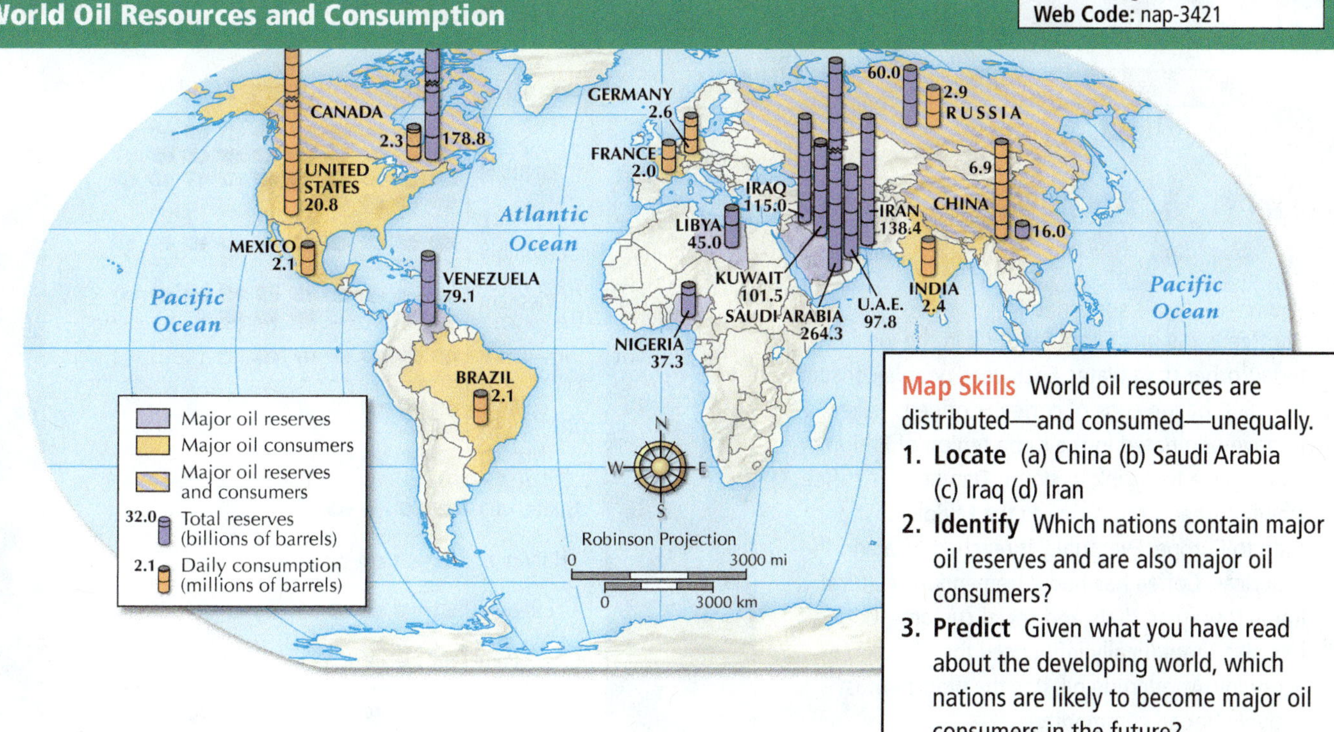

Map Skills World oil resources are distributed—and consumed—unequally.

1. **Locate** (a) China (b) Saudi Arabia (c) Iraq (d) Iran
2. **Identify** Which nations contain major oil reserves and are also major oil consumers?
3. **Predict** Given what you have read about the developing world, which nations are likely to become major oil consumers in the future?

Debt Hurts the Developing World Developing nations borrowed heavily in order to modernize. In the 1980s, bank interest rates rose as the world economy slowed. As demand for their goods fell, poor nations could not repay their debts or even interest on their loans. Their economies stalled as they spent much of their export incomes on payments to foreign creditors.

The debt crisis hurt rich nations, too. Banks were stuck with billions of dollars of bad debts. To ease the crisis, lenders made agreements with debtor nations to lower interest rates or allow more time to repay their loans. Some debts were canceled. In return, debtor nations had to accept market reforms to help improve their economies. Debt has remained a major issue throughout the developing world.

✔ **Checkpoint** How do changes in the supply of oil affect economies around the world?

Global Trade Organizations and Treaties

Many international organizations and treaties connect people and nations around the world. These organizations have various goals, such as supporting development, settling economic issues, and promoting free trade.

International Organizations Expand The United Nations is an international organization whose membership has grown from 50 nations in 1945 to 192 in 2009. As a result, its global role has expanded. The UN has sent peacekeepers to many trouble spots, including Cambodia, Congo, and the Balkans. In addition, the UN deals with economic and social development, human rights, humanitarian aid, and international law.

COFFEE:
From Shrub to Cup

Coffee is the most popular drink in the world today, other than water. Each year, people consume over 500 billion cups of coffee. Coffee is believed to have originated in the Kaffa region of Ethiopia, which gave the drink its name. Demand for coffee slowly spread from Africa to the Middle East and then to Europe. Eventually it reached Asia and the Americas. Coffee has had a tremendous cultural impact, shaping diets and social customs. Coffee has also dramatically influenced the global economy. After crude oil, it is the world's most actively traded commodity.

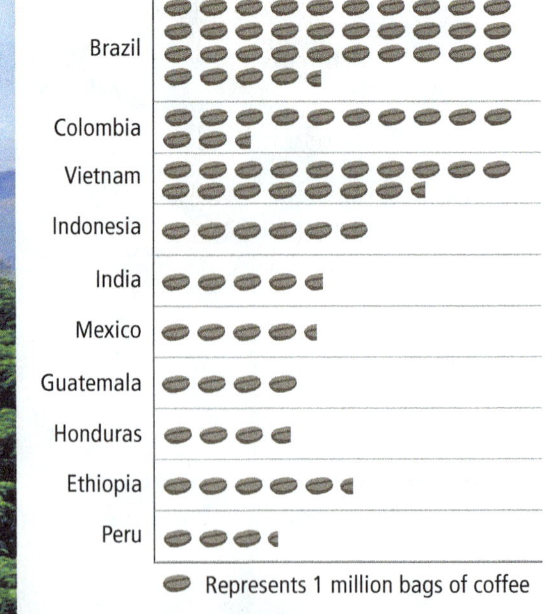

Other organizations deal with economic issues. The World Bank, for example, offers loans and technical advice to developing nations. The International Monetary Fund (IMF) encourages global economic growth, promotes international monetary cooperation, and helps developing nations solve economic problems. It also lends to countries in crisis.

Organizations not affiliated with governments also provide aid. These non-governmental organizations (NGOs) perform a variety of functions, such as monitoring human rights, supplying disaster relief, and providing medical care. The International Red Cross is an example of an NGO.

Treaties Promote Global Trade A variety of international treaties help regulate world trade. The General Agreement on Tariffs and Trade (GATT) was signed in 1947 to expand world trade and reduce tariffs, or taxes on imported goods. In 1995, more than 100 nations joined to form the **World Trade Organization (WTO)** to strengthen GATT. Its goal was to set global rules to ensure that trade flows as smoothly and as freely as possible. The WTO opposes **protectionism,** or the use of tariffs and other restrictions that protect a country's home industries against international competition. The Group of Eight (G-8) is an organization of industrialized nations that meets annually to discuss a wide range of economic and other issues. The G-8 consists of Canada, France, Germany, Great Britain, Italy, Japan, Russia, and the United States.

Regional Trade Many nations have formed regional **blocs,** or groups, to boost trade and meet common needs. Among the largest is the EU (European Union.) In 1994, NAFTA (North American Free Trade Association) set out to ease restrictions and promote trade among the United States, Canada, and Mexico. APEC (Asia-Pacific Economic Cooperation) was formed to further trade among Pacific Rim nations. OPEC, representing oil-producing countries, regulates the production of oil to stabilize the market. Regional trade groups like these work to lower trade barriers

The Fair Trade Movement ▶
The fair trade movement seeks to ensure that coffee growers receive fair prices for their crops and have decent living and working conditions. Coffee that has met these conditions is stamped with the fair trade logo.

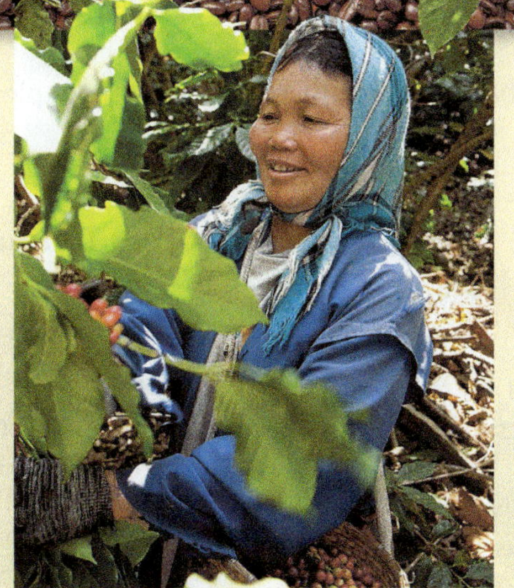

Growing Coffee
A worker in Thailand picks raw coffee beans from a shrub. Less than 10 percent of the money made from coffee actually goes to the grower.

Drinking Coffee
By the time coffee beans are turned into cups of coffee in the developed world, they have passed through the hands of many middlemen and have been re-sold a number of times. The coffee crop that a small farmer earned $8,000 for growing is worth nearly a million dollars to the people who sell it.

Thinking Critically
1. **Chart Skills** What regions are the top 5 coffee producers located in?
2. **Draw Inferences** Why does a crop of coffee become more expensive each time it is sold by middlemen?

and encourage the free exchange of goods and services. Often, regional organizations like the African Union (AU), deal with both economic and political issues.

✔ **Checkpoint**   How does the IMF help developing nations?

Costs and Benefits of Globalization

With advanced communications and increased economic ties, globalization is expected to increase in the years ahead. Yet the debate about the impact of globalization on people and nations around the world continues.

Benefits   Global trade provides consumers with a greater variety of goods and services. And because many people compete to provide these goods and services, prices are generally lower. People in the industrial world, especially, benefited from these changes.

Millions of people worldwide moved from rural areas to cities. There, they often had better access to education and health care. Globalization introduced people to new ideas, technologies, and communications. The money that developing nations earn from trade can be used to improve infrastructure, raise standards of living, and provide better services. Nations that practice free trade often become more democratic.

The Anti-Globalization Movement   Critics point to the costs of free trade and globalization. Generally, anti-globalizers focus on poverty. They claim that rich nations exploit, or take advantage of poor countries by raising their debt and lowering their standard of living. Some anti-globalizers target the World Bank and the IMF. Although these organizations provide aid to ease economic problems, they also require developing nations to make tough reforms and cut costly social programs. Anti-globalizers also oppose the United States, which is seen as the force behind policies they oppose.

Environmentalists claim that industries eager for profits encourage too-rapid development, endangering **sustainability,** or development that balances people's needs today while preserving the environment for future generations.

✔ **Checkpoint**   How has globalization improved the lives of people around the world?

Anti-Globalization in Action
In 1999, an anti-globalization demonstration led to rioting when thousands of protesters disrupted WTO meetings in Seattle, Washington.

SECTION **2 Assessment**

Progress Monitoring *Online*
For: Self-quiz with vocabulary practice
Web Code: naa-3421

Terms, People, and Places

1. What do each of the key terms listed at the beginning of the section have in common? Explain.

Note Taking

2. **Reading Skill: Compare and Contrast**   Use your completed Venn diagram to answer the Focus Question: How is globalization affecting economies and societies around the world?

Comprehension and Critical Thinking

3. **Make Comparisons**   Which countries benefit more from economic interdependence—developed or developing countries? Explain.

4. **Draw Inferences**   Given what you have read in this section, do you think developing nations would support or oppose globalization?

5. **Demonstrate Reasoned Judgment**   Do you think that increased globalization is inevitable? Explain.

● **Writing About History**

Quick Write: Generate Arguments   One of the most effective ways to persuade is to address both sides of the topic you are covering. Create a chart to record facts about globalization. In one column, record the facts that support your position on globalization. In the second column, note arguments that could be used to attack your position.

In This Chapter

What rights are basic to all human beings? The Declaration of Independence lists "life, liberty, and the pursuit of happiness." In 1948, the United Nations Declaration of Human Rights added more, including the rights to own property and to enjoy a basic standard of living. The Grameen Bank has granted loans to many poor women (right) to help them start businesses and provide for their families.

Throughout History

100s B.C. Romans enslave captives taken in war.

1100s A.D. Under King Henry II, England develops an early jury system.

1300s Smaller medieval African societies reach decisions by general agreement.

1800s Women actively seek social and political equality in Britain and the United States.

1980s Trade embargos are used to pressure South Africa to end apartheid.

Continuing Today

Limitation of human rights continues to be an issue in China. Members of the Chinese community in Australia protest severe abuses of freedom of belief and freedom of speech in their homeland.

21st Century Skills

TRANSFER Activities

1. Analyze Throughout history, how have people's rights been limited?

2. Evaluate What role does economic power play in gaining or maintaining human rights?

3. Transfer Complete a Web quest in which you act as a human rights "watch dog"; record your thoughts in the Concept Connector Journal; and learn to make a video. Web Code nah-3408.

A family in Indonesia tries to make their way to shelter after tsunamis destroyed their village in 2004. Aid organizations like CARE (logo above) worked to bring relief to the devastated region.

WITNESS HISTORY ◀)) AUDIO

Giant Waves Arrive

On December 26, 2004, an Indonesian man named Harmi went to the beach with hundreds of other people. An earthquake had hit his village, and people gathered to watch the sea recede from the beach.

66 Suddenly . . . oh my God . . . there was a thundering sound from the sea. I saw the rolls of the waves ten meters (33 feet) high . . . the waves came three times. The worst was the second one, which swallowed thousands of houses in our village. 99

Harmi's village was completely destroyed.

Focus Question How do poverty, disease, and environmental challenges affect people around the world today?

Social and Environmental Challenges

Objectives

- Explain the causes and effects of global poverty, disasters, and disease.
- Analyze whether the basic human rights of people around the world are being upheld.
- Discuss the environmental challenges that have resulted from industrial development.

Terms, People, and Places

tsunami	acid rain
epidemic	deforestation
famine	erosion
refugee	global warming

Note Taking

Reading Skill: Compare Use a chart like this one to compare aspects of globalization.

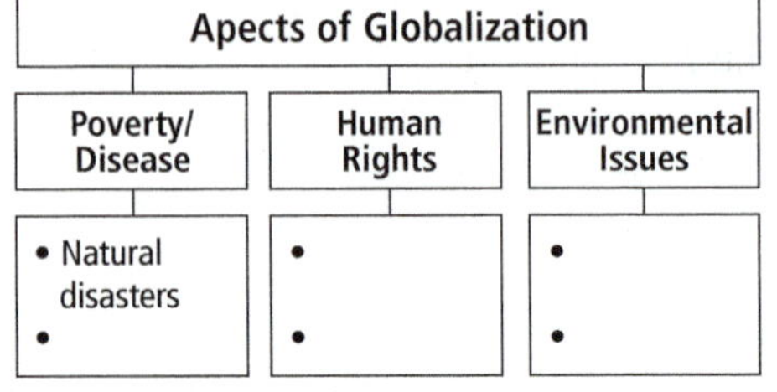

Globalization involves much more than economic links and the spread of technology. It has brought all kinds of social and environmental issues to the world's attention. Poverty, disease, environmental threats, and human rights may originate in countries or regions. But they have global dimensions that often require global solutions.

Global Poverty, Disasters, and Disease

Half of the world's population, or almost 3 billion people, live on less than $2 a day. Almost 1 billion people cannot read or write. About 790 million people in the developing world suffer from hunger—many from extreme hunger. Millions suffer from life-threatening diseases. Although these are problems mainly of the developing world, they affect the nations of the developed world as well.

Causes of Poverty Experts cannot agree on the exact number of people living in poverty worldwide, in part because there are many ways to measure poverty. Experts do agree about some trends, however. First, the gap between rich and poor nations is huge and growing. Second, some progress has been made toward reducing poverty, but it has been uneven. India and China, for example, have enjoyed economic growth, which has meant fewer people overall living in poverty there, but extreme poverty still persists.

Poverty is a complex issue with many causes. Many poor nations owe billions in debt and have no extra money to spend to improve living conditions. Political upheavals, civil war, corruption, and poor planning also <u>inhibit</u> efforts to reduce poverty worldwide. Rapid population growth—especially in India, China, and the nations of Africa and Latin America—has made it harder for countries to provide basic services.

Organizations like the World Bank believe that erasing poverty is essential to global security and peace. In this spirit, they call on poor nations to limit population growth. They also encourage rich nations to forgive the debt of poor nations, making more funds available for education, healthcare, and other services.

Natural Disasters Affect Millions In 2004, a huge underwater earthquake in the Indian Ocean triggered a massive tidal wave, or **tsunami** (tsoo NAH mee). It swept over islands and the coasts of 11 countries ringing the Indian Ocean. More than 160,000 people were killed, mainly in Indonesia, Thailand, Sri Lanka, and India. Millions were left homeless or lost their livelihood.

Natural disasters range from earthquakes, floods, and avalanches to droughts, fires, hurricanes, and volcanic eruptions. They strike all over the world all the time. They cause death, destruction, and unsanitary conditions that often lead to disease. Even a local disaster can disrupt

MALARIA: WHEN A MOSQUITO STRIKES

An African child receives a malaria vaccination.

Workers plan a new sewage project in Pakistan.

the economy of an entire country and have a ripple effect on the global economy. For example, a recent typhoon destroyed Myanmar's rice-producing region, leading to the threat of famine in that country. One benefit of globalization is that news of natural disasters spreads instantly and triggers a quick aid response.

Global Diseases With millions of people on the move daily, diseases can spread rapidly. Still, health experts, working together, can often identify and limit outbreaks of many diseases. In the early 2000s, air travelers spread SARS (severe acute respiratory syndrome), a respiratory disease, from China to more than two dozen countries. Health officials took quick action to stop the SARS outbreak. Other diseases, including the avian flu (bird flu), mad cow disease, West Nile virus, swine flu (H1N1), and influenza have raised concerns about the global spread of disease. Diseases often spread before health officials know they exist. Globalization has meant that health experts around the world cooperate to quickly identify and contain outbreaks of disease.

Some diseases have proved hard to contain. When a disease spreads rapidly, it is called an **epidemic.** HIV/AIDS is an epidemic that began in the 1980s. HIV/AIDS has taken a staggering human and economic toll worldwide, especially in southern Africa and Southeast Asia. An estimated 25 million people have died from HIV/AIDS and as many as 40 million are infected with HIV. By 2010, the treatment and prevention of AIDS had been a global priority for a decade. In some nations, education about how to prevent the transmission of AIDS had lowered infection rates. Despite progress, HIV/AIDS continues to spread, especially in Asia and Eastern Europe.

Ending Hunger and Famine For tens of millions of people, hunger poses a daily threat. A major problem is that food does not get distributed to the people who need it most—especially in countries racked by poverty and civil strife. Hunger escalates into **famine** when large numbers of people in a region or country face death by starvation.

Natural disasters can cause famine. Human activity can also cause famine. War disrupts food distribution. During the 1970s and 1980s, civil wars raging in Ethiopia and Sudan intensified the effects of drought, leading to famine. Each side in the conflict tried to keep relief supplies from reaching the other. In many instances, only the efforts of international aid groups have saved millions of people from starvation.

Global Migration Globalization has led to a vast movement of people around the world. Although some people choose to migrate to find jobs or reunite with their families, millions more are **refugees,** people who are forced to move because of poverty, war, persecution, natural disasters, or other crises.

Many migrants find jobs and homes and create better lives in their new countries. But others face hostility and discrimination. Many people in developed countries resent immigrants, who they claim take away jobs and services from natural-born citizens. Millions of migrants, both legal and illegal, head to Europe, Asia, and North America. Each year, the United States alone receives

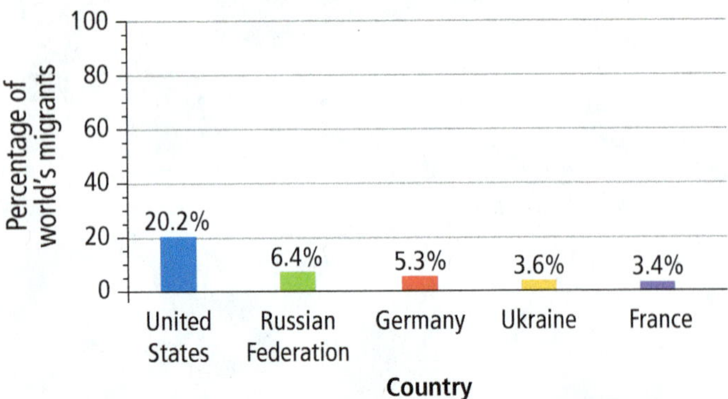

Top Five Destination Countries for International Migrants

Chart Skills In 2005, ten nations received over 50 percent of the world's total migrants. *What characteristics of the top five destination nations might attract migrants?*

SOURCE: *United Nations, Trends in Total Migrant Stock, 2005* about one million legal immigrants and 300,000 or more illegal immigrants. Since World War II, Germany has welcomed large numbers of Turkish, Italian, and Russian immigrants to make up for the part of the labor force that was lost in two world wars.

As migration has grown, so has the smuggling of human beings across borders. Many illegal immigrants pay smugglers large sums to help them reach their destinations. In 2006, the United Nations estimated that human smuggling was a $10 billion-a-year global industry.

✔ **Checkpoint** What are some of the causes of famine and migration?

Human Rights

In 1948, UN members approved the Universal Declaration of Human Rights. It stated that all people are entitled to basic rights "... without distinction of any kind, such as race, colour, sex, language, religion, political or other opinion, national or social origin, property, birth or other status." In 1975, nations signing the Helsinki Accords guaranteed such basic rights as freedom of speech, religion, and the press as well as the rights to a fair trial, to earn a living, and to live in safety. Despite such agreements, human rights abuses—ranging from arbitrary arrest to torture and slavery—occur daily around the world.

The Role of the World Community Human rights abuses are not new, but globalization has brought them to the attention of the world in a new way. And the spread of democracy has forced people to question how human rights abuses can still happen in a modern world. In response, the world community has pressed countries to end abuses. In the 1980s, for example, economic pressure was used against South Africa to end apartheid, its system of legalized segregation.

Sometimes there is no stable government to pressure, or direct pressure does not work. Still, the UN, the United States, and human rights groups monitor and report on human rights violations, from Afghanistan, to Bosnia, to Congo. They even monitor human rights in nations that are part of the developed world, such as Russia.

Women Work for Rights For decades, a global women's movement has focused attention on the needs of women worldwide. The UN Charter supported "equal rights for men and women." By 1950, women had won the right to vote in most European nations, as well as in Japan, China, Brazil, and other countries. In most African nations, both women and men won the vote when their countries gained independence. Women have headed governments in Britain, Israel, India, Pakistan, the Philippines, and elsewhere.

Still, a report to the UN noted that while women represent half of the world's people, "they perform nearly two thirds of all working hours, receive only one tenth of the world's income, and own less than one percent of world property." The UN and other groups thus carefully monitor the human rights of women. They also condemn violence and discrimination against women. More than 165 countries have ratified a new women's human rights treaty.

Women in the Developed and Developing Worlds In the developed world, more and more women now work outside their homes.

An Illegal Crossing
Each year tens of thousands of illegal immigrants, like this family, risk their lives to cross the border between Mexico and the United States. *What factors lead people to risk their lives in illegal border crossings?*

They have gained high-profile jobs as business owners and executives, scientists, and technicians. Yet women often receive less pay for the same job that men do, and many must balance demanding jobs with child-rearing and housework. Still, many women do not have the option of not working, because many families need two incomes just to maintain a decent standard of living. Poor families need two incomes just to survive.

The education gap has been narrowing in developing nations, and women from the middle and elite classes have entered the workforce in growing numbers. Still, women often shoulder a heavy burden of work. In rural areas, especially in Africa where many men have migrated to cities to work, women do much of the farm work in addition to household tasks. In other regions, such as Southeast Asia, young women often leave home in search of work to support the family or to pay for their brothers' education. In many places, cultural traditions still confine women to the home or segregate men and women in the workplace.

Protecting Children Worldwide, children suffer terrible abuses. A 2005 UN report showed that half of the world's children suffer the effects of extreme poverty, armed conflict, and AIDS. Children are also the targets of human rights violations. In some nations, children are forced to serve as soldiers or even slaves. The resulting abuses not only damage children but also hurt a country's hope for the future. In 1989, the UN General Assembly approved the Convention on the Rights of the Child. This human rights treaty sets standards for basic rights for children, including the right to life, liberty, education, and healthcare. But ensuring these rights has proved difficult or even impossible.

In developing countries, tens of millions of children between the ages of 5 and 14 do not attend school. Instead, they work full time. Often, these child laborers work long hours in dangerous, unhealthy conditions for little pay. Many are physically abused by their employers and live in conditions of near slavery. Still, their families need the income the children earn. In some cases, children must work to pay off a family's debt. Human rights groups, the UN, and developed nations have focused a spotlight on child labor in order to end such practices.

Indigenous Peoples Face Challenges Indigenous peoples—including Native Americans, Aborigines in Australia, and Maoris in New Zealand—face discrimination and other abuses. Often, their lands have been forcibly taken. In South America, for example, developers have pushed into once-isolated areas, threatening the ways of life of indigenous peoples. Many Indians have died of diseases carried by the newcomers. During Guatemala's long civil war, the government targeted Mayan villagers, killing tens of thousands. The UN has worked to set standards to protect the rights of indigenous peoples.

✔ **Checkpoint** How are the human rights of children around the world violated?

Development and the Environment

Since earliest times, people have taken what they wanted from the environment. In the past, damage was limited because the world's population was small and technology was simple. Industrialization and the world population explosion have increased the damage done to the environment.

Ending Child Labor
RUGMARK, an organization that works to end child labor, sponsors the education of South Asian students like this girl. The RUGMARK label shown below appears on carpets and rugs that were made without child labor. *What effect might labels like this one have on people's buying habits?*

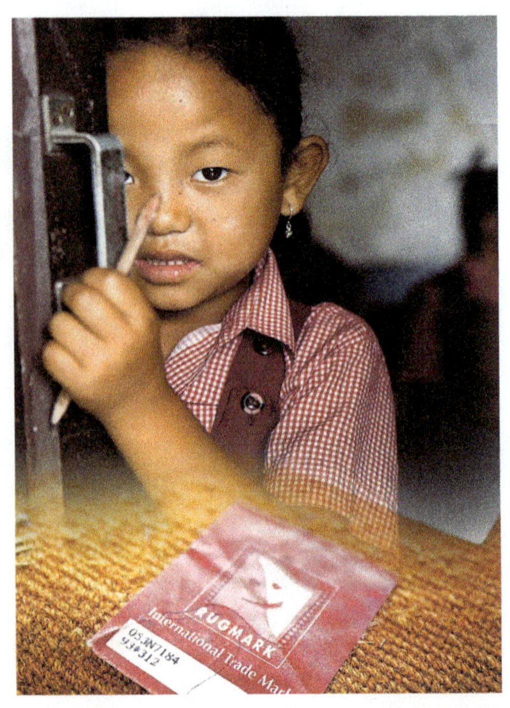

Health of the World Today

In the year 2000, the world population stood at just over 6 billion people. In 2050, it is projected to reach over 9 billion. The world's population in 2000 was sharply divided in terms of health and access to resources. Despite improvements in agriculture, medicine, and technology, huge numbers of people around the world lacked adequate food and access to safe water. Disease threatened some regions more than others. And in certain areas, poverty-stricken people made up the majority of the population.

Global HIV/AIDS Mortality

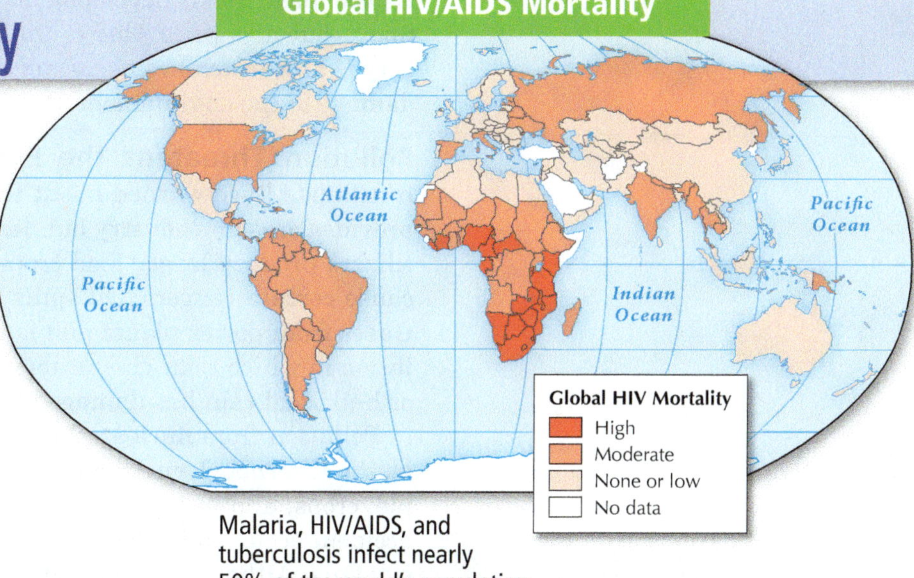

Malaria, HIV/AIDS, and tuberculosis infect nearly 50% of the world's population.

Access to Safe Water

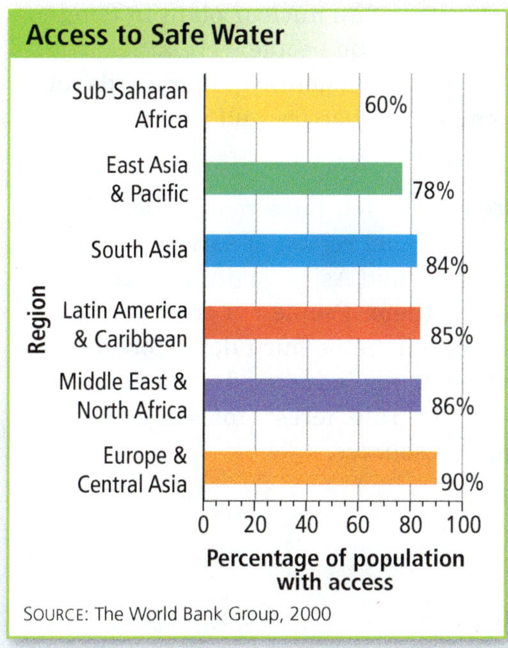

SOURCE: The World Bank Group, 2000

Many people around the world have no access to safe water. Drinking and using unsafe water spreads unsanitary conditions and disease.

World Per Capita GDP

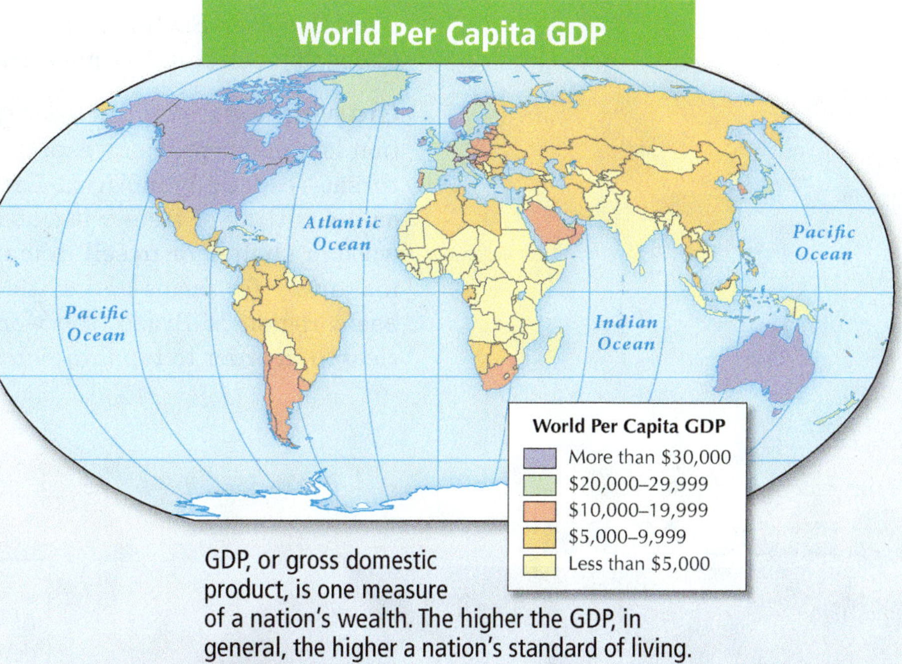

GDP, or gross domestic product, is one measure of a nation's wealth. The higher the GDP, in general, the higher a nation's standard of living.

A United Nation's aid worker carrying children to the safety and care of an orphanage. ▼

History Interactive

For: Interactive world health statistics
Web Code: nap-3431

Thinking Critically

1. **Map Skills** Which regions have high rates of disease and low percentages of their population with access to safe water?
2. **Compare** Compare the HIV/AIDS map and the chart with the map of global GDP. What can a nation's GDP suggest about the health of its people?

As you have read, development improves lives and strengthens economies—but at a price. One of the great challenges of the twenty-first century is how to achieve necessary development without causing permanent damage to the environment.

Pollution Threatens the Environment Since the 1970s, environmentalists have warned about threats to the environment. Strip mining provides ores for industry but destroys land. Chemical pesticides and fertilizers produce larger food crops but harm the soil and water and may cause certain cancers. Oil spills pollute waterways and kill marine life. Gases from power plants and factories produce **acid rain,** a form of pollution in which toxic chemicals in the air fall back to Earth as rain, snow, or hail. Acid rain has damaged forests, lakes, and farmland.

Pollution from nuclear plants is another concern. In 1986, an accident at the Chernobyl nuclear power plant in the Soviet Union exposed people, crops, and animals to deadly radiation over a wide area. A similar accident occurred in 1978 at the Three Mile Island nuclear plant in Pennsylvania. Although the fallout was limited and no people were killed, the accident sparked a great debate about the benefits and hazards of nuclear power. Such accidents have caused industries and governments to develop better safety measures.

Growing Deserts, Shrinking Forests As you have read, desertification is a major problem, especially in the Sahel region of Africa. Another threat—especially in Africa, Latin America, and Asia—is **deforestation,** or the cutting of trees without replacing them. People cut trees for firewood or shelter, or to sell in markets abroad. Some burn down forests to make way for farms and cattle ranches, or for industry. In the Amazon basin region of Brazil, the world's largest rain forest, forests are also cleared in order to tap into rich mineral resources.

BIOGRAPHY

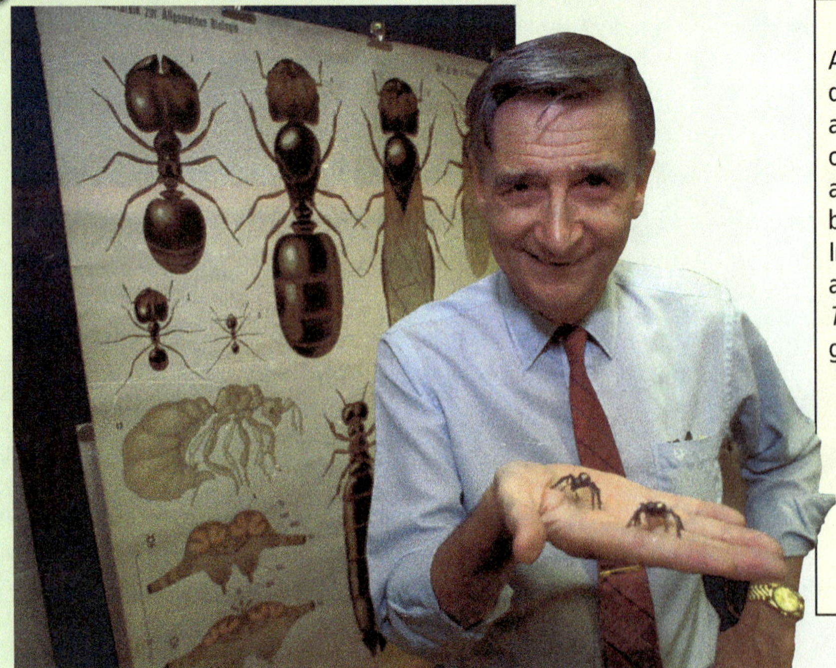

Edward O. Wilson

As a child in Alabama, Edward O. Wilson (1929–) developed a love for nature. His poor eyesight and limited physical strength encouraged him to focus on ants—small creatures that he could hold and look at closely. Wilson never grew out of his "bug period," becoming a renowned professor of biology at Harvard. In recent years, Wilson has increasingly focused his attention on environmental issues. In his 2002 book *The Future of Life,* he writes about how Earth's growing human population is affecting the planet and its resources. Calling the 2000s the "Century of the Environment," he appeals to "science and technology, combined with foresight and moral courage," to meet modern environmental challenges. *Why does Wilson believe that "foresight and moral courage" are needed to preserve the environment?*

Once forests are cleared, rains wash nutrients from the soil, destroying its fertility. Deforestation also causes **erosion,** or the wearing away of land, which encourages flooding. The deforestation of rain forests is particularly worrisome. Rain forests like the Amazon play a key role in absorbing poisonous carbon dioxide from the air and releasing essential oxygen. They are also home to millions of animal and plant species, many of which have become extinct because of deforestation.

Global Warming Another environmental challenge—one that is hotly debated—is **global warming.** Global warming refers to the rise of Earth's surface temperature over time. A rise in Earth's temperature could bring about changes such as the following: a rise in sea level, changes in weather patterns, increased desertification in some areas, and an increase in precipitation in others. Because climates in some areas could become colder, many scientists prefer to call the trend "climate change."

Scientists agree that Earth's temperature has risen slightly over the past century. Many scientists think that this warming comes from gases released into the atmosphere by human activity such as the burning of fossil fuels. These "greenhouse" gases trap warmth in Earth's atmosphere. Some scientists, however, and many policymakers, argue that global warming is due to natural fluctuations in Earth's climate.

The debate over a treaty called the Kyoto Protocol points to a central challenge facing world leaders: Does economic development have to conflict with protecting the environment? The treaty, signed by 140 countries, with the major exceptions of the United States and Australia, went into effect in 2005. Its purpose is to lower the emissions of carbon dioxide and other "greenhouse" gases that contribute to global warming. Many developing nations refuse to sign because they say they must exploit their resources in order to develop fully. The United States has not signed the Kyoto Protocol because it believes the treaty could strain economic growth. Nations that have signed the treaty, however, argue that developed nations must lead the way in slowing emissions.

Vocabulary Builder

fluctuation—(fluk choo AY shun) *n.* swing; rising and falling of something

 **Checkpoint** What kinds of environmental issues do people face today?

Assessment

Terms, People, and Places

1. Place each of the key terms at the beginning of the section into one of the following categories: politics, culture, government, economy, or environment. Write a sentence for each term explaining your choice.

Note Taking

2. **Reading Skill: Compare** Use your completed chart to answer the Focus Question: How do poverty, disease, and environmental challenges affect people around the world today?

Comprehension and Critical Thinking

3. **Synthesize Information** How are global poverty, disease, disasters, and migration linked to each other? How might they be linked to globalization?

4. **Identify Central Issues** Why is protecting human rights not a central issue for many developing countries?

5. **Identify Assumptions** What assumptions can you make about the lack of participation on the part of some nations in the Kyoto Protocol?

● **Writing About History**

Quick Write: Decide on an Organizational Strategy Make a draft of a persuasive essay about social and environmental challenges. Your draft should include a thesis statement, begin with your second-strongest argument, and conclude with your strongest argument. To organize most efficiently, rank your remaining arguments from weakest to strongest.

Aung San Suu Kyi: *Freedom From Fear*

Aung San Suu Kyi, leader of Myanmar's National League for Democracy and winner of the Nobel Peace Prize, has worked courageously for human rights and democracy in her country. Because of her opposition to Myanmar's ruling military junta, she was held under house arrest from 1989 to 1995 and severely restricted thereafter. In this essay, Aung San Suu Kyi describes the need for courage when living under an oppressive government.

▲ Aung San Suu Kyi

Fearlessness may be a gift but perhaps more precious is the courage acquired through endeavor, courage that comes from cultivating the habit of refusing to let fear dictate one's actions, courage that could be described as 'grace under pressure'—grace which is renewed repeatedly in the face of harsh, unremitting[1] pressure.

Within a system which denies the existence of basic human rights, fear tends to be the order of the day. Fear of imprisonment, fear of torture, fear of death, fear of losing friends, family, property or means of livelihood, fear of poverty, fear of isolation, fear of failure. A most insidious[2] form of fear is that which masquerades as common sense or even wisdom, condemning as foolish, reckless, insignificant or futile the small, daily acts of courage which help to preserve man's self-respect and inherent[3] human dignity. It is not easy for a people conditioned by fear under the iron rule of the principle that might is right to free themselves from the enervating[4] miasma[5] of fear. Yet even under the most crushing state machinery courage rises up again and again, for fear is not the natural state of civilized man.

The wellspring[6] of courage and endurance in the face of unbridled power is generally a firm belief in the sanctity of ethical principles combined with a historical sense that despite all setbacks the condition of man is set on an ultimate course for both spiritual and material advancement.... It is man's vision of a world fit for rational, civilized humanity which leads him to dare and to suffer to build societies free from want and fear. Concepts such as truth, justice and compassion cannot be dismissed as trite[7] when these are often the only bulwarks[8] which stand against ruthless power.

▲ Burmese children living in Bangladesh protested for the release of Aung San Suu Kyi on the occasion of the Burmese foreign minister's visit to Bangladesh.

1. **unremitting** (un rih MIT ing) *adj.* not letting up
2. **insidious** (in SID ee us) *adj.* meant to harm
3. **inherent** (in HIHR unt) *adj.* part of one's basic nature
4. **enervating** (EN ur vayt ing) *adj.* weakening or destroying
5. **miasma** (my AZ muh) *n.* harmful atmosphere or influence
6. **wellspring** (WEL spring) *n.* source
7. **trite** (tryt) *adj.* overused; uninteresting
8. **bulwark** (BOOL wurk) *n.* serving as a defense

Thinking Critically

1. **Identify Main Ideas** Why does the author believe that even in harsh, cruel societies courage will rise up again and again?
2. **Apply Information** Give one example of a person refusing to let fear dictate his or her actions.

President Bush emphasizes the importance of national security in a speech to U.S. Coast Guard members in 2003.

Taking a Stand

In the fall of 2002, United States President George W. Bush delivered a speech on international security before the United Nations in New York:

❝ We must choose between a world of fear and a world of progress. We cannot stand by and do nothing while dangers gather. We must stand up for our security and for the permanent rights and for the hopes of mankind. ❞
—George W. Bush, Remarks at the United Nations General Assembly, September 12, 2002

Focus Question What kinds of threats to national and global security do nations face today?

Security in a Dangerous World

Objectives
- Explain why nuclear, biological, and chemical weapons threaten global security.
- Analyze the various terrorist groups and why they are becoming more and more dangerous.
- Describe the various ways in which the United States and other nations have responded to terrorism.

Terms, People, and Places

proliferate	Afghanistan
terrorism	Taliban
al Qaeda	

Note Taking

Reading Skill: Compare and Contrast Use the chart to compare threats to global security.

Threats to Security	
Nuclear Weapons	Nuclear weapons unsecured in former Soviet Union

The end of the Cold War seemed to promise an end to global conflict and the threat of nuclear war. However, since the fall of the Iron Curtain, new and unpredictable threats continue to haunt the world.

The Threat of Modern Weapons

During the Cold War, the United States and the Soviet Union built huge arsenals of nuclear weapons. When the Cold War ended, those weapons still existed. Since then, keeping nuclear, chemical, and biological weapons out of the hands of dangerous groups has become an important issue.

The Nuclear Nonproliferation Treaty In 1968, during a thaw in the Cold War, the United States, the Soviet Union, and 60 other nations signed the Nuclear Nonproliferation Treaty (NPT). The purpose of the treaty was to ensure that nuclear weapons did not **proliferate,** or rapidly spread to nations that had no nuclear weapons. Since then, the treaty has been renewed, with 189 nations agreeing not to develop or possess nuclear weapons.

The International Atomic Energy Agency (IAEA) monitors nations regularly to check that they comply with the treaty. Three nations have not signed the NPT: India, Israel, and Pakistan. All three have nuclear weapons. India and Pakistan's testing of nuclear weapons in 1998 raised fears of a nuclear arms race in Asia. A few signers of the NPT, such as Iran, have tried to sidestep the treaty by acquiring nuclear technology that they claim is being used to develop nuclear power as an energy source.

Russia's Nuclear Weapons During the 1990s, the United States and Russia agreed to reduce their nuclear arsenals. However, after the collapse of the Soviet Union, Russia's nuclear weapons were scattered across a vast territory. With aid from the United States and Europe, Russia dismantled, or took apart, some nuclear weapons. Despite the agreements, however, both the United States and Russia held on to their nuclear stockpiles.

Weapons of Mass Destruction As you have read, weapons of mass destruction (WMDs) include nuclear, biological, and chemical weapons. Nuclear weapons include the atomic bomb. Biological weapons refer mainly to germs that can be released into the air or into water supplies. Chemical weapons are toxins, such as nerve gas and mustard gas.

Recently, however, the danger from WMDs has grown, as terrorist groups and "rogue states"— nations that ignore international law and threaten other nations—try to acquire them. One concern is that terrorists will seize nuclear weapons during transport. Another fear is that terrorists, or those who sympathize with their causes, will gain access to nuclear weapons programs in countries with unstable governments, such as Pakistan.

 **Checkpoint** What was the purpose of the NPT?

Terrorism Threatens Global Security

Since the 1990s, the world has witnessed a growing threat from terrorism. **Terrorism** is the use of violence by groups of extremists to achieve political goals. Terrorists' goals range from getting political prisoners released to gaining territory or autonomy for a particular ethnic group. Terrorists have bombed buildings, slaughtered civilians, police, and soldiers, and assassinated political leaders. Although terrorists have seldom achieved their larger goals, they have inflicted terrible damage and generated widespread fear.

Terrorists use headline-grabbing tactics to draw attention to their demands. They might attack hotels and tourists in Mumbai, bomb commuter trains in Madrid, or blow themselves up as "suicide bombers" to kill Israeli or Iraqi civilians. Terrorism has led to greater international cooperation between governments in an effort to prevent further attacks.

Regional Terrorist Groups Regional terrorist groups have operated in the developed world for decades. For 30 years, the Irish Republican Army (IRA) used terrorist tactics to force Britain out of Northern Ireland. Protestant paramilitary groups loyal to Great Britain responded with the same tactics. During the Cold War, the communist Red Brigade in Italy used violence in an attempt to gain power. The ETA, a Basque terrorist group, wants the Spanish government to grant independence to the Basque region in northern Spain.

In South America, leftist groups like the Shining Path in Peru and FARC in Colombia use kidnappings, murder, and bombings to overthrow national governments. They finance their operations with the sale of illegal drugs. In Asia, terrorist activities were linked to the long conflict between India and Pakistan over Kashmir.

A Risky Situation
Vials of the bacteria that cause plague were left improperly secured in Kazakhstan by Soviet scientists.

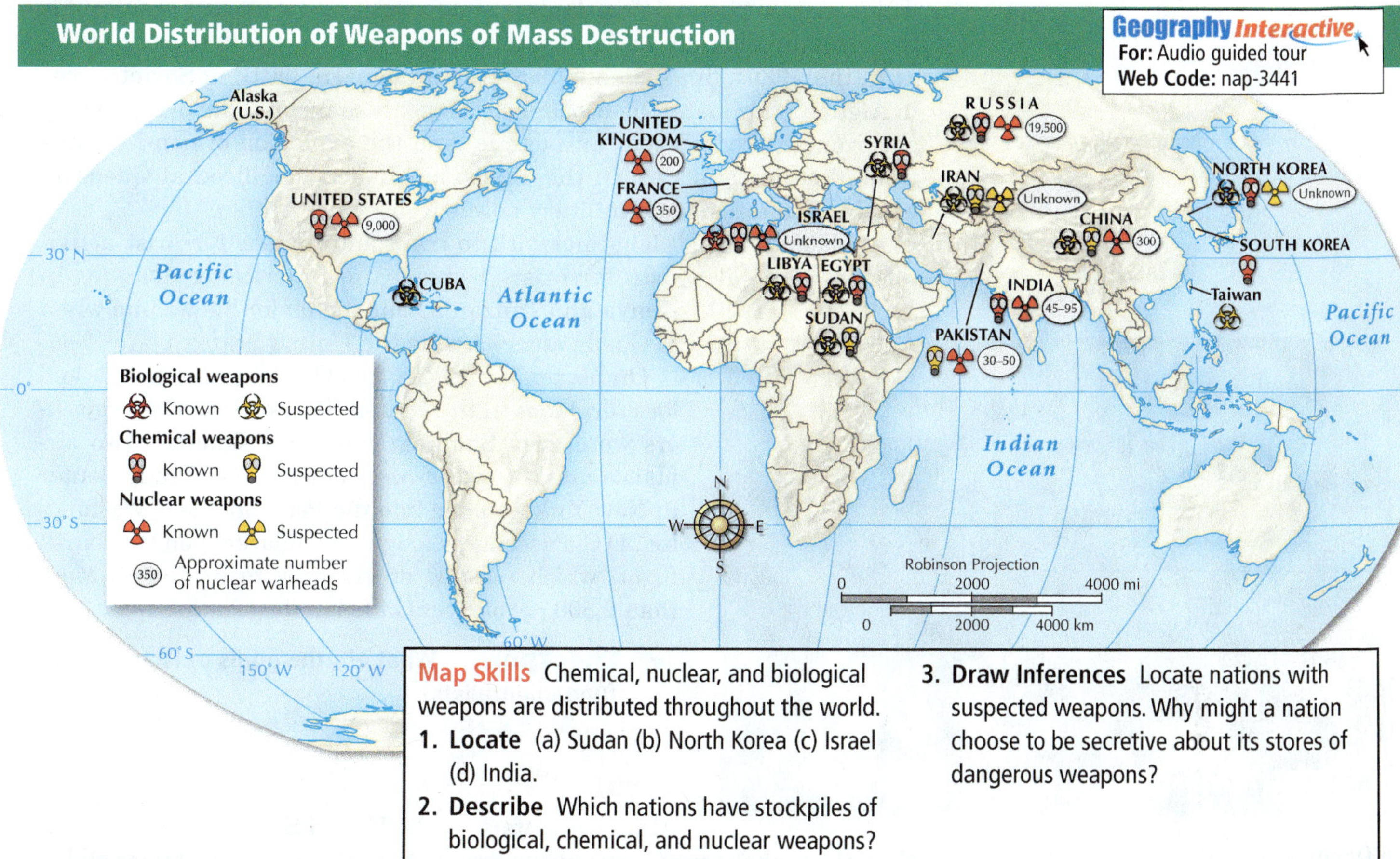

Map Skills Chemical, nuclear, and biological weapons are distributed throughout the world.

1. **Locate** (a) Sudan (b) North Korea (c) Israel (d) India.
2. **Describe** Which nations have stockpiles of biological, chemical, and nuclear weapons?
3. **Draw Inferences** Locate nations with suspected weapons. Why might a nation choose to be secretive about its stores of dangerous weapons?

Conflicts in the Middle East

Decades of conflict between Israel and its neighbors have fueled terrorism. In 1964, a group of Arabs founded the Palestine Liberation Organization (PLO), with the goal of creating an independent Palestinian state. In its early years, the PLO used terrorist methods.

The PLO renounced terrorism in 1988. Meanwhile, other terrorist groups have emerged and continue their calls for the establishment of a Palestinian state and the destruction of Israel. The Al-Aqsa Martyrs Brigade, Hamas, Hezbollah, and Islamic Jihad are among the groups that practice terror to achieve their goals. They found support in poverty-stricken Palestinian refugee camps in Gaza and trained suicide bombers to attack Israeli targets.

Islamic Fundamentalism

By the 1980s, Islamic fundamentalism was on the rise. This conservative reform movement wanted to revive Islamic values and install governments that strictly followed Islamic law, or Sharia. The Islamist movement was partly a response to the rise of secular governments in many Muslim nations and the impact of Western culture. It was also a backlash against foreign support for Israel and the presence of foreign powers in the Middle East. Islamic fundamentalists made Israel or Western nations scapegoats for their problems.

The 1979 Iranian revolution brought an Islamist government to power. Later, an Islamist group called the Taliban gained power in Afghanistan. Fundamentalist movements have also emerged in countries from Algeria to Indonesia. Iran and Saudi Arabia have both provided financial support for terrorist organizations.

Al Qaeda Attacks

Some Islamic fundamentalists turned to terrorism. The most widely known Islamic terrorist organization is **al Qaeda** (ahl KY duh), which means "the Base" in Arabic. The founder and leader of al Qaeda is Osama bin Laden, a wealthy Saudi businessman.

In the 1980s, bin Laden joined Muslim fighters battling Soviet forces in Afghanistan. Later, he broadened his goals to include the overthrow of governments considered "un-Islamic" and the expulsion of non-Muslims from Muslim countries. In the 1990s, bin Laden mobilized al Qaeda to expel U.S. interests and military power from Saudi Arabia.

Al Qaeda built a global network to train and finance terrorist activities. In 1998, al Qaeda terrorists bombed the American embassies in Kenya and Tanzania. But the major blow came when al Qaeda struck inside the United States.

On September 11, 2001, al Qaeda terrorists hijacked four airplanes in the United States. Most of the hijackers were from Saudi Arabia. They slammed two airplanes into the twin towers of the World Trade Center in New York and one into the Pentagon near Washington, D.C. Passengers fought the hijackers on the fourth flight, which crashed on the way to its target. More than 2,500 people were killed in the attacks.

✔ **Checkpoint** What are the goals of Islamic fundamentalists?

Response to Terrorism

Al Qaeda's attack on the United States triggered a startling global shake-up. Governments around the world questioned their ability to keep their citizens safe. U.S. President George W. Bush declared a "war on terror" in general, and against al Qaeda in particular.

New Security Measures After the 2001 attacks, the United States made national security a top priority. To this end, the government strengthened and reorganized its intelligence services and passed new counter terrorism laws. In the United States and elsewhere, there were more rigorous security measures at airports and public buildings. A long-term effort was launched to find out how terrorist groups were funded, with the goal of cutting off terrorists' money supply and limiting their activities. The United States worked with other countries to coordinate intelligence about terrorist groups.

These measures were costly. In addition, some believed the federal government was using the threat of terrorism to increase its power and violate the constitutional rights and freedoms of its citizens. But many felt that the threat was serious enough to justify extreme measures.

The Wars in Afghanistan As part of its "war on terror," the United States made it a priority to find and punish the organizers of the 2001 attacks. Osama bin Laden was based in **Afghanistan.** The government of Afghanistan, an extreme Islamic fundamentalist group called the **Taliban,** refused U.S. demands to surrender the terrorists. The United States then formed a coalition of nations to invade Afghanistan. In 2002, with the help of Afghan warlords, American and allied forces overthrew the Taliban and drove al Qaeda into hiding or flight. Bin Laden and many Taliban leaders escaped capture.

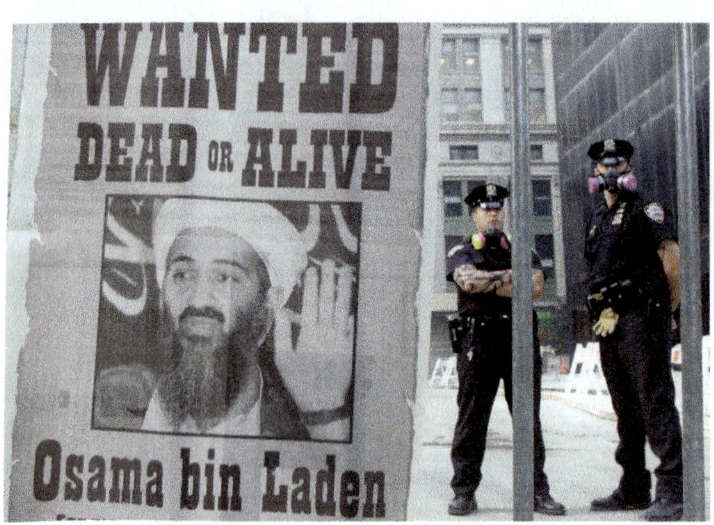

A Dangerous Leader
New York City police stand near a "Wanted" poster in 2001. *How does bin Laden threaten the United States' security?*

Vocabulary Builder

priority—(pry AWR uh tee) *n.* something deemed of greater importance than other things

Coalition forces helped Afghanistan hold elections for a new government. The new government lifted many harsh Taliban laws, such as those that forbid girls and women from getting an education. From hideouts along the Pakistan border, Taliban fighters resisted the new government and its Western allies. The war soon spilled into neighboring Pakistan, where Taliban and al Qaeda fighters took refuge.

War in Iraq In 2003, President Bush urged Congress to agree to an invasion of Iraq, citing intelligence reports that said Iraq was secretly producing WMDs. The Bush administration also suggested that Iraq was involved in the 2001 terrorist attacks against the United States. The war was bitterly debated among Americans and around the world, because no WMDs were found after the U.S. invasion.

A 2008 report by the Senate Intelligence Committee said that prior to the invasion, the Bush administration had repeatedly exaggerated the threat posed by Iraq. The report also revealed that there had been no credible intelligence to support the Bush administration's claims that Iraq was developing nuclear weapons, or that Iraq had longstanding ties to terrorist groups.

Threats From Iran and North Korea When Iran announced a plan to develop nuclear power plants in the early 2000s, the United States and other nations feared that Iran truly intended to develop nuclear weapons. Although Iran insisted its nuclear energy program was for peaceful purposes, the UN Security Council imposed some sanctions on Iran.

For years, North Korea violated its agreement under the Nuclear Nonproliferation Treaty and worked on developing nuclear weapons. Tensions grew as the United States tried to pressure North Korea to stop its nuclear weapons program. In 2003, North Korea withdrew from the NPT. In 2006, it tested a small nuclear bomb.

Many people feared that if Iran or North Korea developed nuclear weapons, that nuclear technology could be passed on to terrorist groups. A nuclear-armed Iran or North Korea also posed threats to their regions and to world peace.

✔ **Checkpoint** Why did the United States invade Iraq?

Iran's Nuclear Plans
Iranians form a chain around a nuclear research facility to show their support for their country's nuclear program. *Why do Western nations object to the program?*

SECTION 4 Assessment

Progress Monitoring Online
For: Self-quiz with vocabulary practice
Web Code: naa-3441

Terms, People, and Places

1. For each term, person, or place listed at the beginning of the section, write a sentence explaining its significance.

Note Taking

2. **Reading Skill: Compare and Contrast** Use your completed chart to answer the Focus Question: What kinds of threats to national and global security do nations face today?

Comprehension and Critical Thinking

3. **Draw Inferences** Why might the United States and Russia be reluctant to fully commit to nuclear disarmament?

4. **Predict Consequences** How might nations around the world react should Middle Eastern nations democratically elect Islamic fundamentalist governments?

5. **Demonstrate Reasoned Judgment** Do you think that "preemptive" wars, or wars waged to prevent other wars or attacks, are sometimes necessary? Explain your answer.

● Writing About History

Quick Write: Draft the Opening Paragraph The paragraph that opens your essay is the place to grab the reader's interest. Remember that if the reader loses interest after reading the first paragraph, he or she is unlikely to continue reading. Draft an opening paragraph about threats to global security, using specific details to grab the reader's interest. An opening such as "There are many threats to global security" is much less compelling than a description of a specific threat.

Buzz Aldrin walks on the moon in 1969. The space capsule that he traveled in is reflected on his visor.

WITNESS HISTORY ◀)) AUDIO

A Giant Leap for Mankind

On July 20, 1969, American astronauts Neil Armstrong and Edwin Aldrin landed on the moon after a four-day trip in the spacecraft *Apollo 11*. Stepping out onto the powdery surface, Armstrong—the first person ever to have walked on the moon—said, "That's one small step for man, one giant leap for mankind." Those words electrified a nation and defined a new era of world history.

Focus Question How have advances in science and technology shaped the modern world?

Advances in Science and Technology

Objectives

- Describe the exploration of space and the practical applications that resulted from it.
- Analyze the development and impact of the computer revolution.
- Explain how advances in medicine and biotechnology have shaped life today.

Terms, People, and Places

artificial satellite
International Space Station (ISS)
personal computer (PC)
Internet
biotechnology
laser
genetics
genetic engineering

Note Taking

Reading Skill: Compare Use the chart to compare the impacts of modern science and technology.

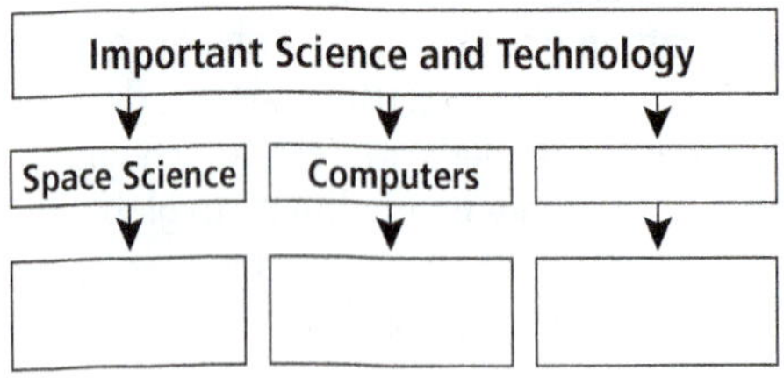

People in the past half century have used various terms to describe the age they live in, including "the atomic age," the "electronic age," and the "automobile age." All of these labels have one thing in common: their connection to modern science and technology. Since 1945, scientific research and technological development have had a transforming effect on human history. Startling new inventions, the computer revolution, and advances in the life sciences have redefined the world we live in and the lives we lead.

Exploring and Making Use of Space

By the second half of the twentieth century, there were few places on Earth that people had not begun to explore. Space was seen as the "final frontier"—an unknown world filled with opportunity. Within a few short decades, people had traveled to this frontier and had used its resources to help develop practical applications that transformed their lives.

The Space Race Begins Rockets are projectiles or vehicles propelled by the ejection of burning gasses from the rear of the rocket. In the early twentieth century, pioneers in rocketry like the American physicist Robert Goddard probed the potential of liquid-fueled rockets. From the beginning, Goddard believed that a rocket could carry people to the moon. At first people met his ideas with disbelief. Increasingly, German scientists took interest in Goddard's work, prompting him to work with great secrecy.

Nevertheless, during World War II German scientists, led by Wernher von Braun, developed Germany's "secret weapon," the V-2 rockets that flew across the English Channel to rain down on London.

During the Cold War, the United States and the Soviet Union competed with each other to build both rocket-propelled weapons and rocketry for the purpose of space exploration. Von Braun, who moved to the United States after World War II, became a leader in the American missiles and space program. In 1957, the space age began when the Soviet Union launched into orbit *Sputnik*, the first **artificial satellite,** or manmade object that orbits a larger body. In 1969, the United States Apollo program landed the first man on the moon. Both superpowers also explored the military uses of space and sent spy satellites to orbit Earth. Since the end of the Cold War, the United States and Russia have cooperated in joint space ventures.

Space Science Develops In the decades since *Sputnik* and *Apollo*, rockets have been launched to other planets and beyond. Robotic space vehicles have penetrated the mists of Venus and the rings of Saturn, landed on Mars, and circled the moons of Jupiter. Rocket missions have various goals. They can take scientific measurements, release permanent satellites or telescopes, and if they are manned, conduct medical or biological experiments. They can also provide information about the composition and formation of the universe itself.

Increasingly, nations have worked together to explore space. For example, Russia, the United States, Canada, Japan, and several countries in Europe are developing the **International Space Station (ISS).**

Traveler's Tales
EYEWITNESS ACCOUNT

An Astronaut Views Earth From Space

Alan Bean is an American astronaut who participated in the United States' Apollo 12 moon-landing project. In 1969, Bean became the fourth person to walk on the moon. Deeply moved by his experience, he began taking art lessons upon his return to Earth to express visually what he had seen. He resigned from NASA in 1981 to devote himself to painting. The excerpt below, taken from a book about the Apollo mission that he wrote and illustrated, describes the view from the moon.

> It was incredible to stand on the moon… and take a moment to reflect on all the dedicated people it took to get us there for America. We were the lucky ones. The stars were not visible because the sunlight reflecting from the bright lunar surface caused the irises of our eyes to contract, just as they do on earth at night when standing on a brightly lit patio. As we looked up, the sky was a deep, shiny black. I guessed that deep, shiny black was the color one sees looking into infinity . . . . I thought: Can all the people we know, all the people we love, who we've seen on TV, or read about in the newspapers, all be up there on that tiny blue-and-white marble? Earth—small but so lovely—was easily the most beautiful object we could see from the moon. It was a wondrous moment.

—*Alan Bean,*
from ***Apollo, 1998***

Thinking Critically
1. **Draw Inferences** Why does Bean call the astronauts the "lucky ones"?
2. **Analyze Information** How does Bean contrast his view of Earth with that of the lunar sky? What point does he make by contrasting these two views?

Construction on the ISS began in 1998. When it is completed in 2010, it will serve as a space laboratory, allowing scientists from many different countries to observe space, conduct research, and develop new space-related technologies.

The Impact of Artificial Satellites The thousands of artificial satellites that orbit Earth have a number of very specific applications. These applications can be divided into three groups—communications, observation, and navigation. Communications satellites relay information that is used in advanced communications, including television, telephone, and high-speed data transmission. Observation satellites observe Earth, providing data to scientists, weather forecasters, and military planners. Navigation satellites beam precise locations to ship captains and others who need to navigate Earth's surface.

By 2000, artificial satellites had revolutionized global communications. Maintaining stationary orbits over specific points on Earth's surface, artificial satellites can transmit phone messages or television pictures anywhere on Earth. Linked to cell phones or computers, they allow people separated by thousands of miles to communicate instantly.

✔ **Checkpoint** What is the International Space Station and what is its significance?

The Computer Revolution

The invention of the computer in the twentieth century caused an unprecedented information revolution. Very few aspects of modern life remain untouched by computers. Computers run businesses and power plants, help scientists conduct advanced research, and when connected to satellites, make global communications possible. The development of computer technology has given rise to the term "Information Age."

Early Computers A computer is a device for making mathematical calculations and for storing, processing, and rapidly manipulating data. Computers have made it possible to preserve vast amounts of data. And when linked up in a vast network, they have brought written communication over enormous distances instantaneously.

The first electronic computers, built in the 1940s, were huge, slow machines. Later, thanks to inventions like the silicon chip, the computer was reduced in size. **Personal computers,** or **PCs,** became widely available in the 1970s for individual users, both at work and at home. By inserting basic programs into the machine, the user could perform complex and difficult tasks quickly and easily.

Over the next few decades, PCs replaced typewriters and account books in homes and businesses worldwide. At the same time, computer technology spread into many different fields. Computerized robots operate in factories. Computers remotely control satellites and probes in space and students use them in school classrooms. And computers increasingly aid scientists and architects in developing models to predict disasters, understand environmental changes, and plan urban development.

The Internet In the 1970s, various branches of the U.S. government along with groups in several American universities led efforts to link computer systems together via cables and satellites. By the 1990s, the "Internet" or "World Wide Web" was well established, again revolutionizing information technology. Using the **Internet,** a person can instantly communicate with other users around the world. The same person can also instantly access vast storehouses of information of all sorts.

By 2000, the Internet had grown to a gigantic network, linking individuals, governments, and businesses around the world. E-commerce, or buying and selling on the Internet, contributed to economic growth. The Internet also began to shape life in developing nations.

Breakthroughs in Medicine

Twentieth-century discoveries in medicine had a major impact on people around the world. For example, in 1952 researcher Jonas Salk (left) developed a vaccine for polio. Polio is a virus that spreads rapidly among people, especially children, causing paralysis. Before Salk's discovery, around 20,000 people in the United States contracted polio each year. Because of Salk's vaccine, the disease is extremely rare in the world today.

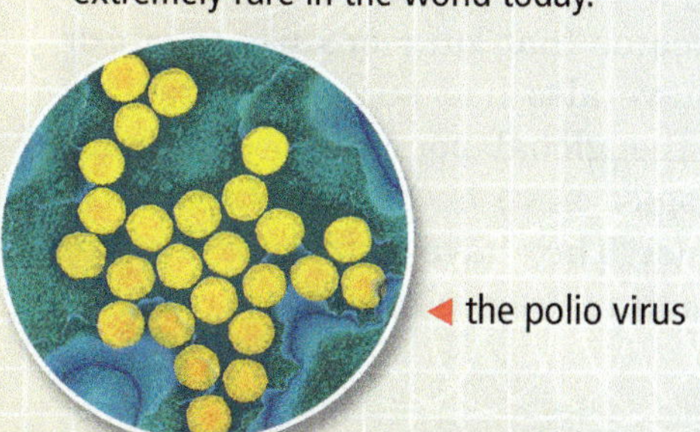
◀ the polio virus

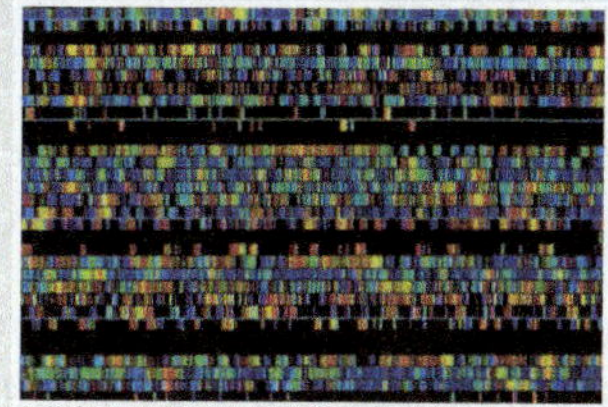
DNA ▶ sequencer

Expanding the Science of Genetics

The study of genes was not new to the twentieth century. The work of James Watson and Francis Crick, (right) however, dramatically transformed the science of genetics. In 1953, the two men discovered the basic structure of DNA—the material in the chromosomes of all cells that determines how every organism functions. This discovery revolutionized the study of heredity and paved the way for genetic engineering.

Thinking Critically
1. **Draw Inferences** Why did Albert Einstein later regret his work on the Manhattan Project?
2. **Cause and Effect** How did the discovery of DNA affect the field of genetics?

◀)) AUDIO

A GLOBAL FOOD EVOLVES

What we now know as corn originally grew as a wild grass in the Americas. Thousands of years ago, ancient peoples began experimenting with this grass, carefully selecting good seeds and nurturing plants. About 7,000 years ago, Native Americans near present-day Mexico City developed small ears of corn, calling them *maize*. Indians throughout the Americas, and then European settlers, constantly experimented with corn to produce bigger and better ears. The experimentation still continues today.

▲ Eventually, Native Americans produced maize, a plant with ears of plump, soft kernels like today's corn. Maize became a staple crop for many Native American groups. They also developed multi-colored ears of corn, like those above, using them for food and in religious activities.

◀ Ancient wild corn was called *teosinte* (tee oh *SIN* tee). Teosinte kernels, hard and nut-like, grew on thick grassy stalks. Over thousands of years Native Americans domesticated teosinte, carefully preserving the seeds of the plants that produced the best ears.

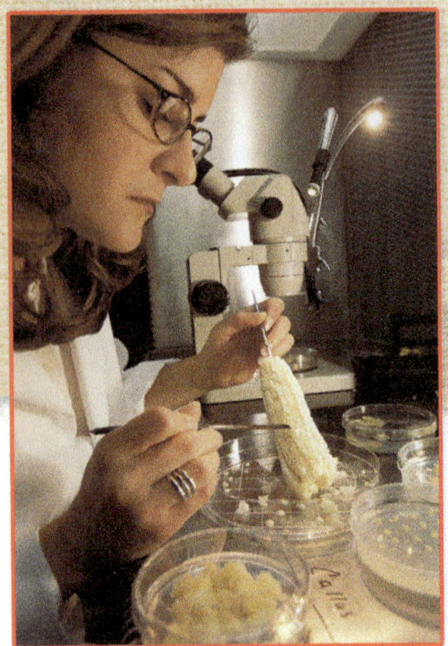

▲ A biotechnology worker cuts into an ear of corn to extract a section of DNA, or genetic material, that will be used to improve the next corn crop. By selecting only specific DNA, scientists can transfer only the genes that will result in desirable crop traits, such as hardiness or resistance to insects.

At the beginning of the twenty-first century, about 6 percent of the world's population could access the Internet. By 2010, it is estimated that about one third of the world's population will have access to the Internet—connecting them to a new world of ideas and information.

✓ **Checkpoint** What impact have personal computers had on people's lives?

Advances in Medicine and Biotechnology

Science and technology have revolutionized our understanding and our control of both human life and other forms of life on this planet. Developments in medicine and **biotechnology,** the application of biological research to industry, engineering, and technology, have resulted in new ways to combat and prevent disease.

Breakthroughs Transform Medicine In the postwar era, pioneers in the life sciences such as Dr. Jonas Salk became household names. Before the Salk vaccine, the paralyzing disease polio had crippled thousands of children and adults—including President Franklin D. Roosevelt. Other medical researchers developed vaccines to help prevent the spread of smallpox and other diseases.

Breakthroughs in surgery also transformed the field of medicine. In the 1970s, surgeons learned to transplant organs, including the human heart, to save lives. **Lasers** made many types of surgery safer and more precise. Lasers are high-energy light beams that surgeons use to cut or repair tissues and organs. Scientists have also had success in treating some cancers, a disease that affects the global population. In recent decades, computers and other technologies have become partners with doctors in diagnosing and treating disease. They have also made it easier for people to share information, thus making diseases easier to treat.

Biotechnology and Genetic Engineering In the past couple of decades, the field of biotechnology has exploded. Biotechnology companies make products including vaccinations, medicines, and industrial bacteria that can be used to treat waste or clean up toxic spills.

Biotechnology is closely related to the fields of genetics and genetic engineering, which have also made dramatic advances in recent years. **Genetics** is the study of genes and heredity, while **genetic engineering** is the manipulation of genetic material to produce specific results. Beginning in the 1950s, genetic researchers, spearheaded by Rosalind Franklin, J. D. Watson, and F.H.C. Crick, examined the chemical code carried by all living things. Their research established the central role of DNA—deoxyribonucleic acid—in the chromosomes that determine human heredity. Their work revealed the "double helix," spiral-shaped DNA that carries hereditary traits from parents to children.

Ongoing genetic research has produced new drug therapies to fight human diseases. Research has also created new strains of fruits and vegetables that are intended to resist disease or thrive in conditions that usually inhibit growth. Genetic cloning, or the process of creating identical organisms from the cell of a host organism, has many practical applications in raising livestock and in biological research.

Biotechnology and genetic engineering have brought benefits, but also debate. Some people believe that genetically modified foods are unnatural and potentially dangerous. The possibility of cloning genetically identical mammals—including human beings—has also raised ethical questions about the role of science in creating and changing life.

Standards of Living Rise As you have read, science and technology have often had a direct and powerful impact on human life. Advances in diagnosing and treating disease and increased agricultural output have raised life expectancies worldwide, as well as standards of living. Yet great challenges still remain, from overpopulation to disasters to corrupt governments. In the decades ahead, people will continue to look for ways to solve global problems, using whatever tools they have.

✔ **Checkpoint** How have scientific advances affected people's standard of living?

SECTION 5 Assessment

Terms, People, and Places

1. What do each of the key terms listed at the beginning of the section have in common? Explain.

Note Taking

2. **Reading Skill: Compare** Use your completed chart to answer the Focus Question: How have advances in science and technology shaped the modern world?

Comprehension and Critical Thinking

3. **Synthesize Information** Considering the history of the Cold War, explain why the United States and Russia competed against each other to achieve dominance in the space race.

4. **Recognize Cause and Effect** What impact has the computer revolution had on globalization?

5. **Express Problems Clearly** Biotechnology has provided many benefits, but many people worry about its long-term effects. Explain why this is so.

● **Writing About History**

Quick Write: Write a Conclusion Write a conclusion that restates your thesis, sums up the supporting details, and leaves readers with a final impression. This final impression can be a memorable statement or even a call to action. As you write a conclusion about science and technology in the modern world, consider what basic impression you want the reader to remember about the topic, even if he or she takes nothing else away from the essay.

Quick Study Guide

■ Key Components of Globalization

- Interdependence: dependence of countries on goods, resources, knowledge, and labor from other parts of the world
- Advances in communications and transportation
- Rise of huge multinational corporations
- Far-reaching effects of financial crisis, shortages of natural resources, and debt
- Rise of global economy with many global organizations and treaties

■ Influential Technology of the Twentieth Century

Technology	Description	Uses
Artificial satellite	Man-made object that orbits a larger body	Space exploration; spying and other military purposes; scientific research; navigation; communications
Computer	Device for storing, processing, and rapidly manipulating data	Creating and preserving data; making businesses and homes run more efficiently; controlling satellites and factories
Internet	Network of world computer systems linked by cables and satellites	Instant communication with users around world; instant data retrieval; means of commerce
Biotechnology	Application of biological research to industry	Vaccinations and medicines; industrial bacteria; genetic engineering

■ Major Challenges to Society Today

- Global poverty, disasters, and disease
- Ensuring human rights for all, including women, children, and indigenous peoples
- Environmental problems including pollution, deforestation, desertification, and climate change
- Threat of misuse of nuclear technology and weapons of mass destruction
- Terrorism

■ Important Industrialized Regions

Region	Description	Role in Global Economy
The United States	Worldís only superpower	Important world leader; largest trading country in world
The European Union	Union of 25 European nations with distinct governments but common economic, political, and cultural institutions	Currently includes over half of European nations and is growing; world's largest trading region
The Pacific Rim	Geographical region that includes the countries that border the Pacific Ocean	With many countries and huge populations, potential to be major player in global economy

■ Recent World Events

1986
Nuclear accident occurs in Chernobyl.

1990
Germany is reunited.

1995
The WTO forms.

1985

1990

1995

1988
Osama bin Laden forms al Qaeda.

1994
NAFTA is created.

 Essential Question Review

To connect prior knowledge with what you have learned in this chapter, answer the questions below in your Concept Connector journal. Use the journal in the Reading and Note Taking Study Guide to record your answers (or go to www.phschool.com **Web Code:** nad-3407). In addition, record information about the following concepts:

- Trade: United States trade in the twentieth century
- Economic systems: Globalization

1. **Technology** Since their introduction, personal computers have become more common around the world. If everyone in the world could have access to a computer and the Internet, how might society, culture, and the economy change?

2. **Trade** The formation of the European Union improved the economy of many nations in Europe and created a sense of unity. But not all people and all member nations were equally happy with the many changes. What were some of the unintended consequences of the formation of the EU?

3. **Cooperation** Is the work of NGOs essential in the 21st century? Think about the work that organizations like the International Red Cross do. Are there situations in which an NGO would be better suited to provide relief than a government or an organization like the United Nations? Why might groups of people in some situations be more likely to welcome aid from an NGO than from a government?

4. **Democracy** Look at the image at the start of this chapter. Artificial satellites can transmit phone messages or television pictures anywhere on earth. Do you think better communication will lead to the spread of democracy? Explain.

■ Connections to Today

1. **Advances in Science: Medical Procedures** In 1954, American doctor Joseph Murray performed the first organ transplant, successfully transplanting a kidney from a man into his twin brother. In 2004, nearly 30,000 organ transplants were performed. Think about the issues that people grappled with decades ago as they considered the ethics of organ transplantation. Then choose a medical procedure that is being debated today. (Possibilities might include stem cell research, genetic cloning, or the use of surrogate mothers.) Research your topic and then write two paragraphs: one that supports the procedure and one that opposes it.

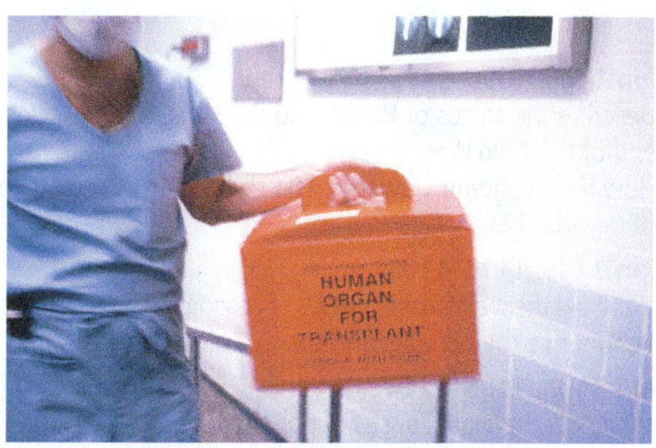

2. **Cultural Diffusion: Spread of Popular Culture** During the 20th century, American popular culture—especially American movies, music, and clothing—influenced people around the world. Consider the factors necessary for cultural diffusion. Why is popular culture from the United States widely influential? Predict which countries' popular culture will become widely influential in the early 21st century.

1997
The Asian financial crisis hits.

Sept. 11, 2001
Al Qaeda attacks the United States.

2000 2005 2010

2000
Vladimir Putin is elected president of Russia.

October 2001
The United States begins war on the Taliban in Afghanistan.

Dec. 26, 2004
Tsunami devastates Southeast Asia.

2007
The United States commits more troops to Iraq and Afghanistan.

Chapter Assessment

Terms, People, and Places

Choose the italicized term in parentheses that best completes each sentence.

1. A *(deficit/default)* is the gap between what a government spends and what it takes in through taxes and other resources.
2. One of the WTO's basic policies is its opposition to *(outsourcing/protectionism)*.
3. *(Famine/Acid rain)* is a particular concern in areas where there has been a natural disaster.
4. The belief that society should be governed by Islamic law is known as *(Islamic fundamentalism/terrorism)*.
5. *(Genetics/Artificial satellites)* have revolutionized communications.

Main Ideas

Section 1 (pp. 1096–1099)
6. Describe the status of Russia and the United States after the end of the Cold War.
7. How has economic power in Asia shifted over the past couple of decades?

Section 2 (pp. 1100–1105)
8. What are the main characteristics of economic interdependence?
9. Summarize the benefits and costs of globalization.

Section 3 (pp. 1106–1114)
10. What are the main causes of poverty?
11. Describe some of the environmental challenges of the 21st century.

Section 4 (pp. 1115–1119)
12. Why are nuclear weapons a particular problem in Russia?
13. What is al Qaeda, and why is it such a threat?

Section 5 (pp. 1120–1125)
14. Summarize the impact of science and technology on modern life.

Chapter Focus Question
15. What are the major issues facing the world today?

Critical Thinking

16. **Analyze Information** Which region do you think will be the most important economically during the next half-century: the EU, the Pacific Rim, or the United States? Explain your answer.
17. **Predict Consequences** What might be the global impact if terrorists cut off supplies of natural gas or another important resource to a large American city?
18. **Geography and History** Consider the space race of the late 1900s. Why have nations throughout history found it important to explore frontiers?
19. **Recognize Cause and Effect** In this chapter you have read about how economic and technological changes have had an impact on people around the world. How might these changes also affect people's values and beliefs?

"Nothing's labeled. How are we supposed to know which fruit has been genetically engineered?"

20. **Analyze Visuals** What point is the cartoonist making about genetically modified foods in the cartoon above?
21. **Recognize Cause and Effect** How does outsourcing jobs affect both the home country and the country where the jobs are outsourced?
22. **Draw Inferences** How can globalization bring about a stronger commitment to human rights? How can it encourage human rights abuses, such as child labor?

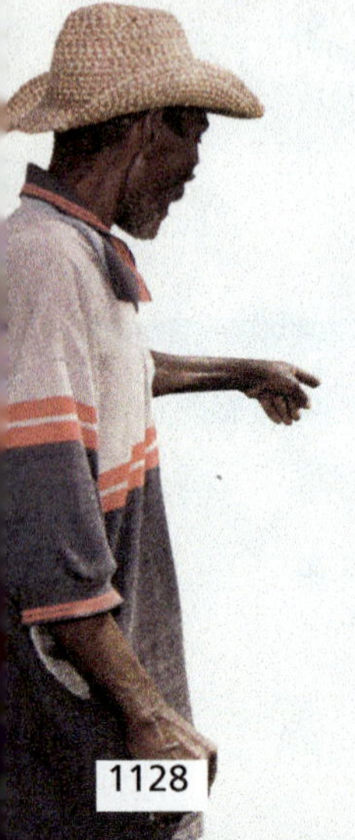

● Writing About History

In this chapter's five Section Assessments, you developed the skills to write a persuasive essay.

Write a Persuasive Essay People strongly debate many of the issues that face the world today. Choose a topic that interests you—and that you have a strong opinion about—and then write a persuasive essay. You may choose your own topic or select from the following: free trade, global warming, the war on terrorism, WMDs, or HIV/AIDS. Consult page SH16 of the Writing Handbook for additional help.

Prewriting
- Do library or Internet research to read about each of the topics listed above.
- Choose a topic that interests you.
- List questions about the topic and gather sources.

Drafting
- Develop your thesis and select persuasive arguments that support it.
- Organize and write the essay, using your second best argument in the introduction and your best argument in the conclusion.
- Be sure to include a personal appeal or an example that many people can relate to.

Revising
- Use the guidelines for revising your report on page SH17 of the Writing Handbook.

Document-Based Assessment

The Use of Alternative Energy

For many scientists, politicians, and citizens, energy consumption is a troubling issue. Most people agree that the world is too dependent on fossil fuels, which are not renewable. However, intense debate surrounds the questions of which alternate energy sources we should focus on and how quickly we need to have them developed.

Document A

U. S. Energy Consumption by Energy Source, 2007

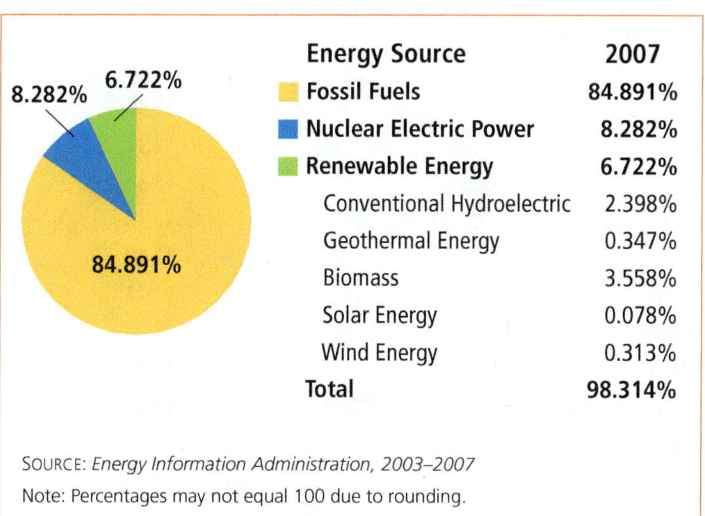

Energy Source	2007
Fossil Fuels	84.891%
Nuclear Electric Power	8.282%
Renewable Energy	6.722%
Conventional Hydroelectric	2.398%
Geothermal Energy	0.347%
Biomass	3.558%
Solar Energy	0.078%
Wind Energy	0.313%
Total	98.314%

SOURCE: *Energy Information Administration, 2003–2007*

Note: Percentages may not equal 100 due to rounding.

Document B

"As we approach the end of the twentieth century there is no single thing we can do that will have as large an impact on the people of the world during the new century than the development of solar power satellites. They will bring prosperity, an opportunity for the poor nations of the earth to achieve true freedom from want, healing of our environment, and open the vast new frontier of space to all of us.

. . . With the development of solar power satellites we will tap directly into the power of the sun and save the world from impending chaos. There will be hope for the future as we enter the twenty-first century."

—From *Sun Power* by Ralph Nansen

Document C

"Renewables are not without their drawbacks. Solar and wind farms cannot generate much electricity on cloudy or still days. As intermittent energy sources, they require vast systems to store the energy they produce, or must rely on the rest of the electrical system for backup. And despite federal subsidies to spur technological innovation, renewable sources have not become economical enough to seriously challenge fossil fuels in an open market."

—From *CQ Researcher*, November 7, 1997

Analyzing Documents

Use your knowledge of global issues and Documents A, B, and C to answer questions 1–4.

1. Which document is supported by the actual U.S. energy consumption data shown in Document A?
   A Document B
   B Document C
   C both Documents B and C
   D neither Document B nor C

2. Which statement best describes the viewpoint of the author of Document B?
   A Biomass generators are a better alternative to fossil fuel than solar powered satellites.
   B Solar powered satellites are the most promising alternative to fossil fuel.
   C Solar powered satellites are not realistic or cost effective as an alternative to fossil fuel.
   D More research must be carried out to determine whether solar powered satellites are a realistic alternative to fossil fuel.

3. According to Document C, all are drawbacks of renewables except which of the following?
   A They are intermittent energy sources.
   B They are not cost-efficient.
   C They rely on traditional electricity sources.
   D They are worse for the environment.

4. **Writing Task** What does our energy future hold? Make some predictions for 50 years in the future. Use information from these documents along with information from the chapter to support your predictions.

Concept Connector Handbooks

The Concept Connector Handbooks provide you with reference information that will make it easier for you to compare key concepts and events across time and place.

■ Atlas and Geography Handbook

■ History Handbook

Spanish doubloons

Lithuanian woman, 1991

Ancient Egypt

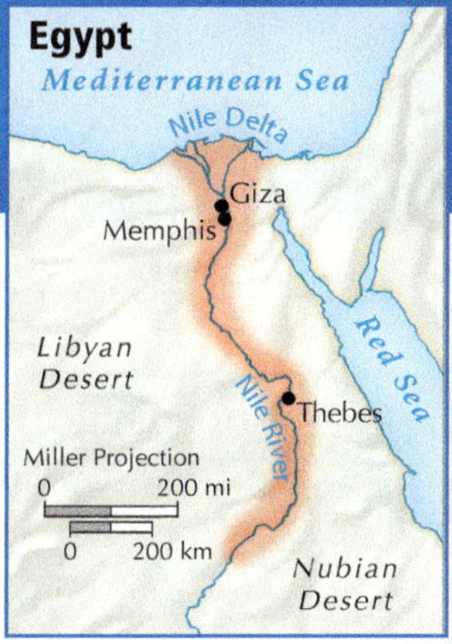

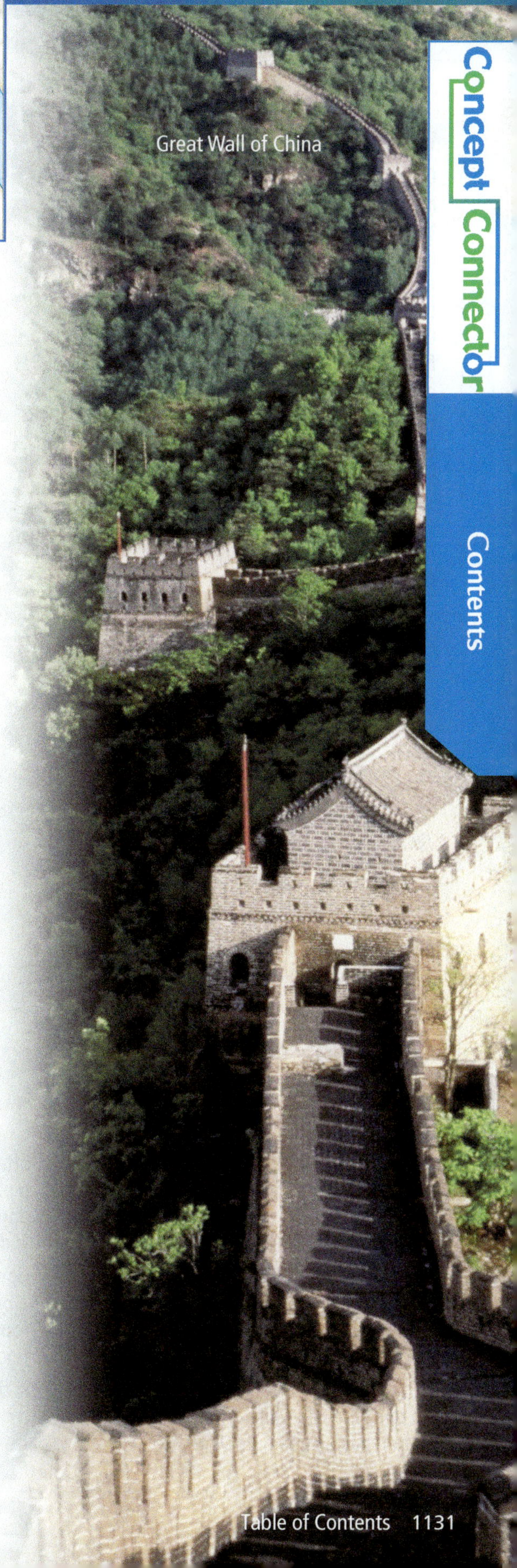
Great Wall of China

Economics Handbook

Science and Technology Handbook

Government and Civics Handbook

Culture Handbook

Detail of the Bayeux Tapestry

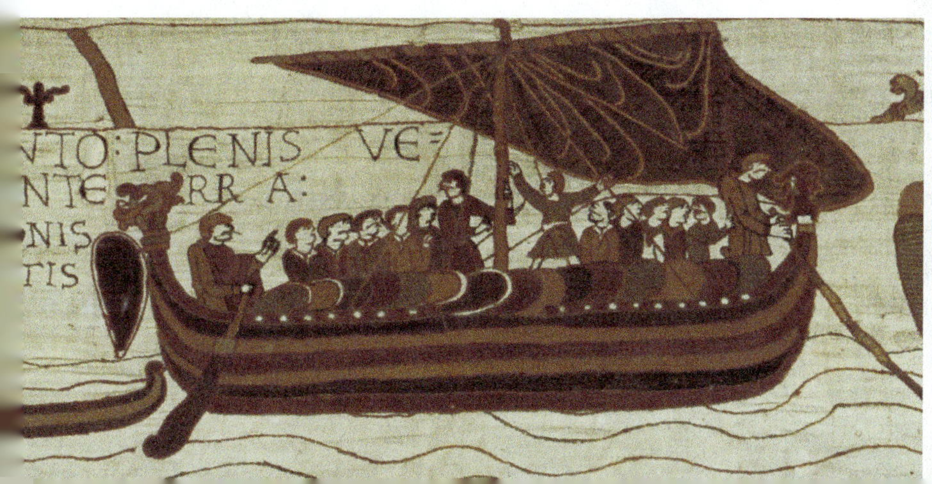

What Is Geography?

Geography is the study of Earth's features, including its people, their surroundings, and the resources available to them. By describing the human environment in different times and places, geographers have added to our knowledge of world history. Often geographers must draw conclusions from limited evidence. For example, studies might turn up common artistic styles or religious rituals in two widely separated groups of people. A geographer might conclude that the groups traded with each other and, in the process, developed shared cultural traits. Geographers use their favorite tool, the map, to show the results of their observations.

Glossary of Geographic Terms

basin
an area that is lower than surrounding land areas; some basins are filled with water

bay
a part of a larger body of water that extends into the land

butte
a small, high, flat-topped landform with cliff-like sides

canyon
a deep, narrow valley with steep sides; often has a stream flowing through it

cataract
a large waterfall or steep rapids

delta
a plain at the mouth of a river, often triangular in shape, formed when sediment is deposited by flowing water

flood plain
a broad plain on either side of a river, formed when sediment settles during floods

glacier
a huge, slow-moving mass of snow and ice

hill
an area that rises above surrounding land and has a rounded top; lower and usually less steep than a mountain

island
an area of land completely surrounded by water

isthmus
a narrow strip of land that connects two larger areas of land

mesa
a high, flat-topped landform with cliff-like sides; larger than a butte

mountain
a landform that rises steeply at least 2,000 feet (610 m) above surrounding land; usually wide at the bottom and rising to a narrow peak or ridge

mountain pass
a gap between mountains

peninsula
an area of land almost completely surrounded by water and connected to the mainland by an isthmus

plain
a large area of flat or gently rolling land

plateau
a large, flat area that rises above the surrounding land; at least one side has a steep slope

river mouth
the point where a river enters a lake or sea

strait
a narrow stretch of water that connects two larger bodies of water

tributary
a river or stream that flows into a larger river

valley
a low stretch of land between mountains or hills; land that is drained by a river

volcano
an opening in the Earth's surface through which molten rock, ashes, and gases from the Earth's interior escape

Atlas and Geography

20°W
0°
20°E
40°E
60°E
80°E
100°E
120°E
140°E
160°E
enland
(nmark)
Arctic Ocean
Arctic Circle
80°N
ICELAND
inset below
60°N
RUSSIA
EUROPE
ASIA
KAZAKHSTAN
MONGOLIA
GEORGIA
AZER.
UZBEK.
KYRGYZSTAN
NORTH
KOREA
JAPAN
40°N
ARMENIA
TURKMEN.
TAJIKZSTAN
CHINA
SOUTH
KOREA
MOROCCO
IRAN
AFGHAN.
IRAQ
Pacific
Ocean
ALGERIA
ISRAEL
JORDAN
BAHRAIN
PAKISTAN
NEPAL
BHUTAN
LIBYA
EGYPT
KUWAIT
QATAR
SAUDI
ARABIA
U.A.E.
OMAN
INDIA
MYANMAR
(BURMA)
TAIWAN
(Claimed by China)
20°N
AFRICA
CHAD
ERITREA
YEMEN
SUDAN
DJIBOUTI
BANGLADESH
LAOS
THAILAND
VIETNAM
CAMBODIA
MARSHALL
ISLANDS
CAMEROON
CEN.
AFR. REP.
ETHIOPIA
SRI
LANKA
PHILIPPINES
KIRIBATI
re inset below
GABON
DEM.
REP. OF
CONGO
UGANDA
KENYA
SOMALIA
MALDIVES
BRUNEI
MALAYSIA
FEDERATED STATES
OF MICRONESIA
0°
CONGO
RWANDA
SINGAPORE
NAURU
BURUNDI
TANZANIA
SEYCHELLES
INDONESIA
PAPUA NEW
GUINEA
SOLOMON
ISLANDS
TUVALU
Atlantic
Ocean
ANGOLA
MALAWI
ZAMBIA
COMOROS
Indian
Ocean
TIMOR
LESTE
OCEANIA
FIJI
VANUATU
ISLANDS
20°S
ZIMBABWE
MOZAMBIQUE
MADAGASCAR
NAMIBIA
BOTSWANA
MAURITIUS
AUSTRALIA
New
Caledonia
(France)
SWAZILAND
SOUTH AFRICA
LESOTHO
NEW
ZEALAND
40°S
N
W   E
S
Robinson Projection
0   1000   2000 miles
0   1000   2000 kilometers
60°S
Southern Ocean
20°W
0°
20°E
40°E
60°E
80°E
100°E
120°E
140°E
160°E
ANTARCTICA

20°W
20°N
Western
Sahara
(Morocco)
ALGERIA
MAURITANIA
N
W   E
S
MALI
NIGER
SENEGAL
GAMBIA
GUINEA-
BISSAU
GUINEA
BURKINA
FASO
BENIN
Atlantic
Ocean
10°N
SIERRA
LEONE
TOGO
GHANA
NIGERIA
IVORY
COAST
LIBERIA
Azimuthal Equidistant
Projection
0   200   400 miles
0   200   400 kilometers
Gulf of Guinea
EQUATORIAL GUINEA
0°

Barents
Sea
SWEDEN
FINLAND
NORWAY
N
W   E
S
Conic Projection
0   200   400 miles
0   200   400 kilometers
IRELAND
UNITED
KINGDOM
North
Sea
DENMARK
ESTONIA
LATVIA
NETHERLANDS
Baltic Sea
LITHUANIA
RUSSIA
BELARUS
RUSSIA
Atlantic
Ocean
BELGIUM
LUX.
GERMANY
POLAND
FRANCE
LIECH.
SWITZ.
CZECH REP.
SLOVAKIA
UKRAINE
Bay of
Biscay
AUSTRIA
HUNGARY
MOLDOVA
ANDORRA
MONACO
SLOVENIA
CROATIA
ROMANIA
PORTUGAL
ITALY
SAN
MARINO
BOS. AND
HERZ.
SERBIA
BULGARIA
Black Sea
SPAIN
Corsica
(France)
MONT.
KOSOVO
Gibraltar
(U.K.)
Melilla
(Spain)
Sardinia
(Italy)
VATICAN
CITY
ALBANIA
TURKEY
Ceuta
(Spain)
Balearic Isands
(Spain)
Sicily
(Italy)
GREECE
CYPRUS
SYRIA
MOROCCO
ALGERIA
TUNISIA
MALTA
Mediterranean
Sea
Crete
(Greece)
LEBANON

EUROPE
ASIA
Atlantic Ocean
Mediterranean Sea
Red Sea
Gulf of Aden
Indian Ocean
Madeira Islands (Portugal)
Strait of Gibraltar
Algiers
Tunis
Tripoli
Alexandria
Cairo
Rabat
Casablanca
TUNISIA
Canary Islands (Spain)
MOROCCO
Tropic of Cancer
Western Sahara (Morocco)
ALGERIA
LIBYA
EGYPT
MAURITANIA
Nouakchott
MALI
Tombouctou
NIGER
CHAD
Khartoum
SUDAN
ERITREA
Asmara
DJIBOUTI
Djibouti
CAPE VERDE
Dakar
Banjul
SENEGAL
GAMBIA
BURKINA FASO
Bamako
Niamey
Lake Chad
Kano
N'Djamena
Addis Ababa
GUINEA-BISSAU
Bissau
Ouagadougou
NIGERIA
ETHIOPIA
Conakry
GUINEA
SIERRA LEONE
Freetown
BENIN
Abuja
CENTRAL AFRICAN REPUBLIC
Bangui
SOMALIA
Monrovia
IVORY COAST
GHANA
TOGO
Porto-Novo
Lagos
Lake Turkana
LIBERIA
Yamoussoukro
Abidjan
Accra
Lomé
CAMEROON
Mogadishu
Gulf of Guinea
Malabo
Yaoundé
Kisangani
UGANDA
KENYA
EQUATORIAL GUINEA
Libreville
Kampala
Lake Victoria
SÃO TOMÉ AND PRÍNCIPE
São Tomé
Equator
GABON
CONGO
DEMOCRATIC REPUBLIC OF THE CONGO
Nairobi
Kigali
Indian Ocean
Brazzaville
Bujumbura
Mombasa
RWANDA
BURUNDI
Kinshasa
Dodoma
Atlantic Ocean
Cabinda (Angola)
Lake Tanganyika
Dar es Salaam
Luanda
TANZANIA
Lake Malawi
SEYCHELLES
Lubumbashi
MALAWI
Moroni
COMOROS
ANGOLA
Lilongwe
Mayotte (France)
ZAMBIA
Lusaka
MOZAMBIQUE
Harare
Mozambique Channel
Antananarivo
NAMIBIA
ZIMBABWE
MADAGASCAR
Tropic of Capricorn
BOTSWANA
Windhoek
Gaborone
Pretoria
Maputo
Johannesburg
Mbabane
Lobamba
SWAZILAND
Bloemfontein
Maseru
Durban
LESOTHO
SOUTH AFRICA
Cape of Good Hope
Cape Town
Cape Agulhas
N W E S
National border
Disputed border
National capital
Other city
Azimuthal Equidistant Projection
0   500   1000 miles
0   500   1000 kilometers

Concept Connector
Atlas and Geography
EUROPE
ASIA
Atlantic Ocean
Madeira Islands
Strait of Gibraltar
Mediterranean Sea
Suez Canal
Sinai Peninsula
Canary Islands
Tropic of Cancer
ATLAS MOUNTAINS
Qattara Depression
Arabian Desert
Red Sea
Cape Verde Islands
Ahaggar Mountains
Tibesti Mountains
LIBYAN DESERT
Nile River
Lake Nasser
NUBIAN DESERT
Gulf of Aden
Senegal R.
Niger River
S A H A R A
S A H E L
Lake Chad
White Nile R.
Blue Nile R.
Lake Tana
ETHIOPIAN HIGHLANDS
Fouta Djallon
Volta R.
Lake Volta
Benue River
Adamawa Highlands
SUDD
Gulf of Guinea
Bioko
Ubangi R.
Congo R.
Lake Albert
Lake Turkana
GREAT RIFT VALLEY
Equator
São Tomé
CONGO BASIN
Lake Victoria
Mt. Kilimanjaro 19,341 ft. (5,895 m)
Atlantic Ocean
N W E S
Serengeti Plain
Lake Tanganyika
Zanzibar
Indian Ocean
Lake Malawi
Comoro Islands
Zambezi R.
Mozambique Channel
Madagascar
Okavango Basin
NAMIB DESERT
KALAHARI DESERT
Limpopo R.
Tropic of Capricorn
Orange R.
Drakensberg
Cape of Good Hope
Cape Agulhas
Elevation
Feet
Meters
More than 13,000
More than 3,960
6,500–13,000
1,980–3,960
1,600–6,500
480–1,980
650–1,600
200–480
0–650
0–200
Below sea level
Below sea level
National border
Disputed border
Azimuthal Equidistant Projection
0   500   1000 miles
0   500   1000 kilometers

International Date Line
National border
National capital
Other city
Two-Point Equidistant Projection
1000 miles
1000 kilometers
500
500
0
0
Arctic Ocean
Bering Sea
East Siberian Sea
Barents Sea
Pacific Ocean
Sea of Okhotsk
Kuril Islands (Russia)
Sakhalin (Russia)
Sea of Japan
JAPAN
Tokyo
Osaka
Ryukyu Islands (Japan)
Vladivostok
NORTH KOREA
Pyongyang
SOUTH KOREA
Seoul
Yellow Sea
Shanghai
East China Sea
Taipei
TAIWAN
Guangzhou
Hong Kong
Philippine Sea
PHILIPPINES
Manila
OCEANIA
New Guinea
INDONESIA
TIMOR-LESTE
Dili
Timor
Arafura Sea
Celebes (Sulawesi)
Borneo
Surabaya
Java
Jakarta
Sumatra
MALAYSIA
BRUNEI
Bandar Seri Begawan
SINGAPORE
Kuala Lumpur
Singapore
South China Sea
VIETNAM
Ho Chi Minh City
Hanoi
LAOS
Vientiane
THAILAND
Bangkok
CAMBODIA
Phnom Penh
Andaman Sea
MYANMAR (BURMA)
Yangon (Rangoon)
Andaman Islands (India)
Nicobar Islands (India)
Bay of Bengal
BANGLADESH
Dhaka
BHUTAN
Thimphu
NEPAL
Kathmandu
Kolkata (Calcutta)
New Delhi
INDIA
Chennai (Madras)
SRI LANKA
Colombo
Mumbai (Bombay)
Lakshadweep (India)
Arabian Sea
MALDIVES
Male
Chagos Archipelago (British Indian Ocean Territory)
Indian Ocean
SEYCHELLES
Victoria
Gulf of Aden
Socotra (Yemen)
YEMEN
Sanaa
Red Sea
Mecca
OMAN
Muscat
UNITED ARAB EMIRATES
Abu Dhabi
QATAR
Doha
BAHRAIN
Manama
SAUDI ARABIA
Riyadh
KUWAIT
Kuwait
IRAQ
Baghdad
Shiraz
IRAN
Tehran
AZERBAIJAN
Baku
ARMENIA
Yerevan
GEORGIA
Tbilisi
Black Sea
TURKEY
Ankara
Istanbul
CYPRUS
Nicosia
LEBANON
Beirut
ISRAEL
Jerusalem
JORDAN
Amman
SYRIA
Damascus
EUROPE
Moscow
Arctic Circle
AFRICA
TURKMENISTAN
Ashgabat
UZBEKISTAN
Tashkent
KAZAKHSTAN
Astana
Aral Sea
Caspian Sea
AFGHANISTAN
Kabul
PAKISTAN
Islamabad
Karachi
TAJIKISTAN
Dushanbe
KYRGYZSTAN
Bishkek
Almaty
Lake Balkhash
Yekaterinburg
Omsk
Novosibirsk
RUSSIA
Yakutsk
Lake Baikal
Irkutsk
MONGOLIA
Ulan Bator
Harbin
Beijing
Tianjin
Xi'an
CHINA
Chongqing
International Date Line
Tropic of Cancer
Equator

Concept Connector
Atlas and Geography
Elevation
Feet
More than 13,000
6,500–13,000
1,600–6,500
650–1,600
0–650
Below sea level
Meters
More than 3,960
1,980–3,960
480–1,980
200–400
0–200
Below sea level
National border
International Date Line
Two-Point Equidistant Projection
0   500   1000 miles
0   500   1000 kilometers
Arctic Ocean
Pacific Ocean
Bering Sea
Sea of Okhotsk
Sea of Japan
Yellow Sea
East China Sea
Philippine Sea
South China Sea
Hainan Sea
Andaman Sea
Bay of Bengal
Indian Ocean
Arabian Sea
Red Sea
Gulf of Aden
Persian Gulf
Caspian Sea
Black Sea
Mediterranean Sea
Barents Sea
Kara Sea
Laptev Sea
East Siberian Sea
International Date Line
Kolyma Range
Kamchatka Peninsula
Cherski Range
Verkhoyansk Range
Stanovoy Range
Amur R.
Sakhalin
Kuril Islands
Hokkaidō
Honshū
Shikoku
Kyūshū
Korean Peninsula
Manchurian Plain
Ryukyu Islands
Taiwan
Luzon
Mindanao
Palawan
Celebes (Sulawesi)
Borneo
Greater Sunda Islands
Java
Sumatra
Lesser Sunda Islands
Timor
Moluccas
Arafura Sea
New Guinea
OCEANIA
Lena R.
Lake Baikal
Mongolian Plateau
North China Plain
GOBI
Huang R.
Chang R.
Mekong R.
Indochina Peninsula
Malay Peninsula
North Siberian Lowland
Central Siberian Plateau
SIBERIA
Altai Mountains
Yenisey R.
Ob R.
North Siberian Plain
Irtysh R.
Lake Balkhash
The Steppes
Tian Shan
Taklimakan Desert
Kunlun Shan
Plateau of Tibet
Mt. Everest 29,035 ft. (8,850 m)
HIMALAYAS
Irrawaddy R.
Ganges R.
Indus R.
Eastern Ghats
Western Ghats
Deccan Plateau
INDIAN PENINSULA
Sri Lanka
Andaman Islands
Nicobar Islands
Maldive Islands
Lakshadweep
Chagos Archipelago
Seychelles
Socotra
URAL MOUNTAINS
EUROPE
Caspian Depression
Aral Sea
Karakum
Thar Desert
Hindu Kush
Plateau of Iran
Zagros Mountains
CAUCASUS MTNS
Tigris R.
Euphrates R.
Syrian Desert
Anatolia
Cyprus
ARABIAN PENINSULA
Ar Rub' al Khālī
AFRICA
Arctic Circle
N
E
S
W

RUSS
Nizhniy Novgo
Rostov-on-Don
Arkhangel'sk
White Sea
Moscow
Sea of Azov
Black Sea
Asia
Donets'k
St. Petersburg
Kiev
UKRAINE
Constanta
TURKEY
FINLAND
Tampere
Gulf of Finland
Tallinn
ESTONIA
Helsinki
Riga
LATVIA
Vilnius
LITHUANIA
Minsk
BELARUS
MOLDOVA
Chişinău
Odessa
Istanbul
ROMANIA
Bucharest
BULGARIA
Sofia
Aegean Sea
GREECE
Gulf of Bothnia
Baltic Sea
RUSSIA
Warsaw
POLAND
Łódź
Prague
Belgrade
Skopje
MACEDONIA
Priština
SERBIA
ALBANIA
Tiranë
SWEDEN
Stockholm
Göteborg
SLOVAKIA
Bratislava
Budapest
HUNGARY
SLOVENIA
Vienna
AUSTRIA
Zagreb
CROATIA
BOSNIA AND HERZEGOVINA
Sarajevo
MONTENEGRO
Podgorica
KOSOVO
Ionian
NORWAY
Oslo
Hamburg
Berlin
DENMARK
Copenhagen
GERMANY
Frankfurt
CZECH REPUBLIC
Munich
Ljubljana
Venice
SAN MARINO
VATICAN CITY
Rome
ITALY
Naples
Tyrrhenian Sea
Bergen
North Sea
NETHERLANDS
Amsterdam
LUXEMBOURG
Vaduz
LIECHTENSTEIN
Bern
SWITZERLAND
Milan
MONACO
Faeroe Islands (Denmark)
Shetland Islands (U.K.)
Scotland
Glasgow
UNITED KINGDOM
Manchester
England
London
Brussels
BELGIUM
Paris
Luxembourg
FRANCE
Lyon
Monaco
Corsica (France)
Sardinia (Italy)
Balearic Isands (Spain)
Wales
English Channel
Northern Ireland
IRELAND
Dublin
N
E
S
W
Bay of Biscay
Toulouse
ANDORRA
Marseille
Andorra la Vella
Barcelona
Valencia
400 miles
Lambert Conformal Conic
200
400 kilometers
200
0
ATLANTIC OCEAN
SPAIN
Madrid
Seville
Melilla
PORTUGAL
Lisbon
Gibraltar (U.K.)
Ceuta
30°W
50°N
20°W
40°N

URAL MOUNTAINS
Pechora R.
Kama R.
Ural R.
N. Dvina R.
Volga R.
Don R.
Volga R.
Volga Upland
Caspian Sea
Caspian Depression
CAUCASUS MTS.
Mt. Elbrus
18,510 ft. (5,642 m)
Central Russian Upland
Sea of Azov
Black Sea
Barents Sea
Kola Peninsula
White Sea
Lake Onega
Lake Ladoga
Dnieper R.
Dniester R.
Danube R.
Sea of Marmara
Bosporus
Dardanelles
ASIA
NORTH EUROPEAN PLAIN
Gulf of Finland
Carpathian Mountains
Transylvanian Alps
Balkan Mountains
BALKAN PENINSULA
Aegean Sea
Crete
Gulf of Bothnia
SCANDINAVIAN PENINSULA
Kjolen Mountains
Gotland
Baltic Sea
Lake Vänern
Lake Vättern
Vistula R.
Oder R.
Elbe R.
Sjælland
Jutland
Great Hungarian Plain
Pindus Mts.
Dinaric Alps
Adriatic Sea
ITALIAN PENINSULA
Apennines
Ionian Sea
Sicily
Maltese Islands
Mediterranean Sea
ARCTIC OCEAN
Jan Mayen
Arctic Circle
Norwegian Sea
North Sea
Rhine R.
Danube R.
Seine R.
ALPS
Mt. Blanc
15,775 ft. (4,808 m)
Lake Geneva
Massif Central
Po R.
Corsica
Sardinia
Tyrrhenian Sea
Balearic Islands
Faeroe Islands
Shetland Islands
Great Britain
English Channel
Thames R.
British Isles
Ireland
Loire R.
Garonne R.
Bay of Biscay
Pyrenees
Ebro R.
AFRICA
Iceland
Denmark Strait
ATLANTIC OCEAN
Douro R.
Meseta
Tagus R.
IBERIAN PENINSULA
Guadalquivir R.
Strait of Gibraltar
Lambert Conformal Conic
400 miles
400 kilometers
200
0
N E S W
Elevation
Feet
More than 13,000
6,500–13,000
1,600–6,500
650–1,600
0–650
Below sea level
Meters
More than 3,960
1,980–3,960
480–1,980
200–400
0–200
Below sea level
National border

International Date Line
Bering Strait
Bering Sea
Beaufort Sea
Alaska (United States)
Gulf of Alaska
Great Bear Lake
Great Slave Lake
Hudson Bay
Baffin Bay
Davis Strait
Greenland (Denmark)
Nuuk
Arctic Circle
Labrador Sea
CANADA
Lake Winnipeg
Vancouver
Great Lakes
Ottawa
Toronto
Chicago
New York
Washington, D.C.
UNITED STATES
Los Angeles
Atlantic Ocean
Houston
Tropic of Cancer
Gulf of Mexico
MEXICO
Mexico City
Nassau
Havana
BAHAMAS
CUBA
DOMINICAN REPUBLIC
HAITI
Puerto Rico (United States)
U.S. Virgin Islands (United States)
JAMAICA
Belmopan
Guatemala City
BELIZE
Kingston
Port-au-Prince
Santo Domingo
Guadeloupe (France)
Martinique (France)
HONDURAS
Tegucigalpa
Caribbean Sea
DOMINICA
BARBADOS
GUATEMALA
San Salvador
NICARAGUA
Managua
TRINIDAD AND TOBAGO
EL SALVADOR
San José
Panama
Caracas
GUYANA
Georgetown
COSTA RICA
PANAMA
VENEZUELA
Paramaribo
French Guiana (France)
Cayenne
Bogotá
COLOMBIA
SURINAME
Equator
Galápagos Islands (Ecuador)
Quito
ECUADOR
Pacific Ocean
PERU
Lima
BRAZIL
Lake Titicaca
La Paz
Brasília
BOLIVIA
Sucre
Tropic of Capricorn
PARAGUAY
Asunción
Rio de Janiero
São Paulo
CHILE
ARGENTINA
URUGUAY
Santiago
Buenos Aires
Montevideo
Rio de la Plata
Atlantic Ocean
Falkland Islands (U.K.)
National border
International Date Line
National capital
Other city
Lambert Azimuthal Equal-Area Projection
0   1000   2000 miles
0   1000   2000 kilometers
N
W   E
S
180°
0°
60°N
45°N
30°N
15°N
0°
15°S
30°S
45°S
165°W
150°W
135°W
120°W
105°W
90°W
75°W
60°W
45°W
30°W
15°W

North and South America: Physical

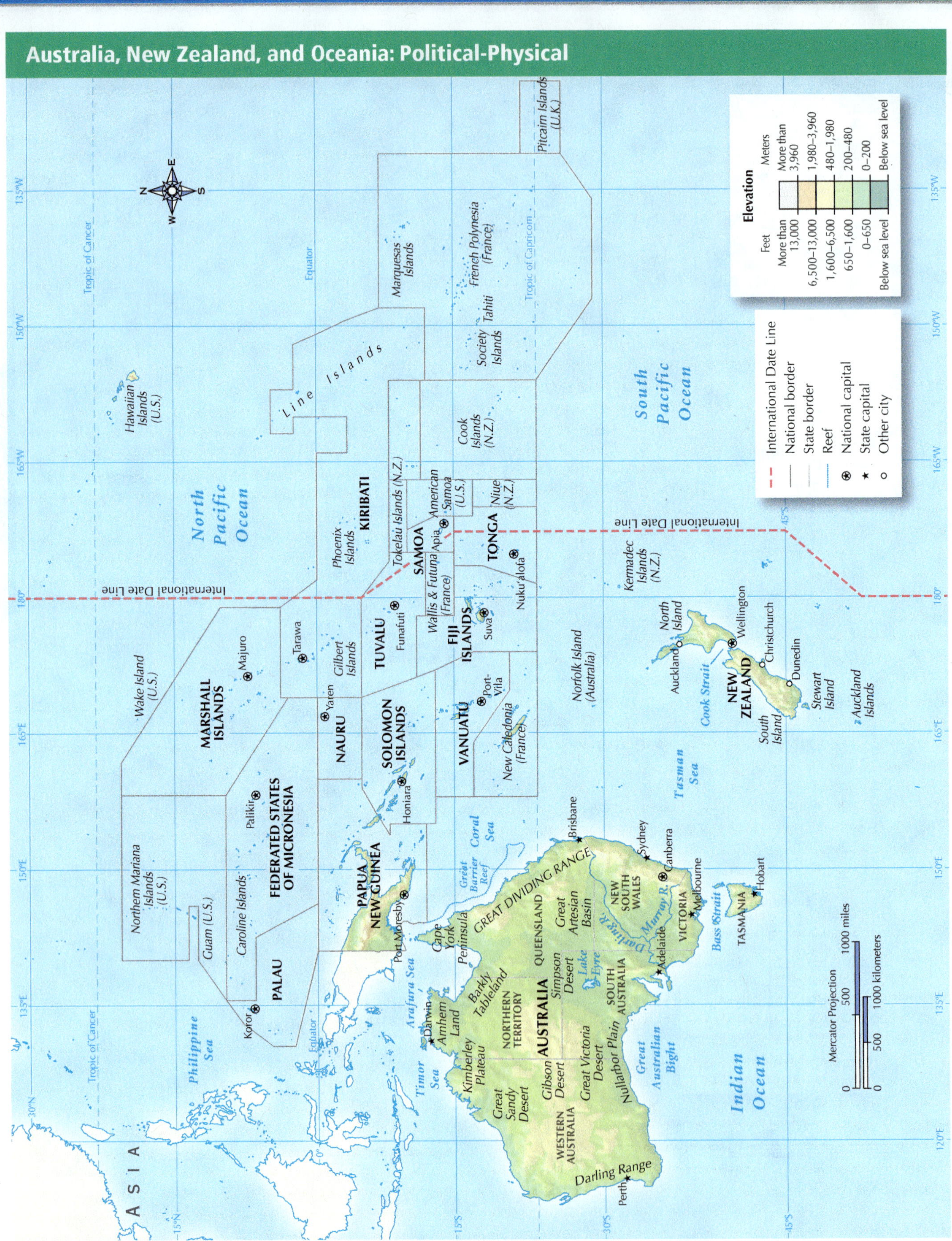
N
E
S
W

Elevation
Meters
Feet
More than 3,960 / More than 13,000
1,980–3,960 / 6,500–13,000
480–1,980 / 1,600–6,500
200–480 / 650–1,600
0–200 / 0–650
Below sea level / Below sea level

International Date Line
National border
State border
Reef
National capital
State capital
Other city

Tropic of Cancer
Equator
Tropic of Capricorn

North Pacific Ocean
South Pacific Ocean
Philippine Sea
Indian Ocean
Tasman Sea
Coral Sea
Arafura Sea
Timor Sea

International Date Line

135°W
150°W
165°W
180°
165°E
150°E
135°E
120°E

15°N
30°N
15°S
30°S
45°S

ASIA

Hawaiian Islands (U.S.)
Line Islands
Marquesas Islands
French Polynesia (France)
Society Islands
Tahiti
Cook Islands (N.Z.)
Pitcairn Islands (U.K.)
Niue (N.Z.)
Phoenix Islands
Tokelau Islands (N.Z.)
KIRIBATI
American Samoa (U.S.)
SAMOA
Apia
Wallis & Futuna (France)
TONGA
Nuku'alofa
Kermadec Islands (N.Z.)
Wake Island (U.S.)
Tarawa
Majuro
Gilbert Islands
MARSHALL ISLANDS
TUVALU
Funafuti
FIJI ISLANDS
Suva
Yaren
NAURU
SOLOMON ISLANDS
Honiara
VANUATU
Port-Vila
New Caledonia (France)
Norfolk Island (Australia)
North Island
Auckland
Wellington
Christchurch
Dunedin
Stewart Island
Auckland Islands
NEW ZEALAND
South Island
Cook Strait
Northern Mariana Islands (U.S.)
Guam (U.S.)
Caroline Islands
FEDERATED STATES OF MICRONESIA
Palikir
PALAU
Koror
PAPUA NEW GUINEA
Port Moresby
Great Barrier Reef
Brisbane
Sydney
Canberra
Melbourne
Adelaide
Hobart
TASMANIA
Bass Strait
VICTORIA
NEW SOUTH WALES
Murray R.
Darling R.
GREAT DIVIDING RANGE
QUEENSLAND
Great Artesian Basin
SOUTH AUSTRALIA
Lake Eyre
Cape York Peninsula
Simpson Desert
AUSTRALIA
NORTHERN TERRITORY
Barkly Tableland
Darwin
Arnhem Land
Kimberley Plateau
Great Sandy Desert
WESTERN AUSTRALIA
Gibson Desert
Great Victoria Desert
Nullarbor Plain
Great Australian Bight
Darling Range
Perth

Mercator Projection
1000 miles
500
0
1000 kilometers
500
0

The Arctic: Physical

Sea of Okhotsk
Cherski Range
Kamchatka Peninsula
Kolyma Range
Kolyma R.
Laptev Sea
East Siberian Sea
Novosibirskiye Ostrova
Severnaya Zemlya
Kara Sea
Novaya Zemlya
Barents Sea
Franz Josef Land
Kola Peninsula
Lake Ladoga
EUROPE
120°E
90°E
60°E
30°E
Gulf of Bothnia
Baltic Sea
SCANDINAVIA
Arctic Ocean
Svalbard
Norwegian Sea
North Sea
International Date Line
Aleutian Islands
Bering Sea
60°N
180°
Chukchi Peninsula
Wrangel Island
Chukchi Sea
Bering Strait
North Pole
North Magnetic Pole
80°N
90°W
Greenland Sea
Jan Mayen
Arctic Circle
Shetland Islands
Faeroe Islands
British Isles
Ireland
St. Lawrence Island
Nunivak Island
Mt. McKinley (Denali) 20,320 ft. (6,194 m)
Alaska
Brooks Range
150°W
Beaufort Sea
120°W
Queen Elizabeth Islands
Ellesmere Island
Greenland
Denmark Str.
Iceland
Atlantic Ocean
Alaska Peninsula
Kodiak Island
Yukon River
Alaska Range
ROCKY MOUNTAINS
Banks Island
Mackenzie River
Amundsen Gulf
Victoria Island
Great Bear Lake
Baffin Bay
Baffin Island
Davis Strait
30°W
Pacific Ocean
Gulf of Alaska
NORTH AMERICA
60°N
Foxe Basin
60°W

Lambert Azimuthal Equal Area Projection
0   400   800 miles
0   400   800 kilometers

Elevation
Feet   Meters
More than 13,000   More than 3,960
6,500–13,000   1,980–3,960
1,600–6,500   480–1,980
650–1,600   200–400
0–650   0–200
Below sea level   Below sea level
National border
International Date Line

Antarctica: Physical

Atlantic Ocean
30°W
60°W
Fimbul Ice Shelf
30°E
60°E
Riiser-Larsen Ice Shelf
QUEEN MAUD LAND
Enderby Land
Southern Ocean
South Shetland Islands
70°S
Weddell Sea
Coats Land
Larsen Ice Shelf
Antarctic Peninsula
Berkner Island
Filchner Ice Shelf
Amery Ice Shelf
Alexander Island
Ronne Ice Shelf
TRANSANTARCTIC MOUNTAINS
Polar Plateau
ANTARCTICA
West Ice Shelf
SOUTH AMERICA
Bellingshausen Sea
Ellsworth Land
Vinson Massif 16,067 ft. (4,897 m)
South Pole
Shackleton Ice Shelf
90°W
90°E
Queen Maud Mts.
WILKES LAND
Amundsen Sea
Marie Byrd Land
Ross Ice Shelf
Indian Ocean
Pacific Ocean
Getz Ice Shelf
Roosevelt Island
Victoria Land
Ross Sea
Southern Ocean
120°W
International Date Line
South Magnetic Pole
120°E
Antarctic Circle
60°S
70°S
Lambert Azimuthal Equal Area Projection
0   400   800 miles
0   400   800 kilometers
150°W
180°
150°E

History

History and Prehistory

You might think of history as everything that has ever happened. For historians, however, history began around 5,000 years ago with the appearance of writing in two civilizations—Sumer and Egypt. Everything before that is prehistory.

Prehistory   3000 B.C.   History

Writing systems appear in Sumer (above) and in Egypt *c.* 3000 B.C.*

* The *c.* before the date is Latin for *circa*, meaning ìaround " or "approximately."

Historians study how people lived in the past. They might examine their tools, weapons, jewelry, and building sites, but they rely mainly on written records. For this reason, we say that history began when writing began.

History is a changing story. A historian living at the time of an event may write what seems like a valid description, but a historian writing 100 years later may describe the same event another way entirely. This is because different generations have different perspectives on, or ways of looking at, history. In addition, as time passes, new evidence may appear to alter the interpretation of an event.

Major Eras in World History

Historians attempt to make sense of vast stretches of history by dividing them into periods. This periodization makes it easier to discuss a group of events by relating them to a broader theme.

Technology Periodization
This model of periodization divides history according to the technology that drove economic progress.

Stone Age
2 million B.C. – 3000 B.C.

Iron Age
1200 B.C. – A.D.1000

2 million B.C. / 10,000 B.C.   5000 B.C.   B.C./A.D.

Agricultural Age
9000 B.C. – A.D.1800

Bronze Age
3300 B.C. – 700 B.C.

Western Periodization
This model of periodization reflects a European perspective. Classical generally refers to the Greek and Roman civilizations. Middle Ages refers to Europe between the fall of Rome and the Renaissance.

Ancient World
4000 B.C. – 1000 B.C.

2 million B.C. / 10,000 B.C.   5000 B.C.   B.C./A.D.

Classical Period
1000 B.C. – A.D. 400

Global Periodization
This model of periodization reflects a more global perspective.

Classical Era
1000 B.C. – 400 B.C.

Spread of Monotheism
A.D. 1 – 750

2 million B.C. / 10,000 B.C.   5000 B.C.   B.C./A.D.

Ancient Civilizations
4000 B.C. – 1000 B.C.

Great Empires
400 B.C. – A.D.400

Your textbook is divided this way, into units. Each unit deals with a period, or era, in world history. There are endless ways to categorize the past, depending on one's point of view. The time-lines below show three different examples of periodization.

Decades, Centuries, and Millenniums

Most nations today use a standard calendar that dates events from the believed birth of Jesus. For dates preceding his birth, this calendar uses the abbreviation B.C. ("before Christ"). For dates after his birth, it uses A.D. (anno Domini, Latin for "in the year of our Lord"). An alternative version of this calendar uses the abbreviations B.C.E. and C.E., meaning "Before the Common Era" and "Common Era."

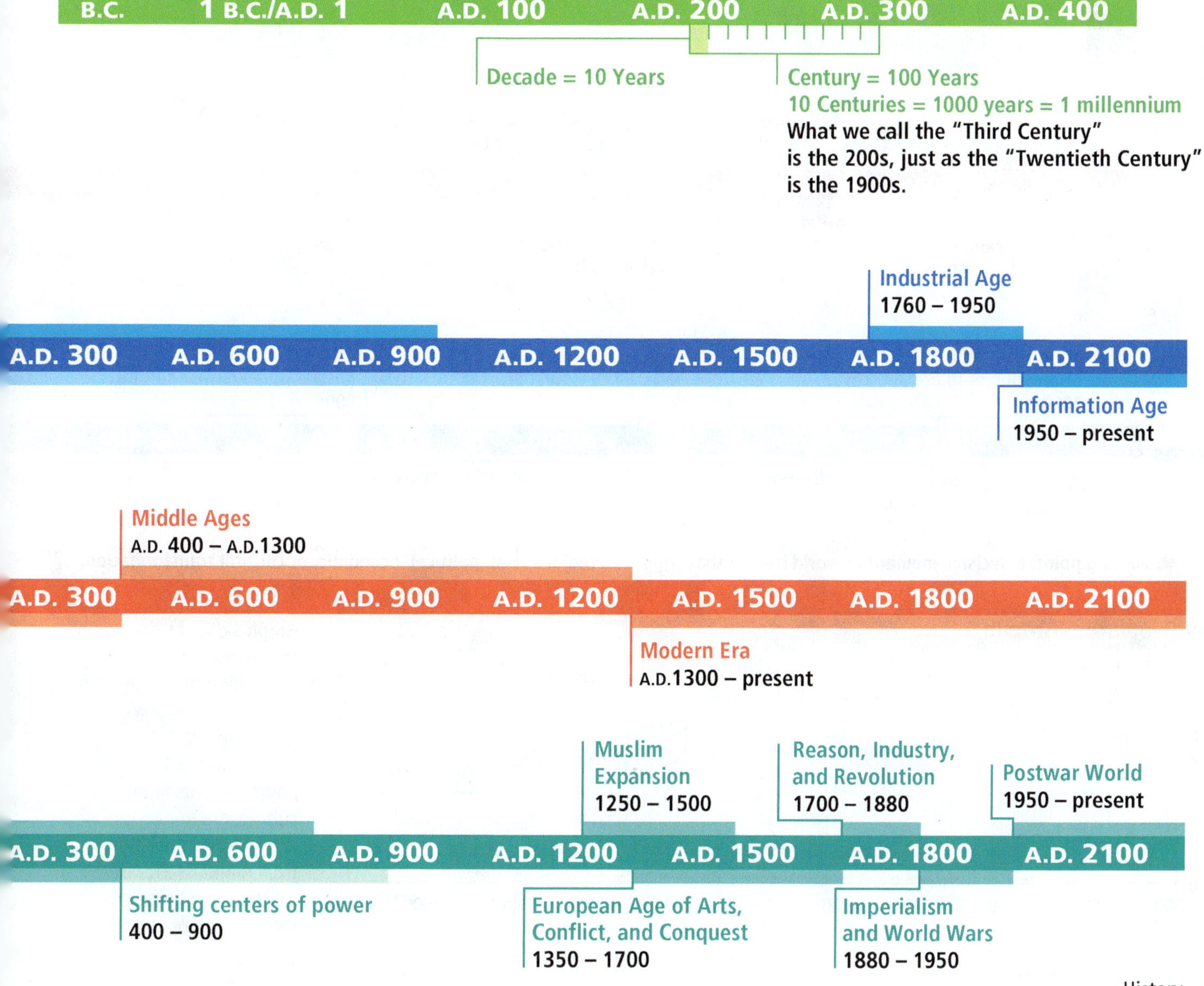

History

World Regional Timelines

Africa

Menes unites Egypt
🔵 3100 B.C.

Bantu migrations begin
2000 B.C.

Romans destroy Carthage
146 B.C.

Islam spreads to North Africa
A.D. 600s

Ghana controls trans-Saharan gold-salt trade
A.D. 800s

| 5000 B.C. | 3000 B.C. | B.C./A.D. | A.D. 300 | A.D. 600 | A.D. 900 |

Great Pyramid and Sphinx at Giza, in Egypt
2550 B.C.

Ironworking flourishes at Meroë, on the Nile River
500 B.C.

Axum converts to Christianity
A.D. 350

East Africa trading cities prosper
A.D. 1000

Europe

Rise of Greek city-states
700s B.C.

| 5000 B.C. | 3000 B.C. | B.C./A.D. | A.D. 300 | A.D. 600 | A.D. 900 |

Western Roman empire falls
🔵 A.D. 476

Asia

Sumerian city-states thrive
3200 B.C.

Persian empire created
539 B.C.

Buddhism introduced to Japan
🔵 500s

| 5000 B.C. | 3000 B.C. | B.C./A.D. | A.D. 300 | A.D. 600 | A.D. 900 |

Indus Valley civilization develops
🔵 2500 B.C.

Gupta Golden Age begins in India
A.D. 320

Muhammad's Hijira from Mecca to Medina
🔵 622

The Americas

Cultivation of maize and cotton
3200 B.C.

Hopewell culture flourishes
A.D. 200s

Mississippian civilization thrives
800s

| 5000 B.C. | 3000 B.C. | B.C./A.D. | A.D. 300 | A.D. 600 | A.D. 900 |

Rise of Olmec civilization
🔵 1400 B.C.

Height of Maya civilization
500s

🔵 Turning point: a decisive moment in world history that triggers a major social, political, economic, or cultural transformation.

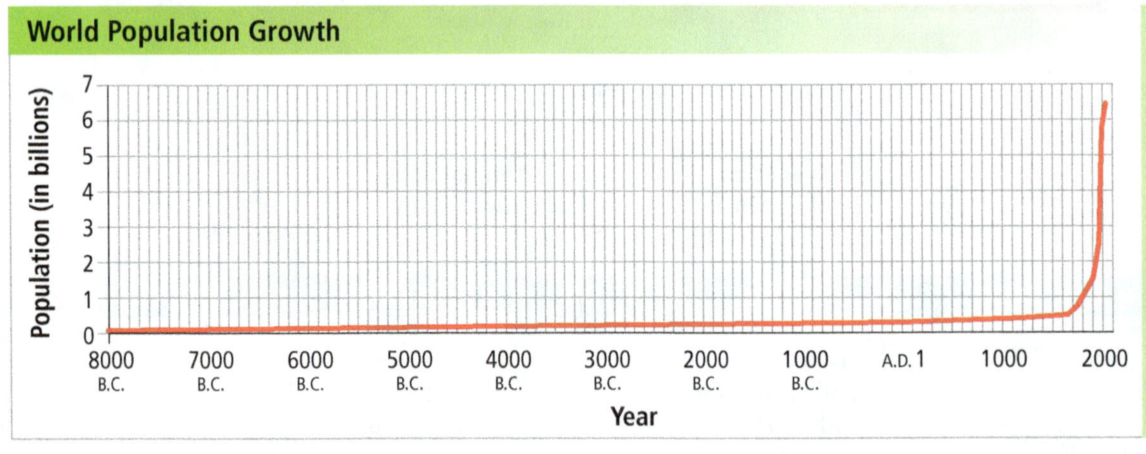

Graph Skills As the graph shows, the world's population gradually rose over many centuries, until it shot up suddenly, starting in the 1700s. Improvements in agriculture, greater control of disease, and the shift from manual labor to machines all helped to increase the population.

Height of
Empire of Mali
A.D. 1250

Atlantic slave
trade grows
1500s

Berlin Conference
carves up Africa
1884

Italy invades
Ethiopia
1935

Apartheid becomes
law in South Africa
1948

A.D. 1200   **A.D. 1500**   **A.D. 1800**   **A.D. 2100**

Great Zimbabwe
constructed
A.D. 1250

Sonni Ali
founds Songhai
1460s

Boers begin
Great Trek
1830s

Suez Canal opens
1869

Mandela wins first multiracial
election in South Africa
1994

English Magna
Carta accepted
A.D. 1215

Renaissance
begins in Italy
mid-1300s

Gutenberg
Bible printed
1456

Industrial Revolution
begins in Britain
1760

Italy
unified
1870

World War I
begins
1914

World War II
begins
1939

Berlin Wall
falls
1989

A.D. 1200   **A.D. 1500**   **A.D. 1800**   **A.D. 2100**

Ottoman Turks conquer
Constantinople
A.D. 1453

French Revolution
begins
1789

Germany
unified
1871

Russian
Revolution
1917

Breakup of
Soviet Union
1991

Voyages of Zheng He
for China
1405–1433

Sepoy Rebellion
in India
1857

Boxer Uprising
in China
1900

People's Republic of China established
1949

Revolution
in Iran
1979

A.D. 1200   **A.D. 1500**   **A.D. 1800**   **A.D. 2100**

Tokugawas gain
power in Japan
1600

Meiji Restoration begins in Japan
1868

Civil war in China
1911

Cultural Revolution
in China
1966

War in
Iraq
2003

Inca empire
founded
1438

Height of
Aztec empire
1500

British found
Jamestown
1607

Bolívar
captures
Bogotá
1819

Mexican
Revolution begins
1910

Panama
Canal
opens
1914

Perón becomes
president of
Argentina
1946

Cuban
Missile
Crisis
1962

A.D. 1200   **A.D. 1500**   **A.D. 1800**   **A.D. 2100**

Columbus reaches
the Caribbean
1492

American
Revolution begins
1775

Act of Union unites Canada
1840

Spanish-American War
1898

Canada,
United States, and
Mexico sign NAFTA
1993

Terrorists
attack U.S.
on 9/11
2001

The Parthenon, Athens, Greece

History

Flag of Giovine
Italia, 1833

Imperialism, Colonialism, Nationalism, and Revolution

Imperialism

A policy of pursuing, often through conquest, the economic and political domination of another state.

Colonialism

A policy of politically dominating a dependent territory or people.

Nationalism

A strong feeling of pride in, or devotion to, one's nation.

Revolution

The overthrow of a government from within.

Conquest and Empire

An empire is a group of states or territories controlled by one ruler. Empires often form in a haphazard way. For example, a small state with a strong army successfully defends itself against one neighboring state after another and incorporates their lands. Or at some point, an able ruler aggressively seeks more territory. Over time, the state expands into an empire. A strong military and able leadership are two factors that go into creating an empire. However, successful empires also must develop a government system that can maintain control of conquered peoples.

Selected Empires in World History

Conquests	Time Span	Location
Roman	509 B.C.–A.D. 180	Mediterranean region, Western Europe, Britain
Arab Muslim	A.D. 624–750	Southwest Asia, North Africa, Spain
Mongol	1206–1294	China, Central Asia, Eastern Europe
Ottoman	1299–1566	Southwest Asia, North Africa, Balkans, Eastern Europe
Spanish	1492–1560	Mexico, Central America, South America, Cuba, Florida

First Landing of Columbus by Frederick Kemmelmeyer

Major Conflicts in World History

This table shows selected major wars and conquests. Hundreds of other conflicts, large and small, have occurred throughout history. The cause of a conflict may be as simple as "I want what you have." For example, the basic need for food—and the land to grow it on—has been a prime cause of war. But most of the time, the reasons for wars are more complex. They can involve intertwining economic, political, religious, and cultural forces.

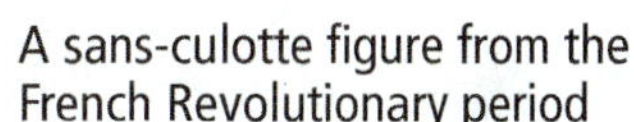

A sans-culotte figure from the French Revolutionary period

Selected Conflicts in World History

Conflict	Time Span	Location	Combatants
Persian Wars	499–448 B.C.	Greece	Greeks vs. Persians
Peloponnesian War	431–404 B.C.	Greece	Athens vs. Sparta
Punic Wars	264–146 B.C.	Mediterranean region	Rome vs. Carthage
Crusades	A.D. 1096–1291	Southwest Asia	Christians vs. Muslims
Hundred Years' War	1337–1443	France	England vs. France
Wars of King Philip II	1571–1588	Europe	Spain vs. Dutch Netherlands; Spain vs. England
Thirty Years' War	1618–1648	Central Europe (German states)	Holy Roman Empire, Spain, Poland, and others vs. Netherlands, Sweden, France, and others
English Civil War	1642–1649	England	Parliament (Roundheads) vs. Charles I and supporters (Cavaliers)
Seven Years' War (includes French and Indian War)	1756–1763	Europe; North America; India	Austria, Russia, and France vs. Prussia and Britain; Britain and its American colonies vs. France and its Native American allies; Britain vs. France
American Revolution	1775–1783	North America	Britain vs. its American colonies
French Revolution	1789–1799	France	Reformers (mainly middle class and peasants) vs. Louis XVI and supporters (mainly nobles and clergy)
Napoleonic Wars (end of the French Revolution)	1799–1815	Europe	France vs. combined European powers
Latin American Wars of Independence	1802–1824	Latin America	Colonies in Latin America vs. France and Spain
American Civil War	1860–1865	United States	North (Unionists) vs. South (Secessionists)
World War I	1914–1918	Europe (mainly France and Russia)	Allied powers vs. Central powers
World War II	1939–1945	North Africa, Europe, East Asia, Pacific Islands	Allies vs. Axis powers
Korean War	1950–1953	Korea	North Korea and China vs. South Korea and United States
Vietnam War	1959–1975	Vietnam	North Vietnam vs. South Vietnam and the United States

Regional Organizations

Through treaties, nations with common regional interests often work together to improve themselves politically, economically, and socially.

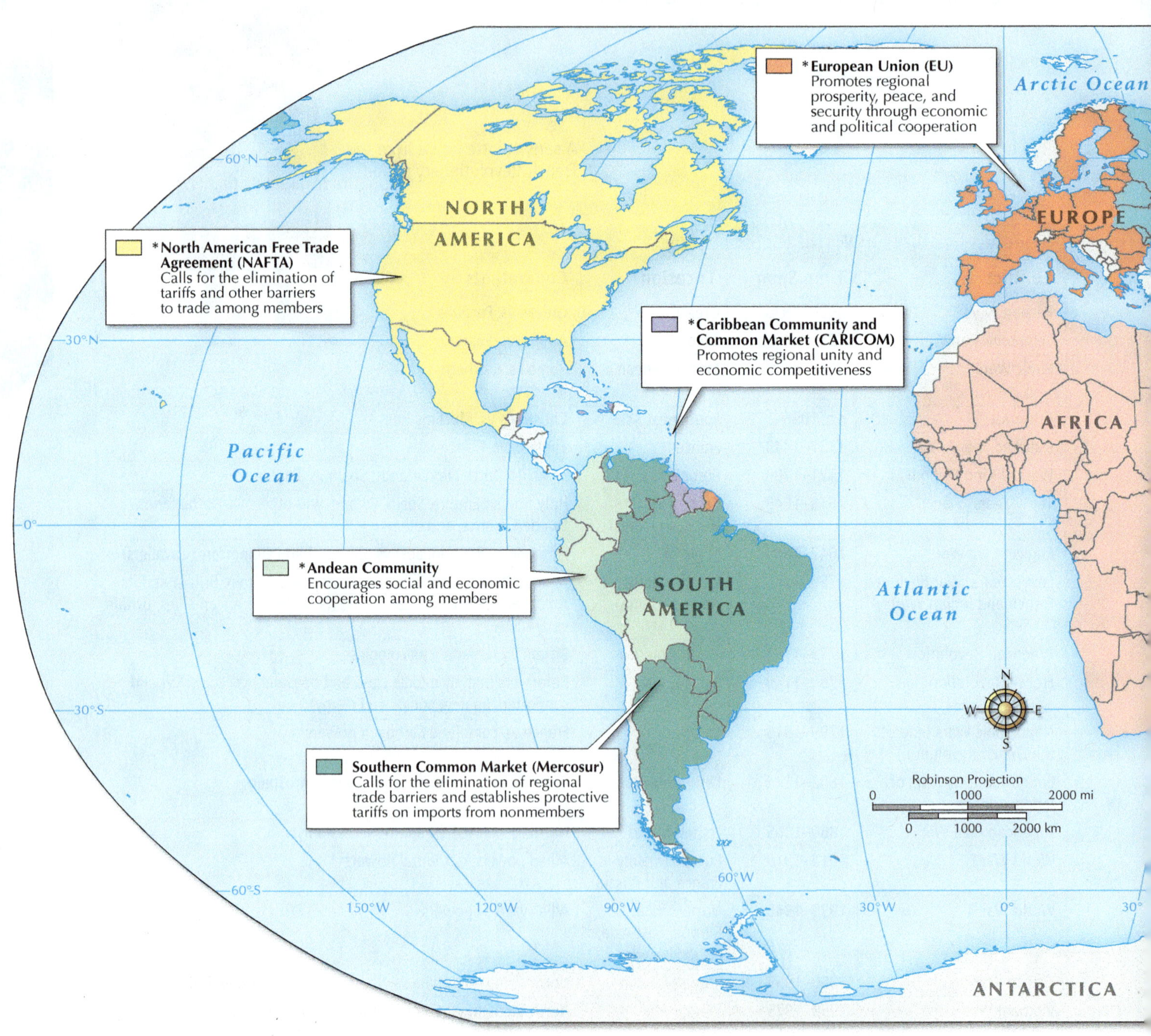

International Organizations

These organizations promote cooperation across regions:

- Arab League
- International Monetary Fund (IMF)
- North Atlantic Treaty Organization (NATO)
- Organization for Economic Cooperation and Development (OECD)
- Organization of American States (OAS)
- Organization of Petroleum Exporting Countries (OPEC)
- United Nations (UN)
- World Trade Organization (WTO)

The United Nations

Of all the organizations in the world, the UN stands out as the main coordinator of international activities. With the support of its 191 member nations, the UN plays a vital, ongoing role in keeping the peace, fighting disease, promoting economic development, and providing humanitarian aid.

International aid poured into Indonesia following the December 2004 tsunami. Here an American navy pilot delivers supplies from the United States Agency for International Development (USAID), an independent federal agency.

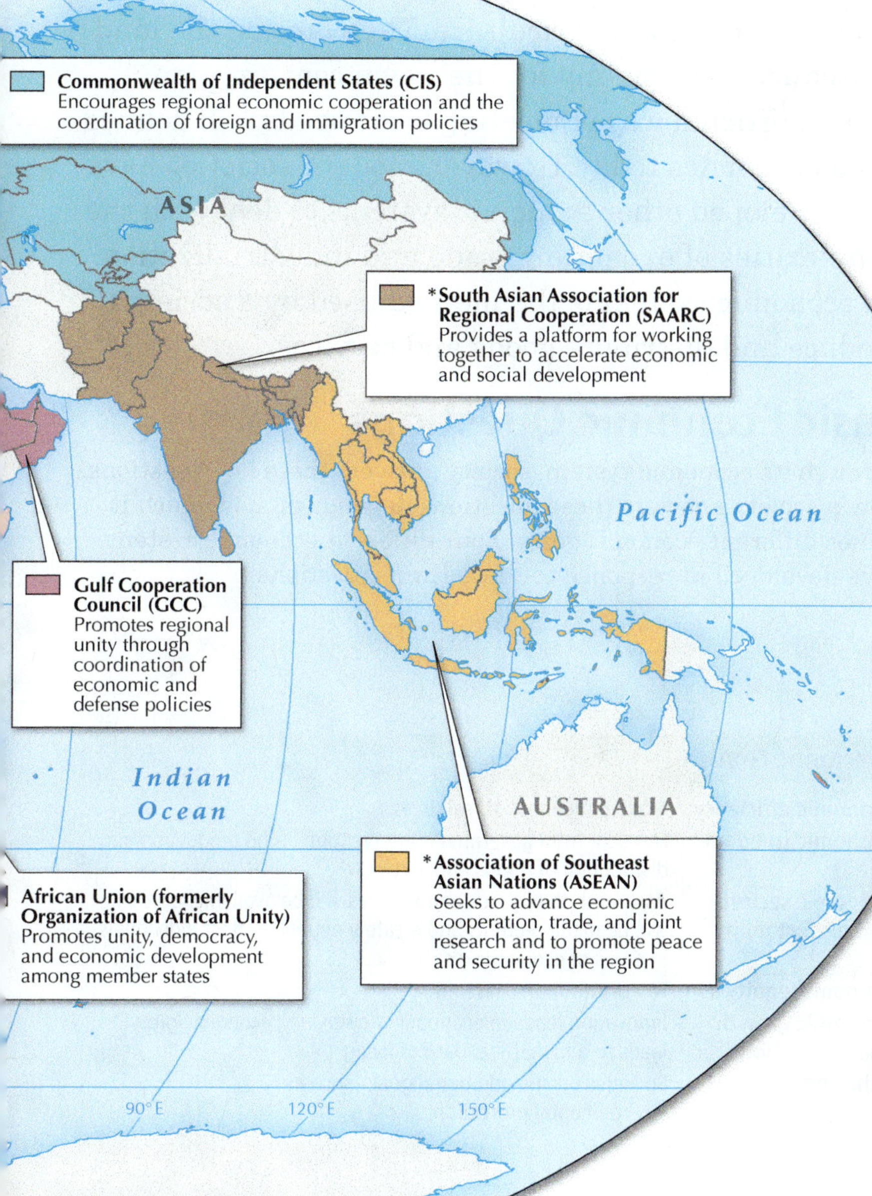

Economics

Three Key Economic Questions		
What goods and services should be produced?	**How should goods and services be produced?**	**Who consumes the goods and services?**
How much of our resources should we devote to national defense, education, public health, or consumer goods? Which consumer goods should we produce?	Should we produce food on large corporate farms or on small family farms? Should we produce electricity with oil, nuclear power, coal, or solar power?	How do goods and services get distributed? The question of who gets to consume which goods and services lies at the very heart of the differences between economic systems. Each society answers the question of distribution based on its combination of social values and goals.

In 1923, due to the collapse of German currency, it was cheaper to paper a wall with Deutsche marks than it was to buy wallpaper.

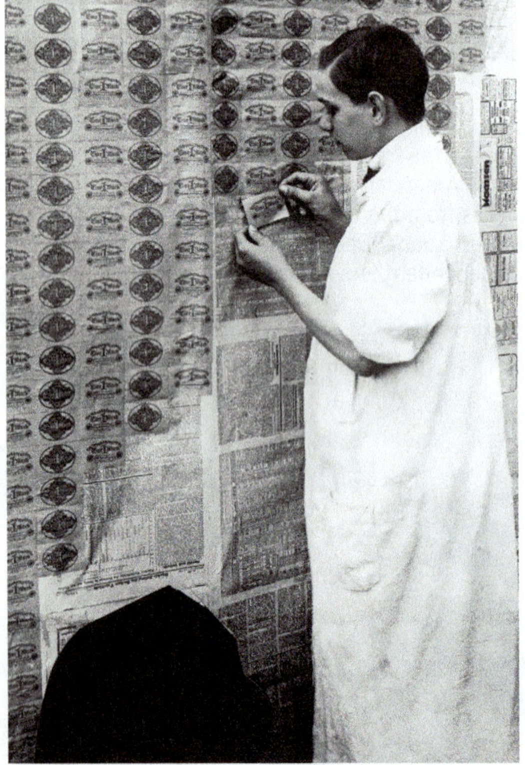

In every society throughout history, people have had access to resources, such as water, fertile land, and human labor. Yet everywhere in the world, people's resources are limited. Economics is the study of how people choose to use their limited resources to meet their wants and needs.

Until modern times, people focused largely on resources related to agriculture. They farmed the land to produce food, mainly for their own consumption. This traditional way of meeting basic needs still defines some economies today. However, modern societies have also developed other economic systems to deal with the complexities of expanding trade and industrialization. An economic system is the method used by a society to produce and distribute goods and services.

Basic Economic Questions

Through its economic system, society answers three key questions. How a society answers these questions depends on how much it values different economic goals. Four different economic systems have developed in response to these three questions.

Economic Goals	
Economic efficiency	Making the most of resources
Economic freedom	Freedom from government intervention in the production and distribution of goods and services
Economic security and predictability	Assurance that goods and services will be available, payments will be made on time, and a safety net will protect individuals in times of economic disaster
Economic equity	Fair distribution of wealth
Economic growth and innovation	Innovation leads to economic growth, and economic growth leads to a higher standard of living.
Other goals	Societies pursue additional goals, such as environmental protection.

Modern Economic Systems

A society's economic system reflects how that society answers the three key economic questions. Different systems produce different results in terms of productivity, the welfare of workers, and consumer choice. This table provides information about the main economic systems in the world today.

A Grameen Bank officer meets with loan recipients in India.

Modern Economic Systems

	Description	Origin	Location Today
Traditional	People make economic decisions based on custom or habit. They produce what they have always produced and just as much as they need, using long-established methods.	Accompanied the rise of agriculture and home crafts	Mainly in rural areas within developing nations
Market (Capitalist, Free-Enterprise)	Economic decisions are made in the marketplace through interactions between buyers and sellers according to the laws of supply and demand. Individual capitalists own the means of production. Government regulates some economic activities and provides such "public goods" as education.	Capitalism has existed since the earliest buying and selling of goods in a market. The market economic system developed in response to Adam Smith's ideas and the shift from agriculture to industry in the 1800s.	Canada, Germany, Japan, United States, and a handful of other nations
Centrally Planned (Command, Socialist, Communist)	Central government planners make most economic decisions for the people. In theory, the workers own the means of production. In practice, the government does. Some private enterprise, but government dominates.	In the 1800s, criticism of capitalism by Karl Marx and others led to calls for distributing wealth according to need. After the 1917 Russian Revolution, the Soviet Union developed the first command economy.	Communist countries, including China, Cuba, North Korea, and Vietnam
Mixed (Social Democratic, Liberal Socialist)	A mix of socialism and free enterprise in which the government plays a significant role in making economic decisions.	The Great Depression of the 1930s ended laissez-faire capitalism in most countries. People insisted that government take a stronger role in fixing economic problems. The fall of communism in Eastern Europe in the 1990s ended central planning in most countries. People insisted on freer markets.	Most nations, including Brazil, France, India, Italy, Poland, Russia, Sweden, and the United Kingdom

Major Trade Organizations

This map shows the major regional trade associations in the world today. In addition, 147 countries belong to the World Trade Organization (WTO). The WTO works to encourage trade by reducing tariffs, promoting international agreements, and mediating trade disputes among member nations.

This illustration represents the cooperation among nations involved in NAFTA.

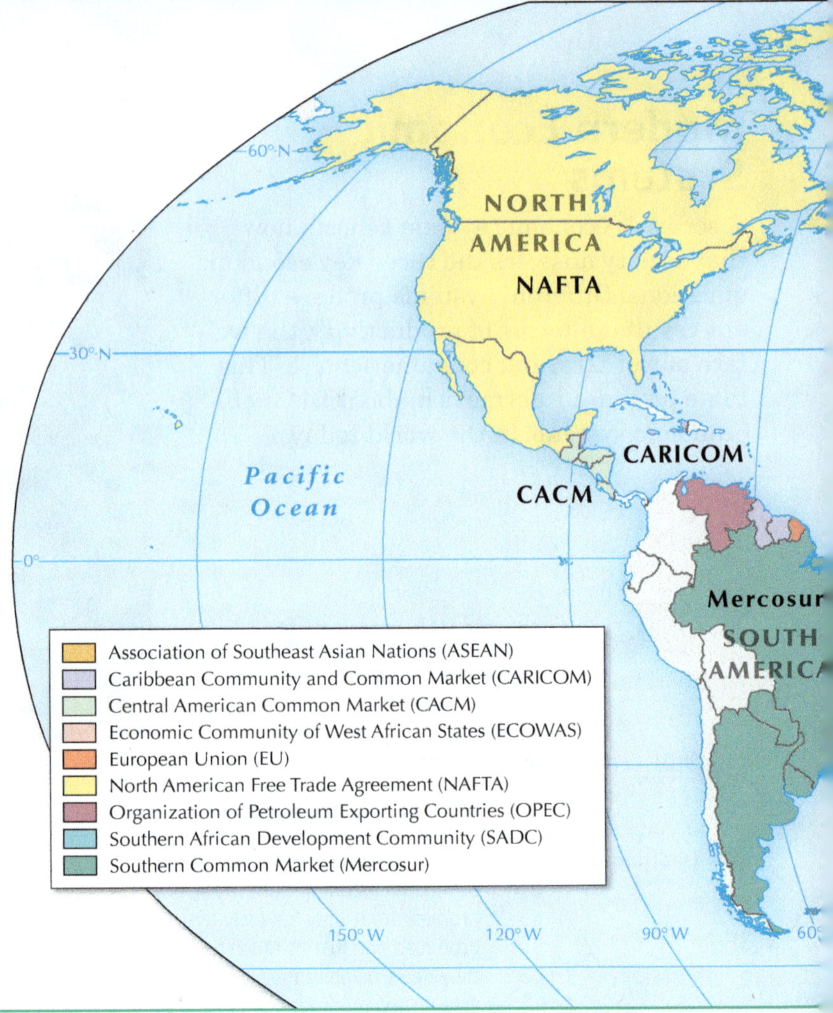

Glossary of Economic Terms

barter
the direct exchange of one set of goods or services for another

budget
a plan for income and spending

capital
any human-made resource that is used to create other goods or services

communism
a political system characterized by a centrally planned economy with all economic and political power resting in the hands of the central government

currency
coins and paper bills used as money

depression
a recession that is especially long and severe

developed nation
industrialized country with a higher average level of material well-being

developing nation
country with limited industrialization and a lower average level of material well-being

economic system
the method used by a society to produce and distribute goods and services

entrepreneur
ambitious leader who combines land, labor, and capital to create and market new goods or services

export
a good that is sent to another country for sale

free enterprise
an economic system that permits the conduct of business with minimal government intervention

goods
physical objects such as clothes or shoes

import
a good that is brought in from another country for sale

industrialization
the extensive organization of an economy for the purpose of manufacturing

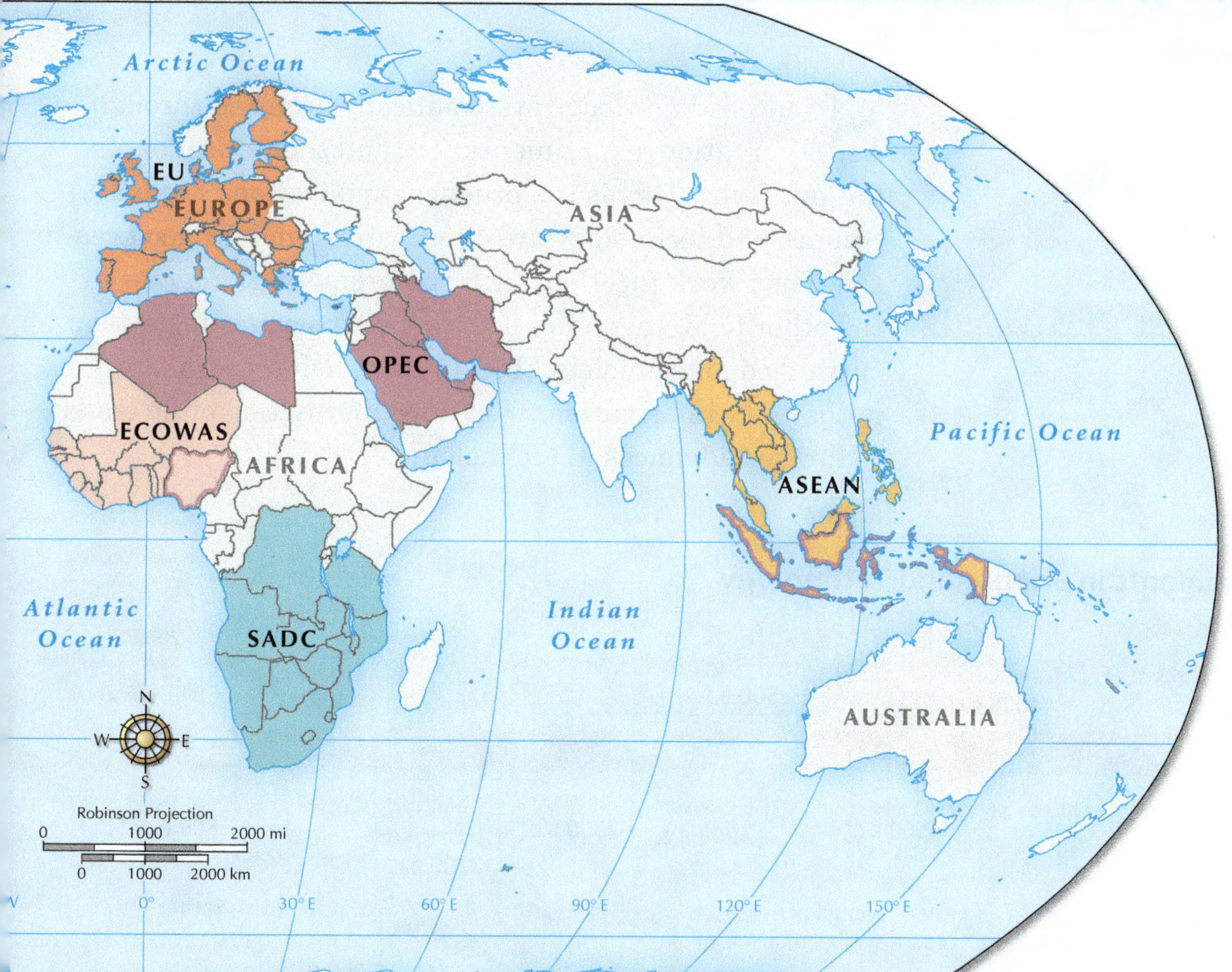

inflation
a general increase in prices

law of demand
economic law that states that consumers buy more of a good when its
price decreases and less when its price
increases

law of supply
tendency of suppliers to offer more of a
good at a higher price

market
an arrangement that allows buyers and
sellers to exchange things

market economy
economic system in which decisions on
production and consumption of goods
and services are based on voluntary
exchange in markets

mixed economy
economic system that combines tradition and the free market with limited
government involvement

opportunity cost
the most desirable alternative given up
as the result of a decision

recession
a prolonged economic contraction

scarcity
limited quantities of resources to meet
unlimited wants

socialism
a social and political philosophy based
on the belief that democratic means
should be used to evenly distribute
wealth throughout a society.

tariff
a tax on imported goods

tax
a required payment to a government

traditional economy
economic system that relies on habit,
custom, or ritual to decide questions of
production and consumption of goods
and services

welfare
government aid to the poor

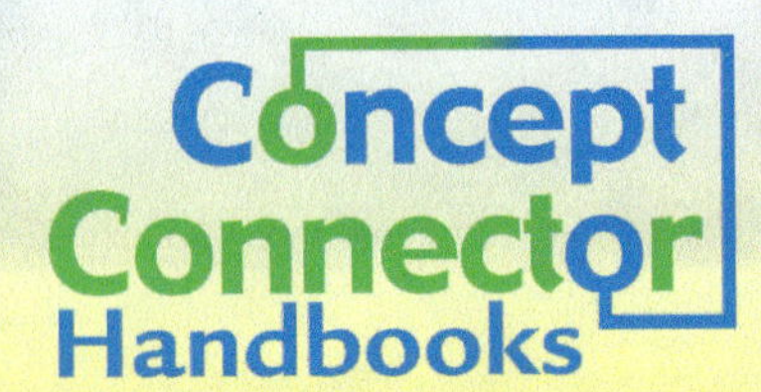

Science and Technology

Science is knowledge systematically acquired through observation, experimentation, and theoretical explanation. Technology is the practical application of science. Science and technology are often paired, and for good reason. They work together, each one promoting progress in the other field. Inventors use the latest science to develop cutting-edge technology that, in turn, helps scientists gather new information. That new information often leads to further advances in technology.

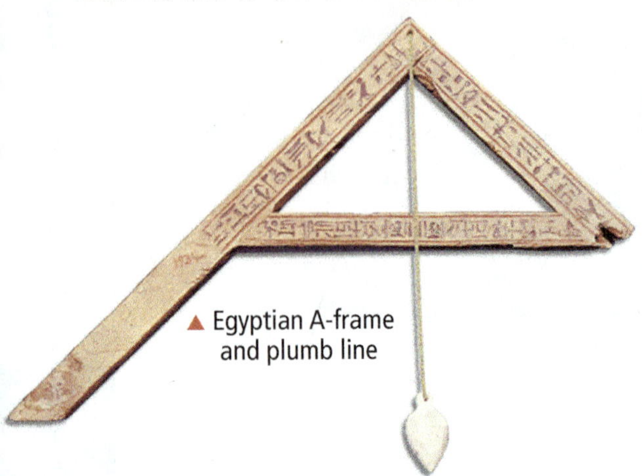

▲ Egyptian A-frame and plumb line

■ Key Developments in Science and Technology

Coin showing Alexander the Great ▶

Science and Technology

Copper tools and ornaments **10,000** B.C.	Light wooden plow **4000** B.C.	Kiln-fired bricks, pots **3500** B.C.

Irrigation **2400** B.C. | Iron weapons **1400** B.C.

10,000 B.C. ———— **5000** B.C. ———— **B.C.** **A.D.**

Widespread domestication of plants and animals **9000–6000** B.C.

Bronze objects **4500** B.C. | Dam **4000** B.C. | Pyramids **2800** B.C.

Plumbing, water pipes, sewer drains **2700** B.C.

Coins **600** B.C.

Medicine

Greek symbol of peace, now a symbol of medicine ▶

Hippocrates, father of medicine, born **460** B.C.

10,000 B.C. ———— **5000** B.C. ———— **B.C.** **A.D.**

Greek physician Galen born A.D. **130**

Communication

Egyptian cursive writing on papyrus ▼

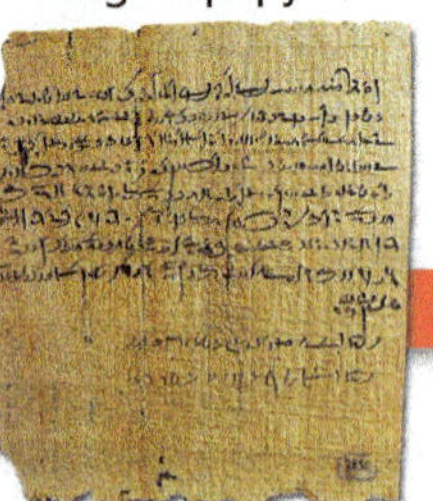

Pictographs **3500** B.C. | Writing **3200** B.C. | Alphabet **1700** B.C. | Paper A.D. **105**

10,000 B.C. ———— **5000** B.C. ———— **B.C.** **A.D.**

Papyrus **2800** B.C.

Transportation

Ancient dugout canoe *c.* **6000** B.C. | Wheeled cart from Sumer *c.* **3500** B.C. | Roman chariot *c.* A.D. **1**

10,000 B.C. ———— **5000** B.C. ———— **B.C.** **A.D.**

Portuguese square-sailed ship ▶

Square-sailed ships **3000** B.C.

◀ Italian compass

▼ Seed drill

Concept Connector

Science and Technology

| Gunpowder c. A.D. 900 | Magnetic compass c. 1100 | Glass lens c. 1300 | Compound microscope 1590 | Lightning rod 1752 | Power loom 1785 |

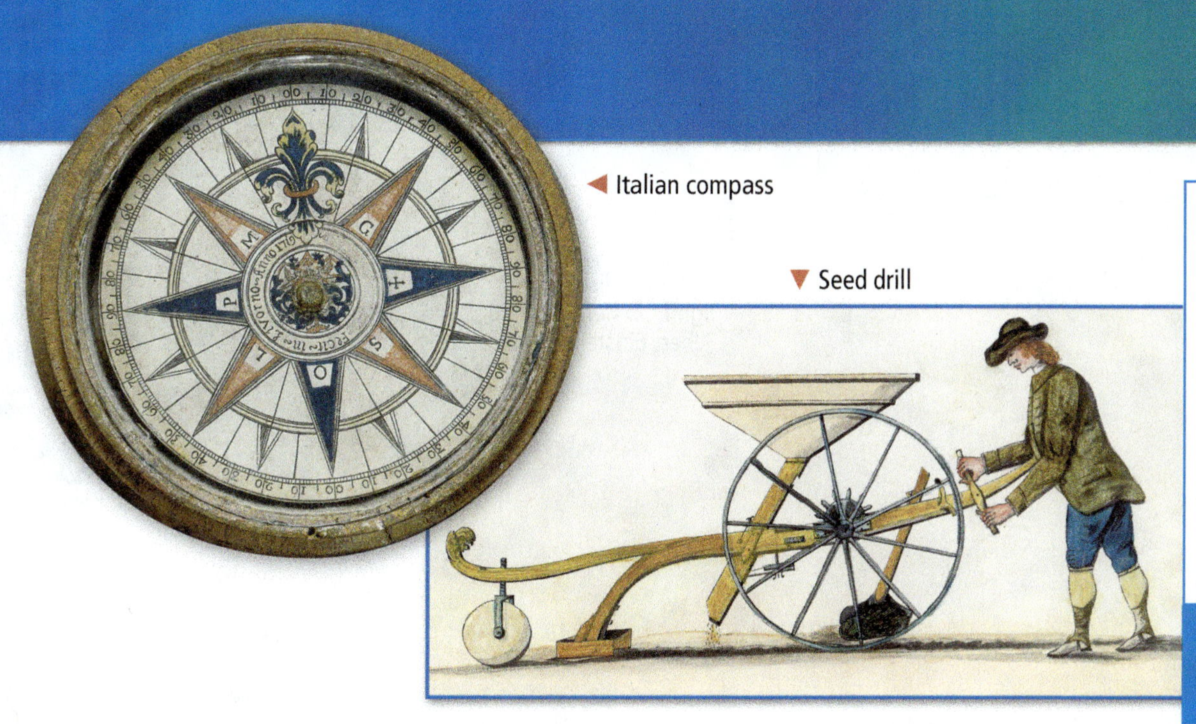

A.D. 1100 — A.D. 1300 — A.D. 1500 — A.D. 1700

| Magnifying glass 1250 | Mechanical clock c. 1400 | Newton formulates Law of gravitation 1687 | Steam engine 1769 |

Bald's *Leechbook*
c. 900

Early vaccination ▶

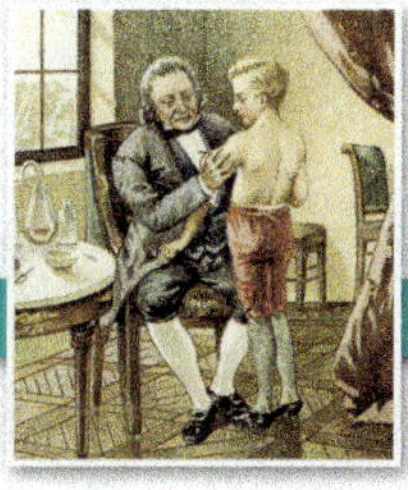

William Harvey's *Circulation of the Blood*
1628

Smallpox vaccine
1796

A.D. 1100 — A.D. 1300 — 1500 — A.D. 1700

Gutenberg Bible ▶

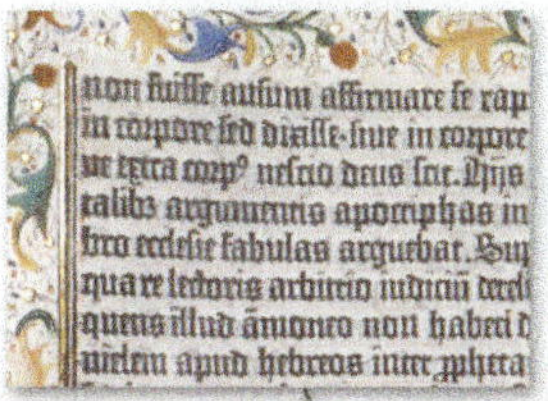

Printing press using moveable type
c. 1450

A.D. 1100 — A.D. 1300 — A.D. 1500 — A.D. 1700

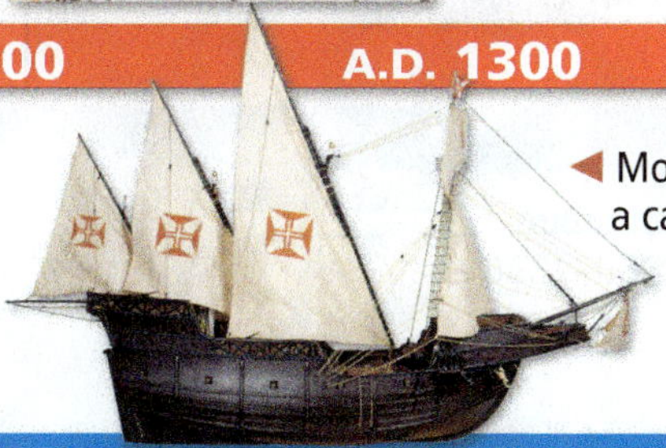

◀ Model of a caravel

Viking ship
800s

Stagecoach
1500s

Hot-air balloon
1783

A.D. 1100 — A.D. 1300 — A.D. 1500 — A.D. 1700

Caravel
1200s

Science and Technology

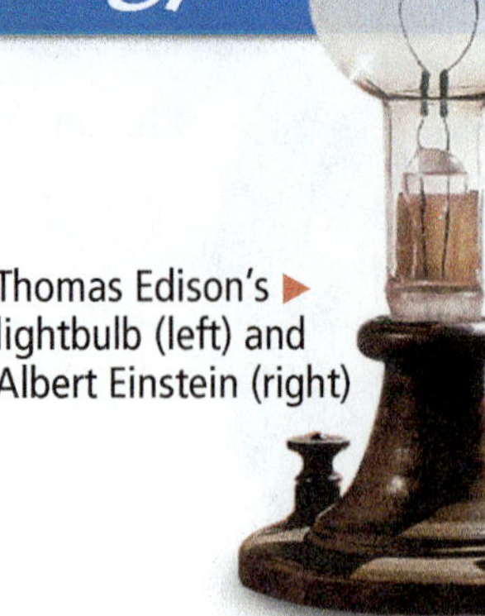

Thomas Edison's ▶
lightbulb (left) and
Albert Einstein (right)

Science and Technology

| Electric motor 1821 | Theory of evolution 1849 | Incandescent lamp 1879 | Quantum theory 1900 | Frozen food 1924 |

A.D. 1800 — **A.D. 1850** — **A.D. 1900**

Canning of food 1809 — Mechanical reaper 1843 — Special Theory of Relativity 1905 — Plastics 1909 — Liquid fuel rocket 1926

Medicine

Anesthesia 1842 — Pasteurization of milk 1865 — Antiseptic surgery 1867 — Diphtheria antitoxin 1891 — Typhus vaccine 1909

A.D. 1800 — **A.D. 1850** — **A.D. 1900**

Government focus on improving hygiene and public sanitation 1850–1950 — Genetics; laws of heredity 1866 — Rabies vaccine 1885 — X-ray 1895 — Penicillin, first antibiotic 1928

Communication

Telegraph 1837 — Radio 1895

A.D. 1800 — **A.D. 1850** — **A.D. 1900**

Telephone 1846 — Early telephone ◀ — Electronic television 1927

Transportation

Steam locomotive 1825 — Biplane 1903

A.D. 1800 — **A.D. 1850** — **A.D. 1900**

Steamboat 1807 — Automobile c. 1860–1890

Daimler motor car ▶

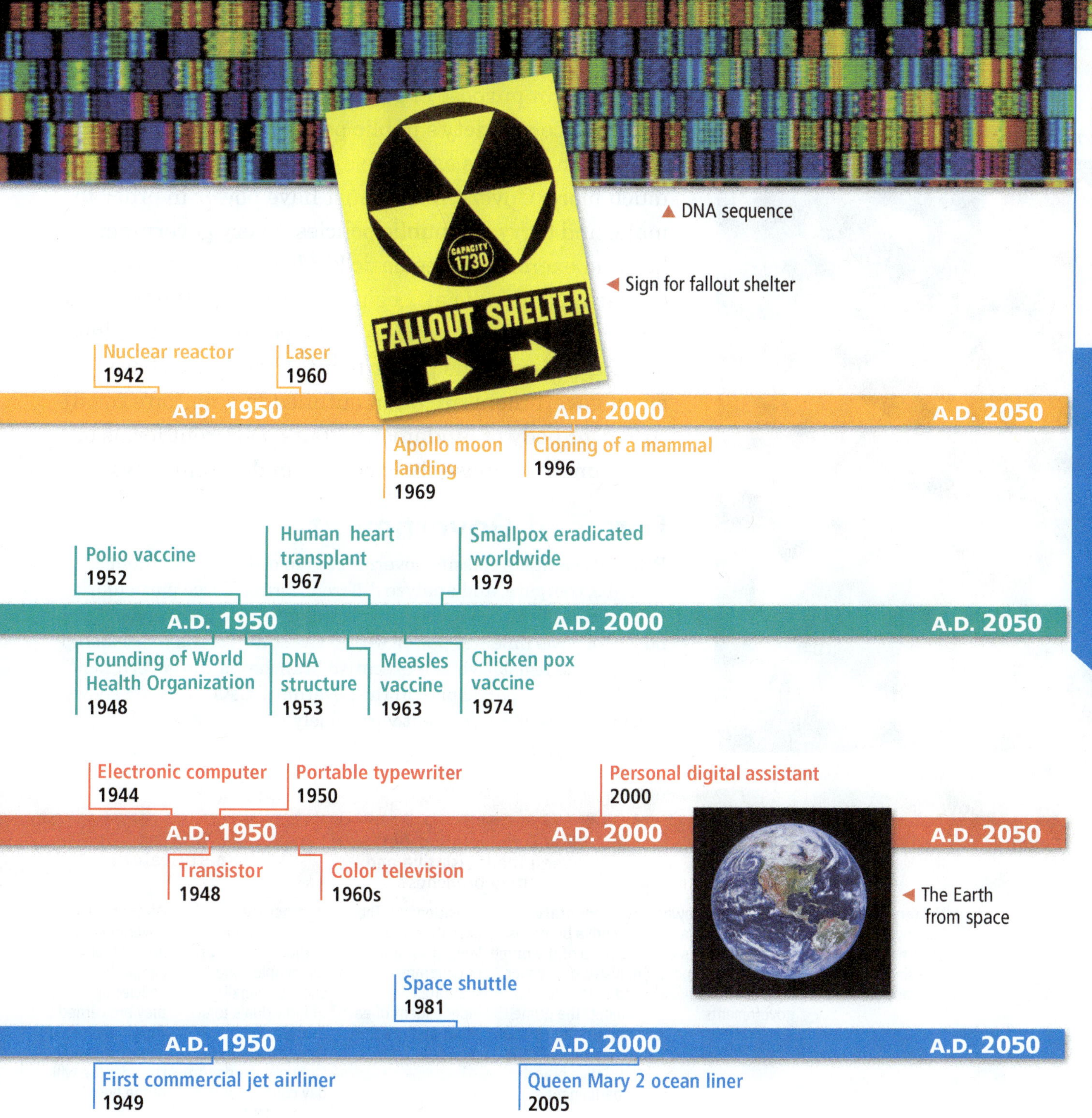
CAPACITY 1730
FALLOUT SHELTER

DNA sequence

Sign for fallout shelter

Nuclear reactor
1942

Laser
1960

A.D. 1950
A.D. 2000
A.D. 2050

Apollo moon
landing
1969

Cloning of a mammal
1996

Polio vaccine
1952

Human heart
transplant
1967

Smallpox eradicated
worldwide
1979

A.D. 1950
A.D. 2000
A.D. 2050

Founding of World
Health Organization
1948

DNA
structure
1953

Measles
vaccine
1963

Chicken pox
vaccine
1974

Electronic computer
1944

Portable typewriter
1950

Personal digital assistant
2000

A.D. 1950
A.D. 2000
A.D. 2050

Transistor
1948

Color television
1960s

The Earth
from space

Space shuttle
1981

A.D. 1950
A.D. 2000
A.D. 2050

First commercial jet airliner
1949

Queen Mary 2 ocean liner
2005

Government and Civics

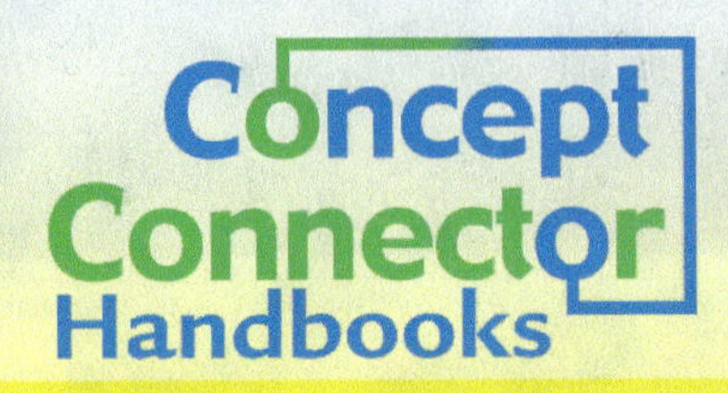

Presidential elections in Ukraine, 2004

The main purpose of government is to create and enforce a society's public policies. Public policies cover such matters as defense, crime, taxation, and much more. Governments must have power in order to make and carry out public policies. Every government has and exercises three basic kinds of power: legislative, executive, and judicial. Legislative refers to the power to make laws. Executive refers to the power to enforce laws. Judicial refers to the power to interpret laws. These powers of government are often outlined in a nation's constitution, or body of fundamental laws. Different forms of government exercise their powers in different ways.

Forms of Government

Political scientists classify governments in order to help them describe, compare, and analyze different forms. Three particularly helpful classifications involve determining (1) the geographic distribution of governmental power within the state, (2) the relationship between the legislative and executive branches of the government, and (3) who can participate in the government. As the chart shows, modern forms of government vary widely.

Forms of Government

Country	Where is the power?		What is the relationship between the legislative and executive branches?		Who can participate?	
	Unitary: All powers held by the government belong to a single, central agency.	**Federal**: The powers of government are divided between a central government and several regional governments.	**Parliamentary**: The executive branch is made up of the prime minister, or premier, and that official's cabinet. The prime minister and cabinet are members of the legislative branch, or parliament.	**Presidential**: The executive and legislative branches of government are separate, independent of each other, and coequal.	**Democracy**: Supreme political authority rests with the people, who choose a small group of individuals to act as their representatives to carry out the day-to-day conduct of government.	**Dictatorship**: The government is not accountable to the people for its policies or for how they are carried out. Those who rule do not represent or consider the will of the people.
Botswana	✓		✓		✓	
Brazil		✓		✓	✓	
Costa Rica	✓		✓		✓	
Cuba	✓		✓			✓
France	✓			✓	✓	
India		✓	✓		✓	
Syria	✓			✓		✓
United States		✓		✓	✓	

Federal vs. Unitary Government

Today, about two dozen nations, including the United States, have a federal system of government. In this kind of system, two levels of government—central and state—divide power between them. In the unitary system, which is more common by far, all powers belong to the central government. One disadvantage of a federal system is its inefficiency. People must obey two sets of laws, which may overlap or even conflict. In a unitary system, one government governs all the people directly, even though it may yield certain powers to the states. On the other hand, a federal system allows for checks on the power of the central government and for some diversity of laws in regions with a distinctive culture, history, or language.

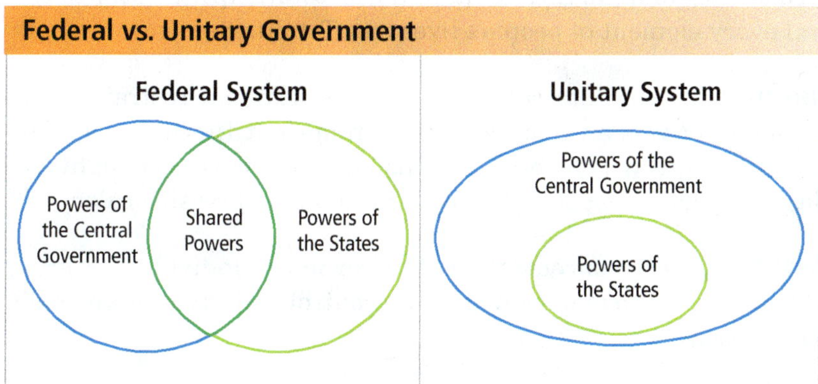

Presidential and Parliamentary Governments

The Presidential Relationship Voters elect the legislature and the chief executive, who is part of the executive branch. The legislative and executive branches are independent and coequal.

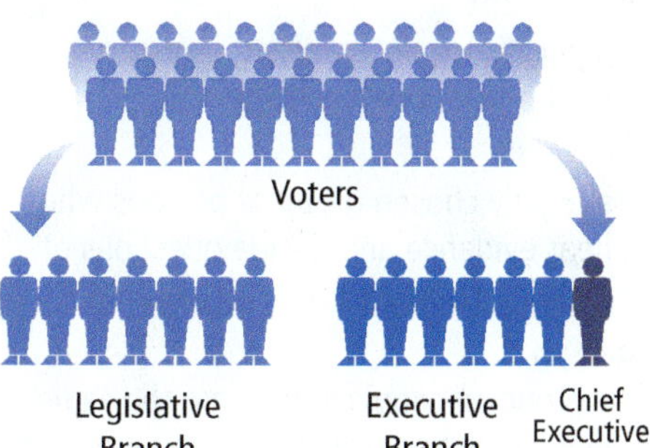

The Parliamentary Relationship Voters elect the legislature. The chief executive is drawn from the legislature.

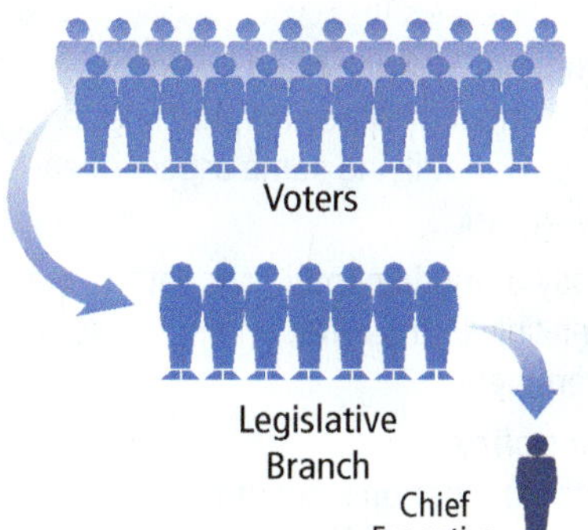

Basic Concepts of Democracy

1. A recognition of the fundamental worth and dignity of every person. At various times, the welfare of one or a few individuals is subordinate to the interests of the many in a democracy. For example, a democratic society may force people to pay a tax or obey traffic signals.

2. A respect for the equality of all persons. The democratic concept of equality insists that all people are entitled to equality of opportunity and equality before the law—not necessarily equal distribution of wealth.

3. A faith in the majority rule and an insistence upon minority rights. In a democracy, the will of the people and not the dictate of the ruling few determine public policy. Unchecked, however, a majority could destroy its opposition and, in the process, destroy democracy. Thus, democracy insists upon majority rule restrained by minority rights.

4. An acceptance of the necessity of compromise. In a democracy, public decision making must be largely a matter of give-and-take among the various competing interests. People must compromise to find the position most acceptable to the largest number. Compromise is the process of blending and adjusting competing views and interests.

5. An insistence upon the widest possible degree of individual freedom. In a democracy, each individual must be as free to do as he or she pleases as far as the freedom of all will allow. Oliver Wendell Holmes once had this to say about the relative nature of each individuals rights: "The right to swing my fist ends where the other man's nose begins."

Louis XIV of France

Catherine the Great of Russia

Forms of Dictatorship

Typically militaristic in character, an authoritarian or dictatorial regime usually acquires political power by force and may turn to foreign aggression to enhance its military strength and prestige. Authoritarianism has taken several related forms throughout history.

Absolutism A system in which the ruler holds complete authority over the government and the lives of the people. Some absolute monarchs ruled according to the principle of divine right. Modern forms of absolutism include military dictatorships that try to control every element of people's lives (see Totalitarianism).

Despotism Absolute rule with no constitutional restraints. The term *despot* was an honorable title in ancient times. Later, absolute monarchs who favored reforms became known as enlightened despots. Today, despot refers to a brutal and oppressive ruler.

Autocracy The concentration of power in one individual or group that uses force to maintain absolute control and smother any political opposition.

Mehmed II of the Ottoman Empire

Glossary of Political Terms

bureaucracy
a large, complex administrative structure that handles the everyday business of government

citizen
a member of a state or nation who is entitled to full civil rights

civil service
those civilian employees who perform the administrative work of government

compromise
an adjustment of opposing principles or systems by modifying some aspect of each

constitution
the body of fundamental laws setting out the principles, structures, and processes of a government

foreign policy
everything a nation's government says and does in world affairs

immigrant
a person legally admitted as a permanent resident of a country

jury
a legally chosen group of persons who hear evidence and decide questions of fact in a court case

nation
a group of people who share the same way of life and live in the same area and under the same central government

Totalitarianism   A form of absolutism in which the government sweeps away existing political institutions and exerts complete control over nearly every aspect of the society. In this system, a supreme leader often becomes the sole source of society's rules.

Communism   An ideology that, in theory, calls for ownership of all land and other productive property by the workers. In practice, a system of repressive, single-party government that completely controls its citizens' lives and stifles all opposition.

Fascism   A form of government that seeks to renew society by demanding citizens' complete devotion to the state. Often led by a dictator who strictly controls industry and labor, denies freedom and individual rights, and uses police and the military to silence opposition.

Adolf Hitler of Germany

Mural of Saddam Hussein

Mao Zedong's
Little Red Book

politics
  the activities of those who run or seek to run a government

rule of law
  idea that all citizens, including government officials, are subject to the law

sovereign
  having supreme power within its own territory

state
  a group of people living in a defined territory who have a government with the power to make and enforce law without the consent of any higher authority

suffrage
  the right to vote

tax
  a charge levied by government on persons or property to meet public needs

treaty
  a formal agreement between two or more sovereign states

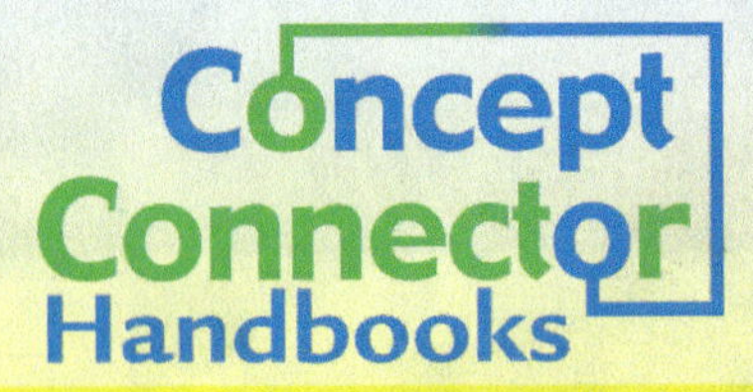

Culture

Culture is a way of life, or a set of values and behaviors, that people in a society learn, share, and pass on from generation to generation. Culture mainly involves what people think, what they do, and what they create. It consists of such elements as language, religion, art, social organization, and technology. Cultures can change over time. Some elements are forgotten, and others are improved or replaced. Still others are picked up from outside cultures. This spread of ideas, customs, and technologies from one culture to another is known as cultural diffusion. Historically, cultures have spread mainly through trade, migration, and conquest.

World Languages

Language is a part of culture. Yet it is also the main tool by which people transmit their culture. Many thousands of languages have arisen since humans first began to communicate. Some 6,800 of those languages still survive. Related languages can be grouped into language families.

Principal Languages of the World	
Language	Speakers* (in millions)
Mandarin (Chinese)	873
Spanish	322
English	309
Hindi	180
Portuguese	177
Bengali	171
Russian	145
Japanese	122
German	95
Wu (Chinese)	77

* estimated number for whom this is their first language

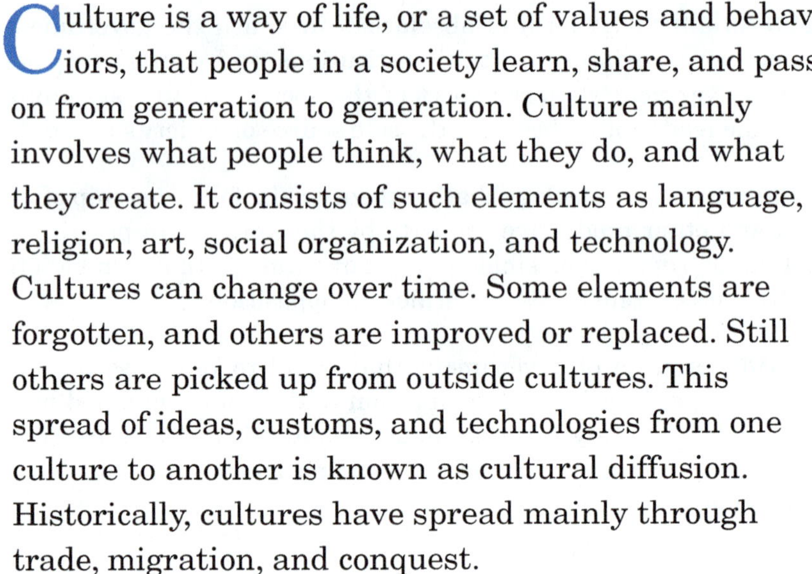

Sign in a Native American language and English (above); fragment of a Dead Sea scroll, written in ancient Hebrew (below)

Major Belief Systems

Most of the world's major belief systems have existed for more than 2,000 years. Today, if the world included only 1,000 people, 330 of them would be Christian, 215 would be Muslim, 149 would be Hindu, 140 would follow no religion, 59 would be Buddhist, 37 would follow Chinese traditional religions, and 41 would hold primal-indigenous beliefs.

Major World Religions/Belief Systems

	Leading Figures; Dates	Key Beliefs	Writings	Number of Followers
Buddhism	Siddhartha Gautama (the Buddha); late sixth to fourth century B.C.	No gods, but buddhas, or "enlightened ones" exist; reincarnation (cycle of birth, death, and rebirth); the Four Noble Truths: (1) suffering is a part of life; (2) selfish desire leads to suffering; (3) desire can be overcome; (4) the Eightfold Path leads away from desire, toward release from the cycle of birth, death, and rebirth	*Tripitaka (The Three Baskets)*; the sutras; the tantras	373 million
Chinese Traditional Religions (blend of Buddhism, Confucianism, and Daoism)	Blending began in the A.D. 900s	Reincarnation (from Buddhism); virtuous way of life (from Confucianism); acting in harmony with nature and avoiding aggressive action (from Daoism)	*Dao de Jing (The Way of Power)*; *Zhuangzi* (named after the greatest interpreter of Daoism); (see also Buddhism and Confucianism)	398 million
Christianity	Jesus of Nazareth; early first century A.D.	One God; to save humans, God sent Jesus, who suffered, died, and rose from the dead; the Trinity: three figures (God the Father, God the Son, and God the Holy Spirit) united as one; love God above all else	The Bible: the Old Testament (Hebrew Bible) and the New Testament; various creeds and statements of faith	2.07 billion
Confucianism	Confucius; around 500 B.C.	No gods; not an organized religion, but a system of moral conduct based on the teachings of Confucius; kindness, love, and respect lead to a virtuous way of life	The *Lun yü (Analects)*; the *Wu-ching (Five Classics)*; the *Ssu Shu (Four Books)*	6.43 million (mainly in Korea)
Hinduism	No founder or central institution; around 1500 B.C.	Brahman, the ultimate God, is the source of all existence; many lesser gods, the main ones being Vishnu and Siva; reincarnation; law of karma (actions in one life affect next life); ahimsa (principle of noninjury or nonviolence)	The Vedas, sutras, epics, and puranas	837 million
Islam	Muhammad; early A.D. 600s	One God, Allah; Five Pillars, or duties: (1) profession of faith; (2) prayer; (3) charity; (4) fasting; (5) pilgrimage to Mecca in Saudi Arabia	Quran	1.25 billion
Judaism	Abraham; around 2000 B.C.	One God; God made a covenant, with Abraham and the Jewish people that if they obey God's commands, God will make Israel a great nation; moral actions are more important than beliefs	Hebrew Bible: The Torah (the "Law"), the Nevi'im (the "Prophets"), and the Ketuvim (the "Writings"); oral tradition, written as the Talmud	14.6 million
primal-indigenous (includes tribal religions, animism, shamanism, and paganism)	Such religions have existed since prehistoric times	May be a high god; nature spirits (powerful life forces inhabiting the elements of nature); communication with spirits through prayers and offerings ensures the support of the spirits	none	238 million
Shinto	No founder; well established by the A.D. 500s	Many gods; Kami (superior, mystical, or divine powers) are the sources of human life; main deity is sun goddess Amaterasu O-mikami; each person is worthy of respect; truthfulness and purification (physical and spiritual) bring the blessings of the kami	No central sacred scripture; chief books: *Kojiki (Records of Ancient Matters)* and *Nihon shoki (Chronicles of Japan)*	2.68 million
Sikhism (combines elements of Hinduism and Islam)	Nanak; around A.D. 1500	One God; reincarnation; meditation can release one from the cycle of reincarnation; law of karma; all humans are equal	*Adi Granth (First Book)*	24.3 million

Culture

The Arts

The arts tell much about a culture. Ancient civilizations produced artists only after they were capable of generating an agricultural surplus. Some people could then be spared from the fields to devote themselves to other pursuits, including the arts. Works of art, from paintings and sculptures to music, dance, and writing, reflect the culture in which the artist lived. Notice the variations among the arts presented in these pictures. Think about what each picture says about the culture that produced it.

▲ Neoclassical bust of Napoleon by Antonio Canova, *c.* 1802

Romantic poet, writer, and artist William Blake's *Songs of Innocence*, 1789 ▼

Major Art Movements

classicism
Greek and Roman art; emphasis on harmony, proportion, balance, and simplicity

byzantine
500s–1400s, Europe, Russia

Romanesque
late eleventh century, Europe

Gothic
1100s–1400s, Europe; cathedral architecture and religious art

Renaissance
c. 1400–1600, Europe; Leonardo, Michelangelo, Raphael

mannerism
c. 1520–1600, Europe; Parmigianino

baroque
seventeenth and early eighteenth centuries, Europe; Bernini, Caravaggio, Rubens

rococo
eighteenth century, Europe; Fragonard

neoclassicism
late eighteenth and early nineteenth centuries, Europe; revival of ancient Greek and Roman art; David, Canova

romanticism
late eighteenth to mid-nineteenth century, Europe, United States; Delacroix, Géricault, Turner, Blake, Hudson River school

Barbizon School
c. 1840–1870, France; landscapes; Rousseau, Corot, Millet

realism
nineteenth century, Europe and United States; Daumier, Courbet, Eakins

impressionism
late nineteenth century, France and United States; Monet, Renoir, Cassatt

pointillism
1880s, France; Seurat, Signac

Costume from Georg Friedrich Handel's baroque opera *Agrippina*, 1709 (right) ▶

Pointillist painting by Georges Seurat, *Porte-en-Bessin*, 1888 (far right) ▶

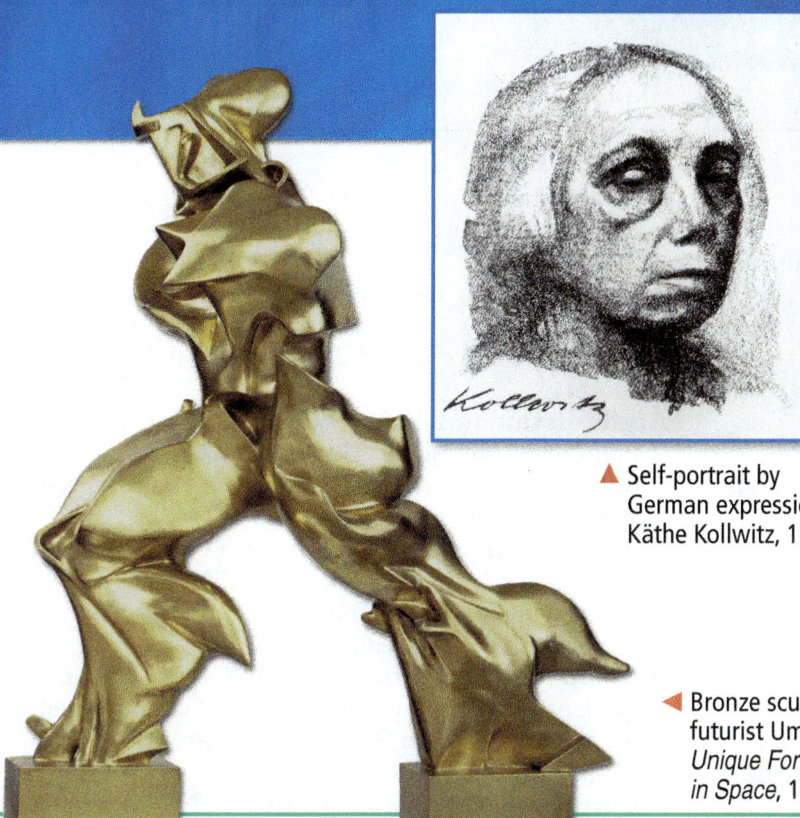

▲ Self-portrait by German expressionist Käthe Kollwitz, 1920

◀ Bronze sculpture by Italian futurist Umberto Boccioni, *Unique Forms of Continuity in Space*, 1913

Poster for ► Émile Zola's realist novel *La Terre*, 1887

postimpressionism
late nineteenth century, France; Cézanne, Van Gogh, Gauguin

art nouveau
late nineteenth century, Europe; decorative arts

cubism
early twentieth century, Europe; Picasso, Braque

fauvism
c. 1905–1908, France; pure, bold colors applied in a spontaneous manner; Matisse

expressionism
c. 1905–1925, northern Europe; Rouault, Kokoschka, Schiele

futurism
c. 1909–1919, Italy; Boccioni

constructivism
c. 1915, Russia; abstract style using non-traditional materials; Rodchenko, Tatlin, Gabo, Pevsner

dadaism
c. 1915–1923, France; rejected accepted aesthetic standards; Duchamp

surrealism
1920s–1930s, Europe; Magritte, Dalí, Miró, Ernst, de Chirico

art deco
1920s–1930s; decorative arts characterized by sleek lines and slender forms

abstract expressionism
1940s, New York City; Pollock, de Kooning, Motherwell, Kline

minimalism
late 1950s, United States; Judd, Martin, Kelly

color field painting
1950s, United States; Newman, Rothko, Frankenthaler

pop art
1950s, United States; Warhol, Lichtenstein, Oldenburg

conceptual art
1960s and 1970s, international; questioned the definition of "art"

Sculpture for a park in Minneapolis by pop artist Claes Oldenburg, *Spoonbridge and Cherry*, 1988 ▼

A

Abbasids dynasty that ruled in Bagdad from 750–1258 (p. 314)

Abbasids dinastía que gobernó Bagdad durante los años 750–1258

abdicate to give up or step down from power (p. 598)

abdicar renunciar de un puesto de poder

abolition movement the campaign against slavery and the slave trade (p. 727)

movimiento por la abolición campaña contra la esclavitud y contra el tráfico de esclavos

absentee landlord one who owns a large estate but does not live there (p. 729)

dueño ausente dueño de una gran propiedad que no vive en ella

absolute monarch ruler with complete authority over the government and lives of the people he or she governs (p. 506)

monarca absoluto gobernante que tiene autoridad absoluta sobre la administración y la vida de los que están bajo su mando

abstract style of art composed of lines, colors, and shapes, sometimes with no recognizable subject matter at all (p. 889)

abstracto estilo de arte compuesto de líneas, colores y formas, y que a veces no tiene un tema reconocible

acculturation the blending of two or more cultures (p. 72)

aculturación mezcla de dos o más culturas

acid rain a form of pollution in which toxic chemicals in the air come back to Earth in the form of rain, snow, or hail (p. 1112)

lluvia ácida forma de polución en la que los productos químicos tóxicos que se encuentran en el aire vuelven a la tierra en la lluvia, nieve o granizo

acropolis highest and most fortified point within a Greek city-state (p. 119)

acrópolis el punto más alto y fortificado de una ciudad-estado griega

acupuncture medical treatment, originated in ancient China, in which needles are inserted into the skin at specific points to relieve pain or treat various illnesses (p. 106)

acupuntura tratamiento médico, originario de China, por el que se introducen agujas en la piel en puntos específicos para aliviar el dolor o como tratamiento de diversas enfermedades

adobe a mixture of clay and plant fibers that becomes hard as it dries in the sun and that can be used for building (p. 196)

adobe mezcla de arcilla y fibras vegetales que se endurece al secarse al sol y se puede usar en la construcción

Adulis strategic trading port of the kingdom of Axum (p. 352)

Adulis puerto comercial estratégico del reino de Axum

Afghanistan an Islamic country in Central Asia; invaded by the Soviet Union in 1979; later home to the radical Islamist Taliban and the terrorist al Qaeda (p. 1119)

Afganistán país islámico en Asia Central; invadido por la Unión Soviética en 1979; más tarde hogar de los radicales islamistas Talibán y de los terroristas de al Qaeda

African National Congress (ANC) the main organization that opposed apartheid and pushed for majority rule in South Africa; later a political party (p. 1049)

Congreso Nacional Africano (ANC, por sus siglas en inglés) principal organización que se opuso al apartheid y que abogó por el gobierno de la mayoría de Sudáfrica; posteriormente, partido político

agribusinesses giant commercial farms, often owned by multinational corporations (p. 1084)

industria agropecuaria inmensas granjas comerciales, generalmente administradas por corporaciones multinacionales

ahimsa Hindu belief in nonviolence and reverence for all life (pp. 77, 866)

ahimsa creencia hindú en la no violencia y en el respeto a todas las formas de vida

aircraft carriers ships that accommodate the taking off and landing of airplanes, and transport aircraft (p. 940)

portaaviones buque dotado de las instalaciones necesarias para el transporte, despegue y aterrizaje de aparatos de aviación

al Qaeda a fundamentalist Islamic terrorist organization led by Saudi Arabian Osama bin Laden (p. 1118)

al Qaeda organización fundamentalista islámica terrorista liderada por el saudí Osama bin Laden

Alexandria an ancient Hellenistic city in Egypt (p. 140)

Alejandría antigua ciudad helenista en Egipto

alliance formal agreement between two or more nations or powers to cooperate and come to one another's defense (pp. 126, 473)

alianza acuerdo formal de cooperación y defensa mutua entre dos o más naciones o potencias

alphabet writing system in which each symbol represents a single basic sound (p. 43)

alfabeto sistema de escritura en el que cada símbolo representa un único sonido

Alsace and Lorraine provinces on the border of Germany and France, lost by France to Germany in 1871; regained by France after WWI (p. 818)

Alsacia y Lorena provincias en la frontera entre Alemania y Francia, que Alemania arrebató a Francia en 1871, y que Francia recuperó después de la Primera Guerra Mundial

Amritsar massacre an incident in 1919 in which British troops fired on an unarmed crowd of Indians (p. 865)

masacre de Amritsar incidente en 1919 en el que las tropas británicas dispararon contra un grupo de indios indefensos

anarchist someone who wants to abolish all government (p. 704)

anarquista persona que quiere abolir toda forma de gobierno

ancien régime old order; system of government in pre-revolution France (p. 572)

ancien regime antiguo orden; sistema de gobierno en la Francia prerevolucionaria

anesthetic drug that prevents pain during surgery (p. 609)

anestesia fármaco que suprime el dolor durante la cirugía

animism the belief that spirits and forces live within animals, objects, or dreams (p. 13)

animismo creencia de que los espíritus y fuerzas pueden vivir en animales, objetos o sueños

annex add a territory to an existing state or country (pp. 594, 694)

anexar agregar un territorio a un estado o país existente

Anschluss union of Austria and Germany (p. 927)

Anschluss unión de Austria y Alemania

anthropology the study of the origins and development of people and their societies (p. 5)

antropología estudio del origen y desarrollo de los pueblos y sus sociedades

anti-ballistic missiles (ABMs) missiles that can shoot down other missiles (p. 968)

misiles anti-balísticos (ABM, por sus siglas) misiles que pueden derribar otros misiles

anti-Semitism prejudice against Jews (p. 230)

antisemitismo prejuicio contra los judíos

apartheid a policy of rigid segregation of non-white people in the Republic of South Africa (pp. 859, 1048)

apartheid política de estricta separación racial en Sudáfrica que fue abolida en 1989

apostle leader or teacher of a new faith or movement (p. 168)

apóstol líder o maestro de una nueva fe o movimiento

appeasement policy of giving in to an aggressor's demands in order to keep the peace (p. 925)

contemporización política de aceptación de las exigencias de un agresor para mantener la paz

apprentice a young person learning a trade from a master (p. 235)

aprendiz persona joven que aprendía un oficio de un maestro

aqueduct in ancient Rome, underground or bridgelike stone structure that carried water from the hills into the cities (p. 164)

acueducto en la antigua Roma, estructura parecida a un puente que llevaba agua desde las colinas hasta las ciudades

archaeology the study of people and cultures through their material remains (p. 5)

arqueología estudio de pueblos y culturas antiguas por medio de sus restos materiales

archipelago chain of islands (p. 387)

archipiélago cadena de islas

aristocracy government headed by a privileged minority or upper class (p. 120)

aristocracia gobierno encabezado por una minoría privilegiada o de clase alta

armada fleet of ships (p. 507)

armada flota de barcos

armistice agreement to end fighting in a war (p. 833)

armisticio acuerdo para dejar de luchar en una guerra

artifact an object made by human beings (p. 4)

artefacto objeto hecho por seres humanos

artificial satellite man-made object that orbits a larger body in space (p. 1121)

satélite artificial objeto artificial que gira en el espacio alrededor de un cuerpo más grande

artisan a skilled craftsperson (p. 20)

artesano trabajador cualificado que hace objetos a mano

Asante kingdom kingdom that emerged in the 1700s in present-day Ghana and was active in the slave trade (p. 454)

reino Asante reino que surgió en el siglo XVIII en el actual Ghana y que tenía comercio de esclavos

Asia Minor the Turkish peninsula between the Black Sea and the Mediterranean Sea (p. 861)

Asia Menor la península turca entre el Mar Negro y el Mar Mediterráneo

assassination murder of a public figure, usually for political reasons (p. 139)

asesinato acto de dar muerte a una figura pública, generalmente por razones políticas

assembly line production method that breaks down a complex job into a series of smaller tasks (p. 663)

cadena de montaje método de producción que divide un trabajo complejo en una serie de tareas menores

assimilate absorb or adopt another culture (p. 139)

asimilar absorber o adoptar otra cultura

atheism belief that there is no god (p. 909)

ateísmo creencia de que no existen dioses

Athens a city-state in ancient Greece (p. 121)

Atenas ciudad-estado en la antigua Grecia

atman in Hindu belief, a person's essential self (p. 77)

atman según la creencia hindú, el ser esencial de una persona

atrocity horrible act committed against innocent people (p. 830)

atrocidad acto brutal cometido en contra de inocentes

autocrat ruler who has complete authority (p. 285)

autócrata gobernante que tiene autoridad total

autocratic having unlimited power (pp. 531, 1020)

autocrático que tiene poder ilimitado

autonomy self-rule (p. 636)

autonomía autogobierno

Axis powers group of countries led by Germany, Italy, and Japan that fought the Allies in World War II (p. 926)

Potencias del Eje grupo de países liderado por Alemania, Italia y Japón que luchó contra los Aliados durante la Segunda Guerra Mundial

Axum trading center, and powerful ancient kingdom in northern present-day Ethiopia (p. 352)

Axum ciudad capital, centro de comercio y poderoso antiguo reino del norte de la presente Etiopía

ayllu in the Inca empire, a close-knit village (p. 198)

ayllu en el imperio Inca, aldea muy unida

B

Baghdad capital city of present-day Iraq; capital of the Muslim empire during Islam's golden age (p. 314)

Baghdad capital del actual Iraq; capital del imperio musulmán durante la época dorada del islam

balance of power distribution of military and economic power that prevents any one nation from becoming too strong (p. 514)

equilibrio de poder distribución del poder military y económico que evita que una nación se vuelva demasiado fuerte

balance of trade difference between how much a country imports and how much it exports (p. 773)

balance commercial diferencia entre lo que importa y exporta un país

Balfour Declaration statement issued by the British government in 1917 supporting the establishment of a homeland for Jews in Palestine (p. 864)

Declaración Balfour declaración hecha por el gobierno británico en 1917 en la que apoyaba la constitución de un estado judío en Palestina

Balkan Peninsula triangular arm of land that juts from southeastern Europe into the Mediterranean (p. 294)

Península Balcánica extensión triangular de tierra que sobresale del sudeste de Europa hasta el Mediterráneo

Bangladesh nation east of India that was formerly part of Pakistan (p. 1017)

Bangladesh país al este de India que antiguamente formaba parte de Pakistán

Bantu root language of West Africa on which some early African migration patterns are based (p. 341)

Bantú lengua madre del África occidental en la que están basados algunos patrones migratorios africanos

baroque ornate style of art and architecture popular in the 1600s and 1700s (p. 551)

barroco estilo artístico y arquitectónico elaborado que se dio en los siglos XVII y XVIII

barter economy economic system in which one set of goods or services is exchanged for another (p. 42)

economía de trueque sistema económico en el que se utiliza el intercambio de mercancías o servicios

Bastille fortress in Paris used as a prison; French Revolution began when Parisians stormed it in 1789 (p. 577)

Bastilla fortificación en París usada como prisión; la Revolución Francesa empezó cuando los parisinos la asaltaron en 1789

Bataan Death March during World War II, the forced march of Filipino and American prisoners of war under brutal conditions by the Japanese military (p. 949)

Jornada de la Muerte desde Baatan episodio acaecido durante la Segunda Guerra Mundial, en el que prisioneros de guerra filipinos y estadounidenses fueron obligado a marchar bajo condiciones brutales por parte de militares japoneses

Battle of Tours battle in 732 in which the Christian Franks led by Charles Martel defeated Muslim armies and stopped the Muslim advance into Europe (pp. 215, 312)

Batalla de Tours batalla en 732 en la que los francos cristianos liderados por Charles Martel derrotaron al ejército musulmán y detuvieron el avance árabe en Europa

Bedouin a desert-dwelling Arab nomad (p. 304)

Beduino nómada árabe que vive en el desierto

Benedictine Rule rules drawn up in 530 by Benedict, a monk, regulating monastic life. The Rule emphasizes obedience, poverty, and chastity and divides the day into periods of worship, work, and study. (p. 227)

Regla Benedictina en 530, reglas establecidas por Benedicto, un monje, para regular la vida monástica. La Regla enfatizaba la obediencia, pobreza y castidad, y divide el día en períodos de adoración, trabajo y estudio.

Biafra region of southeastern Nigeria that launched a failed bid for independence from Nigeria in 1966, launching a bloody war (p. 1030)

Biafra región del sudeste de Nigeria que lanzó un fallido intento de independizarse de Nigeria en 1966, y por el que se desató una cruenta guerra

biotechnology the application of biological research to industry, engineering, and technology (p. 1124)

biotecnología la aplicación de investigaciones biológicas en la industria, la ingeniería y la tecnología

bishop high-ranking Church official with authority over a local area, or diocese (p. 171)

Obispo funcionario eclesiástico de alto nivel con autoridad sobre un área local o diócesis

Black Death an epidemic of the bubonic plague that ravaged Europe in the 1300s (p. 269)

Peste Negra epidemia de la peste bubónica que arrasó Europa en el siglo XIV

Black Shirt any member of the militant combat squads of Italian Fascists set up under Mussolini (p. 899)

Camisa Negra cualquier miembro de las escuadras militantes de combate de los fascistas italianos que estableció Mussolini

blitzkrieg lightning war (p. 930)

blitzkrieg guerra relámpago o guerra intensa y muy breve

bloc a group of nations acting together in support of one another (p. 1103)

bloque grupo de naciones que actúan conjuntamente en apoyo mutuo

Boer War (1899–1902) a war in which Great Britain defeated the Boers of South Africa (p. 758)

Guerra Boer (1899–1902) guerra en la que Gran Bretaña venció a los Boer de Sudáfrica

Boers Dutch people who settled in Cape Town, Africa, and eventually migrated inland (p. 455)

Boers holandeses establecidos en Ciudad del Cabo, África, que con el tiempo emigraron hacia el interior

bourgeoisie the middle class (p. 573)

burguesía clase media

Boxer Uprising anti-foreign movement in China from 1898–1900 (p. 776)

Rebelión Bóxer movimiento en contra de los extranjeros ocurrido en China de 1898 a 1900

boyar landowning noble in Russia under the tsars (p. 531)

boyar noble ruso que poseía tierras en la época de los zares (p. 531)

boycott refuse to buy (p. 866)

boicot negarse a comprar

brahman in the belief system established in Aryan India, the single spiritual power that resides in all things (p. 73)

brahman en el sistema de creencias establecido en la India aria, el único poder espiritual que reside en todas las cosas

bureaucracy system of government that includes different job functions and levels of authority (p. 45)

burocracia sistema de gobierno que incluye diferentes trabajos y niveles de autoridad

bushido code of conduct for samurai during the feudal period in Japan (p. 391)

bushido código de conducta de los samuráis durante el período feudal japonés

C

cabinet parliamentary advisors to the king who originally met in a small room, or "cabinet" (p. 522)

  gabinete miembros del parlamento consejeros del rey que originalmente se reunían en un pequeño cuarto o "gabinete"

cahier notebook used during the French Revolution to record grievances (p. 576)

  memorándum cuaderno usado durante la Revolución Francesa para anotar los agravios

Cahokia in Illinois, the largest earthwork of the Mississippian culture, c. A.D. 700 (p. 204)

  Cahokia en Illinois, el mayor terraplén de la cultura de los mississippianos, construido alrededor del 700 D.C.

calculus a branch of mathematics in which calculations are made using special symbolic notations; developed by Isaac Newton (p. 438)

  cálculo rama de las matemáticas en la que los cálculos se hacen con notaciones simbólicas especiales; fue desarrollado por Isaac Newton

caliph successor to Muhammad as political and religious leader of the Muslims (p. 310)

  califa sucesor de Mahoma como líder religiosoy político de los musulmanes

calligraphy the art of producing beautiful handwriting (pp. 100, 320)

  caligrafía arte de producir una bella escritura a mano

canon law body of laws of a church (p. 229)

  ley canónica serie de leyes de una iglesia

canonize recognize a person as a saint (p. 429)

  canonizar reconocer a una persona como santo

Cape Town seaport city and legislative capital of South Africa; first Dutch colony in Africa (p. 455)

  Ciudad del Cabo ciudad portuaria y capital legislativa de Sudáfrica; fue la primera colonia holandesa en África

capital money or wealth used to invest in business or enterprise (pp. 234, 613)

  capital dinero o bienes que se usan para invertir en negocios o empresas

capital offense crime punishable by death (p. 727)

  ofensa capital crimen que puede castigarse con la muerte

capitalism economic system in which the means of production are privately owned and operated for profit (p. 493)

  capitalismo sistema económico por el que los medios de producción son propiedad privada y se administran para obtener beneficios

cartel a group of companies that join together to control the production and price of a product (p. 666)

  cartel asociación de grandes corporaciones formada para controlar la producción y el precio de un producto

cartographer mapmaker (p. 447)

  cartógrafo persona que hace mapas

caste in traditional Indian society, an unchangeable social group into which a person is born (p. 78)

  casta grupo social en la sociedad tradicional de India, en el que una persona nace y del que no se puede cambiar

Çatalhüyük one of the world's first villages, established in modern-day Turkey around 7000 B.C. (p. 14)

  Çatalhüyük una de las primeras aldeas del mundo establecida en la Turquía actual alrededor del 7000 A.C.

cataract waterfall (pp. 45, 340)

  catarata cascada, caída de agua

caudillo military dictator in Latin America (p. 802)

  caudillo dictador militar en América Latina

celadon porcelain made in Korea with an unusual blue-green glaze (p. 385)

  celadon porcelana hecha en Korea con brillo azulverdoso poco común

censorship restriction on access to ideas and information (p. 551)

  censura restricción en el acceso a ideas o información

census population count (p. 159)

  censo recuento de la población

chancellor the highest official of a monarch, prime minister (pp. 693, 912)

  canciller oficial con más rango dentro de una monarquía, primer ministro

character written symbol in writing systems such as that of the Chinese (p. 100)

  carácter símbolo escrito en los sistemas de escritura como en el chino

charter in the Middle Ages, a written document that set out the rights and privileges of a town (p. 233)

  fuero en la Edad Media, documento escrito que establecía los derechos y privilegios de un pueblo

Chavín a culture that thrived in the Andean region from about 900 B.C. to 200 B.C. (p. 195)

  chavín cultura que tuvo su apogeo en la región andina, desde alrededor de 900 A.C. a 200 A.C.

Chechnya a republic within Russia where rebels have fought for independence (p. 1045)

  Chechenia república dentro del territorio ruso en la que grupos rebeldes luchan por su independencia

Cheka early Soviet secret police force (p. 844)
Cheka una de las primeras fuerzas policiales secretas soviética

chinampas in the Aztec empire, artificial islands used to cultivate crops and made of mud piled atop reed mats that were anchored to the lakebed with willow trees (p. 192)
chinampas en el imperio azteca, islas artificiales que se usaban para la agricultura y que estaban hechas de barro apilado sobre esteras de junco ancladas al fondo del lago con ramas de sauce

chivalry code of conduct for knights during the Middle Ages (p. 222)
caballería código de conducta para los caballeros durante la Edad Media

Choson dynasty Korean dynasty that ruled from 1392 to 1910, the longest-lived of Korea's three dynasties (p. 386)
dinastía Choson dinastía coreana que gobernó desde 1392 a 1910, la que más duró de las tres dinastías coreanas

circumnavigate to travel completely around the world (p. 451)
circunnavegar viajar alrededor del mundo

citizen a native or resident of a town or city (p. 119)
ciudadano nativo o residente de un pueblo o ciudad

city-state a political unit that includes a city and its surrounding lands and villages (p. 23)
ciudad estado unidad polítca compuesta por una diudad y las tierras que la rodean

civil disobedience the refusal to obey unjust laws (p. 866)
desobediencia civil negarse a obedecer leyes injustas

civil law branch of law that deals with private rights and matters (p. 37)
derecho civil cuerpo legal que trata de los derechos y asuntos privados de los individuos

civil servant government official (p. 104)
funcionario público oficial del gobierno

civil war war fought between two groups of people in the same nation (p. 475)
guerra civil guerra en la que luchan dos grupos de personas de una misma nación

civilization a complex, highly organized social order (p. 19)
civilización orden social complejo y altamente organizado

clan group of families with a common ancestor (p. 94)

clan grupo de familias con un antepasado en común

clergy the body of people who conduct Christian services (p. 171)
clero grupo de gente que oficia en los servicios religiosos cristianos

coalition temporary alliance of various political parties (p. 736)
coalición alianza temporal de varios partidos políticos

codify to arrange or set down in writing (p. 37)
codificar organizar o establecer por escrito

Cold War state of tension and hostility between nations aligned with the United States on one side and the Soviet Union on the other that rarely led to direct armed conflict (p. 954)
Guerra Fría estado de tensión y hostilidad entre las naciones alineadas con Estados Unidos, por una parte, y con la Unión Soviética, por la otra, que salvo raras excepciones desembocó en un conflicto armado

collective large farm owned and operated by peasants as a group (p. 905)
granja colectiva granja grande que pertenece a campesinos que la administran en grupo

collective security system in which a group of nations acts as one to preserve the peace of all (p. 836)
seguridad colectiva sistema por el que un grupo de naciones actúa como una para preservar la paz común

collectivization the forced joining together of workers and property into collectives, such as rural collectives that absorb peasants and their land (p. 986)
colectivización unión forzada de trabajadores y propiedad en colectivos, como colectivos rurales que absorben a campesinos y sus tierras

colony territory settled and ruled by people from another land (p. 43)
colonia territorio poblado y gobernado por personas de otro lugar

colossus giant (p. 710)
coloso gigante

Columbian Exchange the global exchange of goods, ideas, plants and animals, and disease that began with Columbus' exploration of the Americas (p. 491)
Intercambio colombino intercambio global de bienes, ideas, plantas, animales y enfermedades que comenzaron con la exploración de las Américas por parte de Colón

comedy in ancient Greece, play that mocked people or social customs (p. 135)

comedia en la antigua Grecia, obra de teatro donde se hacía burla de personas o costumbres

Comintern Communist International, international association of communist parties led by the Soviet Union for the purpose of encouraging worldwide communist revolution (p. 911)

Comintern Internacional Comunista, asociación internacional de partidos comunistas liderada por la Unión Soviética con el propósito de extender por el mundo una revolución comunista

command economy system in which government officials make all basic economic decisions (p. 905)

economía controlada sistema en el que los funcionarios del gobierno toman todas las decisiones económicas básicas

commissar Communist party officials assigned to the army to teach party principles and ensure party loyalty during the Russian Revolution (p. 844)

comisario funcionario del partido comunista asignado al ejército para enseñar los principios del partido y para asegurar la lealtad al mismo durante la revolución rusa

commodity valuable product (p. 347)

mercancía producto valioso

common law a legal system based on custom and court rulings (p. 245)

derecho consuetudinario sistema legal basado en la costumbre y en las sentencias de los tribunales

communism form of socialism advocated by Karl Marx; according to Marx, class struggle was inevitable and would lead to the creation of a classless society in which all wealth and property would be owned by the community as a whole (p. 625)

comunismo forma de socialismo defendido por Karl Marx; según Marx, la lucha de clases era inevitable y llevaría a la creación de una sociedad sin clases en la que toda la riqueza y la propiedad pertenecería a la comunidad como un todo

compact an agreement among people (p. 484)

pacto acuerdo

compromise an agreement in which each side makes concessions; an acceptable middle ground (p. 430)

compromiso acuerdo en el que cada parte hace concesiones; un término medio aceptable

concentration camp detention center for civilians considered enemies of the state (p. 935)

campo de concentración centro de detención de los civiles que se considera enemigos del estado

Concert of Europe a system in which Austria, Russia, Prussia, and Great Britain met periodically to discuss any problems affecting the peace in Europe; resulted from the post-Napoleon era Quadruple Alliance (p. 600)

Concierto de Europa sistema por el cual Austria, Rusia, Prusia y Gran Bretaña se reunían periódicamente para discutir cualquier problema que afectara a la paz en Europa; resultado de la Cuádruple Alianza de la era postnapoleónica

concession special economic rights given to a foreign power (p. 766)

concesión derechos económicos especiales que se dan a un poder extranjero

confederation unification (p. 797)

confederación unificación

Congress of Vienna assembly of European leaders that met after the Napoleonic era to piece Europe back together; met from September 1814 to June 1815 (p. 599)

Congreso de Viena asamblea de líderes europeos que se reunió después de la era napoleónica para reconstruir Europa; se reunieron desde septiembre de 1814 a junio de 1815

conquistador Spanish explorers who claimed lands in the Americas for Spain in the 1500s and 1600s (p. 472)

conquistador los exploradores españoles que apropiaron tierras en América para España en los siglos XVI y XVII

conscription "the draft," which required all young men to be ready for military or other service (p. 829)

conscripción llamado a filas que exigía que todos los hombres jóvenes estuvieran listos para el servicio militar u otro servicio

consensus general agreement (p. 359)

consenso acuerdo general

Constantinople the capital of the eastern Roman empire; capital of the Byzantine and Ottoman empires, now called Istanbul (pp. 174, 282)

Constantinopla capital del Imperio Romano Oriental; capital de los imperios bizantino y otomano, en la actualidad llamada Estambul

constitutional government government whose power is defined and limited by law (p. 522)

gobierno constitucional gobierno cuyo poder está definido y limitado por las leyes

consul in ancient Rome, official from the patrician class who supervised the government and commanded the armies (p. 152)

cónsul funcionario de la clase patricia que en la Roma antigua supervisaba el gobierno y dirigía los ejércitos

containment the U.S. strategy of keeping communism within its existing boundaries and preventing its further expansion (p. 973)

contención estrategia de Estados Unidos de mantener el comunismo dentro de sus fronteras existentes y de prevenir su expansión

Continental System blockade designed by Napoleon to hurt Britain economically by closing European ports to British goods; ultimately unsuccessful (p. 594)

sistema continental bloqueo diseñado por Napoleón para dañar a Gran Bretaña económicamente que consistía en cerrar los puertos europeos a los productos británicos; con el tiempo no tuvo éxito

contraband during wartime, military supplies and raw materials needed to make military supplies that may legally be confiscated by any belligerent (p. 830)

contrabando durante el tiempo de guerra, provisiones militares y materias primas necesarios para fabricar artículos militares, y que pueden ser confiscados legalmente por cualquiera de las partes beligerantes

contras guerrillas who fought the Sandinistas in Nicaragua (p. 1086)

contras grupo guerrillero que luchó contra los sandinistas en Nicaragua

convoy group of merchant ships protected by warships (p. 825)

convoy grupo de barcos mercantes protegidos por barcos de guerra

corporation business owned by many investors who buy shares of stock and risk only the amount of their investment (p. 665)

corporación empresa propiedad de muchos inversores que compran acciones y que sólo arriesgan el monto de su inversión

Council of Trent a group of Catholic leaders that met between 1545 and 1563 to respond to Protestant challenges and direct the future of the Catholic Church (p. 431)

Concilio de Trento grupo de líderes católicos que se reunieron entre 1545 y 1563 para tratar los retos protestantes y liderar el futuro de la Iglesia Católica

coup d'état the forcible overthrow of a government (p. 1025)

golpe de estado derrocamiento por la fuerza de un gobierno

covenant a binding agreement; specifically, in the Jewish tradition, the binding agreement God made with Abraham (p. 58)

convenio acuerdo vinculante; específicamente, en la tradición judía, el acuerdo vinculante hecho entre Dios y Abraham

creole person in Spain's colonies in the Americas who was an American-born descendent of Spanish settlers (pp. 480, 645)

criollo descendiente de colonos españolas nacido en las colonias españolas de América

Crimean War war fought mainly on the Crimean Peninsula between the Russians and the British, French, and Turks from 1853–1856 (p. 711)

Guerra de Crimea guerra librada principalmente en la península de Crimea entre los rusos y los británicos, franceses y turcos entre 1853 y 1856

criminal law branch of law that deals with offenses against others (p. 37)

derecho penal rama de la ley que se ocupa de los delitos contra otros

Crusades a series of wars from the 1000s through 1200s in which European Christians tried to win control of the Holy Land from Muslims (p. 255)

Cruzadas serie de guerras entre el siglo XI y el siglo XIII en las que los cristianos europeos intentaron ganar el control sobre los musulmanes de la Tierra Santa

cult of domesticity idealization of women and the home (p. 675)

culto a lo doméstico idealización de las mujeres y del hogar

cultural diffusion the spread of ideas, customs, and technologies from one people to another (p. 23)

difusión cultural divulgación de ideas, costumbres y tecnología de un pueblo a otro

cultural nationalism pride in the culture of one's country (p. 856)

nacionalismo cultural orgullo de la cultura del país propio

Cultural Revolution a Chinese Communist program in the late 1960s to purge China of nonrevolutionary tendencies that caused economic and social damage (p. 986)

Revolución Cultural programa de la China comunista a finales de la década de 1960 que pretendía eliminar de China todas las tendencias no revolucionarias y que causó daños económicos y sociales

culture the way of life of a society, which is handed down from one generation to the next by learning and experience (p. 5)

cultura forma de vida de una sociedad que se pasa de una generación a la siguiente mediante el aprendizaje y la experiencia

cuneiform in the ancient Middle East, a system of writing that used wedge-shaped marks (p. 33)
  cuneiforme en el antiguo Oriente Medio, sistema de escritura cuyos caracteres tenían forma de cuña

Cuzco capital city of the Inca empire (p. 197)
  Cuzco capital del imperio Inca

Cyrillic relating to the Slavic alphabet derived from the Greek and traditionally attributed to St. Cyril; in modified form still used in modern Slavic languages (p. 290)
  cirílico relativo al alfabeto eslavo, derivado del griego y tradicionalmente atribuido a San Cirilo; todavía en uso, de forma modificada, en las lenguas eslavas modernas

D

dada artistic movement in which artists rejected tradition and produced works that often shocked their viewers (p. 889)
  dadaísmo movimiento artístico en el que los artistas rechazaban la tradición y producían obras que a menudo sorprendían a su público

dalits outcastes or members of India's lowest caste (pp. 72, 1016, 1080)
  dalits (o intocables) los marginados o miembros de las castas más bajas de India

Dardanelles vital strait connecting the Black Sea and the Mediterranean Sea in present-day Turkey (p. 826)
  Dardanelos estrecho de vital importancia que conecta el Mar Negro y el Mar Mediterráneo en la actual Turquía

Darfur a region in western Sudan where ethnic conflict threatened to lead to genocide (p. 1052)
  Darfur región occidental de Sudán donde un conflicto étnico amenaza con provocar un genocidio

D-Day code name for June 6, 1944, the day that Allied forces invaded France during WWII (p. 944)
  Día D nombre en clave del día en que las fuerzas aliadas invadieron Francia durante la Segunda Guerra Mundial (6 de junio de 1944)

decimal system system of numbers based on 10 (p. 88)
  sistema de decimal sistema numérico basado en el número 10

decipher to figure out the meaning of (p. 55)
  descrifrar descubrir el significado de algo

default fail to make payments (p. 1098)
  cese de pagos imposibilidad de realizar pagos

deficit gap between what a government spends and what it takes in through taxes and other sources (p. 1098)
  déficit diferencia entre los gastos de un gobierno y las recaudaciones por impuestos y otras fuentes de ingresos

deficit spending situation in which a government spends more money than it takes in (p. 575)
  gasto deficitario situación en la que un gobierno gasta más de lo que recauda

deforestation the destruction of forest land (pp. 770, 1112)
  deforestación destrucción de tierras forestales

Delhi the third-largest city in India; capital of medieval India (p. 324)
  Delhi tercera ciudad más grande de India; capital de la India medieval

delta triangular area of marshland formed by deposits of silt at the mouth of some rivers (p. 45)
  delta área triangular de tierra pantanosa que se forma con los depósitos de limo en la desembocadura de algunos ríos

demilitarized zone a thin band of territory across the Korean peninsula separating North Korean forces from South Korean forces; established by the armistice of 1953 (p. 990)
  zona desmilitarizada estrecha franja de tierra que cruza la península de Corea y que separa las fuerzas de Corea del Norte y las fuerzas de Corea del Sur; establecida por el armisticio de 1953

democracy government in which the people hold ruling power (p. 121)
  democracia forma de gobierno en el que la soberanía reside en el pueblo

depopulation reduction in the number of people in an area (p. 527)
  despoblación reducción del número de la población en una zona

desertification process by which fertile or semi-desert land becomes desert (pp. 341, 1073)
  desertización proceso por el que la tierra fértil o semifértil se convierte en desierto

détente the relaxation of Cold War tensions during the 1970s (p. 968)
  distensión relajamiento de las tensiones de la Guerra Fría en los años 70

developing world nations working toward development in Africa, Asia, and Latin America (p. 1066)

mundo en desarrollo países en vías de desarrollo de á frica, Asia y Latinoamérica

development the process of building stable governments, improving agriculture and industry, and raising the standard of living (p. 1066)

desarrollo proceso de establecer gobiernos estables, mejorar la agricultura, la industria y las condiciones de vida

dharma in Hindu belief, a person's religious and moral duties (p. 77)

dharma según la creencia hindú, las obligaciones morales y religiosas de un individuo

Diaspora the spreading of the Jews beyond their historic homeland (p. 60)

Diáspora diseminación de los judíos más allá de su patria histórica

dictator ruler who has complete control over a government; in ancient Rome, a leader appointed to rule for six months in times of emergency (p. 152)

dictador dirigente con control absolute sobre el gobierno; en la antigua Roma, líder designado para gobernar durante seis meses en casos de emergencia

Dienbienphu small town and former French army base in northern Vietnam; site of the battle that ended in a Vietnamese victory, the French withdrawal from Vietnam, and the securing of North Vietnam's independence (p. 993)

Dienbienphu pequeño pueblo y antigua base del ejército francés en el norte de Vietnam; lugar de la batalla que terminó con la victoria vietnamita, la expulsión de los franceses de Vietnam y la obtención de la independencia de Vietnam del Norte

diet assembly or legislature (pp. 296, 425, 787)

dieta asamblea o cuerpo legislativo

direct democracy system of government in which citizens participate directly in the day-to-day affairs of government rather than through elected representatives (p. 126)

democracia directa sistema de gobierno en el que los ciudadanos participan directamente en lugar de hacerlo a través de representantes electos en los asuntos diarios del gobierno

disarmament reduction of armed forces and weapons (p. 893)

desarme reducción del ejército y del armamento

discrimination unequal treatment or barriers (p. 978)

discriminación tratamiento desigual o barreras

dissent ideas that oppose those of the government (p. 84)

disentir ideas que se oponen a las del gobierno

dissenter Protestant whose views and opinions differed from those of the Church of England (p. 517)

disidente protestante cuyos puntos de vista y opiniones diferían de los de la Iglesia de Inglaterra

divine right belief that a ruler's authority comes directly from God (p. 506)

derecho divino creencia de que la autoridad de un gobernante proviene directamente de Dios

domesticate to tame animals and adapt crops so they are best suited to use by humans (p. 13)

domesticar domar animales y adaptar plantas con el propósito de adecuarlos para el uso humano

dominion self-governing nation (p. 797)

dominio nación que se gobierna a sí misma

domino theory the belief that a communist victory in South Vietnam would cause noncommunist governments across Southeast Asia to fall to communism, like a row of dominoes (p. 993)

teoría del dominó creencia de que una victoria comunista en Vietnam del Sur podría causar que los gobiernos no comunistas del sudeste de Asia cayeran bajo dominio del comunismo, como una fila de fichas de dominó

dowry in some societies, payment a bride's family makes to the bridegroom and his family; payment a woman brings to a marriage (pp. 89, 372)

dote en algunas sociedades, pago de la familia de la novia al novio y a su familia; pago que una mujer proporciona a sumatrimonio

Dreyfus affair a political scandal that caused deep divisions in France between Royalists and liberals and republicans; centered on the 1894 wrongful conviction of Alfred Dreyfus, a Jewish officer in the French army (p. 737)

Caso Dreyfus escándalo político que causó divisiones profundas en Francia entre los realistas, liberales y republicanos; basado en la in justa condena en 1894 de Alfred Dreyfus, un oficial judío del ejérci to francés

Dual Monarchy the monarchy of Austria-Hungary (p. 706)

monarquía dual monarquía de Austria-Hungría

due process of law the requirement that the government act fairly and in accordance with established rules in all that it does (p. 246)

garantías procesales debidas requisito para que el gobierno actúe justamente y en concordancia con las normas establecidas en todo lo que hace

Duma elected national legislature in Russia (p. 715)
　Duma en Rusia, asamblea legislative nacional electa

Dunkirk port in France from which 300,000 Allied troops were evacuated when their retreat by land was cut off by the German advance in 1940 (p. 931)
　Dunkirk puerto de Francia desde donde fueron evacuadas 300,000 tropas aliadas en 1940 al ser bloqueada su retirada terrestre por el avance del ejército alemán

Dutch East India Company a trading company established by the Netherlands in 1602 to protect and expand its trade in Asia (p. 458)
　Compañía Holandesa de las Indias Orientales compañía de comercio establecida por Holanda en 1602 para proteger y aumentar su comercio con Asia

dynamo a machine used to generate electricity (p. 663)
　dínamo máquina que se usa para generar electricidad

dynastic cycle rise and fall of Chinese dynasties according to the Mandate of Heaven (p. 95)
　ciclo dínastico florecimiento y caída de las dinastías chinas de acuerdo con el Mandato del Cielo

dynasty ruling family (p. 45)
　dinastía familia gobernante

E

earthwork an embankment or other construction made of earth (p. 203)
　terraplén muro de contención u otra construcción hecha de tierra

East Timor a former Portuguese colony, seized by Indonesia, that gained independence in 2002 (p. 1021)
　Timor Oriental antigua colonia portuguesa, ocupada por Indonesia, que obtuvo su independencia en 2002

economic nationalism an emphasis on domestic control and protection of the economy (p. 855)
　nacionalismo económico énfasis en el control nacional y en la protección de la economía

Edict of Nantes law issued by French king Henry IV in 1598 giving more religious freedom to French Protestants (p. 510)
　Edicto de Nantes ley promulgada por el rey francés Enrique IV en 1598 por la que se concedía mayor libertad religiosa a los protestantes frances (p. 510)

Eightfold Path as taught by the Buddha, the path one must follow to achieve nirvana (p. 80)
　Óctuple Sendero como enseñó Buda, el camino que debe seguir todo individuo para conseguir el nirvana

elector one of seven German princes who would choose the Holy Roman emperor (p. 525)
　elector uno de los siete príncipes germanos que elegían al emperador del Sacro Romano

electorate body of people allowed to vote (p. 723)
　electorado conjunto de personas a quienes se permite votar

elite upper class (p. 760)
　élite clase alta

emancipation granting of freedom to serfs or slaves (p. 711)
　emancipación concesión de libertad a esclavos o siervos

emigration movement away from one's homeland (p. 704)
　emigración trasladarse de su propio país a otro

émigré person who flees his or her country for political reasons (p. 582)
　exiliado persona que deja su país por razones políticas

empire a group of states or territories controlled by one ruler (p. 23)
　imperio grupo de estados o territorios controlados por un gobernante

enclosure the process of taking over and consolidating land formerly shared by peasant farmers (p. 610)
　cercamiento proceso de consolidar y apropiarse de una tierra que anteriormente compartían campesinos

encomienda right the Spanish government granted to its American colonists to demand labor or tribute from Native Americans (p. 478)
　encomienda derecho a exigir tributo o trabajo a los natives americanos, que el gobierno español otorgó a sus colonos en América

endangered species species threatened with extinction (p. 1074)
　especies en vías de extinción especies amenazadas de extinción, es decir, de desaparición

engineering application of science and mathematics to develop useful structures and machines (p. 164)
　ingeniería aplicación de las ciencias y matemáticas al desarrollo do máquinas y estructuras útiles

English Bill of Rights series of acts passed by the English Parliament in 1689 that limited the rights of the monarchy and ensured the superiority of Parliament (p. 521)

Declaración de derechos de los ingleses serie de leyes aprobadas por el parlamento inglés en 1689 que limitaba los derechos de la monarquía y establecía la primacía del parlamento

engraving art form in which an artist etches a design on a metal plate with acid and then uses the plate to make multiple prints (p. 419)

grabado forma de arte en la que un artista graba un diseño con ácido en una placa de metal y después la usa para producir múltiples impresiones

enlightened despot absolute ruler who used his or her power to bring about political and social change (p. 553)

déspota ilustrado gobernante absoluto que usa su poder para precipitar cambios políticos y sociales

entente nonbinding agreement to follow common policies (p. 817)

entendimiento acuerdo no vinculante de seguir normas comunes

enterprise a business organization in such areas as shipping, mining, railroads, or factories (p. 613)

empresa entidad empresarial en áreas como transportes, minería, ferrocariles o fábricas

entrepreneur person who assumes financial risk in the hope of making a profit (pp. 493, 613)

empresario persona que asume riesgos financieros con la esperanza de obtener beneficios

Epic of Gilgamesh Mesopotamian narrative poem that was first told in Sumer (p. 30)

El poema de Gilgamesh poema narrativo de Mesopotamia que se contó por primera vez en Sumeria

epidemic outbreak of a rapidly spreading disease (pp. 269, 1108)

epidemia brote de una enfermedad que se extiende rápidamente

erosion the wearing away of land (p. 1113)

erosión el desgaste paulatino de la tierra

estate social class (p. 572)

estado clase social

Estates-General legislative body made up of representatives of the three estates in pre-revolutionary France (p. 575)

Estados Generales cuerpo legislativo formado por representantes de los tres estados en la Francia prerevolucionaria

ethics moral standards of behavior (p. 60)

ética estándar moral de conducta

Ethiopia ancient Greek term for Axumite kingdom; present-day country in East Africa (p. 353)

Etiopía antiguo término griego para el reino de Axumite; también es un país actual del este de África

ethnic cleansing the killing or forcible removal of people of different ethnicities from an area by aggressors so that only the ethnic group of the aggressors remains (p. 1046)

limpieza étnica la matanza o expulsión forzosa de personas de diferentes grupos étnicos de una zona, llevadas a cabo por agresores para que su grupo étnico tenga permanencia exclusiva

ethnic group large group of people who share the same language and cultural heritage (p. 295)

étnico grupo grande de personas que comparten el idioma y la herencia cultural

Etruscans a people who inhabited early Italy (p. 151)

estrucos pueblo que habitaba principalmente al norte the Roma

euro common currency used by member nations of the European Union (p. 1097)

euro moneda común usada por las naciones que pertenecen a la Unión Europea

European Community an international organization dedicated to establishing free trade among its European member nations (p. 982)

Comunidad Europea organización internacional dedicada a establecer un comercio libre entre sus naciones europeas miembros de todos los productos

European Union an international organization made up of over two dozen European nations, with a common currency and common policies and laws (p. 1097)

Unión Europea organización internacional compuesta por más de dos docenas de países, con una misma moneda, y políticas y leyes en común

excommunication exclusion from the Roman Catholic Church as a penalty for refusing to obey Church law (p. 229)

excomunión exclusión de la Iglesia Católica Romana como castigo por rehusar obedecer la ley de la Iglesia

expansionism policy of increasing the amount of territory a government holds (pp. 104, 739)

expansionismo política de aumentar el territorio que posee un gobierno

extraterritoriality right of foreigners to be protected by the laws of their own nation (p. 774)
extraterritorialidad derecho de los extranjeros a recibir protección de las leyes de su propio país

F

faction dissenting group of people (p. 579)
facción grupo de disidentes

famine a severe shortage of food in which large numbers of people starve (p. 1108)
hambruna escasez severa de alimentos por la que perece gran número de personas

fascism any centralized, authoritarian government system that is not communist whose policies glorify the state over the individual and are destructive to basic human rights (p. 901)
fascismo cualquier sistema de gobierno autoritario centralizado no comunista cuya política glorifica al estado or encima del individuo y que destruye los derecho humanos fundamentales

federal republic government in which power is divided between the national, or federal, government and the states (p. 563)
república federal gobierno en el que el poder se divide entre el gobierno nacional o federal y los estados

Federal Reserve central banking system of the United States, which regulates banks (p. 895)
Reserva Federal sistema central de banca de Estados Unidos que regula los bancos

Fertile Crescent region of the Middle East in which civilizations first arose (p. 30)
Medialuna Fértil región de Oriente Medio en la cual surgieron las primeras civilizaciones

feudal contract exchange of pledges between lords and vassals (p. 219)
contrato feudal intercambio de garantías entre los señores y los vasallos

feudalism loosely organized system of government in which local lords governed their own lands but owed military service and other support to a greater lord (pp. 95, 219)
feudalismo sistema de gobierno poco organizado en el que los señores goberna ban sus propias tierras, pero debían servicio militar y otras formas de apoyo a un superior

fief in medieval Europe, an estate granted by a lord to a vassal in exchange for service and loyalty (p. 219)
estado feudal durante la Edad Media, terreno que un señor cedía a un vasallo a cambio de servicio y lealtad

filial piety respect for parents (p. 97)
piedad filial respeto hacia los padres

finance the management of money matters including the circulation of money, loans, investments, and banking (p. 895)
finanzas o gestión de los asuntos monetarios incluyendo la circulación de dinero, préstamos, inversiones y banca

First Sino-Japanese War conflict between China and Japan in 1894–1895 over control of Korea (p. 789)
Primera guerra sino-japonesa conflicto entre China y Japón de 1894 a 1895 por el control de Corea

Flanders a region that included parts of present-day northern France, Belgium, and the Netherlands; was an important industrial and financial center of northern Europe during the Middle Ages and Renaissance (p. 419)
Flandes región que incluye partes de los actuales norte de Francia, Bélgica y Holanda; fue un importante centro industrial y financiero del norte de Europa durante la Edad Media y el Renacimiento

flapper in the United States and Europe in the 1920s, a rebellious young woman (p. 885)
flapper mujer joven y rebelde en los años 20 en Estados Unidos y Europa

Florence a city in the Tuscany region of northern Italy that was the center of the Italian Renaissance (p. 412)
Florencia ciudad de la región de Toscana en el norte de Italia que fue el centro del Renacimiento italiano

flying buttresses stone supports on the outside of a building that allowed builders to construct higher, thinner walls that contained large stained-glass windows (p. 266)
contrafuertes flotantes soportes de piedra en la parte exterior de un edificio que permitía a los constructores construir paredes más finas y más altas que contenían ventanas con vidrieras

Four Noble Truths as taught by the Buddha, the four basic beliefs that form the foundation of Buddhism (p. 80)
Cuatro Verdades Nobles como enseñó Buda, las cuatro creencias básicas que forman la base del budismo

Fourteen Points list of terms for resolving WWI and future wars outlined by American President Woodrow Wilson in January 1918 (p. 833)
Catorce puntos lista de condiciones para resolver la Primera Guerra Mundial y futuras

guerras, esbozada por el presidente estadounidense Woodrow Wilson en enero de 1918

Franks a Germanic tribe that conquered present-
day France and neighboring lands in the 400s
(p. 215)

francos tribu germánica que conquistó la actual
Francia y las tierras colindantes en el siglo V

free trade trade between countries without
quotas, tariffs, or other restrictions (p. 726)

libre comercio comercio entre países, sin cuo-
tas, tasas u otras restricciones

French and Indian War war between Britain
and France in the Americas that happened from
1754 to 1763; it was part of a global war called
the Seven Years' War (p. 486)

Guerra franco-india guerra entre Gran
Bretaña y Francia en América, que duró desde
1754 a 1763; fue parte de una guerra global que
se conoció como la Guerra de los Siete Años

French Indochina Western name for the colonial
holdings of France on mainland Southeast Asia;
present-day Vietnam, Laos, and Cambodia (p. 792)

Indochina francesa nombre occidental para
las colonias de Francia en el sudeste asiático
continental

fresco colorful painting completed on wet plaster
(p. 115)

fresco pintura colorida realizada sobre una
pared de yeso húmedo

friar a medieval European monk who traveled
from place to place preaching to the poor (p. 229)

fraile monje de la Europa medieval que viajaba
de un lugar a otro predicando a los pobres

fundamentalists religious leaders who call for a
return to what they see as the fundamental, or
basic, values of their faiths (p. 1070)

fundamentalistas líderes religiosos que abogan
por el retorno de lo que consideran ser los valores
fundamentales, o básicos, de sus creencias

G

general strike strike by workers in many different industries at the same time (p. 894)

huelga general huelga de trabajadores de mu-
chas industrias diferentes al mismo tiempo

genetic engineering manipulation of living organisms' chemical code in order to produce specific results (p. 1125)

ingeniería genética alteración del código gené-
tico que portan todas las formas de vida con el fin
de producir resultados específicos

genetics a branch of biology dealing with heredity
and variations among plants and animals (p. 1125)

genética rama de la biología que trata sobre la
herencia y las variaciones entre sí de los animales y las plantas

Geneva Swiss city-state which became a Calvinist
theocracy in the 1500s; today a major city in
Switzerland (p. 427)

Ginebra ciudad estado suiza que se convirtió en
una teocracia calvinista en el siglo XVI; en la actualidad es una de las principales ciudades de
Suiza

genocide deliberate attempt to destroy an entire
religious or ethnic group (p. 764)

genocidio intento deliberado de destruir la to-
talidad de un grupo religioso o étnico

gentry wealthy, landowning class (p. 371)

alta burguesía clase social rica, dueña de
tierras

germ theory the theory that infectious diseases
are caused by certain microbes (p. 667)

teoría de los gérmenes teoría de que las enfermedades infecciosas son causadas por ciertos
microbios

Gestapo secret police in Nazi Germany (p. 915)

Gestapo policía secreta de la Alemania nazi

Ghana early West African trading kingdom located
in parts of present-day Mauritania and Mali
(p. 347)

Ghana antiguo reino comerciante de África occidental ubicado en partes de la actual Mauritania
y Mali

ghetto separate section of a city where members
of a minority group are forced to live (p. 433)

gueto área separada de una ciudad donde se fuerza a vivir a los miembros de una minoría

glasnost "openness" in Russian; a Soviet policy of
greater freedom of expression introduced by
Mikhail Gorbachev in the late 1980s (p. 1002)

glasnost "apertura" en ruso; política soviética de
mayor libertad de expresión introducida por
Mikhail Gorbachev a finales de la década de 1980

global warming the rise of Earth's surface temperature over time (p. 1113)

calentamiento global el aumento de la tem-
peratura de la superficie terrestre a través del
tiempo

globalization the process by which national economies, politics, cultures, and societies become integrated with those of other nations around the
world (p. 1100)

globalización proceso mediante el cual las
economías nacionales, la política, la cultura y la

sociedades se integran con las de otros países del mundo

Goa a state in western India; formerly a coastal city that was made the base of Portugal's Indian trade (p. 457)

Goa estado en el oeste de India; antiguamente una ciudad costera que se convirtió en la base del comercio en la India de Portugal

golden age period of great cultural achievement (p. 86)

edad de oro período de grandes logros culturales

Golden Bull of 1222 charter that strictly limited royal power in Hungary (p. 297)

Bula de Oro de 1222 carta constitucional que limitaba rigurosamente el poder de la realeza en Hungría

Golden Horde the Mongol armies that invaded Europe in 1237 and ruled Russia for over two centuries (p. 291)

Horda Dorada los ejércitos mongoles que invadieron Europa en 1237 y que gobernaron Rusia durante más de dos siglos

Golden Temple the Sikh religion's holiest shrine (p. 1017)

Templo Dorado santuario de mayor peso sagrado de la religión sikh

Good Friday Agreement an agreement to end the conflict in Northern Ireland signed in 1998 by Protestants and Catholics (p. 1045)

Acuerdo del Viernes Santo acuerdo firmado por protestantes y católicos en 1998 para poner fin al conflicto en Irlanda del Norte

Good Neighbor Policy policy in which American President Franklin Roosevelt promised that the United States would interfere less in Latin American affairs (p. 856)

Política del Buen Vecino politica con la que el presidente estadounidense Franklin Roosevelt prometio que Estados Unidos interferiria menos en los asuntos de America Latina

Gothic style type of European architecture that developed in the Middle Ages, characterized by flying buttresses, ribbed vaulting, thin walls, and high roofs (p. 266)

estilo gótico tipo de arquitectura europea que se desarrolló en la Edad Media caracterizada por contrafuertes flotantes, bóvedas estriadas, paredes finas y techos altos

gravity force that pulls objects in Earth's sphere to the center of Earth (p. 438)

gravedad fuerza que atrae los objetos dentro de la esfera terrestre al centro de la Tierra

Great Depression a painful time of global economic collapse, starting in 1929 and lasting until about 1939 (p. 895)

Gran Depresión período nefasto de colapso de la economía mundial que empezó en 1929 y duró hasta 1939

Great Leap Forward a Chinese Communist program from 1958 to 1960 to boost farm and industrial output that failed miserably (p. 986)

Gran Salto hacia Adelante programa de la China comunista de 1958 a 1960 para aumentar la producción agrícola e industrial que fracasó miserablemente

Great Schism the official split between the Roman Catholic and Byzantine churches that occurred in 1054 (p. 286)

Gran Cisma división oficial entre las iglesias católica romana y bizantina ocurrida en 1054

Great Zimbabwe powerful East African medieval trade center and city-state located in southeastern present-day Zimbabwe (p. 356)

Gran Zimbabwe poderoso centro de comercio medieval de África oriental y ciudad estado ubicada en el sureste del actual Zimbabwe

Green Revolution the improved seeds, pesticides, mechanical equipment, and farming methods introduced in the developing world beginning in the 1950s (p. 1068)

revolución verde la introducción, en los países en vías de desarrollo durante la década de 1950, de semillas, pesticidas, equipo mecánico y métodos de agricultura perfeccionados

griot professional storyteller in early West Africa (p. 361)

griot antiguo narrador de historias profesional en África occidental

gross domestic product (GDP) the total value of all goods and services produced in a nation within a particular year (p. 984)

producto interior bruto (PIB) valor total de todos los productos y servicios producidos en una nación en un determinado año

Guangzhou a coastal city in southeastern China, also known as Canton (p. 461)

Guangzhou ciudad costera del sudeste de China, también conocida como Cantón

guerrilla a soldier in a loosely organized force making surprise raids (p. 992)

guerrilla pequeños grupos de soldados pertenecientes a una fuerza poco organizada que despliega ataques por sorpresa

guerrilla warfare fighting carried on through hit-and-run raids (p. 597)
guerra de guerrillas lucha que se caracteriza por rápidos ataques y retiradas

guild in the Middle Ages, an association of merchants or artisans who cooperated to uphold standards of their trade and to protect their economic interests (p. 235)
gremio en la Edad Media, asociación de mercaderes o artesanos que cooperaban para mantener los valores de sus oficios y para proteger sus intereses económicos

guillotine device used during the Reign of Terror to execute thousands by beheading (p. 588)
guillotina aparato usado durante el Reinado del Terror para decapitar a miles de personas

Gulag in the Soviet Union, a system of forced labor camps in which millions of criminals and political prisoners were held under Stalin (p. 906)
Gulag en la Unión Soviética, un sistema de campos de trabajo forzado donde millones de criminales y prisioneros políticos fueron detenidos durante el gobierno de Stalin

Guomindang Nationalist party; active in China 1912 to 1949 (p. 870)
Guomindang partido nacionalista, activo en China entre 1912 y 1949

habeas corpus principle that a person cannot be held in prison without first being charged with a specific crime (p. 247)
habeus corpus principio por el que no puede encarcelarse a una persona sin haber sido antes acusada formalmente de un delito específico

hacienda a large plantation (p. 852)
hacienda plantación grande

hajj one of the Five Pillars of Islam, the pilgrimage to Mecca that all Muslims are expected to make at least once in their lifetime (p. 306)
hayyi uno de los Cinco Pilares del Islam, la peregrinación a la Meca que se espera hagan todos los musulmanes por lo menos una vez en la vida

hangul alphabet that uses symbols to represent the sounds of spoken Korean (p. 386)
hangul alfabeto que usa símbolos para representar gráficamente los sonidos del idioma coreano

Hapsburg empire Central European empire that lasted from the 1400s to the 1900s and at its height included the lands of the Holy Roman Empire and the Netherlands (p. 504)

Imperio Habsburgo imperio centroeuropeo que duró desde el siglo XV hasta el siglo XX, y que en su plenitud abarcó los territorios del Sacro Imperio Romano y Holanda

Harappa large ancient city of the Indus civilization, located in present-day Pakistan (p. 70)
Harappa antigua gran ciudad de la civilización del Indo, ubicada en el presente Pakistán

Harlem Renaissance an African American cultural movement in the 1920s and 1930s, centered in Harlem (p. 887)
Renacimiento de Harlem movimiento cultural afroamericano durante las décadas de 1920 y 1930, que estaba centrado en Harlem

hejab headscarves and loose-fitting, ankle-length garments meant to conceal the body (p. 1035)
hejab velos, pañuelos y prendas de vestir amplias y hasta los tobillos cuya finalidad es ocultar el cuerpo

heliocentric based on the belief that the sun is the center of the universe (pp. 142, 434)
heliocéntrico sistema basado en la creencia de que el Sol es el centro del universo

heresy religious belief that is contrary to the official teachings of a church (p. 171)
herejía creencia religiosa contraria a las enseñanzas oficiales de la iglesia

hierarchy system of ranking groups (p. 32)
jerarquía sistema que clasifica a las personas de una sociedad

hieroglyphics system of writing in which pictures called hieroglyphs represent objects, concepts, or sounds (p. 54)
jeroglíficos sistema de escritura cuyos dibujos, llamados jeroglíficos, representan objetos, conceptos o sonidos

hijra Muhammad's journey from Mecca to Medina in 622 (p. 305)
héjira trayecto de Mahoma de la Meca a Medina en el año 622

Hiroshima city in Japan where the first atomic bomb was dropped in August 1945 (p. 951)
Hiroshima ciudad de Japón donde fue lanzada la primera bomba atómica en agosto de 1945

historian a person who studies how people lived in the past (p. 4)
historiador persona que estudia el modo de vida de la gente en el pasado

Holocaust the systematic genocide of about six million European Jews by the Nazis during World War II (p. 936)
Holocausto el genocidio sistemático por parte de los nazis de alrededor de seis millones de

judíos europeos durante la Segunda Guerra Mundial

Holy Land Jerusalem and other places in Palestine where Christians believe Jesus had lived and preached (p. 256)

Tierra Santa Jerusalem y otros lugares en Palestina donde los cristianos creen que Jesús vivió y predicó

Holy Roman Empire empire of west central Europe from 962 to 1806, comprising present-day Germany and neighboring lands (p. 251)

Sacro Imperio Romano imperio de la Europa central occidental desde 962 a 1806, que comprendía la actual Alemania y las tierras aledañas

home rule local self-government (p. 731)

autogobierno autogobierno local

homogeneous society society that has a common culture and language (p. 788)

sociedad homogénea sociedad que tiene un lenguaje y una cultura común

Huari a culture that thrived in the Andean region from about A.D. 600–A.D. 1000 (p. 196)

huari cultura que tuvo su apogeo en la región andina desde alrededor de 600 D.C. a 1000 D.C.

Huguenots French Protestants of the 1500s and 1600s (p. 510)

Hugonotes protestantes franceses de los siglos XVI y XVII

humanism an intellectual movement at the heart of the Renaissance that focused on education and the classics (p. 411)

humanismo movimiento intelectual durante el auge del Renacimiento que se centraba en la educación y los clásicos

humanities study of subjects such as grammar, rhetoric, poetry, and history, that were taught in ancient Greece and Rome (p. 411)

humanidades estudio de asignaturas como la gramática, la retórica, poesía e historia que se enseñaban en las antiguas Grecia y Roma

Huns a nomadic people of central Asia (p. 175)

hunos pueblo nómada del centro de Asia

Hutus the group that forms the majority in Rwanda and Burundi (p. 1051)

Hutus grupo mayoritario de Ruanda y Burundi

hypothesis an unproved theory accepted for the purposes of explaining certain facts or to provide a basis for further investigation (p. 436)

hipótesis teoría sin probar aceptada con el propósito de explicar determinados hechos o de proveer una base para una investigación posterior más profunda

icon holy image of Christ, the Virgin Mary, or a saint venerated in the Eastern Orthodox Church (p. 286)

ícono imagen sagrada de Cristo, la Vírgen María o de un santo venerado por la iglesia ortodoxa oriental

ideology system of thought and belief (pp. 634, 972)

ideología sistema de pensamiento y creencias

illumination the artistic decoration of books and manuscripts (p. 267)

iluminación decoración artística de libros y manuscritos

immunity natural protection, resistance (p. 473)

inmunidad protección natural, resistencia

imperialism domination by one country of the political, economic, or cultural life of another country or region (pp. 156, 750)

imperialismo dominio por parte de un país de la vida política, económica o cultural de otro país o región

import substitution manufacturing goods locally to replace imports (p. 1082)

sustitución de importaciones la producción local de bienes para reemplazar su importación

impressionism school of painting of the late 1800s and early 1900s that tried to capture fleeting visual impressions (p. 684)

impresionismo escuela de pintura de finales del siglo XIX y principios del siglo XX que trataba de captar impresiones visuales fugaces

indemnity payment for losses in war (p. 774)

indemnización compensación como pago por pérdidas de guerra

indigenous original or native to a country or region (pp. 798, 1087)

indígena originario o nativo de un país o región

indulgence in the Roman Catholic Church, pardon for sins committed during a person's lifetime (p. 424)

indulgencia perdón por los pecados cometidos en vida concedido por la Iglesia Católica Romana

inflation economic cycle that involves a rapid rise in prices linked to a sharp increase in the amount of money available (pp. 174, 270, 492)

inflación ciclo económico caracterizado por un rápida subida de los precios ligada a un aumento rápido del dinero disponible

Inquisition a Church court set up to try people accused of heresy (p. 260)

Inquisición tribunal de la Iglesia establecido para juzgar a la gente acusada de herejía

insurgents rebel forces (p. 1059)

insurgentes fuerzas rebeldes

intendant official appointed by French king Louis XIV to govern the provinces, collect taxes, and recruit soldiers (p. 512)

intendente oficial publico nombrado por el rey francés Luis XIV para gobernar las provincias, recaudar impuestos y reclutar soldados

interchangeable parts identical components that can be used in place of one another in manufacturing (p. 663)

repuestos intercambiables componentes idénticos que pueden usarse unos en lugar de otros en el proceso de producción

interdependence mutual dependence of countries on goods, resources, labor, and knowledge from other parts of the world (p. 1100)

interdependencia dependencia mutua de los países con los de otras partes del mundo en cuanto a productos, recursos, mano de obra y conocimientos

interdict in the Roman Catholic Church, excommunication of an entire region, town, or kingdom (p. 229)

interdicto en la Iglesia Católica Romana, excomunión de una región, pueblo o reino

International Space Station (ISS) an artificial structure built and maintained by a coalition of nations with the purpose of research (p. 1121)

Estación Espacial Internacional (ISS, por sus siglas en inglés) estructura artificial construida y mantenida por una coalición de naciones con el fin de llevar a cabo investigaciones

Internet a huge international computer network linking millions of users around the world (p. 1123)

Internet inmensa red internacional de computadoras que une a millones de ususarios en todo el mundo

Inti the Inca sun god (p. 199)

Inti dios sol inca

intifada Palestinian Arab uprisings against the Israeli occupation (p. 1055)

intifadas levantamientos de árabes palestinos en contra de la ocupación israelí

Iroquois League political alliance of five Iroquois groups, known as the Five Nations, in the late 1500s (p. 205)

Liga de los iroqueses alianza política de cinco grupos iroqueses, conocida como las Cinco Naciones, de finales del siglo XVI

Isfahan capital of Safavid empire during the 1600s; located in present-day Iran (p. 333)

Isfahan capital del imperio safavid durante el siglo XVII, situada en actual Irán

Islamist a person who wants government policies to be based on the teachings of Islam (p. 1029)

islamista persona que desea que las políticas del gobierno tengan su fundamento en las enseñanzas del Islam

island-hopping during World War II, Allied strategy of recapturing some Japanese-held islands while bypassing others (p. 950)

salto entre islas estrategia aliada durante la Segunda Guerra Mundial de retomar algunas de las islas ocupadas por los japoneses e ignorar y pasar de largo de otras

Istanbul capital of the Ottoman empire; located in the northwest of present-day Turkey; formerly Constantinople (p. 329)

Estambul capital del imperio otomano; situada en el noroeste de la actual Turquía; anteriormente llamada Constantinopla

J

Jacobin member of a radical political club during the French Revolution (p. 583)

jacobino miembro de un club político radical durante la Revolución Francesa

janizary elite force of the Ottoman army (p. 331)

jenízaro fuerza de élitedel ejército otomano

Jericho the world's first village, established in the modern-day West Bank between 10,000 and 9000 B.C. (p. 14)

Jericó la primera aldea del mundo establecidas en la actual Cisjordania entre alrededor del año 10,000 y 9000 A.C.

Jerusalem capital of the Jewish state of Judea in ancient times and capital of the modern State of Israel; city sacred to Jews, Muslims, and Christians (p. 1056)

Jerusalén capital del estado judío de Judea en la antigüedad, y capital del actual estado de Israel; ciudad sagrada para los judíos, musulmanes y cristianos

jihad in Islam, an effort in God's service (p. 306)

yihad en el Islam, un esfuerzo al servicio de Dios

joint family family organization in which several generations share a common dwelling (p. 89)

familia extendida organización familiar en la que varias generaciones comparten una vivienda

journeyman a salaried worker employed by a guild master (p. 235)

　oficial trabajador asalariado empleado por el maestro del gremio

jury legal group of people sworn to make a decision in a legal case (pp. 126, 245)

　jurado grupo de personas que han prestado juramento para tomar una decisión en un caso legal

Justinian's Code collection of Roman laws organized by the Byzantine emperor Justinian and later serving as a model for the Catholic Church and medieval monarchs (p. 283)

　Código Justiniano recopilación de leyes romanas organizada por el emperador bizantino Justiniano y que luego sirvió como modelo para la iglesia católica y los monarcas medievales

K

Kaaba the most sacred temple of Islam, located at Mecca (p. 305)

　Kaaba el templo más sagrado del islam, ubicado en La Meca

kaiser emperor of Germany (p. 695)

　kaiser emperador de Alemania

kamikaze Japanese pilot who undertook a suicide mission (p. 950)

　kamikaze piloto japonés que emprendía una misión suicida

kana in the Japanese writing system, phonetic symbols representing syllables (p. 390)

　kana en el sistema japonés de escritura, símbolos fonéticos que representan sílabas

karma in Hindu belief, all the actions that affect a person's fate in the next life (p. 77)

　karma según la creencia hindú, todas las acciones que afectan el destino de una persona en su próxima vida

Kashmir a former princely state in the Himalayas, claimed by both India and Pakistan, which have fought wars over its control (p. 1015)

　Cachemira antiguo estado principesco de los Himalayas, reclamado tanto por India como Pakistán, y por cuyo control han librado varias guerras

Katanga a province of the Democratic Republic of the Congo with rich copper and diamond deposits that tried to gain independence from Congo in 1960 (p. 1029)

　Katanga provincia de la República Democrática del Congo con ricos depósitos de cobre y diamantes, que intentó independizarse del Congo en 1960

Kellogg-Briand Pact an international agreement, signed by almost every nation in 1928, to stop using war as a method of national policy (p. 893)

　Pacto de Kellogg-Briand acuerdo internacional firmado por casi todas las naciones en 1928 para erradicar el uso de la guerra como un metodo de politica nacional

Khmer Rouge a political movement and a force of Cambodian communist guerrillas that gained power in Cambodia in 1975 (p. 997)

　Khmer Rouge movimiento político y fuerza guerrillera comunista de Camboya que llegó al poder en ese país en 1975

kibbutz a collective farm in Israel (p. 1033)

　kibbutz en Israel, granja comunitaria

Kiev capital of medieval Russia and of present-day Ukraine (p. 290)

　Kiev capital de la Rusia medieval y de la actual Ucrania

kiva large underground chamber that the Anasazi used for religious ceremonies and political meetings (p. 203)

　kiva gran sala subterránea que usaban los anazasi para ceremonias religiosas y reuniones políticas

knight a European noble who served as a mounted warrior (p. 220)

　caballero noble europeo que servía como guerrero montado

Knossos an ancient Minoan city on the island of Crete (p. 114)

　Cnosos antigua ciudad minoica en la isla de Creta

Kolkata a large city in India, also known as Calcutta (p. 1080)

　Kolkata ciudad grande de India, conocida también como Calcuta

Koryo dynasty Korean dynasty that ruled from 935 to 1392 (p. 385)

　dinastía Koryo dinastía coreana que gobernó desde 935 a 1392

Kosovo a province of Serbia with an Albanian ethnic majority that was the site of an ethnic conflict during the 1990s (p. 1047)

　Kosovo provincia de Serbia de mayoría étnica albanesa que sufrió un conflicto étnico durante la década de 1990

kulak wealthy peasant in the Soviet Union in the 1930s (p. 905)

　campesino adinerado de la Unión Soviética en la década de 1930

Kulturkampf Bismarck's "battle for civilization," intended to make Catholics put loyalty to the state above their allegiance to the Church (p. 698)
Kulturkampf "batalla por civilización" de Bismarck, cuyo objetivo era que los católicos pusieran la lealtod al estado por encima de la lealtad a la Iglesia

L

La Reforma an era of liberal reform in Mexico from 1855 to 1876 (p. 803)
La Reforma era de reforma liberal en México desde 1855 a 1876
labor union workers' organization (p. 618)
sindicato organización de trabajadores
laissez faire policy allowing business to operate with little or no government interference (p. 548)
laissez faire política que permite a los negocios y empresas operar con poca o ninguna interferencia del gobierno
land reform breakup of large agricultural holdings for redistribution among peasants (p. 369)
reforma agraria división de grandes propiedades dedicadas a la agricultura para distribuirlas entre los campesinos
laser a high-energy light beam that can be used for many purposes including surgery, engineering, and scientific research (p. 1124)
láser haz luminoso de alta energía que puede ser usado para muchos fines, entre ellos la cirugía, la ingeniería y la investigación científica
latifundia huge estates bought up by newly wealthy Roman citizens (p. 157)
latifundios grandes propiedades adquiridas por los ciudadanos romanos que se habían vuelto ricos recientemente
lay investiture appointment of bishops by anyone who is not a member of the clergy (p. 252)
investidura nombramiento de obispos por cualquiera que no sea miembro del clero
legion basic unit of the ancient Roman army, made up of about 5,000 soldiers (p. 154)
legión unidad básica del ejército de la antigua Roma, que consistía de unos 5,000 soldados
legislature lawmaking body (p. 122)
asamblea legislativa cuerpo encargado de promover y promulgar las leyes
legitimacy principle by which monarchies that had been unseated by the French Revolution or Napoleon were restored (p. 600)

legitimidad principio por el que las monarquías que habían sido derrocadas por la Revolución Francesa o por Napoleón fueron restituidas
Lend-Lease Act act passed by the U. S. Congress in 1941 that allowed the president (FDR) to sell or lend war supplies to any country whose defense was considered vital to the United States (p. 937)
Ley de Préstamo y Arriendo decreto aprobado por el Congreso de Estados Unidos en 1941 que permitió al presidente (FDR) vender o arrendar materiales de guerra a cualquier país cuya defensa fuese considerada de vital importancia para Estados Unidos
levée morning ritual during which nobles would wait upon French king Louis XIV (p. 512)
recepción matutina ritual de la mañana en el que los nobles atendían al rey Luis XIV
libel knowing publication of false and damaging statements (p. 737)
libelo publicación intencional de declaraciones falsas que perjudican a alguien
liberation theology movement within the Catholic Church that urged the church to become a force for reform, social justice, and put an end to poverty (p. 1085)
teología de la liberación movimiento dentro de la Iglesia Católica que urgía a la iglesia a liderar un llamamiento por la reforma, la justicia social el fin de la pobreza
limited monarchy government in which a constitution or legislative body limits the monarch's powers (p. 522)
monarquía limitada gobierno en el que la constitución o el cuerpo legislativo limitan los poderes de la monarquía
Line of Demarcation line set by the Treaty of Tordesillas dividing the non-European world into two zones, one controlled by Spain and the other by Portugal (p. 450)
Línea de demarcación línea establecida por el Tratado de Tordesillas que dividía el mundo fuera de Europa en dos zonas: una controlada por España y otra por Portugal
lineage group claiming a common ancestor (p. 358)
linaje grupo que reivindica un antepasado en común
literacy the ability to read and write (p. 1066)
alfabetismo capacidad de leer y escribir
literacy rate percentage of people who can read and write (p. 386)
tasa de alfabetización porcentaje de personas que pueden leer y escribir

Liverpool city and one of the largest ports in England; first major rail line linked Liverpool to Manchester in 1830 (p. 615)

Liverpool ciudad y uno de los puertos más grandes de Inglaterra; línea importante de ferrocarril unió Liverpool con Manchester en 1830

loess fine windblown yellow soil (p. 93)

loes tierra fina y amarilla que se llava el viento

logic rational thinking (p. 130)

lógica pensamiento racional

Long March epic march in which a group of Chinese Communists retreated from Guomindang forces by marching over 6,000 miles (p. 871)

Gran Marcha marcha épica en la que un grupo de comunistas chinos marcharon en retirada de las fuerzas del Guomindang por más de 6,000 millas

longbow six-foot-long bow that could rapidly fire arrows with enough force to pierce most armor (p. 272)

arco largo arco de seis pies de largo que podía disparar rápidamente flechas con suficiente fuerza como para agujerear una armadura

Louisiana Purchase territory purchased by Thomas Jefferson from France in 1803 (p. 739)

Compra de Luisiana territorio que Thomas Jefferson compró a Francia en 1803

Luftwaffe German air force (p. 930)

Luftwaffe fuerza aérea alemana

Lusitania British liner torpedoed by a German submarine in May 1915 (p. 830)

Lusitania crucero británico torpedeado por un submarino alemán en mayo de 1915

M

Macao region of southeastern China made up of a peninsula and two islands, a Portuguese territory from the mid-1800s to 1999 (p. 461)

Macao región al sudeste de China formada por una península y dos islas; fue territorio portugués desde mediados del siglo XIX a 1999

Maginot Line massive fortifications built by the French along their border with Germany in the 1930s to protect against invasion (p. 893)

Línea Maginot fortificaciones masivas construídas por los franceses a lo largo de la frontera france sa con Alemania en la década de 1930 para protegerse contra invasiones futuras

Magna Carta the Great Charter approved by King John of England in 1215; it limited royal power and established certain rights of English freemen (p. 246)

Carta Magna carta constitucional aprobada por el Rey Juan de Inglaterra en 1215; limitaba el poder real y establecía ciertos derechos de los ingleses libres

Magyars an ethnic group centered in present-day Hungary (p. 218)

magiar grupo étnico establecido en la actual Hungría

Mahdi a Muslim savior of the faith (p. 762)

Mahdi salvador musulmán de la fe

maize corn (p. 187)

maíz elote

Malacca a state and coastal city in SW Malaysia, was an early center of the spice trade (p. 457)

Malacca estado y ciudad costera en el sudoeste de Malasia; fue uno de los primeros centros del comercio de especias

Mali medieval West African trading empire located in present-day Mali (p. 348)

Mali imperio comerciante de África occidental medieval ubicado en el actual Mali

Malindi a coastal town in SE Kenya (p. 452)

Malindi pueblo costero al sudeste de Kenia

Manchester city in England; one of the leading industrial areas; example of an Industrial Revolution city; first major rail line linked Manchester to Liverpool in 1830 (p. 615)

Manchester ciudad de Inglaterra; una de las principales áreas industriales; ejemplo de ciudad de la Revolución Industrial; la primera línea importante de ferrocarril unió Manchester con Liverpool en 1830

Manchuria historic province in northeastern China; rich in natural resources (p. 876)

Manchuria provincia histórica en el noreste de China; rica en recursos naturales

Manchus people originally from Manchuria, north of China, who conquered the Ming dynasty and ruled China as the Qing dynasty from the mid-1600s to the early 1900s (p. 462)

manchus personas originalmente de Manchuria, al norte de China, que derrotaron a la dinastía Ming y gobernaron como la dinastía Chin desde mediados del siglo XVII a principios del siglo XX

mandate after World War I, a territory administered by a Western power (p. 838)

mandato territorio administrado por un poder occidental después de la Primera Guerra Mundial

Manhattan Project code name for the project to build the first atomic bomb during WWII (p. 950)

Proyecto Manhattan nombre en clave del proyecto para la fabricación de la primera bomba atómica durante la Segunda Guerra Mundial

Manifest Destiny American idea that the United States should stretch across the entire North American continent (p. 739)

Destino Manifiesto idea estadounidense de que Estados Unidos debería extenderse hasta ocupar todo el continente norteamericano

manor during the Middle Ages in Europe, a lord's estate which included one or more villages and the surrounding lands (p. 222)

señorío durante la Edad Media en Europa, propiedad de un señor que incluía uno o más pueblos y sus terrenos adyacentes

Maori indigenous people of New Zealand (p. 800)

maoríe pueblo indígena de Nueva Zelanda

March on Rome planned march of thousands of Fascist supporters to take control of Rome; in response Mussolini was given the legal right to control Italy (p. 899)

Marcha sobre Roma marcha planeada de miles de simpatizantes fascistas sobre Roma para tomar su control; en respuesta a ella a Mussolini se le concedió el derecho legal del control de Italia

Marseilles French port city; troops marched to a patriotic song as they marched from this city, the song eventually became the French national anthem (p. 590)

Marsella ciudad portuaria francesa; las tropas que marcharon al ritmo de una canción patriótica desde esta ciudad inspiraron el himno nacional francés

Marshall Plan massive aid package offered by the U. S. to Europe to help countries rebuild after WWII (p. 955)

Plan Marshall paquete de ayuda a gran escala ofrecido por Estados Unidos a Europa para apoyar la reconstrucción de los países después de la Segunda Guerra Mundial

martyr person who suffers or dies for his or her beliefs (p. 170)

mártir persona que sufre o muere por sus creencias

matrilineal term for a family organization in which kinship ties are traced through the mother (pp. 358, 399)

matrilineal organización familiar en la que los lazos de parentesco se siguen a través de la madre

May Fourth Movement cultural movement in China that sought to reform China and make it stronger (p. 870)

Movimiento del Cuatro de Mayo movimiento cultural de China que se centró en reformar China y hacerla más fuerte

means of production farms, factories, railways, and other large businesses that produce and distribute goods (p. 625)

medios de producción granjas, fábricas, ferrocarriles y otros grandes negocios que producen y distribuyen mercancías

Mecca a city in western Saudi Arabia; birthplace of the prophet Muhammad and most holy city for Islamic people (p. 304)

Meca ciudad en el oeste de Arabia Saudita; lugar de nacimiento del profeta Mahoma y ciudad sagrada para los creyentes islámicos

medieval referring to the Middle Ages in Europe or the period of history between ancient and modern times (p. 214)

medieval se refiere a la Edad Media en Europa, es decir, el período de la historia entre la edad antigua y la edad moderna

Medina a city in western Saudi Arabia; a city where Muhammad preached (p. 305)

Medina ciudad en el oeste de Arabia Saudita; ciudad donde predicó Mahoma

Meiji Restoration in Japan, the reign of emperor Meiji from 1868 to 1912 which was marked by rapid modernization and industrialization (p. 786)

restauración de Meiji en Japón, reino del emperador Meiji desde 1868 a 1912 que fue marcado por la rápida modernización e industrialización

mercantilism policy by which a nation sought to export more than it imported in order to build its supply of gold and silver (p. 494)

mercantilismo política por la que una nación trataba de exportar más de lo que importaba para aumentar sus reservas de o ro y plata

mercenary soldier serving in a foreign army for pay (pp. 177, 527)

mercenario soldado que sirve en un ejército extranjero a cambio de dinero

Meroë capital of the ancient kingdom of Nubia (p. 343)

Meroë capital del antiguo reino de Nubia

Mesa Verde the largest complex of Anasazi cliff-dwellings in the United States Southwest, built between about A.D. 1150 and A.D. 1300 (p. 203)

Mesa Verde el mayor complejo de viviendas anazasi construidas en acantilados en el sudoeste de Estados Unidos, entre alrededor de 1150 D.C. y 1300 D.C.

Mesoamerica region of North America, including Mexico and Central America, in which civilizations with common cultural features developed before Europeans entered the continent (p. 186)

Mesoamérica región de América del Norte, que incluye a México y América Central, en la cual se desarrollaron, antes de la llegada de los europeos al continente, civilizaciones con características culturales similares

Mesopotamia region within the Fertile Crescent that lies between the Tigris and Euphrates rivers (p. 30)

Mesopotamia región del Creciente Fértil que se encuentra entre los ríos Tigris y Éufrates

messiah savior sent by God (p. 167)

mésias salvador enviado por Dios

mestizo person in Spain's colonies in the Americas who was of Native American and European descent (pp. 480, 645)

mestizo persona de las colonias españolas de América descendiente de nativos y europeos

métis people of mixed Native American and French Canadian descent (p. 798)

métis pueblo de descendientes con mezcla de indígenas americanos y franceses canadienses

middle class a group of people, including merchants, traders, and artisans, whose rank was between nobles and peasants (p. 235)

clase media grupo de personas, incluyendo mercaderes, comerciantes y artesanos, cuyo rango estaba entre los nobles y los campesinos

Middle Passage the leg of the triangular trade route on which slaves were transported from Africa to the Americas (p. 487)

Travesía Intermedia parte de la ruta del comercio triangular en la que los esclavos eran transportados desde África a las Américas

militarism glorification of the military (p. 818)

militarismo glorificación de las fuerzas armadas

militias armed groups of citizen soldiers (p. 1058)

milicias grupos armados de soldados-ciudadanos

minaret slender tower of a mosque, from which Muslims are called to prayer (p. 314)

minarete torre esbelta de una mezquita desde la que se convoca a los musulmanes a la oración

Ming dynasty Chinese dynasty in which Chinese rule was restored; held power from 1368 to 1644 (p. 379)

dinastía Ming dinastía china en la que se restauro el gobierno chino; se mantuvo en el poder desde a 1644

missionary someone sent to do religious work in a territory or foreign country (pp. 85, 453)

misioneros personas enviadas para hacer trabajos religiosos en un territorio u otro país

mobilize prepare military forces for war (p. 820)

mobilizar preparar las fuerzas militares para la guerra

Moche a culture that thrived in the Andean region from about 400 B.C. to A.D. 600 (p. 196)

moche cultura preincaica que tuvo su apogeo en la región andina, desde alrededor de 400 A.C. a 600 D.C.

Mohenjo-Daro ancient city of the Indus civilization, located in present-day Pakistan (p. 70)

Mohenjo-Daro antigua ciudad de la civilización del Indo, ubicada en el presente Pakistán

moksha in Hindu belief, the ultimate goal of existence, which is to achieve union with brahman (p. 77)

moksha según la creencia hindú, el objetivo final de la existencia, que es llegar a la unión con el brahman

Moluccas a group of islands in eastern Indonesia; was the center of the spice trade in the 1500s and 1600s (p. 446)

Molucas grupo de islas en el este de Indonesia; fue el centro del comercio de especias en los siglos XVI y XVII

Mombasa a city in southeastern Kenya, located on a small coastal island (p. 452)

Mombasa ciudad al sudeste de Kenia, localizada en una pequeña isla costera

monarchy government in which a king or queen exercises central power (p. 120)

monarquía gobierno en el que el poder reside en el rey o la reina

money economy economic system in which goods or services are paid for through the exchange of a token of an agreed value (p. 42)

economía de dinero sistema económico en el que las mercancías y los servicios se pagan mediante el intercambio de una moneda con un valor establecido

monopoly complete control of a product or business by one person or group (pp. 103, 454)

monopolio control total de un producto o negocio por una persona o grupo

monotheistic believing in one God (p. 57)

monoteísta creencia en un solo Dios

Monroe Doctrine American policy of discouraging European intervention in the Western Hemisphere (p. 805)

Doctrina Monroe política estadounidense de rechazo a la intervención europea en el hemisferio occidental

monsoon seasonal wind that regularly blows from a certain direction for part of the year (p. 69)

monzón viento estacional que regularmente sopla desde una dirección específica durante una parte del año

mosaic picture made from chips of colored stone or glass (p. 162)

mosaico imagen hecha con pedazos de piedras o vidrios de colores

mosque Muslim house of worship; (p. 306)

mezquita templo musulmán

Mothers of the Plaza de Mayo a movement of women who protested weekly in a central plaza in the capital of Argentina against the disappearance or killing of relatives (p. 1088)

Madres de la Plaza de Mayo asociación de mujeres que se reunían semanalmente en una céntrica plaza de la capital de Argentina para protest por la desaparición o asesinato de sus familiares

Mughal Muslim dynasty that ruled much of present-day India from 1526 to 1857 (p. 327)

Mughal dinastía musulmana que gobernó gran parte de la India actual de 1526 a 1857

Mughal empire Muslim empire that ruled most of northern India from the mid-1500s to the mid-1700s; also known as the Mogul or Mongol empire (p. 457)

imperio Mughal imperio musulmán que gobernó la mayor parte del norte de India desde mediados del siglo XVI a mediados del siglo XVIII; también se conoce como imperio Mogul o Mongol

mujahedin Muslim religious warriors (p. 1002)

mujaedin guerreros religiosos musulmanes

mulatto in Spain's colonies in the Americas, person who was of African and European descent (pp. 480, 645)

mulato en las colonias españolas de América descendiente de africanos y europeos

multiethnic made up of several ethnic groups (p. 1046)

multiétnico compuesto de varios grupos étnicos

multinational corporation company with branches in many countries (p. 1101)

corporación multinacional empresa con sucursales en muchos países

Mumbai a large city in India, also known as Bombay (p. 1080)

Mumbai ciudad grande de India, conocida también como Bombay

mummification the preservation of dead bodies by embalming and wrapping them in cloth (p. 53)

momificación práctica de preservar los cuerpos de los muertos embalsamándolos y envolviéndolos en vendas

mutiny revolt, especially of soldiers or sailors against their officers (p. 490)

motín revuelta, especialmente de soldados y marineros contra sus oficiales

mutual-aid societies self-help groups to aid sick or injured workers (p. 670)

sociedades de ayuda mutua grupos de apoyo establecidos para ayudar a los trabajadores enfermos o heridos en accidentes laborales

mystic person who devotes his or her life to seeking direct communion with divine forces (p. 73)

místico persona que dedica su vida a buscar la comunión directa con las fuerzas divinas

Nagasaki a coastal city in southern Japan on the island of Kyushu; city in Japan where the second atomic bomb was dropped in August, 1945 (pp. 465, 951)

Nagasaki ciudad costera en el sur de Japón en la isla de Kyushu; ciudad de Japón donde fue lanzada la segunda bomba atómica en agosto de 1945

Napoleonic Code body of French civil laws introduced in 1804; served as model for many nations' civil codes (p. 593)

Código Napoleónico cuerpo de las leyes civiles francesas presentadas en 1804, que sirvieron como modelo para los códigos civiles de muchos países

nationalism a strong feeling of pride in and devotion to one's country (p. 590)

nacionalismo fuerte sentimiento de orgullo y devoción hacia el país propio

nationalization takeover of property or resources by the government (p. 854)

nacionalización apropiación de propiedades o recursos por parte del gobierno

natural law rules of conduct discoverable by reason (p. 544)

leyes naturales normas de conducta que se pueden descubrir mediante la razón

natural right right that belongs to all humans from birth, such as life, liberty, and property (p. 545)

derecho natural derecho que pertenece a todos los humanos desde el nacimiento: vida, libertad y propiedad

Nazca a culture that thrived in the Andean region from about 200 B.C. to A.D. 600 (p. 196)

Nazca cultura que tuvo su apogeo en la región andina desde alrededor de 200 A.C. a 600 D.C.

Nazi-Soviet Pact agreement between Germany and the Soviet Union in 1939 in which the two nations promised not to fight each other and to divide up land in Eastern Europe (p. 929)

Pacto nazi-soviético acuerdo en 1939 entre Alemania y la Unión Soviética mediante el cual las dos naciones prometen no atacarse mutuamente y dividirse entre sí territorio de Europa del Este

négritude movement movement in which writers and artists of African descent expressed pride in their African heritage (p. 860)

movimiento de la negritud movimiento en el que los escritores y artistas descendientes de africanos expresabansu orgullo por la herencia africana

Neolithic Period the final era of prehistory, which began about 9000 B.C.; also called the New Stone Age (p. 11)

período Neolítico era final de la prehistoria que empezó hacia el 9000 A.C.; también llamado Nueva Edad de Piedra

Neolithic Revolution the period of time during which the introduction of agriculture led people to transition from nomadic to settled life (p. 13)

revolución neolítica período durante el cual el comienzo de la agricultura llevó a la gente a la transición de la vida nómada a la vida sedentaria

neutrality policy of supporting neither side in a war (p. 820)

neutralidad política de mantenerse al margen en una guerra

Neutrality Acts a series of acts passed by the U.S. Congress from 1935 to 1939 that aimed to keep the U. S. from becoming involved in WWII (p. 926)

Leyes de Neutralidad serie de decretos aprobados por el Congreso de Estados Unidos de 1935 a 1939 con el fin de evitar la implicación del país en la Segunda Guerra Mundial

New Deal a massive package of economic and social programs established by FDR to help Americans during the Great Depression (p. 897)

Nuevo Tratado paquete masivo de programas económicos y sociales establecidos por FDR para ayudar a los estadounidenses durante la Gran Depresión

New France French possessions in present-day Canada from the 1500s to 1763 (p. 482)

Nueva Francia posesiones francesas en el actual Canadá desde el siglo XVI a 1763

New Stone Age the final era of prehistory, which began about 9000 B.C.; also called the Neolithic Period (p. 11)

Nueva Edad de Piedra era final de la prehistoria que empezó aproximadamente hacia el 9000 A.C.; también llamado período Neolítico

nirvana in Buddhist belief, union with the universe and release from the cycle of rebirth (p. 80)

nirvana en el budismo, unión con el universo y liberación del ciclo de la reencarnación

no-fly zones in Iraq, areas where the United States and its allies banned flights by Iraqi aircraft after the 1991 Gulf War (p. 1059)

zonas de exclusión del espacio aéreo zonas de Iraq en las que Estados Unidos y sus aliados prohibieron el vuelo a la aviación iraquí después de la Guerra del Golfo en 1991

nomad a person who moves from place to place in search of food (p. 11)

nómada persona que se traslada de un lugar a otro en busca de alimentos

nonalignment political and diplomatic independence from both Cold War powers (p. 1019)

no alineación independencia política y diplomática de ambas potencias de la guerra fría

North Atlantic Treaty Organization (NATO) a military alliance between several North Atlantic states to safeguard them from the presumed threat of the Soviet Union's communist bloc; countries from other regions later joined the alliance (p. 956)

Organización del Tratado del Atlántico Norte (OTAN) alianza militar entre varios estados del Atlántico norte para salvaguardarlos de la supuesta amenaza del bloque comunista liderado por la Unión Soviética; más tarde se incorporarían a la alianza países de otras regiones

Northern Ireland the northern portion of the island of Ireland, a part of the United Kingdom that has had a long religious conflict (p. 1045)

Irlanda del Norte parte norte de la isla de Irlanda y territorio del Reino Unido, que ha sufrido un conflicto religioso durante mucho tiempo

Nubia ancient kingdom in northeastern Africa, also called Kush (p. 343)

Nubia antiguo reino del noreste africano, también llamado Kush

nuclear family family unit consisting of parents and children (p. 357)

familia nuclear unidad familiar que consta de los padres y sus hijos

Nuremberg Germany city where Hitler staged Nazi rallies in the 1930s, and where Nazi war crimes trials were held after WWII (p. 953)

Nuremberg ciudad del sur de Alemania donde Hitler escenificó manifestaciones nazis durante la década de 1930, y donde se celebraron los juicios por crímenes de guerra nazis después de la Segunda Guerra Mundial

Nuremberg Laws laws approved by the Nazi Party in 1935, depriving Jews of German citizenship and taking some rights away from them (p. 915)

Leyes de Nuremberg leyes aprobadas por el partido nazi en 1935, que eliminaba algunos de los derechos de los judíos en Alemania

occupied territories areas controlled by a nation that are part of another entity; Palestinians use this term for certain lands Israel gained after the 1967 war. (p. 1055)

territorios ocupados zonas controladas por una nación que forman parte de otra entidad. Los palestinos usan esta palabra para referirse a los territorios ocupados por Israel después de la guerra de 1967

Old Stone Age the era of prehistory that lasted from 2 million B.C. to about 9000 B.C. (p. 11)

Antigua Edad de Piedra era de la prehistoria que duró desde aproximadamente 2 millones de años A.C. hasta el 9000 A.C.; también llamado período Paleolítico

Olduvai Gorge a gorge in Tanzania in which many hominid remains have been found (p. 8)

desfiladero Olduvai desfiladero en Tanzania donde se han encontrado muchos restos de homínidos

oligarchy government in which ruling power belongs to a few people (pp. 120, 523)

oligarquía gobierno en el que el poder está en manos de unas pocas personas

Olmecs the earliest American civilization, located along the Gulf Coast of Mexico from about 1500 B.C. to 400 B.C. (p. 188)

olmecas la primera civilización americana, ubicada a lo largo de la costa del Golfo de México, desde alrededor de 1500 A.C. a 400 A.C.

one-child policy a Chinese government policy limiting urban families to a single child (p. 1077)

política de un sólo hijo medida del gobierno chino que limita a las familias urbanas a tener únicamente un hijo

Open Door Policy American approach to China around 1900, favoring open trade relations between China and other nations (p. 776)

Política de puertas abiertas política estadounidense con respecto a China a principios del siglo XX, que abogaba por las libres relaciones comerciales entre China y otras naciones

Opium War war between Great Britain and China over restrictions to foreign trade (p. 774)

Guerra del opio guerra librada entre Gran Bretaña y China por las restricciones sobre el comercio exterior

oracle bone in Shang China, animal bone or turtle shell used by priests to predict the future (p. 100)

hueso de oráculo en la China Shang, hueso de animal o caparazón de tortuga usado por los sacerdotes para predecir el futuro

Organization of American States (OAS) a group formed in 1948 to promote democracy, economic cooperation, and human rights in the Americas (p. 1086)

Organización de los Estados Americanos grupo formado en 1948 con el fin de promover la democracia, la cooperación económica y los derechos humanos en las Américas

ostracism practice used in ancient Greece to banish or send away a public figure who threatened democracy (p. 126)

ostracismo en la antigua Grecia, el acto de desterrar o enviar lejos a una figura pública que amenazaba la democracia

Ottomans Turkish-speaking nomadic people who migrated from Central Asia into northwestern Asia Minor (p. 329)

otomanos grupo nómada de habla turca que emigró de Asia Central al noroeste de Asia Menor

outpost a distant military station or a remote settlement (p. 458)

fuerte fronterizo estación militar distante o asentamiento lejano

outsourcing the practice of sending work to companies in the developing world in order to save money or increase efficiency (p. 1100)

subcontratación práctica empresarial de enviar trabajo a compañías de países en vías de desarrollo con el fin de ahorrar dinero o aumentar el rendimiento

overproduction condition in which production of goods exceeds the demand for them (p. 895)

superproducción condición en la que la producción de mercancías excede la demanda

Oyo empire Yoruba empire that arose in the 1600s in present-day Nigeria and dominated its neighbors for a hundred years (p. 455)

imperio Oyo el imperio Yoruba que surgió en el siglo XVII en la actual Nigeria y dominó a sus vecinos durante cien años

P

Pacific Rim vast region of nations, including countries in Southeast Asia, East Asia, and the Americas, that border the Pacific Ocean (p. 1099)
Cuenca del Pacífico vasta región de naciones, que incluye los países del sureste y este asiático y de las Américas, que limitan con el océano Pacífico

pacifism opposition to all war (p. 925)
pacifismo oposición a las guerras

paddy rice field (p. 401)
arrozal campo de arroz

pagoda multistoried Buddhist temple with eaves that curve up at the corners (p. 372)
pagoda templo budista de varios pisos con aleros que se curvan en las esquinas

Paleolithic Period the era of prehistory that lasted from at least 2 million B.C. to about 9000 B.C.; also called the Old Stone Age (p. 11)
período Paleolítico era de la prehistoria que duró desde aproximadamente 2 millones de años A.C. hasta el 9000 A.C.; también llamado la Antigua Edad de Piedra

Pan-Africanism movement which began in the 1920s that emphasized the unity and strength of Africans and people of African descent around the world (p. 859)
Panafricanismo movimiento que empezó en la década de 1920 que se centraba en la unidad y fuerza de los africanos y personas con ascendencia africana en todo el mundo

Panama Canal man-made waterway connecting the Atlantic and Pacific oceans (p. 807)
Canal de Panamá canal artificial que conecta los océanos Atlántico y Pacífico

Pan-Arabism movement in which Arabs sought to unite all Arabs into one state (p. 862)
Panarabismo movimiento en el que los árabes pretendían unir a todos los árabes en un sólo estado

pandemic spread of a disease across a large area, country, continent, or the entire world (p. 834)
pandemia propagación de una enfermedad a una gran área, país, continente o al mundo entero

papal supremacy the claim of medieval popes that they had authority over all secular rulers (p. 228)
supremacía papal demanda de los papas medievales de que ellos tenían autoridad sobre todos los gobernantes laicos

Parthenon the chief temple of the Greek goddess Athena on the Acropolis in Athens, Greece (p. 132)
Partenón el principal templo de la diosa griega Atena, situado en la Acrópolis de Atenas en Grecia

papyrus plant used to make a paper-like writing material in ancient Egypt (p. 54)
papiro planta usada por los antiguos egipcios para hacer un material de escritura parecido al papel

Parliament the legislature of England, and later of Great Britain (p. 247)
Parlamento asamblea legislativa de Inglaterra, y más tarde de Gran Bretaña

parliamentary democracy a form of government in which the executive leaders (usually a prime minister and cabinet) are chosen by and responsible to the legislature (parliament), are also members of it (p. 724)
democracia parlamentaria forma de gobierno en la que la dirección ejecutiva (normalmente un primer ministro y un gabinete) es elegida por la asamblea legislativa (parlamento) y controlada por la misma, además de formar parte de ella

partition a division into pieces (pp. 535, 1015)
partición división en partes

partnership a group of merchants who joined together to finance a large-scale venture that would have been too costly for any individual trader (p. 234)
asociación grupo de mercaderes que se unen para financiar una empresa más grande que hubiera sido demasiado costosa para un solo comerciante

pasha provincial ruler in the Ottoman empire (p. 763)
bajá gobernante provincial del imperio otomano

paternalistic the system of governing a country as a father would a child (p. 756)
paternalista sistema de gobernar un país como un padre lo hace con su hijo

patriarch in the Roman and Byzantine empires, highest church official in a major city (pp. 171, 286)
patriarca en el Imperio Romano y imperio bizantino, el funcionario de rango más alto en la iglesia de una ciudad importante

patriarchal relating to a society in which men hold the greatest legal and moral authority (p. 59)
patriarcal relacionado con una sociedad en la que los hombres tienen la autoridad legal y moral

patrician in ancient Rome, member of the land-holding upper class (p. 152)
patricio miembro de la clase alta terrateniente en la antigua Roma

patrilineal term for a family organization in which kinship ties are traced through the father (p. 358)

patrilineal organización familiar en la que los lazos de parentesco se siguen a través del padre

patron a person who provides financial support for the arts (p. 412)

mecenas persona que proporciona apoyo financiero a la cultura y las artes

Peace of Westphalia series of treaties that ended the Thirty Years' War (p. 527)

Paz de Westfalia serie de tratados por los que se puso fin a la Guerra de los Treinta Años

penal colony place where people convicted of crimes are sent (pp. 727, 798)

colonia penal lugar al que se manda a los condenados por crímenes

peninsulare member of the highest class in Spain's colonies in the Americas (pp. 480, 645)

peninsular miembro de la clase más alta en las colonias españolas de América

peon worker forced to labor for a landlord in order to pay off a debt (p. 478)

peón trabajador forzado a trabajar para un terrateniente para pagar una deuda

peonage system by which workers owe labor to pay their debts (p. 803)

peonaje sistema en el que los trabajadores deben trabajo como pago por sus deudas

perestroika a Soviet policy of democratic and free-market reforms introduced by Mikhail Gorbachev in the late 1980s (p. 1002)

perestroika "reestructuración" en ruso; política soviética de reformas democráticas y de libre mercado que introdujo Mikhail Gorbachev a finales de la década de 1980

personal computer (PC) a small computer meant to be used by individuals or small businesses (p. 1123)

computadora personal (PC, por sus siglas en inglés) pequeña computadora diseñada para uso individual o por parte de pequeñas empresas

perspective artistic technique used to give paintings and drawings a three-dimensional effect (p. 412)

perspectiva técnica artística usada para lograr el efecto de tercera dimensión en dibujos y pinturas

phalanx in ancient Greece, a massive tactical formation of heavily armed foot soldiers (p. 120)

falange en la antigua Grecia, sólida formación táctica de soldados a pie fuertemente armados

pharaoh title of the rulers of ancient Egypt (p. 45)

faraón título de los gobernantes del antiguo Egipto

Philippines a country in southeastern Asia made up of several thousand islands (p. 459)

Filipinas país al sudeste de Asia formado por varios miles de islas

philosophe French for "philosopher"; French thinker who desired reform in society during the Enlightenment (p. 546)

philosophe palabra francesa que significa "filósofo"; pensador francés que abogaba por reformas en la sociedad durante la Ilustración

philosopher someone who seeks to understand and explain life; a person who studies philosophy (p. 130)

filósofo persona que trata de comprender y explicar la vida; persona que estudia la filosofía

philosophy system of ideas (p. 97)

filosofía sistema de ideas

pictograph a simple drawing that looks like the object it represents (p. 22)

pictografía dibujo sencillo que se parece al objeto que representa (also called pictograms)

Pilgrims English Protestants who rejected the Church of England (p. 484)

peregrinos protestantes ingleses que rechazaron la Iglesia de Inglaterra

plantation large estate run by an owner or overseer and worked by laborers who live there (p. 453)

plantación gran propiedad administrada por un dueño o capataz y cultivada por trabajadores que viven en ella

plateau raised area of level land (p. 69)

meseta área elevada de tierra plana

plebeian in ancient Rome, member of the lower class, including farmers, merchants, artisans, and traders (p. 152)

plebeyo en la antigua Roma, miembro de clase baja, que incluía granjeros, mercaderes, artesanos y comerciantes

plebiscite ballot in which voters have a direct say on an issue (p. 593)

plebiscito votación en la que los votantes expresan su opinión sobre un tema en particular

pogrom violent attack on a Jewish community (p. 713)

pogrom ataque violento de una multitud hacia una comunidad judía

polis city-state in ancient Greece (p. 118)

polis ciudad-estado de la antigua Grecia

polytheistic believing in many gods (p. 20)

politeísta creencia en muchos dioses

pope head of the Roman Catholic Church; in ancient Rome, bishop of Rome who claimed authority over all other bishops (p. 171)
papa cabeza de la iglesia Católica Romana; obispo de Roma que afirmaba tener autoridad sobre los otros obispos

popular sovereignty basic principle of the American system of government which asserts that the people are the source of any and all governmental power, and government can exist only with the consent of the governed (p. 560)
soberanía popular principio básico del sistema de gobierno estadounidense en el que se determina que el pueblo es la fuente de todo poder gubernamental, y que el gobierno sólo puede existir con el consentimiento de los gobernados

potlatch among Native American groups of the Northwest Coast, ceremonial gift-giving by people of high rank and wealth (p. 205)
potlatch entre los grupos indígenas de la costa noroeste, ceremonia en que la gente de alto rango o riqueza hacía regalos

predestination Calvinist belief that God long ago determined who would gain salvation (p. 427)
predestinación creencia calvinista de que Dios decidió hace mucho tiempo quién conseguiría la salvación

prehistory the period of time before writing was invented (p. 4)
prehistoria período anterior a la invención de los sistemas de escritura

premier prime minister (p. 736)
premier primer ministro

price revolution period in European history when inflation rose rapidly (p. 492)
revolución del precio período en la historia de Europa en que la inflación aumentó rápidamente

privateer privately owned ship commissioned by a government to attack and capture enemy ships, especially merchant's ships (p. 481)
corsario barco privado comisionado por un gobierno para atacar y capturar barcos enemigos, especialmentelos barcos mercantes

Prohibition a ban on the manufacture and sale of alcohol in the U. S. from 1920 to 1933 (p. 885)
Prohibición restricción de la fabricación y venta de bebidas alcohólicas en Estados Unidos desde 1920 a 1933

proletariat working class (pp. 625, 840)
proletariado clase trabajadora

proliferate to multiply rapidly (p. 1115)
proliferar multiplicarse rápidamente

propaganda spreading of ideas to promote a cause or to damage an opposing cause (p. 830)
propaganda divulgación de ideas para promover cierta causa o para perjudicar una causa opuesta

prophet spiritual leader who interprets God's will (p. 60)
profeta líder espiritual a quien se le atribuye la interpretación de la voluntad de Dios

protectionism the use of tariffs and other restrictions to protect a country's home industries against competition (p. 1103)
proteccionismo el uso de aranceles y otras medidas restrictivas para proteger a las empresas de un país de la competencia

protectorate country with its own government but under the control of an outside power (p. 753)
protectorado país con su propio gobierno pero que está bajo el control de una potencia exterior

provisional temporary (p. 735)
provisional temporal

Prussia a strong military state in central Europe that emerged in the late 1600s (p. 528)
Prusia estado centroeuropeo militarmente poderoso que emergió a finales del siglo XVII

psychoanalysis a method of studying how the mind works and treating mental disorders (p. 888)
psicoanálisis método que estudia el funcionamiento de la mente y trata los trastornos mentales

pueblo Native American village of the United States Southwest (p. 203)
pueblo poblado indígena del sudoeste de Estados Unidos

Pueblo Bonito the largest Anasazi pueblo, built in New Mexico in the A.D. 900s (p. 203)
Pueblo Bonito el mayor poblado anazasi, construido en Nuevo México en el siglo X D.C.

Punjab state in northwestern India with a largely Sikh population (p. 1016)
Punjab estado del noroeste de India de población mayoritariamente sikh

purdah isolation of women in separate quarters (p. 770)
purdah aislamiento de las mujeres en recintos separadas

Puritans members of an English Protestant group who wanted to "purify" the Church of England by making it more simple and more morally strict (p. 517)

puritanos miembros de un grupo de protestantes ingleses que querían "purificar" la Iglesia de Inglaterra, haciéndola más sencilla y moralmente más estricta

Pusan Perimeter a defensive line around the city of Pusan, in the southeast corner of Korea, held by South Korean and United Nations forces in 1950 during the Korean War; marks the farthest advance of North Korean forces (p. 990)

Perímetro de Pusan línea defensiva alrededor de la ciudad de Pusan, en el sudeste de Corea, custodiada por Corea del Sur y las fuerzas de las Naciones Unidas en 1950 durante la Guerra de Corea; marca el mayor avance de las fuerzas de Corea del Norte

putting-out system a system developed in the 18th century in which tasks were distributed to individuals who completed the work in their own homes; also known as cottage industry (p. 614)

sistema de trabajo a domicilio sistema desarrolla do en el siglo XVIII en el que las tareas se distribúan a individuos quienes completaban el trabajo en sus hogares; tambien se conoce como industria familiar

Q

Qajars members of the dynasty that ruled present-day Iran from the late 1700s until 1925 (p. 333)

Qajars miembros de la dinastía que gobernó la zona del actual Irán desde fines del siglo XVIII hasta 1925

Qing dynasty dynasty established by the Manchus in the mid 1600s and lasted until the early 1900s; China's last dynasty (p. 463)

dinastía Chin dinastía establecida por los manchus a mediados del siglo XVII que duró hasta principios del siglo XX; fue la última dinastía china

Quran the holy book of Islam (p. 306)

Corán el libro sagrado del islam

quipu knotted strings used by Inca officials for record-keeping (p. 197)

quipu cuerdas con nudos que usaban los incas como llevar registros

R

racism belief that one racial group is superior to another (p. 680)

racismo creencia de que un grupo racial es superior a otro

radicals those who favor extreme changes (pp. 638, 835)

radicales persona que quiere hacer cambios extremos

rajah in ancient India, the elected warrior chief of an Aryan tribe (pp. 72, 326)

rajah jefe guerrero electo de una tribu aria en la antigua India

realism 19th-century artistic movement whose aim was to represent the world as it is (p. 682)

realismo movimiento artístico del siglo XIX cuyo objetivo era representar el mundo tal como es

Realpolitik realistic politics based on the needs of the state (p. 694)

Realpolitik política realista basada en las necesidades del estado

recession period of reduced economic activity (pp. 640, 977)

recesión periodo de reducción de la actividad económica

Reconquista during the 1400s, the campaign by European Christians to drive the Muslims from present-day Spain (p. 260)

Reconquista durante el siglo XV, campaña por parte de cristianos europeos para expulsar a los musulmanes de la actual España

refugee a person who flees from home or country to seek refuge elsewhere, often because of political upheaval or famine (pp. 713, 1108)

refugiado persona que abandona su hogar o país en busca de refugio en otro lugar, a menudo como consecuencia de inestabilidad política o hambruna

regionalism loyalty to a local area (p. 802)

regionalismo lealtad a un área local

Reich German empire (p. 695)

Reich imperio alemán

Reign of Terror time period during the French Revolution from September 1793 to July 1794 when people in France were arrested for not supporting the revolution and many were executed (p. 587)

Reinado del terror período durante la Revolución Francesa desde septiembre de 1793 a julio de 1794, en el que la gente en Francia era arresta da por no apoyar la revolución; mucha gente fue ejecutada

reincarnation in Hindu belief, the rebirth of the soul in another bodily form (p. 77)

reencarnación según la creencia hindú, renacimiento del alma en otra forma corporal

reparation payment for war damage, or damage caused by imprisonment (p. 834)

indemnización pago por daños causados por guerra o encarcelamiento

repeal cancel (p. 727)

revocar cancelar

republic system of government in which officials are chosen by the people (pp. 151, 583)

república sistema de gobierno en el que los gobernantes son elegidos por el pueblo

revenue money taken in through taxes (p. 483)

rentas públicas dinero que se recauda por impuestos

rhetoric art of skillful speaking (p. 130)

retórica arte de hablar con habilidad

rococo personal, elegant style of art and architecture made popular during the mid-1700s that featured designs with the shapes of leaves, shells, and flowers (p. 551)

rococó estilo de arte y arquitectura elegante y personal que se hizo popular a mediados del siglo XVIII y que incluía diseños con formas de hojas, conchas y flores

romanticism 19th-century artistic movement that appealed to emotion rather than reason (p. 681)

romanticismo movimiento artístico del siglo XIX que apelaba a la emoción más que a la razón

Rosetta Stone stone monument that includes the same passage carved in hieroglyphics, demotic script, and Greek and that was used to decipher the meanings of many hieroglyphs (p. 55)

piedra de Rosetta piedra arquitectónica que incluye el mismo pasaje esculpido con caracteres jeroglíficos, demóticos y en escritura griega que se usó para descifrar el significado de muchos jeroglíficos

Rosie the Riveter popular name for women who worked in war industries during WWII (p. 940)

Rosita la Remachadora nombre popularmente dado a las mujeres que trabajaban en las fábricas de armamento durante la Segunda Guerra Mundial

rotten borough rural town in England that sent members to Parliament despite having few or no voters (p. 722)

"distrito podrido" en Inglaterra, ciudad rural que enviaba miembros al parlamento a pesar de no tener o tener pocos votantes

Ruhr Valley coal-rich industrial region of Germany (p. 913)

Valle del Ruhr región industrial alemana rica en carbón

russification making a nationality's culture more ethnically Russian (p. 908)

rusificación hacer la cultura nacionalista más étnicamente rusa

Russo-Japanese War conflict between Russia and Japan in 1904–1905 over control of Korea and Manchuria (p. 790)

Guerra ruso-japonesa conflicto entre Rusia y Japón de 1904 a 1905 por el control de Corea y Manchuria

S

Sabbath a holy day for rest and worship (p. 60)

sabbat día sagrado para descansar y rendir culto

sacrament sacred ritual of the Roman Catholic Church (p. 225)

sacramento ritual sagrado de la Iglesia Católica Romana

Safavid Shiite Muslim empire that ruled much of present-day Iran from the 1500s into the 1700s (p. 333)

Safávida imperio musulmán chiíta que gobernó la mayor parte del actual Irán desde el siglo XVI hasta el siglo XVIII

Sahara largest desert in the world, covering almost all of North Africa (p. 340)

Sahara desierto más grande del mundo que cubre casi todo el norte de África

salon informal social gathering at which writers, artists, *philosophes,* and others exchanged ideas (p. 551)

salón reuniones sociales informales en las que escritores, artistas, filósofos y otros intercambiaban ideas

samurai member of the warrior class in Japanese feudal society (p. 391)

samurai miembro de la clase guerrera en la sociedad japonesa feudal

Sandinistas a socialist political movement and party that held power in Nicaragua during the 1980s (p. 1086)

sandinistas partido y movimiento político socialista que gobernó Nicaragua durante la década de 1980

sans-culotte working-class man or woman who made the French Revolution more radical; called such because he or she wore long trousers instead of the fancy knee breeches that the upper class wore (p. 583)

sans-culotte hombre o mujer de la clase obrera que hicieron la Revolución Francesa más radical; llamados así porque llevaban pantalones largos a la rodilla como los que llevaba en vez de los pantalones ajustados la clase altas a la rodilla como los que llevaba la clase alta

Sapa Inca the title of the Inca emperor (p. 197)
　Sapa Inca título del emperador inca

sati Hindu custom that called for a widow to join her husband in death by throwing herself on his funeral pyre (p. 768)
　sati costumbre hindú que requería que la esposa se uniera a su marido en la muerte arrojándose a su pira funeraria

satirize make fun of (p. 162)
　satirizar burlarse de algo

savanna grassy plain with irregular patterns of rainfall (pp. 340, 1024)
　sabana planicie con pastizales cuyo régimen de lluvias es irregular

schism permanent division in a church (p. 270)
　cisma división permanente de una iglesia

scholasticism in medieval Europe, the school of thought that used logic and reason to support Christian belief (p. 264)
　escolástica en la Edad Media europea, escuela de pensamiento que usaba la lógica y el razonamiento para apoyar las creencias cristianas

scientific method careful, step-by-step process used to confirm findings and to prove or disprove a hypothesis (p. 436)
　método científico proceso cuidadoso y de varios pasos que se usa para confirmar descubrimientos y para aprobar o desaprobar una hipótesis

scorched-earth policy military tactic in which soldiers destroy everything in their path to hurt the enemy (p. 597)
　política de tierra quemada táctica militar en la que los soldados destruyen todo lo que tienen a su paso para perjudicar al enemigo

scribe in ancient civilizations, a person specially trained to read, write, and keep records (p. 22)
　escriba en las civilizaciones antiguas, persona especialmente educada para leer, escribir y mantener registros

secede withdraw (p. 741)
　separar retirarse

secret ballot votes cast without announcing them publicly (p. 723)
　voto secreto votos que se dan sin hacerlos públicos

sect a subgroup of a major religious group (pp. 82, 428)
　secta subgrupo de un grupo religioso importante

secular having to do with worldly, rather than religious, matters; nonreligious (pp. 228, 1035)

secular que tiene que ver más con asuntos mundanos que religiosos; no religioso

segregation forced separation by race, sex, religion, or ethnicity (pp. 741, 978)
　segregación separación forzada por razón de raza, sexo, religión o etnia

selective borrowing adopting or adapting some cultural traits but discarding others (p. 390)
　préstamo selectivo adoptar o adaptar algunos rasgos culturales y descartar otros

self-determination right of people to choose their own form of government (p. 833)
　autodeterminación derecho de los pueblos a elegir su propia forma de gobierno

sepoy Indian soldier who served in an army set up by the French or English trading companies (pp. 460, 768)
　sepoy soldado indio que sirvió en un ejército establecido por las compañías de comercio francesas o inglesas

serf in medieval Europe, a peasant bound to the lord's land (p. 222)
　siervo en la Europa medieval, campesino vinculado a las tierras del señor

shah king (p. 333)
　sha rey

shantytowns slums of flimsy shacks (p. 1070)
　barrio de chabolas barrios muy pobres de casuchas endebles

Sharia body of Islamic law that includes interpretation of the Quran and applies Islamic principles to everyday life (p. 308)
　Sharía ley canónica del islam que incluye la interpretación del Corán y que aplica los principios islámicos a la vida diaria

Sharpeville a black township in South Africa where the government killed anti-apartheid demonstrators in 1960 (p. 1049)
　Sharpeville municipio sudafricano habitado por personas de raza negra donde el gobierno mató a decenas de manifestantes antiapartheid en 1960

Shiite a member of one of the two major Muslim sects; believe that the descendents of Muhammad's daughter and son-in-law, Ali, are the true Muslim leaders (p. 311)
　chiíta miembro de una de las dos sectas musulmanas principales; creedor de que los descendientes de la hija y el yerno de Mahoma, Alí, son los verdaderos líderes musulmanes

Shinto principal religion in Japan that emphasizes the worship of nature (p. 389)

ENGLISH/SPANISH GLOSSARY

Shinto principal religión de Japón que enfatiza la adoración a la naturaleza

shogun in Japanese feudal society, supreme military commander, who held more power than the emperor (p. 391)

shogún en la sociedad feudal japonesa, jefe militar supremo con más poder que el emperador

shrine altar, chapel, or other sacred place (p. 114)

santuario altar, capilla u otro lugar sagrado

Sikhism religion founded by Nanak that blended Islamic and Hindu beliefs (p. 327)

sikhismo religión fundada por Nanak que incorpora creencias islámicas e hindúes

Sikhs members of an Indian religious minority (p. 1015)

sikhs miembros de una minoría religiosa de India

Silla dynasty Korean dynasty that ruled from 668 to 935 (p. 385)

dinastía Silla dinastía coreana que gobernó desde 668 a 935

Sino-Japanese War war between China and Japan in which Japan gained Taiwan (p. 776)

Guerra Sinojaponesa guerra entre China y Japón por la que Japón obtuvo el control de Taiwán

smelt melt in order to get the pure metal away from its waste matter (p. 611)

refinar fundir mineral para separar el mineral puro de las impurezas

social contract an agreement by which people gave up their freedom to a powerful government in order to avoid chaos (p. 545)

contrato social acuerdo mediante el cual el pueblo cede sus libertades a un gobierno poderoso para evitar el caos

social democracy political ideology in which there is a gradual transition from capitalism to socialism instead of a sudden violent overthrow of the system (p. 626)

democracia social ideología política en la que hay una transición gradual del capitalismo al socialismo en vez de un derrocamiento violento del sistema

social gospel movement of the 1800s that urged Christians to do social service (p. 680)

evangelio social movimiento del siglo XIX que urgía a los cristianos a que hicieran servicios sociales

social mobility the ability to move in social class (p. 318)

movilidad social la capacidad de cambiar de clase social

social welfare programs to help certain groups of people (p. 699)

bienestar social programas para ayudar a ciertos grupos de personas

socialism system in which the people as a whole rather than private individuals own all property and operate all businesses (pp. 625, 1072)

socialismo sistema en el que el pueblo como un todo, en vez de los individuos, son dueños de todas la propiedades y manejan todos los negocios

socialist realism artistic style whose goal was to promote socialism by showing Soviet life in a positive light (p. 908)

realismo socialista estilo artistico cuyo objetivo era promover el socialismo mostrando la vida en la Union Sovietica desde un perspectiva postiva

Solidarity a Polish labor union and democracy movement (p. 1003)

Solidaridad sindicato laboral y movimiento democrático polaco

Song dynasty Chinese dynasty from 960 to 1279; known for its artistic achievements (p. 370)

dinastía Song dinastía china desde 960 a 1279; conocida por sus grandes logros artísticos

Songhai medieval West African kingdom located in present-day Mali, Niger and Nigeria (p. 349)

Songhai reino medieval de África occidental ubicado en el presente Mali, Níger y Nigeria

sovereign having full, independent power (p. 458)

soberano tener poder pleno e independiente

soviet council of workers and soldiers set up by Russian revolutionaries in 1917 (p. 840)

soviet consejo de trabajadores y soldados establecido por los revolucionarios rusos en 1917

Spanish-American War conflict between the United States and Spain in 1898 over Cuban independence (p. 793)

Guerra entre Estados Unidos y España (Guerra hispano-estadounidense) conflicto entre Estados Unidos y España en 1898 por la independencia de Cuba

Sparta city-state in ancient Greece (p. 120)

Esparta antigua ciudad-estado en Grecia

speakeasies illegal bars (p. 885)

speakeasies bares ilegales

sphere of influence area in which an outside power claims exclusive investment or trading privileges (p. 753)

esfera de influencia área sobre la que un poder exterior se reserva privilegios comerciales o la exclusividad de realizar inversiones

St. Petersburg capital city and major port that Peter the Great established in 1703 (p. 532)
San Petersburgo ciudad y capital con un puerto importante, establecida en 1703 por Pedro el Grande

stalemate deadlock in which neither side is able to defeat the other (p. 822)
estancamiento punto muerto en una confrontación, en el que ninguna de las partes puede vencer a la otra

Stalingrad now Volgograd, a city in SW Russia that was the site of a fierce battle during WWII (p. 942)
Stalingrado actual Volgogrado; ciudad del sudoeste de Rusia donde se libró una encarnizada batalla durante la Segunda Guerra Mundial

Stamp Act law passed in 1765 by the British Parliament that imposed taxes on items such as newspapers and pamphlets in the American colonies; repealed in 1766 (p. 559)
Ley del Timbre ley promulgada en 1765 por el Parlamento Británico que imponía gravá menes a artículos como diarios y panfletos en las colonias americanas; revocada en 1766

standard of living measures the quality and availability of necessities and comforts in a society (p. 671)
estándar de vida medida de la calidad y disponibilidad de las necesidades básicas y de los lujos en una sociedad

stela in the ancient world, a tall, commemorative monument that was often decorated (p. 190)
estela en el mundo antiguo, gran monumento monolítico conmemorativo que comúnmente estaba decorado

steppe sparse, dry, treeless grassland (pp. 19, 289, 376)
estepa tierra de pastos escasos y secos sin árboles

stipend a fixed salary given to public office holders (p. 126)
estipendio salario fijo de los funcionarios públicos

stock shares in a company (p. 665)
acciones títulos o valores de una compañía

strait narrow water passage (p. 116)
estrecho paso angosto de agua

stupa large domelike Buddhist shrine (p. 400)
stupa gran altar budista en forma de cúpula

subcontinent large landmass that juts out from a continent (p. 68)
subcontinente gran masa de tierra que sobresale de un continente

suburbanization the movement to built-up areas outside of central cities (p. 977)

suburbanización proceso de construcción en áreas fuera del centro de la ciudad

Sudetenland a region of western Czechoslovakia (p. 927)
Sudetenland región occidental de la antigua Checoslovaquia

Suez Canal a canal linking the Red Sea and Indian Ocean to the Mediterranean Sea, which also links Europe to Asia and East Africa (pp. 734, 1036)
Canal de Suez canal que une el Mar Rojo y el Océano índico con el Mar Mediterráneo, que a la vez une Europa con Asia y África Oriental

suffrage right to vote (p. 586)
sufragio derecho al voto

Sufis Muslim mystics who seek communion with God through meditation, fasting, and other rituals (p. 312)
sufis místicos musulmanes que buscan la comunión con dios mediante la meditación, el ayuno y otros rituals

sultan Muslim ruler (pp. 316, 324, 764)
sultán gobernante musulmán

Sumer site of the world's first civilization, located in southeastern Mesopotamia (p. 30)
Sumeria lugar de la primera civilización del mundo, ubicada en el sureste de Mesopotamia

Sunni a member of one of the largest Muslim sects; Sunnis believe that inspiration came from the example of Muhammad as recorded by his early followers (p. 311)
sunita miembro de una de las dos sectas musulmanas principales; los sunitas creen que la inspiración proviene del ejemplo de Mahoma según fue registrada por sus primeros seguidores

superpower a nation stronger than other powerful nations (p. 966)
superpotencia nación suficientemente poderosa para influir en los actos y políticas de otras naciones poderosas

surplus an amount that is more than needed, excess (pp. 17, 346, 1098)
excedente cantidad de algo superior a lo que se necesita; exceso

surrealism artistic movement that attempts to portray the workings of the unconscious mind (p. 889)
surrealismo movimiento artístico que trata de mostrar el funcionamiento del inconsciente

sustainability the ability to meet the needs of the present without compromising the needs of future generations (p. 1104)

sostenibilidad capacidad de satisfacer las necesidades actuales sin poner en peligro las necesidades de generaciones futuras

sustainable development development that meets the needs of the present without compromising the ability of future generations to meet their own needs (p. 1074)

desarrollo sostenible desarrollo que cubre las necesidades del presente sin perjudicar la capacidad de las generaciones futuras de cubrir sus necesidades

Swahili an East African culture that emerged about 1000 A.D.; also a Bantu-based language, blending Arabic words and written in Arabic script (p. 355)

swahili cultura del este de África que emergió alrededor del año 1000 D.C.; también un idioma basado en el Bantú, que mezcla palabras árabes y usa la escritura árabe

T

Taiping Rebellion peasant revolt in China (p. 775)

Rebelión Taiping revuelta campesina en China

Taliban Islamic fundamentalist faction that ruled Afghanistan for nearly ten years until ousted by the United States in 2002 (p. 1119)

Talibán facción islámica fundamentalista que gobernó Afganistán durante casi diez años hasta que fue expulsada por Estados Unidos en 2002

Taj Mahal a tomb built by Shah Jahan for his wife (p. 328)

Taj Mahal tumba construida por Shah Jahan para su esposa; considerado como uno de los monumentos más importantes del imperio mughal

Tang dynasty Chinese dynasty from 618 to 907 (p. 368)

dinastía Tang dinastía china desde 618 a 907

tariff tax on imported goods (p. 495)

tasa impuesto a mercancías importadas

technology the skills and tools people use to meet their basic needs (p. 8)

tecnología herramientas y destrezas que usan las personas para satisfacer sus necesidades básicas

Tehran capital of the Qajar dynasty and present-day Iran (p. 333)

Teherán capital de la dinastía Qajar y del actual Irán

temperance movement campaign to limit or ban the use of alcoholic beverages (p. 676)

campaña de moderación campaña para limitar o prohibir el uso de bebidas alcohólicas

tenant farmer someone who would pay rent to a lord to farm part of the lord's land (p. 235)

agricultor arrendatario alguien que paga un alquiler a un señor para poder cultivar la tierra de éste

tenement multistory building divided into crowded apartments (p. 618)

apartamento de vecindad edificio de varios pisos dividido en apartamentos donde vive mucha gente

Tennis Court Oath famous oath made on a tennis court by members of the Third Estate in France (p. 576)

Juramento del juego de pelota famoso juramento hecho en una cancha de frontón por los miembros del Tercer Estado en Francia

Tenochtitlán capital city of the Aztec empire, on which modern-day Mexico City was built (pp. 192, 473)

Tenochtitlán capital del imperio azteca, sobre la cual se construyó la actual Ciudad de México

Teotihuacán city that dominated the Valley of Mexico from about A.D. 200 to A.D. 750 and that influenced the culture of later Mesoamerican peoples (p. 193)

Teotihuacán ciudad que dominó el Valle de México desde alrededor de 200 D.C. a 750 D.C., y que influyó en la cultura de los pueblos mesoamericanos posteriores

terrorism deliberate use of random violence, especially against civilians, to achieve political goals (p. 1116)

terrorismo uso deliberado de la violencia indiscriminada, especialmente en contra de civiles, para lograr fines políticos

Tet Offensive a massive and bloody offensive by communist guerrillas against South Vietnamese and American forces on Tet, the Vietnamese New Year, 1968; helped turn American public opinion against military involvement in Vietnam (p. 996)

Ofensiva Tet ofensiva masiva y sangrienta de las guerrillas comunistas contra los sudvietnamitas y las fuerzas estadounidenses durante el Tet, el Nuevo Año vietnamita, en 1968; ayudó a que la opinión pública estadouniden se se volviera en contra de la ocupación militar en Vietnam

theocracy government run by religious leaders (pp. 427, 1036)

teocracia gobierno administrado por líderes religiosos

Third Reich official name of the Nazi party for its regime in Germany; held power from 1933 to 1945 (p. 915)

Tercer Reich nombre oficial del partido nazi durante su mandato en Alemania; mantuvo el poder desde 1933 a 1945

38th parallel an imaginary line marking 38 degrees of latitude, particularly the line across the Korean Peninsula, dividing Soviet forces to the north and American forces to the south after WWII (p. 989)

paralelo 38 línea imaginaria que marca los 38 grados de latitud, en particular la línea a 38 grados de latitud norte que cruza la península coreana, que dividía las fuerzas soviéticas al norte y las fuerzas estadounindenses al sur después de la Segunda Guerra Mundial

Tiahuanaco a culture that thrived in the Andean region from about A.D. 200–A.D. 1000 (p. 196)

tiahuanaco cultura preincaica que tuvo su apogeo en la región andina desde alrededor de 200 D.C. a 1000 D.C.

Tiananmen Square a huge public plaza at the center of China's capital, Beijing (p. 1077)

Plaza de Tiananmen inmensa plaza pública en el centro de Beijing, la capital de China

Tokyo capital of Japan (p. 786)

Tokio capital de Japón

Torah the most sacred text of the Hebrew Bible, including its first five books (p. 57)

Tora el texto más sagrado de la Biblia judía que incluye sus cinco primeros libros

total war channeling of a nation's entire resources into a war effort (p. 829)

estado de guerra canalización de todos los recursos de una nación hacia la guerra

totalitarian state government in which a one-party dictatorship regulates every aspect of citizens' lives (p. 901)

estado totalitario gobierno en el que una dictadura de partido único regula todos los aspectos de la vida de los ciudadanos

tournament a mock battle in which knights would compete against one another to display their fighting skills (p. 221)

torneo batalla simulada en la que los caballeros competían entre ellos para lucir sus destrezas de lucha

trade deficit situation in which a country imports more than it exports (p. 773)

déficit comercial situación en la que un país importa más de lo que exporta

trade surplus situation in which a country exports more than it imports (p. 773)

excedente commercial situación en la que un país exporta más de lo que importa

traditional economy undeveloped economic systems that rely on custom and tradition (p. 17)

economía tradicional sistemas económicos sin desarrollar dependen de costumbres y tradiciones

tragedy in ancient Greece, a play about human suffering often ending in disaster (p. 134)

tragedia en la antigua Grecia, obra teatral que trataba del sufrimiento humano y que a menudo terminaba con un desastre

Treaty of Paris treaty of 1763 that ended the Seven Years' War and resulted in British dominance of the Americas (p. 486)

Tratado de París en 1763, tratado que terminó con la Guerra de los Siete Años y resultó en el dominio británico de las Américas

Treaty of Paris peace treaty made final in 1783 that ended the American Revolution (p. 562)

Tratado de París tratado de paz de 1783 que dio final a la Revolución Americana

Treaty of Tordesillas treaty signed between Spain and Portugal in 1494 which divided the non-European world between them (p. 450)

Tratado de Tordesillas tratado firmado por España y Portugal en 1494 por el que se dividían entre ellos el mundo fuera de Europa

triangular trade colonial trade routes among Europe and its colonies, the West Indies, and Africa in which goods were exchanged for slaves (p. 487)

comercio triangular ruta colonial de comercio entre Europa y sus colonias en las Indias Occidentales y África, en donde las mercancías se cambiaban por esclavos

tribunes in ancient Rome, official who was elected by the plebeians to protect their interests (p. 152)

tribuno en la antigua Roma, funcionario elegido por los plebeyos para proteger sus intereses

tributary state independent state that has to acknowledge the supremacy of another state and pay tribute to its ruler (p. 369)

estado tributario estado independiente que debe reconocer la supremacía de otro estado y pagar tributo a su gobernante

tribute payment that conquered peoples may be forced to pay their conquerors (p. 193)
  tributo pago que los conquistadores podían obligar a pagar a los pueblos conquistados

Trojan War in Greek epic poems and myths, a ten-year war between Mycenae and the city of Troy in Asia Minor (p. 116)
  Guerra de Troya en los mitos y poemas griegos, guerra de diez años de duración entre Micenas y la ciudad de Troya situada en Asia Menor

troubadour a wandering poet or singer of medieval Europe (p. 222)
  trovador poeta o cantante itinerante de la Europa medieval

Truman Doctrine United States policy, established in 1947, of trying to contain the spread of communism (p. 955)
  Doctrina Truman estrategia política establecida en 1947 con el propósito de contener la expansión del comunismo

tsar title of the ruler of the Russian empire (p. 293)
  zar título del regente del imperio ruso

tsunami very large, damaging wave caused by an earthquake or very strong wind (pp. 388, 1107)
  tsunami ola enorme y destructiva causada por un terremoto o vientos muy fuertes

turnpike private road built by entrepreneurs who charged a toll to travelers who used it (p. 614)
  autopista de peaje carretera construida con capital privado; el dueño de la carretera cobra una tarifa a los viajeros por usarla

Tutsis the main minority group in Rwanda and Burundi (p. 1051)
  Tutsis principal minoría de Ruanda y Burundi

Twenty-One Demands list of demands given to China by Japan in 1915 that would have made China a protectorate of Japan (p. 870)
  Veintiuna Exigencias lista de exigencias dadas por Japón a China en 1915 por las que, si hubiera estado de acuerdo, China se habría convertido en un protectorado de Japón

tyrant in ancient Greece, ruler who gained power by force (p. 122)
  tirano en la antigua Grecia, gobernante que llegó al poder por medio de la fuerza

U-boat German submarine (p. 825)
  U-Boat submarino alemán

ultimatum final set of demands (p. 819)
  ultimátum serie final de exigencias

ultranationalist extreme nationalist (p. 876)
  ultranacionalista nacionalista radical

Umayyads members of the Sunni dynasty of caliphs that ruled a Muslim empire from 661 to 750 (p. 312)
  omeyas miembros de la dinastía Sunita de califas que gobernó un imperio musulmán de 661 a 750

United Nations (UN) international organization established after World War II with the goal of maintaining peace and cooperation in the international community (p. 953)
  Naciones Unidas (ONU) organización internacional establecida después de la Segunda Guerra Mundial con el propósito de preservar la paz y la cooperación en la comunidad internacional

universal manhood suffrage right of all adult men to vote (p. 635)
  sufragio universal masculino derecho de todos los hombres adultos a votar

untouchable in India, a member of the lowest caste (p. 866)
  intocable en India, miembro de la casta más baja

urban renewal the process of fixing up the poor areas of a city (p. 668)
  renovación urbana reconstrucción de las áreas pobres de una ciudad

urbanization movement of people from rural areas to cities (pp. 616, 1073)
  urbanización movimiento de personas de las áreas rurales a las ciudades

utilitarianism idea that the goal of society should be to bring about the greatest happiness for the greatest number of people (p. 623)
  utilitarismo idea de que el objetivo de la sociedad debería ser lograr la mayor felicidad para el mayor número de personas

utopian idealistic or visionary, usually used to describe a perfect society (p. 420)
  utópico idealista o visionario, normalmente se usa para describir una sociedad perfecta

V-E Day Victory in Europe Day, May 8, 1945, the day the Allies won WWII in Europe (p. 948)
  Día de la Victoria en Europa (Día del Armisticio) (8 de mayo de 1945) día en que los aliados vencieron en Europa durante la Segunda Guerra Mundial

Valley of Mexico valley in Mexico in which the numerous Mesoamerican civilizations, including the Aztecs, arose (p. 192)
Valle de México valle en México en el cual se desarrollaron numerosas civilizaciones mesoamericanas, incluyendo los aztecas
vanguard group of elite leaders (p. 870)
vanguardia grupo de líderes de la élite
vassal in medieval Europe, a lord who was granted land in exchange for service and loyalty to a greater lord (p. 219)
vasallo durante la Edad Media, señor a quien se le cedía un terreno a cambio de servicio y lealtad al señor más importante
Vedas a collection of prayers, hymns, and other religious teachings developed in ancient India beginning around 1500 B.C. (p. 72)
Vedas con onjunto de oraciones, himnos y otras enseñanzas religiosas desarrolladas en la antigua India a partir de alrededor del siglo XVI a. de C.
veneration special regard (p. 71)
veneración estima especial
vernacular everyday language of ordinary people (pp. 265, 419)
vernáculo lenguaje diario de la gente corriente
Versailles royal French residence and seat of government established by King Louis XIV (p. 512)
Versalles residencia de la realeza francesa y sede de gobierno establecidos por el rey Luis XIV
veto block a government action (p. 152)
veto bloquear una acción del gobierno
viceroy representative who ruled one of Spain's provinces in the Americas in the king's name; one who governed in India in the name of the British monarch (pp. 477, 769)
virrey representante que regía una de las provincias de España en las Américas en nombre del rey; quien gobernaba en India en nombre del monarca británico
Vichy city in central France where a puppet state governed unoccupied France and the French colonies (p. 931)
Vichy ciudad en el centro de Francia desde donde un gobierno títere dirigió la Francia no ocupada y las colonias francesas
Viet Cong communist rebels in South Vietnam who sought to overthrow South Vietnam's government; received assistance from North Vietnam (p. 993)
Vietcong rebeldes comunistas en Vietnam del Sur que buscaban derrotar el gobierno de Vietnam del Sur; recibieron ayuda de Vietnam del Norte
Vikings Scandinavian peoples whose sailors raided Europe from the 700s through the 1100s (p. 218)
vikingo pueblo escandinavo cuyos marineros asaltaron Europa durante los siglos VIII al XII
vizier chief minister who supervised the business of government in ancient Egypt (p. 45)
visir ministro principal que supervisaba los asuntos de gobierno en el antiguo Egipto

W

War of the Austrian Succession series of wars in which various European nations competed for power in Central Europe after the death of Hapsburg emperor Charles VI (p. 528)
Guerra de Sucesión Austriaca serie de guerras en las que diversos países europeos lucharon por la hegemonía en centroeuropa después de la muerte de Carlos IV, emperador Habsburgo
warlord local military ruler (p. 105)
jefe militar cabeza de un ejército local
warm-water port port that is free of ice year-round (p. 532)
puerto de aguas templadas puerto en el que sus aguas nunca se congelan a lo largo del año
Warsaw Pact mutual-defense alliance between the Soviet Union and seven satellites in Eastern Europe set up in 1955 (p. 956)
Pacto de Varsovia alianza de defensa mutua establecida en 1955 entre la Unión Soviética y siete países de Europa del Este pertenecientes a su esfera de influencia
weapons of mass destruction (WMDs) biological, nuclear, or chemical weapons (p. 1059)
armas de destrucción masiva (ADM) armas biológicas, nucleares o químicas
welfare state a country with a market economy but with increased government responsibility for the social and economic needs of its people (p. 982)
estado de bienestar país con una economía de Mercado, pero con un gobierno con mayor responsabilidad sobre las nece sidades económicas de su pueblo
westernization adoption of western ideas, technology, and culture (p. 531)
occidentalización adopción de ideas, tecnología y cultura occidentales
Wittenberg a city in northern Germany, where Luther drew up his 95 theses (p. 425)

Wittenberg ciudad al norte de Alemania donde Lutero redactó sus 95 tesis

women's suffrage right of women to vote (p. 676)
sufragio femenino derecho de las mujeres a votar

World Trade Organization (WTO) international organization set up to facilitate global trade (p. 1103)
Organización Mundial del Comercio (OMC) organización internacional constituida para facilitar el comercio en el ámbito mundial

Y

Yalta Conference meeting between Churchill, Roosevelt, and Stalin in February 1945 where the three leaders made agreements regarding the end of World War II (p. 945)
Conferencia de Yalta reunión mantenida en febrero de 1945 entre Churchill, Roosevelt y Stalin en la que los tres mandatarios alcanzaron un acuerdo con respecto a la finalización de la Segunda Guerra Mundial

Yathrib final destination of Muhammad's hijra and the home of the first community of Muslims; later renamed Medina; located in the northwest of present-day Saudi Arabia (p. 305)
Yathrib destino final de la hégira de Mahoma y hogar de la primera comunidad de musulmanes; posteriormente rebautizada como Medina; ubicada en el noroeste de la actual Arabia Saudita

Yorktown, Virginia location where the British army surrendered in the American Revolution (p. 562)
Yorktown, Virginia lugar donde el ejército británico se rindió en la Revolución Americana

Yuan dynasty Chinese dynasty ruled by the Mongols from 1279 to 1368; best known ruler was Kublai Khan (p. 378)
dinastía Yuan dinastía china gobernada por los mongoles desde 1279 a 1368; su gobernante más conocido fue Kublai Khan

Z

zaibatsu since the late 1800s, powerful banking and industrial families in Japan (p. 788)
zaibatsu familias japonesas de banqueros e industriales poderosos desde finales del siglo XIX

zemstvos local elected assembly set up in Russia under Alexander II (p. 711)
zemstvos asambla local electa que se estableció en Rusia en la época de Alejandro II

Zen the practice of meditation; a school of Buddhism in Japan (p. 394)
zen práctica de meditación; escuela del budismo en Japón

zeppelin large gas-filled balloon (p. 825)
zepelín dirigible, globo grande lleno de gas

ziggurat in ancient Mesopotamia, a large, stepped platform thought to have been topped by a temple dedicated to a city's chief god or goddess (p. 32)
zigurat templo piramidal de la antigua Mesopotamia dedicado al dios o diosa principal de una ciudad

Zionism a movement devoted to rebuilding a Jewish state in Palestine (p. 737)
zionismo movimiento dedicado a la reconstrucción del estado judío en Palestina

A

INDEX

ACKNOWLEDGMENTS

Staff Credits
The people who make up the **World History © 07** team—representing design services, editorial, editorial services, educational technology, marketing, market research, photo research and art development, production services, publishing processes, and rights & permissions—are listed below. Bold type denotes core team members.

Marla Abramson, Leann Davis Alspaugh, Scott Andrews, Helene Avraham, Renee Beach, Eytan Bernstein, Suzanne Biron, Stephanie Bradley, **Peter Brooks,** Kerry Lyn Buckley, Lynn Burke, Kerry Cashman, Geoffrey Cassar, Todd Christy, Lori-Anne Cohen, Alan Dalgleish, Laura Edgerton Riser, Anne Falzone, Tom Ferreira, Lara Fox, Elizabeth Good, Ellen Welch Granter, **Diane Grossman,** Julie Gurdin, **Mary Ann Gundersen,** Mary Hanisco, Salena Hastings, Lance Hatch, Brian Heyward, Margaret Higgins, Katharine Ingram, Tim Jones, Judie Jozokos, Lynne Kalkanajian, Courtney Lane, Ruth Lopriore, **Grace Massey, Constance J. McCarty,** Michael McLaughlin, Claudi Mimo, Xavier Niz, Carrie O'Connor, Mark O'Malley, Linda Punskovsky, **Deborah Nicholls,** Jen Paley, Jonathan Penyack, **Gabriela Perez-Fiato,** Judi Pinkham, Jennifer Ribnicky, Marcy Rose, Rashid Ross, Robyn Salbo, **Colleen Searson,** Greg Slook, Laurel Smith, **Lisa Smith-Ruvalcaba,** Kara Stokes, Ana Sofia Villaveces, Rachel Winter, **Sarah Yezzi**

Vendor
Pronk & Associates Inc.

Maps
XNR Productions, Inc.: SH25, SH27, SH28, SH29, 10, 18, 31, 37, 40–41, 45, 47, 63, 69, 74–75, 81, 85, 93, 103, 105, 119, 125, 127, 138, 151, 156, 164, 169, 174, 178–179, 181, 187, 189, 196, 202, 206, 210–211, 215, 217, 222, 226, 232, 248, 257, 261, 271, 275, 286, 292, 295, 298, 307, 315, 325, 332, 341, 342, 345, 349, 355, 380, 384, 388, 398, 406–407, 413, 432, 443, 447, 454, 462–463, 475, 485, 489, 496–497, 498, 505, 526, 532, 536, 540–541, 554, 558, 565, 595, 599, 613, 640, 647, 649, 656–657, 661, 678–679, 693, 703, 707, 716, 735, 742, 757, 765, 769, 774, 778, 793, 797, 799, 804, 806, 812–813, 821, 827, 830, 841, 852, 853, 860, 863, 872, 876, 879, 892, 907, 928, 934, 940, 943, 946, 949, 955, 957, 958, 961, 962–963, 969, 971, 975, 988, 989, 995, 998, 999, 1011, 1015, 1022, 1027, 1033, 1038, 1041, 1046, 1051, 1056, 1060, 1063, 1067, 1074, 1083, 1097, 1099, 1101, 1107, 1111, 1117, 1131, 1134–1135, 1136, 1137, 1138, 1139, 1140, 1141, 1142, 1143, 1144, 1145, 1152–1153, 1156–1157

Illustrations
Kenneth Batelman 929, 946–947; Kerry Cashman SH13, SH26, SH39, 6–7, 10, 12, 21, 24–25, 34, 39, 42, 47, 49, 52, 54, 58, 62–63, 77, 79, 87, 95, 97, 99, 104–105, 127, 132–133, 140–141, 143, 144–145, 163, 172, 174–175, 180, 180–181, 192, 206–207, 227, 232, 234, 238–239, 247, 259, 264, 272, 274–275, 276–277, 284, 295, 298–299, 307, 321, 323, 334–335, 349, 351, 354–355, 358–359, 362–363, 370, 373, 378–379, 380, 390, 393, 396, 402–403, 414–415, 420–421, 430–431, 436, 437, 440–441, 448–449, 462–463, 466–467, 474–475, 480, 488–489, 496–497, 498–499, 506, 509, 513, 518–519, 534, 536–537, 552, 558, 562, 564–565, 566–567, 574, 581, 588–589, 602–603, 614, 624, 628–629, 640–641, 649, 652–653, 666, 674–675, 675, 677, 683, 686–687, 703, 712–713, 716–717, 724–725, 730, 734–735, 740, 744–745, 765, 768–769, 774–775, 778–779, 786–787, 794, 806, 808-809, 828–829, 828–829, 839, 846–847, 852–853, 853, 860–861, 878–879, 886–887, 894, 894–895, 900–901, 918–919, 932–933, 934–935, 941, 946–947, 946–947, 958–959, 969, 971, 988–989, 994–995, 1008–1009, 1038–1039, 1050, 1054–1055, 1060–1061, 1074, 1078, 108–109, 1084–1085, 1090–1091, 1102–1103, 1107, 1111, 1121, 1122–1123, 1124, 1126–1127, 1132–1133, 1146–1147, 1147, 1148–1149, 1158–1159, 1160–1161, 1163, 1168–1169; Ellen Welch Granter SH2, SH3, SH4, SH9, SH10, SH12, SH13, SH15, SH16, SH17, SH21, SH30, SH41; Kevin Jones Associates 12, 14, 21, 33, 39, 49, 52, 179, 204, 220–221, 582, 614, 635, 664, 712–713; Jen Paley SH5, SH20, SH23, SH37, 4, 5, 8, 11, 17, 20, 22, 24, 30, 33, 36, 44, 49, 50, 54, 57, 59, 62, 68, 76, 84, 92, 101, 108, 114, 118, 119, 124, 130, 137, 144, 150, 155, 159, 161, 166, 171, 173, 175, 180, 186, 188, 195, 201, 202, 206, 214, 216, 219, 225, 231, 238, 244, 246, 247, 251, 255, 262, 269, 271, 276, 282, 289, 294, 296, 298, 304, 306, 307, 310, 311, 317, 322, 324, 326, 329, 334, 340, 346, 352, 357, 362, 368, 376, 383, 387, 397, 402, 410, 418, 423, 426, 428, 434, 440, 446, 452, 457, 461, 466, 472, 477, 480, 482, 487, 491, 493, 496, 497, 498, 504, 506, 510, 516, 522, 525, 530, 534, 544, 550, 554, 555, 557, 563, 566, 569, 572, 578, 585, 592, 602, 608, 609, 612, 616, 617, 622, 628, 634, 637, 638, 642, 645, 652, 660, 662, 667, 670, 674, 675, 681, 686, 689, 692, 696, 700, 705, 710, 716, 722, 726, 730, 733, 739, 744, 750, 754, 762, 767, 772, 773, 778, 779, 784, 788, 791, 796, 801, 804, 806, 808, 809, 824, 826, 828, 833, 838, 839, 840, 843, 852, 853, 854, 855, 858, 865, 869, 870, 874, 878, 884, 886, 891, 895, 897, 898, 901, 904, 905, 906, 912, 917, 918, 924, 927, 929, 930, 934, 935, 938, 939, 947, 948, 952, 953, 958, 959, 961, 968, 972, 976, 985, 992, 1000, 1008, 1014, 1017, 1020, 1022, 1024, 1032, 1035, 1041, 1044, 1045, 1048, 1050, 1051, 1054, 1057, 1060, 1061, 1066, 1067, 1072, 1076, 1077, 1078, 1082, 1085, 1090, 1096, 1100, 1102, 1106, 1108, 1111, 1115, 1120, 1126, 1129, 1148, 1150, 1151, 1154, 1155, 1162, 1163, 1166, 1167; Ted Smykal SH4, SH6, SH7, SH8, SH9, SH10, SH11, SH14, SH15, SH16, SH17, SH18, SH19, SH21, 33, 493, 554, 678–679, 998–999, 1022, 1034–1035, 1089

Photographs
Every effort has been made to secure permission and provide appropriate credit for photographic material. The publisher deeply regrets any omission and pledges to correct errors called to its attention in subsequent editions.

Unless otherwise acknowledged, all photographs are the property of Pearson Education, Inc.

Photo locators denoted as follows: Top (T), Center (C), Bottom (B), Left (L), Right (R), Background (Bkgd)

Cover Art Resource, NY; **Front Matter v** National Geographic Image Collection; **vi** (T) Alan Hills and Barbara Winter ©The British Museum/©DK Images; **vii** (B) Ace Stock Limited/Alamy Images, The Image Works, Inc.; **viii** (B) Musee de la Tapisserie, Bayeux, France/ /Bridgeman Art Library; **ix** (T) Art Resource, NY; **x** (T, B) Victoria & Albert Museum, London/Art Resource, NY; **xi** (T) AKG London Ltd., (B) Science Museum/Science & Society Picture Library; **xii** Mary Evans Picture Library; **xiii** Corbis; **xiv** Kapoor Baldev/Sygma/Corbis; **xv** Alison Wright/Corbis; **xvi** (L) Wanda's Pie in the Sky; **xvii** Alamy Images; **xix** British Museum/The Art Archive; **xx** (Inset) AKG London Ltd., Charles & Josette Lenars/Corbis; **xxi** New York Daily News/Getty Images; **xxiv** bpk, Berlin/Antikensammlung, Staatliche Museen, Berlin, Germany/Art Resource, NY; **xxix** (R) Time & Life Pictures/Getty Images; **SH1** Jose Luis Pelaez, Inc./Corbis; **SH2** IT Stock Free/AGE Fotostock; **SH3** Ed Bock/Corbis; **SH6** Jupiter Images; **SH13** Public Record Office/HIP/The Image Works, Inc.; **SH22** Arthur Tilley/Getty Images; **SH24** Roger Wood/Corbis; **SH29** Getty Images; **SH30** (T) ©DK Images, (B) North Wind Picture Archives; **SH31** Arcadio/Cartoon Web, Cartoon & Writers Syndicate; **SH33** Science Museum/Science & Society Picture Library; **SH36** (L) ©The Granger Collection, NY, (R) Corbis; **SH38** ©Dana White/PhotoEdit; **2** Time & Life Pictures/Getty Images; **3** (T) ©Images of Africa Photobank/Alamy Images, (C) ©MELBA PHOTO AGENCY/Alamy, Reunion des Musees Nationaux/Art Resource, NY; **4** (R) ©Gallo Images/Corbis, (L) Kenneth Garrett/National Geographic Image Collection; **5** ©The Granger Collection, NY; **6** National Geographic Image Collection; **7** (R) ©Caro/Alamy Images, (BL) Michael P. Fogden/Photoshot, (TL) Peabody Museum, Harvard University, (R) Roger M. Richards; **8** Robert F. Sisson/National Geographic Image Collection; **9** Institute of Human Origins; **10** ©Wave Royalty Free/Alamy; **11** BibleLandPictures/Alamy Images; **12** (B) ©DK Images, (C) ©SSPL/The Image Works, Inc., (T) Steve Gorton/©DK Images; **13** Reunion des Musees Nationaux/Art Resource, NY; **16** (CR) ©JM Labat/Photo Researchers, Inc., (BR) DK Images, (BL) Harry Taylor/©DK Images, (CL) Réunion des Musées Nationaux/Art Resource, NY, (T) Sisse Brimberg/National Geographic Image Collection, (BC) Ted Kinsman/Photo Researchers, Inc.; **17** Art Resource, NY; **21** (T) ©Best View Stock/Alamy, (B) Juan Silva/Getty Images; **23** Alinari/Art Resource, NY; **24** ©Gallo Images/Corbis; **25** ©MELBA PHOTO AGENCY/Alamy; **26** (T) Cartoon Stock, (B) Time & Life Pictures/Getty Images; **27** Peter Brown; **28** The Gallery Collection/Corbis; **29** (T) ©The Granger Collection, NY, (C) ©The Trustees of The British Museum/Art Resource, NY, (R) Private Collection/The Art Archive, (B) Staatliche Sammlung Ägyptischer Kunst Munich/Gianni Dagli Orti/The Art Archive; **30** (R) ©Ancient Art & Architecture Collection Ltd/Alamy Images, (L) ©The Trustees of The British Museum/Art Resource, NY; **32** ©DK Images; **33** (C) Ashmolean Museum, University of Oxford, UK/Bridgeman Art Library, (TR, TL) Réunion des Musées Nationaux/Art Resource, NY, (B) The Art Archive; **34** (T, B) ©Planetary Exclusives/Alamy; **35** (T) Ronald Sheridan/Ancient Art & Architecture Collection Ltd.; **36** Réunion des Musées Nationaux/Art Resource, NY, (Bkgrd) The Art Archive/Musée du Louvre Paris/Gianni Dagli Orti/The Kobal Collection; **37** Erich Lessing/Art Resource, NY; **38** ©Topham/Image Works; **39** (T) ©CM Dixon/HIP/The Image Works, Inc., (BR, BL) Erich Lessing/Art Resource, NY; **42** (TR) ©The Granger Collection, NY, (C) ©The Trustees of the

British Museum/Art Resource, NY, (BL) Alan Hills and Barbara Winter ©The British Museum/©DK Images, (TL) Ian O'Leary/©DK Images, (BR) The Granger Collection, NY; **43** Ronald Sheridan/Ancient Art & Architecture Collection Ltd.; **44** Werner Forman/Art Resource, NY; **45** Nik Wheeler/Corbis; **47** Andrea Jemolo/AKG London Ltd.; **48** Dagli Orti/Egyptian Museum Cairo/The Art Archive; **49** ©The Granger Collection, NY; **50** (R) Alistair Duncan/©DK Images, (L) Réunion des Musées Nationaux/Art Resource, NY; **51** ©The Trustees of The British Museum/Art Resource, NY; **52** (B) ©The Trustees of The British Museum/Art Resource, NY, (Border) Egyptian Museum Cairo/Collection Dagli Orti/The Art Archive, (T) Réunion des Musées Nationaux/Art Resource, NY; **53** ©Roger Wood/Corbis; **54** (R) ©The British Museum/Topham/The Image Works, Inc., (C) akg-images/Werner Forman/NewsCom, (L) Werner Forman/AKG London Ltd.; **55** (T) Gianni Dagli Orti/The Art Archive, (B) KENNETH GARRETT/National Geographic Image Collection; **56** (T) ©Oscar Elias/Alamy Images, (B) ©Robert Harding Picture Library Ltd/Alamy Images, (TR) Staatliche Sammlung Ägyptischer Kunst Munich/Gianni Dagli Orti/The Art Archive; **57** West London Synagogue, London, UK/Bridgeman Art Library; **58** (CL) ©Nathan Benn/Corbis, (TL, Bkgrd) ©The Granger Collection, NY, (CR) The Israel Museum, Jerusalem; **61** (B) ©Peter Hvizdak/The Image Works, Inc.; **62** ©Michael S. Yamashita/Corbis; **63** (B) ©Asian Art & Archaeology, Inc/Corbis, (T) Réunion des Musées Nationaux/Art Resource, NY; **64** The Gallery Collection/Corbis; **65** (B) Erich Lessing/Art Resource, NY, (T) Zen Radovan/Z. Radovan, Jerusalem; **66** Eddie Gerald/Eddie Gerald, Hung Chung Chih/Shutterstock, Korobanova/Shutterstock; **67** (T) ©British Library Board. All Rights Reserved., (C) Image copyright ©The Metropolitan Museum of Art/Art Resource, NY, (B) Kamat's Potpourri/CyberCrow Inc.; **68** (R) Ronald Sheridan/Ancient Art & Architecture Collection Ltd., (L) Scala/Art Resource, NY; **70** Getty Images; **71** (B) ©Angelo Hornak/Alamy Images, (B) Copyright J.M. Kenoyer, Courtesy Dept. of Archaeology and Museums, Govt. of Pakistan/Harappa, (C) The Art Archive, (T) The Image Works, Inc.; **73** (R) ©Zhao Xuan/Alamy, (L) Angelo Hornak/Corbis, (R) Photo by Ling Long/Imaginechina; **75** (B) ©Rubin Museum of Art/Art Resource, NY, (T) bpk, Berlin/Museum fuer Asiatische Kunst, Staatliche Museen, Berlin, Germany/Art Resource, NY; **76** (R) ©mark downey/Alamy Images, (L) ©Robert Maass/Corbis; **77** (TC) ©Angelo Hornak/Corbis, (T) ©Lindsay Hebberd/Corbis, (B) ©Sheldan Collins/Corbis, (B) Image copyright ©The Metropolitan Museum of Art/Art Resource, NY; **79** (BL) ©Asia Alan King/Alamy Images,

(BR) ©Greg Martin/SuperStock, (T) Jobon Rendaiji Temple Kyoto/Laurie Platt Winfrey/The Art Archive; **81** Tibor Hirsch/Photo Researchers, Inc.; **82** ©Profimedia International s.r.o./Alamy Images; **83** Corbis; **84** Kamat's Potpourri/CyberCrow Inc.; **87** (TR) ©Corbis Premium RF/Alamy, (Border) ©Karen Kasmauski/Corbis, (B) ©Lindsay Hebberd/Corbis, (TC) ©The Trustees of The British Museum/Art Resource, NY, (TL) Jean-Louis Nou/AKG London Ltd.; **88** H. Hansum/Bucknell University; **90** ©Associated Press; **91** (L) Borromeo/Art Resource, NY, (T) Getty Images, (BR) Sudharak Olwe/Dinodia Photo Library/Dinodia Picture Agency; **92** ©The Granger Collection, NY; **94** (T, B) ©Asian Art & Archaeology, Inc./Corbis; **97** ©The Granger Collection, NY; **98** Réunion des Musées Nationaux/Art Resource, NY; **99** (T) ©inga spence/Alamy Images, (BR, Border) ©The Trustees of The British Museum/Art Resource, NY, (C) Bibliotheque Municipale, Poitiers, France/Giraudon/Bridgeman Art Library, (BL) Bob Gibbons/Photo Researchers, Inc., (BC) Maryann Frazier/Photo Researchers, Inc., (C) Museum of Fine Arts, Boston, Massachusetts, USA/Special Chinese and Japanese Fund/Bridgeman Art Library; **100** (T) ©British Library Board. All Rights Reserved., (B) Ashmolean Museum, University of Oxford, UK/Bridgeman Art Library; **101** (R, L) ©British Library Board. All Rights Reserved.; **102** The Art Archive/Bibliothèque Nationale Paris/The Kobal Collection; **103** Corbis; **104** (Bkgrd) Art Wolfe/Getty Images, Bildarchiv Preussischer Kulturbesitz/Art Resource, NY; **105** ©The Granger Collection, NY; **106** Tek Image/Photo Researchers, Inc.; **107** Victoria & Albert Museum, London/Art Resource, NY; **108** (L) The Image Works, Inc., (R) Werner Forman/Art Resource, NY; **109** ©Bettmann/Corbis; **110** ©Greg Martin/SuperStock; **111** Ashmolean Museum, University of Oxford, UK/Bridgeman Art Library; **112** Erich Lessing/Art Resource, NY; **113** (C) ©akg-images/The Image Works, Inc., (B) ©Alinari Archives/Corbis, (T) Alinari/Art Resource, NY; **114** Scala/Art Resource, NY; **115** (T) Nimatallah/Art Resource, NY; **116** Erich Lessing/Art Resource, NY; **117** ©Kevin Fleming/Corbis; **118** (R) ©akg-images/The Image Works, Inc., (L) Peter Connolly/AKG London Ltd.; **119** ©Elio Ciol/Corbis; **120** Réunion des Musées Nationaux/Art Resource, NY; **121** Ace Stock Limited/Alamy Images; **122** bpk, Berlin/Antikensammlung, Staatliche Museen, Berlin, Germany/Art Resource, NY; **123** ©Steve Vidler/SuperStock; **124** Louvre, Paris, France/Giraudon/Bridgeman Art Library; **125** Scala/Art Resource, NY; **127** (C) ©2004 AAAC/Topham/The Image Works, Inc., (TL) ©Gianni Dagli Orti/Corbis, (TR) AKG London Ltd., (B) Ancient Art and Architecture Collection Ltd./Bridgeman Art Library; **128** bpk, Berlin/Antikensam-

mlung, Staatliche Museen, Berlin, Germany/Art Resource, NY; **129** ©Martin Beddal/Alamy Images, ©The British Museum/Heritage-Images; **130** Alinari/Art Resource, NY; **131** The Metropolitan Museum of Art/Art Resource, NY; **132** (B) ©SuperStock/SuperStock, (T) Erich Lessing/Art Resource, NY, (C) Image copyright ©The Metropolitan Museum of Art/Art Resource, NY; **133** (R) ©Carl & Ann Purcell/Corbis, (BL) ©Neil Setchfield/Lonely Planet Images, (TL) Nick Nicholls ©The British Museum/©DK Images; **134** (BT) ©Ruggero Vanni/Corbis, ©The Granger Collection, NY, (T) Erich Lessing/Art Resource, NY; **135** Nimatallah/Art Resource, NY; **136** Alinari/Art Resource, NY; **137** ©INTERFOTO/Alamy Images; **138** (B) Ancient Art & Architecture Collection Ltd., (T) BibleLandPictures/Alamy Images; **139** bpk, Berlin/Museum fuer Asiatische Kunst, Staatliche Museen, Berlin, Germany/Art Resource, NY; **140** ©The Granger Collection, NY, (Bkgrd) Photoaisa; **141** (C) ©SSPL/The Image Works, Inc., (L) National Archaeological Museum Athens/Gianni Dagli Orti/The Art Archive, (R) Time & Life Pictures/Getty Images; **142** ©Exactostock/SuperStock; **143** (B) ©Hubert Stadler/Corbis, (TL) ©Lebrecht Music and Arts Photo Library/Alamy Images; **144** Réunion des Musées Nationaux/Art Resource, NY; **145** (B) BibleLandPictures/Alamy Images, (T) Michael Ventura Photography; **146** ©Elio Ciol/Corbis; **147** Scala/Art Resource, NY; **148** Villa of the Mysteries Pompeii/Collection Dagli Ort/The Art Archive; **149** (C) ©Iberfoto/The Image Works, Inc., (T) bpk, Berlin/Antikensammlung, Staatliche Museen, Berlin, Germany/Art Resource, NY, (B) The Art Archive/Archaeological Museum Split Croatia/Alfredo Dagli Orti/The Kobal Collection; **150** Musée du Louvre Paris/Dagli Orti/The Art Archive; **151** Galleria di Storia ed Arte Udine/Collection Dagli Orti/The Art Archive; **154** Art Resource, NY; **155** (R) ©Mimmo Jodice/Corbis, (L) Archaeological Museum Venice/Collection Dagli Orti/The Art Archive; **156** Gianni Dagli Orti/Corbis; **157** (B) ©The Trustees of The British Museum/Art Resource, NY, (T) Scala/Ministero per i Beni e le Attività culturali/Art Resource, NY; **158** Gianni Dagli Orti/The Art Archive; **160** ©Iberfoto/The Image Works, Inc.; **161** Mary Evans Picture Library; **162** ©Topham/The Image Works, Inc.; **(BR)** ©Topham/The Image Works, Inc., (TL) Erich Lessing/Art Resource, NY, (CL) Erich Lessing/Art Resource, NY, (BL) Gianni Dagli Orti/The Art Archive, (TR) Metropolitan Museum of Art, New York, USA/Bridgeman Art Library; **164** Jupiterimages/Thinkstock; **166** (R) Art Resource, NY, (L) Scala/Art Resource, NY; **167** (B) ©Nathan Benn/Corbis, (T) Private Collection/The Stapleton Collection/Bridgeman Art Library; **168** Mary Evans Picture Library; **170**

©Christie's Images Ltd./SuperStock; **172** ©The British Library/HIP/The Image Works, Inc.; **173** (L) ©The Granger Collection, NY, (R) Kunstmuseum, Bern, Switzerland/Bridgeman Art Library; **174** (Bkgrd) ©Historical Picture Archive/Corbis, Scala/Art Resource, NY; **175** (L) Pinacoteca Comunale Fermo Ascoli Piceno/Gianni Dagli Orti/The Art Archive, (R) The Art Archive/Archaeological Museum Split Croatia/Alfredo Dagli Orti/The Kobal Collection; **176** Bryan Reinhart/Masterfile Corporation; **179** (T) Image copyright ©The Metropolitan Museum of Art/Art Resource, NY; **180** (T) Gianni Dagli Orti/Corbis, (B) Kamat's Potpourri/CyberCrow Inc.; **181** (T) Scala/Art Resource, NY; **182** Villa of the Mysteries Pompeii/Collection Dagli Ort/The Art Archive; **183** bpk, Berlin/Antikensammlung, Staatliche Museen, Berlin, Germany/Art Resource, NY; **184** ©Charles & Josette Lenars/Corbis; **185** (B) ©Canadian Museum of Civilization, (C) Archaeological Museum Lima/Mireille Vautier/The Art Archive, (T) Werner Forman Archive/National Museum of Anthropology, Mexico City. Location: 12. ©Werner Forman/Topham/The Image Works, Inc.; **186** (C) ©Matthias Kulka/Corbis, (L) John Bigelow Taylor/Art Resource, NY; **187** Archaeological Museum Lima/Mireille Vautier/The Art Archive, (T) Réunion des Musées Nationaux/Art Resource, NY; **188** ©Danny Lehman/Corbis, (TL,) The Art Archive, (BR) The Image Works, Inc., (TR) Werner Forman/Art Resource, NY; **189** (T) Corbis, (T) The Art Archive, (B) Werner Forman Archive/National Museum of Anthropology, Mexico City. Location: 12. ©Werner Forman/Topham/The Image Works, Inc.; **190** Art Resource, NY, Throckmorton Fine Art; **191** (B) ©Danny Lehman/Corbis, (BR) ©Macduff Everton/Corbis, (CL) ©Paul Almasy/Corbis, (CR) ©Peter Arnold, Inc./Alamy Images, (TR) ©Werner Forman/Topham/The Image Works, Inc., (TL) François Guénet/AKG London Ltd., (CR) Museum of Fine Arts, Boston, Massachusetts, USA/Gift of Landon T. Clay/Bridgeman Art Library, Werner Forman Archive/Collection: Edward H. Merrin Gallery, New York. Location: 12. ©Werner Foreman/Topham/The Image Works, Inc.; **192** (B) ©DK Images, (T) ©The Granger Collection, NY, BeBa/Iberfoto/Photoaisa; **193** (L) Archaeological Museum Teotihuacan Mexico/Gianni Dagli Orti/The Art Archive, (R) PRISMA/Ancient Art & Architecture Collection Ltd.; **194** Image copyright ©The Metropolitan Museum of Art/Art Resource, NY; **195** (R) ©Werner Forman/Topham/The Image Works, Inc., (L) Archaeological Museum Lima/Gianni Dagli Orti/The Art Archive; **196** (B) ©Art Directors & TRIP/Alamy Images, (L) Archaeological Museum Lima/Gianni Dagli Orti/The Art Archive; **197** ©The Granger Collection, NY, Corbis, (Inset) Rick Browne/Photo Researchers, Inc.;

198 (B) ©Danny Lehman/Corbis, (T) Ronald Sheridan/Ancient Art & Architecture Collection Ltd., The Image Works, Inc.; **199** (L) ©British Library Board. All Rights Reserved., ©The Trustees of The British Museum/Art Resource, NY, (C) Art Resource, NY, (BR) Corbis, (T) John Bigelow Taylor/Art Resource, NY; **200** (B) Corbis, (T) Photo Researchers, Inc., Photri Images; **201** The Raven and the First Men, by Bill Reid (Haida), 1980. Collection of the UBC Museum of Anthropology, Vancouver, Canada. Photo: Bill McLennan/©University of British Columbia Museum of Anthropology; **202** (B) ©Canadian Museum of Civilization, (TR) ©Richard A. Cooke/Corbis, (TL) ©The Granger Collection, NY, Réunion des Musées Nationaux/Art Resource, NY; **203** George H. H. Huey/Corbis; **204** (T) ©Canadian Museum of Civilization, Art Resource, NY; **205** Art Resource, NY; **206** (B) ©Royalty-Free/Corbis, Francois Guénet/AKG London Ltd., (T) The Art Archive; **207** ©Gianni Dagli Orti/Corbis; **208** (B) ©Charles & Josette Lenars/Corbis, (T) Bodleian Library; **209** The Ann Ronan Picture Library/Heritage-Images; **212** ©The Granger Collection, NY; **213** (T) ©British Library Board. All Rights Reserved., (B) Scala/Art Resource, NY, (C) Snark/Art Resource, NY; **214** (L) Corbis, (R) Reunion des Musee Nationaux/Art Resource, NY; **216** Reunion des Musee Nationaux/Art Resource, NY; **218** The British Library/Topham-HIP/The Image Works, Inc.; **219** BeBa/Iberfoto/Photoaisa; **222** Topham/The Image Works, Inc.; **223** (R) North Wind Picture Archives, (L) The British Library/HIP/The Image Works, Inc.; **224** (R) The British Library/HIP/The Image Works, Inc., (L) Torla Evans ©The Museum of London/©DK Images; **225** (L) ADO/Iberfoto/Photoaisa, (R) HIP/Art Resource, NY; **227** (C) Erich Lessing/Art Resource, NY, (T) Kunsthistorisches Museum, Vienna, Austria/Bridgeman Art Library, (C) Lambeth Palace Library, London, UK/Bridgeman Art Library; **228** Scala/Art Resource, NY; **229** Louvre, Paris, France/Bridgeman Art Library; **230** Musee du Judaisme/RMN/Art Resource, NY; **231** British Library/The Art Archive; **232** (L) Erich Lessing/Art Resource, NY, (R) Judith Miller/Lennox Gallery Ltd/©DK Images; **233** The Pierpont Morgan Library, New York, NY/Art Resource, NY; **234** ©Mary Evans Picture Library/The Image Works, Inc., (R) Bridgeman Art Library; **235** Scala/Art Resource, NY; **237** (C) SuperStock, (T, B) The British Library/The Image Works, Inc.; **239** (T) ©Associated Press, (B) Judith Miller/Lennox Gallery Ltd/©DK Images; **240** ©The Granger Collection, NY; **241** (R) D.Y./Art Resource, NY, (L) Scala/Art Resource, NY; **242** Gianni Dagli Orti/Corbis; **243** (B) ©DK Images, (C) AKG London Ltd., (T) Musée Municipal Vaucouleurs/Dagli Orti/The Art Archive, (B) York Archaeological Trust for Excavation and Research Ltd./ ©DK Images; **244** (R) AKG London Ltd., (L) Archives Nationales Paris/JFB/The Art Archive; **245** Franz-Marc Frei/Corbis; **247** The Royal Collection ©2006 Her Majesty Queen Elizabeth II; **249** The Art Archive/Corbis; **250** (B) ©The Granger Collection, NY, (T) Bridgeman Art Library; **251** (R) Erich Lessing/Art Resource, NY, (L) SEF/Art Resource, NY; **252** Foto Marburg/Art Resource, NY; **253** The British Library/HIP/The Image Works, Inc.; **254** San Francesco Assisi/Dagli Orti/The Art Archive; **255** Scala/Art Resource, NY; **257** (B) Bibliotheque des Arts Decoratifs, Paris, France/Bridgeman Art Library; **258** Galleria degli Uffizi Florence/Dagli Orti/The Art Archive; **259** (BL) Amos Zezmer/Omni Photo Communications, (TL) David Turnley/Corbis, (BR) Ellen Howdon/Courtesy of Glasgow Museum/©DK Images, (TR) Reuters/Corbis, (BR) University Library Coimbra/Dagli Orti/The Art Archive; **261** (T) Biblioteca Nacional Madrid/Laurie Platt Winfrey/The Art Archive, (B) Getty Images; **262** (R) ©DK Images, (L) Corbis, (R) York Archaeological Trust for Excavation and Research Ltd./©DK Images; **263** The British Library/HIP/The Image Works, Inc.; **264** (CR) Araldo de Luca/Corbis, (CL) Dave G. Houser/Corbis, (T) Peter Anderson/Courtesy of Saxon Village Crafts, Battle, East Sussex/DK Images, (B) The Pierpont Morgan Library/Art Resource, NY; **266** (B) Giraudon/Art Resource, NY, (T) Musee de la Tapisserie, Bayeux, France/ /Bridgeman Art Library; **268** (C) ©DK Images, (CR) Michel Setboun/Corbis, (B) Neil Lukas/©DK Images, (T) Vanni/Art Resource, NY; **269** (T, B) The Image Works, Inc.; **270** Musee Conde, Chantilly, France/Bridgeman Art Library; **272** (TR, TL) Geoff Dann/©DK Images, (BL) Snark/Art Resource, NY, (BR) The Board of Trustees of the Armouries/HIP/The Image Works, Inc.; **274** (Inset) ©DK Images, (TR) Bettmann/Corbis, (B) Frank Greenaway/©DK Images, (L) Stock Montage/SuperStock; **275** (L) ©The Granger Collection, NY, (R) Bibliotheque Royale de Belgique, Brussels, Belgium//Bridgeman Art Library; **276** The Board of Trustees of the Armouries/HIP/The Image Works, Inc.; **277** (T) Reuters/Wilson Chu/Corbis, (B) The Image Works, Inc.; **278** Galleria degli Uffizi Florence/Dagli Orti/The Art Archive; **279** Gianni Dagli Orti/Corbis; **280** Art Resource, NY; **281** (C) Art Resource, NY, (B) Bridgeman Art Library, (T) N. Carter/North Wind Picture Archives; **282** (L) ©The Granger Collection, NY, (R) Art Resource, NY; **284** (T) Adrian Zenz/Shutterstock, (Inset) Michele Burgess/PhotoLibrary Group, Inc.; **285** San Vitale, Ravenna, Italy/Bridgeman Art Library; **287** Alamy Images; **288** Giraudon/Art Resource, NY; **289** (L) ©DK Images, (R) Bridgeman Art Library; **290** Museum of History of Sofia, Bulgaria/Archives Charmet/Bridgeman Art Library; **291** Doug Page/Index Stock/PhotoLibrary Group, Inc.; **292** Andy Crawford/Courtesy of the History Museum, Moscow/©DK Images; **293** Tretyakov Gallery, Moscow, Russia/Bridgeman Art Library; **294** (L) Erich Lessing/Art Resource, NY, (R) Historical Museum of Republic of Crimea Simferopol/Dagli Orti (A)/The Art Archive; **295** (L) ©The Granger Collection, NY; **296** ©Pegaz/Alamy Images; **297** Erich Lessing/Art Resource, NY; **298** (B) Art Resource, NY; **299** (B) AKG London Ltd., (T) Elvis Barukcic/©Associated Press; **300** (B) Alamy Images, (T) British Library, London, Great Britain/Art Resource, NY; **301** PRISMA/Ancient Art & Architecture Collection Ltd.; **303** (B) ©DK Images, (C) ©The Granger Collection, NY, (T) Bridgeman Art Library; **304** (R) Art Directors & TRIP Photo Library, (L) Peter Sanders Photography Limited; **305** (T) Fitzwilliam Museum, University of Cambridge, UK/Bridgeman Art Library, (B) Kurt Stier/Corbis; **307** (CR) ©Associated Press, (CC) Prisma/Ancient Art & Architecture Collection Ltd., (TR) Reuters/Corbis, (TL) Steven Rubin/The Image Works, Inc., (B) Trip/Alamy Images; **308** ©The Granger Collection, NY; **309** (BL) ©The Granger Collection, NY, (BR) 2005 Richard l'Anson/Lonely Planet Images, (T) Bridgeman Art Library; **310** Monasterio de El Escorial/Index/Bridgeman Art Library; **311** Gary Cross/©DK Images; **312** Expuesto - Nicolas Randall/Alamy Images; **313** ©The Granger Collection, NY; **314** Snark/Art Resource, NY; **315** (B) José Fuste Raga/zefa/Corbis, (TR) Photographer's Choice/Getty Images, (TL) Roger Wood/Corbis; **316** Peter M. Wilson/Corbis; **317** (Inset) Topkapi Palace Museum, Istanbul, Turkey/Bridgeman Art Library, (Bkgrd) Werner Forman/Art Resource, NY; **318** (T) Peter Harholdt/Corbis, (B) Werner Forman/TopFoto/The Image Works, Inc.; **319** Royal Asiatic Society, London, UK/Bridgeman Art Library; **320** Ancient Art & Architecture Collection Ltd.; **321** (Bkgrd) ©British Library Board. All Rights Reserved., (T) ©The Granger Collection, NY, Bridgeman Art Library, (CL) Kharbine-Tapabor/Boisteselin/The Art Archive, (CC) The British Museum/HIP/The Image Works, Inc., (B) The Image Bank/Getty Images, (CR) University Library, Istanbul, Turkey/Bridgeman Art Library; **323** (TR) BeBa/Iberfoto/Photoaisa, (Bkgrd) Charles & Josette Lenars/Corbis, (B) Corbis, (TL) Victoria & Albert Museum, London/Art Resource, NY; **324** Getty Images; **325** Victoria and Albert Museum London/Eileen Tweedy/The Art Archive; **326** (L) Annie Griffiths Belt/Corbis, (R) Burstein Collection/Corbis; **327** Bridgeman Art Library; **328** Taxi/Getty Images; **329** (L) Moldovita Monastery Romania/Dagli Orti/The Art Archive, (R) Topkapi Palace Museum, Istanbul, Turkey, Giraudon/Bridgeman Art Library; **330** Ancient Art & Architecture Collection Ltd.; **331** (B) Private Collection, Archives Charmet/Bridgeman Art Library, (T) Topkapi Palace Museum, Istanbul, Turkey/Bridgeman Art Library; **332** Nat & Yanna Brandt/Photo Researchers, Inc.; **334** Snark/Art Resource, NY; **335** Getty Images; **336** Bridgeman Art Library; **337** (R) Private Collection/Bridgeman Art Library, (L) rochaphoto/Alamy Images; **338** (B) André Held/AKG London Ltd.; **339** (B) Hamill Gallery of African Art, (T) The Metropolitan Museum/Art Resource, NY, (C) The Nasli M. Heeramaneck Collection, gift of Joan Palevsky/Art Resource, NY; **340** (R) Bibliotheque Nationale, Paris, France/Bridgeman Art Library, (L) GoodShoot/Corbis; **341** David Keith Jones/Images of Africa Photobank/Alamy Images; **342** (R) A van Zandbergen/AfriPics Images, (C) Christopher and Sally Gable/©DK Images, (L) Michele Westmorland/Corbis; **343** (T) ©DK Images, (B) Bildarchiv Preussischer Kulturbesitz/Art Resource, NY; **344** The Nasli M. Heeramaneck Collection, gift of Joan Palevsky/Art Resource, NY; **345** Shizuo Kambayashi/©Associated Press; **346** (L) Nik Wheeler/Corbis, (R) The Metropolitan Museum/Art Resource, NY; **347** (B) Masterfile Corporation, (T) Werner Forman/Art Resource, NY; **348** Werner Forman/Art Resource, NY; **349** (B) Bridgeman Art Library, (C) The Granger Collection, NY, (Bkgrd) Topham/The Image Works, Inc.; **350** Betty Press/Woodfin Camp & Associates; **351** AKG London Ltd., (Bkgrd) Annebicque Bernard/Sygma/Corbis, (R) National Museum Lagos, Nigeria/Held Collection/Bridgeman Art Library, (L) Werner Forman/Corbis; **352** (R) Art Resource, NY, (L) The Metropolitan Museum of Art, Rogers Fund, 1998 (1998.66). Photograph 1998/Art Resource, NY; **353** Mike Andrews/Ancient Art & Architecture Collection Ltd.; **354** AKG London Ltd.; **355** Suzanne Porter/Rough Guides/©DK Images; **356** Alamy Images; **357** ©Images & Stories/Alamy Images; **358** (R) ©The Trustees of the British Museum/Art Resource, NY, (TL, CL, C, Bkgrd) Hamill Gallery of African Art, (Bkgrd) Seattle Art Museum/Seattle Art Museum, (Inset) The Newark Museum/Art Resource, NY; **359** (C) Ellen Howdon/St Mungo, Glasgow Museums/©DK Images, (R) Glen Allison/Mira, (L) Hamill Gallery of African Art; **361** Brian Seed & Associates; **362** (T) ©DK Images, (B) Bibliotheque Nationale, Paris, France/Bridgeman Art Library; **363** (T) Art Resource, NY, (B) Werner Forman/Art Resource, NY; **364** ©Images & Stories/Alamy Images; **365** The Granger Collection, NY; **366** AAAC/Topham/The Image Works, Inc.; **367** (T) China Legacy Images, (C) Rick Browne/Photo Researchers, Inc., (B) Sekai Bunka/Ancient Art & Architecture Collection Ltd.; **368** British Library/The Art Archive; **369** (R) ©The Granger Collection, NY, (L) China Legacy Images; **370** (B) ©SSPL/The Image Works, Inc., (TL, R) China Legacy Images; **372** Norma Joseph/Robert Harding World Imagery; **373** (B) ©The Granger Collection, NY, (T) Bildarchiv Preussischer Kulturbesitz/Art Resource, NY; **374** British Library/The Art Archive; **375** (T) Edifice/Corbis, (BL) Peter Yates/Science Photo Library/Photo Researchers, Inc.; **376** (L) Art Resource, NY, (R) The British Museum/©DK Images; **377** ©The Granger Collection, NY; **378** (R) AKG London Ltd., (L) Bridgeman Art Library, Palazzo Farnese Caprarola/Dagli Orti/The Art Archive, (L) SuperStock; **380** (R) China Legacy Images, (C) Nigel Tudor, (L) Werner Forman/Art Resource, NY; **382** ©ChinaStock; **383** (Bkgrd) Rick Browne/Photo Researchers, Inc.; **385** Steve Vidler/Iberfoto/Photoaisa; **386** Alon Reininger/Contact Press Images; **387** (R) Erich Lessing/Art Resource, NY; **389** The Art Archive; **390** Musee des Beaux-Arts, Angers, France/Bridgeman Art Library; **391** Mary Evans Picture Library; **392** (B) British Museum, London, UK/Bridgeman Art Library; **393** (R, L) Art Resource, NY; **394** ©Catherine Karnow/Corbis; **396** (R) Asian Art & Archaeology, Inc./Corbis; **397** (B) Eric Trachtenberg; **398** (L) British Library, London, UK/Bridgeman Art Library, (B) C. Jopp/Robert Harding World Imagery; **399** Massimo Listri/Corbis; **400** Digital Vision/Getty Images, (Inset) Frank Carter/Lonely Planet Images; **402** Scala/Art Resource, NY; **403** (L) Art Resource, NY, (R) The Art Archive; **404** (L) ©The Granger Collection, NY, (R) AKG London Ltd.; **405** (B) Art Resource, NY, Peter Wilson/©DK Images; **408** Corbis; **409** (C) Art Resource, NY, (T) Arte & Immagini srl/Corbis; **410** (R) Ashley Simmons/Alamy Images, (L) Scala/Art Resource, NY; **411** The Bridgeman Art Library/Getty Images; **412** Archivio di Stato di Siena/Gianni Dagli Orti/The Art Archive; **414** (C, Bkgrd) ©DK Images, (R) Private Collection/Bridgeman Art Library, (L) Scala/Art Resource, NY, The Image Bank/Getty Images; **415** (L) ©DK Images, (R) Mary Evans Picture Library; **416** Mary Evans Picture Library; **417** Iberfoto/Photoaisa; **418** (R) Art Resource, NY, (L) Mary Evans Picture Library; **419** M. C. Esteban/Iberfoto/Photoaisa; 420 Scala/Art Resource, NY; **421** (TR) ©DK Images, (L, C) Erich Lessing/Art Resource, NY, (BR) Susannah Price/©DK Images; **422** (C) ©DK Images, (B) Andrea Pistolesi/Getty Images, (T) Mary Evans Picture Library; **423** (L) AAAC/Topham/The Image Works, Inc., (R) London College of Printing/©DK Images; **424** Bildarchiv Preussischer Kulturbesitz/Art Resource, NY; **425** The Corcoran Gallery of Art/Corbis; **427** Erich Lessing/Art Resource, NY; **428** (R) Art Resource, NY, (L) National Trust Photographic Library/Derrick E. Witty/The Image Works, Inc.; **429** Corbis; **430** ©The Granger Collection, NY, (Bkgrd) Michael Busselle/Corbis; **431** (R) ©The Granger Collection, NY, (L) Mary Evans

Picture Library; **433** Erich Lessing/Art Resource, NY; **434** (R) ©Gustavo Tomsich/Corbis, (L) ©The Granger Collection, NY; **435** (L) ©The Granger Collection, NY, (R) Reuters/Corbis; **436** (BL) Corbis, (TL) Kevin Fleming/Corbis, (R) Maximilian Stock Ltd./Photo Researchers, Inc.; **437** (R) AAAC/Topham/The Image Works, Inc., (L) Glasgow University Library, Scotland/Bridgeman Art Library; **439** (T) Galileo Galilei (1564–1642) before members of the Holy Office in the Vatican in 1633, 1847, Robert-Fleury, Joseph-Nicolas (1797–1890)/Louvre, Paris, France/Peter Willi/Bridgeman Art Library, (B) Gildas Raffenel/epa/Corbis; **440** Scala/Art Resource, NY; **441** (BR) ©The Granger Collection, NY, (BL) Art Resource, NY, Cartoon Stock; **442** (Bkgrd) Corbis, Scala/Art Resource, NY; **444** Instituto Portugues de Museus; **445** (T) Art Resource, NY, (TR) China Legacy Images, (B) Christie's Images/Corbis; **446** (L) Ann Ronan Picture Library/The Image Works, Inc., (R) Bridgeman Art Library; **448** (R) ©National Maritime Museum, London, (L, Bkgrd) ©The Granger Collection, NY; **449** (TR) Alfredo Dagli Orti/The Art Archive, (TL) Antiquarian Images, (BR) Art Resource, NY, (BR) Museu de Marinha; **450** Preussischer Kulturbesitz/Art Resource, NY; **452** (R) Smithsonian Institution, (L) Topham/The Image Works, Inc.; **453** Private Collection/Photo ©Heini Schneebeli/Bridgeman Art Library; **455** Werner Forman/Art Resource, NY; **456** (T) Gift of Ernest Anspach, 1999 (199.295.4) Photograph (c) 2002/Art Resource, NY, (B) Museo de Arte Antiga/The Art Archive; **457** (L) Art Resource, NY, (R) Rainer Daehnhardt/Portuguese Academy of Antique Arms; **458** (R) Maritime Museum of Rotterdam, (L) The Royal Collection ©2006 Her Majesty Queen Elizabeth II; **459** Rijks Museum Amsterdam; **460** ©British Library Board. All Rights Reserved., ©The Granger Collection, NY; **461** (R) Biblioteca Apostolica Vaticana, (L) Ricci Institute; **462** The British Museum/The Image Works, Inc.; **463** (L) ©The Granger Collection, NY, (C) Christie's Images/Corbis, (R) The British Museum/HIP/The Image Works, Inc.; **464** ©The Cleveland Museum of Art, ©The Granger Collection, NY; **465** ©The Granger Collection, NY, Michael Holford; **466** (T) Art Resource, NY, (B) The British Museum/The Image Works, Inc.; **467** ©The Granger Collection, NY; **468** (T) ©The Granger Collection, NY, (B) Instituto Portugues de Museus; **469** (B) ©The Granger Collection, NY, (T) Giraudon/Art Resource, NY; **470** Schalkwijk/Art Resource, NY; **471** (C) Bridgeman Art Library, (T) Erich Lessing/Art Resource, NY, (B) Library of Congress; **472** Biblioteca Medicea-Laurenziana/Florence/Bridgeman Art Library; **473** (B) ©akg-images/The Image Works, Inc., (T) ©The Granger Collection, NY; **474** (Inset) AKG London Ltd., (Bkgrd) Charles & Josette

Lenars/Corbis; **475** ©Frank Nowikowski Photography; **476** Ira Block Photography; **477** Hispanic Society of America; **478** Instituto Portugues de Museus; **479** Danny Lehman/Corbis; **480** Joseph Martin/AKG London Ltd.; **481** Bridgeman Art Library; **482** Lee Snider/Photo Images/Corbis; **483** Bettmann/Corbis; **484** Michael Schwarz/The Image Works, Inc.; **485** (BR) Collection of The New-York Historical Society, (TR) National Museum of the American Indian, Smithsonian Institution, (BC) The Newark Museum/Art Resource, NY, (BL) Victoria & Albert Museum, London/Art Resource, NY; **486** Gunter Marx Stock Photos; **487** (R) Chicago History Museum, (L) Royal Albert Museum/Bridgeman Art Library; **488** (B) Ariadne Van Zandbergen/Lonely Planet Images, Bettmann/Corbis, Corbis, Image Source/Corbis; **489** (B) ©British Library Board. All Rights Reserved., (TR) Library of Congress; **491** The Art Archive; **492** (L) ©Courtesy of the Bancroft Library, University of California, Berkeley, (R) Francis C. Mayer/Corbis; **493** (C) Corbis, (L) Darrell Guiin/Corbis, (R) O'cean/Corbis; **494** (B) Journal-Courier/Steve Warmowski/The Image Works, Inc., Robert Harding World Imagery; **495** Erich Lessing/Art Resource, NY; **496** (CR) ©Julie Habel/Corbis, (L) Carlos Goldin/Corbis, (R) PoodlesRock/Corbis; **497** (TL) Bettmann/Corbis, (BR) Ira Block Photography, (BL) Kim Blaxland/Getty Images, (TR) Liba Taylor/Corbis, (BC) Ron Giling/PhotoLibrary Group, Inc.; **498** Steve Vidler/eStock Photo; **499** (BR) baur/Shutterstock, (TR) RICHARD B. LEVINE/NewsCom, (L) Stock Montage Inc.; **500** (R) ©The Art Gallery Collection/Alamy Images; **501** Mary Evans Picture Library; **502** Erich Lessing/Art Resource, NY; **503** (T) Erich Lessing/Art Resource, NY, (C) Rob Reichenfeld/©DK Images; **504** (R) Bettman/Corbis, (Bkgrd) Bettmann/Corbis, (R) J.Bedmar/Iberfoto/Photoaisa; **506** (Bkgrd) ©National Maritime Museum, London, (L) Bridgeman Art Library, (BR) British Library/Bridgeman Art Library, (TR) J.Bedmar/Iberfoto/Photoaisa; **508** Bridgeman Art Library; **509** (T) Art Resource, NY, (B) Mary Evans Picture Library; **510** Art Resource, NY; **511** ©Lebrecht Music and Arts Photo Library/Alamy Images; **513** (TR) ©Peter Willi/SuperStock, (BL) Reunion des Musees Nationaux/Art Resource, NY, (TL) Scala/Art Resource, NY, (BR) Topham/The Image Works, Inc., (CL) Victoria & Albert Museum/Art Resource, NY; **515** (B) STEPHEN MORRISON/epa/Corbis, (T) The Gallery Collection/Corbis; **516** Art Resource, NY; **517** J. Bedmar/Iberfoto/Photoaisa; **518** (TR) ©The Granger Collection, NY, (L) Corbis, (BR) The British Museum/HIP/The Image Works, Inc.; **519** (BR) ©The Granger Collection, NY, (TR) Bridgeman Art Library, (L) Mary Evans Picture Library; **520** (Bkgrd) HIP/The Image Works, Inc., Rob Reichenfeld/©DK

Images; **521** (B) ©The Granger Collection, NY, (T) Atwater Kent Museum/Bridgeman Art Library; **524** (T) Bettmann/Corbis, (B) The Parliamentary Archives; **525** (R) ©The Board of Trustees of the Armouries/HIP/The Image Works, Inc., (L) Erich Lessing/Art Resource, NY; **528** Photoaisa; **529** Mary Evans Picture Library; **530** (R, L) Corbis; **531** The Granger Collection, NY; **532** (BL) ©The Granger Collection, NY, (TR) AKG London Ltd., (Bkgrd) Sovfoto/Eastfoto; **533** ©Photos 12/Alamy Images; **536** (L) ©The Board of Trustees of the Armouries/HIP/The Image Works, Inc., (R) Mary Evans Picture Library; **537** (T) ©The Granger Collection, NY; **538** Photoaisa; **539** Bridgeman Art Library; **542** Réunion des Musées Nationaux/Art Resource, NY; **543** (C) Bridgeman Art Library, (T) Réunion des Musées Nationaux/Art Resource, NY, (B) The Granger Collection, New York; **544** (T) BeBa/Iberfoto/Photoaisa, (B) Musee Marmottan/©DK Images; **545** ©The Granger Collection, NY; **546** (R) Chateau de Versailles, France, Lauros/Giraudon/Bridgeman Art Library, (L) Réunion des Musées Nationaux/Art Resource, NY; **547** (L) ©The Granger Collection, NY, (R) Corbis; **548** BeBa/Iberfoto/Photoaisa; **549** (T) ©The Granger Collection, NY, (B) Iberfoto/Photoaisa; **550** (Inset) Bettmann/Corbis; **551** ©The Granger Collection, NY; **552** (B) Bridgeman Art Library, (Border, Bkgrd) Russ Lappa, (L) Victoria & Albert Museum, London/Art Resource, NY; **553** (R) ©DK Images, (C) Francis G. Mayer/Corbis, (L) John Heseltine/Corbis; **554** (C) BeBa/Iberfoto/Photoaisa, (R) Bridgeman Art Library, (L) Kurpfalzisches Museum, Heidelberg, Germany/Bridgeman Art Library; **556** (BL) Reuters/Corbis, (Bkgrd) The Art Archive, (TL) Zuma/Corbis; **557** (L) ©The Granger Collection, NY, (R) The Granger Collection, New York; **558** (L) Stock Connection; **559** SuperStock; **560** (L) National Portrait Gallery, Smithsonian Institution/Art Resource, NY, (C) Reunion des Musees Nationaux/Art Resource, NY, (R) The Corcoran Gallery of Art/Corbis; **561** Bridgeman Art Library; **562** The Granger Collection, NY; **564** (Inset) ©Bettmann/Corbis, (Bkgrd) Bettmann/Corbis; **565** (TL) Bettmann/Corbis, (TL) Library of Congress, (TC) MPI/Getty Images; **566** ©The Granger Collection, NY; **567** (B) Bridgeman Art Library, Steven G Artley/Artley Cartoons; **568** (B) ©The Granger Collection, NY, (T) Christie's Images/Corbis; **569** Bettmann/Corbis; **570** Bridgeman-Giraudon/Art Resource, NY; **571** (C, B) Art Resource, NY, (T) Musee de L'Histoire Vivante, Montreuil, France, Archives Charmet/Bridgeman Art Library; **572** (B) ©The Granger Collection, NY, (T) Erich Lessing/Art Resource, NY; **573** Snark/Art Resource, NY; **574** (TR) Giraudon/Art Resource, NY, (B) Musee de la ville de Paris, Musee Carnavalet, Paris, France, Archives Charmet/

ACKNOWLEDGMENTS

Bridgeman Art Library, (TL) Musee du Ranquet, Clermont-Ferrand, France/Giraudon/Bridgeman Art Library; **575** Musee Carnavalet, Paris, France, Lauros/Giraudon/Bridgeman Art Library; **576** (B) Chateau de Versailles, France/Bridgeman Art Library, (T) Giraudon/Art Resource, NY; **577** Rèunion des MusÈes Nationaux/Art Resource, NY; **578** Réunion des Musées Nationaux/Art Resource, NY; **579** Judith Miller/Bill & Myrtle Aquillino/©DK Images; **580** (T) AKG London Ltd., (B) Chateau de Versailles, France, Giraudon/Bridgeman Art Library; **583** Giraudon/Art Resource, NY; **584** Musee de la Ville de Paris, Musee Carnavalet, Paris, France, Giraudon/Bridgeman Art Library; **585** Bibliothèque des Arts Décoratifs Paris/Dagli Orti/The Art Archive; **586** Leonard de Selva/Corbis; **587** Giraudon/Art Resource, NY; **588** (L) Bridgeman Art Library, (C) Hulton Archive/Getty Images, (R) Musée Carnavalet Paris/Dagli Orti/The Art Archive; **589** (TL) Hulton-Deutsch Collection/Corbis, (R) Max Alexander/©DK Images, (BL) Musee de la Revolution Francaise, Vizille, France/Bridgeman Art Library; **590** (B) Art Resource, NY, (T) Bridgeman Art Library; **591** (T) Erich Lessing/Art Resource, NY, (B) Réunion des Musées Nationaux/Art Resource, NY; **592** (B) Private Collection/Bridgeman Art Library, (T) Scala/Art Resource, NY; **593** Giraudon/Art Resource, NY; **595** Art Resource, NY; **596** Musee des Beaux-Arts, Rouen, France Lauros/Giraudon/Bridgeman Art Library; **597** Giraudon/Art Resource, NY; **598** Bibliotheque Nationale, Paris, France, Archives Charmet/Bridgeman Art Library; **600** Giraudon/Art Resource, NY; **601** Randy Faris/Corbis; **602** ©The Granger Collection, NY; **603** (B) Private Collection/Bridgeman Art Library, (T) Riyadh Biji/Reuters/Corbis; **604** (R) ©The Granger Collection, NY, (L) Bridgeman-Giraudon/Art Resource, NY, (R) The Image Works, Inc.; **605** Giraudon/Art Resource, NY; **606** ©NRM/Pictorial Collection/SSPL/The Image Works, Inc.; **607** (C, B) Corbis, (T) National Railway Museum/Science & Society Picture Library; **608** NRM/SSPL/The Image Works, Inc.; **610** ©The Granger Collection, NY; **611** Oxford Scientific Films,Ltd./Photolibrary Group Inc.; **612** (L) Fine Art Photographic Library, London/Art Resource, NY, (R) National Railway Museum/Science & Society Picture Library; **613** Science Museum/Science & Society Picture Library; **616** Mary Evans Picture Library; **617** Hulton Archives/Getty Images; **619** (B) Manchester Archives and Local Studies, (T) Mary Evans Picture Library; **620** ©The Granger Collection, NY; **621** Hulton-Deutsch Collection/Corbis; **622** Hulton-Deutsch Collection/Corbis; **623** (B) ©The Granger Collection, NY, (T) Fine Art Photographic Library/Art Resource, NY; **624** (R) The Stapleton Collection/Bridgeman Art Library, (L) Topham/The Image Works,

Inc.; **626** (T) ©The Granger Collection, NY, (B) Corbis; **627** (B) Daniel Leclair/Reuters/Corbis, (T) Mary Evans Picture Library Ltd /The Image Works, Inc.; **628** (L) AKG London Ltd.; **629** (B) Museo Historico Nacional Buenos Aires/Dagli Orti/The Art Archive, (T) Peter Titmuss/Alamy Images; **630** ©NRM/Pictorial Collection/SSPL/The Image Works, Inc.; **631** Image Select/Art Resource, NY; **632** Simon Bolivar Amphiteatre Mexico/Dagli Orti/The Art Archive; **633** (B) ©The Granger Collection, NY, (C) Gary Ombler/Courtesy of 1er Chasseurs a Cheval de la Lighne, 2e Compagnie/©DK Images, (T) Museo National De Colombia; **634** Hadtorteneti Muzeum, Budapest, Hungary/Archives Charmet/Bridgeman Art Library; **636** (R) ©Mary Evans/GROSVENOR PRINTS/The Image Works, Inc., (L) Georgios Kollidas/Shutterstock; **638** (R) Gary Ombler/Courtesy of 1er Chasseurs a Cheval de la Lighne, 2e Compagnie/©DK Images, (L) North Wind Picture Archives; **639** Musee de la Ville de Paris, Musee Carnavalet, Paris, France, Lauros/Giraudon/Bridgeman Art Library; **640** (Bkgrd) ullstein bild/©The Granger Collection, NY; **641** (R) Louvre, Paris, France/Bridgeman Art Library, (L) Private Collection, Archives Charmet/Bridgeman Art Library, (C, Bkgrd) ullstein bild/©The Granger Collection, NY; **642** Scala/Art Resource, NY; **643** ©The Granger Collection, NY; **644** (T) ©The Granger Collection, NY, (B) Gleb Garanich/Reuters/Corbis; **645** (L) Museo Nacional Bogota/Dagli Orti/The Art Archive, (R) Museo National De Colombia; **646** Chateau de Versailles, France/Bridgeman Art Library; **647** Corbis; **649** (BL) ©The Granger Collection, NY, (TR) Bettmann/Corbis, (BR) Museo Bolivar Caracas/Gianni Dagli Orti/The Art Archive, (TL) The Granger Collection, NY; **650** Miramare Museum Trieste/Dagli Orti/The Art Archive; **651** North Wind Picture Archives; **652** North Wind Picture Archives; **653** (C) Bibliothéque des Art Décoratifs Paris/Marc Charmet/The Art Archive, (B) Masterfile Corporation, (T) Reuters/Corbis; **654** (TR) AGE Fotostock/SuperStock, (BL) Simon Bolivar Amphitheatre Mexico/Dagli Orti/The Art Archive; **658** Lewis W. Hine/George Eastman House/Getty Images; **659** (T) Private Collection/Bridgeman Art Library, (B) The Image Works, Inc., (C) The Women's Library/Mary Evans Picture Library; **660** Mary Evans Picture Library; **661** Lewis B. Hine/AKG London Ltd.; **662** The Image Works, Inc.; **663** (B) Mary Evans Picture Library; **664** (TR) ©SSPL/Science Museum/The Image Works, Inc., (CR) Dagli Orti/The Art Archive, (L) The Image Works, Inc.; **665** Hulton-Deutsch Collection/Corbis; **666** Library of Congress; **667** (T) Bettmann/Corbis, (B) Topham/The Image Works, Inc.; **668** ©Bettmann/Corbis; **669** Hulton-Deutsch Collection/Corbis; **671** Musée de l'Affiche Paris/Dagli Orti/The Art Archive; **672** (T) Leland

J. Prater/Corbis, (B) SSPL/The Image Works, Inc., (C) The Advertising Archive; **673** (TR) Michael Nicholson/Corbis, (TL) Scala/Art Resource, NY, (B) Sirl Schwartzman; **674** (R) The Women's Library/Mary Evans Picture Library, (L) Underwood & Underwood/Corbis; **675** (BR) Corbis, (TL) Museum of London/Topham-HIP/The Image Works, Inc., Museum of London, UK/Bridgeman Art Library, (Bkgrd) Philip de Bay/Corbis; **676** ©Hulton Archive/MPI/Getty Images; **677** Topham/The Image Works, Inc.; **678** (TR) Kevin Schafer/Corbis, (BR) Oriol Alamany/Corbis, (BL) Renee Lynn/Photo Researchers, Inc., (TL) Tui De Roy/Minden Pictures; **679** (BR) ©The Granger Collection, NY, (C) Kevin Schafer/Corbis, (TL) Mary Evans Picture Library, (TR) Michael Nicholson/Corbis, (CL) Tom Brakefield/SuperStock, (BL) Tony Arruza/Corbis; **680** Underwood & Underwood/Corbis; **681** Albert Bierstadt (American, 1830–1902), Hetch Hetchy Canyon Oil on canvas, 1875 Gift of Mrs. E. H. Sawyer and Mrs. A. L. Williston/Mount Holyoke College Art Museum; **682** The Art Archive; **683** Art Resource, NY, (BC) Bettmann/Corbis, (TC) Erich Lessing/Art Resource, NY, (T) Philadelphia Museum of Art, (B) Private Collection, Archives Charmet/Bridgeman Art Library; **684** Erich Lessing/Art Resource, NY; **685** (BL) Art Resource, NY, (T) Réunion des Musées Nationaux/Art Resource, NY, (BR) SuperStock; **686** ©DK Images; **687** Private Collection/Bridgeman Art Library; **688** (T) Christie's Images/SuperStock, (B) Jacqui Hurst/Corbis; **689** North Wind Picture Archives; **690** AKG London Ltd.; **691** (B) ©DK Images, (C) DK Images, (T) Judith Miller Archive/©DK Images; **692** (TR) Judith Miller Archive/©DK Images, (L) PhotoLibrary Group, Inc.; **694** (T) AKG London Ltd.; **696** (R) Alison Harris/©DK Images, (L) Popperfoto/Getty Images; **697** ©The Granger Collection, NY; **698** WEIMAR ARCHIVE/Mary Evans Picture Library; **699** AKG London Ltd.; **700** (L) Alinari/Art Resource, NY; 701 ©Roger-Viollet/The Image Works, Inc.; **703** (B) ©The Granger Collection, NY, (TR) Alinari/Art Resource, NY, (C) Private Collection, Alinari/Bridgeman Art Library, (TL) Private Collection, Ken Welsh/Bridgeman Art Library; **704** Alinari/Art Resource, NY; **705** (R) DK Images, (L) Private Collection, Archives Charmet/Bridgeman Art Library; **708** Mary Evans Picture Library; **709** (B) Brooks Kraft/Sygma/Corbis, (T) The Art Archive/Corbis; **710** North Wind Picture Archives; **711** (T) ©DK Images, (B) Private Collection/Bridgeman Art Library; **712** HIP/Art Resource, NY; **713** ©The Granger Collection, NY; **714** (T) Mary Evans Picture Library, (B) Snark/Art Resource, NY; **716** Corbis; **717** (B) ©The Granger Collection, NY, (T) Musée Carnavalet Paris/Dagli Orti/The Art Archive; **718** (B) AKG London Ltd., (T) Giraudon/Art Resource, NY; **719** Greater London

Council, UK/Bridgeman Art Library; **720** Blackburn Museum and Art Gallery, Lancashire, UK/Bridgeman Art Library; **721** (T) AKG London Ltd., (B) Bettmann/Corbis, (C) Trades Union Congress Library Collections; **722** (L) Hulton Archive/Getty Images, (R) Victoria & Albert Museum, London/Art Resource, NY; **723** ©Birmingham Museums and Art Gallery/Bridgeman Art Library; **724** (R, CL) AKG London Ltd., (L) Corbis, (CR) Palace of Westminster, London, UK/Bridgeman Art Library; **725** (C) Mary Evans Picture Library, (L) Private Collection/Bridgeman Art Library; **726** Bettmann/Corbis; **727** Anti-Slavery International; **728** Mary Evans Picture Library; **729** Trades Union Congress Library Collections; **730** (Bkgrd) ©Dave Ashwin/Alamy, (TR) Holt Studios Int./Photo Researchers, Inc., (CL) Sean Sexton Collection/Corbis, (CR) The Illustrated London News Picture Library, London, UK/Bridgeman Art Library, (B) Trustees of the Watts Gallery, Compton, Surrey, UK/Bridgeman Art Library; **732** (T) Bradford Art Galleries and Museums, West Yorkshire, UK/Bridgeman Art Library, (B) Getty Images; **733** (R) Erich Lessing/Art Resource, NY, (L) Hulton Archive/Getty Images; **734** (Inset, Bkgrd) Hulton Archive/Getty Images; **735** (T) ©The Granger Collection, NY, (B) Musee de la Poste, Paris, France, Archives Charmet/Bridgeman Art Library; **736** ©Dave G. Houser/Corbis; **737** AKG London Ltd.; **738** Musee National de l'Education, Rouen, France, Archives Charmet/Bridgeman Art Library; **739** Stockbyte/Getty Images; **740** (BL, Bkgrd) American Philosophical Society, (BR) Division of Political History/National Museum of American History/Smithsonian Institution, (TR) Kevin R. Morris/Bohemian Nomad Picturemakers/Corbis; **741** New-York Historical Society/Bridgeman Art Library; **744** Mary Evans Picture Library; **745** The Women's Library/Mary Evans Picture Library; **746** (T) ©The Granger Collection, NY, (B) AKG London Ltd.; **747** Musee de la Ville de Paris, Musee Carnavalet, Paris, France, Archives Charmet/Bridgeman Art Library; **748** Hulton-Deutsch Collection/Corbis; **749** (T) ©British Library Board. All Rights Reserved., (B) Bridgeman Art Library, (C) Private Collection/Bridgeman Art Library; **750** (R) AKG London Ltd., (L) Mary Evans Picture Library; **751** National Archives UK; **752** (R, BL) ©The Granger Collection, NY, Roger Viollet/Topham/The Image Works, Inc.; **753** Hulton Archive/Getty Images; **754** AKG London Ltd.; **755** The Royal Collection ©2006 Her Majesty Queen Elizabeth II; **756** (B) AKG London Ltd., (T) Mary Evans Picture Library; **758** ©The Granger Collection, NY; **759** Mary Evans Picture Library; **760** Popperfoto/Getty Images; **761** Mansell/Time Life Pictures/Getty Images; **762** (R) Bridgeman Art Library, (L) Swim Ink 2, LLC/Corbis; **763** AKG London Ltd.; **765** (L) ©The Granger

Collection, NY, (Bkgrd) Public Record Office/HIP/The Image Works, Inc.; **766** Hulton Archive/Getty Images; **767** (R) ©British Library Board. All Rights Reserved., (L) Hulton Archive/Getty Images; **768** (T) Company of Girdlers/Eileen Tweedy/The Art Archive, (C) Photo ©Civil War Archive/Bridgeman Art Library, (TR, BC) Royal Armouries Museum, (BR) The Image Works, Inc.; **769** (R) Mary Evans Picture Library; **770** (T) AFP/Getty Images, (C) Colin Garatt/Corbis, (B) Paul A. Souders/Corbis; **772** (B) Alexander Popov/ITAR-TASS/ABACA-PRESS/NewsCom, Roy Miles Fine Paintings/Bridgeman Art Library; **773** (R) Bridgeman Art Library, (L) Masterfile Corporation; **774** The Image Works, Inc.; **775** (L) Panorama Stock, (R) Private Collection/The Art Archive; **776** Corbis; **777** Time- Life Pictures/Getty Images; **778** (L) Bridgeman Art Library, (R) The Image Works, Inc.; **779** Topham/The Image Works, Inc.; **780** (T) ©The Granger Collection, NY, (B) Time- Life Pictures/Getty Images; **782** Peter Harholdt/Corbis; **783** (T) ©The Granger Collection, NY, (C) Index Stock Imagery/Photolibrary Group, Inc., (B) The Image Works, Inc.; **784** (L) Topham/The Image Works, Inc.; **785** British Museum/The Art Archive; **786** Réunion des Musées Nationaux/Art Resource, NY; **787** (R) ©directphoto.bz/Alamy Images, (L) Index Stock Imagery/PhotoLibrary Group, Inc.; **788** Old Japan; **789** Rykoff Collection/Corbis; **790** Mary Evans Picture Library; **791** (R) Mary Evans Picture Library; **792** (L) Bettmann/Corbis, (R) National Archives; **794** (TR) Getty Images, (TL) Horace Bristol/Corbis, (BR) Ray Moller/Royal Pavilion Museum and Art Galleries, Brighton/©DK Images, (TC) Roy Miles Fine Paintings/Bridgeman Art Library; **796** (R) ©Royalty-Free/Corbis, (L) Art Gallery of Ontario, Toronto, Canada/Bridgeman Art Library; **798** (B) Mary Evans Picture Library, (T) Photolibrary Group, Inc.; **800** (Inset) ©mediacolor's/Alamy Images, (B) Historical Picture Archive/Corbis; **801** (L) National History Museum Mexico City/Gianni Dagli Orti/The Art Archive, (R) Ocean/Corbis; **802** National History Museum Mexico City/Dagli Orti/The Art Archive; **803** (L) National History Museum Mexico City/Dagli Orti/The Art Archive, (R) Private Collection/Bridgeman Art Library; **805** Bettmann/Corbis; **806** (Bkgrd) Corbis, (TR, BC) Office of Imaging, Printing & Photographic Services/Smithsonian Institution, (BR) The Image Works, Inc.; **808** (L) ©DK Images, (R) Werner Forman/Corbis; **809** ©Royalty-Free/Corbis; **810** (R) Asian Art & Archaeology, Inc./Corbis, (L) National History Museum Mexico City/Dagli Orti/The Art Archive; **814** Imperial War Museum/The Art Archive; **815** (C) ©DK Images, (T) Getty Images, (B) SSPL/The Image Works, Inc.; **816** (L) bettmann/Corbis, (R) ullstein bild/©The Granger Collection, NY; **818** Corbis; **819** ©The Granger Collection, NY; **820** Chicago Tribune; **821** Jacques Moreau/Archives Larousse, Paris, France/Bridgeman Art Library; **822** (L) Hulton-Deutsch Collection/Corbis, (R) Imperial War Museum, London/©DK Images; **823** Art Resource, NY; **824** (BR) Foto Marburg/Art Resource, NY, (T) SSPL/The Image Works, Inc., (T) ullstein bild/©The Granger Collection, NY; **825** (T) Popperfoto/Getty Images, (B) The Tank Museum; **827** Bettmann/Corbis; **828** Mary Evans Picture Library; **829** (R) ©The Granger Collection, NY, (L) Bettmann/Corbis; **830** (T) David Pollack/Corbis, (B) Snark/Art Resource, NY; **831** Hulton-Deutsch Collection/Corbis, (T) A. R. Coster/Hulton Archive/Getty Images; **833** Bettmann/Corbis; **834** (L) Corbis; **835** (Bkgrd) Bettmann/Corbis, Corbis; **838** SSPL/The Image Works, Inc.; **839** (L) ©DK Images, (R) AKG London Ltd.; **840** (L) The Image Works, Inc., (R) Wonders Exhibit/©Associated Press; **841** Hulton Archive/Getty Images; **842** (R) AKG London Ltd., (L) Christie's Images, London, UK/Bridgeman Art Library; **843** (L) Novosti/Bridgeman Art Library, (R) Topham/The Image Works, Inc.; **844** Eric Miller/Panos Pictures; **845** Topical Press Agency/Hulton Archive/Getty Images; **846** (C) Art Resource, NY, (L) bettmann/Corbis, (R) Imperial War Museum, London/©DK Images; **847** (L) ©The Granger Collection, NY, (R) Corbis; **848** (T) Eileen Tweedy/The Art Archive, (B) The Image Works, Inc.; **850** Corbis; **851** (C) Bridgeman Art Library, (B) Martin Plomer/©DK Images, (T) Paul Franklin ©Dorling Kindersley, Courtesy of the Castillo de Chapultepec/©DK Images; **852** (R) Bill Manns/The Art Archive, (L) Fernando Bueno/Getty Images; **853** (TR, TL, CC,) Bettmann/Corbis, (TR, CL, B) Corbis; **854** Corbis; **856** Paul Franklin ©Dorling Kindersley, Courtesy of the Castillo de Chapultepec/©DK Images; **857** (B) Schalkwijk/Art Resource, NY, (T) Time Life Pictures/Getty Images; **858** (L) The Advertising Archive; **859** National Library of South Africa; **860** (B) ©The Granger Collection, NY (C) WorldSat International Inc./Photo Researchers, Inc.; **861** (R) Bettmann/Corbis, (L) Harry Thuku/Bettmann/Corbis; **862** ©The Granger Collection, NY; **864** Library of Congress; **865** Underwood & Underwood/Corbis; **866** DAP/The Image Works, Inc.; **868** Hulton-Deutsch Collection/Corbis; **869** (R) Corbis, (L) Panorama Stock; **870** ©The Granger Collection, NY; **871** Bettmann/Corbis; **872** Sovfoto/Eastfoto; **875** (T) ©Random House Inc., (B) Mansell/Time Life Pictures/Getty Images; **877** Hulton/Getty Images; **878** ©The Granger Collection, NY, (L) Corbis; **879** (B) ©The Granger Collection, NY; **880** ©The Granger Collection, NY, (B) Corbis; **881** DPA/The Image Works, Inc.; **882** Time Life Pictures/Getty Images; **883** (C) Library of Congress, (B) ullstein bild/©The Granger Collection, NY; **884** ©Bettmann/Corbis; **885** (R) Culver Pictures/The Art Archive, (L) Drug Enforcement Administration; **886** (TR, L) Bettmann/Corbis, (R) Library of Congress, (BR) Topham/The Image Works, Inc., (L) Underwood & Underwood/Corbis; **888** New York Daily News/Getty Images; **889** Tate Gallery/Art Resource, NY; **890** (BR) Art Resource, NY, (BC) Fogg Art Museum, Harvard University Art Museums, USA/Bequest from the Collection of Maurice Wertheim, Class 1906/Bridgeman Art Library, (T) Roger Viollet/Topham/The Image Works, Inc., (BL) Scala/Art Resource, NY; **891** (R) ©DK Images, (L) Corbis; **892** Bettmann/Corbis; **893** ©The Granger Collection, NY; **894** (R) AKG London Ltd., (L) Archive Holdings Inc/Getty Images, (B) Museum of American Finance; **895** (B) Bettmann/Corbis, (T) Mary Evans Picture Library; **896** (R) Roger-Viollet/Topham/The Image Works, Inc., (L) The Granger Collection, NY; **898** (L) ©DK Images, (R) Mary Evans Picture Library; **899** Time Life Pictures/Getty Images; **900** (R) Imperial War Museum, London/©DK Images, (TL) Museum of the Revolution, Moscow/©DK Images, (BL) Stefano Bianchetti/Corbis, (Inset) ullstein bild/©The Granger Collection, NY; **901** (Bkgrd,) Bettmann/Corbis; **903** Korea News Service/Reuters/Corbis; **904** ullstein bild/©The Granger Collection, NY; **905** ©The Granger Collection, NY; **906** London Express/Getty Images; **907** Rue des Archives/©The Granger Collection, NY; **908** ©DK Images; **909** ©The Granger Collection, NY; **910** akg-images/RIA Nowosti/AKG London Ltd.; **912** Corbis; **913** (B) Bettmann/Corbis, (T) Corbis; **914** Mary Evans Picture Library; **915** United States Holocaust Museum; **916** Feltz/Topham/The Image Works, Inc.; **918** (R, L) ©DK Images; **919** (T) ©Associated Press, (B) Drug Enforcement Administration; **920** Corbis; **922** Time & Life Pictures/Getty Images; **923** (B) The Advertising Archive; **924** (R) Getty Images, (L) London Express/Getty Images; **925** (L) Getty Images; **926** (TC, BC, B) Corbis; **927** (L) Getty Images, (R) Time Life Pictures/Getty Images; **930** (T) Museum of Flight/Corbis, (L) Wanda's Pie in the Sky; **932** (BR) Bettmann/Corbis, (BL) Eric L. Johnson; **933** (B) Bettmann/Corbis; **934** ©Hulton-Deutsch Collection/Corbis, (Bkgrd) United States Holocaust Museum; **935** Topham/The Image Works, Inc.; **936** Panorama Stock; **937** ©Associated Press; **938** ©AP Images; **939** (L) ©The Granger Collection, NY; **940** (L) Bettmann/Corbis, (R) Corbis; **941** (Bkgrd) Bettmann/Corbis, (B) Geoff Dann/Imperial War Museum, London/©DK Images, (R, L) Hulton Archive/Getty Images; **942** Corbis; **944** Bettmann/Corbis; **946** Topham/The Image Works, Inc.; **947** (B) Bettmann/Corbis; **948** (L) ©Associated Press, (R) Painting by Don Troiani, Military & Historical Image Bank; **949** ©Associated Press; **950** ©AP Images; **951** (B) Richard Klune/Corbis, (T) Time Life Pictures/Getty Images; **952** (R) Alfred Eisenstaedt/Time Life Pictures/Getty Images, (L) Imperial War Museum/DK Images; **953** Hulton Deutsch/Corbis; **954** (T) Corbis, (B) Library of Congress; **955** Bettmann/Corbis; **956** The Michael Barson Collection; **957** (T) Bildarchiv Preussischer Kulturbesitz/Art Resource, NY, (B) THOMAS COEX/AFP/Getty Images/NewsCom; **958** (L) Corbis; **960** (T) Eric L. Johnson, (B) Time & Life Pictures/Getty Images; **964** Photos12/Polaris Images; **965** (B) Corbis, (T) Jacques M. Chenet/Corbis; **966** (R) Getty Images, (L) Photos12/Polaris Images; **967** Alamy Images; **968** Bettmann/Corbis; **969** Patrick Robert/Sygma/Corbis; **971** (BR) ©Associated Press, (TR, BL) Bettmann/Corbis, (TL) Keystone/Gamma Rapho; **972** (R) Bob Rowan/Progressive Image/Corbis, (L) Peter Turnley/Corbis; **973** ©Associated Press; **974** Everett Collection, Inc.; **975** (TL) "LET'S GET A LOCK FOR THIS THING"—A 1962 Herblock Cartoon/The Herb Block Foundation, (B) ©Associated Press, (TR) Getty Images; **976** (B) David Seymour/©Magnum Photos, (T) Library of Congress; **977** (B) Bettmann/Corbis, (T) Lambert/Archive Photos/Getty Images; **978** (R) ©Associated Press, (L) ©Owen Franken/Corbis; **979** Bob Adelman/©Magnum Photos; **980** Polaris Images; **981** Brian Rose; **982** Topham/The Image Works, Inc.; **983** (B) Horace Bristol/Corbis; **984** Charles Gupton/Getty Images; **985** (L) Baldwin H. Ward and Kathryn C. Ward/Corbis, (R) Corbis; **986** Bettmann/Corbis; **987** (R) Corbis, (L) Gamma Rapho; **988** Bettmann/Corbis; **990** Bettmann/Corbis; **992** (R) Corbis, (L) Hulton Archive/Getty Images; **993** Time Life Pictures/Getty Images; **994** (TR, BR) ©Associated Press, (Bkgrd) Bettmann/Corbis, (BL) Nathan Benn/Corbis; **996** Russ Lappa; **997** Dirck Halstead/Getty Images; **998** (R) ©Associated Press, (L) Gamma Rapho; **999** (T) ©Associated Press, (B) Hires Chip/Gamma Rapho; **1000** (L) ©Associated Press; **1001** Bettman/Corbis; **1003** (T) ©Mark Richards/PhotoEdit, Inc., Pascal Le Segretain/Sygma/Corbis; **1004** (L) Gamma Rapho, (R) Time Life Pictures/Getty Images; **1005** Ricky Wong/Bloomberg News/Landov LLC; **1007** (B) Jacques Langevin/Sygma/Corbis, (T) Liba Taylor/Corbis; **1008** Corbis; **1009** (L) Bettmann/Corbis, (R) Gamma Rapho; **1010** Photos12/Polaris Images; **1011** Martyn Goddard/Corbis; **1012** Alexis Orand/Gamma Rapho; **1013** (B) ©Associated Press, (T) Andrew England/©Associated Press, (C) PhotoDisc/Getty Images; **1014** (R) ©Associated Press, (L) Henri Cartier-Bresson/©Magnum Photos; **1016** Bettman/Corbis; **1017** Phoenix Art Museum, Arizona, Gift of George P. Bickford/Bridgeman Art Library; **1018** Mike Goldwater/Alamy Images; **1020** (R) Bernard Napthine/Lonely Planet Images, (L) Howard Sochurek//Time Life Pictures/Getty Images; **1021** Getty Images; **1022** ©Hes Mundt/Alamy, (R) Sakchai Lalit/

©Associated Press; **1024** (R) Corbis; **1025** Fredrik Naumann/Panos Pictures; **1026** ©Danita Delimont/Alamy Images; **1028** Keystone/Getty Images; **1029** Ben Curtis/©Associated Press, (B) Plambeck/NewsCom; **1031** (T) Bettmann/Corbis, (B) Mark Kauffman/Time Life Pictures/Getty Images; **1032** (B) Corbis, (R) Patrick Ben Luke Syder/Lonely Planet Images; **1034** (T) Hassan Massoudy/ARS/Banque d'Images, ADAGP//Art Resource, NY, (B) Marco Di Lauro/Getty Images; **1035** (L) Richard Vogel/©Associated Press; **1036** ©AP Images; **1038** (R) Bettmann/Corbis, (TL) Corbis, (BL) Rick Barrentine/Corbis; **1039** (BR) ©AP Images, (BL) Getty Images, (T) Mindaugas Kulbis/©Associated Press; **1040** ©Hes Mundt/Alamy, (T) Henri Cartier-Bresson/©Magnum Photos; **1041** AFP/NewsCom; **1042** Gamma Rapho; **1043** (C) ©Tyler Cody/Alamy Images, (B) Olivier Coret/In Visu/Corbis; **1044** Corbis; **1045** Turesson/Pressens Bild/Gamma Rapho; **1047** OTHoNIEL/Gamma Rapho; **1048** Dieter Telemans/Panos Pictures; **1049** ©Magnum Photos; **1050** (TR) ©Associated Press, (TL) David Turnley/Corbis, (B) Frankenfeld/South Light/Gamma Rapho; **1052** Getty Images; **1053** (B) David Turnley/Corbis, (T) Owen Franken/Corbis; **1054** Nasser Shiyoukhi/©Associated Press; **1055** Ziv Koren/Polaris Images; **1056** ©Associated Press; **1057** (R, L) ©Associated Press; **1058** Laurent Rebours)/©Associated Press; **1059** Wissam Al-Okaili/AFP/Getty Images; **1060** ©Magnum Photos, (TL) ©SSPL/Science Museum/The Image Works, Inc., Bettmann/Corbis; **1061** Michael Evstafiev/AFP/Getty Images; **1062** (T) CARLSON©2004 Milwaukee Sentinel. Reprinted with permission of UNIVERSAL PRESS SYNDICATE. All rights reserved./Universal Press Syndicate, Gamma Rapho; **1064** Tischler Fotografen/PhotoLibrary Group, Inc.; **1065** (C) Evaristo SA/AFP/Getty Images, (B) Paul C. Pet/Corbis; **1066** (L) Zed Nelson/Panos Pictures; **1068** Ron Giling/PhotoLibrary Group, Inc.; **1069** (Inset) Clive Shirley/Panos Pictures; **1070** Mark Henley/Panos Pictures; **1071** (T) Betty Press-Woodfin Camp/AURORA, Richard Hainebach; **1072** Mark Edwards/PhotoLibrary Group, Inc.; **1073** Liba Taylor/Panos Pictures; **1074** (CR) ABPL/Nigel Dennis/Animals Animals/Earth Scenes, (T) Betty Press/Panos Pictures, (B) Cyril Ruoso/Minden Pictures, (CL) Fiona Teede-UNEP/PhotoLibrary Group, Inc.; **1075** William Campbell/Corbis; **1076** (T) Jeff Widener/©Associated Press, (B) Peter Turnley/Corbis; **1077** Greg Baker/©Associated Press; **1078** (L) Eugene Hoshiko/©Associated Press, (R) Findlay Kember/Polaris Images; **1079** Christopher Brown/Polaris Images; **1081** (B) Corbis, (T) Steve Northup/Timepix/Time Life Pictures/Getty Images; **1082** Janet Jarman/Corbis; **1083** (B) David Rochkind/Polaris Images, (T) Russell Gordon/

Das Fotoarchiv./PhotoLibrary Group, Inc.; **1084** (R) Paulo Santos/©Associated Press, (L) Paulo Santos-Interfoto/©Associated Press; **1085** Anders Gunnartz/PhotoLibrary Group, Inc.; **1086** Dado Galdieri/©Associated Press; **1087** (B) Dario Lopez-Mills/©Associated Press; **1088** (L) ALI BURAFI/AFP/Getty Images, (R) Rafael Wollmann/Gamma Rapho; **1089** Barriopedro, EFE/©Associated Press; **1090** (L) Bettmann/Corbis, (R) Image Port/PhotoLibrary Group, Inc.; **1091** Dennis Galante/Corbis; **1092** Jorgen Schytte/PhotoLibrary Group, Inc.; **1093** China Photos/Reuters/Corbis; **1094** Alison Wright/Corbis; **1095** (T) CARE USA, (B) NASA; **1096** (R) ©Matthias Kulka/Corbis, (L) AFP/Getty Images; **1098** Anthony Devlin/©Associated Press; **1100** David Grossman/The Image Works, Inc.; **1102** (Bkgrd) Corel, (Bkgrd) Russell Gordon/Das Fotoarchiv/PhotoLibrary Group, Inc.; **1103** (L) ©simon kolton/Alamy Images, (R) Bananastock/Jupiter Images, (L) Michael Yamashita Photography; **1104** Paul A. Souders/Corbis; **1105** (B) AFP/Getty Images, (T) NewsCom/NewsCom, (C) Rafiqur Rahman/Reuters Media; **1106** (R) CARE USA, (L) Getty Images; **1107** (C) ©Noah Poritz/Photo Researchers, Inc., (L) Andy Crump, TDR, World Health Organization/Photo Researchers, Inc., (R) Caroline Penn/Corbis; **1109** (T) Phil Huber/Black Star; **1110** Demotix Demotix/PhotoLibrary Group, Inc., Russell Sadur/©DK Images; **1111** (B) ©Mike Goldwater/Alamy Images; **1112** ©Associated Press; **1114** (T) Alison Wright/The Image Works, Inc., (B) Shawkat Khan/AFP/Getty Images; **1115** Larry Downing/Reuters/Corbis; **1116** Lynn Johnson/AURORA; **1118** (T) ©Reuters/Corbis; **1119** Raheb Homavandi/Reuters/Landov LLC; **1120** (R) NASA, (L) Photo Researchers, Inc.; **1121** (Bkgrd) Bettmann/Corbis, (Inset) ESA/PLI/Corbis; **1122** (Border) ©James King-Holmes/Photo Researchers, Inc., (R) Bettmann/Corbis, (L) Getty Images, (Bkgrd) Los Alamos National Laboratory/Photo Researchers, Inc.; **1123** (R) ©A. Barrington Brown/Photo Researchers, Inc., (L) ©James King-Holmes/Photo Researchers, Inc., (B) Dr. Linda M. Stannard, University of Cape Town/Photo Researchers, Inc.; **1124** (BL) Jim Richardson/Corbis, (T) R. Gino Santa Maria/Shutterstock; **1126** ©Reuters/Corbis; **1127** (T) Custom Medical Stock Photo, (B) Rafiq Maqbool/©Associated Press; **1128** (B) AFP/Getty Images, (T) Cartoon Stock; **1130** (TR) J.Bedmar/Iberfoto/Photoaisa, (BR) Musee de la Tapisserie, Bayeux, France//Bridgeman Art Library, (BL) Pascal Le Segretain/Sygma/Corbis; **1131** Corbis; **1146** The Art Archive; **1149** Anders Blomqvist/Lonely Planet Images; **1150** (B) ©The Art Gallery Collection/Alamy Images, (T) DK Images; **1151** Giraudon/Art Resource, NY; **1153** ©Associated Press; **1154** Corbis; **1155** Rafiqur Rahman/Reuters Media; **1156** baur/Shutterstock; **1158** (TL) ©The Granger Collection, NY, (TR) Ancient Art &

Architecture Collection Ltd., (B) Art Resource, NY, (CL) Musée du Louvre Paris/Gianni Dagli Orti/The Art Archive; **1159** (TL) ©National Maritime Museum, London, (CL) Art Resource, NY, (TR) Getty Images, (CR) Mary Evans Picture Library/Photo Researchers, Inc., (B) Museu de Marinha; **1160** (C) Dagli Orti/The Art Archive, (TL) Getty Images, (B) The Image Works, Inc.; **1161** (T) ©James King-Holmes/Photo Researchers, Inc., (B) ESA/PLI/Corbis, (C) Getty Images; **1162** Alexander Zemlianichenko/©Associated Press; **1163** (T) Corbis; **1164** (TL, BL) Art Resource, NY, (TR) Bridgeman Art Library; **1165** (BL) Corbis, (BR) Laurent Rebours)/©Associated Press; **1166** (B) ©The Granger Collection, NY, (T) Gunter Marx Stock Photos; **1168** (TL) Art Resource, NY, (BR) Erich Lessing/Art Resource, NY, (TR) Fitzwilliam Museum, University of Cambridge, UK/Bridgeman Art Library, (BL) The Art Archive; **1169** (TC) Copyright ARS, NY./Art Resource, NY, (TR) Historical Picture Archive/Corbis, (B) Jeff Greenberg/eStock Photo, (TL) The Museum of Modern Art/Art Resource, NY.

Text
Grateful acknowledgment is made to the following for copyrighted material:
ACT, Inc. Excerpt from "Writing Test Scores" from *www.act.org*. Copyright © 2005 by Act, Inc. All rights reserved. Used by permission.
Anglo-Norman Text Society c/o Birkbeck College Excerpt from "Test of Skill and Courage" from *History of William Marshall, Volume I - Text & Translation (11. 1-10031)* edited by A.J. Holden, with English translation by S. Gregory and historical notes by D. Crouch. © Anglo-Norman Text Society 2002. All rights reserved. Used by permission.
Ardis Publishing
From "Requiem" from *Selected Poems* by Anna Ahkmatova, translation copyright © 1974 by Robin Kemball. Reprinted with the permission of The Overlook Press (Ardis Publishers).
BBCi c/o BBC News Online
Excerpt "Black Death (Poem: "We see death coming…")" by Dr. Mike Ibeji from *www.bbc.co.uk*. British Broadcasting Corporation © 2002–2005.
Cambridge University Press
From *Hind Swaraj* by Mohandas K. Gandhi (Anthony J. Parel, editor.), copyright © 1997 by Anthony J. Parel, editor. Reprinted with the permission of Cambridge University Press.
The College Board Excerpt from "Scoring Guide" from *www.collegeboard.com*. Copyright © 2005 collegeboard.com. All rights reserved. Used by permission.
Columbia University Press
"3," "The Teachings of Confucius, Government by Personal Virtue, 43 and 97" by Wm. Theodore de Bary, et

al. from *Sources of Chinese Tradition Volume 1*. Copyright © 1960 by Columbia University Press. "55. Nothing Can Be Worse" by Sei Shonagon, translated by Ivan Morris from *The Pillow Book of Sei Shonagon*. Copyright © 1967 by Columbia University Press. Used by permission.
Doubleday A division of Random House, Inc. Excerpt from "Ja Nus Hons Pris" by Richard the 1st of England from *Warriors Of God, Richard The Lionheart And Saladin In The Third Crusade* by James Reston, Jr. Copyright © 2001 by James Reston, Jr. All rights reserved. Used by permission.
Farrar, Straus & Giroux, LLC. Excerpt from "Book Twenty: The Ranging of Powers" from *The Iliad* by Homer, translated by Robert Fitzgerald. Translation copyright © 1974 by Robert Fitzgerald. Reprinted by permission of Farrar, Straus and Giroux, LLC.
The Free Press, A Division of Simon & Schuster, Inc. Excerpts from "The Republic" by Plato from *Greek Philosophy: Thales To Aristotle, Second Edition, Revised and Expanded* edited by Reginald E. Allen. Copyright © 1966, 1985 by Reginald E. Allen. All rights reserved.
Georges Borchardt, Inc. "55 Nothing Can Be Worse" from *The Pillow Book of Sei Shonagon* translated and edited by Ivan Morris. Copyright © 1967, 1991 by Ivan Morris. Used by permission of Georges Borchardt, Inc., on behalf of the Estate of Ivan Morris.
Greenwich Workshop Press "Heavenly Reflections" by Alan Bean with Andrew Chaikin from *Apollo: An Eyewitness Account by Astronaut/Explorer/Artist/Moonwalker*. Copyright © 2009 Alan Bean. Courtesy of The Greenwich Workshop, Inc. Used by permission.
Harcourt Education Ltd. From *On Trial for my Country* by Stanlake Samkange. Reprinted by permission of Harcourt Education Limited.
Henry Holt and Company, Inc. From "Aeneid" by Virgil (Publius Vergilius Maro) from *The Classical Roman Reader, New Encounters With Ancient Rome* edited by Kenneth J. Atchity, copyright ©1997 by Kenneth J. Atchity. Reprinted by permission of Henry Holt and Company.
Houghton Mifflin Company From *Stolen Continents* by Ronald Wright. Copyright © 1992 by Ronald Wright. Reprinted by permission of Houghton Mifflin Company. All rights reserved.
Indiana University Press Song: "Our homes and humble dwellings …" from *The Mexican Corrido as a Source for Interpretive Study of Modern Mexico (1870–1950)* by Merle E.

Simmons. Copyright © 1957 by Merle E. Simmons.

Barbara Levy Literary Agency
From "Suicide in the Trenches" by Siegfried Sassoon from *Collected Poems Of Siegfried Sassoon*. Copyright © 1918, 1920, by E.P. Dutton & Co.; 1936, 1946, 1947, 1948, by Siegfried Sassoon. Copyright © Siegfried Sassoon by kind permission of the Estate of George Sassoon.

Alfred A. Knopf, Inc. From *Gilgamesh* by John Gardner and John Maier, copyright © 1984 by Estate of John Gardner and by John Maier. Used by permission of Alfred A. Knopf, a division of Random House, Inc. All rights reserved under International and Pan-American Copyright Conventions.

National Council of Churches of Christ.
"The Beatitudes: Matthew Chapter 5, Verses 5–9," "The Divine Shepherd: Psalm, Chapter 23," "The Gift of Love: I Corinthians, Chapter 13," "The Sign of the Convenant: Genesis, Chapter 17, Verses 4, 6–8" and "The Ten Commandments: Exodus, Chapter 20, Verses 2–3" from *The New Revised Standard Version of the Bible*. Copyright © 1989 The National Council of the Churches of Christ in the USA. All rights reserved. Used by permission.

New Directions Publishing Corporation
"Brotherhood" by Octavio Paz, translated by Eliot Weingberger, from *Collected Poems 1957–1987*, copyright © 1986 by Octavio Paz and Eliot Weinberger. Reprinted by permission of New Directions Publishing Corp. "Hermandad" by Octavio Paz, from *Collected Poems 1957–1987*, copyright © 1986 by Octavio Paz. Reprinted by permission of New Directions Publishing Corp.

Next Decade Entertainment, Inc.
"Brother Can You Spare a Dime?" by E.Y. "Yip" Harburg and Jay Gorney. Published by Glocca Morra Music (ASCAP) and Gorney Music (ASCAP). Administered by Next Decade Entertainment, Inc. All rights reserved. Used by permission.

W. W. Norton & Company, Inc.
from *The Prince: A Norton Critical Edition, Second Edition* by Niccolo Machiavelli, translated by Robert M. Adams. Copyright © 1992, 1977 by W. W. Norton & Company, Inc. Used by permission of W. W. Norton & Company, Inc. From *The Song of Roland* translated by Frederick Goldin. Copyright © 1978 by W. W. Norton & Company, Inc. Used by permission of W. W. Norton & Company, Inc.

Oxford University Press, Inc.
From *Ancient Greece: A Political, Social And Cultural History* by Sarah B. Pomeroy and Stanley M. Burstein and Walter Donlan et al.. Copyright © 1998 by Sarah Pomeroy, Stanley Burstein, Walter Donlan, and Jennifer T. Roberts. Reprinted by permission of Oxford University Press.

Penguin Books, Ltd. Excerpts from "Prologue" from *The Canterbury Tales* by Geoffrey Chaucer, translated into Modern English by Nevill Coghill. Copyright © 1951 by Nevill Coghill. Copyright © Nevill Coghill, 1958, 1960, 1975, 1977. Excerpts from "2:177" and excerpt "96.1" from *The Koran, With A Parallel Arabic Text* translated with Notes by N.J. Dawood. Copyright © N.J. Dawood, 1956, 1959, 1966, 1968, 1974, 1990, 1993, 1994, 1995, 1998, 2000. All rights reserved. The moral right of the translator has been asserted. Used by permission.

The Estate of Paulette Goddard Remarque c/o Richard Kay/Pryor, Cashamn, Sherman & Flynn
Excerpt from *All Quiet on the Western Front* by Erich Maria Remarque, translated by A.W. Wheen. "Im Western Nichts Neues," copyright 1928 by Ullstein A.G.; Copyright renewed 1956 by Erich Maria Remarque. "All Quiet On The Western Front," copyright 1929, 1930 by Little, Brown and Company; copyright renewed 1957, 1958 by Erich Maria Remarque. All rights reserved. All rights reserved under International and Pan-American Copyright Conventions, including the right to reproduce this book or portions therof. Used by permission.

The Polish Institute of Arts and Sciences of America
"The Bronze Horseman" by Alexander Pushkin. Copyright © The Estate of Waclaw Lednicki. Used by permission of The Estate of Waclaw Lednicki, on behalf of The Polish Institute of Arts and Sciences of America.

The University of Chicago Press
Excerpt from "Antigone" by Sophocles, E. Wyckoff, translator, in *The Complete Greek Tragedies*, D. Grene and R. Lattimore, editors. Copyright © 1954 by The University of Chicago Press. All rights reserved. Used by permission. Excerpt from *The Mahabharata: I The Book Of The Beginning*, translated and edited by J.A.B. van Buitenen. Copyright © 1973 by The University of Chicago Press. All rights reserved. Used by permission. Excerpts from *The Edicts Of Asoka* translated and edited by N.A. Nikam & Richard McKeon. Copyright © 1959 by The University of Chicago Press. Used by permission.

University of California Press, Inc.
Excerpt from "The Bronze Horseman" by Alexander Pushkin, translated by Waclaw Lednicki from *Waclaw Lednicki, Pushkin's Bronze Horseman* (Berkeley, CA: University of California Press, 1955). Used by permission.

University of Oklahoma Press
From "Two: Invasion" by Ralph L. Roys, ed. From *The Book of Chilam Balam of Chumayel*. Copyright © 1992 by Ronald Wright. Used with permission of the University of Oklahoma Press.

Vintage Books
From *Open Letters: Selected Writings 1965–1990* by Vaclav Havel, translated by Paul Wilson, copyright © 1991 by A.G. Brain. Preface/translation copyright © 1985, 1988, 1991 by Paul Wilson. Used by permission of Alfred A. Knopf, a division of Random House, Inc.

The Arthur Waley Estate
From "2, Book II" by Confucius (Arthur Waley, translator.) from *The Analects of Confucius*. Reprinted with permission of The Arthur Waley Estate. From "13, Book II" by Confucius (Arthur Waley, translator.) from *The Analects of Confucius*. Reprinted with permission of The Arthur Waley Estate. From "17, Book II" by Confucius (Arthur Waley, translator.) from *The Analects of Confucius*. Reprinted with permission of The Arthur Waley Estate.

Note: Every effort has been made to locate the copyright owner of material reprinted in this book. Omissions brought to our attention will be corrected in subsequent editions.